Handbook On The Law Of Bailments And Carriers

Armistead Mason Dobie

Handbook On The Law Of Bailments And Carriers

Armistead Mason Dobie

The Hornbook Series

of

Treatises on all the Principal Subjects of the Law

Admiralty — Gustavus H. Robinson.
Agency — Tiffany, 2nd Ed. by Richard R. Powell.
Bailments and Carriers — Armistead M. Dobie.
Bankruptcy — 2nd Ed., Henry C. Black.
Banks and Banking — Francis B. Tiffany.
Bills and Notes — William E. Britton.
Code Pleading — Charles E. Clark.
Common Law Pleading — Shipman, 3rd Ed. by Henry W. Ballantine.
Conflict of Laws —2nd Ed., Herbert F. Goodrich.
Constitutional Law — Henry Rottschaefer.
Construction and Interpretation of Laws — 2nd Ed., Henry C. Black.
Contracts — Clark, 4th Ed. by A. H. Throckmorton.
Corporations — Robert S. Stevens.
Criminal Law — Justin Miller.
Criminal Procedure — Clark, 2nd Ed. by William E. Mikell.
Damages — Charles T. McCormick.
Domestic Relations — Joseph W. Madden.
Elementary Law — Smith, 2nd Ed. by Archie H. McGray.
Equity — Henry L. McClintock.
Equity Pleading and Practice — Walter C. Clephane.
Evidence — 5th Ed., John J. McKelvey.
Executors and Administrators — Simon G. Croswell.
Federal Jurisdiction and Procedure — Armistead M. Dobie.
Insurance — 2nd Ed., William R. Vance.
International Law — 3rd Ed., George G. Wilson.
Judicial Precedents — Henry C. Black.
Legal History — Max Radin.
Municipal Corporations — Roger W. Cooley.
Partnership — Judson A. Crane.
Real Property — William L. Burdick.
Real Property — William E. Burby.
Roman Law — Max Radin.
Sales — Lawrence Vold.
Suretyship and Guaranty — Herschel W. Arant.
Torts — William L. Prosser.
Trusts — 2nd Ed., George G. Bogert.
Wills — Thomas E. Atkinson.

Published and for sale by

WEST PUBLISHING CO. **ST. PAUL 2, MINN.**

T7302

HANDBOOK

ON THE LAW OF

BAILMENTS AND CARRIERS

BY

ARMISTEAD M. DOBIE

PROFESSOR OF LAW IN THE UNIVERSITY OF VIRGINIA
AUTHOR OF DOBIE'S CASEBOOK ON BAILMENTS AND CARRIERS

ST. PAUL
WEST PUBLISHING CO.
1914

(Dob.Bailm.)

PREFACE

THE publishers had contemplated originally a second edition of Hale on Bailments and Carriers rather than a new treatise on the subject. Before the work had progressed far, it seemed best to abandon this plan and issue a new book, in which free use might be made of all suitable material in Mr. Hale's text. Grateful acknowledgment is here made for the substantial aid thus received. Particularly valuable assistance has been derived from Mr. Hale's notes. General acknowledgment seems proper also to the many authors both ancient and modern whose works have been consulted. When specific use has been made of definite excerpts from other authors, proper credit has been duly given. In the present volume, however, both the analysis and treatment are new.

To give an exposition of bailments and carriers in brief compass is a difficult task. Only the more essential aspects of each subject could be treated, and the practical importance of each topic has been duly considered in the apportionment of space. Clearness and accuracy have been sought both in the analysis and in the more detailed discussion. Unusual care has been bestowed upon the notes, especially in the citation of cases supporting each specific principle set forth in the text. No attempt has been made to make these citations exhaustive. The author's effort has been rather directed towards making them both ample and representative. Special emphasis has been placed upon cases in the standard series of selected decisions, and upon the decisions of those courts whose opinions seem to carry the greatest weight. The title of a case is printed in bold type if it is found in Dobie's Cases on Bailments and Carriers, which is a collection of illustrative cases especially prepared to accompany the present volume.

ARMISTEAD M. DOBIE.

UNIVERSITY OF VIRGINIA, October, 1914.

TABLE OF CONTENTS

PART ONE

BAILMENTS

CHAPTER I

DEFINITION AND CLASSIFICATION OF BAILMENTS

CHAPTER II

GENERAL PRINCIPLES COMMON TO ALL BAILMENTS

CHAPTER III

BAILMENTS FOR THE BAILOR'S SOLE BENEFIT

CHAPTER IV

BAILMENTS FOR THE BAILEE'S SOLE BENEFIT

CHAPTER V

BAILMENTS FOR MUTUAL BENEFIT—HIRED USE OF THINGS

CHAPTER VI

BAILMENTS FOR MUTUAL BENEFIT—HIRED SERVICES ABOUT THINGS

CHAPTER VII

BAILMENTS FOR MUTUAL BENEFIT—PLEDGES

CHAPTER VIII

INNKEEPERS

PART TWO

CARRIERS

CHAPTER IX

PRIVATE AND COMMON CARRIERS OF GOODS

CHAPTER X

LIABILITIES OF THE COMMON CARRIER OF GOODS

CHAPTER XI

LIABILITY UNDER SPECIAL CONTRACT

CHAPTER XII

COMMENCEMENT AND TERMINATION OF THE LIABILITY OF THE COMMON CARRIER OF GOODS

CHAPTER XIII

THE RIGHTS OF THE COMMON CARRIER OF GOODS

CHAPTER XIV

QUASI CARRIERS OF GOODS—POST OFFICE DEPARTMENT

CHAPTER XV

ACTIONS AGAINST CARRIERS OF GOODS

PART THREE

CARRIERS OF PASSENGERS

CHAPTER XVI

THE NATURE OF THE RELATION

CHAPTER XVII

COMMENCEMENT AND TERMINATION OF THE RELATION

CHAPTER XVIII

LIABILITIES OF THE COMMON CARRIER OF PASSENGERS

CHAPTER XIX

THE RIGHTS OF THE COMMON CARRIER OF PASSENGERS

CHAPTER XX

THE BAGGAGE OF THE PASSENGER

CHAPTER XXI

ACTIONS AGAINST CARRIERS OF PASSENGERS

SUPPLEMENT

THE INTERSTATE COMMERCE ACT

THE SAFETY APPLIANCE ACTS

THE EMPLOYERS' LIABILITY ACTS

TABLE OF CASES CITED

INDEX

†

HANDBOOK

ON THE LAW OF

BAILMENTS AND CARRIERS

PART ONE

BAILMENTS

CHAPTER I

DEFINITION AND CLASSIFICATION OF BAILMENTS

DEFINITION

1. A bailment is the relation created through the transfer of the possession of goods or chattels, by a person called the bailor to a person called the bailee, without a transfer of ownership, for the accomplishment of a certain purpose, whereupon the goods or chattels are to be dealt with according to the instructions of the bailor.

There are nearly as many definitions of a bailment as there are writers on the subject. The definition given in the black letter is submitted with the intention, not of adding to an already too numerous collection, but rather of furnishing a composite description of some practical utility. Its accuracy, or lack of it, will appear as the general subject is developed and no elaborate attempt to justify it will be made here. Even an extended explication of the terms of the definition will be postponed until the next chapter, which treats of the legal incidents inhering in the bailment relation.

A bailment is usually defined as a delivery,[1] or transfer of the possession, of chattels under certain circumstances; but it is defined above, not as a delivery of goods, but as a *relation* resulting from this delivery. It seems clearer and more accurate to designate delivery as merely one of the essential elements of the definition and to say that, when it and all the other essential elements are present, there springs up a legal relation which we call a bailment. The bailment does not rise to the dignity of a status, such as marriage. As a relation, however, it is upon the same plane as other important legal relations, such as agency, master and servant, or even partnership.

Since the bailment relation is created by a delivery of goods in the sense of a transfer of the possession of the chattels, this necessarily involves one person making the delivery and another to whom the delivery is made. The deliverer, the person actively creating the bailment, is called the bailor; the "deliveree," the person more or less passively accepting the bailment, is called the bailee. Possession is thus transferred by the bailor to the bailee.

Though possession must pass in order that there may be a bailment, such possession must pass alone, and not in connection with, or as an incident to, ownership. If ownership passes, either with or without possession, the transaction then becomes, as we shall see (in section 3), not a bailment, but a gift or sale. So fundamental is this that some writers describe bailments solely in terms of this unique feature. Thus Hammond refers to a bailment as "possession of a chattel lawfully severed from its ownership," while in the sixteenth century St. Germain gives us this happy and naive description of a bailment: "Goods that a man hath in his keeping which be not his own."

Not a few distinguished writers (including Sir William Jones, Story, and Kent), in their definitions, refer to a bailment as the delivery of a thing "in trust."[2] This terminology is somewhat

[1] See definitions given under note 2.

[2] Bailment is defined by Sir William Jones (Jones, Bailm. 1) as being a delivery of goods in trust, on a contract, express or implied, that the trust shall be duly executed, and the goods redelivered as soon as the time or use for which they were bailed shall have elapsed or been performed. According to Judge Story (Story, Bailm. c. 1, § 2) a bailment is "a delivery of a thing in trust, for some special object or purpose, and upon a contract, express or implied, to conform to the object or purpose of the trust." In Kent's Commentaries (2 Kent, Comm. [4th Ed.] lect. 40, p. 558) a bailment is said to be "a delivery of goods on trust, upon a contract, express or implied, that the trust shall be duly executed, and the goods restored by the bailee, as soon as

confusing, however, for in a technical trust the trustee has the legal title to the goods held in trust. In a bailment, as we have just seen, the bailee has merely possession, but not title or ownership.

The motive actuating the bailor in creating the bailment is "the accomplishment of a certain purpose," so it is for the execution of this purpose by the bailee that possession of the goods is transferred to him by the bailor. This is called the bailment purpose, and its nature plays an important part in the classification of bailments.

When the bailment purpose is fully accomplished, the goods are to be dealt with by the bailee "according to the instructions of the bailor." In a majority, perhaps, of the cases, the goods are then to be redelivered to the bailor. Accordingly, some definitions specify such a return to the owner as an essential element in a bailment. It is clear, though, that the instructions of the bailor are decisive of this question, and these instructions frequently indicate that, after the bailment purpose is accomplished, the bailee must deliver the goods to a person other than the bailor. Thus, the carrier must deliver the goods after the carriage of the goods is over, to the consignee. Again, the factor or commission merchant keeps the goods of the bailor for sale to a third person, and on such a sale the factor is to deliver the goods to such third person as the purchaser. There are even cases when the bailor's instructions contemplate that the bailee himself is, on the performance of certain conditions, to keep the goods as their owner.[3]

the purpose of the bailment shall be answered." Numerous other definitions, or unimportant variations on the definitions given, may be found in the reported cases. The essential elements of a bailment are now so well recognized, however, that modern accepted definitions differ rather in the wording than in legal effect. A contract whereby the owner of a sawmill and timber employed another to take possession of the mill and timber and saw the timber into lumber for the owner created the relation of bailor and bailee, both as to the timber and lumber. Chaffin v. State, 5 Ga. App. 368, 63 S. E. 230. See, also, as to what constitutes a bailment, Pribble v. Kent, 10 Ind. 325, 71 Am. Dec. 327; La Farge v. Rickert, 5 Wend. (N. Y.) 187, 21 Am. Dec. 209; Tuttle v. Campbell, 74 Mich. 652, 42 N. W. 384, 16 Am. St. Rep. 652; Bohannon v. Springfield, 9 Ala. 789; Oakley v. State, 40 Ala. 372; Green v. Hollingsworth, 5 Dana (Ky.) 173, 30 Am. Dec. 680; Newhall v. Paige, 10 Gray (Mass.) 366; Dunlap v. Gleason, 16 Mich. 158, 93 Am. Dec. 231; Wadsworth v. Allcott, 6 N. Y. 64; Poe v. Horne, 44 N. C. 398; Henry v. Patterson, 57 Pa. 346; Furlow v. Gillian, 19 Tex. 250; Armour & Co. v. Ross, 78 S. C. 294, 58 S. E. 941, 1135; Blondell v. Consolidated Gas Co., 89 Md. 732, 43 Atl. 817, 46 L. R. A. 187; Chaffin v. State, 5 Ga. App. 368, 63 S. E. 230; Northcutt v. State, 60 Tex. Cr. R. 259, 131 S. W. 1128, 31 L. R. A. (N. S.) 822; Bates v. Bigby, 123 Ga. 727, 51 S. E. 717.

[3] As in the so-called "sale on approval," discussed in section 3.

HISTORICAL

2. Though bailments are practically as old as society, the law of bailments as a part of English jurisprudence has been of comparatively recent development.

Historical Outline

The mere definition of a bailment necessarily shows in itself that bailments must have been more or less frequent even in the most primitive stages of society. Thus, even in the remotest of historical eras, it is easy to imagine a man keeping the goods of another, or carrying them from place to place, or becoming a bailee of the spears of his fellow tribesmen to sharpen them or otherwise repair them. It is, therefore, all the more remarkable that the subject of bailments was so slow to assume a place of importance in English law.

Especially is this true when we consider the part played by bailments in the jurisprudence of the world. Thus, frequent mention is made of bailments, and elaborate provisions are made concerning them, in the wonderful, ancient Babylonian Code of Hammurabi.[4] Even the earliest of the Mosaic Codes, the so-called "JE Code," brief as it is, contains several provisions on the subject.[5] Bailments played a large part in Roman law, and under this remarkable jurisprudence the law of bailments was worked out with a wondrous wealth of detail, particularly in connection with real and consensual contracts.[6] To the Roman law, the English law of bailments is indebted for many of its principles and also in a large measure for its terminology.

Of the earlier English writers, Bracton, in the thirteenth century, wrote of bailments. His work, however, was largely a mere restatement of Roman law, and he made no convincing application of these principles to the practical conditions of his time. Coke[7]

[4] See Cook, The Law of Moses and Code of Hammurabi.

[5] Thus in the twenty-second chapter of the book of Exodus these expressions are found "If a man shall deliver unto his neighbor money or stuff to keep" (verse 7); "If a man borrow aught of his neighbor" (verse 14); "If it be an hired thing" (verse 15).

[6] See Morey, Outlines of Roman Law, pp. 355–358, 365–368; Leage, Roman Private Law, pp. 264–271, 297–300; Sandar's Justinian (Hammond) pp. 405–410, 448–452.

[7] Coke, First Inst. 89a, 89b. See, also, Rolle, Abr. (1668) tit. "Bailment;" Brooke, Abr. (1576). An interesting historical treatment of bailments is found in Holmes, The Common Law, pp. 164–205, and also in 2 Street, Foundations of Legal Liability, pp. 251–269.

(who lived during the last half of the sixteenth and the first half of the seventeenth centuries), in his Institutes, devotes some space to the liability of the bailee, but his treatment was far from satisfactory.

The first real attempt, however, at reducing the law of bailments in English jurisprudence to some degree of order was made by Lord Holt in the celebrated case of COGGS v. BERNARD,[8] decided in 1703. Though the only real point in issue in this case was the liability of a gratuitous bailee specially undertaking the accomplishment of a certain purpose, yet the endeavors of this great judge to give some definite shape and order to a subject whose future importance he saw served to lay the groundwork for, and give a great impetus to, future investigation and research. COGGS v. BERNARD is therefore, considered from a historical standpoint, the leading case on bailments in our jurisprudence.

It was largely due to the labors of Sir William Jones, in the latter half of the eighteenth century, that the subject began first to take definite form, and it is upon his "Essay"[9] that all subsequent works upon bailments have been founded. The treatise of Mr. Justice Story,[10] though, was the first logical and reliable exposition of the modern law of bailments in the form in which it now substantially exists. To Lord Holt, Sir William Jones, and Mr. Justice Story, then, is largely due the state in which we now find the law of bailments, and upon their work every subsequent writer must draw heavily in his treatment of the same subject.

In modern times, the bailment has become, not a mere incidental, personal transaction, but one of tremendous commercial import, and the law of bailments has been developed accordingly, until it is now in practical importance one of the leading subjects in our law. With the increase of commerce and the changed conditions of our marvelously complex life, both in its social and commercial aspects, the law of bailments must and will keep pace.

[8] (1703) COGGS v. BERNARD, 2 Ld. Raym. (Eng.) 909, 1 Smith, Lead. Cas. (7th Am. Ed.) 369, Dobie Cas. Bailments and Carriers, 1. Among the most interesting cases prior to COGGS v. BERNARD are Bonion's Case (1315) Y. B. 8 Edw. II, 275, Fitz. Abr. Detinue, pl. 59; Woodlife's Case (1596) Moore, 462, Owen, 57; the celebrated Southcote's Case (1601) Cro. Eliz. 815, 4 Coke, 836; 2 Bl. Comm. 452; and Williams v. Hide (1628) Palmer, 548, W. Jones, 179.

[9] Jones, Bailm. (1781).

[10] Story, Bailm. (1832).

BAILMENT AND SALE DISTINGUISHED

3. In a sale, ownership or title must pass, while possession either may or may not pass; in a bailment, ownership must not pass, but possession must.

It is easy to state the difference in legal effect between a sale and a bailment; the difficulty lies in the practical application of the test to specific transactions. The sale contemplates the passage of title; the seller divests himself of his ownership in the goods and confers it on the buyer. In a bailment, the owner retains still his ownership and transfers to the bailee something far short of title, viz., mere possession. The seller parts with the goods; they are no longer his but the buyer's. The bailor parts, not with the goods, but merely with possession of the goods, so that they are, after the bailment purpose is accomplished, to be returned to him or to such other person as he may direct.[11]

According to Benjamin,[12] the following is the test: "When the identical thing delivered is to be returned, though, perhaps, in an altered form, it is a bailment and the title is not changed; but when there is no obligation to return the specific article received, and the receiver is at liberty to return another thing, either in the same or some other form, or else to pay merely * * * the title is changed, and the transaction is a sale."[13] Thus, when

[11] Bretz v. Diehl, 117 Pa. 589, 11 Atl. 893, 2 Am. St. Rep. 706; Appeal of Edward, 105 Pa. 103; Dando v. Foulds, 105 Pa. 74; Enlow v. Klein, 79 Pa. 488; Rose v. Story, 1 Pa. 190, 44 Am. Dec. 121; Wheeler & Wilson Manuf'g Co. v. Heil, 115 Pa. 487, 6 Atl. 616, 2 Am. St. Rep. 575; William R. Trigg Co. v. Bucyrus Co., 104 Va. 79, 51 S. E. 174; First Nat. Bank of Concordia v. McIntosh & Peters Live Stock & Commission Co., 72 Kan. 603, 84 Pac. 535. On a sale, however, the seller of the goods may become a bailee by agreeing by the same contract to store them. Oakley v. State, 40 Ala. 372. See, further, as to the distinction between a bailment and a sale, Potter v. Mt. Vernon Roller Mill Co., 101 Mo. App. 581, 73 S. W. 1005; Woodward v. Edmunds, 20 Utah, 118, 57 Pac. 848; Gleason v. Beers' Estate, 59 Vt. 581, 10 Atl. 86, 59 Am. Rep. 757; Singar Mfg. Co. v. Ellington, 103 Ill. App. 517.

[12] Benj. Sales (6th Am. Ed.) p. 5, note; and see cases there cited.

[13] Pierce v. Schenck, 3 Hill (N. Y.) 28; Foster v. Pettibone, 7 N. Y. 433, 57 Am. Dec. 530; Mansfield v. Converse, 8 Allen (Mass.) 182; Barker v. Roberts, 8 Greenl. (Me.) 101; Brown v. Hitchcock, 28 Vt. 452; Irons v. Kentner, 51 Iowa, 88, 50 N. W. 73, 33 Am. Rep. 119. If, however, the identical thing is not to be returned, it is a sale or an exchange, according to the nature of the consideration. South Australian Ins. Co. v. Randell, L. R. 3 P. C. 101; Laflin & R. Powder Co. v. Burkhardt, 97 U. S. 110, 116, 24 L. Ed. 973; Sturm v. Boker, 150 U. S. 312, 330, 14 Sup. Ct. 99, 37 L. Ed. 1093; McCabe v. McKinstry, 5 Dill. 509, Fed. Cas. No. 8,667; Ewing v. French, 1 Blackf. (Ind.) 354; Smith v. Clark, 21 Wend. (N. Y.) 83, 34 Am. Dec. 213; Norton v. Wood-

wheat is delivered by a farmer to a miller to be ground, and the flour made from that identical wheat is to be returned by the miller, the transaction is very clearly a bailment.[14] But when the miller in return for the wheat agrees to deliver merely a specified quantity of flour of a designated grade or brand, then it is equally as clear that the transaction is not a bailment, but a sale or exchange.[15] In the first case, the farmer still owns the wheat and the flour into which it is converted, so that the miller would have no right as against the farmer to destroy such wheat or flour, nor could he dispose of it to another person. In the second case, however, the farmer passes the title to the wheat, and he cannot demand it or its product again; for he has bartered it, and in its place he has a mere right to receive a certain quantity of flour of a certain type. Accordingly, here the miller could destroy the wheat as soon as it was received by him, and the farmer would have no legal right to complain.

ruff, 2 N. Y. 153; Crosby v. Delaware & H. Canal Co., 119 N. Y. 334, 23 N. E. 736; Chase v. Washburn, 1 Ohio St. 244, 59 Am. Dec. 623; Butterfield v. Lathrop, 71 Pa. 225; Andrews v. Richmond, 34 Hun (N. Y.) 20; Austin v. Seligman (C. C.) 21 Blatchf. 507, 18 Fed. 519; Lyon v. Lenon, 106 Ind. 567, 7 N. E. 311; Marsh v. Titus, 3 Hun (N. Y.) 550; Kaut v. Kessler, 114 Pa. 603, 7 Atl. 586; Bailey v. Bensley, 87 Ill. 556; Mack v. Snell, 140 N. Y. 193, 35 N. E. 493, 37 Am. St. Rep. 534. The fact that the bailee agrees to pay a certain sum, if he does not return the property, does not, per se, convert the bailment into a sale. Westcott v. Thompson, 18 N. Y. 363; SATTLER v. HALLOCK, 160 N. Y. 291, 54 N. E. 667, 46 L. R. A. 679, 73 Am. St. Rep. 686, Dobie Cas. Bailments and Carriers, 9; First Nat. Bank of Elgin v. Schween, 127 Ill. 573, 20 N. E. 681, 11 Am. St. Rep. 174; Genobia Aragon De Jaramillo v. United States, 37 Ct. Cl. 208; Fleet v. Hertz, 201 Ill. 594, 66 N. E. 658, 94 Am. St. Rep. 192; Scott Mining & Smelting Co. v. Shultz, 67 Kan. 605, 73 Pac. 903. For a long line of cases distinguishing Bailments and Sales, see 43 Cent. Dig. (Sales) §§ 7–10, columns 36–47; Dec. Dig. (Sales) § 3, pp. 1706–1710. See, also, Tiffany on Sales, § 5.

14 Slaughter v. Green, 1 Rand. (Va.) 3, 10 Am. Dec. 488; Inglebright v. Hammond, 19 Ohio, 337, 53 Am. Dec. 430; Mallory v. Willis, 4 N. Y. 76.

15 Hurd v. West, 7 Cow. (N. Y.) 752, note page 758; Smith v. Clark, 21 Wend. (N. Y.) 83, 34 Am. Dec. 213; Norton v. Woodruff, 2 N. Y. 153; Ewing v. French, 1 Blackf. (Ind.) 353; Buffum v. Merry, 3 Mason, 478, Fed. Cas. No. 2,112; Chase v. Washburn, 1 Ohio St. 251, 59 Am. Dec. 623 (distinguishing Slaughter v. Green and Inglebright v. Hammond, supra); Jones v. Kemp, 49 Mich. 9, 12 N. W. 890. The same rule has been applied to the refining of jeweler's sweepings, Austin v. Seligman (C. C.) 21 Blatchf. 506, 18 Fed. 519; to the sawing of logs into boards, Barker v. Roberts, 8 Greenl. (Me.) 101; Pierce v. Schenck, 3 Hill (N. Y.) 28; to the delivery of hides to be tanned, Jenkins v. Eichelberger, 4 Watts (Pa.) 121, 28 Am. Dec. 691. But see Weir Plow Co. v. Porter, 82 Mo. 23; Caldwell v. Hall, 60 Miss. 330, 44 Am. Rep. 410.

Grain Elevators

The distinction between sales and bailments is most subtle from a legal standpoint and most important from a practical standpoint in the case of grain elevators. Here the question is complicated by the fact that considerations of convenience and economy demand that the grain deposited by each person be not kept separate, but that it be commingled with similar grain of other depositors. The specific contract is in each case controlling, and all relevant surrounding facts and circumstances should be considered in doubtful cases, in order to arrive at the real intention of the parties. The distinction turns about the question of whether the elevator keeper's control of the grain is of such an order as to negative ownership in any one else. The cases cannot be reconciled, but reason and authority would seem to support the doctrines indicated.[16]

The mere fact that the keeper of the elevator by custom or contract has the right to commingle the grain of several depositors, so that no depositor can receive the identical grain deposited, does not make the transaction any the less a bailment. Each depositor is then the owner of a share in the mass, to be determined by the proportion which his own deposit bears to the entire mass, while the keeper remains a mere bailee of the mass.[17]

The situation is more complicated when the keeper has the right to deposit grain of his own in the mass and also to make withdrawals from the mass, and to make substitutions of other grain of like grade for that withdrawn, subject to the proviso that he must at all times keep in his elevator grain equal in quality and quantity to the sum total of all the deposits. This, though, is still a bailment,[18] and the relation attaches to the grain through all the mutations of individual particles in the elevator. The keeper could not here destroy the grain in the elevator, nor could he dispose of

[16] For a discussion of the question and review of the cases, see article on "Grain Elevators" in 6 Am. Law Rev. 450. For cases, see 43 Cent. Dig. (Sales) § 11, columns 48–51, 17 Dec. Dig. (Sales) 4 (5), p. 1710.

[17] Mayer v. Springer, 192 Ill. 270, 61 N. E. 348; Savage v. Salem Mills Co., 48 Or. 1, 85 Pac. 69, 10 Ann. Cas. 1065; State v. Cowdery, 79 Minn. 94, 81 N. W. 750, 48 L. R. A. 92; Bryan v. Congdon, 54 Kan. 109, 37 Pac. 1009; Millhiser Mfg. Co. v. Gallego Mills Co., 101 Va. 579, 44 S. E. 760; Greenleaf v. Dows (C. C.) 8 Fed. 550; Bretz v. Diehl, 117 Pa. 589, 11 Atl. 893, 2 Am. St. Rep. 706.

[18] Sexton v. Graham, 53 Iowa, 181, 4 N. W. 1090; JAMES v. PLANK, 48 Ohio St. 255, 26 N. E. 1107, Dobie Cas. Bailments and Carriers, 14; McGrew v. Thayer, 24 Ind. App. 578, 57 N. E. 262; Andrews v. Richmond, 34 Hun (N. Y.) 20; Odell v. Leyda, 46 Ohio St. 244, 20 N. E. 472; Hall v. Pillsbury, 43 Minn. 33, 44 N. W. 673, 7 L. R. A. 529, 19 Am. St. Rep. 209.

any of the grain save his own without substituting similar grain therefor. This therefore implies, rather than negatives, the ownership of some one other than the elevator keeper.

But when the obligation imposed on the elevator keeper by the receipt of the grain is merely to return grain of a certain quantity and quality, then the transaction cannot be a bailment.[19] The same is true when the keeper has the right to use any and all of the grain on payment therefor, either in money or other grain, without any duty of substitution of other grain therefor in the elevator;[20] and also when the keeper has the option whether he shall return the grain delivered or pay for the grain.[21] In all of these cases, the keeper could destroy the grain when received without impairing the legal rights of the depositor, and this is here inconsistent with the legal notion of a bailment.

It might be remarked that in doubtful cases the older decisions are somewhat inclined to hold the transaction a sale, while the trend of the later cases has decidedly favored the holding that such transactions are bailments and that the essential nature of the transaction, depending on the intention of the parties, is not changed merely by modern methods of handling the storage of grain.

Mutuum

In this connection may be noticed, for the purpose of distinguishing it, the "mutuum" of the Roman law. A mutuum was a delivery of goods which were expected to be consumed by the recipient, and for which other goods of the same kind were to be returned to the owner. It is clear, from what has been said, that, since title to the goods in such cases would immediately vest in

19 The principle here is the same as when a certain amount of the manufactured product (e. g. flour) is to be given for the wheat. See cases cited in note 15. See, also, O'Neal v. Stone, 79 Mo. App. 279.

20 Savage v. Salem Mills Co., 48 Or. 1, 85 Pac. 69, 10 Ann. Cas. 1065; Cloke v. Shafroth, 137 Ill. 393, 27 N. E. 702, 31 Am. St. Rep. 375; Johnston v. Browne, 37 Iowa, 200; Chase v. Washburn, 1 Ohio St. 244, 59 Am. Dec. 623; Rahilly v. Wilson, 3 Dill. 420, Fed. Cas. No. 11,532; McCabe v. McKinstry, 5 Dill. 509, Fed. Cas. No. 8,667.

21 Barnes v. McCrea, 75 Iowa, 267, 39 N. W. 392, 9 Am. St. Rep. 473; O'Neal v. Stone, 79 Mo. App. 279; Potter v. Mt. Vernon Roller Mill Co., 101 Mo. App. 581, 73 S. W. 1005. See, also, cases cited in preceding note. In State v. Rieger, 59 Minn. 151, 60 N. W. 1087, under the contract, the elevator man could exercise his option and acquire the right to use the grain only when the owner had presented the ticket and been paid for the grain. The transaction was held to be a bailment with option to elevator man to convert it into a sale when the ticket was presented.

the recipient, such a transaction would in no sense be a bailment, but is a sale or exchange.[22]

Sale on Approval—Sale or Return

Finally, in this connection should be noted the so-called "sale on approval." Here goods are delivered to a party, but title to the goods does not vest in him until he has in some way manifested his approval. The result is that such person acquires possession forthwith, while he may or may not acquire title by his approval at a later date. It is therefore clear that such a transaction is not in its inception a sale at all, but a mere bailment, and remains such until it is converted into a sale by the approval. The so-called "sale on approval" is therefore a mere bailment, with the option in the bailee by his approval to convert the bailment into a sale.[23]

When, however, the title passes immediately, but the buyer has the option to defeat the sale by returning the article, this is a sale originally and not a bailment. This is usually called a "sale or return." [24]

CLASSIFICATION OF THE ROMAN LAW

4. According to the classification of the Roman law, bailments were divided into six kinds:

(a) Depositum.
(b) Mandatum.
(c) Commodatum.
(d) Mutuum.
(e) Pignus.
(f) Locatio.

[22] In regard to the Roman mutuum, Gaius says: "This chiefly relates to things which are estimated by weight, number, or measure, such as money, wine, oil, corn, bronze, silver, gold. We transfer our property in these, on condition that the receiver shall transfer back to us at a future time, not the same things, but other things of the same nature; wherefore this contract is called 'mutuum,' because thereby meum becomes tuum." Poste Gaius, III. § 90.

[23] Tiffany on Sales, § 45; American Sales Act, § 19, rule 3 (2); Sargent v. Gile, 8 N. H. 325; Goss Printing Press Co. v. Jordan, 171 Pa. 474, 32 Atl. 1031; Hart v. Carpenter, 24 Conn. 427.

Where two colts were delivered for keeping, and to be sold by bailee if possible, if not to be returned, the contract was held to be one of bailment. Middleton v. Stone, 111 Pa. 589, 4 Atl. 523. So an option may reside in the bailor to make the transaction a sale; but, unless the option is exercised, the bailment relation will continue. Weir Plow Co. v. Porter, 82 Mo. 23.

[24] Tiffany on Sales, § 46; American Sales Act, § 19, rule 3 (1); Gay v. Dare, 103 Cal. 454, 37 Pac. 466; Sturm v. Boker, 150 U. S. 312, 14 Sup. Ct. 99, 37 L. Ed. 1093; Robinson v. Fairbanks, 81 Ala. 132, 1 South. 552.

(a) DEPOSITUM—A depositum is a bailment of goods for mere custody, without recompense.

(b) MANDATUM—A mandatum is a bailment of goods for the purpose of having some more or less active services performed about them by the bailee without recompense.

(c) COMMODATUM—A commodatum is a gratuitous bailment of goods for use by the bailee.

(d) MUTUUM—A mutuum is a delivery of goods, involving, not the return of the identical goods lent, but their replacement by other goods of the same kind. At common law, such a transaction is regarded as a sale or exchange, and not a bailment.

(e) PIGNUS—A pignus, pledge, or pawn is a bailment of goods as security for some debt or engagement, accompanied by a power of sale in case of default.

(f) LOCATIO—A locatio, or hiring, is a bailment for reward, and may be:

(1) Locatio rei, or the hired use of a thing.

(2) Locatio operis, or hired services about a thing, which includes:

(i) Locatio operis faciendi, or hired work and labor about a thing.

(ii) Locatio custodiæ, or hired custody of a thing.

(iii) Locatio operis mercium vehendarum, or hired transportation of a thing.

This classification of the Roman law is unquestionably of great value, though it has been severely criticised and is open to a number of objections. Thus it is not strictly a classification at all, but a mere enumeration of different kinds of bailments, with no attempt to arrange them into classes showing their relations to one another. The Roman classification, too, has been criticised as being unnecessarily refined. It is also true that the distinctions and differences it draws afford no satisfactory test of differences in the legal incidents attached to the various kinds of bailments. The terminology has no doubt resulted with us in some inconsistencies and not a few obscurities.

This classification and its terminology, however, have played no small part in shaping and coloring our own law on the subject, so that no writer can afford to ignore it. The relation of the Roman classification and terminology to that adopted by modern writers, as one evidence of the impress of the Roman law on the common law in this connection, will more fully appear as the subject of bailments is developed.

MODERN CLASSIFICATION WITH REFERENCE TO BENEFIT

5. The rights and liabilities of the parties to a bailment depend primarily upon which party the bailment is intended to benefit. Bailments may therefore be divided into three classes:

(a) Bailments for the bailor's sole benefit, including
(1) Depositum, and
(2) Mandatum.

(b) Bailments for the bailee's sole benefit, including
(1) Commodatum.

(c) Bailments for mutual benefit of both bailor and bailee, including
(1) Pignus, and
(2) Locatio.

Bailments are sometimes classified as:
(1) Gratuitous.
(a) Bailments for bailor's sole benefit.
(b) Bailments for bailee's sole benefit.
(2) Nongratuitous.
(a) Bailments for mutual benefit of bailor and bailee.

This classification begins where that of the Roman law ends. It seeks not merely to enumerate or catalogue, but also to arrange, the enumerated classes according to some rational scheme, showing the relations of each class to the others. A basis of classification is therefore sought, not merely because it is arbitrary or convenient, but because it in itself determines the differences and similarities in the legal incidents which the law attaches to bailments of the classes in question. This basis is found in the practical theory of benefit.

Every bailment is created for the sole purpose of benefit to the parties to the transaction. The duties and responsibilities imposed by law upon the bailor or bailee, as the case may be, are accordingly determined by, and are in proportion to, the benefit which such party receives from the bailment. A necessarily exhaustive classification on this theory is therefore made by dividing bailments on the score of benefit into three classes: (a) When the bailor alone receives such benefit. (b) When the bailee alone receives the benefit. (c) When both the bailor and the bailee receive a benefit.

This classification is consistent with that of the Roman law, and no class under the scheme of benefit, cuts across any single class enumerated in the Roman scheme. A comparison of the two classifications will show that the "depositum" and "mandatum" confer a benefit on the bailor alone, so they are both (a) bailments for the bailor's sole benefit; the "commodatum" bestows benefit solely on the bailee, so that it falls under (b) bailments for the bailee's sole benefit; the "pignus" and "locatio" contemplate a benefit to both parties to the relation, and they are therefore included under (c) bailments for the mutual benefit of both the bailor and bailee.

Gratuitous and Nongratuitous Bailments

Bailments are sometimes classified as (1) gratuitous and (2) nongratuitous. By gratuitous is meant gratuitous, on the score of benefit, as to either party. Gratuitous bailments, therefore include (a) bailments for the bailor's sole benefit and (b) bailments for the bailee's sole benefit. Nongratuitous bailments are (c) bailments for the mutual benefit of both the bailor and bailee.

As the general classification of bailments into three great classes on the score of benefit forms the analysis in accordance with which the whole subject of bailments is developed in this book, no further comment on this classification is here required.

CLASSIFICATION OF LOCATIO OPERIS BAILMENTS AS ORDINARY AND EXTRAORDINARY

6. Locatio operis bailments, or hired services about a thing, are sometimes classified as:

(a) Ordinary bailments.

(b) Extraordinary or exceptional bailments.

(1) Innkeepers.

(2) Common carriers of goods.

(3) Post office department.

Generally, the question of benefit alone determines the rights and duties of the parties to the bailment relation. There are some bailments, however, in which other considerations enter into this problem. These are bailments of such a character that they are public in their nature and are so closely connected with the interests of the public that the law has seen fit to single such bailments out and to affix distinctive and unusual rights and duties to the relation.

Thus the innkeeper and common carrier of goods, in professing to serve all who properly apply, pursue a public calling, while the post office department, charged with the transportation of the mails, is a branch of the government. Public policy, therefore, demands in such cases exceptional standards of responsibility not imposed on ordinary bailees. These unique considerations have thus set apart the innkeeper, common carrier of goods, and the post office department. They are therefore made the subject of separate treatment.

7. GRAPHIC CHART

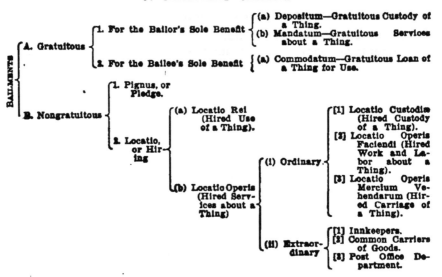

BAILMENTS
- A. Gratuitous
  - 1. For the Bailor's Sole Benefit
    - (a) Depositum—Gratuitous Custody of a Thing.
    - (b) Mandatum—Gratuitous Services about a Thing.
  - 2. For the Bailee's Sole Benefit
    - (a) Commodatum—Gratuitous Loan of a Thing for Use.
- B. Nongratuitous
  - 1. Pignus, or Pledge.
  - 2. Locatio, or Hiring
    - (a) Locatio Rei (Hired Use of a Thing).
    - (b) Locatio Operis (Hired Services about a Thing)
      - (i) Ordinary
        - [1] Locatio Custodiæ (Hired Custody of a Thing).
        - [2] Locatio Operis Faciendi (Hired Work and Labor about a Thing).
        - [3] Locatio Operis Mercium Vehendarum (Hired Carriage of a Thing).
      - (ii) Extraordinary
        - [1] Innkeepers.
        - [2] Common Carriers of Goods.
        - [3] Post Office Department.

CHAPTER II

GENERAL PRINCIPLES COMMON TO ALL BAILMENTS

INTRODUCTORY

8. There are certain circumstances, as we have seen, that are essential to the existence of a bailment, just as there are certain legal incidents or general principles that are common to all bailments.

In addition, the law prescribes certain rights and duties as inhering in the notion of a bailment; but these rights and duties may be varied at will by the agreement of the parties, provided this agreement is not in contravention of positive law or a sound public policy.

It is the purpose of the present chapter to discuss the circumstances essential to the existence of a bailment, the general principles of law common to all bailments, and finally the rights and duties of the parties to a bailment, when these rights and duties are not enlarged or diminished by special contract.

The very definition of a bailment implies that there are certain essential features that are present in all bailments and that the presence of all these features makes the relation a bailment, as distinguished from the various other relations known to the law The plainest of common sense would therefore seem to demand that there should first be a discussion of the general properties that are found alike in all bailments, before we take up the unique features that distinguish one class of bailments from another. This not only makes for clearness and accuracy, but obviates the necessity of a repetition of these general features in the treatment of each of the various classes of bailments.

In addition, the law prescribes certain rights and duties as attaching to the bailor or bailee merely by virtue of the fact that they are parties to the bailment relation, unless the parties have themselves made some different provision for these rights and duties. Certain general observations on this subject, too, should precede any detailed treatment of the rights and duties of the bailor and bailee, as affected by the specific class to which the bailment in question belongs.

General Principles of Contract and Agency Apply

Bailments are in the great majority of instances, though not always, created by express contract.[1] In such cases, the general rules of contract apply and need no discussion here. Thus, as to the competency of the parties to contract,[2] the construction or validity[3] of the contract, the effect of fraud,[4] duress, etc., no unique considerations affect the application of the same general rules that would govern other classes of contracts.

Again, bailment contracts may be, and frequently are, made, not by the parties acting directly, but through the intervention of agents.[5] Here the usual rules of agency can be invoked and the bailment contract, just as any other contract, made in the name of the principal by the agent acting within the scope of his authority is just as binding on the principal as if made by him in person.[6] When the agent, however, accepting the goods, acts

1 Post, §§ 22, 33, 45, 71.

2 Eaton v. Eaton, 37 N. J. Law, 108, 18 Am. Rep. 716; Mutual Life Ins. Co. v. Hunt, 79 N. Y. 541; Fay v. Burditt, 81 Ind. 433, 42 Am. Rep. 142; Scanlan v. Cobb, 85 Ill. 296; Shoulters v. Allen, 51 Mich. 531, 16 N. W. 888; Hagebush v. Ragland, 78 Ill. 40.

3 Singar Manuf'g Co. v. Converse, 23 Colo. 247, 47 Pac. 264; Newhall v. Paige, 10 Gray (Mass.) 366.

4 Camp v. Dill, 27 Ala. 553.

5 City Bank of New Haven v. Perkins, 29 N. Y. 554, 86 Am. Dec. 332; Brown v. Warren, 43 N. H. 430; Boynton v. Payrow, 67 Me. 587; McCready v. Haslock, 3 Tenn. Ch. 13; Lloyd v. Barden, 3 Strob. (S. C.) 343.

6 Scranton v. Baxter, 4 Sandf. (N. Y.) 5; Blake v. Kimball, 106 Mass. 115, 116; Stevens v. Boston & M. R., 1 Gray (Mass.) 277; Macklin v. Frazier, 9 Bush (Ky.) 3; Schouler, Bailm. (2d Ed.) §§ 19, 30, 33; Story, Bailm. § 55; First Nat. Bank of Carlisle v. Graham, 79 Pa. 106, 21 Am. Rep. 49. In the case of Lloyd v. Barden, 3 Strob. (S. C.) 343, it was held that, to charge a bailee with an article lost, it is not necessary that, in every case, the delivery should have been to him individually, or to one expressly or specifically authorized to receive for him; but an agency to receive may be implied in the same manner as such agency may be implied in relation to articles which were to be carried for hire. "The master and owner of a house or warehouse, allowing his servants or clerks to receive for custody the goods of another, and

without authority, the agent himself is then the bailee, and the principal is not bound by the transaction.[7]

Infant Bailees

The subject of parties as bailees who are incompetent to contract requires brief mention here. The typical and most important case is that of an infant. An infant's contracts are, as a rule, voidable at his option,[8] and the bailment contract is no exception to this rule. When the bailment is not one created by contract, as when one finds lost goods and takes them into his possession, the infant may become a bailee by the same acts as a person sui juris.

Again, the infant is liable for his torts.[9] This raises the interesting and often difficult question of the liability of the infant under a bailment created by contract. As to mere failure to carry out the terms of the contract, or even a breach of the bailment contract as a contract, the infant can escape liability by pleading infancy.[10] Further, so long as he keeps within the terms of the bailment, using the bailed chattel only for the purposes agreed on, the infant is not liable for any loss or damage due merely to his want of skill or experience provided he has no wrongful intent.[11]

But it is said that the disability of the infant is to be used by him as a shield and not as a sword. Accordingly, when the infant de-

especially if the practice be general and unlimited, as is the case with banks in relation to special deposits, will be considered the bailee of the goods so received, and will incur the duties and liabilities belonging to that relation. Not so if the servant, secretly, and without the knowledge, express or implied, of the master, he not having authorized or submitted to the practice, receives the goods for such purpose; for no man can be made the bailee of another's property without his consent." Parker, C. J., in Foster v. President, etc., of Essex Bank, 17 Mass. 479, 498, 9 Am. Dec. 168. And see Merchants' Nat. Bank v. State Nat. Bank, 10 Wall. (U. S.) 604, 650, 19 L. Ed. 1008; Elliot v. Abbot, 12 N. H. 549, 37 Am. Dec. 227; Farrar v. Gilman, 19 Me. 440, 36 Am. Dec. 766; McHenry v. Ridgely, 2 Scam. (Ill.) 309, 35 Am. Dec. 110; Everett v. United States, 6 Port. (Ala.) 166, 30 Am. Dec. 584.

7 Meech v. Smith, 7 Wend. (N. Y.) 315. See, also, Foster v. President, etc., of Essex Bank, 17 Mass. 479, 9 Am. Dec. 168.

8 Whitney v. Dutch, 14 Mass. 457, 7 Am. Dec. 229; Sanger v. Hibbard, 104 Fed. 455, 43 C. C. A. 635; Lansing v. Michigan Cent. R. Co., 126 Mich. 663, 86 N. W. 147, 86 Am. St. Rep. 567. For extended collection of cases, see 22 Cyc. p. 620.

9 Vasse v. Smith, 6 Cranch, 226, 3 L. Ed. 207; Saum v. Coffelt, 79 Va. 510; Sikes v. Johnson, 16 Mass. 389; cases collected 22 Cyc. 618, 619.

10 Caswell v. Parker, 96 Me. 39, 51 Atl. 238; Prescott v. Norris, 32 N. H. 101; Slayton v. Barry, 175 Mass. 513, 56 N. E. 574, 49 L. R. A. 560, 78 Am. St. Rep. 510; Monumental Bldg. Ass'n No. 2 v. Herman, 33 Md. 128.

11 Stack v. Cavanaugh, 67 N. H. 149, 30 Atl. 350; Young v. Muhling, 48 App. Div. 617, 63 N. Y. Supp. 181; CHURCHILL v. WHITE, 58 Neb. 22, 78 N. W. 369, 76 Am. St. Rep. 64, Dobie Cas. Bailments and Carriers, 19; Hill v. Becker, 9 Ky. Law Rep. 619.

parts from the purpose for which the bailment was created and to that extent exercises an unlawful dominion over the bailed chattel, he is then guilty of the tort of conversion and his infancy is no defense.[12] Thus an infant, hiring a horse to go to one place, who goes on a much longer journey to another place, is liable in spite of his infancy.[13] Again, for his willful and intentional wrong in beating or otherwise misusing the horse which he had hired, the infant would also be responsible.[14] Nor would a plea of infancy excuse the infant bailee's refusal to surrender the bailed chattel after the termination of the bailment.[15]

Corporations and Partnerships

It is probably already true, or at least soon will be, that in a majority of concrete cases the bailor or bailee is a corporation. The corporation, acting within its corporate powers, has the fullest right to become either a bailor or bailee.[16] Here, of course, resort must be had to the large body of legal doctrines governing these artificial entities that we call corporations.

Partnerships, in a sense, stand midway between individual persons and corporations. Here again the partnership may become a bailor or bailee, with the rights and duties thereto attached.[17] The law of partnership is thus called into play, probably most frequently, in determining here, as elsewhere, to what extent the acts of one of the partners are binding in the partnership.

Liability of the Parties under Special Contract

As we have seen, the law affixes certain rights and duties to the bailment relation, when the parties have not themselves made provisions on the subject.[18] These rights and duties, though, are peculiarly within the control of the bailor and bailee, who may by their contract enlarge or diminish them at will, subject only to the

12 Freeman v. Bowland, 14 R. I. 39, 51 Am. Rep. 340.

13 Towne v. Wiley, 23 Vt. 355, 56 Am. Dec. 85.

14 Moore v. Eastman, 1 Hun (N. Y.) 578; Campbell v. Stakes, 2 Wend. (N. Y.) 137, 19 Am. Dec. 561. See, also, CHURCHILL v. WHITE, 58 Neb. 22, 78 N. W. 369, 76 Am. St. Rep. 64, Dobie Cas. Bailments and Carriers, 19.

15 Eaton v. Hill, 50 N. H. 235, 9 Am. Rep. 189; CHURCHILL v. WHITE, 58 Neb. 22, 78 N. W. 369, 76 Am. St. Rep. 64, Dobie Cas. Bailments and Carriers, 19.

16 Duncomb v. New York, H. & N. R. Co., 84 N. Y. 190; Baldwin v. Canfield, 26 Minn. 43, 1 N. W. 261, 276; Lloyd v. West Branch Bank, 15 Pa. 172, 53 Am. Dec. 581; Combination Trust Co. v. Weed (C. C.) 2 Fed. 24; Chouteau v. Allen, 70 Mo. 290; Lehman v. Tallassee Manuf'g Co 64 Ala. 567.

17 George v. Tate, 102 U. S. 564, 26 L. Ed. 232; Hopkins v. Thomas, 61 Mich. 389, 28 N. W. 147.

18 Story, Bailm. § 10; President, etc., of Conway Bank v. American Exp. Co., 8 Allen (Mass.) 512, 516.

limitation that this contract must not be illegal or against public policy.[19]

Questions in this connection are concerned chiefly with how far the bailee may by contract restrict his liability; the law does not prevent him from thus enlarging it indefinitely.[20] That a bailee would not be permitted by special contract to exempt himself from liability for his fraud or its equivalent, is perfectly clear.[21] The same would also be true as to his active wrongdoing. Nor could he thus contravene a well-settled rule of law, as, for example, by attempting to stipulate that he would not be liable for the acts of his agents, even though committed within the scope of their authority.[22]

The question of the greatest difficulty is whether a bailee may validly contract against responsibility for his negligence, or failure to exercise the proper degree of care, varying in the different classes of bailments, ordinarily imposed upon him by law. That the common carrier[23] and innkeeper,[24] who pursue public callings, cannot do this, is well settled. It would seem, though, that an ordinary bailee may thus relieve himself of responsibility for his negligence,[25] or mere negative failure to exercise a specific degree of care, as distinguished from his fraud or active wrongdoing.

19 Ames v. Belden, 17 Barb. (N. Y.) 515; Kettle v. Bromsall, Willes, 118; Trefftz v. Canelli, L. R. 4 P. C. 277; Parker v. Tiffany, 52 Ill. 286; Remick v. Atkinson, 11 N. H. 256, 35 Am. Dec. 493; Vaughan v. Webster, 5 Har. (Del.) 256. But see, as to a carrier's contract to carry "safely," Austin v. Manchester, S. & L. Ry. Co., 5 Eng. Law & Eq. 329; Shaw v. York & N. M. Ry. Co., 13 Q. B. 347; Wells v. Steam Nav. Co., 8 N. Y. 375; Pennsylvania R. Co. v. McCloskey's Adm'r, 23 Pa. 526. The liability of a bailee, however, is not to be enlarged or restricted by words of doubtful meaning. The intent to vary the liability imposed by law must clearly appear. Trefftz v. Canelli, L. R. 4 P. C. 277; Belden v. Perkins, 78 Ill. 449.

20 Sturm v. Boker, 150 U. S. 312, 14 Sup. Ct. 99, 37 L. Ed. 1093; Reinstein v. Watts, 84 Me. 139, 24 Atl. 719; Rohrabacher v. Ware, 37 Iowa, 85.

21 Story, Bailm. § 32; Hollister v. Nowlen, 19 Wend. (N. Y.) 234, 32 Am. Dec. 455; Coffield v. Harris, 2 Willson, Civ. Cas. Ct. App. (Tex.) § 315; Alexander v. Greene, 3 Hill (N. Y.) 9.

22 Peet v. Railway Co., 10 H. L. Cas. (Eng.) 473, 494.

23 Post, p. 393.

24 Post, § 98.

25 The ordinary bailee is under no legal duty to enter upon the bailment, and, being able to refuse, should be allowed to prescribe his terms, unless, as indicated, he seeks to escape from his fraud or active wrong. Gashweiler v. Wabash, St. L. & P. Ry. Co., 83 Mo. 112, 53 Am. Rep. 558; Wells v. Steam Nav. Co., 8 N. Y. 375, Alexander v. Greene, 3 Hill (N. Y.) 9. Contra, Lancaster County Nat. Bank v. Smith, 62 Pa. 47. On this subject, see also 1 Hutchinson on Carriers, § 40; Bridwell v. Moore, 8 Ky. Law Rep. 535; Memphis & C. R. Co. v. Jones, 2 Head (Tenn.) 517; Coffield v. Harris, 2 Willson, Civ. Cas. Ct. App. (Tex.) § 315.

BAILMENT OF PERSONALTY ONLY

9. The subject-matter of the bailment must be personalty.

Personal property alone can be the subject-matter of a bailment. There can be no bailment of real estate.[26] The relation, in the realm of real property, corresponding to that of bailment in personal property, is that of landlord and tenant, created by a lease; but, owing to striking differences between real and personal property, the two relations present many differences in legal effect.

There are expressions in some of the early cases to the effect that only corporeal personal property could be the subject-matter of a bailment. It is now well settled, however, that there may be a bailment of incorporeal as well as corporeal personalty, of choses in action as well as of choses in possession.[27] Thus there may be a bailment of negotiable notes, bonds, corporate stock, and insurance policies, as well as of horses, watches, or furniture.[28]

Since a bailment requires first a delivery of the goods to the bailee, there can be, technically speaking, no such thing as a bailment of goods not yet in existence.[29] There may be, however, a valid present contract to create a future bailment in goods not then in existence. The bailment relation might then attach to the goods when they did come into existence,[30] subject, perhaps, to the rights of third persons in the goods which may have intervened.

[26] A bailment can exist only as to a chattel, not as to realty. Williams v. Jones, 3 Hurl. & C. 256; Coupledike v. Coupledike, Cro. Jac. 39. And cf. Dewey v. Bowman, 8 Cal. 145.

[27] McLean v. Walker, 10 Johns. (N. Y.) 471; Jarvis v. Rogers, 15 Mass. 389; White v. Phelps, 14 Minn. 27 (Gil. 21), 100 Am. Dec. 190; Appleton v. Donaldson, 3 Pa. 381; Loomis v. Stave, 72 Ill. 623; Cowdrey v. Vandenburgh, 101 U. S. 572, 25 L. Ed. 923. Any kind of personal property, including current money and even a chose in action, if in existence, may be the subject of a bailment. Van Wagoner v. Buckley, 148 App. Div. 808, 133 N. Y. Supp. 599.

[28] Hanna v. Holton, 78 Pa. 334, 21 Am. Rep. 20; Walker v. Staples, 5 Allen (Mass.) 34; Shaw v. Wilshire, 65 Me. 485; Hudson v. Wilkinson, 45 Tex. 444; In re Rawson, 2 Low. 519, Fed. Cas. No. 4,837; Biebinger v. Continental Bank, 99 U. S. 143, 25 L. Ed. 271. Bailments of such property are usually pledges and will be discussed at length under that subject. Post, p. 187.

[29] Gittings v. Nelson, 86 Ill. 591; Smithurst v. Edmunds, 14 N. J. Eq. 408.

[30] Story, Bailm. § 294. Thus, in Macomber v. Parker, 14 Pick. (Mass.) 497, a brickmaker agreed with the lessees of a brickyard in which he was manufacturing bricks that they should hold the bricks to be made as security for money advanced by them. It was held that the bricks were pledged as fast as made. See, also, Cushman v. Hayes, 46 Ill. 145; Smithurst v. Edmunds, 14 N. J. Eq. 408; Appeal of Collins, 107 Pa. 590, 52 Am. Rep. 479; Smith v. Atkins, 18 Vt. 461.

DELIVERY

10. To constitute a bailment, there must be a delivery, actual or constructive, of the goods or chattels.

The term "bailment" is derived from the Norman-French word "bailler," meaning to deliver. Though not every delivery creates a bailment, yet delivery remains the most important element both in the definition and in the practical aspect of a bailment. Delivery, or transfer of possession, is absolutely essential to the creation of the bailment.[31] Where there is no delivery, there can be no bailment. Delivery, therefore, marks the real inception of the bailment, which begins from the time when possession is transferred to the bailee. Accordingly, a mere executory contract to deliver goods, technically speaking, is alone no more effective in creating a bailment than is a mere agreement to marry in creating the marriage. Delivery thus is seen as more vivid and more real than any other aspect of the bailment.

Delivery may be either actual or constructive. Actual delivery contemplates the real physical transfer of the manual control of the goods or chattels by the bailor to the bailee.[32] Thus, where one places his razor in the hands of a barber to be sharpened and returned to him, this is an actual delivery about which there could be little question. A constructive delivery, in its broad sense, consists of such acts which, though falling short of actual delivery, are held, in the contemplation of the law, to be the equivalent of an actual delivery in legal effect.[33] Thus, when goods have been shipped by a carrier, the transfer of the document known as a "bill of lading," which stands for the goods, and is therefore legally equivalent to an actual delivery of the goods, is a constructive de-

[31] Trunick v. Smith, 63 Pa. 18; Houghton v. Lynch, 13 Minn. 85 (Gil. 80); Sherman v. Commercial Printing Co., 29 Mo. App. 31; Northcutt v. State, 60 Tex. Cr. R. 259, 131 S. W. 1128, 31 L. R. A. (N. S.) 822; Bertig v. Norman, 101 Ark. 75, 141 S. W. 201, Ann. Cas. 1913D, 943; Sherman v. Hicks, 14 N. M. 439, 94 Pac. 959.

[32] Owens v. Kinsey, 52 N. C. 245; Fletcher v. Ingram, 46 Wis. 191, 50 N. W. 424; Samuels v. McDonald, 33 N. Y. Super. Ct. 211.

[33] Story, Bailm. § 55; Whitaker v. Sumner, 20 Pick. (Mass.) 399; Tuxworth v. Moore, 9 Pick. (Mass.) 347, 20 Am. Dec. 479. The property may be regarded as in bailee's possession, without any actual removal, if it passes under bailee's exclusive control. Dillenback v. Jerome, 7 Cow. (N. Y.) 294; Blake v. Kimball, 106 Mass. 115. See, also, Schneider v. Dayton, 111 Mich. 396, 69 N. W. 829.

livery.[34] So, also, when the seller of goods continues in possession of them with the buyer's consent, this is a constructive delivery, and is just as effective in making the seller a bailee as if the seller had actually delivered the goods to the buyer, who, in turn, actually redelivered them to the seller.[35]

Actual delivery is, of course, the most perfect form known to the law, and is always the safest. But such a delivery is in many cases either impossible or at least impracticable. In such cases constructive delivery is frequently resorted to. Modern decisions show an increasing tendency to regard constructive delivery with favor and to extend its meaning, particularly when the rights of innocent third parties are not thereby jeopardized. The always prominent question of delivery becomes specially important in pledges, where it is treated, particularly as to certain classes of incorporeal property, at some length.

The control which a servant exercises over the goods of his master, with the latter's consent, does not make the servant a bailee of the goods. The master is here treated as being still in possession of the goods, and the servant's control, falling short of an independent possession, is designated as mere custody. Thus, a butler cleaning his master's silver has merely the custody of the silver, possession still remaining in the master. The question whether a person exercising a measure of control over the goods of another, is a bailee having possession or a servant with mere custody becomes highly important in distinguishing between the common-law crime of larceny and the statutory crime of embezzlement.[36]

ACCEPTANCE

11. A great majority of bailments (though not all) are created by mutual contract of the parties. In every bailment, though, there must be an express or implied acceptance by the bailee of the goods constituting the subject-matter of the bailment.

34 Post, pp. 196, 211–214, 418. 35 Oakley v. State, 40 Ala. 372.

36 See Clark & Marshall on Crimes, §§ 316–317; Rex v. Harvey, 9 Car. & P. 353; Jenkins v. State, 62 Wis. 49, 21 N. W. 232; United States v. Clew, 4 Wash. C. C. 700, Fed. Cas. No. 14819. One holding as servant for another is not bailee. COMMONWEALTH v. MORSE, 14 Mass. 217, Dobie Cas. Bailments and Carriers, 51; Dillenback v. Jerome, 7 Cow. (N. Y.) 294; Ludden v. Leavitt, 9 Mass. 104, 6 Am. Dec. 45; Warren v. Leland, 9 Mass. 265; Waterman v. Robinson, 5 Mass. 303.

Bailment Not Always Created by Contract

While in the overwhelming majority of instances the bailment relation is founded on the mutual agreement of both the bailor and bailee, in exceptional cases bailments may exist without such an agreement. One may become a constructive bailee in the absence of any contract between the parties.[37] It is not essential that the bailee should have obtained possession by the consent of the owner, or even with the intention of holding the goods as a bailee. But, in many cases, the law, from considerations of public policy, imposes the liability of a bailee upon one who has, without private agreement, come into possession of the goods of another.

Thus, the finder of lost goods, who takes them into his possession, becomes a bailee of the goods.[38] A sheriff, levying on the goods of the debtor and taking possession of them, is also a bailee.[39] The same would be true of marine salvors [40] of goods, and also of one who received and retained possession of goods addressed to another.[41] Many writers, in such instances, say that the consent of the parties is implied and that there is thus a contract. The owner might well prefer that the goods should remain lost rather than that they should come into the hands of the particular person who found them. The finder, too, may have been in ignorance of the fact that he had incurred the duties of a bailee. To say that the law, under certain circumstances, imposes an affirma-

[37] Post, §§ 22, 45. A contract inter partes is not essential to a bailment; but it is the element of lawful possession, however created, and duty to account for the thing as the property of another, that creates the bailment. Burns v. State, 145 Wis. 373, 128 N. W. 987, 140 Am. St. Rep. 1081.

[38] One who finds a thing is not compelled to assume its custody; but, if he voluntarily does so, he will be held by the law to be a depositary, and must exercise the care due from such a bailee. In Cory v. Little, 6 N. H. 213, 25 Am. Dec. 458, it was held that one who finds a horse wrongfully in his field may turn it into the highway; and, if it stray away, he will not be responsible for it. In Isaack v. Clark, 2 Bulst. 306, Lord Coke said: "If a man finds goods, an action on the case lies for his ill and negligent keeping of them, but not trover or conversion, because this is but a nonfeasance." According to St. Germain (Doct. & Stud. Dial. 2, c. 38), "if a man finds goods of another, if they be after hurt or lost by willful negligence, he shall be charged to the owner. But, if they be lost by other casualty, * * * I think he be discharged." As to this point, see Dougherty v. Posegate, 3 Iowa, 88; Merry v. Green, 7 Mees. & W. 623, 631; People v. Cogdell, 1 Hill (N. Y.) 94, 37 Am. Dec. 297; People v. Anderson, 14 Johns. (N. Y.) 294, 7 Am. Dec. 462.

[39] Phillips v. Bridge, 11 Mass. 242; Tyler v. Ulmer, 12 Mass. 163; Blake v. Kimball, 106 Mass. 115, 116; Parrott v. Dearborn, 104 Mass. 104; Jenner v. Joliffe, 6 Johns. (N. Y.) 9; Burke v. Trevitt, 1 Mason, 96, 100, Fed. Cas. No. 2,163.

[40] Post, § 45.

[41] Newhall v. Paige, 10 Gray (Mass.) 366.

tive duty upon a person does not necessarily mean that he agrees to perform that duty. An obligation is hardly contractual when imposed without the consent of the parties. It therefore seems a perversion of language to say, in cases such as that indicated, that a bailment is always the result of a contract.

Acceptance by the Bailee

There must, however, be an acceptance by the bailee of the goods forming the subject-matter of the bailment, before there can be any bailment.[42] The law does not insistently thrust the liabilities of a bailee upon one without his knowledge or consent. Such acceptance may be express or implied, but until there is something to show notice or knowledge, until the facts, at least, are known by the person, the law will not constitute him a bailee.[43]

Thus, where goods come into one's possession without his knowledge, he is in no sense a bailee; but if, after acquiring such knowledge, he continues in possession of the goods, the law imposes on him the duties of a bailee in regard to such goods. Accordingly, when a man puts goods in the wagon of another, and the latter drives away, in ignorance of the presence of the goods on his wagon, he is not a bailee of such goods, nor responsible as such. As soon, though, as he discovers the goods, by continuing in possession of them he becomes, in the eyes of the law, a bailee, with the attendant responsibility of a bailee imposed upon him. Again, one seeing a lost watch in the road may pass it by without incurring any responsibility, but by voluntarily taking the watch into his possession, he becomes chargeable as a bailee.[44]

One is not made a bailee against his will or without his consent. Such consent, however, is easily implied when, with his knowledge, the goods of another come into his possession. Indeed, it may be laid down as a general rule that whenever a person knowingly acquires possession of goods, unaccompanied by any right of owner-

[42] Bohannon v. Springfield, 9 Ala. 789; Delaware, L. & W. R. Co. v. Central S. Y. & T. Co., 45 N. J. Eq. 50, 17 Atl. 146, 6 L. R. A. 855; Lloyd v. West Branch Bank, 15 Pa. 172, 53 Am. Dec. 581; Bunnell v. Stern, 122 N. Y. 539, 25 N. E. 910, 10 L. R. A. 481, 19 Am. St. Rep. 519.

[43] Where goods are placed in a carrier's possession without his knowledge or consent, there can be no contract of bailment. Where one checked his trunk on a railway as baggage, paying no compensation therefor except his fare as a passenger, and giving no notice that it contained valuable and costly merchandise, it was held that the want of fair dealing on his part was a full answer to any action upon any implied contract of bailment for hire. Michigan Cent. R. Co. v. Carrow, 73 Ill. 348, 24 Am. Rep. 248. See, also, Sherman v. Hicks, 14 N. M. 439, 94 Pac. 959; Bertig v. Norman, 101 Ark. 75, 141 S. W. 201, Ann. Cas. 1913D, 943.

[44] See note 38, supra.

ship, such acquiring of possession is equivalent to an implied consent, and the law will impose upon such person in possession of the goods the liabilities of a bailee.[45]

WHAT TITLE BAILOR MUST HAVE

12. If the bailor has a special property in, or even lawful possession of, the goods, this is sufficient title to support the bailment.

In order that one may make a valid bailment of a thing, it is not essential that he shall be the owner of it. If the bailor has what is known as a special property in goods, or even lawful possession thereof, this is sufficient. For a bailment requires the transfer, not of ownership, but merely of possession. Accordingly, to create a bailment, it is necessary only that the bailor have a possession that he can transfer to the bailee.

Thus, the finder of lost goods does not, by such finding, acquire the ownership of such goods, yet he has such a possessory right as will enable him to keep the goods as against all but the rightful owner, and the finder may make, subject to the rights of the owner, a valid bailment of the goods.[46] One holding goods without title and wrongfully may make a bailment of them, valid save as against the real owner, and as between the bailor and bailee the rights and duties of the bailment relation would attach;[47] or, as against all but the owner, even a thief may make a bailment of stolen goods, and, since the bailee is estopped to deny his bailor's title, the bailee would, as between the bailor and bailee, be compelled to restore the goods to his bailor, the thief.

[45] Schouler, Bailm. (2d Ed.) § 3; Wolf v. Shannon, 50 Ill. App. 396; Jones v. Maxwell, 1 Lack. Leg. N. (Pa.) 191.

[46] Thus, in the case of Armory v. Delamirie, 1 Strange, 505, it appeared that a boy found a jewel, and took it to a jeweler's shop, to find what it was. The jeweler refused to return the jewel, and, in an action in trover, it was held that the finder of a chattel, though he does not by such finding acquire an absolute property or ownership, yet he has such a property as will enable him to keep it against all but the rightful owner, and consequently he may maintain trover. And see Rooth v. Wilson, 1 Barn. & Ald. 59. The finder of a bank note, as against a bailee to whom he delivers it, has such a possessory interest in the note as entitles him to recover it from the bailee, in the absence of any claim by the rightful owner. Tancil v. Seaton, 28 Grat. (Va.) 601, 26 Am. Rep. 380.

[47] Taylor v. Plumer, 3 Maule & S. (Eng.) 562; Learned v. Bryant, 13 Mass. 224.

INTEREST OF BAILOR AND BAILEE IN THE BAILED GOODS

13. The general property or ownership in the bailed goods remains in the bailor, while the bailee acquires at least a possessory interest, and in many cases a special property, in such goods.

Bailor's Interest

A bailment is a transfer of possession unaccompanied by ownership. The person owning the goods before the bailment therefore continues to own them afterwards. Since the ownership of the goods remains unaffected by the bailment, the bailor, if he was, as is usually the case, the owner of the goods, continues to bear that relation toward them.[48] Indeed, as we have already seen, particularly in distinguishing a bailment from a sale, the severance of ownership and possession is of the very essence of the bailment. This ownership is an independent property right which the bailor, even without the bailee's consent, may freely transfer to a third person.[49] Such third person, however, would acquire the ownership, just as the bailor held it, subject to all the rights of the bailee. This ownership of the bailor is, of course, unaffected by any wrongful disposal of the goods by the bailee to a third person.[50] For the bailor could, in such a case, assert his ownership against the third person with as much force as he could against the bailee. This ownership, consisting of the residuary right in the goods remaining after the rights of the bailee are

[48] Story, Bailm. § 93; Henry v. Patterson, 57 Pa. 346, 352; Prichett v. Cook, 62 Pa. 193; Laflin & R. Powder Co. v. Burkhardt, 97 U. S. 110, 24 L. Ed. 973.

[49] And notice to the bailee of such transfer of title is a sufficient constructive delivery to hold the property as against attaching creditors of the bailor, or one claiming as a bona fide purchaser. Erwin v. Arthur, 61 Mo. 386; Gerber v. Monie, 56 Barb. (N. Y.) 652. Thus, where the owner of a lot of cotton in the hands of the surveyor of a port, seized by him, to await an examination in regard to charges, sold the same, and gave his vendee an order on the surveyor for the cotton, and also notified the surveyor of such sale, it was held that such action on the part of the vendor passed all his rights to his vendee, who could maintain an action of replevin for the cotton, as against a subsequent attaching creditor of his vendor, whether the surveyor had consented or not to the delivery, after the termination of his own right of possession. Hodges v. Hurd, 47 Ill. 363.

[50] Benner v. Puffer, 114 Mass. 376; Austin v. Dye, 46 N. Y. 500; Davis v. Bigler, 62 Pa. 242, 1 Am. Rep. 393; Baehr v. Clark, 83 Iowa, 313, 49 N. W. 840, 13 L. R. A. 717.

satisfied, the bailor may also protect by appropriate action, when it is wrongfully interfered with either by the bailee or by third parties.[51]

Bailee's Interest

The bailee acquires, by virtue of the bailment, an interest in the goods bailed that amounts at least to a possessory right or interest.[52] In many cases, the bailee's interest rises to the dignity of a special property in the goods, which is a right against the goods, an in rém claim, which he can assert as against all the world, including the bailor.[53]

Even when the bailee's interest is only a mere possessory right, this constitutes what is known in fire insurance as an insurable interest upon which a valid policy may be taken out. The bailee, too, can protect by appropriate action his interest against wrongful interference.[54] As the nature of this interest, as well as the ap-

[51] Strong v. Adams, 30 Vt. 221, 73 Am. Dec. 305. And see BURDICT v. MURRAY, 3 Vt. 302, 21 Am. Dec. 588, Dobie Cas. Bailments and Carriers, 84; Root v. Chandler, 10 Wend. (N. Y.) 110, 25 Am. Dec. 546; Cannon v. Kinney, 3 Scam. (Ill.) 9; Long v. Bledsoe, 3 J. J. Marsh. (Ky.) 307; Overby v. McGee, 15 Ark. 459, 63 Am. Dec. 49; Walker v. Wilkinson, 35 Ala. 725, 76 Am. Dec. 315; White v. Brantley, 37 Ala. 430; Lotan v. Cross, 2 Camp. 464. Where the bailor is entitled to possession at any time, he may maintain trespass against a third person for injury to the bailed property. Walcot v. Pomeroy, 2 Pick. (Mass.) 121; Bradley v. Davis, 14 Me. 44, 47, 30 Am. Dec. 729; Dallam v. Fitler, 6 Watts & S. (Pa.) 323, 325; Staples v. Smith, 48 Me. 470; Hart v. Hyde, 5 Vt. 328; Freeman v. Rankins, 21 Me. 446; Gauche v. Mayer, 27 Ill. 134; Shloss v. Cooper, 27 Vt. 623; Hayward Rubber Co. v. Duncklee, 30 Vt. 29; Holly v. Huggeford, 8 Pick. (Mass.) 73, 19 Am. Dec. 303. See post, §§ 28, 39, 48, 61. But, when the bailment is for a definite time, the bailor cannot maintain trespass, because he has no right to possession until the expiration of such period. Walcot v. Pomeroy, 2 Pick. (Mass.) 121, 122; Muggridge v. Eveleth, 9 Metc. (Mass.) 233; Lunt v. Brown, 13 Me. 236; Lewis v. Carsaw, 15 Pa. 31; Hume v. Tufts, 6 Blackf. (Ind.) 136; Putnam v. Wyley, 8 Johns. (N. Y.) 432, 5 Am. Dec. 346; Bell v. Monahan, Dud. (S. C.) 38, 31 Am. Dec. 548; McFarland v. Smith, Walk. (Miss.) 172; Lacoste v. Pipkin, 13 Smedes & M. (Miss.) 589; Soper v. Sumner, 5 Vt. 274; Clark v. Carlton, 1 N. H. 110; WILSON v. MARTIN, 40 N. H. 88, Dobie Cas. Bailments and Carriers, 85; Corfield v. Coryell, 4 Wash. C. C. 371, Fed. Cas. No. 3,230; Ward v. McCauley, 4 Term R. 489.

[52] Smith v. Jones, 8 Ark. 109; COMMONWEALTH v. MORSE, 14 Mass. 217, Dobie Cas. Bailments and Carriers, 51; Sibley v. Story, 8 Vt. 15.

[53] The question of when the bailee has a mere possessory interest in the bailed chattels and when a special property is discussed in detail as to the various classes of bailments.

[54] Shaw v. Kaler, 106 Mass. 448; Hopper v. Miller, 76 N. C. 402; Knight v. Davis Carriage Co., 71 Fed. 662, 18 C. C. A. 287; CHAMBERLAIN v. WEST, 37 Minn. 54, 33 N. W. 114, Dobie Cas. Bailments and Carriers, 59; Walsh v. United States Tent & Awning Co., 153 Ill. App. 229.

propriate action by which it may be protected, varies in different bailments, an accurate discussion of this subject must be left to the detailed treatment of the various specific classes of bailments.

ESTOPPEL OF BAILEE TO DENY BAILOR'S TITLE

14. The bailee is estopped, by virtue of the bailment, from denying the title of the bailor at the time of the delivery of the goods to the bailee.

The bailee is not permitted to dispute the bailor's title, at the time of the delivery of the goods to him, by setting up in himself an adverse title to the goods as of that time.[55] The possession of the bailee was acquired from the bailor, and by thus assuming possession of the goods the bailee estops himself from setting up that he had title to the goods when he received them from the

[55] Plummer v. Hardison, 6 Ala. App. 525, 60 South. 502; Britton v. Aymar, 23 La. Ann. 63, 65; Peebles v. Farrar, 73 N. C. 342; Foltz v. Stevens, 54 Ill. 180; Maxwell v. Houston, 67 N. C. 305; Thompson v. Williams, 30 Kan. 114, 1 Pac. 47; Marvin v. Ellwood, 11 Paige (N. Y.) 365. Where one borrows property, without alleging any right to it, he is estopped from setting up a claim to it on behalf of his wife. Pulliam v. Burlingame, 81 Mo. 111, 51 Am. Rep. 229. See, also, Hentz v. The Idaho, 93 U. S. 575, 23 L. Ed. 978; Osgood v. Nichols, 5 Gray (Mass.) 420; Thompson v. Williams, 30 Kan. 114, 1 Pac. 47; Tribble v. Anderson, 63 Ga. 31; Shellhouse v. Field, 49 Ind. App. 659, 97 N. E. 940. For extended note on this subject, see 19 Ann. Cas. 521. The bailee sued by the bailor for conversion of the property cannot set up title of a third person thereto, except by authorization of that person. Bondy v. American Transfer Co., 15 Cal. App. 746, 115 Pac. 965. Where plaintiff acquired possession of a mileage book from defendant for the purpose of riding thereon, agreeing to return the balance of the mileage, plaintiff was estopped to deny his obligation to return the book to defendant because defendant was not the original purchaser, who was alone entitled to use the book for transportation. Cook v. Bartlett, 115 App. Div. 829, 100 N. Y. Supp. 1032. By the acceptance of a bailment the bailee admits the title of his bailor, and is estopped thereafter from disputing it. Atlantic & B. R. Co. v. Spires, 1 Ga. App. 22, 57 S. E. 973. In an action against a bailee for conversion, defendant is estopped from denying the title of his bailors, no paramount title having intervened. Barker v. S. A. Lewis Storage & Transfer Co., 79 Conn. 342, 65 Atl. 143, 118 Am. St. Rep. 141. A bailee is estopped to deny the bailor's title or ownership of the property bailed at the time of bailment, but is not estopped, when sued for conversion, from showing that the title held by the bailor at the time of bailment has been acquired by himself, or has passed to another. Shellhouse v. Field, 49 Ind. App. 659, 97 N. E. 940. While a bailee can in no case set up a claim in himself to the goods as against the bailor when the goods are claimed by a third person, he may refuse to deliver them at his peril. Atlantic & B. R. Co. v. Spires, 1 Ga. App. 22, 57 S. E. 973.

bailor. The bailee's very act of accepting possession from the bailor is in itself an admission of the bailor's title, which the bailee would not be permitted, while still holding possession, to deny by asserting title in himself.

A bailee may show, however, that, since the goods were delivered to him, the bailor has sold them to another. On a valid sale by the bailor, when the bailee has notice of the sale, the bailee must account to the buyer.[56] The rule that a bailee cannot attorn to a stranger has no application to such a case; the purchaser from the bailor is not a stranger. The estoppel extends only to a denial by the bailee that the bailor had title at the time he delivered the goods to the bailee. So, when a person borrowed a gun from another, thus becoming a bailee, and then such person afterwards refused to return the gun, claiming that it belonged to him when he borrowed it, it was held that such person, as a bailee, must first return the gun to his bailor before he could claim title to the gun in himself at the time the bailment was created.[57]

One claiming title to a chattel held by another cannot obtain possession of it under the guise of a bailment and then excuse himself from returning it by repudiating the bailment by virtue of which he acquired his possession and by setting up a hostile title to the chattel in himself. Having acquired his possession solely in the rôle of a bailee, he must continue in that rôle, and, as the rôle requires, surrender possession of the chattel to the bailor.

This estoppel is limited in time to the moment when the goods were delivered to the bailee.[58] Thus, though the bailee cannot claim that he was then the owner of the goods, he can claim that he acquired the ownership of the goods by virtue of a transfer by the bailor of such ownership to him at a period subsequent to the creation of the bailment; for this claim, instead of repudiating the bailor's title at the creation of the bailment, affirms that the bailor

[56] Roberts v. Noyes, 76 Me. 590; Marvin v. Ellwood, 11 Paige (N. Y.) 365; Smith v. Hammond, 6 Sim. 10; National Exch. Bank of Boston v. McLoon, 73 Me. 498, 40 Am. Rep. 388.

[57] SIMPSON v. WRENN, 50 Ill. 222, 99 Am. Dec. 511, Dobie Cas. Bailments and Carriers, 22. And see Bursley v. Hamilton, 15 Pick. (Mass.) 40, 25 Am. Dec. 423, where it was held that an owner of property giving a receipt for it to an officer who had seized it under process could not set up title in himself when sued by the officer without first restoring the property to the officer. Contra, Learned v. Bryant, 13 Mass. 224. It is said that a purchaser from the bailor has the same right as the bailor to assert the estoppel against the bailee.

[58] Roberts v. Noyes, 76 Me. 590; Burnett v. Fulton, 48 N. C. 486; Kingsman v. Kingsman (Eng.) 6 Q. B. D. 122; Marvin v. Ellwood, 11 Paige (N. Y.) 365.

had title even subsequent to this time, which title the bailee claims was transferred to him by the bailor.[59]

Again, the bailee may, of course, claim his full rights as a bailee against the bailor. When he has a special property in the goods, he may sue the bailor, and recover his possession of the goods, wrongly interrupted by the bailor.[60] The estoppel applies only when the bailee seeks to claim an interest beyond that of a bailee, as that of owner. In asserting his rights as the bailor's bailee, the bailee, instead of denying, is affirming the bailment and the fullest right of the bailor to create it.

Finally, in this connection, while the bailee cannot set up title for himself at the time of the inception of the bailment, he must, at his peril, respect the rights of third persons superior to those of his bailor. As we shall see, the bailee is an insurer as to delivery of the goods to the right person. Accordingly, when he has notice of the paramount claim of a third person, the bailee must deliver the goods to him and not to the bailor. Thus the estoppel, as of the time of the beginning of the bailment, is limited to the bailee's setting up title in himself adverse to the bailor; the estoppel does not apply, as of the same time, to the bailee's respecting, as he must, the paramount title of the third party brought to his notice.[61] There is no inconsistency between the rule that the bailee, having received possession from the bailor, cannot retain the possession thus gained by repudiating its source, and the rule that the adverse claimant or third party, as the real owner of the chattel, can disregard an unauthorized bailment as not being binding on him and can seize the chattel in the hands of the bailee.

[59] The bailee cannot, however, during the continuance of the bailment purchase the adverse outstanding title of a third person, and then set up such title before surrendering possession of the goods to the bailor. Nudd v. Montanye, 38 Wis. 511, 20 Am. Rep. 25.

[60] SIMPSON v. WRENN, 50 Ill. 222, 99 Am. Dec. 511, Dobie Cas. Bailments and Carriers, 22; BURDICT v. MURRAY, 3 Vt. 302, 21 Am. Dec. 588, Dobie Cas. Bailments and Carriers, 84.

[61] Hentz v. The Idaho, 93 U. S. 575, 23 L. Ed. 978; Mullins v. Chickering, 110 N. Y. 513, 18 N. E. 377, 1 L. R. A. 463; DAVIS v. DONOHOE-KELLY BANKING CO., 152 Cal. 282, 92 Pac. 639, Dobie Cas. Bailments and Carriers, 29; Atlantic & B. R. Co. v. Spires, 1 Ga. App. 22, 57 S. E. 973; Kelly v. Patchell, 5 W. Va. 585; Thompson v. Williams, 30 Kan. 114, 1 Pac. 47.

BAILOR MUST NOT EXPOSE BAILEE TO DANGER WITHOUT WARNING

15. It is the duty of the bailor to warn the bailee of any hidden defects in the articles bailed or any latent danger attendant upon the execution of the bailment, provided the bailor knows, or should have known, of such defect or danger.

The law places upon the bailor the duty of warning the bailee of any hidden defects in the bailed goods, or any latent danger involved in the bailment purpose, provided actual or constructive knowledge of such defect or danger can be attributed to the bailor.[62] The bailor must not knowingly expose the bailee without warning to dangers or perils of which the latter is ignorant. Thus, if the bailor of a horse, knowing the horse to be wild and vicious, fails to inform an ignorant bailee of this fact, the bailor is liable in damages to the bailee for injuries sustained by the bailee as a result of this dereliction of duty.[63]

It is sometimes said that the bailor is liable to the bailee for all damages sustained by the latter, without fault on his part, the proximate cause of which was the performance of the bailment purpose. This, however, is much too broad. No such liability is imposed on the bailor by the bailment contract, in the absence of a special stipulation. Nor does the law impose any such responsibility as inherent in the bailment relation. If the danger was clear to both parties, it is assumed by the bailee in undertaking the bailment. The same would be true if the bailee alone knew of the danger. If the danger was not known to the bailor, and there was no fault on his part in not knowing it, he incurs no such responsibility.

Accordingly, in the absence of knowledge, actual or constructive, of the defect or danger, the bailor incurs no responsibility for damages suffered by the bailee in executing the bailment.[64] The law is reasonable in not imposing upon the bailor the duty of disclosing

[62] Story, Bailm. §§ 390–391a; Hadley v. Cross, 34 Vt. 586, 80 Am. Dec. 699; Horne v. Meakin, 115 Mass. 326; Reading v. Price, 3 J. J. Marsh. (Ky.) 61, 19 Am. Dec. 162; Kissam v. Jones, 56 Hun, 432, 10 N. Y. Supp. 94.

[63] Story, Bailm. § 391a; Campbell v. Page, 67 Barb. (N. Y.) 113; Huntoon v. Trumbell (C. C.) 12 Fed. 844; Kissam v. Jones, 56 Hun, 432, 10 N. Y. Supp. 94. For note on liability of owner of vicious animals to disclose such propensities to bailee, see 18 Ann. Cas. 814.

[64] COPELAND v. DRAPER, 157 Mass. 558, 32 N. E. 944, 19 L. R. A. 283, and note, 34 Am. St. Rep. 314, Doble Cas. Bailments and Carriers, 25.

what he neither knows nor should know. In the absence, then, of a breach of duty, or a contract specially imposing liability on the bailor for damages resulting from the carrying out of the bailment purpose, what legal reason is there, or what consideration of public policy, for imposing on the bailor the unusual responsibility involved in the broad rule given above?

Hence, if neither party knows nor ought to know, there is no liability on the bailor. The same result follows when both parties know or ought to know, or when this is true of the bailee alone. The legal duty of disclosure, for a breach of which he is responsible, rests on the bailor only when he knows or ought to know, and the bailee neither knows nor ought to know.

CARE TO BE EXERCISED BY THE BAILEE

16. In performing the bailment purpose, the bailee must exercise due care, or that degree of care which is determined by, and commensurate with, the particular class to which the specific bailment belongs.

The degree of care which the bailee must exercise is, from a practical standpoint, by far the most important of the duties imposed by the law upon the bailee. In practice, the question is always considered in connection with the class of bailments under which the particular bailment falls. The subject is therefore discussed at some length under each class of bailments considered; but a brief discussion of some of the basic principles underlying the whole subject will not be out of order here.

When the point is not covered by a stipulation in the bailment contract the law imposes on the bailee in all ordinary bailments (as distinguished from extraordinary bailments) the duty of exercising due care. As due care is too indefinite, the law goes further and, in each of the three great classes of bailments classified in the score of benefit, sets up a more definite standard of care as applicable only to bailments of that class. When the class to which the particular bailment belongs is determined, the standard of care applicable to that class is fixed, and the question then asked is whether the bailee has fulfilled the duty imposed on him by law and exercised that particular degree of care.[65] If the ques-

[65] 2 Jagg. Torts, 88; Hall v. Chicago, B. & N. R. Co., 46 Minn. 439, 49 N. W. 239; Meredith v. Reed, 26 Ind. 334; Barnum v. Terpening, 75 Mich. 557, 42 N. W. 967; Grand Trunk R. Co. v. Ives, 144 U. S. 408, 12 Sup. Ct. 679, 36 L. Ed. 485; Michigan Cent. R. Co. v. Coleman, 28 Mich. 440; Pennsylvania

tion be answered in the affirmative, the bailee is not responsible for any loss or injury that occurs to the bailed goods, and such loss must fall on the bailor. If, however, the question be answered in the negative, the bailee is then guilty of a breach of a legal duty, and is therefore responsible to the bailor for all damages directly and proximately flowing from the breach.

As we have just seen, by classifying the bailment on the score of benefit, a certain degree of care is arrived at as the measure of the bailee's duty, and the bailee is liable only for a breach of his duty as so measured. This breach of a legal duty is called negligence, and the ordinary bailee is therefore said to be liable only for his negligence.[66] Or it is said that his liability is reckoned in terms of negligence. This is to distinguish the liability of the ordinary bailee from that of certain of the extraordinary bailees who are liable (with specific exceptions) for any loss or injury to the goods regardless of how the loss or injury occurred, and regardless of any fault or dereliction of duty on their part. These extraordinary bailees are said to be liable as insurers; or it is said that their liability is reckoned in terms of insurance.

In fixing the degrees of care, thus establishing standards of duty, any breach of which is negligence, the controlling factor is the

Co. v. O'Shaughnessy, 122 Ind. 588, 23 N. E. 675; Smith v. New York Cent. R. Co., 24 N. Y. 222; Perkins v. New York Cent. R. Co., 24 N. Y. 196, 82 Am. Dec. 281; McAdoo v. Richmond & D. R. Co., 105 N. C. 140, 11 S. E. 316; Storer v. Gowen, 18 Me. 174; Lane v. Boston & A. R. Co., 112 Mass. 455; Hinton v. Dibbin, 2 Q. B. 646; Wyld v. Pickford, 8 Mees. & W. 442; Preston v. Prather, 137 U. S. 604, 11 Sup. Ct. 162, 34 L. Ed. 788; GRAY v. MERRIAM, 148 Ill. 179, 35 N. E. 810, 32 L. R. A. 769, 39 Am. St. Rep. 172, Dobie Cas. Bailments and Carriers, 43. On negligence as a breach of duty to use commensurate care, see 2 Jagg. Torts, 810; City of Terre Haute v. Hudnut, 112 Ind. 542, 13 N. E. 686; Brown v. Congress & B. St. Ry. Co., 49 Mich. 153, 13 N. W. 494; Blyth v. Birmingham Waterworks Co., 11 Exch. 781, 784; Cooley on Torts (Student's Edition) § 338; Faris v. Hoberg, 134 Ind. 269, 33 N. E. 1028, 39 Am. St. Rep. 261.

[66] Wood v. McClure, 7 Ind. 155; Watkins v. Roberts, 28 Ind. 167; Carpenter v. Branch, 13 Vt. 161, 164, 37 Am. Dec. 587; BELLER v. SCHULTZ, 44 Mich. 529, 7 N. W. 225, 38 Am. Rep. 280, Dobie Cas. Bailments and Carriers, 57; Cass v. Boston & L. R. Co., 14 Allen (Mass.) 448; Chenowith v. Dickinson, 8 B. Mon. (Ky.) 156, 158; Abraham v. Nunn, 42 Ala. 51; Yale v. Oliver, 21 La. Ann. 454; Levy v. Bergeron, 20 La. Ann. 290; Waller v. Parker, 5 Cold. (Tenn.) 476; James v. Greenwood, 20 La. Ann. 297; Britton v. Aymar, 23 La. Ann. 63; McGinn v. Butler, 31 Iowa, 160; Watkins v. Roberts, 28 Ind. 167; Shiells v. Blackburne, 1 H. Bl. (Eng.) 158; Drudge v. Leiter, 18 Ind. App. 694, 49 N. E. 34, 63 Am. St. Rep. 359. A bailee who receives plumes to be dyed is not an insurer thereof. Johnson v. Chicago Feather Co., 172 Ill. App. 81. See, also, Whitlock v. Auburn Lumber Co., 145 N. C. 120, 58 S. E. 909, 12 L. R. A. (N. S.) 1214; O'ROURKE v. BATES, 73 Misc. Rep. 414, 133 N. Y. Supp. 392, Dobie Cas. Bailments and Carriers, 172.

intended benefit to be derived from the bailment. The degree of care exacted of the bailee varies directly with the benefit accruing to the bailee from the bailment. When the bailor receives all the benefit from the bailment, and the bailee none, this standard of care is the lowest. When the bailor receives none of the benefit and the bailee all, the highest standard of care is exacted. When the benefit is mutual, accruing to both bailor and bailee, the standard is naturally higher than in the first case mentioned and lower than in the second case. Accordingly we say that in bailments for the bailor's sole benefit the bailee must exercise only slight care;[67] in bailments for the bailee's sole benefit, great care;[68] and in bailments for the mutual benefit of both the bailor and bailee, ordinary care.[69]

It is thus clear that the bailee is always liable for his negligence, which is a breach of legal duty. But it is impossible to determine the presence or absence of negligence without first outlining the duty, which is here done by classifying the bailment, thus arriving at the degree or standard of care which it is the bailee's duty to exercise. By comparison with this standard the conduct of the bailee is then to be judged. It therefore follows that the same acts of the bailee might be negligence when judged by the standard of duty prescribed in one class of bailments and might not be negligence judged by the standard of another class. Thus, let us suppose that the conduct of the bailee is equivalent, under the circumstances, to ordinary care. Now, in a bailment for the bailor's sole benefit, the bailee's duty is only slight care, and therefore in exercising ordinary care (a higher degree than slight care) the bailee has more than fulfilled the duty imposed on him, and he is therefore not guilty of negligence, and hence not liable. But, in a bailment for the bailee's sole benefit, the bailee's duty is great care (a higher degree than ordinary care) and in exercising only ordinary care the bailee has committed a breach of his duty, and he is therefore guilty of negligence in the premises and hence liable. Measured, then, by his duty to exercise a certain degree of care, any failure by the bailee, however slight, to live up to that standard, is negligence, rendering him liable for direct and proximate damages flowing therefrom.

[67] CONNER v. WINTON, 8 Ind. 315, 65 Am. Dec. 761, Dobie Cas. Bailments and Carriers, 54; Belmont Coal Co. v. Richter, 31 W. Va. 858, 8 S. E. 609. See post, § 29.

[68] Wilcox v. Hogan, 5 Ind. 546; FORTUNE v. HARRIS, 51 N. C. 532, Dobie Cas. Bailments and Carriers, 61. See post, § 40.

[69] Wood v. Remick, 143 Mass. 453, 9 N. E. 831; Standard Brewery v. Bemis & Curtis Malting Co., 171 Ill. 602, 49 N. E. 507. See post, §§ 58, 65.

Ever since Lord Holt's decision in COGGS v. BERNARD, however, writers and judges have fallen into the use of the extremely unfortunate terminology known as "grades or degrees of negligence."[70] Thus it is said that, in bailments for the bailor's sole benefit the bailee is responsible only for great or gross negligence, by which is meant failure to exercise even slight care; in bailments for the bailee's sole benefit, it is said that the bailee is responsible even for slight negligence, by which is meant failure to exercise great care; and in bailments for the mutual benefit of both bailor and bailee, it is said the bailee is liable for ordinary negligence, by which is meant the failure to exercise ordinary care.

This distinction of three grades or degrees of negligence, in order to determine the liability of the bailee, has become so interwoven with the law of bailments that it is impossible to disregard it. It has been, however, severely and justly criticised as unscientific, inaccurate, and misleading. Negligence, as we have already seen, is the breach of a legal duty. For any negligence, or breach of such duty, resulting in damage, the bailee is liable, regardless of the fact whether the negligence be slight, ordinary, or great. Therefore, when negligence is given its real meaning as a juristic concept, a statement that the bailee is not liable for slight negligence or ordinary negligence is a misnomer, a contradiction in terms, a legal absurdity. It is therefore logical to apply the adjectives of comparison ("slight," "ordinary," and "great") to the term "diligence" or "care," and not to the correlative term "negligence." If the degrees were applied to the terms "neglect," "fault," or "carelessness," there would be much less objection, but even this terminology is not to be commended.

It remains, in this connection, only to explain briefly what is meant by the acceptable terms "slight care," "ordinary care," and "great care." To judge ordinary care, a theoretical man is set up, the man of ordinary prudence, and ordinary care is that degree of care which this man of ordinary prudence is accustomed to exercise in his own affairs under similar circumstances;[71] to

[70] Degrees of negligence are not recognized in some cases. Bigelow, Torts, § 265; First Nat. Bank of Lyons v. Ocean Nat. Bank, 60 N. Y. 278, 19 Am. Rep. 181; Hall v. Chicago, B. & N. R. Co., 46 Minn. 439, 49 N. W. 239; Gill v. Middleton, 105 Mass. 479, 7 Am. Rep. 548. See, also, as to degrees of negligence, The New World v. King, 16 How. (U. S.) 474, 14 L. Ed. 1019; New York Cent. R. Co. v. Lockwood, 17 Wall. (U. S.) 382, 21 L. Ed. 627; Wilson v. Brett, 11 Mees. & W. 113; Grill v. Iron Screw Collier Co., L. R. 1 C. P. 612.

[71] The Farmer v. McCraw, 26 Ala. 189, 72 Am. Dec. 718; United States v. Yukers, 60 Fed. 641, 9 C. C. A. 171; Hoffman v. Tuolumne County Water Co., 10 Cal. 413; Spokane Truck & Dray Co. v. Hoefer, 2 Wash. 45, 25 Pac. 1072, 11 L. R. A. 689, 26 Am. St. Rep. 842; Austin & N. W. Ry. Co. v. Beatty,

judge slight care is set up the man of less than ordinary prudence;[72] while great care is judged by the man of more than ordinary prudence.[73] By just how much the man of less than ordinary prudence falls below the man of ordinary prudence, as well as how far above this same ordinary prudent man is the man of great prudence cannot be stated with any accuracy or definiteness. The force and application of these comparative standards will appear in the treatment of the several classes of bailments.

Finally, it might be remarked that the whole scheme of degrees of diligence, as well as the methods of judging them, has been criticised as being neither accurate nor philosophical. But by the overwhelming weight of authority the scheme, though admittedly far from perfect, still obtains, and continual resort is had to it as the best method yet suggested in order to arrive at a practical solution of the question of the liability of the bailee for loss of, or injury to, the goods constituting the subject-matter of the bailment.[74]

PRESUMPTION OF NEGLIGENCE FROM LOSS OR INJURY

17. The burden of proof as to negligence rests primarily upon the bailor, but he makes out a prima facie against the bailee by showing the loss of, or injury to, the goods.

There is no little confusion among the decisions in regard to the burden of proof in cases where the bailee is sued by the bailor for loss of, or injury to, the bailed goods. It seems accurate, according to the weight of authority, and also on principle, to say that, since the negligence of the bailee is a fact upon which the bailor's right to recover is based, the burden of proof as to such negligence

73 Tex. 592, 11 S. W. 858; Marsh v. Benton County, 75 Iowa, 469, 471, 39 N. W. 713. See Story, Bailm. § 11; Jones, Bailm. § 6.

72 According to Judge Story, "slight diligence is that which persons of less than common prudence, or, indeed, of any prudence at all, take of their own concerns." Story, Bailm. § 16. And see Vaughan v. Menlove, 3 Bing. N. C. 468, 475.

73 Scranton v. Baxter, 4 Sandf. (N. Y.) 5; Wood v. McClure, 7 Ind. 155; BENNETT v. O'BRIEN, 37 Ill. 250, Dobie Cas. Bailments and Carriers, 56; Hagebush v. Ragland, 78 Ill. 40; Kennedy v. Ashcraft, 4 Bush (Ky.) 530; Lane v. Cameron, 38 Wis. 603; Cullen v. Lord, 39 Iowa, 302; Stewart v. Davis, 31 Ark. 518, 25 Am. Rep. 576.

74 See Van Zile, Bailm. & Carr. § 94.

rests at the outset on the plaintiff bailor, and remains on him all during the trial. But by proving that the goods were delivered to the bailee in good condition and that they were returned in a damaged condition or not returned at all, the plaintiff thereby makes out a prima facie case of negligence, and thus imposes upon the defendant bailee the duty of going forward with the evidence under penalty of losing the suit.[75] Hence a mere showing of loss or injury will entitle the plaintiff bailor to recover, unless this is offset by evidence adduced by the defendant bailee. The bailee, though, may overcome the prima facie case, thus made out on the part of the bailor, by proving affirmatively that he exercised that degree of care which the bailment in question called for, or that the loss or injury was due to causes in no way connected with the lack of proper care on his part.[76] Such a showing

[75] Boies v. Hartford & N. H. R. Co., 37 Conn. 272, 9 Am. Rep. 347; Funkhouser v. Wagner, 62 Ill. 59; Goodfellow's Ex'rs v. Meegan, 32 Mo. 280, 284; BENNETT v. O'BRIEN, 37 Ill. 250, Dobie Cas. Bailments and Carriers, 56; Vaughan v. Webster, 5 Har. (Del.) 256; Safe Deposit Co. of Pittsburgh v. Pollock, 85 Pa. 391, 27 Am. Rep. 660; Wintringham v. Hayes, 144 N. Y. 1, 38 N. E. 999, 43 Am. St. Rep. 725; Claflin v. Meyer, 75 N. Y. 260, 31 Am. Rep. 467; Coleman v. Livingston, 36 N. Y. Super. Ct. 32; Golden v. Romer, 20 Hun (N. Y.) 438; McDaniels v. Robinson, 26 Vt. 316, 62 Am. Dec. 574; Wilson v. Southern Pac. R. Co., 62 Cal. 164; Thompson v. St. Louis & S. F. Ry. Co., 59 Mo. App. 37; BELLER v. SCHULTZ, 44 Mich. 529, 7 N. W. 225, 38 Am. Rep. 280, Dobie Cas. Bailments and Carriers, 57; Beardslee v. Richardson, 11 Wend. (N. Y.) 25, 25 Am. Dec. 596; McCarthy v. Wolfe, 40 Mo. 520; Cross v. Brown, 41 N. H. 283; Collins v. Bennett, 46 N. Y. 490; Lamb v. Western R. Corp., 7 Allen (Mass.) 98; Massillon Engine & Thresher Co. v. Akerman, 110 Ga. 570, 35 S. E. 635; HUNTER v. RICKE BROS., 127 Iowa, 108, 102 N. W. 826, Dobie Cas. Bailments and Carriers, 27; Jackson v. McDonald, 70 N. J. Law, 594, 57 Atl. 126; Shropshire v. Sidebottom, 30 Mont. 406, 76 Pac. 941; Davis v. A. O. Taylor & Son, 92 Neb. 769, 139 N. W. 687; Seybolt v. New York, L. E. & W. R. Co., 95 N. Y. 562, 568, 47 Am. Rep. 75. See Alden v. Pearson, 3 Gray (Mass.) 342; Platt v. Hibbard, 7 Cow. (N. Y.) 497; Burnell v. New York Cent. R. Co., 45 N. Y. 184, 6 Am. Rep. 61; Schwerin v. McKie, 51 N. Y. 180, 10 Am. Rep. 581; Fairfax v. New York Cent. & H. R. R. Co., 67 N. Y. 11; Travelers' Indemnity Co. v. Fawkes, 120 Minn. 353, 139 N. W. 703, 45 L. R. A. (N. S.) 331; Nutt v. Davison, 54 Colo. 586, 131 Pac. 390, 44 L. R. A. (N. S.) 1170. The rule that, where property bailed is not returned, the law presumes negligence in the bailee, and the burden is on him of showing that the loss is not due to his negligence, is the same whether the bailment is gratuitous or not. Pregent v. Mills, 51 Wash. 187, 98 Pac. 328. Where a horse in the hands of a blacksmith to be shod is returned to the owner with his foot injured, and the blacksmith makes no explanation other than that he dropped the horse's foot on a drawing knife, such evidence will support a finding of negligence. Powell v. Hill (Tex. Civ. App.) 152 S. W. 1125. See, also, Johnson v. Perkins, 4 Ga. App. 633, 62 S. E. 152.

[76] McLoughlin v. New York Lighterage & Transp. Co., 7 Misc. Rep. 119, 27 N. Y. Supp. 248; HUNTER v. RICKE BROS., 127 Iowa, 108, 102 N. W.

will then prevent a recovery by the bailor for the loss or injury, the loss or injury then falling on the bailor under the principle res perit domino.[77] Proof of loss or injury, standing alone, accordingly constitutes as to negligence the preponderance of evidence required in civil causes to make out a case.

The justification for this rule is found in the fact that experience shows, in the great majority of cases, that the exercise by the bailee of the particular degree of care which the bailment demands will be sufficient to prevent the loss of, or injury to, the bailed goods. Another, and perhaps a stronger, reason is that the bailee, in possession and control of the goods, has the fullest opportunities of knowing just how the loss or injury occurred, while just the opposite is true of the bailor.

The rule given above is sometimes termed the modern rule, because it has the overwhelming support of the modern cases. There are quite a few cases, most of them old, though, holding that proof of loss or injury alone does not even make out a prima

826, Doble Cas. Bailments and Carriers, 27. See, also, cases cited in preceding note. When a bailor shows that goods were delivered to the bailee in good condition and have been lost, destroyed, or returned in a damaged condition, negligence of the bailee is shown prima facie, and the burden rests upon him to show that the loss resulted from a cause prima facie exonerating him from negligence, and, when he shows loss by burglary, fire, etc., the burden shifts to the bailor to show negligence. Yazoo & M. V. R. Co. v. Hughes, 94 Miss. 242, 47 South. 662, 22 L. R. A. (N. S.) 975. Where a horse is delivered in good condition to a blacksmith to shoe, and shortly thereafter is found badly cut, a presumption of negligence by the blacksmith arises, authorizing a recovery for the injury, unless rebutted to the satisfaction of the jury. Johnson v. Perkins, 4 Ga. App. 633, 62 S. E. 152. An unreasonable, improbable, or impossible explanation of an injury to property of bailor while in the hands of bailee may be equivalent to an admission of liability, and, in any event, such an explanation, as well as no explanation, may be held by the jury to be a failure by bailee to show proper diligence. Johnson v. Perkins, 4 Ga. App. 633, 62 S. E. 152.

[77] Bailee may make out a prima facie defense by showing that the injury or loss occurred under circumstances not in themselves imputing any fault to him. This then imposes on the bailor plaintiff the duty to bring forward evidence to prove some negligence of the bailee defendant, as that the bailee was negligent in exposing the property to the risk of harm, or in failing to avoid or minimize injury to the goods after the danger was known. HUNTER v. RICKE BROS., 127 Iowa, 108, 102 N. W. 826, Doble Cas. Bailments and Carriers, 27; Standard Brewery v. Bemis & Curtis Malting Co., 171 Ill. 602, 49 N. E. 507; Seals v. Edmondson, 71 Ala. 509; Beardslee v. Perry, 14 Mo. 88; Schwerin v. McKie, 51 N. Y. 180, 10 Am. Rep. 581; First Nat. Bank of Carlisle v. Graham, 85 Pa. 91, 27 Am. Rep. 628; Cochran v. Dinsmore, 49 N. Y. 249; Cox v. O'Riley, 4 Ind. 368, 58 Am. Dec. 633; Boies v. Hartford & N. H. R. Co., 37 Conn. 272, 9 Am. Rep. 347; Logan v. Mathews, 6 Pa. 417; Tompkins v. Saltmarsh, 14 Serg. & R. (Pa.) 275; Malaney v. Taft, 60 Vt. 571, 15 Atl. 326, 6 Am. St. Rep. 135.

facie case against the bailee, on the ground that the law tends to presume one diligent rather than negligent, and that therefore the bailor plaintiff must go further and connect such loss or injury with some negligent act or omission on the part of the bailee defendant.[78]

BAILEE MUST ACT IN GOOD FAITH

18. The bailee must at all times exercise good faith in carrying out the purpose of the bailment. For his fraud or positive wrong he is always liable.

A bailment is not a technical trust, nor is the relation one of the closest confidence or uberrimæ fidei as it is called in the law; but the relation ordinarily involves, to a limited extent, at least, the reposal of some confidence in the bailee. Ample warrant is therefore found for holding the bailee to a standard of strict honesty and good faith in the execution of the bailment purpose. For reasons much stronger than in the case of his negligence, the bailee is held liable for the consequences of his fraud or willful wrongdoing.[79] As we have seen, the courts are unanimous in

[78] Tompkins v. Saltmarsh, 14 Serg. & R. (Pa.) 275; Schmidt v. Blood, 9 Wend. (N. Y.) 268, 24 Am. Dec. 143; James v. Orrell, 68 Ark. 284, 57 S. W. 931, 82 Am. St. Rep. 293; 2 Kent, Comm. (4th Ed.) Lect. 40, p. 587; Adams v. Inhabitants of Carlisle, 21 Pick. (Mass.) 146; Harrington v. Snyder, 3 Barb. (N. Y.) 380; Finucane v. Small, 1 Esp. 315; Butt v. Great Western R. Co., 11 C. B. 140; Smith v. First Nat. Bank in Westfield, 99 Mass. 605, 97 Am. Dec. 59; Cross v. Brown, 41 N. H. 283; Carsley v. White, 21 Pick. (Mass.) 254, 32 Am. Dec. 259; Brind v. Dale, 8 Car. & P. 207; Foote v. Storrs, 2 Barb. (N. Y.) 326; Browne v. Johnson, 29 Tex. 40, 43. This is the English rule. Finucane v. Small, 1 Esp. 315; Cooper v. Barton, 3 Camp. 5, note; Harris v. Packwood, 3 Taunt. 264; Gilbart v. Dale, 5 Adol. & E. 543.

[79] Corotinsky v. Cooper, 26 Misc. Rep. 138, 55 N. Y. Supp. 570; Kahaley v. Haley, 15 Wash. 678, 47 Pac. 23; Chew v. Louchheim, 80 Fed. 500, 25 C. C. A. 596; Martin v. Cuthbertson, 64 N. C. 328; Lane v. Cameron, 38 Wis. 603; Cullen v. Lord, 39 Iowa, 302; Line v. Mills, 12 Ind. App. 100, 39 N. E. 870; Fisher v. Kyle, 27 Mich. 454; Ross v. Southern Cotton-Oil Co. (C. C.) 41 Fed. 152; Wintringham v. Hayes, 144 N. Y. 1, 38 N. E. 999, 43 Am. St. Rep. 725; Townsend v. Rich, 58 Minn. 559, 60 N. W. 545; Foster v. President, etc., of Essex Bank, 17 Mass. 479, 9 Am. Dec. 168; Sodowsky's Ex'r v. McFarland, 3 Dana (Ky.) 204; Calhoun v. Thompson, 56 Ala. 166, 28 Am. Rep. 754; McMahon v. Sloan, 12 Pa. 229, 231, 51 Am. Dec. 601. Bailee pledging another's property without authority is guilty of conversion; and both bailee and pledgee are liable in trover, whether pledgee knew real state of title or not. Thrall v. Lathrop, 30 Vt. 307, 73 Am. Dec. 306. Bailees for special purpose have no right to sell property bailed, and, upon such sale, bailment is determined, and real owner may replevy it from vendee. Emerson v. Fisk, 6

refusing to permit the bailee to contract against such liability. Negligence is more or less negative, and may, of course, consist in a mere omission or failure to take such steps as due care demands. Fraud or willful wrongdoing, however, is positive, involving a measure of moral turpitude.

The bailee is, of course, liable, irrespective of the question of negligence or fraud, for any absolute breach of the bailment contract.[80] Such breaches, however, are usually accompanied by positive wrong on the part of the bailee.

REDELIVERY OF BAILED GOODS BY THE BAILEE

19. The bailee must redeliver the goods, unless legally excused, at the termination of the bailment, according to the bailor's directions. When he has notice of the claim of a third person adverse to the bailor, the bailee is an insurer as to his delivery to the right person.

As is indicated in the definition of a bailment, it is the normal duty of the bailee to redeliver the goods according to the directions of the bailor, and these directions usually, but not always, contemplate a redelivery to the bailor. If, in such a case, the bailee in good faith delivers the goods to the bailor, without notice of any adverse claim, the bailee will not be responsible.[81] The

Greenl. (Me.) 200, 19 Am. Dec. 206. Bailment requires on the part of the bailee the utmost good faith as to every matter wherein the interest of the bailor may be affected. Morris Storage & Transfer Co. v. Wilkes, 1 Ga. App. 751, 58 S. E. 232. See, also, Haines v. Chappell, 1 Ga. App. 480, 58 S. E. 220.

[80] These are usually cases of conversion of the bailed goods by the bailee. See preceding note. A bailee is liable in an action of tort for an injury to bailed property occurring during a use of it by him, or by others with his consent, which was neither expressly nor impliedly authorized by the contract of bailment, even though the injury was the result of accident, and not of negligence. Palmer v. Mayo, 80 Conn. 353, 68 Atl. 369, 15 L. R. A. (N. S.) 428, 125 Am. St. Rep. 123, 12 Ann. Cas. 691.

[81] Nanson v. Jacob, 93 Mo. 331, 6 S. W. 246, 3 Am. St. Rep. 531; PARKER v. LOMBARD, 100 Mass. 405, Dobie Cas. Bailments and Carriers, 31. So, in Strickland v. Barrett, 20 Pick. (Mass.) 415, B., who was a mortgagor in possession of certain goods, conspired with H. to remove them out of the reach of the mortgagee, and employed the defendant to assist in removing them; and it was held that defendant was not liable in trover, unless he knew of the intent to deprive the plaintiff of his property. And where one received a gun as a pledge from a person in possession of it, and restored it to him before any demand by the owner, this was not found to be a conversion. Leonard v. Tidd, 3 Metc. (Mass.) 6. See, also, Loring v. Mulcahy, 3 Allen (Mass.) 575. Nelson v. Iverson, 17 Ala. 216. And see Brown v. Thayer, 12 Gray (Mass.) 1.

goods to be redelivered are the identical goods delivered to the bailee, either in the same or in an altered form, together with the profits or increase of such goods, though, in the case of stock certificates, mere evidences of certain rights in the corporation, any one of which is as good as another similar one, the identical certificate need not be returned.[52]

The bailee is an insurer as to his delivery to the right person. In other words, he is absolutely responsible for a delivery to the wrong person, regardless of the question of the bailee's good faith or negligence in making the delivery.[53] He therefore acts at his own peril and is liable for any mistake that he may make. Thus he will be responsible for delivery on a forged order, however perfect the forgery, and whatever precautions he may have taken to discover it.[54] A bailee, accepting goods to be delivered to a third person on the happening of a certain event, must at his own peril decide whether the event has happened.[55] Of course, the bailee is not liable when he delivers the goods to the right person, though the delivery is made on insufficient or even false evidence.[56]

As we have just seen, the bailee is justified in following the

[52] Atkins v. Gamble, 42 Cal. 86, 10 Am. Rep. 282.

[53] ESMAY v. FANNING, 9 Barb. (N. Y.) 176, Dobie Cas. Bailments and Carriers, 36; Wear v. Gleason, 52 Ark. 364, 12 S. W. 756, 20 Am. St. Rep. 186; Nelson v. King, 25 Tex. 655; Ganley v. Troy City Nat. Bank, 98 N. Y. 487; Bank of Oswego v. Doyle, 91 N. Y. 32, 42, 43 Am. Rep. 634; Willard v. Bridge, 4 Barb. (N. Y.) 361; Graves v. Smith, 14 Wis. 5, 80 Am. Dec. 762; Jenkins v. Bacon, 111 Mass. 373, 15 Am. Rep. 33; Dufour v. Mepham, 31 Mo. 577; Jeffersonville R. Co. v. White, 6 Bush. (Ky.) 251; Alabama & T. R. R. Co. v. Kidd, 35 Ala. 209. But see Lancaster County Nat. Bank v. Smith, 62 Pa. 47. In some jurisdictions the question of negligence has been considered in the matter of delivery. See Manhattan Bank v. Walker, 130 U. S. 267, 9 Sup. Ct. 519, 32 L. Ed. 959; Lancaster County Nat. Bank v. Smith, 62 Pa. 47; Heugh v. London & N. W. Ry. Co., L. R. 5 Exch. 51. When property in the custody of a bailee for hire is demanded by a third person under color of process, it is the bailee's duty to ascertain whether the process is such as required him to surrender, and, if the proceeding is illegal or void, he must refuse to surrender the property and adopt such means for reclaiming it, if taken, as a prudent man would had his own been taken under a claim of right without legal process. Morris Storage & Transfer Co. v. Wilkes, 1 Ga. App. 751, 58 S. E. 232.

[54] Kowing v. Manly, 49 N. Y. 192, 10 Am. Rep. 346; Lichtenhein v. Boston & P. R. Co., 11 Cush. (Mass.) 70; Hall v. Boston & W. R. Corp., 14 Allen (Mass.) 439, 92 Am. Dec. 783; Forsythe v. Walker, 9 Pa. 148; Collins v. Burns, 63 N. Y. 1; Dufour v. Mepham, 31 Mo. 577; McGinn v. Butler, 31 Iowa, 160; Stephenson v. Price, 30 Tex. 715; Willard v. Bridge, 4 Barb. (N. Y.) 361; Alabama & T. R. R. Co. v. Kidd, 35 Ala. 209.

[55] Carle v. Bearce, 33 Me. 337, 340; Chase v. Gates, 33 Me. 363; Trefftz v. Canelli, L. R. 4 P. C. 277, 282; Lafarge v. Morgan, 11 Mart. (La.) 462.

[56] Chattahoochee Nat. Bank v. Schley, 58 Ga. 369, 374.

instructions of his bailor and redelivering the goods to the bailor, when no adverse claim is brought to his attention. Upon notice of such adverse claim by the third party, the legality of this claim must be determined by the bailee on his own responsibility. He cannot disregard the claim, and if he does, and redelivers to the bailor, the bailee is responsible to the adverse claimant if his claim prove a just one.[87] Again, if the bailee yield to the claim by delivering the goods to the third person, he thereby becomes liable to the bailor, should such claim turn out to have no foundation in law.[88]

When such adverse claim is made, the bailee, unless he is perfectly sure of its validity, should refuse to deliver the goods to the third party and should call in his bailor to defend against such adverse claim.[89] If there be privity between the bailor and third person, the safest course for the bailee to pursue is to file a bill of interpleader in a court of equity, asking that the bailor and third person be brought into court and have the question of the ownership of the goods decided.[90] But, as we have seen, when the bailee himself undertakes to pass upon the merits of the opposing claims, he is absolutely responsible for a wrong decision. The bailee incurs no liability by surrendering the goods under valid process of law or the decree of a court of competent jurisdiction;[91] but,

[87] Wilson v. Anderton, 1 Barn. & Adol. (Eng.) 450.

[88] Calhoun v. Thompson, 56 Ala. 166, 28 Am. Rep. 754; POWELL v. ROBINSON, 76 Ala. 423, Dobie Cas. Bailments and Carriers, 33.

[89] Schouler, Bailm. (2d Ed.) § 60; Story, Bailm. § 111; Bliven v. Hudson River R. Co., 35 Barb. (N. Y.) 188; POWELL v. ROBINSON, 76 Ala. 423, Dobie Cas. Bailments and Carriers, 33.

[90] Bechtel v. Sheafer, 117 Pa. 555, 11 Atl. 889; Ball v. Liney, 48 N. Y. 6, 13, 8 Am. Rep. 511; Banfield v. Haeger, 7 Abb. N. C. (N. Y.) 318. See, also, De Zouche v. Garrison, 140 Pa. 430, 21 Atl. 450; Hatfield v. McWhorter, 40 Ga. 269; note 91 Am. St. Rep. 608. But when no privity exists, the bailee cannot, in the absence of statute, compel them to interplead. Marvin v. Ellwood, 11 Paige (N. Y.) 365; First Nat. Bank of Morristown v. Bininger, 26 N. J. Eq. 345; Bartlett v. His Imperial Majesty, The Sultan (C. C.) 23 Fed. 257; Bechtel v. Sheafer, 117 Pa. 555, 11 Atl. 889.

[91] Stiles v. Davis, 1 Black (U. S.) 101, 17 L. Ed. 33; French v. Star Union Transp. Co., 134 Mass. 288; Britton v. Aymar, 23 La. Ann. 63; Ohio & M. Ry. Co. v. Yohe, 51 Ind. 181, 19 Am. Rep. 727; Bliven v. Hudson River R. Co., 36 N. Y. 403; Robinson v. Memphis & C. R. Co. (C. C.) 16 Fed. 57; Burton v. Wilkinson, 18 Vt. 186, 46 Am. Dec. 145. When property is taken from a bailee's custody by valid legal process, the bailee must notify the bailor of the taking within a reasonable time, in order to protect himself from being charged with the conversion of the property. Medina Gas & Electric Light Co. v. Buffalo Loan, Trust & Safe Deposit Co., 119 App. Div. 245, 104 N. Y. Supp. 625; MacDonnell v. Buffalo Loan, Trust & Safe Deposit Co., 193 N. Y. 92, 85 N. E. 801.

if he can reasonably do so, the bailee must notify the bailor of the commencement of any such legal proceedings, in order to give the bailor opportunity to make a suitable defense.[92]

It is, of course, a perfect defense for the bailee to show, when sued by the bailor, that he surrendered the goods, even without suit, to the person rightfully entitled to receive them.[93] As we have seen, the estoppel of the bailee to deny his bailor's title has no reference to such a case. This rule of estoppel applies only when the bailee sets up the adverse title for the purpose of keeping the goods himself, and not to cases in which the bailee has yielded to the superior rights of another. The estoppel provided for in the rule ceases when the bailment on which it is founded is terminated by what is equivalent to an eviction by title paramount.[94]

[92] Scrantom v. Farmers' & Mechanics' Bank of Rochester, 24 N. Y. 424, 427; POWELL v. ROBINSON, 76 Ala. 423, Dobie Cas. Bailments and Carriers, 33.

[93] Gerber v. Monie, 56 Barb. (N. Y.) 652. But he takes the risk of showing that such person had a good title. Foltz v. Stevens, 54 Ill. 180; Dodge v. Meyer, 61 Cal. 405; Maxwell v. Houston, 67 N. C. 305. The bailee may show in defense that the bailor obtained the property from the real owner feloniously or by fraud. Bates v. Stanton, 1 Duer (N. Y.) 79; King v. Richards, 6 Whart. (Pa.) 418, 37 Am. Dec. 420; Kelly v. Patchell, 5 W. Va. 585. Where a bailee is sued in trover by the real owner, and compelled to pay the value of the goods, he may assert the title thus acquired in defense to an action of his bailor. Cook v. Holt, 48 N. Y. 275.

[94] Western Transp. Co. v. Barber, 56 N. Y. 544; Burton v. Wilkinson, 18 Vt. 186, 46 Am. Dec. 145; Wallace v. Matthews, 39 Ga. 617, 99 Am. Dec. 473; Bliven v. Hudson River R. Co., 36 N. Y. 403; King v. Richards, 6 Whart. (Pa.) 418, 37 Am. Dec. 420; Stephenson v. Price, 30 Tex. 715, 717. A bailee cannot, in an action brought against him by his bailor, set up the title of a third person, except by the authorization of that person. Dodge v. Meyer, 61 Cal. 405. A bailee may not set up the claim of the true owner when the true owner has abandoned such claim. Betteley v. Reed, 3 Gale & D. 561. Although, in certain cases, a bailee may set up the jus tertii, yet, if he accepts the bailment with full knowledge of an adverse claim, he cannot afterwards set up the existence of such a claim as against his bailor. Ex parte Davies, In re Sadler, 19 Ch. Div. 86. One borrowing property on promise to return it cannot release himself from his promise by purchasing a title adverse to that of the lender. Nudd v. Montanye, 38 Wis. 511, 20 Am. Rep. 25. A bailee is not permitted to dispute the title of his bailor, but he may show that the bailor has assigned his title to another, since the property was intrusted to him. If legally assigned, and the bailee has notice of the fact, the bailee must account to the assignee. The rule that a bailee should not attorn to a stranger does not apply; the assignee is not a stranger. Roberts v. Noyes, 76 Me. 590. See, also, Biddle v. Bend, 6 Best. & S. 225, 233; Shelbury v. Scotsford, Yelv. (3d Ed. Translated) 23; Betteley v. Reed, 4 Q. B. 511, 517; DAVIS v. DONOHOE-KELLY BANKING CO., 152 Cal. 282, 92 Pac. 639, Dobie Cas. Bailments and Carriers, 29.

TERMINATION OF THE BAILMENT

20. The bailment may be terminated by:
1. Act of the parties.
(a) By full performance of the bailment purpose or expiration of the time for which the bailment was created.
(b) By mutual consent of the parties in all cases, and in some bailments at the option of one of the parties.
(c) By the bailee's wrong, at the option of the bailor.
2. By operation of law.
(a) By death of bailor or bailee, in some instances.
(b) By change of legal status of the parties, in some cases.
(c) By destruction of the bailed goods.

The question of the termination of the bailment is discussed at some length under each separate class of bailments; but a brief statement is here made applicable alike to all bailments. In this connection, it might be noted that in many works on bailments not a little inaccuracy is found as to the termination of the bailment, as a result of attempts to formulate broad rules applicable to all bailments, which fail to notice essential distinctions between the various classes of bailments. As to the various ways in which the termination of the bailment may be effected, a clear distinction is seen between those ways which are (1) the positive acts of the parties themselves, and those ways in which (2) the law declares the bailment ended as a result of changed conditions brought about usually without regard to their effect on the bailment.

Performance or Expiration of Time

When the purpose of the bailment is fully accomplished,[95] or when the time expires for which the bailment was created,[96] the bailment in all cases comes to an end. The bailment thus ceases by natural limitations imposed upon it in its inception. This is, of course, true of all bailments.

[95] Lay's Ex'r v. Lawson's Adm'r, 23 Ala. 377; Chattahoochee Nat. Bank v. Schley, 58 Ga. 369; Morse v. Androscoggin R. Co., 39 Me. 285; New York, L. E. & W. R. Co. v. New Jersey Electric Ry. Co., 60 N. J. Law, 338, 38 Atl. 828; Ouderkirk v. Central Nat. Bank of Troy, 119 N. Y. 263, 23 N. E. 875.

[96] Cobb v. Wallace, 5 Cold. (Tenn.) 539, 98 Am. Dec. 435; Benje v. Creagh's Adm'r, 21 Ala. 151.

Consent of the Parties

The parties who created the bailment can alike destroy it. Any bailment can therefore be terminated by the mutual consent of both bailor and bailee.[97] The relation concerns the parties thereto; the law, therefore, has no reason for keeping alive the relation when both the parties concerned wish to bring it to an end. The same result is reached when, without expressly consenting to the termination of the relation, both bailor and bailee consent to the assuming of some relation towards the goods which is inconsistent with the continuance of the bailment.

Some bailments may be terminated at the option of the bailor alone, some may be ended if the bailee so chooses, while still others can rightfully be terminated by neither party without the consent of the other. The termination of the bailment at the option of one of the parties can be accurately discussed only in connection with the specific classes of bailments.

Bailee's Wrong

It is a general rule, applicable to all bailments, that the active wrong of the bailee does not of itself operate to bring the bailment to an end, but merely gives the bailor the right to terminate the bailment if he so desires. Thus, when the bailee transcends the contemplated purpose of the bailment and uses the bailed goods for a purpose utterly different from that stipulated in the bailment contract, or when the bailee grossly misuses the goods, this immediately confers on the bailor the option of terminating the bailment.[98]

Death or Change of Legal Status in the Parties

The effect of death, or a change of legal status on the part of the bailor or bailee, such as bankruptcy or insanity, varies widely according to the nature of the bailment. Under each of the three great classes of bailments, the question is treated at some length. Any attempt to formulate any general rules on the subject, common to all bailments, would tend to confusion rather than clearness.[99]

97 Story, Bailm. §§ 418, 418a; New York, L. E. & W. R. Co. v. New Jersey Electric Ry. Co., 60 N. J. Law, 338, 38 Atl. 828; Minturn v. Stryker, 1 Edm. Sel. Cas. (N. Y.) 356.

98 Wentworth v. McDuffie, 48 N. H. 402; Green v. Hollingsworth, 5 Dana (Ky.) 173, 30 Am. Dec. 680; BARRINGER v. BURNS, 108 N. C. 606, 13 S. E. 142, Dobie Cas. Bailments and Carriers, 38.

99 Story, Bailm. §§ 277, 418, 419; Schouler, Bailm. & C. §§ 56, 61, 156.

Destruction of the Bailed Goods

This necessarily terminates any bailment, for after such destruction [100] there is then nothing to which the relation can attach. A bailment without an existing subject-matter is a legal absurdity. The rights and liabilities of the bailor and bailee, upon such a destruction, depend upon various considerations subsequently to be discussed.

[100] New York, L. E. & W. R. Co. v. New Jersey Electric Ry. Co., 60 N. J. Law, 338, 38 Atl. 828; Masterson v. International & G. N. R. Co. (Tex. Civ. App. 1900) 55 S. W. 577.

CHAPTER III

BAILMENTS FOR THE BAILOR'S SOLE BENEFIT

DEPOSITUM AND MANDATUM

21. Bailments for the sole benefit of the bailor include
(a) Depositum and
(b) Mandatum.

Introductory

The distinctive feature of bailments for the bailor's sole benefit lies, of course, in the fact that all the benefit arising from the bailment relation accrues to the bailor, while the bailee receives no compensation or reward. Such bailments are usually divided into two classes: Gratuitous bailments of goods for mere custody, and gratuitous bailments of goods for the purpose of having active services performed concerning the goods.[1]

The terminology employed to designate these classes is far from satisfactory. To call the gratuitous bailment for mere custody "depositum" and the gratuitous bailment for active services "mandatum" is objectionable, because these terms (as used in Roman law, from which they were borrowed), are not limited to, or synonymous with, the bailment relations to which they are applied.[2]

1 Story, Bailm. § 3.

2 See Morey, Outlines of Roman Law, p. 369; Sandars' Justinian (Hammond) p. 457. The term "mandate" is sometimes used in a sense not denoting a bailment relation at all. "The Roman mandate in fact—a term apparently derived from the fiction of giving one's right hand as symbolical of giving to another authority to act—meant in the vernacular simply to constitute a gratuitous agency. A wide, sweeping class of trusts was this, not confined to personalty, nor to things specific as distinguishable from property in the mass, nor necessarily occupied with property at all. An unpaid carrier was for the time being a mandatary; but so, too, was an unpaid oral messenger or a naked attorney." Schouler, Bailm. p. 30.

On the other hand, the use of the apparently cognate English words "deposit" and "mandate" is still more unfortunate, for these terms not only have indefinite meanings, but they also apply to legal relations which are not bailments at all.[3] Accordingly, it is believed that the Roman terms are clearer, if it is understood that they are to be used merely to designate the two classes of bailments for the bailor's sole benefit with no attempt to give to the terms their exact and scientific meanings under the Roman law.

The two classes of bailments may well be treated together, for the degree of diligence required and the other important legal consequences are the same in each case; the only substantial differences in the rights and duties of the parties being such as naturally and obviously result from the difference in the purpose of the bailments.

Depositum

A depositum has already been defined[4] as a bailment of goods for mere custody, without recompense. The bailor reaps all the benefit by having his goods kept without payment therefor. The bailee receives no benefit from the bailment; he keeps the goods purely as a gratuitous favor to the bailor. There are various other definitions of a depositum,[5] but it is sufficient here to indicate that essentially it is the bailment relation resulting from the delivery of a thing to be kept by the bailee without reward, and, further, that there are no duties demanded of the bailee towards the thing en-

[3] Thus the ordinary "deposit" of money in a bank is not a bailment, while the word "mandate" signifies, in appellate proceedings, the precept or order of the higher court directing the action to be taken, or the disposition to be made of the case, by the lower court. Black's Law Dictionary, "Mandate."

[4] Ante, p. 11.

[5] A deposit is defined by Sir William Jones (Jones, Bailm. § 36) as being a naked bailment of goods, to be kept for the bailor without reward, and to be returned when he shall require it; but Judge Story (Story, Bailm. § 41) suggests as a correction that it is "a bailment of goods to be kept by the bailee without reward, and delivered according to the object or purpose of the original trust." In his reason for this amendment, Judge Story embodies the fact emphasized in the definition of bailment as laid down in the first pages of this book; namely, that, on the termination of a bailment, the thing may either be returned to the bailor, or be delivered over to some third party, specified by the bailor. The definition given by Pothier (Pothier, Traité de Dépot, note 1) is that a deposit is a contract by which one of the contracting parties gives a thing to another to keep, who is to do so gratuitously, and obliges himself to return it when he shall be requested. Ulpian (Com. Dig. lib. 16, tit. 36 [1]) gives as a definition: "Depositum est quod custodiendum alicui datum est" (it is a deposit because it is given to some one to keep). See, also, Whiting v. Chicago, M. & St. P. Ry. Co., 5 Dak. 90, 37 N. W. 222; Bunnell v. Stern, 122 N. Y. 539, 25 N. E. 910, 10 L. R. A. 481, 19 Am. St. Rep. 519.

trusted to him which are not involved in merely keeping it for the bailor.[6]

In the depositum, the bailor is usually called the "depositor" and the bailee the "depositary." The most important depositaries from a legal standpoint are finders of lost goods[7] and banks receiving special deposits.[8] An ordinary deposit of money in a bank, though, must not be confused with this last type of bailments. Such a deposit is not a bailment, for the identical money need not be returned, but is rather in the nature of a commercial loan, and accordingly the relation which it creates is that of debtor and creditor, and not that of bailor and bailee.[9] But where gold, bonds, stocks, or other things of value, or even money, is deposited with a bank on the understanding that the identical thing deposited is to be

[6] Thibaud v. Thibaud's Heirs, 1 La. 493. A., as the agent of B., deposits a sum of money with C., with a request that he will keep it until B. returns home (he being absent at the time), and then pay it to him, which C. agrees to do. Held, that C. is a depositary, and not liable to be sued for the money by B. until after a request to pay it. Montgomery v. Evans, 8 Ga. 178. If a person consents that a deposit of money shall be made in his name in a bank, for the purpose of accommodating the owner, with no control over it other than to draw it out when the owner should direct, he will not be held liable for its safe-keeping. Dustin v. Hodgen, 38 Ill. 352.

[7] Cory v. Little, 6 N. H. 213, 25 Am. Dec. 458; Dougherty v. Posegate, 3 Iowa, 88. The finder of property on land is a bailee thereof without reward. The owner is liable to the finder, however, for the necessary expenses of preserving the property if the owner reclaims it. Chase v. Corcoran, 106 Mass. 286. A receiptor is primarily liable as a bailee without hire. Thus, in Brown v. Cook, 9 Johns. (N. Y.) 361, a constable, having taken goods on an execution against B., delivered them to C., who gave a receipt for them, promising to deliver them to the constable on demand. The constable suffered the execution to expire without making any demand for the goods. In an action brought by the constable against C., it was held that he was a mere naked bailee, and that no action would lie against him until after a demand and refusal of the goods. If a chattel be taken from one who receipts and promises in writing to redeliver it, by another who has a paramount title, the bailee is discharged. Edson v. Weston, 7 Cow. (N. Y.) 278. See, also, Cornell v. Dakin, 38 N. Y. 253; Murgoo v. Cogswell, 1 E. D. Smith (N. Y.) 359; Parker v. Evans, 23 Mo. 67; Bobo v. Patton, 6 Heisk. (Tenn.) 172, 19 Am. Rep. 593.

[8] Post, p. 55.

[9] Commercial Bank of Albany v. Hughes, 17 Wend. (N. Y.) 94; Carroll v. Cone, 40 Barb. (N. Y.) 220; Phœnix Bank v. Risley, 111 U. S. 125, 4 Sup. Ct. 322, 28 L. Ed. 374. "The primary relation of a depositor in a savings bank to the corporation is that of creditor, and not that of a beneficiary of a trust. The deposit when made becomes the property of the corporation. The depositor is a creditor for the amount of the deposit, which the corporation becomes liable to pay, according to the terms of the contract under which it is made." Andrews, J., in People v. Mechanics' & Traders' Sav. Inst., 92 N. Y. 7, 9. And see Chapman v. White, 6 N. Y. 412, 417, 57 Am. Dec. 464. See, also, Vandagrift v. Masonic Home of Missouri, 242 Mo. 138, 145 S. W. 448; Reid v. Charlotte Nat. Bank, 159 N. C. 99, 74 S. E. 746.

returned, this transaction is called a "special deposit," and constitutes a bailment.[10]

Mandatum

Perhaps the most celebrated definition of a mandatum is that of Lord Holt in COGGS v. BERNARD[11]: "A delivery of goods or chattels to somebody who is to carry them or do some act about them gratis, without any reward for such work or carriage." In other words, the mandatum is a bailment of goods for the purpose of having some more or less active services (beyond mere custody) performed about them by the bailee, who receives no recompense for these services.[12] The performance of these services by the bailee is a gratuitous favor on his part, while the bailor receives, without paying therefor, the benefit of having these services performed about his goods.

Depositum and Mandatum Distinguished

Great stress was formerly laid on the distinction between a mandatum and a depositum, as to their respective purposes. This, according to Sir William Jones,[13] was the fact that a mandatum lay

[10] Foster v. President, etc., of Essex Bank, 17 Mass. 479, 9 Am. Dec. 168; First Nat. Bank of Carlisle v. Graham, 79 Pa. 106, 21 Am. Rep. 49; Scott v. National Bank of Chester Valley, 72 Pa. 471, 13 Am. Rep. 711; First Nat. Bank of Lyons v. Ocean Nat. Bank, 60 N. Y. 278, 19 Am. Rep. 181; Preston v. Prather, 137 U. S. 604, 11 Sup. Ct. 162, 34 L. Ed. 788; Griffith v. Zipperwick, 28 Ohio St. 388.

[11] 2 Ld. Raym. 909, Dobie Cas. Bailments and Carriers, 1. And see CONNER v. WINTON, 8 Ind. 315, 65 Am. Dec. 761, Dobie Cas. Bailments and Carriers, 54.

[12] This definition is practically adopted by Sir William Jones (Jones, Bailm. 117) when he says that a mandate is a bailment of goods without reward, to be carried from place to place, or to have some act performed about them. According to Kent (Comm. 12th Ed. 568), "a mandate is when one undertakes, without recompense, to do some act for another, in respect to the thing bailed." A mandate is a contract by which one commits a lawful business to the management of another who undertakes to perform the service gratuitously. Richardson v. Futrell, 42 Miss. 525; McCauley v. Davidson, 10 Minn. 418, 421 (Gil. 335); Eddy v. Livingston, 35 Mo. 487, 492, 88 Am. Dec. 122; Bronnenburg v. Charman, 80 Ind. 475, 477. Where one carried gold dust as a favor from California to New Orleans, to be delivered to a third person, and the mandator gave the mandatary the privilege of converting the gold dust into coin, such a conferring of power did not change the relationship of bailor and bailee into that of debtor and creditor. Goodenow v. Snyder, 3 G. Greene (Iowa) 599. Delivery of a horse to a farrier, who gratuitiously offers to cure him, is bailment of the horse, and the farrier becomes a mandatary. CONNER v. WINTON, 8 Ind. 315, 65 Am. Dec. 761, Dobie Cas. Bailments and Carriers, 54. See, also, Funkhouser v. Ingles, 17 Mo. App. 232; Devalcourt v. Dillon, 12 La. Ann. 672.

[13] Jones, Bailm. 53.

in feasance, and a depositum merely in custody. Judge Story [14] and many others have clearly pointed out, though, that for practical purposes the importance of the distinction is almost negligible. This is true, since the mere custody of a thing involves the performance of some services, while the services demanded in a mandatum require the custody of the thing in order that they may be performed. The true distinction between them is that in the case of a depositum the principal object of the parties is the custody of the thing, and the service and labor are merely accessorial; in the case of a mandatum, the labor and service are the principal objects of the parties, and the custody of the thing is merely accessorial.[15]

NATURE OF THE RELATION

22. Bailments for the sole benefit of the bailor may be created
(a) By contract, or
(b) By operation of law.

By Contract

Bailments for the sole benefit of the bailor are in the great majority of cases created by express contract. The bailee usually expressly agrees either to keep the thing deposited, or to perform some active services about it, as the case may be.[16] When the bailment is thus created by express contract, the ordinary rules of contracts, both as to their construction and validity, are applicable and require no further discussion here.[17]

By Operation of Law

It has been seen that bailments may be created by operation of law, independently of any express contract between the parties.[18] Such a bailment is called a quasi or constructive bailment. It is usually for the sole benefit of the bailor and is substantially in legal contemplation a depositum. If the law, however, in a particu-

14 Story, Bailm. § 140. "In cases of deposit," says he, "something almost always remains to be done, besides a mere passive custody. If the deposit is perishable, labor must be performed to keep it in proper order. If it is a living animal, as a horse, suitable food and exercise must be given to it. In the next place, in mandates there is commonly custody; the possession of the thing being generally indispensable to the performance of the act intended by the parties, so that in each contract there is custody, and labor and service to be performed."

15 Story, Bailm. § 140.

16 Lethbridge v. Phillips, 2 Starkie (Eng.) 544; Foster v. President, etc., of Essex Bank, 17 Mass. 479, 9 Am. Dec. 168; Eddy v. Livingston, 35 Mo. 487, 88 Am. Dec. 122.

17 Ante, p. 16.

18 Ante, p. 23.

lar bailment awards the bailee compensation, as in the case of salvage for property saved at sea, the bailment is then one for mutual benefit.[19] As has been seen, however, it is a general rule that the law will not impose the liabilities of a bailee on one unless he voluntarily accepts possession of the goods. No man can be made a bailee of another's property without his express or implied consent. The finder of lost goods, for example, is under no obligation whatsoever to take them into his custody; but if he does voluntarily assume the care of them, he thereby becomes burdened with the liabilities of a depositary.[20]

Involuntary Deposits

An exception to the general principle that the duties of a bailee are never by law thrust upon a person without his consent is found in a somewhat anomalous class of bailments, which Story aptly calls "involuntary deposits." These arise whenever the goods of one person have by an unavoidable casualty or accident been lodged upon the land of another person, as where lumber floating in a river is cast upon the land of another person by a sudden freshet and left there, or where goods are blown upon the land of another by a tempest.[21] The rights and duties of the parties in this class of cases are not very well settled, as they are not of frequent occurrence. But it would seem that the owner of the land is a quasi bailee, with liabilities similar to those of a finder of lost property. He cannot, when there is no fault on the part of the owner of goods, refuse to deliver the goods to their owner and decline to permit the latter to remove them.[22] But if the goods are cast upon another's land through the negligence or wrong of the owner, the owner has no right, at least without making compensation, to enter to remove them.[23] Even here, though, the landowner would have no right to use the goods or otherwise dispose of them. So, also, it seems that the owner of the goods would be liable if he fails to remove his goods after due notice, even though they were cast there originally without his fault.

19 Story, Bailm. § 622; Abbott, Shipp. (5th Ed.) pt. 3, c. 10, §§ 1, 2; In re Cargo ex Schiller, 2 Rob. Div. (Eng.) 145; post, p. 103.

20 Ante, note 7.

21 Walker v. Norfolk & W. R. Co., 67 W. Va. 273, 67 S. E. 722; Anthony v. Haney, 8 Bing. (Eng.) 186; Mitten v. Faudrye, Poph. (Eng.) 161 (same case as Millen v. Hawery, Latch [Eng.] 13); Nicholson v. Chapman, 2 H. Bl. (Eng.) 254.

22 Cases in preceding note; Read v. Smith, 2 N. B. (Can.) 288.

23 Anthony v. Haney, 8 Bing. (Eng.) 186. And see Jaggard, Torts, 149.

ABSENCE OF COMPENSATION TO BAILEE

23. The distinguishing feature of bailments for the bailor's sole benefit is the entire absence of any compensation (direct or indirect, express or implied) to the bailee.

Absence of Intended Compensation

In this class of bailments it is of the very essence of the contract that the proposed custody or services be gratuitous.[24] A person becomes a bailee for hire when he takes goods into his possession for a compensation, and the nature and amount of the compensation are immaterial.[25] The law will not inquire into the adequacy of the compensation, its relative value in connection with the services rendered, or the certainty of its being realized by the bailee. These questions are all left to the parties, who are the sole judges of the benefits or advantages to be derived from their contracts It is sufficient to make the bailment one for hire if the consideration be of any value, however slight, and even a mere contingent benefit will suffice.[26] The real question is: Was the bailment contract made with reference to a consideration moving to the bailee?

The intent of the parties is of course the important thing. This

[24] Wilson v. Wilson, 16 La. Ann. 155; Lafourche & Terrebonne Nav. Co. v. Collins, 12 La. Ann. 119; Mariner v. Smith, 5 Heisk. (Tenn.) 203; Pattison v. Syracuse Nat. Bank, 4 Thomp. & C. (N. Y.) 96; Lobenstein v. Pritchett, 8 Kan. 213. But see Waterman v. Gibson, 5 La. Ann. 672. A mandatary cannot recover on a quantum meruit. Wilson v. Wilson, 16 La. Ann. 155; Preston v. Prather, 137 U. S. 604, 11 Sup. Ct. 162, 34 L. Ed. 788; First Nat. Bank v. Graham, 100 U. S. 699, 25 L. Ed. 750; WOODRUFF v. PAINTER, 150 Pa. 91, 24 Atl. 621, 16 L. R. A. 451, 30 Am. St. Rep. 786, Dobie Cas. Bailments and Carriers, 40; Devalcourt v. Dillon, 12 La. Ann. 672. The bailment was none the less gratuitous by virtue of the fact that one motive of the bailee was that the bailment might assist to hold trade in a town in which he carried on business. Bissell v. Harris & Co., 1 Neb. (Unof.) 535, 95 N. W. 779.

[25] If there be compensation, express or implied, certain or uncertain in amount, the contract is a contract for hire. Newhall v. Paige, 10 Gray (Mass.) 366; Ouderkirk v. Central Nat. Bank, 52 Hun, 1, 4 N. Y. Supp. 734; Hollister v. Central Nat. Bank, 52 Hun, 610, 4 N. Y. Supp. 737; Keller v. Rhoads, 39 Pa. 513, 80 Am. Dec. 539; GRAY v. MERRIAM, 148 Ill. 179, 35 N. E. 810, 32 L. R. A. 769, 39 Am. St. Rep. 172, Dobie Cas. Bailments and Carriers, 43; Vogel & Son v. Braudrick, 25 Okl. 259, 105 Pac. 197.

[26] Newhall v. Paige, 10 Gray (Mass.) 366. And see Chamberlin v. Cobb, 32 Iowa, 161; Francis v. Shrader, 67 Ill. 272; White v. Humphery, 11 Q. B. 43; VIGO AGRICULTURAL SOC. v. BRUMFIELD, 102 Ind. 146, 1 N. E. 382, 52 Am. Rep. 657, Dobie Cas. Bailments and Carriers, 42; Prince v. Alabama State Fair, 106 Ala. 340, 17 South. 449, 28 L. R. A. 716; WOODRUFF v. PAINTER, 150 Pa. 91, 24 Atl. 621, 16 L. R. A. 451, 30 Am. St. Rep. 786, Dobie Cas. Bailments and Carriers, 40.

is a question of fact, to be determined in view of all the surrounding facts and circumstances.[27] The general principles as to the consideration of contracts are applicable here as elsewhere. When the bailment contract expressly provides for a consideration, there is usually little difficulty. The cases that give trouble are those in which the consideration, if any, is implied. Due weight must then be given to any surrounding facts and circumstances that tend to throw light on the real intent of the parties. Thus, in doubtful cases, the fact that the bailment was in the line of the bailee's business, for which he regularly received compensation, that the bailee was a stranger to the bailor, or that the bailment involved the expenditure of much time and trouble, would tend to prove that a consideration was intended;[28] while the fact that the bailment was outside of the bailee's regular business, that the bailee was a relative or intimate friend of the bailor, or that the bailment involved only little time and slight trouble, might indicate that no compensation was expected.[29] Of course, where a consideration is express, or would otherwise be implied, the bailee could not escape the duties of a bailee for hire by a secret and uncommunicated mental reservation not to charge for his services.[30]

This question is a practical and often a close one when a patron on the premises of another, in a transaction involving a financial consideration, makes use of facilities supplied for his convenience

[27] Lobenstein v. Pritchett, 8 Kan. 213; Mariner v. Smith, 5 Heisk. (Tenn.) 203; Pattison v. Syracuse Nat. Bank, 4 Thomp. & C. (N. Y.) 96; Kincheloe v. Priest, 89 Mo. 240, 1 S. W. 235, 58 Am. Rep. 117. In Height v. State (Tex. Cr. App.) 150 S. W. 908, a bailment of a piano in consideration of the right of the bailee's child to use the piano, was held to be a bailment of hiring, and not gratuitous. See, also, Vogel & Son v. Braudrick, 25 Okl. 259, 105 Pac. 197.

[28] Pattison v. Syracuse Nat. Bank, 4 Thomp. & C. (N. Y.) 96; Kirtland v Montgomery, 1 Swan (Tenn.) 452; Second Nat. Bank v. Ocean Nat. Bank, 11 Blatchf. 362, Fed. Cas. No. 12,602; Rea's Adm'x v. Trotter, 26 Grat. (Va.) 585. If a package containing money be handed to the captain of a steamboat, which is in the habit of charging freight for carrying remittances of money, without informing him of its contents, and the package is lost, the owners of the vessel are not liable. Mechanics' & Traders' Bank v. Gordon, 5 La. Ann. 604. Public officers who receive property in the course of their official duty are held to be bailees for hire. Aurentz v. Porter, 56 Pa. 115; Browning v. Hanford, 5 Denio (N. Y.) 586; Witowski v. Brennan, 41 N. Y. Super. Ct. Rep. 284; Moore v. Westervelt, 27 N. Y. 234; Wood v. Bodine, 32 Hun (N. Y.) 354.

[29] Dart v. Lowe, 5 Ind. 131; Lafourche & Terrebonne Nav. Co. v. Collins, 12 La. Ann. 119. A mere volunteer, under no legal obligation to take and store goods, who accepts the temporary custody of them without any agreement on the subject, has no lien on them for storage. Rivara v. Ghio, 3 E. D. Smith (N. Y.) 264.

[30] Second Nat. Bank v. Ocean Nat. Bank, 11 Blatchf. 362, Fed. Cas. No. 12,602; Kirtland v. Montgomery, 1 Swan (Tenn.) 452.

by such other person in connection with this transaction. Thus where a customer in a tailor's shop leaves his clothes in a dressing-room to try on the clothes made by the tailor,[31] or where the patron of a restaurant[32] or barber-shop[33] hangs up his hat or overcoat. If it is conceded that there is sufficient delivery to constitute a bailment, the courts, in the absence of exceptional circumstances, usually hold the bailment one for mutual benefit, on the ground that the price paid in the principal transaction includes also the services incidental thereto.[34]

Special Bank Deposits

Special bank deposits, or the gratuitous deposit of gold, stocks, even money, or other things of value, with a bank, on the understanding that the identical things deposited are to be returned, constitute, perhaps, the most important class of bailments for the bailor's sole benefit.[35] Such deposits are not uncommon, though

[31] Rea v. Simmons, 141 Mass. 561, 6 N. E. 699, 55 Am. Rep. 492. See, also, Bunnell v. Stern, 122 N. Y. 539, 25 N. E. 910, 10 L. R. A. 481, 19 Am. St. Rep. 519; WOODRUFF v. PAINTER, 150 Pa. 91, 24 Atl. 621, 16 L. R. A. 451, 30 Am. St. Rep. 786, Dobie Cas. Bailments and Carriers, 40.

[32] Ultzen v. Nicols, 1 Q. B. 92; Buttman v. Dennett, 9 Misc. Rep. 462, 30 N. Y. Supp. 247; Simpson v. Rourke, 13 Misc. Rep. 230, 34 N. Y. Supp. 11; Goff v. Wanamaker, 25 Wkly. Notes Cas. (Pa.) 358.

[33] Dilberto v. Harris, 95 Ga. 571, 23 S. E. 112. See, also, Trowbridge v. Schriever, 5 Daly (N. Y.) 11.

[34] See cases cited in three preceding notes. See, also, the following cases, all involving the liability of keepers of bathing houses: Tombler v. Koelling, 60 Ark. 62, 28 S. W. 795, 27 L. R. A. 502, 46 Am. St. Rep. 146; Levy v. Appleby, 1 City Ct. R. (N. Y.) 252; Bird v. Everard, 4 Misc. Rep. 104, 23 N. Y. Supp. 1008; Sulpho-Saline Bath Co. v. Allen, 66 Neb. 295, 92 N. W. 354, 1 Ann. Cas. 21; Walpert v. Bohan, 126 Ga. 532, 55 S. E. 181, 6 L. R. A. (N. S.) 828, 115 Am. St. Rep. 114, 8 Ann. Cas. 89.

[35] Smith v. First Nat. Bank in Westfield, 99 Mass. 605, 97 Am. Dec. 59; First Nat. Bank of Carlisle v. Graham, 79 Pa. 106, 21 Am. Rep. 49; First Nat. Bank of Allentown v. Rex, 89 Pa. 308, 33 Am. Rep. 767; Lancaster County Nat. Bank v. Smith, 62 Pa. 47; Scott v. National Bank of Chester Valley, 72 Pa. 471, 13 Am. Rep. 711; De Haven v. Kensington Nat. Bank, 81 Pa. 95; Dearborn v. Union Nat. Bank of Brunswick, 61 Me. 369; Maury v. Coyle, 34 Md. 235; First Nat. Bank v. Graham, 100 U. S. 699, 25 L. Ed. 750; GRAY v. MERRIAM, 148 Ill. 179, 35 N. E. 810, 32 L. R. A. 769, 39 Am. St. Rep. 172, Dobie Cas. Bailments and Carriers, 43; Manhattan Bank v. Walker, 130 U. S. 267, 9 Sup. Ct. 519, 32 L. Ed. 959; Pattison v. Syracuse Nat. Bank, 80 N. Y. 82, 36 Am. Rep. 582; Mutual Acc. Ass'n of the Northwest v. Jacobs, 141 Ill. 261, 31 N. E. 414, 16 L. R. A. 516, 33 Am. St. Rep. 302; Giblin v. McMullen, L. R. 2 P. C. 317; Bank of Blackwell v. Dean, 9 Okl. 626, 60 Pac. 226; Moreland v. Brown, 86 Fed. 257, 30 C. C. A. 23. See Morse, Banks and Banking, §§ 189–203. In the absence of any explanatory evidence, an instrument signed by a depositary, by which he acknowledges that a third person has deposited with him for "safe-keeping" a certain number of dollars in gold coin, which depositary is to "return whenever called for," will be held a special deposit

not so numerous as formerly, owing to the tremendous development of safe-deposit companies, which for a compensation make a specialty of providing facilities for this class of business. There is great conflict among the courts as to many of the rules of law governing special deposits, and the confusion is further heightened by the judges, owing to their loose and inaccurate use of language.

Certain principles, however, seem to be well established. Corporations doing a general banking business have an implied power to receive such special deposits, even though they are gratuitous, for safe-keeping.[36] Even as to a national bank, a contract creating such a deposit is not beyond its corporate powers.[37] Though such a deposit is within the powers of a banking corporation, in order that the deposit may be binding in the bank, it must be created by the board of directors, or by some officer of the bank with the authorization of the directors, either express or implied,[38] as in the case of the cashier habitually receiving such deposits, while the directors, knowing of such habit, allow it to continue.[39] Since the reception of deposits for safe-keeping, however, lies rather outside of the ordinary business of a bank, no officer, either ministerial or executive, without the express or implied authority of the directors, can bind the bank (though he may render himself personally liable) by contracts for such bailments.

The degree of care which the bank must exercise in the case of special deposits is by many courts placed at ordinary care,[40] while others, with better reason, it would seem, require (as in the case

Wright v. Paine, 62 Ala. 340, 34 Am. Rep. 24. By a subsequent contract a special deposit may be turned into a general one. Chiles v. Garrison, 32 Mo. 475. An agreement that the depositary shall pay interest on the deposit makes the transaction of special deposit one of open account. Howard v. Roeben, 33 Cal. 399.

[36] Foster v. President, etc., of Essex Bank, 17 Mass. 479, 9 Am. Dec. 168; Marine Bank of Chicago v. Chandler, 27 Ill. 525, 81 Am. Dec. 249; Scott v. National Bank of Chester Valley, 72 Pa. 471, 13 Am. Rep. 711; Lancaster County Nat. Bank v. Smith, 62 Pa. 54; First Nat. Bank of Muskogee v. Tevis, 29 Okl. 714, 119 Pac. 218.

[37] First Nat. Bank v. Graham, 100 U. S. 699, 25 L. Ed. 750.

[38] Lloyd v. West Branch Bank, 15 Pa. 172, 53 Am. Dec. 581; First Nat. Bank of Lyons v. Ocean Nat. Bank, 60 N. Y. 278, 19 Am. Rep. 181; Chattahoochee Nat. Bank v. Schley, 58 Ga. 369; Foster v. President, etc., of Essex Bank, 17 Mass. 479, 9 Am. Dec. 168; Scott v. National Bank of Chester Valley, 72 Pa. 471, 13 Am. Rep. 711.

[39] First Nat. Bank of Carlisle v. Graham, 79 Pa. 106, 21 Am. Rep. 49; Chattahoochee Nat. Bank v. Schley, 58 Ga. 369; First Nat. Bank of Muskogee v. Tevis, 29 Okl. 714, 119 Pac. 218.

[40] First Nat. Bank of Mansfield v. Zent, 39 Ohio St. 105; Maury v. Coyle, 34 Md. 235.

of other bailments for the bailor's sole benefit) only slight care[41] When the act resulting in the loss of, or injury to, the thing deposited is the act of an officer of a corporation, the corporation is not responsible therefor (according to well-known principles of agency), unless such act is within the scope of the employment of such officer, or unless the directors or other supervising corporate authority with knowledge of his unfitness either employed or retained such officer. When the act of the officer is not a mere negative or careless one, but rather a fraudulent or felonious one (as where the cashier steals the thing deposited), the question of the liability of the bank, in the absence of negligence in employing or retaining the officer, is a much-mooted one. The question, of course, is one of agency. In a leading American case, Foster v. President, etc., of Essex Bank,[42] the bank was held not liable. This case, though frequently followed, has in other cases been severely criticised.[43] Where the cashier is the officer charged with the supervision of the thing deposited, and has therefore access to the safe in which it is kept, it would seem that the modern conception, at least, of the scope of an agent's employment is broad enough to render the bank liable.

[41] First Nat. Bank of Muskogee v. Tevis, 29 Okl. 714, 119 Pac. 218; First Nat. Bank v. Graham, 100 U. S. 699, 25 L. Ed. 750; Chattahoochee Nat. Bank v. Schley, 58 Ga. 369; Ouderkirk v. Central Nat. Bank of Troy, 119 N. Y. 263, 23 N. E. 875; Foster v. President, etc., of Essex Bank, 17 Mass. 479, 9 Am. Dec. 168; Pattison v. Syracuse Nat. Bank, 80 N. Y. 82, 36 Am. Rep. 582. The language of the courts in defining the terms used to designate the measure of care here is frequently inaccurate, wrong and even contradictory.

[42] 17 Mass. 497, 9 Am. Dec. 168.

[43] The doctrine of Foster v. President, etc., of Essex Bank was criticised in Preston v. Prather, 137 U. S. 604, 11 Sup. Ct. 162, 34 L. Ed. 788. The court, in speaking of thefts by bank employés of special deposits made in the bank, said: "The doctrine of exemption from liability in such cases was at one time carried so far as to shield the bailees from the fraudulent acts of their own officers and employés, although their employment embraced a supervision of the property, such acts not being deemed within the scope of their employment." And that case was followed in GRAY v. MERRIAM, 148 Ill. 179, 35 N. E. 810, 32 L. R. A. 769, 39 Am. St. Rep. 172, Dobie Cas. Bailments and Carriers, 43. And see L'Herbette v. Pittsfield Nat. Bank, 162 Mass. 137, 38 N. E. 368, 44 Am. St. Rep. 354; Scott v. National Bank of Chester Valley, 72 Pa. 471, 13 Am. Rep. 711; First Nat. Bank of Allentown v. Rex, 89 Pa. 308, 33 Am. Rep. 767. See 2 Street, Foundations of Legal Liability, pp. 276, 277.

RIGHTS AND DUTIES OF THE PARTIES

24. The rights and duties of the bailor and bailee depend primarily upon the special contract in each case. The principles discussed, however, are, unless varied by the special contract, common to all bailments for the bailor's sole benefit. The utter absence of benefit to the bailee is ample warrant for making the bailee's duties as slight as is consistent with the nature and purpose of the bailment.

In General

The rights and duties of the parties are, of course, primarily dependent upon the contract they have made.[44] The instructions of the bailor accompanying the delivery and the terms of acceptance imposed by the bailee are binding upon both parties. Subject only to the limitation that their contract must not be in violation of positive law or against public policy, the parties may by contract vary their rights and liabilities at will.[45]

The rights and duties of the bailor and bailee in this class of bailments, in the absence of special contract, may well be considered together. In the transaction, the more active and important part is played by the bailee. In the discussion of his rights and duties, those of the bailor will incidentally appear.

The prime determinant, to be kept constantly in view in working out the rights and correlative duties of the parties, is, of course, the fact that the bailor alone derives any benefit from the transaction. It follows, accordingly, that the burdens as far as is consistent with the essential nature of the bailment, should rest with the bailor, and the gratuitous undertaking of the bailee should be made as light for him as is possible. This will clearly appear in the discussion of the rights and duties of the parties to such a bailment contained in the succeeding sections of this chapter.

EXPENSES OF CARRYING OUT THE BAILMENT

25. The bailor must indemnify the bailee against necessary expenses reasonably incurred in the performance of the bailment. For the payment of such expenses, the bailee has implied authority to bind the bailor by a contract with a third person.

[44] Ferguson v. Porter, 3 Fla. 27; McCauley v. Davidson, 10 Minn. 418 (Gil. 335); Fellowes v. Gordon, 8 B. Mon. (Ky.) 415; Archer v. Walker, 38 Ind. 472.

[45] Ante, pp. 18-19.

Bailor must Indemnify Bailee against Expense

While the bailee, in bailments for the sole benefit of the bailor, is not entitled to any compensation for his services, he is entitled to recover his actual disbursements and expenses necessarily incurred in carrying out the bailment.[46] This is naturally implied in the undertaking. The law does not presume that the bailee, in thus undertaking a gratuitous task, intended to assume the additional burden of making any pecuniary expenditures. Particularly in doubtful cases, the bailee should, if possible, secure the bailor's consent before the expense is incurred. It is equally immaterial, however, either that the expenses were greater than those that the owner himself would have paid, if these expenses were reasonably incurred, or that the bailor has not derived the expected benefit from the execution of the bailment, if such failure was in no way caused by the fault of the bailee.[47] So, also, the bailee can claim indemnity from the bailor against liability on contracts entered into by the bailee in his own name, which are necessarily incidental to the performance of the bailment.[48] At common law the bailee had no lien on the goods forming the subject-matter of the bailment for such expenses, but might claim and recover them in an action.[49]

Reward Offered for Recovery of Lost Goods

When the owner of lost property offers a specific sum of money as a reward for its return, the finder has a lien for the amount of the reward and can retain the goods until this reward is paid.[50] If no particular sum was offered, but merely a liberal reward, then there is no lien.[51] Many cases hold that the finder cannot

46 Story, Bailm. §§ 121, 154; Devalcourt v. Dillon, 12 La. Ann. 672; Harter v. Blanchard, 64 Barb. (N. Y.) 617; Bacon v. Fourth Nat. Bank (City Ct. N. Y.) 9 N. Y. Supp. 435; Chase v. Corcoran, 106 Mass. 286. Where the purchaser of goods shipped them back to the seller without any notification, or any previous agreement in regard thereto, and the seller, in order to protect the goods, stored them, he became a gratuitous bailee, and the buyer was liable to the seller for necessary storage charges actually paid. Smith v. F. W. Heitman Co., 44 Tex. Civ. App. 358, 98 S. W. 1074. Courts are indisposed to extend, by inference, the perils of an unprofitable trust; and so it is that every bailee without reward is regarded as having assumed the least responsibility consistent with his actual undertaking. Christian v. First Nat. Bank, 155 Fed. 705, 84 C. C. A. 53.

47 Story, Bailm. § 197.

48 See Story, Bailm. § 198.

49 Nicholson v. Chapman, 2 H. Bl. (Eng.) 254; Reeder v. Anderson's Adm'rs, 4 Dana (Ky.) 193; Amory v. Flyn, 10 Johns. (N. Y.) 102, 6 Am. Dec. 316; Etter v. Edwards, 4 Watts (Pa.) 63; Chase v. Corcoran, 106 Mass. 286.

50 Wentworth v. Day, 3 Metc. (Mass.) 352, 37 Am. Dec. 145; Cummings v. Gann, 52 Pa. 484.

51 Wilson v. Guyton, 8 Gill (Md.) 213.

even claim the reward offered, unless he performed the services with knowledge of the reward.[52] When no reward is offered, the courts agree that no compensation can be claimed merely for finding the goods, though the finder could claim reasonable expenses necessarily involved in keeping the goods.[53]

Bailee may Bind Bailor by Contract

Instead of paying out money and seeking reimbursement, the bailee may make the contract (necessary to carry out the bailment) with the third person in the name of the bailor, and the latter will be bound thereon. In other words, inhering in the relation of a bailment for the bailor's sole benefit is an implied agency on the part of the bailee to bind the bailor as principal by such contracts as are involved in performing the object for which the bailment was created. Thus, where a horse, which was pastured by a bailee without reward, broke his leg, it was held that the bailee had implied authority to contract, in behalf of the bailor, with a competent farrier for the care and keeping of the horse, and to bind the bailor by such contract until the latter could be informed of the injury, and had time and opportunity to make other provision for the care of the horse.[54]

LIABILITY FOR NONFEASANCE AND MISFEASANCE

26. A person is not liable for his nonfeasance in failing to enter upon a bailment, though he has gratuitously promised to do so. Once the bailment is begun, however, the bailee is liable for his misfeasance in the defective performance of the bailment.

A clear distinction should be noted between an actual bailment (that is, when the relation is really established by the delivery of the goods to the bailee) and a mere executory contract contemplating the creation of a bailment in the future. In the first case, the party actually becomes a bailee; in the second, he merely agrees to become a bailee at a later date. The second case is no more a bailment than a mere promise to marry is a marriage.

Nonfeasance

In the second case, since there is no bailment, but a mere executory contract, the general principles of contract apply. It will

[52] Howland v. Lounds, 51 N. Y. 604, 10 Am. Rep. 654.

[53] Watts v. Ward, 1 Or. 86, 62 Am. Dec. 299; Amory v. Flyn, 10 Johns. (N. Y.) 102, 6 Am. Dec. 316.

[54] Harter v. Blanchard, 64 Barb. (N. Y.) 617.

readily be seen that the promise of the person that he will become a bailee (since he will receive no benefit, even if a bailment is afterwards created) is without consideration, and therefore unenforceable. Such person, then, can break his executory contract with impunity and incur no legal liability. By nonfeasance, then, which imposes no liability, is meant the utter failure even to enter upon the performance of the bailment. No legal responsibility thus rests on one who declines to become a bailee, though he has gratuitously agreed to do so.[55]

Misfeasance

If, however, the goods have been delivered to the person, then a bailment is actually created; and this task, once entered upon, must be completed according to its terms, including both duties created by contract and those created by law.[56] Thus any performance must be a proper performance, and for a defective performance the bailee is liable in damages. A consideration is here found in the fact of the actual intrusting by the bailor of his goods to the bailee; the acceptance of the bailment, thus resulting in a loss of possession to the bailor during the continuance of the bailment, prevents the bailor from making other arrangements as to the goods, which he might well have done had there been merely nonfeasance, or a failure to create the bailment at all. For misfeasance, or a defective performance, the bailee is thus liable, and the misfeasance may, of course, consist in a negative act, such as the failure to take proper precautions to protect the goods in the possession of the bailee.

Here there is liability imposed on one who is an actual bailee. When the bailment relation once attaches, the law imposes on the bailee certain duties, which he must perform or answer for the consequences. Though these duties vary in the particular classes

[55] Nonfeasance of gratuitous undertaking creates no liability. Morrison v. Orr, 3 Stew. & P. (Ala.) 49, 23 Am. Dec. 319; French v. Reed, 6 Bin. (Pa.) 308; Smedes v. Utica Bank, 20 Johns. (N. Y.) 372; Ainsworth v. Backus, 5 Hun (N. Y.) 414; THORNE v. DEAS, 4 Johns. (N. Y.) 84, Dobie Cas. Bailments and Carriers, 47; Rutgers v. Lucet, 2 Johns. Cas. (N. Y.) 92; McGee v. Bast, 6 J. J. Marsh. (Ky.) 453; Elsee v. Gatward, 5 Term R. (Eng.) 143.

[56] See cases in preceding note, and see discussions and cases cited in section 29. See, also, Walden v. Karr, 88 Ill. 49; Graves v. Ticknor, 6 N. H. 537; First Nat. Bank of Carlisle v. Graham, 79 Pa. 106, 21 Am. Rep. 49; Knowing v. Manly, 49 N. Y. 192, 10 Am. Rep. 346; Whitney v. Lee, 8 Metc. (Mass.) 92; Clark v. Gaylord, 24 Conn. 484; Wilkinson v. Verity, L. R. 6 C. P. (Eng.) 206. For applications of this principle to common-law agencies, see Fellowes v. Gordon, 8 B. Mon. (Ky.) 415; McGee v. Bast, 6 J. J. Marsh. (Ky.) 453; Ferguson v. Porter, 3 Fla. 27; Wilkinson v. Coverdale, 1 Esp. (Eng.) 75; Park v. Hammond, 4 Camp. 344; Balfe v. West, 13 C. B. 466.

of bailments, for a defective performance of the particular duty attached to the bailment in question, the bailee is equally responsible in a bailment from which he receives no benefit as in one from which he derives the sole benefit.

USE OF BAILED CHATTELS BY BAILEE

27. The bailee has no right to any beneficial use of the thing bailed. This he may use only in so far as such use is incidental to the carrying out of the purpose for which the bailment was created.

In this class of bailments, the bailee has no right to the beneficial use of the goods bailed to him; for, if he had such a right, since this right would be a benefit accruing to the bailee, the bailment would become one for the mutual benefit of the bailor and bailee.[57] It may happen, however, that the proper keeping of the property involves a certain measure of use, such as exercising a horse. The bailee may in such case keenly enjoy riding the horse, but as long as his use of the animal is limited to such as is necessary for its preservation, such enjoyment is entirely adventitious, as being incidental to his duties as bailee, and hence would not change the character of the bailment into one for mutual benefit.[58] Any attempt, however, by the bailee to act in regard to the thing as its owner, such as disposing of it to a third person, or even to the extent of making an unauthorized use of it, would constitute a conversion, rendering him at once liable to the owner.[59]

INTEREST OF BAILOR AND BAILEE

28. The general property or ownership in the thing bailed remains in the bailor. The bailee has not even a special property therein, but merely a possessory interest. Either party, however, may maintain an appropriate action for an injury to, or conversion of, the thing bailed.

[57] Alvord v. Davenport, 43 Vt. 30; Boston & C. Smelting Co. v. Reed, 23 Colo. 523, 48 Pac. 515; Persch v. Quiggle, 57 Pa. 247. The finder of a lottery ticket is not entitled to receive payment on it. If paid, with notice of the holder's possession by finding, it can be collected again by the rightful owner. McLaughlin v. Waite, 5 Wend. (N. Y.) 404, 21 Am. Dec. 232. See Height v. State (Tex. Cr. App.) 150 S. W. 908.

[58] Mores v. Conham, Owen (Eng.) 123; Anon., 2 Salk. (Eng.) 522.

[59] Dale v. Brinckerhoff, 7 Daly (N. Y.) 45; King v. Bates, 57 N. H. 446.

Nature of Bailee's Interest

There is no little confusion in the books as to the nature of the interest of the bailee in a bailment for the bailor's sole benefit. Does this consist merely of a "possessory interest," or does it rise to the dignity of a "special property" in the bailed goods? Much of this confusion is no doubt due to an inaccurate use of terms.

If by the term "special property" is meant "something in the nature of an estate carved out of the general ownership in a thing," a right in rem, in other words, a fixed right inhering in a thing or definitely attached to it, then it would seem that the precarious interest of the gratuitous bailee is certainly not a special property.[60] It is clear, though, that such a bailee has a lawful custody and possession of the thing, which he can protect when such possession is interfered with by third persons.[61] The real special property is in the thing, and can be asserted, regardless of persons (being available equally against one as against another), against all the world. But in the bailment in question, the bailor can at any time terminate the bailment and recover the goods.[62] This seems utterly inconsistent with the notion that the bailee's interest in the goods amounts to a special property. The bailee here, then, has a possessory interest, but not a special property, in the bailed goods. This distinction will become clearer when the bailee in mutual benefit bailments is contrasted with the bailee in gratuitous bailments as to their comparative interests in the goods forming the subject-matter of the bailment.

[60] COMMONWEALTH v. MORSE, 14 Mass. 217, Dobie Cas. Bailments and Carriers, 51; Norton v. People, 8 Cow. (N. Y.) 137; Sibley v. Story, 8 Vt. 15; Hartop v. Hoare, 3 Atk. (Eng.) 44, 2 Strange, 1187. In Faulkner v. Brown, 13 Wend. (N. Y.) 63, Savage, C. J., asserts that the bailee in such a bailment has a special property in the goods, but it was necessary here only to hold that the bailee had rightful possession of the goods.

[61] But if the depositary has no property whatever in the goods, yet his possession is sufficient ground for a suit against a tort-feasor. Poole v. Symonds, 1 N. H. 289, 8 Am. Dec. 71; Thayer v. Hutchinson, 13 Vt. 504, 37 Am. Dec. 607; Sutton v. Buck, 2 Taunt. (Eng.) 302; Burton v. Hughes, 2 Bing. 173. A depositary may sue one who has converted the property, though the former may not be responsible to the owner. CHAMBERLAIN v. WEST, 37 Minn. 54, 33 N. W. 114, Dobie Cas. Bailments and Carriers, 59. A receiptor to whom a sheriff has intrusted for safe-keeping property attached by him on a writ against a third person may maintain trover against a wrongdoer. Thayer v. Hutchinson, 13 Vt. 504, 37 Am. Dec. 607; Compare Dillenback v. Jerome, 7 Cow. (N. Y.) 294; Norton v. People, 8 Cow. (N. Y.) 137. A finder or other depositary may maintain trover against a person converting the article. Armory v. Delamirie, 1 Strange (Eng.) 505; New York & H. R. Co. v. Haws, 56 N. Y. 175; Brown v. Shaw, 51 Minn. 266, 53 N. W. 633.

[62] Post, p. 72.

The reason often given for the statement that a bailee in a bailment for the bailor's sole benefit has a special property in the goods is that he may maintain the common-law action of trover against one who disturbs his possession by a conversion of the goods, and that, to maintain trover, the plaintiff must have either an absolute or special property in the goods, rather than a mere interest.[63] This test, however, is far from conclusive. Trover is not exclusively founded on a property in goods.[64] It might be remarked that, even if it were, the bailee would bring trover because he had a property in the goods; he would not have such a property because he could bring trover. Such a test could not be applied in those progressive states which by the adoption of "code pleading" have abolished the many futile distinctions between common-law forms of action.

Right of Bailor and Bailee to Sue

As has been seen, the general property or ownership in the thing bailed remains in the bailor, though possession passes to the bailee. Accordingly, it is held that either the bailor or bailee may sue third persons for any interference with the bailee's possession or any injury to the thing bailed.[65] When the bailee sues such third person, in spite of the precarious nature of his possession, it is held that he may recover the full amount of damage to the thing bailed, holding as a kind of trustee for the bailor, and this, even when the bailee would not himself be liable to the bailor for such wrongful act. A full recovery by either bailor or bailee is a bar to a subsequent action by the other.[66] A tendency is clear, however, in recent times to regard the interests of the bailor and bailee as separate and to permit each to sue only for injury to his own interest, and not to recover damages to be held as trustee for the other.[67]

[63] See cases cited in note 61.

[64] But possession is sufficient. 1 Street, Foundations of Legal Liability, p. 251.

[65] Fish v. Skut, 21 Barb. (N. Y.) 333; Tremont Coal Co. v. Manly, 60 Pa. 384. And see Rooth v. Wilson, 1 Barn. & Ald. 58; Thorp v. Burling, 11 Johns. (N. Y.) 285; Cary v. Hotailing, 1 Hill (N. Y.) 311, 37 Am. Dec. 323; Ash v. Putnam, 1 Hill (N. Y.) 302. A gratuitous bailee may maintain an action for the loss of bailed property against a wrongdoer, and the fact that the bailee is not liable to the bailor is no defense. Abrahamovitz v. New York City Ry. Co., 54 Misc. Rep. 539, 104 N. Y. Supp. 663. Where goods have been illegally taken from a bailee in possession, the latter has a right to recover as against the wrongdoer the market value of the goods, and the bailee will then be liable over to the bailor for such interest as he may have in the goods. McCrossan v. Reilly, 33 Pa. Super. Ct. 628.

[66] Green v. Clarke, 12 N. Y. 343; Chesley v. St. Clair, 1 N. H. 189; Abrahamovitz v. New York City R. Co., 54 Misc. Rep. 539, 104 N. Y. Supp. 663.

[67] See article, 25 Harvard Law Review, 655.

DEGREE OF CARE TO BE EXERCISED BY THE BAILEE

29. The bailee owes the duty of exercising only slight care as to the bailed goods. For the violation of this duty, which is negligence, the bailee is liable for any loss or injury directly and proximately resulting therefrom.

In bailments of the class under discussion, since the sole benefit accrues to the bailor, the duty owed by the bailee is placed at merely slight care and the law holds the bailee liable only when loss of the goods or injury to them is fairly attributable to the bailee's failure to exercise even this slight care.[68] As soon as the legal duty is stated,

[68] Depositum: See Dunn v. Branner, 13 La. Ann. 452; Chase v. Maberry, 3 Har. (Del.) 266; Dougherty v. Posegate, 3 Iowa, 88; Green v. Hollingsworth, 5 Dana (Ky.) 173, 30 Am. Dec. 680; Mechanics' & Traders' Bank v. Gordon, 5 La. Ann. 604; Foster v. President, etc., of Essex Bank, 17 Mass. 479, 9 Am. Dec. 168; Edson v. Weston, 7 Cow. (N. Y.) 278; Sodowsky's Ex'r v. McFarland, 3 Dana (Ky.) 204; Whitney v. Lee, 8 Metc. (Mass.) 91; McKay v. Hamblin, 40 Miss. 472; Montieth v. Bissell's Adm'r, Wright (Ohio) 411; Spooner v. Mattoon, 40 Vt. 300, 94 Am. Dec. 395; Davis v. Gay, 141 Mass. 531, 6 N. E. 549; Henry v. Porter, 46 Ala. 293; Hale v. Rawallie, 8 Kan. 136; De Lemos v. Cohen, 28 Misc. Rep. 579, 59 N. Y. Supp. 498.

Mandatum: See Kemp v. Farlow, 5 Ind. 462; McNabb v. Lockhart, 18 Ga. 495; Skelley v. Kahn, 17 Ill. 170; CONNER v. WINTON, 8 Ind. 315, 65 Am. Dec. 761, Dobie Cas. Bailments and Carriers, 54; Jourdan v. Reed, 1 Iowa, 135; Storer v. Gowen, 18 Me. 174; Lampley v. Scott, 24 Miss. 528; McLean v. Rutherford, 8 Mo. 109; Stanton v. Bell, 9 N. C. 145, 11 Am. Dec. 744; Sodowsky's Ex'r v. McFarland, 3 Dana (Ky.) 204; Tompkins v. Saltmarsh, 14 Serg. & R. (Pa.) 275; Anderson v. Foresman, Wright (Ohio) 598; TRACY v. WOOD, 3 Mason, 132, Fed. Cas. No. 14,130, Dobie Cas. Bailments and Carriers, 52; Lobenstein v. Pritchett, 8 Kan. 213.

And, generally, First Nat. Bank of Lyons v. Ocean Nat. Bank, 60 N. Y. 278, 19 Am. Rep. 181; Lancaster County Nat. Bank v. Smith, 62 Pa. 47; Griffith v. Zipperwick, 28 Ohio St. 388; Green v. Birchard, 27 Ind. 483; Knowles v. Atlantic & St. L. R. Co., 38 Me. 55, 61 Am. Dec. 234; Dinsmore v. Abbott, 89 Me. 373, 36 Atl. 621; Jenkins v. Bacon, 111 Mass. 373, 15 Am. Rep. 33; Eddy v. Livingston, 35 Mo. 487, 88 Am. Dec. 122; Belmont Coal Co. v. Richter, 31 W. Va. 858, 8 S. E. 609; King v. Exchange Bank, 106 Mo. App. 1, 78 S. W. 1038; Smith v. Elizabethport Banking Co., 69 N. J. Law, 288, 55 Atl. 248.

One to whom a picture was sent without his knowledge is not liable for an accidental injury to it. Lethbridge v. Phillips, 2 Starkie (Eng.) 544. Bailee liable only for gross negligence is still liable for actual conversion of the property. Graves v. Smith, 14 Wis. 5, 80 Am. Dec. 762. Where a hotel clerk received and signed a return receipt for a registered letter delivered to him by a letter carrier for a guest of the hotel, and the letter was lost through his negligence, he was held liable. Joslyn v. King, 27 Neb. 38, 42 N. W. 756, 4 L. R. A. 457, 20 Am. St. Rep. 656. Where one gratuitously undertakes to carry a letter containing money from one city to another, he is liable for nondelivery. Beardslee v. Richardson, 11 Wend. (N. Y.) 25, 25 Am. Dec. 596;

it follows that any breach of this duty by the bailee is negligence, which renders him liable for damages proximately ensuing. This measure of slight care as the criterion of the liability of the bailee receiving no benefit from the relation was laid down by Lord Holt in the celebrated case of COGGS v. BERNARD[69] (1703), and has since been very generally followed.

What constitutes slight care, however, is a question of no little difficulty. It cannot be answered by any exact rule that will

Graves v. Ticknor, 6 N. H. 537. A ring deposited with defendant to be illegally raffled for was lost by his gross carelessness. Held, that he was liable. Woolf v. Bernero, 14 Mo. App. 518. An agreement by an agent of a carrier to have goods forwarded to their proper destination, from a point on a connecting line to which they were carried through the mistake of the shipper in addressing them, makes such carrier merely a gratuitous bailee of the goods. Treleven v. Northern Pac. R. Co., 89 Wis. 598, 62 N. W. 536. A common carrier is not liable, as a trespasser, to the owner of merchandise which it has refused to receive, as being badly packed, and which is destroyed, without negligence on its part, while being separated by it from other freight with which it has been improperly mixed, and which it is such carrier's duty to transport. Gulf, C. & S. F. Ry. Co. v. Insurance Co. of North America (Tex. Civ. App.) 28 S. W. 237. Where the defendant was to carry gold dust from California to Iowa gratuitously, there dispose of it, and turn the proceeds over to plaintiff's wife, he was held liable only for gross negligence. Jourdan v. Reed, 1 Iowa, 135. Where a person was to take abroad bonds gratuitously, and deposit them for sale for another person, he was held liable only for gross negligence. Carrington v. Ficklin's Ex'rs, 32 Grat. (Va.) 670.

On a deposit or bailment of money, to be kept without recompense, if the bailees, without authority, attempt to transmit the money to the bailor, at a distant point, by mail or private conveyance, and the money is lost, they are responsible. Stewart v. Frazier, 5 Ala. 114. If the bailee delegates his trust without the consent of the bailor, he is liable regardless of the question of negligence. Colyar v. Taylor, 1 Cold. (Tenn.) 372. Where plaintiff gave money to defendant to keep for him, it constituted a bailment, and on loss of the money defendant would be liable to restore it only in case of gross negligence on his part. Patriska v. Kronk, 57 Misc. Rep. 552, 109 N. Y. Supp. 1092. A deposit of $1,000, made by plaintiff with his brother, placed in an envelope marked as plaintiff's property and put in a safe, is a gratuitous bailment, entailing no liability except for gross negligence. Stevens v. Stevens, 132 Mo. App. 624, 112 S. W. 35. Even if an agreement between plaintiff and defendant that defendant should provide storage and insurance for plaintiff's piano constituted merely a gratuitous agency, the defendant was obligated to act in good faith, without negligence, and to obey the instructions of the plaintiff, as principal, to procure insurance. Schroeder v. Mauzy, 16 Cal. App. 443, 118 Pac. 459.

[69] 2 Ld. Raym. 909, Dobie Cas. Bailments and Carriers, 1. Many of the cases cited in the preceding note and in succeeding notes use the unfortunate term "gross negligence" in stating the liability of the gratuitous bailee, and others go even further and define gross negligence in such terms as to make it the equivalent of a failure to use ordinary (instead of slight) care.

furnish a reliable test in all cases. But the question is one of fact, to be determined according to the peculiar circumstances of each particular case by the jury, under proper instructions from the court.[70]

It is clear, though, that by slight care is meant some care, and that slight care is less than ordinary care (demanded of bailees in mutual benefit bailments), which is itself less than the great care which is demanded of the bailee, when the bailment is solely for his benefit. By just how much slight care is less than ordinary care cannot be exactly stated, since degrees of care do not vary by definite units, nor are they capable of being judged by mathematical standards.

Judge Story[71] describes slight care as that degree of care which men habitually careless or of little prudence generally take in their own concerns. This sets up, then, a theoretical man, who is accustomed to take less care than the ordinary man usually takes about his concerns, by whose habitual conduct slight care is judged. Though slight care is the least exacting and most lenient standard by which the legal responsibility of a bailee is judged, yet the failure to exercise even that care by no means implies fraud, bad faith, or willful wrong on the bailee's part. Witness, for example, the stock case of a man carelessly leaving a purse filled with gold on a table in the public room of an inn.

Slight care is necessarily a term with a meaning of intense

[70] Lancaster County Nat. Bank v. Smith, 62 Pa. 47; Griffith v. Zipperwick, 28 Ohio St. 388; Doorman v. Jenkins, 2 Adol. & E. (Eng.) 256; Carrington v. Ficklin's Ex'rs, 32 Grat. (Va.) 670; Third Nat. Bank of Baltimore v. Boyd, 44 Md. 47, 22 Am. Rep. 35; Gulledge v. Howard, 23 Ark. 61; Skelley v. Kahn, 17 Ill. 170; Storer v. Gowen, 18 Me. 174; Kirtland v. Montgomery, 1 Swan (Tenn.) 452. See also State's Prison v. Hoffman & Bros., 159 N. C. 564, 76 S. E. 3; McKenny Transfer Co. v. Mayer Bros. Co., 170 Ill. App. 607; Baker v. Bailey, 103 Ark. 12, 145 S. W. 532, 39 L. R. A. (N. S.) 1085; Schroeder v. Mauzy, 16 Cal. App. 443, 118 Pac. 459.

[71] Bailm. § 16. In Tompkins v. Saltmarsh, 14 Serg. & R. (Pa.) 275, gross negligence was defined as the omission of that degree of care which even the most inattentive and thoughtless men take of their own concerns. Ordinary negligence was defined as the want of that diligence which the generality of mankind use in their own concerns. These definitions were approved in First Nat. Bank of Carlisle v. Graham, 79 Pa. 106, 117, 21 Am. Rep. 49. The amount of care which gratuitous bailees, under the same circumstances, are accustomed to take of similar goods is a good test. Brown, Carriers, § 28; TRACY v. WOOD, 3 Mason, 132, Fed. Cas. No. 14,130, Dobie Cas. Bailments and Carriers, 52; GRAY v. MERRIAM, 148 Ill. 179, 35 N. E. 810, 32 L. R. A. 769, 39 Am. St. Rep. 172, Dobie Cas. Bailments and Carriers, 43; Preston v. Prather, 137 U. S. 604, 11 Sup. Ct. 162, 34 L. Ed. 788; Bland v. Womack, 6 N. C. 373; Anderson v. Foresman, Wright (Ohio) 598.

relativity, varying with an infinite variety of circumstances,[72] such, for example, as the value of the goods or the people among whom the goods are kept. Thus, the same acts of the bailee might exceed slight care in the bailment of a number of bricks, and yet fall far short of the same degree of care when not bricks, but bars of gold, are being kept; or precautions as to the same bar of gold, adequate when it is exhibited before a church sewing society, would show an utter lack of care when the gold is shown before a company composed largely of thugs and thieves.

It has been frequently said that the bailee is not liable for a loss or injury where he takes the same care of the thing bailed as he does of his own goods.[73] Such a rule is objectionable for many reasons.[74] The law does not put a premium on carelessness by

[72] See cases cited in notes 68, 70. See, also, Tompkins v. Saltmarsh, 14 Serg. & R. (Pa.) 275; Eddy v. Livingston, 35 Mo. 487, 88 Am. Dec. 122; TRACY v. WOOD, 3 Mason, 132, Fed. Cas. No. 14,130, Dobie Cas. Bailments and Carriers, 52. Express or implied notice that the article is of unusual value is quite important. Joslyn v. King, 27 Neb. 38, 42 N. W. 756, 4 L. R. A. 457, 20 Am. St. Rep. 656. H. offered to invest a sum of money for D. in the purchase of an annuity. He laid out the money in securities wholly insufficient, and of no value whatever. Held, that it does not necessarily follow from these circumstances that H. was guilty of gross or corrupt negligence. Dartnell v. Howard, 4 Barn. & C. (Eng.) 345. If a depositary fails to procure suitable means for the extinguishment of fires, he cannot be held liable for an accidental fire which destroyed the chattel deposited. Clark v. Eastern R. Co., 139 Mass. 423, 1 N. E. 128. If the deposit is taken away by superior force, the depositary may make this a defense. Watkins v. Roberts, 28 Ind. 167. If a person intrusted with money by his superior to give to a third person gives it to a boy whom he has seen but a few times, and who has but recently entered the employ of said third person, and the boy absconds, the mandatary is guilty of gross negligence, and is liable to his superior for damages. Skelley v. Kahn, 17 Ill. 170. Where the speculations in stocks and bonds, on margins, of a bank cashier, of which the president had knowledge, were such that the president must have known the cashier's dishonesty, the bank is liable for bonds deposited with it as a gratuitous bailee which the cashier converted to his own use. Merchants' Nat. Bank of Savannah v. Guilmartin, 93 Ga. 503, 21 S. E. 55, 44 Am. St. Rep. 182.

[73] Anderson v. Foresman, Wright (Ohio) 598. Where money is paid by a judgment debtor to the judge, and the latter places it in his desk with his own money and then notifies the judgment creditor that the money is ready for him, and the latter neglects for two days to call for it, during which time the money is stolen, it was held that the judge was not guilty of gross negligence, and hence was not liable. Montieth v. Bissell's Adm'r, Wright (Ohio) 411. See, also, Knowles v. Atlantic & St. L. R. Co., 38 Me. 55, 59, 61 Am. Dec. 234. It is a suspicious circumstance when a bailee claims to have lost the bailed chattels and to have saved his own when both were together. Bland v. Womack, 6 N. C. 373.

[74] First Nat. Bank of Carlisle v. Graham, 79 Pa. 106, 21 Am. Rep. 49; Giblin v. McMullen, 21 Law T. (N. S.) 214; TRACY v. WOOD, 3 Mason, 132, Fed. Cas. No. 14,130, Dobie Cas. Bailments and Carriers, 52; Doorman v. Jen-

permitting a man to take risks with the goods of another simply because he is willing to take such risks with his own. Slight care refers, not to the particular acts of a specific individual, but "looks to the general conduct and character of a whole class of persons." [75] The most that can be said is that taking the same care of the bailed goods as the bailee takes of his own raises a presumption, prima facie at best (rebuttable by other evidence), that he did take slight care of the bailed goods.[76] In other words, taking the same care of bailed goods as of one's own is not an operative fact (one which in itself determines liability), but merely an evidential fact, tending to prove such an operative fact.

Knowledge of Bailee's Character or Manner of Keeping Goods

It is held that where the bailor knows the general character and habits of the bailee, and the place where or the manner in which the goods deposited are to be kept by him, the bailor, creating the bailment in the light of this knowledge, must be presumed to assent in advance that his goods shall be thus treated; and if, under such circumstances, they are damaged or lost, it is by reason of his own fault or folly, and he cannot recover damages.[77] The basis of this doctrine is not contributory negligence, but rather that such knowledge and implied assent work an estoppel against the bailor.

kins, 2 Adol. & E. (Eng.) 256. See, also, Just. Inst. lib. 3, tit. 15, § 3; COGGS v. BERNARD, 2 Ld. Raym. 909, 914, Dobie Cas. Bailments and Carriers, 1; Foster v. President, etc., of Essex Bank, 17 Mass. 479, 500, 9 Am. Dec. 168. Where a bailee of money alleges that it was stolen from him, the fact that other money belonging to defendant was stolen at the same time is not conclusive against the allegation of gross negligence. Patriska v. Kronk, 57 Misc. Rep. 552, 109 N. Y. Supp. 1092.

[75] Story, Bailm. § 64. "Notwithstanding the weight of these authorities, they do not seem to me to express the general rule in its true meaning. The depositary is, as has been seen, bound to slight diligence only; and the measure of that diligence is that degree of diligence which persons of less than common prudence, or indeed of any prudence at all, take of their own concerns. The measure, abstractly considered, has no reference to the particular character of an individual, but it looks to the general conduct and character of a whole class of persons."

[76] Cases cited in note 74.

[77] Knowles v. Atlantic & St. L. R. Co., 38 Me. 55, 61 Am. Dec. 234; President, etc., of Conway Bank v. American Express Co., 8 Allen (Mass.) 512; Arthur v. St. Paul & D. R. Co., 38 Minn. 95, 35 N. W. 718; Parker v. Union Ice & Salt Co., 59 Kan. 626, 54 Pac. 672, 68 Am. St. Rep. 383. These principles were applied in the case of a bailor consenting that the hay should be stored in a certain wharf of the bailee. The wharf broke down from overloading No additional incumbrance had been placed on the wharf after the arrival of the hay. It was held that the bailee was not liable. Knowles v. Atlantic & St. L. R. Co., 38 Me. 55, 61 Am. Dec. 234. Where knowledge of a general custom in regard to such bailment can be imputed to the bailor, he is pre-

Bailments Demanding Skill

Somewhat as a corollary to the proposition just stated is the doctrine that, when the bailee expressly holds himself out as possessing special skill or knowledge (or such holding out is involved in the situation of the parties or the nature of the bailment), he is to be judged, on the question of his negligence, by the standard he has himself held out, even though he receives no recompense.[78] Thus, if the bailee hold himself out as a veterinarian, the care exercised ordinarily by veterinarians (and not the care of persons unskilled in curing the diseases of horses) is the criterion to be used.[79]

Quasi Bailments by Conversion

In quasi bailments, where one comes into possession of goods through a wrong, as by conversion, he is strictly liable, irrespective of the question of negligence. By wrongfully taking possession of the goods, he becomes an insurer against loss, regardless of the care and attention that he bestows upon the goods.[80] As the liability of the bailee here is measured, not in terms of negligence, but in terms of *insurance,* the bailee becomes absolutely responsible for loss or damage, regardless of the degree of care he exercised or the manner in which such loss or injury occurred.

sumed to have consented that his goods should be kept in accordance with such custom.

Cf. President, etc., of Conway Bank v. American Express Co., 8 Allen (Mass.) 512; Kelton v. Taylor, 11 Lea (Tenn.) 264, 47 Am. Rep. 284.

[78] One who, without any benefit to himself, rides a horse, at the owner's request, for the purpose of exhibiting him for sale, is bound to use such skill as he possesses, and, if proved to be skilled in horses, is equally liable with a borrower for an injury done to the horse. Wilson v. Brett, 11 Mees. & W. (Eng.) 113, 12 Law J. Exch. 264. Where the profession of the bailee implies skill, a want of skill is imputable as gross negligence. Stanton v. Bell, 9 N. C. 145, 11 Am. Dec. 744; Gill v. Middleton, 105 Mass. 477, 7 Am. Rep. 548; Eddy v. Livingston, 35 Mo. 487, 493, 88 Am. Dec. 122; Shiells v. Blackburne, 1 H. Bl. (Eng.) 158, in which Lord Loughborough says: "I agree with Sir William Jones, that where a bailee undertakes to perform a gratuitous act, from which the bailor alone is to receive benefit, there the bailee is liable only for gross negligence; but if a man gratuitously undertakes to do a thing to the best of his skill, where his situation or profession is such as to imply skill, an omission of that skill is imputable to him as gross negligence." Isham v. Post, 141 N. Y. 100, 35 N. E. 1084, 23 L. R. A. 90, 38 Am. St. Rep. 766; The New World v. King, 16 How. 469, 14 L. Ed. 1019.

[79] Where a farrier, without reward, offers to cure a horse of a swelling on the hock joint, and he makes the puncture so unskillfully that the horse becomes worthless, this act is equivalent to gross negligence. CONNER v. WINTON, 8 Ind. 315, 65 Am. Dec. 761, Dobie Cas. Bailments and Carriers, 54.

[80] For a full discussion of the reasons of this strict liability, see post, § 47.

TERMINATION OF BAILMENT

30. Bailments for the sole benefit of the bailor may be terminated by:

(1) Act of the parties.

(a) By performance of the bailment purpose, or expiration of the time for which the bailment was created.

(b) By mutual consent of both bailor and bailee.

(c) At the option of either bailor or bailee, except that, when the bailment was created for a definite time or purpose, the bailee, having once entered upon the performance of the bailment, must complete it.

(d) By bailee's wrong, at the option of the bailor.

(2) Operation of law.

(a) By death of bailor or bailee (in some cases).

(b) By change in the legal status of bailor or bailee (in some cases).

(c) By destruction of the subject-matter of the bailment.

Termination by Full Performance or Expiration of Time

Of course, upon the accomplishment of the bailment purpose, or the expiration of the time for which the bailment was created,[31] the bailment, expiring by inherent limitation, comes to a natural end. It then remains for the bailee to redeliver the goods to the bailor, or otherwise deal with them according to the terms of the bailment contract. If the bailee retains possession of the goods, after the bailment is thus ended, a new quasi bailment springs up; or, on the bailee's wrongful refusal to surrender the goods, the bailor may treat this as a conversion and may sue accordingly.

Termination by Mutual Consent of Bailor and Bailee

These bailments, like any other bailments, may also be terminated at any time by the mutual assent of both the bailor and bailee.[32] The bailment contract, like all other contracts, is always under control of the parties who made it. The parties cannot tie their own hands. The power that created may likewise destroy. So a gratuitous bailment may by mutual consent be changed into one for mutual benefit, and vice versa, or an entirely different arrangement may in like manner be substituted for the bailment relation.[33]

[31] This is common to all bailments. See ante, p. 44.

[32] True of all bailments. See ante, p. 45.

[33] As where, after making a special deposit of money, the parties agree that the depositary shall pay the depositor interest thereon. This has been

Termination at Option of Bailor or Bailee

The bailor may at any time terminate the bailment. This arbitrary right follows from the fact that the bailee, having no beneficial interest in the continuance of the bailment as against the bailor, cannot legally object when it is thus ended.[84]

When the bailment is general or indefinite as to its time and purpose, the bailee may at any time terminate the bailment by giving notice to the bailor.[85] Thus the bailee would have this right where he was keeping the bailor's horse, with no under-

held to change the bailment relation into one of debtor and creditor. Howard v. Roeben, 33 Cal. 399; Hathaway v. Brady, 26 Cal. 581; Chiles v. Garrison, 32 Mo. 475; Rankin v. Craft, 1 Heisk. (Tenn.) 711; Cicalla v. Rossi, 10 Heisk. (Tenn.) 67.

[84] Thus, if a deposit is made to be restored at a future time, it may be immediately demanded back by the depositor; for, as the depositary has no interest in the custody, he can have no right to retain the thing against the will of the depositor. If the bailee was to derive a benefit from the custody, the bailment would not belong to this class. Graves v. Ticknor, 6 N. H. 537; Beardslee v. Richardson, 11 Wend. (N. Y.) 25, 25 Am. Dec. 596. So also in the case of mandates, where the thing is to be delivered to a third person, if the latter has no vested interest in it, the bailor may revoke the bailment at any time. On this principle, it was said in a New Hampshire case that a party who deposits money with another, to be appropriated for the benefit of a third person, being under no legal obligation to so appropriate it, has a right to countermand the appropriation, and recall the money at any time before it has been actually appropriated, or before such an arrangement has been entered into between the depositary and the person for whose benefit it was deposited as creates a privity between them and amounts to an appropriation of it. Anything short of this is immaterial and unimportant, so far as concerns the depositor's right to recall and recover back his money. Winkley v. Foye, 33 N. H. 171, 66 Am. Dec. 715. Where the bailor wishes to terminate the bailment, he should make a demand, as a demand and a refusal are ordinarily evidence of conversion. If the bailee improperly refuses to redeliver the goods when demanded, he henceforth holds them at his own peril. If, therefore, they are afterwards lost, either by negligence or inevitable accident, he is liable. The demand fixes liability. Emerick v. Chesrown, 90 Ind. 47; Zuck v. Culp, 59 Cal. 142; Stewart v. Frazier, 5 Ala. 114; Hosmer v. Clarke, 2 Greenl. (Me.) 308; Montgomery v. Evans, 8 Ga. 178; McLain v. Huffman, 30 Ark. 428; Jackman v. Partridge, 21 Vt. 558; Brown v. Cook, 9 Johns. (N. Y.) 361; Magee v. Scott, 9 Cush. (Mass.) 148, 55 Am. Dec. 49. However, when the circumstances show that a demand would be wholly futile, none need be made. A demand and a refusal are not the only evidence of a conversion. First Nat. Bank v. Dunbar, 118 Ill. 625, 9 N. E. 186; Kellogg v. Olson, 34 Minn. 103, 24 N. W. 364; Huntsman v. Fish, 36 Minn. 148, 30 N. W. 455; Derrick v. Baker, 9 Port. (Ala.) 362.

[85] A bailee without hire is ordinarily not bound to keep articles deposited with him. He may terminate the bailment by giving the bailor notice to remove the goods, and allowing him a reasonable time in which to do so. If, upon tender of the goods, the owner refuses to take them away, the bailee may place them off from his premises. Dale v. Brinckerhoff, 7 Daly (N. Y.) 45; Roulston v. McClelland, 2 E. D. Smith (N. Y.) 60; De Lemos v. Cohen, 28 Misc. Rep. 579, 59 N. Y. Supp. 498.

standing that he was to keep the horse for a definite time or until a specific purpose was accomplished. But when the custody of the goods was clearly undertaken for a fixed time, or where the bailment was created for the performance of definite services or a specific purpose, then the bailee, after he has once entered upon the execution of the bailment, no longer has the right to terminate the bailment before it has been fully performed.[86] Thus, when the bailee actually receives the horse on the understanding that it shall be kept *a month,* or that he will *shoe* the horse, even though he receives no recompense therefor, then the bailee cannot refuse to go forward with the uncompleted bailment without being responsible in damages to the bailor. These distinctions follow from what has already been said to the effect that a bailment for the bailor's sole benefit, once entered upon by the bailee, must be completed according to its terms. But, when the relation is indefinite or general both in time and purpose, it is by its terms a bailment at will, and as such terminable at the option of the bailor as well as of the bailee.

Termination by Bailee's Wrong

It has already been pointed out, as a principle common to all bailments, that the wrong of the bailee does not operate of itself to terminate the bailment (though statements to the contrary may be found in some of the books), but that it merely gives the bailor the right to terminate the bailment.[87] Since, in the case of bailments for the bailor's sole benefit, the bailor already has arbitrarily such a right, the bailee's wrong here confers no new right but rather affords a strong reason why the old right should be exercised. When, as is frequently the case, the wrong consists in an unlawful dominion by the bailee over the goods, the bailor may (as in other cases) sue for conversion.[88]

[86] Story, Bailm. § 202. Goddard, Bailm. & Carr. § 54. See ante, § 26, "Nonfeasance." Cases are very rare here, but the rule stated seems sound on principle, and the bailee, having lulled the bailor into a false sense of security as to the definite time or purpose of the bailment, and having prevented the bailor from making other arrangements, should be compelled to complete such a bailment when he has once entered upon its performance.

[87] See ante, p. 45; King v. Bates, 57 N. H. 446; Crump v. Mitchell, 34 Miss. 449; McMahon v. Sloan, 12 Pa. 229, 51 Am. Dec. 601; Wilkinson v. Verity, L. R. 6 C. P. 206.

Thus, where a bailee wrongfully disposes of the property to a third person, the statute of limitations does not run against an action on the bailment contract until the breach is discovered. Wilkinson v. Verity, L. R. 6 C. P. 206; Crump v. Mitchell, 34 Miss. 449; McMahon v. Sloan, 12 Pa. 229, 51 Am. Dec. 601. In case of such a conversion, the bailor may, however, treat the bailment as terminated, and recover the property itself from whomever is in possession. King v. Bates, 57 N. H. 446.

[88] Ante, p. 62; post, p. 105.

Termination by Death

The cases are few, and far from clear, on the subject of the effect that the death of the bailor or bailee has on the termination of bailments for the bailor's sole benefit. It is usually held that the death of the bailor terminates the bailment.[89] This is certainly true when the bailment is for an indefinite time or purpose, and a quasi bailment arises until the goods are delivered to the bailor's personal representatives. It would seem, however, that when the bailment is for a definite time or purpose, so that the bailor has a right to insist on the completion of the bailment, this right should pass ordinarily to the personal representative of the bailor after the latter's death.

When the bailment involves a personal trust or confidence imposed in the bailee, then clearly the death of the bailee terminates the bailment. It is equally clear that in bailments for an indefinite time or purpose, since neither party can insist on the completion of the bailment, this is terminated when the bailee dies.[90] If, however, the bailment involves no personal trust in the bailee (so that his personal representatives can complete it), and if, in addition, the bailment is for a definite time or purpose (so that the bailor can insist in the completion of the bailment), then it would seem that the death of the bailee does not of itself operate to terminate the bailment.

Termination by Change of Legal Status of Parties—Bankruptcy

The effect of bankruptcy of the parties in terminating a bailment of the class in question is also far from clear. It would seem that the bankruptcy of the bailor would operate to terminate the bailment,[91] the rights of the bankrupt bailor ordinarily passing to his trustee. But it seems that the bankruptcy of the bailee does not terminate ipso facto such a bailment, since his bankruptcy does not incapacitate the bailee from continuing the bailment,

[89] See Farrow v. Bragg's Adm'r, 30 Ala. 261; Morris v. Lowe, 97 Tenn. 243, 36 S. W. 1098; Goddard, Bailm. & Carr. § 31; Van Zile, Bailm. & Carr. § 82.

[90] If there are joint mandataries, the death of one of them dissolves the contract as to all, for, by the general rule of the common law, an authority to two cannot be executed except by both. Sinclair v. Jackson ex dem. Field, 8 Cow. (N. Y.) 543. As to whether this rule would apply in cases of bailments not requiring the united advice, confidence, and skill of all, Judge Story (Bailm. § 211) seems doubtful. Where the authority of the bailees is joint and several, the death of one does not revoke the authority of the others to act.

[91] See Ex parte Newhall, 2 Story, 360, Fed. Cas. No. 10,159; Parker v. Smith, 16 East (Eng.) 382; Minett v. Forrester, 4 Taunt. (Eng.) 541. See Loveland, Bankruptcy (3d Ed.) § 153; National Bankruptcy Act (Act July 1, 1898, c. 541, 30 Stat. 565 [U. S. Comp. St. 1901, p. 3451]) § 70; Collier, Bankruptcy 9th Ed.) § 1000 et seq.

and since the trustee of the bankrupt bailee could not take over the goods, which are owned by the bailor. The bailee's bankruptcy, however, would tend to make the bailor himself exercise his right of terminating the bailment, but this right the bailor always has in bailments for his benefit alone.

Same—Marriage of Woman

The marriage of a woman at common law wrought so tremendous a change in her as a juristic personality that the marriage of a woman, whether bailor or bailee, would probably immediately terminate the bailment.[92] Under modern emancipation statutes, however (which place the married woman substantially on the same plane, as to contract relations, with the feme sole), there seems to be no reason why the marriage of a woman (whether bailor or bailee) should affect the bailment relation.

Same—Insanity

It would seem that what has just been said as to the bailor, and his personal representative on the bailor's death, is also applicable to the bailor and his committee on the bailor's insanity. On the insanity of the bailee, incapacitating him by an unusual and unforeseen misfortune from carrying out the bailment, the bailment, it seems, would immediately be terminated.[93]

Termination by Destruction of the Bailed Goods

This necessarily, as has been shown,[94] terminates all bailments.

REDELIVERY OF THE BAILED GOODS

31. At the termination of the bailment, the bailee must deliver up the bailed goods, according to the terms of the bailment contract.

Unless otherwise provided for, the normal place of delivery is the place in which the goods are kept by the bailee.

The rights and duties of the parties, as to the redelivery of the goods forming the subject-matter of the bailment, when the bailment is terminated, are, in general, the same here as in other classes of bailments.[95] Particularly is this true as to what goods

[92] See Story, Ag. §§ 488–500; Story, Bailm. § 206; Poth. Contrat de Mandat, note 111; 2 Rop. Husb. & Wife, 69, 73; 2 Kent, Comm. (4th Ed.) lect. 41, p. 645; Story, Ag. § 481.

[93] See Story, Ag. § 481; Goddard, Bailm. & Carr. § 82; Van Zile, Bailm. & Carr. § 83.

[94] Ante, p. 46.

[95] Ante, § 19.

are to be delivered [96] and as to whom such delivery should be made.[97] Only the place of delivery requires separate treatment in this connection.

Place of Delivery

If the bailment contract expressly provides where the bailed goods shall be redelivered, or if the intention of the parties as to the place of delivery can be gathered from the contract, that, of course, governs. When the contract is silent on this point, however, much will depend on the particular circumstances of each case, while recourse is often had to custom and usage to ascertain the proper place of delivery.

Unless some other place is expressly agreed upon, or may be thus implied from custom, usage, or the circumstances of the transaction, it would seem that the place in which the goods are kept by the bailee should be considered the proper place for the redelivery.[98] This is worked out on the theory that the bailee, deriving no benefit from the transaction, should be given as little trouble as possible. Under such circumstances, it seems fairer and more natural that the bailor (receiving all the benefit) should come to such place for the goods rather than that the bailee (receiving no benefit) should have added to his burdens that of delivering the goods at some other place, such as the residence or store of the bailor.

[96] If an animal deposited brings forth young, the latter must also be restored to the owner. He must deliver it in the state in which he received it, with the profits and the increase, and if he fails in either of these respects he is liable. Game v. Harvie, Yel. (Eng.) 50; Civ. Code La. 1838, art. 2919.

[97] Burton v. Baughan, 6 Car. & P. (Eng.) 674; Chattahoochee Nat. Bank v. Schley, 58 Ga. 369. A mere depositary is not liable to an action, until refusal to deliver up on demand. West v. Murph, 3 Hill (S. C.) 284; Hill v. Wiggin, 31 N. H. 292; Brown v. Cook, 9 Johns. (N. Y.) 361; Phelps v. Bostwick, 22 Barb. (N. Y.) 314; Duncan v. Magette, 25 Tex. 245; Jackman v. Partridge, 21 Vt. 558. A. deposited money with B., to be paid to C. when A. should have satisfied himself of a fact connected with the deposit. Held, that no duty rested upon B. to inquire whether the fact had occurred; and in a suit by C. against B. to recover the money, evidence was inadmissible to show that A. had declared himself satisfied of the fact, unless such declaration had been made known to B. before the suit. Carle v. Bearce, 33 Me. 337. Where one as a bailee without hire receives money to deliver to another, there is an implied contract that he shall deliver it, or return it, or account for it in a reasonable time. Graves v. Ticknor, 6 N. H. 537.

[98] This point seems to have been seldom litigated. See, in general, Scott v. Crane, 1 Conn. 255; Slingerland v. Morse, 8 Johns. (N. Y.) 474; Mason v. Briggs, 16 Mass. 453. A demand for the return may be made elsewhere. Dunlap v. Hunting, 2 Denio (N. Y.) 643, 43 Am. Dec. 763; Scott v. Crane, 1 Conn. 255.

CHAPTER IV

BAILMENTS FOR THE BAILEE'S SOLE BENEFIT

INTRODUCTORY—COMMODATUM

32. A bailment for the sole benefit of the bailee is a bailment of goods for beneficial use by the bailee, without recompense to the bailor. In short, it is a gratuitous loan for use. Such bailments correspond to the Roman commodatum.

In this class of bailments (the opposite of the class just considered), the sole benefit, consisting of the beneficial use of the bailed article, is received by the bailee, and the bailor is wholly without reward. Such a bailment contemplates the gratuitous loan of a chattel, to be used temporarily by the bailee for his own sole benefit, and then to be returned according to the bailor's directions.[1] The fact that the sole benefit of the bailment accrues to

[1] According to Sir William Jones (Bailm. 118), "lending for use is a bailment of a thing for a certain time, to be used by the borrower without paying for it." The civil-law definition is that it is the grant of a thing to be used by the grantee gratuitously for a limited time, and then to be specifically returned. Story, Bailm. § 219. In the words of Chancellor Kent (2 Comm., 13th Ed., 573), it is "a bailment or loan of an article for a certain time, to be used by the borrower without paying for the use." According to Ayliffe (Pand. bk. 4, tit. 16, p. 516), "it is a grant of something made in a gratuitous manner for some certain use, and for a certain term of time, expressed or implied, to the end that the same species should be again returned or restored again to us, and not another species of the same kind or nature; and this in as good a plight as when delivered to us." In COGGS v. BERNARD, 2 Ld. Raym. 909, 913, Dobie Cas. Bailments and Carriers, 1, Lord Holt says that a commodatum arises "when goods or chattels that are useful are lent to a friend, gratis, to be used by him."

Of the modern authors, the definition of Schouler is worthy of attention. In this he says: "We may define the bailment as one for the temporary bene-

the bailee constitutes, of course, the distinguishing characteristic of the bailment in question, and from this can be deduced the specific rules of law applicable to this bailment, which differ from the broad principles which apply alike to all classes of bailments.

In the modern classification of bailments, bailments for the bailee's sole benefit correspond exactly with the Roman commodatum.[2] The English term "loan" or "lending," however, is not an exact translation of the Roman "commodatum." The word "loan" is broad enough to include both the commodatum and mutuum of the Roman law, while it has already been seen[3] that a mutuum, or the loan of goods for consumption by the borrower, involving the return of similar goods, is thus either a sale or exchange, and not a bailment at all. A delivery of goods to another to be consumed in the use, without compensation therefor, would be a gift. The ordinary commercial loan of money, at interest, involves compensation on the part of the borrower and creates the relation of debtor and creditor, without in any way touching the principles of law which control the bailment relation. The term "loan," therefore, when used to designate a bailment of this class, must be understood to mean a gratuitous loan, which contemplates the return of the specific thing loaned.

ficial use, gratis, of a chattel which the borrower must return." A loan of property on condition that it shall be turned into a sale if certain payments are made does not subject the property in hands of the bailee to levy for the debts of the bailee. Clark v. Jack, 7 Watts (Pa.) 375. Where a slave is placed by his owner in the possession of a third person, "to take care of him, keep him until called for, and pay nothing for his hire during the time he might have him," this is a mere deposit, and does not amount to a contract of hiring. Farrow v. Bragg's Adm'r, 30 Ala. 261. For transactions held to be loans, and not gifts or sales, see Smith v. Jones, 8 Ark. 109; Boswell v. Clarksons, 1 J. J. Marsh. (Ky.) 47. And see Morris v. Caldwell, 3 J. J. Marsh. (Ky.) 693; Breeding v. Thrielkeld, 6 J. J. Marsh. (Ky.) 378; Hinson v. Hinson, 10 La. Ann. 580; Williams v. McGrade, 13 Minn. 174 (Gil. 165); Collier v. Poe, 16 N. C. 55; Hurd v. West, 7 Cow. (N. Y.) 752; Otis v. Wood, 3 Wend. (N. Y.) 498. See, also, Francis v. Shrader, 67 Ill. 272; Chamberlin v. Cobb, 32 Iowa, 161; Carpenter v. Branch, 13 Vt. 161, 37 Am. Dec. 587; BELLER v. SCHULTZ, 44 Mich. 529, 7 N. W. 225, 38 Am. Rep. 280, Dobie Cas. Bailments and Carriers, 57; Apczynski v. Butkiewicz, 140 Ill. App. 375; Archer v. Walker, 38 Ind. 472.

The delivering of a chattel by the owner to another to be used by the latter during life, and then returned, is not an attempt to create a remainder or a reversion in the property, but is a mere loan, the title remaining in the lender. Booth v. Terrell, 16 Ga. 20.

[2] "Commodatum is a bailment where a chattel is lent by its owner to the bailee for the express purpose of conferring a benefit upon the latter, without any corresponding advantage to its owner." Halsbury, Laws of Eng. vol. 1, p. 537.

[3] Ante, p. 11.

NATURE OF THE RELATION

33. In addition to the circumstances common to all bailments, it is essential to the creation of a bailment for the bailee's sole benefit—

(a) That it be created by contract.

(b) That it be without intended compensation to the bailor.

(c) That it be for the exclusive use of the bailee.

Must be Created by Contract

It follows from the very definition of this class of bailments that the relation cannot be created except by contract. Only by the owner's consent can one acquire the right to use gratuitously for his own benefit the goods of another. The use of goods is an important advantage resulting from ownership and unless the owner has by contract given another the right to use the goods, the law will not deprive the owner of such use gratuitously for the mere purpose of conferring it on another person. The contract creating such a bailment is governed by the rules of law that govern contracts in general.[4] Where possession is obtained under a contract that is invalid (but not fraudulent), a quasi bailment in the nature of a depositum is created by operation of law.

Must be without Intended Compensation to the Bailor

Absence of intended compensation to the bailor for the use of his chattel by the bailee is of the very essence of bailments of this class.[5] The fact that the benefit flowing from the transaction accrues solely to the bailee is what distinguishes it from all other bailments and determines largely the measure of the bailee's duties. If any compensation, even though indirect or contingent, is to be paid to the bailor in any manner for the use of the bailed goods, such bailments would fall under another class—those for mutual benefit. Much that has been said as to what constitutes

[4] See Vasse v. Smith, 6 Cranch, 226, 3 L. Ed. 207; Campbell v. Stakes, 2 Wend. (N. Y.) 137, 19 Am. Dec. 561; Eaton v. Hill, 50 N. H. 235, 9 Am. Rep. 189; Jennings v. Rundall, 8 Term R. (Eng.) 335; Green v. Greenback, 4 E. C. L. 377; Campbell v. Stakes, 2 Wend. (N. Y.) 137, 19 Am. Dec. 561; Hagebush v. Ragland, 78 Ill. 40; State v. Bryant, 74 N. C. 124; Clark, Cr. Law, 250; Poth. Pret. & Usage, notes 13, 15; Story, Bailm. § 229.

[5] Where valuable property is used for a considerable time, a hiring and not a loan will be presumed. Rider v. Union India Rubber Co., 28 N. Y. 379; Cullen v. Lord, 39 Iowa, 302. See, also, Davis v. Breon, 1 Ariz. 240, 25 Pac. 537; Dunham v. Kinnear, 1 Watts (Pa.) 130; Plimpton v. Gleason, 57 Vt. 604.

a compensation (in regard to bailments for bailor's sole benefit)[6] is applicable here mutatis mutandis.

Though, in the case of a commodatum, there is imposed on the bailee the duty of bearing the ordinary expenses incidental to the preservation of the property during the time of the bailment,[7] this fact does not operate to change the gratuitous nature of the bailment. Thus, if a horse is gratuitously lent to a friend for a journey, he must bear the expenses of food and shelter for the horse during that journey, and even of getting the horse shod, if necessary; for these are burdens naturally incident to the use of a horse.[8] However, where a horse or other chattel is lent in distinct consideration of its keep, the bailment is one for hire.[9] The question, depending on the construction of the bailment contract, is whether such expense was the consideration for, or a mere incident of, the bailment. Where the use of the property was the principal thing contemplated by the parties in creating the bailment, and the keep merely incidental, the bailment is a gratuitous loan. Where the custody and care of the property was also an object aimed at by the bailor in creating the bailment, then, the bailment is one for hire.

Must be for Exclusive Use of Bailee

From what has just been said, it is clear that in gratuitous loans, not only must the use be the principal rather than the mere incidental object of the bailment, but this use must also be exclusively for the bailee's benefit. If the use is for the joint benefit of the borrower and the lender, the bailment is no longer a gratuitous loan, but the benefit then becomes mutual and the bailment then falls into another class—those for the benefit of both bailor and bailee.

[6] Ante, p. 53.

[7] Post, p. 81.

[8] BENNETT v. O'BRIEN, 37 Ill. 250, Dobie Cas. Bailments and Carriers, 56; and the bailment here was held to be still a gratuitous one.

[9] Carpenter v. Branch, 13 Vt. 161, 37 Am. Dec. 587. "Where the owner of an article of property is anxious to avoid the expense and trouble of caring for it, at a season of the year when its use is not more than equivalent to the expense of keeping, and at his solicitation another agrees to keep it for its use, the lender is as much accommodated by the transaction as the borrower, and the benefit is mutual." Chamberlin v. Cobb, 32 Iowa, 161. In Neel v. State, 33 Tex. Cr. R. 408, 26 S. W. 726, it was held that an agreement whereby a person undertakes to make a horse gentle, and fit for the use of the owner's family, in consideration of permission to ride it, is a contract of hiring, and not a gratuitous loan. See, also, Height v. State (Tex. Cr. App.) 150 S. W. 908, where the bailee agreed to keep the piano in consideration of the right of bailee's child to use the piano, which was held to be a mutual benefit bailment, and not gratuitous.

RIGHTS AND DUTIES OF THE PARTIES

34. The rights and duties of the bailor and bailee, here as in the case of other bailments, may be varied by special contract; but when these rights and duties are not covered by the contract of the parties, they will be implied by law from the nature of the bailment.

The discussion that follows is a treatment of the rights and duties of the parties to a bailment for the bailee's sole benefit.[10] The ensuing discussion is concerned with the rights and duties of the parties where there is no express contract; or when there is such a contract, the discussion may be regarded as furnishing general principles of construction which will control in the absence of any direct provision in the contract as to the specific point in question. Here, as elsewhere, the parties may by contract vary their liabilities indefinitely and arbitrarily, provided their contract is neither in violation of positive law nor against public policy.[11] Of course, when a particular right or duty of the parties is clearly covered by a valid stipulation in the bailment contract, such stipulation must be given full effect.

EXPENSES OF THE BAILMENT

35. The bailee must bear the ordinary expenses incidental to preserving the property while in use, but for any extraordinary expense the bailor is liable

Ordinary and Extraordinary Expenses

The bailee must bear the usual and ordinary expenses incident to the use of the thing loaned or necessary to its due preservation.[12] As the bailee alone derives benefit from the use of the goods, it follows that he should bear the expenses which such

10 "It is surprising how little in the way of decision in our courts is to be found in our books upon the obligations which a mere lender of a chattel for use contracts towards the borrower." Coleridge, J., in Blakemore v. Bristol & E. Ry. Co., 8 El. & Bl. (Eng.) 1035, 1050. And see Clapp v. Nelson, 12 Tex. 370, 62 Am. Dec. 530. For this scarcity of legal authority Mr. Schouler (Bailm. § 65) suggests as a reason that, when honor does not hold the borrower to his duty, delicacy restrains the lender from pursuing legal remedies.

11 Ante, p. 18.

12 Harrington v. Snyder, 3 Barb. (N. Y.) 380; Handford v. Palmer, 2 Brod. & Bing. (Eng.) 359; 1 Domat, book 1, title 5, § 3, art. 4.

use necessarily entails. Thus where domestic animals, such as horses or cattle, are lent, the bailee must bear the expense of feeding and caring for these, and, as has been seen, the merely incidental benefit which the bailor receives in being relieved of such burden is not sufficient to change the gratuitous nature of the bailment.[13]

But where extraordinary and unusual expenses become necessary for the preservation of the goods, these must be borne by the bailor.[14] Thus, where a horse unexpectedly became dangerously sick, the bailor should bear the expenses of a veterinarian, called in by the bailee to attend the horse. If the bailee has advanced such expenses, the bailor must reimburse him; and it seems that the bailee may, under an implied agency, bind the bailor by contract in the latter's name when, under the peculiar circumstances of the particular case, such expenses are reasonable and necessary for the proper preservation of the bailed object.[15]

FRAUD IN PROCURING THE LOAN

36. Fraud in procuring the loan renders the borrower liable as an insurer.

Any fraud practised by the borrower to procure the loan vitiates the contract; for in such case the owner, owing to the fraud, has not legally consented to the taking and use of his property. The pretended borrower is no better than a trespasser. He is therefore absolutely liable for the goods entirely irrespective of the question of negligence. As far as the safety of the goods is concerned, he is an insurer.[16] The fraud may be either an express misrepresentation or a fraudulent concealment of a fact under circumstances such as to impose on the bailee the duty of disclosing the fact to the bailor;[17] though in the first case the liability is much clearer.

13 BENNETT v. O'BRIEN, 37 Ill. 250, Dobie Cas. Bailments and Carriers, 56.

14 Harter v. Blanchard, 64 Barb. (N. Y.) 617; Story, Bailm. §§ 273, 274; Jones, Bailm. p. 65. Pothier and Domat seem to place such expenses on the lender. This is not free from doubt, though. See, for example, 1 Halsbury, Laws of England, p. 539, note (i), in which it is said: "But it is thought that this is not the law of England."

15 If, as seems to be the case, these extraordinary expenses fall on the bailor, this would follow as in the cases of bailments for the bailor's sole benefit.

16 Though not directly in point, see Campbell v. Stakes, 2 Wend. (N. Y.) 137, 19 Am. Dec. 561; Cary v. Hotailing, 1 Hill (N. Y.) 311, 37 Am. Dec. 323.

17 Judge Story (Bailm. § 243) gives as an illustration of the doctrine of

USE OF BAILED CHATTELS BY THE BAILEE

37. The borrower may use the bailed goods only for the purpose, at the place, and in the manner contemplated by the contract.

The terms of the bailment contract prescribe the use of the bailed chattels by the bailee. This contract is at the same time the authority for, and the limitation of, the use of the goods on the bailee's part. Articles lent for one purpose cannot be used for another. The lender has a perfect right to fix the conditions upon which he is willing to lend his property. Where the lender has fixed the time, place, or mode of use, any departure from such limitations is a wrong, and renders the borrower absolutely and strictly liable as an insurer for all damage to the chattels bailed, regardless of the question of negligence.[18] This principle is one of general application to all bailments; but, in the case of gratuitous loans, since the bailee alone receives a benefit, it applies with peculiar force and strictness. For example, to take a case supposed by Lord Holt,[19] if a man lends another his horse to go west-

tacit fraud the following, taken originally from Pothier: If a soldier were to borrow the horse of a friend for a battle, expected to be fought the next morning, and were to conceal from the lender the fact that his own horse was as fit for the service, if the borrowed horse were slain in the engagement, the borrower would be responsible, for the natural presumption created by the concealment is that the horse of the borrower is unfit, or that he has none. But, if the borrower had frankly stated that fact, then the loss must be borne by the lender.

18 Collins v. Bennett, 46 N. Y. 490; Scranton v. Baxter, 4 Sandf. (N. Y.) 5; Buchanan v. Smith, 10 Hun (N. Y.) 474; WHEELOCK v. WHEELWRIGHT, 5 Mass. 104, Dobie Cas. Bailments and Carriers, 66; Isaack v. Clark, 2 Bulst. (Eng.) 306; Cullen v. Lord, 39 Iowa, 302; Kennedy v. Ashcraft, 4 Bush (Ky.) 530; Stewart v. Davis, 31 Ark. 518, 25 Am. Rep. 576; Martin v. Cuthbertson, 64 N. C. 328; Booth v. Terrell, 16 Ga. 25; Lay's Ex'r v. Lawson's Adm'r, 23 Ala. 377; Woodman v. Hubbard, 25 N. H. 67, 57 Am. Dec. 310; Grant v. Ludlow's Adm'r, 8 Ohio St. 1. If, after a conversion, the owner receives the property back, he can still recover for any damage he has sustained; that is, the value of the property when received goes in mitigation of damages. Murray v. Burling, 10 Johns. (N. Y.) 172; Bowman v. Teall, 23 Wend. (N. Y.) 306, 35 Am. Dec. 562; Gibbs v. Chase, 10 Mass. 125; WHEELOCK v. WHEELWRIGHT, 5 Mass. 104, Dobie Cas. Bailments and Carriers, 66; Todd v. Figley, 7 Watts (Pa.) 542; Bayliss v. Fisher, 7 Bing. 153; Syeds v. Hay, 4 Term R. (Eng.) 260, 264. See, also, post, p. 105; BELLER v. SCHULTZ, 44 Mich. 529, 7 N. W. 225, 38 Am. Rep. 280, Dobie Cas. Bailments and Carriers, 57.

19 In COGGS v. BERNARD, 2 Ld. Raym. 909, 915, 916, Dobie Cas. Bailments and Carriers, 1. And see De Tollenere v. Fuller, 1 Mill, Const. (S. C.) 117, 12 Am. Dec. 616; Vaughan v. Menlove, 3 Bing. N. C. 468, 475.

ward or for a month, and the bailee goes northward or keeps the horse above a month, the bailee will be chargeable if any accident happens on the northern journey or after the expiration of the month, whether due to his negligence or not, because he has made use of the horse contrary to the contract under which it was lent to him, and from this contract alone all his rights as to the use of the horse were derived.[20] By accepting the horse under the contract, the bailee thereby effectively consents to its terms and accepts all the limitations on his use that such contract prescribes.

A gratuitous loan is to be regarded as strictly personal to the bailee, unless, from the bailment contract or the circumstances surrounding the loan, a different intention can fairly and reasonably be presumed.[21] Hence the borrower has ordinarily no right to lend the goods to another,[22] or to permit a third person to participate in the use of them. Where the contract is silent on the point, it may at times be difficult to say whether the surrounding facts would imply the right of the bailee to permit any use of the goods by such third person. The presumed intention of the parties, of course, is controlling, and each case must rest on its own facts.[23]

[20] Stewart v. Davis, 31 Ark. 518; Hart v. Skinner, 16 Vt. 138, 42 Am. Dec. 500.

[21] BRINGLOE v. MORRICE, 1 Mod. 210, 3 Salk. (Eng.) 271, Dobie Cas. Bailments and Carriers, 58; Scranton v. Baxter, 4 Sandf. (N. Y.) 5. See, also, Gwilliam v. Twist, 2 Q. B. (Eng.) (1895) 84.

[22] Wilcox v. Hogan, 5 Ind. 546.

[23] Scranton v. Baxter, 4 Sandf. (N. Y.) 5; Wilcox v. Hogan, 5 Ind. 546. In BRINGLOE v. MORRICE, 1 Mod. 210, 3 Salk. (Eng.) 241, Dobie Cas. Bailments and Carriers, 58, the plaintiff had loaned his horse to defendant to ride for pleasure, and it was held that the defendant had no right to permit his servant to ride the horse. But in Camoys v. Scurr, 9 C. & P. (Eng.) 383, it was held that one in possession of a horse for the purpose of trying it with a view to a purchase was entitled to put a competent person on the horse for the purpose of trying it, and was not limited to merely trying it himself. So, also, if a horse should be loaned for the bailee's use for a fixed time, it is a fair presumption that the parties intended that the bailee might use the horse through his servants. Every case must rest on its own facts. Ray v. Tubbs, 50 Vt. 688, 28 Am. Rep. 519. One who borrows a vehicle having a seat for two may take another person with him, unless otherwise stipulated. Harrington v. Snyder, 3 Barb. (N. Y.) 380. The bailee is not liable for depreciation due to the contemplated use. BELLER v. SCHULTZ, 44 Mich. 529, 7 N. W. 225, 38 Am. Rep. 280, Dobie Cas. Bailments and Carriers, 57; Parker v. Gaines (Ark.) 11 S. W. 693. "Thus the loan of a traction engine, a threshing machine, or some other piece of machinery must, in the majority of cases, of necessity imply both superintendence and use by some person other than the actual and responsible borrower." 1 Halsbury, Laws of England, p. 540. See, also, for hypothetical cases Story, Bailm. § 234.

INTEREST OF THE BAILEE

38. When the loan is neither for a definite time nor for a specific purpose, clearly the bailee has merely a possessory interest as to the chattels bailed. But when the loan is created for a definite time or for a definite purpose, the bailee (it would seem), having once entered upon the bailment, has a special property in the goods.

There is much of the same confusion of ideas in regard to the nature of the borrower's interest in the goods lent under a commodatum that exists as to the bailee's interest in a depositum or mandatum. Some authors claim that the borrower has a special property in the subject of the loan;[24] others maintain that he has merely a possessory interest.[25] It would seem that, in order to determine the true rule as to the interest of the bailee in the chattels bailed, a distinction must be made between (a) those loans which are created for a definite time or a specific purpose, and (b) those which are created for an indefinite time or an indefinite purpose.[26]

Under (b), the loan (being neither for a definite time nor for a specific purpose) is terminable at any time at the option of the bailor. Now the idea of a special property in a thing (as we have seen) involves the idea of a right to the thing which can be asserted against the world. Therefore, in these indefinite bailments (b), the right of the bailee can hardly be said to rise above the dignity of a mere possessory interest.

24 See Schouler, Bailm. § 81; Goddard, Bailm. & Carr. § 58. Both of these writers recognize the distinction between the bailment for an indefinite time and the bailment for a definite time or specific purpose, contending for the special property (or its legal equivalent) only as to bailments of the latter type. Direct authority in such cases seems lacking. The cases usually cited are usually (if bailments at all) either bailments for the bailor's sole benefit or bailments for hire. Many writers lay down general rules as to gratuitous bailments, making no distinction between bailments in which the bailee receives all the benefit and those in which he receives none.

25 2 Kent, Comm. 574: "The borrower has no special property in the thing loaned, though his possession is sufficient for him to protect it by an action of trespass against a wrongdoer." See, also, Van Zile, Bailm. & Carr. § 105. LITTLE v. FOSSETT, 34 Me. 545, 56 Am. Dec. 671, Dobie Cas. Bailments and Carriers, 71, quotes the above passage from Kent, though that case was one of hiring.

26 This distinction, with the attendant difference as to the nature of the bailee's interest here, seems right on principle. Authority in decided cases, when this question was necessarily passed on by the court as a controlling question, is lamentably scarce. See note 24.

Under (a), however, the bailment being either for a definite time or a specific purpose, the bailee (having once entered upon the bailment) has rights in the goods, which he can assert, not only against third persons, but even against the bailor. The bailee can then as against all the world retain possession of the goods until the expiration of the time or the accomplishment of the bailment purpose. It therefore seems proper to say here that the bailee has a special property in the goods. His right is in the thing and exists as an in rem right, without regard to persons.

Of course a mere agreement by the owner to make a loan of the goods to another, even for a definite time or purpose (unaccompanied by any delivery of the goods), is not a bailment at all. It is a mere executory contract, and as long as it remains such, as it is not based upon any consideration, it is unenforceable.[27]

RIGHT OF BAILOR AND BAILEE TO BRING SUIT

39. Either the borrower bailee or the lender bailor may, in an appropriate action, sue third persons for wrongful interference with the bailed chattels.

The right of the bailor or bailee to bring suit for a wrongful interference with the bailed chattels is but a phase of, or a deduction from, the principles discussed in the preceding section. The bailee borrower may maintain, by virtue of his interest, an appropriate action against a third party for the wrongful disturbance of his possession,[28] and it is generally held that the bailee's action

[27] The bailee here cannot enforce the executory contract for a gratuitous loan, just as the bailor cannot enforce such a contract looking to a bailment for the bailor's sole benefit. In both cases there is a mere executory contract, unsupported by a consideration, and no bailment at all. See THORNE v. DEAS, 4 Johns. (N. Y.) 84, Dobie Cas. Bailments and Carriers, 47; Crosby v. German, 4 Wis. 373; Elsee v. Gatward, 5 Term R. (Eng.) 143; Shillibeer v. Glyn, 2 Mees. & W. (Eng.) 143.

[28] CHAMBERLAIN v. WEST, 37 Minn. 54, 33 N. W. 114, Dobie Cas. Bailments and Carriers, 59; Paddock v. Wing, 16 How. Prac. (N. Y.) 547; Hurd v. West, 7 Cow. (N. Y.) 753; Hendricks v. Decker, 35 Barb. (N. Y.) 298; Barker v. Miller, 6 Johns. (N. Y.) 195; Duncan v. Spear, 11 Wend. (N. Y.) 54; Badlam v. Tucker, 1 Pick. (Mass.) 389, 11 Am. Dec. 202; Nicolls v. Bastard 2 Cromp., M. & R. (Eng.) 859; Burton v. Hughes, 2 Bing. (Eng.) 173; Sutton v. Buck, 2 Taunt. (Eng.) 302; Rooth v. Wilson, 1 Barn. & Ald. (Eng.) 59. As to trover by the bailee, see Waterman v. Robinson, 5 Mass. 303; Burton v. Hughes, supra; Armory v. Delamirie, 1 Strange (Eng.) 505; Ogle v. Atkinson, 5 Taunt. (Eng.) 759. The bailee may sue and recover, although he is not liable to the bailor. Where a bailee received a horse from the owner with the understanding that he might use him, and, if satisfied with him, pur-

here may be either in trespass or trover; and, at least when the bailee has a special property in the goods, there seems to be no reason why the action of replevin should not lie.

An action may also be maintained by the bailor lender.[29] A complete recovery by either the bailor or bailee is a bar to any action by the other.[30] Any excess beyond his own interest that the bailee recovers is held by him, of course, as trustee for the bailor. What was said, however, under bailments for bailor's sole benefit,[31] in regard to modern authority casting doubt on this last proposition, and advocating the doctrine that the interests of the bailor and bailee (which are separable and can be separately valued) should be protected by separate suits brought by each to recover only his own loss, is more strongly applicable here, since the bailee's interest is much more real.

chase him, held, that such bailee had a sufficient right of property in the horse to maintain an action against a party to whom he had let the horse, for injuries resulting from overdriving. Harrison v. Marshall, 4 E. D. Smith (N. Y.) 271. And see White v. Philbrick, 5 Greenl. (Me.) 147, 17 Am. Dec. 214; Campbell v. Phelps, 1 Pick. (Mass.) 62, 11 Am. Dec. 139; Adams v. Broughton, 2 Strange (Eng.) 1078; Lamine v. Dorrell, 2 Ld. Raym. (Eng.) 1216; Broome v. Wooter, Yel. (Eng.) 67j. Cf. LITTLE v. FOSSETT, 34 Me. 545, 56 Am. Dec. 671, Dobie Cas. Bailments and Carriers, 71, with Lockhart v. Western & A. R. R., 73 Ga. 472, 54 Am. Rep. 883. See, also, Baggett v. McCormack, 73 Miss. 552, 19 South. 89, 55 Am. St. Rep. 554; Gillette v. Goodspeed, 69 Conn. 363, 37 Atl. 973; The Winkfield (Eng.) C. A. (1902) 42.

29 ORSER v. STORMS, 9 Cow. (N. Y.) 687, 18 Am. Dec. 543, Dobie Cas. Bailments and Carriers, 60; Thorp v. Burling, 11 Johns. (N. Y.) 285; Hurd v. West, 7 Cow. (N. Y.) 753; Putnam v. Wyley, 8 Johns. (N. Y.) 432, 5 Am. Dec. 346; Hoyt v. Gelston, 13 Johns. (N. Y.) 141; Booth v. Terrell, 16 Ga. 21, 25; Smith v. Milles, 1 Term R. (Eng.) 475, 480; Lotan v. Cross, 2 Camp. (Eng.) 464; Nicolls v. Bastard, 2 Cromp., M. & R. (Eng.) 659. And see Roberts v. Wyatt, 2 Taunt. (Eng.) 268, 275. In ORSER v. STORMS, 9 Cow. (N. Y.) 687, 18 Am. Dec. 543, Dobie Cas. Bailments and Carriers, 60, it was held that one who had a right to personal property loaned for an indefinite time might maintain trespass for the taking of it. The court said: "The first question to be considered is whether the plaintiff had such a property in the cattle as to be able to maintain trespass. For this purpose he must have had the actual or constructive possession at the time; and the latter is when he has such a right as to be entitled to reduce the goods to actual possession at any time. * * * In my opinion, the plaintiff had the right to bring this action." See, also, Pulliam v. Burlingame, 81 Mo. 111, 51 Am. Rep. 229. As holding that a lender for a fixed time has not such constructive possession, see Putnam v. Wyley, 8 Johns. (N. Y.) 432, 5 Am. Dec. 346; Hoyt v. Gelston, 13 Johns. (N. Y.) 142; Buck v. Aikin, 1 Wend. (N. Y.) 466, 19 Am. Dec. 535. The bailor may maintain trespass against one who wrongfully takes the goods from the bailee even by legal process. Root v. Chandler, 10 Wend. (N. Y.) 110, 25 Am. Dec. 546.

30 Faulkner v. Brown, 13 Wend. (N. Y.) 63; Hall v. Tuttle, 2 Wend. (N. Y.) 475, 479; Flewellin v. Rave, 1 Bulst. (Eng.) 68.

31 Ante, p. 64.

DEGREE OF CARE TO BE EXERCISED BY THE BAILEE

40. The bailee in a gratuitous loan is held to the exercise of great or extraordinary care or diligence.

As the comparative benefit accruing to the bailee is, in the class of bailments under consideration, greater than in either of the other two classes, it is only fair to exact of the bailee a correspondingly higher degree of care. If in bailments for the bailor's sole benefit only slight care is exacted of the bailee, and if in mutual benefit bailments the standard is set higher at ordinary care, it seems natural to continue the progressive scale, and, in bailments for the bailee's sole benefit, to require a degree of care that is, in turn, greater than ordinary care. And so the bailee's duty here is fixed at great care [32] or extraordinary diligence, the two terms being used interchangeably.

[32] Scranton v. Baxter, 4 Sandf. (N. Y.) 5; Phillips v. Coudon, 14 Ill. 84; BENNETT v. O'BRIEN, 37 Ill. 250, Dobie Cas. Bailments and Carriers, 56; Hagebush v. Ragland, 78 Ill. 40; Howard v. Babcock, 21 Ill. 259; Green v. Hollingsworth, 5 Dana (Ky.) 173, 30 Am. Dec. 680; FORTUNE v. HARRIS, 51 N. C. 532, Dobie Cas. Bailments and Carriers, 61; Ross v. Clark, 27 Mo. 549; Wood v. McClure, 7 Ind. 155; Carpenter v. Branch, 13 Vt. 161, 37 Am. Dec. 587; Vaughan v. Menlove, 3 Bing. (N. C.) 468, 475. If bailment be for exclusive benefit of bailee, greatest care and attention is necessary to discharge him in case of loss; hence bailee of negress was held liable when he sent her where smallpox was known to be raging, and she sickened and died of that disease. De Tollenere v. Fuller, 1 Mill, Const. (S. C.) 117, 12 Am. Dec. 616. In Watkins v. Roberts, 28 Ind. 167, which was a suit for the value of a borrowed horse, the answer was that the horse was borrowed to go to a certain place and return, and that while on his way, and without fault or negligence on his part, the borrower was met by soldiers, who took the horse by force. The answer was held good. In De Fonclear v. Shottenkirk, 3 Johns. (N. Y.) 170, where it was shown that a slave was delivered to a party on trial, and that, upon being allowed to go on an errand, he ran away, it was held that the bailee was not responsible. Where a horse loaned by plaintiff to defendant was carried to defendant's house, and placed in the common horse lot, so used for many years, though it was somewhat slanting, and the horse, being nearly blind, and the weather being wet, slipped and fell upon a stump, breaking its thigh, held, that these facts did not import such negligence as to render defendant liable for the loss of the property. FORTUNE v. HARRIS, 51 N. C. 532, Dobie Cas. Bailments and Carriers, 61. Owner of a flag lent it to his employer, helped to hoist it on employer's building, and left it flying when he went away. It was afterwards injured by a hailstorm. Held, in absence of proof of negligence, that borrower was not liable. BELLER v. SCHULTZ, 44 Mich. 529, 7 N. W. 225, 38 Am. Rep. 280, Dobie Cas. Bailments and Carriers, 57. One who, at owner's request, takes a drive in a sulky, is liable for injury to it occasioned by his want of common prudence. Carpenter v. Branch, 13 Vt. 161, 37 Am. Dec. 587. In a suit

The duty of gratuitous borrowers of goods, however, is measured in terms of care, and they are responsible only for negligence, which is the failure to exercise the requisite degree of care. They are never (in spite of the fact that theirs is all the benefit accruing from the bailment) absolutely responsible as insurers for loss or injury, unless they have made themselves thus liable either by specific contract or by their positive wrong.[33] In the absence, then, of such contract or positive wrong, the gratuitous borrower, who has exercised such great care or extraordinary diligence, is not responsible for loss of, or damage to, the goods lent.[34] And it then is immaterial how such loss or damage occurred. He is not liable for loss or damage due to inevitable accident, vis major, or the ordinary wear and tear,[35] unless he negligently or willfully exposed the goods to the danger of such loss, or negligently failed to avert the danger after it became imminent.[36]

brought by the lender against the borrower of a horse, which died in the possession of the latter, after the plaintiff proved the character of the bailment and the death of the horse in the bailee's hands, it devolved on the latter to show he had exercised the degree of care required by the nature of the bailment. BENNETT v. O'BRIEN, 37 Ill. 250, Dobie Cas. Bailments and Carriers, 56. And see Logan v. Mathews, 6 Pa. 417; Bush v. Miller, 13 Barb. (N. Y.) 481; Beardslee v. Richardson, 11 Wend. (N. Y.) 25, 25 Am. Dec. 596; Platt v. Hibbard, 7 Cow. (N. Y.) 497, note; Doorman v. Jenkins, 2 Adol. & E. (Eng.) 256, 259; Marsh v. Horne, 5 Barn. & C. (Eng.) 322; Harris v. Packwood, 3 Taunt. (Eng.) 264. If an injury happen to property in the hands of the borrower, the interference of the lender to remedy the evil will not release the bailee from responsibility for negligence. Todd v. Figley, 7 Watts (Pa.) 542; Eastman v. Sanborn, 3 Allen (Mass.) 594, 81 Am. Dec. 677. And see Bayliss v. Fisher, 7 Bing. (Eng.) 153. See, generally, BENNETT v. O'BRIEN, 37 Ill. 250, Dobie Cas. Bailments and Carriers, 56; Phillips v. Condon, 14 Ill. 84; Moore v. Westervelt, 27 N. Y. 234, 243; ESMAY v. FANNING, 9 Barb. (N. Y.) 176, Dobie Cas. Bailments and Carriers, 36. A gratuitous bailee for his own benefit is bound to the exercise of extraordinary care. Apczynski v. Butkiewicz, 140 Ill. App. 375. "As he [borrower bailee] alone receives benefit from the contract, he is liable for negligence, however slight; and he is bound to exercise the utmost degree of care in regard to the chattel bailed." 1 Halsbury, Laws of England, p. 538.

[33] Archer v. Walker, 38 Ind. 472. But see Watkins v. Roberts, 28 Ind. 167; BELLER v. SCHULTZ, 44 Mich. 529, 7 N. W. 225, 38 Am. Rep. 280, Dobie Cas. Bailments and Carriers, 57; Apczynski v. Butkiewicz, 140 Ill. App. 375. See, also, cases cited in preceding note.

[34] Casey v. Suter, 36 Md. 1; World's Columbian Exposition Co. v. Republic of France, 91 Fed. 64, 33 C. C. A. 333; Wilson v. Rockland Mfg. Co., 2 Har. (Del.) 67. See, also, cases cited in note 32.

[35] Hyland v. Paul, 33 Barb. (N. Y.) 245; Watkins v. Roberts, 28 Ind. 167; Wood v. McClure, 7 Ind. 155; FORTUNE v. HARRIS, 51 N. C. 532, Dobie Cas. Bailments and Carriers, 61; Abraham v. Nunn, 42 Ala. 51; Yale v. Oliver, 21 La. Ann. 454; Blakemore v. Bristol & E. Ry. Co. (Eng.) 8 E. & B. 1035; Pomfret v. Ricroft, 1 Saund. (Eng.) 321, 323.

[36] See Read v. Spaulding, 30 N. Y. 630, 86 Am. Dec. 426; Bowman v. Teall,

Lord Holt [37] said that the borrower is bound to "the strictest care and diligence; * * * that, if the bailee be guilty of the least neglect, he will be answerable." This was substantially the rule of the Roman Law, where "exactissima diligentia" marked the degree of diligence exacted.[38] The rule at common law requires such diligence as a person of more than ordinary prudence would bestow upon his own property under like circumstances.

Extraordinary care, then, is about as far above ordinary care as slight care is below it; [39] while the same considerations and difficulties apply in judging how far the great care is above ordinary care as in judging how far below it is the slight care. Much that was formerly said in that connection [40] is equally applicable here. Each, in an individual case, is a question of fact for the jury. Just as the conduct of that hypothetical being, the ordinarily prudent man, in caring for his own goods under like circumstances is the more or less concrete criterion by which ordinary care is judged, so we judge slight care by the man of less than ordinary prudence and extraordinary care by the man of more than ordinary diligence. Up to this extraordinarily careful man, then, must the gratuitous borrower measure or else be guilty of negligence.

Here, as in the case of bailments for the bailor's sole benefit, the doctrine of estoppel can be invoked against the bailor to prevent his recovering damages when loss or injury to the goods is the result of conditions (such as the character of the bailee and the place or manner in which the goods are to be kept) which were well known to the bailor at the time the bailment was created.[41] Here, too, is equally applicable what was there said as to

23 Wend. (N. Y.) 310, 35 Am. Dec. 562; Wing v. New York & E. R. Co., 1 Hilt. (N. Y.) 235; Davis v. Garrett, 6 Bing. (Eng.) 716.

[37] In COGGS v. BERNARD, 2 Ld. Raym. (Eng.) 909, 915, Dobie Cas. Bailments and Carriers, 1.

[38] See Story, Bailm. § 238.

[39] See Mason v. St. Louis Union Stock Yards Co., 60 Mo. App. 93; Whiting v. Chicago, M. & St. P. Ry. Co., 5 Dak. 90, 37 N. W. 222. See, also, cases cited in note 32.

[40] Ante, §§ 16, 29.

[41] A borrower's character, habits, and skill, so far as known to the lender, may be considered in determining what care or skill was expected by the parties. The lender cannot require greater skill on the part of the borrower than he had a right to presume the borrower was capable of bestowing. If a spirited horse be lent to a raw youth, and the owner knew him to be such, the circumspection of an experienced rider cannot be required; and what would be negligence in the one would not be so in the other. Mooers v. Larry, 15 Gray (Mass.) 451; Knowles v. Atlantic & St. L. R. Co., 38 Me. 55, 61 Am. Dec. 234; Eastman v. Patterson, 38 Vt. 146; Beale v. South Devon Ry. Co., 12 Wkly. Rep. (Eng.) 1115; Wilson v. Brett, 11 Mees. & W. (Eng.) 113;

express or implied representations as to the bailee's possession of special knowledge or peculiar skill.[42]

TERMINATION OF THE BAILMENT

41. The gratuitous loan for use may be terminated by:
- **(1) Acts of the parties.**
  - **(a) Accomplishment of the bailment purpose or expiration of the time for which the bailment was created.**
  - **(b) Mutual consent of both bailor and bailee.**
  - **(c) Positive wrong of bailee, at the option of the bailor.**
  - **(d) Option of either bailor or bailee, under certain circumstances.**
- **(2) Operation of law.**
  - **(a) Destruction of the bailed goods.**
  - **(b) Death of bailor or bailee, under certain circumstances.**
  - **(c) Change in legal status of bailor or bailee, under certain circumstances.**

Termination by Causes Terminating All Bailments

The termination of bailments in general by consent of both bailor and bailee, by the accomplishment of the bailment purpose or expiration of time, by positive wrong of the bailee, or by destruction of the bailed goods has already been discussed.[43] As this discussion is true of all bailments, including the loan for use, no further statement here is either necessary or desirable. So we proceed to discuss those cases in which the loan for use presents distinctive features not common to all bailments.

Termination by Option of Bailor or Bailee

As the sole benefit of the transaction accrues to the bailee, and the bailor, therefore, has no interest in having the bailment relation continued, it would seem that the bailee may terminate the bailment at any time.[44]

In a bailment for a definite time or specific purpose, the bailee (having once entered upon the bailment) has, as we have seen, a special property in the goods, which he can assert against all the world, including the bailor.[45] Such a bailment, therefore, can-

FORTUNE v. HARRIS, 51 N. C. 532, Dobie Cas. Bailments and Carriers, 61; Story, Ballm. § 245; 2 Kent, Comm. 575, and note.

[42] Ante, p. 70.

[43] Ante, § 20.

[44] Just as in bailments for the bailor's sole benefit, the bailment may at any time be terminated by the bailor.

[45] Ante, p. 86.

not be terminated at the mere option of the bailor.[46] When the bailment is not for a definite time or specific purpose, however, the rights of the bailee are at best a more or less precarious possessory interest as against the bailor, though such interest, during its continuance, however, is complete in so far as third persons are concerned. Here, from what has been said, such indefinite bailment can accordingly be terminated at any time at the bailor's option.[47]

Termination by Death

First, as to the death of the bailor. When the bailment is for a definite time or specific purpose, the special property of the bailee in the goods is not affected by the bailor's death, but the bailee can assert his right to keep the goods until the expiration of such time or the accomplishment of such purpose as against the personal representative of the bailor.[48] In indefinite bailments, however, the mere possessory interest of the bailee is terminated by the death of the bailor, and the right to reclaim the goods immediately vests in the bailor's personal representative.

We have already had occasion to discuss the personal nature of the loan for use, and we have seen that the bailee has ordinarily no right to transfer his interest and give another the right to use the goods which he himself has. Hence, on the death of the bailee, the very object for which the loan was created, namely, to

[46] The better view is that, when the loan is for a definite time, the lender cannot terminate the loan before that time. This was the rule of the civil law. The detriment to the borrower in failing to make other arrangements for his needs is a sufficient consideration to bind the lender to his promise. The borrower's distinct wrong or violation of the contract gives the lender a right to recall the loan. See Root v. Chandler, 10 Wend. (N. Y.) 110, 25 Am. Dec. 546; Hoyt v. Gelston, 13 Johns. (N. Y.) 142; BRINGLOE v. MORRICE, 1 Mod. (Eng.) 210, Dobie Cas. Bailments and Carriers, 58. See, also, Story, Bailm. §§ 258, 271, 277; Schouler, Bailm. 87.

[47] Putnam v. Wyley, 8 Johns. (N. Y.) 432, 5 Am. Dec. 346; ORSER v. STORMS, 9 Cow. (N. Y.) 687, 18 Am. Dec. 543; Dobie Cas. Bailments and Carriers, 60; Neff v. Thompson, 8 Barb. (N. Y.) 213; Green v. Hollingsworth, 5 Dana (Ky.) 173, 30 Am. Dec. 680; Pulliam v. Burlingame, 81 Mo. 111, 116, 51 Am. Rep. 229; Clapp v. Nelson, 12 Tex. 370, 62 Am. Dec. 530; Lyle v. Perry, 1 Dyer, 486; Smith v. Milles, 1 Term R. 480; Taylor v. Lendey, 9 East, 49; Clark's Case, 2 Leon. 30. Where loan is for indefinite time, lender must make demand before bringing suit. Payne v. Gardiner, 29 N. Y. 146. Until a demand and refusal to return property loaned for an indefinite time, the statute of limitations does not begin to run against the bailor. Payne v. Gardiner, 29 N. Y. 146; Kelsey v. Griswold, 6 Barb. (N. Y.) 436; Huntington v. Douglass, 1 Rob. (N. Y.) 204; Bruce v. Tilson, 25 N. Y. 194; Roberts v. Berdell, 61 Barb. (N. Y.) 37; Roberts v. Sykes, 30 Barb. (N. Y.) 173.

[48] It seems that this would logically follow from the bailee's special property in the goods, if that be conceded.

confer a personal favor or benefit on such bailee, necessarily no longer exists. The passing of the interest of a person after his death to his representative is sometimes called an assignment by operation of law. These considerations would seem to justify the rule, even in bailments for a definite time or specific purpose, that the loan for use (which is gratuitous) is terminated on the death of the bailee.[49]

Termination by Change of Legal Status of Parties—Bankruptcy

The bankruptcy of the bailor, if the loan is an indefinite one (so that the bailee has only a possessory interest), it would seem, terminates the bailment; the bailor's right to the goods passing to the bankrupt's trustee. The federal Bankrupt Act (Act July 1, 1898, c. 541, 30 Stat. 544 [U. S. Comp. St. 1901, p. 3418]), however, recognizes and preserves valid liens, and the term "lien" is given a very broad meaning. The special property of the bailee (in bailments for definite time or specific purpose), then, it would seem, is not affected by the bankruptcy of the bailor,[50] provided, of course, the bailment is not in any way fraudulent under the Act.

The bankruptcy of the bailee, by transferring the administration of his business affairs to his trustee and indicating that he is unable to meet his financial obligations, renders him unable to perform properly the duties of a bailee, and at least (it would seem) gives the bailor the right to terminate the bailment if the bailee's bankruptcy does not operate of itself to bring the bailment to an end. It hardly seems fair to presume that the bailor intended the continuance of the gratuitous personal benefit conferred on the bailee, after the bankruptcy of the latter.

Same—Insanity

The insanity of the bailor probably terminates an indefinite loan (in which the bailee has only a possessory interest), and the right to the goods loaned passes to the insane person's committee. The bailor's insanity, it would seem, does not affect the special property of the bailee, where the loan is definite as to time or specific as to purpose, provided, of course, that the bailment was created while the bailor was sane. The bailee's insanity renders him utterly unfit to perform any of the duties of a bailee, and it seems that it would therefore operate as an immediate termination of all loans for use. It would scarcely seem fair to infer that the bailor contemplated continuing gratuitous benefit on the bailee during the latter's insanity, with all the attendant risks.

49 See Farrow v. Bragg's Adm'r, 30 Ala. 261; Smiley v. Allen, 13 Allen (Mass.) 465; Morris v. Lowe, 97 Tenn. 243, 36 S. W. 1098.

50 See 1 Loveland on Bankruptcy (4th Ed.) §§ 310, 435.

Same—Marriage of Woman

The marriage of a woman at common law, owing to the tremendous change wrought as to her legal status, whether she be bailor or bailee, would probably terminate the gratuitous loan. Under modern emancipation acts, however, which practically give the rights of a feme sole to a married woman, her marriage would hardly affect a bailment.

REDELIVERY OF THE BAILED GOODS

42. The general principles affecting the delivery of goods by the bailee on the termination of the bailment are the same here as in other classes of bailments.

The place of delivery, in the absence of any contrary provision, should be the bailor's house, factory, or store.

The primary duty of the bailee, on the termination of the bailment, is the redelivery of the goods forming the subject-matter of the now extinct bailment. In general, the rules of law affecting the various aspects of such redelivery as to a gratuitous loan for use are those applicable to bailments in general.[51] Brief mention should be made, however, of one distinctive feature of the gratuitous loan, the place of delivery.

Place of Delivery

In regard to the place at which, on the termination of the gratuitous loan, the goods should be returned by the borrower, only

[51] See ante, p. ——. The thing borrowed is not only to be returned, but everything that is accessorial to it. Thus, the young of an animal, born during the time of the loan, is to be restored; and the income of stock, which has been lent to the borrower to enable him to pledge it, as a temporary security, also belongs to the lender. ORSER v. STORMS, 9 Cow. (N. Y.) 687, 18 Am. Dec. 543, Dobie Cas. Bailments and Carriers, 60; Hasbrouck v. Vandervoort, 4 Sandf. (N. Y.) 74; Booth v. Terrell, 16 Ga. 20, 25; Allen v. Delano, 55 Me. 113, 92 Am. Dec. 573. When no time has been fixed for a termination of the loan, the return must be made in a reasonable time. Wilcox v. Hogan, 5 Ind. 546; Green v. Hollingsworth, 5 Dana (Ky.) 173, 30 Am. Dec. 680; Ross v. Clark, 27 Mo. 549; Lay's Ex'r v. Lawson's Adm'r, 23 Ala. 377. The bailee is liable for breach of contract if he fails to return at the time specified. Fox v. Pruden, 3 Daly (N. Y.) 187; Clapp v. Nelson, 12 Tex. 370, 62 Am. Dec. 530. The borrower is bound to return the article loaned at the time stipulated, or, if no time is fixed, in a reasonable time; and whether it had become his duty to return it or not, where a loss occurred, is a question of fact, to be found by a jury. Green v. Hollingsworth, 5 Dana (Ky.) 173, 30 Am. Dec. 680. Where there has been a temporary exchange of articles of property, there is no principle that requires that the one shall be returned to the former owner before the other can be recovered. Hoell v. Paul, 49 N. C. 75.

general principles can be laid down. When the bailment contract covers this point, that will, of course, be controlling. If, however, no particular place is pointed out by the contract, and no specific place can be reasonably inferred from custom, usage, or the circumstances of the transaction, the normal place of delivery would be the dwelling, factory, or store of the lender.[52] The reason for this is that, since the bailor receives no benefit from the bailment, his convenience (rather than that of the bailee, receiving all the benefit) should be consulted and as little trouble as possible should be given to him. It therefore seems reasonable that the bailee should bring the goods to the bailor rather than that the bailor should be compelled to go for them to the bailee.

If the bailor has in the meantime removed his domicile to another place, the bailee is not bound to return the thing at the new residence; but he is bound only to return it at the former residence, unless, indeed, there is but a trifling difference in the distance between them. The common law seems not to have laid down any definite or special rules on the subject, but has left the decision to be determined by the varying and particular circumstances of each individual case according to the presumed intention of the parties. A demand by the bailor for the return of the goods (as is true of other bailments) need not be made at the place of delivery.

[52] The plaintiff loaned his carriage, in June, to the defendant, it being then stored at a stable in the city in which both parties resided; and, in December following, the defendant returned it to the same stable, after the stable keeper had ceased to be plaintiff's agent. Held a conversion. It should have been returned to plaintiff at his residence. ESMAY v. FANNING, 9 Barb. (N. Y.) 176, 5 How. Prac. (N. Y.) 228, Dobie Cas. Bailments and Carriers, 36. And see Rutgers v. Lucet, 2 Johns. Cas. (N. Y.) 92.

CHAPTER V

BAILMENTS FOR MUTUAL BENEFIT—HIRED USE OF THINGS

CLASSIFICATION OF MUTUAL BENEFIT BAILMENTS[1]

43. Bailments for the mutual benefit of the bailor and bailee may be thus classified:

1. Locatio, or hiring.

A. Locatio rei, the hired use of a thing.

B. Locatio operis, hired services about a thing.

(1) Ordinary bailments for hire.

(a) Locatio operis faciendi, hired services about a thing.

(b) Locatio custodiæ, the hired custody of a thing.

(c) Locatio operis mercium vehendarum, or the hired carrying of a thing.

(2) Extraordinary bailments for hire.

(a) Innkeepers.

(b) Common carriers of goods.

(c) Post office department.

2. Pignus, or pledge.

The general principles applicable to gratuitous bailments are in the main equally applicable to mutual benefit bailments. The fundamental distinction between these classes of bailments is that in the latter both the bailor and the bailee contemplate receiving

[1] This classification is practically that of Goddard, Bailm. & Carr. § 64.

some benefit or advantage from the bailment. On this fact depend many important differences in the rights and liabilities of the parties. The question of what constitutes a benefit sufficient to make the bailment one for mutual benefit (rather than a gratuitous one) has already been discussed.[2]

Bailments of this class are the usual bailments of commerce and may be created for an almost infinite variety of purposes. Since the great majority of bailments fall within this class, the practical importance of the questions involved justifies a very much more elaborate and detailed discussion than has been given to the subject of gratuitous bailments.

For the purpose of indicating subdivisions in the analysis of mutual benefit bailments, the names of the corresponding classes in the Roman law have been used; for these make up the natural and logical divisions of the subject, and this terminology has the advantage of familiarity.

The first great division of mutual benefit bailments is into two large classes—(1) Locatio, or hiring; and (2) pignus, or pledge. The pledge differs from all other bailments in that the bailment exists, not for itself alone, but merely as incidental to, and security for, the performance of the principal obligation. Pledges are discussed at some length in chapter 7.

The locatio or hiring bailments are first divided into (A) locatio rei, or the hired use of a thing; and (B) locatio operis, or hired services about a thing. Locatio operis bailments are in turn divided into (1) ordinary bailments for hire; and (2) extraordinary bailments for hire, including innkeepers, common carriers of goods, and the post office department. In these extraordinary bailments, considerations of public policy involve such unique distinctions that they are keenly differentiated from other bailments. They are accordingly discussed separately, and not in connection with the other bailments of the various classes.[3]

The classes of ordinary bailments of the hiring of services about a thing can be all treated together, as the distinctions are largely for convenience alone. As we have already seen, custody ordinarily involves services, and services on the bailed chattel require its custody in order that they may be performed. The carrying of a thing from one place to another is only a specific kind of service about a chattel, involving (when performed by a private and not a common carrier) no unique principles of the law of bailments.

[2] Ante, §§ 23, 33. It is immaterial whether the benefit is in fact ultimately received or not. It is essential, however, that the bailment be constituted with the intention of securing such benefit. This benefit, while commonly money on one part at least, may be anything else of value.

[3] Post, chapters 8-15.

After a brief discussion of locatio, or hiring, in general, this chapter will be devoted to the first great class of locatio bailments, viz., locatio rei, the hired use of things; while chapter 6 is concerned with locatio operis, or hired services about a thing, excluding the extraordinary bailments, which will be subsequently treated.

LOCATIO OR HIRING—IN GENERAL

44. Locatio, or hiring, is a bailment in which compensation is to be given either by the bailee to the bailor for the use of a thing (locatio rei) or by the bailor to the bailee for labor and services about a thing (locatio operis).

Bailments of hiring were called in the Roman law "locatio," or "locatio-conductio," both expressions being used to signify the same relation. It is a bailment whereby either the use of a thing or the services and labor of a person about a thing are given for a reward.[4] At the common law it may be defined as a bailment of a personal chattel, where a compensation is to be given for the use of the thing, or for labor or services about it.[5]

It is clear that these definitions or descriptions of locatio practically amount simply to throwing together the two definitions of locatio rei and locatio operis.

The terms used in the Roman and French law to designate the parties to locatio bailments are confusing rather than illumi-

[4] Ayliffe, Pand. bk. 4, tit. 7, p. 460; Wood, Inst. bk. 3, pp. 235, 236, c. 5; 1 Domat, bk. 1, tit. 4, § 1, art. 1.

[5] Pothier (Contrat de Louage, note 1) defines it to be a contract by which one of the contracting parties engages to allow the other to enjoy or use the thing hired, during the stipulated period, for a compensation, which the other party engages to pay. A definition substantially the same will be found in other writers. Lord Holt in COGGS v. BERNARD, 2 Ld. Raym. 909, 913, Dobie Cas. Bailments and Carriers, 1, has defined it to be "when goods are left with the bailee to be used by him for hire." The objection to this, as well as to the definition of Pothier, is that it is incomplete, and covers only cases of the hire of a thing (locatio rei), and excludes all cases of the hire of labor and services, and of the carriage of goods. Mr. Bell defines it, with great exactness, thus: "Location is, in general, defined to be a contract, by which the temporary use of a subject, or the work or service of a person, is given for an ascertained hire." 1 Bell, Comm. (4th Ed.) §§ 198, 385; Id. (5th Ed.) pp. 255, 451. See, also, 2 Kent, Comm. lect. 40 (4th Ed.) p. 585; 1 Bell, Comm. (5th Ed.) pp. 255, 451; 1 Bell, Comm. (4th Ed.) §§ 198, 385. See, also, Monthly Law Mag. (London) for April, 1839, pp. 217-219; Story, Bailm. § 368; 1 Domat, bk. 3, tit. 4, § 1, art. 1. See, also, Code Civil of France, arts. 1709, 1710; Sohm Inst. (Ledlie's Transl., 2d Ed.) 419; 2 Street, Foundations of Legal Liability, p. 284.

nating, and as they are on that account seldom used by English or American writers, they can be omitted here.[6] Some explanation of the terms "letter" and "hirer" in this connection, however, is essential. The hirer is the one who receives the immediate benefit from the bailment itself, and accordingly pays a compensation therefor; while the letter, in the eyes of the law, suffers a loss or detriment from the actual fulfillment of the bailment purpose, he therefore receives the compensation as his reward for such detriment.

In a locatio rei bailment, the bailee is the hirer; the bailor, the letter. Thus, where one procures a horse from a livery stable to ride, he (bailee) clearly receives the immediate benefit from the bailment (i. e., the delivery of the horse), for which he pays the livery stable keeper (bailor). On the contrary, in a locatio operis bailment, the bailee is the letter; the bailor, the hirer. For example, one who boards his horse at a stable (bailor) receives the benefit from the bailment (here the caring for the horse), and therefore pays the compensation to the stable keeper (bailee). It will thus be seen that the terms "hirer" and "letter" do not invariably refer to either the bailor and the bailee. In locatio rei, the bailee hires the use of the thing; in locatio operis, the bailor hires services about the thing.

SAME—NATURE OF THE RELATION

45. Locatio bailments, or bailments of hiring, may be created:
- **(a) By contract.**
- **(b) By operation of law.**

Locatio bailments are divided into two classes.
- **(a) Locatio rei, or the hiring of the use of a thing.**
- **(b) Locatio operis, or the hiring of services about a thing.**

[6] We are accustomed, in the common law, to use words corresponding to those of the Roman law, almost in the same promiscuous manner. Thus, letting ("locatio") and hiring ("conductio") are precise equivalents, used for the purpose of distinguishing the relative situation of different parties to the same contract. The letter, called in the civil law "locator," and in the French law "locateur," "loueur," or "bailleur," is he who, being the owner of the thing, lets it out to another for hire or compensation; and the hirer, called in the civil law "conductor," and in the French law "conducteur," "preneur," "locataire," is he who pays the compensation, having the benefit of the use of the thing. See, also, Story, Bailm. § 369; Wood, Inst. bk. 3, p. 236, c. 5; Poth. Contrat de Louage, note 1; 1 Domat, bk. 1, tit. 4, § 1, art. 2; Heinecc. Pand. lib. 19, tit. 2, § 818; Jones, Bailm. 90; Wood, Inst. Civ. Law, 236.

The locatio, or bailment of hiring, is, of course, governed by the principles common to all bailments. A mutual benefit bailment is distinguished from the gratuitous bailments by the fact that the bailment is undertaken or created for a recompense or consideration. What constitutes such a consideration has already been sufficiently discussed[7]

Establishment of the Relation by Contract

It follows naturally from the requirement of a contemplated consideration, to be paid by one party and received by the other, that the very great majority of bailments for hire are founded on special contracts, and these are the usual bailments of commerce. In such cases, as elsewhere, the general rules of contract apply.[8]

[7] Ante, §§ 23, 33. Apart from the fact that they are undertaken for a consideration, bailments for hire differ very little from gratuitous bailments either in their manner of creation, or in their purposes. Thus, in the case of a simple deposit, if a price is to be paid for the keeping, the character of the bailment is changed. It is no longer a depositum, but becomes a locatio custodiæ, or a hiring of custody. So, also, if a loan for use is gratuitous, it is a commodatum, but, if it be for a price, it is a locatio rei, or the hiring of a thing; and what would be a mandate, if it were not for the consideration, is a hiring of work and labor, or the hiring of carriage.

In every bailment of letting for hire, a contemplated price or compensation for the hire is essential, though the amount may not be stipulated. Herryford v. Davis, Use of Jackson & S. Co., 102 U. S. 235, 26 L. Ed. 160. In the absence of an agreement to the contrary, the law implies an agreement to pay a reasonable sum for the use of a thing. Cullen v. Lord, 39 Iowa, 302; Gray v. Missouri River Packet Co., 64 Mo. 47; Schouler, Bailm. (2d Ed.) § 98. Where a bailee takes a horse to care for, and is to have the use of the horse in consideration of his keep, the bailment is one for hire. Chamberlin v. Cobb, 32 Iowa, 161. See, also, Francis v. Shrader, 67 Ill. 272; White v. Humphery, 11 Q. B. Div. 43; Gaff v. O'Neil, 2 Cin. R. (Ohio) 246. Where one entering a clothing house for the purchase of a suit deposits his watch, at the direction of the salesman, in a drawer, preparatory to trying on some clothes, the jury are warranted in finding that such deposit is a necessary incident of the business, in which case the clothier becomes a bailee for hire, bound to exercise ordinary diligence. WOODRUFF v. PAINTER, 150 Pa. 91, 24 Atl. 621, 16 L. R. A. 451, 30 Am. St. Rep. 786, Dobie Cas. Bailments and Carriers, 40. A merchant who sells ready-made cloaks at retail, and provides mirrors for the use of customers while trying them on, and clerks to aid in the process, thereby impliedly invites his customers to take off their wraps and lay them down in the store, and is bound to exercise some care over such wraps. Where such merchant provides no place for keeping such wraps, and does not notify customers to look out for their wraps themselves, nor give any direction to his clerks on the subject, he is liable for the loss of a wrap laid on the counter by a customer while trying on a cloak, since his acts show that he exercised no care whatever. Bunnell v. Stern, 122 N. Y. 539, 25 N. E. 910, 10 L. R. A. 481, 19 Am. St. Rep. 519. Story, Bailm. § 375; Schouler, Bailm. (2d Ed.) § 90.

[8] Not only fraud or duress, but even mistake in regard to the subject-matter

There is, however, one instance of illegal contract, of such frequent occurrence, that it calls for brief consideration. This is the hiring of horses for use on Sunday, contrary to statute. The rule is that neither party can set up the illegal contract, either as the basis of an action or as a defense. But if a party can make out a case without relying on such contract, then he can recover. Thus, where the bailor sues to recover the stipulated price for the use of the horse, he cannot recover; for, to make out his case, he must set up the illegal contract of hiring. But if the bailor sues for a conversion when the bailee's use of the horse is outside of the contract, he can recover. Here the bailor sues for the bailee's wrongful dealing with an article not his own in a way inconsistent with the ownership of the bailor. The bailor's right of action is not based on the contract, and, since the illegal contract furnishes no excuse or defense, the bailor could recover; and the same is true, it is believed, when the bailor sues the bailee for mere negligence.[9]

of the bailment, its purpose, or the recompense, may avoid the contract. Thus, if I agree to hire a certain horse, and the bailor understands me to mean a different horse, there is no contract, for there is no mutual assent. The contract must not involve the execution of an unlawful purpose, or be against good morals and public policy. Thus, a contract for a bailment of furniture to be used for purposes of prostitution is void. So, also, are contracts to supply tools to commit burglary with, or goods to aid a public enemy, or for the purpose of smuggling. See Clark, Contr. 289, 346; Story, Bailm. §§ 372, 378, 379; Schouler, Bailm. (2d Ed.) §§ 91, 92.

[9] As to conversion, see Schouler, Bailm. (2d Ed.) § 140; Hall v. Corcoran, 107 Mass. 251, 9 Am. Rep. 30; Stewart v. Davis, 31 Ark. 518, 25 Am. Rep. 576. "The illegal letting may or may not appear. If it does, it simply explains the defendant's possession, and proves that it was by the owner's permission, at least for a certain purpose. It may give the defendant an opportunity to injure the horse, but it does not cause the injury; nor does it contribute to it, in such a sense as to make the plaintiff a party to the wrongful act. If it does not appear, before the defendant can avail himself of it as a defense, it becomes necessary for him to prove the illegal contract to which he was a party, and his own illegal conduct in traveling upon the Sabbath. But he can no more avail himself of that as a defense than the plaintiff can as a cause of action. Either party whose success depends upon proving his own violation of law must fail." Frost v. Plumb, 40 Conn. 111, 113, 16 Am. Rep. 18. See, also, DOOLITTLE v. SHAW, 92 Iowa, 348, 60 N. W. 621, 26 L. R. A. 366, 54 Am. St. Rep. 542, Dobie Cas. Bailments and Carriers, 67; Woodman v. Hubbard, 25 N. H. 67, 57 Am. Dec. 310. For other cases, see 45 Cent. Dig. "Sunday," § 52.

It seems that, when the bailor sues the bailee for negligence (even when there has been no conversion), the fact of the bailment being a Sunday one should be no defense, as the negligence and not the Sunday bailment is the proximate cause of the injury. Frost v. Plumb, 40 Conn. 111, 113, 16 Am.

We have already seen, in the case of gratuitous bailments, that, before the bailment is actually entered upon by the bailee, no rights accrue for breaches of the bailment contract, since it is without consideration.[10] In the case of locatio (and all other mutual benefit bailments), since the contract is supported by a consideration, mutual rights are acquired as soon as the contract is made. For nonfeasance, or a mere breach of this contract, then, either party is liable.[11]

Establishment of the Relation by Operation of Law

Though the very great majority of bailments for hire rest upon express contract between the parties, there are a few classes of quasi bailments for hire which may arise independently of the bailor's consent.[12] Such are cases of possession of property by

Rep. 18; Newbury v. Luke, 68 N. J. Law, 189, 52 Atl. 625; Hinkel & Edelen v. Pruitt, 151 Ky. 34, 151 S. W. 48. But there are cases to the contrary. Way v. Foster, 1 Allen (Mass.) 408; Hall v. Corcoran, 107 Mass. 258, 9 Am. Rep. 30.

[10] Ante, §§ 26, 38.

[11] Story, Bailm. §§ 384, 436; 2 Kent, Comm. 570; Schouler, Bailm. (2d Ed.) § 100. See THORNE v. DEAS, 4 Johns. (N. Y.) 84, Dobie Cas. Bailments and Carriers, 47; Elsee v. Gatward, 5 Term R. 143; Balfe v. West, 13 C. B. 466. "In cases of nondelivery of the thing by the letter, whether it arises from his mere refusal, or from his subsequent sale or transfer thereof to another person, or from his having stipulated for the delivery of a thing of which he is not the owner, and over which he has not any control, a right of action accrues to the hirer. But by the French law, if the nondelivery is prevented by inevitable casualty or superior force, as if it perishes, no such action lies; for in that law the rule is, 'Impossibilium nulla obligatio est.' But in all these cases the hirer may, if he chooses, treat the contract as rescinded; and, if he has paid any consideration therefor, he may recover it back. On the other hand, if the letter offers to deliver the thing in an injured or broken or altered state from what it was at the time of the hiring, the hirer is not bound to receive it, but he is entitled to insist upon rescinding the contract. And in such a case it will make no difference whether the injury or deterioration was by inevitable accident, or by any other cause." Story, Bailm. § 384. Such a contract, having the elements of contractual validity, can be sued on by one party to the contract, upon a breach of the contract by the other party. The legal incidents of such a suit are governed by the general rules of law applicable to contracts.

[12] "Nor should it be thought that bailments for mutual benefit necessitate a contract and mutual terms. * * * There may exist what we call a 'quasi bailment,' namely, one whose conditions are satisfied with the voluntary acceptance of possession by one who expects a reward for his service." Schouler, Bailm. (2d Ed.) § 94. The acceptance may be either actual or constructive, but unless there is something to show bailment, knowledge, and intent, no bailment can be inferred. Schouler, Bailm. (2d Ed.) § 100; Spangler v. Eicholtz, 25 Ill. 297; Cox v. Reynolds, 7 Ind. 257; Rodgers v. Stophel, 32 Pa. 111, 72 Am. Dec. 775; Feltman v. Gulf Brewery, 42 How. Prac. (N. Y.) 488.

captors,[13] by revenue officers,[14] by prize agents,[15] by officers of courts,[16] and by marine salvors.[17] Thus, in the last case, if a disabled ship is abandoned in a storm by the crew, and is towed into port by another vessel, by the rules of admiralty, the owner of the towing vessel is treated as a quasi bailee and is entitled to compensation for the services rendered.

Locatio Rei and Locatio Operis Bailments

As we have seen, in locatio rei the bailee is benefited by the bailment and pays a compensation therefor; while in locatio operis, the benefit of the bailment accrues to, and the compensation is paid by, the bailor. As a result of this, any attempt to treat together the rights and duties of the parties in both classes is apt to be confusing. The two will therefore be considered separately. The rest of the present chapter will be devoted to locatio rei, while chapter 6 will discuss locatio operis.

LOCATIO REI, OR THE HIRED USE OF A THING

46. Where things are hired for use, the rights and duties of the parties, as in other bailments, are controlled primarily by the bailment contract; but, when not thus controlled, they are implied by law.

As in all other classes of bailments, the parties may determine for themselves the nature and extent of their mutual rights and

[13] Story, Bailm. § 614; The Betsey, 1 W. Rob. Adm. 93, 96. Captors are bound to exercise ordinary care. The Maria, 4 W. Rob. Adm. 348, 350; The Anne, 3 Wheat. 435, 4 L. Ed. 428; The George, 1 Mason, 24, Fed. Cas. No. 5,328; The Lively, 1 Gall. 315, Fed. Cas. No. 8,403.

[14] Burke v. Trevitt, 1 Mason, 96, 101, Fed. Cas. No. 2,163.

[15] Story, Bailm. § 619; The Rendsberg, 6 C. Rob. Adm. (Eng.) 142.

[16] Story, Bailm. §§ 124–135, 620. See, generally, Burke v. Trevitt, 1 Mason, 96, 101, Fed. Cas. No. 2,163; Browning v. Hanford, 5 Hill (N. Y.) 588, 592, 40 Am. Dec. 369; Trotter v. White, 26 Miss. 88, 93. Ordinary diligence is the measure of liability. Cross v. Brown, 41 N. H. 283; Blake v. Kimball, 106 Mass. 115; Aurentz v. Porter, 56 Pa. 115; Burke v. Trevitt, 1 Mason, 96, Fed. Cas. No. 2,163; The Rendsberg, 6 C. Rob. Adm. (Eng.) 142. The same rules apply to receivers and other depositaries appointed by courts. Story, Bailm. § 621; Knight v. Plimouth, 3 Atk. (Eng.) 480; Beauchamp v. Silverlock, 2 Rep. Ch. (Eng.) 5; Horsely v. Chaloner, 2 Ves. Sr. (Eng.) 83; Rowth v. Howell, 3 Ves. (Eng.) 566; Wren v. Kirton, 11 Ves. (Eng.) 377. As to sheriffs and constables (the case most frequently occurring), see Snell v. State, to Use of Greenfield, 2 Swan (Tenn.) 344; Vance v. Vanarsdale, 1 Bush (Ky.) 504; Cresswell v. Burt, 61 Iowa, 590, 16 N. W. 730; Bridges v. Perry, 14 Vt. 262; Fletcher v. Circuit Judge of Kalkaska, 81 Mich. 186, 45 N. W. 641.

[17] Salvors are entitled to compensation for their services. This compensation is called "salvage," and renders the bailment one for hire. Story, Bailm.

liabilities by any special contract, not against public policy or in violation of law. The discussion that follows treats of these rights and duties when they are not controlled by the special contract of the parties to the bailment. In locatio rei, the bailee is the hirer of the use of the thing; the bailor is the letter. The use of the terms "bailor" and "bailee," however, seems preferable.

SAME—USE OF BAILED CHATTELS BY THE BAILEE

47. The bailee is entitled to the beneficial use of the thing hired; but such use is limited to the time, purpose, and manner for which the thing was hired.

The bailee acquires the right, and the exclusive right, to the use of the thing hired during the time of the bailment.[18] This right is good against the world, and not even the owner can disturb the bailee in the lawful enjoyment of it.[19] For this is the benefit accruing to the bailee, for which he pays the stipulated compensation. Nor can a creditor of the bailor, during the term of hire, attach the goods and take them from the custody of the bailee;[20] since the bailor's creditor can in such case claim no higher right than that of the bailor. If, during such time, the thing is redelivered to the owner for a temporary purpose only, he is bound to deliver it back afterwards to the bailee.[21] As long as the bailee keeps within the terms of the bailment, this right is clear and presents little difficulty.

§ 622; Abbott, Shipp. (5th Ed.) pt. 3, c. 10, §§ 1, 2; In re Cargo ex Schiller, 2 Prob. Div. (Eng.) 145. See, also, Seven Coal Barges, 2 Biss. 297, Fed. Cas. No. 12,677; The Fannie Brown (D. C.) 30 Fed. 215; The Mulhouse, Fed. Cas. No. 9,910; Nickerson v. John Perkins, 3 Ware, 87, Fed. Cas. No. 10,252.

18 Harris v. Maury, 30 Ala. 679; Schoyer v. Leif, 11 Colo. App. 49, 52 Pac. 416; Harrington v. Snyder, 3 Barb. (N. Y.) 380; Zell v. Dunkle, 156 Pa. 353, 27 Atl. 38; Ledbetter v. Thomas, 130 Ala. 299, 30 South. 342.

19 Story, Bailm. § 395; HICKOK v. BUCK, 22 Vt. 149, Dobie Cas. Bailments and Carriers, 63; Camp v. Dill, 27 Ala. 553; Bower v. Coker, 2 Rich. (S. C.) 13.

20 HARTFORD v. JACKSON, 11 N. H. 145, Dobie Cas. Bailments and Carriers, 64. Lessee has a right to property leased during lease, paramount to any right of lessor or his creditors; and, in enjoyment of this right, they cannot disturb him with impunity. They cannot take the property out of his possession. Smith v. Niles, 20 Vt. 315, 49 Am. Dec. 782. See, also, Truslow v. Putnam, 4 Abb. Dec. (N. Y.) 425; Anderson v. Heile, 64 S. W. 849, 23 Ky. Law Rep. 1115.

21 Roberts v. Wyatt, 2 Taunt. (Eng.) 268.

Conversion and Misuser

The bailee must respect the limitations on his use imposed by the contract of hiring; his use of the thing is limited strictly to the time, purpose, and manner therein set out. He therefore has no right to use the thing during a longer time, or for a different purpose, or in another manner from that specified by the bailment contract.[22] Thus, if a horse is hired as a saddle horse, the hirer has no right to use the horse in a cart, or as a beast of burden.[23] So, if a carriage and horses are hired for a journey to Boston, the hirer has no right to use them for making a journey to New

[22] Story, Bailm. § 413. Compare "Gratuitous Loans," ante, p. 89. And see Cullen v Lord, 39 Iowa, 302; Kennedy v. Ashcraft, 4 Bush (Ky.) 530; Stewart v. Davis, 31 Ark. 518, 25 Am. Rep. 576; Martin v. Cuthbertson, 64 N. C. 328. If hiring be general, any prudent use of the thing is permissible. Horne v. Meakin, 115 Mass. 326; McLauchlin v. Lomas, 3 Strob. (S. C.) 85; Harrington v. Snyder, 3 Barb. (N. Y.) 380. See, also, Ledbetter v. Thomas, 130 Ala. 299, 30 South. 342; Mayer v. Springer, 192 Ill. 270, 61 N. E. 348; Hall v. Corcoran, 107 Mass. 251, 9 Am. Rep. 30; Markoe v. Tiffany & Co., 163 N. Y. 565, 57 N. E. 1116; Direct Nav. Co. v. Davidson, 32 Tex. Civ. App. 492, 74 S. W. 790; McCurdy v. Wallblom Furniture & Carpet Co., 94 Minn. 326, 102 N. W. 873, 3 Ann. Cas. 468; Bac. Abr. "Bailment," C; Id. "Trover," C, D, E; Wilbraham v. Snow, 2 Saund. (Eng.) 47a, 47f, 47g, note by Williams & Patteson; Isaack v. Clark, 2 Bulst. (Eng.) 306, 309; Wilkinson v. King, 2 Camp. (Eng.) 335; Loeschman v. Machin, 2 Starkie (Eng.) 311; Youl v. Harbottle, Peake (Eng.) 49; Rotch v. Hawes, 12 Pick. (Mass.) 136, 22 Am. Dec. 414; WHEELOCK v. WHEELWRIGHT, 5 Mass. 104, Dobie Cas. Bailments and Carriers, 66; Cooper v. Willomatt, 1 Man., G. & S. (Eng.) 672; Harrington v. Snyder, 3 Barb. (N. Y.) 380; Crocker v. Gullifer, 44 Me. 491, 69 Am. Dec. 118; Cobb v. Wallace, 5 Cold. (Tenn.) 539, 98 Am. Dec. 435; Wentworth v. McDuffie, 48 N. H. 402; De Tollenere v. Fuller, 1 Mill, Const. (S. C.) 117, 121, 12 Am. Dec. 616; Jones, Bailm. 68, 69, 121; COGGS v. BERNARD, 2 Ld. Raym. (Eng.) 909, 917, Dobie Cas. Bailments and Carriers, 1; Buchanan v. Smith, 10 Hun (N. Y.) 474; Fisher v. Kyle, 27 Mich. 454; Lane v. Cameron, 38 Wis. 603; Ray v. Tubbs, 50 Vt. 688, 28 Am. Rep. 519. Where a horse meets with an injury through his own fault, but while the bailee is misusing it, the bailee is liable. Lucas v. Trumbull, 15 Gray (Mass.) 306. An infant is not liable on a contract of hire, but, if he uses the property in any other than the stipulated way, he is liable for conversion. Jennings v. Rundall, 8 Term R. (Eng.) 335; Homer v. Thwing, 3 Pick. (Mass.) 492. Cf. Whelden v. Chappel, 8 R. I. 230. For collection of cases, see 6 Cent. Dig. "Bailments," §§ 64–74; 3 Dec. Dig. "Bailments," § 16; 3 Am. & Eng. Enc. of Law, pp. 752–759; 3 Ann. Cas. 470; 12 Ann. Cas. 692; 38 Cyc. 1997. See, also, Story, Bailm. §§ 413–413d; Schouler, Bailm. §§ 139–142; Goddard, Bailm. & Carr. §§ 115–119; Van Zile, Bailm. & Carr. 124–126; 1 Street, Foundations of Legal Liability, p. 231 et seq.; Id. p. 257; 2 Street, Foundations of Legal Liability, pp. 286–288; note 26 L. R. A. 366.

[23] Jones, Bailm. 68, 88. See Wilbraham v. Snow, 2 Saund. (Eng.) 47a, 47g, and note; Lockwood v. Bull, 1 Cow. (N. Y.) 322, 13 Am. Dec. 539; McNeill v. Brooks, 1 Yerg. (Tenn.) 73.

York.[24] Again, if horses are hired for a week, the hirer has no right to use them for a month.[25]

Where the bailee transcends the bailment contract, along any of the lines indicated, there can be no question that he has committed an actionable wrong, and that he can be held liable for any damages proximately connected with his breach. But whether in such cases there is a conversion, rendering the bailee absolutely responsible, is a question on which there is much confusion and conflict.[26]

Where the bailee undertakes to act as the unqualified owner of the thing hired, as where he attempts to sell it to a third person, this is a clear case of conversion.[27] When the bailee keeps within the bailment contract, but merely fails to exercise the ordinary care in the use of the thing imposed on him by the nature of the bailment, it is just as clear that this is mere negligence and is in no sense a conversion.[28] Between these two, however, lie many cases as to which it is difficult to speak authoritatively.

[24] Jones, Bailm. 68. And see COGGS v. BERNARD, 2 Ld. Raym. (Eng.) 909, 915, Doble Cas. Bailments and Carriers, 1; Rotch v. Hawes, 12 Pick. (Mass.) 136, 22 Am. Dec. 414; Homer v. Thwing, 3 Pick. (Mass.) 492; WHEELOCK v. WHEELWRIGHT, 5 Mass. 104, Doble Cas. Bailments and Carriers, 66. Where a person who had hired a horse and buggy to drive to a specified place loaned them to defendant to drive to a different place, and while driving there he collided with a trolley pole and street car, destroying the horse and buggy, defendant, if he knew the purpose for which they had been hired, was liable to the owner, even if the collision was accidental and without negligence on his part. Palmer v. Mayo, 80 Conn. 353, 68 Atl. 369, 15 L. R. A. (N. S.) 428, 125 Am. St. Rep. 123, 12 Ann. Cas. 691.

[25] Jones, Bailm. 68; COGGS v. BERNARD, 2 Ld. Raym. (Eng.) 909, 915, Doble Cas. Bailments and Carriers, 1. And see WHEELOCK v. WHEELWRIGHT, 5 Mass. 104, Doble Cas. Bailments and Carriers, 66; Stewart v. Davis, 31 Ark. 518, 25 Am. Rep. 576.

[26] See cases and authorities cited in note 22.

[27] Schwartz v. Clark, 136 Ill. App. 150; Short v. Lapeyreuse, 24 La. Ann. 45; Geneva Wagon Co. v. Smith, 188 Mass. 202, 74 N. E. 299; Howard v. Seattle Nat. Bank, 10 Wash. 280, 38 Pac. 1040, 39 Pac. 100; Bryant v. Kenyon, 123 Mich. 151, 81 N. W. 1093; Sargent v. Gile, 8 N. H. 325; Lovejoy v. Jones, 30 N. H. 164; Swift v. Moseley, 10 Vt. 208, 33 Am. Dec. 197; Sanborn v. Colman, 6 N. H. 14, 23 Am. Dec. 703; Johnson v. Willey, 46 N. H. 75; Rodgers v. Grothe, 58 Pa. 414; Cooper v. Willomatt, 1 C. B. 672; Marner v. Bankes (C. P.) 16 Wkly. Rep. 62. But a bailee may have an assignable interest, which interest he may lawfully transfer. Post, p. 114.

[28] Thus, in an action for conversion of a horse, it appeared that defendant had hired the horse for a journey, and had carried, in addition to his own weight, $2,000 in specie, weighing 160 pounds. The court said: "If, however, an excessive weight be put on the horse, it will not amount to a conversion, but will be an abuse of the animal, for which, if injured by it, the owner may recover damages in an action on the case. By the contract of hiring, the hirer is bound to use the horse in a moderate and prudent manner. If the

Now conversion implies the assertion of a right of dominion over personalty inconsistent with the ownership of another.[29] It involves an interference with that dominion which is incident to the ownership of goods. It is something entirely apart from, and disassociated with, injury to chattels. As soon as a conversion takes place, the owner is thereby immediately vested with the right to sue the wrongdoer for the entire value of the goods converted.[30] It would thus seem clear that not every wrongful

hiring be to ride, he must not ride immoderately; if to work, he must not work the animal unreasonably—or, in either case, he will be liable, in action on the case, for the damages resulting from his misconduct, but not for a conversion, because the immoderate use of the animal during the time and in the mode stipulated by the contract does not amount to the assertion of ownership and of a right distinct and different from that acquired by the contract. It may have resulted from ignorance or carelessness, without any design whatever to exceed the authority given by the owner." McNiell v. Brooks, 1 Yerg. (Tenn.) 73.

Conversion will not lie against a bailee, because of his omission to place the horse in a barn at night, whereby it escaped or was stolen; there being no exercise of dominion by him, but merely a negligent omission to comply with his contract of bailment. Rosenberg v. Diele, 61 Misc. Rep. 610, 114 N. Y. Supp. 24. See, also, Forehead v. Jones, 84 Ga. 508, 10 S. E. 1090; Berman v. Kling, 81 Conn. 403, 71 Atl. 507; Cohen v. Koster, 133 App. Div. 570, 118 N. Y. Supp. 142; Ross v. Johnson, 5 Burr. (Eng.) 2825, 98 Eng. Reprint, 483.

29 "A conversion consists in an illegal control of the thing converted, inconsistent with the plaintiff's right of property." Perley, J., in Woodman v. Hubbard, 25 N. H. 67, 71, 57 Am. Dec. 310. See, also, Spooner v. Holmes, 102 Mass. 503, 3 Am. Rep. 491, collecting cases; Direct Nav. Co. v. Davidson, 32 Tex. Civ. App. 492, 74 S. W. 790. "The assertion of a title to, or an act of dominion over, personal property inconsistent with the right of the owner." Bigelow, Torts, 428 (quoted in Ramsby v. Beezley, 11 Or. 49, 51, 8 Pac. 288). "Any distinct act or dominion wrongfully exerted over one's property in denial of his right, or inconsistent with it." Cooley, Torts, 448 (quoted in Hossfeldt v. Dill, 28 Minn. 469, 475, 10 N. W. 781).

30 This right of an owner to recover as damages the value of the property converted is itself regarded as in the nature of property. It vests in him the instant the wrong is committed; the subsequent verdict and judgment serve merely to define its extent, and he cannot be deprived of it without his consent. 2 Bl. Comm. 438; Suth. Dam. § 7; Cooley, Const. Lim. 449; Westervelt v. Gregg, 12 N. Y. 211, 62 Am. Dec. 160; Dash v. Van Kleeck, 7 Johns. (N. Y.) 477, 5 Am. Dec. 291; Streubel v. Milwaukee & M. R. Co., 12 Wis. 67; Thornton v. Turner, 11 Minn. 336 (Gil. 237).

The owner cannot be compelled to accept the property in mitigation of damages. Green v. Speery, 16 Vt. 390, 42 Am. Dec. 519; Hart v. Skinner, 16 Vt. 138, 42 Am. Dec. 500; Shotwell v. Wendover, 1 Johns. (N. Y.) 65. But where the conversion is merely technical, and the property is in the same condition, it has been held that the plaintiff may be compelled to accept its return in mitigation of damages. Hart v. Skinner, 16 Vt. 138, 42 Am. Dec. 500; Churchill v. Welsh, 47 Wis. 39, 1 N. W. 398; Cook v. Loomis, 26 Conn. 483; Stevens v. Low, 2 Hill (N. Y.) 132.

detention or illegal control of the chattels of another amounts to a conversion. An act of the bailee, then, to constitute a conversion, must amount to an unauthorized assumption of dominion over the chattel, both hostile to, and exclusive of, the owner. The holding of the bailee must be entirely adverse to the bailor, since the former's possession was entirely lawful in its beginning.

This brings us to the debated question whether a bailee, who has intentionally deviated, however slightly, from the bailment contract as to the time, purpose, or manner of the use of the hired chattel, is thereby ipso facto guilty of a conversion. This seems to be the holding of a majority of the courts,[31] though a respectable minority hold the opposite view.[32] The majority holding, how-

[31] COGGS v. BERNARD, 2 Ld. Raym. 909, 915, Dobie Cas. Bailments and Carriers, 1 (dictum of Lord Holt). And see Disbrow v. Tenbroeck, 4 E. D. Smith (N. Y.) 397; WHEELOCK v. WHEELWRIGHT, 5 Mass. 104, Dobie Cas. Bailments and Carriers, 66; Rotch v. Hawes, 12 Pick. (Mass.) 136, 22 Am. Dec. 414; Woodman v. Hubbard, 25 N. H. 67, 57 Am. Dec. 310; Morton v. Gloster, 46 Me. 520; Crocker v. Gullifer, 44 Me. 491, 69 Am. Dec. 118; Fish v. Ferris, 5 Duer (N. Y.) 49; McNeill v. Brooks, 1 Yerg. (Tenn.) 73; Wentworth v. McDuffie, 48 N. H. 402; Lucas v. Trumbull, 15 Gray (Mass.) 306; Harrington v. Snyder, 3 Barb. (N. Y.) 380; Buchanan v. Smith, 10 Hun (N. Y.) 474; Perham v. Coney, 117 Mass. 102; Lane v. Cameron, 38 Wis. 603; Malone v. Robinson, 77 Ga. 719; Murphy v. Kaufman, 20 La. Ann. 559; Fisher v. Kyle, 27 Mich. 454; Welch v. Mohr, 93 Cal. 371, 28 Pac. 1060; Freeman v. Boland, 14 R. I. 39, 51 Am. Rep. 340; Evertson v. Frier (Tex. Civ. App. 1898) 45 S. W. 201; Hall v. Corcoran, 107 Mass. 251, 9 Am. Rep. 30. See, also, Raynor v. Sheffler, 79 N. J. Law, 340, 75 Atl. 748.

[32] Thus in DOOLITTLE v. SHAW, 92 Iowa, 348, 60 N. W. 621, 26 L. R. A. 366, 54 Am. St. Rep. 562, Dobie Cas. Bailments and Carriers, 67, the court said: "To constitute a conversion in a case like that at bar, there must be some exercise of dominion over the thing hired, in repudiation of, or inconsistent with, the owner's rights. We hold that the mere act of deviating from the line of travel which the hiring covered, or going on beyond the point for which the horse was hired, are acts which, in and of themselves, do not necessarily imply an assertion of title or right of dominion over the property inconsistent with, or in defiance of, the bailor's interest therein." This rule seems to do substantial justice, though it is opposed to the weight of authority.

In Harvey v. Epes, 12 Grat. (Va.) 153, the bailment contract was one for the hire of slaves for a year, to work in a certain county. They were taken by the hirer, without the owner's consent, to another county, but employed in the same kind of work, and while there died. The court, in an elaborate opinion, held that the removal of the slaves to a county other than that to which they were hired to work in was not of itself a conversion. It said: "Upon the whole, I am of the opinion that, in the case of a bailment for hire for a certain term, * * * the use of the property by the hirer, during the term, for a different purpose or in a different manner from that which was intended by the parties, will not amount to a conversion for which trover will lie, unless the destruction of the property be thereby occasioned, or at least unless the act be done with intent to convert the property, and thus to

ever, is criticised by Judge Story;[83] Mr. Schouler[84] conceives the "leaven of common sense" as fighting against it; while Mr. Street[85] more strongly characterizes it as "a judicial blunder" and as "among eccentric doctrines which have become inbedded in the law of conversion."

destroy or defeat the interest of the bailor therein. * * * A bailment upon hire is not conditional in its nature, any more than any other contract, and, in the absence of an express provision to that effect, the bailee will not, in general, forfeit his estate by a violation of any of the terms of the bailment. * * * If he merely uses the property in a manner or for a purpose not authorized by the contract, and without destroying it, or without intending to injure or impair the reversionary interest of the bailor therein, such misuser does not determine the bailment, and therefore is not a conversion for which trover will lie."

In Carney v. Rease, 60 W. Va. 676, 55 S. E. 729, Brannon, J., said: "The doctrine of Harvey v. Epes is considered as sound in a note by Freeman in 12 Am. Dec. 621. I consider the other rule extreme and hard. See DOOLITTLE v. SHAW, supra, citing the Harvey Case and holding its principles. President Lincoln, as counsel, successfully maintained this position in Johnson v. Weedman, 4 Scam. (Ill.) 495." See cases cited in note mentioned 12 Am. Dec. 621. See, also, Farkas v. Powell, 86 Ga. 800, 13 S. E. 200, 12 L. R. A. 397, in which this language was used: "We can see no good reason to hold the hirer liable for an injury to the horse which occurred without his fault, after he had returned with it within the limits of his original contract, although he had been guilty of a technical conversion by riding it three miles beyond the point to which it was hired to go, the extra distance not causing or contributing to the injury. We have been unable to find any case, the facts of which are like the facts in this. Nearly all the cases which hold the hirer liable when he has deviated from the terms of his contract are cases in which he was negligent in fact, or willfully and wantonly misconducted himself, or had overdriven the horse, or destroyed or ruined the property while beyond the limit or in the course of deviation from the purpose of hiring." As examples the court cited Mayor, etc., of City of Columbus v. Howard, 6 Ga. 213; Gorman v. Campbell, 14 Ga. 137; Collins v. Hutchins, 21 Ga. 270; Lewis v. McAfee, 32 Ga. 465; Malone v. Robinson, 77 Ga. 719. See, also, Weller & Co. v. Camp, 169 Ala. 275, 52 South. 929, 28 L. R. A. (N. S.) 1106.

[83] Story, Bailm. §§ 409, 413–413d.

[84] Schouler, Bailm. (2d Ed.) §§ 140, 141.

[85] 1 Street, Foundations of Legal Liability, p. 257. The same author (volume 2, p. 287) continues: "As an application of the doctrine of conversion the position assumed is clearly untenable, for the general principle underlying conversion is that where possession has a lawful inception, no act will amount to a conversion unless it is of such character as conclusively to show an intention on the part of the bailee to hold adversely and to the exclusion of the rightful owner. Another circumstance which shows that the doctrine of conversion is not the true basis of the exceptional liability fastened upon the bailee in this situation is the fact that the rule in question cannot be invoked merely for the purpose of vesting the general property in the bailee, thus making him an unwilling purchaser of the animal. It is applied only in order to fix liability upon the bailee in case of actual loss. There is no case where a bailee, being willing and able to return the animal sound within a

To hold that one hiring a horse to ride to Q., who rides a mile beyond Q., or who turns off from the road to Q. to see a friend, or who takes a different ride to R. (the same distance as Q.), commits a conversion with its attendant responsibilities, seems indeed a harsh and unfair doctrine. There is little wonder, then, that courts have endeavored to escape from it. Thus, it has been suggested[36] that a fair interpretation of the contract of hiring might enlarge the scope of discretionary use permitted to the bailee, who might then deviate from such contract, subject only to the possibility of having to pay an increased compensation. Other courts have held (without invoking the principle just mentioned) that a mere deviation from the agreed line of travel, or going beyond the point stipulated, are acts that do not of themselves imply an assertion of dominion over the chattel inconsistent with the owner's interest, and hence do not necessarily constitute a conversion.[37]

In most of the cases in which the general question under discussion has arisen, the owner has sought to hold the bailee liable, not for the full value of the chattel but rather for damage to the thing hired on the theory that the latter's conversion has made him an insurer absolutely responsible for loss or damage, regardless of the question of negligence.[38] Now there may be many reasons for thus imposing so strict a responsibility on the erring bailee, such as the quasi trust reposed in him by the bailor; but these considerations do not demand that the bailee should be adjudged guilty of a technical conversion. When the action, then, is simply for damage to the chattel, it approximates more closely an action of trespass on the case for a misuser or abuse of the chattel, than an action of conversion for what is now called "the disseisin" of the chattel. When the bailor sues to hold the bailee responsible as insurer (by virtue of the conversion) for damages suffered, after he has received back the damaged chattel, he recovers the amount of damage done to the chattel; when he sues for the value of the chattel, his recovery is reduced by the value of the damaged chattel when he received it back.[39] On

proper time, has been held liable in trover merely because he traveled in the wrong direction or went beyond the destination stated."

[36] Schouler, Bailm. (2d Ed.) § 141.

[37] Harvey v. Epes, 12 Grat. (Va.) 153, and DOOLITTLE v. SHAW, 92 Iowa, 348, 60 N. W. 621, 26 L. R. A. 366, 54 Am. St. Rep. 562, Dobie Cas. Bailments and Carriers, 67, are the leading cases holding this view. See notes 32 and 35.

[38] See cases cited in note 32. See, also, note 35.

[39] Plummer v. Reeves, 83 Ark. 10, 102 S. W. 376; Gove v. Watson, 61 N. H. 136; Stillwell v. Farwell, 64 Vt. 286, 24 Atl. 243; Irish v. Cloyes, 8 Vt. 30,

whichever of these theories, then, the bailor proceeds, after receiving back the injured chattel, practically the measure of damages is the same. Of course, in a technical conversion, a right to sue for the full value of the chattel accrues to the bailor (and can be taken from him only by his consent); so that he can refuse to receive back the damaged chattel and recover its full value.[40]

It should be noted, in conclusion of this subject, that, as has been already indicated, when there has been no deviation from the contract of hiring, but mere negligence (or failure to exercise ordinary care) even the courts holding to the strict deviation theory concede that this is in no sense a conversion, in that there is no unwarranted assumption of dominion by the bailee. Thus, where a horse is hired for a ride to Q., and the bailee, while riding to Q. without deviation, rides the horse too fast, the bailee has not committed any conversion, but is merely negligent.[41] Again there are some acts, such as an unauthorized sale,[42] or the consumption (as of food) or tortious destruction of the hired chattel,[43] which amount to a conversion per se. On the other hand, a deviation, for example, is most equivocal, and the intent must

30 Am. Dec. 446; Ewing v. Blount, 20 Ala. 694; 2 Sedg. Dam. § 494; Renfro's Adm'x v. Hughes, 69 Ala. 581; Davenport v. Ledger, 80 Ill. 574; Carter v. Roland, 53 Tex. 540; Kinnear v. Robinson, 2 Han. (N. B.) 73; Jamison v. Hendricks, 2 Blackf. (Ind.) 94, 18 Am. Dec. 131; WHEELOCK v. WHEELWRIGHT, 5 Mass. 104, 106, Dobie Cas. Bailments and Carriers, 66; Sparks v. Purdy, 11 Mo. 219; Yale v. Saunders, 16 Vt. 243; Brady v. Whitney, 24 Mich. 154; Cook v. Loomis, 26 Conn. 483. Acceptance of the property may or may not show a waiver of the tort, according to circumstances. Certainly, an acceptance without knowledge of the tort would not be a waiver. See Lucas v. Trumbull, 15 Gray (Mass.) 306; Austin v. Miller, 74 N. C. 274; Reynolds v. Shuler, 5 Cow. (N. Y.) 323. See 47 Cent. Dig. "Trover and Conversion," § 277.

40 See cases cited in note 30.

41 See note 28. But in Wentworth v. McDuffie, 48 N. H. 402, it was held that the bailor of a mare may maintain trover against the bailee, if the bailee willfully and intentionally drove the mare at such an immoderate and violent rate of speed as seriously to endanger her life; he being aware of the danger at the time, and the death of the mare being caused thereby. "The act of the bailee in willfully and intentionally driving the horse at such an immoderate rate of speed as he knew would seriously endanger the life of the horse is at least as marked an assumption of ownership, and as substantial an invasion of the bailor's right of property, as the act of driving the horse at a moderate speed one mile beyond the place named in the contract of hiring." Id.

42 See cases cited in note 27.

43 Barrett v. Mobile, 129 Ala. 179, 30 South. 36, 87 Am. St. Rep. 54; Atchison, T. & S. F. Ry. Co. v. Tanner, 19 Colo. 559, 36 Pac. 541; Turnbull v. Widner, 103 Mich. 509, 61 N. W. 784.

be ascertained. For, if such deviation was unintentional on the part of the bailee, then clearly it could not be considered a conversion.[44]

SAME—INTEREST OF THE BAILEE—RIGHT TO BRING SUIT

48. The interest of the bailee in the thing hired amounts to a special property, which he by appropriate action can, protect either against the bailor or third parties. When the injury is to his reversionary interest, or when the bailment is for an indefinite period, the bailor can sue third persons for injury to the thing hired.

The bailee acquires the right, as against the world, to hold and use the hired chattel during the time stipulated in the contract of hiring.[45] His interest is therefore clearly a special property.[46] This the bailee can, of course, protect by appropriate action, when it is tortiously interfered with either by third persons or the bailor.[47] While in a suit against the bailor the bailee recovers merely for the injury to his own interest, in a suit against a third party for the destruction of the chattel it is generally held that

[44] Where one unintentionally deviates from the line of travel, as where the hirer of a horse loses his way, he is not liable for conversion. To constitute conversion there must be an intention to exercise dominion over the property. Spooner v. Manchester, 133 Mass. 270, 43 Am. Rep. 514. Merely stopping along the road is not sufficient to constitute conversion. Evans v. Mason, 64 N. H. 98, 5 Atl. 766.

[45] Ante, p. 104.

[46] Jones, Ballm. 85, 86; Bac. Abr. "Bailment," C; Lee v. Atkinson, Yel. 172; 2 Bl. Comm. 395, 396; 2 Kent, Comm. (4th Ed.) lect. 40, p. 586; Wilbraham v. Snow, 2 Saund. (Eng.) 47, and note by Williams; Eaton v. Lynde, 15 Mass. 242; LITTLE v. FOSSETT, 34 Me. 545, 56 Am. Dec. 671, Doble Cas. Bailments and Carriers, 71.

[47] LITTLE v. FOSSETT, 34 Me. 545, 56 Am. Dec. 671, Dobie Cas. Bailments and Carriers, 71; Croft v. Alison, 4 Barn. & Ald. 590; Bac. Abr. "Trespass," C; Id. "Trover," C; Ludden v. Leavitt, 9 Mass. 104, 6 Am. Dec. 45; Warren v. Leland, 9 Mass. 265; Hall v. Pickard, 3 Camp. 187; Nicolls v. Bastard, 2 Cromp., M. & R. 659, 660; Bliss v. Schaub, 48 Barb. (N. Y.) 339; Woodman v. Town of Nottingham, 49 N. H. 387, 6 Am. Rep. 526; Rindge v. Inhabitants of Coleraine, 11 Gray (Mass.) 158; Hare v. Fuller, 7 Ala. 717; McGill v. Monette, 37 Ala. 49; Hopper v. Miller, 76 N. C. 402; White v. Bascom, 28 Vt. 268. An auctioneer, who, as agent of the owner, sells and delivers goods on a condition which is not complied with, may maintain replevin therefor. Tyler v. Freeman, 3 Cush. (Mass.) 261. See, also, Moore v. Winter, 27 Mo. 380; City of Chicago v. Pennsylvania Co., 119 Fed. 497, 57 C. C. A. 509; Brewster v. Warner, 136 Mass. 57, 49 Am. Rep. 5.

the bailee can recover the full value of the chattel, holding the surplus over his own interest for the bailor, and this[48] will be a bar to a subsequent action by the bailor.

As to actions by the bailor against third persons for damage to the hired chattel, when the bailment is for a definite period the bailor cannot bring such action (such right existing only in the bailee) unless such damage affects the bailor's reversionary interest in the chattel.[49] Since the bailor is entitled to receive the chattel at the end of the bailment, however, if such injury is so serious or permanent as to affect the chattel after its return to him, then the bailor may to that extent recover from such third persons.[50] When the bailment is for an indefinite time, so that the bailor may terminate it at his option, then, for any injury to the chattel, he, as well as the bailee, may bring suit against the third person committing such injury.[51]

[48] LITTLE v. FOSSETT, 34 Me. 545, 56 Am. Dec. 671, Dobie Cas. Bailments and Carriers, 71; White v. Webb, 15 Conn. 302; American Dist. Tel. Co. of Baltimore v. Walker, 72 Md. 454, 20 Atl. 1, 20 Am. St. Rep. 479; Gillette v. Goodspeed, 69 Conn. 363, 37 Atl. 973; Waggoner v. Snody, 98 Tex. 512, 85 S. W. 1134; Walsh v. United States Tent & Awning Co., 153 Ill. App. 229. If a bailee has sued for and collected the entire damage done to personal property in his possession, the true owner of such property may by assumpsit, recover of such bailee the amount so collected. Walsh v. United States Tent & Awning Co., 153 Ill. App. 229.

[49] Clarke v. Poozer, 2 McMul. (S. C.) 434; Swift v. Moseley, 10 Vt. 208, 33 Am. Dec. 197. But see Mears v. London & S. W. Ry. Co. (Eng.) 11 C. B. (N. S.) 850; Eldridge v. Adams, 54 Barb. (N. Y.) 417. Unless bailee has absolute right to retain bailed property for definite time, trespass may be brought against wrongdoer to property, either in name of bailor or bailee, Strong v. Adams, 30 Vt. 221, 73 Am. Dec. 305; or trover, Drake v. Redington, 9 N. H. 243. See, also, Hurd v. West, 7 Cow. (N. Y.) 752; Halyard v. Dechelman, 29 Mo. 459, 77 Am. Dec. 585; Howard v. Farr, 18 N. H. 457; Swift v. Moseley, 10 Vt. 208, 33 Am. Dec. 197; Clarke v. Poozer, 2 McMul. (S. C.) 434. A bailee for a definite term may maintain trespass against his bailor for a wrongful retaking of the property. BURDICT v. MURRAY, 3 Vt. 302, 21 Am. Dec. 588, Dobie Cas. Bailments and Carriers, 84. See Angus v. McLachlan, 23 Ch. Div. 330. In trover by a bailee against his bailor, the measure of damages is the value of the bailee's special interest in the goods; but in trover against a stranger the bailee recovers the entire value of the goods, and must hold the excess over his special interest in trust for the bailor. Benjamin v. Stremple, 13 Ill. 466. See, also, Soper v. Sumner, 5 Vt. 274; Lexington & O. R. Co. v. Kidd, 7 Dana (Ky.) 245; Gordon v. Harper, 7 T. R. (Eng.) 9.

[50] New Jersey Electric Ry. Co. v. New York, L. E. & W. R. Co., 61 N. J. Law, 287, 41 Atl. 1116, 43 L. R. A. 849. See Schouler, Bailm. (2d Ed.) § 154; Howard v. Farr, 18 N. H. 457; White v. Griffin, 49 N. C. 139. See, also, Lexington & O. R. Co. v. Kidd, 7 Dana (Ky.) 245; Mears v. London & S. W. Ry. Co. (Eng.) 11 C. B. (N. S.) 850.

[51] Bac. Abr. "Trespass," C; Id. "Trover," C; 2 Bl. Comm. 396; Gordon v. Harper, 7 Term R. (Eng.) 9; Pain v. Whittaker, 1 Ryan & M. (Eng.) 99;

SAME—ASSIGNABILITY OF THE BAILEE'S INTEREST

49. Where the bailment is for a definite time, and is not personal to the bailee, the bailee's interest in the hired chattel is assignable.

When the bailment is personal to the bailee by virtue of confidence reposed in him personally, this by its very terms forbids any assignment of his interest by the bailee.[52] Again, when the bailment is not for a definite time, but is one at will, terminable at the pleasure of either party, the interest of the bailee is too elusive and indefinite to be capable of assignment.[53] An attempt, in either of these two cases, by the bailee to transfer his interest to a third person, would confer on the latter no property in the hired chattel. It would, on the other hand, give the bailor the right to put an end to the bailment and bring trover or trespass against such transferee, who took possession of the chattel.[54]

But when the hiring is for a definite time, and when also there is no personal confidence reposed in the bailee, so that the bailment is not a personal one, then the bailee's interest is assignable and he can transfer it to a third person.[55] Such third person, as

Wilbraham v. Snow, 2 Saund. (Eng.) 47a, notes by Williams, etc.; Nicolls v. Bastard, 2 Cromp. M. & R. (Eng.) 659; Lacoste v. Pipkin, 13 Smedes & M. (Miss.) 589. See, also, Story, Bailm. § 394; Flewellin v. Rave, 1 Bulst. (Eng.) 68, 69; William v. Gywn, 2 Saund. (Eng.) 46, 47, and note.

[52] Crocker v. Gullifer, 44 Me. 491, 69 Am. Dec. 118; BAILEY v. COLBY, 34 N. H. 29, 66 Am. Dec. 752, Dobie Cas. Bailments and Carriers, 73. See, also, Dunlap v. Gleason, 16 Mich. 158, 93 Am. Dec. 231.

[53] BAILEY v. COLBY, 34 N. H. 29, 66 Am. Dec. 752, Dobie Cas. Bailments and Carriers, 73.

[54] BAILEY v. COLBY, 34 N. H. 29, 66 Am. Dec. 752, Dobie Cas. Bailments and Carriers, 73.

[55] "A party may lease his farm for years, with the stock and tools upon it; the whole lease, it can hardly be doubted, may be assigned. A party may let furnished lodgings for a term; the lessee has an assignable interest in the furniture. * * * So a party who should lease his livery stable, with his stock of horses and carriages, for a term of years, could hardly complain if the lessee should assign his interest, unless some restriction was introduced in the lease." BAILEY v. COLBY, 34 N. H. 29, 36, 37, 66 Am. Dec. 752, Dobie Cas. Bailments and Carriers, 73. The hirer's transfer of his beneficial interest alone, made with due reservation of the bailor's permanent ownership, should be upheld, unless the use was strictly personal or precarious. Vincent v. Cornell, 13 Pick. (Mass.) 294, 23 Am. Dec. 683; Nash v. Mosher, 19 Wend. (N. Y.) 431. See Fenn v. Bittleston, 7 Exch. 152; Day v. Bassett, 102 Mass. 445; Putnam v. Wyley, 8 Johns. (N. Y.) 432, 5 Am. Dec. 346.

A factor may pledge the goods to the extent of his own lien thereon, if he avowedly confines his pledge to that, and does not exceed his interest. Man

the bailee's assignee, would take in general the same interest that the bailee had.[56] The original bailee, however, continues liable to the original bailor for any damage to, or the loss of, the hired chattel, due to the negligence of the assignee, his servants or agents. The basis of this rule is sometimes said to be lack of privity between the original bailor and the bailee's assignee; and sometimes, with more reason, the rule is grounded on the general rules governing principal and agent and master and servant.[57]

SAME—BAILOR'S WARRANTY OF TITLE OR INTEREST

50. The bailor warrants that he has sufficient title or interest in the hired chattel to make the bailment.[58]

In the very act of creating the bailment, the bailor impliedly warrants that his title or interest in the thing hired is sufficient to enable him to make the bailment in question.[59] This is anal-

v. Shiffner, 2 East, 523–529; McCombie v. Davies, 7 East, 6; Urquhart v. McIver, 4 Johns. (N. Y.) 103; Whitwell v. Wells, 24 Pick. (Mass.) 25, 31. And see ante, §§ 47, 48. Hirer of personal property cannot, by sale thereof, though to a purchaser in good faith, pass title. Russell v. Favier, 18 La. 585, 36 Am. Dec. 662.

[56] BAILEY v. COLBY, 34 N. H. 29, 66 Am. Dec. 752, Dobie Cas. Bailments and Carriers, 73.

[57] Goddard, Bailm. & Carr. § 120.

[58] It is frequently said that the bailor, in a hiring for use, warrants that the hired thing is suitable for the purpose of the hiring. Harrington v. Snyder, 3 Barb. (N. Y.) 380; Leach v. French, 69 Me. 389, 392, 31 Am. Rep. 296. See, also, Horne v. Meakin, 115 Mass. 326. It is believed, though, that this states the case too strongly against the bailor and that his liability is not an absolute warranty, but merely a duty to disclose to the bailee any defects which he knew or by the exercise of due care might have known. COPELAND v. DRAPER, 157 Mass. 558, 32 N. E. 944, 19 L. R. A. 283, 34 Am. St. Rep. 314, Dobie Cas. Bailments and Carriers, 25. See, ante, p. 31. See, also, Van Zile, Bailm. & Carr. § 123; Goddard, Bailm. & Carr. § 113. In favor of the warranty theory, see 1 Halsbury, Laws of England, p. 550; Sutton v. Temple, 12 M. & W. (Eng.) 52; Mowbray v. Merryweather, 2 Q. B. 640. If he gives him no notice of any vicious propensity of the horse, except to tell him, in answer to an inquiry, that the horse is all right, except a little "skeery," when he knows that the horse has a vicious habit, he will be liable for any injuries sustained by reason of such vicious habit. Kissam v. Jones, 56 Hun, 432, 10 N. Y. Supp. 94. See, also, Hadley v. Cross, 34 Vt. 586, 80 Am. Dec. 699. Plaintiff cannot recover hire of slave, if he knew slave was unsound, and fraudulently concealed it from defendant, providing the latter, within reasonable time after discovering fraud, offered to return slave and rescind contract. Reading v. Price, 3 J. J. Marsh. (Ky.) 61, 19 Am. Dec. 162.

[59] Goddard, Bailm. & Carr. § 113; Van Zile, Bailm. & Carr. § 121; Schouler, Bailm. (2d Ed.) § 151; Story, Bailm. §§ 383, 387. "A pledgor, by the act

ogous to the covenant of the lessor of lands for quiet enjoyment by the lessee,[60] the implied warranty of title by one purporting to make a sale of personalty,[61] and the implied warranty of authority of an agent who undertakes to make a contract with a third party binding on his principal.[62]

In a hiring for use, the bailor stipulates that the bailee shall have the exclusive use of the chattel for the agreed time. Manifestly, then, in creating the very bailment, the bailor impliedly warrants that he has sufficient title or interest in the chattel to confer such use on the bailee for such time. If, therefore, the bailee's use is disturbed by a superior title in a third person, the bailor is liable for the amount of damage which the bailee thereby suffers. Such warranty applies only against the claims of third persons that rest on a real legal basis. When his possession is disturbed by the mere tortious acts of third persons, the bailee's remedy is against them alone.[63]

SAME—LIABILITY FOR INJURIES TO THIRD PERSONS

51. For injuries to third persons, due to the negligent use of the hired chattel, the bailee alone is responsible.

The bailee has the exclusive use of the hired chattel; he alone exercises entire control over it. Naturally, then, when a third person is injured, owing to the negligent use of the chattel, he must proceed solely against the bailee; he has no remedy against the bailor.[64] The bailor, by creating the bailment, has severed from

of pledging, impliedly warrants that he is the general owner of the property pledged; and he is liable to the pledgee in damages, if the property, or any part of it, is taken from the latter under a superior title." Jones, Pledges, § 52. See Goldstein v. Hort, 30 Cal. 372; Mairs v. Taylor, 40 Pa. 446; Cass v. Higenbotam, 27 Hun (N. Y.) 406.

[60] Tayl. Landl. & Ten. § 308; 1 Schouler, Pers. Prop. (2d Ed.) § 29.

[61] Williston, Sales, § 216; American Sales Act, § 13.

[62] Mechem, Agency, §§ 544, 545.

[63] Baugher v. Wilkins, 16 Md. 35, 77 Am. Dec. 279; Playter v. Cunningham, 21 Cal. 229; Surget v. Arighi, 11 Smedes & M. (Miss.) 87, 49 Am. Dec. 46.

[64] McColligan v. Pennsylvania Ry. Co., 214 Pa. 229, 63 Atl. 792, 6 L. R. A. (N. S.) 544, 112 Am. St. Rep. 739; New Jersey Electric Ry. Co. v. New York, L. E. & W. R. Co., 61 N. J. Law, 287, 41 Atl. 1116, 43 L. R. A. 849; Sproul v. Hemmingway, 14 Pick. (Mass.) 1, 25 Am. Dec. 350; Schular v. Hudson River R. Co., 38 Barb. (N. Y.) 653; Carter v. Berlin Mills Co., 58 N. H. 52, 42 Am. Rep. 572; Stevens v. Armstrong, 6 N. Y. 435; Rapson v. Cubitt, 9 Mees. & W. (Eng.) 710. And see Powles v. Hider, 6 El. & Bl. (Eng.) 207; Venables v. Smith, 2 Q. B. Div. (Eng.) 279. Compare King v. Spurr, 8 Q. B. Div. (Eng.) 104. The owner of a boat, who leases it to another to be used as a

himself the use of the chattel within the limits of the contract of hiring; he also thereby relieves himself from responsibility to third persons resulting solely from such use.

Nor does the bailee so represent or stand for the bailor as to create the relation here of master and servant or principal and agent, thus rendering the acts of the bailee legally those of the bailor.[65] The bailor does not employ the bailee, but rather the bailee hires the use of a chattel, obtaining the benefits of such use and assuming its burdens. Therefore, when the bailee or his servant is negligent in the use of the chattel, the bailor cannot be connected therewith so as to render him liable to third persons for the resulting damage.

SAME—EXPENSES ABOUT THE BAILED CHATTELS

52. The bailee must bear ordinary expenses incidental to the use of the thing; but for extraordinary expenses the bailor is responsible.

Custom, or the contract of hiring, will ordinarily determine which party is to bear the various expenses connected with the bailment.[66] When both of these are silent, it is a fair presumption that the bailee, who bargains for the use of the chattel, should bear the expenses necessarily and reasonably incident to such use, as, for example, feed for a horse.[67] The compensation, it seems, is ordinarily fixed on this assumption. The express or presumed intention must govern; and, as bearing upon this point, in doubtful cases the bailment purpose, and the rate and nature of the recompense must be duly considered.

It would seem a fair presumption that the parties intended the bailor to bear any unforeseen and extraordinary expense, which permanently enhances the value of the property, or preserves it from loss,[68] provided, of course, the expense was not necessitated

ferry, is not liable for an accident occurring on the boat while in use of the latter. Claypool v. McAllister, 20 Ill. 504. And see Tuckerman v. Brown, 17 Barb. (N. Y.) 191.

[65] McColligan v. Penn. Ry. Co., 214 Pa. 229, 63 Atl. 792, 6 L. R. A. (N. S.) 544, 112 Am. St. Rep. 739; New Jersey Electric Ry. Co. v. New York, L. E. & W. R. Co., 61 N. J. Law, 287, 41 Atl. 1116, 43 L. R. A. 849, and other cases cited in preceding note.

[66] Handford v. Palmer, 2 Brad. & B. (Eng.) 359, 5 Moore, 74.

[67] Schouler, Bailm. § 392; Handford v. Palmer, 2 Brad. & B. (Eng.) 359, 5 Moore, 74.

[68] Harrington v. Snyder, 3 Barb. (N. Y.) 380.

by the bailee's fault. Thus, when the horse becomes sick unexpectedly, the expense of a veterinarian should be borne by the bailor.[69] It is generally held that, in the absence of such a stipulation in the contract, the bailor is under no obligation to pay the expenses of keeping the thing (such as a machine) in repair.[70]

SAME—DEGREE OF CARE TO BE EXERCISED BY THE BAILEE

53. The degree of diligence exacted of the bailee in the use of the hired chattel is placed at ordinary care.

Since a locatio rei is a bailment for the mutual benefit of the bailor and bailee, the bailee must exercise ordinary care in using and keeping the hired chattel.[71] The legal duty of the bailee having been thus fixed, any breach of that duty is negligence, which renders the bailee liable to the bailor for any damage thereby proximately occasioned. Ordinary care, however, in the absence of

[69] One who hires a horse is not liable for expense of caring for it, if it becomes sick in his hands without his fault; but the owner is liable therefor to third person, who, with his knowledge, cares for it at request of hirer. Leach v. French, 69 Me. 389, 31 Am. Rep. 296.

[70] Gleason v. Smith, 39 Hun (N. Y.) 617; Central Trust Co. v. Wabash, St. L. & P. R. Co. (C. C.) 50 Fed. 857; Sutton v. Temple, 12 M. & W. (Eng.) 52; Herman v. Nye, 6 Q. B. D. (Eng.) 685; 1 Halsbury, Laws of England, p. 552. A provision in a lease of a machine, binding the lessee to keep the same in working order, requires the lessee to have some one in charge of the machine capable of managing it, and imposes on him the duty of exercising reasonable attention to keep the same in good working order. J. T. Stark Grain Co. v. Automatic Weighing Mach. Co., 81 Ark. 609, 99 S. W. 1103. Where a lease of machinery contained a covenant on the part of the lessor to repair the then existing plant so that the same may be successfully operated, the lessor is bound to repair all the machinery which then comprises the plant, but he is not required to furnish additional machinery or larger pumps. Sharpless v. Zelley, 37 Pa. Super. Ct. 102.

[71] See Jones, Bailm. p. 88; Story, Bailm. §§ 398, 399; Domat, Civ. Law, lib. 1, tit. 4, § 3, para. 3, 4; 1 Bell, Comm. (7th Ed.) pp. 481, 483. See, also, cases infra; Collins v. Bennett, 46 N. Y. 490; Chamberlin v. Cobb, 32 Iowa, 161; Millon v. Salisbury, 13 Johns. (N. Y.) 211; Handford v. Palmer, 2 Brad. & B. (Eng.) 359; Clark v. U. S., 95 U. S. 539, 24 L. Ed. 518. See, on this subject generally, the following recent cases: GANNON v. CONSOLIDATED ICE CO., 91 Fed. 539, 33 C. C. A. 662, Dobie Cas. Bailments and Carriers, 81; WISECARVER v. LONG & CAMP, 120 Iowa, 59, 94 N. W. 467, Dobie Cas. Bailments and Carriers, 78; Bradbury v. Lawrence, 91 Me. 457, 40 Atl. 332; Alden v. Grande Ronde Lumber Co., 46 Or. 593, 81 Pac. 385; Phillips v. International Text Book Co., 26 Pa. Super. Ct. 230; SINISCHALCHI v. BASLICO (Sup.) 92 N. Y. Supp. 722, Dobie Cas. Bailments and Carriers, 80.

the bailee's active wrongdoing or special contract, is the full measure of the bailee's duty.[72] When this duty has, therefore, been fulfilled, the bailee is not responsible for any loss or damage to the bailed chattel, regardless of how it happened. When loss of damage occurs, then, the apposite inquiry is: Was such loss or damage due to the bailee's negligence—that is, to the failure of the bailee to exercise ordinary care?

Ordinary care or diligence, as we have already seen,[73] is that degree of care which men of ordinary prudence would exercise under like circumstances. This ordinarily prudent man is the standard, and by means of comparison with him the whole scheme of the requisite care to be exacted of bailees has been evolved. Slight care, it has been pointed out, is that exercised by men of less than ordinary prudence; while great care is that expected of men of more than ordinary prudence. The ordinary care of the mutual benefit bailee is higher in the scale of care than the slight care of the bailee in a bailment for the bailor's sole benefit; it is correspondingly lower than the great care exacted of the bailee when the bailment is solely for the bailee's benefit.

Here should be emphasized what has been already said in other

[72] One who leased moving picture films for use was a bailee, and as such only bound to exercise ordinary care in using the films. MILLER v. MILOSLOWSKY, 153 Iowa, 135, 133 N. W. 357, Dobie Cas. Bailments and Carriers, 79. In an action to recover damages for injuries to a horse alleged to have happened while the horse was in the defendant's possession as a bailee for hire, the court commits no error in charging as follows: "The rule of law is that he is obliged to use ordinary diligence and care in order to preserve the property, and if you find in this case that he has not used ordinary diligence and care, but that the animal was hurt because he did not use ordinary diligence and care, then the plaintiff is entitled to recover. On the other hand, if you find that he did use ordinary diligence and care, your verdict should be for the defendant." Brannan v. Haldeman, 35 Pa. Super. Ct. 286. A contract of hire of chattels being one of mutual benefit, the hirer, in the absence of any agreement to the contrary, is only bound to exercise ordinary diligence in taking care of the property, and it is error to charge the jury Civ. Code 1895, § 2895, defining "extraordinary diligence," and section 2900, defining "gross neglect"; such instructions being calculated to mislead or confuse the jury in applying the facts to the proper rule of diligence. Evans & Pennington v. Nail, 1 Ga. App. 42, 57 S. E. 1020. As to effect of special contract on the bailee's liability, see Rapid Safety Fire Extinguisher Co. of New York v. Hay-Budden Mfg. Co., 77 App. Div. 643, 79 N. Y. Supp. 1145; Direct Nav. Co. v. Davidson, 32 Tex. Civ. App. 492, 74 S. W. 790. Where a bailee on hire of a horse agrees to return it in as good condition as when received, or pay for it, he is liable where the horse died while in his possession, though without fault on his part. Grady v. Schweinler, 16 N. D. 452, 113 N. W. 1031, 14 L. R. A. (N. S.) 1089, 125 Am. St. Rep. 674, 15 Ann. Cas. 161.

[73] Ante, §§ 16, 29, 40.

connections on ordinary care. The term is one of intense relativity,[74] and the question whether the bailee has exercised such care can never be accurately answered, apart from the peculiar circumstances of each individual case. The nature of the chattel, its value, weight, whether it is animate or inanimate, and a thousand other considerations, enter into the problem, which is, in each particular instance, an intensely practical one, to be worked out in harmony with the dictates of sound common sense.[75] Again,

[74] Where plaintiff rented a truck to defendant D., who placed the same in charge of an experienced driver, and the truck was injured in a collision with a street car, owing to the negligence of the motorman, without any negligence on the part of the driver, the bailees were not liable to plaintiff for the damages sustained. Littlefield v. New York City Ry. Co., 51 Misc. Rep. 637, 101 N. Y. Supp. 75. A bailee of a horse and wagon for hire is liable for the value thereof, if he fails to exercise reasonable care to protect it from theft. Kleiner v. Cohn, 75 Misc. Rep. 116, 132 N. Y. Supp. 779. Defendants hired a horse and wagon from plaintiff, which was taken to their place of business at 8 o'clock a. m., and from 8 until 11 o'clock the driver worked in defendants' factory, during which time no watch was kept over the wagon, except that every 10 or 15 minutes one of defendants' workmen would look from the fifth-story window to see if the horse and wagon was still there. The horse and wagon was stolen. *Held*, that defendants were negligent in not keeping a better watch to protect the horse and wagon. Id. Where, from its nature, the hirer must know that the thing is liable to deterioration or injury, this fact demands from him the exercise of greater diligence than in the case of a thing not supposed to be liable to injury from use. Beale v. South Devon Ry. Co., 12 Wkly. R. (Eng.) 1115; Wilson v. Brett, 11 Mees. & W. (Eng.) 113. See FORTUNE v. HARRIS, 51 N. C. 532, Dobie Cas. Bailments and Carriers, 61; Rooth v. Wilson, 1 Barn. & Ald. (Eng.) 59. As to bailor's failure to inform bailee of special circumstances, see Bradley v. Cunningham, 61 Conn. 485, 23 Atl. 932, 15 L. R. A. 679. As to bailee's failure to provide appliances to avoid consequences of an accident, see Stacy v. Knickerbocker Ice Co., 84 Wis. 614, 54 N. W. 1091.

[75] Since the whole duty of the bailee, in this class of cases, is to exercise good faith and ordinary diligence in carrying out the contract, he is not liable when the thing is lost or injured by overwhelming force or inevitable accident. Story, Bailm. §§ 408–412; Watkins v. Roberts, 28 Ind. 167; McEvers v. The Sangamon, 22 Mo. 187; Field v. Brackett, 56 Me. 121; Hyland v. Paul, 33 Barb. (N. Y.) 241; Ames v. Belden, 17 Barb. (N. Y.) 513; Reeves v. Constitution, Gilp. 579, Fed. Cas. No. 11,659. Even if the loss is not strictly inevitable, there is no liability if there has been no omission of reasonable diligence on the part of the bailee. Thus, a warehouseman is not responsible for the destruction of goods, deposited there for hire, by rats or mice, if he has used the ordinary precautions to guard against the loss. Cailiff v. Danvers, Peake (Eng.) 114. See, also, Menetone v. Athawes, 3 Burrows (Eng.) 1592; Longman v. Galini, Abb. Shipp. (Eng.) pt. 3, c. 4, § 8; Id. (5th Ed.) p. 259, note d; 1 Bell, Comm. (5th Ed.) pp. 453, 455, 458; Id. (4th Ed.) § 394; Reeves v. The Constitution, Gilp. 579, Fed. Cas. No. 11,659. So, if the owner of slaves lets them to the master of a vessel for a voyage, and they run away in a foreign port, the master who has acted in good faith and with reasonable care is not responsible for their loss, although he might

what has already been said in connection with the estoppel of the bailor when he has knowledge of the bailee's character, skill, or manner of keeping the chattel is equally applicable here.[76] Accordingly, when a horse is hired to a one-armed man, the bailor cannot expect the care that a man with two arms might exercise.

Thus, in the case of the most frequent instances of locatio rei, the hiring of a horse,[77] ordinary care demands that the hirer supply him with suitable food during the time of the hiring.[78] If the hired horse becomes exhausted, the hirer should abstain, temporarily at least, from using him.[79] If the horse falls seriously sick during the journey, the hirer ought to procure the aid of a veterinarian, if one can be obtained within a reasonable time or distance.[80]

Of course, in the class of bailments now under consideration, the skill of the hirer is not such an important element, nor one demanding the same consideration from the bailor, as in those bailments where services are hired about or upon a chattel. In the latter case, the bailor creates the bailment for the express purpose of securing the services of the bailee; in the former, the use of the thing hired is the prime object of the bailment, while any services rendered by the bailee are merely incidental to his use.

have exercised a higher power of restraint or confinement over them. Beverly v. Brooke, 2 Wheat. 100, 4 L. Ed. 194. Where, however, the bailee's negligence exposed the thing hired to danger of injury in the way in which it was injured, or contributed to such injury, he is liable. Buis v. Cook, 60 Mo. 391; Eastman v. Sanborn, 3 Allen (Mass.) 594, 81 Am. Dec. 677; Edwards v. Carr, 13 Gray (Mass.) 234; Wentworth v. McDuffie, 48 N. H. 402; SINISCHALCHI v. BASLICO (Sup.) 92 N. Y. Supp. 722, Dobie Cas. Bailments and Carriers, 80.

76 Ante, pp. 69, 90; Schouler, Bailm. § 138. But see, also, Mooers v. Larry, 15 Gray (Mass.) 451.

77 As to what constitutes ordinary diligence on the part of the hirer of a horse, see Eastman v. Sanborn, 3 Allen (Mass.) 594, 81 Am. Dec. 677; Cross v. Brown, 41 N. H. 283; Banfield v. Whipple, 10 Allen (Mass.) 27, 87 Am. Dec. 618; Edwards v. Carr, 13 Gray (Mass.) 234; Wentworth v. McDuffie, 48 N. H. 402; Rowland v. Jones, 73 N. C. 52; Ray v. Tubbs, 50 Vt. 688, 28 Am. Rep. 519; Buis v. Cook, 60 Mo. 391; McNeill v. Brooks, 1 Yerg. (Tenn.) 73; Harrington v. Snyder, 3 Barb. (N. Y.) 380; Jackson v. Robinson, 18 B. Mon. (Ky.) 1; Thompson v. Harlow, 31 Ga. 348; United Tel. Co. v. Cleveland, 44 Kan. 167, 24 Pac. 49.

78 Handford v. Palmer, 2 Brod. & B. (Eng.) 359, 5 Moore, 74; Eastman v. Sanborn, 3 Allen (Mass.) 594, 81 Am. Dec. 677.

79 Bray v. Mayne, 1 Gow. (Eng.) 1. See Thompson v. Harlow, 31 Ga. 348; Graves v. Moses, 13 Minn. 335 (Gil. 307); Vaughan v. Webster, 5 Har. (Del.) 256.

80 Story, Bailm. § 105; Dean v. Keate, 3 Camp. (Eng.) 4. See, also, Thompson v. Harlow, 31 Ga. 348.

Liability of Joint Bailees

Where two persons jointly hire a thing for use, and it is injured during such use by the hirers, both may be made to answer for the misconduct or negligence of either one.[81] In a case, however, in which only one hires a thing—as, for instance, a wagon—and invites another to share in its use, and such other person does so, but without exercising any control, and simply as a passenger, only he who has hired the wagon is responsible.[82]

SAME—LIABILITY OF BAILEE FOR ACTS OF HIS AGENTS OR SERVANTS

54. The bailee is liable for the negligence of his agents and servants within the scope of their employment, and also for the negligent acts of those whom he permits to use the thing hired.

The bailee is responsible, not only for his personal negligence, but he may be held liable for the negligence of his agents or servants.[83] Thus, by the doctrine of "qui facit per alium facit per se" or "respondeat superior," the agent or servant becomes a mere instrumentality by which the principal or master accomplishes his ends; so that the act of the agent or servant becomes the act of the principal or master, who becomes responsible for the consequences, whether beneficial or not, flowing from such acts.[84]

If, therefore, a hired horse is ridden by the servant of the hirer so immoderately that the horse is injured or killed thereby, the hirer is personally responsible.[85] So, if the servant of the hirer negligently leaves open the door of the hirer's stable and the hired

[81] Davey v. Chamberlain, 4 Esp. (Eng.) 229; O'Brien v. Bound, 2 Speers (S. C.) 495, 42 Am. Dec. 384.

[82] Davey v. Chamberlain, 4 Esp. (Eng.) 229; O'Brien v. Bound, 2 Speers (S. C.) 495, 42 Am. Dec. 384; Dyer v. Erie Ry. Co., 71 N. Y. 228; Story, Bailm. § 399. But see, also, Banfield v. Whipple, 10 Allen (Mass.) 27, 87 Am. Dec. 618.

[83] Pothier, Contrat de Louage, notes 193, 428; 2 Kent, Comm. (4th Ed.) lect. 40, pp. 586, 587; Pothier, Pand. lib. 19, tit. 2, note 31. Pothier holds the hirer responsible for the default or negligence of his boarders, guests, and undertenants. Pothier, Contrat de Louage, note 193; 1 Domat, bk. 1, tit. 4, § 2, art. 6. See, also, 1 Bell, Comm. (4th Ed.) § 389; 1 Bell, Comm. (5th Ed.) pp. 454, 455.

[84] Schouler, Bailm. (2d Ed.) § 145; Jaggard, Torts, 239–280; Mechem on Agency, §§ 703, 704.

[85] Jones, Bailm. 89; 1 Bl. Comm. 430, 431; 1 Domat, bk. 1, tit. 4, § 2, art. 5; 1 Bell, Comm. (5th Ed.) p. 455; 1 Bell, Comm. (4th Ed.) § 389.

horse is stolen by thieves, the hirer is responsible therefor.[66] So, if furnished lodgings are rented, and the renter's servants, children, guests, or boarders negligently injure or deface the furniture, he is responsible therefor.[67] So, if the injury is done by subagents employed by the hirer, responsibility for the negligent acts of the subagents rests upon the hirer.[68]

In order that this may be true, however, the agent or servant must be acting within the scope of his employment.[69] The relation of agency or service is limited strictly to the employment, and when the so-called agent or servant goes outside of the scope of such employment, he is no longer in legal contemplation an agent or servant. The term "scope of employment" is used in a broad sense, however, and contemplates the general course of the work of such agent or servant. Scope of employment, however, should be judged in relation to the specific act causing the loss or damage; and, if that particular act lies beyond such scope, the principal or master is not liable. But, if that specific act does lie within such scope, the principal or master is responsible, even though he may have in terms forbidden that particular act. Thus, the hirer of an automobile directs his chauffeur to drive the car alone to a certain place, but forbids the chauffeur from driving more than 20 miles an hour. The chauffeur, while proceeding to such place, wrecks the car, by negligently driving it at the rate of 50 miles an hour. The hirer is responsible to his bailor for the damage. The trend of modern decisions has been to broaden appreciably the meaning of "scope of employment"; but when the agent or servant steps entirely aside from the course of his employment, his act then becomes his own act, for which he alone,

[66] Jones, Bailm. 89; COGGS v. BERNARD, 2 Ld. Raym. (Eng.) 909, Dobie Cas. Bailments and Carriers, 1; President, etc., of Salem Bank v. President, etc., of Gloucester Bank, 17 Mass. 1, 9 Am. Dec. 111.

[67] Jones, Bailm. 89; Pothier, Contrat de Louage, note 193.

[68] Story, Ag. §§ 308, 311, 452, 457; Randelson v. Murray, 8 Nev. & P. (Eng.) 239, 8 Adol. & E. (Eng.) 109; Bush v. Steinman, 1 Bos. & P. (Eng.) 404, 409; Hilliard v. Richardson, 3 Gray (Mass.) 349, 63 Am. Dec. 743; Laugher v. Pointer, 5 Barn. & C. (Eng.) 547, 553, 554; Boson v. Sandford, 2 Salk. (Eng.) 440, 441; Milligan v. Wedge, 12 Adol. & E. (Eng.) 737; Quarman v. Burnett, 6 Mees. & W. (Eng.) 499; Story, Bailm. § 401.

[69] See McDonald v. Snelling, 14 Allen (Mass.) 290, 92 Am. Dec. 768; Philadelphia & R. R. Co. v. Derby, 14 How. 468, 14 L. Ed. 502; Ward v. London General Omnibus Co., 42 L. J. (Eng. C. P.) 265; 1 Halsbury, Laws of England, p. 553. See, also, Hofer v. Hodge, 52 Mich. 372, 18 N. W. 112, 50 Am. Rep. 256; Maxwell v. Eason, 1 Stew. (Ala.) 514; McCaw v. Kimbrel, 4 McCord (S. C.) 220; Hall v. Warner, 60 Barb. (N. Y.) 198; Smith v. Bouker, 49 Fed. 954, 1 C. C. A. 481; American Dist. Tel. Co. of Baltimore v. Walker, 72 Md. 454, 20 Atl. 1, 20 Am. St. Rep. 479.

and not the agent or master, is responsible. The question under discussion more properly belongs to the subject of agency or master and servant.[90]

Again, the bailee becomes responsible for the negligence of those whom he admits to the use of the thing hired. Such persons become, in a sense, the servants of the bailee, for whose negligent acts, resulting in loss or damage to the hired chattel, he can be held responsible by the bailor. Thus, if one hires furniture which he places in his room, and admits a third person to the enjoyment and use of such furniture, the bailor might hold the bailee for damage resulting from the negligent use of such furniture by the third person.[91] If the hirer, however, had used due care to protect the furniture from use by third persons, as by securely locking the door of his room, and such third person had, by breaking down the door, entered the room and misused the furniture without the hirer's consent, then the third person (here a mere trespasser) alone, and not the hirer, would be liable to the bailor.[92]

SAME—COMPENSATION OF THE BAILOR

55. The bailee must make compensation to the bailor according to the terms of the contract of hiring.

As the benefit of the bailment to the bailor consists in receiving the stipulated reward, it is the primary duty of the bailee to pay the agreed compensation to the bailor.[93] When the bailment is

[90] Jagg. Torts, 279; Storey v. Ashton, L. R. 4 Q. B. (Eng.) 476; Vanderbilt v. Richmond Turnpike Co., 2 N. Y. 479, 51 Am. Dec. 315; Evansville & C. R. Co. v. Baum, 26 Ind. 70; Cheshire v. Bailey, [1905] 1 K. B. (Eng.) 237. See, also, Sanderson v. Collins, [1904] 1 K. B. (Eng.) 628, distinguishing the rather extreme case of Coupe Co. v. Maddick, [1891] 2 Q. B. 413. See 1 Halsbury, Laws of England, p. 553.

[91] Schouler, Bailm. § 146; cases cited in note 89. See, also, Smith v. Read, 6 Daly (N. Y.) 33; Holder v. Soulby, 8 C. B. N. S. (Eng.) 254; Dansey v. Richardson, 3 El. & Bl. (Eng.) 144; GANNON v. CONSOLIDATED ICE CO., 91 Fed. 539, 33 C. C. A. 662, Dobie Cas. Bailments and Carriers, 81.

[92] Schouler, Bailm. § 146.

[93] Knickerbocker Trust Co. v. Ryan, 227 Pa. 245, 75 Atl. 1073; Cullen v. Lord, 39 Iowa, 302; Armijo v. Abeytia, 5 N. M. 533, 25 Pac. 777; Cushman v. Somers, 60 Vt. 613, 15 Atl. 315; Wilcox & Gibbs Sewing Mach. Co. v. Himes, 67 Hun, 648, 21 N. Y. Supp. 760; Moneyweight Scale Co. v. Woodward, 29 Pa. Super. Ct. 142; Van De Vanter v. Redelsheimer, 58 Wash. 38, 107 Pac. 847; Rogers v. McKenzie, 73 N. C. 487; Wright v. Melville, 3 C. & P. (Eng.) 542; 1 Halsbury, Laws of England, p. 552. Where a contractor to "shoot" a gas well for the owner caused a charge of nitroglycerine to so

fully completed, this ordinarily presents little difficulty. The contract is, as a rule, quite definite as to the compensation, which is usually, but not necessarily, in money. If the bailment is one of hiring, but the contract does not fix the compensation, then, as in other similar cases, the bailee must pay a reasonable price.[94] What is reasonable is a question of fact, to be solved in the light of the particular circumstances of each case.

When, however, the contract of hiring was for a definite time, and the bailment is only partially completed, owing to the destruction (or damage rendering the chattel unfit for the use, thus practically amounting to destruction) of the hired chattel, the question of compensation has not been satisfactorily worked out in the rather few cases in which it has been presented.[95] Here the inquiry as to who (bailor or bailee) was at fault in bringing about the destruction is a prime factor in the problem.

First, when the destruction is the fault of neither, it would seem (in the absence of a clear stipulation to the contrary) that neither bailor nor bailee can be sued for failure to complete the bailment, which has, of course, become impossible. But the bailee is liable pro tanto for such use of the chattel as he had prior to its destruction, paying for such use its reasonable worth.[96]

The next case is when the destruction is due to the fault of

explode as to damage the well, and then obtained from the owner drilling tools to repair the damage, on an agreement to pay reasonable compensation for such tools, and the contractor used the tools therefor, its promise to pay a reasonable compensation was supported by a valid consideration. Independent Torpedo Co. v. J. E. Clark Oil Co., 48 Ind. App. 124, 95 N. E. 592. One contracting to pay a reasonable compensation for the use of another's drilling tools to repair a gas well is liable to pay a reasonable compensation for the time he has possession and use of the tools, and his liability is not limited to days of actual service; the word "use" applying to one's service, employment, or conversion to some purpose (quoting 8 Words and Phrases, pp. 7226, 7227). Id.

94 Cullen v. Lord, 39 Iowa, 302; Rider v. Union India Rubber Co., 28 N. Y. 379.

95 See, on this subject, Story, Bailm. & Carr. §§ 416-417a; Schouler, Bailm. & Carr. §§ 160-161; Goddard, Bailm. & Carr. § 123; 5 Cyc. 192. Cases on this subject are very rare. In Gleason v. Smith, 39 Hun (N. Y.) 617, the boiler broke down and bailor refused to repair it, but it was held the bailee must pay the agreed rent.

96 Williams v. Holcombe, 4 N. C. 33; WILKES v. HUGHES, 37 Ga. 361, Dobie Cas. Bailments and Carriers, 82 (death of slave); Bacot v. Parnell, 2 Bailey (S. C.) 424. See, also, George v. Elliott, 2 Hen. & M. (Va.) 5; Collins v. Woodruff, 9 Ark. 463; see Harrington v. Snyder, 3 Barb. (N. Y.) 380; Warth v. Mack, 79 Fed. 915, 25 C. C. A. 235, though here this contingency was covered by the contract. See, also, authorities in preceding note. That the bailor is not liable for nonperformance, see Stewart v. Stone, 127 N. Y. 500, 28 N. E. 595, 14 L. R. A. 215.

the bailor. Here it would seem that, in spite of the bailor's fault, the bailee should pay pro tanto for such use as he received, while the bailee should have a right of action against the bailor for the latter's wrong, resulting in the destruction of the chattel, before the expiration of the time agreed. Hence the bailee should be liable for the reasonable worth of his actual use, minus such damages as he has suffered from the wrong of the bailor.[97] If such damage was greater than the reasonable worth of the bailee's use, then the bailee should recover such excess.

Finally, the destruction may have been due to the fault of the bailee. Here the bailee should not be allowed to set up his own fault as an excuse, and the bailor recovers the full compensation.[98] If the chattel is only damaged, and is returned to the bailor, the bailee is entitled as an offset to the value (if any) of such use to the bailor, or to such person as he may have hired it, as could be made of the chattel during the remaining time of the bailment period.[99]

SAME—TERMINATION OF THE BAILMENT

56. Locatio rei may be terminated by—

1. Act of the parties.

(a) Accomplishment of the bailment purpose or expiration of the time for which bailment was created.

(b) Mutual consent of bailor and bailee.

(c) Bailee's wrong, at option of bailor.

2. Operation of law.

(a) Destruction of hired chattel.

Ordinarily death or change of legal status of the parties does not terminate a bailment of this class.

[97] See authorities cited in note 95. Such cases will be rare, since the bailee's use and control of the goods afford scant opportunity for destruction by the bailor's fault. In HICKOK v. BUCK, 22 Vt. 149, Dobie Cas. Bailments and Carriers, 63, the bailor took the mare from the bailee; but there the bailee was plaintiff and the bailor defendant in an action of trover, and it was held that plaintiff could recover.

[98] See authorities cited in note 95; Bigbee v. Coombs, 64 Mo. 529. In HARTFORD v. JACKSON, 11 N. H. 145, Dobie Cas. Bailments and Carriers, 64, the bailor's creditors attached the property. Since the creditors had no right thus to disturb the bailee's possession, which is good against the world, it was held that the bailee was liable to the bailor for the agreed compensation. But see Muldrow v. Wilmington & M. R. Co., 13 Rich. (S. C.) 69, in which it was held that on the death of a slave during the time, due to bailee's negligence, the rent should be apportioned.

[99] See Johnson v. Meeker, 96 N. Y. 93, 48 Am. Rep. 609, in which bailee abandoned the hired barge.

Act of the Parties

. The termination of locatio rei by the three events set out under the head of "acts of the parties" is clear, and, as such bailments, in this respect, present no distinctive features, no further discussion of these is needed.[1]

It should be noted, however, in connection with the consent of the parties, that though locatio rei may be terminated by consent of both parties, neither the bailor nor the bailee alone has the right to terminate the bailment.[2] This is true because there is a legal consideration moving from each party, on which he can base his rights against the other party. Of course, when the bailment is made terminable at the option of either party, it is a bailment at will, and either bailor or bailee may terminate it, and this is the case when it is indefinite as to time.[3]

Operation of Law

The destruction of the hired chattel necessarily ends the bailment, leaving the parties to work out their various rights, depending upon the circumstances surrounding such destruction.[4]

Since the bailee has a special property in the chattel, ordinarily, the death of the bailor does not terminate the bailment, and the bailee may hold such chattel, according to the terms of the contract of hiring, as against the personal representative of the bailor.[5] In like manner, unless the bailment was a personal one, involving confidence reposed, it is not terminated by the bailee's death, but his rights pass to his personal representative.[6] When, however,

1 Ante, § 20.

2 This follows from the fact that the bailment contract is binding on both the parties, and neither can rescind without the other's consent. The very idea of the bailee's special property in a bailment for a definite time precludes the idea of the bailor's right to end the bailment. See ante, p. 112.

3 Here, while the rights of each continue while the bailment continues, the failure to specify the time during which the bailment is to continue is equivalent to an agreement that either bailor or bailee has the option to end the bailment. See Learned-Letcher Lumber Co. v. Fowler, 109 Ala. 169, 19 South. 396; Gleason v. Morrison, 20 Misc. Rep. 320, 45 N. Y. Supp. 684; New York, L. E. & W. R. Co. v. New Jersey Electric Ry. Co., 60 N. J. Law, 338, 38 Atl. 828; Puffer & Sons Mfg. Co. v. Baker, 104 N. C. 148, 10 S. E. 254; Drake v. Redington, 9 N. H. 243.

4 See ante, p. 46.

5 This follows from the nature of the bailee's special property in the goods. It is well settled as to pledges that the pledgor's (bailor's) death does not affect the bailee's (pledgee's) special property in the goods pledged (bailed). Fulton v. National Bank of Denison, 26 Tex. Civ. App. 115, 62 S. W. 84. See Van Zile, Bailm. & Carr. § 82.

6 This is a general rule of contracts. See McKeown v. Harvey, 40 Mich. 226; Bambrick v. Webster Groves Presbyterian Church Ass'n, 53 Mo. App. 225

the bailment is a personal one, the death of the bailee causes the bailment to cease.[7]

The effect of a change of legal status is, in some cases, far from clear. Since bankruptcy does not sever contractual relations, it would seem that neither the bankruptcy of the bailor nor that of the bailee operates, of itself, to terminate the bailment.[8] There seem to be few cases involving such a change of legal status as insanity. Probably the insanity of the bailor would not have a greater effect than his death, and the bailment which would continue against his personal representative ought to continue against his committee. Certainly, when the bailment is a personal one, it would be terminated by the bailee's insanity. When the bailment is not personal, the question is more doubtful. It would seem, in such case, that the bailment would not be terminated, but that the insane bailee's rights and liabilities would pass to his committee. The question, as it very seldom arises, is not of great practical importance.

SAME—REDELIVERY OF THE BAILED GOODS

57. As in other bailments, the bailee should, on the termination of the bailment, redeliver the bailed goods, together with any increase or profit, according to the directions of the bailor.

The principles governing the bailee's duty to redeliver, already discussed in connection with other classes of bailments, are equally applicable here, and will not be repeated.[9] The place of redelivery will usually be determined by contract, custom, or usage.

[7] This rule also applies to contracts in general. See Marvel v. Phillips, 162 Mass. 399, 38 N. E. 1117, 26 L. R. A. 416, 44 Am. St. Rep. 370.

[8] See Remington on Bankruptcy, § 451.

[9] See ante, § 19. See, also, Syeds v. Hay, 4 Term R. (Eng.) 260, per Buller, J.; Pothier, Contrat de Louage, note 197; Pothier, Pand. lib. 19, tit. 2, notes 27, 28, 29. See, also, Schouler, Bailm. (2d Ed.) § 158; Cobb v. Wallace, 5 Cold. (Tenn.) 539, 98 Am. Dec. 435; European & Australian Royal Mail Co. v. Royal Mail Steam Packet Co., 8 Jur. N. S. (Eng.) 136; Erwin v. Arthur, 61 Mo. 386; Stephenson v. Hart, 4 Bing. (Eng.) 476; Stephens v. Elwall, 4 Maule & S. (Eng.) 259; Youl v. Harbottle, Peake (Eng.) 68; Devereux v. Barclay, 2 Barn. & Ald. (Eng.) 702; Willard v. Bridge, 4 Barb. (N. Y.) 361; Pothier, Contrat de Louage, notes 197, 198, 200; Pothier, Pand. lib. 19, tit. 2, notes 27, 28, 29; 1 Domat, bk. 1, tit. 4, § 2, note 11; Cooper v. Barton, 3 Camp. (Eng.) 5, note; Millon v. Salisbury, 13 Johns. (N. Y.) 211; Reynolds v. Shuler, 5 Cow. (N. Y.) 323.

CHAPTER VI

BAILMENTS FOR MUTUAL BENEFIT—HIRED SERVICES ABOUT THINGS

CLASSIFICATION

58. Locatio operis bailments, or hired services about a thing, are divided into:

(1) Ordinary bailments for hire.

(a) Locatio operis faciendi, or hired services about a thing.

(b) Locatio custodiæ, or the hired custody of a thing.

(c) Locatio operis mercium vehendarum, or the hired carrying of a thing from one place to another.

(2) Extraordinary bailments for hire.

(a) Innkeepers.

(b) Common carriers of goods.

(c) Post Office Department.

This classification of locatio operis bailments has already been given, and briefly discussed, in the classification of mutual benefit bailments in general.[1] The classification of the ordinary locatio operis bailments is largely one of convenience, based upon differences in the nature of the services hired. Such ordinary bailments, then, may be divided into three classes:

(1) Locatio operis faciendi, or the hire of active labor and

[1] Ante, § 43.

services upon a thing. Examples of this are the hiring of jewelers to set jewels, or watchmakers to repair watches. This bailment is in many respects analogous to a mandatum, differing only in the fact that the services are rendered for a reward.

(2) Locatio custodiæ, or the hired custody of a thing. This is simply the receiving of goods on deposit, with a reward to the bailee for such custody. It differs from a depositum in that here the bailee who undertakes the custody of the goods receives a compensation. While it is true that the custody of goods necessarily involves some physical labor and services, there are yet differences between these two classes of locatio operis bailments. The distinction lies in the fact that in locatio operis faciendi the performance of specific services about the goods constitutes the principal undertaking contemplated by the parties, and the bailee's custody is merely incidental, existing solely in order that these services might be performed. On the other hand, in locatio custodiæ the custody of the thing by the bailee is itself the principal undertaking. The bailee is charged solely with keeping the goods, and renders no services unless they are involved in such custody.[2] Thus a watchmaker charged with repairing a watch (locatio operis faciendi) has custody of the watch only in order that he may render the specific services involved in making the repairs. In the case of a warehouseman, charged with the storage of goods, the custody is paramount; he has only to keep the goods, performing the more or less inactive services implied by, and involved in, such custody. The distinction between locatio operis faciendi and locatio custodiæ (both mutual benefit bailments) is precisely the same as the difference between the mandatum and depositum (both bailments for the sole benefit of the bailor).[3]

(3) Locatio operis mercium vehendarum, or the hired transportation of goods. These are simply a particular type of bailment of the class just discussed, the services here consisting in the carrying of the goods from one place to another. It should be carefully remembered, though, that what is said in the present chapter on locatio operis bailments in general is applicable only

[2] Story, Bailm. § 422; Jones, Bailm. 98.

[3] Ante, p. 50. Where plaintiff in consideration of a purchase of goods and reimbursement of expenses, agreed to receive, care for, and ship other goods purchased elsewhere, it was a bailee for hire, and not a gratuitous bailee as affecting the degree of care required of it. Michigan Stove Co. v. Pueblo Hardware Co., 51 Colo. 160, 116 Pac. 340. Upon receiving an automobile for repairs, to be made for the mutual benefit of the owner and the repairer, the repairer becomes a bailee for hire, responsible for loss by fire only by failure to exercise ordinary care. Ford Motor Co. v. Osburn, 140 Ill. App. 633.

to the private carrier of goods and not to the distinctive common carrier.

There are no essential legal differences between the three classes of bailments just enumerated, convenience constituting the basis of such classification. The same rules, accordingly, control the rights and duties of the parties in all three classes. These rules, applicable to all these three classes of the ordinary locatio operis bailments, are discussed in the present chapter.

The extraordinary bailments of locatio operis, we have seen,[4] are as a class sharply differentiated, owing to considerations of public policy, from all other bailments. Not only is this true, but these extraordinary bailments present keen distinctions and differences among themselves. The (a) innkeeper,[5] (b) common carrier of goods,[6] and (c) post office department[7] will therefore be discussed separately and in great detail. Of these, the common carrier of goods is by far the most important bailee known to our civilization, so that the rights and duties of this bailee are treated with appropriate detail and at corresponding length.

RIGHTS AND DUTIES OF THE PARTIES—IN GENERAL

59. In the hiring of work and labor about a thing, as in other bailments, the rights and duties of the parties are primarily controlled by the bailment contract. When not thus controlled, these rights and duties are implied by law; the distinctive features of the bailments in question being the performance of more or less active services about the goods by the bailee, who receives a compensation for such services.

Here, as elsewhere, the bailor and bailee may determine by contract the exact extent and nature of their rights and duties.[8] Such contract will, of course, be valid, unless it is in violation of law or against public policy.[9]

[4] Ante, § 43.

[5] See post, chapter 8.

[6] See post, chapters 9–14.

[7] See post, chapter 15.

[8] Upon a bailment of goods for work and labor to be done thereon by the bailee, the contract between the parties arises immediately upon the delivery of the goods to the bailee, and he cannot afterwards impose conditions, nor limit his liability resulting from such bailment. Dale v. See, 51 N. J. Law, 378, 18 Atl. 306, 5 L. R. A. 583, 14 Am. St. Rep. 688.

[9] See ante, pp. 18–19. As to whether bailee may by contract relieve himself from liability for negligence is not settled. That he cannot, see Patterson v.

In locatio operis, the bailor is the person receiving the immediate benefit from the carrying out of the bailment (i. e., the performance of the work and labor); while the compensation or reward (usually, but not necessarily, in money) is received by the bailee. The bailor has now become the hirer, and the bailee is now the letter, of the services. From this distinction flow most of the legal consequences that distinguish locatio operis from locatio rei.

PERFORMANCE OF THE AGREED SERVICES BY THE BAILEE

60. The bailee must in good faith perform the agreed services about the chattel.

In bailments for hired services about a chattel, the primary duty of the bailee is to perform the agreed services in good faith;[10] for the bailment is created by the bailor for the express purpose of securing the performance by the bailee of the services in question, and it is only in consideration of such services that the stipulated compensation[11] is to be paid.

For any breach or failure in this respect the bailee must respond to the bailor in damages. Since the bailment contract is based on a consideration, the bailee is liable if he refuses to enter upon the bailment, a pure nonfeasance. He is equally liable when he does enter upon the bailment, but fails without legal excuse to perform the services as agreed. What these particular services are depends on the specific bailment contract, and such services may

Wenatchee Canning Co., 59 Wash. 556, 110 Pac. 879; Hoyt v. Clinton Hotel Co., 35 Pa. Super. Ct. 297. In favor of the validity of such contracts (which is believed to be the better doctrine), see section 106, and cases there cited in note 13. These concern the private carrier for hire, but he is merely an ordinary locatio operis bailee and liable accordingly.

[10] This amounts simply to stating that the bailee must perform a valid bailment contract into which he has entered. He contractually undertakes to perform certain services; the bailor agrees by contract to pay the stipulated compensation for such performance. The bailment contract thereby imposes on each the duty of performing his peculiar part of the transaction. See 1 Halsbury, Laws of England, p. 559. Where a United States collector selling goods under distraint agrees with the purchaser to ship the goods to a third person, and to send the purchaser the bill of lading, he is liable for a breach of this agreement. Sprinkle v. Brimm, 144 N. C. 401, 57 S. E. 148, 12 L. R. A. (N. S.) 679.

[11] See post, § 62.

be of almost infinite variety. The questions arising in this connection depend upon, and are governed by, the general rules of contract.[12]

INTEREST OF THE BAILEE—RIGHT TO BRING SUIT

61. The bailee has a special property in the bailed goods which he can protect by appropriate action, either against the bailor or third parties. The bailor can sue third parties for any injury to his reversionary interest in the bailed chattels

In locatio operis, the bailee can keep the goods, pending the accomplishment of the bailment purpose, in order that he may earn the stipulated compensation. This right of the bailee to undisturbed possession is good against all the world, and therefore the bailee has clearly a special property in the thing about which the services are to be performed[13] It is a distinctive feature of locatio operis bailments that the bailee must frequently add material of his own to the bailed goods in order to carry out the bailment purpose. His special property in the bailed goods thereby assumes an added importance.

This special property of the bailee in the goods he can protect by appropriate action against the bailor or against third persons wrongfully interfering with it. Thus the bailee can bring trespass or trover against such third parties.[14] It is generally held

[12] See, also, post, §§ 62, 65.

[13] See Story, Bailm. § 422a; Schouler, Bailm. (2d Ed.) § 110; Engel v. Scott & Holston Lumber Co., 60 Minn. 39, 61 N. W. 825; Eaton v. Lynde, 15 Mass. 242; Grandy v. Kittredge, 8 Cush. (Mass.) 562; Morse v. Androscoggin R. Co., 39 Me. 285; BURDICT v. MURRAY, 3 Vt. 302, 21 Am. Dec. 588, Dobie Cas. Bailments and Carriers, 84. This special property of the bailee is, of course, an insurable interest in the goods, which the bailee may protect by fire insurance. Fire Ins. Ass'n v. Merchants' & Miners' Transp. Co., 66 Md. 339, 7 Atl. 905, 59 Am. Rep. 162; Sheppard v. Peabody Ins. Co., 21 W. Va. 368. The bailee may insure the goods for their full value, holding any excess beyond his own interest for the bailor. Waring v. Indemnity Fire Ins. Co., 45 N. Y. 606, 6 Am. Rep. 146.

[14] Atlantic Coast Line R. Co. v. Partridge, 58 Fla. 153, 50 South. 634; Mizner v. Frazier, 40 Mich. 592, 29 Am. Rep. 562; National Surety Co. v. United States, 129 Fed. 70, 63 C. C. A. 512; Shaw v. Kaler, 106 Mass. 448; BURDICT v. MURRAY, 3 Vt. 302, 21 Am. Dec. 588, Dobie Cas. Bailments and Carriers, 84; Evans v. Nichol, 4 Scott, N. R. 43. But see Morse v. Androscoggin R. Co., 39 Me. 285; In re Phœnix Bessemer Steel Co., 4 Ch. Div. (Eng.) 112. Thus, where a bailee of yarn was to procure it to be made into cloth for a commission, it was held that he had a special property in the

that the bailee can recover full damages for the loss or injury in such case, holding the excess beyond his own interest in trust for the bailor; and such a recovery is a bar to any subsequent action by the bailor.[15]

For any tortious injury by a third person to the bailed chattel, so serious as to affect his reversionary interest, the bailor has a right to sue such third party.[16] When the wrongful act affects only the possession of the bailee, however, and not this reversionary interest of the bailor, the latter should have no right to sue the third party; such right being then limited to the bailee.[17] The doctrine that the rights of the bailor and bailee should be separately valued and that each should sue solely for the damage to his own interest, previously referred to,[18] finds in the locatio operis bailments unusually strong support.[19]

COMPENSATION OF THE BAILEE

62. Upon complete performance of the bailment, the bailee is entitled to the agreed compensation. When the work is completed, but not according to the bailment contract, or when the work is left uncompleted, various considerations affect both the right and measure of a recovery by the bailee.

yarn, and that he might maintain an action against any one who should wrongfully take it from his own possession, or from that of his servant, to whom he had delivered it to be woven. Eaton v. Lynde, 15 Mass. 242.

15 National Surety Co. v. United States, 129 Fed. 70, 63 C. C. A. 512; Moran v. Portland Steam Packet Co., 35 Me. 55; Hare v. Fuller, 7 Ala. 717; Union Pac. R. Co. v. Meyer, 76 Neb. 549, 107 N. W. 793, 14 Ann. Cas. 634; Leoncini v. Post (Com. Pl.) 13 N. Y. Supp. 825.

16 This seems to follow from the general principle that one having a reversionary interest in personal property may sue one not in possession of such property, whose wrong causes such serious and permanent injury to the property as to diminish the value of such reversionary interest. This right is said to exist on the part of the reversioner in personal, just as in real, property. See New Jersey Electric Ry. Co. v. New York, L. E. & W. R. Co., 61 N. J. Law, 287, 41 Atl. 1116, 43 L. R. A. 849; Shearm. & Redf. Neg. § 119; Pollock, Torts, p. 432; Mears v. London & S. W. Ry. Co., 11 C. B. N. S. 850; Lexington & O. R. Co. v. Kidd, 7 Dana (Ky.) 245; White v. Griffin, 49 N. C. 139; Howard v. Farr, 18 N. H. 457; Hawkins v. Phythian, 8 B. Mon. (Ky.) 515.

17 WILSON v. MARTIN, 40 N. H. 88, Dobie Cas. Bailments and Carriers, 85; Cowing v. Snow, 11 Mass. 415.

18 Ante, pp. 64, 87.

19 Since here the bailee's interest is a very real one, which can readily be given a money value.

In locatio operis, the primary right of the bailee is to receive the stipulated compensation. The reward is the benefit accruing to the bailee, in consideration of which he performs the services. The receipt of the compensation by the bailee distinguishes locatio operis from all other bailments. This whole problem of the bailee's compensation is variously affected by questions of whether the services have been completely performed, and, if so, whether or not they were performed according to the bailment contract, and whether, when the services are not completed, this is due to destruction of the bailed chattel without fault of the parties, or to some fault on the part of the bailor or bailee.

There is much confusion and uncertainty in the cases, due in many instances to a failure to make the distinctions just indicated. The real question involved is also often obscured by the subtle, but often useless, niceties of common-law forms of action in states which still cling to this outworn system of pleading. The decided trend of modern decisions has been towards allowing compensation to the bailee for value conferred on the bailed chattel, with damages to the bailor for any harm caused by the bailee's departure from the bailment contract. The treatment of compensation, accordingly, conforms to the following analysis: [20]

1. Work fully completed
   - (a) According to mutual intent of the parties.
   - (b) Not according to such mutual intent.
2. Work not fully completed, owing to
   - (a) Destruction of the thing bailed, without fault of either party.
   - (b) Fault of bailor, preventing completion of the work.
   - (c) Fault of bailee, in abandoning the work while incomplete.

In this connection, it should be noted that, when the person is to furnish materials out of which a thing is to be made and deliver the completed thing to another, this is not a bailment, but an agreement to sell.[21] Again, where one is called on to perform

[20] This analysis is practically that of Goddard (Bailm. & Carr. § 129), whose brief treatment of this topic is yet one of the clearest to be found in the books.

[21] In such a case the title remains in the maker seller, with the attendant risk of loss, until after the completion of the article. See McConihe v. New York & E. R. Co., 20 N. Y. 495, 75 Am. Dec. 420; Merritt v. Johnson, 7 Johns. (N. Y.) 473, 5 Am. Dec. 289; Atkinson v. Bele, 8 Barn. & Cress. (Eng.) 277; Laflin & R. Powder Co. v. Burkhardt, 97 U. S. 110, 24 L. Ed. 973. However, when an owner leaves an old article with another to be repaired, this is nev-

services about goods not delivered into his possession, this is not a bailment, but a mere contract of service, as where one is engaged to paint a ship in the owner's possession. These cases belong to sales and contracts, but not to bailments. The analogies, though, are helpful.

Work Fully Completed—According to Mutual Intent of the Parties

If the work be fully completed, according to the terms of the bailment contract, so that there has been a full performance of all his duties by the bailee, he is then entitled to full compensation.[22] If the amount is fixed in the contract, this is, of course, the measure of the bailee's recovery. If the amount is not so fixed, then the bailee recovers a reasonable price for his services.[23]

If the work be completed, but the chattel is destroyed, without fault, in the bailee's possession, before he redelivers it to the bailor, the bailee can still recover. This is placed on the doctrine of accession, by which the labor and material pass to the chattel as they are added; and the doctrine res perit domino makes the chattel perish to the owner, in its condition at the time it is destroyed.[24] Of course, the bailee may change this by stipulating, expressly or by clear implication, that he shall be entitled to compensation only when he has redelivered the goods to the bailor.[25] Courts, though, lean strongly against such a construction of the agreement.

ertheless a bailment, though the value of the repairs may far exceed the value of the article when delivered. Gregory v. Stryker, 2 Denio (N. Y.) 628. See, also, Schouler, Bailm. & Carr. (2d Ed.) § 111.

[22] Where a person fully performed his duties under a contract of storage of a boat and to furnish materials for repairs, and the owner accepted the boat after such repairs, the bailee should be allowed recovery for his services. Webster v. Beebe, 2 Boyce (Del.) 161, 77 Atl. 769. This practically amounts only to saying that one who has fully performed his part of the contract can look to the other party for a full performance on the part of the latter.

[23] Dougherty v. Whitehead, 31 Mo. 257; Sumpter v. Hedges (1898) 1 Q. B. (Eng.) 673. Of course, if the services are performed by the bailee without any express or implied promise of payment on the part of the bailor, the bailee can recover nothing for his services. As was said by Pollock, C. B., in Taylor v. Laird, 25 L. J. (Ex.) 329, 332: "Suppose I clean your property without your knowledge; have I then a claim on you for payment? One cleans another's shoes; what can the other do but put them on? Is that evidence of a contract to pay for the cleaning." See 1 Halsbury, Laws of England, p. 557.

[24] KAFKA v. LEVENSOHN, 18 Misc. Rep. 202, 41 N. Y. Supp. 368, Dobie Cas. Bailments and Carriers, 87; Rothoser v. Cosel, 39 Misc. Rep. 337, 79 N. Y. Supp. 855; Halyard v. Dechelman, 29 Mo. 459, 77 Am. Dec. 585. See, also, 2 Kent, Comm. 590–591; Story, Bailm. § 421.

[25] KAFKA v. LEVENSOHN, 18 Misc. Rep. 202, 41 N. Y. Supp. 368, Dobie Cas. Bailments and Carriers, 87.

Same—Not According to Mutual Intent of the Parties

The next case is where the work has been fully completed, but not according to the terms of the contract, as where there has been a deviation from such contract, or an improper execution thereof, or where the work has not been completed within the stipulated time.

If such deviation was with the assent of the bailor, or was occasioned by his fault, then the bailee can recover on a quantum meruit the reasonable value of the services which he performed.[26] Even though this deviation is due to the fault of the bailee, he may still, as before, recover the reasonable worth of the services; but this is now reduced by the damages which his deviation has caused to the bailor.[27] Of course, in such a case, if the damage equals the worth of the service, the bailee recovers nothing.[28] When the work is well and properly done according to the contract, save that it is not completed within the stipulated time, it would seem that the bailee should here recover the contract price (rather than reasonable worth) for the services, diminished by the damage suffered by the bailor owing to the bailee's failure to complete the work in time.[29]

When the departure from the contract consists in the bailee's doing more than was called for by the agreement, instead of less, he cannot recover any extra compensation, in the absence of the bailor's acquiescence or consent. Thus, where, without such consent, the bailee does finer work or uses more valuable materials than the agreement calls for, he cannot recover more than the stip-

[26] See, in general, 1 Bell, Comm. (5th Ed.) pp. 455, 456; 1 Bell, Comm. (4th Ed.) §§ 391, 393; Bank of Columbia v. Patterson, 7 Cranch, 299, 3 L. Ed. 351; Robson v. Godfrey, 1 Starkie (Eng.) 275; Id., 1 Holt, 236; Pepper v. Burland, Peake (Eng.) 103.

[27] Cases involving bailments here seem to be rare. See, in general, the following cases: Farnsworth v. Garrard, 1 Camp. (Eng.) 38; Duncan v. Blundell, 3 Starkie (Eng.) 6; Basten v. Butter, 7 East (Eng.) 479; Linningdale v. Livingston, 10 Johns. (N. Y.) 36; Jennings v. Camp, 13 Johns. (N. Y.) 94, 97, 7 Am. Dec. 367; Grant v. Button, 14 Johns. (N. Y.) 377; Jewell v. Schroeppel, 4 Cow. (N. Y.) 564; Chapel v. Hickes, 2 Cromp. & M. (Eng.) 214; Id., 4 Tyrw. (Eng.) 43; Cutler v. Close, 5 Car. & P. (Eng.) 337; Thornton v. Place, 1 Moody & R. (Eng.) 218; Taft v. Inhabitants of Montague, 14 Mass. 282, 7 Am. Dec. 215; Feeter v. Heath, 11 Wend. (N. Y.) 477.

[28] See cases cited in preceding note; also, Hillyard v. Crabtree's Adm'r, 11 Tex. 264, 62 Am. Dec. 475; Mack v. Snell, 140 N. Y. 193, 35 N. E. 493, 37 Am. St. Rep. 534; Jones v. Foreman, 93 Iowa, 198, 61 N. W. 846; Higman v. Camody, 112 Ala. 267, 20 South. 480, 57 Am. St. Rep. 33.

[29] See Jewell v. Schroeppel, 4 Cow. (N. Y.) 564. See, also, Littler v. Holland, 3 Term. R. (Eng.) 590; Philips v. Rose, 8 Johns. (N. Y.) 392; Dubois v. Delaware & H. Canal Co., 4 Wend. (N. Y.) 285.

ulated compensation.[30] His attempt to impose added financial burdens on an unwilling bailor will not be countenanced by the law.

It need hardly be added that in the case of services complete, but different from the contract, as well as when the services are not completed, the bailor can render himself liable for the full compensation by waiving his right to a perfect performance and accepting such incomplete or different performance in lieu thereof.[31] Whether there has been such a waiver—in other words, whether the bailor accepts as a full or merely a part performance—is to be determined from the facts of each case.[32]

Work Not Completed—Destruction of Thing Bailed Without Fault of Either Party

By the doctrine of accession, already discussed, when the bailee adds materials of his own to the bailed chattel, the title to such accessorial material passes to the bailor, as the owner of the principal thing. The bailee's labor and services are also viewed as being added to the thing as soon as they are bestowed thereon. When, therefore, the chattel is destroyed without fault, the bailee can recover pro tanto for all his materials used and labor bestowed on the chattel.[33] As has just been pointed out, the thing perishes

[30] 1 Bell, Comm. (5th Ed.) pp. 455, 456; 1 Bell, Comm. (4th Ed.) §§ 391, 393; Wilmot v. Smith, 3 Car. & P. (Eng.) 453; Lovelock v. King, 1 Moody & R. (Eng.) 60; Burn v. Miller, 4 Taunt. (Eng.) 745, 749.

[31] Linningdale v. Livingston, 10 Johns. (N. Y.) 36; Burn v. Miller, 4 Taunt. (Eng.) 745, 749; Dubois v. Delaware & H. Canal Co., 4 Wend. (N. Y.) 285; Hollinsead v. Mactier, 13 Wend. (N. Y.) 276.

[32] The cases that present difficulty are those in which the waiver is not express, but it is sought to imply such a waiver. Where the article is of small bulk and can easily be rejected if unsatisfactory, and when the bailee is close at hand, a waiver might well be implied when no objection is made by the bailor; whereas, if the article is bulky and the bailee in such a place and at such a distance that such rejection would be much more difficult, such a waiver would be less readily implied.

[33] Poth. Cont. de Louage, note 433. See, also, Story, Bailm. § 426; Gillett v. Mawman, 1 Taunt. (Eng.) 137. This was decided in an early English case, in an action by a shipwright for work and labor done, and for materials provided, in repairing the defendant's vessel. Before the completion of this work with only three hours' work remaining to be done, the ship was burned by an accidental fire. It was held that the shipwright was entitled to recover for his labor and materials. This decision was based upon the maxim that in such a case "res perit domino." Menetone v. Athawes, 3 Burrows (Eng.) 1592. Mr. Bell has deduced the following as the true rules on the subject: If the work is independent of any materials or property of the employer, the manufacturer has the risk, and the unfinished work perishes to him. If he is employed in working up the materials, or adding his labor to the property of the employer, the risk is with the owner of the thing with which

to the owner in its condition at the time it perishes. Neither party is here liable to the other, because the bailment contract cannot be completely carried out.

As before, the bailee can recover nothing, when by an entire contract he has stipulated that he shall receive no compensation whatever unless he has completely performed; but courts hesitate thus to construe the contract.[84]

Same—Fault of Bailor Preventing Completion of Work

When the completion of the work is prevented by the bailor's wrong, the question of compensation should present no complications. The suit is brought by the bailee, in no way at fault, under an unfinished bailment upon which he is ready and willing to proceed, but is prevented from doing so by the fault of the bailor. The law in such case endeavors to make the bailee whole again. This is done by allowing the bailee to recover from the bailor, not only the reasonable worth of the services already performed, but also full damages for all the loss that he has suffered as the result of the bailor's wrongful breach of the bailment contract.[85] The bailee is thus placed in practically the same position as that which he would have occupied had he been permitted to complete the bailment. He is paid for the work already done, and receives also the profits he would have earned had he been permitted to complete the bailment.

Same—Fault of Bailee in Abandoning the Work While Incomplete

The principles laid down by the courts in this situation are many, varied, and utterly irreconcilable. The conflict is in a way an outgrowth of the widespread controversy which has raged around the great case of BRITTON v. TURNER,[86] involving the

the labor is incorporated. If the work has been performed in such a way as to afford a defense to the employer against a demand for the price, if the accident had not happened (as, if it was defectively or improperly done), the same defense will be equally available to him after the loss. 1 Bell, Comm. p. 456.

[84] Story, Bailm. § 426; Brumby v. Smith, 3 Ala. 123; Appleby v. Myers, L. R. 2 C. P. 651, 656. Though generally, where, while work is doing on a thing belonging to an employer, the thing perishes by internal defect or inevitable accident without the workman's fault, he is entitled to compensation for the work actually done, where plaintiff worked on defendants' material under an agreement that defendants would pay therefor only after delivery in good order at their store, he may not recover for work done on material destroyed on his premises, though he is blameless for the loss. Stern v. Rosenthal, 56 Misc. Rep. 643, 107 N. Y. Supp. 772.

[85] See Story, Bailm. § 441; Schouler, Bailm. § 111.

[86] 6 N. H. 481, 26 Am. Dec. 713, and note, Dobie Cas. Bailments and Car-

general right of one to recover on a contract which he has not fully performed. That there can be no recovery on the contract itself is generally conceded, but the battle of the cases rages around the right of a recovery on a quantum meruit for the worth of the services actually performed. Even when such a recovery is granted, the other party is always allowed to diminish the recovery by any damages that he has suffered, flowing from the breach. The particular question with which we are concerned, and about which there is such direct conflict, is this: When a bailment is not completed, owing to the fault of the bailee, can the bailee recover the excess of the reasonable value of his services performed over the damage caused to the bailor by the bailee's failure to complete the bailment?[87] Some courts answer generally in the affirmative;[88] others give a negative reply and refuse the bailee any

riers, 88. See, also, Cutter v. Powell, 6 Term R. (Eng.) 320, 3 R. R. 185, and a collection of the cases, involving the entirety of contracts based on Cutter v. Powell, in 2 Hughes on Procedure, 892. In Cutter v. Powell, however, as opposed to BRITTON v. TURNER, the contract was not broken by the party, but he died leaving it unperformed in part. In BRITTON v. TURNER, a laborer who agreed to work a specified time for an extra sum abandoned the contract after working a part of the time. He was permitted to recover on a quantum meruit the value of his services in excess of the damage caused to his employer by such breach of contract. The doctrine of this great case is believed to be sound.

[87] Neither BRITTON v. TURNER, supra, nor Cutter v. Powell, supra, involved a bailment. Indeed, most of the cases cited are contracts of service, and not bailments at all. The analogy is a good one, however, and the right of the party breaking the contract to recover is governed by the same principles, whether or not a technical bailment be created.

[88] See BRITTON v. TURNER, supra; Larkin v. Buck, 11 Ohio St. 568; McClay v. Hedge, 18 Iowa, 66; Hillyard v. Crabtree's Adm'r, 11 Tex. 264, 62 Am. Dec. 475; McDonough v. Evans Marble Co., 112 Fed. 634, 50 C. C. A. 403 (this case speaks of the doctrine permitting a recovery as "the more modern rule"); Duncan v. Baker, 21 Kan. 99; Bedow v. Tonkin, 5 S. D. 432, 59 N. W. 222; Watson v. Kirby, 112 Ala. 436, 20 South. 624. These are cases of contracts of service, not bailments. Mr. Parsons, in his great work on Contracts (volume 2 [6th Ed.] 38, 39), thus approves the rule of BRITTON v. TURNER: "BRITTON v. TURNER permits the servant to recover on a quantum meruit. His right to recover is carefully guarded in this case by principles which seem to protect the master from all wrong. * * * So guarded, it might seem that the principles of this case are better adapted to do adequate justice to both parties and *wrong to neither* than those of the numerous cases which rest upon the somewhat technical rule of the entirety of the contract." Mr. Page, however (3 Page, Cont. § 1604), after discussing the cases following BRITTON v. TURNER, remarks: "In studying the principles here discussed, as enforced by the courts, one is sometimes driven to inquire whether a special contract means anything."

recovery;[39] others give a qualified answer,[40] holding that it depends on whether the bailment contract is a general or special one, or whether the abandonment of the bailee was or was not willful or malicious, and so on.

Thus some of the older cases hold that the bailee must here stand rigidly by the contract, and that, when he is in fault in not completing it, he should not be permitted to recover.[41] This rule was applied, even though a great part of the work had been completed, conferring a substantial benefit on the bailor, who was thereby gratuitously enriched. This doctrine, emphasizing the technical unity and entirety of contracts, is too extreme for a large majority of the modern courts.

Other courts, modifying the severity of this rule, have permitted the bailee to recover on the quantum meruit when the contract is a general one of hiring, but have refused such a recovery when the contract is a special one, explicitly stating the way the bailment services are to be performed and agreeing on a specified price.[42] It has been a generally held technical rule that,

[39] Olmstead v. Beale, 19 Pick. (Mass.) 528; Forman v. The Leddesdale, [1900] App. Cas. (Eng.) 190; Hansbrough v. Peck, 5 Wall. 497, 18 L. Ed. 520; Scheible v. Klein, 89 Mich. 376, 50 N. W. 857; Elliott v. Caldwell, 43 Minn. 357, 45 N. W. 845, 9 L. R. A. 52; Van Clief v. Van Vechten, 130 N. Y. 571, 20 N. E. 1017; Harris v. Sharples, 202 Pa. 243, 51 Atl. 965, 58 L. R. A. 214; Vicksburg Water Supply Co. v. Gorman, 70 Miss. 360, 11 South. 680. See 3 Page, Contracts, § 1603.

[40] STEEPLES v. NEWTON, 7 Or. 110, 33 Am. Rep. 705, Dobie Cas. Bailments and Carriers, 91; Dermott v. Jones, 2 Wall. 1, 17 L. Ed. 762; Id., 23 How. 220, 16 L. Ed. 442; Barrett v. Raleigh Coal & Coke Co., 51 W. Va. 416, 41 S. E. 220, 90 Am. St. Rep. 802; Walsh v. Fisher, 102 Wis. 172, 78 N. W. 437, 43 L. R. A. 810, 72 Am. St. Rep. 865. See 3 Page on Cont. § 1602; Ellis v. Hamlen, 3 Taunt. (Eng.) 53; McMillan v. Vanderlip, 12 Johns. (N. Y.) 165, 7 Am. Dec. 299.

[41] Cutter v. Powell, 6 Term R. (Eng.) 320, 2 Smith, Lead. Cas. 1212, is the extreme case, in which a seaman died before completing the voyage and time contracted for. It was held that his personal representatives could recover nothing. Such cases, however, are now rare.

[42] Farnsworth v. Garrard, 1 Camp. (Eng.) 38; Basten v. Butter, 7 East (Eng.) 479; Cutler v. Close, 5 Car. & P. (Eng.) 337; Thornton v. Place, 1 Moody & R. (Eng.) 218; Grant v. Button, 14 Johns. (N. Y.) 377; Ellis v. Hamlen, 3 Taunt. (Eng.) 53; Cousins v. Paddon, 2 Cromp., Mees. & R. (Eng.) 547; Burn v. Miller, 4 Taunt. (Eng.) 745, 747; Taft v. Inhabitants of Montague, 14 Mass. 282, 7 Am. Dec. 215; Jewell v. Schroeppel, 4 Cow. (N. Y.) 564; Sickels v. Pattison, 14 Wend. (N. Y.) 257, 28 Am. Dec. 527; Sinclair v. Bowles, 9 Barn. & C. (Eng.) 92; Clark v. Smith, 14 Johns. (N. Y.) 326; Raymond v. Bearnard, 12 Johns. (N. Y.) 274, 7 Am. Dec. 317; Jennings v. Camp. 13 Johns. (N. Y.) 94, 7 Am. Dec. 367; Faxon v. Mansfield, 2 Mass. 147; McMillan v. Vanderlip, 12 Johns. (N. Y.) 165, 7 Am. Dec. 299; Champlin v. Butler, 18 Johns. (N. Y.) 169.

when a special contract is open and subsisting, one cannot recover on an implied contract, unless he can show an excuse for his departure from such special contract.

When the bailee's recovery is based upon considerations of whether or not his abandonment was voluntary, or willful or malicious, this substitutes a criterion of morality and public policy for contractual technicality.[43] Courts denying a recovery when the abandonment was willful hold that it contravenes sound morality to permit a person to obtain any recovery for work done under a contract which he has voluntarily abandoned with no excuse for such conduct.[44]

It is submitted, though the weight of authority seems now against it, that the question propounded should be answered in the affirmative, without any of the qualifications mentioned. The ground of the bailee's recovery is not based upon, but is rather in spite of, the specific contract. He recovers for a benefit conferred on the bailor's goods, a step in line toward the realization of what the bailor desired, on the principle that the bailor should not be permitted to enjoy such benefit without paying therefor its reasonable worth, and that therefore the law implies that he will make a reasonable compensation therefor. The broken contract does not help the bailee to recover, but retards his recovery. The bailee seeks no benefit from his contractual breach, but such breach imposes on him the burden for all loss thereby occasioned. Again, the fullest remedy is given to the bailor for the wrong done to him, for he is credited with all his loss flowing from the wrong; he is awarded full compensatory damages. Beyond this, the law goes only in very few cases. Should the law, then, for the bailee's breach, gratuitously enrich the bailor, and punish the bailee by causing him to forfeit the value of all his work, labor, and materials? It is believed that it should not.

Finally, it should be noted that the parties may stipulate clearly, in express terms, that the bailee is to receive no compensation unless he completely performs the bailment contract. Under such an agreement, the bailee, to whose fault is due the failure to

[43] Barrett v. Raleigh Coal & Coke Co., 51 W. Va. 416, 41 S. E. 220, 90 Am. St. Rep. 802; Walsh v. Fisher, 102 Wis. 172, 78 N. W. 437, 43 L. R. A. 810, 72 Am. St. Rep. 865; STEEPLES v. NEWTON, 7 Or. 110, 33 Am. Rep. 705, Dobie Cas. Bailments and Carriers, 91; Gallagher v. Sharpless, 134 Pa. 134, 19 Atl. 491; Dermott v. Jones, 2 Wall. 1, 17 L. Ed. 762; Homer v. Shaw, 177 Mass. 1, 58 N. E. 160; Posey v. Garth, 7 Mo. 94, 37 Am. Dec. 183.

[44] Hogan v. Titlow, 14 Cal. 255; Kohn v. Fandel, 29 Minn. 470, 13 N. W. 904; Hartman v. Meighan, 171 Pa. 46, 33 Atl. 123; Fairfax Forrest Min. & Mfg. Co. v. Chambers, 75 Md. 604, 23 Atl. 1024; Bonesteel v. Mayor, etc., of City of New York, 22 N. Y. 162; Thrift v. Payne, 71 Ill. 408.

complete the bailment, could recover nothing. The bailee, having made such a contract with full knowledge, could not complain; nor does such an agreement contravene a sound public policy. This would afford the bailor a desired method of securing himself against any abandonment of the bailment before it had been perfectly performed.

EXPENSES OF THE BAILMENT

63. The bailee must bear the expenses ordinarily incident to the execution of the bailment. Extraordinary expenses fall on the bailor.

The rules here are in their practical application similar to those obtaining in locatio rei, or the hired use of chattels.

In bailment for hired services, it is a fair prima facie presumption that the parties intended the expenses ordinarily incidental to the execution of the bailment contract to be borne by the bailee, who is presumed to have fixed his compensation high enough to cover these expenses.[45]

This presumption, though, would hardly apply in the case of extraordinary expenses incurred reasonably in some unforeseen or extreme emergency, particularly when made for the preservation of the bailed goods. These expenses, when not due to the bailee's fault, should be borne by the bailor.[46]

THE LIEN OF THE BAILEE ON THE BAILED CHATTELS

64. The bailee performing services about a chattel has a lien on such chattel to secure the payment of his proper compensation.

Lien

It may safely be laid down as a general rule that every bailee for hire who performs services about the goods of another has a lien on such goods to secure his proper compensation, and he can

[45] Story, Bailm. §§ 425, 426, 441; Schouler, Bailm. (2d Ed.) § 114; 2 Kent, Comm. 590; Whitlock v. Heard, 13 Ala. 776, 48 Am. Dec. 73; Menetone v. Athawes, 3 Burrows (Eng.) 1592.

[46] Schouler, Bailm. (2d Ed.) § 114; Story, Bailm. § 426c. If it reasonably can be done, it would seem that the bailee should secure the sanction of the bailor to such expenditure. See Small v. Robinson, 69 Me. 425, 31 Am. Rep. 299. The expenditure must be a proper one in any case to be recoverable by the bailee. See Enos v. Cole, 53 Wis. 235, 10 N. W. 377.

hold the goods until this compensation is paid.[47] Of common-law liens, this is, from the viewpoint of commercial policy, among the most important, as it is, from the standpoint of historical jurisprudence, among the most interesting.

The right of lien at common law seems originally to have been confined to those persons who, from the nature of their occupation, were under a legal obligation to receive the goods of others.[48] Such, for example, were common carriers and innkeepers. This doctrine was next extended to include cases in which the chattel had acquired additional value by the labor and skill of an artisan.[49] By further extensions it has come to include practically every case in which a bailee for hire performs services about the chattel.[50]

[47] Hensel v. Noble, 95 Pa. 345, 40 Am. Rep. 659; Pine Bluff Iron Works v. Boling & Bro., 75 Ark. 469, 88 S. W. 306; Drummond Carriage Co. v. Mills, 54 Neb. 417, 74 N. W. 966, 40 L. R. A. 761, 69 Am. St. Rep. 719; Holderman v. Manier, 104 Ind. 118, 3 N. E. 811; Caroway v. Cochran, 71 W. Va. 698, 77 S. E. 278; Pacific Aviation Co. v. Wells Fargo & Co., 64 Or. 530, 128 Pac. 438; Bass v. Upton, 1 Minn. 408 (Gil. 292); Low v. Martin, 18 Ill. 286; STEINMAN v. WILKINS, 7 Watts & S. (Pa.) 466, 42 Am. Dec. 254, Dobie Cas. Bailments and Carriers, 93. Wharfingers: Brookman v. Hamill, 43 N. Y. 554, 3 Am. Rep. 731; Ex parte Lewis, 2 Gall. 483, Fed. Cas. No. 8,310; Holderness v. Collinson, 7 Barn. & C. (Eng.) 212; Lenckhart v. Cooper, 3 Bing. N. C. (Eng.) 99; Dresser v. Bosanquet, 4 Best & S. (Eng.) 460. See Cowper v. Andrews, Hob. (Eng.) 39, 41a; Case of an Hostler, Yel. (Eng.) 67. And see the learned and valuable note of Mr. Justice Metcalf to this case, in his edition of Yelverton (page 67a), and the authorities therein collected and commented upon; Green v. Farmer, 4 Burrows (Eng.) 2214; Close v. Waterhouse, 6 East (Eng.) 523, note 2; 2 Kent, Comm. (5th Ed.) 635; Grinnell v. Cook, 3 Hill (N. Y.) 485, 491, 38 Am. Dec. 663; Oakes v. Moore, 24 Me. 214, 41 Am. Dec. 379; WILSON v. MARTIN, 40 N. H. 88, Dobie Cas. Bailments and Carriers, 85. "Whenever a party has expended labor and skill in the improvement of a chattel bailed to him, he has a lien upon it." Bevan v. Waters, Moody & M. (Eng.) 235; Scarfe v. Morgan, 4 Mees. & W. (Eng.) 270, 278; Harris v. Woodruff, 124 Mass. 205, 26 Am. Rep. 658; Morgan v. Congdon, 4 N. Y. 552; Mathias v. Sellers, 86 Pa. 486; Farrington v. Meek, 30 Mo. 578, 77 Am. Dec. 627; McIntyre v. Carver, 2 Watts & S. (Pa.) 392, 37 Am. Dec. 519.

[48] WILSON v. MARTIN, 40 N. H. 88, Dobie Cas. Bailments and Carriers, 85.

[49] See the following English cases: Jackson v. Cummins, 5 Mees. & W. 342, 348; Scarfe v. Morgan, 4 Mees. & W. 270; Bevan v. Waters, Moody & W. 235; Id., 3 Car. & P. 520; Forth v. Simpson, 13 Q. B. 680. See, also, Story, Bailm. (9th Ed.) § 453a; Harris v. Woodruff, 124 Mass. 205, 26 Am. Rep. 658; STEINMAN v. WILKINS, 7 Watts & S. (Pa.) 466, 42 Am. Dec. 254, Dobie Cas. Bailments and Carriers, 93; 1 Jones, Liens (2d Ed.) § 742; Morgan v. Congdon, 4 N. Y. 552; King v. Humphreys, 10 Pa. 217; Eaton v. Lynde, 15 Mass. 242; BURDICT v. MURRAY, 3 Vt. 302, 21 Am. Dec. 588, Dobie Cas. Bailments and Carriers, 84.

[50] See cases cited in note 47.

This steady increase in the favor with which the bailee's lien has met, as shown in "the struggle of the judicial mind to escape from the confines of the earlier precedents," [51] has necessarily resulted in some lack of harmony between the earlier and the later decisions. The truth is that the common-law lien of the bailee is a creature of policy, justified by its own inherent justice and expediency.[52] The lien of the bailee was regarded with high favor by Lord Kenyon [53] and Chief Justice Best [54] among the earlier judges, and modern judges have been active in recognizing the equitable and commercial considerations upon which the lien is based.

Agisters and Livery Stable Keepers

By the great weight of authority this common-law lien was denied to livery stable keepers [55] and also to agisters,[56] or those who make a business of taking cattle to be fed or pastured. For these exceptions, though, no entirely satisfactory reason has ever been given. One theory is that the lien exists only when the chattel has been enhanced in value by the skill and labor of the bailee.[57] Other bailees, such as the warehouseman,[58] have a lien, however, whose labors add nothing to the value of the chattel. Nor can it strictly be said that the agister who fattens cattle for the market adds nothing to their value. Another reason, and a more serious one, has been urged to explain why there can be no common-law lien here.[59] A bailee has a lien on goods only so long as he re-

[51] Gilson, C. J., in STEINMAN v. WILKINS, 7 Watts & S. (Pa.) 466, 467, 42 Am. Dec. 254, Dobie Cas. Bailments and Carriers, 93.

[52] Schouler, Bailm. (2d Ed.) § 126; STEINMAN v. WILKINS, 7 Watts & S. (Pa.) 466, 42 Am. Dec. 254, Dobie Cas. Bailments and Carriers, 93.

[53] See Kirkman v. Shawcross, 6 Term R. (Eng.) 14, 17.

[54] See Jacobs v. Latard, 5 Bing. (Eng.) 130, 132.

[55] Jackson v. Cummins, 5 Mees. & W. (Eng.) 350; Parsons v. Gingell, 4 C. B. (Eng.) 545; Smith v. Dearlove, 6 C. B. (Eng.) 132; Miller v. Marston, 35 Me. 153, 56 Am. Dec. 694; Wallace v. Woodgate, 1 Car. & P. (Eng.) 575; Hickman v. Thomas, 16 Ala. 666; McDonald v. Bennett, 45 Iowa, 456; Mauney v. Ingram, 78 N. C. 96; Judson v. Etheridge, 1 Cromp. & M. (Eng.) 742.

[56] Grinnell v. Cook, 3 Hill (N. Y.) 485, 491, 38 Am. Dec. 663; Goodrich v. Willard, 7 Gray (Mass.) 183; Miller v. Marston, 35 Me. 153, 56 Am. Dec. 694; Lewis v. Tyler, 23 Cal. 364; Wills v. Barrister, 36 Vt. 220; Millikin v. Jones, 77 Ill. 372; Allen v. Ham, 63 Me. 532 (by statute); Chapman v. Allen, Cro. Car. (Eng.) 271.

[57] Story, Bailm. 453a; Scarfe v. Morgan, 1 Mees. & W. (Eng.) 270; Jackson v. Cummins, 5 Mees. & M. (Eng.) 342; Grinnell v. Cook, 3 Hill (N. Y.) 485, 491, 38 Am. Dec. 663.

[58] Post, p. 164.

[59] Grinnell v. Cook, 3 Hill (N. Y.) 485, 38 Am. Dec. 663; Bevan v. Waters, 3 Car. & P. (Eng.) 520, 522; Jones v. Thurloe, 8 Mod. (Eng.) 172; Jones v.

tains uninterrupted possession. When horses are kept at a livery stable, the owner takes and uses them at pleasure. As to the agister, in the case of milch cows, the owner has occasional possession for the purpose of milking them. Either the agister or the livery stable keeper could, of course, secure a lien by special contract.[60]

Very generally now the agister and livery stable keeper have liens by statute. It may therefore be stated as a well-established rule that the modern bailee, performing services about a chattel, has a lien thereon for his compensation, regardless of the nature of the services.

Consent of the Owner

Inasmuch as the lien of a bailee arises from his employment to render the services, it follows that the employment must be by the owner, whose goods are to be affected by the lien, or by his consent, express or implied.[61] Thus a thief could not, by giving a stolen watch to a watchmaker for repairs, create a valid lien on the watch against the owner in favor of the watchmaker.

It must not, however, be inferred that the consent of the owner to such a bailment must in all cases be given under such circumstances or in such a manner as would create a personal liability on his part to pay the charges of the bailee. When the goods are improved and enhanced in value by the workman's labor, authority to have it done on the footing of a workman's lien may well be implied from circumstances which would not raise an implication of a contract on the owner's part to pay the workman's charges. Accordingly the bailee may sometimes, in somewhat anomalous

Pearle, 1 Strange (Eng.) 556; Sweet v. Pym, 1 East (Eng.) 4; Jackson v. Cummins, 5 Mees. & W. (Eng.) 342, 350; Cross, Liens, 25, 36, 332.

60 See cases cited in notes 53–57.

61 1 Jones, Liens, § 733; Clark v. Hale, 34 Conn. 398; White v. Smith, 44 N. J. Law, 105, 43 Am. Rep. 347; Hill v. Burgess, 37 S. C. 604, 15 S. E. 963. Cf. McIntyre v. Carver, 2 Watts & S. (Pa.) 392, 37 Am. Dec. 519. The bailee cannot assert his lien against the true owner of the goods who has never consented to such bailment. Small v. Robinson, 69 Me. 425, 31 Am. Rep. 299; Globe Works v. Wright, 106 Mass. 207; Gilson v. Gwinn, 107 Mass. 126, 9 Am. Rep. 13; Hollingsworth v. Dow, 19 Pick. (Mass.) 228; Robinson v. Baker, 5 Cush. (Mass.) 137, 51 Am. Dec. 54; Lloyd v. Kilpatrick, 71 Misc. Rep. 19, 127 N. Y. Supp. 1096; Johnson v. Hill, 3 Starkie (Eng.) 172; Sargent v. Usher, 55 N. H. 287, 20 Am. Rep. 208; Hanch v. Ripley, 127 Ind. 151, 26 N. E. 70, 11 L. R. A. 61. Thus a coach maker to whom a carriage had been delivered for repairs by the owner's servant was denied a lien where the carriage had been broken by the negligence of the servant, without the knowledge of the master, and had been taken by the servant to the coach maker for repairs, without any orders from his master. Hiscox v. Greenwood, 4 Esp. (Eng.) 174.

cases, have a lien on the goods for his services, though he yet may be unable to recover from the owner of the goods the compensation which the lien secures. So, without an in personam claim against the owner, the bailee may have a valid in rem claim against the owner's goods. Thus, where a wife allowed her husband to use her wagon, and he delivered the wagon for certain necessary repairs to a wheelwright, who charged them to the husband, supposing the wagon to be his, it was held that the wheelwright had a lien on the wagon for his charges, as against the wife.[62]

Subcontractors or Servants of the Bailee

The lien is strictly personal to the bailee, who has contracted with the owner to perform the services. It does not attach in favor of a workman who is hired by the original bailee to do the work. In such case both the possession and lien are in the master or contractor.[63] Subcontractors have no lien, because there is no privity between them and the owner.[64] So far as the bailee's own lien is concerned, therefore, it is immaterial whether he perform the work personally or (as he has the right in a proper case) through agents or servants.[65] It is not an essential element of the bailee's lien that he perform the services himself.

Priority of Lien

The question of the priority of the bailee's lien over other liens, both prior and subsequent to it in time, on the same goods, is of no little practical importance. As to subsequent liens, it is clear that, once the bailee's lien has validly attached, the bailor cannot create any incumbrances thereafter which will take precedence over the bailee. His lien is good against the world, and no later act of the bailor can postpone it to the claims of third persons.[66] As a general rule the bailee's lien must yield to mortgages or other valid incumbrances created by the bailor before the commencement of the bailment.[67] The mortgage, for example, when no estoppel or con-

[62] White v. Smith, 44 N. J. Law, 105, 43 Am. Rep. 347.

[63] Gluckman v. Kleiman, 3 Misc. Rep. 97, 22 N. Y. Supp. 549; Wright v. Terry, 23 Fla. 160, 2 South. 6; Quillian v. Central Railroad & Banking Co., 52 Ga. 374. And see White v. Smith, 44 N. J. Law, 105, 43 Am. Rep. 347.

[64] Meyers v. Bratespiece, 174 Pa. 119, 34 Atl. 551; Jacobs v. Knapp, 50 N. H. 71; Gross v. Eiden, 53 Wis. 543, 11 N. W. 9; 1 Jones, Liens, § 721.

[65] Jones, Liens, § 738; Hall v. Tittabawassee Boom Co., 51 Mich. 377, 16 N. W. 770; Webber v. Cogswell, 2 Can. Sup. Ct. 15.

[66] See, on liens in general, Rankin v. Scott, 12 Wheat. 177, 6 L. Ed. 592; Weinprender v. His Creditors, 5 La. 349; Parker v. Kelly, 10 Smedes & M. (Miss.) 184; Puryear v. Taylor, 12 Grat. (Va.) 401.

[67] A recorded chattel mortgage on a horse is superior to a subsequent lien of a livery stable keeper, acquired under Mill. & V. Code Tenn. § 2760, where the horse is placed in the stable after the making of the mortgage, without

sent is invoked against the mortgagee and no questions of recordation appear, ordinarily takes precedence over subsequent claims. As a rule, the bailee's lien attaches to the goods in their incumbered condition at the time the bailment is created. The bailment of a mortgaged chattel gives rise to a lien on a mortgaged chattel, unless the mortgagee expressly or impliedly,[68] yields his precedence.

There are exceptional cases, however, when the lien of a prior mortgage must yield to the lien of the bailee. These are cases in which the mortgagor, in possession of the chattel, delivers it to the bailee for repairs that are necessary to preserve it and to keep up its efficiency as a means of enabling the mortgagor to pay off the mortgage debt. The bailment, in thus adding to the value of the mortgaged chattel, and increasing its earning power, is therefore manifestly to the advantage of the mortgagee. It is accordingly held that the necessities of the case authorize the mortgagor in possession to create such a bailment, rendering himself alone liable for the bailee's compensation in personam, but rendering the mortgaged chattel liable in rem. Thus, when a mortgaged canal boat foundered, the mortgagor took the boat to a shipwright for repairs, without which the boat could not have been used and would have been almost useless as security for the mortgage debt. It was held that the shipwright's lien on the boat was valid and took priority over the mortgage.[69]

the knowledge of the mortgagee, though the stable keeper had no notice in fact of the mortgage. McGhee v. Edwards, 87 Tenn. 506, 11 S. W. 316, 3 L. R. A. 654. See, also, Bissell v. Pearce, 28 N. Y. 252, in which the prior mortgage took precedence over the bailee's lien arising out of special contract. See, further, Denison v. Shuler, 47 Mich. 598, 11 N. W. 402, 41 Am. Rep. 734; Baumann v. Post, 16 Daly, 385, 12 N. Y. Supp. 213; Pickett v. McCord, 62 Mo. App. 467; Hanch v. Ripley, 127 Ind. 151, 26 N. E. 70, 11 L. R. A. 61.

68 The mortgagee's authority for the creation of a lien may be implied from the mortgagor's being allowed to remain in possession of the chattel and to use it for profit. Watts v. Sweeney, 127 Ind. 116, 26 N. E. 680, 22 Am. St. Rep. 615; Hammond v. Danielson, 126 Mass. 294; Loss v. Fry, 1 City Ct. R. (N. Y.) 7; Beall v. White, 94 U. S. 382, 24 L. Ed. 173; Scott v. Delahunt, 5 Lans. (N. Y.) 372; Id., 65 N. Y. 128.

69 Scott v. Delahunt, 65 N. Y. 128. In the leading case on this subject Williams v. Allsup, 10 C. B. N. S. (Eng.) 417, the shipwright's lien for repairs was permitted to take precedence over the lien of the prior mortgage. In that case Erle, C. J., used this language: "I put my decision on the ground that, the mortgagee having allowed the mortgagor to continue in the apparent ownership of the vessel, making it a source of profit, and a means of earning wherewithal to pay off the mortgage debt, the relation so created by implication entitles the mortgagor to do all that may be necessary to keep her in an efficient state for that purpose. The case states

Bailee's Lien is Usually a Special Lien, Not a General Lien

The bailee's lien for services about chattels is ordinarily a special lien,[70] and not a general one. By a special lien is meant that it secures only the debt created by services about the specific goods upon which the lien is claimed. Such a lien does not cover debts for services on other goods besides those held under the lien. Such special lien, however, extends to every portion of the goods delivered under one contract.[71] The whole lien extends to each and every part of the goods subject to it. If not discharged or waived, it remains attached to any part of the goods remaining in the possession of the bailee. A delivery of part of the goods does not discharge the lien either wholly or even pro tanto. Such a delivery, unless it clearly appears that the intention of the parties was otherwise, releases from the operation of the lien only the part delivered. Accordingly, the goods remaining in the bailee's possession are charged with the burden of the whole lien.[72]

Where there is an entire contract for repairing several articles for a gross sum, even though these articles are delivered at different times, the artisan has a lien on each of the articles in his

that the vessel had been condemned as unseaworthy by the government surveyor, and so was in a condition to be utterly unable to earn freight, or be an available security or any source of profit at all. Under these circumstances, the mortgagor did that which was obviously for the advantage of all parties interested; he puts her into the hands of the defendant to be repaired; and, according to all ordinary usage, the defendant ought to have a right of lien on the ship, so that those who are interested in the ship, and who will be benefited by the repairs, should not be allowed to take her out of his hands without paying for them." See, also, in that case, the opinions of Willes and Byles, JJ. See, also, opinion of Gray, C. J., in Hammond v. Danielson, 126 Mass. 294, applying the doctrine of Williams v. Allsup, to a hack.

70 Honig v. Knipe, 25 Mo. App. 574; Miller v. Marston, 35 Me. 153, 155, 56 Am. Dec. 694; Mathias v. Sellers, 86 Pa. 486, 27 Am. Rep. 723; Moulton v. Greene, 10 R. I. 330; Nevan v. Roup, 8 Iowa, 207; Rushforth v. Hadfield, 6 East (Eng.) 519; Green v. Farmer, 4 Burrows (Eng.) 2214. Charge for keeping goods held to preserve a lien cannot be added to the sum for which a lien is claimed. Somes v. British Empire Shipping Co., 8 H. L. Cas. (Eng.) 338; Lord v. Collins, 76 Me. 443. See, also, Harley v. Epps, 69 Ga. 611; McIntyre v. Carver, 2 Watts & S. (Pa.) 392, 37 Am. Dec. 519.

71 When the contract and the work are entire, the lien extends to each part, and may be enforced to the extent of the entire price upon any portion remaining in the possession of the bailee after a partial delivery. Schmidt v. Blood, 9 Wend. (N. Y.) 268, 24 Am. Dec. 143; Morgan v. Congdon, 4 N. Y. 552; Hensel v. Noble, 95 Pa. 345, 40 Am. Rep. 659; STEINMAN v. WILKINS, 7 Watts & S. (Pa.) 466, 42 Am. Dec. 254, Dobie Cas. Bailments and Carriers, 93; Myers v. Uptegrove, 3 How. Prac. N. S. (N. Y.) 316.

72 New Haven & Northampton Co. v. Campbell, 128 Mass. 104, 35 Am. Rep. 360.

possession for such amount as he may be entitled for services bestowed on any or all of the articles embraced in the contract.[73] Nor will a payment of part of the contract price release a part of the goods from the lien; but the bailee may retain all the goods until the entire debt is paid.

A general lien, as opposed to a special lien, is the right to hold goods as security for a general balance arising from a series of transactions either in the same line of business or of the same nature.[74] Unlike the special lien, the general lien is not highly favored by the law.[75] The lien of the bailee is therefore a special one, unless a general lien is given by special contract or by well-defined custom and common usage.[76] Wharfingers and factors are among the bailees to whom long-established usage has given such a general lien.[77] This does not mean that the factor, for example, could retain goods of his principal for all debts due to him by the principal; but the factor's general lien gives him the right to hold the goods in his possession as factor only as security for the general balance due him from a series of contracts of factorage similar to the contract under which he secured possession of the goods to which his general lien attaches.[78]

[73] Hensel v. Noble, 95 Pa. 345, 40 Am. Rep. 659; Blake v. Nicholson, 3 Maule & S. 167; Partridge v. Dartmouth College, 5 N. H. 286; McFarland v. Wheeler, 26 Wend. (N. Y.) 467; Lane v. Old Colony & F. R. R. Co., 14 Gray (Mass.) 143; Chase v. Westmore, 5 Maule & S. (Eng.) 180; Myers v. Uptegrove, 3 How. Prac. N. S. (N. Y.) 316; Moulton v. Greene, 10 R. I. 330; Ruggles v. Walker, 34 Vt. 468; STEINMAN v. WILKINS, 7 Watts & S. (Pa.) 466, 42 Am. Dec. 254, Dobie Cas. Bailments and Carriers, 93.

[74] See Black, Law Dict. (2d Ed.) p. 726.

[75] McKenzie v. Nevius, 22 Me. 150, 38 Am. Dec. 291; Brooks v. Bryce, 21 Wend. (N. Y.) 16.

[76] Schouler, Bailm. (2d Ed.) § 122; 2 Kent, Comm. 634; Story, Ag. § 355; Jarvis v. Rogers, 15 Mass. 389. As to what constitutes a contract for a general lien on the part of a bailee, see Firth v. Hamill, 167 Pa. 382, 31 Atl. 676. The fact that plaintiff had not paid for suits which a tailor made for him did not give the tailor a lien upon other suits which plaintiff delivered to him to be pressed. Owcharoffsky v. Lambert (Sup.) 135 N. Y. Supp. 599.

[77] It is also said that calico printers, fullers, packers, and also bankers and insurance brokers, have general liens by custom and usage. See 3 Wait, Act. & Def. 301; 4 Wait, Act. & Def. 319, 320; 7 Wait, Act. & Def. 215; Hanna v. Phelps, 7 Ind. 21, 63 Am. Dec. 410; Tucker v. Taylor, 53 Ind. 93; Mooney v. Musser, 45 Ind. 115; East v. Ferguson, 59 Ind. 169; Shaw v. Ferguson, 78 Ind. 547; Bunnell v. Davisson, 85 Ind. 557; Spears v. Hartly, 3 Esp. (Eng.) 81. And see Weldon v. Gould, 3 Esp. (Eng.) 268; Savill v. Barchard, 4 Esp. (Eng.) 53; Naylor v. Mangles, 1 Esp. (Eng.) 109; Rushforth v. Hadfield, 6 East (Eng.) 519; Id., 7 East (Eng.) 224; Moet v. Pickering, 8 Ch. Div. (Eng.) 372.

[78] As to the limitations of general liens, see Story, Ag. § 379; Spring v. South Carolina Ins. Co., 8 Wheat. 268, 5 L. Ed. 614; McKenzie v. Nevius,

Waiver and Termination of the Lien

The bailee never has a lien when it is dispensed with by the special contract, and no lien arises when it is obvious that none was intended by the parties.[79] This may result from a contract expressly stipulating that there should be no lien, or from a bailment contract clearly inconsistent with the existence of the lien; as, for example, where payment was to be made in medical services as they were needed by the bailee,[80] or where a term of credit was provided for,[81] thus postponing payment after the completion of the bailment.

Where a valid lien actually arises, the bailee may lose it by a waiver thereof, just as he may voluntarily relinquish his other rights. Such a waiver may be express, or it may be established by evidence showing any acts or conduct of the bailee incon-

22 Me. 138, 38 Am. Dec. 291; Olive v. Smith, 5 Taunt. (Eng.) 57; Castling v. Aubert, 2 East (Eng.) 325.

79 WILES LAUNDRY CO. v. HAHLO, 105 N. Y. 234, 11 N. E. 500, 59 Am. Rep. 496, Dobie Cas. Bailments and Carriers, 95; Rollins v. Sidney B. Bowman Cycle Co., 96 App. Div. 365, 89 N. Y. Supp. 289; Stoddard Woolen Manufactory v. Huntley, 8 N. H. 441, 31 Am. Dec. 198; Trust v. Pirsson, 1 Hilt. (N. Y.) 292; Bailey v. Adams, 14 Wend. (N. Y.) 201; Murphy v. Lippe, 35 N. Y. Super. Ct. 542; Mount v. Williams, 11 Wend. (N. Y.) 77. Insolvency of bailor will not revive lien when it has been waived by special agreement. Fieldings v. Mills, 2 Bosw. (N. Y.) 489. Where credit may be claimed by custom, no lien arises. Raitt v. Mitchell, 4 Camp. (Eng.) 146; Crawshay v. Homfray, 4 Barn. & Ald. (Eng.) 50. If the inconsistent agreement is antecedent to the possession, no lien is created. If it is made afterwards, the lien is waived. 1 Jones, Liens, § 1002; Raitt v. Mitchell, 4 Camp. (Eng.) 146, 149; Crawshay v. Homfray, 4 Barn. & Ald. (Eng.) 50; Bailey v. Adams, 14 Wend. (N. Y.) 201; Dunham v. Pettee, 1 Daly (N. Y.) 112; Trust v. Pirsson, 1 Hilt. (N. Y.) 292; Chandler v. Belden, 18 Johns. (N. Y.) 157, 9 Am. Dec. 193; BURDICT v. MURRAY, 3 Vt. 302, 21 Am. Dec. 588, Dobie Cas. Bailments and Carriers, 84; Pinney v. Wells, 10 Conn. 104; Darlington v. Chamberlain, 20 Ill. App. 443; Lee v. Gould, 47 Pa. 398; Pulis v. Sanborn, 52 Pa. 368. But it must affirmatively appear that the lien is dispensed with. Where the contract is silent on the subject, the law confers a lien. Hazard v. Manning, 8 Hun (N. Y.) 613.

80 Morrill v. Merrill, 64 N. H. 71, 6 Atl. 602.

81 Hale v. Barrett, 26 Ill. 195, 79 Am. Dec. 367; Robinson v. Larrabee, 63 Me. 116; Tucker v. Taylor, 53 Ind. 93; McMaster v. Merrick, 41 Mich. 505, 2 N. W. 895; Dunham v. Pettee, 1 Daly (N. Y.) 112. "The operation of a lien is to place the property in pledge for the payment of the debt; and where the party agrees to give time for payment, or agrees to receive payment in a particular mode, inconsistent with the existence of such a pledge, it is evidence, if nothing appears to the contrary, that he did not intend to rely upon the pledge of the goods, in relation to which the debt arose, to secure the payment." Per Parker, J., in Stoddard Woolen Manufactory v. Huntley, 8 N. H. 441, 31 Am. Dec. 198. See, also, Fielding v. Mills, 2 Bosw. (N. Y.) 489.

sistent [82] with the continuance of the lien. A lien is strictly personal, and continuous possession on the part of the bailee is essential to its continuance. Accordingly, when the bailee voluntarily parts with possession, his lien is waived.[83] Nor, in such case, will it be revived by the bailee's subsequently reassuming the interrupted possession.[84] Again, a wrongful pledge or sale of the chattel by the bailee [85] will destroy his lien.

Since the lien exists solely to secure the payment of the bailee's compensation, such payment, of course, terminates the lien,[86] and a proper tender of payment would have the same effect.[87] A re-

[82] Schouler, Bailm. (2d Ed.) § 123. Bailee forfeits his lien by receipting to stranger and acknowledging that he holds goods for him, or by refusing to deliver goods to his principal on other grounds, omitting to mention his lien. Holbrook v. Wight, 24 Wend. (N. Y.) 169, 35 Am. Dec. 607. See, also, Sensenbrenner v. Mathews, 48 Wis. 250, 3 N. W. 599, 33 Am. Rep. 809; Miller v. Marston, 35 Me. 153, 56 Am. Dec. 694; White v. Gainer, 2 Bing. (Eng.) 23; Brackett v. Pierson, 114 App. Div. 281, 99 N. Y. Supp. 770.

[83] Burrow v. Fowler, 68 Ark. 178, 56 S. W. 1061; Block v. Dowd, 120 N. C. 402, 27 S. E. 129; Holderman v. Manier, 104 Ind. 118, 3 N. E. 811; Tucker v. Taylor, 53 Ind. 93; Nevan v. Roup, 8 Iowa, 207; McDougall v. Crapon, 95 N. C. 292; Kitteridge v. Freeman, 48 Vt. 62; In re Merrick, 91 Mich. 342, 51 N. W. 890; King v. Indian Orchard Canal Co., 11 Cush. (Mass.) 231; Stickney v. Allen, 10 Gray (Mass.) 352. Delivery of goods to third party, with agreement that lien continues, forfeits lien, unless third person is under control of bailee. Walther v. Wetmore, 1 E. D. Smith (N. Y.) 7. A tailor does not lose his lien by allowing the customer to try on the clothes made for him, provided it is done in the tailor's presence. Hughes v. Lenny, 5 Mees. & W. (Eng.) 183, 187. There is no common-law lien for work, done in manufacturing materials into clothing, unless the claimant has possession, actual or constructive, of the materials, and the lien is lost by the claimant voluntarily and unconditionally parting with such possession or control. Danzer v. Nathan, 145 App. Div. 448, 129 N. Y. Supp. 966.

[84] Hartley v. Hitchcock, 1 Starkie (Eng.) 408; Howes v. Ball, 7 Barn. & C. (Eng.) 481; Nevan v. Roup, 8 Iowa, 207; Robinson v. Larrabee, 63 Me. 116; Hale v. Barrett, 26 Ill. 195, 79 Am. Dec. 367.

[85] Rodgers v. Grothe, 58 Pa. 414; Davis v. Bigler, 62 Pa. 242, 1 Am. Rep. 303. The lien is also waived by claiming possession under an adverse title. Everett v. Saltus, 15 Wend. (N. Y.) 474; Holbrook v. Wight, 24 Wend. (N. Y.) 169, 35 Am. Dec. 607; Mexal v. Dearborn, 12 Gray (Mass.) 336. Lien acquired by partnership not lost by dissolution and assignment by one partner of his interest to the other. Busfield v. Wheeler, 14 Allen (Mass.) 139. See, also, Whitlock v. Heard, 13 Ala. 776, 48 Am. Dec. 73; Nash v. Mosher, 19 Wend. (N. Y.) 431; Samuel v. Morris, 6 Car. & P. (Eng.) 620.

[86] Pine Bluff Iron Works v. Boling & Bro., 75 Ark. 469, 88 S. W. 306. This is obviously true of liens in general. See Stephens v. Moodie (Tex. Civ. App.) 30 S. W. 490; Moore v. Hitchcock, 4 Wend. (N. Y.) 292; Stansbury v. Patent Cloth Mfg. Co., 5 N. J. Law, 433.

[87] Pine Bluff Iron Works v. Boling & Bro., 75 Ark. 469, 88 S. W. 306; Stephenson v. Lichtenstein, 72 N. J. Law, 113, 59 Atl. 1033. This is true of liens in general. See Eslow v. Mitchell, 26 Mich. 500; Mitchell v. Roberts-

fusal by the bailee to surrender the goods after such payment or tender is equivalent to conversion. Of course, by agreement of both the bailor and bailee, the lien may be terminated, though the bailment is allowed to continue.[88]

Enforcement of the Lien

At common law a lien is the mere right to retain the possession of goods until the satisfaction of a demand. On default in payment by the bailor, the title to the goods did not vest in the bailee and become absolute at law, as in the case of the mortgage; nor did the bailee have (as has the pledgee) a power of sale as to the goods held under his lien.[89] The bailee's right to sue the bailor personally for the agreed compensation was not affected by the lien, but only by holding could the lien be made effective.

The power of sale could be given by special contract. The bailee has now this power by statute in practically all of the states.[90]

(C. C.) 17 Fed. 776; Tompkins v. Batie, 11 Neb. 147, 7 N. W. 747, 38 Am. Rep. 361.

[88] Bailey v. Adams, 14 Wend. (N. Y.) 201.

[89] 1 Jones, Liens, § 1033; Jones v. Pearle, 1 Strange (Eng.) 557; Lickbarrow v. Mason, 6 East (Eng.) 21, note; Thames Iron Works Co. v. Patent Derrick Co., 1 Johns. & H. (Eng.) 93; Busfield v. Wheeler, 14 Allen (Mass.) 139; Rodgers v. Grothe, 58 Pa. 414; Briggs v. Boston & L. R. Co., 6 Allen (Mass.) 246, 83 Am. Dec. 626. In Doane v. Russell, 3 Gray (Mass.) 382, Chief Justice Shaw says: "If it be said that a right to retain the goods, without the right to sell, is of little or no value, it may be answered that it is certainly not so adequate a security as a pledge with a power of sale; still, it is to be considered that both parties have rights which are to be regarded by the law, and the rule must be adapted to general convenience. In the greater number of cases, the lien for work is small in comparison with the value, to the owner, of the article subject to lien; and in most cases it would be for the interest of the owner to satisfy the lien and redeem the goods, as in the case of the tailor, the coachmaker, the innkeeper, the carrier, and others; whereas, many times, it would cause great loss to the general owner to sell the suit of clothes or other articles of personal property. But, further, it is to be considered that the security of this lien, such as it is, is superadded to the holder's right to recover for his services by action."

[90] "In most of the states there are statutes giving to mechanics, artisans, and others who bestow labor on personal property a lien therefor. The purpose of these statutes is, in general, to extend the common-law lien in respect of the persons who can acquire such lien, and to give an effectual remedy for its enforcement, either by sale after notice, or by attachment and sale under execution. In a few states the lien is extended so that it may be availed of within a limited time after the property has been delivered to the owner. But, generally, these statutes, in most respects, are merely declaratory of the common law, and must be interpreted in accordance with its principles. Especially is this so as regards the necessity of retaining possession of the property in order to retain a lien upon it." Jones, Liens, 749; McDearmid v. Foster, 14 Or. 417, 12 Pac. 813; McDougall v. Crapon, 95 N. C. 292. "The lien under the statute is of the same nature it

Such statutes, being in derogation of the common law, must be strictly construed and followed, particularly when the statute conferring the right of sale prescribes the manner and method of its exercise. Of course, a sale of the goods, without warrant either in the bailment contract or statute, constitutes a conversion.[91]

THE DEGREE OF CARE TO BE EXERCISED BY THE BAILEE

65. The degree of diligence required of the bailee in fulfilling the purpose of the bailment is placed at ordinary care.

In the ordinary locatio operis bailments, as in other bailments for the mutual benefit of the bailor and bailee, the degree of diligence exacted of the bailee is ordinary care. The failure on his part to exercise this degree of care[92] is, of course, negligence,

formerly was, and the same circumstances must combine to create it. There must be a possession of the thing; otherwise, there cannot, without a special agreement to that effect, be any lien. The term 'lien,' as used in the statute, means the same it ever did—the right to hold the thing until the payment of the reasonable charges for making, altering, repairing, or bestowing labor upon it. Possession of the article is a requisite essential." McDearmid v. Foster, 14 Or. 417, 12 Pac. 813, per Thayer, J.

[91] Jones v. Pearle, 1 Strange (Eng.) 556; Mulliner v. Florence, 3 Q. B. Div. (Eng.) 484; Doane v. Russell, 3 Gray (Mass.) 382; Case v. Fogg, 46 Mo. 44; Jones v. Thurloe, 8 Mod. (Eng.) 172; Jesurun v. Kent, 45 Minn. 222, 47 N. W. 784. But in an action for such conversion the bailee may set off the amount of his lien. Briggs v. Boston & L. R. Co., 6 Allen (Mass.) 246, 83 Am. Dec. 626; Rodgers v. Grothe, 58 Pa. 414, 416.

[92] Where plaintiff delivered to cotton ginners certain cotton in controversy to be ginned and stored for hire, the ginners were bailees for hire, chargeable with the exercise of ordinary care. Hackney v. Perry, 152 Ala. 626, 44 South. 1029. Storage of cotton delivered to a compress company being an incident to its compression, the company was bound to use ordinary care in such storage. Loeb Compress Co. v. I. G. Bromberg & Co. (Tex. Civ. App.) 140 S. W. 475. See STUDEBAKER BROS. MFG. CO. v. CARTER, 51 Tex. Civ. App. 331, 111 S. W. 1086, Dobie Cas. Bailments and Carriers, 98; MICHIGAN STOVE CO. v. PUEBLO HARDWARE CO., 51 Colo. 160, 116 Pac. 340, Dobie Cas. Bailments and Carriers, 97; CONNER v. WINTON, 8 Ind. 315, 65 Am. Dec. 761, Dobie Cas. Bailments and Carriers, 54. An agreement to carry or deliver property for a reward, made by one who is not a common carrier, creates the duty to exercise reasonable care, but does not impose a liability on him for losses not occasioned by the ordinary negligence of himself or servants. American Dist. Tel. Co. of Baltimore v. Walker, 72 Md. 454, 20 Atl. 1, 20 Am. St. Rep. 479. When one delivers logs at a custom sawmill, to be sawed at agreed price, the owner of the mill becomes bound to exercise ordinary care in keeping and manufacturing the logs, and, in case of their loss, to prove that it was without his fault. Gleason v. Beers'

which renders the bailee liable to the bailor for all damages proximately flowing therefrom.

What has been said in other connections as to ordinary care applies here with added force. In locatio operis the bailment is created by the bailor for the express purpose of securing more or less active services about the chattel and (which is true of no other class of bailments) the bailee receives a compensation for such services. The question, therefore, of the bailee's skill and care assumes here a greater practical importance than in any other class of bailments.

Here, as in other mutual benefit bailments, the criterion of ordinary care is that degree of care exercised by the man of ordinary prudence under similar circumstances.[99] Here, too, the term is

Estate, 59 Vt. 581, 10 Atl. 86, 59 Am. Rep. 757. Cotton ginner is held only to ordinary diligence and care in custody of cotton delivered to him to be ginned. Kelton v. Taylor, 11 Lea (Tenn.) 264, 47 Am. Rep. 284. As to liability of banks as collecting agents, see German Nat. Bank v. Burns, 12 Colo. 539, 21 Pac. 714, 13 Am. St. Rep. 247, and note; National Butchers' & Drovers' Bank v. Hubbell, 117 N. Y. 384, 22 N. E. 1031, 7 L. R. A. 852, 15 Am. St. Rep. 515; Allen v. Merchants' Bank of City of New York, 22 Wend. (N. Y.) 215, 34 Am. Dec. 289, 307, and extended note. The relation between an owner intrusting goods to the custody of another to have work done on the goods is that of bailor and bailee for mutual benefit, and the bailee need only exercise ordinary care for the protection of the goods. Goldstein v. Blumberg (Sup.) 130 N. Y. Supp. 163. See, also, Fairmont Coal Co. v. Jones & Adams Co., 134 Fed. 711, 67 C. C. A. 265; Union Compress Co. v. Nunnally, 67 Ark. 284, 54 S. W. 872; Standard Brewery v. Bemis & Curtis Malting Co., 171 Ill. 602, 49 N. E. 507; Ashford v. Pittman, 160 N. C. 45, 75 S. E. 943.

[99] Firemen's Fund Ins. Co. v. Schreiber, 150 Wis. 42, 135 N. W. 507, 45 L. R. A. (N. S.) 314, Ann. Cas. 1913E, 823; Saunders v. Hartsook, 85 Ill. App. 55; American Dist. Tel. Co. of Baltimore v. Walker, 72 Md. 454, 20 Atl. 1, 20 Am. St. Rep. 479; Dale v. See, 51 N. J. Law, 378, 18 Atl. 306, 5 L. R. A. 583, 14 Am. St. Rep. 688. One in whose hands property is placed to safely care for, for a consideration, is not liable for its seizure and sale under attachment, he having had nothing to do therewith, except to surrender it to the sheriff on his demanding it by virtue of the attachment in his hands. Fite v. Briedenback, 127 Ky. 504, 105 S. W. 1182, 32 Ky. Law Rep. 400. Where cotton was injured by the negligence of a compress company while still in its actual possession, the fact that there had been a constructive delivery to a railroad company by delivery of the compress receipts did not relieve the compress company from liability for its negligence. Gulf Compress Co. v. Jones Cotton Co., 172 Ala. 645, 55 South. 206. Plaintiff showing bailment of a trunk for hire and nondelivery on demand, defendant has the burden of showing loss under conditions consistent with due care. Nathan v. Woolverton, 149 App. Div. 791, 134 N. Y. Supp. 469. A bale of cotton, after being ginned and tagged, was rolled out on the platform, the attached tag containing the bale number, and a duplicate, containing the number, weight, and name of the owner, was given the person who brought it, and when the owner called for it next morning it could not be found. There were notices around the gin stating the company would not be liable for cotton after

one of intense relativity.[94] Here, too, is frequently invoked the doctrine of estoppel against the bailor, having knowledge of the bailee's character, or the conditions under which the bailment is to be carried out.[95] Of special importance, too, is the doctrine that one holding himself out as possessing unusual skill is to be judged accordingly.[96] Such holding out may be by express terms in an individual instance, or it may be by simply undertaking to perform work necessarily involving skill, or holding one's self out as belonging to a class of bailees implying special skill,[97] such as watch-

ginned and baled, of which the owner knew, as well as that it was the general custom to dispose of baled cotton as defendant had done. Held, in a suit by the owner for the missing bale, that it was error to peremptorily instruct for plaintiff. Batesville Gin Co. v. Whitten (Miss.) 48 South. 616.

[94] See cases cited in notes 92, 93. Showing that a watchman employed by a bailee was addicted to drink, without showing causal connection with a fire which caused loss of goods, will not entitle the bailor to recover for the goods. Gibbons v. Yazoo & M. V. R. Co., 130 La. 671, 58 South. 505. In an action to recover the value of theatrical costumes delivered to the defendant to be cleaned, and not returned by him, an affidavit of defense is sufficient which avers that the defendant employed a competent man to do the work, that the process employed was the best known to the trade, that special care was used, that notwithstanding that every care and precaution was taken in the handling and cleaning of the costumes, the materials used in cleaning were in some unaccountable way ignited, and a fire resulted, destroying some of the costumes and damaging others, and that an offer was made to the plaintiff to repair the damaged goods and put them in as good condition as before, but that plaintiff refused such offer. Gingerbread Man Co. v. Schumacher, 35 Pa. Super. Ct. 652. See, also, Union Compress Co. v. Nunnally, 67 Ark. 284, 54 S. W. 872; Standard Brewery v. Hales & Curtis Malting Co., 70 Ill. App. 363; Vroman v. Kryn (Sup.) 86 N. Y. Supp. 94; Russell v. Koehler, 66 Ill. 459; Smith v. Meegan, 22 Mo. 150, 64 Am. Dec. 259.

[95] See ante, p. 69; Jones, Bailm. 63, 98–100; Story, Bailm. § 435; 1 Bell, Comm. (5th Ed.) p. 459; Knowles v. Atlantic & St. L. R. Co., 38 Me. 55, 61 Am. Dec. 234; Stearns v. Farrand, 29 Misc. Rep. 292, 60 N. Y. Supp. 501. A bailment contract ordinarily imports that the bailee may use the usual means of executing the bailment. Firemen's Fund Ins. Co. v. Schreiber, 150 Wis. 42, 135 N. W. 507, 45 L. R. A. (N. S.) 314, Ann. Cas. 1913E, 823. See note 97.

[96] Lincoln v. Gay, 164 Mass. 537, 42 N. E. 95, 49 Am. St. Rep. 480; Stanton v. Bell, 9 N. C. 145, 11 Am. Dec. 744; Kuehn v. Wilson, 13 Wis. 104; Hillyard v. Crabtree's Adm'r, 11 Tex. 264, 62 Am. Dec. 475; Smith v. Meegan, 22 Mo. 150, 64 Am. Dec. 259; Baird v. Daly, 57 N. Y. 236, 15 Am. Rep. 488; Moneypenny v. Hartland, 1 Car. & P. (Eng.) 352; Id., 2 Car. & P. (Eng.) 378; Duncan v. Blundell, 3 Starkie (Eng.) 6; Gamber v. Wolaver, 1 Watts & S. (Pa.) 60; Farnsworth v. Garrard, 1 Camp. (Eng.) 28; Moore v. Mourgue, Cowp. (Eng.) 479. See, also, Mack v. Snell, 140 N. Y. 193, 35 N. E. 493, 37 Am. St. Rep. 534; McKibben v. Bakers, 1 B. Mon. (Ky.) 120; Zell v. Dunkle, 156 Pa. 353, 27 Atl. 38; Horner v. Cornelius, 5 C. B. (Eng.) at page 246, Willes, J.; 1 Halsbury, Laws of England, p. 559.

[97] See cases in last note. Lincoln v. Gay, for example, involved a dressmaker. But even when the particular business or employment requires skill,

makers, tailors, and cabinet makers. The doctrine is "spondet peritiam artis"—he promises the skill of his art. Thus one undertaking to clean a delicate and expensive lace garment is not to be judged by the same practical standard as one cleaning an ordinary pair of shoes; nor one retouching the colors of an ivory miniature by the skill of one who paints doors and window blinds. Practical common sense is always to be used in solving the problem of what, under an infinite variety of controlling circumstances, does or does not constitute ordinary care.[98]

The parties can, of course, stipulate for a higher or lower degree of care, or the bailee may by his active wrong become an insurer.[99] In the absence of such contract or wrong, the bailee is liable for loss or damage only when it is due to his failure to exercise ordinary care.[1] Thus for loss or damage by act of God, or other inevitable

if the bailee is known not to possess it, or he does not exercise the particular art or employment to which it belongs, and he makes no pretension to skill in it, there, if the bailor, with full notice, trusts him with the undertaking, the bailee is bound only for a reasonable exercise of the skill which he possesses, or of the judgment which he can employ; and, if any loss ensues from his want of due skill, he is not chargeable. Thus, if a person will knowingly employ a common mat maker to weave or embroider a fine carpet, he must impute the bad workmanship to his own folly.

[98] See, further, Keith v. Bliss, 10 Ill. App. 424; Gamber v. Wolaver, 1 Watts & S. (Pa.) 60; Lienan v. Dinsmore, 3 Daly (N. Y.) 365; Clark v. Evershaw, Gow (Eng.) 30; Lanphier v. Phipes, 8 Car. & P. (Eng.) 475. Usage may be shown to qualify liability of bailee. Kelton v. Taylor, 11 Lea (Tenn.) 264, 47 Am. Rep. 284. In Brown v. Hitchcock, 28 Vt. 452, 457, it was shown that the defendant received from the plaintiff a quantity of palm leaf, agreeing to manufacture the same into hats, or to return it to plaintiff on demand. While in the hands of the defendant, the leaf was injured by heat and mildew. Isham, J., said: "We perceive no objection to the admission of the testimony in relation to the usage and custom in packing leaf for market, as also the necessity and custom of taking the leaf from the sacks and exposing it to air to prevent its becoming injured and worthless. Its object was simply to ascertain the character and degree of care which the defendant should have exercised, and that which he did exert over the property while it was in his possession."

[99] Russell v. Koehler, 66 Ill. 459. As in other classes of bailments. See ante, pp. 18–19, 83, 110; Story, Bailm. § 431; Schouler, Bailm. (2d Ed.) § 105. As to when such contracts extend the common-law duty of ordinary care, see Shaw v. Davis, 7 Mich. 318; Chicago, St. L. & N. O. R. Co. v. Pullman Southern Car Co., 139 U. S. 79, 11 Sup. Ct. 490, 35 L. Ed. 97; Phillips v. Hughes (Tex. Civ. App.) 33 S. W. 157.

[1] Story, Bailm. § 437; Norway Plains Co. v. Boston & M. R. R., 1 Gray (Mass.) 263, 61 Am. Dec. 423; Francis v. Dubuque & S. C. R. Co., 25 Iowa, 60, 95 Am. Dec. 769; McCullom v. Porter, 17 La. Ann. 89; Waller v. Parker, 5 Cold. (Tenn.) 476; Cowles v. Pointer, 26 Miss. 253; Johnson v. Smith, 54 Minn. 319, 56 N. W. 37; SAFE-DEPOSIT CO. OF PITTSBURGH v. POLLOCK, 85 Pa. 391, 27 Am. Rep. 660, Dobie Cas. Bailments and Carriers, 101;

calamity, the bailee would be responsible only when his negligence exposed the goods to such act, or when he was negligent in failing to minimize the loss flowing therefrom, after the act had occurred.[2]

The bailor is, of course, denied a recovery when the damage is attributable to his own fault, as when it is due to the plan outlined by the bailor, or when he furnishes defective materials.[3]

DELEGATION OF THE SERVICES BY THE BAILEE TO A THIRD PERSON

66. Unless the contract or the nature of the bailment requires the personal services of the bailee, he may have the work completely performed by third persons, or he may employ them to assist him in the undertaking.

It is difficult in a locatio operis bailment to say that the carrying out of the bailment purpose either is or is not personal to the

Chenowith v. Dickinson, 8 B. Mon. (Ky.) 156; Abraham v. Nunn, 42 Ala. 51; Smith v. Frost, 51 Ga. 336; Yale v. Oliver, 21 La. Ann. 454. A bailee for hire is not an insurer as to the conduct of his employés, but is responsible for ordinary care in the selection of his agents, in retaining them in his employ, and for wrongful acts within the scope of the employment. Firemen's Fund Ins. Co. v. Schreiber, 150 Wis. 42, 135 N. W. 507, 45 L. R. A. (N. S.) 314, Ann. Cas. 1913E, 823. A want of ordinary care in one particular, on the part of a warehouseman, does not render him responsible for a loss occasioned by other causes not connected with that particular. Gibson v. Hatchett, 24 Ala. 201. See, also, 2 Jag. Torts, "Connection as Cause," 929, 975. But see Powers v. Mitchell, 3 Hill (N. Y.) 545; Francis v. Castleman, 4 Bibb (Ky.) 282; Claflin v. Meyer, 43 N. Y. Super. Ct. 1; McGinn v. Butler, 31 Iowa, 160. See Stevens v. Boston & M. R. R., 1 Gray (Mass.) 277.

[2] Leck v. Maestaer, 1 Camp. (Eng.) 138; Smith v. Meegan, 22 Mo. 150, 64 Am. Dec. 259; James v. Greenwood, 20 La. Ann. 297. See, also, Story, Bailm. § 444; Platt v. Hibbard, 7 Cow. (N. Y.) 497; Schmidt v. Blood, 9 Wend. (N. Y.) 268, 24 Am. Dec. 143; Chenowith v. Dickinson, 8 B. Mon. (Ky.) 156; Claflin v. Meyer, 43 N. Y. Super. Ct. 1. One who undertakes to repair a boat, and places her upon marine railways upon bank of river for that purpose, is bound to use at least ordinary care for preservation thereof. He is liable in damages for her destruction if he launches her into river at time and under circumstances of great danger, which he ought to have foreseen, and which caused destruction of boat in spite of her owner's efforts to save her. This, although the loss was occasioned by breaking up of the ice, and 12 days after launching. Smith v. Meegan, 22 Mo. 150, 64 Am. Dec. 259.

[3] Story, Bailm. § 431; Schouler, Bailm. (2d Ed.) § 105. Where the employer supersedes the judgment of the workman, and insists that his own plan be followed, the workman is not liable for any losses resulting from pursuing such method. Duncan v. Blundell, 3 Starkie (Eng.) 6. See, also, Vroman v. Kryn (Sup.) 86 N. Y. Supp. 94, when bailor prescribed the type of machine by which the bailee was to polish the diamonds.

bailee. In the absence of special contract, this depends on the nature and circumstances of the particular bailment. For example, of the cases just mentioned, cleaning the shoes would ordinarily not be personal, and the bailee could intrust the work to a third person; quite the contrary would be true as to retouching the miniature. The more valuable the bailed chattel, the more difficult and delicate the work, the more unique the skill required, and especially the greater the play for the individuality of the bailee, the stronger is the showing that the bailment is a personal one, involving confidence reposed in the individual bailee.[4]

SPECIFIC BAILMENTS

67. There are a few classes of locatio operis bailees or semi-bailees whose business so vitally affects the public that they require some brief special mention. Such are (1) warehousemen; (2) wharfingers; (3) factors; (4) safe-deposit companies; and (5) officers in charge of public funds.

SAME—WAREHOUSEMEN

A warehouseman is a bailee who receives goods and merchandise to be stored in his warehouse for hire.[5] This is therefore a locatio custodiæ bailment, one involving the hiring of the custody of a thing rather than active labor and services about it. The storing of goods in warehouses is among the most common of all commercial bailments and it has assumed a tremendous practical importance.

[4] See Rodgers v. Grothe, 58 Pa. 414; Firemen's Fund Ins. Co. v. Schreiber, 150 Wis. 42, 135 N. W. 507, 45 L. R. A. (N. S.) 314, Ann. Cas. 1913E, 823. See, also, 1 Halsbury Laws of England, p. 560; Van Zile, Bailm. & Carr. § 154. Custom and usage, of course, play an important part here. Frequently the size and variety of the work (as in the case of extensive repairs to a ship) would conclusively show that the bailee could not personally perform all the services himself, but must delegate it in whole or part to others for whose work, while acting within the scope of their employment, the bailee is, of course, responsible.

[5] See 2 Bouv. Law Dict. 799; Black, Law Dict. (2d Ed.) p. 1218. In the Uniform Warehouse Receipts Act (adopted in a number of states), a warehouseman is defined as "a person lawfully engaged in the business of storing goods for profit." There are also other statutory definitions. See, for example, Ky. St. § 4768 (Act July 6, 1893); Burns' Rev. St. Ind. 1894, § 8720. See, further, Sinsheimer v. Whitely, 111 Cal. 378, 380, 43 Pac. 1109, 52 Am. St. Rep. 192; Geilfuss v. Corrigan, 95 Wis. 651, 659, 70 N. W. 306, 37 L. R. A. 166, 60 Am. St. Rep. 143; United States v. Oregon R. & Navigation Co. (C. C.) 159 Fed. 975, 977; 48 Cent. Dig. "Warehousemen," § 4.

The nature of the warehouseman's business, as well as his methods of conducting it, vary as widely as the nature of the goods intrusted to him. A great number of cases are concerned with the storage of grain; but, since the common carrier, as to goods in his hands, is a mere warehouseman before the technical carriage relation attaches and after it ends,[6] this, too, has made the rights and duties of warehousemen the subject of frequent study by the courts.

Though warehousemen of grain were declared by the United States Supreme Court to be "clothed with a public interest,"[7] it is generally held that the warehouseman, in the absence of statute, does not pursue a "public calling" in the strict sense in which that term is used of common carriers and innkeepers, and hence ordinarily he is not obliged by law, in the absence of statute, to receive goods tendered to him for storage.[8] The warehouseman is, therefore, said to pursue a quasi public calling. The validity of statutes making his calling strictly a public one, and imposing on him the duty to serve all the public, has been frequently upheld.[9]

Even the owners of so-called "bonded warehouses," in which goods are stored until the payment of the duties prescribed by the federal government, remain in a sense private warehousemen and liable as such for their negligence, or failure to exercise ordinary care, in protecting such goods.[10]

Warehouseman Required to Exercise Only Ordinary Care

In spite of his quasi public calling, the warehouseman is held to the same standard of diligence as other bailees in mutual benefit bailments, the exercise of ordinary care.[11] The warehouseman is

[6] See post, §§ 136, 139, 144.

[7] Munn v. Illinois, 94 U. S. 113, 24 L. Ed. 77.

[8] Delaware, L. & W. R. Co. v. Central Stock-Yard & Transit Co., 46 N. J. Eq. 280, 19 Atl. 185; Nash v. Page, 80 Ky. 539, 44 Am. Rep. 490.

[9] As to how far warehousemen pursue a public calling and how far they may be regulated, see Bank of Rome v. Haselton, 15 Lea (Tenn.) 216, upholding Tennessee Warehouse Act of 1879 (Laws 1879, c. 236); Hannah v. People ex rel. Attorney General, 198 Ill. 77, 64 N. E. 776 (police power of state); Ratcliff v. Wichita Union Stockyards Co., 74 Kan. 1, 86 Pac. 150, 6 L. R. A. (N. S.) 834, and note, 118 Am. St. Rep. 298, 10 Ann. Cas. 1016 (rates to be charged); Central Elevator Co. v. People ex rel. Moloney, 174 Ill. 203, 51 N. E. 254, 43 L. R. A. 658 (method of doing business).

[10] See Rev. St. §§ 2954–3008 (U. S. Comp. St. 1901, pp. 1941–1984); Macklin v. Frazier, 9 Bush (Ky.) 3; Claflin v. Meyer, 75 N. Y. 260, 31 Am. Rep. 467.

[11] Warehousemen are only ordinary bailees for hire, and are bound only to common care and diligence, and are liable only for want of such diligence or care. Edw. Bailm. 254; Jones, Bailm. 97; Story, Bailm. § 444; Cailiff v. Danvers, Peake (Eng.) 155; Foote v. Storrs, 2 Barb. (N. Y.) 326, 328; Bogert v. Haight, 20 Barb. (N. Y.) 251; Myers v. Walker, 31 Ill. 353; Buckingham v. Fisher, 70 Ill. 121; Hatchett v. Gibson, 13 Ala. 587; Dimmick v. Milwaukee

therefore liable only for negligence as thus judged. The rules as to negligence and the burden of proving it [12] that govern bailments in general, and the tests by which ordinary care is determined in other mutual benefit bailments, are all applicable here.[13]

The place of storage is of great practical importance,[14] as well as the precautions to protect the goods against damage from such

& St. P. Ry. Co., 18 Wis. 471; McCullom v. Porter, 17 La. Ann. 89; Blin v. Mayo, 10 Vt. 56, 59, 33 Am. Dec. 175; Taylor v. Secrist, 2 Disn. (Ohio) 299; Cowles v. Pointer, 26 Miss. 253; Rodgers v. Stophel, 32 Pa. 111, 72 Am. Dec. 775; Ducker v. Barnett, 5 Mo. 97; Mechanics' & T. Co. v. Kiger, 103 U. S. 352, 26 L. Ed. 433. A warehouseman is not liable as a common carrier, but only for ordinary diligence. Ducker v. Barnett, 5 Mo. 97; Cincinnati & C. Air Line R. Co. v. McCool, 26 Ind. 140; Holtzclaw v. Duff, 27 Mo. 392; Titsworth v. Winnegar, 51 Barb. (N. Y.) 148; Knapp v. Curtis, 9 Wend. (N. Y.) 60. The duty of warehousemen imposes on them the exercise of ordinary care only, or, in other words, the care and diligence which good and capable warehousemen are accustomed to show under similar circumstances. Lancaster Mills v. Merchants' Cotton-Press Co., 89 Tenn. 1, 14 S. W. 317, 24 Am. St. Rep. 586. Whatever a diligent man would deem necessary, under any given circumstances, for the preservation of his own property, must be done by the individual, or corporation, or city, that undertakes, for hire, the preservation of property for the public. Willey v. Allegheny City, 118 Pa. 490, 12 Atl. 453, 4 Am. St. Rep. 608. See, also, the following modern cases: Denver Public Warehouse Co. v. Munger, 20 Colo. App. 56, 77 Pac. 5; Charlotte Trouser Co. v. Seaboard Air Line R. Co., 139 N. C. 382, 51 S. E. 973; Louisville & N. R. Co. v. United States, 39 Ct. Cl. 405; Wiley v. Locke, 81 Kan. 143, 105 Pac. 11, 24 L. R. A. (N. S.) 1117, 19 Ann. Cas. 241; Baltimore Refrigerating & Heating Co. v. Kreiner, 109 Md. 361, 71 Atl. 1066.

12 Davis v. Hurt, 114 Ala. 146, 21 South. 468; Taussig v. Bode & Haslett, 134 Cal. 260, 66 Pac. 259, 54 L. R. A. 774, 86 Am. St. Rep. 250; Geo. C. Bagley Elevator Co. v. American Exp. Co., 63 Minn. 142, 65 N. W. 264; Evans v. New York & P. S. S. Co. (D. C.) 163 Fed. 405; Hoeveller v. Myers, 158 Pa. 461, 27 Atl. 1081; Marks v. New Orleans Cold Storage Co., 107 La. 172, 31 South. 671, 57 L. R. A. 271, 90 Am. St. Rep. 285.

13 Security Storage & Trust Co. v. Denys, 119 Md. 330, 86 Atl. 613; Buffalo Grain Co. v. Sowerby, 195 N. Y. 355, 88 N. E. 569; Baltimore & O. R. Co. v. Schumacher, 29 Md. 168, 96 Am. Dec. 510; Sibley Warehouse & Storage Co. v. Durand & Kasper Co., 200 Ill. 354, 65 N. E. 676; Mayer v. Brensinger, 180 Ill. 110, 54 N. E. 159, 72 Am. St. Rep. 196; Muskogee Crystal Ice Co. v. Riley Bros., 24 Okl. 114, 108 Pac. 629. In Chenowith v. Dickinson, 8 B. Mon. (Ky.) 156, it appeared that 900 barrels of salt were stored in a frame warehouse, on an alley. Two hundred and forty barrels were stolen, in quantities ranging from 20 to 25 barrels a day, so that the entire 240 barrels were taken at about 10 different times, running through a period of one month. It was held that the defendants were negligent in failing to exercise any further care or supervision after placing the salt in the warehouse.

14 Moulton v. Phillips, 10 R. I. 218, 14 Am. Rep. 663; Walden v. Finch, 70 Pa. 460. See Hickey v. Morrell, 102 N. Y. 454, 7 N. E. 321, 55 Am. Rep. 824. Cf. Hallock v. Mallett, 55 N. Y. Super. Ct. 265. The law does not require a warehouseman to construct his buildings secure from all possible contingencies. If they are reasonably and ordinarily safe against ordinary

agencies as fire,[15] theft,[16] heat or cold,[17] and dampness. Modern improvements have made tremendous strides in devising and perfecting such protective methods, and with these the warehouseman must keep pace. He need not be among the first to try every new device; he must not be among the last to abandon such as are old and outworn. Particularly is this true when perishable goods are received in "cold storage,"[18] a business which modern

and common occurrences, it is sufficient. Cowles v. Pointer, 26 Miss. 253. See, also, Schouler, Bailm. (2d Ed.) § 102; Hatchett v. Gibson, 13 Ala. 587; Jones v. Hatchett, 14 Ala. 743; Chenowith v. Dickinson, 8 B. Mon. (Ky.) 156; Moulton v. Phillips, 10 R. I. 218, 14 Am. Rep. 663. The bailee may show that the bailor approved of the place of storage, and that the goods were damp when delivered, and liable to mildew; and the bailor, that the goods were in the ordinary trade condition, and that the bailee knew they should have been aired and dried. Brown v. Hitchcock, 28 Vt. 452. Where a bailee to store cotton for hire permitted it to remain with the roping off, the bagging torn, the cotton loose, and the under bales in the mud, whereby it was much injured, held, that it was a want of ordinary care. Morehead v. Brown, 51 N. C. 367.

15 McLane, Swift & Co. v. Botsford Elevator Co., 136 Mich. 664, 99 N. W. 875, 112 Am. St. Rep. 384; Walker v. Eikleberry, 7 Okl. 599, 54 Pac. 553. A warehouseman who agrees to store the property in a fireproof building is liable for any loss caused by his failure to do so. Vincent v. Rather, 31 Tex. 77, 98 Am. Dec. 516. See, also, Jones v. Hatchett, 14 Ala. 743; Hatchett v. Gibson, 13 Ala. 587. In Hamilton v. Elstner, 24 La. Ann. 455, the warehouseman was held liable for failure to remove the goods to a place of safety after knowledge of danger from the fire.

16 Lockwood v. Manhattan Storage & Warehouse Co., 28 App. Div. 68, 50 N. Y. Supp. 974; Murray v. International S. S. Co., 170 Mass. 166, 48 N. E. 1093, 64 Am. St. Rep. 290; Moore v. Mayor, etc., of City of Mobile, 1 Stew. (Ala.) 284; COGGS v. BERNARD, 2 Ld. Raym. (Eng.) 909, Dobie Cas. Bailments and Carriers, 1; Vere v. Smith, 1 Vent. (Eng.) 121; Coke, Inst. 89a; Southcote v. Bennet, 4 Coke (Eng.) 83b; Lamb v Western R. Corp., 7 Allen (Mass.) 98; Cass v. Boston & L. R. Co., 14 Allen (Mass.) 448; Claflin v. Meyer, 75 N. Y. 260, 31 Am. Rep. 467; Platt v. Hibbard, 7 Cow. (N. Y.) 497; Schmidt v. Blood, 9 Wend. (N. Y.) 268, 24 Am. Dec. 143; Williamson v. New York, N. H. & H. R. Co. (Super. Ct.) 4 N. Y. Supp. 834; Williams v. Holland, 22 How. Prac. (N. Y.) 137; Berry v. Marix, 16 La. Ann. 248. Warehousemen not chargeable with negligence are not answerable for goods intrusted to them, in case of robbery, or when embezzled by their storekeeper or servant; and the onus of showing negligence is on the owner. Schmidt v. Blood, 9 Wend. (N. Y.) 268, 24 Am. Dec. 143; Moore v. Mayor, etc., of City of Mobile, 1 Stew. (Ala.) 284.

17 Rudell v. Grand Rapids Cold Storage Co., 136 Mich. 528, 99 N. W. 756; Sutherland v. Albany Cold Storage & Warehouse Co., 171 N. Y. 269, 63 N. E. 1100, 89 Am. St. Rep. 815. As to rats, see Cailiff v. Danvers, 1 Peake (Eng.) 155. The constant presence of a terrier dog is sufficient precaution, Taylor v. Secrist, 2 Disn. (Ohio) 299, 301; or of a cat, Cailiff v. Danvers, 1 Peake (Eng.) 155; Aymar v. Astor, 6 Cow. (N. Y.) 266, 267. But see, contra, Laveroni v. Drury, 16 Jur. (Eng.) 1024, 22 L. J. Exch. 2.

18 See, in general, the following cold storage cases: Baltimore Refrigerating

methods of refrigeration and temperature control have raised to a state of unusual efficiency.

The warehouseman, as is the case with other bailees, is not in general required by ordinary care to take out fire insurance on the goods.[19] He can do so, however, for the full value of the goods, holding any excess beyond his own interest in trust for the bailor.

Warehouse Receipts—Usage—Lien

It is the custom of warehousemen, on receiving goods to be stored, to issue a receipt or delivery order upon the presentation of which the goods are to be surrendered to the bailor or his order. These instruments are called "warehouse receipts," and in their general nature and legal incidents they are similar to the carrier's bills of lading.[20] They are issued primarily in order that, as a symbol or representative of the goods, they might furnish the bailor an effective and simple method of dealing with the goods,[21] as by a sale or pledge. They are not, strictly speaking, negotiable; but a transfer of the warehouse receipt, in general, confers the same measure of title that an actual delivery of the goods which it represents would confer.[22] Warehouse receipts are discussed in other connections, and what is said as to bills of lading, in regard to their transfer and the rights conferred on their transferee, is, in general, equally true of warehouse receipts.[23]

The part that custom and usage may play in affecting the rights and duties of bailees is accentuated in the case of warehousemen. Such usages may and do explain and qualify the warehouseman's

& Heating Co. v. Kreiner, 109 Md. 361, 71 Atl. 1066 (failure to construct proper ice box and cold storage cellar); Greenwich Warehouse Co. v. Maxfield, 8 Misc. Rep. 308, 28 N. Y. Supp. 732 (freezing of fruit stored); LEIDY v. QUAKER CITY COLD STORAGE & WAREHOUSE CO., 180 Pa. 323, 36 Atl. 851, Dobie Cas. Bailments and Carriers, 100 (poultry molded by moisture).

19 Atwater v. Hannah & Co., 116 Ga. 745, 42 S. E. 1007.

20 See post, pp. 196, 214. See 35 Am. Bar Ass'n Rep. (1910) 1116, as to Uniform Warehouse Receipts Act and its adoption in various states. See also, McClain v. Merchants' Warehouse Co., 115 Fed. 295, 53 C. C. A. 155; Canadian Bank of Commerce v. McCrea, 106 Ill. 281, 292; Millhiser Mfg. Co. v. Gallego Mills Co., 101 Va. 579, 44 S. E. 760; Miller v. Browarsky, 130 Pa. 372, 373, 18 Atl. 643.

21 Livingston v. U. Anderson & Son, 2 Ga. App. 274, 58 S. E. 505; Citizens' Banking Co. v. Peacock, 103 Ga. 171, 29 S. E. 752; Bush v. Export Storage Co. (C. C.) 136 Fed. 918; Friedman v. Peters, 18 Tex. Civ. App. 11, 44 S. W. 572.

22 McNeil v. Hill, 16 Fed. Cas. No. 8,914; Millhiser Mfg. Co. v. Gallego Mills Co., 101 Va. 579, 44 S. E. 760; Solomon v. Bushnell, 11 Or. 277, 3 Pac. 677, 50 Am. Rep. 475; Gibson v. Stevens, 8 How. 384, 12 L. Ed. 1123.

23 See post, pp. 196, 211-214, 418.

contract to a highly appreciable extent, but custom and usage are never permitted to contradict a positive rule of law.

The warehouseman's lien is a special and not a general one.[24] It is therefore controlled by the rules applicable to special liens, which have been previously discussed.[25]

In general, the liability of the warehouseman begins only when the goods have been delivered on his premises, and expressly or impliedly received by him.[26] It has been held that as soon as the goods arrive, and the crane of the warehouse is applied to raise them into the warehouse, the liability of the warehouseman begins.[27] If a warehouseman consents to take charge of goods before they reach the warehouse, he is liable from the moment that he thus takes charge. The liability[28] of a warehouseman ends with his delivery of the goods to the person rightfully entitled to them. Thus, where wheat is discharged into a vessel through a pipe controlled by the vessel, the warehouseman's liability ends with the discharge into the pipe.[29] The liability of the warehouseman also ceases when the goods are taken from his possession without fault on his part, or lost by means for which he is not responsible.[30]

The general principle of bailments, that the bailee must return to the bailor the identical goods delivered, of course, applies to the warehouseman.[31] In practice, however, the actual working of the rule is often done away with as to warehousemen, when the

[24] Schumacher v. Chicago & N. W. R. Co., 207 Ill. 199, 69 N. E. 825; J. I. Case Plow Works v. Union Iron Works, 56 Mo. App. 1; Reidenback v. Tuck (Sup.) 85 N. Y. Supp. 352; Wesling v. Noonan, 31 Miss. 599.

[25] Ante, § 64.

[26] Burr v. Daugherty, 21 Ark. 559; Vincent v. Rather, 31 Tex. 77, 98 Am. Dec. 516; Rodgers v. Stophel, 32 Pa. 111, 72 Am. Dec. 775; Blin v. Mayo, 10 Vt. 56, 33 Am. Dec. 175. See, also, Titsworth v. Winnegar, 51 Barb. (N. Y.) 148. A warehouseman cannot have possession of another's property, with its accompanying duties and responsibilities, forced upon him against his will. Delaware, L. & W. R. Co. v. Central S. Y. & T. Co., 45 N. J. Eq. 50, 17 Atl. 146, 6 L. R. A. 855. A warehouseman is responsible for the safety and security of goods after delivery in the warehouse on Sunday, the safe-keeping of goods being a work of necessity. Powhatan Steamboat Co. v. Appomattox R. Co., 24 How. 247, 16 L. Ed. 682.

[27] Thomas v. Day, 4 Esp. (Eng.) 262. See, also, De Mott v. Laraway, 14 Wend. (N. Y.) 225, 28 Am. Dec. 523; Randleson v. Murray, 8 Adol. & E. (Eng.) 109; Merritt v. Old Colony & N. R. Co., 11 Allen (Mass.) 80; Jeffersonville R. Co. v. White, 6 Bush (Ky.) 251, 252.

[28] Ducker v. Barnett, 5 Mo. 97.

[29] The R. G. Winslow, 4 Biss. 13, Fed. Cas. No. 11,736.

[30] Sessions v. Western R. Corp., 16 Gray (Mass.) 132. Cf. Smith v. Frost, 51 Ga. 336.

[31] United States v. Oregon R. & Navigation Co. (C. C.) 159 Fed. 975; Hale v. Milwaukee Dock Co., 29 Wis. 482, 9 Am. Rep. 603.

bailors expressly or impliedly (as by custom) consent to have their goods (generally grain) mixed in a common mass of similar goods, and each bailor has the right to withdraw from the uniform mass the quantity he deposited.[32] Under such an arrangement, as we have already seen, the transaction is none the less a bailment because the bailor does not receive back the identical grain deposited, and each bailor remains the owner of a share in the mass determined by the percentage that the amount his deposit is of the entire mass.[33]

SAME—WHARFINGERS

A wharfinger is one who owns or keeps a wharf for the purpose of receiving and shipping merchandise to or from it for hire.[34] The control of their own wharves by modern transportation companies has greatly diminished the practical importance of the wharfinger. He is in no sense a common carrier, fulfilling neither word of the term. The liabilities of wharfingers are thus substantially similar to those of warehousemen. They are therefore, like the latter, responsible only for ordinary care in securing the goods from loss or damage.[35]

The responsibility of a wharfinger begins and ends when he acquires, and when he ceases to have, the custody of the goods in that capacity.[36] His liability thus begins when the goods are delivered on the wharf and he has either expressly or impliedly received them. This is frequently governed by custom or usage, which plays an unusually important part in this business. A mere delivery of goods at a wharf is not necessarily a delivery of them to the wharfinger, but there must be some act or assent on his part, which may be either express or implied, to the custody of the goods.[37] Where goods are in the wharfinger's possession, to be sent on board of a vessel for a voyage, as soon as he delivers the

[32] Bretz v. Diehl, 117 Pa. 589, 11 Atl. 893, 2 Am. St. Rep. 706; Hutchison v. Commonwealth, 82 Pa. 472; Chase v. Washburn, 1 Ohio St. 244, 59 Am. Dec. 623.

[33] Ante, p. 8.

[34] Black, Law Dict. (2d Ed.) p. 1226; Rodgers v. Stophel, 32 Pa. 111, 113, 72 Am. Dec. 775; Chapman v. State, 104 Cal. 690, 694, 38 Pac. 457, 43 Am. St. Rep. 158.

[35] Buckingham v. Fisher, 70 Ill. 121; Blin v. Mayo, 10 Vt. 56, 33 Am. Dec. 175; Foote v. Storrs, 2 Barb. (N. Y.) 326; Cox v. O'Riley, 4 Ind. 368, 58 Am. Dec. 633.

[36] Rodgers v. Stophel, 32 Pa. 111, 72 Am. Dec. 775; Blin v. Mayo, 10 Vt. 56, 33 Am. Dec. 175.

[37] Buckman v. Levi, 3 Camp. (Eng.) 414; Gibson v. Inglis, 4 Camp. (Eng.) 72; Packard v. Getman, 6 Cow. (N. Y.) 757, 16 Am. Dec. 475.

possession and care of them to the proper officers of the vessel, although they are not actually removed from his wharf, he is deemed exonerated from any further responsibility, and the goods are deemed to be in the constructive possession of the officers of the ship.[38]

A wharfinger, like other depositaries for hire, has a lien on the goods for his wharfage.[39] By inveterate custom, the wharfinger seems to have been among the few favored bailees to whom the law gives a general, as opposed to a special, lien.[40]

SAME—SAFE-DEPOSIT COMPANIES

Safe-deposit companies make a business of renting to the public for a compensation the control of drawers, boxes, safes, or even rooms in their vaults.[41] In these drawers, boxes, or safes, the persons renting them keep such valuables as papers or corporeal chattels of small bulk. During the time for which the drawer or box is rented, the renter alone has access to the drawer or box, to the exclusion even of the officers of the safe-deposit company. The property kept in the drawer or box is usually unknown to the company; in fact, this very secrecy is one of the elements highly desired by the depositor, and for which he pays the compensation. Secrecy and security are, indeed, the distinctive advantages accruing to the renter.

The company has control of the vault in which the drawer or box is situated. Its chief duty is to prevent any person other than the renter from having access to such drawer or box, and to

[38] "When the responsibility of the ship begins, that of the wharfinger ends." Lord Ellenborough in Cobban v. Downe, 5 Esp. (Eng.) 41. A wharfinger who has illegally detained goods, which the owner has since agreed to accept and send for, is not liable for their destruction by fire, without his fault, after the owner has had a reasonable time to remove them. Carnes v. Nichols, 10 Gray (Mass.) 369. See, also, Merritt v. Old Colony & N. R. Co., 11 Allen (Mass.) 80, 83; Gass v. New York, P. & B. R. Co., 99 Mass. 227, 96 Am. Dec. 742.

[39] Johnson v. The McDonough, Gilp. 101, Fed. Cas. No. 7,395; Ex parte Lewis, 2 Gall. 483, Fed. Cas. No. 8,310; Vaylor v. Mangles, 1 Esp. (Eng.) 109; Spears v. Hartly, 3 Esp. (Eng.) 81; Holderness v. Collinson, 7 Barn. & C. (Eng.) 212. See, generally, Brookman v. Hamill, 43 N. Y. 554, 3 Am. Rep. 731; Lenckhart v. Cooper, 3 Bing. N. C. (Eng.) 99; Barry v. Longmore, 4 Perry & D. (Eng.) 344. And see Sage v. Gittner, 11 Barb. (N. Y.) 120.

[40] Taylor v. Margles, 1 Esp. (Eng.) 109; Spears v. Hartley, 3 Esp. (Eng.) 81; Dresser v. Bosanquet, 4 Best & S. (Eng.) 460; Holderness v. Collinson, 7 Barn. & C. (Eng.) 212, 14 E. C. L. 30.

[41] Bouv. Law Dict.; Cent. Dict.

protect the contents thereof as well from personal as from impersonal destructive agencies, such as theft, fire, flood, etc. To this end, the company usually employs elaborate instrumentalities, both animate and inanimate.

The phenomenal development of this business, particularly in the important financial centers of the country, has compelled the courts to discuss the nature of the relation between the renter of the box, drawer, etc., and the company. That cases of loss or damage have so seldom been before the courts is a striking testimony to the efficiency of the companies in safeguarding the property in their vaults. At one time courts and writers seem to have taken it for granted that the relation was one of bailment and adjudged accordingly.[42] Judge Sharswood, however, in an early case,[43] pointed out that the contents of the safe remained in the possession of the renter. If this be true, and it can hardly be gainsaid, there has been no transfer of possession, and hence no delivery. Without a delivery, there can be no bailment.

In some of the cases holding the relation to be that of bailment, it was not at all necessary to the decision in the case to pronounce the defendant a bailee, as it was clearly liable for a breach of its contract undertaking. This was true, for example, in Roberts v. Stuyvesant Safe-Deposit Co.,[44] where the company was held liable for permitting property to be removed from a vault rented by it to the plaintiff, under color of legal process, which, in fact, did not authorize the officers of the law to seize the property. In another case,[45] the company agreed to "keep a constant and adequate guard over and upon the burglar-proof safe," and it was held that the mere disappearance of the plaintiff's bonds constituted a prima facie case against the company. The correctness of these decisions

[42] Roberts v. Stuyvesant Safe Deposit Co., 123 N. Y. 57, 25 N. E. 294, 9 L. R. A. 438, 20 Am. St. Rep. 718; Schouler, Bailm. (2d Ed.) § 96; Lawson, Bailm. § 44. The relation was also held to be that of bailor and bailee in the following cases, both citing the Roberts Case: Mayer v. Brensinger, 180 Ill. 110, 54 N. E. 159, 72 Am. St. Rep. 196; Cussen v. Southern California Sav. Bank, 133 Cal. 534, 65 Pac. 1099, 85 Am. St. Rep. 221. See, also, Lockwood v. Manhattan Storage & Warehouse Co., 28 App. Div. 68, 50 N. Y. Supp. 974, 72 Am. St. Rep. 206, note; Guaranty Trust Co. v. Diltz, 42 Tex. Civ. App. 26, 91 S. W. 596.

[43] Gregg v. Hilson, 8 Phila. (Pa.) 91. Said Sharswood, J.: "The contents of the safe are in actual possession of the renter of the safe. They have not been deposited with or demised to the company." See, also, United States v. Graff, 67 Barb. (N. Y.) 304.

[44] 123 N. Y. 57, 25 N. E. 294, 9 L. R. A. 438, 20 Am. St. Rep. 718.

[45] SAFE DEPOSIT CO. OF PITTSBURGH v. POLLOCK, 85 Pa. 391, 27 Am. Rep. 660, Dobie Cas. Bailments and Carriers, 101.

seems hardly open to question, but whether the transactions involved were bailments is quite another question.[46]

In view of the considerations mentioned, it seems that the relation in question is not that of bailor and bailee, nor that of landlord and tenant, nor yet that of master and servant, but is rather an anomalous combination of the three.[47] The similarity between safe-deposit companies and bailees seems to lie in the fact that the former by express contract assume certain duties which, in the case of the latter, are imposed by law, when there is no express contract, as being implicit in the bailment relation.

It should be noted, though, that when (as is usually the case) ordinary care is the measure of the company's duty, either as arising from express contract or being implied from custom and usage, this term here involves a high measure of diligence and watchfulness.[48] This follows from the fact that the very nature of the business implies that the property in the drawers or boxes is usually of small bulk and comparatively great value, thus offering an unusual temptation to the most skilled criminals.

SAME—FACTORS OR COMMISSION MERCHANTS

The factor, or commission merchant, as he is frequently called, is one who makes a business of selling goods sent to him by others

[46] In Jones v. Morgan, 90 N. Y. 4, 43 Am. Rep. 131, it appeared that plaintiff had rented a room in a storehouse from defendant, who contracted to guard it. The door to the room had two locks, the key of one of which was kept by plaintiff. The property was stolen from the room, and, in an action for damages, plaintiff contended that the defendant was a bailee, while the defendant claimed that the relation was that of landlord and tenant. The court said that the relation was one of bailment, though it was not necessary to a decision of the case. The case was likened to that of one who hires a box in a safe-deposit company. The defendant was held liable on his contract, irrespective of whether it created a bailment. In Peers v. Sampson, 4 Dowl. & R. (Eng.) 636, where a room was hired in which to store goods, the key being kept by the hirer, it was held that the owner of the house was not liable for a theft of the goods by his servant, on the ground that the goods had never been delivered to him for safe-keeping. See, also, East India Co. v. Pullen, 1 Strange (Eng.) 690.

[47] See Van Zile, Bailm. & Carr. § 196: "It would appear that the relation is not that of bailor and bailee in the full meaning of that relation, but that it answers more nearly to that of landlord and tenant, or of leasing space in the deposit vault or banking house." Says Street (2 Found. Leg. Liab. p. 291): "It is clear that this is not a bailment. The company does not have possession, and there is no delivery. The liability of the company must therefore be determined entirely by the contract and usages of business incident to carrying it out."

[48] See cases cited in preceding notes.

for that purpose.[49] He differs from the broker, in that he has possession of the goods to be sold.[50] Thus the factor is at the same time a bailee in possession of the goods,[51] and also an agent authorized to make a binding sale of them to a third person. In his rôle of bailee, the factor is governed by the general principles of bailments, which here present in their application no unique difficulty. As an agent with a power of sale, the factor gives more trouble (both to judges and to those with whom he deals); but the questions raised here belong more properly to a work on Agency.[52]

Just as other bailees for mutual benefit, to which class the factor belongs by virtue of his commission, the factor is bound to use good faith and ordinary care; but, if these be exercised, he is not responsible for either loss of, or damage to, the goods.[53]

The factor is also in the favored class of bailees having a general lien. He can therefore hold the goods of his bailor in his possession to secure a general balance due to him from such bailor arising out of a series of factorage transactions.[54]

SAME—OFFICERS CHARGED WITH THE CUSTODY OF PUBLIC FUNDS

Public officers, charged with the custody of public funds, fall within the definition of bailees for hire.[55] In England these seem

49 Black, Law Dict. p. 476; Howland v. Woodruff, 60 N. Y. 80; In re Rabenau (D. C.) 118 Fed. 474; Ruffner v. Hewitt, 7 W. Va. 585. In some states factors are defined by statute. See, for example, Civ. Code Cal. § 2026.

50 Delafield v. Smith, 101 Wis. 664, 78 N. W. 170, 70 Am. St. Rep. 938; Edwards v. Hoeffinghoff (C. C.) 38 Fed. 641.

51 Substantially a warehouseman.

52 See Mechem on Agency, §§ 986a–1052.

53 Ives v. Freisinger, 70 N. J. Law, 257, 57 Atl. 401; Roberts v. Cobb, 76 Minn. 420, 79 N. W. 540; Weaver v. Poyer, 70 Ill. 567; Dunbar v. Gregg, 44 Ill. App. 527; Bogert v. Dorsey, 14 La. 430; Jervis v. Hoyt, 2 Hun (N. Y.) 637. They are at liberty to act according to the general usages of trade, and to give credit on sales, wherever that is customary. They are bound, however, in all cases, to follow the lawful instructions of their principals. If they act with reasonable diligence and good faith, they are protected. In cases of unforeseen emergency and necessity, they may even act contrary to the general tenor of the instructions of their principal, if those instructions are manifestly applicable to ordinary circumstances only. But good faith alone is not sufficient. There must be reasonable skill, and a careful obedience to orders, on their part.

54 Johnson v. Clark, 20 Ind. App. 247, 50 N. E. 762; Cator v. Merrill, 16 La. Ann. 137; Matthews v. Menedger, 2 McLean, 145, Fed. Cas. No. 9,289; Winne v. Hammond, 37 Ill. 99; Archer v. McMechan, 21 Mo. 43.

55 "They are nothing but bailees. To call them anything else, when they are expressly forbidden to touch or use the public money, except as directed,

to be held responsible only as bailees, and they are therefore not held liable for the loss of funds due to act of God or irresistible force.[56] This view is also held in many of the states of this country.[57]

According, however, to the weight of authority in the United States, the public officer becomes an insurer of the safety of the public funds in his possession, and is thereby absolutely responsible for any loss, even though he is guilty of no fault or neglect.[58] This absolute liability is based partly on considerations of public policy, and partly on the language of the officer's official bond. Some writers see in the theory of absolute liability a reversion to the primitive theory under which the bailee was liable as a debtor.[59]

Many of the more recent cases tend to soften the rigor of the doctrine of holding the public officer an insurer and adopt the saner English rule, holding the officer liable only for his negligence.[60] There are also statutes (both state [61] and federal [62]) passed for the relief of officers in no wise negligent.

would be an abuse of terms." United States v. Thomas, 15 Wall. 347, 21 L. Ed. 89. See, also, Wilson v. People, 19 Colo. 199, 34 Pac. 944, 22 L. R. A. 449, 41 Am. St. Rep. 243; State v. Houston, 78 Ala. 576, 56 Am. Rep. 59; Marx v. Parker, 9 Wash. 473, 37 Pac. 675, 43 Am. St. Rep. 849; Story, Bailm. § 620; 2 Street, Found. Leg. Liab. pp. 292, 293. See, for an excellent note on the liability of public officers for loss of public money (with extensive collection of authorities), 17 Ann. Cas. 929.

56 Walker v. British Guarantee Ass'n, 18 Q. B. 277, 83 E. C. L. 277.

57 Wilson v. People, 19 Colo. 199, 34 Pac. 944, 22 L. R. A. 449, 41 Am. St. Rep. 243; Healdsburg v. Mulligan, 113 Cal. 205, 45 Pac. 337, 33 L. R. A. 461; INHABITANTS OF CUMBERLAND COUNTY v. PENNELL, 69 Me. 357, 31 Am. Rep. 284, Dobie Cas. Bailments and Carriers, 106; State v. Copeland, 96 Tenn. 296, 34 S. W. 427, 31 L. R. A. 844, 54 Am. St. Rep. 840; Roberts v. Board of Com'rs of Laramie County, 8 Wyo. 177, 56 Pac. 915.

58 The leading case is UNITED STATES v. PRESCOTT, 3 How. 578, 11 L. Ed. 734, Dobie Cas. Bailments and Carriers, 104, holding a receiver of public money liable who was robbed without any lack of care on his part; and any claim that the Thomas Case, 15 Wall. 337, 21 L. Ed. 89, had relaxed this rule was negatived in Smythe v. United States, 188 U. S. 156, 23 Sup. Ct. 279, 47 L. Ed. 425. See, also, State v. Wood, 51 Ark. 205, 10 S. W. 624; Town of Cicero v. Grisko, 240 Ill. 220, 88 N. E. 478; Inhabitants of Hancock v. Hazzard, 12 Cush. (Mass.) 112, 59 Am. Dec. 171; Tillinghast v. Merrill, 151 N. Y. 135, 45 N. E. 375, 34 L. R. A. 678, 56 Am. St. Rep. 612; Commonwealth v. Baily, 129 Pa. 480, 10 Atl. 764; Van Tress v. Territory, 7 Okl. 353, 54 Pac. 495.

59 2 Street, Found. Leg. Liab. p. 293, note 4.

60 See cases cited in note 57; also, State v. Houston, 78 Ala. 576, 56 Am. Rep. 59; York County v. Watson, 15 S. C. 1, 40 Am. Rep. 675; City of Living-

61 See McSurely v. McGrew, 140 Iowa, 163, 118 N. W. 415, 132 Am. St. Rep. 248; Board of Education v. McLandsborough, 36 Ohio St. 227, 38 Am. Rep. 582.

62 See note 62 on following page.

TERMINATION OF THE BAILMENT

68. Locatio operis bailments may be terminated by—
(1) Act of the parties.
(a) Accomplishment of the bailment purpose.
(b) Mutual consent of bailor and bailee.
(c) Bailee's wrong, at option of bailor.
(2) Operation of law.
(a) Destruction of bailed goods.
Ordinarily, neither death nor change in the legal status of the parties terminates the bailment.

Act of the Parties

The termination of locatio operis under this head presents no difficulty, and what is said as to locatio rei applies equally here.[63] It is equally true, here as there, that neither bailor nor bailee has a right to terminate the bailment without the consent of the other.

Operation of Law

Here the analogies of locatio rei also apply. The destruction of the bailed goods necessarily [64] terminates the bailment. The death of the bailor does not terminate the bailment, nor does the death of the bailee, unless the bailment is a personal one. It would also seem that neither the bankruptcy of the bailor nor that of the bailee would, of itself, terminate the bailment. The insanity of the bailor, it would seem, would not terminate the bailment any more than his death; nor would the insanity of the bailee, it seems, unless the bailment were personal.

ston v. Woods, 20 Mont. 91, 49 Pac. 437. Some cases seem to take a middle ground, and exempt the officer when the loss is due to act of God or public enemy. See Adams v. Lee, 72 Miss. 281, 16 South. 243; Thompson v. Board of Trustees of Township 16, 30 Ill. 99; Union Dist. Tp. v. Smith, 39 Iowa, 9, 18 Am. Rep. 39.

[62] See Rev. St. §§ 1059, 1062, 2 Fed. St. Ann. pp. 59, 62, Act May 9, 1866, c. 75, §§ 1, 2, 14 Stat. 44 (U. S. Comp. St. 1901, pp. 734, 737); Judicial Code (Act March 3, 1911, c. 231) § 145 (3), 36 Stat. 1137 (U. S. Comp. St. Supp. 1911, p. 199), conferring jurisdiction on the Court of Claims to hear cases for relief of disbursing officers losing money without fault. See, also, United States v. Clark, 96 U. S. 37, 24 L. Ed. 696; Glenn's Case, 4 Ct. Cl. 501; Penrose v. United States, 42 Ct. Cl. 29.

[63] Ante, § 56.

[64] Ante, § 20.

REDELIVERY OF THE BAILED GOODS

69. As in other bailments, upon the termination of the bailment, the duty rests upon the bailee to redeliver the goods according to the directions of the bailor.

Redelivery by the bailee on the termination of a locatio operis bailment is governed by the principles applicable to other classes of bailments, which have already been sufficiently discussed.[65]

[65] Ante, § 19.

CHAPTER VII

BAILMENTS FOR MUTUAL BENEFIT—PLEDGES

DEFINITIONS AND DISTINCTIONS

70. A pledge or pawn is a bailment to secure the payment of a debt, or the performance of an engagement, accompanied by a power of sale in case of default.

Historical

The practice of giving possession of a chattel by the owner to another to secure a debt or to insure the performance of some engagement is of great antiquity, and laws governing such pawns or pledges are to be found among all the nations of ancient times. Thus more or less elaborate provisions on this subject are found in the Israelitic code of Moses,[1] the monumental Babylonian code

[1] Thus provisions are found in the earliest of these codes, in the Book of the Covenant, a part of the so-called JE Code. "If thou at all take thy neighbor's raiment to pledge, thou shalt deliver it unto him by that the sun goeth down." Exodus, xxii, 26. Further humanitarian restrictions are found in the code of Deuteronomy. Deut. xxiv, 6, 10-13.

of Hammurabi[2] and in other codes of the Orient.[3] In England, the law of pledges was of little practical importance until 1546, when, for the first time, the taking of interest on money loans was made legal. Since then, however, the English law of pledges has received a tremendous development, and to-day, both in England and the United States, the pledge is among the most frequent and important of commercial transactions.

Pawnbrokers are those who make a business of loaning money on the security of corporeal property,[4] rather than incorporeal property, such as corporate stock. In many countries, as in France, the business of pawnbroking is carried on as a public institution, so that money may be borrowed by the poor at a reasonable rate of interest. In England and in the United States, however, it is carried on, just as any other enterprise, by individuals; but in almost all of the states of this country the business is to a greater or less degree regulated by special statutes.[5]

Definitions

As in the case of other bailments, many and various definitions of a pledge or pawn have been given. Those that follow are among the most important. Lord Holt[6] defines it as existing "when goods or chattels are delivered to another, to be a security to him for money borrowed of him by the bailor." By Sir William Jones[7] it is defined to be "a bailment of goods by a debtor to his creditor, to be kept by him till his debt is discharged." Both of these definitions, however, are faulty in two respects. First, they fail to recognize the fact that the pledge need not be solely to secure the payment of money, but it may be created for the purpose of insuring the performance of any other lawful engagement on the part of the bailor, or even to secure the undertaking of a third party, on whose account the bailor has made the bailment; and, secondly, neither states that there is in a pledge an implied power of sale

[2] See Cook, The Laws of Moses and the Code of Hammurabi, p. 232 et seq. According to Lee, Historical Jurisprudence, p. 30, "the Babylonians pledged property of every description."

[3] Pledges were known to the early law of Egypt. See Lee, Historical Jurisprudence, pp. 71–74. The same is true of India. Lee, pp. 146–150.

[4] City of Chicago v. Hulbert, 118 Ill. 632, 8 N. E. 812, 59 Am. Rep. 400; Schaul v. City of Charlotte, 118 N. C. 733, 24 S. E. 526. See, also, Rev. St. Ohio 1880, § 4387.

[5] These statutes usually cover the rate of interest which a pawnbroker may charge and the formalities of a sale of the pledged article. A typical statute is that of Virginia. Pollard's Va. Code 1904, vol. 2, pp. 2232–2235.

[6] In COGGS v. BERNARD, 2 Ld. Raym. (Eng.) 909, 913, Dobie Cas. Bailments and Carriers, 1.

[7] Bailm. § 35.

on default. This implied power of sale is an important element in distinguishing a pledge from other transactions that lie close to it, such, for example, as a lien. The definitions of more modern writers are given in the notes.[8]

In a number of states, pledges have been defined by statute. Thus, in California, "a pledge is a deposit of personal property by way of security for the performance of another act."[9] And this definition has been copied by the codes of North Dakota,[10] South Dakota,[11] and Montana.[12] Other definitions are found in other codes.[13]

Lien, Pledge, and Chattel Mortgage Distinguished

Pledges are most nearly allied to liens and to chattel mortgages. It therefore becomes necessary to distinguish clearly between them.

The lien and pledge are similar, in that the general property or ownership of the goods does not pass either to the lienholder or to the pledgee, but in each case a special property in the goods does.

8 Thus Story (Bailm. § 286) defines a pledge broadly as "a bailment of personal property as security for some debt or engagement." Substantially similar is Mr. Schouler's definition, as "the bailment of a chattel as security for some debt or engagement." Judge L. A. Jones (Jones on Collateral Securities [3d Ed.] § 1) defines a pledge as "a deposit of personal property as security, with an implied power of sale on default." See, also, Black, Law Dict. "Pledge," p. 905; 31 Cyc. 785, and note, giving various definitions.

In the Roman law a pledge or pawn is called "pignus," but it was the rule of the civil law that a pledge could never be sold, unless authorized by special agreement, except under a judicial sentence; and this appears to be the law at this day in many countries in Europe, and it was the rule in the old English law in the time of Glanville. Lib. 10, cc. 1, 6; Hart v. Ten Eyck, 2 Johns. Ch. (N. Y.) 62. In the Roman law, also, a pawn (pignus) was distinguished from a hypothecation (hypotheca), in this: That in the former alone was the possession delivered to the pledgee; in the latter, it was retained by the pledgor, and was thus not a bailment at all. However, the words "pignus" and "hypotheca" seem often to have been confounded. See, also, Jackson v. Kincaid, 4 Okl. 554, 46 Pac. 587; FIRST NAT. BANK OF PARKERSBURG v. HARKNESS, 42 W. Va. 156, 24 S. E. 548, 32 L. R. A. 408, Dobie Cas. Bailments and Carriers, 109; Farson v. Gilbert, 114 Ill. App. 17.

9 Civ. Code Cal. 1906, § 2986.

10 Rev. Codes N. D. 1905, §§ 6193, 6194.

11 Civ. Code, § 2104.

12 Civ. Code 1895, §§ 3890, 3891 (Rev. Codes, §§ 5774, 5775).

13 Thus in Georgia (Code Ga. 1882, § 2138), the following definition is given: "A pledge or pawn is property deposited with another as security for the payment of a debt. Delivery of the property is essential to this bailment, but promissory notes and evidences of debt may be delivered in pledge. The delivery of title deeds creates no pledge." The Louisiana law is that "the pledge is a contract by which one debtor gives something to his creditor as a security for his debt." Rev. Civ. Code La. 1870, art. 3133. See, also, 1 Stimson, Am. Stat. Law, p. 520.

The two transactions, however, present two striking points of difference: First, the rights of the lienholder are personal to him, and he may not transfer them to a third person;[14] while, in the case of a pledgee, his interest is freely assignable, even without the consent of the pledgor.[15] Secondly, though the lienholder can hold the goods against all the world, until the debt secured by the lien is paid, his rights at common law are limited to such a holding, and he has (in the absence of a statute to that effect) no power to sell the goods to which his lien attaches;[16] while one of the most important incidents of the pledge is the power of the pledgee to sell the goods on the default of the pledgor.[17]

In the case of a chattel mortgage, the legal title to the thing passes to the mortgagee,[18] either with or (what is probably more frequent) without possession passing to the mortgagee. But this legal title of the mortgagee will be defeated on the payment of the debt within the stipulated time by the mortgagor.[19] In the case of a pledge, the title to the goods remains in the pledgor,[20] while possession of the goods [21] and a special property [22] therein pass to

[14] Upon this point it was said by Lord Ellenborough, C. J., in McCombie v. Davies, 7 East (Eng.) 6, that "nothing could be clearer than that liens were personal, and could not be transferred to third persons by any tortious pledge of the principal's goods." If the one having the lien parts with the possession of the goods, unless, indeed, to one who is his own agent, and with the intent that such agent shall have merely the custody of them, he thereby loses his lien. See the opinions of Cockburn, C. J., in Donald v. Suckling, L. R. 1 Q. B. (Eng.) 585, 617, and Buller, J., in the celebrated case of Lickbarrow v. Mason, 6 East (Eng.) 21.

[15] See post, § 77.

[16] Chief Justice Gibbs, in Pothonier v. Dawson, Holt, N. P. (Eng.) 383, 385, said: "Undoubtedly, as a general proposition, a right of lien gives no right to sell the goods. But, when goods are deposited by way of security to indemnify a party against a loan of money [a pledge], * * * the lender's rights are more extensive than such as accrue under an ordinary lien in the course of trade." In order to sell, the lienor must resort to a judicial proceeding and sell under a decree from the court.

[17] See post, § 88.

[18] Walker v. Smith, 5 B. & Ald. (Eng.) 439; Hyams v. Bamberger, 10 Utah, 3, 36 Pac. 202; FIRST NAT. BANK OF PARKERSBURG v. HARKNESS, 42 W. Va. 156, 24 S. E. 548, 32 L. R. A. 408, Dobie Cas. Bailments and Carriers, 109; Palmer v. Mutual Life Ins. Co. of New York, 114 Minn. 1, 130 N. W. 250, Ann. Cas. 1912B, 957.

[19] Jones, Chattel Mortgages (5th Ed.) § 426; Lickbarrow v. Mason, 6 East (Eng.) 22; Sheridan v. Presas, 18 Misc. Rep. 180, 41 N. Y. Supp. 451; Union Trust Co. v. Rigdon, 93 Ill. 458.

[20] This is involved in the definition of a pledge, and constitutes the chief distinction between a pledge and a sale. Unless the title thus remained in the pledgor, the pledge would not be a bailment. See, also, Harding v. Eldridge, 186 Mass. 39, 71 N. E. 115.

[21] Post, § 74.

[22] Post, § 79.

the pledgee. However, until the expiration of the time within which the pledgor may regain possession of the goods by the payment of his debt or the performance of his engagement, the pledgee is nothing more than a bailee of the goods.[23] In other words, the situation (before default by the debtor) is this: In a chattel mortgage, a defeasible title must pass, and possession of the chattel either may or may not pass; in a pledge, no title passes, but possession and a special property in the chattel must pass. Again: After default by the debtor in a chattel mortgage, the title of the mortgagee (hitherto defeasible) now becomes absolute at law[24] (though the mortgagor ordinarily has a right in equity to redeem); but, in a pledge, default by the debtor never confers an absolute title in the chattel on the pledgee, but merely operates to give him the right to sell the chattel.[25]

In cases in which it is not clear whether the transaction in question is a mortgage or a pledge, it will, if the facts will bear out such

[23] Post, § 76.

[24] Lickbarrow v. Mason, 6 East (Eng.) 21, 25; Sims v. Canfield, 2 Ala. 555; Brown v. Bement, 8 Johns. (N. Y.) 96; McLean v. Walker, 10 Johns. (N. Y.) 471; Eastman v. Avery, 23 Me. 248; Day v. Swift, 48 Me. 368; Gleason v. Drew, 9 Greenl. (Me.) 79, 82; Haven v. Low, 2 N. H. 13, 9 Am. Dec. 25; Ash v. Savage, 5 N. H. 545; Lewis v. Stevenson, 2 Hall (N. Y.) 76, 98; Homes v. Crane, 2 Pick. (Mass.) 607, 610; Ward v. Sumner, 5 Pick. (Mass.) 59, 60; Bonsey v. Amee, 8 Pick. (Mass.) 236.

[25] Said Willes, J., distinguishing the lien, chattel mortgage, and pledge in Halliday v. Holgate, L. R. 36 Ch. (Eng.) 299, 302: "There are three kinds of security: The first, a simple lien; the second, a mortgage, passing the property out and out; the third, a security intermediate between a lien and a mortgage, viz., a pledge, where by contract a deposit of goods is made the security for a debt, and the right to the property vests in the pledgee so far as is necessary to secure the debt." See, also, Palmer v. Mutual Life Ins. Co. of New York, 114 Minn. 1, 130 N. W. 250, Ann. Cas. 1912B, 957; Hyams v. Bamberger, 10 Utah, 3, 36 Pac. 202; FIRST NAT. BANK OF PARKERSBURG v. HARKNESS, 42 W. Va. 156, 24 S. E. 548, 32 L. R. A. 408, Dobie Cas. Bailments and Carriers, 109; Jones v. Smith, 2 Ves. Jr. (Eng.) 372; Ryall v. Rolle, 1 Atk. (Eng.) 165; Cortelyou v. Lansing, 2 Caines, Cas. (N. Y.) 200; Barrow v. Paxton, 5 Johns. (N. Y.) 258, 4 Am. Dec. 354; Strong v. Tompkins, 8 Johns. (N. Y.) 98; McLean v. Walker, 10 Johns. (N. Y.) 471; Wilson v. Little, 2 N. Y. 443, 51 Am. Dec. 307; Haskins v. Kelly, 1 Rob. (N. Y.) 160; Parshall v. Eggart, 52 Barb. (N. Y.) 367; Winchester v. Ball, 54 Me. 558; Walcott v. Keith, 22 N. H. 196; Whittle v. Skinner, 23 Vt. 531; Wright v. Ross, 36 Cal. 414; Heyland v. Badger, 35 Cal. 404; Dewey v. Bowman, 8 Cal. 145; Waldie v. Doll, 29 Cal. 556; Goldstein v. Hort, 30 Cal. 372; Gay v. Moss, 34 Cal. 125; Ponce v. McElvy, 47 Cal. 154; Meyerstein v. Barber, L. R. 2 C. P. (Eng.) 38, 51; Id., L. R. 4 H. L. 317; Ratcliff v. Davies, Cro. Jac. (Eng.) 244; Tannahill v. Tuttle, 3 Mich. 104, 61 Am. Dec. 480; Bryson v. Rayner, 25 Md. 424, 90 Am. Dec. 69.

a construction, be held to be a pledge.[26] This is sometimes a nice question, and in solving it the courts will look to the real intention and understanding of the parties rather than to the name used by the parties themselves to designate the transaction. Since in a pledge possession must pass, while in a chattel mortgage it either may or may not pass, where personal property is given as security for a debt or engagement, accompanied by a change of possession, the law strongly favors the conclusion that it was intended as a pledge and not as a mortgage.[27]

Sale and Pledge Distinguished

The distinction between a sale, in which the title or ownership of goods passes, and a bailment, in general, was pointed out at some length in the first chapter.[28] An absolute bill of sale, however, accompanied by a delivery of the goods, may be shown, even by parol evidence, to be only a pledge, if such was the intention of the parties.[29] The necessity of distinguishing between a sale and a

[26] Bank of British Columbia v. Marshall (C. C.) 11 Fed. 19; Woodworth v. Morris, 56 Barb. (N. Y.) 97.

[27] Luckett v. Townsend, 3 Tex. 119, 49 Am. Dec. 723; Wilson v. Brannan, 27 Cal. 258, 271; Lewis v. Varnum, 12 Abb. Prac. (N. Y.) 305, 308; Warren v. Emerson, 1 Curt. 239, 241, Fed. Cas. No. 17,195; West v. Crary, 47 N. Y. 423, 425; Woodworth v. Morris, 56 Barb. (N. Y.) 97, 104; Bank of British Columbia v. Marshall (C. C.) 11 Fed. 19. A pledge need not be recorded as a chattel mortgage. First Nat. Bank of Cincinnati v. Kelly, 57 N. Y. 34; Parshall v. Eggert, 54 N. Y. 18; Griffin v. Rogers, 38 Pa. 382; McCready v. Haslock, 3 Tenn. Ch. 13; Shaw v. Wilshire, 65 Me. 485; Harris v. Birch, 9 Mees. & W. (Eng.) 591; Ward v. Sumner, 5 Pick. (Mass.) 59; Wright v. Bircher, 5 Mo. App. 322; Langdon v. Buel, 9 Wend. (N. Y.) 80; Atwater v. Mower, 10 Vt. 75.

[28] Ante, § 3.

[29] Barber v. Hathaway, 169 N. Y. 575, 61 N. E. 1127; Skenandoa Cotton Mills v. Lefferts, 59 Hun, 620, 13 N. Y. Supp. 33; Thompson v. Dolliver, 132 Mass. 103; Oakland Cemetery Ass'n v. Lakins, 126 Iowa, 121, 101 N. W. 778, 3 Ann. Cas. 559; Keeler v. Commercial Printing Co., 16 Wash. 526, 48 Pac. 239; Walker v. Staples, 5 Allen (Mass.) 34; Whitaker v. Sumner, 20 Pick. (Mass.) 399; Hazard v. Loring, 10 Cush. (Mass.) 267; Kimball v. Hildreth, 8 Allen (Mass.) 167; Bright v. Wagle, 3 Dana (Ky.) 252; Ex parte Fitz, 2 Lowell, 519, Fed. Cas. No. 4,837; Newton v. Fay, 10 Allen (Mass.) 505; Jones v. Rahilly, 16 Minn. 320 (Gil. 283); Shaw v. Wilshire, 65 Me. 485; Morgan v. Dod, 3 Colo. 551; Blodgett v. Blodgett, 48 Vt. 32. See, also, Colburn v. Commercial Security Co., 172 Ill. App. 510. But there may be a conditional bill of sale, which will be a mortgage when such is the intention of the parties. Brown v. Bement, 8 Johns. (N. Y.) 96; Clark v. Henry, 2 Cow. (N. Y.) 324; Milliken v. Dehon, 27 N. Y. 364; Homes v. Crane, 2 Pick. (Mass.) 607; Fraker v. Reeve, 36 Wis. 85; Wood v. Dudley, 8 Vt. 430; Murdock v. Columbus Ins. & Banking Co., 59 Miss. 152; Gregory v. Morris, 96 U. S. 619, 24 L. Ed. 740; Laflin & R. Powder Co. v. Burkhardt, 97 U. S. 110, 24 L. Ed. 973. In the same way, a bill of sale, with an agreement to repurchase, may be either a pledge or chattel mortgage, according to the circumstances and intention

pledge often arises when goods or securities are assigned by a debtor to a creditor.[30] Here, in doubtful cases, the law always leans towards the presumption that the transfer was intended by the debtor merely as a pledge created as security for the indebtedness and not as an absolute transfer of title to the goods in payment of the debt.[31]

Collateral Security

The term "collateral security" has come into quite frequent use of late to designate pledges of incorporeal personalty, and, when so used, it distinguishes in general the business of the banker from that of the pawnbroker.[32] As thus used, the term is convenient and unobjectionable. Unfortunately, however, it is loosely applied to mortgages either of realty or personalty, and is often improperly used in still other senses.[33]

THE NATURE OF THE RELATION

71. In addition to those circumstances that are essential to any bailment, for the establishment of a pledge there must be:
(a) Mutual assent of the parties.
(b) A debt or engagement secured.

Pledges must Arise out of Contract

Pledges cannot be created by operation of law, as such a situation is precluded by their very nature. They can therefore arise only by the mutual assent of the parties, express or implied.[34] As a pledge is, of course, a bailment, what has already been said

of the parties. Hines v. Strong, 46 How. Prac. (N. Y.) 97; Bright v. Wagle, 3 Dana (Ky.) 252.

30 Standen v. Brown, 83 Hun, 610, 31 N. Y. Supp. 535.

31 Delaware County Trust, Safe Deposit & Title Ins. Co. v. Haser, 199 Pa. 17, 48 Atl. 694, 85 Am. St. Rep. 763; Butler v. Rockwell, 14 Colo. 125, 23 Pac. 462; Jones v. Johnson, 3 Watts & S. (Pa.) 276, 38 Am. Dec. 760; Perit v. Pittfield, 5 Rawle (Pa.) 166; Leas v. James, 10 Serg. & R. (Pa.) 307; Eby v. Hoopes, 1 Penny. (Pa.) 175.

32 Jones, Collateral Securities (3d Ed.) § 1; Brooklyn City & N. R. Co. v. National Bank of the Republic, 102 U. S. 14, 26 L. Ed. 61; In re Athill, L. R. 16 Ch. D. (Eng.) 211, 223; Mitchell v. Roberts (C. C.) 17 Fed. 776.

33 Penney v. Lynn, 58 Minn. 371, 59 N. W. 1043; Chambersburg Ins. Co. v. Smith, 11 Pa. 120, 127. This broad definition is also given by Black, Bouvier, Webster, and Worcester.

34 Mead v. Bunn, 32 N. Y. 275; Taylor v. Jones, 3 N. D. 235, 55 N. W. 593; Wilkinson v. Misner, 158 Mo. App. 551, 138 S. W. 931; Farson v. Gilbert, 114 Ill. App. 17.

of contracts creating a bailment is equally applicable here.[35] In connection with pledges, the general rules of agency, partnership, and corporations also are frequently applied.

Nature of the Debt or Engagement Secured

In a pledge, unlike all other bailments, the bailment is created, not for itself alone, but in order to secure the performance of some other undertaking. This undertaking which the pledge is created to secure is determined by the contract of the parties and varies accordingly. It is immaterial whether the debt or engagement for which the security is given is that of the pledgor, or of some other person; for, if there is an assent by all the proper parties, it is equally binding in each case.[36] It may be delivered as security for a future[37] as well as for a past[38] debt or engagement; for one or for many debts and engagements;[39] upon condition, or absolutely; for a limited time, or for an indefinite period.[40] A pledge may

[35] Ante, § 8.

[36] A liability for another on a contract still in force is a sufficient consideration for a pledge, and the ratio of the consideration to the value of the thing pledged is of no importance. Jewett v. Warren, 12 Mass. 300, 7 Am. Dec. 74. When a third person pledges his property as security for the payment of a debt or obligation of another, such property will occupy the same position as that of surety of the debtor, and any change in the contract of suretyship which would discharge a surety will release and discharge property so held as collateral. Price v. Dime Sav. Bank, 124 Ill. 317, 15 N. E. 754, 7 Am. St. Rep. 367. The drawer of a note can pledge property to secure an accommodation acceptor, and also to protect the future holder of the note. Britton v. Harvey, 47 La. Ann. 259, 16 South. 747.

[37] Brown v. James, 80 Neb. 475, 114 N. W. 491; Moors v. Washburn, 147 Mass. 344, 17 N. E. 884; Didier v. Patterson, 93 Va. 534, 25 S. E. 661; Leonard v. Kebler's Adm'r, 50 Ohio St. 444, 34 N. E. 659; Merchants' Nat. Bank of Savannah v. Demere, 92 Ga. 735, 19 S. E. 38; Clymer v. Patterson, 52 N. J. Eq. 188, 27 Atl. 645. Or for future advances. Merchants' Nat. Bank of Whitehall v. Hall, 83 N. Y. 338, 38 Am. Rep. 434; Stearns v. Marsh, 4 Denio (N. Y.) 227, 47 Am. Dec. 248; Badlam v. Tucker, 1 Pick. (Mass.) 389, 398, 11 Am. Dec. 202; Jewett v. Warren, 12 Mass. 300, 7 Am. Dec. 74; Macomber v. Parker, 14 Pick. (Mass.) 497; Holbrook v. Baker, 5 Greenl. (Me.) 309, 17 Am. Dec. 236; Eichelberger v. Murdock, 10 Md. 373, 69 Am. Dec. 140; Wolf v. Wolf, 12 La. Ann. 529; Smithurst v. Edmunds, 14 N. J. Eq. 408; D'Wolf v. Harris, 4 Mason, 515, Fed. Cas. No. 4,221; Conard v. Atlantic Ins. Co., 1 Pet. 386, 448, 7 L. Ed. 189.

[38] Conard v. Atlantic Ins. Co., 1 Pet. (U. S.) 386, 448, 7 L. Ed. 189; Stearns v. Marsh, 4 Denio (N. Y.) 227, 47 Am. Dec. 248; Badlam v. Tucker, 1 Pick. (Mass.) 389, 398, 11 Am. Dec. 202; Holbrook v. Baker, 5 Greenl. (Me.) 309, 17 Am. Dec. 236; D'Wolf v. Harris, 4 Mason, 515, Fed. Cas. No. 4,221; Hanover Nat. Bank v. Brown (Tenn. Ch. App.) 53 S. W. 206.

[39] Mechanics' & Traders' Bank v. Livingston, 6 Misc. Rep. 81, 26 N. Y. Supp. 25; Jones v. Merchants' Nat. Bank, 72 Hun, 344, 25 N. Y. Supp. 660.

[40] Shirras v. Caig, 7 Cranch, 34, 3 L. Ed. 260; Hendricks v. Robinson, 2 Johns. Ch. (N. Y.) 283, 309; Stevens v. Bell, 6 Mass. 339.

also be made a continuing security, which will apply to any future transaction between the parties that is within the limits of the original pledge agreement.[41] The contract secured by the pledge is not confined to an engagement for the payment of money; but a pledge is susceptible of being applied to any other lawful contract whatever. Pledges to secure contracts other than for the payment of money, however, are quite rare.

In all cases the pledge is understood to be a security both for the whole and for every part of the debt or engagement, unless it is otherwise stipulated between the parties. The payment or discharge of a part of the debt or engagement, therefore, still leaves it a perfect pledge for the residue.[42] The pledge may, however, be created to secure a part only of a debt.[43]

When new agreements are made, which are clearly intended by the parties, either tacitly or expressly, to be attached to the pledge, the pledgee has, of course, a title and right of possession as to the pledged goods coextensive with the new engagements.[44] But neither the mere existence of a former debt [45] between the parties nor the creation of a future one [46] authorizes the pledgee to detain

[41] Fidelity Mut. Life Ins. Co. v. Germania Bank, 74 Minn. 154, 76 N. W. 968; Merchants' Nat. Bank of Whitehall v. Hall, 83 N. Y. 338, 38 Am. Rep. 434; Norton v. Plumb, 14 Conn. 512.

[42] Baldwin v. Bradley, 69 Ill. 32; Ellis v. Conrad Seipp Brewery Co., 207 Ill. 291, 69 N. E. 808; Williams v. National Bank of Baltimore, 72 Md. 441, 20 Atl. 191.

[43] Fridley v. Bowen, 103 Ill. 633, 637.

[44] Moors v. Washburn, 147 Mass. 344, 17 N. E. 884; Smith v. Denison, 101 Ill. 531.

[45] Jarvis v. Rogers, 15 Mass. 389; Allen v. Megguire, 15 Mass. 490; Robinson v. Frost, 14 Barb. (N. Y.) 536; President, etc., of Neponset Bank v. Leland, 5 Metc. (Mass.) 259; James' Appeal, 89 Pa. 54; Russell v. Hadduck, 3 Gilman (Ill.) 233, 238, 44 Am. Dec. 693; Baldwin v. Bradley, 69 Ill. 32; St. John v. O'Connel, 7 Port. (Ala.) 466; Gilliat v. Lynch, 2 Leigh (Va.) 493; Mahoney v. Caperton, 15 Cal. 314; Bank of Metropolis v. New England Bank, 1 How. 234, 11 L. Ed. 115; Boughton v. United States, 12 Ct. Cl. 330; Thompson v. Dominy, 14 Mees. & W. (Eng.) 403; Vanderzee v. Willis, 3 Brown, Ch. (Eng.) 21; Brandao v. Barnett, 3 C. B. (Eng.) 519, 530; In re Meadows, 28 Law J. Ch. (Eng.) 891; Walker v. Birch, 6 Term R. (Eng.) 258; Rushforth v. Hadfield, 7 East (Eng.) 224; Green v. Farmer, 4 Burrows (Eng.) 2214; Buckley v. Garrett, 60 Pa. 333, 100 Am. Dec. 564; Philler v. Jewett, 166 Pa. 456, 31 Atl. 204. Where a judgment is given as collateral security for a note which is afterwards paid, a parol agreement between the creditor and the agent of the debtor to continue such judgment as security for certain other notes of the debtor is valid against subsequent judgment creditors of such debtor without notice. Merchants' Nat. Bank v. Mosser, 161 Pa. 469, 29 Atl. 1.

[46] Midland Co. v. Huchberger, 46 Ill. App. 518; Searight v. Carlisle Deposit Bank, 162 Pa. 504, 29 Atl. 783; Baldwin v. Bradley, 69 Ill. 32; Adams v. Sturges, 55 Ill. 468; Gilliat v. Lynch, 2 Leigh (Va.) 493. Of course, such new loan is secured by the goods already pledged when the new loan was made

the pledged goods as a security for such past or future debt, when the goods have been put into his hands for another debt or contract, unless there is some just presumption that such was the intention of the parties. If the debt secured bears interest, the pledge secures the payment not only of the principal but also of such interest.[47] And when a pledge is made it continues effectual until the debt secured is paid or discharged, notwithstanding the evidence of the debt is changed from a promissory note to a judgment of a court of record thereon.[48] Ordinarily the pledge secures any renewal of the original debt.[49]

Legality of the Debt or Engagement Secured

Even though the debt which the pledge is given to secure is void on account of illegality of consideration, the pledge is nevertheless effectual. The pledgee, of course, cannot recover on the debt itself, yet he can retain the pledge until the debt is paid.[50] This is on the ground, not that the law in such case confers a positive right on the pledgee, but rather denies the pledgor, under the principle "in pari delicto potior est conditio defendentis," the privilege of setting up an illegal transaction to which he was himself a party, in order to recover goods, the possession of which he has transferred to another by virtue of such illegal transaction.[51]

The pledgor cannot, therefore, recover possession of the goods without paying the debt, because in order to establish his case he would have to set up his own wrong. When, however, the pledgor pays or tenders the amount of the illegal debt to the pledgee, the latter must deliver up the goods.[52] The pledgee would not be al-

on the credit of the pledge. Van Blarcom v. Broadway Bank, 9 Bosw. (N. Y.) 532; Id., 37 N. Y. 540; Smith v. Dennison, 101 Ill. 531; Buchanan v. International Bank, 78 Ill. 500.

47 Boardman v. Holmes, 124 Mass. 438; Charles v. Coker, 2 S. C. 122; Hamilton v. Wagner, 2 A. K. Marsh. (Ky.) 331.

48 Robinson & Co. v. Stiner, 26 Okl. 272, 109 Pac. 238; Fisher v. Fisher, 98 Mass. 303; Jenkins v. International Bank, 111 Ill. 462; Everman v. Hyman, 3 Ind. App. 459, 29 N. E. 1140; Jones v. Scott, 10 Kan. 33.

49 Cotton v. Atlas Nat. Bank, 145 Mass. 43, 12 N. E. 850; Miller v. McCarty, 47 Minn. 321, 50 N. W. 235, 28 Am. St. Rep. 375; First Nat. Bank of Emmetsburg v. Gunhus, 133 Iowa, 409, 110 N. W. 611, 9 L. R. A. (N. S.) 471.

50 King v. Green, 6 Allen (Mass.) 139.

51 Taylor v. Chester, L. R. 4 Q. B. (Eng.) 309 (pledge to secure debt contracted for wine and suppers supplied in a bawdyhouse); King v. Green, 6 Allen (Mass.) 139 (pledge of watch to secure payment of an illegal debt incurred for use of horse and wagon on Sunday). See, also, Curtis v. Leavitt, 15 N. Y. 9; Beecher v. Ackerman, 1 Abb. Prac. N. S. (N. Y.) 141; Roosevelt v. Dreyer, 12 Daly (N. Y.) 370.

52 Jones, Collateral Securities, § 354. See, also, the opinion of Mellor, J., in Taylor v. Chester, cited in the preceding note, though there the pledgor was suing to recover the pledged article without payment of the debt secured.

lowed to retain the goods, on the ground that the debt for which the goods were pledged was an illegal one; for the pledgee would then, in his turn, be compelled to set up his own wrong as the basis of his asserted right.

THE TITLE OF THE PLEDGOR

72. The pledgor need not be the absolute owner of the goods; but ordinarily he can pledge, just as he can sell, any assignable interest that he has.

In the absence of statute, unauthorized attempts by factors or other agents to pledge the owner's goods will confer no rights as against such owner.

Pledgor Need Not be Absolute Owner

It is not necessary that the pledgor be the absolute owner of the thing pledged.[53] He may have only a limited interest therein, such as a life interest.[54] But when a thing is pledged by one having only such a limited interest, the pledgee acquires no right to sell the pledged goods on default, because to do so would divest the rights of the ultimate owner.[55] He can, however, sell whatever interest the pledgor has, and the purchaser in such case gets a mere right to hold the goods as long as the pledgor could have held them.[56] Even a pledgee may make a subpledge of his interest as pledgee.[57]

However, one who has only a lien on a thing cannot make a valid pledge of it. If he attempts to do so, his pledgee cannot hold the thing against the owner, even for the amount of the lien.[58] This results from the rule that a lien is a personal right to retain possession, and cannot be assigned. In some states it is specifically provided by statute that a lienholder may pledge property in his

[53] McCombie v. Davies, 7 East (Eng.) 5; Eddy v. Fogg, 192 Mass. 543, 78 N. E. 549; Kelly v. Richardson, 100 Ala. 584, 13 South. 785. But a partner cannot pledge partnership property as security for his private debts. Oliphant v. Markham, 79 Tex. 543, 15 S. W. 569, 23 Am. St. Rep. 363. A joint owner in possession may pledge his own interest, but not that of the co-owner, without the latter's consent. Frans v. Young, 24 Iowa, 375.

[54] Hoare v. Parker, 2 Term R. (Eng.) 376; Robertson v. Wilcox, 36 Conn. 426, 430.

[55] Robertson v. Wilcox, 36 Conn. 426.

[56] Eddy v. Fogg, 192 Mass. 543, 78 N. E. 549; Jones on Collateral Securities (3d Ed.) § 60.

[57] Lewis v. Mott, 36 N. Y. 395; Jarvis v. Rogers, 15 Mass. 389; McCombie v. Davies, 7 East (Eng.) 5, 7.

[58] McCombie v. Davies, 7 East (Eng.) 5.

possession, to the extent of his lien, and a like result might follow when a statute in general terms makes liens assignable.[59]

Factors[60]

Factors are agents employed by the owner to sell the goods which the owner delivers to them.[61] Since the factor has authority from his principal to sell, a sale of the goods by the factor passes a good title to the goods, according to the rules of agency. But the factor, ordinarily, has no authority to make a pledge of the goods delivered to him.[62] Therefore, in such a case, his attempt to pledge the goods (being in excess of his authority) confers no rights on the pledgee as against the owner of the goods. But the authority to make a valid pledge may be conferred on the factor by the doctrine of estoppel, as when the owner in any way holds out the factor as one having such authority.[63] The rights of the parties

[59] See Civ. Code Cal. 1906, § 2990; Rev. Codes N. D. 1905, § 6197; Civ. Code S. D. § 2108.

[60] For discussion of pledges by factors, see Jones, Collateral Securities (3d Ed.) §§ 327-353.

[61] Black, Law Dictionary, p. 476; Howland v. Woodruff, 60 N. Y. 80; In re Rabenau (D. C.) 118 Fed. 474. See, also, Civ. Code Cal. § 2026.

[62] Morsch v. Lessig, 45 Colo. 168, 100 Pac. 431; Kennedy v. Strong, 14 Johns. (N. Y.) 128; Rodriguez v. Hefferman, 5 Johns. Ch. (N. Y.) 417; Newbold v. Wright, 4 Rawle (Pa.) 195; Kinder v. Shaw, 2 Mass. 398; Gray v. Agnew, 95 Ill. 315; Kelly v. Smith, 1 Blatchf. 290, Fed. Cas. No. 7,675; Van Amringe v. Peabody, 1 Mason, 440, Fed. Cas. No. 16,825; Warner v. Martin, 11 How. 209, 13 L. Ed. 667; First Nat. Bank of Macon v. Nelson, 38 Ga. 391, 95 Am. Dec. 400; Wright v. Solomon, 19 Cal. 64, 79 Am. Dec. 196; Merchants' Nat. Bank of Memphis v. Trenholm, 12 Heisk. (Tenn.) 520; McCreary v. Gaines, 55 Tex. 485, 40 Am. Rep. 818; Paterson v. Tash, 2 Strange (Eng.) 1178; Daubigny v. Duval, 5 Term R. (Eng.) 604; Newsom v. Thornton, 6 East (Eng.) 17; Graham v. Dyster, 2 Starkie (Eng.) 21; Martini v. Coles, 1 Maule & S. (Eng.) 140; Shipley v. Kymer, Id. 484; Solly v. Rathbone, 2 Maule & S. (Eng.) 298; Cockran v. Irlam, Id. 301, note; Boyson v. Coles, 6 Maule & S. (Eng.) 14; Fielding v. Kymer, 2 Brod. & B. (Eng.) 639; Queiroz v. Trueman, 3 Barn. & C. (Eng.) 342; Bonito v. Mosquera, 2 Bosw. (N. Y.) 401. But cf. Hutchinson v. Bours, 6 Cal. 384; Leet v. Wadsworth, 5 Cal. 404; Wright v. Solomon, 19 Cal. 64, 79 Am. Dec. 196; Miller v. Schneider, 19 La. Ann. 300, 92 Am. Dec. 535; McCreary v. Gaines, 55 Tex. 485, 40 Am. Rep. 818; First Nat. Bank of Macon v. Nelson, 38 Ga. 391, 95 Am. Dec. 400.

[63] Leet v. Wadsworth, 5 Cal. 404, in which the factor purchased the goods in his own name, stored them, and paid storage in his own name. For other cases in which the owner, by clothing the factor with the indicia of ownership, lost his right to take the goods from the pledgee of the factor, see Calais S. B. Co. v. Scudder, 2 Black 372, 17 L. Ed. 282; Babcock v. Lawson, 4 Q. B. Div. (Eng.) 394. Where an agent fraudulently misappropriates negotiable collaterals deposited with him on a loan of the principal's money, the borrower offering to pay the loan at maturity, the principal is liable to him for the value of the collaterals at that time. Reynolds v. Witte, 13 S. C. 5, 36 Am. Rep. 678. A clerk or salesman has no power to pawn his employer's

in all the cases given are governed by the general principles of agency.

In a number of states, however, the rules of the common law as to factors have been changed by statute. These enactments, commonly known as "Factors' Acts,"[64] were passed for the protection of innocent third persons, and frequently enable such innocent third parties dealing with factors to take pledges of goods held by the latter, and, by so doing, acquire rights superior to those of the owner.[65] Even under these statutes, the real owner may recover the goods pledged by the factor by paying to the pledgee the amount of money he has advanced, or otherwise fulfilling the undertaking secured by the factor's pledge of the goods. Factors' Acts protect only the innocent third person, and do not affect the remedies of the owner against the factor.[66] As the various acts differ greatly in scope and effect, the specific statute should in all cases be carefully consulted.

WHAT MAY BE PLEDGED

73. Unless public policy or some statute forbids, any assignable interest in personal property, corporeal or incorporeal, may be pledged.

assets as security for his own debts. Oliphant v. Markham, 79 Tex. 543, 15 S. W. 569, 23 Am. St. Rep. 363. But, for cases where it was held that the pledgor did not have sufficient indicia of ownership, see Agnew v. Johnson, 22 Pa. 471, 62 Am. Dec. 303; Gallaher v. Cohen, 1 Browne (Pa.) 43; Branson v. Heckler, 22 Kan. 610; Cox v. McGuire, 26 Ill. App. 315. An administrator or executor may make as to an innocent third person a valid pledge of the goods of the estate. Pickens v. Yarborough's Adm'r, 26 Ala. 417, 62 Am. Dec. 728; Carter v. Manufacturers' Nat. Bank of Lewistown, 71 Me. 448, 36 Am. Rep. 338; Leitch v. Wells, 48 N. Y. 585; Hutchins v. President, etc., of State Bank, 12 Metc. (Mass.) 421; Bayard v. Farmers' & Mechanics' Bank of Philadelphia, 52 Pa. 232; Appeal of Wood, 92 Pa. 379, 37 Am. Rep. 694; Petrie v. Clark, 11 Serg. & R. (Pa.) 377, 14 Am. Dec. 636; Russell v. Plaice, 18 Beav. (Eng.) 21; Vane v. Rigden, L. R. 5 Ch. App. (Eng.) 663.

64 See Jones, Collateral Securities (3d Ed.) §§ 333–340. For specimens of factors' acts, see Civ. Code Cal. 1906, § 2368; Rev. Laws Mass. 1902, c. 68, §§ 1–6; 3 Birdseye's C. & G. Consol. Laws N. Y. 1909, p. 3232, § 182; Gen. Code Ohio, §§ 8358–8362; Purdon's Dig. Pa. (13th Ed.) pp. 1608–1610; St. Wis. 1898, §§ 3345–3347.

65 Jones, Collateral Securities, § 333; Allen v. St. Louis Nat. Bank, 120 U. S. 20, 7 Sup. Ct. 460, 30 L. Ed. 573; Wisp v. Hazard, 66 Cal. 459, 6 Pac. 91; New York Security & Trust Co. v. Lipman, 157 N. Y. 551, 52 N. E. 595; Cole v. Northwestern Bank, L. R. 10 C. P. (Eng.) 354; Henry v. Philadelphia Warehouse Co., 81 Pa. 76.

66 Stollenwerck v. Thacher, 115 Mass. 224.

Any legal or equitable interest whatever in any form of personal property may be pledged, provided the interest can be put, by actual delivery or by written transfer, into the hands, or within the power, of the pledgee, so as to make such interest available to him for the satisfaction of the debt or engagement secured.[67] Goods at sea may be pledged by a transfer of the muniments of title, as by a written assignment of the bill of lading. This is equivalent to a transfer of possession, because it is a delivery of the symbols of the goods and the means of obtaining possession of them.[68] And debts and choses in action are also capable, by means of a written assignment, of being conveyed in pledge.[69]

The common law, unlike the Roman law,[70] permits a debtor to pledge any of his goods, and it is immaterial whether or not these are necessary articles, such as one's household furniture or even the tools of one's trade. Thus even goods expressly exempted by statute from execution may be pledged by the owner as security for the payment of his debts.[71] By pledging his property, the owner expressly waives the benefit of the exemption, as far as the pledge in question is concerned. As a pledge is a bailment, it applies only to personalty and there can be no pledge of real estate.

On the ground of public policy, the pay and pensions of soldiers and sailors cannot be pledged. This has been frequently held in England,[72] in the absence of a statute. In the United States, there are also statutes to the same effect.[73] National banks are prohibited from lending money on their own stock.[74]

Future Property

The general rule is that property not yet in existence or not yet acquired cannot be pledged.[75] This may be the subject of

[67] In re Pleasant Hill Lumber Co., 126 La. 743, 52 South. 1010.

[68] Story, Bailm. § 293.

[69] Wilson v. Little, 2 N. Y. 443, 51 Am. Dec. 307. But a chose in action growing out of a personal tort is not assignable, and therefore cannot be pledged. Pindell v. Grooms, 18 B. Mon. (Ky.) 501.

[70] See Story, Bailm. § 293.

[71] Kyle v. Sigur, 121 La. 888, 46 South. 910; Frost v. Shaw, 3 Ohio St. 270; Jones v. Scott, 10 Kan. 33.

[72] McCarthy v. Goold, 1 Ball & B. 387; Lidderdale v. Montrose, 4 T. R. 248.

[73] As to pay, Rev. St. § 1291 (U. S. Comp. St. 1901, p. 918). As to pensions, Rev. St. § 4745 (U. S. Comp. St. 1901, p. 3278).

[74] Act June 3, 1864, c. 106, 13 Stat. 99. First Nat. Bank v. Lanier, 11 Wall. 369, 20 L. Ed. 172; Bullard v. National Eagle Bank, 18 Wall. 589, 21 L. Ed. 923; Hagar v. Union Nat. Bank, 63 Me. 509.

[75] In re Pleasant Hill Lumber Co., 126 La. 743, 52 South. 1010; Gittings v. Nelson, 86 Ill. 591; Owens v. Kinsey, 52 N. C. 245; Smithurst v. Edmunds, 14 N. J. Eq. 408. For a pledge of an interest in a partnership not yet in existence, see Appeal of Collins, 107 Pa. 590, 52 Am. Rep. 479.

an agreement to pledge, but not of a pledge. Any attempt to pledge such property can create only contract rights or rights in personam, as distinguished from rights in rem; for manifestly there could be no in rem rights without a res. The pledge, however, may take effect when the property is acquired or comes into existence, provided the rights of innocent third persons have not in the meantime intervened.[76]

According to the analogy of a doctrine frequently held in the case of sales, many courts hold that property which is potentially in existence, such as crops in the ground [77] and wool to be raised from sheep which are already owned, may be pledged, with the rights of the pledgee attaching to such property as its potential existence merges into actual existence. Thus, under this rule, a man may pledge all the wool that he may take from his flocks in a certain year, but not all the wool that shall grow upon sheep that he may thereafter buy.[78]

The American Sales Act,[79] however, abolishes the distinction as to sales between future goods and goods having a potential existence, and a like doctrine is probably advisable in the case of pledges.

Incorporeal Property

Not only corporeal property (that which may be seen and touched and which is ordinarily valuable for itself rather than for what it represents), but also incorporeal property, may be the subject of a pledge. In fact, by far the most important pledge transactions in the commercial world have to do with this latter class of property. Examples of incorporeal property frequently pledged are the ordinary negotiable instruments, such as bills of exchange and promissory notes,[80] nonnegotiable instruments, such as in-

[76] Sequeira v. Collins, 153 Cal. 426, 95 Pac. 876; Macomber v. Parker, 14 Pick. (Mass.) 497; Goodenow v. Dunn, 21 Me. 86; Smith v. Atkins, 18 Vt. 461; Ayers v. South Australian Banking Co., L. R. 3 P. C. (Eng.) 548.

[77] Smith v. Atkins, 18 Vt. 461. But an attempt to pledge crops not yet planted is ineffectual against a landlord's lien. Gittings v. Nelson, 86 Ill. 591.

[78] Smithurst v. Edmunds, 14 N. J. Eq. 408.

[79] American Sales Act, § 5; Williston, Sales, §§ 127-137.

[80] Casey v. Cavaroc, 96 U. S. 467, 24 L. Ed. 779; Atkinson v. Foster, 134 Ill. 472, 25 N. E. 528; American Exch. Nat. Bank of New York v. Federal Nat. Bank of Pittsburg, 226 Pa. 483, 75 Atl. 683, 27 L. R. A. (N. S.) 666, 134 Am. St. Rep. 1071, 18 Ann. Cas. 444; Eddy v. Fogg, 192 Mass. 543, 78 N. E. 549; Wilson v. Little, 2 N. Y. 443, 447, 51 Am. Dec. 307; McLean v. Walker, 10 Johns. (N. Y.) 471; White v. Phelps, 14 Minn. 27 (Gil. 21), 100 Am. Dec. 190; Appleton v. Donaldson, 3 Pa. 381; Loomis v. Stave, 72 Ill. 623; Sanders v. Davis, 13 B. Mon. (Ky.) 433; Morris Canal & Banking Co. v. Fisher, 9 N. J. Eq. 667, 64 Am. Dec. 423; Fennell v. McGowan, 58 Miss. 261; William-

surance policies[81] and corporate stock,[82] and such well-known quasi negotiable instruments as the ordinary bills of lading[83] and warehouse receipts.[84]

DELIVERY

74. Delivery is absolutely essential to the creation of a pledge. Such delivery may be either—

(a) Actual; or

(b) Constructive.

Delivery with intention to create a pledge is sufficient to establish a pledge of any kind of property except corporate stock.

As a pledge is primarily a bailment, there can, of course, be no pledge without a delivery (in the sense in which it has already

son v. Culpepper, 16 Ala. 211, 50 Am. Dec. 175; President, etc., of Louisiana State Bank v. Gaiennie, 21 La. Ann. 555. A man may pledge his own note. Green v. Sinker, Davis & Co., 135 Ind. 434, 35 N. E. 262. A promissory note of a third person, deposited by a debtor with his creditor as collateral security for a debt, is a pledge in which the pawnee has merely a special property, the general ownership remaining in the pawnor. Garlick v. James, 12 Johns. (N. Y.) 146, 7 Am. Dec. 294. Coupon bonds payable to the bearer may be pledged by the party issuing them, because they are securities usually sold in the stock market, and understood by the parties to be designed for that use, and not because the party's ordinary bond or mortgage, deposited as a collateral, could be so regarded. Morris Canal & Banking Co. v. Fisher, 9 N. J. Eq. 667, 64 Am. Dec. 423.

81 Life insurance policies: Tateum v. Ross, 150 Mass. 440, 23 N. E. 230; Grant's Adm'rs v. Kline, 115 Pa. 618, 9 Atl. 150; Gilman v. Curtis, 66 Cal. 116, 4 Pac. 1094; Collins v. Dawley, 4 Colo. 138, 34 Am. Rep. 72. Fire insurance policies: Stout v. Yaeger Mill. Co. (C. C.) 13 Fed. 802; Merrill v. Colonial Mut. Fire Ins. Co., 169 Mass. 10, 47 N. E. 439, 61 Am. St. Rep. 268; East Texas Fire Ins. Co. v. Coffee, 61 Tex. 287.

82 Thompson v. Holladay, 15 Or. 34, 14 Pac. 725; Barse Live-Stock Co. v. Range Valley Cattle Co., 16 Utah, 59, 50 Pac. 630; Hasbrouck v. Vandervoort, 4 Sandf. (N. Y.) 74; Wilson v. Little, 2 N. Y. 443, 51 Am. Dec. 307; Fisher v. Brown, 104 Mass. 259, 6 Am. Rep. 235; Rozet v. McClellan, 48 Ill. 345, 95 Am. Dec. 551; Heath v. Silverthorn Lead Mining & Smelting Co., 39 Wis. 147; Appeal of Conyngham, 57 Pa. 474. It may be pledged by the corporation itself. Brewster v. Hartley, 37 Cal. 15, 99 Am. Dec. 237.

83 Lickbarrow v. Mason, 1 H. Bl. (Eng.) 357; Douglass v. People's Bank of Kentucky, 86 Ky. 176, 5 S. W. 420, 9 Am. St. Rep. 276; NEILL v. ROGERS BROS. PRODUCE CO., 41 W. Va. 37, 23 S. E. 702, Dobie Cas. Bailments and Carriers, 122; First Nat. Bank of Cincinnati v. Kelly, 57 N. Y. 34; Petitt v. First Nat. Bank of Memphis, 4 Bush (Ky.) 334.

84 Babcock v. Lawson, 5 Q. B. D. (Eng.) 284; Ammon v. Gamble-Robinson Commission Co., 111 Minn. 452, 127 N. W. 448; People's Sav. Bank v. Bates, 120 U. S. 556, 7 Sup. Ct. 679, 30 L. Ed. 754; Gibson v. Stevens, 8 How. 384, 12 L. Ed. 1123; Yenni v. McNamee, 45 N. Y. 614, 620; Vogelsang's Adm'r v. Fisher, 128 Mo. 386, 31 S. W. 13.

been used, viz., a transfer of possession) of the goods.[85] The pledge exists only, and takes its beginning, from the time of such delivery. An agreement to deliver, however, does not (and cannot) create a pledge; it is, at best, merely a contract to create a pledge at some future time.[86]

The question as to the exact time when the pledge begins, involving the distinction between delivery and a contract to deliver, is not of primary importance as between the pledge parties.[87] This for the reasons, first, that the contract to deliver, being based on a consideration, is enforceable at law; and, secondly, since, between the pledge parties, their rights are frequently worked out just as if there had been a complete delivery, creating a pledge, by virtue of the maxim "Equity treats that as done which ought to be done." [88]

When, however, the rights of third parties are called into question (either where there has never been a delivery, or where these rights attach before such delivery), then somewhat different con-

[85] Boney & Harper Milling Co. v. J. C. Stevenson Co., 161 N. C. 510, 77 S. E. 676; Porter v. Shotwell, 105 Mo. App. 177, 79 S. W. 728; Robertson v. Robertson, 186 Mass. 308, 71 N. E. 571; Dunn v. Train, 125 Fed. 221, 60 C. C. A. 113; Farson v. Gilbert, 114 Ill. App. 17; AMERICAN CAN CO. v. ERIE PRESERVING CO., 183 Fed. 96, 105 C. C. A. 388, Dobie Cas. Bailments and Carriers, 114; Fletcher v. Howard, 2 Aikens (Vt.) 115, 16 Am. Dec. 686; Succession of Lanaux, 46 La. Ann. 1036, 15 South. 708, 25 L. R. A. 577; Cortelyou v. Lansing, 2 Caines, Cas. (N. Y.) 200; Barrow v. Paxton, 5 Johns. (N. Y.) 259, and note, 4 Am. Dec. 354; Brown v. Bement, 8 Johns. (N. Y.) 97; Ceas v. Bramley, 18 Hun (N. Y.) 187; Campbell v. Parker, 9 Bosw. (N. Y.) 322, 329; Haskins v. Kelly, 1 Rob. (N. Y.) 160, 172; Milliman v. Neher, 20 Barb. (N. Y.) 37, 40; Muller v. Pondir, 6 Lans. (N. Y.) 472, 480; Nevan v. Roup, 8 Iowa, 207; Gleason v. Drew, 9 Greenl. (Me.) 79, 82; Walcott v. Keith, 22 N. H. 196; Propst v. Roseman, 49 N. C. 130; Corbett v. Underwood, 83 Ill. 324, 25 Am. Rep. 392; Casey v. Cavaroc, 96 U. S. 467, 24 L. Ed. 779. Plaintiff leased a machine to defendant for certain work, under an agreement that plaintiff should receive one-fourth of the profits of the work, and pay one-fourth of the losses. Afterwards it was agreed that defendant should have a lien on the machine as security for plaintiff's agreement to pay one-fourth of the losses. It was then delivered to defendant. Held, that there was a pledge of the machine to defendant. Clark v. Costello, 79 Hun, 588, 29 N. Y. Supp. 937.

[86] Cameron v. Orleans & J. R. Co., 108 La. 83, 32 South. 208; Copeland v. Barnes, 147 Mass. 388, 18 N. E. 65; Nisbit v. Macon Bank & T. Co. (C. C.) 12 Fed. 686; Rowell v. Claggett, 69 N. H. 201, 41 Atl. 173; Hitchcock v. Hassett, 71 Cal. 331, 12 Pac. 228; In re Automobile Livery Service Co. (D. C.) 176 Fed. 792.

[87] Keiser v. Topping, 72 Ill. 226; Tuttle v. Robinson, 78 Ill. 332; City Fire Ins. Co. v. Olmsted, 33 Conn. 476.

[88] But the mere contract to deliver the goods in pledge does not give the contract pledgee a lien on such goods. Hitchcock v. Hassett, 71 Cal. 331, 12 Pac. 228; Davenport v. City Bank of Buffalo and Marcy, 9 Paige (N. Y.) 12.

siderations apply.[89] The delivery not only creates a pledge, but serves to give notice to the world of the rights of the pledgee in the pledged goods; but a mere agreement to deliver in no way serves this last purpose. Accordingly, as to innocent purchasers from the owner and those who innocently acquire in rem rights to the goods, such as attaching creditors, in both cases, if this in rem right precedes the delivery to the pledgee, the latter's rights must yield.[90] There is no little confusion as to the comparative rights of the general creditors of the intending pledgor and the intending pledgee before delivery. In such a case neither the creditor nor the intended pledgee has an in rem claim to the goods; but it would seem that, certainly before the creditors acquire a lien on the goods by an attachment or execution, the intending pledgee has in the absence of fraud the superior right to take possession of the goods and hold them against such general creditors.[91]

Actual and Constructive Delivery—Symbolical Delivery

It has been said: "In all cases the essence of delivery is that the deliveror, by some apt and manifest act, puts the deliveree in the same position of control over the thing, either directly or through a custodian, which he himself held immediately before that act."[92] The question of what acts constitute a sufficient delivery to create a pledge, either when considered generally or with reference to specific kinds of property, is not an easy one. Mr. Schouler's phrase, "the modern mosaic of pledge delivery,"[93] is both accurate and happy.

The most perfect form of delivery, known as actual delivery,

[89] Nisbit v. Macon Bank & T. Co. (C. C.) 12 Fed. 686; AMERICAN CAN CO. v. ERIE PRESERVING CO., 183 Fed. 96, 105 C. C. A. 388, Dobie Cas. Bailments and Carriers, 114; Rowell v. Claggett, 69 N. H. 201, 41 Atl. 173; Copeland v. Barnes, 147 Mass. 388, 18 N. E. 65.

[90] Cameron v. Orleans & J. R. Co., 108 La. 83, 32 South. 208; Parshall v. Eggert, 54 N. Y. 18; American Pig Iron Storage Warrant Co. v. German, 126 Ala. 194, 28 South. 603, 85 Am. St. Rep. 21; Nisbit v. Macon Bank & T. Co. (C. C.) 12 Fed. 686; AMERICAN CAN CO. v. ERIE PRESERVING CO., 183 Fed. 96, 105 C. C. A. 388, Dobie Cas. Bailments and Carriers, 114; Rowell v. Claggett, 69 N. H. 201, 41 Atl. 173; Casey v. National Park Bank, 96 U. S. 492, 493, 24 L. Ed. 789; Cotton v. Arnold, 118 Mo. App. 596, 95 S. W. 280.

[91] See Schouler, Bailm. § 199. "As between the pledge parties and general creditors, such transactions can only be attacked by the latter for fraud upon them; and if there be a bona fide pledge contract, ineffectual for want of delivery, the pledgee may, at any time, take full possession and maintain his priority over them." Parshall v. Eggert, 54 N. Y. 18; Succession of Hiligsberg, 1 La. Ann. 340. See, also, Jones, Collateral Securities (3d Ed.) § 38; Prouty v. Barlow, 74 Minn. 130, 76 N. W. 946.

[92] Pollock, Possession, p. 46.

[93] Schouler, Bailm. § 199.

consists in the real physical transfer of the manual control of the goods by the pledgor to the pledgee,[94] as where the pledgor takes a watch from his pocket and puts it in the hands of the pledgee. About such a delivery there could be no question, and, when it is possible and practicable, it is always safest for the pledgee to resort to such a delivery. To constitute a valid delivery of part of a larger quantity of goods, the part to be pledged should be separated from the rest and delivered.[95]

In some cases, however, an actual delivery is not necessary for the creation of a pledge;[96] in other cases, an immediate actual delivery is either impracticable or impossible.[97] Here all that is necessary is what is called a "constructive delivery." This is a term of comprehensive meaning, and includes those acts which, though not conferring manual control of the goods (or approximating real possession in that sense), are yet held by law to be the equivalent in legal effect to such acts of real delivery.[98] Thus, when property is in the possession of a third person, an actual delivery to the pledgee will not be required; but an order by the pledgor upon the keeper is sufficient to constitute a constructive delivery.[99] Where goods are lying in a warehouse, notice to the warehouse keeper, when all the other essential requisites of a pledge are proved, is equivalent to a delivery; for after such notice

[94] Black, Law Dict. pp. 349, 350. Of course, an effective delivery may be made by an agent of the pledgor. Cartwright v. Wilmerding, 24 N. Y. 521. Or such delivery may be made to an agent of the pledgee. City Bank of New Haven v. Perkins, 29 N. Y. 554, 86 Am. Dec. 332; Johnson v. Smith, 11 Humph. (Tenn.) 396; McCready v. Haslock, 3 Tenn. Ch. 13; Brown v. Warren, 43 N. H. 430; Tibbetts v. Flanders, 18 N. H. 284; Boynton v. Payrow, 67 Me. 587; Weems v. Delta Moss Co., 33 La. Ann. 973.

[95] Collins v. Buck, 63 Me. 459; Sholes v. Western Asphalt Block & Tile Co., 183 Pa. 528, 38 Atl. 1029.

[96] FIRST NAT. BANK OF PARKERSBURG v. HARKNESS, 42 W. Va. 156, 24 S. E. 548, 32 L. R. A. 408, Dobie Cas. Bailments and Carriers, 109; Dubois v. Spinks, 114 Cal. 289, 294, 46 Pac. 95; Jewett v. Warren, 12 Mass. 300, 7 Am. Dec. 74.

[97] Goods during shipment by land or water furnish excellent examples of this.

[98] Black, Law Dict. p. 350, and cases cited. As to what will not be effective as a constructive delivery, see Thurber v. Oliver (C. C.) 26 Fed. 224 (delivery of samples of goods); Brown v. Warren, 43 N. H. 430 (owning the shop in which the goods are used). In Huntington v. Sherman, 60 Conn. 463, 466, 22 Atl. 769, the court, in a case similar to Brown v. Warren, supra, said: "The circumstances ordinarily furnishing a basis for constructive delivery are wholly wanting; the goods are not at sea, nor in a warehouse, nor were they too ponderous to be readily moved, nor were they placed within the power and control of the plaintiffs."

[99] Whitaker v. Sumner, 20 Pick. (Mass.) 399; Tuxworth v. Moore, 9 Pick. (Mass.) 347, 349, 20 Am. Dec. 479.

the keeper ceases to be the agent of the pledgor, and becomes the agent of the pledgee; and thus the goods are placed under the effective control of the pledgee, practically to the same extent that they would be by an actual delivery.[1] The pledgee may himself be in possession when the pledge is created, as where goods already pledged are, by agreement of the parties, made security for a further loan.[2] Or possession may be held by the pledgee jointly with others. Actual delivery is not necessary in such cases. The delivery of the key to the warehouse in which the goods are stored has been held to be an effective delivery of the goods.[3]

When the goods are cumbersome or inaccessible, a delivery is often effected by the physical transfer of some symbol or representative of the goods, which is conventionally recognized as standing for the goods and furnishing a method of dealing with them. Thus, a transfer of the bill of lading[4] of goods in the course of shipment would constitute such a delivery. This form of constructive delivery is called a symbolic delivery.[5]

Incorporeal Property

A pledge of incorporeal property is made by delivery, just as in other cases—that is, the delivery of the evidence or symbol, as the most apt delivery of which this kind of property is capable, creates a pledge of the property—and such a delivery is necessary.[6] Though a pledge of this kind of property is generally made by an assignment in writing, and should be so made, such an as-

[1] Whitaker v. Sumner, 20 Pick. (Mass.) 399, 403; Hathaway v. Haynes, 124 Mass. 311; First Nat. Bank of Cincinnati v. Kelly, 57 N. Y. 34; Cartwright v. Wilmerding, 24 N. Y. 521; Michigan Cent. R. Co. v. Phillips, 60 Ill. 190; Western Union R. Co. v. Wagner, 65 Ill. 197; Burton v. Curyea, 40 Ill. 325, 89 Am. Dec. 350; Newcomb v. Cabell, 10 Bush (Ky.) 460; Whitney v. Tibbits, 17 Wis. 369; Dows v. National Exch. Bank, 91 U. S. 618, 23 L. Ed. 214; First Nat. Bank of Cincinnati v. Bates (D. C.) 1 Fed. 702; Freiburg v. Dreyfus, 135 U. S. 478, 10 Sup. Ct. 716, 34 L. Ed. 206; Harris v. Bradley, 2 Dill. 284, Fed. Cas. No. 6,116.

[2] Herber v. Thompson, 47 La. Ann. 800, 17 South. 318; Van Blarcom v. Broadway Bank, 37 N. Y. 540; Brown v. Warren, 43 N. H. 430; Clark v. Costello, 79 Hun, 588, 29 N. Y. Supp. 937.

[3] Hilton v. Tucker, 39 Ch. D. (Eng.) 669; Ryall v. Rolle, 1 Atk. (Eng.) 165.

[4] Moors v. Wyman, 146 Mass. 60, 15 N. E. 104; Gibson v. Stevens, 8 How. 384, 12 L. Ed. 1123; Peters v. Elliott, 78 Ill. 321; Meyerstern v. Barber, 36 L. J. C. P. (Eng.) 48. The same is true of warehouse receipts. In re Cincinnati Iron Store Co., 167 Fed. 486, 93 C. C. A. 122; Hoor v. Barker, 8 Cal. 609; National Exch. Bank v. Wilder, 34 Minn. 149, 24 N. W. 699.

[5] Black, Law Dict. p. 350.

[6] Jones, Collateral Securities (3d Ed.) § 80; Casey v. Cavaroc, 96 U. S. 467, 24 L. Ed. 779; Atkinson v. Foster, 134 Ill. 472, 25 N. E. 528; Farm Inv. Co. v. Wyoming College and Normal School, 10 Wyo. 240, 68 Pac. 561; Cotton v. Arnold, 118 Mo. App. 596, 95 S. W. 280.

signment is not absolutely necessary,[7] except in the case of corporate stocks, mentioned later in this section. Thus, a negotiable instrument may be pledged by a simple delivery, without any indorsement, even though it be payable "to order."[8] And it has long been settled that if a nonnegotiable note is transferred by delivery, in good faith and for a valuable consideration, this is a valid pledge, which the courts of law will recognize and protect, even though the pledgee cannot maintain an action at law thereon in his own name. And the same principle applies to other choses in action.[9] An equitable interest in a judgment may be pledged by the delivery of the execution thereon to the pledgee.[10] Where there is a pledge of a nonnegotiable chose in action, no notice to the debtor is necessary to the validity of the pledge.[11]

Applying the rules of the preceding paragraphs to some special cases, we find that a delivery of a savings bank book, with the intention that the deposit in the bank represented by the book should be held as collateral security for the payment of a debt,

[7] Bank of Chadron v. Anderson, 6 Wyo. 518, 48 Pac. 197; Sharmer v. McIntosh, 43 Neb. 509, 61 N. W. 727; Crain v. Paine, 4 Cush. (Mass.) 483, 50 Am. Dec. 807; Dickey v. Pocomoke City Nat. Bank, 89 Md. 280, 43 Atl. 33; Bank of Woodland v. Duncan, 117 Cal. 412, 49 Pac. 414. But see American Exch. Bank of New York v. Federal Nat. Bank of Pittsburg, 226 Pa. 483, 75 Atl. 683, 27 L. R. A. (N. S.) 666, 134 Am. St. Rep. 1071, 18 Ann. Cas. 444, holding that there must be a written assignment to pledge a book account, though in the note to this case in 27 L. R. A. (N. S.) 666, many cases are cited holding oral assignments of book accounts valid.

[8] Bank of Chadron v. Anderson, 6 Wyo. 518, 48 Pac. 197; Van Riper v. Baldwin, 19 Hun (N. Y.) 344; Morris v. Preston, 93 Ill. 215; Tucker v. New Hampshire Sav. Bank in Concord, 58 N. H. 83, 42 Am. Rep. 580.

[9] Jones v. Witter, 13 Mass. 304, 307; Grover v. Grover, 24 Pick. (Mass.) 261, 263, 35 Am. Dec. 319; Norton v. Piscataqua Fire & Marine Ins. Co., 111 Mass. 532, 535; Kingman v. Perkins, 105 Mass. 111; Dix v. Cobb, 4 Mass. 508; Williams v. Ingersoll, 89 N. Y. 508, 518; Stout v. Yaeger Mill. Co. (C. C.) 13 Fed. 802; McArthur v. Magee, 114 Cal. 126, 45 Pac. 1068; Hewins v. Baker, 161 Mass. 320, 37 N. E. 441; Grant's Adm'r v. Kline, 115 Pa. 618, 9 Atl. 150.

[10] Crain v. Paine, 4 Cush. (Mass.) 483, 485, 50 Am. Dec. 807; Dunn v. Snell, 15 Mass. 481; Thayer v. Daniels, 113 Mass. 129. See, also, Mulford v. Waller, 3 Abb. Dec. (N. Y.) 330.

[11] Jones, Collateral Securities (3d Ed.) § 136; Thayer v. Daniels, 113 Mass. 129. But see, contra, the English cases of Dearle v. Hall, 3 Russ. 1; Meux v. Bell, 1 Hare, 73. The rule in England would seem to be that, as between successive purchasers of a chose in action, he will have the preference who first gives notice to the debtor, even if he be a subsequent purchaser. Such, however, has not been the rule adopted in this country, where it is held that the assignment of a chose in action is complete upon the mutual assent of the assignor and assignee, and does not gain additional validity, as against third persons, by notice to the debtor.

is a valid pledge.[12] So the delivery of a note and mortgage as security for a debt, even without an assignment in writing, is entitled to protection in a court of law.[13] And where the directors of a corporation placed the company's policies of insurance in the hands of two of its directors, without any formal assignment, to secure loans made and to be made by such directors and others to the corporation, it was held that there was a sufficient delivery of these policies to sustain the pledge.[14]

Corporate Stock

What is necessary to constitute a valid pledge of stock in a corporation has been the subject of much discussion and many conflicting decisions. Indeed, formerly there was doubt whether it could be the subject of a pledge at all, though this is now well settled in the affirmative.[15] It seems, also, well settled that, in the absence of statutory provisions, to pledge corporate stock, some written transfer or contract is necessary, as against third parties.[16] A mere handing over of the stock certificate to the pledgee is not sufficient.[17] There must be either a transfer on the books of the company, or a power of attorney authorizing such a transfer,[18] or some assignment or contract in writing by which the holder may assert title and compel a transfer when desired.[19]

The safest method of delivery is an actual transfer of the stock

[12] Taft v. Bowker, 132 Mass. 277; Boynton v. Payrow, 67 Me. 587.

[13] Crain v. Paine, 4 Cush. (Mass.) 483, 50 Am. Dec. 807; Adler v. Sargent, 109 Cal. 42, 41 Pac. 799; Kamena v. Huelbig, 23 N. J. Eq. 78; Prescott v. Hull, 17 Johns. (N. Y.) 284.

[14] Stout v. Yeager Mill. Co. (C. C.) 13 Fed. 802.

[15] Hasbrouck v. Vandervoort, 4 Sandf. (N. Y.) 74; Gilpin v. Howell, 5 Pa. 41, 45 Am. Dec. 720; Barse Live Stock Co. v. Range Valley Cattle Co., 16 Utah, 59, 50 Pac. 630; Newton v. Fay, 10 Allen (Mass.) 505. See, also, cases cited in the succeeding notes of this section.

[16] Nisbit v. Macon Bank & T. Co. (C. C.) 12 Fed. 686; Succession of Lanaux, 46 La. Ann. 1036, 15 South. 708, 25 L. R. A. 577; First Nat. Bank of Waterloo v. Bacon, 113 App. Div. 612, 98 N. Y. Supp. 717.

[17] Wagner v. Marple, 10 Tex. Civ. App. 505, 31 S. W. 691.

[18] A pledge of stock by a transfer in blank on the back of the certificate, which is pinned to the note secured, is valid in respect to form. McClintock v. Central Bank of Kansas, 120 Mo. 127, 24 S. W. 1052.

[19] Nisbit v. Macon Bank & T. Co. (C. C.) 12 Fed. 686. And see article on Law of Collateral Security, by Leonard A. Jones, in 14 Am. Law Rev. (Feb., 1880) 97, 128. A broker carrying stocks upon margins is a pledgee. The purchaser is regarded as pledgor of the stock which the broker holds as a pledge for the advances made by him in purchasing the stock. Baker v. Drake, 66 N. Y. 518, 23 Am. Rep. 80; Stenton v. Jerome, 54 N. Y. 480; Vaupell v. Woodward, 2 Sandf. Ch. (N. Y.) 143; McNeil v. Tenth Nat. Bank, 55 Barb. (N. Y.) 59; Thompson v. Toland, 48 Cal. 99; Worthington v. Tormey, 34 Md. 182; Hatch v. Douglas, 48 Conn. 116, 40 Am. Rep. 154.

certificate to the pledgee, with a written indorsement thereon, accompanied by a formal transfer of the stock on the books of the corporation. The pledgee is then fully protected, both as against the pledgor and as against third persons claiming through him. In the absence of a statute, or provision in the corporate charter or by-laws, requiring a transfer on the books of the corporation, however, this is not necessary, and a good delivery in pledge may be made by the mere transfer of the stock certificate to the pledgee, with the proper indorsement written thereon.[20]

It is usually provided by statute, or by the charter or by-laws of the corporation, that no transfer of stock is valid unless made on the books of the corporation. The entry of the transaction on the corporation's books, where stock is sold or pledged, is required, not for the transfer of the title, but for the protection of the parties and others dealing with the corporation, and to enable it to know who are its stockholders,[21] entitled as such to participate in the control and the profits of the corporation. In such cases, it seems that a pledge transfer not so recorded is invalid as to bona fide purchasers of the stock.[22] The effect of the unrecorded pledge transfer as against the creditors of the pledgor has resulted in inconsistent holdings by the various courts passing on the question. In some of the cases, the courts deny the validity of the transfer as against such creditors;[23] while in Massachusetts a like result is reached when the recorded transfer is required by statute or the corporate charter, but when such a provision is found only in the corporate by-laws, then the pledgee takes precedence (even though the transfer is not recorded in the company's books) as against the creditors of the pledgor.[24] Since a state statute and

[20] Cecil Nat. Bank v. Watsontown Bank, 105 U. S. 217, 26 L. Ed. 1039; Sibley v. Quinsigamond Nat. Bank, 133 Mass. 515; Johnson v. Underhill, 52 N. Y. 203; Merchants' Nat. Bank v. Richards, 6 Mo. App. 454; CORNICK v. RICHARDS, 3 Lea (Tenn.) 1, Dobie Cas. Bailments and Carriers, 117.

[21] Johnston v. Laflin, 103 U. S. 800, 26 L. Ed. 532; Chouteau Spring Co. v. Harris, 20 Mo. 382; Parker v. Bethel Hotel Co., 96 Tenn. 252, 34 S. W. 209, 31 L. R. A. 706; Scott v. Pequonnock Nat. Bank (C. C.) 15 Fed. 494.

[22] New York & N. H. R. Co. v. Schuyler, 34 N. Y. 30; Johnston v. Laflin, 103 U. S. 800, 26 L. Ed. 532.

[23] See Colt v. Ives, 31 Conn. 25, 81 Am. Dec. 161; Van Zile on Bailm. & Carr. p. 231.

[24] Boston Music Hall Ass'n v. Cory, 129 Mass. 435; Fisher v. President, etc., of Essex Bank, 5 Gray (Mass.) 373. See, also, Smith v. Crescent City Live-Stock Landing & Slaughter House Co., 30 La. Ann. 1378; CORNICK v. RICHARDS, 3 Lea (Tenn.) 1, Dobie Cas. Bailments and Carriers, 117; Jones on Collateral Securities (3d Ed.) §§ 158-162; Otis v. Gardner, 105 Ill. 436; Shipman v. Ætna Ins. Co., 29 Conn. 245; Merchants' Nat. Bank v. Richards, 74 Mo. 77.

the charter of a corporation are public acts of a state, with which those dealing with a corporation are charged with notice, while the by-laws of the corporation are mere rules enacted by a private corporation for its own government, the Massachusetts rule has much to commend it, and is believed to be sound.

Bills of Lading

A bill of lading issued by a carrier is at the same time both a receipt for the goods delivered to the carrier and also a contract containing the terms of the agreement for the transportation of the goods.[25] It is one of the most important of commercial documents, and we shall have frequent occasion to refer to it, in many connections. The bill of lading forms a convenient means of dealing with goods that are in the course of shipment by the carrier.

Though the safest delivery of a bill of lading in pledge is by a delivery of the bill to the pledgee with the proper indorsement, usually in blank, an indorsement is not essential; and a delivery of the bill of lading with the intention of pledging it is entirely sufficient, without any indorsement at all.[26]

Warehouse Receipts

Warehouse receipts are issued by warehousemen, stating that certain goods have been deposited with the warehouseman, and are held by him subject to the order of the person making the deposit.[27] Like a bill of lading, to which in legal effect it is practically similar, the warehouse receipt is a symbol of the goods, and the transfer of such a receipt is equivalent to a delivery of the goods.[28] Like the bill of lading, it is not strictly negotiable, and may also be pledged by a mere delivery of the receipt with that intention without any indorsement.[29]

[25] The Delaware, 14 Wall. 600, 20 L. Ed. 779; Gage v. Jaqueth, 1 Lans. (N. Y.) 210. Civ. Code Cal. § 2126.

[26] Gibson v. Stevens, 8 How. 384, 12 L. Ed. 1123; First Nat. Bank of Cairo v. Crocker, 111 Mass. 163, 167; First Nat. Bank of Green Bay v. Dearborn, 115 Mass. 219, 15 Am. Rep. 92; Michigan Cent. R. Co. v. Phillips, 60 Ill. 190; Haille v. Smith, Bos. & P. (Eng.) 563; Holbrook v. Wight, 24 Wend. (N. Y.) 169, 173, 35 Am. Dec. 607; Grosvenor v. Phillips, 2 Hill (N. Y.) 147; Bank of Rochester v. Jones, 4 N. Y. 497, 55 Am. Dec. 290; Gibson v. Stevens, 8 How. 384, 12 L. Ed. 1123; Allen v. Williams, 12 Pick. (Mass.) 297; Peters v. Elliott, 78 Ill. 321.

[27] Miller v. Browarsky, 130 Pa. 372, 18 Atl. 643; Merchants' Warehouse Co. v. McClain (C. C.) 112 Fed. 789.

[28] Bush v. Export Storage Co. (C. C). 136 Fed. 918; FIRST NAT. BANK OF PARKERSBURG v. HARKNESS, 42 W. Va. 156, 24 S. E. 548, 32 L. R. A. 408, Dobie Cas. Bailments and Carriers, 109; Young v. Lambert, L. R. 3 P. C. (Eng.) 142; Western Union R. Co. v. Wagner, 65 Ill. 197.

[29] Danforth v. McElroy, 121 Ala. 106, 25 South. 840; Gibson v. Stevens,

In the absence of statute, it is generally held that a warehouseman may issue a warehouse receipt for goods of his own which he has in store, and may make a valid pledge by the delivery of such receipt.[30]

RIGHTS AND DUTIES OF THE PLEDGOR

75. Unless varied by a special contract, the principal rights and duties of the pledgor are as follows:

(a) He impliedly warrants his title or interest.

(b) His interest is assignable.

(c) At common law the pledgor's interest seems not to have been subject to judicial sale, but this is now changed in most states by statute.

(d) He can sue third persons for injuries to the pledged goods.

(e) He has a right to redeem the pledged goods, which continues until it is lost:

(1) By a valid sale of the goods by the pledgee after the default of the pledgor.

(2) By a subsequent release by the pledgor of his right of redemption.

(3) By the running of the statute of limitations.

The rights and liabilities of the parties to a pledge may be varied, as in other bailments, by a special contract containing such terms as they see fit to insert.[31] In the absence of such agreements, the law annexes certain conditions to a pledge, which control the rights of the pledgor and pledgee and their duties to each other and to third persons.

Warranty of Title or Interest by the Pledgor

In the very act of creating a pledge, the pledgor impliedly warrants that he has sufficient title, interest, or authority as to the

8 How. 384, 12 L. Ed. 1123; Wilkes v. Ferris, 5 Johns. (N. Y.) 335, 4 Am. Dec. 364; Hoor v. Barker, 8 Cal. 609; St. Louis Nat. Bank v. Ross, 9 Mo. App. 399.

30 Milhiser Mfg. Co. v. Gallego Mills Co., 101 Va. 579, 44 S. E. 760; National Exch. Bank v. Wilder, 34 Minn. 149, 24 N. W. 699; Merchants' Bank of Detroit v. Hibbard, 48 Mich. 118, 11 N. W. 834, 42 Am. Rep. 465; Alabama State Bank v. Barnes, 82 Ala. 607, 2 South. 349. But see, contra, Franklin Nat. Bank v. Whitehead, 149 Ind. 560, 49 N. E. 592, 39 L. R. A. 725, 63 Am. St. Rep. 302; Jones, Collateral Securities, §§ 325a, 326.

31 St. Losky v. Davidson, 6 Cal. 643; Lee v. Baldwin, 10 Ga. 208; Lawrence v. McCalmont, 2 How. 426, 451, 11 L. Ed. 326; Drake v. White, 117 Mass. 10.

goods to make the pledge in question.[32] It is frequently said that the pledgor impliedly warrants his title to be that of absolute owner;[33] but this is true only when the particular pledge was such that only an absolute owner could have made it, or when the pledge is itself a practical affirmation of ownership on the part of the pledgor. When the pledgor purports to pledge merely a specific interest in the goods, he then impliedly warrants only that he has the right to pledge such interest. The pledgor, by virtue of this implied warranty, is accordingly liable to the pledgee for the amount of any liens or incumbrances on the goods which the pledgee is obliged to discharge in order to perfect his interest.[34]

Of course, one can undertake to pledge only such interest (if any) in the goods as he has, without specifying the extent of that interest, and there will then be no such implied warranty on his part. The pledgor's warranty here is analogous to that of the seller in sales of personalty.

One assuming to own goods, and pledging them, is estopped from afterwards denying such ownership at the time the pledge was created; and a subsequent acquisition of title by the pledgor, as between the parties to the contract, inures to the benefit of the pledgee, without any new delivery or ratification of the pledge on the part of the pledgor.[35]

Assignment of His Interest by the Pledgor

The owner of a chattel, which he has pledged, still retains his ownership or general property in the chattel, qualified by, and subject to, the special property and rights of the pledgee in the chattel, created by the pledge.[36] This qualified general property in the chattel the owner may transfer to a third person by sale or assignment.[37] Such third person then succeeds to the rights of the owner, without affecting the right or interest of the pledgee in the chattel.[38] The assignee may tender the amount of the debt

[32] Edwards, Bailm. p. 192; Jones, Collateral Securities, § 52; Mairs v. Taylor, 40 Pa. 446; Goldstein v. Hort, 30 Cal. 372.

[33] Story, Bailm. § 354; Jones, Collateral Securities, § 52.

[34] Cass v. Higenbotam, 27 Hun (N. Y.) 406.

[35] Goldstein v. Hort, 30 Cal. 372.

[36] See ante, § 72; post, § 78.

[37] Brent v. Miller, 81 Ala. 309, 8 South. 219; Brown v. Hotel Ass'n, 63 Neb. 181, 88 N. W. 175; Fletcher v. Howard, 2 Aikens (Vt.) 115, 16 Am. Dec. 686; Bush v. Lyon, 9 Cow. (N. Y.) 52; Whitaker v. Sumner, 20 Pick. (Mass.) 399; Tuxworth v. Moore, 9 Pick. (Mass.) 347, 20 Am. Dec. 479; Fettyplace v. Dutch, 13 Pick. (Mass.) 388, 23 Am. Dec. 688; Cooper v. Ray, 47 Ill. 53; Ratcliff v. Vance, 2 Mill, Const. (S. C.) 239.

[38] Taggart v. Packard, 39 Vt. 628; Shinkle v. Vickery, 130 Fed. 424, 64 C. C. A. 626; Citizens' Nat. Bank of Ft. Scott v. Bank of Commerce, 80 Kan.

secured and demand the return of the pledged chattel; and if this is refused by the pledgee, such assignee may enforce his rights by an action of replevin or trover or conversion.[39] After the pledgee has received notice of an assignment of the pledgor's interest, the pledgee holds the goods for the benefit of the assignee, and cannot lawfully surrender them to the pledgor, even on payment of the amount secured.[40] If, on default, the pledgee sells the pledged goods, he holds the surplus proceeds, after the satisfaction of the debt, on behalf of the assignee.[41]

Sale of Pledgor's Interest on Judicial Process

At common law, the interest remaining in a pledgor of goods was not subject to attachment,[42] garnishment,[43] or seizure and sale on execution.[44] This rule has been changed by statute in most of the states. In some states this result is brought about by express enactments specifically providing that the pledgor's interest shall be liable to judicial sale;[45] in other states the terms of the statutes providing what interests shall be subject to judicial sale are so

205, 101 Pac. 1005; Carothers Warehouse Bldg. Ass'n v. McConnell, 30 Okl. 394, 121 Pac. 191.

[39] Durfee v. Harper, 22 Mont. 354, 56 Pac. 582; Id., 22 Mont. 373, 56 Pac. 589; Franklin v. Neate, 13 Mees. & W. (Eng.) 480; Ratcliff v. Vance, 2 Mill, Const. (S. C.) 239. Refusal to deliver pledged stock to the pledgor's assignee is not justified by its attachment under a writ against such pledgor, subsequent to such assignment. Loughborough v. McNevin, 74 Cal. 250, 14 Pac. 369, 15 Pac. 773, 5 Am. St. Rep. 435.

[40] Duell v. Cudlipp, 1 Hilt. (N. Y.) 166.

[41] Van Blarcom v. Broadway Bank, 37 N. Y. 540.

[42] Ætna Ins. Co. v. Bank of Wilcox, 48 Neb. 544, 67 N. W. 449; Mapleton Bank v. Standrod, 8 Idaho, 740, 71 Pac. 119, 67 L. R. A. 656; Badlam v. Tucker, 1 Pick. (Mass.) 389, 11 Am. Dec. 202; Jennings v. McIlroy, 42 Ark. 236, 48 Am. Rep. 61; Tannahill v. Tuttle, 3 Mich. 104, 61 Am. Dec. 480; Wilkes v. Ferris, 5 Johns. (N. Y.) 336, 4 Am. Dec. 364; Marsh v. Lawrence, 4 Cow. (N. Y.) 461; Stief v. Hart, 1 N. Y. 20, 28; Pomeroy v. Smith, 17 Pick. (Mass.) 85; Hunt v. Holton, 13 Pick. (Mass.) 216; Srodes v. Caven, 3 Watts (Pa.) 258. Where a sheriff violates the law, in seizing goods pledged, under an attachment against the pledgor, in an action against him by the pledgee he will be liable to the latter for the entire value of the goods. Treadwell v. Davis, 34 Cal. 601, 94 Am. Dec. 770.

[43] Drake, Attachment, § 539; Hall v. Page, 4 Ga. 428, 48 Am. Dec. 235; Winslow v. Fletcher, 53 Conn. 390, 4 Atl. 250, 55 Am. Rep. 122; Roby v. Labuzan, 21 Ala. 60, 56 Am. Dec. 237; Kergin v. Dawson, 1 Gilman (Ill.) 86; Patterson v. Harland, 12 Ark. 158.

[44] Soule v. White, 14 Me. 436; Thompson v. Stevens, 10 Me. 27; Briggs v. Walker, 21 N. H. 72; Dowler v. Cushwa, 27 Md. 354, 366; Badlam v. Tucker, 1 Pick. (Mass.) 389, 11 Am. Dec. 202; Treadwell v. Davis, 34 Cal. 601, 94 Am. Dec. 770.

[45] For examples of such statutes, see Civ. Code Ga. 1910, § 3524; 1 Burns' Ann. St. Ind. 1908, § 764; Rev. Laws Mass. 1902, c. 167, §§ 69-72;

broad that they include the interest of a pledgor by implication.[46] These statutes, of course, do not permit the creditor to interfere with the rights of the pledgee;[47] for he has a special property in the goods pledged, and is not bound to deliver them up to the pledgor until the debt is paid, or the undertaking performed, for the security of which the pledge was created, and a creditor of the pledgor, standing in the latter's shoes, cannot in this respect have any greater rights than the pledgor himself.

Action by Pledgor against Third Persons

The general rules governing the right of a bailor in a mutual benefit bailment to sue third persons are applicable here; also what has been said as to the doctrine (generally held) that a complete recovery by either bailor (pledgor) or bailee (pledgee) will bar an action by the other.[48] The modern criticisms on the rule permitting one to recover for injuries caused to the other (resulting in no damage to the litigant) receive an added force in the case of pledges, when (as is rare in other bailments) the interest of the bailee (pledgee) is, from a practical standpoint, frequently greater than that of the bailor (pledgor).[49] Mr. Schouler maintains that, for damage by third persons intermeddling with the pledged goods, the courts practically favor an action by the pledgee rather than one by the pledgor, which might wholly or in part oust the pledgee of his security.[50] Very few of the points here involved have been satisfactorily worked out by the courts. Certainly, however, the pledgee has the same right to sue third persons as other mutual benefit bailees; and it would seem that the pledgor has at least the same right as other mutual benefit bailors to protect by suit his reversionary interest in the goods.[51]

Pledgor's Right to Redeem

The right of redemption, or of again securing the pledged goods on the payment of the debt or performance of the engagement

Comp. Laws Mich. 1897, § 10318. See Jones, Collateral Securities, §§ 375–392a.

[46] See Petty v. Overall, 42 Ala. 145, 94 Am. Dec. 634; Arizona Civ. Code 1901, par. 2565; Reichenbach v. McKean, 95 Pa. 432; Horner v. Dennis, 34 La. Ann. 389; First Nat. Bank of Memphis v. Pettit, 9 Heisk. (Tenn.) 447.

[47] Jones, Collateral Securities, § 374; McClintock v. Central Bank of Kansas City, 120 Mo. 127, 24 S. W. 1052.

[48] See ante, pp. 112, 134. See, also, Einstein v. Dunn, 171 N. Y. 648, 63 N. E. 1116; Adams v. O'Connor, 100 Mass. 515, 1 Am. Rep. 137; Miller v. McKenzie, 11 Ga. App. 494, 75 S. E. 820; Gamson v. Pritchard, 210 Mass. 296, 96 N. E. 715.

[49] See Schouler, Bailm. § 223.

[50] Schouler, Bailm. § 223.

[51] See cases cited in note 48; Usher v. Van Vranken, 48 App. Div. 413,

secured, is, of course, the most important of the pledgor's rights.[52] Practically, this is the only real interest remaining in the pledgor, and his other rights are all incidental thereto. This important right continues in the pledgor until it is lost by one of the methods now to be discussed.

(1) The usual way in which this right of redemption is lost is by a valid sale of the pledged goods by the pledgee.[53] The same result follows from the rightful collection of money claims or negotiable paper.[54] Since this power of sale inheres in the pledge relation, a proper sale by the pledgee confers title to the goods on the purchaser at the sale, and the pledgor's right to redeem is thus forever lost.[55]

(2) A stipulation inserted in the original pledge contract, providing that, if the debt be not paid or the engagement secured be not strictly fulfilled at the time and in the mode prescribed, the pledge shall be irredeemable, is void, upon the ground of public policy, as tending to the oppression of debtors.[56] However, after the pledge

68 N. Y. Supp. 104; Gregg v. Bank of Columbia, 72 S. C. 458, 52 S. E. 195, 110 Am. St. Rep. 633.

52 Hart v. Burton, 7 J. J. Marsh. (Ky.) 322; Hughes v. Johnson, 38 Ark. 285; Jennings v. Wyzanski, 188 Mass. 285, 74 N. E. 347; White River Sav. Bank v. Capital Sav. Bank & Trust Co., 77 Vt. 123, 59 Atl. 197, 107 Am. St. Rep. 154; Chambers v. Kunzman, 59 N. J. Eq. 433, 45 Atl. 599; Roberts v. Sykes, 30 Barb. (N. Y.) 173. When no time for redemption is fixed, the pledgor may redeem at any time. Cortelyou v. Lansing, 2 Caines, Cas. (N. Y.) 200, 204. In an action in equity to redeem a pledge, payment of the amount for which the pledge was given should be directed before the return of the pledge is ordered. Smith v. Anderson, 8 Tex. Civ. App. 188, 27 S. W. 775. And see, further, as to redemption in equity, Bartlett v. Johnson, 9 Allen (Mass.) 530; Appeal of Conyngham, 57 Pa. 474; Brown v. Runals, 14 Wis. 693; Chapman v. Turner, 1 Call (Va.) 280, 288, 1 Am. Dec. 514; Flowers v. Sproule, 2 A. K. Marsh. (Ky.) 54; Merrill v. Houghton, 51 N. H. 61; White Mountains R. R. v. Bay State Iron Co., 50 N. H. 57; Hasbrouck v. Vandervoort, 4 Sandf. (N. Y.) 74; Jones v. Smith, 2 Ves. Jr. (Eng.) 372.

53 See post, § 88. See, also, Swann v. Baxter, 36 Misc. Rep. 233, 73 N. Y. Supp. 336; Jennings v. Wyzanski, 188 Mass. 285, 74 N. E. 347.

54 Polhemus v. Prudential Realty Corp., 74 N. J. Law, 570, 67 Atl. 303; Naef v. Potter, 127 Ill. App. 106, affirmed in 226 Ill. 628, 80 N. E. 1084, 11 L. R. A. (N. S.) 1034.

55 Post, § 88.

56 Ritchie v. McMullen, 79 Fed. 522, 25 C. C. A. 50; Sherman v. Mutual Life Ins. Co., 53 Wash. 523, 102 Pac. 419; Vickers v. Battershall, 84 Hun, 496, 32 N. Y. Supp. 314; Luckett v. Townsend, 3 Tex. 119, 49 Am. Dec. 723. The Roman law treated a similar stipulation (called in that law "lex commissoria") in the same manner, holding it to be a mere nullity. However, the Roman law allowed the parties to agree that upon default in payment the creditor might take the pledge at a stipulated price, provided it was its reasonable value, and the transaction was bona fide. Story, Bailm. § 345.

contract is entered into and the pledge created by delivery, the pledgor may by a subsequent agreement release his right of redemption to the pledgee, just as he may transfer it to a third person, and such a contract is valid.[57] In other words, this right of redemption cannot be strangled in its inception; but, once existent, it may be either transferred to a third person or released to the pledgee.

(3) The right of redemption may also be lost by the bar of the statute of limitations. Where the pledgee remains in possession of the pledged goods, the statute of limitations does not ordinarily begin to run against the pledgor until after a tender of the debt for which the pledge was given, and a refusal by the pledgee to restore the pledged goods upon demand by the pledgor.[58] Until then the pledgor has no cause of action, for until such tender and refusal the holding of the pledgee is rightful and the pledgor has no right either to demand the goods or sue for their recovery. Similarly the statute begins to run when the pledgee unequivocally repudiates the pledgor's interest in the goods.[59] Mere delay on the part of the pledgor (in the absence of such demand or refusal) to claim a redemption of the pledged goods will not suffice to cut off the right of the pledgor to redeem, unless this case is expressly included within the terms of the particular statute of limitations.[60] The fact that the debt secured is barred by the statute does not bar the pledgor's right to redeem;[61] nor, on the other hand, does this fact entitle the pledgor to recover the pledged goods without

[57] Beatty v. Sylvester, 3 Nev. 228; Rutherford v. Massachusetts Mut. Life Ins. Co. (C. C.) 45 Fed. 712; Small v. Saloy, 42 La. Ann. 183, 7 South. 450.

[58] Whelan's Ex'r v. Kinsley's Adm'r, 26 Ohio St. 131; Jones v. Thurmond's Heirs, 5 Tex. 318; Cross v. Eureka L. & Y. Canal Co., 73 Cal. 302, 14 Pac. 885, 2 Am. St. Rep. 808; Brown v. Bronson, 93 App. Div. 312, 87 N. Y. Supp. 872.

[59] University of North Carolina v. State Nat. Bank, 96 N. C. 280, 3 S. E. 259; Gilmer v. Morris (C. C.) 43 Fed. 456; Waterman v. Brown, 31 Pa. 161.

[60] Reynolds v. Cridge, 131 Pa. 189, 18 Atl. 1010; Chouteau v. Allen, 70 Mo. 290; Roberts v. Sykes, 30 Barb. (N. Y.) 173; Whelan's Ex'r v. Kinsley's Adm'r, 26 Ohio St. 131; Hancock v. Franklin Ins. Co., 114 Mass. 155; Moses v. St. Paul, 67 Ala. 168; Kemp v. Westbrook, 1 Ves. Sr. (Eng.) 278. Where an article pledged is a specific chattel, there is an ample remedy at law, by replevin, if the pledgee retains the possession, or by trover or assumpsit in case he has parted with it. Bryson v. Rayner, 25 Md. 424, 90 Am. Dec. 69. The pledgor may estop himself, when the elements of estoppel are present, from setting up the statute. Lance v. Bonnell, 58 N. J. Eq. 259, 43 Atl. 288; Waterman v. Brown, 31 Pa. 161.

[61] Brewster v. Hartley, 37 Cal. 15, 99 Am. Dec. 237; Kemp v. Westbrook, 1 Ves. (Eng.) 278; Hartranft's Estate, 153 Pa. 530, 26 Atl. 104, 34 Am. St. Rep. 717; Hancock v. Franklin Ins. Co., 114 Mass. 155.

paying the debt, for the obligation to pay continues, even though the remedy is barred.[62]

Again, though the pledgee may not, because of the statute, then sue on the barred debt, he may either retain the pledged goods until the debt is paid or else sell them and retain the amount of the debt out of the proceeds of the sale.[63] If, as is not usually the case, the pledgor, seeking to redeem, has to invoke the powers of a court of equity,[64] he might be met with the defense of laches (or that he has unduly delayed in asserting his rights), under the maxim "Æquitas vigilantibus non dormientibus subvenit," even though the period prescribed by the statute of limitations has not yet run.

RIGHTS AND DUTIES OF THE PLEDGEE AS AFFECTED BY PLEDGOR'S DEFAULT

76. The rights and duties of the pledgee depend largely upon whether or not there has been a default by the pledgor.

As has already been seen, a pledge is a bailment that is incidental to a debt or other undertaking, which the pledge is created to secure. Until there has been a default by the pledgor in the payment of this debt or the performance of this undertaking, the pledgee is little more than an ordinary mutual benefit bailee. But when the debt becomes due, or the time for the performance of the undertaking arrives and the pledgor is in default, the pledgee has unique rights not possessed at all by mutual benefit bailees in general. We shall accordingly proceed to discuss the pledgee's rights before a default by the pledgor, and later take up his rights after such a default.

62 Jones v. Merchants' Bank of Albany, 6 Rob. (N. Y.) 162; In re Oakley, 2 Edw. Ch. (N. Y.) 478; Spect v. Spect, 88 Cal. 437, 26 Pac. 203, 13 L. R. A. 137, 22 Am. St. Rep. 314.

63 Jones v. Thurmond's Heirs, 5 Tex. 318.

64 As to the need of resorting to a court of equity by the pledgor, see Jones, Collateral Securities, § 556. As to redemption in equity, see, also, Merrill v. Houghton, 51 N. H. 61; Appeal of Conyngham, 57 Pa. 474; Bartlett v. Johnson, 9 Allen (Mass.) 530.

RIGHTS AND DUTIES OF THE PLEDGEE BEFORE DEFAULT—ASSIGNABILITY OF THE PLEDGEE'S INTEREST

77. The interest of the pledgee is assignable.

Unlike the interest of the lienholder, the interest which the pledgee acquires is transferable.[65] He may make an absolute assignment of all his interest in the goods pledged,[66] or he may assign his interest conditionally, to secure payment of his own debt; that is, he may subpledge it,[67] or he may even deliver it to a bailee to hold for him.[68] The transfer of the pledged goods in any one of these ways would be a legal disposition of them authorized by the nature of the pledgee's interest.[69]

The subpledgee (or assignee of the original pledgee) can in turn claim the possession of the goods originally pledged, both as against the original pledgor and the original pledgee; but such subpledgee (or assignee of the pledgee) can acquire, ordinarily, only the rights of the original pledgee.[70]

[65] Hawkins v. Fourth Nat. Bank, 150 Ind. 117, 49 N. E. 957; Brittan v. Oakland Bank of Savings, 124 Cal. 282, 57 Pac. 84, 71 Am. St. Rep. 58; Boswell v. Thigpen, 75 Miss. 308, 22 South. 823; Rand v. Barrett, 66 Iowa, 731, 24 N. W. 530; Talty v. Freedman's Sav. & T. Co., 93 U. S. 321, 23 L. Ed. 886.

[66] Jarvis v. Rogers, 15 Mass. 389, 408; Whitaker v. Sumner, 20 Pick. (Mass.) 399; Bush v. Lyon, 9 Cow. (N. Y.) 52; Ferguson v. Union Furnace Co., 9 Wend. (N. Y.) 345; Thompson v. Patrick, 4 Watts (Pa.) 414; Appeal of Ashton, 73 Pa. 153; Goss v. Emerson, 23 N. H. 38; Bailey v. Colby, 34 N. H. 29, 66 Am. Dec. 752; Warner v. Martin, 11 How. 209, 13 L. Ed. 667; Calkins v. Lockwood, 17 Conn. 154, 42 Am. Dec. 729; Belden v. Perkins, 78 Ill. 449; Bradley v. Parks, 83 Ill. 169. The consent of the pledgor to the assignment is not necessary. Curtis v. Leavitt, 15 N. Y. 9. A pledgee of negotiable instruments may assign them. Chapman v. Brooks, 31 N. Y. 75; Duncomb v. New York, H. & N. R. Co., 84 N. Y. 190; Id., 88 N. Y. 1; Baldwin v. Ely, 9 How. 580, 599, 13 L. Ed. 266; Merchants' Nat. Bank v. State Nat. Bank, 10 Wall. 604, 19 L. Ed. 1008.

[67] Interurban Const. Co. v. Hayes, 191 Mo. 248, 89 S. W. 927; Drake v. Cloonan, 99 Mich. 121, 57 N. W. 1098, 41 Am. St. Rep. 586; Meyer v. Moss, 110 La. 132, 34 South. [illegible]; Lewis v. Mott, 36 N. Y. 395; Jarvis v. Rogers, 15 Mass. 389; National Bank of Pulaski v. Winston, 5 Baxt. (Tenn.) 685; McCombie v. Davies, 7 East, 5, 7. One to whom securities have been pledged to secure the payment of a note may, on negotiating the note, transfer the securities, without being liable to a suit for conversion by the pledgor. Waddle v. Owen, 43 Neb. 489, 61 N. W. 731. Nor is the consent of the original pledgor necessary. Cumming v. McDade, 118 Ga. 612, 45 S. E. 479; Coleman v. Anderson, 98 Tex. 570, 86 S. W. 730.

[68] Ingersoll v. Van Bokkelin, 7 Cow. (N. Y.) 670.

[69] Goss v. Emerson, 23 N. H. 38.

[70] Norton v. Baxter, 41 Minn. 146, 42 N. W. 865, 4 L. R. A. 305, 16 Am. St. Rep. 679; Williams v. Ashe, 111 Cal. 180, 43 Pac. 595; Interurban Const.

SAME—RELATIVE TITLE ACQUIRED BY THE PLEDGEE

78. The rights and interest of the pledgee are ordinarily neither more nor less valid than those of the pledgor.
EXCEPTIONS: (1) Agency by estoppel.
(2) Negotiable instruments.

When a valid pledge of goods is created, the pledgee acquires rights which neither the pledgor and those in privity with him nor third parties can dispute.[71] As to third persons, by virtue of the general principle of jurisprudence that a person can confer no greater interest in goods than he himself has, the pledgee's interest is only as valid as that of the pledgor.[72] If the pledgor has a title good against all the world, the pledgee's rights are equally as valid. If the pledgor's title is defective, the pledgee holds the pledged goods subject to the same defect. By a pledge the pledgee acquires no better rights in the goods than the pledgor had.[73] To this rule there is an exception (apparent, at least) in the case of agency by estoppel, and another exception in the case of negotiable paper.

Agency by Estoppel

We have already discussed instances of this kind in the case of factors, who, having no real authority as between the owner and themselves to pledge goods intrusted to them, may yet create pledges of the goods (valid against the owner) to third persons, when such owner has, by clothing the factor with the indicia of title or otherwise holding him out as having the power to pledge the goods, estopped himself from denying such authority in the factor.[74] The principle is of general application, both in the field of pledges and elsewhere, and requires no further discussion here.

Negotiable Instruments

When a person takes negotiable paper before maturity, without notice of any defenses to such paper, in the usual course of busi-

Co. v. Hayes, 191 Mo. 248, 89 S. W. 927; Jenckes v. Rice, 119 Iowa, 451, 93 N. W. 384; Waddle v. Owen, 43 Neb. 489, 61 N. W. 731.

[71] See post, § 79.

[72] Duell v. Cudlipp, 1 Hilt. (N. Y.) 166; Taylor v. Turner, 87 Ill. 296; Agnew v. Johnson, 22 Pa. 471, 62 Am. Dec. 303; Hooper v. Ramsbottom, 4 Camp. (Eng.) 121; Gottlieb v. Hartman, 3 Colo. 53; Hartop v. Hoare, 3 Atk. (Eng.) 44; Patton v. Joliff, 44 W. Va. 88, 28 S. E. 740; Worthington v. Vette, 77 Mo. App. 445.

[73] Swett v. Brown, 5 Pick. (Mass.) 178; Reeves v. Smith, 1 La. Ann. 379; Agnew v. Johnson, 22 Pa. 471, 62 Am. Dec. 303; Gallaher v. Cohen, 1 Browne (Pa.) 43.

[74] Ante, pp. 184–185.

ness, as collateral security, and makes advances at the time upon the credit of such paper, he is considered by all the authorities as a bona fide holder for value, within the rule for the protection of holders of commercial paper.[75] Such a negotiation cuts off previous equities (as distinguished from absolute defenses, which are not thus cut off) which might have been set up against the pledgor or other prior parties, so that the pledgee thus acquires a better title than his bailor had.[76] This is really what is meant by "negotiable" as applied to written instruments.

As to whether a pledgee who takes negotiable instruments merely as security for a pre-existing debt is a holder for value, the cases are in conflict. The question is important, since, unless he is a holder for value, previous equities are not cut off, but may be set up against him just as they could be set up against the pledgor, or other prior parties.

When the instrument is received in whole or part payment of

[75] Swift v. Tyson, 16 Pet. 1, 10 L. Ed. 865; Brooklyn City & N. R. Co. v. National Bank of the Republic, 102 U. S. 14, 26 L. Ed. 61; American Exchange Nat. Bank v. New York Belting & Packing Co., 148 N. Y. 698, 43 N. E. 168; Des Moines Nat. Bank v. Chisholm, 71 Iowa, 675, 33 N. W. 234; Best v. Crall, 23 Kan. 482, 33 Am. Rep. 185; Bell v. Bell, 12 Pa. 235; Bowman v. Van Kuren, 29 Wis. 209, 219, 9 Am. Rep. 554; Curtis v. Mohr, 18 Wis. 615; Bond v. Wiltse, 12 Wis. 611; Jenkins v. Schaub, 14 Wis. 1; Kinney v. Kruse, 28 Wis. 183; Dix v. Tully, 14 La. Ann. 456; Warner v. Fourth Nat. Bank, 115 N. Y. 251, 22 N. E. 172; Nelson v. Eaton, 26 N. Y. 410, 416; Exchange Bank v. Butner, 60 Ga. 654; Griswold v. Davis, 31 Vt. 390; Worcester Nat. Bank v. Cheeney, 87 Ill. 602. One who receives, as collateral security to a loan then made, negotiable bonds not yet matured, without knowledge of any defense to such bonds, is entitled to protection, as a purchaser thereof, to the extent of the amount of such loan. Hayden v. Lincoln City Electric Ry. Co., 43 Neb. 680, 62 N. W. 73.

[76] Allaire v. Hartshorne, 21 N. J. Law, 665, 47 Am. Dec. 175; Youngs v. Lee, 12 N. Y. 551; First Nat. Bank v. Fowler, 36 Ohio St. 524, 38 Am. Rep. 610; Zellweger v. Caffe, 5 Duer (N. Y.) 87, 91; Farwell v. Importers' & Traders' Nat. Bank, 16 Wkly. Dig. (N. Y.) 20; Fisher v. Fisher, 98 Mass. 303; Stoddard v. Kimball, 6 Cush. (Mass.) 469; Draper v. Saxton, 118 Mass. 427; Buchanan v. International Bank, 78 Ill. 500, 504; Stotts v. Byers, 17 Iowa, 303; Crosby v. Roub, 16 Wis. 616, 84 Am. Dec. 720; Helmer v. Commercial Bank of B. M. Webster, 28 Neb. 474, 44 N. W. 482; Haydon v. Nicoletti, 18 Nev. 290, 3 Pac. 473; Duncomb v. New York, H. & N. R. Co., 84 N. Y. 190; Richardson v. Crandall, 48 N. Y. 348, 364; Bank of New York v. Vanderhorst, 32 N. Y. 553; Miller v. Pollock, 99 Pa. 202; Munn v. McDonald, 10 Watts (Pa.) 270; Stotts v. Byers, 17 Iowa, 303; Crosby v. Roub, 16 Wis. 616, 84 Am. Dec. 720; Lyon v. Ewings, 17 Wis. 61; Bowman v. Van Kuren, 29 Wis. 209, 219, 9 Am. Rep. 554; Hotchkiss v. National Shoe & Leather Bank, 21 Wall. 354, 22 L. Ed. 645; Tiffany v. Boatman's Sav. Inst., 18 Wall. 375, 21 L. Ed 868; Michigan Ins. Bank v. Eldred, 9 Wall. 544, 19 L. Ed. 763.

the debt,[77] when any previously held securities are surrendered,[78] or when any indulgence or forbearance[79] is granted to the debtor, in consideration of the pledge of the instrument, then the courts agree that the pledgee is a holder for value. The dispute, then, is limited to the case when the pledgee takes the instrument, without surrendering any of his former rights, solely as security for the pre-existing debt.[80]

The view supported by the great weight of authority, and the sounder reason, declares the pledgee in such cases to be a holder for value.[81] This is the rule of the United States Supreme Court,[82]

[77] Mayer v. Heidelbach, 123 N. Y. 332, 25 N. E. 416, 9 L. R. A. 850; American Exch. Nat. Bank v. New York Belting & Packing Co., 74 Hun, 446, 26 N. Y. Supp. 822; Ward v. Howard, 88 N. Y. 74; Chrysler v. Renois, 43 N. Y. 209; Brown v. Leavitt, 31 N. Y. 113; Youngs v. Lee, 12 N. Y. 551; Mix v. National Bank of Bloomington, 91 Ill. 20, 33 Am. Rep. 44; Bardsley v. Delp, 88 Pa. 420; Norton v. Waite, 20 Me. 175; Brush v. Scribner, 11 Conn. 388, 29 Am. Dec. 303; Dixon v. Dixon, 31 Vt. 450, 76 Am. Dec. 128; Kellogg v. Fancher, 23 Wis. 21, 99 Am. Dec. 96; McKnight v. Knisely, 25 Ind. 336, 87 Am. Dec. 364; Mayberry v. Morris, 62 Ala. 116.

[78] Goodwin v. Conklin, 85 N. Y. 21; Phœnix Ins. Co. v. Church, 81 N. Y. 218, 37 Am. Rep. 494; Park Bank v. Watson, 42 N. Y. 490, 1 Am. Rep. 573; Salina Bank v. Babcock, 21 Wend. (N. Y.) 499.

[79] Central Sav. Bank v. Smith, 43 Colo. 90, 95 Pac. 307; Atlanta Guano Co. v. Hunt, 100 Tenn. 89, 42 S. W. 482; Mechanics' & Farmers' Bank of Albany v. Wixson, 42 N. Y. 438; Traders' Bank of Rochester v. Bradner, 43 Barb. (N. Y.) 379; Burns v. Rowland, 40 Barb. (N. Y.) 368; Watson v. Randall, 20 Wend. (N. Y.) 201.

[80] As to ordinary chattels the cases hold, in the absence of a statute, that a pledge of these merely as security for, and not in payment of, pre-existing debts does not constitute the pledgee a holder for value. Chartered Bank v. Henderson, L. R. 5 P. C. (Eng.) 501; Goodwin v. Massachusetts Loan & Trust Co., 152 Mass. 189, 25 N. E. 100; Sleeper v. Davis, 64 N. H. 59, 6 Atl. 201, 10 Am. St. Rep. 377.

[81] Jones, Collateral Securities (3d Ed.) §§ 107-121; Sackett v. Johnson, 54 Cal. 107; Tomblin v. Callen, 69 Iowa, 229, 28 N. W. 573; Wilkins v. Usher, 123 Ky. 696, 97 S. W. 37, 29 Ky. Law Rep. 1232; Birket v. Elward, 68 Kan. 295, 74 Pac. 1100, 64 L. R. A. 568, 104 Am. St. Rep. 405, 1 Ann. Cas. 272; Herman v. Gunter, 83 Tex. 66, 18 S. W. 428, 29 Am. St. Rep. 632; Hotchkiss v. Fitzgerald Patent Prepared Plaster Co., 41 W. Va. 357, 23 S. E. 576; Barney v. Earle, 13 Ala. 106; Brush v. Scribner, 11 Conn. 388, 29 Am. Dec. 303; Meadow v. Bird, 22 Ga. 246; Conkling v. Vail, 31 Ill. 166; McKnight v. Knisely, 25 Ind. 336, 87 Am. Dec. 364; Homes v. Smyth, 16 Me. 177, 33 Am. Dec. 650; Blanchard v. Stevens, 3 Cush. (Mass.) 162, 50 Am. Dec. 723; Thacher v. Pray, 113 Mass. 291, 18 Am. Rep. 480; Outhwite v. Porter, 13 Mich. 533; Stevenson v. Hyland, 11 Minn. 198 (Gil. 128); Struthers v. Kendall, 41 Pa.

[82] Swift v. Tyson, 16 Pet. 1, 10 L. Ed. 865; Oates v. First Nat. Bank, 100 U. S. 239, 25 L. Ed. 580; RAILROAD CO. v. NATIONAL BANK OF THE REPUBLIC, 102 U. S. 14, 25, 26 L. Ed. 61, Dobie Cas. Bailments and Carriers, 119.

and is also the rule adopted by the Negotiable Instruments Law.[83] The basis of this rule has been said to be sound business policy and commercial convenience; while a technical consideration has been found in the fact of the undertaking by the pledgee to fix the liability of parties secondarily liable on the instrument by taking the proper steps at maturity, such as presentment, demand, and notice, on penalty of becoming liable himself for any loss resulting from his neglect to take such steps.[84] The doctrine declaring the pledgee here a holder for value is in line, not only with the trend of modern decisions, but also with modern statutory definitions of "value," as in the American Sales Act.[85] This doctrine has been denied, though, by the courts of New York,[86] Ohio,[87] and many other states.[88]

A pledgee of a negotiable instrument to secure future advances is protected, as a bona fide holder, for all advances made before he

214, 80 Am. Dec. 610; Dixon v. Dixon, 31 Vt. 450, 76 Am. Dec. 128. See, also, Bridgeport City Bank v. Welch, 29 Conn. 475; Manning v. McClure, 36 Ill. 490; President, etc., of Washington Bank v. Lewis, 22 Pick. (Mass.) 24; Fisher v. Fisher, 98 Mass. 303; Armour v. McMichael, 36 N. J. Law, 92; Cobb v. Doyle, 7 R. I. 550. This rule is also the established rule in England. Poirier v. Morris, 2 El. & Bl. 89; Bosanquet v. Dudman, 1 Stark. 1; Price v. Price, 16 M. & W. 232.

[83] Section 25: "An antecedent or pre-existing debt constitutes value."

[84] RAILROAD CO. v. NATIONAL BANK OF THE REPUBLIC, 102 U. S. 25, 26 L. Ed. 61, Dobie Cas. Bailments and Carriers, 119. And see Penn Bank v. Frankish, 91 Pa. 339; Goodman v. Simmonds, 19 Mo. 106; Grant v. Kidwell, 30 Mo. 455; Brainard v. Reavis, 2 Mo. App. 490; First Nat. Bank v. Strauss, 66 Miss. 479, 6 South. 233, 14 Am. St. Rep. 579; Maitland v. Citizens' Nat. Bank, 40 Md. 540, 17 Am. Rep. 620; Straughan v. Fairchild, 80 Ind. 598; Continental Nat. Bank v. Townsend, 87 N. Y. 10. See, also, cases cited in note 81.

[85] Section 76: "Value. * * * An antecedent or pre-existing claim, whether for money or not, constitutes value where goods or documents of title are taken either in satisfaction thereof or as security therefor." See Williston, Sales, § 620.

[86] The leading case is Bay v. Coddington, 5 Johns. Ch. (N. Y.) 54, 9 Am. Dec. 268; Coddington v. Bay, 20 Johns. (N. Y.) 637, 11 Am. Dec. 342, opinion by Chancellor Kent. See, also, Stalker v. McDonald, 6 Hill (N. Y.) 93, 40 Am. Dec. 389; Weaver v. Barden, 49 N. Y. 286; Prentiss v. Graves, 33 Barb. (N. Y.) 621; Stevens v. Brennan, 79 N. Y. 254.

[87] Roxborough v. Messick, 6 Ohio St. 448, 67 Am. Dec. 346; City of Cleveland v. State Bank, 16 Ohio St. 236, 88 Am. Dec. 445; Pitts v. Foglesong, 37 Ohio St. 676, 41 Am. Rep. 540.

[88] Boyd v. Breck, 29 Ala. 703; Ryan v. Chew, 13 Iowa, 589; Nutter v. Stover, 48 Me. 163; Williams v. Little, 11 N. H. 66; Farmers' Nat. Bank of Tecumseh v. McCall, 25 Okl. 600, 106 Pac. 866, 26 L. R. A. (N. S.) 217; Altoona Second Nat. Bank v. Dunn, 151 Pa. 228, 25 Atl. 80, 31 Am. St. Rep. 742; Nichol v. Bate, 10 Yerg. (Tenn.) 429; Atlanta Guano Co. v. Hunt, 100 Tenn. 89, 42 S. W. 482.

receives notice of any defenses to the instrument,[89] or, if he is under a binding contract to make further advances, he is protected for advances so made after notice, up to the amount he is so bound to advance.[90]

A pledgee of negotiable paper can ordinarily pass a good title thereto, though he transfers it in violation of the rights of the pledgor.[91] In other words, he has the power, though he may not have the right. But not if the transferee has notice of the character in which the pledgee holds the paper.[92] Such notice may be given by an indorsement on the instrument that it is transferred to the pledgee as collateral security.[93]

Nonnegotiable Instruments

But a pledgee of a nonnegotiable instrument or chose in action can acquire only the rights of the pledgor, and takes the instrument subject to all the equities which existed against the pledgor.[94] So, too, a pledgee, in such cases, can transfer to a third person no better title than he himself has.[95]

In the case of a bona fide purchaser for value of a nonnegotiable chose in action, from one upon whom the owner has, by assignment, conferred the apparent absolute ownership, where the pur-

89 Kerr v. Cowen, 17 N. C. 356; Buchanan v. International Bank, 78 Ill. 500; Matthews v. Rutherford, 7 La. Ann. 225.

90 Kerr v. Cowen, 17 N. C. 356, 358.

91 Spaulding v. Kendrick, 172 Mass. 71, 51 N. E. 453; Currie v. Bowman, 25 Or. 364, 35 Pac. 848; Merchants' Nat. Bank of St. Paul v. Allemania Bank, 71 Minn. 477, 74 N. W. 203; Colt v. Humbert, 5 Cal. 260, 63 Am. Dec. 128; Ballard v. Burgett, 40 N. Y. 314, 318; McNeil v. Tenth Nat. Bank, 46 N. Y. 325, 7 Am. Rep. 341; Sargent v. Metcalf, 5 Gray (Mass.) 306, 66 Am. Dec. 368; Stoddard v. Kimball, 6 Cush. (Mass.) 469; Fisher v. Fisher, 98 Mass. 303; Wheeler v. Guild, 20 Pick. (Mass.) 545, 32 Am. Dec. 231; Valette v. Mason, 1 Ind. 288; Trustees of Iowa College v. Hill, 12 Iowa, 462; Patterson v. Deering, 1 A. K. Marsh. (Ky.) 326. In this respect, a pledge of negotiable paper differs from a pledge of ordinary corporeal chattels, for as to the latter, in general, the pledgee can convey no greater interest than he himself has.

92 Vinton v. King, 4 Allen (Mass.) 562; National Bank of North America v. Kirby, 108 Mass. 497; Patterson v. Deering, 1 A. K. Marsh. (Ky.) 326.

93 Haskell v. Lambert, 16 Gray (Mass.) 592; Costelo v. Crowell, 127 Mass. 293, 34 Am. Rep. 367; Robins v. May, 11 Adol. & E. (Eng.) 213.

94 Works v. Meritt, 105 Cal. 467, 38 Pac. 1109; Moore v. Metropolitan Nat. Bank, 55 N. Y. 41, 14 Am. Rep. 173; Fullerton v. Sturges, 4 Ohio St. 529.

95 Cowdrey v. Vandenburgh, 101 U. S. 572, 25 L. Ed. 923; International Bank v. German Bank, 71 Mo. 183, 36 Am. Rep. 468; Weirick v. Mahoning County Bank, 16 Ohio St. 297; People ex rel. Hurd v. Johnson, 100 Ill. 537, 39 Am. Rep. 63; Isett v. Lucas, 17 Iowa, 503, 507, 85 Am. Dec. 572; Burtis v. Cook, 16 Iowa, 194. The payee of a nonnegotiable note, secured by mortgage, who transfers the note and mortgage as collateral security for a debt, is not liable to the transferee for any deficiency arising on foreclosure of the mortgaged premises. Haber v. Brown, 101 Cal. 445, 35 Pac. 1035.

chase is made upon the faith of such apparent ownership, such purchaser acquires here, as in the case of sales of corporeal chattels (under the doctrine of agency by estoppel), a title valid even as against the owner.[96] For the same reason, an innocent pledgee from one having such indicia of ownership would also (to the extent of his interest as pledgee) take free from the claims of the real owner.[97] It will thus be seen that the doctrine of agency by estoppel (applicable to all classes of property) is not the same principle as negotiability, though either may operate to the benefit of the innocent purchaser or pledgee from one who exceeds his right or actual authority in making such sale or pledge.

Certificates of Corporate Stock

Certificates of stock in a corporation are not regarded as negotiable instruments in the sense in which that term is properly used, viz., that a negotiation cuts off latent equities and thus confers on the transferee a better title than that of the transferror.[98] They do not run to bearer or to the order of the party named in the certificate, nor do they contain words of negotiability. They are not, like checks, the immediate representative of money; they were not designed, like promissory notes, to circulate in place of money; nor, like corporate bonds, are they promises by the corporation to pay money. Certificates of stock are simply the muniments and evidence of the holder's title to a given share in the property and franchises of the corporation of which he is a member.[99]

[96] Combes v. Chandler, 33 Ohio St. 178; Moore v. Metropolitan Nat. Bank, 55 N. Y. 41, 14 Am. Rep. 173, overruling Bush v. Lathrop, 22 N. Y. 535. See, also, Mechanics' Nat. Bank v. Comins, 72 N. H. 12, 55 Atl. 191, 101 Am. St. Rep. 650.

[97] International Bank v. German Bank, 71 Mo. 183, 36 Am. Rep. 468; Weirick v. Mahoning County Bank, 16 Ohio St. 297; Combes v. Chandler, 33 Ohio St. 178; Weyh v. Boylan, 85 N. Y. 394, 39 Am. Rep. 669; Appeal of Ashton, 73 Pa. 153; Cowdrey v. Vandenburgh, 101 U. S. 572, 25 L. Ed. 923; Merchants' Banking Co. of London v. Phœnix Bessemer Steel Co., 5 Ch. Div. (Eng.) 205, 217; Goodwin v. Robarts, L. R. 10 Exch. (Eng.) 76. The pledgee, however, must be without notice. Swan v. Produce Bank, 24 Hun (N. Y.) 277.

[98] George H. Hammond & Co. v. Hastings, 134 U. S. 401, 10 Sup. Ct. 727, 33 L. Ed. 960; Sewall v. Boston Water Power Co., 4 Allen (Mass.) 277, 81 Am. Dec. 701; Weaver v. Barden, 49 N. Y. 286; Barstow v. Savage Min. Co., 64 Cal. 388, 1 Pac. 349, 49 Am. St. Rep. 705. The assignment of shares of railroad stock as collateral security for a pre-existing debt, not contracted on the faith of the security, confers upon the assignee no better title than his assignor had, and he takes subject to equities. City of Cleveland v. State Bank, 16 Ohio St. 236, 88 Am. Dec. 445.

[99] President, etc., of Mechanics' Bank v. New York & N. H. R. Co., 13 N. Y. 599; Wilson v. Little, 2 N. Y. 443, 447, 51 Am. Dec. 307; Appeal of Roberts, 85 Pa. 84; Weston v. Bear River & Auburn Water & Mining Co., 5 Cal. 186, 63 Am. Dec. 117; Pinkerton v. Manchester & L. R. R., 42 N. H. 424, 447; City

Pledges of corporate stock, then, being subject in general to the same rules as pledges of other nonnegotiable instruments and pledges of corporeal property, it follows that a pledge of stock certificates ordinarily confers on the pledgee no higher rights than those of the pledgor.[1] Here, as elsewhere, a pledge by one having a void title is invalid;[2] while a pledge of goods by one having a voidable title, before his title is avoided, like a sale under similar circumstances, confers valid rights on the pledgee.[3]

All that has been said in the previous section about agency by estoppel in general and about clothing one with the indicia of title (for example, by transferring the stock certificate with a blank indorsement thereon) is equally true here, and in practice finds frequent application.[4] In this connection, and elsewhere, we find, too, the law as to pledges of stock closely interwoven with the principles of agency and corporations.

Bills of Lading

A bill of lading is a symbol of, and stands for, the goods that it represents. Accordingly, a pledge or other transfer of the bill of lading confers the same rights (and no greater ones) as an

Fire Ins. Co. v. Olmsted, 33 Conn. 476, 480; Platt v. Hawkins, 43 Conn. 139; Platt v. Birmingham Axle Co., 41 Conn. 255, 267; Shropshire Union Railway & Canal Co. v. Reg., L. R. 7 H. L. (Eng.) 496; Shipman v. Ætna Ins. Co., 29 Conn. 245; Hall v. Rose Hill & E. Road Co., 70 Ill. 673.

1 Pratt v. Taunton Copper Mfg. Co., 123 Mass. 110, 25 Am. Rep. 37; Davis v. Bank of England, 2 Bing. (Eng.) 393.

2 Machinists' Nat. Bank v. Field, 126 Mass. 345; Bercich v. Marye, 9 Nev. 312; Tayler v. Great Indian Peninsula Ry. Co., 4 De Gex & J. (Eng.) 559.

3 McNeil v. Tenth Nat. Bank, 46 N. Y. 325, 7 Am. Rep. 341; Moore v. Miller, 6 Lans. (N. Y.) 396; Crocker v. Crocker, 31 N. Y. 507, 88 Am. Dec. 291; Appeal of Wood, 92 Pa. 379, 37 Am. Rep. 694; Appeal of Burton, 93 Pa. 314; Appeal of Pennsylvania R. Co., 86 Pa. 80; Otis v. Gardner, 105 Ill. 436; Walker v. Detroit Transit Ry. Co., 47 Mich. 338, 11 N. W. 187; Strange v. Houston & T. C. R. Co., 53 Tex. 162; Mount Holly, L. & M. Turnpike Co. v. Ferree, 17 N. J. Eq. 117; Thompson v. Toland, 48 Cal. 112; Stone v. Marye, 14 Nev. 362; Borland v. Clark, 26 Kan. 349.

4 Otis v. Gardner (1883) 105 Ill. 436; Strange v. Houston & T. C. R. Co., 53 Tex. 162; Fraser v. City Council of Charleston, 11 S. C. 486. And see cases cited in preceding note. One who pledges stock is not thereby estopped to assert his claims against the corporation for money owing him, and therefore his assignee for the benefit of creditors can enforce such claims, though it render the stock worthless. Janney v. Merchants' & Planters' Nat. Bank of Montgomery, 98 Ala. 515, 13 South. 761; Appeal of Wood, 92 Pa. 379, 37 Am. Rep. 694; Bentinck v. Bank, 3 Reports, 120, [1893] 2 Ch. (Eng.) 120; Persch v. Quiggle, 57 Pa. 247; Jarvis v. Rogers, 13 Mass. 105. The owner of stock certificates, fraudulently pledged by one holding them as trustee, is not estopped from claiming them of the pledgee, by standing by, after having notified the pledgee of his claim, and demanding the stock, and without protest witnessing the pledgee pay an assessment theretofore made on

actual delivery of the goods under similar circumstances.[5] A thief cannot make a valid pledge or sale of the stolen goods, even by an actual delivery of such goods; no more could he make a valid sale or pledge by shipping the goods and transferring the bill of lading, which represents them. This necessarily leads to the conclusion, then, that the bill of lading is no more negotiable (strictly speaking) than the goods for which it stands.[6] Therefore, ordinarily, the pledgee of such bill of lading acquires rights no more valid than those of the pledgor. Since the bill of lading, however, is one of the best examples that the law knows of indicia of title, this results in the frequent application of the principle of estoppel as

the stock. Shaw v. Spencer, 100 Mass. 382, 97 Am. Dec. 107, 1 Am. Rep. 115. Where a bank wrongfully pledged stock deposited with it, the facts that the stock was issued in the name of the owner, and that the power of attorney to transfer it was a detached paper, and not acknowledged before a notary public, as required by the rules of the stock exchange, do not charge the pledgees with notice of the defect in the pledgor's title. Smith v. Savin, 141 N. Y. 315, 36 N. E. 338. The law of estoppel here has been developed to such an extent as to render sales or pledges of corporate stock almost as effective to confer good title on bona fide buyers and pledgees as a like sale or pledge of negotiable instruments. Moore v. Metropolitan Nat. Bank, 55 N. Y. 41, 14 Am. Rep. 173; Mt. Holly, L. & M. Turnpike Co. v. Ferree, 17 N. J. Eq. 117; Walker v. Detroit Transit Ry. Co., 47 Mich. 338, 11 N. W. 187.

5 The subject of bills of lading as collateral security is discussed at length in Jones, Collateral Securities (3d Ed.) §§ 227–279. The Carlos F. Roses, 177 U. S. 655, 20 Sup. Ct. 803, 44 L. Ed. 929; Rowley v. Bigelow, 12 Pick. (Mass.) 307, 23 Am. Dec. 607; FORBES v. BOSTON & L. R. CO., 133 Mass. 154, Dobie Cas. Bailments and Carriers, 236; Hathaway v. Haynes, 124 Mass. 311; First Nat. Bank of Green Bay v. Dearborn, 115 Mass. 219, 15 Am. Rep. 92; First Nat. Bank of Cairo v. Crocker, 111 Mass. 163; Allen v. Williams, 12 Pick. (Mass.) 297; De Wolf v. Gardner, 12 Cush. (Mass.) 19, 59 Am. Dec. 165; Bank of Rochester v. Jones, 4 N. Y. 497, 55 Am. Dec. 290; Holbrook v. Wight, 24 Wend. (N. Y.) 169, 35 Am. Dec. 607; Cayuga County Nat. Bank v. Daniels, 47 N. Y. 631; Farmers' & Mechanics' Nat. Bank of Buffalo v. Logan, 74 N. Y. 568; First Nat. Bank of Cincinnati v. Kelly, 57 N. Y. 34; Holmes v. German Security Bank, 87 Pa. 525; Peters v. Elliott, 78 Ill. 321, 326; Michigan Cent. R. Co. v. Phillips, 60 Ill. 190; Taylor v. Turner, 87 Ill. 296; Security Bank of Minnesota v. Luttgen, 29 Minn. 363, 13 N. W. 151; Emery v. Irving Nat. Bank, 25 Ohio St. 360, 18 Am. Rep. 299; Adoue v. Seeligson, 54 Tex. 593; McCants v. Wells, 4 S. C. 381; First Nat. Bank of Peoria v. Northern R. R., 58 N. H. 203; Gibson v. Stevens, 8 How. 384, 12 L. Ed. 1123; Shaw v. North Pennsylvania R. Co., 101 U. S. 557, 564, 25 L. Ed. 892; Dows v. National Exchange Bank, 91 U. S. 618, 23 L. Ed. 214.

6 Pollard v. Vinton, 105 U. S. 7, 26 L. Ed. 998; Kirkpatrick v. Kansas City, St. J. & C. B. R. Co., 86 Mo. 341; Barnard v. Campbell, 55 N. Y. 462, 14 Am. Rep. 289; Allen v. Williams, 12 Pick. (Mass.) 297; Davenport Nat. Bank v. Homeyer, 45 Mo. 145, 100 Am. Dec. 363; Canadian Bank of Commerce v. McCrea, 106 Ill. 281; Burton v. Curyea, 40 Ill. 320, 89 Am. Dec. 350; Evansville & T. H. R. Co. v. Erwin, 84 Ind. 457, 466; The Idaho, 93 U. S. 575, 23 L. Ed. 978.

already indicated, and many writers and judges have therefore said that bills of lading are quasi negotiable.[7]

Bills of lading constitute such a convenient method of dealing with goods which (being in the hands of the carrier) are physically inaccessible that they are of tremendous commercial importance,[8] and commercial customs and usages have naturally lent to them certain distinctive characteristics. In many states statutes have been passed changing the common-law incidents of bills of lading.[9] Some of the statutes, using an exceedingly unfortunate terminology, have declared them negotiable in the same manner that promissory notes or bills of exchange are negotiable.[10] It has been held, however, that these statutes could not have been intended to change totally the character of the bill of lading and put it on the same

[7] Barnard v. Campbell, 55 N. Y. 456, 14 Am. Rep. 289; Newhall v. Central Pac. R. Co., 51 Cal. 345, 21 Am. Rep. 713.

[8] Among the most frequent and important of the commercial transactions involving bills of lading is the taking by the consignor of goods of the bill of lading to his order and the drawing of a draft on the consignee for the purchase price. This draft is then attached to the bill of lading and sent to a bank in the consignee's city. In such case, the bill of lading is ordinarily to be regarded as security for the acceptance of the draft by the consignee rather than for its payment. Dows v. National Exch. Bank, 91 U. S. 618, 630, 23 L. Ed. 214; National Bank of Commerce v. Merchants' Nat. Bank, 91 U. S. 92, 23 L. Ed. 208; Mears v. Waples, 4 Houst. (Del.) 62; Landfear v. Blossman, 1 La. Ann. 148, 45 Am. Dec. 76. As to the rights of the pledgee of the bill of lading as against attaching creditors, see NEILL v. ROGERS BROS. PRODUCE CO., 41 W. Va. 37, 23 S. E. 702, Dobie Cas. Bailments and Carriers, 122. The consignee is therefore entitled to the delivery of the bill of lading when he accepts the draft. National Bank of Commerce v. Merchants' Nat. Bank, 91 U. S. 92, 23 L. Ed. 208; Schuchardt v. Hall, 36 Md. 590, 11 Am. Rep. 514; Security Bank of Minnesota v. Luttgen, 29 Minn. 363, 13 N. W. 151; Marine Bank of Chicago v. Wright, 48 N. Y. 1; Cayuga County Nat. Bank v. Daniels, 47 N. Y. 631. When the consignor of goods takes a bill of lading, which he pledges, the pledgee acquires rights superior to those of the consignee. Richardson v. Nathan, 167 Pa. 513, 31 Atl. 740; Hieskell v. Farmers' & Mechanics' Nat. Bank, 89 Pa. 155, 33 Am. Rep. 745; Bank of Rochester v. Jones, 4 N. Y. 497, 501, 55 Am. Dec. 290. On the other hand, when the consignee has the bill of lading, and pledges it, the consignor cannot subsequently stop the goods in transitu without paying the pledgee the amount secured to him. Kemp v. Falk, 7 App. Cas. (Eng.) 573; Spalding v. Ruding, 6 Beav. (Eng.) 376. If a bill of lading consists of more than one part, a pledgee advancing money on one of the set has a better title than a subsequent purchaser taking the goods or a duplicate bill. Skilling v. Bollman, 6 Mo. App. 76. And see Hieskell v. Farmers' & Mechanics' Nat. Bank, 89 Pa. 155, 33 Am. Rep. 745; Meyerstein v. Barber, L. R. 2 C. P. (Eng.) 38; Id., L. R. 4 H. L. 317, 331.

[9] For such statutes, and cases construing them, see Jones, Collateral Securities (3d Ed.) §§ 233–240.

[10] For specimens of such statutes, see Rev. Laws La. 1897, § 2485; Code Pub. Gen. Laws Md. 1904, art. 14, § 1; Rev. St. Mo. 1909, §§ 11956, 11957.

footing as promissory notes or bills of exchange.[11] Owing to essential distinctions between a note or bill of exchange, on the one hand, and the bill of lading, on the other, any other holding would have led to strange, if not impossible, consequences.

Warehouse Receipts

The general nature of warehouse receipts has already been discussed.[12] Like bills of lading, they stand for the goods they represent, they are not negotiable, and their transfer is legally equivalent to a delivery of such goods.[13] So close is their legal parallel to bills of lading that they require no further discussion here.[14]

SAME—SPECIAL PROPERTY OF PLEDGEE IN PLEDGED GOODS—RIGHT TO BRING SUIT

79. The pledgee has a special property in the pledged goods, involving the right to possession of them, and this he can protect by an appropriate action.

The courts agree that the pledgee's interest in the pledged goods rises to the dignity of a special property.[15] Involved in this is the right to the possession of the goods, which the pledgee can assert

[11] Shaw v. North Pennsylvania R. Co., 101 U. S. 557, 25 L. Ed. 892; Tiedeman v. Knox, 53 Md. 612, 614; Douglas v. People's Bank of Kentucky, 86 Ky. 175, 5 S. W. 420, 9 Am. St. Rep. 276; Jones, Collateral Securities (3d Ed.) § 241.

[12] Ante, pp. 163, 196.

[13] On warehouse receipts as collateral security, see Jones, Collateral Securities (3d Ed.) §§ 280–326; Burton v. Curyea, 40 Ill. 320, 89 Am. Dec. 350; Western Union R. Co. v. Wagner, 65 Ill. 197; Second Nat. Bank of Toledo v. Walbridge, 19 Ohio St. 419, 2 Am. Rep. 408; Gibson v. Chillicothe Branch of State Bank of Ohio, 11 Ohio St. 311; Newcomb v. Cabell, 10 Bush (Ky.) 460; Stewart v. Phœnix Ins. Co., 9 Lea (Tenn.) 104; Horr v. Barker, 8 Cal. 603; St. Louis Nat. Bank v. Ross, 9 Mo. App. 399; Fourth Nat. Bank v. St. Louis Cotton Compress Co., 11 Mo. App. 333; Gibson v. Stevens, 8 How. 384, 12 L. Ed. 1123; Chicago Dock Co. v. Foster, 48 Ill. 507; Ditson v. Randall, 33 Me. 202; Fourth Nat. Bank v. St. Louis Cotton Compress Co., 11 Mo. App. 333; Western Union R. Co. v. Wagner, 65 Ill. 197; Hoyt v. Baker, 15 Abb. Prac. N. S. (N. Y.) 405; McCombie v. Spader, 1 Hun (N. Y.) 193; Paddon v. Taylor, 44 N. Y. 371; Barnard v. Campbell, 55 N. Y. 456, 14 Am. Rep. 289; FIRST NAT. BANK OF PARKERSBURG v. HARKNESS, 42 W. Va. 156, 24 S. E. 548, 32 L. R. A. 408, Dobie Cas. Bailments and Carriers, 109; Bush v. Export Storage Co., 136 Fed. 918.

[14] Just as is the case of bills of lading, many state statutes have been passed declaring warehouse receipts negotiable. These statutes are collected in Jones, Collateral Securities (3d Ed.) §§ 283–295.

[15] Dickey v. Pocomoke City Nat. Bank, 89 Md. 280, 43 Atl. 33; First Nat. Bank of Chicago v. Bayley, 115 Mass. 228; Moreland v. Houghton, 94 Mich. 548, 54 N. W. 285; Marts v. Cumberland Mut. Fire Ins. Co., 44 N. J. Law, 478.

as against the world, including the pledgor.[16] This right, too, continues until the payment of the debt or the performance of the undertaking secured by the pledge.[17]

This possession the pledgee can protect by the appropriate action, when it is tortiously interfered with either by the pledgor or by third parties. Thus, he may bring detinue or replevin to recover his lost possession,[18] or trover for the conversion of the goods.[19] When the pledgee sues third persons in trover, he can (it is generally held) recover the full value of the goods,[20] when he holds any excess beyond his own interest on behalf of the pledgor. But when the action is against the pledgor, the pledgee then, of course, recovers only for his own interest, usually the amount of the debt.[21]

SAME—RIGHT TO USE THE PLEDGED GOODS

80. The pledgee has ordinarily no right to use the pledged goods.

Ordinarily, in the absence of any agreement or assent by the pledgor, the pledgee has no right to use the thing pledged,[22] and any

16 Robinson & Co. v. Ralph, 74 Neb. 55, 103 N. W. 1044; Mitchell v. McLeod, 127 Iowa, 733, 104 N. W. 349; Coleman v. Shelton, 2 McCord Eq. (S. C.) 126, 16 Am. Dec. 639; Yeatman v. Savings Inst., 95 U. S. 764, 24 L. Ed. 589; Mitchell v. Brown, 6 Cold. (Tenn.) 505; Printup v. Johnson, 19 Ga. 73; Kittera's Estate, 17 Pa. 416. A pledgee may hold more than one security as collateral for the same debt. Union Bank v. Laird, 2 Wheat. (U. S.) 390, 4 L. Ed. 269.

17 Caven v. Harsh, 186 Pa. 132, 40 Atl. 321; Ætna Ins. Co. v. Bank of Wilcox, 48 Neb. 544, 67 N. W. 449; Bartlett v. Johnson, 9 Allen (Mass.) 530.

18 Noles v. Marable, 50 Ala. 366; Gamson v. Pritchard, 210 Mass. 296, 96 N. E. 715.

19 Miller v. McKenzie, 11 Ga. App. 494, 75 S. E. 820; Easton v. Hodges (C. C.) 18 Fed. 677; Einstein v. Dunn, 171 N. Y. 648, 63 N. E. 1116; United States Exp. Co. v. Meints, 72 Ill. 293; Treadwell v. Davis, 34 Cal. 601, 94 Am. Dec. 770; Roeder v. Green Tree Brewery Co., 33 Mo. App. 69; Brownell v. Hawkins, 4 Barb. (N. Y.) 491. The pledgee of a promissory note may maintain an action against a pledgor for the conversion of the note, where the latter has obtained the note, though without fraud, under an agreement that he is to return it or another note, which agreement he refuses to comply with. Way v. Davidson, 12 Gray (Mass.) 465, 74 Am. Dec. 604.

20 Adams v. O'Connor, 100 Mass. 515, 1 Am. Rep. 137; Ullman v. Barnard, 7 Gray (Mass.) 554; Pomeroy v. Smith, 17 Pick. (Mass.) 85; Lyle v. Barker, 5 Bin. (Pa.) 457; Baldwin v. Bradley, 69 Ill. 32; Benjamin v. Stremple, 13 Ill. 466; United States Exp. Co. v. Meints, 72 Ill. 293; Treadwell v. Davis, 34 Cal. 601, 94 Am. Dec. 770; Soule v. White, 14 Me. 436.

21 Treadwell v. Davis, 34 Cal. 601, 94 Am. Dec. 770; Lyle v. Barker, 5 Bin. (Pa.) 457, 460; Ingersoll v. Van Bokkelin, 7 Cow. (N. Y.) 681; Hays v Riddle, 1 Sandf. (N. Y.) 248; Hurst v. Coley (C. C.) 15 Fed. 645.

22 By the civil law there are two kinds of pledges,—the pawn and anti-

such use of it is wrongful.[23] The advantage accruing to the pledgee from the transaction consists solely in the right to hold the goods merely as a security, and no beneficial use by the pledgee is contemplated.

In some of the older cases [24] it was said that the pledgee could make any use of the pledged goods which did not thereby injure them or impair their value; but this is clearly erroneous, and has been repudiated by practically all of the late cases. Of course (as in bailments for bailor's sole benefit[25]), when the proper custody of the thing involves use (for example, exercising a horse), this use is treated as merely incidental to the custody, and is not such a beneficial use as is forbidden to the pledgee, and thus does not render him absolutely liable as an insurer for loss or injury to the thing pledged.

SAME—PROFITS OF THE THING PLEDGED

81. The pledgee can hold the profits and increase of the thing pledged, but he must account for these to the pledgor.

A pledgee is entitled to hold the profits and increase of the thing pledged as a part of his security, but these must be applied towards the payment of the debt secured.[26] Of course, if the debt is paid in full from other funds, the pledgee must restore such profits and increase along with the thing pledged. Thus it is the duty of the

chresis. A thing is said to be pawned when a movable thing is given as security. The antichresis is when the security given consists in immovables. Rev. Civ. Code La. 1870, tit. 20, art. 3135. In the antichresis the creditor acquires the right of reaping the fruits or other revenues of the immovables given to him in pledge, on condition of deducting annually their proceeds from the interest, if any be due to him, and afterwards from the principal of his debt. Rev. Civ. Code La. 1870, tit. 20, art. 3176; Livingston v. Story, 11 Pet. 351, 9 L. Ed. 746.

[23] Scott v. Reed, 83 Minn. 203, 85 N. W. 1012; Champlain Const. Co. v. O'Brien (C. C.) 104 Fed. 930; Hawkins v. Hubbard, 2 S. D. 631, 51 N. W. 774; Stearns v. Marsh, 4 Denio (N. Y.) 227, 47 Am. Dec. 248; McArthur v. Howett, 72 Ill. 358, 360.

[24] COGGS v. BERNARD, 2 Ld. Raym. (Eng.) 909, Dobie Cas. Bailments and Carriers, 1; Thompson v. Patrick, 4 Watts (Pa.) 414.

[25] Ante, p. 62. Of course, the pledgee may lawfully use the pledged chattels on the express or implied consent of the pledgor. Lawrence v. Maxwell, 53 N. Y. 19; Damon v. Waldteufel, 99 Cal. 234, 33 Pac. 903.

[26] Lathrop v. Adkisson, 87 Ga. 339, 13 S. E. 517; Sokup v. Letellier, 123 Mich. 640, 82 N. W. 523; Felton v. Brooks, 4 Cush. (Mass.) 203, 206; Merrifield v. Baker, 9 Allen (Mass.) 29; McCrea v. Yule, 68 N. J. Law, 465, 53 Atl. 210.

pledgee to render a due account of the milk received from cows,[27] of the young of animals,[28] of the profits from the labor of a slave,[29] of the dividends from corporate stock,[30] and of the interest received from coupons [31] on a bond. It is, in general, the duty of the pledgee to make the pledged goods yield a profit, if this can reasonably be done. When there is such a duty, express or implied, the pledgee is liable for such profits as the pledged goods might have earned, but failed to do so, owing to his neglect.[32]

In the case of corporate stocks, not only is the pledgee entitled to the dividends (to be accounted for just as other profits), but it is usually held that, if the stock stands on the company's books in his name, the pledgee may vote it.[33] In many states, this right is specifically controlled by statute; the statutory trend being in favor of the pledgor.[34]

[27] COGGS v. BERNARD, 2 Ld. Raym. 909, Dobie Cas. Bailments and Carriers, 1.

[28] Jones, Collateral Securities, § 396.

[29] Geron v. Geron, 15 Ala. 558, 50 Am. Dec. 143; Houton v. Holliday, 6 N. C. 111, 5 Am. Dec. 522; Woodard v. Fitzpatrick, 9 Dana (Ky.) 117, 120.

[30] BOYD v. CONSHOHOCKEN WORSTED MILLS, 149 Pa. 363, 24 Atl. 287, Dobie Cas. Bailments and Carriers, 124; McCrea v. Yule, 68 N. J. Law 465, 53 Atl. 210; Hunsaker v. Sturgis, 29 Cal. 142; Hagar v. Union Nat. Bank, 63 Me. 509; Herrman v. Maxwell, 47 N. Y. Super. Ct. 347; Merchants' Nat. Bank v. Richards, 6 Mo. App. 454, 464; Gaty v. Holliday, 8 Mo. App. 118; Kellogg v. Stockwell, 75 Ill. 68, 71; Fairbanks v. Merchants' Nat. Bank of Chicago, 30 Ill. App. 28.

[31] Androscoggin R. Co. v. Auburn Bank, 48 Me. 335.

[32] Where corporate bonds were pledged to secure a debt, it was the duty of the pledgee, in the event that there was either waste or misappropriation of the properties covered by the deed of trust securing the bonds, to use reasonable diligence to secure the fruits thereof and to preserve and care for their payment. State Nat. Bank v. Syndicate Co. of Eureka Springs, Ark. (C. C.) 178 Fed. 359. But when money is deposited as a pledge, while the pledgee holds it as such, he is not chargeable with interest to be paid by himself. Story, Bailm. § 339. Ordinarily, however, if the pledgee does let the money out at interest, he must account therefor. Gilson v. Martin, 49 Vt. 474; Hunsaker v. Sturgis, 29 Cal. 142; Merrifield v. Baker, 9 Allen (Mass.) 29.

[33] Commonwealth v. Dalzell, 152 Pa. 217, 25 Atl. 535, 34 Am. St. Rep. 640; In re Argus Printing Co., 1 N. D. 434, 48 N. W. 347, 12 L. R. A. 781, 26 Am. St. Rep. 639; Ex parte Willcocks, 7 Cow. (N. Y.) 402, 17 Am. Dec. 525; In re Barker, 6 Wend. (N. Y.) 509; Becher v. Wells Flouring Mill Co. (C. C.) 1 Fed. 276. Some cases hold, even though the stock stands on the corporate books in the pledgee's name, that the pledgor has the right to vote it. State v. Smith, 15 Or. 98, 14 Pac. 814, 15 Pac. 137, 386; People ex rel. Allen v. Hill, 16 Cal. 113. See, also, McDaniels v. Flower Brook Mfg. Co., 22 Vt. 274. See, on this subject, Cook on Corp. § 612; 3 Thomp. Comm. on Corp. § 3872.

[34] For examples of statutes favorable to the pledgor's right to vote stock see Civ. Code Ariz. 1901, par. 782; Laws Md. 1908, c. 240, § 22; 1 Brightly's Dig. Pa. 1894, p. 416, § 62; Comp. St. Wyo. 1910, § 3994.

SAME—EXPENSES ABOUT THE THING PLEDGED

82. The pledgee can charge the pledgor with expenses necessarily incurred as to the pledged goods.

Expenses of the Pledge

The pledgee is entitled to be reimbursed for expenses incurred by him which were reasonably necessary in keeping and caring for the pledged goods.[85] The term "expenses" is used in a broad sense, and includes the premiums paid by the pledgee on an insurance policy held in pledge,[86] money paid in removing the lien of an incumbrance superior to the lien of the pledge,[87] and assessments on corporate stock.[88] These expenses are added to the debt for which the pledge stands as security.

Liability of Pledgee of Stock to Corporate Creditors

A few words seem appropriate here as to the liability of the pledgee to creditors of the corporation for unpaid stock subscriptions, and also as to the liability imposed on stockholders by statute. The decisions are not entirely harmonious, but it seems that, if there is an absolute transfer to the pledgee on the corporate books, then the pledgee is liable to the creditors just as if he were the absolute owner of the stock.[89] But if the transfer on the books is to

[85] Furness v. Union Nat. Bank, 147 Ill. 570, 35 N. E. 624; Hickson Lumber Co. v. Pollock, 139 N. C. 174, 51 S. E. 855; Bank of Staten Island v. Silvie, 89 App. Div. 465, 85 N. Y. Supp. 760; Hills v. Smith, 28 N. H. 369; Starrett v. Barber, 20 Me. 457; Hendricks v. Robinson, 2 Johns. Ch. (N. Y.) 283; Fagan v. Thompson (C. C.) 38 Fed. 467. One of two joint pledgees cannot recover from the other compensation for caring for and selling the pledged property, where there was no agreement therefor. Central Trust Co. of New York v. New York Equipment Co., 87 Hun, 421, 34 N. Y. Supp. 349.

[86] These expenses, to be recoverable by the pledgee, must not be unreasonable. Iowa Nat. Bank v. Cooper (Iowa) 101 N. W. 459; Raley v. Ross, 59 Ga. 862.

[87] Furness v. Union Nat. Bank, 147 Ill. 570, 35 N. E. 624. One who takes notes as collateral security for a debt is entitled, as against the owner thereof, to be allowed the cost of realizing on them, including a reasonable attorney's fee. Gregory v. Pike, 15 C. C. A. 33, 67 Fed. 837. But, for a case in which attorney's fees were not allowed the pledgee in defending an action against the real owner, see Work v. Tibbits, 87 Hun, 352, 34 N. Y. Supp. 308.

[88] McCalla v. Clark, 55 Ga. 53; Mabb v. Stewart, 147 Cal. 413, 81 Pac. 1073.

[89] 3 Thomp. Comm. on Corp. § 2937; 1 Cook, Corp. § 247; Germania Nat. Bank v. Case, 99 U. S. 628, 25 L. Ed. 448; Pullman v. Upton, 96 U. S. 328, 24 L. Ed. 818; Johnson v. Underhill, 52 N. Y. 203; In re Empire City Bank, 18 N. Y. 199; Adderly v. Storm, 6 Hill (N. Y.) 624; Holyoke Bank v. Burnham, 11 Cush. (Mass.) 183; Crease v. Babcock, 10 Metc. (Mass.) 525; Hale v. Walker, 31 Iowa, 344, 7 Am. Rep. 137; Magruder v. Colston, 44 Md. 349, 22 Am. Rep. 47; Wheelock v. Kost, 77 Ill. 296; Appeal of Aultman, 98 Pa. 505.

him as "pledgee," or otherwise indicates that he holds the stock merely as collateral, then the pledgee is not so liable.[40] Where the pledgee does not appear on the books of the company as a stockholder, though he holds the stock certificate, again the pledgee is not liable to the creditors of the corporation.[41] In some states, statutes have been passed exempting the pledgee from such liability on stock held by him as collateral.[42]

SAME—DEGREE OF CARE REQUIRED OF THE PLEDGEE

83. The pledgee must exercise ordinary care or diligence about the pledged goods.

In General

Apart from the somewhat anomalous case of commercial paper, this subject presents no unique difficulty. Since the pledge is a bailment for the mutual benefit of both parties (the pledgor bailor and pledgee bailee), the pledgee is held to the usual standard of diligence in such cases and is bound to exercise ordinary care.[43]

[40] Pauly v. State Loan & T. Co., 165 U. S. 606, 17 Sup. Ct. 465, 41 L. Ed. 844; Beal v. Essex Sav. Bank, 67 Fed. 816, 15 C. C. A. 128; May v. Genesee County Savings Bank, 120 Mich. 330, 79 N. W. 630.

[41] Henkle v. Salem Mfg. Co., 39 Ohio St. 547; Prouty v. Prouty & Barr Boot & Shoe Co., 155 Pa. 112, 25 Atl. 1001.

[42] Colorado, Gen. Laws 1877, p. 150, § 210; Dakota, Laws 1879, p. 14, c. 9; Indiana, 1 Rev. St. 1876, p. 371, §§ 8, 9, and Rev. St. 1881, § 3008 (Burns' Ann. St. 1894, § 3431); Maryland, Code 1878, art. 40, § 61; Massachusetts, Pub. St. 1882, c. 105, § 25; Missouri, Rev. St. 1879, §§ 934, 935; New York, 2 Rev. St. 1881 (7th Ed.) p. 1548, § 11; Ohio, Rev. St. 1880, § 3259; Washington, 1 Hill's Ann. St. & Codes 1891, § 1512; Wisconsin, Rev. St. 1878, p. 532, § 1827; Wyoming, Comp. Laws 1876, c. 34, art. 1, §§ 16, 17. And see Beal v. Essex Sav. Bank, 15 C. C. A. 128, 67 Fed. 816; Pauly v. State Loan & Trust Co., 7 C. C. A. 422, 58 Fed. 666; Borland v. Nevada Bank of San Francisco, 99 Cal. 89, 33 Pac. 737, 37 Am. St. Rep. 32.

[43] Mansur-Tebbetts Implement Co. v. Carey, 1 Ind. T. 572, 45 S. W. 120; MINNEAPOLIS & N. ELEVATOR CO. v. BETCHER, 42 Minn. 210, 44 N. W. 5, Dobie Cas. Bailments and Carriers, 128; O'Kelly v. Ferguson, 49 La. Ann. 1230, 22 South. 783; Commercial Bank of New Orleans v. Martin, 1 La. Ann. 344, 45 Am. Dec. 87; Cooper v. Simpson, 41 Minn. 46, 42 N. W. 601, 4 L. R. A. 194, 16 Am. St. Rep. 667; Girard Fire & Marine Ins. Co. v. Marr, 46 Pa. 504; Erie Bank v. Smith, 3 Brewst. (Pa.) 9; Third Nat. Bank of Baltimore v. Boyd, 44 Md. 47, 22 Am. Rep. 35; St. Losky v. Davidson, 6 Cal. 643; Scott v. Crews, 2 S. C. 522; Petty v. Overall, 42 Ala. 145, 94 Am. Dec. 634; Wells v. Wells, 53 Vt. 1; Cutting v. Marlor, 78 N. Y. 454; Ouderkirk v. Central Nat. Bank of Troy, 119 N. Y. 263, 23 N. E. 875; Hollister v. Central Nat. Bank of Troy, 119 N. Y. 634, 23 N. E. 878; Damon v. Waldteufel, 99 Cal. 234, 33 Pac. 903; Cutting v. Marlor, 78 N. Y. 454. Where a life insurance policy is assigned to secure the assignee against a contingent liability, de-

The duty and liability of the pledgee are closely analogous to those of the bailee in locatio custodiæ bailments. The general question of care in mutual benefit bailments has already been sufficiently discussed,[44] and what has been said on that subject is equally applicable to pledges.

Negotiable Paper

Though the theoretical standard, ordinary care, is the same in pledges of negotiable paper as in other classes of property, the practical application of this standard to pledges of negotiable paper presents some unique features. In the case of the ordinary pledge of corporeal goods, only passive custody is usually demanded of the pledgee, who ultimately returns the pledged article in the same form in which it is received. Negotiable paper, however, is valuable, not for itself, but because it is either a promise or order to pay money, and into money it should ultimately be converted.

Accordingly, at the maturity of the paper, ordinary care demands that the pledgee (even though the debt secured by the paper is not due) should proceed to take such action as is necessary to collect the note.[45] Again, there are many parties to negotiable paper, who are only secondarily liable thereon (indorsers, for example); and to fix their liability certain steps (such as presentment, demand, and notice) must be taken. It is not ordinary care, usually, unless the pledgee proceeds to take these steps; and if he fails, without reasonable excuse, thus to proceed, and an indorser is released from liability, thereby causing loss, the pledgee is respon-

pendent on the life of the assured, and such assignee is paid by a third person a sum sufficient to pay the premiums while such contingency exists, but he does not agree to pay them, he is not liable in damages to the assured's estate for permitting the policy to lapse by failure to apply the money received to the payment of such premiums. Killoran v. Sweet, 72 Hun, 194, 25 N. Y. Supp. 295. Where a creditor holds as security logs, which he is to manufacture into lumber, sell the lumber, and apply the net proceeds on the debt, he must use reasonable diligence to secure the best net results, account for the proceeds, and show what expenditures were necessarily or reasonably incurred. Second Nat. Bank of Grand Forks v. Sproat, 55 Minn. 14, 56 N. W. 254. If a theft of the pawn was occasioned by his negligence, he is responsible; if without any negligence, he is discharged from liability. Petty v. Overall, 42 Ala. 145, 94 Am. Dec. 634. A pledgee is responsible, also, for the negligence of his servants as well as his own negligence. But he would not be responsible for the negligence of an attorney employed to collect negotiable instruments held in pledge if he used reasonable care in selecting the attorney. Commercial Bank of New Orleans v. Martin, 1 La. Ann. 344, 45 Am. Dec. 87.

44 Ante, §§ 53, 65.

45 Richardson v. Ashby, 132 Mo. 238, 33 S. W. 806; C. H. Larkin Co. v. Dawson, 37 Tex. Civ. App. 345, 83 S. W. 882; Joliet Iron & Steel Co. v. Scioto Fire Brick Co., 82 Ill. 548, 25 Am. Rep. 341; Hamilton's Ex'r v. Hamilton,

sible in damages.[46] Although no steps are necessary to fix the liability of parties primarily liable on a negotiable instrument (such as the maker of a note), yet if the pledgee negligently delays collection and the parties become insolvent, the pledgee would, of course, be liable.[47] The pledgee will also be liable for neglecting to put the collateral in suit, when an ordinarily prudent man would sue, if any loss results from the neglect.[48] In suing on the instrument the pledgee collects the full amount of the instrument,[49] and holds any balance, over and above the amount secured to him, on behalf of the pledgor, unless there were equities existing against the pledgor, in which case the pledgee can collect only the amount of his own interest.[50] Where there is danger of loss, the pledgee

84 S. W. 1156, 27 Ky. Law Rep. 298; Mauck v. Atlanta Trust & Banking Co., 113 Ga. 242, 38 S. E. 845; Daugherty v. Wiles (Tex. Civ. App.) 156 S. W. 1089.

[46] Swift v. Tyson, 16 Pet. 1, 10 L. Ed. 865; 1 Am. Lead. Cas. Eq. 411, 423, note; Smith v. Miller, 43 N. Y. 171, 3 Am. Rep. 690; Wheeler v. Newbould, 16 N. Y. 392; McLughan v. Bovard, 4 Watts (Pa.) 308; Sellers v. Jones, 22 Pa. 423; Muirhead v. Kirkpatrick, 21 Pa. 237; Betterton v. Roope, 3 Lea (Tenn.) 215, 31 Am. Rep. 633; ALEXANDRIA, L. & H. R. CO. v. BURKE, 22 Grat. (Va.) 254, Dobie Cas. Bailments and Carriers, 135; Foote v. Brown, 2 McLean, 369, Fed. Cas. No. 4,909; Lee v. Baldwin, 10 Ga. 208. And see Goodall v. Richardson, 14 N. H. 567.

[47] C. H. Larkin Co. v. Dawson, 37 Tex. Civ. App. 345, 83 S. W. 882; Hazard v. Wells, 2 Abb. N. C. (N. Y.) 444; Barrow v. Rhinelander, 3 Johns. Ch. (N. Y.) 614; Muirhead v. Kirkpatrick, 21 Pa. 237; Bank of U. S. v. Peabody, 20 Pa. 454; Sellers v. Jones, 22 Pa. 423; Lyon v. Huntingdon Bank, 12 Serg. & R. (Pa.) 61; Lamberton v. Windom, 12 Minn. 232 (Gil. 151), 90 Am. Dec. 301; Noland v. Clark, 10 B. Mon. (Ky.) 239; Roberts v. Thompson, 14 Ohio St. 1, 82 Am. Dec. 465; Reeves v. Plough, 41 Ind. 204.

[48] Ex parte Mure, 2 Cox, Ch. 63; Williams v. Price, 1 Sim. & S. 581; Wakeman v. Gowdy, 10 Bosw. (N. Y.) 208; Hoard v. Garner, 10 N. Y. 261; Lyon v. Huntingdon Bank, 12 Serg. & R. (Pa.) 61; Lamberton v. Windom, 12 Minn. 232 (Gil. 151), 90 Am. Dec. 301; Slevin v. Morrow, 4 Ind. 425, 426; Whitin v. Paul, 13 R. I. 40. But see 1 Am. Lead. Cas. 404. The same rule applies to securities, not negotiable, held as collateral; for instance, a judgment. Hanna v. Holton, 78 Pa. 334, 21 Am. Rep. 20. If a pledgee, without the consent of the debtor, renews or extends a note pledged as collateral, or surrenders such note and takes new security, he must account to his debtor as if he had collected it in full. Haas v. Bank of Commerce, 41 Neb. 754, 60 N. W. 85. Particularly is this true when pledgee allows the note to be barred by the statute of limitations. Farm Inv. Co. v. Wyoming College and Normal School, 10 Wyo. 240, 68 Pac. 561.

[49] No demand by the pledgee on the maker is necessary in such case to enable him to sue. White v. Phelps, 14 Minn. 27 (Gil. 21), 100 Am. Dec. 190.

[50] Williams v. Smith, 2 Hill (N. Y.) 301; City Bank v. Taylor, 60 Iowa, 66, 14 N. W. 128; Steere v. Benson, 2 Ill. App. 560; Valette v. Mason, 1 Ind. 288; Mayo v. Moore, 28 Ill. 428; Ehrler v. Worthen, 47 Ill. App. 550; Barmby v. Wolfe, 44 Neb. 77, 62 N. W. 318; Haas v. Bank of Commerce, 41 Neb. 754, 60 N. W. 85. So, in the case of a note given for the pledgor's accommodation.

should immediately proceed to collect the collateral, though the pledge debt is not then due.[51]

Ordinarily the pledgee of negotiable paper (or even of nonnegotiable choses in action) has no right, without the consent of the pledgor, to compromise and take less than what is due on the instrument, and in such case the pledgee might be held responsible for the difference between the amount received under the compromise and face value of the instrument pledged.[52] To this rule there are exceptions, however, as, for example, when the maker of a note is insolvent and the compromise was an advantageous one for the pledgor, since the amount secured was more than could have been collected by suing on the instrument.[53]

SAME—REDELIVERY OF THE PLEDGED GOODS

84. The pledgee must, on redemption by the pledgor, redeliver the identical things pledged, except in cases of certificates of corporate stock.

Redelivery of Things Pledged

When the pledge is redeemed by payment of the debt or performance of the undertaking secured, it is the duty of the pledgee to redeliver the goods pledged, together with all their increase and profits.[54] This duty is fulfilled only by a delivery of the identical

Atlas Bank v. Doyle, 9 R. I. 76, 98 Am. Dec. 368, 11 Am. Rep. 219; Doud v. Reid, 53 Mo. App. 553. Where the debt for which a note was pledged is paid pending an action on the note by the pledgee, the latter may continue the action, subject to all equitable defenses, holding the proceeds as trustee for the pledgor. First Nat. Bank of Johnson City v. Mann, 94 Tenn. 17, 27 S. W. 1015, 27 L. R. A. 565. Where notes held as collateral are impounded in an equity suit, the pledgee is still entitled to control the same, so far as necessary to bring an action at law thereon, and have the proceeds paid into court. Gregory v. Pike, 15 C. C. A. 33, 67 Fed. 837.

51 Seeley v. Wickstrom, 49 Neb. 730, 68 N. W. 1017; Field v. Sibley, 74 App. Div. 81, 77 N. Y. Supp. 252.

52 Powell v. Ong, 92 Ill. App. 95; Hawks v. Hinchcliff, 17 Barb. (N. Y.) 492; Grant v. Holden, 1 E. D. Smith (N. Y.) 545; Gage v. Punchard, 6 Daly (N. Y.) 229; Garlick v. James, 12 Johns. (N. Y.) 146, 7 Am. Dec. 294; Zimpleman v. Veeder, 98 Ill. 613; Union Trust Co. v. Rigdon, 93 Ill. 458; Depuy v. Clark, 12 Ind. 427; Wood v. Matthews, 73 Mo. 477, 479; Stevens v. Hurlbut Bank, 31 Conn. 146.

53 When the compromise yields more than could have been realized from a suit, then the pledgor is benefited rather than injured by the transaction. It would seem though that the burden of showing this would rest on the pledgee making the compromise. See Powell v. Ong, 92 Ill. App. 95.

54 Whittaker v. Amwell Nat. Bank, 52 N. J. Eq. 400, 29 Atl. 203; Dean v. Lawham, 7 Or. 422; Davenport v. Tarlton, 1 A. K. Marsh. (Ky.) 244; Woodard

thing pledged,[55] with the exception of certificates of corporate stock.[56]

Since the certificate is merely evidence of certain rights in the corporation, the return of a similar (though not the identical) certificate, showing that the pledgor is entitled to the same rights, results in no loss to the pledgor.[57] And the nature of the whole transaction is foreign to the idea that the specific stock certificate should be an object of personal attachment or should have any unique value in the estimation of the pledgor. There are a few cases, however, holding the contrary view.[58]

Conversion by the Pledgee

As it is the duty of the pledgee to redeliver the pledged goods upon redemption, if he wrongfully sells or otherwise disposes of them, he is guilty of a conversion.[59] The pledgor, in such a case, is not limited to his (1) right to sue either the pledgee [60] or the

v. Fitzpatrick, 9 Dana (Ky.) 117; Hunsaker v. Sturgis, 29 Cal. 142; Geron v. Geron, 15 Ala. 558, 50 Am. Dec. 143; Houton v. Holliday, 6 N. C. 111, 5 Am. Dec. 522.

[55] The pledgee must redeliver the identical article pledged, where it is distinctive in its character, and for a failure to do so renders himself liable in trover. Ball v. Stanley, 5 Yerg. (Tenn.) 199, 26 Am. Dec. 263. And equity may be invoked for this purpose where the law fails. Bryson v. Rayner, 25 Md. 424, 90 Am. Dec. 69. See, also, the cases cited in note 59.

[56] Gilpin v. Howell, 5 Pa. 41, 45 Am. Dec. 720; Horton v. Morgan, 19 N. Y. 170, 75 Am. Dec. 311; Gruman v. Smith, 81 N. Y. 25; Stewart v. Drake, 46 N. Y. 449; Worthington v. Tormey, 34 Md. 182; Atkins v. Gamble, 42 Cal. 86, 10 Am. Rep. 282; Hawley v. Brumagim, 33 Cal. 394. And, as to redelivery of the identical bonds deposited in pledge, see Stuart v. Bigler's Assignees, 98 Pa. 80.

[57] Hubbell v. Drexel (C. C.) 11 Fed. 115; Lecroy v. Eastman, 10 Mod. (Eng.) 499, 88 Eng. Reprint, 285; Hayward v. Rogers, 62 Cal. 348.

[58] See 2 Thompson, Comm. Corp. §§ 2651-2653; Fay v. Gray, 124 Mass. 500; Langton v. Waite, L. R. 6 Eq. (Eng.) 165; Allen v. Dubois, 117 Mich. 115, 75 N. W. 443, 72 Am. St. Rep. 557.

[59] Radigan v. Johnson, 174 Mass. 68, 54 N. E. 358; Romero v. Newman, 50 La. Ann. 80, 23 South. 493; Toplitz v. Bauer, 161 N. Y. 325, 55 N. E. 1059; Brown v. First Nat. Bank, 132 Fed. 450, 66 C. C. A. 293; Richardson v. Ashby, 132 Mo. 238, 33 S. W. 806. The pledgee may recoup the amount of his debt when sued for the conversion of the pledged property, or for any tort with respect thereto. Stearns v. Marsh, 4 Denio (N. Y.) 227, 47 Am. Dec. 248. Where assignors for benefit of creditors, before the assignment, convert stock pledged to them as security, the pledgor is not entitled to payment in full for his claim for the value of the stock converted out of the assigned estate, on the ground that the conversion was a breach of trust, which entitled him to follow the proceeds specifically. In re Jamison & Co.'s Estate, 163 Pa. 143, 29 Atl. 1001. The fact that the transferee of pledged securities converts them does not render the original pledgee liable in trover. Waddle v. Owen, 43 Neb. 489, 61 N. W. 731.

[60] Harrell v. Citizens' Banking Co., 111 Ga. 846, 36 S. E. 460; Hurst v. Coley (C. C.) 15 Fed. 645; Hays v. Riddle, 1 Sandf. (N. Y.) 248.

purchaser[61] for the conversion; but the pledgor may (2) recover the goods from such purchaser or any other party into whose hands they may have come,[62] or (3) waive the tort and sue the pledgee in assumpsit for such purchase money, while the latter may use the amount of the pledged debt as an offset.[63]

The question of the measure of damages, when the pledgor sues the pledgee for conversion of the pledged goods, is not without difficulty. The usual measure in cases of conversion is the fair value of the goods at the time of the conversion;[64] and this, ordinarily, in the case in question, would be both fair and easy to apply, allowing the pledgee to offset the amount of the debt secured.[65] When, however, the pledged goods are subject, like corporate stocks, to rapid fluctuations in value, and particularly when some time elapses before the pledgor learns of the conversion, then different considerations apply, and this measure might work either undue advantage or great prejudice to the pledgor.

Some courts, however, have clung to the old rule of the value of the goods at the time of the conversion, even though it might compel the pledgor practically to stand by a sale made at a low price, at a time when he would never have consented to sell.[66] Other courts fix the damages at the value of the goods at the time of the pledgor's demand.[67] This is objectionable in allowing the pledgor, by postponing demand, thus to speculate as to the rise or fall in the value of the goods. Still more objectionable is the rule that the pledgor can recover the highest value between the time of the con-

[61] Gregg v. Bank of Columbia, 72 S. C. 458, 52 S. E. 195, 110 Am. St. Rep. 633; Usher v. Van Vranken, 48 App. Div. 413, 63 N. Y. Supp. 104.

[62] Johnson v. Succession of Robbins, 20 La. Ann. 569; Winston v. Rawson, 38 Ill. App. 193; German Sav. Bank of Baltimore City v. Renshaw, 78 Md. 475, 28 Atl. 281.

[63] Union Nat. Bank v. Post, 192 Ill. 385, 61 N. E. 507; Mayo v. Peterson, 126 Mass. 516; Brown v. First Nat. Bank, 132 Fed. 450, 66 C. C. A. 293; Hinckley v. Pfister, 83 Wis. 64, 53 N. W. 21.

[64] Dimock v. United States Nat. Bank, 55 N. J. Law, 296, 25 Atl. 926, 39 Am. St. Rep. 643; Robinson v. Hurley, 11 Iowa, 410, 79 Am. Dec. 497; Blood v. Erie Dime Savings & Loan Co., 164 Pa. 95, 30 Atl. 362; Loomis v. Stave, 72 Ill. 623; Belden v. Perkins, 78 Ill. 449; Fowle v. Ward, 113 Mass. 548, 18 Am. Rep. 534; Newcomb-Buchanan Co. v. Baskett, 14 Bush (Ky.) 658; Rosenzweig v. Frazer, 82 Ind. 342; Hudson v. Wilkinson, 61 Tex. 606; Grimes v. Watkins, 59 Tex. 140.

[65] Stearns v. Marsh, 4 Denio (N. Y.) 227, 47 Am. Dec. 248.

[66] Fisher v. George S. Jones Co., 108 Ga. 490, 34 S. E. 172; Third Nat. Bank of Baltimore v. Boyd, 44 Md. 47, 22 Am. Rep. 35; Sterling v. Garritee, 18 Md. 468; Union Trust Co. v. Rigdon, 93 Ill. 458.

[67] Pinkerton v. Manchester & L. R. R., 42 N. H. 424; Reynolds v. Witte, 13 S. C. 5, 36 Am. Rep. 678; Baltimore City Pass. Ry. Co. v. Sewell, 35 Md. 238, 6 Am. Rep. 402; Fowle v. Ward, 113 Mass. 548, 18 Am. Rep. 534.

version and the trial[68] for this would tempt the pledgor to postpone unduly bringing suit, in the hope that the value might reach in the future a higher figure than it had yet done.

The fairest rule, which is most consonant with reason, fixes the damages at the highest value of the goods within a reasonable time after the pledgor learns of the conversion.[69] This is the rule in New York[70] (where such transactions are most frequent), and has the support of the United States Supreme Court.[71] This involves no speculative elements, but contemplates restoring the pledgor to the position in which he would have been, had not his rights been violated, and presumes that, after learning of the conversion, the pledgor would act reasonably to restore himself to that position.

RIGHTS AND DUTIES OF THE PLEDGEE AFTER DEFAULT—IN GENERAL

85. Default by the pledgor in the debt or engagement secured confers unique rights on the pledgee, who then becomes more than a mere bailee. The pledgee's chief concern then becomes the realization of such debt or the performance of such engagement, and the methods of dealing with the pledged goods to encompass this end.

In General

The rights and duties of the pledgor were considered in some detail without distinctive reference to the question of default on the obligation secured.[72] As to the pledgee, however, so great a

[68] See Gregg v. Columbia Bank, 72 S. C. 458, 52 S. E. 195, 110 Am. St. Rep. 633, holding that the court may instruct the jury that they may fix the damages as the value at the time of the conversion or as the highest value up to the time of the trial. As to the measure of the highest intermediate value between the conversion and demand, see Bank of Montgomery v. Reese, 26 Pa. 143; Page v. Fowler, 39 Cal. 412, 2 Am. Rep. 462; Wilson v. Little, 2 N. Y. 443, 51 Am. Dec. 307.

[69] Smith v. Savin, 141 N. Y. 315, 36 N. E. 338; Baker v. Drake, 53 N. Y. 211, 13 Am. Rep. 507; Wright v. Bank of Metropolis, 110 N. Y. 237, 18 N. E. 79, 1 L. R. A. 289, 6 Am. St. Rep. 356; GALIGHER v. JONES, 129 U. S. 193, 200-202, 9 Sup. Ct. 335, 32 L. Ed. 658, Dobie Cas. Bailments and Carriers, 126. The rule of higher intermediate value is discussed at great length, with an elaborate review of the cases, in 2 Sedgwick, Damages (9th Ed.) c. 22, §§ 507-525. See, also, Jones, Collateral Securities (3d Ed.) §§ 750-757a.

[70] Baker v. Drake, 53 N. Y. 211, 13 Am. Rep. 507; Wright v. Bank of Metropolis, 110 N. Y. 237, 18 N. E. 79, 1 L. R. A. 289, 6 Am. St. Rep. 356.

[71] GALIGHER v. JONES, 129 U. S. 193, 200-202, 9 Sup. Ct. 335, 32 L. Ed. 658, Dobie Cas. Bailments and Carriers, 126.

[72] Ante, § 75.

change is wrought in his position and attitude by the default of the pledgor that the pledgee's duties and rights must necessarily be treated as revolving about this important fact.

Those rights and duties accruing before default have just been considered.[73] Those arising on the pledgor's default in the obligation secured next demand attention. It is then that the distinctive features of the pledge, and the peculiar rights that accrue to pledgees apart from other bailees, are brought into being. These questions naturally turn about the pledgee's dealing with the pledged goods to protect himself from the consequences of such default, for it is in contemplation of that contingency that the pledge relation owes its very inception. The pledgee's rights are varied, but cumulative.[74]

SAME—HOLDING THE PLEDGED GOODS

86. The pledgee may, if he so sees fit, continue to hold the pledged goods as security, without taking any other action.

After the pledgor is in default as to the debt secured or the undertaking to be performed, the pledgee may ordinarily continue to hold the pledged goods as security for such payment or performance. He may be content with this right, without taking any other action.[75] Whether, besides holding the goods, he shall pursue any other of his remedies, is a matter which he may decide. Such additional remedies are cumulative, and he has his option as to whether he shall resort to any of them. Simply holding the pledged goods, as the lienor does, is the least effective of his remedies; but still the pledgee, if he so wishes, may elect that remedy, and that alone, and decline to sell, even though so requested by the pledgor.[76]

[73] Ante, §§ 77–84.

[74] Emes v. Widdowson, 4 Car. & P. (Eng.) 451; Beckwith v. Sibley, 11 Pick. (Mass.) 482; Barnes v. Bradley, 56 Ark. 105, 19 S. W. 319; Mitchell v. Roberts (C. C.) 17 Fed. 776; Whitwell v. Brigham, 19 Pick. (Mass.) 117.

[75] Robinson v. Hurley, 11 Iowa, 410, 79 Am. Dec. 479; Rozet v. McClellan, 48 Ill. 345, 95 Am. Dec. 551. A contract may make it the duty of the pledgee to sell within a specified time, and his failure to do so is then such breach of duty as will render him answerable to the pledgor. Cooper v. Simpson, 41 Minn. 46, 42 N. W. 601, 4 L. R. A. 194, 16 Am. St. Rep. 667.

[76] Simonton v. Sibley, 122 U. S. 220, 7 Sup. Ct. 1351, 30 L. Ed. 1225; Furness v. Union Nat. Bank, 147 Ill. 570, 35 N. E. 624; MINNEAPOLIS & N. ELEVATOR CO. v. BETCHER, 42 Minn. 210, 44 N. W. 5, Dobie Cas. Bailments and Carriers, 128. Hence the pledgee is not liable for depreciation in value of the pledged goods, though he might have avoided this by selling

But the duty of exercising ordinary care as to the pledged goods may require a sale by the pledgee,[77] as in the case of perishable goods. And, in exceptional cases, where the goods may decrease in value, a court of equity might force the pledgee to sell. Subject to these qualifications, however, the pledgor cannot compel a sale; his only right is to redeem by paying the debt or performing the engagement secured.[78]

SAME—SUIT ON THE DEBT OR ENGAGEMENT SECURED

87. The pledgee, without in any way impairing his rights in the pledged goods, may bring suit against the pledgor on the debt or undertaking secured.

The pledge is a security for the debt, not a substitute therefor. It is a cumulative remedy, conferring added rights, without impairing those already existing. Accordingly, the pledgee creditor can bring suit personally on the debt against the pledgor debtor, without affecting his lien and rights in the pledged goods.[79] Nor is

promptly on default. O'Neill v. Whigham, 87 Pa. 394; Rozet v. McClellan, 48 Ill. 345, 95 Am. Dec. 551; Field v. Leavitt, 37 N. Y. Super. Ct. 215.

[77] Franklin, etc., Inst. v. Preetorious, 6 Mo. App. 470; Field v. Leavitt, 37 N. Y. Super. Ct. 215.

[78] Colquitt v. Stultz, 65 Ga. 305; Newsome v. Davis, 133 Mass. 343; Mueller v. Nichols, 50 Ill. App. 663.

[79] Savings Bank v. Middlekauf, 113 Cal. 463, 45 Pac. 840; Lormer v. Bain, 14 Neb. 178, 15 N. W. 323; Ketcham v. Provost, 156 App. Div. 477, 141 N. Y. Supp. 437; Emes v. Widdowson, 4 Car. & P. (Eng.) 151; Commercial Sav. Bank v. Hornberger, 140 Cal. 16, 73 Pac. 625; Butterworth v. Kennedy, 5 Bosw. (N. Y.) 143; Rogers v. Ward, 8 Allen (Mass.) 387, 85 Am. Dec. 710; Darst v. Bates, 95 Ill. 493; Whitwell v. Brigham, 19 Pick. (Mass.) 117; Beckwith v. Sibley, 11 Pick. (Mass.) 482; Sonoma Val. Bank v. Hill, 59 Cal. 107; Jones v. Scott, 10 Kan. 33; SMITH v. STROUT, 63 Me. 205, Dobie Cas. Bailments and Carriers, 129; Ehrlick v. Ewald, 66 Cal. 97, 4 Pac. 1062; Grand Island Sav. & Loan Ass'n v. Moore, 40 Neb. 686, 59 N. W. 115; Ambler v. Ames, 1 App. D. C. 191. The person holding collateral securities is not bound to resort to them before suing upon his principal claim; but, when that claim is satisfied, he may be compelled to release or reassign the collaterals. Wallace v. Finnegan, 14 Mich. 170, 90 Am. Dec. 243. If a pawn is lost or injured, the pledgor can set off against the debt for which it stood as security the loss or injury attributable to any want of necessary care and diligence upon the pledgee's part. Crocker v. Monrose, 18 La. 553, 36 Am. Dec. 660; Cooper v. Simpson, 41 Minn. 46, 42 N. W. 601, 4 L. R. A. 194, 16 Am. St. Rep. 667. Of course, when the contract specifies that the pledgee is to look alone to the pledged goods for the debt, then the pledgor cannot be personally sued. Archibald v. Argall, 53 Ill. 307; Wilhelm v. Schmidt, 84 Ill. 183; Cornwall v. Gould, 4 Pick. (Mass.) 444; Beckwith v. Sibley, 11 Pick. (Mass.) 482; Bigelow v. Walker, 24 Vt. 149, 58 Am. Dec. 156.

the pledge affected by the pledgee's obtaining a judgment against the pledgor for the amount of the debt.[80] Though the debt may be merged in the judgment, the obligation to pay still remains in a new form and evidenced by a higher security; but the property pledged for its payment still remains liable therefor. The pledgee in a suit on the debt may even, as in other cases, attach the pledged goods; but by so doing, it seems, he waives the lien of the pledge, and substitutes therefor the in rem rights of an attaching creditor.[81] When the judgment is fully satisfied, however, this is equivalent to a payment of the debt, which, of course, immediately extinguishes the pledge.[82]

In this connection it might be noted that so independent are the pledge and the debt secured (as far as the pledgee is concerned) that the pledge may be (and frequently is) terminated without at all affecting the debt. Thus a valid tender of the amount of the debt, or a redelivery of the goods to the pledgor, would terminate the pledge;[83] but neither the tender by the pledgor nor the redelivery by the pledgee would extinguish the debt, which would still continue.[84]

Since the right to sue on the debt is an independent one, which can be exercised by the pledgee without proceeding against the goods pledged, the pledgor, when thus sued, cannot set off the value of such goods, and thereby reduce the amount of the pledgee's recovery.[85] The existence of such a right on the pledgor's part would practically negative all that has just been said in regard to the relation between the debt and the pledge. When there has been a conversion of the pledged goods by the pledgee, this, of course, gives a right of action to the pledgor. Whether the pledgor can set this up in defense, by way of set-off or recoupment, when sued

[80] Fairbank v. Merchants' Nat. Bank of Chicago, 132 Ill. 120, 22 N. E. 524; Barnes v. Bradley, 56 Ark. 105, 19 S. W. 319; Black v. Reno (C. C.) 59 Fed. 917; SMITH v. STROUT, 63 Me. 205, Dobie Cas. Bailments and Carriers, 129; Jones v. Scott, 10 Kan. 35; Charles v. Coker, 2 S. C. 122. Even securing an execution on the judgment and arresting the debtor does not affect the pledgee's right to hold the pledged goods. SMITH v. STROUT, 63 Me. 205, Dobie Cas. Bailments and Carriers, 129.

[81] Citizens' Bank v. Dows, 68 Iowa, 460, 27 N. W. 459; SMITH v. STROUT, 63 Me. 205, Dobie Cas. Bailments and Carriers, 129; Sensenbrenner v. Matthews, 48 Wis. 250, 3 N. W 599, 33 Am. Rep. 809; Legg v. Willard, 17 Pick. (Mass.) 140, 28 Am. Dec. 282; Whitaker v. Sumner, 20 Pick. (Mass.) 399; Buck v. Ingersoll, 11 Metc. (Mass.) 226. Contra: Arendale v. Morgan, 5 Sneed (Tenn.) 703.

[82] Post, § 89.

[83] Post, § 89.

[84] Jones, Collateral Securities (3d Ed.) § 592; Mitchell v. Roberts (C. C.) 17 Fed. 776.

[85] Winthrop Sav. Bank v. Jackson, 67 Me. 570, 24 Am. Rep. 56.

on the debt by the pledgee, is a question depending largely on the pleading, practice, and the statutes of the various states. The liberalizing trend of modern procedural law, though, has been toward allowing this to be done.[86] In those states which permit this to be done, it is generally held that the pledgee, when suing on the debt, must produce the pledged goods or account for their nonproduction.[87]

SAME—SALE OF THE PLEDGED GOODS

88. The pledgee may sell the pledged goods:
(1) At common law, upon notice to the pledgor.
(2) By a proceeding in equity, when his common-law right of sale is not clear, or is disputed, or when an accounting is necessary.
(3) Under a power of sale given by the pledge contract.
(4) Under a power of sale given by statute, which either may or may not take away the right to sell at common law or under the pledge contract, according to the language of the particular statute.

Sale at Common Law

Perhaps the most frequent procedure, upon the pledgor's default, is a sale of the pledged goods by the pledgee under the power of sale existing at common law by virtue of the pledge.[88] An assignee of the pledgee's interest has the same right to sell that the pledgee has.[89] Where the pledgor is not the owner of the goods, and pledg-

[86] Stearns v. Marsh, 4 Denio (N. Y.) 227, 47 Am. Dec. 248; Cass v. Higenbotam, 27 Hun (N. Y.) 406, 408; Bigelow v. Walker, 24 Vt. 149, 58 Am. Dec. 156; Bank of British Columbia v. Marshall (C. C.) 11 Fed. 19; Donnell v. Wyckoff, 49 N. J. Law, 48, 7 Atl. 672; Haskell v. Africa, 68 N. H. 421, 41 Atl. 73.

[87] Jones, Collateral Securities (3d Ed.) § 596; Ocean Nat. Bank of City of New York v. Fant, 50 N. Y. 474; Smith v Rockwell, 2 Hill (N. Y.) 482; Stuart v. Bigler's Assignees, 98 Pa. 80; Spalding v. Bank of Susquehanna County, 9 Pa. 28.

[88] Mauge v. Heringhi, 26 Cal. 577; Vaupell v. Woodward, 2 Sandf. Ch. (N. Y.) 143; Garlick v. James, 12 Johns. (N. Y.) 146, 7 Am. Dec. 294; De Lisle v. Priestman, 1 Browne (Pa.) 176; Cushman v. Hayes, 46 Ill. 145; Union Trust Co. v. Rigdon, 93 Ill. 458; Robinson v. Hurley, 11 Iowa, 410, 79 Am. Dec. 497; Kemp v. Westbrook, 1 Ves. (Eng.) 278; Union Cattle Co. v. International Trust Co., 149 Mass. 492, 21 N. E. 962; Sharpe v. National Bank of Birmingham, 87 Ala. 644, 7 South. 106; McDowell v. Chicago Steel Works, 124 Ill. 491, 16 N. E. 854, 7 Am. St. Rep. 381.

[89] Ante, § 77; Jones, Collateral Securities (3d Ed) § 418; Donald v. Suckling, L. R. 1 Q. B. (Eng.) 585; Talty v. Freedman's Sav. & T. Co., 93 U. S. 321, 23 L. Ed. 886.

es merely his interest therein, then, of course, the pledgee can sell only the pledgor's limited interest.[90]

This common-law sale is a general right, but does not extend to pledges of commercial paper.[91] It is contemplated that the proper method of realizing on negotiable bills and notes is by collecting them [92] rather than selling them. In such a case, the pledgee should hold the bills or notes, collect them as they fall due, and apply the proceeds towards the payment of the debt secured.[93] The pledgee would not be justified in selling such paper at less than its value, either at a private or public sale, unless so authorized by the pledge contract.[94] But negotiable bonds, which (especially in the case of

[90] Harding v. Eldridge, 186 Mass. 39, 71 N. E. 115.

[91] For remedies on pledges of negotiable paper, see Jones, Collateral Securities (3d Ed.) c. 17; Stevens v. Wiley, 165 Mass. 402, 43 N. E. 177; Boswell v. Thigpen, 75 Miss. 308, 22 South. 823; E. F. Hallack Lumber & Mfg. Co. v. Gray, 19 Colo. 149, 34 Pac. 1000.

[92] ALEXANDRIA, L. & H. R. CO. v. BURKE, 22 Grat. (Va.) 254, Doble Cas. Bailments and Carriers, 135; Union Trust Co. v. Rigdon, 93 Ill. 458; Zimpleman v. Veeder, 98 Ill. 613; Fletcher v. Dickinson, 7 Allen (Mass.) 23, 25; Brookman v. Metcalf, 5 Bosw. (N. Y.) 429; Brown v. Ward, 3 Duer (N. Y.) 660; Lamberton v. Windom, 12 Minn. 232 (Gil. 151), 90 Am. Dec. 301; Morris Canal & Banking Co. v. Lewis, 12 N. J. Eq. 323; In re Litchfield Bank, 28 Conn. 575; Whitteker v. Charleston Gas Co., 16 W. Va. 717; Hunt v. Nevers, 15 Pick. (Mass.) 500, 26 Am. Dec. 616; Joliet Iron & Steel Co. v. Scioto Fire Brick Co., 82 Ill. 548, 25 Am. Rep. 341; Wheeler v. Newbould, 16 N. Y. 392; Fletcher v. Dickinson, 7 Allen (Mass.) 23, 25. So a savings bank book cannot be sold by a pledgee. Boynton v. Payrow, 67 Me. 587 An ordinary note and mortgage pledged cannot be sold. Morris Canal & Banking Co. v. Fisher, 9 N. J. Eq. 667, 64 Am. Dec. 423.

[93] Cleghorn v. Minnesota Title Insurance & Trust Co., 57 Minn. 341, 59 N. W. 320, 47 Am. St. Rep. 615; Handy v Sibley, 46 Ohio St. 9, 17 N. E. 329; Zimpleman v. Veeder, 98 Ill. 613. See ante.

[94] Powell v. Ong, 92 Ill. App. 95; Union Trust Co. v. Rigdon, 93 Ill. 458; Fletcher v. Dickinson, 7 Allen (Mass.) 23, 25; Washburn v. Pond, 2 Allen (Mass.) 474; Stearns v. Marsh, 4 Denio (N. Y.) 227, 47 Am. Dec. 248; Hunter v. Hamilton, 52 Kan. 195, 34 Pac. 782. A power of sale does not deprive the pledgee of the right to sue on the paper. Nelson v. Eaton, 26 N. Y. 410; Nelson v. Edwards, 40 Barb. (N. Y.) 279; Nelson v. Wellington, 5 Bosw. (N. Y.) 178. Where negotiable paper is pledged as collateral security for a loan, and the lender is authorized to sell the collaterals in case the loan is not paid at maturity, such authority does not limit the rights of the lender to a sale of the collateral, so as to prevent him from suing thereon. Holland Trust Co. v. Waddell, 75 Hun, 104, 36 N. Y. Supp. 980. Though a pledgee cannot, without express authority, sell commercial paper pledged as collateral security, a court may, under proper circumstances, order a judicial sale of it. Cleghorn v. Minnesota Title Insurance & Trust Co., 57 Minn. 341, 59 N. W. 320, 47 Am. St. Rep. 615. The foreclosure and sale of a negotiable instrument held as a pledge is authorized, when the maker resides in a remote country or a different state, and it does not appear that he has any property within the jurisdiction subject to seizure and sale. Donohoe v. Gamble, 38 Cal. 341,

corporations) are more formal instruments and run for much longer periods than ordinary commercial paper, can be sold before their maturity, at a common-law sale, without authority to that effect in the pledge contract.[95]

Though this common-law sale is not dependent on express authority in the pledge contract,[96] and requires no judicial proceedings,[97] yet the sale must be a public one,[98] because in that way a better price is ordinarily secured and less opportunity for fraud or unfair dealing is afforded to the pledgee. Since the sale of stocks, bonds, etc., on the Stock Exchange or Boards of Trade and similar institutions is ordinarily more advantageous than a sale at public auction, the sounder view seems to be that such a sale is proper,[99] though there are cases holding the contrary.[1]

Due notice both of the time and place of the sale must be seasonably given to the pledgor.[2] The purpose of this requirement is

99 Am. Dec. 399. Where a bond and mortgage having several years to run are assigned as collateral security for a loan due in three months, but the assignment does not provide for a sale of the security, the lender, on maturity of the loan, may sue in equity to procure a sale. Porter v. Frazer, 6 Misc. Rep. 553, 27 N. Y. Supp. 517. Where a mortgage and note were assigned as collateral security, with authority in the assignee, on default, to sell the mortgage, the pledgee was authorized to sell the note or debt. Watson v. Smith, 60 Minn. 206, 62 N. W. 265.

95 Jones, Collateral Securities (3d Ed.) § 657a; Duffield v. Miller, 92 Pa. 286; Morris Canal & Banking Co. v. Lewis, 12 N. J. Eq. 323; Newport & C. Bridge Co. v. Douglass, 12 Bush. (Ky.) 673; ALEXANDRIA, L. & H. R. CO. v. BURKE, 22 Grat. (Va.) 254, Dobie Cas. Bailments and Carriers, 135; Brown v. Tyler, 8 Gray (Mass.) 135, 69 Am. Dec. 239.

96 Jerome v. McCarter, 94 U. S. 734, 24 L. Ed. 136; Lockwood v. Ewer, 9 Mod. (Eng.) 275.

97 Lockwood v. Ewer, 2 Atk. (Eng.) 303, 9 Mod. 275; Pothonier v. Dawson, Holt (Eng.) 385; Guinzburg v. H. W. Downs Co., 165 Mass. 467, 43 N. E. 195, 52 Am. St. Rep. 525; McDowell v. Chicago Steel Works, 124 Ill. 491, 16 N. E. 854, 7 Am. St. Rep. 381.

98 Bryson v. Rayner, 25 Md. 424, 90 Am. Dec. 69; Jeanes' Appeal, 116 Pa. 573, 11 Atl. 862, 2 Am. St. Rep. 624; King v. Texas Banking & Ins. Co., 58 Tex. 669; Pogue v. Hillman, 85 Ohio St. 463, 98 N. E. 1131; Williams v. Hahn, 113 Cal. 475, 45 Pac. 815; Rankin v. McCullough, 12 Barb. (N. Y.) 103.

99 MARYLAND FIRE INS. CO. v. DALRYMPLE, 25 Md. 242, 89 Am. Dec. 779, Dobie Cas. Bailments and Carriers, 130; Brown v. Ward, 3 Duer (N. Y.) 660. See, also, as to sales at board of trade rooms, Fitzpatrick v. Bank of Forrest City, 95 Ark. 542, 129 S. W. 795; Earle v. Grant, 14 R. I. 228; Stern v. Simons, 77 Conn. 150, 58 Atl. 696.

1 Hagan v. Continental Nat. Bank, 182 Mo. 319, 81 S. W. 171; Brass v. Worth, 40 Barb. (N. Y.) 648; Dykers v. Allen, 7 Hill (N. Y.) 497, 42 Am. Dec. 87.

2 National Bank of Illinois v. Baker, 128 Ill. 533, 21 N. E. 510, 4 L. R. A. 586; Sell v. Ward, 81 Ill. App. 675; Stearns v. Marsh, 4 Denio (N. Y.) 227, 47 Am. Dec. 248; Luckett v. Townsend, 3 Tex. 119, 49 Am. Dec. 723; Wilson

in order that the pledgor may exert himself in procuring the attendance of prospective buyers and thus enhance the price obtained, and that the pledgor may have an opportunity to attend the sale and see that it is fairly conducted. Further, the pledgor has the right to redeem the pledged goods by paying the debt secured at any time before the sale is actually made.[3] Accordingly, when the pledgor is otherwise fully informed on the subject, no matter from what source, a further and more formal notice by the pledgee is unnecessary.[4] The only question is, Did the pledgor have actual notice of the time and place of sale? The safest course, of course, is to have formal written notice served on the pledgor, for then the fact of notice can easily be proved; otherwise, the pledgee may find difficulty in proving that the pledgor was actually informed of the time and place of the sale a reasonable time before such sale was to take place.[5]

In making the sale the pledgee acts in a quasi fiduciary capacity and must in all respects exercise the utmost fairness and good faith.[6] The courts will closely scrutinize such sales, particularly

v. Little, 2 N. Y. 443, 51 Am. Dec. 307; E. F. Hallack Lumber & Manuf'g Co. v. Gray, 19 Colo. 149, 34 Pac. 1000; Smith v. Savin, 141 N. Y. 315, 36 N. E. 338; Wheeler v. Newbould, 16 N. Y. 392; Garlick v. James, 12 Johns. (N. Y.) 146, 7 Am. Dec. 294; Indiana & I. C. Ry. Co. v. McKernan, 24 Ind. 62; Small v. Housman, 208 N. Y. 115, 101 N. E. 700; Colton v. Oakland Bank of Savings, 137 Cal. 376, 70 Pac. 225; Green v. Lafayette County Bank, 128 Mo. 559, 30 S. W. 319. When the pledgor's liability on the debt or obligation secured is not fixed until a demand on him, such demand or notice must be given by the pledgee in addition to the notice of sale. Garlick v. James, 12 Johns. (N. Y.) 146, 7 Am. Dec. 294; Moffat v. Williams, 5 Colo. App. 184, 36 Pac. 914; Milliken v. Dehon, 27 N. Y. 364; Wilson v. Little, 1 Sandf. (N. Y.) 351. Consent that the pledgee may sell without giving notice does not relieve him from the necessity of demanding payment of the debt before he sells. Wilson v. Little, 2 N. Y. 443, 51 Am. Dec. 307. The sale of stock pledged as collateral, made in default of payment of a demand for a larger sum than that for which the stock was pledged, is a conversion of such stock, though, immediately prior to such sale, the pledgee offer to accept the amount justly due, plaintiff not having a reasonable time within which to comply with such offer. Blood v. Erie Dime Savings & Loan Co., 164 Pa. 95, 30 Atl. 362. The notice must be to the pledgor or his agent, or to some one authorized to receive notice. Notice given to an agent having no authority over the pledge is not sufficient. Washburn v. Pond, 2 Allen (Mass.) 474. Of course, the pledgor may waive any notice. Williams v. United States Trust Co. of New York, 133 N. Y. 660, 31 N. E. 29; Carson v. Iowa City Gaslight Co., 80 Iowa, 638, 45 N. W. 1068; Dullnig v. Weekes, 16 Tex. Civ. App. 1, 40 S. W. 178.

[3] Milliken v. Dehon, 27 N. Y. 364, 369; ante, § 75.

[4] ALEXANDRIA, L. & H. R. CO. v. BURKE, 22 Grat. (Va.) 254, Dobie Cas. Bailments and Carriers, 135; Earle v. Grant, 14 R. I. 228.

[5] ALEXANDRIA, L. & H. R. CO. v. BURKE, 22 Grat. (Va.) 254, Dobie Cas. Bailments and Carriers, 135.

[6] FOOTE v. UTAH COMMERCIAL & SAVINGS BANK, 17 Utah, 783, 54

to ascertain whether the time and place were proper, and generally to see that the pledgor's rights are properly protected.[7] Thus, when the pledged goods are susceptible of division, and when, by a sale of part of the goods, a sufficient amount can be realized, it then becomes the duty of the pledgee to make such division and to sell only such portion of the goods.[8]

The pledgee cannot become the purchaser at the sale.[9] If he does, the sale is voidable as to the pledgor, and the pledgor has the right to treat it as a valid sale,[10] or to treat it as void.[11] If the pledgor elects to treat the sale as void, then the title to the pledge remains precisely as if no sale had been made, with the lien of the pledgee still on it for the amount of his debt.[12]

The interest of the pledgee in the goods pledged is only coextensive with the debt secured. Therefore, on a sale in any of the methods indicated in this section, any surplus remaining in the hands of the pledgee, after the satisfaction of his claims (i. e., the debt and necessary expenses of keeping and selling the pledged goods) be-

Pac. 104, Dobie Cas. Bailments and Carriers, 138; Perkins v. Applegate, 85 S. W. 723, 27 Ky. Law Rep. 522; Schaaf v. Fries, 77 Mo. App. 346.

7 Kinnaird v. Dudderrar, 54 S. W. 847, 21 Ky. Law Rep. 1230; Sparhawk v. Drexel, Fed. Cas. No. 13,204; Barber v. Hathaway, 47 App. Div. 165, 62 N. Y. Supp. 329.

8 Fitzgerald v Blocher, 32 Ark. 742, 29 Am. Rep. 8.

9 Sharpe v. National Bank of Birmingham, 87 Ala. 644, 7 South. 106; Lord v. Hartford, 175 Mass. 320, 50 N. E. 609; Winchester v. Joslyn, 31 Colo. 220, 72 Pac. 1079, 102 Am. St. Rep. 30; Stokes v. Frazier, 72 Ill. 428; Killian v. Hoffman, 6 Ill. App. 200; MARYLAND FIRE INS. CO. v. DALRYMPLE, 25 Md. 242, 89 Am. Dec. 779, Dobie Cas. Bailments and Carriers, 130. But the pledgee may be given power to purchase by express contract. Chouteau v. Allen, 70 Mo. 290; Hamilton v. Schaack, 16 Wkly. Dig. (N. Y.) 423. The holder of collateral security cannot appropriate it in satisfaction of the debt at his own option. Diller v. Brubaker, 52 Pa. 498, 91 Am. Dec. 177. Where a pledgee is an agent or trustee, and is authorized by the pledgor to purchase the pledge in his own right in case of sale, a purchase by the pledgee in his own right is valid, as between him and the pledgor. Manning v. Shriver, 79 Md. 41, 28 Atl. 899.

10 Faulkner v. Hill, 104 Mass. 188; Killian v. Hoffman, 6 Ill. App. 200; Holston Nat. Bank v. Wood, 125 Tenn. 6, 140 S. W. 31.

11 Duncomb v. New York, H. & N. R. Co., 84 N. Y. 190; Glidden v. Mechanics' Nat. Bank, 53 Ohio St. 588, 42 N. E. 995, 43 L. R. A. 737; Leahy v. Lobdell, Farwell & Co., 80 Fed. 665, 26 C. C. A. 75; Hyams v. Bamberger, 10 Utah, 3, 36 Pac. 202.

12 Bank of Old Dominion v. Dubuque & P. R. Co., 8 Iowa, 277, 74 Am. Dec. 302; Bryson v. Rayner, 25 Md. 424, 90 Am. Dec. 69; MARYLAND FIRE INS. CO. v. DALRYMPLE, 25 Md. 242, 89 Am. Dec. 779, Dobie Cas. Bailments and Carriers, 130; Hyams v. Bamberger, 10 Utah, 3, 36 Pac. 202; Stokes v. Frazier, 72 Ill. 428. But the pledgor may ratify such a purchase. Hill v.

longs to the pledgor.[13] This surplus in no sense belongs to the pledgee, but is held by him strictly in trust for the pledgor.[14] The pledgee's interest is at best a special one for a special purpose; that purpose fulfilled, any residuum naturally reverts to the pledgor. Should the sale of the pledged goods fail to realize an amount as large as the amount of the debt, the pledgee may bring a personal suit against the pledgor for the deficiency.[15]

Sale in Equity

The common-law sale just considered, requiring no judicial proceedings, is ordinarily adequate for the pledgee, and is simple and inexpensive. Resort should be had to it, then, in all clear cases. But when there are intervening or conflicting rights,[16] when the rights and powers of the pledgee are in any way questioned or denied,[17] when notice cannot be given to the pledgor[18] (upon which depends the validity of the common-law sale), then the safest course for the pledgee to pursue is to proceed by a bill in equity to obtain a decree from a court of chancery ordering the sale of the pledged goods. Such a decree would show due regard, in case of conflicting claims, for the rights of all concerned.

Finigan, 62 Cal. 426; Carroll v. Mullanphy Sav. Bank, 8 Mo. App. 249. Pledgor has a right of election to treat the purchase of the pledged property by the pledgee at his own sale as invalid, but loses such right by failing to exercise it within a reasonable time after being informed of the purchase. Hill v. Finigan, 77 Cal. 267, 19 Pac. 494, 11 Am. St. Rep. 279. Pledgor's election to treat the purchase of the pledged property by the pledgee at his own sale as valid cannot afterwards be retracted; nor can an election to disaffirm the sale be retracted or renewed at a later date, for the purpose of increasing the damages. Hill v. Finigan, 77 Cal. 267, 19 Pac. 494, 11 Am. St. Rep. 279.

13 Hirsch v. Mayer, 165 N. Y. 236, 59 N. E. 89; Union Nat. Bank v. Post, 192 Ill. 385, 61 N. E. 507; Whittaker v. Amwell Nat. Bank, 52 N. J. Eq. 400, 29 Atl. 203.

14 Fletcher v. Harmon, 78 Me. 465, 7 Atl. 271; Ponce v. McElvy, 47 Cal. 154; Du Casse v. Keyser, 28 La. Ann. 419; Graydon v. Church, 7 Mich. 36.

15 Mauge v. Heringhi, 26 Cal. 577; Jones, Collateral Securities (3d Ed.) § 597.

16 Halle v. National Park Bank of New York, 140 Ill. 413, 29 N. E. 727; Homer v. Savings Bank of New Haven, 7 Conn. 478; Merchants' & Farmers' State Bank v. Sheridan, 156 Ill. App. 25.

17 STOKES v. DIMMICK, 157 Ala. 237, 48 South. 66, Dobie Cas. Bailments and Carriers, 139; Boynton v. Payrow, 67 Me. 587; Briggs v. Oliver, 68 N. Y. 336, 339; Vaupell v. Woodward, 2 Sandf. Ch. (N. Y.) 143; Stokes v. Frazier, 72 Ill. 428; Sitgreaves v. Farmers' & Mechanics' Bank, 49 Pa. 359; Robinson v. Hurley, 11 Iowa, 410, 79 Am. Dec. 497; Arendale v. Morgan, 5 Sneed (Tenn.) 703.

18 Indiana & I. C. Ry. Co. v. McKernan, 24 Ind. 62; Stearns v. Marsh, 4 Denio (N. Y.) 227, 47 Am. Dec. 248.

Where an accounting,[19] or other distinctive equitable remedy, or ground of equitable jurisdiction,[20] is present, a court of chancery will also assume jurisdiction. But when none of the considerations herein discussed apply, resort cannot be had to equity, since there is an adequate remedy at law.[21] The court decrees a sale, not an absolute foreclosure vesting absolute title in the pledgee.[22]

Sale under Power Given by the Pledge Contract

The parties may, at the time of creating the pledge relation, provide that, on default by the pledgor, the pledgee shall have power to sell the pledged goods on such terms as they see fit.[23] Unless unduly oppressive or otherwise illegal, such contracts are controlling and will be duly enforced. Thus the time and manner of making the sale[24] may be thus fixed, the pledgor may dispose with the otherwise necessary notice,[25] or a private instead of a public sale may be permitted.[26] Again, it may be stipulated that the pledgee shall have the right to purchase the goods at such sale.[27]

Sale under Statutes

In a number of states, sales of pledged goods have been made the subject of statutory regulation.[28] Some of these statutes provide a cumulative remedy by affording an additional method of selling the pledged goods, the pledgee retaining besides the statutory method

19 Durant v. Einstein, 5 Rob. (N. Y.) 423; Appeal of Conyngham, 57 Pa. 474; Conde v. Rodgers, 74 App. Div. 147, 77 N. Y. Supp. 518.

20 Evans v. Goodwin, 132 Pa. 136, 19 Atl. 49; Thornton v. Thornton, 31 Grat. (Va.) 212; San Pedro Lumber Co. v. Reynolds, 111 Cal. 588, 44 Pac. 309.

21 Dupuy v. Gibson, 36 Ill. 197; Thames Ironworks & Shipbuilding Co. v. Patent Derrick Co., 1 Johns. & Hen. (Eng.) 93, 99.

22 Carter v. Wake, 4 Ch. D. (Eng.) 605; but the court may in its decree permit the pledgee to bid at the sale.

23 Lowe v. Ozmun, 3 Cal. App. 387, 86 Pac. 729; Nelson v. Wellington, 5 Bosw. (N. Y.) 178; Goldsmidt v. Trustees of First Methodist Episcopal Church in Worthington, 25 Minn. 202; Chapman v. Gale, 32 N. H. 141; In re Mertens, 144 Fed. 818, 75 C. C. A. 548.

24 Mowry v. Wood, 12 Wis. 413; Lowe v. Ozmun, 3 Cal. App. 387, 86 Pac. 729.

25 Williams v. United States Trust Co. of New York, 133 N. Y. 660, 31 N. E. 29; Union Nat. Bank of New Orleans v. Forsyth, 50 La. Ann. 770, 53 South. 917; McDowell v. Chicago Steel Works, 124 Ill. 491, 16 N. E. 854, 7 Am. St. Rep. 381.

26 Carson v. Iowa City Gaslight Co., 80 Iowa, 638, 45 N. W. 1068; Jeanes' Appeal, 116 Pa. 573, 11 Atl. 862, 2 Am. St. Rep. 624.

27 Barry v. American White Lead & Color Works, 107 La. 236, 31 South. 733; Appleton v. Turnbull, 84 Me. 72, 24 Atl. 592; Hiscock v. Varick Bank of New York, 206 U. S. 28, 27 Sup. Ct. 681, 51 L. Ed. 945.

28 See Jones, Collateral Securities (3d Ed.) §§ 616–630, for an analysis of these statutes in many of the states, with citations of cases construing them.

those methods existing in the absence of statute.[29] Other statutes, however, are exclusive in their operation, taking away completely the power to sell at common law or under the power given by the pledge contract, leaving the statutory method as the only way in which the sale can be made. General observations on these statutes would avail little here. The specific statute should in each case be carefully consulted and then scrupulously followed.

TERMINATION OF THE PLEDGE

89. The pledge may be terminated by:

1. Act of parties.

(a) By performance of the obligation secured, or tender thereof, by the pledgor.

(b) By valid sale of the pledged chattel by pledgee on pledgor's default.

(c) By consent of the pledgee.

(d) By redelivery of the pledged article to the pledgor.

(e) By conversion or like wrong of the pledgee, at the pledgor's option.

2. Operation of law.

(a) Destruction of the pledged chattel.

Neither death nor other change in the legal status of the parties terminates the pledge.

Of all bailments, the pledge, perhaps, presents the least difficulty as to its termination. The special property of the pledgee is undisputed,[30] while his power of sale, binding on the pledgor when exercised, rises to the dignity of a power coupled with an interest,[31] and is therefore governed by the rules of agency applicable thereto.

Acts of the Parties—Performance or Tender

The usual way of putting an end to the pledge by the pledgor is the payment of the debt or performance of the engagement secured. The debt includes (as we have seen) expenses necessarily incurred by the pledgee in keeping the pledged chattel.[32] On such payment or performance, the whole reason for the creation and continued

[29] This is the situation, unless the statutory intention is clear in excluding all remedies save that granted by the statute. Taft v. Church, 162 Mass. 527, 39 N. E. 283. See, also, Jones v. Dimmick (Ala.) 59 South. 623.

[30] Ante, § 79.

[31] Henry v. Eddy, 34 Ill. 508; Chapman v. Gale, 32 N. H. 141; De Wolf v. Pratt, 42 Ill. 198; Renshaw v. Creditors, 40 La. Ann. 37, 3 South. 403.

[32] Ante, § 82.

existence of the pledge ceases. The pledge, therefore, immediately terminates.[33] Payment need not be in money,[34] and anything that is the legal equivalent of payment operates to terminate the pledge.[35]

A proper tender of performance or payment also serves to terminate the pledge as effectively as an actual performance or payment.[36] As the pledgee holds the pledged goods solely in order to enforce payment or performance, after a tender, which offers to him the fullest fruits of the transaction to which he can be entitled, the pledgee's holding is no longer a rightful one.[37] Any other rule might indefinitely obstruct the pledgor's right of redemption. To constitute a good tender, it is not necessary that the money be paid, nor even, when the pledgor's offer is refused by the pledgee, that the pledgor actually produce the money.[38] The

[33] Tate v. Security Trust Co., 63 N. J. Eq. 559, 52 Atl. 313; Gage v. McDermid, 150 Ill. 598, 37 N. E. 1026; Merrifield v. Baker, 9 Allen (Mass.) 29; Wilson v. Shocklee, 92 Ark. 370, 123 S. W. 403; Herrmann v. Central Car Trust Co., 101 Fed. 41, 41 C. C. A. 176. But part payment does not discharge the lien on the pledged goods. Herman Goepper & Co. v. Phœnix Brewing Co., 115 Ky. 708, 74 S. W. 726; Williams v. National Bank of Baltimore, 72 Md. 441, 20 Atl. 191.

[34] Strong v. Wooster, 6 Vt. 536; Bacon v. Lamb, 4 Colo. 578.

[35] Leighton v. Bowen, 75 Me. 504; Lathrop v. Adkisson, 87 Ga. 339, 13 S. E. 517; Hermann v. Central Car Trust Co., 101 Fed. 41, 41 C. C. A. 176. A pledgee may, by his misconduct with respect to the thing pledged, become liable to the pledgor for depreciation or loss in value in consequence of his negligence, but when the value of the thing pledged is lost through the negligence of the pledgee, it does not operate, ipso facto, as a satisfaction or extinction of the debt to the extent of the loss. Cooper v. Simpson, 41 Minn. 46, 42 N. W. 601, 4 L. R. A. 194, 16 Am. St. Rep. 667. Money collected by a creditor on a note received as collateral security, which the creditor has power to convert into money, operates, pro tanto, as payment of the secured debt. Hunt v. Nevers, 15 Pick. (Mass.) 500, 26 Am. Dec. 616.

[36] Ryall v. Rowles, 1 Atk. (Eng.) 165; Latta v. Tutton, 122 Cal. 279, 54 Pac. 844, 68 Am. St. Rep. 30; Moyer v. Leavitt, 82 Neb. 310, 117 N. W. 698, 130 Am. St. Rep. 682; Hathaway v. Fall River Nat. Bank, 131 Mass. 14.

[37] Haskins v. Kelly, 1 Rob. (N. Y.) 160; McCalla v. Clark, 55 Ga. 53; Mitchell v. Roberts (C. C.) 17 Fed. 776; Humphrey v. County Nat. Bank of Clearfield, 113 Pa. 417, 6 Atl. 155; Loughborough v. McNevin, 74 Cal. 250, 14 Pac. 369, 15 Pac. 773, 5 Am. St. Rep. 435; Norton v. Baxter, 41 Minn. 146, 42 N. W. 865, 4 L. R. A. 305, 16 Am. St. Rep. 679; Hicks v. National Life Ins. Co., 9 C. C. A. 215, 60 Fed. 690; Hyams v. Bamberger, 10 Utah, 3, 36 Pac. 202. Pledgee is answerable for depreciation in value of pledged property, after he has refused to accept a valid tender of the debt, and a demand for the possession of the property; and this is equally true whether an action is brought against him as for a conversion, or a bill is filed against him to redeem from the pledge. Loughborough v. McNevin, 74 Cal. 250, 14 Pac. 369, 15 Pac. 773, 5 Am. St. Rep. 435.

[38] Hazard v. Loring, 10 Cush. (Mass.) 267.

pledgee's wrongful refusal to surrender the pledged goods on demand, after tender of performance, makes him liable for conversion.[39] It has already been pointed out that a tender of payment, though it extinguishes the lien of the pledge, is not a discharge of the debt.[40]

Same—Sale by the Pledgee

A valid sale of the pledged goods, in any of the ways pointed out, terminates the pledge.[41] This necessarily follows, since such sale confers title on the purchaser,[42] and the rights of pledgor and pledgee attach to the purchase price of the goods.[43] But, as has been pointed out,[44] if the pledgee himself (in the absence of a stipulation to that effect in the pledge contract) attempts to become the purchaser at the sale of the goods, the pledgor may treat the sale as of no effect and the pledge as still continuing.

Same—Consent of the Pledgee

The pledgee's special property in the goods, of course, prevents the pledgor from terminating the pledge at his option alone.[45] But since the pledge is created for the benefit of the pledgee alone (the debt or engagement secured forming the benefit or advantage to the pledgor), the pledge may at any time be terminated by the consent of the pledgee. This may be done by an express release of his rights by the pledgee,[46] or by a waiver,[47] either express or implied from any conduct inconsistent with the continuance of the lien of the pledge. A release of the debt secured terminates a

[39] Loughborough v. McNevin, 74 Cal. 250, 14 Pac. 369, 15 Pac. 773, 5 Am. St. Rep. 435; Ball v. Stanley, 5 Yerg. (Tenn.) 199, 26 Am. Dec. 263; Hyams v. Bamberger, 10 Utah, 3, 36 Pac. 202.

[40] Ante, p. 228; Ball v. Stanley, 5 Yerg. (Tenn.) 199, 26 Am. Dec. 263; Mitchell v. Roberts (C. C.) 17 Fed. 776.

[41] Kemp v. Westbrook, 1 Ves. (Eng.) 278; Sharpe v. National Bank of Birmingham, 87 Ala. 644, 7 South. 106; Boynton v. Payrow, 67 Me. 587.

[42] Carson v. Iowa City Gaslight Co., 80 Iowa, 638, 45 N. W. 1068; Wheelwright v. St. Louis, N. O. & O. Canal & Transp. Co. (C. C.) 56 Fed. 164; Potter v. Thompson, 10 R. I. 1.

[43] Louisville Banking Co. v. W. H. Thomas & Sons Co., 68 S. W. 2, 24 Ky. Law Rep. 115; McDougall v. Hazelton Tripod-Boiler Co., 88 Fed. 217, 31 C. C. A. 487.

[44] Ante, p. 233.

[45] Ante, § 79; De Wolf v. Pratt, 42 Ill. 198.

[46] Hermann v. Central Car Trust Co., 101 Fed. 41, 41 C. C. A. 176; Union & Planters' Bank v. Smith, 107 Tenn. 476, 64 S. W. 756; In re Dyott's Estate, 2 Watts & S. (Pa.) 463.

[47] Hickok v. Cowperthwait, 137 App. Div. 94, 122 N. Y. Supp. 78; Valley Nat. Bank v. Jackaway, 80 Iowa, 512, 45 N. W. 881; Whitaker v. Sumner 20 Pick. (Mass.) 399.

pledge just as performance or payment would, unless the pledgee expressly reserves his rights to the pledged goods.[48]

Same—Redelivery of Pledged Chattel to Pledgor

Just as delivery (in the sense of a transfer of possession) is necessary to bring a pledge into being, so the continued life of the pledge is absolutely dependent upon continued possession by the pledgee. Redelivery of the pledged goods to the pledgor will therefore terminate the pledge.[49] But when such a redelivery is for a mere temporary purpose, as for shoeing a horse which has been pledged and is owned by the blacksmith, or for repairing a carriage which has been pledged and is owned by the carriage maker, this does not amount to an interruption of the pledgee's possession. The owner is in these cases but a mere special bailee for the creditor, and the pledge is not thereby ended.[50] So, when the debtor is employed in the creditor's service, his temporary use of the pledged article in the creditor's business does not effect a restoration of the possession to the debtor, as the article is then regarded as being still in the creditor's possession.

Same—Conversion or Like Wrong of Pledgee

As in the case of other bailments, it is usually held that the conversion of the pledged goods or like wrong by the pledgee gives the pledgor the option to terminate the pledge and recover either the pledged goods [51] or damages for the conversion.[52]

[48] Beacon Trust Co. v. Robbins, 173 Mass. 261, 53 N. E. 868.

[49] Harper v. Goodsell, L. R. 5 Q. B. (Eng.) 422; Wilkie v. Day, 141 Mass. 68, 6 N. E. 542; McFall v. Buckeye Grangers' Warehouse Ass'n, 122 Cal. 468, 55 Pac. 253, 68 Am. St. Rep. 47; Shaw v. Wilshire, 65 Me. 485; Britton v. Harvey, 47 La. Ann. 259, 16 South. 747; First Nat. Bank of Superior v. Bradshaw, 91 Neb. 210, 135 N. W. 830, 39 L. R. A. (N. S.) 886.

[50] In Reeves v. Capper, 5 Bing. N. C. (Eng.) 136, a sea captain pledged his chronometer for a debt. He was afterwards employed by the pledgee as master of one of his ships, and the chronometer was placed in his charge, to be used on the voyage. It was held that the possession of the pledge was not lost. See, also, Matthewson v. Caldwell, 59 Kan. 126, 52 Pac. 104; Cooley v. Minnesota Transfer Ry. Co., 53 Minn. 327, 55 N. W. 141, 39 Am. St. Rep. 609; Casey v. Cavaroc, 96 U. S. 467, 24 L. Ed. 779; Hays v. Riddle, 1 Sandf. (N. Y.) 248; Way v. Davidson, 12 Gray (Mass.) 465, 74 Am. Dec. 604; Macomber v. Parker, 14 Pick. (Mass.) 497; Thayer v. Dwight, 104 Mass. 254; Walker v. Staples, 5 Allen (Mass.) 34, 35; Hutton v. Arnett, 51 Ill. 198; Cooper v. Ray, 47 Ill. 53; Martin v. Reid, 11 C. B. N. S. (Eng.) 730. But see Bodenhammer v. Newsom, 50 N. C. 107, 69 Am. Dec. 775.

[51] Johnson v. Succession of Robbins, 20 La. Ann. 569; Merchants' Bank of Canada v. Livingston, 17 Hun (N. Y.) 321, affirmed 79 N. Y. 618.

[52] Glidden v. Mechanics' Nat. Bank, 53 Ohio St. 588, 42 N. E. 995, 43 L. R. A. 737; Baltimore Marine Ins. Co. v. Dalrymple, 25 Md. 269.

Operation of Law—Destruction of Pledged Chattel

This, by operation of law, necessarily terminates the pledge, as there is then nothing to which the relation can attach, even though it be theoretically considered as still existing. The liability of the pledgee for damages in such case would turn on the question of negligence, already discussed.[53]

Same—Death or Change of Legal Status

The pledge creates in the pledgee not only a special property in the pledged goods, but a right to sell and reimburse himself to the extent of the debt, which is known in agency as a "power coupled with an interest." [54] This is not affected by death of the parties. On the pledgor's death,[55] the power can be exercised by the pledgee against his personal representative; on the pledgee's death,[56] the power is exercisable by his personal representative. In like manner, neither marriage, insanity, nor bankruptcy of the parties will terminate the pledge.[57] The lien and right of sale continue either for or against the representative of the pledgor or pledgee whose legal status is changed, such as his committee in insanity or his trustee in bankruptcy.

Same—Redelivery on Termination of the Pledge

As in the case of other bailments, the pledgee must, on the termination of the pledge, redeliver to the pledgor the identical goods pledged, together with the profits and the increase thereof. What has been said as to redelivery on redemption,[58] is also applicable here, when the pledge is terminated by any of the methods just discussed.

[53] Ante, § 83.

[54] Ante, p. 214.

[55] Drostes' Estate, 9 Wkly. Notes Cas. (Pa.) 224; BELL v. MILLS, 123 Fed. 24, 59 C. C. A. 104, Dobie Cas. Bailments and Carriers, 142; Warrior Coal & Coke Co. v. National Bank of Augusta, Ga. (Ala.) 53 South. 997.

[56] Chapman v. Gale, 32 N. H. 141; Henry v. Eddy, 34 Ill. 508.

[57] Renshaw v. Creditors, 40 La. Ann. 37, 3 South. 403; Jerome v. McCarter, 94 U. S. 734, 24 L. Ed. 136; Yeatman v. New Orleans Sav. Inst., 95 U. S. 764, 24 L. Ed. 589; Dayton Nat. Bank v. Merchants' Nat. Bank, 37 Ohio St. 208; Dowler v. Cushwa, 27 Md. 354. Where a deposit with a correspondent has, long prior to the commission of an act of insolvency by a national bank, been pledged to secure loans made to the insolvent by its correspondent, neither the subsequent insolvency of the bank nor the appointment of a receiver destroys the lien of the correspondent on the deposit. Bell v. Hanover Nat. Bank (C. C.) 57 Fed. 821.

[58] Ante, § 84.

CHAPTER VIII

INNKEEPERS

DEFINITION AND DISTINCTIONS

90. The innkeeper is one who holds himself out to the public to furnish either lodging alone, or lodging and some other form of entertainment, to transients for hire.

This definition excludes:

(a) Persons furnishing only occasional entertainment.

(b) Keepers of mere restaurants and eating houses.

(c) Keepers of boarding houses or lodging houses.

(d) Sleeping car companies and steamship companies.

Historical [1]

The innkeeper is, of course, the keeper of an inn, and the inn, or house for the entertainment of travelers, dates back in all civilized countries to the remotest antiquity. The inn of medieval England is the fountainhead of most of our law on the subject, and these inns sprang up in great numbers, on all the much traveled roads, to furnish shelter and entertainment to the wayfarer, who either

[1] The history of inns, the derivation of the word "hotel," and the various terms applied in different times and countries to public houses of entertainment, with references to original sources, are discussed in an interesting manner by Daly, J., in Cromwell v. Stephens, 2 Daly (N. Y.) 15, 17. For a brief, but admirable, historical introduction to the subject of innkeepers, see Beale, Innkeepers, §§ 1-6.

could not or did not resort to the monasteries or the hospitality of private individuals.

The increase of travel naturally increased the number and importance of the inns; while the establishment of inns, in which the traveler could be protected from the perils of thieves and highwaymen, also reacted upon and stimulated travel. Thus, out of the social and economic relation of the inn to the life of the English, there soon developed a body of legal principles controlling the ever increasingly important relation of the innkeeper to those whom he served or purported to serve.

The term "tavern," or alehouse, as it was sometimes called, originally meant a house at which no lodging was furnished, but only food and drink, chiefly the latter. The tavern, therefore, catered primarily to the inhabitants of the neighborhood in which it was situated. The word "hotel," of French origin, has in popular use almost supplanted "inn," and is used and understood all over the world. "Inn" and "innkeeper" still remain the accepted legal terminology generally used by judges and writers. With us, the words "tavern," "inn," and "hotel" are used without any distinction in legal meaning.[2]

It is clear that the innkeeper was a bailee only as to goods brought within the inn (infra hospitium), and often not then; but convenience and custom justify here a treatment of the general rights and duties of the innkeeper, even when they are in no way connected with the subject of bailments.

Definition

The definitions of an innkeeper, given by courts and text writers, have been many and varied, some of which are given and criticised in the notes.[3] At the outset, however, it should be noted that the

[2] See, on the use of these terms, Black, Law Dictionary, "Inn" and "Hotel." See, also, Foster v. State, 84 Ala. 451, 4 South. 833; Bonner v. Welborn, 7 Ga. 296; People v. Jones, 54 Barb. (N. Y.) 311; City of St. Louis v. Siegrist, 46 Mo. 593; Lewis v. Hitchcock (D. C.) 10 Fed. 4; Kopper v. Willis, 9 Daly (N. Y.) 460, 462; Wardell, Inns, 15; Civ. Code Ga. 1882, § 2114; Cromwell v. Stephens, 2 Daly (N. Y.) 15, 17; Halsbury, Laws of England, § 633, pp. 302–306.

[3] The definition given by Best, J., in the old English case of Thompson v. Lacy, 3 Barn. & Ald. (Eng.) 283, 287, is as follows: "An inn is a house, the owner of which holds out that he will receive all travelers and sojourners who are willing to pay a price adequate to the sort of accommodation provided, and who come in a situation in which they are fit to be received." It is not necessary, of course, that the innkeeper own the inn. He may lease it. The definition of an inn given by Justice Bayley in Jones v. Osborn, 2 Chit. (Eng.) 484, 486, "a house where a traveler is furnished with everything which he has occasion for while on his way," is comprehensive enough to

person operating and controlling the inn is the innkeeper, and not one who manages the inn as his agent, nor one who, owning the inn, leases it to him.[4]

The definition of the black letter text, "The innkeeper is one who holds himself out to the public to furnish either lodging alone, or lodging with some other form of entertainment, to transients for hire," is substantially that of Prof. Goddard.[5] It will be seen that this definition involves four elements: (1) A public holding out by the innkeeper (2) as one ready to furnish lodging at least (3) to transients (4) for hire. Of these in their turn.

(1) The real test of the innkeeper is his holding out that he will serve the public in general and entertain any proper person applying for a proper purpose, who is willing to pay for the entertainment received.[6] Without this distinctive public profession, a person is not, strictly speaking, an innkeeper. To make one an innkeeper, and render him liable accordingly, no particular form of holding out is necessary, and it may be in any of the many means of conveying information, and may be either express or im-

include every description of an inn; but a house that does not fill the full measure of this definition may be an inn. "An innkeeper is called in the law 'communis hospitator,' the which signifies the nature of his office and employment." Luton v. Bigg, Skin. (Eng.) 291. For other cases defining an innkeeper, see Wintermute v. Clark, 5 Sandf. (N. Y.) 242, 247; People v. Jones, 54 Barb. (N. Y.) 311; Walling v. Potter, 35 Conn. 183; Kisten v. Hildebrand, 9 B. Mon. (Ky.) 72, 75, 48 Am. Dec. 416; Mateer v. Brown, 1 Cal. 221, 227, 52 Am. Dec. 303; Dansey v. Richardson, 3 El. & Bl. (Eng.) 144; Doe v. Laming, 4 Camp. (Eng.) 77; Com. v. Wetherbee, 101 Mass. 214; Rafferty v. New Brunswick Fire Ins. Co., 18 N. J. Law, 480, 38 Am. Dec. 525; Gray v. Com., 9 Dana (Ky.) 300, 35 Am. Dec. 136; FAY v. PACIFIC IMP. CO., 93 Cal. 253, 26 Pac. 1099, 28 Pac. 943, 16 L. R. A. 188, 27 Am. St. Rep. 198, Dobie Cas. Bailments and Carriers, 146; Birmingham Ry., Light & Power Co. v. Drennen, 175 Ala. 338, 57 South. 876; Pettit v. Thomas, 103 Ark. 593, 148 S. W. 501, 42 L. R. A. (N. S.) 122; Hill v. Memphis Hotel Co., 124 Tenn. 376, 136 S. W. 997.

4 See cases cited in preceding note; also Dixon v. Birch, L. R. 8 Exch. (Eng.) 135; Winter v. State, 30 Ala. 22; Nantasket Beach Steamboat Co. v. Shea, 182 Mass. 147, 65 N. E. 57.

5 See Goddard, Bailm. & Carr. § 163, which gives the definition: "The innkeeper is one who holds himself out to furnish lodging, or lodging and other entertainment, to transients for hire."

6 Lane v. Cotton, 12 Mod. (Eng.) 472; Luton v. Bigg, Skin. (Eng.) 291; JOHNSON v. CHADBOURN FINANCE CO., 89 Minn. 310, 94 N. W. 874, 99 Am. St. Rep. 571, Dobie Cas. Bailments and Carriers, 159. So true is this that one, though not technically an innkeeper, may incur the liability of one by thus holding himself out to the public. Pinkerton v. Woodward, 33 Cal. 557, 91 Am. Dec. 657; Howth v. Franklin, 20 Tex. 798, 73 Am. Dec. 218; Dickerson v. Rogers, 4 Humph. (Tenn.) 179, 40 Am. Dec. 642. See, also, cases cited in note 3.

plied.[7] What is subsequently said as to the holding out that is distinctive of the common carrier, as opposed to the private carrier, is, mutatis mutandis, also applicable here.

(2) The distinctive thing furnished by the innkeeper, which sets him apart from other persons serving the public, is lodging.[8] No other form of entertainment will make one an innkeeper; but, to constitute one an innkeeper, he must furnish lodging. If he does, he need not furnish anything else, though the furnishing of other entertainment in addition to lodging renders one none the less an innkeeper. Thus, those who operate hotels on the so-alled "European plan" are innkeepers, though they supply meals à la carte, or even not at all.[9] The nature and extent of the accommodations furnished by an establishment, apart from lodging, have, accordingly, nothing to do with its character as an inn.[10]

(3) The innkeeper is such only as to transients, as we shall subsequently see,[11] and then only (4) when the accommodations are furnished to them for hire. The technical innkeeping relation does

[7] Lyon v. Smith, Morris (Iowa) 185; FAY v. PACIFIC IMP. CO., 93 Cal. 253, 26 Pac. 1099, 28 Pac. 943, 16 L. R. A. 188, 27 Am. St. Rep. 198, Dobie Cas. Bailments and Carriers, 146. In Howth v. Franklin, 20 Tex. 798, 73 Am. Dec. 218, it was held that one uniformly entertaining travelers for hire, though he often declared that he did not keep an inn, might be considered an innkeeper by a jury. See, also, Pettit v. Thomas, 103 Ark. 593, 148 S. W. 501, 42 L. R. A. (N. S.) 122.

[8] Block v. Sherry, 43 Misc. Rep. 342, 87 N. Y. Supp. 160; Sheffer v. Willoughby, 163 Ill. 518, 45 N. E. 253, 34 L. R. A. 464, 54 Am. St. Rep. 483; Regina v. Rymer, 2 Q. B. D. (Eng.) 136.

[9] JOHNSON v. CHADBOURN FINANCE CO., 89 Minn. 310, 94 N. W. 874, 99 Am. St. Rep. 571, Dobie Cas. Bailments and Carriers, 159; Bullock v. Adair, 63 Ill. App. 30; Krohn v. Sweeney, 2 Daly (N. Y.) 200; Pinkerton v. Woodward, 33 Cal. 557, 91 Am. Dec. 657; Willard v. Reinhardt, 2 E. D. Smith (N. Y.) 148; Wintermute v. Clark, 5 Sandf. (N. Y.) 243; Bernstein v. Sweeny, 33 N. Y. Super. Ct. 271; Taylor v. Monnot, 4 Duer (N. Y.) 116; Kisten v. Hildebrand, 9 B. Mon. (Ky.) 72, 48 Am. Dec. 416. One who holds himself out to the world as an innkeeper may be regarded as such, though the only eating department of his establishment is a restaurant in the basement, connected with the house by a stairway, and conducted by the innkeeper and two other persons jointly, who share the profits. Pinkerton v. Woodward, 33 Cal. 557, 91 Am. Dec. 657.

[10] City of St. Louis v. Siegrist, 46 Mo. 593; Curtis v. State, 5 Ohio, 324; Com. v. Wetherbee, 101 Mass. 214; Pinkerton v. Woodward, 33 Cal. 557, 91 Am. Dec. 657. Where a building is divided into suites or flats, each suite rented to families for housekeeping purposes, heat, hot and cold water, and janitor's services being furnished to each suite by the proprietor, but where no board, lodging, or accommodation for transient patrons is provided, the house is not an inn. Davis v. Gay, 141 Mass. 531, 6 N. E. 549.

[11] Post, § 91.

not exist, as we shall also see, as to those persons who come to the inn without payment at the personal invitation of the innkeeper.[12]

Persons Furnishing only Occasional Entertainment

From what has been said it is clear that one who, without a holding out to the public, furnishes only occasional entertainment, is not an innkeeper, even though he receives pay for such entertainment.[13] Thus it was well said by Mason, C. J., speaking for the court in Lyon v. Smith:[14] "To render a person liable as a common innkeeper it is not sufficient to show that he occasionally entertains travelers. Most of the farmers in a new country do this, without supposing themselves answerable for the horses or other property of their guests which may be stolen or otherwise lost without any fault of their own. Nor is such the rule in older countries, where it would operate with far less injustice, and be less opposed to good policy, than with us. To be subjected to the same responsibilities attaching to innkeepers, a person must make tavern keeping, to some extent, a regular business—a means of livelihood; he should hold himself out to the world as an innkeeper. It is not necessary that he should have a sign or a license, provided that he has in any other manner authorized the general understanding that his was a public house, where strangers had a right to require accommodation. The person who occasionally entertains others for a reasonable compensation is no more subject to the extraordinary responsibility of an innkeeper than is he liable as a common carrier who, in certain special cases, carries the property of others from one place to another for hire."

There is no reason why one may not be an innkeeper at certain seasons of the year and not at other times.[15] This is the relation in which the proprietors of hotels at our summer resorts stand to those whom they entertain, though they keep their houses open only during a few months of the year. During these months their

[12] Post, p. 253.

[13] See, also, Howth v. Franklin, 20 Tex. 798, 73 Am. Dec. 218; State v. Matthews, 19 N. C. 424; Kisten v. Hildebrand, 9 B. Mon. (Ky.) 74, 48 Am. Dec. 416. See, too, in general, Parker v. Flint, 12 Mod. (Eng.) 254, and Bonner v. Welborn, 7 Ga. 296; Parkhurst v. Foster, 1 Ld. Raym. (Eng.) 479, Carth. 417; Bac. Abr. tit. "Inns & Innkeepers," B; Farnworth v. Packwood, Holt, N. P. (Eng.) 209, 1 Starkie, 249; Mason v. Grafton, Hob. (Eng.) 245b; Dr. & Stud. 137b; Calye's Case, 8 Coke (Eng.) 32a; Overseers of Poor of Town of Crown Point v. Warner, 3 Hill (N. Y.) 150; State v. Chamblyss, Cheves (S. C.) 220, 34 Am. Dec. 593.

[14] Morris (Iowa) 184, 186.

[15] This emphasizes the personal nature of the innkeeping relation as attaching to a person by virtue of his holding out, and combats the idea of its being impersonally attached to a particular building.

holding out may well bring them within the definition of an innkeeper as given above. At other seasons of the year, however, during which they make no profession of taking all suitable persons who may apply, they may yet furnish entertainment to some persons, as to whom they are not innkeepers at all, but merely boarding house keepers.

Keepers of Restaurants and Eating Houses

The furnishing of food alone, without lodging, does not make one an innkeeper. A mere restaurant (however elaborate or however extended may be its patronage) or eating house for meals cannot be considered an inn.[16] The idea of a "temporary home for the guest"[17] and a place for storing his baggage, so characteristic of the inn, is completely lacking in such establishments.

The innkeeper may, of course, in the same building conduct a restaurant, to which he may invite, not only his guests, but the public in general. In such case, "if the restaurant is entirely distinct from the rooms proper to the inn,"[18] his liability to a mere patron of the restaurant is that of restaurant keeper only.[19]

Though not an innkeeper, when the goods of the customer (such as his coat or hat) are delivered to the restaurant keeper or his servants, this is a mutual benefit bailment, and the keeper must use ordinary care to protect them.[20]

Keepers of Lodging Houses and Boarding Houses

Keepers of lodging houses and boarding houses are not innkeepers, nor subject to their liabilities.[21] These satisfy the defini-

16 Sheffer v. Willoughby, 163 Ill. 518, 45 N. E. 253, 34 L. R. A. 464, 54 Am. St. Rep. 483; People v. Jones, 54 Barb. (N. Y.) 311; La Salle Restaurant & Oyster House v. McMasters, 85 Ill. App. 677; Lewis v. Hitchcock (D. C.) 10 Fed. 4. See, also, on innkeepers and restaurant keepers, Carpenter v. Taylor, 1 Hilt. (N. Y.) 193; Queen v. Rymer, 2 Q. B. Div. (Eng.) 136; The Civil Rights Bill, 1 Hughes (U. S.) 541, 543, Fed. Cas. No. 2,774; Bonner v. Welborn, 7 Ga. 296; Willard v. Reinhardt, 2 E. D. Smith (N. Y.) 148; Walling v. Potter, 35 Conn. 183; Kisten v. Hildebrand, 9 B. Mon. (Ky.) 73, 48 Am. Dec. 416; Doe v. Laming, 4 Camp. (Eng.) 77; Kelly v. Excise Com'rs of New York, 54 How. Prac. (N. Y.) 332.

17 Van Zile, Bailm. & Carr. § 333.

18 Beale, Innkeepers, § 21.

19 Krohn v. Sweeney, 2 Daly (N. Y.) 200. As to the liabilities of the restaurant keeper, see Sheffer v. Willoughby, 163 Ill. 518, 45 N. E. 253, 34 L. R. A. 464, 54 Am. St. Rep. 483; Partaze v. West, 7 Ala. App. 599, 61 South. 42.

20 See ante, p. 55.

21 FAY v. PACIFIC IMP. CO., 93 Cal. 253, 26 Pac. 1099, 28 Pac. 943, 16 L. R. A. 188, 27 Am. St. Rep. 198, Dobie Cas. Bailments and Carriers, 146; Beall v. Beck, 2 Fed. Cas. No. 1,161, 3 Cranch, C. C. 666; Pullman Palace Car Co. v. Lowe, 28 Neb. 239, 44 N. W. 226, 6 L. R. A. 809, 26 Am. St. Rep. 325; Parker v. Fleat, 12 Mod. (Eng.) 254; Birmingham Ry., Light & Power

tion as to the accommodations offered, but not as to the essential profession to serve the public. The proprietor of such a house does not hold himself out to the public as prepared to provide accommodations for all who may apply. On the other hand, he reserves the right to select arbitrarily whom he will, and whom he will not, entertain. Accordingly he is not bound to receive any person unless he chooses to do so,[22] which is not true, as we shall see, of the innkeeper. The boarding house keeper is, therefore, not held to the high responsibility of the innkeeper, but is ordinarily liable only for failure to exercise ordinary care as to the goods of the boarder, being thus placed in the same position as other bailees in mutual benefit bailments.[23]

It is frequently said[24] that in a boarding house the boarder is under an express contract at a certain rate for a certain time, while at an inn there is no such express engagement, but that the guest, being on his way, is entertained from day to day, according to his business, on an implied contract. This, however, is not an accurate test of the nature of the relation. One who purports to keep merely a boarding house may occasionally entertain transient persons both for an indefinite time and with no express contract, without either acquiring the character, or being under the responsibilities, of an innkeeper. And, as we shall see, the innkeeper continues as such to the transient guest, though the latter makes a specific contract as to the length of his stay, accommodations to be received, and the price he is to pay.[25]

Sleeping Car Companies and Steamship Companies

Sleeping car companies are held not to occupy the relation of innkeepers to those who occupy berths on their cars.[26] Various

Co. v. Drennen, 175 Ala. 338, 57 South. 876; Burdock v. Chicago Hotel Co., 172 Ill. App. 185.

22 Pinkerton v. Woodward, 33 Cal. 557, 91 Am. Dec. 657; Willard v. Reinhardt, 2 E. D. Smith (N. Y.) 148; Commonwealth v. Cuncannon, 3 Brewst. (Pa.) 344. See cases cited in preceding note.

23 They are liable for the goods of their lodgers or boarders only as ordinary bailees for hire. Smith v. Read, 52 How. Prac. (N. Y.) 14; Vance v. Throckmorton, 5 Bush (Ky.) 41, 96 Am. Dec. 327; Manning v. Wells, 9 Humph. (Tenn.) 746, 51 Am. Dec. 688; Johnson v. Reynolds, 3 Kan. 257; Wiser v. Chesley, 53 Mo. 547; Dansey v. Richardson, 3 El. & Bl. (Eng.) 144; Holder v. Soulby, 8 C. B. N. S. (Eng.) 254.

24 See, for example, Willard v. Reinhardt, 2 E. D. Smith (N. Y.) 148; Bostick v. State, 47 Ark. 126, 14 S. W. 476.

25 See post, p. 256; Pettit v. Thomas, 103 Ark. 593, 148 S. W. 501, 42 L. R. A. (N. S.) 122.

26 See Beale, Innkeepers, § 341; Pullman Palace Car Co. v. Adams, 120 Ala. 581, 24 South. 921, 45 L. R. A. 767, 74 Am. St. Rep. 53; Pullman's Palace Car Co. v. Hall, 106 Ga. 765, 32 S. E. 923, 44 L. R. A. 790, 71 Am. St. Rep.

grounds are given for this holding. Thus, the sleeping car company does not, like an innkeeper, undertake to serve the traveling public indiscriminately, but only a certain limited class—those who have already paid their fare, and are provided with a first-class ticket, entitling them to ride to a particular place.[27] The innkeeper, as we shall see, is obliged to receive and care for the goods of the traveler which he may choose to take with him upon the journey; while the sleeping car company is not bound to care for the goods of the traveler and notoriously refuses to do so.[28] Again, the innkeeper's liability had its origin in the fact that the traveler was often compelled to resort to the inn for necessary protection. But the traveler is not thus compelled to resort to the sleeping car; he may remain in the ordinary car, and the legal duty of protection is owed to him by the carrier.[29]

Again, it is the policy of the law to keep within its technical limits rather than to extend the rigorous and unusual liability of the innkeeper. There are cases, however, that refuse to accept the cumulative force of these reasons, and hold the sleeping car company an innkeeper and liable accordingly.[30] Though not a carrier itself, either private or common, the close relation between the sleeping car and the train of which it is a part renders it more convenient to discuss the rights and duties of sleeping car companies under the subject of carriers.[31]

The weight of authority also holds that steamship companies are not innkeepers.[32] Even though a room on the boat be given

293; Whicher v. Boston & A. R. Co., 176 Mass. 275, 57 N. E. 601, 79 Am. St. Rep. 314; Pullman Palace Car Co. v. Smith, 73 Ill. 360, 24 Am. Rep. 258; LEWIS v. NEW YORK CENT. SLEEPING CAR CO., 143 Mass. 267, 273, 9 N. E. 615, 58 Am. Rep. 135, Doble Cas. Bailments and Carriers, 295; Woodruff Sleeping & Parlor Coach Co. v. Diehl, 84 Ind. 474, 481, 43 Am. Rep. 102; Blum v. Southern Pullman Palace Car Co., 1 Flip. 500, Fed. Cas. No. 1,574; Pullman Palace Car Co. v. Gaylord, 6 Ky. Law Rep. 279; Welch v. Pullman Palace Car Co., 16 Abb. Prac. N. S. (N. Y.) 352; Pullman Car Co. v. Gardner, 3 Penny. (Pa.) 78; Tracy v. Pullman Palace Car Co., 67 How. Prac. (N. Y.) 154. But see, contra, Pullman Palace Car Co. v. Lowe, 28 Neb. 239, 44 N. W. 226, 6 L. R. A. 809, 26 Am. St. Rep. 325.

27 Welch v. Pullman Palace Car Co., 16 Abb. Prac. N. S. (N. Y.) 352, 357. But that they are bound to receive any one who applies for a berth, see NEVIN v. PULLMAN PALACE CAR CO., 106 Ill. 222, 46 Am. Rep. 688, Doble Cas. Bailments and Carriers, 297.

28 Pullman Palace Car Co. v. Smith, 73 Ill. 360, 24 Am. Rep. 258.

29 Pullman Palace Car Co. v. Smith, 73 Ill. 360, 24 Am. Rep. 258.

30 Pullman Palace Car Co. v. Lowe, 28 Neb. 239, 44 N. W. 226, 6 L. R. A. 809, 26 Am. St. Rep. 325; Lise v. Pullman, etc., Co., 1 Quebec Super. Ct. 9.

31 See post, § 165.

32 Clark v. Burns, 118 Mass. 275, 19 Am. Rep. 456; The Crystal Palace v. Vanderpool, 16 B. Mon. (Ky.) 302; Adams v. New Jersey Steamboat Co., 151

into the control of the passenger, this is merely incidental to the carriage, and the rights and duties of the steamboat owner can best be worked out along the line of his real occupation as a carrier. As they are usually common carriers, however, their liability as such for the goods of the passenger given into their charge is fully as great as, and, according to many courts, even greater than, the corresponding liability of the innkeeper.

License as Innkeeper [33]

An innkeeper cannot set up his failure to procure a license as a defense to his technical innkeeping liability.[34] The mere possession of a license does not make one an innkeeper at common law, nor does the lack of it prevent him from being one. It is his holding out and business that fix the status of a party in this respect. A license, as a matter between him and the state or municipality, saves the innkeeper from the penalty of pursuing that calling without a license;[35] but the want of it does not save him from his exceptional liability to his guests.

WHO ARE GUESTS

91. A guest is a transient, who patronizes the inn as such, with the consent of the innkeeper.

It is as important to determine who are guests as it is to decide who are innkeepers; for, as the exceptional liabilities, which will be subsequently discussed, are imposed only on those who are strictly innkeepers, so these liabilities exist solely in favor of those whose legal relation is that of guests, and not in favor of

N. Y. 163, 45 N. E. 369, 34 L. R. A. 682, 56 Am. St. Rep. 616; McKee v. Owen, 15 Mich. 115, decided by a divided court.

[33] The right to keep an inn was not a franchise at common law and required no license. Rex v. Collins, Palmer (Eng.) 367, 373; Overseers of Poor of Town of Crown Point v. Warner, 3 Hill (N. Y.) 150. Inns are public places of entertainment and have been made the subject of frequent statutory regulation. White v. Holman, 44 Or. 180, 74 Pac. 933, 1 Ann. Cas. 843; Bostick v. State, 47 Ark. 126, 14 S. W. 476. Mr. Beale collects the American statutes in an appendix to Beale, Innkeepers, pp. 307–534.

[34] Norcross v. Norcross, 53 Me. 163; State v. Wynne, 8 N. C. 451; Dickerson v. Rogers, 4 Humph. (Tenn.) 179, 40 Am. Dec. 642.

[35] State v. Johnson, 65 Me. 362. It is held that the innkeeper failing to take out the statutory license cannot recover compensation for entertainment he has furnished. Randall v. Tuell, 89 Me. 443, 36 Atl. 910, 38 L. R. A. 143. Nor has he any lien on the guest's goods. Stanwood v. Woodward, 38 Me. 192.

boarders, or other persons resorting to the inn.[36] He alone, then, can hold the innkeeper to his rigorous liability who is technically a guest. That the plaintiff is not a guest is therefore always a defense to the strict liability as an innkeeper for loss or damage to the goods.

It is clear that the definition of "guest" involves three elements, which require separate treatment in the order named: First, a transient; second, patronizing the inn as such; third, consent of the innkeeper.[37]

Transients

As only transients can become guests, the single most important element, in determining who are guests, is that they first must be transients.[38] Other terms are also used by the courts, such

[36] See Mowers v. Fethers, 61 N. Y. 34, 19 Am. Rep. 244; Grinnell v. Cook, 3 Hill (N. Y.) 485, 38 Am. Dec. 663; Ingalsbee v. Wood, 36 Barb. (N. Y.) 452, 455; Hulett v. Swift, 33 N. Y. 571, 88 Am. Dec. 405; Miles v. International Hotel Co., 167 Ill. App. 440; Ticehurst v. Beinbrink, 72 Misc. Rep. 365, 129 N. Y. Supp. 838.

[37] As we proceed with the discussion of the subject, the inadequacy of the following definitions of a guest will become apparent: Every one who is received into an inn and has entertainment there, for which the innkeeper has compensation by way of remuneration or reward for his services, is a guest. Comegys, C. J., in Russell v. Fagan, 7 Houst. (Del.) 389, 8 Atl. 258, 260. A guest is one who comes without any bargain for time, remains without one, and may go when he pleases. 2 Pars. Cont. 151. A guest is one who patronizes an inn as such. Walling v. Potter, 35 Conn. 183. Any one away from home, receiving accommodations at an inn as a traveler, is a guest, and entitled to hold the innkeeper responsible as such. Wintermute v. Clark, 5 Sandf. (N. Y.) 242, 247, adopted in Pullman Palace Car Co. v. Lowe, 28 Neb. 239, 44 N. W. 226, 6 L. R. A. 809, 26 Am. St. Rep. 325. Guests are those who are bona fide (really) traveling, and make the use of an inn, and not mere neighbors and friends who visit the house occasionally. Tidswell, Innkeepers' Legal Guide, 1. A guest is "a stranger who comes from a distance and takes his lodgings at a place." Webst. Dict. See, also, a valuable article in 14 Cent. Law J. 206; Hall v. Pike, 100 Mass. 495; Norcross v. Norcross, 53 Me. 163; Pinkerton v. Woodward, 33 Cal. 557, 91 Am. Dec. 657; Hancock v. Rand, 17 Hun (N. Y.) 279; Phillips v. Henson, 30 Moak, Eng. R. 19; Thompson v. Ward, L. R. 6 C. P. (Eng.) 327; Bradley v. Baylis, 8 Q. B. Div. (Eng.) 195; Ness v. Stephenson, 9 Q. B. Div. (Eng.) 245; Hickman v. Thomas, 16 Ala. 666; Ullman v. State, 1 Tex. App. 220, 28 Am. Rep. 405; Dickerson v. Rogers, 4 Humph. (Tenn.) 179, 40 Am. Dec. 642; LUSK v. BELOTE, 22 Minn. 468, Dobie Cas. Bailments and Carriers, 148. See, too, the following recent cases on the general subject of who are guests: R. L. Polk & Co. v. Melenbacker, 136 Mich. 611, 99 N. W. 867; CRAPO v. ROCKWELL, 48 Misc. Rep. 1, 94 N. Y. Supp. 1122, Dobie Cas. Bailments and Carriers, 149; Pettit v. Thomas, 103 Ark. 593, 158 S. W. 501, 42 L. R. A. (N. S.) 122; Ticehurst v. Beinbrink, 72 Misc. Rep. 365, 129 N. Y. Supp. 838; Vigeant v. Nelson, 140 Ill. App. 644; De Lapp v. Van Closter, 136 Mo. App. 475, 118 S. W. 120.

[38] FAY v. PACIFIC IMP. CO., 93 Cal. 253, 26 Pac. 1099, 28 Pac. 943, 16

as "traveler,"[39] or "wayfarer";[40] but their meaning is essentially the same. No entirely satisfactory definition of a transient seems to have been formulated, but the term is opposed to the notion of residing in a place, and carries with it nothing that is in any marked degree permanent. It rather conveys the idea of a mere temporary sojourner, the period of whose stay is brief or uncertain.[41]

One who has his permanent abode in the inn falls without the transient category, so that, whatever may be his relation to the keeper of the inn, he is not a guest.[42] So, too, a railroad conductor, running on regular trips between fixed termini, who staid at each end of his route at a hotel in a room which he rented by the month, is not a transient.[43] But officers of the army and navy and soldiers

L. R. A. 188, 27 Am. St. Rep. 128, Doble Cas. Bailments and Carriers, 146; Jalie v. Cardinal, 35 Wis. 118; Curtis v. Murphy, 63 Wis. 4, 22 N. W. 825, 53 Am. Rep. 242; Manning v. Wells, 9 Humph. (Tenn.) 746, 51 Am. Dec. 688; Neal v. Wilcox, 49 N. C. 146, 67 Am. Dec. 266; Horner v. Harvey, 3 N. M. (Johns.) 197, 5 Pac. 329; Russell v. Fagan, 7 Houst. (Del.) 389, 8 Atl. 258; Clute v. Wiggins, 14 Johns. (N. Y.) 175, 7 Am. Dec. 448; Beale v. Posey, 72 Ala. 323; Burgess v. Clements, 4 Maule & S. (Eng.) 306. See, also, Burdock v. Chicago Hotel Co., 172 Ill. App. 185.

39 Beale v. Morris, Cro. Jac. (Eng.) 224; Thompson v. Lacy, 3 B. & Ald. (Eng.) 283.

40 Calye's Case, 8 Coke (Eng.) 32, "wayfaring men."

41 CRAPO v. ROCKWELL, 48 Misc. Rep. 1, 94 N. Y. Supp. 1122, Doble Cas. Bailments and Carriers, 149; Shoecraft v. Bailey, 25 Iowa, 553; Moore v. Long Beach Development Co., 87 Cal. 483, 26 Pac. 92, 22 Am. St. Rep. 265. Notwithstanding one who sues for lost baggage may have paid for his lodging by the week, yet, if he has not established a permanent abode and has done nothing to divest himself of his status as a traveler, he is a "guest" within the meaning of the law and may hold the owner of his lodging house to the liability of an innkeeper. Moon v. Yarian, 147 Ill. App. 383.

42 Meacham v. Galloway, 102 Tenn. 415, 52 S. W. 859, 46 L. R. A. 319, 73 Am. St. Rep. 886; Haff v. Adams, 6 Ariz. 395, 59 Pac. 111; Johnson v. Reynolds, 3 Kan. 257; Ewart v. Stark, 8 Rich. (S. C.) 423. The fact that an hotel has a rule to charge a guest a less rate per diem by the week than by the day, and that, if a guest had been there longer than a week, he got the benefit of the rule, does not show that one who had been at the hotel more than a week was a "boarder," rather than a "guest," it not being shown that he had any notice of the rule, or any knowledge of the charges, or that any arrangement for a permanent stay had been made. Magee v. Pacific Imp. Co., 98 Cal. 678, 33 Pac. 772, 35 Am. St. Rep. 199. Plaintiff registered at a hotel and secured a room, which she occupied a number of months, and then moved to another room in the same hotel. During the time of her stay at the hotel, she was absent for about three weeks at one time, during which time the room was reserved for her and the rent paid by her. During the entire period of her absence and the time of her stay at the hotel it was her only place of residence. Held, that her status was that of a lodger, and not a guest at an inn. Gray v. Drexel Arms Hotel, 146 Ill. App. 604.

43 Horner v. Harvey, 3 N. M. (Johns.) 197, 5 Pac. 329.

and sailors, who have no permanent residence which they can call home, but who are "liable to the call of their superiors at any moment," may well be regarded as transients when stopping at public inns or hotels.[44]

A townsman or neighbor may be a traveler, and therefore a guest at an inn, as well as one who comes from a distance.[45] If he resides permanently at an inn, his relation to the innkeeper is that of a boarder;[46] but if he resides away from it, whether far or near, and comes to it for entertainment in the rôle of a traveler, and receives it as such, he is subjected to all the duties of a guest, and entitled to all the rights and privileges of one.[47] In short, any one receiving entertainment for hire at an inn as a transient with the innkeeper's consent, is a guest, and is entitled to hold the innkeeper responsible as such.

Patronizing the Inn as Such

The second requisite of the guest is that he must patronize the inn as an inn; that is, he must resort to it for the legitimate purposes and entertainment that characterize the inn.[48] Thus one who went to a hotel with a prostitute, whom he fraudulently registered as his wife, for the purpose of sexual intercourse, is not a guest.[49] Nor is one who, in order to secure a safe place to de-

[44] Hancock v. Rand, 94 N. Y. 1, 46 Am. Rep. 112, a leading case. See, also, Metzger v. Schnabel, 23 Misc. Rep. 698, 52 N. Y. Supp. 105 (involving a foreign army officer temporarily in this country).

[45] Curtis v. Murphy, 63 Wis. 4, 22 N. W. 825, 53 Am. Rep. 242; Walling v. Potter, 35 Conn. 183.

[46] See Meacham v. Galloway, 102 Tenn. 415, 52 S. W. 859, 46 L. R. A. 319, 73 Am. St. Rep. 886; Haff v. Adams, 6 Ariz. 395, 59 Pac. 111.

[47] The cases are numerous where persons obviously living near by were held guests, thus: A driver of cattle along the road, in Hilton v. Adams, 71 Me. 19. One who came with a horse and wagon to attend the trial of a case brought against him by the innkeeper, in Read v. Amidon, 41 Vt. 15, 98 Am. Dec. 560. One who came to market, in Bennet v. Mellor, 5 Term R. (Eng.) 273. So, it does not appear that the party was a traveler in Farnworth v. Packwood, 1 Starkie (Eng.) 249. See, also, McDonald v. Edgerton, 5 Barb. (N. Y.) 560; Parker v. Flint, 12 Mod. (Eng.) 254 (case 455); Hancock v. Rand, 94 N. Y. 1, 46 Am. Rep. 112; Orchard v. Bush [1898] 2 Q. B. (Eng.) 284.

[48] Toub v. Schmidt, 60 Hun, 409, 15 N. Y. Supp. 616; Read v. Amidon, 41 Vt. 15, 98 Am. Dec. 560; Lynar v. Mossop, 36 Q. B. U. C. (Can.) 230. See, also, Baker v. Bailey, 103 Ark. 12, 145 S. W. 532, 39 L. R. A. (N. S.) 1085.

[49] Curtis v. Murphy, 63 Wis. 4, 22 N. W. 825, 53 Am. Rep. 242. In this case Cole, C. J., said that "while the definition of a guest has been somewhat extended beyond its original meaning, it does not include every one who goes to an inn for convenience to accomplish some purpose. If a man and woman go together to, or meet by concert at, an inn or hotel in the town or city where they reside, and take a room for no other purpose than to have illicit intercourse, can it be that the law protects them as guests? Is the

posit his money, hired a room at the inn, which he had no intention of occupying.[50] A neighbor or friend who comes to an inn on the social invitation of the innkeeper, to be entertained gratuitously, is not a guest;[51] for, not paying for what he receives, he is entertained by the keeper of the inn purely in his private, and not in his public, capacity. Of course, one who goes to an inn merely to call upon a guest does not by so doing become a guest himself.[52]

The transient, resorting to the inn as such (when accepted by the innkeeper), is none the less a guest though the entertainment he receives is limited to a single meal,[53] or even if an unexpected alteration of his plans might result in his ultimately receiving no entertainment at all. Though no one is an innkeeper unless he holds himself out to furnish lodging, it is not essential that a person must take lodgings in order that he may be a guest.[54] Nor need one be entertained at an inn any definite length of time to make

extraordinary rule of liability which was originally adopted from considerations of public policy to protect travelers and wayfarers, not merely from the negligence, but the dishonesty, of innkeepers and their servants, to be extended to such persons? * * * Then, for a like reason, it would protect a thief who takes a room at an inn and improves the opportunity thus given to enter the rooms and steal the goods of guests and boarders."

[50] W., the keeper of a gambling house, closed his night's business at 2 o'clock a. m., having a sum of money upon his person, and, not being ready to retire for the night, and not wishing to carry his money upon his person at that time of the night, visited an inn, for the purpose of depositing his money for safe-keeping; found the inn in charge of a night clerk; inquired if he could have lodging for the night; was told that he could; stated that he did not desire to go to his room at that time, but wished to leave some money with the clerk, and would return in about half an hour. The clerk told him he would reserve a good room for him. He did not register his name. It was not upon any book of the inn. No room was assigned him. He left his package of money with the clerk, received a check for it, and departed. He returned in about three hours to have a room assigned him and retire for the balance of the morning. The clerk had absconded with the money. Held, W. was not a guest of the inn at the time he deposited his money with the clerk, and the innkeeper was not liable for its loss. Arcade Hotel Co. v. Wiatt, 44 Ohio St. 32, 4 N. E. 398, 58 Am. Rep. 785. A person engaging and paying for a room at a hotel does not thereby become a guest, when he has no intention of occupying the room. Bunn v. Johnson, 77 Mo. App. 596.

[51] Anonymous, 1 Rolle, Abr. 3 Pl. 4; Southcote v. Stanley, 1 H. & N. (Eng.) 247; Bac. Abr. "Inns and Innkeepers"; 5 Comyn, Dig. "Action on Case for Negligence," B, 2.

[52] Gastenhofer v. Clair, 10 Daly (N. Y.) 265, 266. Cf. Kopper v. Willis, 9 Daly (N. Y.) 460; Bennet v. Mellor, 5 Term R. (Eng.) 273.

[53] Orchard v. Bush [1898] 2 Q. B. 284; Read v. Amidon, 41 Vt. 15, 98 Am. Dec. 560.

[54] Overstreet v. Moser, 88 Mo. App. 72; Kopper v. Willis, 9 Daly (N. Y.) 460.

him a guest.[55] Thus, even the purchasing of liquor has been held sufficient,[56] under some circumstances, to make one the guest of the innkeeper; for it is not the nature or amount of entertainment, but the character under which the person receives it, which determines the relation of the parties.

To make one a guest, the entertainment must be given by the innkeeper in his capacity as the keeper of an inn.[57] Thus, if for pay the innkeeper agreed to furnish a banquet for a society, members of the society attending the banquet are not guests of the innkeeper,[58] for he is here not strictly an innkeeper, but a club caterer, and the two employments, as to their nature and attendant responsibility, are separate and distinct.

The authorities seem to be divided on the question whether the transient must be personally entertained at the inn, in order to be a guest. The point is generally raised in connection with the innkeeper's responsibility for loss of, or damage to, a horse sent to the inn by a person who does not himself resort to the inn. It would seem, though there are cases to the contrary,[59] that if a person was not personally entertained at the inn and never intended to be, then he does not become a guest merely by sending his horse to the inn to be cared for.[60] If, however, a person intends to become a guest at the inn, and sends his horse there in advance (the horse being accepted on that understanding by the innkeeper), then the owner of the horse, it seems, would become a guest (in so far, at least,

[55] Kopper v. Willis, 9 Daly (N. Y.) 460, 465.

[56] McDonald v. Edgerton, 5 Barb. (N. Y.) 560, 562; Fitch v. Casler, 17 Hun (N. Y.) 126, 127. See, also, Bennet v. Mellor, 5 T. R. (Eng.) 273. For comments on this last case, see Strauss v. County Hotel & Wine Co., 12 Q. B. Div. (Eng.) 27; McDonald v. Edgerton, 5 Barb. (N. Y.) 560; Kopper v. Willis, 9 Daly (N. Y.) 460, 465; McDaniels v. Robinson, 26 Vt. 316, 332, 62 Am. Dec. 574.

[57] Carter v. Hobbs, 12 Mich. 52, 83 Am. Dec. 762; Fitch v. Casler, 17 Hun (N. Y.) 126 (ball held at the inn in both of these cases, and persons attending ball held not to be guests, even though they bought liquor at the inn).

[58] AMEY v. WINCHESTER, 68 N. H. 447, 39 Atl. 487, 39 L. R. A. 760, 73 Am. St. Rep. 614, Dobie Cas. Bailments and Carriers, 153.

[59] See Russell v. Fogan, 7 Houst. (Del.) 389, 8 Atl. 258; Yorke v. Grenaugh, 2 Ld. Raym. (Eng.) 866; Mason v. Thompson, 9 Pick. (Mass.) 280, 20 Am. Dec. 471. It is said that the basis of this liability is the compensation received by the innkeeper for keeping the horse. So that as to inanimate goods, for the keeping of which no compensation is charged, this alone would not create the relation of innkeeper and guest. As to this last, see McDaniels v. Robinson, 28 Vt. 387, 67 Am. Dec. 720.

[60] Healey v. Gray, 68 Me. 489, 28 Am. Rep. 80; Neale v. Crocker, 8 U. C. C. P. (Can.) 224; Ingallsbee v. Wood, 33 N. Y. 577, 88 Am. Dec. 409.

as the innkeeper's responsibility for the horse is concerned) from the time that the horse is accepted.[61]

Consent of the Innkeeper

The third element in the definition of a guest is acceptance as such by the innkeeper. The latter has the power to refuse to accept any person as a guest, and upon such refusal such person does not, and cannot, become a guest.[62] The innkeeper is liable, as we shall see, when he refuses, without lawful excuse, to accept a person as a guest;[63] but his refusal, though wrongful, is none the less effective in preventing the establishing of the relation of innkeeper and guest. The innkeeper thus has the power, but not the right, to determine who his guests shall be.

Not even a transient, patronizing the inn as such, can make himself a guest without the innkeeper's consent. Of course, that consent may be given either by the innkeeper himself or by an agent or servant intrusted with the duty of receiving and rejecting travelers. Frequently there is no formal bargain, and there need be none; for the acceptance of a person as a guest will readily be implied from appropriate acts, as where he calls for refreshment which is furnished to him by a servant who has the discretion either to give or to withhold it.[64] Again, when the porter of an inn is sent to the station for that purpose, the porter, merely by assuming control of a traveler's baggage, may accept him as a guest.[65]

[61] See Grinnell v. Cook, 3 Hill (N. Y.) 485, 38 Am. Dec. 663. See, also, Coykendall v. Eaton, 55 Barb. (N. Y.) 188. For an interesting case in this connection, see Brewer v. Caswell, 132 Ga. 563, 64 S. E. 674, 23 L. R. A. (N. S.) 1107, 131 Am. St. Rep. 216, 16 Ann. Cas. 936. See Flint v. Illinois Hotel Co., 149 Ill. App. 404, where the innkeeper was held liable as such for goods sent in advance by an intending guest, who actually became a guest.

[62] Bird v. Bird, 1 And. (Eng.) 29; White's Case, 2 Dyer (Eng.) 158b. Both of these cases arose in the sixteenth century. See, also, Gastenhofer v. Clair, 10 Daly (N. Y.) 265, 266; Strauss v. County Hotel & Wine Co., 12 Q. B. Div. (Eng.) 27. See, also, cases cited in note 37.

[63] Post, § 94.

[64] Gastenhofer v. Clair, 10 Daly (N. Y.) 265.

[65] Sasseen v. Clark, 37 Ga. 242; Coskery v. Nagle, 83 Ga. 696, 10 S. E. 491, 6 L. R. A. 483, 20 Am. St. Rep. 333; Dickinson v. Winchester, 4 Cush. (Mass.) 114, 50 Am. Dec. 760; Richards v. London, etc., Ry. Co., 7 C. B. (Eng.) 839, 62 E. C. L. 839. See, also, Strauss v. County, etc., Co., 12 Q. B. D. (Eng.) 27. Tulane Hotel Co. v. Holohan, 112 Tenn. 214, 79 S. W. 113, 105 Am. St. Rep. 930, 2 Ann. Cas. 345. In these last two cases the person, after he had delivered his baggage to the porter, decided not to become a guest at the inn and received no entertainment there. In both cases it was held that he had not become a guest. There was a similar holding in Baker v. Bailey, 103 Ark. 12, 145 S. W. 532, 39 L. R. A. (N. S.) 1085, where one sent his baggage to a hotel and then went to the hotel merely to write letters and wait for a train.

No one, however, can become a guest until he has first given the innkeeper an opportunity, either in person or through an authorized representative, to receive or to reject him. Only after the innkeeper has elected to receive him is a person entitled to the privileges of a guest. Accordingly, a man cannot make himself a guest merely by slipping into the dining room of a hotel and ordering a dinner of a waiter who has no discretion whatever, and who brings what is ordered under the belief that the person who gives the order is in the dining room by permission of the innkeeper.[66] In such case, the act of the waiter is in no sense equivalent to an acceptance by the innkeeper, but is rather a mechanical act performed on the false supposition that the person has already been accepted as a guest by the innkeeper.

Special Agreement

The guest does not lose that character merely by making an arrangement for a definite time, or at definite rates, provided he still remains a transient.[67]

Neither the length of his stay nor any agreement he may make as to the price of board is sufficient in itself to deprive a person of his character as a guest, provided that he still fulfills the definition of a guest.[68] A transient who enters an inn as a guest does not cease to be a guest, provided he remain a transient, by agreeing to remain a given time, or by ascertaining the price that will be charged, or by paying in advance for the entertainment.[69] Thus, a guest for a single night might make a special contract as to the price to be paid for his lodging, without in any way affecting his character as a guest.

Whether a person is a guest, then, depends upon his fulfilling the three elements of the definition. A special contract, though, might show conclusively, and is always evidence to prove, that one

[66] Gastenhofer v. Clair, 10 Daly (N. Y.) 265.

[67] LUSK v. BELOTE, 22 Minn. 468, Dobie Cas. Bailments and Carriers, 148; Moon v. Yarlan, 147 Ill. App. 383; Magee v. Pacific Imp. Co., 98 Cal. 678, 33 Pac. 772, 35 Am. St. Rep. 199; Pettit v. Thomas, 103 Ark. 593, 148 S. W. 501, 42 L. R. A. (N. S.) 122; Norcross v. Norcross, 53 Me. 169; Hancock v. Rand, 94 N. Y. 1, 46 Am. Rep. 112; Lima v. Dwinelle, 7 Alb. Law J. (N. Y.) 44; Berkshire Woolen Co. v. Proctor, 7 Cush. (Mass.) 417; Hall v. Pike, 100 Mass. 495; Walling v. Potter, 35 Conn. 183, 185; Richmond v. Smith, 8 Barn. & C. (Eng.) 9, 11; Kisten v. Hildebrand, 9 B. Mon. (Ky.) 72, 48 Am. Dec. 416; Parker v. Flint, 12 Mod. (Eng.) 254, 255; Allen v. Smith, 12 C. B. N. S. (Eng.) 638.

[68] Pinkerton v. Woodward, 33 Cal. 557, 91 Am. Dec. 657; Shoecraft v. Bailey, 25 Iowa, 553.

[69] Ross v. Mellin, 36 Minn. 421, 32 N. W. 172; Jalie v. Cardinal, 35 Wis. 118.

or more of these elements is lacking, thereby establishing that the person is not a guest. Thus, where the person agrees, in consideration of a special rate, to remain at the inn an extended period of time, this could negative the idea of his being a transient; or the special agreement might show that, even when his stay is very short, the person is not to patronize the inn as such, but for other purposes. A guest, then, is a (1) transient (2) who patronizes the inn as such (3) with the consent of the innkeeper; and all the surrounding facts and circumstances that are relevant, including the special agreement where there is one, are to be taken into consideration in solving this question of fact.

It is clear, from what has been said, that the same establishment may have a double character, being both a boarding house and an inn. Thus, it would be an inn as to transients patronizing it; while as to those living there as residents, under special contracts showing them not to be transients, it would be a mere boarding house.[70] Under such circumstances, the keeper of the inn would be liable, as an innkeeper to his guests, as a boarding house keeper to his boarders.

DURATION OF THE RELATION

92. The relation of innkeeper and guest begins when the guest is accepted as such, and continues until it is terminated in one of the ways subsequently to be considered.

When a transient applies to the innkeeper for entertainment and is accepted by the latter, he immediately becomes a guest.[71] Some of the cases contain expressions to the effect that "taking the room is the decisive act to create the relation;"[72] but it is clear, from what has already been said in discussing who are guests, that it is by no means essential that one be assigned a room in order to create the relation.[73] The relation dates from the innkeeper's ac-

[70] Cromwell v. Stephens, 2 Daly (N. Y.) 15; Seward v. Seymour, Anthon Law Stud. (N. Y.) 51; LUSK v. BELOTE, 22 Minn. 468, Dobie Cas. Bailments and Carriers, 148.

[71] Pinkerton v. Woodward, 33 Cal. 557, 91 Am. Dec. 657; Ross v. Mellin, 36 Minn. 421, 32 N. W. 172; Healey v. Gray, 68 Me. 489, 28 Am. Rep. 80.

[72] McDaniels v. Robinson, 26 Vt. 316, 324, 62 Am. Dec. 574. And see, as giving color to this view, Arcade Hotel Co. v. Wiatt, 44 Ohio St. 32, 4 N. E. 398, 58 Am. Rep. 785.

[73] Since merely buying liquor has, as we have seen, been held sufficient to make one a guest. Kopper v. Willis, 9 Daly (N. Y.) 460; McDonald v. Edgerton, 5 Barb. (N. Y.) 560; Fitch v. Casler, 17 Hun (N. Y.) 126, 127; Atkinson v. Sellers, 5 C. B. N. S. (Eng.) 442, 448; Bennet v. Mellor, 5 Term R.

ceptance, and that is the decisive factor. Its inception has nothing essentially to do with the receipt of any specific form of entertainment. The request for entertainment at the inn may be, and in fact often is, implied from the conduct of the intending guest, and he may be received as a guest in the same way. The personal assent of the innkeeper to receiving the guest, as we have seen, is not necessary; it may be given by an employé or agent authorized to do so.[74]

The relation of innkeeper and guest, once established, continues until terminated in one of the ways later to be discussed.[75] The mere temporary absence of the guest from the inn, however, does not terminate the relation;[76] while the mere lapse of time in no way affects it, provided only that the guest still retains his character as a transient.[77]

RIGHTS AND DUTIES OF INNKEEPER—IN GENERAL

93. The duties of the innkeeper consist primarily of—
(a) The duty to receive guests.
(b) The duty to care for the comfort and safety of the guest.
(c) The duty to care for the goods of the guest.
The rights of the innkeeper turn chiefly about his compensation and his lien on the goods of the guest to secure that compensation.

Analysis

The rights and duties of the innkeeper will be considered according to the following analysis:

(a) The duty to receive guests.
(b) The duty to care for the comfort and safety of the guest.
(c) The liability for the goods of the guest.
  (1) The nature of the liability.
  (2) For what goods liable.
  (3) Limitation of the liability.

(Eng.) 273. See, also, cases cited in notes 53 and 54, holding persons guests who did not take lodgings.

74 Gastenhofer v. Clair, 10 Daly (N. Y.) 265; Pinkerton v. Woodward, 33 Cal. 557, 91 Am. Dec. 657. See cases cited in notes 64, 65.

75 Post, § 104.

76 Brown Hotel Co. v. Burckhardt, 13 Colo. App. 59, 56 Pac. 188; Hays v. Turner, 23 Iowa, 214; Day v. Bother, 2 H. & C. (Eng.) 14.

77 Jalie v. Cardinal, 35 Wis. 118. See, also, cases cited in notes 67 and 68.

(d) The right of compensation and lien.
  (1) Compensation.
  (2) Lien.
    (i) Nature and extent of the lien.
    (ii) Waiver of the lien.
    (iii) Enforcement of the lien.
(e) The liability of the innkeeper as an ordinary bailee.
  (1) As an ordinary bailee for hire.
  (2) As a gratuitous bailee.

In General

The innkeeper has been defined and distinguished from those whose occupations seem to lie closest to him. Attention has also been directed to the question of who is a guest, and it has been seen that the innkeeper is technically such only as to one who is his guest. We next proceed to discuss the nature and extent of the rights and duties implied by law as inhering in the relation of innkeeper and guest, and this discussion turns about the analysis given above. This discussion forms naturally the most important part of the law of innkeepers.

SAME—THE DUTY TO RECEIVE GUESTS

94. The innkeeper is bound, provided he has accommodations for them, to receive as guests all proper persons who come to his inn, and who are able and willing to pay for their entertainment.

In General

The innkeeper by holding out his house as a public place to which travelers may resort thereby surrenders some of the rights which he would otherwise have over it.[78] He, according to Lord Holt, "has made profession of a trade which is for the public good, and has thereby exposed and vested an interest of himself in all the King's subjects that will employ him." [79] By becoming, in a sense, a public servant, the innkeeper acquires certain unique

[78] The ground upon which these restrictions are imposed is that persons engaged in this vocation are in some sense servants of the public, and in conducting their business they exercise a privilege conferred upon them by the public, and they have secured to them by the law certain privileges and rights which are not enjoyed by the members of the public generally. Bowlin v. Lyon, 67 Iowa, 536, 25 N. W. 766, 56 Am. Rep. 355. And cf. Beale v. Posey, 72 Ala. 323, 330; De Wolf v. Ford, 193 N. Y. 397, 86 N. E. 527, 21 L. R. A. (N. S.) 860, 127 Am. St. Rep. 969.

[79] Lane v. Cotton, 12 Mod. (Eng.) 472.

privileges, and owes to the public unique duties. Holding out the inn as a public place of entertainment for travelers, he cannot refuse to serve proper persons who come under that character, in a proper manner, and at suitable times, so long as he has the means of accommodation for them.[80] Subject to the limitations about to be discussed, as was said in a leading English case:[81] "The innkeeper is not to select his guests. He has no right to say to one, You shall come into my inn, and to another, You shall not, as every one coming and conducting himself in a proper manner has a right to be received; and for this purpose innkeepers are a sort of public servants." The innkeeper, therefore, holding himself out to serve the public indifferently, must, in the absence of a good excuse, live up to his holding out.

This duty to receive as guests all proper persons who apply is imposed by law, and for any violation of it by the innkeeper there are remedies both criminal and civil. For a wrongful refusal to receive a person as a guest, it is held that the innkeeper may be indicted and held criminally liable.[82] The person whom he wrongfully declined to receive may bring a civil action[83] against the innkeeper and recover such damages as he suffered in consequence of the wrong. In exceptional cases, even punitive damages[84] may sometimes be recovered

Excuses for Refusal to Receive Guests

Of course, the innkeeper's duty is commensurate with his facilities and he is not liable for refusal to accept a guest, when

[80] Cornell v. Huber, 102 App. Div. 293, 92 N. Y. Supp. 434; Willis v. McMahon, 89 Cal. 156, 26 Pac. 649; Watkins v. Cope, 84 N. J. Law, 143, 86 Atl. 545; Kirkman v. Shawcross, 6 Term R. (Eng.) 14, 17; Rex v. Ivens, 7 Car. & P. (Eng.) 213. That he cannot refuse accommodation to an infant or a married woman traveling alone, see Watson v. Cross, 2 Duv. (Ky.) 147. An innkeeper is not bound to receive and keep horses or other property of a person who is neither a traveler nor a guest. Grinnell v. Cook, 3 Hill (N. Y.) 485, 38 Am. Dec. 663.

[81] Rex v. Ivens, 7 Car. & P. (Eng.) 213.

[82] Commonwealth v. Mitchell, 2 Pars. Eq. Cas. (Pa.) 431; Id., 1 Phila. (Pa.) 63; Kisten v. Hildebrand, 9 B. Mon. (Ky.) 72, 48 Am. Dec. 416; Rex v. Ivens, 7 Car. & P. (Eng.) 213. See admirable summing up of Coleridge, J., in this last case.

[83] Watson v. Cross, 2 Duv. (Ky.) 147, 148; Hawthorn v. Hammond, 1 Car. & K. (Eng.) 404; Cornell v. Huber, 102 App. Div. 293, 92 N. Y. Supp. 434; Willis v. McMahon, 89 Cal. 156, 26 Pac. 649; McHugh v. Schlosser, 159 Pa. 480, 28 Atl. 291, 23 L. R. A. 574, 39 Am. St. Rep. 699. The last two cases cited are also interesting as to the elements of damages recoverable against the innkeeper. See, also, on that subject, Malin & Browder v. McCutcheon, 33 Tex. Civ. App. 387, 76 S. W. 586.

[84] McCarthy v. Niskern, 22 Minn. 90 (person turned away with abusive and insulting language).

his inn is full and his accommodations are exhausted.[85] Again, he is not obliged to receive one who is not able and willing to pay for his entertainment,[86] and such payment may be demanded in advance.[87] Even his public profession does not demand that he make the inn a common receptacle for all comers, regardless of their character and condition. And, by virtue of his duty properly to care for and protect his guests, it is imperative that certain persons should be excluded from the inn. The innkeeper violates no duty, unless the one he declined to receive was a proper person.

Accordingly it has been held that the innkeeper is justified in refusing to receive one who is drunk,[88] or disorderly,[89] or suffering from a contagious disease,[90] or filthy,[91] persons of evil reputation,[92] thieves or common brawlers,[93] persons coming to the inn for an illegal purpose,[94] and prizefighters,[95] who violate the criminal laws against prizefighting. But it has been held that an innkeeper cannot refuse to accept a person because he lives in the same town, if he is a traveler,[96] one whose costume is uncon-

[85] Browne v. Brandt, [1902] 1 K. B. (Eng.) 696, 71 L. J. K. B. 367. Gordon v. Sieber, 25 Q. B. D. (Eng.) 491. Commonwealth v. Mitchell, 2 Pars. Eq. Cas. (Pa.) 431; Id., 1 Phila. (Pa.) 63.

[86] Markham v. Brown, 8 N. H. 523, 31 Am. Dec. 209; Thompson v. Lacy, 3 Barn. & Ald. (Eng.) 283, 286; Watson v. Cross, 2 Duv. (Ky.) 147; Pinkerton v. Woodward, 33 Cal. 557, 91 Am. Dec. 657; Grinnell v. Cook, 3 Hill (N. Y.) 485, 38 Am. Dec. 663. The price of accommodation need not be tendered unless it is demanded or the refusal to receive is on that ground. Rex v. Ivens, 7 Car. & P. (Eng.) 213. But see Fell v. Knight, 8 Mees. & W. (Eng.) 269, 276.

[87] Bac. Abr. "Inns and Innkeepers," C; Beale, Innkeepers, § 244; Mulliner v. Florence, 3 Q. B. D. (Eng.) 484, 47 L. J. Q. B. 700; Fell v. Knight, 8 M. & W. (Eng.) 276.

[88] Markham v. Brown, 8 N. H. 523, 31 Am. Dec. 209; Rex v. Ivens, 7 Car. & P. (Eng.) 213.

[89] Beale v. Posey, 72 Ala. 323; Goodenow v. Travis, 3 Johns. (N. Y.) 427.

[90] Beale, Innkeepers, § 93; Levy v. Corey, 1 City Ct. R. Supp. (N. Y.) 57.

[91] State v. Steele, 106 N. C. 766, 11 S. E. 478, 8 L. R. A. 516, 19 Am. St. Rep. 573; Markham v. Brown, 8 N. H. 523, 31 Am. Dec. 209.

[92] Goodenow v. Travis, 3 Johns (N. Y.) 427.

[93] Markham v. Brown, 8 N. H. 523, 31 Am. Dec. 209; Bac. Abr. "Inns," A; 1 Hawk. P. C. c. 78, § 1.

[94] Markham v. Brown, 8 N. H. 523, 528, 31 Am. Dec. 209.

[95] NELSON v. BOLDT (C. C.) 180 Fed. 779, Dobie Cas. Bailments and Carriers, 155, an interesting case, in which "Bat" Nelson, a notorious prize fighter, was ejected from the Bellevue Stratford Hotel in Philadelphia and was denied a recovery.

[96] In such cases, the fact that the person presenting himself is an inhabitant is important only in so far as it may tend to prove that he is not a transient. See note 45 for cases in which such townsmen were held to be guests. The note to Walling v. Potter, 9 Am. Law Reg. (N. S.) 618, to the

ventional, but decent,[97] or a married woman or infant traveling alone.[98] Nor can he refuse to receive a militiaman, because other men wearing the same uniform have conducted themselves improperly in the inn.[99]

The question whether an innkeeper, in this country, can legally refuse to accept a negro has caused much comment.[1] Such refusal has been justified on the ground that an innkeeper can exclude persons who will be objectionable to his guests, or subject them to annoyance.[2] Mr. Beale says that this is too broad and "that it is not likely, however, that the law would permit an innkeeper to tender his house for the use only of members of a certain race or to persons of a certain color." [3] The question is complicated further by state statutes [4] forbidding race distinctions in hotels, by "civil rights acts," both state and federal,[5] and by the fact that it would not be unnatural to expect different holdings on the general question in different parts of the country.

Duty to Receive the Goods of the Guest

As an incident of the innkeeper's duty to receive the guest, he must also receive into the inn the goods of the latter.[6] If this were not true, the right of the guest to demand that he be received might prove a very futile one, and particularly was this true of the early times when the inn was a haven of refuge for the traveler. If the goods are dangerous in themselves, or would be a

effect that the innkeeper need not receive a townsman, is not supported by reason or authority.

[97] Reg. v. Sprague, 63 J. P. (Eng.) 233.

[98] Watson v. Cross, 2 Duv. (Ky.) 147.

[99] Atwater v. Sawyer, 76 Me. 539, 49 Am. Rep. 634.

[1] See Beale, Innkeepers, §§ 65, 92; Stephenson, Race Distinctions in American Law, p. 124.

[2] See State v. Steele, 106 N. C. 766, 11 S. E. 478, 8 L. R. A. 516, 19 Am. St. Rep. 573.

[3] Beale, Innkeepers, § 65.

[4] For references to the codes of particular states which have passed such statutes, and for citations to cases construing such state statutes and upholding their constitutionality, see 7 Cyc. "Civil Rights," pp. 165–167.

[5] See, on this subject, 7 Cyc. "Civil Rights," pp. 163–165. The leading case on this subject is, of course, the Civil Rights Cases, 109 U. S. 3, 3 Sup. Ct. 18, 27 L. Ed. 835. Here the first and second sections of the celebrated Civil Rights Act of March 1, 1875 (18 Stat. 335, c. 114 [U. S. Comp. St. 1901, p. 1260]), were declared unconstitutional by the United States Supreme Court, as being authorized neither by the thirteenth nor fourteenth amendments to the United States Constitution.

[6] Beale, Innkeepers, § 68; ROBINS & CO. v. GRAY, [1895] 2 Q. B. (Eng.) 501, Dobie Cas. Bailments and Carriers, 164; Threfall v. Borwick, L. R. 10 Q. B. (Eng.) 210; Mulliner v. Florence, 3 Q. B. D. (Eng.) 484; 17 Halsbury, Laws of England, pp. 307, 308.

nuisance, clearly the innkeeper need not receive them. There must also be some reasonable limitations on the amount and value of the goods, but it seems that the innkeeper cannot refuse to receive the goods because they are not solely for the use of the traveler on the journey or do not come within the technical definition of baggage.[7] Ordinarily the innkeeper cannot question the traveler's title to the goods before receiving them, unless he knew, or had good reason to believe, they were stolen.[8]

Duty to Receive Persons Coming to See the Guest

When there is any duty resting on the innkeeper to receive into the inn persons coming to see the guest, such duty springs from the right of the guest to have such persons admitted, and these persons have accordingly no basis of their own upon which they can claim admission to the inn.[9] Thus the innkeeper should receive a stranger who comes to make a mere social call on the guest, at the previous request of the latter.[10] The same is true of one coming by previous engagement on a mission of business with the guest.[11] But the landlord may exclude unbidden solicitors who resort to the inn, seeking to obtain the patronage of the guest.[12] Whether the innkeeper can discriminate in this last case, allowing certain persons the privilege and denying the same privilege to others, is not entirely clear. It would seem that he can thus discriminate, provided he does not thereby violate his duty to care properly for the comfort and welfare of the guest.[13]

SAME—THE DUTY TO CARE FOR THE COMFORT AND SAFETY OF THE GUEST

95. The innkeeper must exercise reasonable care to provide for the comfort and safety of his guest.

7 See cases cited in preceding note.

8 ROBINS & CO. v. GRAY, [1895] 2 Q. B. (Eng.) 501, Dobie Cas. Bailments and Carriers, 164.

9 See, on this subject, Beale, Innkeepers, §§ 82–88.

10 Beale, Innkeepers, § 84. See, too, a qualification of such right in Commonwealth v. Mitchell, 2 Pars. Eq. Cas. (Pa.) 43; Id., 1 Phila. (Pa.) 63.

11 Markham v. Brown, 8 N. H. 523, 31 Am. Dec. 209; State v. Steele, 106 N. C. 766, 11 S. E. 478, 8 L. R. A. 516, 19 Am. St. Rep. 573.

12 State v. Steele, 106 N. C. 766, 11 S. E. 478, 8 L. R. A. 516, 19 Am. St. Rep. 573.

13 This question is discussed in Beale, Innkeepers, § 87, 1 Wyman, Public Service Corporations, § 493, and Markham v. Brown, 8 N. H. 523, 31 Am. Dec. 209. An exception is found to the innkeeper's right thus to discriminate when it touches the travel of the guest, and it is held he cannot permit one line of stagecoaches to solicit the right to take away departing guests, and exclude all other lines.

By virtue of the relation, the law imposes upon the innkeeper the duty of exercising reasonable care in looking after the comfort and safety of the guest.[14] The innkeeper, however, is in no sense an insurer in this respect.[15] This duty of the innkeeper is manifest along three practical lines. He must see to the (1) physical condition of the inn; (2) the food supplied to his guests; and the (3) safety of the guests from attack or similar harm.

Thus (1) he must use ordinary care to see that elevators [16] are kept in good condition, and that proper protection against fire [17] and due precautions as to sanitation [18] are taken. With equal care, (2) he must look to the quantity and wholesomeness of the food served.[19] The person of the guest should be (3) with like care protected from assault or attack by persons [20] in the inn, whether servants, other guests, or strangers. When the landlord has used ordinary care, he has fulfilled his duty and the guest has no right to demand more. Accordingly, in the matter of accommo-

[14] Hilton v. Adams, 71 Me. 19; Stott v. Churchill, 157 N. Y. 692, 51 N. E. 1094; Stringfellow v. Grunewald, 109 La. 187, 33 South. 190; Gilbert v. Hoffman, 66 Iowa, 205, 23 N. W. 632, 55 Am. Rep. 263; WEEKS v. McNULTY, 101 Tenn. 495, 48 S. W. 809, 43 L. R. A. 185, 70 Am. St. Rep. 693, Dobie Cas. Bailments and Carriers, 156; Curran v. Olson, 88 Minn. 307, 92 N. W. 1124, 60 L. R. A. 733, 97 Am. St. Rep. 517; Clancy v. Barker, 71 Neb. 83, 98 N. W. 440, 103 N. W. 446, 69 L. R. A. 642, 115 Am. St. Rep. 559, 8 Ann. Cas. 682.

[15] WEEKS v. McNULTY, 101 Tenn. 495, 48 S. W. 809, 43 L. R. A. 185, 70 Am. St. Rep. 693, Dobie Cas. Bailments and Carriers, 156; Stringfellow v. Grunewald, 109 La. 187, 33 South. 190; Clancy v. Barker, 131 Fed. 161, 66 C. C. A. 469, 69 L. R. A. 653.

[16] Stott v. Churchill, 157 N. Y. 692, 51 N. E. 1094; Bremer v. Pleiss, 121 Wis. 61, 98 N. W. 945. Other cases as to defective premises are Morris v. Zimmerman, 138 App. Div. 114, 122 N. Y. Supp. 900 (fall of plaster); Hotel Ass'n of Omaha v. Walters, 23 Neb. 280, 36 N. W. 561 (defective railing); Burchmore v. Antlers Hotel Co., 54 Colo. 314, 130 Pac. 846 (defective chair), and Ritter v. Norman, 71 Wash. 563, 129 Pac. 103, 43 L. R. A. (N. S.) 657 (dark stairway).

[17] WEEKS v. McNULTY, 101 Tenn. 495, 48 S. W. 809, 43 L. R. A. 185, 70 Am. St. Rep. 693, Dobie Cas. Bailments and Carriers, 156; Acton v. Reed, 104 App. Div. 507, 93 N. Y. Supp. 911.

[18] Gilbert v. Hoffman, 66 Iowa, 205, 23 N. W. 632, 55 Am. Rep. 263; Patrick v. Springs, 154 N. C. 270, 70 S. E. 395, Ann. Cas. 1912A, 1209. There are statutes in many states on this point. For a case construing such a statute, see Hubbell v. Higgins, 148 Iowa, 36, 126 N. W. 914, Ann. Cas. 1912B, 822.

[19] Stringfellow v. Grunewald, 109 La. 187, 33 South. 190; Atwater v. Sawyer, 76 Me. 539, 49 Am. Rep. 634.

[20] Protection from other guests: Rommel v. Schambacher, 120 Pa. 579, 11 Atl. 779, 6 Am. St. Rep. 732; Curran v. Olson, 88 Minn. 307, 92 N. W. 1124, 60 L. R. A. 733, 97 Am. St. Rep. 517. Protection from assaults by servants: Clancy v. Barker, 131 Fed. 161, 66 C. C. A. 469, 69 L. R. A. 653; Overstreet v. Moser, 88 Mo. App. 72.

dations, all the law demands is that they be reasonable and proper. The innkeeper is not bound to provide for a guest the precise room or rooms that the latter may select.[21]

SAME—LIABILITY FOR THE GOODS OF THE GUEST

96. At common law, by the weight of authority, the innkeeper is liable as an insurer of the guest's goods brought within the inn, unless the loss or damage was due to act of God, public enemy or fault of the guest. Many cases, however, hold the innkeeper prima facie responsible; but he can escape liability by showing that the loss or injury was due to inevitable accident or irresistible force. A third line of cases allow the innkeeper exemption from responsibility on his showing that he was guilty of no negligence.

The Nature of the Liability—The Three Theories

In a discussion of the liability of the innkeeper for the goods brought by the guest into the inn, it should be noted at the outset that this liability is not dependent upon the existence of a strict bailment relation.[22] Indeed, there is no practical difference in the measure of the innkeeper's liability between the case when by a delivery a technical bailment is created, and the case when the possession of the goods still remains in the guest, provided, in the latter case, the goods may be said to be in the general control of the innkeeper and not in the exclusive custody of the guest. Accordingly the innkeeper's liability can be worked out independently of the subject of bailments and can be grounded in public policy and based on the general custom of the realm.[23]

There is grave conflict as to the extent of the innkeeper's exceptional liability for loss of, or injury to, the goods of the guest. Three rules[24] have been suggested: (a) The rule of strict insurance; (b) the rule of superior force; (c) the rule of prima facie responsibility.

21 De Wolf v. Ford, 193 N. Y. 397, 86 N. E. 527, 21 L. R. A. (N. S.) 860, 127 Am. St. Rep. 969; Fell v. Knight, 8 Mees. & W. (Eng.) 269. See, also, Reg. v. Sprague, 63 J. P. (Eng.) 233.

22 See Beale, Innkeepers, § 182, pointing out how this distinction was not made by many eminent writers and judges.

23 See opinion of Cochrane, J., in CRAPO v. ROCKWELL, 48 Misc. Rep. 1, 94 N. Y. Supp. 1122, Dobie Cas. Bailments and Carriers, 149.

24 These three rules are explained in SIBLEY v. ALDRICH, 33 N. H. 553, 66 Am. Dec. 745, Dobie Cas. Bailments and Carriers, 158.

By (a) the rule of strict insurance, the innkeeper, like the common carrier, is an insurer as to the goods, with certain exceptions, against either loss or injury. Under (b) the rule of superior force, the innkeeper is prima facie liable for all loss or injury; but he may exempt himself from liability by showing that such loss or injury was due either to inevitable accident or to irresistible force. The (c) rule of prima facie liability permits the innkeeper to escape responsibility for loss or injury by a simple showing on his part that he was guilty of no negligence.

The weight of authority, certainly if dicta are included, and particularly the older cases, would seem to favor the first rule, that of strict insurance; but the second rule, that of superior force, it is believed, best commends itself to sound reason and most closely conforms to the spirit of modern legislation.

Under (a) the doctrine of strict insurance, innkeepers are practically under the same liability as common carriers. They are insurers of the goods of their guests brought within the inn, and are liable for loss or injury, unless caused by the act of God, public enemy, act of the law, inherent nature of the goods, or the neglect or fault of the owner or his servants. This very strict liability, it is said, was necessary, in order to protect travelers against any collusion between the innkeeper or his servants on the one hand and thieves or robbers on the other, and to compel him to take care that no improper persons be admitted into his house. Upon proof of loss, the burden of bringing the case within the exceptions to his liability rests upon the innkeeper; and proof of the strictest care on his part avails him nothing, if it falls short of this. The innkeeper was absolutely responsible for loss or injury, unless he could show that it was due to one of the specific exceptions. In the absence of such a showing, proof even that no human effort could have averted such loss or injury did not help the innkeeper. Of course, in modern times there does not exist (as there formerly did) either the same necessity of resorting to an inn for protection against thieves and robbers, or even the same danger of collusion between such lawless persons and the innkeeper. Those courts, however, that cling to the rigor of the old rule making the innkeeper an insurer insist that sufficient other conditions still exist to make the rule a salutary one of sound public policy.[25]

[25] Among the earliest English cases holding the innkeeper an insurer are Richmond v. Smith (1828) 8 B. & C. 9, and Morgan v. Ravey (1861) 6 H. & N. 265. In 2 Kent, Comm. 574, it is said: "An innkeeper, like a common carrier, is an insurer of the goods of his guest." See, also, Lucia v. Omel, 53 App. Div. 641, 66 N. Y. Supp. 1136; Cunningham v. Bucky, 42 W. Va. 671, 26 S. E. 442, 35 L. R. A. 850, 57 Am. St. Rep. 878; Pettit v. Thomas, 103 Ark.

The second rule, the doctrine of superior force, proceeds on the ground that the doctrine of strict insurance places on the innkeeper an unfair and unnecessarily severe responsibility. The superior force rule regards the innkeeper as essentially human, and therefore proclaims that he should not be held responsible for what it was impossible for him to prevent, whether the unpreventable loss or injury was due to divine or human, public or private, animate or inanimate, agencies. Thus Redfield, C. J.,[26] said, as to the rule holding the innkeeper an insurer: "This may be too strongly expressed if applied to all cases of goods taken from the custody of the innkeeper. For it may be done by superior force, and without his fault, and still not the force of a public enemy." The essential fairness of the superior force rule (less severe than that of strict insurance, more severe than that of prima facie liability) lies in the fact that the innkeeper's exceptional calling is recognized by placing his responsibility higher than that of an ordinary bailee, while the rule refuses to make him responsible for conditions which it was impossible for him to control. Such a rule, if fairly enforced, affords little or no temptation to the innkeeper to relax his precautions as to the safety of the goods of his guest.[27]

593, 148 S. W. 501, 42 L. R. A. (N. S.) 122; CRAPO v. ROCKWELL, 48 Misc. Rep. 1, 94 N. Y. Supp. 1122, Dobie Cas. Bailments and Carriers, 149; LUSK v. BELOTE, 22 Minn. 468, Dobie Cas. Bailments and Carriers, 148; Shaw v. Berry, 31 Me. 479, 52 Am. Dec. 628; Mason v. Thompson, 9 Pick. (Mass.) 280, 20 Am. Dec. 471; Hulett v. Swift, 33 N. Y. 571, 88 Am. Dec. 405; SIBLEY v. ALDRICH, 33 N. H. 553, 66 Am. Dec. 745, Dobie Cas. Bailments and Carriers, 158; Dunbier v. Day, 12 Neb. 596, 12 N. W. 109, 41 Am. Rep. 772; Morgan v. Ravey, 6 Hurl. & N. (Eng.) 265; Grinnell v. Cook, 3 Hill (N. Y.) 485, 38 Am. Dec. 663; Burgess v. Clements, 4 Maule & S. (Eng.) 306; Richmond v. Smith, 8 Barn. & C. (Eng.) 9; Kent v. Shuckard, 2 Barn. & Adol. (Eng.) 803; Armistead v. White, 6 Eng. Law & Eq. 349; Mateer v. Brown, 1 Cal. 221, 52 Am. Dec. 303; Norcross v. Norcross, 53 Me. 163; Burrows v. Trieber, 21 Md. 320, 83 Am. Dec. 590; Manning v. Wells, 9 Humph. (Tenn.) 746, 51 Am. Dec. 688; Thickstun v. Howard, 8 Blackf. (Ind.) 535, 537; Sasseen v. Clark, 37 Ga. 242; Purvis v. Coleman, 21 N. Y. 111, 112, 117; Gile v. Libby, 36 Barb. (N. Y.) 70, 74; Ingalsbee v. Wood, 36 Barb. (N. Y.) 452, 458; Washburn v. Jones, 14 Barb. (N. Y.) 193, 195; McDonald v. Edgerton, 5 Barb. (N. Y.) 560, 564; Taylor v. Monnot, 4 Duer (N. Y.) 116; Stanton v. Leland, 4 E. D. Smith (N. Y.) 88, 94; Piper v. Manny, 21 Wend. (N. Y.) 282, 284; Clute v. Wiggins, 14 Johns. (N. Y.) 175, 7 Am. Dec. 44; Berkshire Woolen Co. v. Proctor, 7 Cush. (Mass.) 417, 427; Towson v. Havre-de-Grace Bank, 6 Har. & J. (Md.) 47, 14 Am. Dec. 254; 1 Smith, Lead. Cas. (Hare & W. Notes) 307; Fuller v. Coats, 18 Ohio St. 343, 349, 350 (and see Palace Hotel Co. v. Medart, 87 Ohio St. 130, 100 N. E. 317, Ann. Cas. 1913E, 860, as to qualification of the common-law rule by statute).

[26] McDaniels v. Robinson, 26 Vt. 316, 62 Am. Dec. 574.

[27] JOHNSON v. CHADBOURN FINANCE CO., 89 Minn. 310, 94 N. W. 874, 99 Am. St. Rep. 571, Dobie Cas. Bailments and Carriers, 159; Merritt v. Clag-

The third doctrine, that of prima facie liability, is, of course, the most favorable to the innkeeper, and permits him, as in the case of the ordinary bailee, to excuse himself by a simple showing that he was not guilty of negligence. It will readily be seen that this showing is much less onerous than is the superior force rule, for here the innkeeper is not obliged to show that the loss or injury was due to a force either inevitable or irresistible, but simply that he used due care to avert injury from the force. If he used due care in the premises, he is not liable, though the accident was not inevitable nor the force irresistible.[28]

Finally, in this connection, it might be observed that under all the doctrines a prima facie case is made out against the innkeeper by showing loss of, or injury to, the goods.[29] The rules differ, then, in the showing that the innkeeper must make to offset the prima facie case thus made out. Under the rule of strict insurance, he must bring the case within a few arbitrary exceptions without regard to his own care or caution. The superior force rule requires him to show that the agency causing the loss or injury was irresistible or inevitable, regardless of its nature. The doctrine of prima facie liability requires only that he show the absence of negligence on his part, that is, that he exercised due care under the conditions of the particular case.

Accidental Fires

Though the rule of strict insurance may seem to be most consistent with the theory on which an exceptional liability is imposed

horn, 23 Vt. 177; Howth v. Franklin, 20 Tex. 798, 73 Am. Dec. 218; McDaniels v. Robinson, 26 Vt. 316, 62 Am. Dec. 574; Kisten v. Hildebrand, 9 B. Mon. (Ky.) 72, 48 Am. Dec. 416; Woodworth v. Morse, 18 La. Ann. 156; Cutler v. Bonney, 30 Mich. 259, 18 Am. Rep. 127. The cases are not clear in announcing the exact limits of the innkeeper's liability, and a great many fail to distinguish between the rule of superior force and the rule of prima facie liability, so that one rule is really laid down by the case which the court either fails to designate or designates inaccurately. See JOHNSON v. CHADBOURN FINANCE CO., supra.

28 This is often referred to as the rule of Calye's Case, 8 Coke (Eng.) 63, decided in 1574, holding "the innkeeper shall not be charged, unless there be a default in him or his servants in the well and safe keeping of the custody of their guest's goods and chattels within his common inn." See Edwards, Bailm. 406; Dawson v. Chamney, 5 Q. B. (Eng.) 164; METCALF v. HESS, 14 Ill. 129, Dobie Cas. Bailments and Carriers, 160; Johnson v. Richardson, 17 Ill. 302, 63 Am. Dec. 369; Laird v. Eichold, 10 Ind. 212, 71 Am. Dec. 323; Burnham v. Young, 72 Me. 273; Trieber v. Burrows, 27 Md. 130; Hulbert v. Hartman, 79 Ill. App. 289.

29 Johnson v. Richardson, 17 Ill. 302, 63 Am. Dec. 369; Baehr v. Downey, 133 Mich. 163, 94 N. W. 750, 103 Am. St. Rep. 444; Eden v. Drey, 75 Ill. App. 102; Sasseen v. Clark, 37 Ga. 242; Watt v. Kilbury, 53 Wash. 446, 102 Pac. 403.

on innkeepers, the rule seems hardly able to bear the test of reason in cases in which the goods of the guest are destroyed by an accidental fire, in no way due to the innkeeper's own negligence or that of his servants. In such cases, the courts have been unusually slow to apply the doctrine of strict insurance, when the innkeeper could not be held responsible under either of the other two rules.[30] The contrary was held in New York, in Hulett v. Swift;[31] but it is worthy of note that a statute was passed soon after, exempting innkeepers from liability for such fires. And so, by statutes in a number of states, innkeepers are answerable to their guests, in case of loss or injury by fire, only when they fail to exercise ordinary and reasonable care in the custody of their baggage or other goods.

Loss by Robbery, Riots, and Theft

Much that has been said on the subject of accidental fires is applicable to cases of robbery or riot from without the inn, when the innkeeper is in no way at fault, though such cases have been rare in the courts.[32]

But this unwillingness to hold the innkeeper liable, on the part of courts claiming to uphold the doctrine of strict insurance, is not manifest where the theft is committed by some person, whether guest or servant, within the inn. Against such loss the innkeeper is expected to provide carefully, and both in the selection of his servants and in admitting guests to the inn he becomes in a measure responsible for their conduct. Accordingly, for such losses, the innkeeper is usually liable under all three of the rules, unless some fault can be traced to the guest whose goods were thus stolen.[33]

[30] JOHNSON v. CHADBOURN FINANCE CO., 89 Minn. 310, 94 N. W. 874, 99 Am. St. Rep. 571, Dobie Cas. Bailments and Carriers, 159; Cutler v. Bonney, 30 Mich. 259, 18 Am. Rep. 127; Merritt v. Claghorn, 23 Vt. 177. And see Vance v. Throckmorton, 5 Bush (Ky.) 42, 96 Am. Dec. 327; Mowers v. Fethers, 61 N. Y. 34, 19 Am. Rep. 244.

[31] 33 N. Y. 571, 88 Am. Dec. 405. See, also, FAY v. PACIFIC IMP. CO., 93 Cal. 253, 26 Pac. 1099, 28 Pac. 943, 16 L. R. A. 188, 27 Am. St. Rep. 198, Dobie Cas. Bailments and Carriers, 146; Pettit v. Thomas, 103 Ark. 593, 148 S. W. 501, 42 L. R. A. (N. S.) 122.

[32] See Rev. Civ. Code La. art. 2939; Woodworth v. Morse, 18 La. Ann. 156. In most of the cases before the courts the evidence has tended to show negligence on the innkeeper's part, which is sufficient to hold the innkeeper liable under any of the rules. Pinkerton v. Woodward, 33 Cal. 557, 91 Am. Dec. 657; Woodward v. Birch, 4 Bush (Ky.) 510. And see Mateer v. Brown, 1 Cal. 221, 231, 52 Am. Dec. 303.

[33] Woodworth v. Morse, 18 La. Ann. 156; Wies v. Hoffman House, 28 Misc. Rep. 225, 59 N. Y. Supp. 38; Shultz v. Wall, 134 Pa. 262, 19 Atl. 742, 8 L. R. A. 97, 19 Am. St. Rep. 686; McDaniels v. Robinson, 26 Vt. 316, 62 Am. Dec.

Act of God or the Public Enemy

No case seems to extend the innkeeper's liability beyond that of the common carrier and to hold him responsible for any loss or injury due, without fault on his part, either to an act of God or the public enemy.[34] The meaning of the two terms will be fully explained under carriers of goods.

Inherent Nature of the Goods

Another well-recognized exception to the innkeeper's liability (even when he is held as an insurer) is in cases of loss or injury caused solely by the inherent nature of the goods.[35] Thus, when fruits perish, or volatile liquids evaporate, or horses sicken and die, without fault on the part of the innkeeper, he is in no wise held responsible for such loss or damage, even by courts holding the doctrine of strict insurance. This is sometimes considered as falling under the act of God.

Public Authority

Nor would the innkeeper be liable, even under the doctrine of strict insurance, when the goods were taken from the inn by public authority.[36] It is hardly necessary to point out the inconsistency of a system of law that ordered a person to surrender goods and then held him responsible for yielding to its mandate. Accordingly, when the goods of the guest are affected with contagious diseases, and are taken by public power and burned, or when they are seized in execution, attachment, or similar process, the innkeeper must surrender the goods, and incurs no responsibility by so doing.

Fault of Guest or His Servant or Companion

An innkeeper is not liable for the loss of the goods of the guest, when the loss is due to the fault or negligence of the guest himself,[37] or that of his servants or companions.[38] Thus an un-

574; Dunbier v. Day, 12 Neb. 596, 12 N. W. 109, 41 Am. Rep. 772; Spring v. Hager, 145 Mass. 186, 13 N. E. 479, 1 Am. St. Rep. 451.

[34] Mason v. Thompson, 9 Pick. (Mass.) 283, 20 Am. Dec. 471; Richmond v. Smith, 8 B. & C. (Eng.) 9. But if the innkeeper is negligent in failing to protect the goods from the act of God, he is liable. Scheffer v. Corson, 5 S. D. 233, 58 N. W. 555.

[35] Howe Machine Co. v. Pease, 49 Vt. 477; METCALF v. HESS, 14 Ill. 129, Dobie Cas. Bailments and Carriers, 160.

[36] This principle is applicable to bailments in general (as we have seen), and (as we shall see) even forms an exception to the rigid insuring liability of the common carrier of goods. See ante, § 16; post, p. 338.

[37] Watson v. Loughran, 112 Ga. 837, 38 S. E. 82; Purvis v. Coleman, 21 N. Y. 111; Fowler v. Dorlon, 24 Barb. (N. Y.) 384; LANIER v. YOUNG-

[38] Houser v. Tully, 62 Pa. 92, 1 Am. Rep. 390; Calye's Case, 8 Coke (Eng.) 32.

necessary display of money or valuables, or leaving them where they would tempt thieves, may be such negligence.[39] But failure to lock or bolt his door is not necessarily negligence on the part of the guest.[40] It is evidence, however, from which a jury under varying circumstances either may or may not find the guest guilty of negligence.[41] Nor is the innkeeper exonerated because a theft is committed by a fellow guest, with whom the owner of the stolen goods had consented to occupy the same room.[42]

As usually invoked, the rule is simply an application of the great doctrine of contributory negligence. Accordingly, there

BLOOD, 73 Ala. 587, Dobie Cas. Bailments and Carriers, 162; Spring v. Hager, 145 Mass. 186, 13 N. E. 479, 1 Am. St. Rep. 451; Walsh v. Porterfield, 87 Pa. 376; Mason v. Thompson, 9 Pick. (Mass.) 280, 20 Am. Dec. 471; Berkshire Woolen Co. v. Proctor, 7 Cush. (Mass.) 417; Jalie v. Cardinal, 35 Wis. 118, 130; Hadley v. Upshaw, 27 Tex. 547, 86 Am. Dec. 654; Burrows v. Trieber, 21 Md. 320, 83 Am. Dec. 590; Elcox v. Hill, 98 U. S. 218, 25 L. Ed. 103; Morgan v. Ravey, 6 Hurl. & N. (Eng.) 265; Cashill v. Wright, 6 El. & Bl. (Eng.) 891; Oppenheim v. Hotel Co., L. R. 6 C. P. (Eng.) 515. But see Rubenstein v. Cruikshanks, 54 Mich. 199, 19 N. W. 954, 52 Am. Rep. 806. An innkeeper is liable for the safe-keeping of the valise and box of a peddler, his guest, although he was not notified of the nature and value of their contents, and the peddler was too drunk to take proper care of it. Rubenstein v. Cruikshanks, 54 Mich. 199, 19 N. W. 954, 52 Am. Rep. 806. Evidence of gross neglect of the owner of property, to exempt the innkeeper from liability for its loss, must be confined to the period while he was a guest at the innkeeper's house. Burrows v. Trieber, 21 Md. 320, 83 Am. Dec. 590.

39 Cunningham v. Bucky, 42 W. Va. 671, 26 S. E. 442, 35 L. R. A. 850, 57 Am. St. Rep. 878; Armistead v. Wilde, 17 Q. B. (Eng.) 261; Cashill v. Wright, 6 El. & Bl. (Eng.) 891. Whether or not this is negligence would depend on the circumstances of the particular case.

40 Fuller v. Coats, 18 Ohio St. 343; Smith v. Wilson, 36 Minn. 334, 31 N. W. 176, 1 Am. St. Rep. 669; Buddenburg v. Benner, 1 Hilt. (N. Y.) 84; Classen v. Leopold, 2 Sweeney (N. Y.) 705; Gile v. Libby, 36 Barb. (N. Y.) 70; Murchison v. Sergent, 69 Ga. 206, 47 Am. Rep. 754; Bohler v. Owens, 60 Ga. 185; LANIER v. YOUNGBLOOD, 73 Ala. 587, 594, Dobie Cas. Bailments and Carriers, 162; Spring v. Hager, 145 Mass. 186, 13 N. E. 479, 1 Am. St. Rep. 451; Batterson v. Vogel, 10 Mo. App. 235; Profilet v. Hall, 14 La. Ann. 524; Spice v. Bacon, 36 Law T. N. S. (Eng.) 896; Herbert v. Markwell, 45 Law T. N. S. (Eng.) 649; Morgan v. Ravey, 2 Fost. & F. (Eng.) 283, 6 Hurl. & N. 265; Oppenheim v. Hotel Co., L. R. 6 C. P. (Eng.) 515; Mitchell v. Woods, 16 Law T. N. S. (Eng.) 676.

41 Bohler v. Owens, 60 Ga. 185; Spring v. Hager, 145 Mass. 186, 13 N. E. 479, 1 Am. St. Rep. 451; Murchison v. Sergent, 69 Ga. 206, 47 Am. Rep. 754; Oppenheim v. Hotel Co., L. R. 6 C. P. (Eng.) 515; Spice v. Bacon, 36 Law T. N. S. (Eng.) 896; Herbert v. Markwell, 45 Law T. N. S. (Eng.) 649.

42 Olson v. Crossman, 31 Minn. 222, 17 N. W. 375; Gile v. Libby, 36 Barb. (N. Y.) 70; Buddenburg v. Benner, 1 Hilt. (N. Y.) 84. If the fellow guest be the companion of the guest, and shares the room at the instance of the guest, then the innkeeper is not liable. See Calye's Case, 8 Coke (Eng.) 32; Horslow's Case, Y. B. 22 Hen. VI, 21, pl. 38.

must first be fault or negligence on the part of the guest, or some one whose conduct is chargeable to him, and next this must have contributed to the loss.[43] Thus, when the guest gave detailed instructions to the innkeeper as to the method of caring for the goods, and loss occurs as a result of following such instructions, there can be no recovery.[44]

The question of what acts on the part of the guest constitute negligence, and whether they contributed to the loss, is one of fact for the jury, to be determined by the facts of each case,[45] unless both the facts and the inference to be drawn from the facts are so clear that the judge can take the question from the jury and decide it himself as a matter of law.[46] The case probably most frequently before the courts is the guest's failure to lock or bolt the door of his room.[47] It is impossible to say this is, or is not, negligent, without stating the facts of the individual case. Thus the value of the property kept in the room, knowledge of such value by persons about the inn, the character of such persons, the location of the room rendering unobserved access to it easy or difficult, and many other considerations, might enter into the problem. The same might be said as to a guest's publicly exhibiting his money or other valuables.[48] In the absence of statute or unique circumstances, it is ordinarily held that the guest's retention of valuables in his possession,[49] or the failure of the guest to inform the innkeeper of the value of a package deposited with him,[50] is not of itself such negligence as will bar a recovery by the guest for loss of, or damage to, the goods.

[43] LANIER v. YOUNGBLOOD, 73 Ala. 587, Doble Cas. Bailments and Carriers, 162; Armistead v. Wilde, 7 Q. B. (Eng.) 261.

[44] Owens v. Geiger, 2 Mo. 39, 22 Am. Dec. 435.

[45] Jefferson Hotel Co. v. Warren, 128 Fed. 565, 63 C. C. A. 193; Hadley v. Upshaw, 27 Tex. 547, 86 Am. Dec. 654. The burden of proving this rests on the innkeeper. If, in spite of such negligence on the guest's part, the innkeeper might, by the exercise of reasonable care, still have averted the loss, the innkeeper is liable. Watson v. Loughran, 112 Ga. 837, 38 S. E. 82. As to what is contributory negligence on the part of the guest, see Eden v. Drey, 75 Ill. App. 102; Baehr v. Downey, 133 Mich. 163, 94 N. W. 750, 103 Am. St. Rep. 444.

[46] LANIER v. YOUNGBLOOD, 73 Ala. 587, Doble Cas. Bailments and Carriers, 162.

[47] See cases in notes 40 and 41.

[48] See cases cited in note 39.

[49] Smith v. Wilson, 36 Minn. 334, 31 N. W. 176, 1 Am. St. Rep. 669; Murchison v. Sergent, 69 Ga. 206, 47 Am. Rep. 754.

[50] Baehr v. Downey, 133 Mich. 163, 94 N. W. 750, 103 Am. St. Rep. 444; Bowell v. De Wald, 2 Ind. App. 303, 28 N. E. 430, 50 Am. St. Rep. 240; Coskery v. Nagle, 83 Ga. 696, 10 S. E. 491, 6 L. R. A. 483, 20 Am. St. Rep. 333.

Reasonable Regulations of the Innkeeper

To enable the innkeeper duly to discharge his duty to the public and to safeguard the goods of the traveler from loss, while in a house ever open to the public, it may become necessary for the innkeeper to provide special means, and to make necessary regulations and requirements to be observed by the guest. When such means are proper and such regulations are reasonable, and when they are brought to the actual notice of the guest, the innkeeper will not be responsible for any loss due to a failure on the part of a guest to comply with such regulations.[51]

It should be noted that the innkeeper cannot reduce his responsibility simply by a regulation to that effect, though he may require certain conduct on the part of the guest with a penalty of exemption of the innkeeper from liability for loss resulting from the guest's failure to conduct himself as directed.[52] The validity of the regulation is first dependent upon its reasonableness,[53] and next, to be binding on a particular guest, it must be brought to his notice.[54] Thus a regulation requiring guests to deposit clothing at the office would be clearly unreasonable.[55] Posting the notice in the guest's room, on the question of bringing the notice to the attention of the guest, is not conclusive.[56] Such notices, too, are to be construed strictly against the innkeeper.[57]

The particular regulation most frequently before the courts requires that property of small bulk and great value be left at the office of the inn for deposit in the safe.[58] In most states statutes have been passed (which will subsequently be discussed) imposing this same duty on the guest.[59]

[51] Fuller v. Coats, 18 Ohio St. 343; Purvis v. Coleman, 21 N. Y. 111; Berkshire Woollen Co. v. Proctor, 7 Cush. (Mass.) 417; Cashill v. Wright, 6 El. & Bl. (Eng.) 891.

[52] Stanton v. Leland, 4 E. D. Smith (N. Y.) 88.

[53] Fuller v. Coats, 18 Ohio St. 343; Watson v. Loughran, 112 Ga. 837, 38 S. E. 82.

[54] Van Wyck v. Howard, 12 How. Prac. (N. Y.) 147.

[55] Stanton v. Leland, 4 E. D. Smith (N. Y.) 88.

[56] Bodwell v. Bragg, 29 Iowa, 232.

[57] Pope v. Hall, 14 La. Ann. 324; Milford v. Wesley, Wils. (Ind.) 119; Brown Hotel Co. v. Burckhardt, 13 Colo. App. 59, 56 Pac. 188.

[58] Fuller v. Coats, 18 Ohio St. 343; Stanton v. Leland, 4 E. D. Smith (N. Y.) 88; Profilet v. Hall, 14 La. Ann. 524; Milford v. Wesley, 2 Wils. (Ind.) 119.

[59] Post, § 98.

SAME—SAME—TO WHAT GOODS THE INNKEEPER'S LIABILITY EXTENDS

97. The innkeeper's liability as such extends to all the goods of the guest brought within the inn, except—

EXCEPTIONS: (a) Goods for show or for sale.

(b) Goods retained in the exclusive custody of the guest.

Goods of Guests Only

Innkeepers are liable as such for goods deposited with them only by guests of their inns.[60] The keeper of an inn may, of course, incur a liability as bailee for the safe-keeping of goods which he has voluntarily undertaken to keep for others than guests, and the extent of this liability is subsequently considered.[61] The exceptional liability, however, imposed by law on the innkeeper, is limited to the goods of those who are technically guests. It is sufficient, though, if the guest have a special property, or even a possessory interest, in the goods, such as that of a bailee or an agent. He need not be the owner of the goods to impose the exceptional responsibility on the innkeeper.[62]

More Than is Necessary for Traveling

The liability of an innkeeper for a loss by his guest ordinarily extends to all the movable goods and money which are placed

[60] In Tulane Hotel Co. v. Holohan, 112 Tenn. 214, 79 S. W. 113, 105 Am. St. Rep. 930, 2 Ann. Cas. 345, where the goods were received on the presumption that one would become a guest, but he did not, it was held that the technical innkeeping responsibility did not arise. See, also, Strauss v. County Hotel Co., 12 Q. B. D. (Eng.) 27; Miles v. International Hotel Co., 167 Ill. App. 440; Towson v. Havre de Grace Bank, 6 Har. & J. (Md.) 47, 14 Am. Dec. 254; McDaniels v. Robinson, 28 Vt. 387, 67 Am. Dec. 720; Grinnell v. Cook, 3 Hill (N. Y.) 485, 38 Am. Dec. 663. If a servant is robbed of his master's money or goods while a guest at an inn, the master may maintain an action against the innkeeper. Towson v. Havre de Grace Bank, supra. This principle applies to one who hires a horse and chaise from the owner, and intrusts them to an innkeeper. Mason v. Thompson, 9 Pick. (Mass.) 280, 20 Am. Dec. 471. A guest who is a mere depositary of the goods he brings with him may maintain an action against the innkeeper for their loss. Kellogg v. Sweeney, 1 Lans. (N. Y.) 397. Plaintiff's stallion stood at defendant's inn certain days each week, under an agreement, made for the season, for serving mares. Plaintiff had the key to the stall, and fed and cared for the horse. Defendant furnished the oats for the horse, and meals for the plaintiff, at a price less than the ordinary rates to travelers. Held, that defendant's custody was not that of innkeeper, and that, therefore, he was not liable for the destruction of the barn and horse by fire without negligence on his part. Mowers v. Fethers, 61 N. Y. 34, 19 Am. Rep. 244.

[61] See post, § 103.

[62] Kellogg v. Sweeney, 1 Lans. (N. Y.) 397.

within the inn.[63] It is sometimes claimed that an innkeeper is liable only for such an amount of money as is necessary for the reasonable expenses of the guest, and for such goods as are necessary for the journey in question.[64] This distinction is sought to be maintained upon the analogy to the case of a carrier of passengers, who is liable only for money or articles convenient to the traveler on his journey as these alone come within the technical definition of baggage, and not for goods or merchandise, as such.[65] A brief consideration of the nature of the passenger's baggage, the methods of handling it on fast trains, and its relation to freight, will show that the analogy is not a happy one. Accordingly this contention is not supported by the cases, and innkeepers have frequently been held liable both for goods and money, which could not be included within the technical definition of baggage.[66]

But as to the amount of goods or money for which an innkeeper may be held liable, it would seem that, though this is not confined to baggage, there must be some limit, and that the innkeeper cannot be held liable as such for any very extraordinary amount of goods or any extremely unusual sum of money that the guest may see fit to bring to the inn. It is not clear just what such limit would be, but this would probably be governed by consider-

[63] Smith v. Wilson, 36 Minn. 334, 31 N. W. 176, 1 Am. St. Rep. 669; Eden v. Drey, 75 Ill. App. 102; Berkshire Woollen Co. v. Proctor, 7 Cush. (Mass.) 417; Towson v. Havre de Grace Bank, 6 Har. & J. (Md.) 47, 14 Am. Dec. 254; Wilkins v. Earle, 44 N. Y. 172, 4 Am. Rep. 655; Johnson v. Richardson, 17 Ill. 302, 305, 63 Am. Dec. 369. Cf. Simon v. Miller, 7 La. Ann. 360; Weisenger v. Taylor, 1 Bush (Ky.) 275, 89 Am. Dec. 626. But it is otherwise by statute in Maine. See Noble v. Milliken, 74 Me. 225, 43 Am. Rep. 581.

[64] This limitation is held proper in the following cases: Profilet v. Hall, 14 La. Ann. 524; Treiber v. Burrows, 27 Md. 130; Pettigrew v. Barnum, 11 Md. 434, 69 Am. Dec. 212; Sasseen v. Clark, 37 Ga. 242.

[65] See post, § 197.

[66] Eden v. Drey, 75 Ill. App. 102; Taylor v. Monnot, 4 Duer (N. Y.) 116; Kellogg v. Sweeney, 1 Lans. (N. Y.) 397; Wilkins v. Earle, 44 N. Y. 172, 4 Am. Rep. 655; Needles v. Howard, 1 E. D. Smith (N. Y.) 54; Pinkerton v. Woodward, 33 Cal. 557, 91 Am. Dec. 657; Berkshire Woollen Co. v. Proctor, 7 Cush. (Mass.) 417; Rubenstein v. Cruikshanks, 54 Mich. 199, 19 N. W. 954, 52 Am. Rep. 806; Smith v. Wilson, 36 Minn. 334, 31 N. W. 176, 1 Am. St. Rep. 669; Quinton v. Courtney, 2 N. C. 40; Sasseen v. Clark, 37 Ga. 242; Kent v. Shuckard, 2 Barn. & Adol. (Eng.) 803; Armistead v. White, 6 Eng. Law & Eq. 349. In Clute v. Wiggins, 14 Johns. (N. Y.) 175, 7 Am. Dec. 448, the guest recovered for certain bags of wheat and barley. In Piper v. Manny, 21 Wend. (N. Y.) 282, the recovery was for a tub of butter. In Sneider v. Geiss, 1 Yeates (Pa.) 34, the innkeeper was held liable for 230 Spanish milled dollars. In Hulett v. Swift, 33 N. Y. 571, 88 Am. Dec. 405, the plaintiff recovered the value of his horses, wagon, and a load of buckskin goods.

ations of practical common sense, and would be a question for the jury under proper instructions from the court.[67]

Goods Arriving Before or After the Guest

If the innkeeping relation be actually established, the high responsibility of the innkeeper is the same, whether the goods be in the possession of the guest when he arrives at the inn, whether the property be conveyed to the inn before his arrival, or at a subsequent time during his stay at the inn.[68] Indeed, the same responsibility attaches to the innkeeper, even if the guest did not own the goods when he arrived, but purchased them and had them sent to the inn after his arrival. Provided the goods are brought to the inn, or accepted outside the inn, by the innkeeper or his servants, as the goods of a guest, the innkeeper's unusual liability is in no way affected by the relation in time which the arrival of the goods bears to the arrival of the guest. Of course, this particular responsibility continues only so long as the relation of innkeeper and guest actually exists.

Goods Received within the Inn

The liability of the innkeeper does not attach, unless the goods are brought within the inn (infra hospitium), or otherwise placed within his control or custody.[69] It is not necessary, though, that the goods should be placed in his special keeping; but it is sufficient if they are properly deposited in the inn or intrusted to the care of his servants.[70] The innkeeper's liability, however, extends to goods in all parts of the inn, and even to the outbuildings connected with the inn.[71]

67 Mateer v. Brown, 1 Cal. 221, 52 Am. Dec. 303.

68 Flint v. Illinois Hotel Co., 149 Ill. App. 404; Pinkerton v. Woodward, 33 Cal. 557, 91 Am. Dec. 657; Mateer v. Brown, 1 Cal. 221, 52 Am. Dec. 303. But see Tulane Hotel Co. v. Holohan, 112 Tenn. 214, 79 S. W. 113, 105 Am. St. Rep. 930, 2 Ann. Cas. 345, where the owner sent the goods to the inn, but did not himself go to the inn.

69 Mason v. Thompson, 9 Pick. (Mass.) 280, 20 Am. Dec. 471; Piper v. Manny, 21 Wend. (N. Y.) 282; Albin v. Presby, 8 N. H. 408, 29 Am. Dec. 679; Minor v. Staples, 71 Me. 316, 36 Am. Rep. 318; Norcross v. Norcross, 53 Me. 163; Bennet v. Mellor, 5 Term R. (Eng.) 273; Kent v. Shuckard, 2 Barn. & Adol. (Eng.) 803; Vance v. Throckmorton, 5 Bush (Ky.) 41, 96 Am. Dec. 327; Windham v. Mead, 4 Leon. (Eng.) 96; Hawley v. Smith, 25 Wend. (N. Y.) 642; Maloney v. Bacon, 33 Mo. App. 501.

70 Labold v. Southern Hotel Co., 54 Mo. App. 567; Curtis v. Murphy, 63 Wis. 4, 22 N. W. 825, 53 Am. Rep. 242; 2 Kent, Comm. 593; Story, Bailm. § 479; McDonald v. Edgerton, 5 Barb. (N. Y.) 560; Rockwell v. Proctor, 39 Ga. 105.

71 Albin v. Presby, 8 N. H. 408, 410, 29 Am. Dec. 679; Burrows v. Trieber, 21 Md. 320, 83 Am. Dec. 590; McDonald v. Edgerton, 5 Barb. (N. Y.) 560; Bennet v. Mellor, 5 Term R. (Eng.) 273; Richmond v. Smith, 8 Barn. & C.

When the goods of the guest come into the control of the innkeeper or his servants outside the inn, his high responsibility begins immediately upon such control, even before the goods reach the inn. Thus, as we have seen, when the innkeeper sends his porter to the station to receive the baggage of travelers, the innkeeping liability dates from such delivery to the porter.[72] If the goods are once intrusted to the innkeeper or his servants, or properly deposited within the inn, the innkeeper, of course, remains liable as such, if, on his own initiative, the goods are kept outside the inn.[73] A different result would follow, though, if the goods were put outside the inn, either by the guest himself or by virtue of his instructions.[74]

An innkeeper who also keeps a sea-bathing house, separate from the inn, is not liable as an innkeeper for goods and clothes of his guests, left there while the guests were bathing;[75] but he is in such

(Eng.) 9. But see Sanders v. Spencer, 3 Dyer (Eng.) 266b. In Clute v. Wiggins, 14 Johns. (N. Y.) 175, 7 Am. Dec. 448, the guest put his sleigh, loaded with wheat, into an outhouse appurtenant to the inn, where loads of the kind were usually received, but without specially committing it to the innkeeper. The grain was stolen in the night, and the innkeeper was held liable for the loss. It would be otherwise if a traveler, on arriving at an inn, should place his loaded wagon under an open shed, not appurtenant to the inn, and near the highway, and make no request to the innkeeper to take it into his custody.

72 Ante, p. —; Sasseen v. Clark, 37 Ga. 242; Dickinson v. Winchester, 4 Cush. (Mass.) 114, 50 Am. Dec. 760. An innkeeper employing a transportation company to furnish an omnibus and wagon to receive guests of the hotel at a railway depot, and to transport them and their baggage to the hotel, is liable if the baggage of a guest delivered to such company is by it lost before reaching the hotel. Coskery v. Nagle, 83 Ga. 696, 10 S. E. 491, 6 L. R. A. 483, 20 Am. St. Rep. 333.

73 Piper v. Manny, 21 Wend. (N. Y.) 282; Cohen v. Manuel, 91 Me. 274, 39 Atl. 1030, 40 L. R. A. 491, 64 Am. St. Rep. 225. An innkeeper is responsible for the safe-keeping of a load of goods belonging to a traveler who stops at his inn for the night, if the carriage containing the goods be deposited in a place designated by the servant of the innkeeper, although such place be an open uninclosed space near the public highway. Hilton v. Adams, 71 Me. 19. But see Albin v Presby, 8 N. H. 408, 29 Am. Dec. 679. So, an innkeeper, on a fair day, upon being asked by a traveler, then driving a gig, of which he was the owner, "whether he had room for the horse," put the horse into the stable of the inn, received the traveler, with some goods, into the inn, and placed the gig in the open street, without the inn yard, where he was accustomed to place the carriages of his guests on fair days. The gig having been stolen from thence, held, that the innkeeper was answerable. Jones v. Tyler, 28 E. C. L. (Eng.) 138.

74 Windham v. Mead, 4 Leon (Eng.) 96; Hawley v. Smith, 25 Wend. (N. Y.) 642.

75 Minor v. Staples, 71 Me. 316, 36 Am. Rep. 318.

case a mere bailee, and responsible accordingly.[76] One may be an innkeeper without being a bath-house keeper, or he may be a bath-house keeper without being an innkeeper, or the same person may engage in both employments, without incurring the liability of an innkeeper in transactions falling within his employment as the keeper of a bath-house. In like manner, a livery stable keeper may also be a common carrier of passengers; but by so doing he does not become responsible in the one capacity for liabilities incurred in the other. This does not apply to bathrooms attached to or kept within hotels, but to separate buildings, erected upon the seashore, and used solely as places in which those who bathe in the sea change their garments, and leave their clothes and other valuables while so bathing.

Exceptions to Innkeeper's Extraordinary Liability—Goods for Show or for Sale

A well-defined exception to the innkeeper's extraordinary liability exists when the guest applies for a room for the purpose of displaying goods for show or for sale.[77] Thus, when the guest takes to his room, not merely goods for safe-keeping and articles for his personal use, but merchandise, such as watches and jewelry, for the purpose of show or sale, he is then using the inn, not only as an inn, but also as a showroom or salesroom. It is accordingly not contemplated that the exceptional responsibility imposed on the innkeeper by the common law should be stretched to cover such cases.

The guest here, by becoming an active seller or exhibitor, and inviting the public to come and go in the room in which the goods are exhibited, materially increases the risk of their loss, and the innkeeper is therefore, as to such goods, properly absolved from his special liability.[78]

Same—Goods in Exclusive Possession of Guest

An innkeeper may be relieved from responsibility by showing that the guest whose goods have been lost or injured took them

[76] Tombler v. Koelling, 60 Ark. 62, 28 S. W. 795, 27 L. R. A. 502, 46 Am. St. Rep. 146; Bird v. Everard, 4 Misc. Rep. 104, 23 N. Y. Supp. 1008.

[77] 2 Kent, Comm. 596; Story, Bailm. § 476; Fisher v. Kelsey, 121 U. S. 383, 7 Sup. Ct. 929, 30 L. Ed. 930, affirming (C. C.) 16 Fed. 71; Myers v. Cottrill, 5 Biss. 465, Fed. Cas. No. 9,985; Burgess v. Clements, 4 Maule & S. (Eng.) 306; Mowers v. Fethers, 61 N. Y. 34, 19 Am. Rep. 244; Becker v. Haynes (C. C.) 29 Fed. 441. Nor is the rule changed by the fact that the guest sleeps in the room with the articles. Myers v. Cottrill, supra. But for personal goods of the guest (not for show or sale) in the same room the innkeeper is liable as such.

[78] Scheffer v. Corson, 5 S. D. 233, 58 N. W. 555; Carter v. Hobbs, 12 Mich. 52, 83 Am. Dec. 762; Farnsworth v. Packwood, 1 Starkie (Eng.) 249.

into his exclusive custody; for the innkeeper's responsibility is co-extensive only with his control of the goods.[79] The rule is, of course, the same when the guest intrusts his goods to another guest or inmate,[80] or excludes the innkeeper completely from control of the goods by any special arrangement inconsistent with such control.[81]

As we have already seen, however, it is not necessary, in order to impose liability on the innkeeper as such, that the goods be actually delivered to the innkeeper, so that a bailment is created. All that the law requires is that they be in his general control.[82] A strong showing must therefore be made as to the guest's exclusive custody, in order that the innkeeper may escape from his high responsibility; and a large measure of personal control over the goods may be exercised by the guest, provided it be not exclusive of the innkeeper's general control, without abating the latter's liability. Thus the retention of needed money or valuables on the person of the guest is not ordinarily such exclusive possession as will excuse the innkeeper,[83] nor is the fact that the guest directs his goods to be kept in a certain part of the inn,[84] or that he ordered them taken for his personal use to his bedroom.[85]

SAME—SAME—LIMITATION OF THE INNKEEPER'S LIABILITY

98. The liability of the innkeeper as to the goods of the guest may be limited:

(a) By contract.

(b) By statutes, which usually limit his liability:

(1) In some states, for losses above a certain amount.

(2) In a great many states, on his giving notice, for goods not delivered to the innkeeper to be put in his safe.

79 Vance v. Throckmorton, 5 Bush (Ky.) 41, 96 Am. Dec. 327; Weisenger v. Taylor, 1 Bush (Ky.) 275, 276, 89 Am. Dec. 626.

80 Sneider v. Geiss, 1 Yeates (Pa.) 34; Houser v. Tully, 62 Pa. 92, 1 Am. Rep. 390.

81 Vance v. Throckmorton, 5 Bush (Ky.) 41, 96 Am. Dec. 327.

82 FAY v. PACIFIC IMP. CO., 93 Cal. 253, 26 Pac. 1099, 28 Pac. 943, 16 L. R. A. 188, 27 Am. St. Rep. 198, Dobie Cas. Bailments and Carriers, 146; Read v. Amidon, 41 Vt. 15, 98 Am. Dec. 560; Burrows v. Trieber, 21 Md. 320, 83 Am. Dec. 590.

83 Jalie v. Cardinal, 35 Wis. 118; Smith v. Wilson, 36 Minn. 334, 31 N. W. 176, 1 Am. St. Rep. 669.

84 Fuller v. Coats, 18 Ohio St. 343; Packard v. Northcraft, 2 Metc. (Ky.) 439.

85 Fuller v. Coats, 18 Ohio St. 343; Epps v. Hinds, 27 Miss. 657, 61 Am. Dec. 528; Shaw v. Ray, 1 Cr. & Dix, C. C. (Ireland) 84.

By Contract

The exceptional liability of the innkeeper, like that of the common carrier may, no doubt, be restricted, in a measure at least, by an express contract with the guest.[86] Though there are few cases on the subject, it would seem that such contracts should be valid, provided they do not contravene a sound public policy. On principle, he should be permitted to reduce his liability by express contract to that of an ordinary bailee for hire.[87] But, by virtue of his public profession and calling, he would hardly be permitted, if the analogy of the common carrier counts for anything, to exempt himself from the consequences of his negligence; and surely he could not contract away his liability arising out of his own fraud or active wrongdoing. Nor could he thus relieve himself from all responsibility for the acts of his servants.

The innkeeper, though, cannot reduce his liability, on the theory of an implied contract, by merely posting notices in a room, even though the guest occupy the room.[88] Nor could he limit his responsibility by a mere printed heading in the register of an inn, even though the guest sign this register, unless the attention of the guest is directed to such heading or notice and he indicates his assent thereto.[89]

[86] On this point, Mr. Schouler says: "The right of mitigating this responsibility by special contract with the particular guest receives, thus far, but slight attention from our courts; yet, if analogies can serve us, they tend plainly to the conclusion that any innkeeper may make a qualified or limited acceptance of his guest's property, though not, in America at least, to the extent of divesting himself of all responsibility for the acts of servants, fellow lodgers, or others about the inn, nor certainly so as to excuse misconduct or the want of ordinary care on his own part." Schouler, Bailm. (2d Ed.) § 309. The right is also recognized by Kent (2 Comm. 594), Van Zile (Bailm. & Carr. § 372), and Goddard (Bailm. & Carr. § 186). Mr. Beale, however (Beale, Innkeepers, § 211), seems to question the right; and though the question was not involved in Lane v. Cotton, 1 Salk. (Eng.) 17, Holt, C. J., said that innkeepers are "bound to keep safely, and answer all neglects of those that act under them; and so they would be, though they expressly caution against it."

[87] See the following cases, bearing on the right of the innkeeper thus to limit his liability by contract: Sanders v. Spencer, 3 Dyer (Eng.) 266b; Richmond v. Smith, 8 B. & C. (Eng.) 9, 15 E. C. L. 144; Van Wyck v. Howard, 12 How. Prac. (N. Y.) 147; Fuller v. Coats, 18 Ohio St. 343; McDaniels v. Robinson, 26 Vt. 316, 62 Am. Dec. 574; Pinkerton v. Woodward, 33 Cal. 557, 91 Am. Dec. 657.

[88] Bodwell v. Bragg, 29 Iowa, 232. And see Burbank v. Chapin, 140 Mass. 123, 2 N. E. 934.

[89] Remaley v. Leland, 29 N. Y. Super. Ct. 358; Bernstein v. Sweeny, 33 N. Y. Super. Ct. 271; Olson v. Crossman, 31 Minn. 222, 17 N. W. 375. And see Murchison v. Sergent, 69 Ga. 206, 47 Am. Rep. 754.

We have already seen that the guest must conform to the regulations of the innkeeper, provided these are reasonable and are brought to the actual notice of the guest.[90] This, however, is not on the theory of an implied contract, but rather on the score that the failure of the guest to comply with the regulations, resulting in loss or injury as to the goods, constitutes such contributory negligence on his part as to bar a recovery against the innkeeper.

Though it is sometimes said that an innkeeper's liability may be limited by custom,[91] yet this can be true only on the theory of an implied contract. Therefore a guest is not bound by a custom of which he was ignorant, for his assent thereto cannot properly be presumed.[92]

By Statute—Losses Above a Certain Amount

By statutes in a few states, the liability of innkeepers is limited to a specific amount,[93] or to such things as is usual and prudent for a guest to retain on his person or in his room,[94] or to such goods as are needed by the guest for present use.[95] These statutes simply prescribe a maximum, either in money or in restrictive classes of goods, beyond which the innkeeper's liability does not extend.

Same—Posting Notices Requiring Delivery of Certain Property to Innkeeper

In most states, the statutes limiting the responsibility of the innkeeper provide that an innkeeper may avoid liability as such for the loss of goods not intrusted to his special care by posting notices, in the manner prescribed by the statutes, stating that he has a safe for the deposit of money and valuables and will not be responsible for goods falling within these classes unless they are deposited

[90] Ante, p. 273.

[91] Albin v. Presby, 8 N. H. 408, 29 Am. Dec. 679.

[92] Berkshire Woollen Co. v. Proctor, 7 Cush. (Mass.) 417. When the proprietor of an hotel employs a servant to receive and keep the property of guests while at meals, his liability for the default of this servant in the custody of property so received is not affected by the fact that he has also provided a check room for the safe-keeping of such property. Labold v. Southern Hotel Co., 54 Mo. App. 567.

[93] See Rev. Laws Mass. 1902, c. 102, § 10; Pub. Acts Mich. 1905, No. 42, § 1; Stimson, Am. St. Law, § 4392; Civ. Code Cal. § 1859. The subject of statutory limitations on the innkeeper's liability by statute is admirably discussed in Beale, Innkeepers, c. 31, on which the above treatment is largely based. In an appendix to this work, the statutes of the various states affecting innkeepers are reproduced in full.

[94] Such statutes are frequently qualifications of statutes of the type discussed below. See, for example, Starr & C. Ann. St. Ill. 1896, c. 71, par. 2; Code Iowa 1897, § 3138.

[95] See Rev. St. Me. 1903, c. 29, § 5; Stimson, Am. St. Law, § 4392.

with him.[96] As these statutes differ greatly in their wording, and in the construction placed on them by the courts of the various states, the particular statute and the decisions construing it should always be consulted. A few general observations on these statutes, however, may not be amiss.

Such statutes, being in derogation of the common law, must be strictly construed.[97] The requirements of the particular statute as to the posting of the notice (such as the nature of the notice, type in which it is to be printed, method of posting, etc.) must be strictly complied with by the innkeeper, or he cannot claim the exemption or limitation granted by the statute.[98] Thus, by the better rule (though there are cases to the contrary),[99] even actual notice to the guest is not sufficient if the required statutory notice has not been posted.[1] Again, when the statute requires the innkeeper to have a safe or vault for the deposit of valuables, the innkeeper must provide one or else no advantage accrues to him from the statute.[2]

Under most of the statutes, even if the innkeeper has complied with all the statutory provisions, the innkeeper is not relieved of all liability as to goods not deposited with him. He is not an insurer as to such goods, however, but is liable for loss or damage only as an ordinary bailee for hire; that is, when such loss or damage is due to his negligence or that of his servants.[3] But the effect of such statutes, it is usually held, is to place upon the guest the burden of proving such negligence.[4] For goods deposited with the innkeeper he remains responsible, just as at common law.[5]

96 For specimens of these statutes, see Code Ala. 1896, §§ 2541, 2542; Rev. Code Del. 1852, amended 1893, p. 409 (14 Del. Laws, c. 417, p. 390, § 1); Comp. St. Ky. 1894, § 2176; Rev. Laws Minn. 1905, § 2810. See, also, 1 Stim. Am. St. Law, § 4392.

97 Ramaley v. Leland, 43 N. Y. 539, 3 Am. Rep. 728; LANIER v. YOUNGBLOOD, 73 Ala. 587, Dobie Cas. Bailments and Carriers, 162; Briggs v. Todd, 28 Misc. Rep. 208, 59 N. Y. Supp. 23.

98 Porter v. Gilkey, 57 Mo. 235 (size of type); CHAMBERLAIN v. WEST, 37 Minn. 54, 33 N. W. 114, Dobie Cas. Bailments and Carriers, 59; Olson v. Crossman, 31 Minn. 222, 17 N. W. 375; LANIER v. YOUNGBLOOD, 73 Ala. 587, Dobie Cas. Bailments and Carriers, 162; Beale v. Posey, 72 Ala. 323; Spice v. Bacon, 36 Law T. N. S. (Eng.) 896, 2 Ex. D. 463.

99 Purvis v. Coleman, 21 N. Y. 111. Cf. Shultz v. Wall, 134 Pa. 262, 19 Atl. 742, 8 L. R. A. 97, 19 Am. St. Rep. 686.

1 Batterson v. Vogel, 8 Mo. App. 24; LANIER v. YOUNGBLOOD, 73 Ala. 587, Dobie Cas. Bailments and Carriers, 162; Porter v. Gilkey, 57 Mo. 235.

2 Dunbier v. Day, 12 Neb. 596, 12 N. W. 109, 41 Am. Rep. 772.

3 Medewar v. Hotel Co., [1891] 2 Q. B. (Eng.) 11, 64 L. T. 851; Faucett v. Nichols, 4 Thomp. & C. (N. Y.) 597; Beale v. Posey, 72 Ala. 323, 331.

4 Elcox v. Hill, 98 U. S. 218, 25 L. Ed. 103; Burnham v. Young, 72 Me. 273.

5 Wilkins v. Earle, 44 N. Y. 172, 4 Am. Rep. 655. The same is true, though the deposit is not made, if this is waived by the innkeeper. Friedman v. Breslin, 169 N. Y. 574, 61 N. E. 1129.

The question of what goods must be deposited with the innkeeper is one of no little difficulty. By some statutes, goods needed for the personal use of the guest need not be deposited, but may be retained in the guest's room, or on his person, without diminishing the innkeeper's responsibility.[6] Other statutes enumerate the classes of goods to be deposited, which are usually of small bulk and relatively large value.[7] When this enumeration does not include articles of personal use, of course no deposit of such articles is necessary to fix the common-law liability of the innkeeper.[8] When the enumeration does include such articles, however, the decisions are in conflict. Some cases hold that money for current expenses and personal articles are still impliedly exempted, and the innkeeper remains responsible as at common law.[9] Other cases, probably the greater number, insist that there is no such implied exception, and that the guest has his choice of depositing the goods and insisting on the technical innkeeping liability, or of not depositing them, in which case the innkeeper is, like an ordinary bailee, liable only for negligence.[10] Perhaps the wording of the individual statutes may account in a measure for much of this conflict.

SAME—THE RIGHT OF COMPENSATION AND LIEN—THE COMPENSATION OF THE INNKEEPER

99. The innkeeper is entitled to his compensation and may require payment in advance. His charges, however, must be reasonable.

The innkeeper is, of course, entitled to his proper compensation, as this is the sole advantage that he derives from the innkeeping relation.[11] Owing to his intimate association with, and his im-

[6] See, for example, Rev. Code Del. 1852, amended 1893, p. 409 (14 Del. Laws, c. 417, p. 390, § 1); Code Iowa 1897, § 3138; Laws Neb. 1905, c. 81, § 2.

[7] See, for example, Comp. St. Ky. 1894, § 2176; Voorhies' Rev. Civ. Code La. 1889, art. 2969; Rev. Laws Minn. 1905, § 2810. For cases construing such provisions, see Rains v. Maxwell House Co., 112 Tenn. 219, 79 S. W. 114, 64 L. R. A. 470, 2 Ann. Cas. 488; Briggs v. Todd, 28 Misc. Rep. 208, 59 N. Y. Supp. 23.

[8] Treiber v. Burrows, 27 Md. 130.

[9] Maltby v. Chapman, 25 Md. 310; Murchison v. Sergent, 69 Ga. 206, 47 Am. Rep. 754.

[10] Hyatt v. Taylor, 42 N. Y. 258; Rains v. Maxwell House Co., 112 Tenn. 219, 79 S. W. 114, 64 L. R. A. 470, 2 Ann. Cas. 488; Lang v. Arcade Hotel Co., 9 Ohio Dec. 372.

[11] Newton v. Trigg, 1 Shower (Eng.) 268; Baldwin v. Webb, 121 Ga. 416, 49 S. E. 265. See, also, Roche v. Road Driver's Ass'n of New York (Sup.) 96 N. Y. Supp. 205.

portance to, the public, the law requires of the innkeeper, as it does of the common carrier, that his charges be reasonable.[12] Were it not for this qualification, the innkeeper might also evade his duty to receive as guests all proper persons who apply by fixing his compensation so high that the intending guest could not possibly pay it. In the absence of statutes,[13] which are rare in this country, regulating his compensation, the innkeeper may fix his charges as he sees fit, provided that they are reasonable. In determining whether the charges are reasonable in a particular case, the character of the accommodations furnished, the locality of the inn, and various other considerations apply,[14] while evidence as to the charges made for similar accommodations at neighboring inns is relevant and important.[15]

Compelled by law to serve indifferently all proper persons who apply, the innkeeper, like the common carrier, is permitted by law to require payment of his charges in advance.[16] He can therefore demand his compensation as soon as the relation of innkeeper and guest is established.[17] This right, however, is not as a rule exercised by the innkeeper, though many make a practice of enforcing it as to guests who come to the inn without baggage.

Criminal Statutes Protecting Innkeeper's Compensation

The innkeeper is further protected as to his compensation by criminal statutes in most of the states, designed to deter unscrupulous persons from securing entertainment at an inn without payment therefor.[18] Even under these statutes, however, the mere failure to pay the charges of the innkeeper is not made criminal unless it is in some way connected with fraud.[19] Under most of the statutes, it is made a crime to obtain the entertainment with intent to defraud the innkeeper of his charges, in connection with

12 Roche v. Road Driver's Ass'n of New York (Sup.) 96 N. Y. Supp. 205; Newton v. Trigg, 1 Shower (Eng.) 268; Baldwin v. Webb, 121 Ga. 416, 49 S. E. 265.

13 See Banks v. Oden, 1 A. K. Marsh. (Ky.) 546; Com. v. Shortridge, 3 J. J. Marsh. (Ky.) 638.

14 Proctor v. Nicholson, 7 C. & P. (Eng.) 67.

15 Cross v. Wilkins, 43 N. H. 332.

16 Fell v. Knight, 8 M. & W. (Eng.) 276; Mulliner v. Florence, 3 Q. B. D. (Eng.) 484, 47 L. J. Q. B. 700.

17 Medawar v. Grand Hotel Co., [1891] 2 Q. B. (Eng.) 11, 60 L. J. Q. B. 209.

18 See Beale, Innkeepers, c. 32. The constitutionality of such statutes is now well established. State v. Benson, 28 Minn. 424, 10 N. W. 471; State v. Yardley, 95 Tenn. 546, 32 S. W. 481, 34 L. R. A. 656. As penal statutes, they are to be strictly construed. Hutchinson v. Davis, 58 Ill. App. 358.

19 People v. Nicholson, 25 Misc. Rep. 266, 55 N. Y. Supp. 447; People v. Klas, 79 Misc. Rep. 452, 141 N. Y. Supp. 212.

some false pretence.[20] Many statutes also make it a crime for the guest, who has not paid the innkeeper, to remove his baggage surreptitiously from the inn, either apart from, or in connection with, obtaining the entertainment with fraudulent intent.[21] The individual statutes should in all cases be carefully consulted. Usually the statutes include keepers of boarding houses and lodging houses.[22]

SAME—SAME—THE INNKEEPER'S LIEN—ITS NATURE AND EXTENT

100. The innkeeper has a lien, to secure his proper compensation, on all the property within the inn belonging to the guest.

In General

As a further incident of his duty to entertain the public, the common law gives to the innkeeper a lien on the goods of the guest within the inn to secure the payment of his proper charges.[23] The innkeeper can thus retain (until his compensation is paid) the goods brought by the guest to the inn; but he cannot detain the person of the guest, nor could he "strip the guest of his clothes."[24] Since the innkeeper is compelled to receive even persons incompetent to contract, such as married women and infants, his lien is valid in such cases.[25] The lien is similar in its various legal incidents to other common-law liens; but the lien arises on goods brought to the inn by the guest, even though they are never actually delivered to the innkeeper, but are retained by the guest in his own possession. Even property which is exempt from execution and attachment, if brought to the inn, is subject to the innkeeper's lien.[26] As a general rule, then, if the goods

[20] State v. Kingsley, 108 Mo. 135, 18 S. W. 994; Chauncey v. State, 130 Ala. 71, 30 South. 403, 89 Am. St. Rep. 17; Ex parte Williams, 121 Cal. 328, 53 Pac. 706; State v. Black, 75 Wis. 490, 44 N. W. 635.

[21] State v. Engle, 156 Ind. 339, 58 N. E. 698; Commonwealth v. Morton, 6 Luz. Leg. Reg. (Pa.) 207; Commonwealth v. Billig, 25 Pa. Super. Ct. 477.

[22] Commonwealth v. Gough, 3 Kulp. (Pa.) 148.

[23] Horace Waters & Co. v. Gerard, 189 N. Y. 302, 82 N. E. 143, 24 L. R. A. (N. S.) 958, 121 Am. St. Rep. 886, 12 Ann. Cas. 397; R. L. Polk & Co. v. Melenbacker, 136 Mich. 611, 99 N. W. 867; Nance v. O. K. Houck Piano Co. (Tenn.) 155 S. W. 1172; Murray v. Marshall, 9 Colo. 482, 13 Pac. 589, 59 Am. Rep. 152; Manning v. Hollenbeck, 27 Wis. 202; COOK v. KANE, 13 Or. 482, 11 Pac. 226, 57 Am. Rep. 28, Dobie Cas. Bailments and Carriers, 166.

[24] Sunbolf v. Alford, 3 M. & W. (Eng.) 248, 7 L. J. Ex. 60.

[25] Watson v. Cross, 2 Duv. (Ky.) 147.

[26] Swan v. Bournes, 47 Iowa, 501, 29 Am. Rep. 492.

are brought to the inn and are owned by the guest, the innkeeper can detain them as security for his unpaid charges. In most of the states, provision is made by statute for the lien of the innkeeper.[27]

Goods Not Owned by the Guest

There is grave conflict among the courts as to whether the innkeeper has a lien on goods brought to the inn by a guest who is not the owner.[28] When the guest has no actual or apparent right to deposit the goods at the inn, and the innkeeper knows that the guest's possession is wrongful, then clearly it would seem that there is no lien.[29] On the other hand, it seems only fair that the lien should exist, when the guest in charge of the goods is the servant, agent, or bailee of the owner, using the goods about the owner's business, so that authority from the owner to subject the goods to the lien might reasonably be presumed.[30] The lien should also exist, even when no such actual authority on the part of the guest exists, if the owner has so clothed the guest in possession of the goods with the indicia of ownership, that the doctrine of estoppel can be invoked against the owner.[31]

The English courts,[32] however, and in general the American

[27] For specimens of such statutes, see Pub. Acts Mich. 1897, No. 145; Comp. Laws Mich. 1897, §§ 5317-5323; Ballinger's Ann. Codes & St. Wash. § 5975; Rev. St. Tex. 1895, art. 3318; Laws S. D. 1893, c. 102, amending Civ. Code 1887, § 3686.

[28] The question is discussed at some length, with analyses of the cases, in Beale, Innkeepers, §§ 261-265; Van Zile, Bailm. & Carr. §§ 379-383. See, also, the notes in 3 Ann. Cas. 626, and 12 Ann. Cas. 404.

[29] Beale, Innkeepers, § 262, "where the possession of the guest is wrongful, and is known to the innkeeper to be so; and to this extent the doctrine [that the innkeeper has no lien on knowledge that the guest has no title to the goods] is undoubtedly correct." In Gump v. Showalter, 43 Pa. 507, the court denied the right of the innkeeper as to a statutory lien and right of sale on a horse stolen by the guest, but it did not appear that the innkeeper had notice of the theft. In Johnson v. Hill, 3 Stark (Eng.) 172, 3 E. C. L. Rep. 641, the innkeeper's lien was made to depend on "whether the defendant [innkeeper] knew, at the time when the horse was delivered into his custody, that P. [the guest] was not the owner of the property, but a mere wrongdoer." In Black v. Brennan, 5 Dana (Ky.) 311, the innkeeper was given a lien on a stolen horse, when he had no knowledge of this fact.

[30] ROBINS & CO. v. GRAY, [1895] 2 Q. B. (Eng.) 501, Dobie Cas. Bailments and Carriers, 164, a leading case on the whole subject; Manning v. Hollenbeck, 27 Wis. 202; R. L. Polk & Co. v. Melenbacker, 136 Mich. 611, 99 N. W. 867.

[31] This seems to follow from the application of the general principle of estoppel. See, also, R. L. Polk & Co. v. Melenbacker, 136 Mich. 611, 99 N. W. 867.

[32] ROBINS & CO. v. GRAY, [1895] 2 Q. B. (Eng.) 501, Dobie Cas. Bailments and Carriers, 164; Robinson v. Walter, 3 Bulst. 269; Snead v. Watkins, 1 C. B. N. S. 267; Gordon v. Selber, 25 Q. B. D. 491.

courts,[33] hold that the innkeeper can claim his lien on whatever goods are brought to the inn by the guest, regardless of the question of actual ownership, if the goods are honestly received by the innkeeper on the strength of the innkeeping relation; and this, even though the guest may have stolen the goods, provided, of course, that the innkeeper is ignorant of this fact.[34] This unusual rule is put on the ground that, since the innkeeper is obliged to receive all persons, with their goods, without inquiries as to the guest's title to the goods, incurring also an exceptional liability as to such goods, he should, as a compensation for the burden thus imposed on him, have a lien on all the goods that come into his control in his character of innkeeper, as belonging to the guest, regardless of the question of the real ownership of the goods.

The American cases, as indicated, have, in general, accepted the English rule, in the absence of statute,[35] though individual judges have protested that the innkeeper should have no such lien on the goods of a third person merely because brought by the guest to

[33] Black v. Brennan, 5 Dana (Ky.) 310; Grinnell v. Cook, 3 Hill (N. Y.) 485, 488, 38 Am. Dec. 663.

[34] The English rule established by ROBINS & CO. v. GRAY, [1895] 2 Q. B. 501, Dobie Cas. Bailments and Carriers, 164 (when guest is not known by the innkeeper to be unlawfully in possession of the goods) gives the innkeeper his lien, even though he knows that the guest is not the owner of the goods. A number of the American cases giving the innkeeper a lien on the goods of another brought by the guest to the inn qualify the rule by requiring that the innkeeper (to have his lien) must have no notice of the ownership of such other person. Singer Mfg. Co. v. Miller, 52 Minn. 516, 518, 55 N. W. 56, 21 L. R. A. 229, 38 Am. St. Rep. 568; COOK v. KANE, 13 Or. 482, 11 Pac. 226, 57 Am. Rep. 28, Dobie Cas. Bailments and Carriers, 166; Covington v. Newberger, 99 N. C. 523, 6 S. E. 205.

[35] See Beale, Innkeepers, § 265. Under statutes the American courts have shown a decided tendency to limit the statutory lien, and to hold that it does not extend to the goods of third persons in the possession of the guest, even when the language of the statute seemed merely to be declaratory of the common law. WERTHEIMER-SWARTS SHOE CO. v. HOTEL STEVENS CO., 38 Wash. 409, 80 Pac. 563, 107 Am. St. Rep. 864, 3 Ann. Cas. 625, Dobie Cas. Bailments and Carriers, 169; Torrey v. McClellan, 17 Tex. Civ. App. 371, 43 S. W. 64; McClain v. Williams, 11 S. D. 227, 76 N. W. 930, 49 L. R. A. 610, 74 Am. St. Rep. 791; WYCKOFF v. SOUTHERN HOTEL CO., 24 Mo. App. 382, Dobie Cas. Bailments and Carriers, 168. The language of the statute was so broad, "belonging to or under the control of their guests," that the statutory lien was held, in Brown Shoe Co. v. Hunt, 103 Iowa, 586, 72 N. W. 765, 39 L. R. A. 291, 64 Am. St. Rep. 198, to cover goods of a third person in the control and possession of the guest. See, also, Lurch v. Wilson, 62 Misc. Rep. 259, 114 N. Y. Supp. 789, awarding the statutory lien to the innkeeper, when the innkeeper had no notice that the property was that of a third person until after the property had been put within the inn.

the inn.[36] This protest certainly seems more in keeping with the analogies of our law, for there is something foreign to the spirit of our jurisprudence in the idea that a mere thief can create in stolen goods, as to which he has no interest whatsoever, a lien in favor of the innkeeper, which shall be paramount to the title of the rightful and innocent owner of the goods. Another answer to the English rule is that the innkeeper has a means of protecting himself, in that he can always demand his compensation in advance. It is worthy of note, too, in the substantially similar case of the common carrier, no lien exists against the lawful owner, when the wrongdoer makes an unauthorized shipment of the goods.[37]

For What Charges

An innkeeper's lien covers all proper charges for the guest's entertainment, including extras, such as wines furnished a guest, as well as the amounts due for board and lodging.[38] The lien is not a general one, as that term is technically used, though each article belonging to the guest is liable for the whole amount due. Thus, there is a lien on a guest's horse, not only for the charges incurred for the horse itself, but for the entertainment of the guest, as well.[39]

The innkeeper, since his lien is not a general one, cannot hold the goods of the guest brought to the inn at a subsequent visit. for unpaid charges incurred by the guest on a previous stay at the inn.[40]

Boarding House Keepers

This lien was limited at common law to the innkeeper, and did not exist in favor of the keeper of a boarding house.[41] There are statutes, however, in most of the states, giving this lien to the

[36] Opinion of Thompson, J., in WYCKOFF v. SOUTHERN HOTEL CO., 24 Mo. App. 382, 390, 391, Dobie Cas. Bailments and Carriers, 168; dissenting opinion of Thayer, J., in COOK v. KANE, 13 Or. 482, page 491, 11 Pac. 226, 57 Am. Rep. 28, Dobie Cas. Bailments and Carriers, 166. In Domestic Sewing-Machine Co. v. Watters, 50 Ga. 573, it was held, in order that the innkeeper may have a lien on the goods of a third person, that services must be performed about the specific article to which the lien attaches.

[37] See post, p. 476. See, also, Fitch v. Newberry, 1 Doug. (Mich.) 1, 40 Am. Dec. 33; Clark v. Lowell & L. R. Co., 9 Gray (Mass.) 231.

[38] Proctor v. Nicholson, 7 Car. & P. (Eng.) 67; Watson v. Cross, 2 Duv. (Ky.) 147.

[39] Mulliner v. Florence, L. R. 3 Q. B. Div. (Eng.) 484.

[40] Jones v. Thurloe, 8 Mod. (Eng.) 172.

[41] Singer Mfg. Co. v. Miller, 52 Minn. 516, 55 N. W. 56, 21 L. R. A. 229, 38 Am. St. Rep. 568; Pollock v. Landis, 36 Iowa, 651; Hursh v. Byers, 29 Mo. 469; Nance v. O. K. Houck Piano Co. (Tenn.) 155 S. W. 1172.

boarding house keeper, thus placing him, in this respect, on an equality with the innkeeper.[42] When the keeper of an inn has in the inn both guests and boarders, the lien exists, in the absence of statute, only against the guests,[43] for as to the boarders the relation of the keeper of the inn is legally that of a boarding house keeper.

SAME—SAME—SAME—THE WAIVER OF THE LIEN

101. The innkeeper may waive his lien by voluntarily parting with possession of the goods, or by any other conduct inconsistent with the continuance of the lien.

Waiver of the Lien

The principles of law governing the waiver of the lien of the ordinary bailee for hire, which have already been discussed,[44] are also in general applicable to the lien of the innkeeper. Thus, as a lien exists only by virtue of possession, when an innkeeper permits his guest to take the goods away, the lien is gone. A surrender of the possession of the goods by the innkeeper to the guest, save for a mere temporary purpose,[45] is an effective waiver of the lien;[46] and, once waived, the lien is not revived by the innkeeper subsequently again securing possession of the goods.[47] But, where the innkeeper is induced to part with the possession of the goods through false and fraudulent representations made by the guest, he does not thereby waive his lien.[48] In such case, the innkeeper can reassert his lien by again assuming possession of the goods, subject, however (it would seem), to the intervening rights of any innocent third parties.

Just as other common-law liens, that of the innkeeper may be waived by any conduct inconsistent with its continuance. There is no lien when credit[49] is extended to the guest for the charges; while the lien is, of course, extinguished by payment, or even

[42] Barnett v. Walker, 39 Misc. Rep. 323, 79 N. Y. Supp. 859; Cady v. McDowell, 1 Lans. (N. Y.) 484; Cross v. Wilkins, 43 N. H. 332; Smith v. Colcord, 115 Mass. 70; Nance v. O. K. Houck Piano Co. (Tenn.) 155 S. W. 1172.

[43] Singer Mfg. Co. v. Miller, 52 Minn. 516, 55 N. W. 56, 21 L. R. A. 229, 38 Am. St. Rep. 568.

[44] Ante, p. 151. See, also, post, p. 478.

[45] Allen v. Smith, 12 C. B. N. S. (Eng.) 638, 6 L. T. 459; Caldwell v. Tutt, 10 Lea (Tenn.) 258, 43 Am. Rep. 307.

[46] Danforth v. Pratt, 42 Me. 50; Grinnell v. Cook, 3 Hill (N. Y.) 486, 38 Am. Dec. 663.

[47] Manning v. Hollenbeck, 27 Wis. 202.

[48] Manning v. Hollenbeck, 27 Wis. 202.

[49] Jones v. Thurloe, 8 Mod. (Eng.) 172.

tender [50] of the amount of the compensation. The innkeeper does not lose his lien, however, by merely taking security [51] for the payment of the guest's bill, nor by levying an execution or attachment [52] on the goods covered by the lien.

SAME—SAME—SAME—THE ENFORCEMENT OF THE LIEN

102. At common law, the innkeeper had by virtue of his lien no right to sell the goods, but this right is now very generally given by statute.

Though the innkeeper could hold the goods under his lien until his proper charges were paid, the lien, like other common-law liens, conferred on him no right to sell the goods in order to make the lien effective.[53] Besides holding the goods, his only remedy, in the absence of statute, was to obtain from a court of equity an order to sell the goods by a proceeding in equity to foreclose the lien.[54] By statutes, however, the right to sell the goods under his lien is very generally given, either by statutes specially affecting the innkeeper or those applying to lienholders in general.[55] Any excess, over and above his compensation and the expenses of the sale, remaining in the innkeeper's hands is held in trust for the guest.

SAME—THE LIABILITY OF THE INNKEEPER AS AN ORDINARY BAILEE

103. An innkeeper may under certain circumstances be an ordinary bailee of goods in his charge. His liability is that

(1) Of an ordinary bailee for hire:

(a) For goods of a guest kept for show or sale.

[50] Gordon v. Cox, 7 Car. & P. (Eng.) 172. And see Allen v. Smith, 12 C. B. N. S. (Eng.) 644, where it is said that an innkeeper, by demanding more than is due, makes a tender unnecessary. Where an innkeeper owes his guest for labor more than she owes for board, he has no lien upon her trunk. Hanlin v. Walters, 3 Colo. App. 519, 34 Pac. 686.

[51] Angus v. McLachlan, L. R. 23 Ch. Div. (Eng.) 330.

[52] Lambert v. Niklass, 45 W. Va. 527, 31 S. E. 951, 44 L. R. A. 561, 72 Am. St. Rep. 828.

[53] Case v. Fogg, 46 Mo. 44; Fox v. McGregor, 11 Barb. (N. Y.) 41, 43; Jones v. Pearle, 1 Strange (Eng.) 556.

[54] Fox v. McGregor, 11 Barb. (N. Y.) 41, 43; Black v. Brennan, 5 Dana (Ky.) 310.

[55] 1 Stimson, Am. Statute Law, § 4393. See, also, Brooks v. Harrison, 41 Conn. 184; Coates v. Acheson, 23 Mo. App. 255.

(b) For goods held under his lien for charges.
(c) For goods of boarders.
(2) Of a gratuitous bailee:
(a) For goods left at the inn for an unreasonable time by a departing guest.
(b) For goods deposited by one not a guest, to be kept without compensation.

In General

An innkeeper may be an ordinary bailee of goods, and liable only as such, without being subject to the exceptional liability of an innkeeper as such. This is generally the case whenever goods in his possession are not being kept by him in his technical innkeeping relation. His rights and liabilities are then measured by the rules applicable to the different classes of ordinary bailments. The cases most frequently arising in this connection have been enumerated in the black letter text.

As an Ordinary Bailee for Hire

As to goods kept by the guest for show or sale,[56] as to goods retained by the keeper of the inn under his lien,[57] and as to the goods of those who reside at the inn as boarders, rather than as guests,[58] it will readily be seen that the keeper of the inn is not

[56] Scheffer v. Corson, 5 S. D. 233, 58 N. W. 555; Williams v. Norvell-Shapleigh Hardware Co., 29 Okl. 331, 116 Pac. 786, 35 L. R. A. (N. S) 350, Ann. Cas. 1913A, 448; Fisher v. Kelsey, 121 U. S. 383, 7 Sup. Ct. 929, 30 L. Ed. 930; Myers v. Cottrill, 5 Biss. 465, Fed. Cas. No. 9,985; Mowers v. Fethers, 61 N. Y. 34, 19 Am. Rep. 244; Needles v. Howard, 1 E. D. Smith, (N. Y.) 54, 61; Carter v. Hobbs, 12 Mich. 52, 83 Am. Dec. 762; Neal v. Wilcox, 49 N. C. 146, 67 Am. Dec. 266.

[57] Murray v. Marshall, 9 Colo. 482, 13 Pac. 589, 59 Am. Rep. 152; Giles v. Fauntleroy, 13 Md. 126; Murray v. Clarke, 2 Daly (N. Y.) 102; Angus v. Maclachlan, 23 Ch. D. (Eng.) 330, 52 L. J. Ch. 587.

[58] Haff v. Adams, 6 Ariz. 395, 59 Pac. 111; Hutchinson v. Donovan, 76 Mo. App. 391; LUSK v. BELOTE, 22 Minn. 468, Dobie Cas. Bailments and Carriers, 148; Lawrence v. Howard, 1 Utah, 143. And see Mowers v. Fethers, 61 N. Y. 34, 19 Am. Rep. 244. So, as to person receiving entertainment at a ball. Carter v. Hobbs, 12 Mich. 52, 83 Am. Dec. 762. An hotel keeper in whose safe a regular boarder deposits money for safe-keeping is, at most, a bailee for hire, and is not liable therefor where his night clerk steals the money from the safe, in the absence of any proof of want of ordinary care in employing him. Taylor v. Downey, 104 Mich. 532, 62 N. W. 716, 29 L. R. A. 92, 53 Am. St. Rep. 472. An innkeeper is not liable for loss of boarder's baggage and other valuables by fire, not shown to have been caused by the negligence of the innkeeper or his servants. Moore v. Long Beach Development Co., 87 Cal. 483, 26 Pac. 92, 22 Am. St. Rep. 265. He is not responsible, except as an ordinary bailee for hire, for the safe-keeping of a horse left in his stable for the night by one who is neither a lodger nor a guest, the stable having been consumed by fire, without negligence on his part. Ingallsbee v.

technically an innkeeper. But in all these cases the innkeeper receives a compensation for his custody or control. The standard by which his liability is measured is therefore that of an ordinary bailee for hire, and, in such cases, the keeper of the inn owes merely the duty of ordinary care and is responsible for loss or injury only for his negligence, which is here his failure to live up to his duty by exercising less than that degree of diligence.[59]

As a Gratuitous Bailee

When the custody of the keeper of the inn is outside of his technical relation as innkeeper, and when he receives no recompense, either express or implied, he is in the position of a mere gratuitous bailee, and as such bound to use only slight care.[60] The most important class of these cases is that of a guest leaving goods with the innkeeper for more than a reasonable length of time after his departure from the inn. Until the lapse of such reasonable time, as we shall see, the exceptional responsibility of the innkeeper continues;[61] but, after the expiration of such time, the keeper of the inn is a mere gratuitous bailee and liable accordingly.[62] The innkeeper is also liable merely as a gratuitous bailee when goods are left in his charge by one who does not become a guest at all, and when there is no agreement, either express or implied, that the innkeeper shall receive any compensation for the care of such goods.[63]

Wood, 33 N. Y. 577, 88 Am. Dec. 409. An innkeeper is not an insurer of the safety of baggage delivered to him to be held as a pledge for money loaned, or for accommodation, by a guest, after he has severed his personal connection with the hotel by surrendering his room and paying his bill. Wear v. Gleason, 52 Ark. 364, 12 S. W. 756, 20 Am. St. Rep. 186.

59 See cases cited in notes 56–58.

60 Doorman v. Jenkins, 2 A. & E. (Eng.) 256, 4 L. J. K. B. 29.

61 Post, § 104.

62 Johnson v. Reynolds, 3 Kan. 257; Miller v. Peeples, 60 Miss. 819, 45 Am. Rep. 423; O'Brien v. Vaill, 22 Fla. 627, 1 South. 137, 1 Am. St. Rep. 219; Whitemore v. Haroldson, 2 Lea (Tenn.) 312. But see Murray v. Marshall, 9 Colo. 482, 13 Pac. 589, 59 Am. Rep. 152; Adams v. Clem, 41 Ga. 65, 5 Am. Rep. 524; George v. Depierris, 17 Misc. Rep. 400, 39 N. Y. Supp. 1082. Of course, if there is a compensation, express or implied, for such keeping of the goods by the keeper of the inn, he is a bailee for hire, and as such bound to exercise ordinary care.

63 Wiser v. Chesley, 53 Mo. 547; Stewart v. Head, 70 Ga. 449; Lawrence v. Howard, 1 Utah, 142; Baker v. Bailey, 103 Ark. 12, 145 S. W. 532, 39 L. R. A. (N. S.) 1085. It is usually held that a clerk at a hotel has no authority as such to receive deposits, so as to impose the liability of a gratuitous bailee on the innkeeper. Booth v. Litchfield, 201 N. Y. 466, 94 N. E. 1078, 35 L. R. A. (N. S.) 710; Oxford Hotel Co. v. Lind, 47 Colo. 57, 107 Pac. 222, 28 L. R. A. (N. S.) 495, and note, 18 Ann. Cas. 983.

THE TERMINATION OF THE RELATION

104. The relation of innkeeper and guest may be terminated—

(a) By the innkeeper for the guest's misconduct or default in payment of reasonable charges for his entertainment.

(b) By the guest at any time, by signifying an intention to do so.

When the relation is terminated, the innkeeper's exceptional liability for the guest's goods is at an end, except that it continues for a reasonable time thereafter to enable the guest to remove his goods.

Termination of the Relation

An innkeeper has no right to terminate his relation as such to his guest except for misconduct on the part of the guest,[64] or for the guest's failure to pay the innkeeper his reasonable charges.[65] It will thus be seen that the innkeeper's obligation is not limited to receiving guests, but he must also continue to keep them until the guest forfeits his right to remain such either by misconduct or default in paying the innkeeper.

Such misconduct must in general be of a nature that would have justified the innkeeper in originally refusing to receive the guest. Thus the innkeeper can terminate the relation as to a guest who is drunk and disorderly and eject the latter from the inn.[66] The innkeeper, too, would be justified in sending from the inn one who becomes affected with a contagious disease, if this can be safely and properly done.[67] This is not strictly speaking misconduct, but the innkeeper finds his justification in the duty of protection which he owes to all his guests. The right of the guest to continue as such is, of course, conditioned on his fulfilling his duty of paying the innkeeper's reasonable compensation. For any default, therefore, in this respect, the innkeeper can immediately ter-

[64] Commonwealth v. Mitchel, 2 Pars. Eq. Cas. (Pa.) 431; Markham v. Brown, 8 N. H. 523, 31 Am. Dec. 209; Howell v. Jackson, 6 Car. & P. (Eng.) 723; Moriarty v. Brooks, Id. 684; State v. Steele, 106 N. C. 766, 11 S. E. 478, 8 L. R. A. 516, 19 Am. St. Rep. 573; The Six Carpenters' Case, 8 Coke (Eng.) 290.

[65] Lawrence v. Howard, 1 Utah, 142. See Schouler, Bailm. (2d Ed.) § 326; Doyle v. Walker, 26 Up. Can. (Canada) Q. B. 502.

[66] McHugh v. Schlosser, 159 Pa. 480, 28 Atl. 291, 23 L. R. A. 574, 39 Am. St. Rep. 699.

[67] Levy v. Corey, 1 City Ct. R. Supp. (N. Y.) 57; McHugh v. Schlosser, 159 Pa. 480, 28 Atl. 291, 23 L. R. A. 574, 39 Am. St. Rep. 699. Such removal must be in an appropriate and becoming manner, that does not endanger the life or health of the sick guest.

minate the relation.[68] When the guest ceases to be a transient, he necessarily ceases to be a guest, and in such case the innkeeper need not keep the guest, just as he would not be bound to receive him as a guest.[69]

The guest can terminate the relation whenever he chooses.[70] Of course, if in so doing he breaks a contract with the innkeeper, he would thereby become liable to the innkeeper for any damages flowing from the breach.[71] But if he does not notify the innkeeper of his intention to terminate the relation, he continues liable for any reasonable charges which accrue.[72] The mere temporary absence, however, of a guest from the inn does not terminate the relation of innkeeper and guest.[73] But the relation is terminated when the guest pays his bill, and his name is stricken from the register of guests, thus freeing him from liability as a guest, and he cannot thereafter, and while he is not a guest, claim the rights of one.[74] The expectation to become a guest at a later date does not continue the relation,[75] terminated at his instance, and for his advantage, by settling his account for entertainment. An innkeeper is chargeable as such because of the profit derived from the entertainment of the guest; so that the right to charge is ordinarily the criterion of the innkeeper's liability. Therefore, when the liability of the guest to be charged as such ceases, his claim on

[68] See cases cited in note 65.

[69] Lamond v. Richard, [1897] 1 Q. B. (Eng.) 541, 66 L. J. Q. B. 315, 76 L. T. 141; Whiting v. Mills, 7 Up. Can. Q. B. (Canada) 450.

[70] O'Brien v. Vaill, 22 Fla. 627, 1 South. 137, 1 Am. St. Rep. 219; Glenn v. Jackson, 93 Ala. 342, 9 South. 259, 12 L. R. A. 382; Hays v. Turner, 23 Iowa, 214.

[71] Sonneborn v. Steinan (Sup.) 85 N. Y. Supp. 334 (this was a case involving a boarding house keeper, but the same principle is equally applicable to innkeepers). This is merely saying that one may sue for the breach of a valid contract and recover compensatory damages.

[72] Miller v. Peeples, 60 Miss. 819, 45 Am. Rep. 423.

[73] Towson v. Havre de Grace Bank, 6 Har. & J. (Md.) 47, 14 Am. Dec. 254; Whitemore v. Haroldson, 2 Lea (Tenn.) 312; McDonald v. Edgerton, 5 Barb. (N. Y.) 560; Allen v. Smith, 12 C. B. N. S. (Eng.) 638. One does not cease to be a guest of an innkeeper by going out to dine or lodge with a friend, or by any other temporary absence. Grinnell v. Cook, 3 Hill (N. Y.) 485, 38 Am. Dec. 663. Where a person takes a room at an inn and leaves his effects there, and makes the inn his principal abiding place, he does not cease to be a guest merely because he is occasionally absent from the inn and sometimes takes his meals elsewhere. McDaniels v. Robinson, 26 Vt. 316, 62 Am. Dec. 574; Id., 28 Vt. 387, 67 Am. Dec. 720.

[74] Miller v. Peeples, 60 Miss. 819, 45 Am. Rep. 423; O'Brien v. Vaill, 22 Fla. 627, 1 South. 137, 1 Am. St. Rep. 219.

[75] Miller v. Peeples, 60 Miss. 819, 45 Am. Rep. 423; Glenn v. Jackson, 93 Ala. 342, 9 South. 259, 12 L. R. A. 382.

the innkeeper as such expires, subject only to the guest's right (as indicated in the next paragraph) to hold the innkeeper responsible as such for the baggage of the guest for such time as may be reasonable to enable the guest to effect its removal. What constitutes such a reasonable time is a question to be determined by the circumstances of each particular case.[76]

Innkeeper's Liability for the Guest's Goods after the Innkeeping Relation is Terminated

The innkeeper's exceptional liability for the baggage of his guest does not cease immediately on the latter's leaving the inn, but this continues until the guest has had a reasonable time to effect a removal of the baggage.[77] This is in accord with the rule obtaining in the case of the common carrier and the passenger.[78] Here, too, as there, a reasonable time is usually a short time, for the guest (or ex-guest) as well as the passenger must act with suitable dispatch.[79] After the lapse of such reasonable time, the innkeeper becomes (as we have just seen) a mere gratuitous bailee and liable only as such. But if a guest, intending to leave the inn, intrusts his baggage to the porter of the inn, whose duty it is to deliver the baggage at the depot, the relationship of innkeeper and guest, as to such baggage, continues until its delivery at the designated place.[80]

76 Miller v. Peeples, 60 Miss. 819, 45 Am. Rep. 423; Maxwell v. Gerard, 84 Hun, 537, 32 N. Y. Supp. 849. By leaving a horse with an innkeeper after the guest has departed, the relation of innkeeper and guest is not continued so as to render the former liable as such for a sum of money left with him by the latter while stopping at his house. McDaniels v. Robinson, 28 Vt. 387, 67 Am. Dec. 720.

77 Baehr v. Downey, 133 Mich. 163, 94 N. W. 750, 103 Am. St. Rep. 444; Murray v. Marshall, 9 Colo. 482, 13 Pac. 589, 59 Am. Rep. 152; Kaplan v. Titus, 140 App. Div. 416, 125 N. Y. Supp. 397; Murray v. Clarke, 2 Daly (N. Y.) 102; Adams v. Clem, 41 Ga. 65, 5 Am. Rep. 524.

78 Post, p. 639.

79 See Wharton, Negligence, § 687; Murray v. Marshall, 9 Colo. 482, 13 Pac. 589, 59 Am. Rep. 152.

80 Glenn v. Jackson, 93 Ala. 342, 9 South. 259, 12 L. R. A. 382; Sasseen v. Clark, 37 Ga. 242; Dickenson v. Winchester, 4 Cush. (Mass.) 114, 50 Am. Dec. 760. And so, where baggage is taken to the wrong boat by the innkeeper's servant, and so lost. Giles v. Fauntleroy, 13 Md. 126.

PART TWO

CARRIERS

CHAPTER IX

PRIVATE AND COMMON CARRIERS OF GOODS

CARRIERS

105. The carrier, by far the most important of bailees, is one who undertakes to transport goods or persons from one place to another.

From modest beginnings, the carrier has experienced a tremendous development, until no other bailee can now compare with him in practical importance. Improved methods of transportation, making the world in a sense a single market, have been largely responsible, along with other civilizing factors, in making the carrier's position so lofty and so dignified. Practical importance and commercial necessity, then, would alone justify an extended and detailed discussion of the legal incidents that attend the relation existing between the carrier and those with whom he deals.

The carrier is defined simply as one who undertakes to transport either goods or persons, or both, from place to place.[1] More simply still, the carrier is one who undertakes to carry. Carriers have been variously classified according to many grounds of division. Thus carriers have been independently divided[2] into (a) carriers by land and carriers by water, according to the element in which their business is done; (b) carriers for hire and carriers without hire, according to the presence or absence of a compensation; (c)

[1] Black, Law Dict. p. 172; Van Zile, Bailm. & Carr. § 392. "Any person who carries goods or passengers, for hire or gratuitously, by land or water, is a carrier." 4 Halsbury, Laws of England, p. 2.

[2] The comparative importance of, and the distinctive legal incidents depending upon, these classifications, will appear as the subject is further developed.

initial carriers and connecting carriers, according to whether they initiate or merely continue the transportation; (d) private carriers and common carriers, according to the private or public nature of their calling; and (e) carriers of goods and carriers of passengers, according to what they carry.

Of these classifications, we are chiefly concerned with the last two. Carriers by land and carriers by water are governed in general by the same principles of law, though differences in the nature of their employment may be the occasion of practical differences in the application of these rules to concrete cases.[3] As all common carriers of goods are carriers for hire, and as private carriers for hire are very rare, resort is not frequently had to the classification based on the reward or its absence. Whether the carrier is an initial or connecting carrier is important in practice chiefly in determining which may be sued when loss or damage is suffered. The distinction between private and common carriers is highly important, though nearly all modern transportation is in the hands of the common carrier, to whom, practically, the whole treatment of carriers is devoted. Carriers of goods and carriers of passengers differ so widely that this analysis is the basis for the division of the treatment of the whole subject and the two are treated separately. Carriers of passengers are not bailees at all, but, for convenience sake, they are discussed in detail after carriers of goods.

PRIVATE CARRIERS OF GOODS

106. The private carrier is one who, without engaging in such business as a public employment, undertakes by special contract to transport goods in particular instances from one place to another.[4]

[3] Though, as is said here, the general principles of the law of carriers apply equally, whether the transportation is by land or water, there are many unique rules governing the transportation of goods and passengers by water. These rules form the body of law known as admiralty. The admiralty jurisdiction of the federal government has resulted in the regulation of carriers by sea in ways that are unheard of as to carriers by land. The bulk of admiralty litigation is tried in the United States District Court.

[4] 1 Hutch. Carr. § 35. And see Pennewill v. Cullen, 5 Har. (Del.) 238. See, also, 4 Halsbury, Laws of England, p. 4; Allen v. Sackrider, 37 N. Y. 341. One who is employed to tear down a house for another and deliver the brick and lumber at another place is simply a private carrier for hire. McBurnie v. Stelsly, 97 S. W. 42, 29 Ky. Law Rep. 1191. There are two kinds of carriers, a common carrier and a private carrier; a private carrier being one who acts in a particular case for hire or reward. O'ROURKE v. BATES, 73 Misc. Rep. 414, 133 N. Y. Supp. 392, Dobie Cas. Bailments and Carriers, 172.

Private and Common Carriers of Goods

The private carrier of goods bears substantially the same relation to the common carrier of goods that the boarding house keeper bears to the innkeeper. The nature of the business carried on by the private and common carrier may be the same; but the former pursues it as a private, the latter as a public, calling. The private carrier, unlike the common carrier, does not hold himself out as ready and willing to serve indifferently all who apply. He is a carrier who carries, not by virtue of a public profession, but according to the special contracts which he makes in individual cases. He is therefore not obliged by law to accept and transport the goods of whatever persons may apply. He may pick and choose as to those with whom he will do business, and arbitrarily in specific instances may refuse to carry the goods which are offered [5] to him. Though formerly numerous, private carriers of goods are now comparatively rare.

Private Carriers of Goods are Ordinary Bailees

The private carrier of goods, making no public profession, is an ordinary bailee, and subject to the same rules governing other ordinary bailees.[6] He is vested with no exceptional rights and incurs no extraordinary responsibilities.

When the private carrier transports goods without a contemplated reward, the bailment resulting from such gratuitous carriage is simply a mandatum.[7] The rights and duties of the bailor and the private carrier as bailee are governed by the rules applicable in general to bailments of that class. In chapter III, "Bailments for the Bailor's Sole Benefit," these rights and duties have been already sufficiently considered. Since a compensation, as we shall see,[8] is one of the essential elements in the relation of common carrier, the mere fact alone that the carriage of the goods is gratuitous necessarily stamps the carrier, as to that particular transaction, as a private carrier.

When there is an intended compensation for the carriage of the goods by the private carrier, the bailment is an ordinary one of the hiring of services about a chattel, or, as this particular bailment is called in the Roman terminology, "locatio operis mercium vehen-

[5] Piedmont Mfg. Co. v. Columbia & G. R. Co., 19 S. C. 353.

[6] COGGS v. BERNARD, 2 Ld. Raym. (Eng.) 909, Dobie Cas. Bailments and Carriers, 1; Varble v. Bigley, 14 Bush (Ky.) 698, 29 Am. Rep. 435.

[7] The private carrier being then a mere mandatary, carrying without a reward, is liable, just as other bailees in bailments for the bailor's sole benefit, only for his failure to exercise even slight care. Beauchamp v. Powley, 1 Moody & R. (Eng.) 38.

[8] Post, § 107.

darum." The principles discussed in chapter VI, "B. Mutual Benefit—Hired Services About Things," are the plicable here.

Liability for Negligence

As in other cases of bailments for hired services, a private carrier for hire must exercise ordinary diligence in the performance of his undertaking.[9] By ordinary care or diligence is again meant such care or diligence as the man of ordinary prudence is accustomed to exercise in the conduct of his own affairs under similar circumstances.[10] Ordinary care is here, as elsewhere, a purely relative term, to be judged according to the peculiar circumstances of each individual case.

Unlike the common carrier, the private carrier of goods for hire is not an insurer, unless he has made himself so by special contract,[11] or by his positive wrong; and he is therefore, like other ordinary bailees, liable for loss of, or damage to, the goods only when it is due to his negligence.[12]

Though there is conflict on the point, it seems that, though this privilege is denied to the common carrier, the private carrier of goods, like other ordinary bailees, may by special contract stipulate against liability for his negligence, but not against his active wrong doing or fraud.[13] The private carrier of goods may by con-

[9] 1 Hutch. Carr. § 37; Story, Bailm, § 399; Ang. Carr. § 47; Ames v. Belden, 17 Barb. (N. Y.) 513, 517; Samms v. Stewart, 20 Ohio, 70, 73, 55 Am. Dec. 445; Wyld v. Pickford, 8 Mees. & W. (Eng.) 443; Jaminet v. American Storage & Moving Co., 109 Mo. App. 257, 84 S. W. 128; Central of Georgia R. Co. v. Glascock & Warfield, 117 Ga. 938, 43 S. E. 981.

[10] United States v. Power, 6 Mont. 271, 273, 12 Pac. 639.

[11] Wells v. Steam Nav. Co., 2 N. Y. 204.

[12] White v. Bascom, 28 Vt. 268; Varble v. Bigley, 14 Bush (Ky.) 698, 29 Am. Rep. 435; Pennewill v. Cullen, 5 Har. (Del.) 238; Forsythe v. Walker, 9 Pa. 148; Baird v. Daly, 57 N. Y. 236, 246, 15 Am. Rep. 488; Bush v. Miller, 13 Barb. (N. Y.) 481, 488; Stannard v. Prince, 64 N. Y. 300; Roberts v. Turner, 12 Johns. (N. Y.) 232, 7 Am. Dec. 311; Platt v. Hibbard, 7 Cow. (N. Y.) 497; Brown v. Denison, 2 Wend. (N. Y.) 593; Holtzclaw v. Duff, 27 Mo. 392; Beck v. Evans, 16 East (Eng.) 244.

[13] Cleveland, C., C. & St. L. R. Co. v. Henry, 170 Ind. 94, 83 N. E. 710; Wells v. Steam Nav. Co., 2 N. Y. 204; Alexander v. Greene, 3 Hill (N. Y.) 9. See ante, p. 19. In 1 Hutch. Carr. § 40, it is said: "Negligence being in the nature of an omission simply of that degree of care which, under all the circumstances, is the bailee's duty, without any criminality of purpose, and being, at least within a certain degree, entirely consistent with good faith, the private carrier may, by contract with his employer, exonerate himself from liability on account of his inattention or want of diligence or skill in the execution of the trust. He may, stipulate that he shall in no event be liable, except for fraud or its equivalent."

tract increase his responsibility indefinitely.[14] Such private carrier, however, cannot by contract make himself a common carrier. He may assume the liability of the common carrier, but he cannot by mere special agreement change the nature of his relation to the public. In spite of contracts enlarging his liability, the private carrier of goods remains a private carrier and should be sued in that character.[15]

Lien

Though authority on the subject is scant, the private carrier for hire should, on principle at least, have a lien on the goods carried for his compensation.[16] Whatever may have been the early rule on the subject, when only those pursuing a public calling and later those who conferred additional value in the goods had a lien, according to the modern doctrine, when the lien is given generally to bailees for hire, no satisfactory reason can be advanced for denying it to the private carrier for hire. That there are expressions in the books denying him the lien, however, cannot be gainsaid.[17]

COMMON CARRIERS OF GOODS

107. The common carrier of goods is one who holds himself out, in the exercise of a public calling, to carry goods, for hire, for whomsoever may employ him.

From this definition, it appears that the essential characteristics of the common carrier of goods are:

(a) He must carry as a public employment by virtue of his general holding out.

(b) He must carry for hire, and not gratuitously.

14 Wells v. Steam Nav. Co., 2 N. Y. 204; Robinson v. Dunmore, 2 Bos. & P. (Eng.) 416.

15 1 Hutch. Carr. § 45; Robinson v. Dunmore, 2 Bos. & P. (Eng.) 416; Kimball v. Rutland & B. R. Co., 26 Vt. 247, 62 Am. Dec. 567.

16 1 Hutch. Carr. § 46. "Upon general principles, there seems to be no reason why a private carrier should not have a lien for performing services similar to those rendered by a public carrier." 1 Jones, Liens, § 276. Even if it be conceded that no such lien existed at common law, the private carrier might well claim a lien by virtue of general provisions in modern statutes favoring and extending the liens of bailees in general.

17 See Fuller v. Bradley, 25 Pa. 120, though it is open to very serious question whether, in this case, the so-called carrier was not a mere servant, hired for his services and the use of his boat, and not a bailee at all. In Riddle, Dean & Co. v. New York, L. E. & W. R. Co., 1 Interst. Com. Comm'n R. 594, 604, this language was used: "The compensation of the common carrier is assured to him by a lien upon the goods, a right which is not enjoyed by a private carrier." In Thompson v. New York Storage Co., 97 Mo. App. 135, 70 S. W. 938, the court said: "We have searched the books and found no case allowing a lien to a private carrier." See, also, Van Zile, Bailm. & Carr. § 404.

As the result of his public profession, the law imposes on him, as as a legal duty, that:

(c) He must carry, with limitations subsequently to be discussed, for all those who choose to employ him, and is liable in an action for his refusal thus to carry.

Public Employment

In an English case,[18] decided in the reign of Queen Anne, a common carrier of goods was said to be "any man undertaking, for hire, to carry the goods of all persons indifferently." The most commonly accepted judicial definition, in this country, is that of Parker, C. J., in Dwight v. Brewster,[19] "One who undertakes, for hire or reward, to transport the goods of such as choose to employ him, from place to place." In another English case [20] it was said: "The criterion is whether he carries for particular persons only, or whether he carries for every one. If a man hold himself out to do it for every one who asks him, he is a common carrier; but if he does not do it for every one, but carries for you or me only, that is a matter of special contract."

The same underlying idea is found in all of these cases. Whether one is a common or private carrier is to be tested primarily by his holding out. If he professes to serve indifferently all who choose to employ him, then he is a common carrier.[21] In the absence of

[18] Gisbourn v. Hurst, 1 Salk. (Eng.) 249.

[19] 1 Pick. (Mass.) 50, 53, 11 Am. Dec. 133.

[20] Ingate v. Christie, 3 Car. & K. 61. Other English cases to the same effect are: COGGS v. BERNARD, 2 Ld. Raym. 909, 1 Smith, Lead. Cas. Eq. 283, and notes, Dobie Cas. Bailments and Carriers, 1; Lane v. Cotton, 1 Ld. Raym. 646, 651; Forward v. Pittard, 1 Term R. 27; Nugent v. Smith, 1 C. P. Div. 19; Palmer v. Grand Junction Ry. Co., 4 Mees. & W. 749; Riley v. Horne, 5 Bing. 217, 220; Benett v. Peninsular & O. Steamboat Co., 6 C. B. 775.

[21] Fish v. Clark, 2 Lans. (N. Y.) 176, 49 N. Y. 122; Allen v. Sackrider, 37 N. Y. 341; Fish v. Chapman, 2 Ga. 349, 46 Am. Dec. 393; Piedmont Mfg. Co. v. Columbia & G. R. Co., 19 S. C. 353; Orange County Bank v. Brown, 3 Wend. (N. Y.) 158, 161; Satterlee v. Groat, 1 Wend. (N. Y.) 272; Chevallier v. Straham, 2 Tex. 115, 47 Am. Dec. 639; Samms v. Stewart, 20 Ohio, 70, 55 Am. Dec. 445; Harrison v. Roy, 39 Miss. 396; Mershon v. Hobensack, 22 N. J. Law, 372; Verner v. Sweitzer, 32 Pa. 208; McClures v. Hammond, 1 Bay (S. C.) 99, 1 Am. Dec. 598; The Dan (D. C.) 40 Fed. 691; Doty v. Strong, 1 Pin. (Wis.) 313, 40 Am. Dec. 773; Honeyman v. Oregon & C. R. Co., 13 Or. 352, 10 Pac. 628, 57 Am. Rep. 20; Jackson Architectural Iron Works v. Hurlbut, 158 N. Y. 34, 52 N. E. 665, 70 Am. St. Rep. 432; Caye v. Pool's Assignee, 108 Ky. 124, 55 S. W. 887, 49 L. R. A. 251, 94 Am. St. Rep. 348; Hahl v. Laux, 42 Tex. Civ. App. 182, 93 S. W. 1080; W. C. Agee & Co. v. Louisville & N. R. Co., 142 Ala. 344, 37 South. 680; United States v. Ramsey, 197 Fed. 144, 116 C. C. A. 568, 42 L. R. A. (N. S.) 1031; Kettenhofen v. Globe Transfer & Storage Co., 70 Wash. 645, 127 Pac. 295.

such a profession, his undertaking is not a public one, and as a private carrier he serves such employer by virtue of a special contract, into which he, of his own choice, voluntarily entered. As has been indicated, the common and private carrier of goods, in the field of transportation, correspond, respectively, to the innkeeper and boarding house keeper, in the field of furnishing entertainment.

Indeed, the common carrier-innkeeper and private carrier-boarding house keeper analogy is quite a close one. The same considerations as those already discussed, of what express declarations, what course of dealing, what conduct, will constitute such a public holding out as to render one an innkeeper,[22] are equally applicable, mutatis mutandis, in working out the question of who is, or is not, a common carrier and responsible accordingly.

Like the innkeeper, the common carrier of goods need not be engaged in the business of transportation either continuously or exclusively.[23] He may profess (though this is unusual) to serve

[22] Ante, § 90. Just as the innkeeper need not own the house in which the inn is conducted, to constitute one a common carrier, it is not essential that the person or corporation undertaking such service own the means of transportation. Blakiston v. Davies, Turner & Co., 42 Pa. Super. Ct. 390; J. H. Cownie Glove Co. v. Merchants' Dispatch Transp. Co., 130 Iowa, 327, 106 N. W. 749, 4 L. R. A. (N. S.) 1060.

[23] The Niagara v. Cordes, 21 How. 7, 16 L. Ed. 41; Dwight v. Brewster, 1 Pick. (Mass.) 50, 53, 11 Am. Dec. 133. "It is true that common carriers undertake generally, and not as a casual occupation, and for all people indifferently; but, in order to make them such, it is not necessary that this should be their exclusive business, or that they should be continuously or regularly employed in it. They may combine it with another and several avocations, and yet be common carriers, subject to the extraordinary liabilities which have been imposed upon them in consequence of the public nature of their employment." Moss v. Bettis, 4 Heisk. (Tenn.) 661, 13 Am. Rep. 1. All persons who transport goods from place to place for hire, for such persons as see fit to employ them, whether usually or occasionally, whether as a principal, or an incidental and subordinate, occupation, are common carriers, and incur all their responsibilities. Chevallier v. Straham, 2 Tex. 115, 47 Am. Dec. 639. "The distinctive characteristic of a common carrier is that he transports goods for hire for the public generally, and it is immaterial whether this is his usual or occasional occupation, his principal or subordinate pursuit. * * * There are no grounds, in reason, why the occasional carrier, who, periodically, in every recurring year, abandons his other pursuits, and assumes that of transporting goods for the public, should be exempted from any of the risks incurred by those who make the carrying business their constant or principal occupation. For the time being, he shares all the advantages arising from the business, and, as the extraordinary responsibilities of a common carrier are imposed by the policy, and not the justice, of the law, this policy should be uniform in its operation, imparting equal benefits, and inflicting the like burdens upon all who assume the capacity of public carriers, whether temporarily or permanently, periodically or continuously." Id.

the public only during certain months or at certain seasons of the year, and hence be a common carrier only during such months or seasons. Thus a farmer may hold himself out as willing to carry goods for the public only at certain seasons of the year, as when his crops are laid by. He would thus be a common carrier only during such seasons, and if, during another season, he undertook to carry the goods of another merely in that particular instance, he would be, as to that specific undertaking, a private, and not a common, carrier of goods.

When the carrier of goods for hire professes to serve the public indifferently, he is none the less a common carrier, though he may be making his first trip,[24] or though the termini between which he carries are not definitely fixed,[25] or though he does not make regular trips.[26] Again, one carrying goods for hire under a public holding out cannot change his character, or evade his responsibility, as a common carrier merely by assuming some other name, such as "forwarder,"[27] or "dispatch company."[28] It is the holding out that is determinative of the nature of the relation, and any name assumed can at best be merely evidential in showing what was the nature of such holding out.[29]

Anomalous Doctrine of Pennsylvania and Tennessee

This test has received the very general approval, but not the universal assent, of the courts. A few cases, but not many, have held one a common carrier of goods in the absence of a holding out to serve the public. The leading case holding this view is unquestionably Gordon v. Hutchinson,[30] in which the opinion was written by

[24] Fuller v. Bradley, 25 Pa. 120; Steele v. McTyer's Adm'r, 31 Ala. 667, 70 Am. Dec. 516.

[25] Tuckerman v. Stephens & C. Transp. Co., 32 N. J. Law, 320; Farley v. Lavary, 107 Ky. 523, 54 S. W. 840, 21 Ky. Law Rep. 1252, 47 L. R. A. 383; Liver Alkali Co. v. Johnson, L. R. 7 Exch. (Eng.) 367.

[26] Pennewill v. Cullen, 5 Har. (Del.) 238.

[27] Bank of Kentucky v. Adams Exp. Co., 93 U. S. 174, 23 L. Ed. 872; Southern Exp. Co. v. McVeigh, 20 Grat. (Va.) 264; Lee v. Fidelity Storage & Transfer Co., 51 Wash. 208, 98 Pac. 658. An alleged forwarding agent who receives goods for transit, issues bills of lading, and makes contracts in its own name with a railroad company for carriage, is, as to a person with whom it contracts for the delivery of goods, a common carrier, and liable as such. Ingram v. American Forwarding Co., 162 Ill. App. 476.

[28] Stewart v. Merchants' Despatch Transp. Co., 47 Iowa, 229, 29 Am. Rep. 476; Merchants' Despatch Transp. Co. v. Joesting, 89 Ill. 152; Merchants' Dispatch & Transp. Co. v. Cornforth, 3 Colo. 280, 25 Am. Rep. 757.

[29] J. H. Cownie Glove Co. v. Merchants' Dispatch Transp. Co., 130 Iowa, 327, 106 N. W. 749, 4 L. R. A. (N. S.) 1060; Read v. Spalding, 5 Bosw. (N. Y.) 395; Christenson v. American Exp. Co., 15 Minn. 270 (Gil. 208), 2 Am. Rep. 122.

[30] 1 Watts & S. (Pa.) 285, 37 Am. Dec. 464.

the brilliant, but sometimes erratic, Chief Justice Gibson. The same doctrine has been laid down in Tennessee,[31] though there limited to transportation by river. This unique repudiation of the public profession test, however, seems to be limited, happily, to these two states.

The Carriage Must be for Hire

To render one a common carrier, it is essential that the carriage should have been undertaken for a valuable consideration.[32] Where no consideration is intended in a particular case for the carriage of goods, the carrier, though he may be regularly engaged in the business of carrying goods for hire for the public generally, is not, as to that particular shipment, a common carrier. No carrier professes to serve all who apply without compensation, and the extraordinary responsibility imposed by law on the common carrier of goods always contemplates a reward. Compensation, as an essential element, is therefore found in all definitions of the common carrier of goods. If the element of compensation is lacking, then, as we have seen,[33] the carrier, necessarily a private one, is a bailee in an ordinary mandatum, and his rights and responsibilities are worked out accordingly.

The compensation, referred to as necessary to make one a common carrier of goods, may be either direct or indirect, and either paid or promised, expressly or impliedly. As in other cases, the intention of the parties governs, as gathered from the surrounding facts and circumstances. If the carriage is incident to some other service, for which compensation is paid or to be paid, no separate or special added compensation is necessary. Thus, where the carrier received grain to be carried for a compensation, and agreed to return the empty sacks without additional charge, he was nevertheless held to be a common carrier even as to the empty sacks.[34]

[31] Moss v. Bettis, 4 Heisk. (Tenn.) 661, 13 Am. Rep. 1; Craig v. Childress, Peck (Tenn.) 270, 14 Am. Dec. 751; Johnson v. Friar, 4 Yerg. (Tenn.) 48, 26 Am. Dec. 215; Gordon v. Buchanan, 5 Yerg. (Tenn.) 71; Turney v. Wilson, 7 Yerg. (Tenn.) 340, 27 Am. Dec. 515. These cases are commented on in 1 Hutch. Carr. §§ 52, 53.

[32] Littlejohn v. Jones, 2 McMul. (S. C.) 365, 366, 39 Am. Dec. 132; Self v. Dunn, 42 Ga. 528, 5 Am. Rep. 544; Citizens' Bank v. Nantucket Steamboat Co., 2 Story, 16, Fed. Cas. No. 2,730; Central R. & Banking Co. v. Lampley, 76 Ala. 357, 52 Am. Rep. 334.

[33] Ante, p. 298.

[34] Pierce v. Milwaukee & St. P. Ry. Co., 23 Wis. 387. See, also, Spears v. Lake Shore & M. S. R. Co., 67 Barb. (N. Y.) 513. Where a carrier undertakes to transport and sell goods, and return the money, the return of the money is not gratuitous. Harrington v. McShane, 2 Watts (Pa.) 443, 27 Am. Dec. 321; Kemp v. Coughtry, 11 Johns. (N. Y.) 107.

Action for Refusal to Carry

Involved in the holding out by the common carrier that he will serve the public is the duty on his part of making good this holding out by accepting, according to its tenor, the goods of all persons, properly tendered to him for transportation.[85] As a corollary to the proposition that he pursues a public calling, the common carrier is legally liable when, without sufficient excuse, he declines to receive and transport goods that are properly offered to him for carriage. The nature of this duty, the limitations on it, as well as the remedies for breach of it, will subsequently be considered.[86]

This legal duty of the carrier of goods to carry for all alike, with the attendant liability for a breach of this duty by a refusal to carry, has been frequently suggested as the true test by which the private or common character can be told.[87] If this duty exists, it is said, he is a common carrier; if it does not exist, he is a mere private carrier. As a practical test, however, it is worthless. The duty results from the public calling; the carrier does not pursue a public calling by virtue of, or owing to, the duty. He owes the duty because he is a common carrier; he is not a common carrier because he owes the duty. Again, in order to determine whether or not one is liable for his refusal to carry, it is essential to solve first the question whether or not one is a common carrier. The intending shipper, suing to recover for a breach of the duty, must first prove that the defendant is a common carrier of goods, in order to show that any such duty exists. A test, then, which requires, before it can even be applied, that the truth or falsity of the proposition for which it is a test be first determined by other means, is necessarily lacking in practical utility.

85 Nugent v. Smith, 1 C. P. Div. (Eng.) 19; Doty v. Strong, 1 Pin. (Wis.) 313, 40 Am. Dec. 773; Wheeler v. San Francisco & A. R. Co., 31 Cal. 46, 89 Am. Dec. 147; Piedmont Mfg. Co. v. Columbia & G. R. Co., 19 S. C. 353; Maybin v. South Carolina R. Co., 8 Rich. Law (S. C.) 240, 64 Am. Dec. 753; Ayres v. Chicago & N. W. Ry. Co., 71 Wis. 372, 37 N. W. 432, 5 Am. St. Rep. 226; Avinger v. South Carolina Ry. Co., 29 S. C. 265, 7 S. E. 493, 13 Am. St. Rep. 716.

86 Post, §§ 109–114, 159.

87 Thus, in Fish v. Chapman, 2 Ga. 349, 354, 46 Am. Dec. 393, it is said: "One of the obligations of a common carrier, as we have seen, is to carry the goods of any person offering to pay his hire. With certain specific limitations, this is the rule. If he refuse to carry, he is liable to be sued, and to respond in damages to the person aggrieved; and this is, perhaps, the safest test of his character." See, also, Piedmont Mfg. Co. v. Columbia & G. R. Co., 19 S. C. 353; Nugent v. Smith, L. R. 1 C. P. Div. (Eng.) 19.

Illustrations—Who are and Who are Not Common Carriers of Goods

In accordance with the principles just explained, it has been held, by virtue of their public profession, that ferrymen,[38] bargemen, lightermen, and owners of canal boats [39] or steamboats,[40] are common carriers of goods; also proprietors of land vehicles, such as stagecoaches,[41] hacks, cabs, omnibuses, and carts,[42] for the nature

[38] Wyckoff v. Queens County Ferry Co., 52 N. Y. 32, 11 Am. Rep. 650; Le Barron v. East Boston Ferry Co., 11 Allen (Mass.) 312, 87 Am. Dec. 717; Lewis v. Smith, 107 Mass. 334; White v. Winnisimmet Co., 7 Cush. (Mass.) 156; Fisher v. Clisbee, 12 Ill. 344; Pomeroy v. Donaldson, 5 Mo. 36; Whitmore v. Bowman, 4 G. Greene (Iowa) 148; Miller v. Pendleton, 8 Gray (Mass.) 547; Claypool v. McAllister, 20 Ill. 504; Sanders v. Young, 1 Head (Tenn.) 219, 73 Am. Dec. 175; Wilson v. Hamilton, 4 Ohio St. 722; Harvey v. Rose, 26 Ark. 3, 7 Am. Rep. 595; Powell v. Mills, 37 Miss. 691; Griffith v. Cave, 22 Cal. 535, 83 Am. Dec. 82; May v. Hanson, 5 Cal. 360, 63 Am. Dec. 135; Littlejohn v. Jones, 2 McMul. (S. C.) 365, 39 Am. Dec. 132; Hall v. Renfro, 3 Metc. (Ky.) 51; Babcock v. Herbert, 3 Ala. 392, 37 Am. Dec. 695; Self v. Dunn, 42 Ga. 528, 5 Am. Rep. 544.

[39] Spencer v. Daggett, 2 Vt. 92; Harrington v. Lyles, 2 Nott & McC. (S. C.) 88; Bowman v. Teall, 23 Wend. (N. Y.) 306, 309, 35 Am. Dec. 562; Parsons v. Hardy, 14 Wend. (N. Y.) 215, 28 Am. Dec. 521; De Mott v. Laraway, 14 Wend. (N. Y.) 225, 28 Am. Dec. 523. Compare Fish v. Clark, 49 N. Y. 122. See, also, Humphreys v. Reed, 6 Whart. (Pa.) 435; Fuller v. Bradley, 25 Pa. 120; Arnold v. Halenbake, 5 Wend. (N. Y.) 33; Hyde v. Trent & M. Nav. Co., 5 Term R. (Eng.) 389; Trent Nav. Co. v. Ward, 3 Esp. (Eng.) 127.

[40] Morse v. Slue, 1 Vent. (Eng.) 190; Reed v. Wilmington Steamboat Co., 1 Marv. (Del.) 193, 40 Atl. 955; Reasor v. Paducah & I. Ferry Co., 152 Ky. 220, 153 S. W. 222, 43 L. R. A. (N. S.) 820; 2 Kent, Comm. 599; Harrington v. McShane, 2 Watts (Pa.) 443, 27 Am. Dec. 321; Benett v. Peninsular & O. Steamboat Co., 6 C. B. (Eng.) 775; Crouch v. Railway Co., 14 C. B. (Eng.) 255, 284; Clark v. Barnwell, 12 How. 272, 13 L. Ed. 985; The Delaware, 14 Wall. 579, 20 L. Ed. 779; Hastings v. Pepper, 11 Pick. (Mass.) 41; Gage v. Tirrell, 9 Allen (Mass.) 299; Elliott v. Rossell, 10 Johns. (N. Y.) 1, 6 Am. Dec. 306; Williams v. Branson, 5 N. C. 417, 4 Am. Dec. 562; Crosby v. Fitch, 12 Conn. 410, 31 Am. Dec. 745; Parker v. Flagg, 26 Me. 181, 45 Am. Dec. 101; Swindler v. Hilliard, 2 Rich. Law (S. C.) 286, 45 Am. Dec. 732; McGregor v. Kilgore, 6 Ohio, 358, 27 Am. Dec. 260; Hollister v. Nowlen, 19 Wend. (N. Y.) 234, 32 Am. Dec. 455; Cole v. Goodwin, 19 Wend. 251, 32 Am. Dec. 470; Jones v. Pitcher, 3 Stew. & P. (Ala.) 135, 24 Am. Dec. 716. A ship is a common carrier, though it does not ply on any definite route, or between fixed termini, where it is let to any one who applies, under a special agreement. Liver Alkali Co. v. Johnson, L. R. 9 Exch. (Eng.) 338, 7 Exch. 267.

[41] Story, Bailm. §§ 496, 499; Verner v. Sweitzer, 32 Pa. 208. Hackney coach, Bonce v. Dubuque St. Ry. Co., 53 Iowa, 278, 5 N. W. 177, 36 Am. Rep. 221. Omnibus, Parmelee v. Lowitz, 74 Ill. 116, 24 Am. Rep. 276; Dibble v. Brown, 12 Ga. 217, 56 Am. Dec. 460; Parmelee v. McNulty, 19 Ill. 556.

[42] Cabs, drays, etc., see Story, Bailm. § 496; Richards v. Westcott, 2 Bosw. (N. Y.) 589; Verner v. Sweitzer, 32 Pa. 208; Powers v. Davenport, 7 Blackf. (Ind.) 497, 43 Am. Dec. 100; McHenry v. Philadelphia, W. & B. R. Co., 4 Har. (Del.) 448. In Robertson v. Kennedy, 2 Dana (Ky.) 431, 26 Am. Dec. 466,

of the vehicle has nothing to do with the relation. When carrying passengers under a public holding out, these and other carriers are common carriers of goods as to the passengers' baggage. So called baggage transfer men,[43] who do nothing but carry trunks to and from railroad stations and steamboat wharves, are none the less common carriers of goods; also owners of express wagons, who carry goods only within the limits of a single city.[44]

Express companies[45] have been held to be common carriers of

the court said: "Every one who pursues the business of transporting goods for hire for the public generally is a common carrier. * * * Draymen, cartmen, and porters, who undertake to carry goods for hire, as a common employment, from one part of a town to another, come within the definition. So, also, does the driver of a slide with an ox team. The mode of transporting is immaterial." See, also, Ingate v. Christie, 3 Car. & K. (Eng.) 61; Sales v. Western Stage Co., 4 Iowa, 547; Hollister v. Nowlen, 19 Wend. (N. Y.) 234, 32 Am. Dec. 455; Walker v. Skipwith, Meigs (Tenn.) 502, 33 Am. Dec. 161; Frink v. Coe, 4 G. Greene (Iowa) 555, 61 Am. Dec. 141; Powell v. Mills, 30 Miss. 231, 64 Am. Dec. 158. But see Brind v. Dale, 8 Car. & P. (Eng.) 207; Moses v. Boston & M. R. R., 24 N. H. 71, 55 Am. Dec. 222; Charles v. Lasher, 20 Ill. App. 36; Farley v. Lavary, 107 Ky. 523, 54 S. W. 840, 49 L. R. A. 383; Lawson v. Judge of Recorder's Court of City of Detroit, 175 Mich. 375, 141 N. W. 623, 45 L. R. A. (N. S.) 1152.

43 Verner v. Sweitzer, 32 Pa. 208; Richards v. Westcott, 2 Bosw. (N. Y.) 589. See, also, Parmelee v. McNulty, 19 Ill. 556; Norfolk & W. R. Co. v. Old Dominion Baggage Co., 99 Va. 111, 37 S. E. 784, 50 L. R. A. 722; Hedding v. Gallagher, 72 N. H. 377, 57 Atl. 225, 64 L. R. A. 811.

44 Richards v. Westcott, 2 Bosw. (N. Y.) 589; Jackson Architectural Iron Works v. Hurlbut, 158 N. Y. 34, 52 N. E. 665, 70 Am. St. Rep. 432; Caye v. Pool's Assignee, 108 Ky. 124, 55 S. W. 887, 49 L. R. A. 251, 94 Am. St. Rep. 348. A parcel delivery company is a common carrier. Johnson Express Co. v. City of Chicago, 136 Ill. App. 368. A telegraph company, furnishing messengers for the delivery of packages, does not assume the liability of a common carrier, but only agrees that the messenger furnished shall be a suitable person for the work. Murray v. Postal Telegraph-Cable Co., 96 N. E. 316, 210 Mass. 188, Ann. Cas. 1912C, 1183. The mode employed in transporting goods is immaterial, and persons who are engaged in the business of transporting goods from place to place in a city, in drays or transfer wagons, may be common carriers. ARKADELPHIA MILLING CO. v. SMOKER MERCHANDISE CO., 100 Ark. 37, 139 S. W. 680, Dobie Cas. Bailments and Carriers, 175.

45 Bennett v. Northern Pac. Exp. Co., 12 Or. 49, 6 Pac. 160; Grogan v. Adams' Exp. Co., 114 Pa. 523, 7 Atl. 134, 60 Am. Rep. 360; Southern Exp. Co. v. Ashford, 126 Ala. 591, 28 South. 732; United States Exp. Co. v. Backman, 28 Ohio St. 144; BUCKLAND v. ADAMS EXP. CO., 97 Mass. 124, 93 Am. Dec. 68, Dobie Cas. Bailments and Carriers, 177; Lowell Wire Fence Co. v. Sargent, 8 Allen (Mass.) 189; Bank of Kentucky v. Adams Exp. Co., 93 U. S. 174, 23 L. Ed. 872; Sweet v. Barney, 23 N. Y. 335; American Exp. Co. v. Hockett, 30 Ind. 250, 95 Am. Dec. 691; Gulliver v. Adams Exp. Co., 38 Ill. 503; Verner v. Sweitzer, 32 Pa. 208; Christenson v. American Exp. Co., 15 Minn. 270 (Gil. 208), 2 Am. Rep. 122; Sherman v. Wells, 28 Barb. (N. Y.) 403; Baldwin v. American Exp. Co., 23 Ill. 197, 74 Am. Dec. 190; Southern Exp. Co. v. Newby, 36 Ga. 635, 91 Am. Dec. 783; Hayes v. Wells, Fargo &

goods, though they employ, except as to local deliveries, the conveyances of other common carriers, usually railroads. Railroad companies [46] are the best, as they are by far the most important, example of common carriers. Street railways [47] usually carry only passengers; but they may, and sometimes do, become common carriers of goods. Receivers and trustees [48] operating railroads are common carriers, as are also, according to the weight of authority, carriers of live stock.[49]

A railroad company is none the less a common carrier when the shipper loads a whole car, which is made part of one of the company's trains,[50] or even when a single shipper makes up a whole train, if such car or train is placed in the control or charge of the agents or employés of the railroad company.[51] But when the train is chartered by the railroad company to a person who controls the train, the railroad company furnishing merely the motive power and permitting the use of its tracks, the company is then no longer a common carrier.[52] Again, in the transportation under spe-

Co., 23 Cal. 185, 83 Am. Dec. 89. See Roberts v. Turner, 12 Johns. (N. Y.) 232, 7 Am. Dec. 311; Hooper v. Wells, Fargo & Co., 27 Cal. 11, 85 Am. Dec. 211.

46 Memphis News Pub. Co. v. Southern Ry. Co., 110 Tenn. 684, 75 S. W. 941, 63 L. R. A. 150; Thompson-Houston Electric Co. v. Simon, 20 Or. 60, 25 Pac. 147, 10 L. R. A. 251, 23 Am. St. Rep. 86; Norway Plains Co. v. Boston & M. R. Co., 1 Gray (Mass.) 263, 61 Am. Dec. 423; Thomas v. Boston & P. R. Corp., 10 Metc. (Mass.) 472, 43 Am. Dec. 444; Root v. Great Western R. Co., 45 N. Y. 524; Fuller v. Naugatuck R. Co., 21 Conn. 557, 570; Rogers Locomotive & Machine Works v. Erie Ry. Co., 20 N. J. Eq. 379; Noyes v. Rutland & B. R. Co., 27 Vt. 110; Contra Costa Coal Mines R. Co. v. Moss, 23 Cal. 323. Railway companies are, perhaps, the most common instances of common carriers, and it would be useless to multiply citations. The railroad company is also liable as a common carrier of goods as to the baggage of its passengers. Macrow v. Railway Co., L. R. 6 Q. B. (Eng.) 612; Hannibal & St. J. R. Co. v. Swift, 12 Wall. 262, 20 L. Ed. 423.

47 1 Hutch. Carr. § 78; Levi v. Lynn & B. R. Co., 11 Allen (Mass.) 300, 87 Am. Dec. 713.

48 Rogers v. Wheeler, 2 Lans. (N. Y.) 486, 43 N. Y. 598; Faulkner v. Hart, 44 N. Y. Super. Ct. 471; Sprague v. Smith, 29 Vt. 421, 70 Am. Dec. 424; Beers v. Wabash, St. L. & P. R. Co. (C. C.) 34 Fed. 244; Bartlett v. Keim, 50 N. J. Law, 260, 13 Atl. 7.

49 Post, § 119.

50 Ohio & M. R. Co. v. Dunbar, 20 Ill. 623, 71 Am. Dec. 291; Central R. & Banking Co. v. Anderson, 58 Ga. 393; Fordyce v. McFlynn, 56 Ark. 424, 19 S. W. 961.

51 See, in general, as to carrier's handling a whole train, Hannibal & St. J. R. Co. v. Swift, 12 Wall. 262, 20 L. Ed. 423; Chicago, B. & Q. R. Co. v. Curtis, 51 Neb. 442, 71 N. W. 42, 66 Am. St. Rep. 456; East Tennessee & G. R. Co. v. Whittle, 27 Ga. 535, 73 Am. Dec. 741.

52 East Tennessee & G. R. Co. v. Whittle, 27 Ga. 535, 73 Am. Dec. 741; Ohio & M. R. Co. v. Dunbar, 20 Ill. 624, 71 Am. Dec. 291; Kimball v. Rutland &

cial contract of special circus trains, made up of specially designed cars owned by the circus proprietor, and largely regulated by his employés, the railroad company is held not to be a common carrier.[53]

The following are held not to be common carriers of goods: Sleeping and parlor car companies,[54] since they do not control the train of which their cars are a part, but these are expressly included within the definition of common carriers under the federal Interstate Commerce Act;[55] owners of tugs and other towboats,[56] as a rule, since they furnish only motive power and the property

R. R. Co., 26 Vt. 247, 62 Am. Dec. 567; Davis v. Chicago, St. P., M. & O. Ry. Co., 45 Fed. 543; American Exp. Co. v. Ogles, 36 Tex. Civ. App. 407, 81 S. W. 1023. But see Mallory v. Tioga R. Co., 39 Barb. (N. Y.) 488; Hannibal & St. J. R. Co. v. Swift, 12 Wall. 262, 20 L. Ed. 423.

53 COUP v. WABASH, ST. L. & P. R. CO., 56 Mich. 111, 22 N. W. 215, 56 Am. Rep. 374, Dobie Cas. Bailments and Carriers, 181; Chicago, M. & St. P. R. Co. v. Wallace, 66 Fed. 506, 14 C. C. A. 257, 30 L. R. A. 161; Robertson v. Old Colony Ry. Co., 156 Mass. 525, 31 N. E. 650, 32 Am. St. Rep. 482. See, generally, as to the liability of a railroad hauling cars for another company, Peoria & P. Union Ry. Co. v. United States Rolling Stock Co., 136 Ill. 643, 27 N. E. 59, 29 Am. St. Rep. 348.

54 Pullman Palace Car Co. v. Smith, 73 Ill. 360, 24 Am. Rep. 258; Pullman Car Co. v. Gardner, 3 Penny. (Pa.) 78; Blum v. Southern Pullman Palace Car Co., 1 Flip. 500, Fed. Cas. No. 1,574; Woodruff Sleeping & Parlor Coach Co. v. Diehl, 84 Ind. 474, 43 Am. Rep. 102; Pullman Palace Car Co. v. Lowe, 28 Neb. 239, 44 N. W. 226, 6 L. R. A. 809, 26 Am. St. Rep. 325; Barrott v. Pullman's Palace Car Co., 51 Fed. 796; Pullman Palace Car Co. v. Freudenstein, 3 Colo. App. 540, 34 Pac. 578. See articles, 25 Am. Law Rev. 569, and 20 Am. Law Rev. 159. See "Innkeepers," ante, p. 247; "Carriers," post, p. 520.

55 Interstate Commerce Act Feb. 4, 1887, c. 104, § 1, 24 Stat. 379 (U. S. Comp. St. 1901, p. 3154).

56 See 1 Hutch. Carr. § 92; THE NEAFFIE, 1 Abb. (U. S.) 465, Fed. Cas. No. 10,063, 5 Myers, Fed. Dec. 19, Dobie Cas. Bailments and Carriers, 179; Brown v. Clegg, 63 Pa. 51, 3 Am. Rep. 522; Hays v. Millar, 77 Pa. 238, 18 Am. Rep. 445; Leonard v. Hendrickson, 18 Pa. 40, 55 Am. Dec. 587; Hays v. Paul, 51 Pa. 134, 88 Am. Dec. 569; Wells v. Steam Nav. Co., 2 N. Y. 204, 8 N. Y. 375; Caton v. Rumney, 13 Wend. (N. Y.) 387; Alexander v. Greene, 3 Hill (N. Y.) 9; Arctic Fire Ins. Co. v. Austin, 54 Barb. (N. Y.) 559; Merrick v. Brainard, 38 Barb. (N. Y.) 574; Eastern Transp. Line v. Hope, 95 U. S. 297, 24 L. Ed. 477; The Webb, 14 Wall. 406, 20 L. Ed. 774; Varble v. Bigley, 14 Bush (Ky.) 698, 29 Am. Rep. 435; The New Philadelphia, 1 Black, 62, 17 L. Ed. 84; The Oconto, 5 Biss. 460, Fed. Cas. No. 10,421; Abbey v. The Robert L. Stevens, 22 How. Prac. (N. Y.) 78, Fed. Cas. No. 8; Wooden v. Austin, 51 Barb. (N. Y.) 9; The Margaret, 94 U. S. 494, 24 L. Ed. 146; Symonds v. Pain, 6 Hurl. & N. (Eng.) 709; The Julia, 14 Moore P. C. (Eng.) 210. But see, contra, Bussey v. Mississippi Val. Transp. Co., 24 La. Ann. 165, 13 Am. Rep. 120; Clapp v. Stanton, 20 La. Ann. 495, 96 Am. Dec. 417; Smith v. Pierce, 1 La. 349; White v. The Mary Ann, 6 Cal. 462, 65 Am. Dec. 523; Walston v. Myers, 50 N. C. 174. See, also, Ashmore v. Pennsylvania Steam Towing & Transp. Co., 28 N. J. Law, 180. In Bussey v. Mississippi Val.

towed is not placed in their exclusive custody or control; telephone and telegraph companies,[57] since they do not carry at all. So, also, log driving and booming companies[58] and agisters and drovers[59] of cattle; postmasters, mail contractors, and carriers of the mail,[60] their contract being with the government alone; livery stable keepers,[61] who merely hire horses and vehicles; warehousemen and wharfingers;[62] bridge,[63] canal,[64] and turnpike com-

Transp. Co., supra, it was suggested that a steam towboat might be employed in two very different ways, and that possibly this fact would explain the conflict of opinion. In the first place, it may be employed as a mere means of locomotion, under the entire control of the towed vessel, or the owner of the towed vessel and goods therein may remain in possession and control of the property thus transported, to the exclusion of the bailee, or the towing may be casual, merely, and not a regular business between fixed termini; and it might well be said that, under such circumstances, a towboat is not the common carrier. But a second and quite different method of employing a towboat is where she plies regularly between the fixed termini, towing for hire, and for all persons, barges laden with goods, and taking into her full possession and control, and out of the control of the bailor, the property thus transported. Such a case seems to satisfy every requirement in the definition of a common carrier.

57 Breese v. United States Tel. Co., 48 N. Y. 132, 8 Am. Rep. 526; Hibbard v. Western Union Tel. Co., 33 Wis. 558, 14 Am. Rep. 775; Grinnell v. Western Union Tel. Co., 113 Mass. 299, 18 Am. Rep. 485; Marr v. Western Union Tel. Co., 85 Tenn. 529, 3 S. W. 496; Fowler v. Western Union Tel. Co., 80 Me. 381, 15 Atl. 29, 6 Am. St. Rep. 211. But see Central Union Telephone Co. v. Bradbury, 106 Ind. 1, 5 N. E. 721; Gwynn v. Citizens' Tel. Co., 69 S. C. 434, 48 S. E. 460, 67 L. R. A. 111, 104 Am. St. Rep. 819; Pacific Tel. Co. v. Underwood, 37 Neb. 315, 55 N. W. 1057, 40 Am. St. Rep. 490. These are common carriers under the Interstate Commerce Act (Act Feb. 4, 1887, c. 104, 24 Stat. 379 [U. S. Comp. St. 1901, p. 3154]) § 1. See Johnson on Interstate Commerce (2d Ed.) § 133.

58 Mann v. White R. L. & B. Co., 46 Mich. 38, 8 N. W. 550, 41 Am. Rep. 141.

59 1 Hutch. Carr. § 99; Story, Bailm. § 443.

60 Lane v. Cotton, 1 Ld. Raym. (Eng.) 646; Dunlop v. Munroe, 7 Cranch, 242, 3 L. Ed. 329; Wiggins v. Hathaway, 6 Barb. (N. Y.) 632; Schroyer v. Lynch, 8 Watts (Pa.) 453; Central R. & Banking Co. v. Lampley, 76 Ala. 357, 52 Am. Rep. 334; Boston Ins. Co. v. Chicago, R. I. & P. Ry. Co., 118 Iowa, 423, 92 N. W. 88, 59 L. R. A. 796; BANKERS' MUT. CASUALTY CO. v. MINNEAPOLIS, ST. P. & S. S. M. R. CO., 117 Fed. 434, 54 C. C. A. 608, 65 L. R. A. 397, Dobie Cas. Bailments and Carriers, 267; Id., 187 U. S. 648, 23 Sup. Ct. 847, 47 L. Ed. 348.

61 COPELAND v. DRAPER, 157 Mass. 558, 32 N. E. 944, 19 L. R. A. 283, 34 Am. St. Rep. 314, Dobie Cas. Bailments and Carriers, 25; Stanley v. Steele, 77 Conn. 688, 60 Atl. 640, 69 L. R. A. 561, 2 Ann. Cas. 342.

62 Chattock v. Bellamy, 64 L. J. Q. B. (Eng.) 250; Schloss v. Wood, 11 Colo. 287, 17 Pac. 910; 1 Hutch. Carr. § 71.

63 Kentucky & I. Bridge Co. v. Louisville & N. R. Co. (C. C.) 37 Fed. 567, 616; Grigsby v. Chappell, 5 Rich. Law (S. C.) 443.

64 Exchange Fire Ins. Co. v. Delaware & H. Canal Co., 10 Bosw. (N. Y.) 180; Pennsylvania Canal Co. v. Burd, 90 Pa. 281; Watts v. Canal Co., 64 Ga. 88.

panies,[65] which furnish a thoroughfare by means of which others transport goods, but which are not themselves engaged in transportation; irrigation companies,[66] which merely furnish water for irrigation purposes.

[65] Lake Superior & M. R. Co. v. United States, 93 U. S. 442, 444, 23 L. Ed. 965.

[66] Wyatt v. Larimer & W. Irr. Co., 1 Colo. App. 480, 29 Pac. 906.

CHAPTER X

LIABILITIES OF THE COMMON CARRIER OF GOODS

INTRODUCTORY OUTLINE

108. The most important liabilities imposed by law upon the common carrier of goods are:

(a) His duty to carry for all.

(b) His duty to furnish equal facilities to all.

(c) His liability for loss of, or damage to, the goods.

(d) His liability for deviation and delay.

Mention has been made in several places of the common carrier of goods as one of the extraordinary bailees, and in the last chapter the nature of the relation and its distinctive features have been brought out. The rights and liabilities incident to the relation would seem to be next in order. The present chapter will be devoted solely to a discussion of the liabilities of the common carrier of goods, when these are neither enlarged nor diminished by special agreement. The common carrier's liability under special contract will be the subject of chapter XI, while chapter XII will discuss the somewhat unique rights which are possessed by the common carrier of goods as a partial return, at least, for the unusual liabilities imposed on him by the common law.

DUTY TO CARRY FOR ALL

109. It is the duty of the common carrier of goods to accept and transport all goods offered, subject to the following limitations:

(1) The nature of his holding out.

(2) The extent of his facilities.

(3) The nature and condition of the goods.

(4) The payment of his charges in advance.

(5) The shipper's authority to deliver.

The duty of the common carrier of goods to carry for all has already been briefly discussed in connection with the question of who are common carriers.[1] This duty is imposed by law as the result of the carrier's public profession, but it is subject to the limitations above set out which will now be considered in detail.

For a violation of this legal duty, the carrier may be sued at law by the intending shipper, who may recover for the damage proximately resulting from such refusal.[2] In a few cases, under peculiarly aggravating circumstances, exemplary damages have been allowed.[3] In many cases, it has been held that an injunction or peremptory writ of mandamus will issue to compel the common carrier, in the discharge of this clear legal duty, to accept and transport the goods which have been properly tendered to him.[4]

1 Ante, § 107.

2 Reid v. Southern Ry. Co., 153 N. C. 490, 69 S. E. 618; Ayres v. Chicago & N. Ry. Co., 71 Wis. 372, 37 N. W. 432, 5 Am. St. Rep. 226; Atchison, T. & S. F. Ry. Co. v. Denver & N. O. Ry. Co., 110 U. S. 667, 4 Sup. Ct. 185, 28 L. Ed. 291; Chicago & A. Ry. Co. v. Suffern, 129 Ill. 274, 21 N. E. 824; St. Louis, A. & T. Ry. Co. v. Neel, 56 Ark. 279, 19 S. W. 963; Seasongood v. Tennessee & O. R. Transp. Co., 54 S. W. 193, 21 Ky. Law Rep. 1142, 49 L. R. A. 270; Houston, E. & W. T. Ry. Co. v. Campbell, 91 Tex. 551, 45 S. W. 2, 43 L. R. A. 225; Riley v. Horne, 5 Bing. (Eng.) 217; Crouch v. London, etc., Ry. Co., 14 C. B. (Eng.) 255; Beech Creek Ry. Co. v. Olanta Coal Mining Co., 158 Fed. 36, 85 C. C. A. 148; Louisville & N. Ry. Co. v. Higdon, 149 Ky. 321, 148 S. W. 26. It has been said (Pozzi v. Shipton, 1 Per. & D. [Eng.] 4, 12) that the carrier may be indicted, but there seem to be no records of convictions in such cases.

3 Avinger v. South Carolina Ry. Co., 29 S. C. 265, 7 S. E. 493, 13 Am. St. Rep. 716.

4 Southern Exp. Co. v. Rose, 124 Ga. 581, 53 S. E. 185, 5 L. R. A. (N. S.) 619; CHICAGO & N. W. RY. CO. v. PEOPLE ex rel. HEMPSTEAD, 56 Ill. 365, 8 Am. Rep. 690, Dobie Cas. Bailments and Carriers, 183; Atwater v. Delaware, L. & W. R. Co., 48 N. J. Law, 55, 2 Atl. 803, 57 Am. Rep. 543; Sandford v. Catawissa, W. & E. R. Co., 24 Pa. 378, 64 Am. Dec. 667; People v. New York Cent. & H. R. R. Co., 28 Hun (N. Y.) 543; Menacho v. Ward (C. C.)

SAME—DUTY COEXTENSIVE WITH THE HOLDING OUT

110. As the common carrier's duty to carry is coextensive with his holding out, he is not obliged to accept goods of a kind he does not profess to carry, nor for carriage over any other route nor by any other means than those indicated by his profession.

The duty of the common carrier of goods to carry for all who offer arises from the public profession he has made, and is in turn limited by it. This public profession, therefore, not only furnishes the basis of the duty, but also defines its extent. Accordingly, as to the duty to accept goods for transportation, the carrier is a common carrier only within the limits that he has himself prescribed.[5] If the transportation sought by the individual shipper is outside of these limits, the carrier has a perfect right, without incurring any liability, to refuse to accept the goods for shipment.

Thus a person may profess to carry a particular class of goods only, as, for instance, cattle or dry goods, in which case he could not be compelled to carry any other kind of goods; or he may limit his obligation to carrying from one place to another, as from Manchester to London, and then he would not be compelled to carry either beyond these termini or to or from intermediate places.[6] As we have seen, the wagoner may confine his activities as a com-

27 Fed. 529; Chicago, B. & Q. Ry. Co. v. Burlington, C. R. & N. Ry. Co. (C. C.) 34 Fed. 481. Where an action for damages is an adequate remedy, mandamus will not lie. People v. New York, L. E. & W. R. Co., 22 Hun (N. Y.) 533; People v. Babcock, 16 Hun (N. Y.) 313.

5 Lake Shore & M. S. R. Co. v. Perkins, 25 Mich. 329, 12 Am. Rep. 275; Tunnel v. Pettijohn, 2 Har. (Del.) 48; Knox v. Rives, 14 Ala. 249, 48 Am. Dec. 97; Powell v. Mills, 30 Miss. 231, 64 Am. Dec. 158; Carr v. Lancashire, etc., Ry. Co., 7 Exch. (Eng.) 707; Batson v. Donovan, 4 B. & Ald. (Eng.) 21. Where a carrier holds itself out as only engaged in the carriage of specified articles, it is under no obligation to carry other things. Louisville & N. R. Co. v. Higdon, 149 Ky. 321, 148 S. W. 26.

6 Johnson v. Railway Co., 4 Exch. (Eng.) 367; Central R. & Banking Co. v. Lampley, 76 Ala. 357, 52 Am. Rep. 334; Honeyman v. Oregon & C. R. Co., 13 Or. 352, 10 Pac. 628, 57 Am. Rep. 20; Kimball v. Rutland & B. R. Co., 26 Vt. 247, 62 Am. Dec. 567; Pitlock v. Wells, Fargo & Co., 109 Mass. 452; Citizens' Bank v. Nantucket Steamboat Co., 2 Story, 16, 33, Fed. Cas. No. 2,730; Sewall v. Allen, 6 Wend. (N. Y.) 335, 346; Kuter v. Michigan Cent. R. Co., 1 Biss. 35, Fed. Cas. No. 7,955. Carriers of money: Shelden v. Robinson, 7 N. H. 157, 26 Am. Dec. 726; Kemp v. Coughtry, 11 Johns. (N. Y.) 107, 109; Emery v. Hersey, 4 Greenl. (Me.) 407, 16 Am. Dec. 268; Harrington v. McShane, 2 Watts (Pa.) 443, 27 Am. Dec. 321; Merwin v. Butler, 17 Conn. 138; Dwight v. Brewster, 1 Pick. (Mass.) 50, 11 Am. Dec. 133.

mon carrier to a single city, or baggage transfer men may engage as common carriers solely in the business of transporting trunks to and from railroad stations and steamboat wharves.[7] The carrier may also by his profession limit the means of transportation. Thus the wagoner could not be compelled to carry by railroad, nor must the carrier by land accept goods for transportation by water.[8]

Again, even apart from a definite profession by the carrier, common sense would impose certain limitations on his duty to accept goods for transportation. Thus he is not compelled to accept goods tendered at an unreasonable hour, or at an unreasonable place,[9] or even when tendered an unreasonably long time before the goods are to be shipped.[10] But to the extent of his public profession the common carrier must carry for all who offer.

SAME—DUTY LIMITED BY THE EXTENT OF THE CARRIER'S FACILITIES

111. The early rule seems to have been that the common carrier's duty was strictly limited by his facilities, however insufficient they were; but the modern rule requires the common carrier of goods to provide sufficient facilities to handle all the traffic which can reasonably be anticipated.

By the early common law the duty of the carrier to accept goods for transportation seems to have been strictly limited to his facilities, however crude and insufficient these might have been.[11] Thus it was said that the carter was not bound to supply more carts than he was in the habit of employing, when these were not sufficient to carry the goods tendered to him.[12] And it was further held that he was not obliged to accept goods for transportation

[7] Ante, § 107.

[8] 1 Hutch. Carr. § 60; Pittsburgh, C. & St. L. Ry. Co. v. Morton, 61 Ind. 539, 28 Am. Rep. 682; Pitlock v. Wells, Fargo & Co., 109 Mass. 452.

[9] Pickford v. Railway Co., 12 Mees. & W. (Eng.) 766; Lane v. Cotton, 1 Ld. Raym. (Eng.) 646, 652; Louisville, N. A. & C. Ry. Co. v. Flanagan, 113 Ind. 488, 14 N. E. 370, 3 Am. St. Rep. 674; Cronkite v. Wells, 32 N. Y. 247.

[10] Palmer v. Railway Co., 35 Law J. C. P. (Eng.) 289; Garton v. Railway, Co., 28 Law J. C. P. (Eng.) 306; Lane v. Cotton, 1 Ld. Raym. (Eng.) 646.

[11] Jackson v. Rogers, 2 Stow. (Eng.) 327; Batson v. Donovan, 4 B. & Ald. (Eng.) 21; Riley v. Horne, 5 Bing. (Eng.) 217; Tunnel v. Pettijohn, 2 Har. (Del.) 48.

[12] Wood, Browne, Carr. § 73; Johnson v. Ry. Co., 4 Exch. (Eng.) 367, 373.

when the vehicles which he employed were already full.[13] In other words, the carrier might provide as many or as few facilities as he saw fit, the law imposed no obligation on him in this respect, and these facilities constituted the limit of his duty to accept goods to be carried.

However well these rules may have worked at a time when the wagoner and carter were the chief instruments of commerce on land, they are clearly unsuited to modern economic conditions. The part played by the railroad to-day in the development of any community, and the unique privileges (such as the power of eminent domain) which it enjoys, would emphatically forbid the lax rules under which the wagoner pursued his calling.

It is now held, therefore, that the common carrier of goods must provide facilities sufficient to handle the volume of traffic which, under the circumstances, might reasonably be anticipated.[14] For his failure in this respect the carrier is correspondingly liable in damages to the shipper. To that extent, too, the carrier cannot plead the lack of facilities as an excuse for his failure to accept and transport the goods offered to him. The nature and extent of the equipment which the carrier must furnish is accordingly based on, and determined by, the reasonable demands of the traffic under the particular conditions in question. The carrier, however, is not required to provide facilities adequate for any demands that may be made upon him, and particularly is he excused from liability for his failure to provide for an unusual influx of goods, an unexpected accumulation of freight, or an extraordinary press of business.[15] Any such requirement would be abnormal, and

[13] See cases cited in note 11.

[14] Missouri & N. A. Ry. Co. v. Sneed, 85 Ark. 293, 107 S. W. 1182; Peet v. Chicago & N. W. Ry. Co., 20 Wis. 594, 91 Am. Dec. 446; Galena & C. U. R. Co. v. Rae, 18 Ill. 488, 68 Am. Dec. 574; Chicago & A. Ry. Co. v. Davis, 159 Ill. 53, 42 N. E. 382, 50 Am. St. Rep. 143; Baker v. Boston & M. Ry. Co., 74 N. H. 100, 65 Atl. 386, 124 Am. St. Rep. 937, 12 Ann. Cas. 1072; Western New York & P. Ry. Co. v. Penn Refining Co., Limited, of Oil City, Pa., 137 Fed. 343, 70 C. C. A. 23; Atlantic Coast Line R. Co. v. Wharton, 207 U. S. 328, 28 Sup. Ct. 121, 52 L. Ed. 230. For an elaborate treatment of the common carrier's duty to provide adequate facilities, with copious citations, see 1 Wyman Public Service Corporations, c. 23. Where the shipper applies for cars, to be furnished at a certain time and place, the carrier, if unable to furnish the cars, must so notify the shipper. Ayres v. Chicago & N. W. Ry. Co., 71 Wis. 372, 37 N. W. 432, 5 Am. St. Rep. 226; Newport News & M. V. R. Co. v. Mercer, 96 Ky. 475, 29 S. W. 301.

[15] Toledo, W. & W. Ry. Co. v. Lockhart, 71 Ill. 627; Galena & C. U. R. Co. v. Rae, 18 Ill. 488; Faulkner v. Railroad Co., 51 Mo. 311; Condict v. Railway Co., 54 N. Y. 500; Chicago, St. L. & P. R. Co. v. Wolcott, 141 Ind. 467, 39 N. E. 451; ST. LOUIS SOUTHWESTERN RY. CO. v. CLAY COUNTY

would impose an unreasonable, and often even an impossible, condition upon the carrier. But if the carrier by the exercise of reasonable diligence could have provided adequate facilities to handle this press of business, then the carrier should not be excused for his failure in this respect.[16]

Though the rule imposing upon the common carrier the duty of furnishing reasonable facilities ample for handling traffic which reasonably might have been foreseen is held by modern cases to be a duty derived from the common law, many states have passed statutes on the subject.[17] The same duty, however, is recognized by the federal Interstate Commerce Act,[18] while the right of enforcing this duty by mandamus is specifically conferred on the United States courts.[19]

SAME—DUTY LIMITED BY THE NATURE OR CONDITION OF THE GOODS

112. The common carrier is not obliged to accept for transportation goods of a dangerous or suspicious nature, or goods in such condition as to be unfit for shipment.

The high degree of responsibility as to the goods in his charge is sufficient in itself to excuse the carrier from accepting goods

GIN CO., 77 Ark. 357, 92 S. W. 531, Dobie Cas. Bailments and Carriers, 185; Wallace v. Pecos & N. T. Ry. Co., 50 Tex. Civ. App. 296, 110 S. W. 162; Yazoo & M. V. Ry. Co. v. McKay, 91 Miss. 138, 44 South. 780. It is the duty of a railroad company to provide cars sufficient to transport goods offered in the usual and ordinary course of business, but it is not bound to anticipate and prepare for an exceptional and extraordinary press of business. Southern Ry. Co. v. Atlanta Sand & Supply Co., 135 Ga. 35, 68 S. E. 807. See, also, Montana, W. & S. Ry. Co. v. Morley (D. C.) 198 Fed. 991.

16 Hansley v. Jamesville & W. R. Co., 117 N. C. 565, 23 S. E. 443, 32 L. R. A. 543, 53 Am. St. Rep. 600; Ayres v. Chicago & N. W. Ry. Co., 71 Wis. 372, 37 N. W. 432, 5 Am. St. Rep. 226; Illinois Cent. Ry. Co. v. Cobb, 64 Ill. 128; Dallenbach v. Illinois Cent. Ry. Co., 164 Ill. App. 310.

17 See Oliver & Son v. Chicago, R. I. & P. Ry. Co., 89 Ark. 466, 117 S. W. 238; Murphy Hardware Co. v. Southern Ry. Co., 150 N. C. 703, 64 S. E. 873, 22 L. R. A. (N. S.) 1200, 17 Ann. Cas. 481. Some of these statutes, imposing stringent and unreasonable duties on the carrier, have been declared void by the federal courts. See Houston & T. C. Ry. Co. v. Mayes, 201 U. S. 321, 26 Sup. Ct. 491, 50 L. Ed. 772; St. Louis, I. M. & S. Ry. Co. v. Hampton (C. C.) 162 Fed. 693.

18 Interstate Commerce Act Feb. 4, 1887, c. 104, §§ 1, 3, 23, 24 Stat. 379, 380 (U. S. Comp. St. 1901, pp. 3154, 3155, 3171).

19 See the deficiency appropriation bill of October 22, 1913, abolishing the Commerce Court (which formerly exercised this jurisdiction), and conferring on the United States District Court the powers formerly possessed by the Commerce Court.

which are likely to injure other goods which he is transporting. The carrier, therefore, owes no duty to accept goods which are from their very nature dangerous.[20] Thus the common carrier is justified in refusing to receive such highly explosive substances as dynamite or nitro-glycerine.[21] The same is true of goods affected with contagious diseases, goods prohibited by law from being carried,[22] or goods the transportation of which might precipitate a dangerous riot.[23] When the carrier has reasonable grounds for suspicion that the goods are dangerous, he may refuse to receive such goods, unless he is permitted to open such goods or otherwise acquaint himself with their real nature.[24] Ordinarily, he has no right to insist upon being informed as to the contents of packages offered to him for shipment.[25]

Even though the goods are not dangerous by nature, the carrier may refuse to receive them if, in their then condition, they are unfit for shipment. The carrier may also refuse to accept goods which are improperly packed for shipping.[26] Thus the carrier could refuse eggs merely placed in an open basket, or liquids packed in vessels so fragile that they are certain to be broken in transportation.

20 The Nith (D. C.) 36 Fed. 86; California Powder Works v. Atlantic & P. Ry. Co., 113 Cal. 329, 45 Pac. 691, 36 L. R. A. 648.

21 Nitro-Glycerine Case, 15 Wall. 524, 21 L. Ed. 206.

22 Milwaukee Malt Extract Co. v. Chicago, R. I. & P. Ry., 73 Iowa, 98, 34 N. W. 761; State v. Goss, 59 Vt. 266, 9 Atl. 829, 59 Am. Rep. 706.

23 Edwards v. Sherratt, 1 East (Eng.) 604; Porcher v. Northeastern R. Co., 14 Rich. (S. C.) 181, 184; Pearson v. Duane, 4 Wall. 605, 18 L. Ed. 447.

24 Nitro-Glycerine Case, 15 Wall. 524, 21 L. Ed. 206; Brass v. Maitland, 6 El. & Bl. (Eng.) 485; Crouch v. Railroad Co., 14 C. B. (Eng.) 285, 291; Riley v. Horne, 5 Bing. (Eng.) 217, 222.

25 Nitro-Glycerine Case, 15 Wall. 524, 21 L. Ed. 206; Crouch v. Railroad Co., 14 C. B. (Eng.) 285, 291; Dinsmore v. Louisville, N. A. & C. R. Co. (C. C.) 3 Fed. 593. The right of the company to have parcels opened extends only to those suspected to contain dangerous articles. They have no general right, in all cases, and under all circumstances, to be informed of the contents tendered to be carried. Crouch v. Railway Co., 14 C. B. (Eng.) 255. Where a customer negligently fails to inform the carrier of the dangerous nature of a parcel, he will be liable for damages caused by it. Farrant v. Barnes, 31 Law J. C. P. (Eng.) 137, 11 C. B. (N. S.) 553.

26 Elgin, J. & E. Ry. Co. v. Bates Mach. Co., 98 Ill. App. 311, affirmed 200 Ill. 636, 66 N. E. 326, 93 Am. St. Rep. 218; Vicksburg Liquor & Tobacco Co. v. United States Exp. Co., 68 Miss. 149, 8 South. 332; Union Exp. Co. v. Graham, 26 Ohio St. 595. Goods packed so defectively as to entail upon the carrier extra care and risk may be refused. Munster v. Railway Co., 27 Law J. C. P. (Eng.) 308, 312; Hart v. Baxendale, 16 Law T. N. S. (Eng.) 396.

SAME—DUTY LIMITED BY THE CARRIER'S RIGHT TO DEMAND PAYMENT IN ADVANCE

113. The common carrier may refuse to carry the goods offered unless the transportation charges are paid in advance.

Since the common carrier of goods cannot choose with whom he will deal, but must carry indifferently for all who apply, it is but just that his compensation should be absolutely assured to him. Therefore the law treats him as it does the innkeeper, and not only gives him a lien upon the goods carried for his reasonable charges, but also authorizes him to require payment in advance.[27] The detailed consideration of this subject will be postponed to the chapter dealing with the rights of the common carrier of goods.[28]

Payment in advance is treated here solely as an excuse for the common carrier's refusal to carry the goods offered to him. This duty on the part of the carrier to carry for all falls away when the carrier demands the payment of his reasonable charges in advance, and this is refused by the shipper.[29] If such prepayment is not made on demand, the carrier is then under no obligation whatsoever to transport the goods. The money is not required to be paid down however, until the carrier receives the goods which he is bound to carry.[30] A carrier should therefore first accept the goods, and then demand payment as a condition precedent to transporting them.[31] The right to exact payment in advance may, of course, be waived,[32] and is waived by any conduct on the part of the carrier inconsistent with the continuance of the right,[33] such as an actual acceptance of the goods for carriage without a demand for prepayment of the charges.

[27] Fitch v. Newberry, 1 Doug. (Mich.) 1, 40 Am. Dec. 33; Pickford v. Railway Co., 8 Mees. & W. (Eng.) 372; Wyld v. Pickford, 8 Mees. & W. (Eng.) 443.

[28] See post, § 147.

[29] Wilder v. St. Johnsbury & L. C. R. Co., 66 Vt. 636, 30 Atl. 41; Illinois Cent. Ry. Co. v. Frankenberg, 54 Ill. 88, 5 Am. Rep. 92. But, unless the carrier demands prepayment, failure on the shipper's part to tender the charges will not justify the carrier's refusal to transport the goods. Galena & C. U. Ry. Co. v. Rae, 18 Ill. 488, 68 Am. Dec. 574.

[30] Pickford v. Ry. Co., 8 Mees. & W. (Eng.) 372.

[31] 1 Hutch. Carr. § 150.

[32] Louisville & N. R. Co. v. Allgood, 113 Ala. 163, 20 South. 986; Hannibal & St. J. Ry. Co. v. Swift, 12 Wall. 262, 20 L. Ed. 423.

[33] Grand Rapids & I. Ry. Co. v. Diether, 10 Ind. App. 206, 37 N. E. 39, 1069, 53 Am. St. Rep. 385; Southern Indiana Exp. Co. v. United States Exp. Co. (C. C.) 88 Fed. 659.

SAME—DUTY LIMITED TO AN OFFER OF THE GOODS BY THE OWNER OR HIS AGENT

114. The common carrier may refuse to accept goods offered for transportation by one who is neither the owner of the goods nor the owner's authorized agent.

Common carriers are bound to accept goods for transportation only when they are offered by their lawful owner or his agent with authority to make the shipment.[84] If the goods are innocently accepted by the common carrier from a person not the owner, and who has no such authority from the owner, then not only is the contract of carriage not binding personally against the owner, but such contract, as against the owner, does not even bind the goods. The owner could therefore demand the goods from the carrier, defeating the latter's lien.[85] The carrier, acting in good faith, it is usually held, does not become liable for conversion merely by innocently shipping the goods.[86] The carrier may become liable for conversion by refusing to deliver the goods to their rightful owner. When, however, the carrier, with knowledge of the situation, receives and transports the goods, the carrier then becomes an active participant in the wrong and is liable accordingly. From these considerations it is clear that the carrier, in refusing to accept goods for transportation, finds more than ample justification in the fact that the one offering the goods is neither the owner nor his authorized agent.[87]

DUTY TO FURNISH EQUAL FACILITIES TO ALL

115. Not only must the common carrier of goods serve the public, but he must serve the public impartially, without any preference or discrimination among shippers as to the facilities which are furnished.

84 Drake v. Nashville, C. & St. L. Ry. Co., 125 Tenn. 627, 148 S. W. 214; Fitch v. Newberry, 1 Doug. (Mich.) 1, 40 Am. Dec. 33; Gurley v. Armstead, 148 Mass. 267, 19 N. E. 389, 2 L. R. A. 80, 12 Am. St. Rep. 555.

85 Fitch v. Newberry, 1 Doug. (Mich.) 1, 40 Am. Dec. 33; Gurley v. Armstead, 148 Mass. 267, 19 N. E. 389, 2 L. R. A. 80, 12 Am. St. Rep. 555.

86 Gurley v. Armstead, 148 Mass. 267, 19 N. E. 389, 2 L. R. A. 80, 12 Am. St. Rep. 555.

87 A common carrier need not receive for transportation goods from any person other than the owner or his duly authorized agent. Drake v. Nashville, C. & St. L. R. Co., 125 Tenn. 627, 148 S. W. 214.

It is the purpose of the present section to discuss the question of preference or discrimination among shippers in regard to the carrier's facilities or the nature of the service. Discrimination in the rates charged for the service is left for subsequent consideration.[38]

The duty of the common carrier of goods is not limited to serving the public, but he must serve them impartially.[39] He does not perform his full duty, then, as to two shippers, by serving them both. He must go further, and not prefer the one to the other as to the way in which he serves them. The service must be disinterested, with nothing in it of favoritism.[40] This is true, not only as to the facilities furnished by the carrier and the general nature of the service, but is equally applicable to the highly important element of time. Shippers should be served in the order of their application. The carrier violates its duty of impartiality by withholding cars from one shipper and furnishing them sooner to one who subsequently applied.[41]

[38] Post, § 148.

[39] ST. LOUIS SOUTHWESTERN R. CO. v. CLAY COUNTY GIN CO., 77 Ark. 357, 92 S. W. 531, Dobie Cas. Bailments and Carriers, 185; Memphis News Pub. Co. v. Southern R. Co., 110 Tenn. 684, 75 S. W. 941, 63 L. R. A. 150; Loraine v. Pittsburg, J., E. & E. Ry. Co., 205 Pa. 132, 54 Atl. 580, 61 L. R. A. 502; Strough v. New York Cent. & H. R. R. Co., 181 N. Y. 533, 73 N E. 1133; New England Exp. Co. v. Maine Cent. R. Co., 57 Me. 188, 2 Am. Rep. 31; International Exp. Co. v. Grand Trunk Railway of Canada, 81 Me. 92, 16 Atl. 370; Houston & T. C. Ry. Co. v. Smith, 63 Tex. 322; McDuffee v. Portland & R. R. R., 52 N. H. 430, 13 Am. Rep. 72; Messenger v. Pennsylvania R. Co., 37 N. J. Law, 531, 18 Am. Rep. 754; CHICAGO & N. W. RY. CO. v. PEOPLE ex rel. HEMPSTEAD, 56 Ill. 365, 8 Am. Rep. 690, Dobie Cas. Bailments and Carriers, 183.

[40] In State ex rel. Cumberland Telephone & Telegraph Co. v. Texas & P. Ry. Co., 52 La. Ann. 1850, 28 South. 284, mandamus was held proper to compel the carrier to furnish to one telephone and telegraph company the facilities extended to its rival. See, also, Loraine v. Pittsburg, J., E. & E. Ry. Co., 205 Pa. 132, 54 Atl. 580, 61 L. R. A. 502, when the discrimination was due to the selfish private interests of the president of the railroad; CHICAGO & N. W. RY. CO. v. PEOPLE ex rel. HEMPSTEAD, 56 Ill. 365, 8 Am. Rep. 690, Dobie Cas. Bailments and Carriers, 183, involving delivery to some grain elevators and not to others.

[41] Rhodes v. Northern Pac. Ry. Co., 34 Minn. 87, 24 N. W. 347; Nichols v. Oregon Short Line Ry. Co., 24 Utah, 83, 66 Pac. 768, 91 Am. St. Rep. 778; Houston & T. C. Ry. Co. v. Smith, 63 Tex. 322; Great Western Ry. Co. of Canada v. Burns, 60 Ill. 284; CHICAGO & N. W. R. CO. v. PEOPLE ex rel. HEMPSTEAD, 56 Ill. 365, 8 Am. Rep. 690, Dobie Cas. Bailments and Carriers, 183; Chicago & A. R. Co. v. People ex rel. Koerner, 67 Ill. 11, 16 Am. Rep. 599; Wibert v. New York & E. R. Co., 12 N. Y. 245; Keeney v. Grand Trunk R. Co. of Canada, 47 N. Y. 525.

It is said that the discrimination resulting from a refusal to serve one shipper differs from the discrimination when the carrier serves one shipper better than another only in degree and not in kind.[42] The public nature of the common carrier's calling forbids any partiality in his service which might easily be used to foster monopolies or to crush the business of individuals or even communities.[43] Not merely absolute fairness is required in each case, but comparative fairness when that case is contrasted with another. As was said of railroad companies in an Indiana case:[44] "Every one constituting a part of the public for whose use they are constructed is entitled to an equal and impartial participation in the use of the facilities for transportation which they afford."

In the rule that no favors, no distinctions, are permissible between shippers as to the carrier's facilities, the word "facilities" is used in its broadest sense. It includes, not only rolling stock, but stational facilities, warehouses, docks, pens for facilitating the loading of animals, as well as the many and varied appliances and instrumentalities used in his vast business by the modern carrier.

[42] "That is not, in the ordinary legal sense, a public highway, in which one man is unreasonably privileged to use a convenient path, and another is unreasonably restricted to the gutter; and that is not a public service of common carriage, in which one enjoys an unreasonable preference or advantage, and another suffers an unreasonable prejudice or disadvantage. A denial of the entire right of service, by a refusal to carry, differs, if at all, in degree only, and the amount of damage done, and not in the essential legal character of the act, from a denial of the right in part by an unreasonable discrimination in terms, facilities, or accommodations. Whether the denial is general, by refusing to furnish any transportation whatever, or special, by refusing to carry one person or his goods; whether it is direct, by expressly refusing to carry, or indirect, by imposing such unreasonable terms, facilities, or accommodations as render carriage undesirable; whether unreasonableness of terms, facilities, or accommodations operate as a total or a partial denial of the right; and whether the unreasonableness is in the intrinsic, individual nature of the terms, facilities, or accommodations, or in their discriminating, collective, and comparative character—the right denied is one and the same common right, which would not be a right if it could be rightfully denied, and would not be common, in the legal sense, if it could be legally subjected to unreasonable discrimination, and parceled out among men in unreasonably superior and inferior grades at the behest of the servant from whom the service is due." McDuffee v. Portland & R. R. R., 52 N. H. 430, 450, 13 Am. Rep. 72.

[43] As to the service of communities and the distribution of facilities between different stations and parts of the carrier's lines, see Ballentine v. North Missouri R. Co., 40 Mo. 491, 93 Am. Dec. 315; Ayres v. Chicago & N. W. Ry. Co., 71 Wis. 372, 37 N. W. 432, 5 Am. St. Rep. 226; Martin v. Great Northern Ry. Co., 110 Minn. 118, 124 N. W. 825; Chicago, St. L. & P. R. Co. v. Wolcott, 141 Ind. 267, 39 N. E. 451, 50 Am. Rep. 320.

[44] Louisville, E. & St. L. Con. Ry. Co. v. Wilson, 132 Ind. 517, 32 N. E. 311, 18 L. R. A. 105.

The shipper, then, can in this respect demand, not only service from the common carrier, but service that is fair, equal, and impartial, involving no invidious distinctions, differences, favors, or preferences.

The common law on this subject has been fortified and extended by statutes, both state and federal. Thus it is expressly prohibited by section 3 of the Interstate Commerce Act (Act Feb. 4, 1887, c. 104, 24 Stat. 379 [U. S. Comp. St. 1901, p. 3154]) in the broadest and clearest terms, and not a few cases have been brought before the Interstate Commerce Commission involving such preferences, either as between individual shippers or communities.[45]

"The Express Cases"

The question has been frequently before the courts, resulting in conflicting decisions, as to the legal right of a railroad company to grant by contract to one express company the exclusive use of its passenger trains for the carrying on of the express company's business, and a denial of this privilege to all other express companies. In several of the earlier cases, in Maine,[46] New Hampshire,[47] and Pennsylvania,[48] this right on the part of the railroad was denied, as giving an undue preference.[49]

The United States Supreme Court, however, in what are known as the "Express Cases,"[50] upheld the right, and this is now the accepted doctrine. The Supreme Court held that the duty was owed to the public to provide facilities for the proper handling of express business, and not to the express companies to provide them with equal facilities for handling their business. "While railroad companies must furnish the public with an express service, such companies are not obliged to furnish express facilities to

[45] For an extended discussion of the provisions of section 3 of this act, see Judson on Interstate Commerce (2d Ed.) §§ 227–287.

[46] New England Exp. Co. v. Maine Cent. Ry. Co., 57 Me. 188, 2 Am. Rep. 31; International Exp. Co. v. Grand Trunk Railway Co. of Canada, 81 Me. 92, 16 Atl. 370.

[47] McDuffee v. Portland & R. R. R., 52 N. H. 430, 13 Am. Rep. 72.

[48] Sandford v. Catawissa, W. & E. Ry. Co., 24 Pa. 378, 64 Am. Dec. 667.

[49] This seems to be the English doctrine. Parker v. Ry. Co., 7 M. & G. 253; Pickford v. Ry. Co., 10 M. & W. 399. See, also, in support of this doctrine, 1 Wyman, Pub. Serv. Corporations, §§ 477–480.

[50] Memphis & L. R. R. Co. v. Southern Exp. Co., 117 U. S. 1, 6 Sup. Ct. 542, 628, 29 L. Ed. 791. Two justices, Miller and Field, dissented. The Express Cases overruled what had been the doctrine declared by the inferior federal courts. See Southern Exp. Co. v. Memphis & L. R. R. Co. (C. C.) 2 McCrary, 570, 8 Fed. 799; Wells, Fargo & Co. v. Northern Pac. Ry. Co. (C. C.) 23 Fed. 469.

all applying for them, but that they perform their whole duty to the public at large, and to each individual, when they afford the public all reasonable accommodations. If this is done, the railroad company owes no duty to the public as to the particular agencies it shall select for that purpose."

The inconveniences have also been pointed out which would follow if railroads were compelled to furnish equal facilities on their passenger trains to all express companies which duly applied for the privilege. Accordingly, if the public, to whom the carrier's duty is owed, is efficiently served, the discontented express company should not be heard to complain merely because it is not permitted to perform the service.[51]

LIABILITY OF THE CARRIER FOR LOSS OF, OR DAMAGE TO, THE GOODS

116. The common carrier is an insurer of goods carried in that capacity against all loss or damage except that caused by:

EXCEPTIONS:

(1) The act of God.

(2) The public enemy.

(3) The act of the shipper.

(4) Public authority.

(5) The inherent nature of the goods.

Even when the loss is caused by one of the excepted perils against which the common carrier is not an insurer, he is nevertheless liable if he fails to use reasonable care either to avoid such peril or to minimize the loss after the goods are actually exposed to the peril.

[51] Pfister v. Central Pac. Ry. Co., 70 Cal. 169, 11 Pac. 686, 59 Am. Rep. 404; Sargent v. Boston & L. R. Co., 115 Mass. 416. In Atlantic Exp. Co. v. Wilmington & W. R. Co., 111 N. C. 463, 16 S. E. 393, 18 L. R. A. 393, 32 Am. St. Rep. 805, it was held that a statute providing that it shall be unlawful for any common carrier to give any unreasonable preference to any particular person, company, or locality, or any particular description of traffic, or to subject any person, company, or locality, or any particular description of traffic to any undue disadvantage, did not change or enlarge the duty imposed on railroad companies by the common law, under which they are not obliged, because they furnish facilities to one express company, to furnish other express companies with facilities for doing an express business on their roads, the same in all respects as they provide for themselves, or afford to any particular express company, where such railroad companies have never held themselves out as common carriers of express companies. A regulation concerning freight rates, which provides that no railroad company shall, by reason of any contract, with any express or other company, refuse to act as

By the common law the common carrier is, with certain exceptions, an insurer of the goods intrusted to him. According to the very early cases,[52] the only exceptions to the common carrier's liability as an insurer of the safe delivery of the goods were: (1) The act of God; and (2) the public enemy. To these, however, native justice and the genius of our jurisprudence have added: (3) The act of the shipper; (4) public authority; and (5) inherent nature of the goods.[53]

As we have already seen, the ordinary bailee is required to exercise a certain degree of care, and he is liable only for a failure to exercise this degree of care. His liability is therefore confined to a breach of duty, or negligence. Considerations of public policy seemed to demand a higher measure of responsibility on the part of the common carrier of goods. He is accordingly, with the exceptions mentioned, held liable at all hazards for loss or damage, regardless of how inevitable was the accident causing it or what degree of care he has exercised. He is, with the exceptions in question, an *insurer* of the safe delivery of the goods. The common carrier's responsibility is thus measured by an entirely dif-

a common carrier, to transport any article proper for transportation by the train for which it is offered, does not require railroad companies to furnish an express company with facilities for carrying on its business on their roads, but simply requires them to transport articles. Id.

[52] COGGS v. BERNARD, 2 Ld. Raym. (Eng.) 909, Dobie Cas. Bailments and Carriers, 1; Riley v. Horne, 5 Bing. (Eng.) 217. The common law duty is similarly phrased in many modern cases, though all five of the exceptions are recognized. A carrier is not only liable at common law for loss occurring through the negligence of itself or its servants or agents, but, in addition, is liable for loss occurring from fire, robbery, accident not attributable to negligence, or any cause other than the act of God or of public enemies. Oregon Short Line Ry. Co. v. Blyth, 19 Wyo. 410, 118 Pac. 649, 119 Pac. 875, Ann. Cas. 1913E, 288. A common carrier must use strictest care and deliver safely at the destination; he being regarded as an insurer, excusable from liability only for an act of God or public enemies. Klair v. Philadelphia, B. & W. R. Co., 2 Boyce (Del.) 274, 78 Atl. 1085.

[53] 1 Hutch. Carr. § 265; Van Zile, Bailm. & Carr. § 466; Goddard, Bailm. & Carr. § 231. A carrier, being an insurer, may not escape liability for nonperformance of the contract of transportation, except by showing that a failure to transport or deliver arose from an act of God or the public enemy, or public authority, act of the shipper, or from the intrinsic nature of the property itself. Wells v. Great Northern Ry. Co., 59 Or. 165, 114 Pac. 92, 116 Pac. 1070, 34 L. R. A. (N. S.) 818, 825. See, also, J. H. Cownie Glove Co. v. Merchants Dispatch Transp. Co., 130 Iowa, 327, 106 N. W. 749, 4 L. R. A. (N. S.) 1060, 114 Am. St. Rep. 419; Southern Ry. Co. v. Levy, 144 Ala. 614, 39 South. 95; Central of Georgia Ry. Co. v. Lippman, 110 Ga. 665, 36 S. E. 202, 50 L. R. A. 673; Lacey v. Oregon Ry. & Nav. Co., 63 Or. 596, 128 Pac. 999; Henry Bromschwig Tailors' Trimming Co. v. Missouri, K. & T. Ry. Co., 165 Mo. App. 350, 147 S. W. 175.

ferent type of standard from that of the ordinary bailee. The former's liability, we say, is measured in terms of insurance; the latter's liability, in terms of negligence. Hence, when loss or injury occurs, the only defense open to the common carrier of goods is to show that such loss or injury was due to one of the five excepted perils.

Reason of the Rule

The reason for the rule imposing so stringent a liability upon common carriers of goods is thus stated by Lord Holt in the great case of COGGS v. BERNARD:[54] "The law charges this person [the common carrier] thus intrusted to carry goods against all acts but acts of God and the enemies of the king. For, though the force be ever so great, as if an irresistible multitude of people should rob him, nevertheless he is chargeable. And this is a politic establishment, contrived by the policy of the law for the safety of all persons, the necessity of whose affairs oblige them to trust these sorts of persons, that they may be safe in their ways of dealing; for else these carriers might have an opportunity of undoing all persons that had any dealings with them, or combining with thieves, etc., and yet doing it in such a clandestine manner as would not be possible to be discovered. And this is the reason the law is founded upon on that point."

Speaking on the same subject, Chief Justice Best, in Riley v. Horne,[55] said: "When goods are delivered to a carrier, they are usually no longer under the eye of the owner. He seldom follows or sends any servant with them to the place of their destination. If they should be lost or injured by the grossest negligence of the carrier or his servants, or stolen by them, or by thieves in collusion with them, the owner would be unable to prove either of these causes of loss. His witnesses must be the carrier's servants, and they, knowing that they could not be contradicted, would excuse their masters and themselves. To give due security to property, the law has added to that responsibility of a carrier which immediately arises out of his contract to carry for a reward—namely, that of taking all reasonable care of it—the responsibility of an insurer."

Though these reasons are by no means so cogent as when these opinions were written, owing to rapid advances in civilization and methods of transportation, yet, as the power and importance of the carrier have grown apace, other considerations have justified the expediency and practical wisdom of the common-law rule.[56]

[54] 2 Ld. Raym. (Eng.) 909, 918, Doble Cas. Bailments and Carriers, 1.

[55] 5 Bing (Eng.) 217.

[56] Roberts v. Turner, 12 Johns. (N. Y.) 232; Thomas v. Boston & P. R. Corp., 10 Metc. (Mass.) 472, 43 Am. Dec. 444; Hollister v. Nowlen, 19 Wend. (N. Y.)

This remains, accordingly, in the absence of statute or special contract, the test of the liability of the common carrier of goods.[57]

Retention of Custody by Shipper

Where the shipper does not put the goods in the exclusive custody and control of the carrier, but, on the contrary, the shipper himself or his servant accompanies them and retains possession of them, then the extraordinary liability of a common carrier does not attach.[58] The unusual liability is imposed on the common carrier only when there is a bailment of the goods. If, therefore, the shipper retains possession of the goods, there is no real delivery to the carrier, and without such a delivery to him the carrier is not clothed with his extraordinary responsibility. This liability presupposes a trust reposed in the carrier by vesting him with possession of the goods.[59] Then, too, to be thus responsible, the carrier must be given a control over the goods commensurate with his responsibility.

Thus, where one who shipped goods by boat, put a guardian on board, who locked the hatches, and went with the goods to see that they were delivered safely, the owner of the boat was held not liable as a common carrier, because there was no trust reposed in the carrier, and the goods were to be considered as having been in the possession of the shipper's servant rather than in the pos-

234, 32 Am. Dec. 455; Elkins v. Boston & M. R. Co., 23 N. H. 275; Moses v. Boston & M. R. R., 24 N. H. 71, 55 Am. Dec. 222; Henry Bromschwig Tailors' Trimming Co. v. Missouri, K. & T. Ry. Co., 165 Mo. App. 350, 147 S. W. 175.

[57] Fish v. Chapman, 2 Ga. 349, 46 Am. Dec. 393; Williams v. Grant, 1 Conn. 487, 7 Am. Dec. 235; MERRITT v. EARLE, 29 N. Y. 115, 86 Am. Dec. 292, Dobie Cas. Bailments and Carriers, 188; Parsons v. Hardy, 14 Wend. (N. Y.) 215, 28 Am. Dec. 521; Colt v. McMechen, 6 Johns. (N. Y.) 160, 5 Am. Dec. 200; Wood v. Crocker, 18 Wis. 345; Welsh v. Pittsburg, Ft. W. & C. R. Co., 10 Ohio St. 65, 75 Am. Dec. 490; Parker v. Flagg, 26 Me. 181, 45 Am. Dec. 101; Blumenthal v. Brainerd, 38 Vt. 402, 91 Am. Dec. 349; Hooper v. Wells, Fargo & Co., 27 Cal. 11, 85 Am. Dec. 211; Adams Exp. Co. v. Darnell, 31 Ind. 20, 99 Am. Dec. 582; Gulf, C. & S. F. Ry. Co. v. Levi, 76 Tex. 337, 13 S. W. 191, 8 L. R. A. 323, 18 Am. St. Rep. 45; Daggett v. Shaw, 3 Mo. 264, 25 Am. Dec. 439; Farley v. Lavary, 107 Ky. 523, 54 S. W. 840, 21 Ky. Law Rep. 1252, 47 L. R. A. 383; McFadden v. Missouri Pac. Ry. Co., 92 Mo. 343, 4 S. W. 689, 1 Am. St. Rep. 721; The Niagara v. Cordes, 21 How. 7, 16 L. Ed. 41.

[58] Tower v. Utica & S. R. R. Co., 7 Hill (N. Y.) 47, 42 Am. Dec. 36; East India Co. v. Pullen, 1 Strange (Eng.) 690. Thus, where a steerage passenger in a ship retained exclusive possession and custody of his trunk, and trusted to his own care and vigilance to protect it against loss, the shipowner was held not to be liable as a common carrier. Cohen v. Frost, 2 Duer (N. Y.) 335.

[59] 1 Hutch. Carr. § 110.

session of the carrier.[60] In Wyckoff v. Queens County Ferry Co.[61] it was said: "A ferryman is not a common carrier of the property retained by a passenger in his own custody and under his own control, and liable as such for all losses and injuries except those caused by the act of God or the public enemies. * * * The liability of a common carrier, in all its extent, only attaches when there is an actual bailment."

But the mere fact that the owner or his servant accompanies the goods, or is active in watching over them, does not of itself negative the carrier's liability as an insurer, if the goods have been delivered to the carrier, so that their custody and control are vested in him.[62] When, however, possession is retained by the shipper, there is no bailment, and the carrier is liable, not as an insurer, but solely for any loss or damage that is due to his negligence.

Act of God

Where goods have been lost or injured by what is known in legal phraseology as the "act of God," the common carrier is not liable.[63] While the authorities are unanimous in recognizing the exception, they are consistent neither in the definiton nor in the application of the term. The meaning of "act of God" in this connection, however, is a practical rather than a philosophical, speculative or theological question.

Upon this point there are at least two well-defined theories. According to the so-called "passive theory" the term "act of God" includes all occurrences due to natural causes without the intervention of any human agency. As the broader and saner rule, this has the support of a large majority of the cases,[64] and is regarded

[60] East India Co. v. Pullen, 1 Strange (Eng.) 690.

[61] 52 N. Y. 32, 11 Am. Rep. 650.

[62] Hollister v. Nowlen, 19 Wend. (N. Y.) 234, 32 Am. Dec. 455; Brind v. Dale, 8 Car. & P. (Eng.) 207; Robinson v. Dunmore, 2 Bos. & P. (Eng.) 416. This question frequently arises in shipments of live stock. See post, § 119.

[63] Forward v. Pittard, 1 T. R. (Eng.) 27; Fish v. Chapman, 2 Ga. 349, 46 Am. Dec. 393; Blythe v. Denver & R. G. R. Co., 15 Colo. 333, 25 Pac. 702, 11 L. R. A. 615, 22 Am. St. Rep. 403; Fergusson v. Brent, 12 Md. 9, 71 Am. Dec. 582; Ferguson v. Southern Ry. Co., 91 S. C. 61, 74 S. E. 129; Herring v. Chesapeake & W. R. Co., 101 Va. 778, 45 S. E. 322; Wald v. Pittsburg, C. & St. L. R. Co., 162 Ill. 545, 44 N. E. 888, 35 L. R. A. 356, 53 Am. St. Rep. 332.

[64] Williams v. Grant, 1 Conn. 487, 7 Am. Dec. 235; Smyrl v. Niolen, 2 Bailey (S. C.) 421, 23 Am. Dec. 146; Faulkner v. Wright, Rice (S. C.) 107; MERRITT v. EARLE, 29 N. Y. 115, 86 Am. Dec. 292, Dobie Cas. Bailments and Carriers, 188; Trent Nav. Co. v. Ward, 3 Esp. (Eng.) 127; McArthur v. Sears, 21 Wend. (N. Y.) 190; Ewart v. Street, 2 Bailey (S. C.) 157, 23 Am. Dec. 131; Backhouse v. Sneed, 5 N. C. 173; Nugent v. Smith, 1 C. P. Div. (Eng.) 423; Turney v. Wilson, 7 Yerg. (Tenn.) 340, 27 Am. Dec. 515; Hays v. Kennedy, 41 Pa. 378, 80 Am. Dec. 627.

with favor by most of the text-writers.[65] The narrower "active theory" limits the term to more or less violent disturbances of the elemental forces of nature, such as lightning or earthquakes, and does not include the gradual and more or less orderly changes in the physical world.[66]

As we shall later see, even when loss or injury is due to a cause admitted to be an act of God, this will not excuse the common carrier if he has been negligent in exposing the goods to the peril or in failing to minimize the loss after the act has occurred.[67] The suddenness and violence of the act, and particularly its unexpectedness, are therefore of frequent practical importance in determining whether or not the carrier was negligent in failing either to anticipate the act or to escape its consequences. The more sudden and unexpected the act, the more difficult it is for the carrier to anticipate it by exercising ordinary care; the more violent the act, the harder it is for the carrier to avoid the loss or minimize the injury.

Under either theory, however, "act of God" is a much narrower term than "inevitable accident." [68] An accident may be inevitable, whether due to divine or human agency. "Inevitable accident," therefore admits of an occurrence due to human agency; "act of God" is limited to causes operating in the physical universe, disassociated from any act of man. "Act of God," too, is not synonymous with, and should therefore not be confused with, the phrase

[65] 1 Hutch. Carr. § 170; 2 Kent, Comm. 597; Story, Bailm. §§ 489, 490, 511; Goddard, Bailm. & Carr. § 232; Van Zile, Bailm. & Carr. § 469.

[66] Probably the leading case in support of this view is Friend v. Woods, 6 Grat. (Va.) 189, 52 Am. Dec. 119, in which the cases of Williams v. Grant and Smyrl v. Niolon (see note 64) are expressly repudiated. In Fish v. Chapman, 2 Ga. 349, 46 Am. Dec. 393, the court used this language: "By the act of God is meant any accident produced by physical causes that are irresistible, such as lightning, storms, perils of the sea, earthquakes, inundations, sudden death, or illness." See, also, Gleeson v. Virginia Midland R. Co., 140 U. S. 435, 11 Sup. Ct. 859, 35 L. Ed. 458; Hays v. Kennedy, 41 Pa. 378, 80 Am. Dec. 627, discussing the absolute and relative meaning of "act of God." In the great majority of cases the questions involved do not require that a distinction be made between the active and passive theories.

[67] Post, § 117; Bason v. Charleston & C. Steamboat Co., Harp. (S. C.) 262; Adams Exp. Co. v. Jackson, 92 Tenn. 326, 21 S. W. 666; Nelson v. Great Northern Ry. Co., 28 Mont. 297, 72 Pac. 642; Ferguson v. Southern Ry. Co., 91 S. C. 61, 74 S. E. 129.

[68] Forward v. Pittard, 1 Term R. (Eng.) 27; Nugent v. Smith, 1 C. P. Div. (Eng.) 19; MERRITT v. EARLE, 29 N. Y. 115, 86 Am. Dec. 292, Dobie Cas. Bailments and Carriers, 188. Cf. Fish v. Chapman, 2 Ga. 349, 46 Am. Dec. 393; Central Line of Boats v. Lowe, 50 Ga. 509; Hays v. Kennedy, 41 Pa. 378, 80 Am. Dec. 627.

"perils of the sea," so often found in marine bills of lading and insurance policies.[69]

Same—Proximate and Exclusive Cause

The courts have been very zealous in refusing to excuse the carrier on the score of an act of God, when there has been any admixture of human agency.[70] As we have just seen, the underlying idea of the phrase "act of God" is the total absence of any act of man. The act of God, then, on which the carrier bases his exemption from liability, must be the proximate cause of the loss or injury, not a remote cause, and the exclusive cause, rather than a mere contributing cause.[71]

Thus, where a vessel was driven against a concealed anchor in a river and was sunk, the carrier was held liable, because a human agency contributed to the accident by placing the anchor where it was at the time it was struck.[72] So, also, when the carrier's vessel was lost by striking the mast of a sunken boat.[73] Again, the master of a vessel, on a snowy night, grounded his ship, owing to his mistaking the light on a schooner for the lighthouse beacon, which was not burning through some neglect.[74] In holding the carrier responsible, Cowen, J., said: "I have sought in vain for any case to excuse the loss of the carrier where it arises from human action or neglect, or any combination of such action or neglect."

Same—Goods Exposed to Act of God by Unreasonable Delay

The courts are fairly evenly divided on the question of the common carrier's liability for loss or damage due to an act of God, to which the goods would not have been exposed, save for the car-

[69] Friend v. Woods, 6 Grat. (Va.) 189, 52 Am. Dec. 119; Hays v. Kennedy, 41 Pa. 378, 80 Am. Dec. 627; The Majestic, 166 U. S. 375, 17 Sup. Ct. 597, 41 L. Ed. 1039.

[70] Ante, pp. 328–329.

[71] King v. Shepherd, 3 Story, 356, Fed. Cas. No. 7,804; Green-Wheeler Shoe Co. v. Chicago, R. I. & P. Ry. Co., 130 Iowa, 123, 106 N. W. 498, 5 L. R. A. (N. S.) 882, 8 Ann. Cas. 45; Hart v. Allen, 2 Watts (Pa.) 114; Alabama Great Southern R. Co. v. Quarles, 145 Ala. 436, 40 South. 120, 5 L. R. A. (N. S.) 867, 117 Am. St. Rep. 54, 8 Ann. Cas. 308; Packard v. Taylor, 35 Ark. 402, 37 Am. Rep. 37; Michaels v. New York Cent. R. Co., 30 N. Y. 564, 86 Am. Dec. 415; Ewart v. Street, 2 Bailey (S. C.) 157, 23 Am. Dec. 131; Sprowl v. Kellar, 4 Stew. & P. (Ala.) 382; Blythe v. Denver & R. G. R. Co., 15 Colo. 333, 25 Pac. 702, 11 L. R. A. 615, 22 Am. St. Rep. 403.

[72] Trent Nav. Co. v. Ward, 3 Esp. (Eng.) 127.

[73] MERRITT v. EARLE, 29 N. Y. 115, 86 Am. Dec. 292, Dobie Cas. Bailments and Carriers, 188.

[74] McArthur v. Sears, 21 Wend. (N. Y.) 190. A like decision was reached when a boat was lost by running on a piece of timber projecting from a wharf which was not visible at ordinary tides. New Brunswick Steamboat & Canal Transp. Co. v. Tiers, 24 N. J. Law, 697, 64 Am. Dec. 394.

rier's negligent and unreasonable delay. If the casualty could have been foreseen and avoided by the exercise of reasonable care, or if, by exercising like care, the casualty could have been avoided after the danger became apparent, then the courts agree in pronouncing the common carrier liable.[75] For, even as to the excepted perils, the carrier must use reasonable care to avert or minimize loss of, or injury to, the goods resulting from such perils.

The conflict of authority arises, when, though the loss or injury would not have occurred but for the negligent delay, the carrier, by the exercise of reasonable care, could not have anticipated the operation of the act of God, and could not have avoided the loss or injury after the danger became apparent. By what is believed to be the weight of authority, the carrier in such cases is not liable, on the ground that the act of God and not the delay was the proximate cause of the loss or injury.[76] This seems sound, for the delay is, from a practical standpoint, a mere condition of such loss or injury rather than a cause. The carrier, as to the delay, was negligent, it is true; but the loss or injury did not result either naturally or proximately from such negligence. The law, in fixing responsibility, looks not to a more or less remote condition, but to a present, operating, and efficient proximate cause.

A great many courts, however, under such circumstances, hold the carrier liable.[77] These cases decline to distinguish between

[75] Grier v. St. Louis Merchants' Bridge Terminal Ry. Co., 108 Mo. App. 565, 84 S. W. 158; Baltimore & O. Ry. Co. v. Keedy, 75 Md. 320, 23 Atl. 643.

[76] Denny v. New York Cent. R. Co., 13 Gray (Mass.) 481, 74 Am. Dec. 645; Michigan Cent. R. Co. v. Burrows, 33 Mich. 6; Hoadley v. Northern Transportation Co., 115 Mass. 304, 15 Am. Rep. 106; Morrison v. Davis, 20 Pa. 171, 57 Am. Dec. 695; Memphis & C. R. Co. v. Reeves, 10 Wall. 176, 19 L. Ed. 909; McClary v. Sioux City & P. R. Co., 3 Neb. 44, 19 Am. Rep. 631. And see Caldwell v. Southern Express Co., 1 Flip. 88, Fed. Cas. No. 2,303; Collier v. Valentine, 11 Mo. 299, 49 Am. Dec. 81; Northern Pac. Ry. Co. v. Kempton, 138 Fed. 792, 71 C. C. A. 246; Scheffer v. Washington City, V. M. & G. S. Ry. Co., 105 U. S. 249, 26 L. Ed. 1070; Herring v. Chesapeake & W. R. Co., 101 Va. 778, 45 S. E. 322; Read v. St. Louis, K. C. & N. R. Co., 60. Mo. 199; Gulf, C. & S. F. R. Co. v. Darby, 28 Tex. Civ. App. 229, 67 S. W. 129; Moffatt Commission Co. v. Union Pac. Ry. Co., 113 Mo. App. 544, 88 S. W. 117; Yazoo & M. V. R. Co. v. Millsaps, 76 Miss. 855, 25 South. 672, 71 Am. St. Rep. 536.

[77] Read v. Spaulding, 30 N. Y. 630, 86 Am. Dec. 426; Michaels v. New York Cent. R. Co., 30 N. Y. 564, 86 Am. Dec. 415; Condict v. Grand Trunk R. Co., 54 N. Y. 500; Hewett v. Chicago, B. & Q. R. Co., 63 Iowa, 611, 19 N. W. 790; Read v. St. Louis, K. C. & N. R. Co., 60 Mo. 199; McGraw v. Baltimore & O. R. Co., 18 W. Va. 361, 41 Am. Rep. 696; Pruitt v. Hannibal & St. J. R. Co., 62 Mo. 527; Michigan Cent. R. Co. v. Curtis, 80 Ill. 324; Southern Exp. Co. v. Womack, 1 Heisk. (Tenn.) 256; Wald v. Pittsburg, C., C. & St. L. R. Co., 162 Ill. 545, 44 N. E. 888, 35 L. R. A. 356, 53 Am. St. Rep.

the negligent delay and act of God as to their comparative nearness or efficiency in the scale of causation in producing the loss or injury. The carrier is accordingly held responsible as his negligence contributed, in a measure at least, to the loss of, or injury to, the goods. The basis of the carrier's liability here is sometimes placed on the score that the carrier's negligent delay has the same effect as a wrongful deviation, which, as we shall see, renders the carrier absolutely liable even for loss or injury resulting from the excepted perils.[78] But this unusual responsibility is imposed only as the result of the exercise by the carrier of some unlawful act of dominion over the goods, inconsistent with another's ownership, equivalent to a conversion. It seems clear that a mere negligent delay by the carrier falls far short of this.

Illustrations—What is, and What is Not, an Act of God

Lightning,[79] tempest,[80] earthquake,[81] extraordinary flood,[82] unusual snowstorm,[83] severe gale[84] of wind, are clearly acts of God under either the active or passive theories. Under the broader passive theory, the carrier was excused on the basis of an act of God, where his vessel struck on a hidden rock,[85] the position of which

332; Bibb Broom Corn Co. v. Atchison, T. & S. F. R. Co., 94 Minn. 269, 102 N. W. 709, 69 L. R. A. 509, 110 Am. St. Rep. 361, 3 Ann. Cas. 450; Green-Wheeler Shoe Co. v. Chicago, R. I. & P. R. Co., 130 Iowa, 123, 106 N. W. 498, 5 L. R. A. (N. S.) 882, 8 Ann. Cas. 45; Alabama Great Southern R. Co. v. Quarles et al., 145 Ala. 436, 40 South. 120, 5 L. R. A. (N. S.) 867, 117 Am. St. Rep. 54, 8 Ann. Cas. 308.

78 See 1 Hutch. Carr. § 301.

79 Forward v. Pittard, 1 Term R. (Eng.) 27, 33.

80 Gillett v. Ellis, 11 Ill. 579.

81 Slater v. South Carolina Ry. Co., 29 S. C. 96, 6 S. E. 936.

82 Long v. Pennsylvania Ry. Co., 147 Pa. 343, 23 Atl. 459, 14 L. R. A. 741, 30 Am. St. Rep. 732; Wald v. Pittsburg, C., C. & St. L. Ry. Co., 162 Ill. 545, 44 N. E. 888, 35 L. R. A. 356, 53 Am. St. Rep. 332; Ferguson v. Southern Ry. Co., 91 S. C. 61, 74 S. E. 129; Lovering v. Buck Mountain Coal Co., 54 Pa. 291; Nashville & C. R. Co. v. David, 6 Heisk. (Tenn.) 261, 19 Am. Rep. 594; Davis v. Wabash, St. L. & P. R. Co., 89 Mo. 340, 1 S. W. 327; Norris v. Savannah, F. & W. R. Co., 23 Fla. 182, 1 South. 475, 11 Am. St. Rep. 355; Smith v. Western Ry. of Alabama, 91 Ala. 455, 8 South. 754, 11 L. R. A. 619, 24 Am. St. Rep. 929. A flood such as has occurred but twice in a generation is an act of God. Pearce v. The Thomas Newton (D. C.) 41 Fed. 106.

83 Black v. Chicago, B. & Q. R. Co., 30 Neb. 197, 46 N. W. 428; Feinberg v. Delaware, L. & W. R. Co., 52 N. J. Law, 451, 20 Atl. 33; Chapin v. Chicago, M. & St. P. R. Co., 79 Iowa, 582, 44 N. W. 820.

84 Blythe v. Denver & R. G. R. Co., 15 Colo. 333, 25 Pac. 702, 11 L. R. A. 615, and notes, 22 Am. St. Rep. 403. See, also, Miltimore v. Chicago & N. W. R. Co., 37 Wis. 190; New England & S. S. S. Co. v. Paige, 108 Ga. 296, 33 S. E. 969; Gulf, C. & S. F. Ry. Co. v. Compton (Tex. Civ. App.) 38 S. W. 220.

85 Williams v. Grant, 1 Conn. 487, 7 Am. Dec. 235.

had not before been known or charted, and also when his boat was sunk by a snag lodged[86] in the river by a freshet. In a state holding to the active theory, however, these two cases were expressly repudiated, and the carrier was held liable when his boat ran on a bar formed by a rise and an ice gorge at the mouth of a tributary river.[87] The United States Supreme Court refused to excuse the carrier for injury to goods due to a landslide in a railroad cut caused by a loosening of the superficial earth owing to an ordinary rain, holding that the carrier was negligent in not foreseeing and providing against such ordinary occurrences.[88] The celebrated Johnstown flood of 1889, due to the unexpected breaking of a dam, was held to be an act of God.[89]

Fires, not caused by lightning,[90] and boiler explosions,[91] are held not to be acts of God, owing to the interposition of human agency. The same reason is assigned for similar holdings in cases involving the shifting of buoys[92] and collisions on land.[93] Collisions at sea are likewise held not to be acts of God, but the carrier may be excused when such collision is due to the action of a tempest. In such case, the tempest, and not the collision, is treated as the act of God proximately causing the loss or injury.[94]

[86] Smyrl v. Niolon, 2 Bailey (S. C.) 421, 23 Am. Dec. 146.

[87] Friend v. Woods, 6 Grat. (Va.) 189, 52 Am. Dec. 119.

[88] Gleeson v. Virginia Midland R. Co., 140 U. S. 435, 11 Sup. Ct. 859, 35 L. Ed. 458.

[89] Long v. Pennsylvania Ry. Co., 147 Pa. 343, 23 Atl. 459, 14 L. R. A. 741, 30 Am. St. Rep. 732; Wald v. Pittsburg, C., C. & St. L. R. Co., 162 Ill. 545, 44 N. E. 888, 35 L. R. A. 356, 53 Am. St. Rep. 332.

[90] Forward v. Pittard, 1 Term R. (Eng.) 27, 33; Condict v. Grand Trunk R. Co., 54 N. Y. 500; Miller v. Steam Nav. Co., 10 N. Y. 431; Parsons v. Monteath, 13 Barb. (N. Y.) 353; Patton's Adm'rs v. Magrath, Dud. (S. C.) 159, 31 Am. Dec. 552; Gilmore v. Carman, 1 Smedes & M. (Miss.) 279, 40 Am. Dec. 96; Moore v. Michigan Cent. R. Co., 3 Mich. 23; Cox v. Peterson, 30 Ala. 608, 68 Am. Dec. 145; Hyde v. Trent Nav. Co., 5 Term R. (Eng.) 389. Contra, Hunt v. Morris, 6 Mart. O. S. (La.) 676, 12 Am. Dec. 489. The Chicago fire was held not to be an act of God in Chicago & N. W. R. Co. v. Sawyer, 69 Ill. 285, 18 Am. Rep. 613. Carriers using steam are liable for losses by fire. Garrison v. Memphis Ins. Co., 19 How. 312, 15 L. Ed. 656; New Jersey Steam Nav. Co. v. Merchants' Bank, 6 How. 344, 12 L. Ed. 465; Hale v. New Jersey Steam Nav. Co., 15 Conn. 539, 39 Am. Dec. 398; Patton's Adm'rs v. Magrath, Dud. (S. C.) 159, 31 Am. Dec. 552.

[91] The Mohawk, 8 Wall. 153, 19 L. Ed. 406; Bulkley v. Naumkeag & Cotton Co., 24 How. 386, 16 L. Ed. 599.

[92] Reaves v. Waterman, 2 Spear (S. C.) 197, 42 Am. Dec. 364.

[93] 1 Hutch. Carr. § 281.

[94] 1 Hutch. Carr. § 281. In river navigation, ordinarily collisions are like those on land, due to human agency, and thus do not excuse the carrier as acts of God. Plaisted v. Boston & K. Steam Nav. Co., 27 Me. 132, 46 Am. Dec. 587; Mershon v. Hobensack, 22 N. J. Law, 372.

A casual inspection of the cases will show that exemption from liability owing to an act of God is much more frequent in the case of carriers by water than in the case of carriers by land.

Public Enemy

Common carriers are not insurers against losses caused by the acts of the public enemy.[95] The term "public enemy" means an organized military or naval force, with which the country of the carrier is at war,[96] and pirates,[97] who are regarded as the common enemies of all mankind (hostes humani generis). Losses by thieves and robbers, strikers, rioters, and the like, however numerous, powerful, or well organized these may be, do not fall within the exception.[98] Common carriers are liable for losses caused by a mere rebellion or insurrection,[99] unless it assumes the proportions of a civil war, and involves the recognition of belligerent rights by the combatants, as in the case of the American Revolution or the late war between the states.[1] A formal declaration of war is not

[95] Russell v. Niemann, 17 C. B. N. S. (Eng.) 163; Hubbard v. Harnden Exp. Co., 10 R. I. 244. This exception is clearly recognized in all the cases defining the common carrier's liability.

[96] 1 Hutch. Carr. § 315; Lawson, Bailm. § 129; Story, Bailm. §§ 512, 526; Ang. Carr. § 200; Russell v. Niemann, 17 C. B. (N. S.) 163. See, also, Seligman v. Armijo, 1 N. M. 459.

[97] Lawson, Bailm. § 129; Story, Bailm. § 526; Pickering v. Barkley, Style. (Eng.) 132. But see The Belfast v. Boon, 41 Ala. 50.

[98] COGGS v. BERNARD, 2 Ld. Raym. (Eng.) 909, 918, Dobie Cas. Bailments and Carriers, 1; The Belfast v. Boon, 41 Ala. 50; Boon v. The Belfast, 40 Ala. 184, 88 Am. Dec. 761; Lewis v. Ludwick, 6 Cold. (Tenn.) 368, 98 Am. Dec. 454; Schieffelin v. Harvey, 6 Johns. (N. Y.) 170, 5 Am. Dec. 206; Watkinson v. Laughton, 8 Johns. (N. Y.) 213; Morse v. Slue, 1 Vent. (Eng.) 190. Indians on the warpath are public enemies. Holladay v. Kennard, 12 Wall. 254, 20 L. Ed. 390. Strikers are not a "public enemy," within the meaning of the exception. Missouri Pac. Ry. Co. v. Nevill, 60 Ark. 375, 30 S. W. 425, 28 L. R. A. 80, 46 Am. St. Rep. 208. Their interference may excuse a delay, however, for the carrier is not an insurer of prompt delivery. GREISMER v. LAKE SHORE & M. S. R. CO., 102 N. Y. 563, 7 N. E. 828, 55 Am. Rep. 837, Dobie Cas. Bailments and Carriers, 206; Pittsburgh, Ft. W. & C. R. Co. v. Hazen, 84 Ill. 36, 25 Am. Rep. 422; Lake Shore & M. S. Ry. Co. v. Bennett, 89 Ind. 457; Pittsburgh, C., C. & St. L. Ry. Co. v. Hollowell, 65 Ind. 188, 32 Am. Rep. 63; Hass v. Kansas City Ft. S. & G. R. Co., 81 Ga. 792, 7 S. E. 629; Gulf, C. & S. F. Ry. Co. v. Levi, 76 Tex. 337, 13 S. W. 191, 8 L. R. A. 323, 18 Am. St. Rep. 45; Baltimore & O. R. Co. v. O'Donnell, 49 Ohio St. 489, 32 N. E. 476, 21 L. R. A. 117, 34 Am. St. Rep. 579.

[99] Missouri Pac. Ry. Co. v. Nevill, 60 Ark. 375, 30 S. W. 425, 28 L. R. A. 80, 46 Am. St. Rep. 208; Forward v. Pittard, 1 Term R. (Eng.) 27, 29. But see Nesbite v. Luskington, 4 Term R. (Eng.) 783.

[1] Mauran v. Alliance Insurance Co., 6 Wall. 1, 18 L. Ed. 836; Nashville & C. R. Co. v. Estes, 10 Lea (Tenn.) 749; The Prize Cases, 2 Black, 635, 17 L. Ed. 459; Hubbard v. Harnden Exp. Co., 10 R. I. 244; Lewis v. Ludwick,

necessary however, if actual hostilities exist.[2] If, after entering into a contract of carriage, war breaks out between the country of the carrier and that to which the goods are to be carried, the carrier's nonperformance of the contract of carriage will be excused.[3]

Various reasons are assigned for exempting the common carrier from liability for loss or damage due to the public enemy.[4] Thus it is said to be based on the absence of any real danger of collusion between the carrier and public enemy to defraud the shipper, and also the fact that, if the carrier were liable, he would have no recourse at law against the public enemy to recoup the loss thus suffered. With the spread of peace, and the decline of war through the recognition of its inherent barbarism, this exception becomes of historical rather than practical importance.

Act of the Shipper

To the two original exemptions of the common carrier just discussed—(1) act of God; and (2) public enemy—the courts were not slow in adding three others—(3) act of shipper; (4) public authority; (5) inherent nature of the goods—as based on the clearest principles of justice. Few things could be more directly opposed to the spirit of our law than to allow one to recover for damages brought about by his own wrong or fault. The common carrier of goods is therefore not liable for loss or damage due either to the fraud or to the negligence of the shipper.[5]

Same—Concealing Value of the Goods

It cannot be said that the law imposes upon the shipper the positive duty, in all cases, to disclose the value of the goods to the carrier. The shipper, however, at least owes the negative

6 Cold. (Tenn.) 368, 98 Am. Dec. 454. In the war between the states the Confederate forces were neither robbers on land nor pirates by sea. Fifield v. Insurance Co. of State of Pennsylvania, 47 Pa. 166, 86 Am. Dec. 523; Mauran v. Alliance Ins. Co., 6 Wall. 1, 18 L. Ed. 836. But see Dole v. Merchants' Mutual Marine Ins. Co., 51 Me. 465, contra.

[2] The Prize Cases, 2 Black, 635, 17 L. Ed. 459.

[3] The Prize Cases, 2 Black, 635, 17 L. Ed. 459; Griswold v. Waddington, 16 Johns. (N. Y.) 438; Esposito v. Bowden, 7 El. & Bl. (Eng.) 762; Reid v. Hoskins, 5 El. & Bl. (Eng.) 729, affirmed 6 El. & Bl. (Eng.) 953.

[4] 1 Hutch. Carr. § 315; COGGS v. BERNARD, 2 Ld. Raym. (Eng.) 909, Dobie Cas. Bailments and Carriers, 1.

[5] While carriers in the absence of stipulation to the contrary are insurers of goods entrusted to them for shipment, they will not be so held where loss or damage results from the negligence of the shipper. Currie v. Seaboard Air Line Ry., 156 N. C. 432, 72 S. E. 493. A common carrier is not liable for the loss of goods caused by the shipper's act, whether it be one of negligence or accident. American Lead Pencil Co. v. Nashville, C. & St. L. Ry., 124 Tenn. 57, 134 S. W. 613, 32 L. R. A. (N. S.) 323. See, also, Broadwood v. Southern Exp. Co., 148 Ala. 17, 41 South. 769; Becker v. Pennsylvania Ry. Co., 109 App. Div. 230, 96 N. Y. Supp. 1.

duty, in this respect, not to deceive the carrier.[6] When asked the value of the goods, the shipper must be truthful under penalty at least of recovering no greater value than that set by him upon the goods.[7] Nor can the shipper deceive the carrier, whether intentionally or not, by the form, appearance, or nature of the package in which the goods are shipped.[8]

Thus, under the exception now under discussion, the carrier was excused from liability for the loss of money delivered to him by the shipper, the money being concealed in a bag filled with hay.[9] There was a similar decision when a diamond ring was shipped in a small paper box, tied with a string, with nothing to inform the carrier that the box contained goods of exceptional value.[10] Likewise it was held there could be no recovery for the loss of silverware delivered, without notice to the carrier, in a basket, the appearance of which indicated that its contents were merely household goods, and where the shipper remained silent when he heard the agent of the carrier designate the shipment as one of household goods.[11]

The carrier's compensation, his methods of handling the goods, and his precautions as to their safety are directly connected with the value of the goods.[12] The shipper cannot deceive the carrier in this respect, even innocently, and then recover as if there had been no deception.[13]

6 As by placing money in a box, together with articles of small value. Chicago & A. R. Co. v. Thompson, 19 Ill. 578; Magnin v. Dinsmore, 62 N. Y. 35, 20 Am. Rep. 442; Earnest v. Express Co., 1 Woods, 573, Fed. Cas. No. 4,248.

7 Phillips v. Earle, 8 Pick. (Mass.) 182.

8 Warner v. Western Transportation Co., 5 Rob. (N. Y.) 490; Orange County Bank v. Brown, 9 Wend. (N. Y.) 85, 24 Am. Dec. 129; Pardee v. Drew, 25 Wend. (N. Y.) 459; Chicago & A. R. Co. v. Thompson, 19 Ill. 578; Great Northern R. Co. v. Shepherd, 8 Exch. 30, 14 Eng. Law & Eq. Rep. 367; SHACKT v. ILLINOIS CENT. R. CO., 94 Tenn. 658, 30 S. W. 742, 28 L. R. A. 176, Dobie Cas. Bailments and Carriers, 190. So, where a box contains glass, the carrier should be informed of it. American Exp. Co. v. Perkins, 42 Ill. 458. See, also, generally, Relf v. Rapp, 3 Watts & S. (Pa.) 21, 37 Am. Dec. 528; Hollister v. Nowlen, 19 Wend. (N. Y.) 234, 32 Am. Dec. 455; Hayes v. Wells, Fargo & Co., 23 Cal. 185, 83 Am. Dec. 89; St. John v. Southern Express Co., 1 Woods, 612, Fed. Cas. No. 12,228.

9 Gibbon v. Paynton, 4 Burrows (Eng.) 2298.

10 Everett v. Southern Exp. Co., 46 Ga. 303. And see Sleat v. Fagg, 5 Barn. & Ald. (Eng.) 342.

11 SCHACKT v. ILLINOIS CENT. R. CO., 94 Tenn. 658, 30 S. W. 742, 28 L. R. A. 176, Dobie Cas. Bailments and Carriers, 190.

12 Batson v. Donovan, 4 Barn. & Ald. (Eng.) 21; Cole v. Goodwin, 19 Wend. (N. Y.) 251, 32 Am. Dec. 470; Magnin v. Dinsmore, 62 N. Y. 35, 20 Am. Rep. 442; Oppenheimer v. United States Express Co., 69 Ill. 62, 18 Am. Rep. 596; Graves v. Lake Shore & M. S. R. Co., 137 Mass. 33, 50 Am. Rep. 282.

13 Michalitschke Bros. & Co. v. Wells, Fargo & Co., 118 Cal. 683, 50 Pac.

Same—When Goods are Negligently Packed or Marked by the Shipper

It is the duty of the shipper to see that the goods are properly marked so as to indicate the destination and the consignee. For results traceable to his own fault in this respect, the shipper and not the carrier is liable. Thus a recovery was denied the shipper when goods were missent owing to the negligence of the shipper in marking the goods.[14] The shipper's negligent marking was also held to excuse the carrier when there was a misdelivery of the goods and they were subsequently lost without fault on the carrier's part,[15] or even when, owing to such marking, the goods were delivered to the wrong person.[16]

A similar result is reached when loss or injury is due to the improper loading or packing of the goods by the shipper.[17] Thus, when a large machine was injured, owing to the method of loading it and fastening it to the car, adopted by the shipper, no liability attached to the carrier.[18] So, also, when fragile or brittle goods were so badly packed that they were broken in ordinary transit, without fault of the carrier, the carrier was not liable.[19]

Same—General Negligence of Shipper

In general, it may be said that the carrier is not liable, when he is not at fault, for loss or damage resulting from the fault or negligence of the shipper, or the improper performance of any duty which the latter assumes.[20] Thus, when the goods are injured

847; Gorham Manufacturing Co. v. Fargo, 35 N. Y. Super. Ct. 434; The Ionic, 5 Blatch. 538, Fed. Cas. No. 7,059; Relf v. Rapp, 3 Watts & S. (Pa.) 21, 37 Am. Dec. 528.

14 Congar v. Chicago & N. W. R. Co., 24 Wis. 157, 1 Am. Rep. 164; The Huntress, 2 Ware (Dav. 82) 89, Fed. Cas. No. 6,914; Erie R. Co. v. Wilcox, 84 Ill. 239, 25 Am. Rep. 451; Southern Exp. Co. v. Kaufman, 12 Heisk. (Tenn.) 161; Finn v. Western R. Corp., 102 Mass. 283.

15 Treleven v. Northern Pac. Ry. Co., 89 Wis. 598, 62 N. W. 536.

16 Lake Shore & M. S. Ry. Co. v. Hodapp, 83 Pa. 22. But if the carrier knows, or could reasonably be expected to ascertain, the proper direction, he could be held liable in spite of the misdirection. O'Rourke v. Chicago, B. & Q. Ry. Co., 44 Iowa, 526; Mahon v. Blake, 125 Mass. 477.

17 Klauber v. American Exp. Co., 21 Wis. 21, 91 Am. Dec. 452; Goodman v. Oregon Ry. & Nav. Co., 22 Or. 14, 28 Pac. 894; Shriver v. Sioux City & St. P. Ry. Co., 24 Minn. 506, 31 Am. Rep. 353; Zerega v. Poppe, Abb. Adm. 397, Fed. Cas. No. 18,213.

18 Ross v. Troy & B. Ry. Co., 49 Vt. 364, 24 Am. Rep. 144.

19 See American Exp. Co. v. Perkins, 42 Ill. 458. Here, too, the carrier was not informed the shipment consisted of fragile goods, easily broken in transit.

20 Roderick v. Baltimore & O. Ry. Co., 7 W. Va. 54; Payne v. Ralli (D. C.) 74 Fed. 563; HART v. CHICAGO & N. W. RY. CO., 69 Iowa, 485, 29 N. W. 597, Dobie Cas. Bailments and Carriers, 195. This is particularly true when the shipper attends to the loading or unloading of the goods. Miltimore

owing solely to the method of transportation, the carrier is not liable when the shipper himself specifically directed how the goods should be carried.[21] So, also, when the horse was killed in shipment owing to the intermeddling of the shipper in leaving a car window open.[22] In like manner, when the shipper retains a measure of control over the goods, or accompanies the goods, either in person or through an agent, under an agreement to care for them, the carrier is not responsible for any loss or injury due solely to the shipper's negligent performance of the duties thus assumed by him.[23]

Public Authority

The carrier is, of course, subject to the police power of the state, and must yield obedience to the mandates of its courts. He is therefore properly excused for all resulting loss or damage when, in recognition of such sovereignty, he yields to the paramount public authority.[24] It would be an absurd inconsistency for the law to require the carrier, out of respect for its authority, to give up the shipper's goods, and then to hold the carrier responsible in damages for obeying its express mandate.

Accordingly, when intoxicating liquors, or goods infected with contagious diseases, are seized and destroyed by the state under the police power, the carrier is not liable.[25] The carrier, before

v. Chicago & N. W. R. Co., 37 Wis. 190; Rixford v. Smith, 52 N. H. 355, 13 Am. Rep. 42; Ross v. Troy & B. R. Co., 49 Vt. 364, 24 Am. Rep. 144; Betts v. Farmers' Loan & Trust Co., 21 Wis. 80, 91 Am. Dec. 460; East Tennessee, V. & G. R. Co. v. Johnston, 75 Ala. 596, 51 Am. Rep. 489. But see McCarthy v. Louisville & N. R. Co., 102 Ala. 193, 14 South. 370, 48 Am. St. Rep. 29; Jackson Architectural Iron Works v. Hurlbut, 158 N. Y. 34, 52 N. E. 665, 70 Am. St. Rep. 432; Pennsylvania Co. v. Kenwood Bridge Co., 170 Ill. 645, 49 N. E. 215.

21 White v. Winnisimmet Co., 7 Cush. (Mass.) 155; Wilson v. Hamilton, 4 Ohio St. 722; Western & A. R. Co. v. Exposition Cotton Mills, 81 Ga. 522, 7 S. E. 916, 2 L. R. A. 102.

22 Hutchinson v. Chicago, St. P., M. & O. Ry. Co., 37 Minn. 524, 35 N. W. 433.

23 Gleason v. Goodrich Transportation Co., 32 Wis. 85, 14 Am. Rep. 716; South & N. A. R. Co. v. Henlein, 52 Ala. 606, 23 Am. Rep. 578; McBeath v. Wabash, St. L. & P. Railroad Co., 20 Mo. App. 445. See Bryant v. Southwestern Railroad Co., 68 Ga. 805.

24 1 Hutch. Carr. § 324; Kohn v. Richmond & D. Ry. Co., 37 S. C. 1, 16 S. E. 376, 24 L. R. A. 100, 34 Am. St. Rep. 726. This exception is universally recognized, though it is sometimes omitted in stating the exceptions to the carrier's common-law liability as an insurer. See, for example, Henry Bromschwig Tailors' Trimming Co. v. Missouri, K. & T. Ry. Co., 165 Mo. App. 350, 147 S. W. 175.

25 Wells v. Maine Steamship Co., 4 Cliff. 228, Fed. Cas. No. 17,401; Bliven v. Hudson River R. Co., 35 Barb. 191; Id., 36 N. Y. 407. The carrier is pro-

yielding, however, should satisfy himself as to the authority of the officer seizing the goods.[26] In like manner, the carrier is excused when the goods are taken from him by legal process, such as execution or attachment against the owner,[27] sued out in an ordinary civil action, provided such process is fair on its face.[28] When the goods are seized under public authority, or any legal proceedings are instituted against them, it is the duty of the carrier to give seasonable notice of such seizure or proceedings, if that is practicable, to the shipper or owner of the goods, in order that such shipper

tected if he yields to the paramount public authority, if it is de facto, whether or not it is de jure. Thus a yielding to the Confederate government was held an excuse. Nashville & C. Ry. Co. v. Estes, 10 Lea (Tenn.) 749.

[26] Bennett v. American Exp. Co., 83 Me. 236, 22 Atl. 159, 13 L. R. A. 33, 23 Am. St. Rep. 774.

[27] This subject is discussed at length in 2 Hutch. Carr. §§ 738-748. See Stiles v. Davis, 1 Black, 101, 17 L. Ed. 33; Bliven v. Hudson River Railroad Co., 36 N. Y. 403; Pingree v. Detroit, L. & N. R. Co., 66 Mich. 143, 33 N. W. 298, 11 Am. St. Rep. 479; Furman v. Chicago, R. I. & P. R. Co., 57 Iowa, 42, 10 N. W. 272; Id., 62 Iowa, 395, 17 N. W. 598; Id., 68 Iowa, 219, 26 N. W. 83; Id., 81 Iowa, 540, 46 N. W. 1049; Ohio & M. R. Co. v. Yohe, 51 Ind. 181, 19 Am. Rep. 727; French v. Star Union Transportation Co., 134 Mass. 288; Jewett v. Olsen, 18 Or. 419, 23 Pac. 262, 17 Am. St. Rep. 745; The M. M. Chase (D. C.) 37 Fed. 708; Savannah, G. & N. A. R. Co. v. Wilcox, 48 Ga. 432. But see Bingham v. Lamping, 26 Pa. 340, 67 Am. Dec. 418; McAlister v. Chicago, R. I. & P. R. Co., 74 Mo. 351; Mierson v. Hope, 2 Sweeny (N. Y.) 561. The remedy of the owner for an illegal seizure of his goods for the debt of another is not against the carrier, but against the officer making the seizure, or against the plaintiff, if he directed the seizure. Lawson, Bailm. 131; Stiles v. Davis, 1 Black, 101, 17 L. Ed. 33. But it has been held, in Massachusetts, that the carrier is not excused unless the proceedings be against the owner of the goods. Edwards v. White Line Transit Co., 104 Mass. 159, 6 Am. Rep. 213. See, also, Bingham v. Lamping, 26 Pa. 340, 67 Am. Dec. 418.

[28] Merz v. Chicago & N. W. Ry. Co., 86 Minn. 33, 90 N. W. 7; Edwards v. White Line Transit Co., 104 Mass. 159, 6 Am. Rep. 213; Kiff v. Old Colony & N. R. Co., 117 Mass. 591, 19 Am. Rep. 429; Gibbons v. Farwell, 63 Mich. 344, 29 N. W. 855, 6 Am. St. Rep. 301; Savannah, G. & N. A. R. Co. v. Wilcox, 48 Ga. 432. But it was held in McAlister v. Chicago, R. I. & P. R. Co., 74 Mo. 351, that a regular writ, issued under a statute afterwards declared unconstitutional, was sufficient to protect the carrier. The carrier is liable if he surrenders to an officer without a warrant. Bennett v. American Express Co., 83 Me. 236, 22 Atl. 159, 13 L. R. A. 33, 23 Am. St. Rep. 774. "Whatever may be a carrier's duty to resist a forcible seizure without process, he cannot be compelled to assume that regular process is illegal, and to accept all the consequences of resisting officers of the law. If he is excusable for yielding to a public enemy, he cannot be at fault for yielding to actual authority what he may yield to usurped authority." Campbell, C. J., in Pingree v. Detroit, L. & N. R. Co., 66 Mich. 143, 33 N. W. 298, 11 Am. St. Rep. 479.

or owner may take such steps as he may see fit to protect his interests.[29]

Inherent Nature of the Goods

The common carrier is not an insurer against losses caused by the inherent nature, vice, defect, or infirmity of the goods.[30] Thus, the carrier, when not himself at fault, is not liable for the decay of fruit, the evaporation of liquids, the bursting of a hogshead of molasses due to fermentation, and the like.[31] This exception from liability is said to rest on the same principle as the act of God, and, indeed, to be but an illustration of it. "Men are too apt to hear God in the thunder and storm, and ignore his existence in the still,

[29] Thomas v. Northern Pac. Exp. Co., 73 Minn. 185, 75 N. W. 1120; Jewett v. Olsen, 18 Or. 419, 23 Pac. 262, 17 Am. St. Rep. 745; Bliven v. Hudson River Ry. Co., 36 N. Y. 403.

[30] Lester v. Railway Co. [1903] 1 K. B. (Eng.) 878, 72 L. J. K. B. 385; Lawrence v. Denbreens, 1 Black, 170, 17 L. Ed. 89; Rixford v. Smith, 52 N. H. 355, 13 Am. Rep. 42; McGraw v. Baltimore & O. Ry. Co., 18 W. Va. 361, 41 Am. Rep. 696; R. E. FUNSTEN DRIED FRUIT & NUT CO. v. TOLEDO, ST. L. & W. RY. CO., 163 Mo. App. 426, 143 S. W. 839, Dobie Cas. Bailments and Carriers, 196.

[31] Currie v. Seaboard Air Line R. Co., 156 N. C. 432, 72 S. E. 493; R. E. FUNSTEN DRIED FRUIT & NUT CO. v. TOLEDO, ST. L. & W. RY. CO., 163 Mo. App. 426, 143 S. W. 839, Dobie Cas. Bailments and Carriers, 196; BEARD v. ILLINOIS CENT. R. CO., 79 Iowa, 518, 44 N. W. 800, 7 L. R. A. 280, 18 Am. St. Rep. 381, Dobie Cas. Bailments and Carriers, 199; Gulf, C. & S. F. Ry. Co. v. Levi, 76 Tex. 337, 13 S. W. 191, 8 L. R. A. 323, 18 Am. Rep. 45; Cragin v. New York Cent. R. R. Co., 51 N. Y. 61, 10 Am. Rep. 559; Louisville, N. O. & T. Ry. Co. v. Bigger, 66 Miss. 319, 6 South. 234; Illinois Cent. R. Co. v. Brelsford, 13 Ill. App. 251; The Howard v. Wissman, 18 How. 231, 15 L. Ed. 363; The Collenberg, 1 Black, 170, 17 L. Ed. 89; Swetland v. Boston & A. R. Co., 102 Mass. 276; Warden v. Greer, 6 Watts (Pa.) 424; Powell v. Mills, 37 Miss. 691; EVANS v. FITCHBURG R. CO., 111 Mass. 142, 15 Am. Rep. 19, Dobie Cas. Bailments and Carriers, 201. Peaches were delayed by an extraordinary freshet, and, as they showed signs of decay, the carrier sold them for the best attainable price, for the benefit of the owner. It was held, in an action for damages, that the carrier was not liable for the loss, as it was owing to the inherent qualities of the freight, that it was not bound to seek another route, and that it was justified in selling the property. American Exp. Co. v. Smith, 33 Ohio St. 511, 31 Am. Rep. 561, and note. Where potatoes were wet when shipped, and decayed on the voyage, the carrier is not liable. The Howard v. Wissman, 18 How. 231, 15 L. Ed. 363. See, also, The Collenberg, 1 Black, 170, 17 L. Ed. 89; Brown v. Clayton, 12 Ga. 564. Where the leakage is from an inherent defect of a cask, the carrier is not liable. Hudson v. Baxendale, 2 Hurl. & N. (Eng.) 575. A carrier is not liable for loss of molasses caused by its fermentation and expansion, nor for leakage from secret defects in the casks. Warden v. Greer, 6 Watts (Pa.) 424. Nor where the fermentation of the molasses caused the cask to burst. Faucher v. Wilson, 68 N. H. 338, 38 Atl. 1002, 39 L. R. A. 431.

small voice of the calm. But the acts of God are not always cataclysms, and 'natural decay' may as reasonably be classed under this head as 'tempests' or 'lightnings.'"[32] However, it is usual to treat this class of exceptions separately. This exception, as we shall see,[33] is of unusual importance in shipments of live stock.

SAME—LIABILITY AS AFFECTED BY THE CARRIER'S NEGLIGENCE

117. Though, as we have seen, the liability imposed by law upon the common carrier of goods is that of an insurer, the question of the carrier's negligence is important in determining his liability:

(1) Under the excepted perils;

(2) When the carrier's relation to the goods is that of warehouseman;

(3) When the carrier has by special contract reduced his liability to that of an ordinary bailee for hire.

Excepted Perils

As is indicated in the black letter text under section 116, it is the duty of the common carriers to use reasonable care to avoid loss or injury, even from causes against which they are not insurers. Outside of the excepted perils, the common carrier of goods is an insurer and absolutely liable for all loss or damage. Within any of the excepted perils, the insuring liability falls away; but even here the duty of exercising reasonable care still remains with the carrier. The common carrier then escapes liability only when the loss or damage is due to an excepted peril without any concurring negligence on his part.[34] This qualification is a general one applicable to all the excepted perils.

The qualification is of particular importance, however, in connection with the act of God. The common carrier must use reason-

[32] Wood, Browne, Carr. § 106.

[33] Post, § 119.

[34] Campbell v. Morse, Harp. (S. C.) 468 (attempt to cross a swollen stream with an insufficient team); Bell v. Reed, 4 Bin. (Pa.) 127, 5 Am. Dec. 398 (putting to sea in unseaworthy vessel). See, also, Nelson v. Great Northern Ry. Co., 28 Mont. 297, 72 Pac. 642; Jones v. Minneapolis & St. L. Ry. Co., 91 Minn. 229, 97 N. W. 893, 103 Am. St. Rep. 507; Ferguson v. Southern Ry. Co., 91 S. C. 61, 74 S. E. 129 (all of these cases involved an act of God); Holladay v. Kennard, 12 Wall. 254, 20 L. Ed. 390 (public enemy); McCarthy v. Louisville & N. Ry. Co., 102 Ala. 193, 14 South. 370, 48 Am. St. Rep. 29 (negligence of shipper); BEARD v. ILLINOIS CENT. RY. CO., 79 Iowa, 518, 44 N. W. 800, 7 L. R. A. 280, 18 Am. St. Rep. 381, Dobie Cas. Bailments and Carriers, 199 (inherent nature of goods).

able care, first, to avoid the act of God, and, next, if overtaken by such act, to minimize the loss resulting therefrom. If the carrier fail to exercise reasonable care or ordinary diligence in either of these respects, and the goods are damaged by an act of God, the carrier's negligence is treated as the proximate cause of such damage, and the carrier is accordingly held liable.[35] Thus, if the carrier is negligent in exposing the goods to the act of God, as where he puts to sea in an unseaworthy vessel,[36] or attempts to cross a swollen stream after sundown with an insufficient team,[37] he is liable for the resulting loss. Again, though overtaken by the act of God, without any negligence on his part, the carrier must use ordinary care to render the loss as light as possible; and, if he is negligent in not doing so, he is liable for all losses which he might, by the exercise of reasonable care, have prevented.[38]

Precisely similar considerations obtain as to the public enemy. The carrier remains liable for goods captured by the public enemy when, by the exercise of reasonable care, the capture could have been avoided.[39] Thus, if the carrier, with the choice of two

[35] See cases cited in first part of preceding note. See, also, Wolf v. American Express Co., 43 Mo. 421, 97 Am. Dec. 406; Pruitt v. Hannibal & St. J. R. Co., 62 Mo. 527; Davis v. Wabash, St. L. & P. R. Co., 89 Mo. 340, 1 S. W. 327; Elliott v. Russell, 10 Johns. (N. Y.) 1, 6 Am. Dec. 306; Adams Exp. Co. v. Jackson, 92 Tenn. 326, 21 S. W. 666; Grier v. St. Louis Merchants Bridge Terminal Ry. Co., 108 Mo. App. 565, 84 S. W. 158; Jones v. Minneapolis & St. L. Ry. Co., 91 Minn. 229, 97 N. W. 893, 103 Am. St. Rep. 507; Ferguson v. Southern Ry. Co., 91 S. C. 61, 74 S. E. 129.

[36] Bell v. Reed, 4 Bin. (Pa.) 127, 5 Am. Dec. 398. Or when the carrier negligently exposed the goods to a flood, warning of which had been duly given. Wabash Ry. Co. v. Sharpe, 76 Neb. 424, 107 N. W. 758, 124 Am. St. Rep. 823.

[37] Campbell v. Morse, Harp. (S. C.) 468.

[38] Craig v. Childress, Peck (Tenn.) 270, 14 Am. Dec. 751; Day v. Ridley, 16 Vt. 48, 42 Am. Dec. 489. The carrier need exercise only reasonable care. Nashville & C. R. Co. v. David, 6 Heisk. (Tenn.) 261, 19 Am. Rep. 594; Morrison v. Davis, 20 Pa. 171, 57 Am. Dec. 695; Memphis & C. R. Co. v. Reeves, 10 Wall. 176, 19 L. Ed. 909; Black v. Chicago, B. & Q. R. Co., 30 Neb. 197, 46 N. W. 428; Gillespie v. St. Louis, K. C. & N. R. Co., 6 Mo. App. 554; Nugent v. Smith, 1 C. P. Div. (Eng.) 423; The Generous, 2 Dods. (Eng.) 322. But see The Niagara v. Cordes, 21 How. (U. S.) 7; King v. Shepherd, 3 Story, 349, Fed. Cas. No. 7,804. See, also, Smith v. Western Ry. of Alabama, 91 Ala. 455, 8 South. 754, 11 L. R. A. 619, 24 Am. St. Rep. 929; Milwaukee & St. P. R. Co. v. Kellogg, 94 U. S. 475, 24 L. Ed. 256; Blythe v. Denver & R. G. R. Co., 15 Colo. 333, 25 Pac. 702, 11 L. R. A. 615, 22 Am. St. Rep. 403; Baltimore & O. R. Co. v. Sulphur Spring Independent School Dist., 96 Pa. 65, 42 Am. Rep. 529; Denny v. New York Cent. R. Co., 13 Gray (Mass.) 481, 74 Am. Dec. 645; Collier v. Valentine, 11 Mo. 299, 49 Am. Dec. 81. Where goods are wet by a storm, the carrier must open and dry them. Chouteaux v. Leech, 18 Pa. 224, 57 Am. Dec. 602.

[39] Forward v. Pittard, 1 Term R. (Eng.) 27; Parker v. James, 4 Camp.

routes, along one of which he knew that the armies of the enemy were encamped, chose this route, and the goods were taken by such enemy, the carrier would be responsible.[40]

Even when there has been some negligence on the part of the shipper, if there is also negligence on the part of the carrier, so that the loss or injury would not have occurred, had it not been for this fault of the carrier, then the carrier remains liable.[41] Yielding to public authority, too, will not excuse the carrier when he is negligent in surrendering the goods by virtue of process illegal on its face.[42] And, when he sets up loss or damage due to inherent nature of the goods to shield him from liability, the loss or damage must not have been due to his failure to exercise ordinary care under the circumstances.[43]

Carriers as Warehousemen—Carrier's Liability Under Special Contract

As we shall subsequently see, the relation of the carrier to the goods in his possession is sometimes technically not that of common carrier, but that of a warehouseman.[44] In such cases, then, again the insuring liability of the common carrier falls away, and the carrier's liability, like that of other warehousemen, is measured in terms of negligence, and the carrier is liable only for his failure

(Eng.) 112; Clark v. Pacific R. R. Co., 39 Mo. 184, 90 Am. Dec. 458; Southern Exp. Co. v. Womack, 1 Heisk. (Tenn.) 256.

[40] Express Co. v. Kenitze, 8 Wall. 342.

[41] Guillaume v. General Transportation Co., 100 N. Y. 491, 3 N. E. 489; Mahon v. Blake, 125 Mass. 477; McCarthy v. Louisville & N. Ry. Co., 102 Ala. 193, 14 South. 370, 48 Am. St. Rep. 29.

[42] Merriman v. Great Northern Exp. Co., 63 Minn. 543, 65 N. W. 1080; Nickey v. St. Louis, I. M. & S. Ry. Co., 35 Mo. App. 79 (surrender of goods to person who exhibited merely a telegram from a sheriff); Kiff v. Old Colony & N. Railway Co., 117 Mass. 591, 19 Am. Rep. 429; Bennett v. American Exp. Co., 83 Me. 236, 22 Atl. 159, 13 L. R. A. 33, 23 Am. St. Rep. 774.

[43] BEARD v. ILLINOIS CENT. R. CO., 79 Iowa, 518, 44 N. W. 800, 7 L. R. A. 280, 18 Am. St. Rep. 381, Dobie Cas. Bailments and Carriers, 199; Harris v. Northern Indiana Railroad Co., 20 N. Y. 232; Ohio & M. R. Co. v. Dunbar, 20 Ill. 624, 71 Am. Dec. 291; Welch v. Pittsburg, Ft. W. & C. R. Co., 10 Ohio St. 65, 75 Am. Dec. 490; Powell v. Pennsylvania R. Co., 32 Pa. 414, 75 Am. Dec. 564; Smith v. New Haven & N. R. Co., 12 Allen (Mass.) 531, 90 Am. Dec. 166; CONGER v. HUDSON RIVER R. CO., 6 Duer (N. Y.) 375, Dobie Cas. Bailments and Carriers, 204. As to whether a carrier may or must give perishable property precedence in transportation, see Swetland v. Boston & A. R. Co., 102 Mass. 276; Peet v. Chicago & N. W. R. Co., 20 Wis. 594, 91 Am. Dec. 446; Tierney v. New York Cent. & H. R. Co., 76 N. Y. 305; Marshall v. New York Cent. R. Co., 45 Barb. (N. Y.) 502. See, also, McGraw v. Baltimore & O. Ry. Co., 18 W. Va. 361, 41 Am. Rep. 696.

[44] Post, §§ 136, 144.

to exercise ordinary care.[45] Cases of the carrier as a warehouseman are of frequent occurrence, and here again the question of what constitutes negligence is practical and important.

As we shall see in the next chapter, the common carrier of goods is permitted by special contract to reduce his liability from that of an insurer to that of an ordinary bailee, in which case he is again responsible only for negligence. Such special contracts are now so common that it is probably no exaggeration to say that in the majority of shipments the liability of the carrier turns upon the question of negligence.

What is Negligence on the Part of the Common Carrier of Goods

The question of negligence, then, is so often of primary importance, in spite of the common carrier's common-law liability as an insurer, as to demand at least brief consideration. Negligence, ordinarily, as to the common carrier of goods, is judged, as in the case of ordinary bailees for hire, by the standard of the amount of care which men of ordinary prudence are accustomed to exercise under similar circumstances.[46] The term "negligence" is again an intensely relative one, to be decided in accordance with the infinite variety of facts that present themselves in individual cases.[47]

In this connection, the nature of the goods is always a prime determinant.[48] Many goods can be transported in open cars, ex-

[45] Watts v. Boston & L. Ry. Corp., 106 Mass. 466; Basnight v. Atlantic & N. C. Ry. Co., 111 N. C. 592, 16 S. E. 323; Rogers v. Wheeler, 52 N. Y. 262; Michigan Cent. Ry. Co. v. Mineral Springs Mfg. Co., 16 Wall. 318, 21 L. Ed. 297; E. O. Stanard Milling Co. v. White Line Cent. Transit Co., 122 Mo. 258, 26 S. W. 704; Allam v. Pennsylvania Ry. Co., 183 Pa. 174, 38 Atl. 709, 39 L. R. A. 535; Mulligan v. Northern Pac. Ry. Co., 4 Dak. 315, 29 N. W. 659; Southern Exp. Co. v. Holland, 109 Ala. 362, 19 South. 66.

[46] Jackson Architectural Iron Works v. Hurlbut, 158 N. Y. 34, 52 N. E. 665, 70 Am. St. Rep. 432; Swetland v. Boston & A. Ry. Co., 102 Mass. 276; Gillespie v. St. Louis, K. C. & N. Ry. Co., 6 Mo. App. 554; Morrison v. Davis, 20 Pa. 171, 57 Am. Dec. 695; Memphis & C. Ry. Co. v. Reeves, 10 Wall. 176, 19 L. Ed. 909; Nugent v. Smith, 1 C. P. Div. (Eng.) 423; The Generous, 2 Dods. (Eng.) 322; Nashville & C. Ry. Co. v. David, 6 Heisk. (Tenn.) 261, 19 Am. Rep. 594. But see The Niagara v. Cordes, 21 How. 7, 16 L. Ed. 41; King v. Shepherd, 3 Story, 349, Fed. Cas. No. 7,804; Atlanta & W. P. Ry. Co. v. Jacobs Pharmacy Co., 135 Ga. 113, 68 S. E. 1039.

[47] Chouteaux v. Leech, 18 Pa. 224, 57 Am. Dec. 602 (drying wet goods); Kinnick v. Chicago, R. I. & P. Ry. Co., 69 Iowa, 665, 29 N. W. 772 (live stock); Peet v. Chicago & N. W. Ry. Co., 20 Wis. 594, 91 Am. Dec. 446 (preference as to perishable goods); McFadden v. Missouri Pac. Ry. Co., 92 Mo. 343, 4 S. W. 689, 1 Am. St. Rep. 721 (placing car bedded with straw so close to engine as to be dangerous, owing to sparks).

[48] Shaw v. Railroad Co., 18 Law J. Q. B. (Eng.) 181, 13 Q. B. 347; Root v. New York & N. E. R. Co., 83 Hun, 111, 31 N. Y. Supp. 357. Where fires are burning along the track, it is negligence to carry cotton on open cars. In-

posed to the elements. Ordinary care demands that many other goods be protected from rain or sunshine.[49] Live animals require food and water.[50] Some articles suffer none when they are a long

surance Co. of North America v. St. Louis, I. M. & S. R. Co. (C. C.) 3 McCrary, 233, 9 Fed. 811, 11 Fed. 380. Where a package is too large for a closed car, it is not negligence to carry it on an open car, provided reasonable diligence is used to protect it from the weather. Burwell v. Raleigh & G. R. Co., 94 N. C. 451. Where the shipper, with full knowledge, selects the vehicle, the carrier is not liable for loss caused by its insufficiency. Carr v. Schafer, 15 Colo. 48, 24 Pac. 873. The carrier must not carry goods in the same car so near that the proximity is, by the nature of the goods, likely to result in damage. The Colonel Ledyard, 1 Spr. 530, Fed. Cas. No. 3,027 (flour injured by the effluvium of turpentine); Alston v. Herring, 11 Exch. (Eng.) 822 (cambric goods injured by sulphuric acid).

[49] Where butter shipped to New Orleans in warm weather is carried in a common car, without ice or other protection, the carrier is liable for its deterioration by heat. BEARD v. ILLINOIS CENT. R. CO., 79 Iowa, 518, 44 N. W. 800, 7 L. R. A. 280, 18 Am. St. Rep. 381, Dobie Cas. Bailments and Carriers, 199 (citing Hewett v. Chicago, B. & Q. R. Co., 63 Iowa, 611, 19 N. W. 790); Sager v. Portsmouth S. & P. & E. R. Co., 31 Me. 228, 50 Am. Dec. 659; Hawkins v. Great Western R. Co., 17 Mich. 57, 97 Am. Dec. 179; Id., 18 Mich. 427; Ogdensburg & L. C. R. Co. v. Pratt, 22 Wall. 123, 22 L. Ed. 827; Wing v. New York & E. R. Co., 1 Hilt. (N. Y.) 235; Merchants' Dispatch & Transportation Co. v. Cornforth, 3 Colo. 280, 25 Am. Rep. 757; Boscowitz v. Adams Express Co., 93 Ill. 523, 34 Am. Rep. 191; Steinweg v. Erie R. Co., 43 N. Y. 123, 3 Am. Rep. 673; Alabama & V. R. Co. v. Searles, 71 Miss. 744, 16 South. 255. "Having accepted the butter for transportation defendant cannot escape liability for not safely transporting it on the ground that it did not have cars sufficient for the purpose." BEARD v. ILLINOIS CENT. R. CO., supra. And see Helliwell v. Grand Trunk R. Co. of Canada (C. C.) 7 Fed. 68. Where a carrier allows ice in which poultry is packed to melt, without renewing it, he is liable if the poultry is spoiled by heat. Peck v. Weeks, 34 Conn. 145. See, also, Sherman v. Inman Steamship Co., 26 Hun (N. Y.) 107.

[50] South & North Alabama R. Co. v. Henlein, 52 Ala. 606, 23 Am. Rep. 578. Cf. Great Northern R. Co. v. Swaffield, L. R. 9 Exch. (Eng.) 132. A carrier has the duty to feed and water stock during transportation, and cannot transfer it to the shipper by a custom requiring him to go along on the same train with the stock to feed and water them at his own risk and expense. Missouri Pac. R. Co. v. Fagan, 72 Tex. 127, 9 S. W. 749, 2 L. R. A. 75, 13 Am. St. Rep. 776. Where the shipper agrees to accompany live stock and attend to their wants, the carrier must allow him reasonable opportunity and facilities for so doing, or the carrier will be liable. Smith v. Michigan Cent. R. Co., 100 Mich. 148, 58 N. W. 651, 43 Am. St. Rep. 440; Dawson v. St. Louis, K. C. & N. R. Co., 76 Mo. 514; Wabash, St. L. & P. Ry. Co. v. Pratt, 15 Ill. App. 177; Ft. Worth & D. C. R. Co. v. Daggett, 87 Tex. 322, 28 S. W. 525; Nashville, C. & St. L. Ry. Co. v. Heggie, 86 Ga. 210, 12 S. E. 363, 22 Am. St. Rep. 453; Duvenick v. Missouri Pac. R. Co., 57 Mo. App. 550; Taylor, B. & H. Ry. Co. v. Montgomery (Tex. App.) 16 S. W. 178; Gulf, C. & S. F. R. Co. v. Gann, 8 Tex. Civ. App. 620, 28 S. W. 349. "It is the duty of railway companies to provide suitable places for feeding and watering live stock transported over their lines; and if this is not done they are re-

time in transportation. Fruit and other perishable goods must be carried with expedition, and may require icing and refrigeration.[51]

Proper care on the carrier's part applies not only to its track, its cars, and other vehicles used in actual transportation, but to its other equipment and instrumentalities, whether inanimate or human, and to all the facilities necessary for the business in which he is engaged.[52] When the carrier adopts a car for the purposes of his

sponsible for any loss entailed or that occurs from such neglect or failure. The carrier is primarily bound to provide feed and water for stock shipped over its line of railroad. [Citing Illinois Cent. R. Co. v. Adams, 42 Ill. 474, 92 Am. Dec. 85; Toledo, W. & W. Ry. Co. v. Thompson, 71 Ill. 434; Dunn v. Hannibal & St. J. R. Co., 68 Mo. 268; Harris v. Northern Indiana R. Co., 20 N. Y. 232; Cragin v. New York Cent. R. Co., 51 N. Y. 61, 10 Am. Rep. 559.] In Missouri, it is held that a railroad company which transports live stock ought not only to have proper facilities and machinery for unloading the stock shipped over the company's line of road whenever, in the course of the transit, it may be necessary to unload them for exercise and refreshment, but also that it is the company's duty to unload, feed, and water them at their journey's end, as well as along the route, if there be delay in delivering them to the consignee, in order to discharge the carrier from liability, if the health or necessity of the animals require this to be done. Dunn v. Hannibal & St. J. Railroad Co., 68 Mo. 268." Gulf, C. & S. F. Ry. Co. v. Wilhelm (Ky.) 16 S. W. 109. See, also, Bryant v. Southwestern R. Co., 68 Ga. 805. A car containing a horse should be set on a side track at the request of the owner of the horse or his agent, when the persons in charge of the train are informed that the horse is frightened by the transportation, and is acting badly, and in danger of being killed or hurt, if it can reasonably be done. Coupland v. Housatonic R. Co., 61 Conn. 531, 23 Atl. 870, 15 L. R. A. 534. There is no obligation on a railroad company to lay out, for reloading, a car hired at a certain price for the trip, and partly filled with horses, because one of them has got down in the car, when the owner is with them, and, under the contract, is chargeable with their care, and can, if he chooses, abandon the contract altogether, or make a new one for a longer time. Illinois Cent. R. Co. v. Peterson, 68 Miss. 454, 10 So. 48, 14 L. R. A. 550.

51 See cases cited in note 49; Chicago, I. & L. Ry. Co. v. Reyman, 166 Ind. 278, 76 N. E. 970; Merchants' Dispatch & Transportation Co. v. Cornforth, 3 Colo. 280, 25 Am. Rep. 757; Tucker v. Pennsylvania R. Co., 11 Misc. Rep. 366, 32 N. Y. Supp. 1. Contra, where the shipper selects the vehicle. Carr v. Schafer, 15 Colo. 48, 24 Pac. 873.

52 Rooth v. Railroad Co., 36 Law J. Exch. (Eng.) 83; Mason v. Missouri Pac. R. Co., 25 Mo. App. 473. Carriers of live stock must furnish proper yards and other appliances to enable the stock to be received, loaded, unloaded, and delivered to the consignee. Covington Stockyard Co. v. Keith, 139 U. S. 128, 11 Sup. Ct. 469, 35 L. Ed. 73; McCullough v. Wabash Western R. Co., 34 Mo. App. 23; Cooke v. Kansas City, Ft. S. & M. R. Co., 57 Mo. App. 471. A carrier cannot require extra compensation for such facilities. Covington Stockyard Co. v. Keith, supra; Beckford v. Crutwell, 5 Car. & P. (Eng.) 242. Where a railroad company negligently fails to provide a spark consumer, and goods are damaged by sparks from the engine, the carrier is liable, though by contract it was exempt from liability for loss by fire.

own transit he cannot escape, when liable for negligence, by pleading that the car belongs to another.[53]

Of course, the common carrier of goods is liable for damage resulting from his breach of a contract between himself and the shipper.

SAME—BURDEN OF PROOF

118. The plaintiff makes out a prima facie case of liability against the common carrier by showing the loss of, or injury to, the goods. The carrier can overcome this only by showing that such loss or injury was due to one of the excepted perils. According to the weight of authority, the burden of showing negligence on the part of the carrier in connection with the excepted perils then rests upon the plaintiff.

The liability at common law of the common carrier of goods for loss or injury, with its limitations and the qualifications of such limitations, has been discussed at some length. There remains the question, of great practical importance, of the person on whom the law places the burden of showing by affirmative evidence these various incidents. The plaintiff must show first that the carrier is a common carrier[54] though this is quite easy as to the great modern carriers, and next a delivery of the goods to such common carrier,[55] in order to fix the liability of the carrier as that of an insurer, with the well-known exceptions thereto.

All that the plaintiff is then required to show is loss of, or damage to, the goods while in the carrier's possession. Delivery to the carrier, and his failure to redeliver the goods, after the lapse of sufficient time for the completion of the transportation, is satisfactory proof, in the first instance, of loss.[56] Delivery of the goods

Steinweg v. Erie R. Co., 43 N. Y. 123, 3 Am. Rep. 673. See, also, Empire Transportation Co. v. Wamsutta Oil Refining & Mining Co., 63 Pa. St. 14, 3 Am. Rep. 515.

[53] Combe v. Railway Co., 31 Law T. N. S. (Eng.) 613.

[54] Ringgold v. Haven, 1 Cal. 108; Citizens' Bank v. Nantucket Steamboat Co., 2 Story, 16, Fed. Cas. No. 2,730.

[55] Hipp v. Southern Ry. Co., 50 S. C. 129, 27 S. E. 623; United States v. Pacific Exp. Co. (D. C.) 15 Fed. 867; Pitlock v. Wells, Fargo & Co., 109 Mass. 452; Michigan S. & N. Ry. Co. v. McDonough, 21 Mich. 165, 4 Am. Rep. 466; Blanchard v. Isaacs, 3 Barb. (N. Y.) 388; Truax v. Philadelphia, W. & B. Ry. Co., 3 Houst. (Del.) 233.

[56] Griffiths v. Lee, 1 Car. & P. (Eng.) 110; Tucker v. Cracklin, 2 Stark. (Eng.) 385; Cooper v. Georgia Pac. Ry. Co., 92 Ala. 329, 9 South. 159, 25 Am. St. Rep. 59; The Priscilla (D. C.) 106 Fed. 739; Browning v. Goodrich Transp. Co., 78 Wis. 391, 47 N. W. 428, 10 L. R. A. 415, 23 Am. St. Rep.

to the carrier in good condition, and a redelivery of them by the latter in a damaged condition, is sufficient proof of injury.[57] If the evidence in the case ceases here, the plaintiff recovers against the carrier.

After the proof indicated in the preceding paragraphs, the carrier, unless he can disprove the facts thus established by the plaintiff, can escape liability only by showing that such loss or injury was due to one of the five excepted perils.[58] When the liability of the common carrier of goods remains as at common law, no other evidence is relevant or in any way affects the issue between the parties. The burden, then, of proximately connecting the loss or injury with one of the excepted causes is clearly upon the carrier.

The cases are in direct conflict, however, as to the duty of proving or disproving the carrier's negligence in connection with the excepted peril. As we have just seen, after the plaintiff's prima facie case, the carrier must show that one of the excepted perils was responsible for the loss or injury. The mooted point is: Must he also go further and show that there was no negligence on his part, in connection with the excepted peril, to which the loss or injury may be attributed? Is the carrier required to absolve himself by proving his own lack of negligence, or is such negligence a positive fact to be proved by the plaintiff?[59]

The preponderance of authority seems to favor the rule, which seems to be sound, that the burden of proving the carrier's negli-

414; Grier v. St. Louis Merchants' Bridge Terminal R. Co., 108 Mo. App. 565, 84 S. W. 158; Saleeby v. Central R. Co. of New Jersey, 99 App. Div. 163, 90 N. Y. Supp. 1042; Mouton v. Louisville & N. R. Co., 128 Ala. 537, 29 South. 602; J. H. Cownie Glove Co. v. Merchants' Dispatch Transp. Co., 130 Iowa, 327, 106 N. W. 749, 4 L. R. A. (N. S.) 1060, 114 Am. St. Rep. 419.

57 Marquette, H. & O. R. Co. v. Langton, 32 Mich. 251; The Vincenzo, 10 Ben. 228, Fed. Cas. No. 16,948; Bonfiglio v. Lake Shore & M. S. Ry. Co., 125 Mich. 476, 84 N. W. 722; The La Kroma (D. C.) 138 Fed. 936; Morris v. Wier, 20 Misc. Rep. 586, 46 N. Y. Supp. 413; Heck v. Missouri Pac. Ry. Co., 51 Mo. App. 532; Pennsylvania R. Co. v. Naive, 112 Tenn. 239, 79 S. W. 124, 64 L. R. A. 443; Uber v. Chicago, M. & St. P. Ry. Co., 151 Wis. 431, 138 N. W. 57.

58 Read v. St. Louis, K. C. & N. R. Co., 60 Mo. 206; Wallingford v. Columbia & G. R. Co., 26 S. C. 258, 2 S. E. 19; J. H. Cownie Glove Co. v. Merchants' Dispatch Transp. Co., 130 Iowa, 327, 106 N. W. 749, 4 L. R. A. (N. S.) 1060, 114 Am. St. Rep. 419; Slater v. South Carolina Ry. Co., 29 S. C. 96, 6 S. E. 936. Sometimes the plaintiff's own showing may show clearly the carrier's exemption from responsibility. Davis v. Wabash, St. L. & P. Ry. Co., 89 Mo. 340, 1 S. W. 327.

59 See 3 Hutch. Carr. 1354–1357, with very elaborate citation of cases.

gence rests upon the plaintiff.[60] Under this rule, which obtains in England, New York, and the United States Supreme Court, the carrier prevails, in the absence of further proof by the plaintiff, when he shows that the loss or injury was the result of one of the excepted causes, under circumstances which do not of themselves import negligence on his part. These cases proceed on the ground that loss or injury from an excepted peril raises no presumption that the carrier has been negligent, but rather a presumption that he has performed his duty in the premises. It is therefore held that the carrier's negligence is a positive fault, which the plaintiff must prove.

Very many courts, however, are not so kind to the carrier and hold that, to offset the plaintiff's prima facie case, the carrier must prove, not only that the loss or injury was due to an excepted peril, but also that he exercised reasonable diligence or ordinary care in the premises to avoid such peril and to escape its consequences.[61] In other words, the carrier must prove an excepted

[60] This rule obtains in England, and is supported by the United States courts and those of New York, Pennsylvania, Wisconsin, Tennessee, Missouri, Rhode Island, Maine, Louisiana, Kansas, and other states. Muddle v. Stride, 9 Car. & P. (Eng.) 380; The Glendamoch, L. R. (1894) P. (Eng.) 226, 63 L. J. P. 89; Lamar Mfg. Co. v. St. Louis & S. F. R. Co., 117 Mo. App. 453, 93 S. W. 851; Witting v. St. Louis & S. F. Ry. Co., 101 Mo. 631, 14 S. W. 743, 10 L. R. A. 602, 20 Am. St. Rep. 636; Davis v. Wabash, St. L. & P. Ry. Co., 89 Mo. 340, 1 S. W. 327; Read v. St. Louis, K. C. & N. R. Co., 60 Mo. 199 (cf. Hill v. Sturgeon, 28 Mo. 323); Steers v. Liverpool, N. Y. & P. S. S. Co., 57 N. Y. 1, 15 Am. Rep. 453; Lamb v. Camden & A. R. & Transp. Co., 46 N. Y. 271, 7 Am. Rep. 327; Cochran v. Dinsmore, 49 N. Y. 249; Patterson v. Clyde, 67 Pa. 500; Colton v. Cleveland & P. R. Co., 67 Pa. 211, 5 Am. Rep. 424; Farnham v. Camden & A. R. Co., 55 Pa. 53; Goldey v. Pennsylvania R. Co., 30 Pa. 242, 72 Am. Dec. 703; cf. Pennsylvania R. Co. v. Miller, 87 Pa. 395; Hays v. Kennedy, 41 Pa. 378, 80 Am. Dec. 627; Whitesides v. Russell, 8 Watts & S. (Pa.) 44; Little Rock, M. R. & T. R. Co. v. Corcoran, 40 Ark. 375; Little Rock, M. R. & T. Ry. Co. v. Harper, 44 Ark. 208; Kansas Pac. Ry. Co. v. Reynolds, 8 Kan. 623; Kallman v. United States Exp. Co., 3 Kan. 205; Kelham v. The Kensington, 24 La. Ann. 100; Smith v. North Carolina R. Co., 64 N. C. 235; Hubbard v. Harnden Exp. Co., 10 R. I. 244; Louisville & N. R. Co. v. Manchester Mills, 88 Tenn. 653, 14 S. W. 314; Memphis & C. R. Co. v. Reeves, 10 Wall. 176, 19 L. Ed. 909; Western Transp. Co. v. Downer, 11 Wall. 129, 20 L. Ed. 160; Christie v. The Craigton (D. C.) 41 Fed. 62; Mitchell v. U. S. Exp. Co., 46 Iowa, 214; Sager v. Portsmouth, S. P. & E. R. Co., 31 Me. 228, 50 Am. Dec. 659; National Rice Mill Co. v. New Orleans & N. E. R. Co., 132 La. 615, 61 South. 708.

[61] Among the states upholding this rule are Connecticut, California, Minnesota, Mississippi, Nebraska, Ohio, Kentucky, Texas, North Carolina, Georgia, and Alabama. Mears v. New York, N. H. & H. R. Co., 75 Conn. 171, 52 Atl. 610, 56 L. R. A. 884, 96 Am. St. Rep. 192; Wilson v. California Cent. R. Co., 94 Cal. 166, 29 Pac. 861, 17 L. R. A. 685; Louisville & N. R. Co. v.

cause plus the absence of negligence on his part in connection therewith. Loss or injury by an excepted cause, according to these cases, involves a prima facie presumption of negligence, which, if not overcome by a showing on the part of the carrier, is sufficient to hold him liable. Mere proof, then, that the loss or injury was due to an excepted peril, stopping there, would avail the carrier nothing. This rule has the merit of convenience, as the carrier is in the better position to know all the facts; but it seems to be unduly severe upon the carrier.

It should be noted that, according to the generally accepted modern terminology, the burden of proof does not shift. But the duty of going forward with the evidence may, and frequently does, shift from one party to another,[62] as we have seen above, during the trial. A failure in the duty thus imposed may therefore result in the loss of the suit by the delinquent party.

CARRIERS OF LIVE STOCK

119. Carriers of live stock are none the less common carriers whenever carriers of other goods would be. The exception relieving the common carrier, in the absence of his negligence, from liability for loss or damage due to the inherent nature of the goods, here becomes of striking importance, owing to the vitality of the freight.

Brown, 90 S. W. 567, 28 Ky. Law Rep. 772; Bosley v. Baltimore & O. R. Co., 54 W. Va. 563, 46 S. E. 613, 66 L. R. A. 871; Hinkle v. Southern Ry. Co., 126 N. C. 932, 36 S. E. 348, 78 Am. St. Rep. 685; Central of Georgia Ry. Co. v. Hall, 124 Ga. 322, 52 S. E. 679, 4 L. R. A. (N. S.) 898, 110 Am. St. Rep. 170, 4 Ann. Cas. 128; South & N. A. R. Co. v. Henlein, 52 Ala. 606, 23 Am. Rep. 578; Steele v. Townsend, 37 Ala. 247, 79 Am. Dec. 49; Berry v. Cooper, 28 Ga. 543; Chicago, St. L. & N. O. R. Co. v. Moss, 60 Miss. 1003, 45 Am. Rep. 428; Chicago, St. L. & N. O. R. Co. v. Abels, 60 Miss. 1017; Gains v. Union Transp. & Ins. Co., 28 Ohio St. 418; United States Express Co. v. Backman, 28 Ohio St. 144; Graham v. Davis, 4 Ohio St. 362, 62 Am. Dec. 285; Union Express Co. v. Graham, 26 Ohio St. 595; Slater v. South Carolina Ry. Co., 29 S. C. 96, 6 S. E. 936; Swindler v. Hilliard, 2 Rich. (S. C.) 286, 45 Am. Dec. 732; Baker v. Brinson, 9 Rich. (S. C.) 201, 67 Am. Dec. 548; Missouri Pac. Ry. Co. v. China Manuf'g Co., 79 Tex. 26, 14 S. W. 785; Ryan v. Missouri, K. & T. Ry. Co., 65 Tex. 13, 57 Am. Rep. 589; Brown v. Adams Exp. Co., 15 W. Va. 812; Shriver v. Sioux City & St. P. R. Co., 24 Minn. 506, 31 Am. Rep. 353; Chicago, B. & Q. R. Co. v. Manning, 23 Neb. 552, 37 N. W. 462; Ferguson v. Southern Ry., 91 S. C. 61, 74 S. E. 129.

[62] See, as to this, 4 Wigmore, Evidence, §§ 2483–2498. See, also, Insurance Co. of North America v. Lake Erie & W. R. Co., 152 Ind. 333, 53 N. E. 382; Cau v. Texas & P. R. Co., 194 U. S. 427, 24 Sup. Ct. 663, 48 L. Ed. 1053; Louisville & N. R. Co. v. Manchester Mills, 88 Tenn. 653, 14 S. W. 314; Schal-

Though there are a few decisions to the contrary,[63] the overwhelming weight of authority holds that the carrier of live stock is none the less a common carrier of goods.[64] He is therefore sub-

ler v. Chicago & N. W. R. Co., 97 Wis. 31, 71 N. W. 1042; Long v. Pennsylvania R. Co., 147 Pa. 343, 23 Atl. 459, 14 L. R. A. 741, 30 Am. St. Rep. 732. These last cases are concerned with the carrier's exemption by contract; but the burden of proof is usually the same as to negligence and an excepted peril, whether such peril be one excepted by law or one excepted by contract.

[63] Michigan, S. & N. I. R. Co. v. McDonough, 21 Mich. 165, 4 Am. Rep. 466, the leading case in support of this view, has been followed by other Michigan cases. Lake Shore & M. S. R. Co. v. Perkins, 25 Mich. 329, 12 Am. Rep. 275; McKenzie v. Michigan Cent. R. Co., 137 Mich. 112, 100 N. W. 260. This doctrine was upheld in the Kentucky cases of Louisville, C. & L. R. Co. v. Hedger, 9 Bush, 645, 15 Am. Rep. 740, and Louisville & N. R. Co. v. Wathen, 66 S. W. 714, 23 Ky. Law Rep. 2128. But the doctrine of these cases seems to be repudiated in the later cases of Cincinnati, N. O. & T. P. R. Co. v. Sanders & Russell, 118 Ky. 115, 80 S. W. 488, 25 Ky. Law Rep. 2333, and Chesapeake & O. R. Co. v. Magowan, 147 Ky. 422, 144 S. W. 80.

[64] This is the rule in England. Blower v. Railway Co., L. R. 7 C. P. 655; Kendall v. Railway Co., L. R. 7 Exch. 373. With the exceptions mentioned in the preceding note, the American courts are practically unanimous. Fordyce v. McFlynn, 56 Ark. 424, 19 S. W. 961; Cooper v. Raleigh & G. R. Co., 110 Ga. 659, 36 S. E. 240; Waldron v. Fargo, 170 N. Y. 130, 62 N. E. 1077; Hart v. Pennsylvania R. Co., 112 U. S. 331, 5 Sup. Ct. 151, 28 L. Ed. 717; Ficklir v. Wabash R. Co., 117 Mo. App. 221, 93 S. W. 847; Atlantic Coast Line R. Co. v. Hinely-Stephens Co., 64 Fla. 175, 60 South. 749; MAYNARD v. SYRACUSE, B. & N. Y. R. CO., 71 N. Y. 180, 27 Am. Rep. 28, Dobie Cas. Bailments and Carriers, 213; Cragin v. New York Cent. R. Co., 51 N. Y. 61, 10 Am. Rep. 559; Penn v. Buffalo & E. R. Co., 49 N. Y. 204, 10 Am. Rep. 355; CONGER v. HUDSON RIVER R. CO., 6 Duer (N. Y.) 375, Dobie Cas. Bailments and Carriers, 204; Clarke v. Rochester & S. R. Co., 14 N. Y. 570, 67 Am. Dec. 205; Harris v. Northern Indiana R. Co., 20 N. Y. 232; St. Louis & S. E. Ry. Co. v. Dorman, 72 Ill. 504; Ohio & M. R. Co. v. Dunbar, 20 Ill. 624, 71 Am. Dec. 291; Chicago, R. I. & P. R. Co. v. Harmon, 12 Ill. App. 54; Ayres v. Chicago & N. W. Ry. Co., 71 Wis. 372, 37 N. W. 432, 5 Am. St. Rep. 226; EVANS v. FITCHBURG R. CO., 111 Mass. 142, 15 Am. Rep. 19, Dobie Cas. Bailments and Carriers, 201; Rixford v. Smith, 52 N. H. 355, 13 Am. Rep. 42; Kinnick v. Chicago, R. I. & P. R. Co., 69 Iowa, 665, 29 N. W. 772; McCoy v. Keokuk & D. M. R. Co., 44 Iowa, 424; German v. Chicago & N. W. R. Co., 38 Iowa, 127; Powell v. Pennsylvania R. Co., 32 Pa. 414, 75 Am. Dec. 564; Atchison & N. R. Co. v. Washburn, 5 Neb. 117; Porterfield v. Humphreys, 8 Humph. (Tenn.) 497; Wilson v. Hamilton, 4 Ohio St. 722; Welsh v. Pittsburg, Ft. W. & C. R. Co., 10 Ohio St. 65, 75 Am. Dec. 490; South & N. A. R. Co. v. Henlein, 52 Ala. 606, 23 Am. Rep. 578; Kimball v. Rutland & B. R. Co., 26 Vt. 247, 62 Am. Dec. 567; Moulton v. St. Paul, M. & M. R. Co., 31 Minn. 85, 16 N. W. 497, 47 Am. Rep. 781; Agnew v. The Contra Costa, 27 Cal. 425, 87 Am. Dec. 87; Lindsley v. Chicago, M. & St. P. R. Co., 36 Minn. 539, 33 N. W. 7, 1 Am. St. Rep. 692; Gulf, C. & S. F. Ry. Co. v. Trawick, 68 Tex. 314, 5 S. W. 567, 2 Am. St. Rep. 494; Brown v. Wabash, St. L. & P. R. Co., 18 Mo. App. 569; McFadden v. Missouri Pac. R. Co., 92 Mo. 343, 4 S. W. 689, 1 Am. St. Rep. 721. "It is claimed there is

ject to the liabilities and entitled to the rights which the law attaches to that relation. The question is naturally an important one, particularly in determining his liability for loss or injury. Is this to be measured, as in the case of common carriers, as that of an insurer, with the specified exceptions, or is it to be measured, like that of the ordinary bailee for hire, in terms of negligence, in which case he would be responsible only for his failure to exercise ordinary care.

In Michigan [65] it was held that the carrier of live stock was not a common carrier, and not liable as such, on the ground that "the transportation of cattle and live stock by common carriers by land was unknown to the common law when the duties and responsibilities of common carriers were fixed, making them insurers." But as was said in a leading case in Kansas: [66] "The transportation of thousands of other kinds of property, either by land or water, was unknown to the common law, and yet such kinds of property are now carried by common carriers * * * every day." The Michigan doctrine, based on so slender a thread of reasoning, has been generally repudiated, and one who would be held a common carrier under the accepted tests is none the less so merely because the nature of the goods which he is carrying happens to be live stock.[67]

We have already seen that, to impose the unusual responsibility on the common carrier, the goods must be put in his possession and control; in other words, there must be a delivery to him, so as to constitute a bailment.[68] When this is done, the carrier is

a difference between live stock and other property as to the responsibility assumed by a carrier in its transportation; that the voluntary motion of the stock introduces an element of danger into the transportation against which neither reason nor authority require that the carrier insure; that, inasmuch as it is customary that the shipper, or some one for him, accompany the stock, there is only a qualified or partial delivery to the carrier; and also that proof that a railroad company has suitable cars, and is engaged in the business of carrying cattle, is not proof that it is a common carrier as to such cattle, because, to insure their safe transportation, requires yards and stables, with conveniences for feeding, both at the termini and along the route, as well as a corps of experienced stockmen to take care of them in the transit. These last, as it seems to us, are duties incident to the employment, and not elements to determine its character. Engaging in the business of transporting cattle, it becomes a duty to provide every suitable facility therefor. Not the manner of doing the work, but the fact of engaging in the business, is the test laid down in the books for determining the character of the carrier." Kansas Pac. Ry. Co. v. Reynolds, 8 Kan. 623.

[65] Michigan S. & N. I. R. Co. v. McDonough, 21 Mich. 165, 4 Am. Rep. 466.

[66] Kansas Pac. Ry. Co. v. Nichols, 9 Kan. 235, 12 Am. Rep. 494.

[67] See cases cited in note 64.

[68] See ante, p. 327; post, § 136.

an insurer, though the shipper or his servant may accompany the goods and assume certain duties towards them; but for any loss or injury, resulting from a failure to attend to the duties thus assumed, the carrier is, of course, not responsible.[69] These principles are of frequent application in shipments of live stock, when it is not unusual for a shipper to send with the animals a servant to feed, water, and otherwise take care of them. The carrier must also give such servant reasonable opportunity to perform the duties which he has thus assumed.[70]

Inherent Vice, Disease, or Condition of Animals

Carriers of live stock are liable as insurers, just as other common carriers of goods, subject to the same five exceptions.[71] In this case, though, the last of these exceptions, inherent nature of the goods, far outshadows all the others in practical importance. This is often stated in such a way as to indicate that the exemption of the carrier of live stock in this respect is by virtue of some rule inapplicable to other carriers. The rules are the same in each case; the difference results from the application of the rule to different sets of facts. Animals are alive; most freight is inanimate. In this vitality is found an added element of danger in the transportation of animals. Accordingly, if the cases were counted, the results would probably show that, in the case of live stock, the carrier has occasion to resort more frequently to the inherent nature of the goods than to all the other four exceptions added together.

The carrier's liability is therefore especially contingent upon the inherent vice, disease, or condition of the animals[72] shipped. "Liv-

[69] South & N. A. R. Co. v. Henlein, 52 Ala. 606, 23 Am. Rep. 578; Cragin v. New York Cent. R. Co., 51 N. Y. 61, 10 Am. Rep. 559; Duvenick v. Missouri Pac. Ry. Co., 57 Mo. App. 550; Central R. R. v. Bryant, 73 Ga. 722; Betts v. Farmers' Loan & Trust Co., 21 Wis. 80, 91 Am. Dec. 460; Gannell v. Ford, 5 L. T. (N. S.) (Eng.) 604.

[70] Dunn v. Hannibal & St. J. R. Co., 68 Mo. 268; Harris v. Northern Indiana R. Co., 20 N. Y. 232; Johnson v. Alabama & V. Ry. Co., 69 Miss. 191, 11 South. 104, 30 Am. St. Rep. 534.

[71] See cases cited in note 64.

[72] Richardson v. Chicago & N. W. Ry. Co., 61 Wis. 596, 21 N. W. 49; Illinois Cent. R. Co. v. Scruggs, 69 Miss. 418, 13 South. 698; Louisville, N. O. & T. Ry. Co. v. Bigger, 66 Miss. 319, 6 South. 234; Smith v. New Haven & N. R. Co., 12 Allen (Mass.) 531, 90 Am. Dec. 166; Penn v. Buffalo & E. R. Co., 49 N. Y. 204, 10 Am. Rep. 355. Where the carrier has used due care, and provided a suitable car, and the injuries were caused by the peculiar character and propensities of the horse, such as fright and bad temper, the carrier is not liable. EVANS v. FITCHBURG R. CO., 111 Mass. 142, 15 Am. Rep. 19, Dobie Cas. Bailments and Carriers, 201. It is the duty of the owner, delivering property to a carrier which he knows requires peculiar care in its safe transportation, to make known the necessity in order that

ing animals have excitabilities and volitions of their own, which greatly increase the risks and difficulties of management. They are carried in a mode entirely opposed to their instincts or habits; they may be made uncontrollable by fright, or notwithstanding every precaution, may destroy themselves in attempting to break

the proper precaution may be used. Wilson v. Hamilton, 4 Ohio St. 722. In Clarke v. Rochester & S. R. Co., 14 N. Y. 570, 67 Am. Dec. 205, it was held that common carriers of cattle are liable, not only for a safe and careful conveyance of the car containing them, but also for any injury which can be prevented by foresight, vigilance, and care, although arising from the conduct of the animal, and they are not relieved of this responsibility by the fact that the owner of the cattle was present, and aided in loading them, and was allowed a passage for himself in the train which carried the cattle. See, also, Rixford v. Smith, 52 N. H. 355, 13 Am. Rep. 42; Goldey v. Pennsylvania R. Co., 30 Pa. 242, 72 Am. Dec. 703; McDaniel v. Chicago & N. W. R. Co., 24 Iowa, 412. The carrier is not relieved from his liability merely because delay, which occasions damage to the property, is the result of an unavoidable accident, but is bound, notwithstanding the accident, to use the highest degree of care during the delay for the safety of the deposit. Kinnick v. Chicago, R. I. & P. R. Co., 69 Iowa, 665, 29 N. W. 772. Where there is no misrepresentation or deceit on the part of the shipper of live stock, a common carrier waives all exceptions to the defects in loading by accepting stock so loaded for transportation, and assumes all the liabilities of a common carrier with reference to the property. Id. "No doubt the horse was the immediate cause of its own injuries, i. e. no person got into the box and injured it. It slipped, or fell, or kicked, or plunged, or in some way hurt itself. If it did so from no cause other than its inherent propensities, its proper vice—that is, from fright, or temper, or struggling to keep its legs—the defendants are not liable. But, if it so hurt itself from the defendants' negligence or any misfortune happening to the train, though not through any negligence of the defendants (as, for instance, from the horse box leaving the line, through some obstruction maliciously laid upon it), then the defendants, as insurers, would be liable. If perishable articles, say soft fruits, are damaged by their own weight and the inevitable shaking of the carriage, they are injured through their own intrinsic qualities. If, through pressure of other goods carried with them, or by an extraordinary shock or shaking, whether through negligence or not, the carrier is liable." Kendall v. Railway, L. R. 7 Exch. (Eng.) 373. A railroad company is not responsible for injuries inflicted upon one horse by another while they were being carried in the company's car, if the injuries were caused by the fault or neglect of the owner of the horses, in attaching their halters, or not removing their shoes. EVANS v. FITCHBURG R. CO., 111 Mass. 142, 15 Am. Rep. 19, Dobie Cas. Bailments and Carriers, 201. A shipper must disclose peculiarities affecting the risk (Wilson v. Hamilton, 4 Ohio St. 722; Missouri Pac. R. Co. v. Fagan [Tex. Civ. App.] 27 S. W. 887), but need not disclose facts apparent to observation (McCune v. B., C. R. & N. R. Co., 52 Iowa, 600, 3 N. W. 615; Estill v. New York, L. E. & W. R. Co. [C. C.] 41 Fed. 849). A carrier of live stock cannot stipulate for exemption from liability for his own negligence. Moulton v. St. Paul, M. & M. Ry. Co., 31 Minn. 85, 16 N. W. 497, 47 Am. Rep. 781; Kansas City, St. J. & C. B. R. Co. v. Simpson, 30 Kan 645, 2 Pac. 821, 46 Am. Rep. 104. A carrier of live stock held not lia-

loose, or may kill each other." [73] Animals have active wants that must be attended to; they are susceptible to heat and cold; disease and their inherent propensities frequently kill or injure many of them. The vitality of the freight, then, becomes a tremendous factor in determining the liability of the carrier.

This vitality of the animals, or their peculiar nature, or inherent propensities, or proper vice, as it is variously called, obviously plays a double rôle in this connection: First, it involves a different type of physical facilities and a unique kind of service, far more exacting than in the case of inanimate freight, in order that the carrier may fulfill his duty of exercising ordinary care.[74] Secondly, even when the carrier has exercised ordinary care, there are still, as has been indicated, many more injuries and losses here than in the case of inanimate freight. All of these considerations must be given due weight when the rule is applied that the carrier, who has used ordinary care in the premises and is hence guilty of no negligence, is not liable for any loss or injury as to the animals which can be traced to their inherent nature.[75]

Statutes

Statutes have been passed in many of the states, and also by the federal Congress, affecting the transportation of live stock.

ble for any "gaunting, scratching, biting," etc. Hanley v. Chicago, M. & St. P. Ry. Co., 154 Iowa, 60, 134 N. W. 417. See, also, Gilbert Bros. v. Chicago, R. I. & P. R. Co. (Iowa) 136 N. W. 911; Klair v. Philadelphia, B. & W. R. Co. 2 Boyce (Del.) 274, 78 Atl. 1085; Chicago, I. & L. R. R. Co. v. Woodward, 164 Ind. 360, 72 N. E. 558, 73 N. E. 810; Maslin v. Baltimore & O. R. Co., 14 W. Va. 180, 35 Am. Rep. 748; Winslow v. Chicago & A. R. Co., 170 Mo. App. 617, 157 S. W. 96.

[73] EVANS v. FITCHBURG R. CO., 111 Mass. 142, 15 Am. Rep. 19, Dobie Cas. Bailments and Carriers, 201.

[74] Gulf, C. & S. F. Ry. Co. v. Trawick, 80 Tex. 370, 15 S. W. 568, 18 S. W. 948; Covington Stockyard Co. v. Keith, 139 U. S. 128, 11 Sup. Ct. 469, 35 L. Ed. 73; Betts v. Chicago, R. I. & P. Ry. Co., 92 Iowa, 343, 60 N. W. 623, 26 L. R. A. 248, 54 Am. St. Rep. 558; Pratt v. Ogdensburg & L. C. R. Co., 102 Mass. 557; Coupeland v. Housatonic R. Co., 61 Conn. 531, 23 Atl. 870, 15 L. R. A. 534. A carrier of live stock must furnish all necessary facilities for their rest, exercise, and refreshment, though the time and place thereof must be left to its own judgment. St. Louis Southwestern Ry. Co. v. Mitchell, 101 Ark. 289, 142 S. W. 168, 37 L. R. A. (N. S.) 546. A carrier of live stock must afford proper facilities for having the stock watered and attended to during transportation. Harden v. Chesapeake & O. Ry. Co., 157 N. C. 238, 72 S. E. 1042.

[75] Cragin v. New York Cent. R. Co., 51 N. Y. 61, 10 Am. Rep. 559; Giblin v. National Steamship Co., 8 Misc. Rep. 22, 28 N. Y. Supp. 69; Armstrong v. United States Exp. Co., 159 Pa. 640, 28 Atl. 448. It has been held that this increased hazard in transporting live stock can properly be taken into account by the carrier in fixing his rates. New Orleans Live Stock Exchange v. Texas & P. Ry. Co., 10 Interst. Com. Rep. 327. See, also, Judson, Interstate Commerce (2d Ed.) § 186.

The most important of these is the federal statute requiring that cattle shall not be confined, in interstate shipments, for more than twenty-eight consecutive hours without being unloaded for rest, water, and feeding.[76] There are also various federal statutes as to the transportation of diseased cattle.[77]

THE HARTER ACT AS TO CARRIERS BY WATER—LIMITED LIABILITY ACT

120. The Harter Act, passed by the federal Congress, has materially lessened the liability of carriers by water who have complied with its provisions. The amount of the liability of a vessel owner is further limited by the Limited Liability Act.

The Harter Act,[78] passed by Congress in 1893, has wrought such a change in the liability of carriers by water that it calls for some brief mention here. The language of the act is broad and applies to "all vessels transporting merchandise to and from any port of the United States, situated upon any navigable waters, inland or otherwise, over which the federal government has jurisdiction." [79]

The first section [80] of the act forbids any contract relieving the "manager, agent, master, or owner" of the vessel "from liability for loss or damage arising from negligence * * * in proper loading,[81] stowage,[82] custody, care, or proper delivery of any and all lawful merchandise or property committed to its or their charge."

[76] Rev. St. § 4386 (U. S. Comp. St. 1901, pp. 2995, 2996). See Judson, Interstate Commerce (2d Ed.) §§ 546–558.

[77] See these statutes collected in 1 Fed. St. Annotated, under title "Animals."

[78] Act Feb. 13, 1893, c. 105, 27 Stat. 445. For complete text of act, see U. S. Comp. Stat. 1901, p. 2946, 4 Fed St. Annotated, pp. 854–864, with many annotations. For discussion of the act, with its first three sections in full, see 1 Hutch. Carr. §§ 345–387, on which the brief discussion given above is based. The title of the act is "An act relating to navigation of vessels, bills of lading, and to certain obligations, duties and rights in connection with the carriage of property."

[79] In re Piper Aden Goodall Co. (D. C.) 86 Fed. 670. See, further, as to the extent of the Harter Act, The E. A. Shores, Jr. (D. C.) 73 Fed. 342; The Germanic, 196 U. S. 589, 25 Sup. Ct. 317, 49 L. Ed. 610.

[80] As to this section, see Bethel v. Mellor & Rittenhouse Co. (D. C.) 131 Fed. 129; The Southmark, 191 U. S. 1, 24 Sup. Ct. 1, 48 L. Ed. 65; Calderon v. Atlas S. S. Co., 170 U. S. 272, 18 Sup. Ct. 588, 42 L. Ed. 1033.

[81] For meaning of this word here, see 1 Hutch. Carr. § 350; Insurance Co. of North America v. North German Lloyd Co. (D. C.) 106 Fed. 973; Nord-Deutscher Lloyd v. President, etc., of Insurance Co. of North America, 110 Fed. 420, 49 C. C. A. 1.

[82] For two senses in which this word is used, see 1 Hutch. Carr. §§ 351–

The second section[53] forbids similar contracts, lessening the obligation of the owners "to exercise due diligence [to] properly equip, man, provision, and outfit said vessel seaworthy and capable of performing her intended voyage," or lessening "the obligations of the master, officers, agents or servants to carefully handle and stow her cargo, and to care for and properly deliver same." These two sections, therefore, to which the courts have given full effect, are limitations, as to the incidents mentioned, on the power of the shipowner to limit his liability by contract.

The third section, however, materially limits the common-law liability of the shipowner. The first part of this section provides what such owner must do to secure exemption from liability; the second part defines precisely what is the extent of the exemption thus secured. Thus it is first provided that the owner "shall exercise due diligence[54] to make the said vessel seaworthy and properly manned, equipped and supplied." If this is done, it is provided that neither the vessel nor the owner, agent, or charterer shall be liable for loss or damage due[55] (1) to any of the five excepted perils in the case of the common carrier; (2) to faults or errors in navigation or in the management of said vessel; (3) to saving or attempting to save life or property at sea, or any deviation in rendering such service; or (4) to dangers of the sea or other navigable waters.

Of these exemptions, the second is by far the most striking, under which, if the owner is duly diligent as outlined, he escapes liability for even the negligent acts of his own agents and servants, within the scope of their authority, when such negligent acts were committed "in the navigation or management of the vessel."[56] Thus the duly diligent owner escaped liability for an accumulation of water in the bilges, owing to a failure to make proper use of the pump,[57] and negligently leaving a sea cock open,[58] as faults in

359; Corsar v. J. D. Spreckels & Bros. Co., 141 Fed. 260, 72 C. C. A. 378; The Victoria (D. C.) 114 Fed. 962.

[53] As to the effect of sections 1 and 2 on the shipowner's implied warranty of seaworthiness, see 1 Hutch. Carr. §§ 362–364.

[54] As to what is due diligence, see 1 Hutch. Carr. §§ 380–381; The Manitoba (D. C.) 104 Fed. 145; International Nav. Co. v. Farr & B. Mfg. Co., 181 U. S. 218, 21 Sup. Ct. 591, 45 L. Ed. 830; Nord-Deutcher Lloyd v. President, etc., of Insurance Co. of North America, 110 Fed. 420, 49 C. C. A. 1; The Colima (D. C.) 82 Fed. 665; The Abbazia (D. C.) 127 Fed. 495.

[55] This is not the order in which the exemptions are given in the act.

[56] For scope of this exception, see The Rosedale (D. C.) 88 Fed. 328; Id., 92 Fed. 1021, 35 C. C. A. 167; The Guadaloupe (D. C.) 92 Fed. 671; The Etona (D. C.) 64 Fed. 880; The Nettie Quill (D. C.) 124 Fed. 669.

[57] The Merida, 107 Fed. 146, 46 C. C. A. 208.

[58] The Wildcroft, 130 Fed. 521, 65 C. C. A. 145.

the "management of the vessel"; and also for failure to heed a light showing the position of a reef,[89] and for the mistake of the captain in entering a bay at low tide and thus stranding the ship,[90] as faults of navigation.

Limited Liability Act[91]

Under section 4283 of the Revised Statutes of the United States (U. S. Comp. St. 1901, p. 2943), the liability of the vessel owner for loss or damage[92] is limited in amount to "the interest of such owner in such vessel[93] and her freight,"[94] provided only the loss or damage occurred "without the privity or knowledge of such owner."[95] Under this statute, then, the owner is protected from losing any more than the amount of his interest, even though the damage to the injured cargo, or the value of the lost cargo, may far exceed in amount the interest of the owner.

CARRIER'S LIABILITY FOR DEVIATION AND DELAY—DEVIATION

121. When the carrier, without necessity or reasonable excuse, deviates from the usual or agreed route, he becomes absolutely liable for the goods, without any exception whatsoever.

A material deviation from the usual or agreed route, without justification or excuse, by the carrier, is the assumption of an unlawful dominion over the goods, and is therefore equivalent to a

[89] The E. A. Shores, Jr. (D. C.) 73 Fed. 342.

[90] In re Meyer (D. C.) 74 Fed. 881.

[91] Act March 3, 1851, c. 43, 9 Stat. 635. For text of act, see U. S. Comp. St. 1901, p. 2943; 1 Hutch. Carr. p. 361, note. For text and extensive annotations, see 4 Fed. St. Annotated, pp. 839–849.

[92] The limitation applies equally to cases of personal injury and death, and to cases of loss of, or damage to, property. Butler v. Boston & S. S. S. Co., 130 U. S. 552, 9 Sup. Ct. 612, 32 L. Ed. 1017 (death of passenger); Craig v. Continental Ins. Co., 141 U. S. 643, 12 Sup. Ct. 97, 35 L. Ed. 886 (death of member of crew).

[93] The City of Norwich, 118 U. S. 491, 6 Sup. Ct. 1150, 30 L. Ed. 134; The Benefactor, 103 U. S. 247, 26 L. Ed. 466; In re La Bourgogne (D. C.) 117 Fed. 261; Matter of Wright, 10 Ben. 14, Fed. Cas. No. 18,066.

[94] Sumner v. Caswell (D. C.) 20 Fed. 253; The Main v. Williams, 152 U. S. 122, 14 Sup. Ct. 486, 38 L. Ed. 381; In re Meyer (D. C.) 74 Fed. 897.

[95] The Republic, 61 Fed. 109, 9 C. C. A. 386; Craig v. Continental Ins. Co., 141 U. S. 643, 12 Sup. Ct. 97, 35 L. Ed. 886; Parsons v. Empire Transp. Co., 111 Fed. 208, 49 C. C. A. 302; The Annie Faxon, 75 Fed. 314, 21 C. C. A. 366; In re Leonard (D. C.) 14 Fed. 55.

conversion.[96] This, therefore, imposes upon the carrier an absolute liability which recognizes no exception, not even the five excepted perils.[97] For any loss or injury, the carrier is responsible, utterly regardless of how it happened or what was its cause. Even the pure act of God affords him no excuse.[98]

It is said in such cases that if the loss was due to an act of God, and the carrier can go further and show that such loss or injury would have occurred just the same, had there been no deviation, even this will not excuse him.[99] As the unnecessary deviation was an active wrong, the carrier must bear its consequences, whatever they may be. It is said that he shall not be allowed to qualify or apportion his wrong.

Of course, this perilous responsibility rests upon the carrier only for a wrongful deviation, one for which there is no necessity or excuse. When the deviation was necessary or justifiable, the carrier incurs no liability by it.[1] Indeed, there might be cases when the carrier, in not making a deviation, would thereby convict himself of negligence. In all of these cases, the consent of the shipper to such deviation can readily be presumed. Thus, the deviation was necessary and excusable when the carrier's vessel would otherwise have been captured by the public enemy, or when the deviation was

96 See discussion of this question as to conversion by the ordinary bailee for hire, ante, § 47. See, also, Maghee v. Camden & A. R. Transp. Co., 45 N. Y. 514, 6 Am. Rep. 124; Richmond & D. R. Co. v. Benson, 86 Ga. 203, 12 S. E. 357, 22 Am. St. Rep. 446 (carrier held liable for destruction of goods by act of God, after the carrier's wrongful refusal to deliver the goods); Baltimore & O. R. Co. v. O'Donnell, 49 Ohio St. 489, 32 N. E. 476, 21 L. R. A. 117, 34 Am. St. Rep. 579; Louisville & N. R. Co. v. Barkhouse, 100 Ala. 543, 13 South. 534; Crosby v. Fitch, 12 Conn. 410, 31 Am. Dec. 745; Powers v. Davenport, 7 Blackf. (Ind.) 497, 43 Am. Dec. 100; Davis v. Garrett, 6 Bing. (Eng.) 716; Merchants' Despatch Transp. Co. v. Kahn, 76 Ill. 520.

97 S. D. Seavey Co. v. Union Transit Co., 106 Wis. 394, 82 N. W. 285; Louisville & C. Packet Co. v. Rogers, 20 Ind. App. 594, 49 N. E. 970; Parker v. James, 4 Camp. (Eng.) 12; Galveston, H. & S. A. R. Co. v. Breaux (Tex. Civ. App.) 150 S. W. 287.

98 Davis v. Garrett, 6 Bing. (Eng.) 716; Galveston, H. & S. A. R. Co. v. Breaux (Tex. Civ. App.) 150 S. W. 287.

99 See cases cited in note 97; 1 Hutch. Carr. § 295. See, also, opinion of Tindal, C. J., in Davis v. Garrett, 6 Bing. (Eng.) 716.

1 Hand v. Baynes, 4 Whart. (Pa.) 204, 33 Am. Dec. 54; Johnson v. New York Cent. R. Co., 33 N. Y. 610, 88 Am. Dec. 416. Taking another vessel in tow, when not in distress, constitutes a deviation. Natchez Ins. Co. v. Stanton, 2 Smedes & M. (Miss.) 340, 41 Am. Dec. 592; Johnson v. New York Cent. R. Co., 33 N. Y. 610, 88 Am. Dec. 416. And see International & G. N. R. Co. v. Wentworth, 8 Tex. Civ. App. 5, 27 S. W. 680. But the burden of proving such necessity rests on the carrier. Le Sage v. Great W. Ry. Co., 1 Daly (N. Y.) 306.

made to escape a destructive and dangerous storm, or serious danger from icebergs.[2]

In each of the following cases there was no justification or excuse, and the carrier was held liable: When there was a deviation by the vessel from the usual course, and the loss was caused by a tempest;[3] when the contract was for transportation by land, and the goods were sent by water,[4] and destroyed by the act of God; when the shipper stipulated that the goods were to be sent by one line of boats, and they were sent by another line.[5]

SAME—DELAY

121½. In the absence of special contract, the common carrier is bound to use only reasonable care or ordinary diligence in completing the transportation without delay. The carrier is therefore liable for delay only when it is due to his negligence.

When the carrier specially agrees to transport and deliver the goods within a prescribed time, he is, of course, bound by his contract, and is liable for his failure to live up to its terms.

When the common carrier receives goods for transportation, there is an implied undertaking on his part that they are to be carried and delivered within a reasonable time.[6] But the carrier

[2] See Van Zile, Bailm. & Carr. § 499; Crosby v. Fitch, 12 Conn. 410, 31 Am. Dec. 745; Johnson v. New York Cent. R. Co., 33 N. Y. 610, 88 Am. Dec. 416; Maghee v. Camden & A. R. Transp. Co., 45 N. Y. 514, 6 Am. Rep. 124.

[3] Davis v. Garrett, 6 Bing. (Eng.) 716. The same principle applies to carriers by land. See Powers v. Davenport, 7 Blackf. (Ind.) 497, 43 Am. Dec. 100; Phillips v. Brigham, 26 Ga. 617, 71 Am. Dec. 237; Lawrence v. McGregor, Wright (Ohio) 193.

[4] Ingalls v. Brooks, 1 Edm. Sel. Cas. (N. Y.) 104; Philadelphia & R. R. Co. v. Beck, 125 Pa. 620, 17 Atl. 505, 11 Am. St. Rep. 924. So, where the agreement was to send by canal, and they were sent by sea. Hand v. Baynes, 4 Whart. (Pa.) 204, 33 Am. Dec. 54.

[5] Johnson v. New York Cent. R. Co., 33 N. Y. 610, 88 Am. Dec. 416; Cox v. Foscue, 37 Ala. 505, 79 Am. Dec. 69. So, if the agreement is to send by steam, and the goods are sent by sail. Wilcox v. Parmelee, 3 Sandf. (N. Y.) 610. A carrier must follow instructions as to the selection of carriers beyond his own route. Johnson v. New York Cent. R. Co., supra. If the owner of the designated line of boats refuses to receive the goods, the carrier should so notify the owner and await instructions. Goodrich v. Thompson, 44 N. Y. 324. And see Fisk v. Newton, 1 Denio (N. Y.) 45, 43 Am. Dec. 649.

[6] Ryland & Rankin v. Chesapeake & O. R. Co., 55 W. Va. 181, 46 S. E. 923; The Prussia (D. C.) 100 Fed. 484; Denman v. Chicago, B. & Q. R. Co., 52

is not an insurer, in this regard, as he is in case of loss or damage.[7] He is liable for delay only when this is due to his failure to exercise ordinary care or reasonable diligence to transport and deliver the goods within a reasonable time.[8] His primary duty, then, is to carry safely, as to which he is with certain exceptions an insurer. On this primary duty is ingrafted another, the duty of using ordinary care to carry promptly; but as to this he is liable only when he fails to deliver within a reasonable time, and when, in addition, this failure is due to his negligence.[9] When loss or

Neb. 140, 71 N. W. 967; Denny v. New York Cent. R. Co., 13 Gray (Mass.) 481, 74 Am. Dec. 645; Cincinnati, I., St. L. & C. Ry. Co. v. Case, 122 Ind. 310, 23 N. E. 797; Pittsburg, C., C. & St. L. R. Co. v. Knox, 177 Ind. 344, 98 N. E. 295; CONGER v. HUDSON RIVER R. CO., 6 Duer (N. Y.) 375, Dobie Cas. Bailments and Carriers, 204; Bibb Broom Corn Co. v. Atchison, T. & S. F. R. Co., 94 Minn. 269, 102 N. W. 709, 69 L. R. A. 509, 110 Am. St. Rep. 361, 3 Ann. Cas. 450.

7 Taylor v. Railway Co., L. R. 1 C. P. (Eng.) 385; Philadelphia, W. & B. R. Co. v. Lehman, 56 Md. 209, 40 Am. Rep. 415; CONGER v. HUDSON RIVER R. CO., 6 Duer (N. Y.) 375, Dobie Cas. Bailments and Carriers, 204; Scovill v. Griffith, 12 N. Y. 509; Michigan Cent. R. Co. v. Burrows, 33 Mich. 6; Empire Transp. Co. v. Wallace, 68 Pa. 302, 8 Am. Rep. 178; Kinnick v. Chicago, M. & St. P. R. Co., 69 Iowa, 665, 29 N. W. 772; Savannah, F. & W. Ry. Co. v. Pritchard, 77 Ga. 412, 1 S. E. 261, 4 Am. St. Rep. 92; Johnson v. East Tennessee, V. & G. Ry. Co., 90 Ga. 810, 17 S. E. 121. But see Vicksburg & M. R. Co. v. Ragsdale, 46 Miss. 458. Goods received on Sunday must be transported within a reasonable time. Philadelphia, W. & B. R. Co. v. Lehman, 56 Md. 209, 40 Am. Rep. 415. The rule that a carrier is an insurer of safe delivery held not to apply to liability for delay of transportation; reasonable care only being required to avoid delay. Delaney v. United States Express Co., 70 W. Va. 502, 74 S. E. 512.

8 Southern Ry. Co. v. Wilcox, 99 Va. 394, 39 S. E. 144; International & G. N. Ry. Co. v. Hynes, 3 Tex. Civ. App. 20, 21 S. W. 622; Johnson v. East Tennessee, V. & G. Ry. Co., 90 Ga. 810, 17 S. E. 121; R. E. FUNSTEN DRIED FRUIT & NUT CO. v. TOLEDO, ST. L. & W. R. CO., 163 Mo. App. 426, 143 S. W. 839, Dobie Cas. Bailments and Carriers, 196; Ruppel v. Allegheny Valley Ry. Co., 167 Pa. 166, 31 Atl. 478, 46 Am. St. Rep. 666; Philadelphia, W. & B. R. Co. v. Lehman, 56 Md. 209, 40 Am. Rep. 415; Taylor v. Railroad Co., L. R. 1 C. P. (Eng.) 385; Rawson v. Holland, 59 N. Y. 611, 17 Am. Rep. 494; Michigan Southern & N. I. R. Co. v. Day, 20 Ill. 375, 71 Am. Dec. 278; Rathbone v. Neal, 4 La. Ann. 563, 50 Am. Dec. 579. A carrier of live stock is not liable for delay in the transportation thereof, unless the delay was occasioned by its negligence, and a carrier acting in good faith and to protect the shipment is not negligent. Otrich v. St. Louis, I. M. & S. R. Co., 154 Mo. App. 420, 134 S. W. 665; CONGER v. HUDSON RIVER R. CO., 6 Duer (N. Y.) 375, Dobie Cas. Bailments and Carriers, 204. See, also, Cleveland, C., C. & St. L. Ry. Co. v. Heath, 22 Ind. App. 47, 53 N. E. 198; Bibb Broom Corn Co v. Atchison, T. & S. F. R. Co., 94 Minn. 269, 102 N. W. 709, 69 L. R. A. 509, 110 Am. St. Rep. 361, 3 Ann. Cas. 450; St. Louis & S. F. R. Co. v. Dean (Tex. Civ. App.) 152 S. W. 1127.

9 Taylor v. Railway Co., L. R. 1 C. P. (Eng.) 385; CONGER v. HUDSON RIVER R. CO., 6 Duer (N. Y.) 375, Dobie Cas. Bailments and Carriers, 204.

damage occurs, the only defense that the carrier can make is one of the excepted perils. When delay occurs, the carrier can set up the exercise of ordinary care as a perfect defense. The law thus prefers safety, by imposing an extraordinary responsibility on the common carrier as to this, to promptness, as to which the carrier incurs merely the responsibility of the ordinary bailee for hire. When the safety of the goods demands a delay, this is then not merely an act for which the carrier is excused, but such delay becomes a positive duty.[10]

An unreasonable delay, due to the clear negligence of the carrier, does not, however, amount to a conversion.[11] Conversion involves the assertion of unlawful dominion over the goods. The owner of the goods is therefore bound to receive the goods, however long the delay.[12] He cannot refuse to accept them and recover their value from the carrier. The remedy of the owner, in such cases, is to sue the carrier for damages.[13] The measure of his recovery is the amount of damage that he has suffered, proximately and naturally resulting from the delay.[14]

10 Crosby v. Fitch, 12 Conn. 410, 31 Am. Dec. 745, in which it was held that, when the safer passage was obstructed by ice, the shipmaster should have waited until it was open, instead of venturing out in the open sea. See, also, Davis v. Garrett, 6 Bing. (Eng.) 716; International & G. N. Ry. Co. v. Wentworth, 8 Tex. Civ. App. 5, 27 S. W. 680.

11 Scovell v. Griffith, 12 N. Y. 509; Hackett v. B. C. & M. R. R., 35 N. H. 390.

12 Rubin v. Wells Fargo Exp. Co. (Sup.) 85 N. Y. Supp. 1108; Goldbowitz v. Metropolitan Exp. Co. (Sup.) 91 N. Y. Supp. 318; Illinois Cent. R. Co. v. Johnson & Fleming, 116 Tenn. 624; 94 S. W. 600; Ryland & Rankin v. Chesapeake & O. R. Co., 55 W. Va. 181, 46 S. E. 923; Baumbach v. Gulf, C. & S. F. Ry. Co., 4 Tex. Civ. App. 650, 23 S. W. 693; St. Louis, I. M. & S. Ry. Co. v. Mudford, 44 Ark. 439.

13 Lowe v. East Tennessee, V. & G. Ry. Co., 90 Ga. 85, 15 S. E. 692; Pruitt v. Hannibal & St. J. R. Co., 62 Mo. 527; Wells, Fargo & Co.'s Express v. Fuller, 13 Tex. Civ. App. 610, 35 S. W. 824; Ormsby v. Union Pac. R. Co. (C. C.) 4 Fed. 706; Felton v. McCreary-McClellan Live Stock Co., 59 S. W. 744, 22 Ky. Law Rep. 1058; Ward v. New York Cent. R. Co., 47 N. Y. 29, 7 Am. Rep. 405.

14 See post, § 162. Such as deterioration of goods or loss of market. Murrell v. Pacific Exp. Co., 54 Ark. 22, 14 S. W. 1098, 26 Am. St. Rep. 17; Scott v. Boston & New Orleans S. S. Co., 106 Mass. 468; Scovill v. Griffith, 12 N. Y. 509; Ruppel v. Allegheny Valley Ry. Co., 167 Pa. 166, 31 Atl. 478, 46 Am. St. Rep. 666; Hudson v. Northern Pac. Ry. Co., 92 Iowa, 231, 60 N. W. 608, 54 Am. St. Rep. 550; Fox v. Boston & M. R. Co., 148 Mass. 220, 19 N. E. 222, 1 L. R. A. 702; Pereira v. Central Pac. R. Co., 66 Cal. 92, 4 Pac. 988; Douglass v. Hannibal & St. J. R. Co., 53 Mo. App. 473; The Caledonia, 157 U. S. 124, 15 Sup. Ct. 537, 39 L. Ed. 644. The shipper may recover expenses to which he has been put by the delay. Black v. Baxendale, 1 Exch. (Eng.) 410; Gulf, C. & S. F. Ry. Co. v. Hume, 87 Tex. 211, 27 S. W.

Delay, however, even when in no way due to the negligence of the carrier, does not release the carrier from his duty of completing the carriage of the goods.[15] The contract of carriage is in no sense discharged by such delay. Accordingly, when the cause of delay is removed, the carrier must again use ordinary care to complete the transportation and promptly carry the goods to their destination.[16]

In the cases that follow, the common carrier, who was in no way negligent, was held not liable for delay. In all of these cases, it might be noted, the carrier would have been liable for loss of, or damage to, the goods if similarly caused. When delay was caused by a collision on land,[17] mobs or strikers,[18] destruction of part of

110; Swift River Co. v. Fitchburg R. Co., 169 Mass. 326, 47 N. E. 1015, 61 Am. St. Rep. 288; Baltimore & O. R. Co. v. O'Donnell, 49 Ohio St. 489, 32 N. E. 476, 21 L. R. A. 117, 34 Am. St. Rep. 579. Special damages for a carrier's delay in transportation cannot be recovered where the carrier had no notice at the time of contract of the special facts; not even those accruing from delay occurring after it is given such notice. Hassler v. Gulf, C. & S. F. Ry. Co. (Tex. Civ. App. 1911) 142 S. W. 629. Illinois Cent. R. Co. v. Southern Seating & Cabinet Co., 104 Tenn. 568, 58 S. W. 303, 50 L. R. A. 729, 78 Am. St. Rep. 933; Deming v. Grand Trunk Co., 48 N. H. 455, 2 Am. Rep. 267; St. Louis, I. M. & S. Ry. Co. v. Mudford, 48 Ark. 502, 3 S. W. 814. Special damages for delay in shipment of goods are recoverable when the carrier has notice that delay in delivery will result in such damages. Mills v. Southern Ry. Co., 90 S. C. 366, 73 S. E. 772.

15 St. Louis, I. M. & S. R. Co. v. Jones (Tex. Civ. App.) 29 S. W. 695.

16 Hadley v. Clarke, 8 Term R. (Eng.) 259. Palmer v. Lorillard, 16 Johns. (N. Y.) 348; Spann v. Erie Boatman's Transp. Co., 11 Misc. Rep. 680, 83 N. Y. Supp. 566; Vicksburg & M. R. Co. v. Ragsdale, 46 Miss. 458.

17 CONGER v. HUDSON RIVER R. CO., 6 Duer (N. Y.) 375, Dobie Cas. Bailments and Carriers, 204.

18 See 1 Hutch. Carr. § 657; Pittsburgh, C. & St. L. Ry. Co. v. Hollowell, 65 Ind. 188, 32 Am. Rep. 63. But see Blackstock v. New York & E. R. Co., 20 N. Y. 48, 75 Am. Dec. 372. Where the employés of a railroad company suddenly refuse to work, and are discharged, and delay results from the failure of the company to promptly supply their places, the company is liable for any damage caused by such delay; but, where the places of the striking employés are promptly supplied by other competent men, and the strikers then prevent the new employés from doing duty by lawless and irresistible violence, the company is not liable for delay caused solely by such lawless violence. Pittsburgh, Ft. W. & C. R. Co. v. Hazen, 84 Ill. 36, 25 Am. Rep. 422; Pittsburgh, C. & St. L. R. Co. v. Hollowell, supra; GREISMER v. LAKE SHORE & M. S. R. CO., 102 N. Y. 563, 7 N. E. 828, 55 Am. Rep. 837, Dobie Cas. Bailments and Carriers, 206; Gulf, C. & S. F. Ry. Co. v. Levi, 76 Tex. 337, 13 S. W. 191, 8 L. R. A. 323, 18 Am. St. Rep. 45; Haas v. Kansas City, Ft. S. & G. R. Co., 81 Ga. 792, 7 S. E. 629; International & G. N. R. Co. v. Tisdale, 74 Tex. 8, 11 S. W. 900, 4 L. R. A. 545; Lake Shore & M. S. Ry. Co. v. Bennett, 89 Ind. 457; Missouri Pac. R. Co. v. Levi (Tex. App.) 14 S. W. 1062; Southern Pac. R. Co. v. Johnson (Tex. App.) 15 S. W. 121;

the carrier's track by fire,[19] or a scow running into the carrier's boat,[20] the carrier exercising ordinary diligence was excused.[21]

What is a Reasonable Time

We have just seen that the carrier must use ordinary care to deliver the goods within a reasonable time. What is a reasonable time, in this connection, is a question of fact for the jury, to be determined in the light of the particular circumstances of each case.[22] These, of course, may present an almost infinite variety. Thus, the nature of the goods, the distance they are to be carried,

Bartlett v. Pittsburgh, C. & St. L. Ry. Co., 94 Ind. 281. But cf. Read v. St. Louis, K. & C. & N. R. Co., 60 Mo. 199.

19 Michigan Cent. R. Co. v. Burrows, 33 Mich. 6.

20 Parsons v. Hardy, 14 Wend. (N. Y.) 215, 28 Am. Dec. 521.

21 For other cases in which the carrier's delay was excused, see Bowman v. Teall, 23 Wend. (N. Y.) 306, 35 Am. Dec. 562; Beckwith v. Frisby, 32 Vt. 559 (freezing of navigable waters); Bennett v. Byram, 38 Miss. 17, 75 Am. Dec. 90; Silver v. Hale, 2 Mo. App. 557 (low stage of river); Pruitt v. Hannibal & St. J. R. Co., 62 Mo. 527; Ballentine v. North Missouri R. Co., 40 Mo. 491, 93 Am. Dec. 315; Briddon v. Railroad Co., 28 L. J. Exch. (Eng.) 51 (heavy snow). But where a carrier accepted an automobile for shipment, it is liable for an unreasonable delay in the shipment, and its temporary inability to secure a car large enough to hold the automobile will not exonerate it. Grigsby v. Texas & P. Ry. Co. (Tex. Civ. App.) 137 S. W. 709. See, generally, Vicksburg & M. R. Co. v. Ragsdale, 46 Miss. 458; Livingston v. New York Cent. & H. R. R. Co., 5 Hun (N. Y.) 562; Taylor v. Railroad Co., L. R. 1 C. P. (Eng.) 385. A carrier need not incur heavy expense, or use extraordinary exertions, to hasten the transportation of goods. Reasonable diligence is all that is required. Empire Transportation Co. v. Wallace, 68 Pa. 302, 8 Am. Rep. 178.

22 Cartwell v. Pacific Express Co., 58 Ark. 487, 25 S. W. 503; Hosley v. Baltimore & O. R. Co., 54 W. Va. 563, 46 S. E. 613, 66 L. R. A. 871; Coffin v. New York Cent. R. Co., 64 Barb. (N. Y.) 379; Wibert v. New York & E. R. Co., 12 N. Y. 245; Nudd v. Wells, 11 Wis. 407; Parsons v. Hardy, 14 Wend. (N. Y.) 215, 28 Am. Dec. 521; Michigan Southern & N. I. R. Co. v. Day, 20 Ill. 375, 71 Am. Dec. 278; Bennett v. Byram, 38 Miss. 17, 75 Am. Dec. 90; East Tennessee & G. R. Co. v. Nelson, 1 Cold. (Tenn.) 272; Gerhard's Adm'r v. Neese, 36 Tex. 635; McGraw v. Baltimore & O. R. Co., 18 W. Va. 361, 41 Am. Rep. 696; Petersen v. Case (C. C.) 21 Fed. 885; St. Louis, I. M. & S. Ry. Co. v. Heath, 41 Ark. 476; Ormsby v. Union Pac. R. Co. (C. C.) 2 McCrary, 48, 4 Fed. 706; St. Clair v. Chicago, B. & Q. Ry. Co., 80 Iowa, 304, 45 N. W. 570. Where an unusual contingency has arisen, which, unexpectedly, largely increases the business, and thereby prevents the handling of freight with the usual promptness and dispatch, the criterion of reasonable diligence is not the usual average speed in ordinary times, but the average running time under the extraordinary and unusual circumstances existing at the time. Michigan Cent. R. Co. v. Burrows, 33 Mich. 6. For cases where delay has been held unreasonable, see Missouri Pac. Ry. Co. v. Hall, 14 C. C. A. 153, 66 Fed. 868; Cartwright v. Rome, W. & O. R. Co., 85 Hun, 517, 33 N. Y. Supp. 147; Davis v. Jacksonville Southeastern Line, 126 Mo. 69, 28 S. W. 965.

the mode of transportation, the weather, the season of the year, the amount of traffic handled by the carrier, are all important considerations, to which due weight should be given.

Delivery Within Time Stipulated

The carrier may here, as elsewhere, enlarge his liability by contract. Accordingly, when the carrier agrees to transport goods within a specified time, he is absolutely liable if he fails to do so.[23] He here assumes a strict responsibility by his own affirmative contract, and he must therefore live up to it. In such a case, when the tenor of his contract is for delivery at or before a definite time, without any exceptions, he would then be liable for delay beyond that time, though due to an inevitable accident, or even to the act of God.[24] The contract is the measure of his responsibility, so that it is simply a question of construing the contract. Of course, there could be no recovery for delay that is due to the shipper's own wrong.[25]

[23] Fox v. Boston & M. R. Co., 148 Mass. 220, 19 N. E. 222, 1 L. R. A. 702, Pereira v. Central Pac. R. Co., 66 Cal. 92, 4 Pac. 988; Chicago & A. R. Co. v. Thrapp, 5 Ill. App. 502; Deming v. Grand Trunk R. R. Co., 48 N. H. 455, 2 Am. Rep. 267; Place v. Union Express Co., 2 Hilt. (N. Y.) 19; Harrison v. Missouri Pac. Ry. Co., 74 Mo. 364, 41 Am. Rep. 318; Parmelee v. Wilks, 22 Barb. (N. Y.) 539; Harmony v. Bingham, 12 N. Y. 99, 62 Am. Dec. 142; Cantwell v. Pacific Express Co., 58 Ark. 487, 25 S. W. 503. Cf. Atchison, T. & S. F. Ry. Co. v. Bryan (Tex. Civ. App.) 28 S. W. 98; International & G. N. Ry. Co. v. Wentworth, 87 Tex. 311, 28 S. W. 277. So, where a vendor of goods agrees absolutely to deliver them by a certain time, impossibility of obtaining them will not excuse him. Gilpins v. Consequa, Pet. C. C. 85, Fed. Cas. No. 5,452; Youqua v. Nixon, Pet. C. C. 221, Fed. Cas. No. 18,189. Nor impossibility of delivering them. Bryan v. Spurgin, 5 Sneed (Tenn.) 681. The contract may be implied from acceptance of the goods with knowledge that they are intended to be at their destination on a given day. Chicago & A. R. Co. v. Thrapp, 5 Ill. App. 502; Grindle v. Eastern Express Co., 67 Me. 317, 24 Am. Rep. 31; Philadelphia, W. & B. R. Co. v. Lehman, 56 Md. 209, 40 Am. Rep. 415. But see United States Exp. Co. v. Root, 47 Mich. 231, 10 N. W. 351.

[24] Harmony v. Bingham, 12 N. Y. 99, 62 Am. Dec. 142; Id., 1 Duer, 209

[25] Fowler v. Liverpool & G. W. Steam Co., 87 N. Y. 190; Stoner v. Chicago G. W. Ry. Co., 109 Iowa, 551, 80 N. W. 569.

CHAPTER XI

LIABILITY UNDER SPECIAL CONTRACT

HISTORICAL AND INTRODUCTORY

122. Though the common-law liability of the common carrier of goods was that of an insurer (with certain exceptions), this rigorous responsibility may be modified by special contract between the shipper and the carrier.

Contracts Enlarging the Liability of the Carrier

The courts are unanimous in holding that the common carrier of goods may by special contract indefinitely enlarge and extend his common-law liability.[1] The carrier cannot be compelled by law to enter into such contracts, but if he voluntarily enters into them the law will not hesitate to give them effect. Such contracts, increasing the liability imposed by the common law, are in no sense

[1] Southern Express Co. v. Glenn, 16 Lea (Tenn.) 472, 1 S. W. 102; Gaither v. Barnett, 2 Brev. (S. C.) 488; McCauley v. Davidson, 10 Minn. 418 (Gil. 335); Id., 13 Minn. 162 (Gil. 150); Strohn v. Detroit & M. R. Co., 23 Wis. 126, 99 Am. Dec. 114; Redpath v. Vaughan, 52 Barb. (N. Y.) 489. As the common carrier's liability at common law is so rigorous, the courts require clear language to indicate an intention to increase this responsibility. They are therefore slow to infer such an intention from mere general expressions. Gage v. Tirrell, 9 Allen (Mass.) 299; Price v. Hartshorn, 44 Barb. 655; Id., 44 N. Y. 94, 4 Am. Rep. 645.

opposed to public policy. Hence, if they possess the usual requisites of contractual validity, they are valid and binding.[2]

Thus the carrier may by contract constitute himself an insurer, even against the risks ordinarily excepted by the common law, such as the act of God or the public enemy.[3] More usual stipulations are that the carrier will carry by a certain route,[4] that the goods will be carried by land or by water,[5] that only specified cars or other instrumentalities will be used in transporting the goods,[6] or the manner of carrying the goods may be specified in detail.[7] Again, the carrier may by contract absolutely insure the delivery of the goods at the destination by a specified time.[8] In all these cases, the carrier, having fully and freely entered into the contract, is bound to perform it fully or respond in damages for his breach of it.

Contracts Limiting the Liability of the Carrier—In England

Though the insuring liability of the common carrier of goods was fixed as inhering in the relation, and seems not to have been regarded originally as a matter of contract, yet in comparatively early times we find a recognition of the carrier's right to diminish this unusual responsibility by contract.

The earliest judicial reference to this right seems to have been a declaration of Lord Coke in Southcote's Case.[9] Lord Hale, in Morse v. Slue,[10] apparently conceded the right. The tremendous importance of the right, however, was not immediately recognized by the carrier, for it was not until after the middle of the eighteenth century that any further cases of importance on the subject were decided. The cases of Gibbon v. Paynton[11] (1769), Forward v. Pittard[12] (1785), and the judgment of Lord Ellenborough in Nicholson v. Willan[13] (1804), place the right upon a fairly sound ju-

2 See cases cited in preceding note.

3 Price v. Hartshorn, 44 Barb. 655; Id., 44 N. Y. 94, 4 Am. Rep. 645; Gage v. Tirrell, 9 Allen (Mass.) 299; Miller v. Chicago & A. Ry. Co., 62 Mo. App. 252.

4 Maghee v. Camden & A. R. Transp. Co., 45 N. Y. 522, 6 Am. Rep. 124; Steel v. Flagg, 5 Barn. & Ald. (Eng.) 342; Goodrich v. Thompson, 44 N. Y. 324.

5 Merrick v. Webster, 3 Mich. 268.

6 Mathis v. Southern Ry. Co., 65 S. C. 271, 43 S. E. 684, 61 L. R. A. 824.

7 New York Cent. & H. R. R. Co. v. Standard Oil Co., 20 Hun (N. Y.) 39; Penn v. Buffalo & E. R. Co., 49 N. Y. 204, 10 Am. Rep. 355.

8 Shelby v. Missouri Pac. Ry. Co., 77 Mo. App. 205; Rudell v. Ogdensburgh Transit Co., 117 Mich. 568, 76 N. W. 381, 44 L. R. A. 415.

9 4 Coke (Eng.) 83 b (1601).

10 1 Vent. (Eng.) 190 (1671).

11 4 Burr. (Eng.) 2298.

12 1 T. R. (Eng.) 27.

13 5 East (Eng.) 507.

dicial basis. Later cases unanimously recognized both the existence of this right and its tremendous practical importance.[14] A number of English statutes, also sanctioned such contractual limitations on the old insuring liability. Of these the most important, perhaps, is the Railway and Canal Traffic Act of 1854, which limited these contracts to such as a court or judge should deem "to be just and reasonable."

Same—In the United States

With us the earliest cases were Hollister v. Nowlen[15] (1838) and Cole v. Goodwin,[16] both of which repudiated the right (previously recognized in England) of the carrier to limit his liability by public notices, and Gould v. Hill,[17] holding that the carrier's exceptional responsibility could not be diminished even by special contract. Very soon after the decision in Gould v. Hill, however, the United States Supreme Court repudiated the ruling of the earlier case and held, in New Jersey Steam Navigation Co. v. Merchants' Bank,[18] that the carrier could limit his common-law liability by a special contract to that effect.

After this ruling of the United States Supreme Court, the decision in Gould v. Hill was repudiated even by the New York court which handed it down.[19] In due time this right of the carrier was recognized by the highest courts of all the states. It is now, then, the rule, approved by both state and federal courts, that the common carrier of goods, in the absence of a statute prohibiting it, may restrict by means of a special contract his liability as an insurer of the safe delivery of the goods,[20] which high responsibility is placed upon him by the rules of the common law.

The extraordinary liability of common carriers is said to have

[14] Smith v. Horne, 8 Taunt. 144; Wyld v. Rickford, 8 M. & W. 443; Brooke v. Pickwick, 4 Bing. 218; McCance v. London, etc., Ry. Co., 3 H. & C. 343, 34 L. J. Exch. 39; Peck v. North, etc., Ry. Co., 10 H. L. Cas. 473, 32 L. J. Q. B. 241; Mayhew v. Eames, 3 B. & C. 601.

[15] 19 Wend. (N. Y.) 234, 32 Am. Dec. 455.

[16] 19 Wend. (N. Y.) 251, 32 Am. Dec. 470.

[17] 2 Hill (N. Y.) 623.

[18] 6 How. 344, 12 L. Ed. 465.

[19] Parsons v. Monteath, 13 Barb. (N. Y.) 353; Dorr v. New Jersey Steam Nav. Co., 11 N. Y. 485, 62 Am. Dec. 125.

[20] SOUTHERN EXP. CO. v. CALDWELL, 21 Wall. 264, 22 L. Ed. 556, Dobie Cas. Bailments and Carriers, 226; Merchants' Despatch Transp. Co. v. Leysor, 89 Ill. 43; Ormsby v. Union Pac. Ry. Co. (C. C.) 4 Fed. 706; Ullman v. Chicago & N. W. R. Co., 112 Wis. 150, 88 N. W. 41, 88 Am. St. Rep. 949; Hoadley v. Northern Transportation Co., 115 Mass. 304, 15 Am. Rep. 106; Allam v. Pennsylvania Ry. Co., 183 Pa. 174, 38 Atl. 709, 39 L. R. A. 535; St. Louis, I. M. & S. R. Co. v. Bone, 52 Ark. 26, 11 S. W. 958; Lacey v. Oregon R. & Nav. Co., 63 Or. 596, 128 Pac. 999.

been originally imposed by public policy, because of the danger of collusion between the carrier and robbers. The improved state of society, the better administration of the laws, and the rapidity and comparative safety of modern modes of transportation, are all factors that have, in the course of time, rendered less imperative the strict application of the rule holding the carrier up to the rigid responsibility of an insurer. Hence a contract exempting a carrier from liability as an insurer, and substituting for it some less rigorous responsibility, came to be considered as just and reasonable, and no longer against public policy. But the uneven terms upon which the parties deal, often enabling the carrier practically to dictate his own terms, still make it a matter of public policy that some limitation be put upon the carrier's power thus to limit his liability. The American courts, however, as we shall see, have differed greatly as to the nature and extent of such limitations.

METHOD OF LIMITING LIABILITY

123. The limitation of the carrier's common-law liability can be effected only by means of a contract assented to by the shipper. Notices limiting liability are ineffectual, unless the shipper assents to the terms of such notice; and such assent cannot be inferred merely because the shipper, after he has knowledge of the notice, delivers the goods to the carrier for shipment.

Notices

When the power of the carrier to limit his insuring liability is conceded, a question of paramount importance is the method by which such limitations can be effected. The effect of a notice, published by the carrier and brought home to the shipper, has resulted in a sharp difference of opinion between the English and American courts.

English Rule

In England the custom, resorted to by the carrier, of posting notices in public which purport to limit the carrier's responsibility, met with favor at the hands of the courts. It was there accordingly held that merely by general notice to that effect the carrier could restrict his common-law liability, when the shipper knew of such notice.[21] The evils of such a practice, however, led to the pas-

[21] Gibbon v. Paynton, 4 Burr. 2298; Riley v. Horne, 5 Bing. 217; Mayhew v. Eames, 3 B. & C. 601; Lesson v. Holt, 1 Starkie, 186; Phillips v. Edwards, 3 H. & N. 813; Maving v. Todd, 1 Starkie, 72; Nicholson v. Willan, 5 East, 507; London & N. W. Ry. Co. v. Dunham, 18 C. B. 826.

sage in 1854 of the Railway and Canal Traffic Act. Under this act the carrier was prohibited from limiting his liability by "notice, condition or declaration"; but the right of the carrier to diminish his responsibility by a contract signed by the shipper was expressly recognized.

American Rule

But in this country the rule is well established that notices limiting the liability of the carrier are of no avail unless assented to by the shipper,[22] in which case a contract is established.[23] The American rule finds its justification in the essential nature of a common carrier's duty to the public. It is a common carrier's duty to carry for all who offer, and it cannot divest itself of this duty by any ex parte act of its own, short of ceasing to be a common carrier.[24] The fact that a restrictive notice is shown to have been actually received or seen by the owner of the goods will not of itself raise the presumption that he assents to its terms, since it is as reasonable to infer that he intends to hold the carrier to his full common-law liability as that he assents to a limitation of this liability, and the burden of proof is upon the carrier to establish the contract limiting his liability, if he claims that one exists.[25]

[22] Western Transp. Co. v. Newhall, 24 Ill. 466, 76 Am. Dec. 760; Dorr v. New Jersey Steam Navigation Co., 11 N. Y. 485, 62 Am. Dec. 125; McMillan v. Michigan S. & N. I. R. Co., 16 Mich. 79, 93 Am. Dec. 208; Blumenthal v. Brainerd, 38 Vt. 402, 91 Am. Dec. 349; Little v. Boston & M. R. R., 66 Me. 239; Hale v. New Jersey Steam Nav. Co., 15 Conn. 539, 39 Am. Dec. 398; Piedmont Mfg. Co. v. Columbia & G. R. Co., 19 S. C. 353; Hartwell v. Northern Pacific Exp. Co., 5 Dak. 463, 41 N. W. 732, 3 L. R. A. 342; Brown v. Adams Exp. Co., 15 W. Va. 812; Georgia R. Co. v. Gann, 68 Ga. 350; Central of Ga. R. Co. v. Hall, 124 Ga. 322, 52 S. E. 679, 4 L. R. A. (N. S.) 898, 110 Am. St. Rep. 170, 4 Ann. Cas. 128.

[23] Gott v. Dinsmore, 111 Mass. 45, 52; Fibel v. Livingston, 64 Barb. (N. Y.) 179; Southern Exp. Co. v. Crook, 44 Ala. 468, 4 Am. Rep. 140; Brown v. Adams Exp. Co., 15 W. Va. 812; Farmers' & Mechanics' Bank v. Champlain Transp. Co., 23 Vt. 186, 56 Am. Dec. 68; Blumenthal v. Brainerd, 38 Vt. 402, 91 Am. Dec. 349; BLOSSOM v. DODD, 43 N. Y. 264, 3 Am. Rep. 701, Dobie Cas. Bailments and Carriers, 208; Davidson v. Graham, 2 Ohio St. 131; Rome R. Co. v. Sullivan, 14 Ga. 277; Gerry v. American Exp. Co., 100 Me. 519, 62 Atl. 498.

[24] See Hollister v. Nowlen, 19 Wend. (N. Y.) 234, 32 Am. Dec. 455; Cole v. Goodwin, 19 Wend. (N. Y.) 251, 32 Am. Dec. 470; Jones v. Voorhees, 10 Ohio, 145; BENNETT v. DUTTON, 10 N. H. 481, 487, Dobie Cas. Bailments and Carriers, 322; New Jersey Steam Nav. Co. v. Merchants' Bank, 6 How. 382, 12 L. Ed. 465; Moses v. Boston & M. R. R., 24 N. H. 71, 55 Am. Dec. 222; Kimball v. Rutland & B. R. Co., 26 Vt. 256, 62 Am. Dec. 567; Dorr v. New Jersey Steam Navigation Co., 4 Sandf. (N. Y.) 137; Id., 11 N. Y. 485, 62 Am. Dec. 125; Michigan Cent. R. Co. v. Hale, 6 Mich. 243; Slocum v. Fairchild, 7 Hill (N. Y.) 292.

[25] McMillan v. Michigan S. & N. I. R. Co., 16 Mich. 79, 111, 93 Am. Dec.

"Conceding that there may be a special contract for a restricted liability," says Bronson, J., in a leading American case,[26] "such a contract cannot, I think, be inferred from a general notice brought home to the employer. The argument is that where a party delivers goods to be carried, after seeing a notice that the carrier intends to limit his responsibility, his assent to the terms of the notice may be implied. But this argument entirely overlooks a very important consideration. Notwithstanding the notice, the owner has a right to insist that the carrier shall receive the goods subject to all the responsibilities incident to his employment. If the delivery of the goods under such circumstances authorizes an implication of any kind, the presumption is as strong, to say the least, that the owner intended to insist on his legal rights, as it is that he was willing to yield to the wishes of the carrier. If a coat be ordered from a mechanic after he has given the customer notice that he will not furnish the article at a less price than $100, the assent of the customer to pay that sum, though it be double the value, may, perhaps, be implied; but if the mechanic had been under a legal obligation, not only to furnish the coat, but to do so at a reasonable price, no such implication could arise. Now, the carrier is under a legal obligation to receive and convey the goods safely, or answer for the loss. He has no right to prescribe any other terms; and a notice can, at the most, only amount to a proposal for a special contract, which requires the assent of the other party. Putting the matter in the most favorable light for the carrier, the mere delivery of goods after seeing a notice cannot warrant a stronger presumption that the owner intended to assent to a restricted liability on the part of the carrier, than it does that he intended to insist on the liabilities imposed by law; and a special contract cannot be implied where there is such an equipoise of probabilities."

The American rule, then, is that, though the carrier can modify his responsibility by contract, he cannot do so by notice.[27] When, however, the shipper does more than deliver the goods to the carrier with knowledge of the notice, and actually assents to the terms of the notice, then the shipper is bound.[28] This is on the theory, of course, that the proposal contained in the notice, when accepted by the shipper, ripens into a contract. The limitation, in such a case, is not by notice, but by contract, and the notice is

208 (per Cooley, J.); New Jersey Steam Nav. Co. v. Merchants' Bank, 6 How. 344, 383, 12 L. Ed. 465 (per Nelson, J.).

[26] Hollister v. Nowlen, 19 Wend. (N. Y.) 234, 245, 32 Am. Dec. 455.

[27] See cases cited in note 22.

[28] See cases cited in note 23.

merely a means by which the contract is made. The assent of the shipper thus converts an ex parte notice of the carrier into a contract agreed to by both parties to the transaction, and the limitations of the carrier's liability are thus validly effected by contract.

SAME—NOTICE OF THE CARRIER'S REGULATIONS

124. Regulations of the carrier, enacted for the proper conduct of the carrier's business, are binding on the shipper, when they are reasonable and notice of them is brought home to the shipper, even without his assent.

In order that the carrier may properly perform the manifold duties imposed upon him, the law gives him the right to establish regulations for the conduct of his business.[29] It will be seen that this right is given, not on the basis of the bestowal of an arbitrary privilege upon the carrier, but rather as a method of enabling him to serve the public more efficiently and more expeditiously.

When such regulations are reasonable, and when they are brought to the notice of the shipper, he is bound by, and must conform to, them. When loss or damage is due to the shipper's failure to conform to such reasonable regulations, of which he has knowledge, he is barred of a recovery against the carrier.[30]

The shipper who has failed to comply with the regulations loses his right to recover from the carrier on the ground that the fault of the shipper contributed to the loss or damage. As such regulations are not attempts on the part of the carrier to limit his liability, no assent to the notice or regulation is necessary.[31] The notice is in no sense a proposal for a contract, but merely informs the shipper of the rules under which the carrier's business is conducted. The validity of the regulation is derived, not from the assent of the shipper, but from its reasonableness.[32] The shipper who does business with the carrier must do so in conformity with the latter's known reasonable rules, and any departure therefrom will be at his peril.

[29] Harp v. Choctaw, O. & G. R. Co., 125 Fed. 445, 61 C. C. A. 405; Robinson v. Baltimore & O. R. Co., 129 Fed. 753, 64 C. C. A. 281; BULLARD v. AMERICAN EXP. CO., 107 Mich. 695, 65 N. W. 551, 33 L. R. A. 66, 61 Am. St. Rep. 358, Dobie Cas. Bailments and Carriers, 244.

[30] Western Transp. Co. v. Newhall, 24 Ill. 466, 76 Am. Dec. 760; Boscowitz v. Adams Exp. Co., 93 Ill. 523, 34 Am. Rep. 191; McMillan v. Michigan S. & N. I. R. Co., 16 Mich. 79, 93 Am. Dec. 208.

[31] Oppenheimer v. United States Exp. Co., 69 Ill. 62, 18 Am. Rep. 596; Western Transp Co. v. Newhall, 24 Ill. 466, 76 Am. Dec. 760.

[32] Pennsylvania Coal Co. v. Delaware & H. Canal Co., 31 N. Y. 91.

Notices of reasonable regulations, which for the reasons just stated are valid without assent, and notices limiting liability, which are not valid without assent, are severable; and, though contained in the same paper, the latter may be rejected and the former enforced.[33]

Regulations Requiring Shipper to Disclose the Value of the Goods Shipped

Among the regulations of the carrier which have been most frequently before the courts are those in various forms requiring the shipper to reveal the value of the goods shipped. If the shipper does nothing to mislead the carrier, and the latter makes no inquiries, the shipper is not bound to state the character or value of the goods.[34] But, if the carrier inquires, the shipper must answer truly.[35] The carrier may make such an inquiry in the case of each individual shipper, or the carrier may by means of public notices dispense with the necessity of such special inquiries.[36]

Thus a regulation of the carrier may provide that the goods are accepted as not exceeding in value a specific amount unless the shipper discloses a value in excess of such amount. The carrier has a right to graduate his charges according to the value of the goods, which value largely determines the measure of the carrier's risk, as well as the nature of the precautions the carrier must take to deliver the goods safely.[37] If the shipper, with full knowledge of such regulation, is silent as to the value of the goods, the shipper would be bound by the terms of such notice and could not recover an amount in excess of that fixed in the notice.[38]

[33] Oppenheimer v. United States Express Co., 69 Ill. 62, 18 Am. Rep. 596; Moses v. Boston & M. R. R., 24 N. H. 71, 55 Am. Dec. 222; The Majestic, 9 C. C. A. 161, 60 Fed. 624, 23 L. R. A. 746.

[34] Faulk v. Columbia, N. & L. Ry. Co., 82 S. C. 369, 64 S. E. 383; NEW YORK C. & H. R. R. CO. v. FRALOFF, 100 U. S. 24, 25 L. Ed. 531, Dobie Cas. Bailments and Carriers, 364; Southern Exp. Co. v. Crook, 44 Ala. 468, 4 Am. Rep. 140; Camden & A. R. Co. v. Baldauf, 16 Pa. 67, 55 Am. Dec. 481. See ante, p. 335.

[35] Phillips v. Earle, 8 Pick. 182. See ante, p. 336.

[36] Batson v. Donovan, 4 Barn. & Ald. (Eng.) 21, 28.

[37] Gibbon v. Paynton, 4 Burrows (Eng.) 2298 (per Lord Mansfield, and Aston, J.); Tyly v. Morrice, Carth. (Eng.) 485 (per Holt, C. J.); Southern Exp. Co. v. Newby, 36 Ga. 635, 91 Am. Dec. 783; Batson v. Donovan, 4 Barn. & Ald. (Eng.) 21.

[38] Orange County Bank v. Brown, 9 Wend. (N. Y.) 85, 115, 24 Am. Dec. 129.

SAME—FORM OF THE CONTRACT

125. While the limitation of the carrier's liability must be by contract, it is not essential that this contract should be in any special form.

Acceptance by the shipper of a bill of lading, or similar instrument purporting generally to contain the contract between the carrier and shipper, creates a contract binding on both parties.

While the carrier's limitation of liability must be made through a contract, and not merely by notice brought home to the shipper, this contract requires no special form.[39] It can be made in any way in which contracts are usually made. Such contracts may be oral or written, express or implied, and the general rules as to the formation of contracts are applicable.[40]

Bills of Lading

In the overwhelming majority of cases, the contract between the shipper and carrier is contained in the bill of lading. This well-known instrument, by its very character, gives notice to the shipper or other person dealing with it that, besides being a receipt for the goods delivered, it is a contract embodying the stipulations and terms under which the carrying of the goods is undertaken.[41] Per-

See, also, Fish v. Chapman, 2 Ga. 349, 46 Am. Dec. 393; Cole v. Goodwin, 19 Wend. (N. Y.) 251, 32 Am. Dec. 470; Judson v. Western R. Corp., 6 Allen (Mass.) 486, 83 Am. Dec. 646; Magnin v. Dinsmore, 62 N. Y. 35, 20 Am. Rep. 442; Hopkins v. Westcott, 6 Blatchf. 64. Fed. Cas. No. 6,692; New Jersey Steam Nav. Co. v. Merchants' Bank, 6 How. 344, 12 L. Ed. 465; Farmers' & Mechanics' Bank v. Champlain Transp. Co., 23 Vt. 186, 56 Am. Dec. 68. Where the effect of failure to inform the bailee of the contents of sealed packages is to prevent him from exercising the care he would otherwise have given, the bailee is liable only for positive misfeasance. Gibbon v. Paynton, 4 Burrows (Eng.) 2298.

39 The shipper's assent must be clear, however, and the burden of proving this rests on the carrier. Coats v. Chicago, R. I. & P. R. Co., 134 Ill. App. 217; Adams Express Co. v. Adams, 29 App. D. C. 250; MURPHY v. WELLS FARGO & CO. EXPRESS, 99 Minn. 230, 108 N. W. 1070, Dobie Cas. Bailments and Carriers, 218; Central of Georgia R. Co. v. City Mills Co., 128 Ga. 841, 58 S. E. 197.

40 American Transp. Co. v. Moore, 5 Mich. 368; Bates v. Weir, 121 App. Div. 275, 105 N. Y. Supp. 785; Missouri, K. & T. R. Co. v. Patrick, 144 Fed. 632, 75 C. C. A. 434.

41 BLOSSOM v. DODD, 43 N. Y. 264, 3 Am. Rep. 701, Dobie Cas. Bailments and Carriers, 208; Piedmont Mfg. Co. v. Columbia & G. R. Co., 19 S. C. 353; Wells, Fargo & Co.'s Express Co. v. Fuller, 4 Tex. Civ. App. 213, 23 S. W. 412; McMillan v. Michigan S. & N. I. R. Co., 16 Mich. 79, 93 Am. Dec. 208;

sons receiving these instruments, and others of like character and tenor, are therefore presumed by law to know that they do contain the terms upon which the goods are to be carried.[42]

If, therefore, at the time the goods are delivered to the carrier, the shipper accepts a bill of lading from the carrier, then the law presumes, in the absence of fraud or deception on the part of the carrier, the assent of the shipper to the terms, conditions, and restrictions contained in the bill of lading.[43] Though the bill of lading is signed only by the carrier, it becomes binding on the shipper without any signature or further assent on his part other than that implied from his receiving it and acting upon it.[44]

The bill of lading is binding in such cases, not only without the signature or other express assent to the terms therein contained, but even though the shipper has neither read nor understood the terms of the bill of lading.[45] For the reasons indicated in the pre-

Montague v. The Henry B. Hyde (D. C.) 82 Fed. 681; Cox v. Central Vermont R. Co., 170 Mass. 129, 49 N. E. 97; Schaller v. Chicago & N. W. Ry. Co., 97 Wis. 31, 71 N. W. 1042.

[42] Courteen v. Kanawha Dispatch, 110 Wis. 610, 86 N. W. 176, 55 L. R. A. 182; Davis v. Central Vermont R. Co., 66 Vt. 290, 29 Atl. 313, 44 Am. St. Rep. 852; Merrill v. American Exp. Co., 62 N. H. 514; Graves v. Adams Exp. Co., 176 Mass. 280, 57 N. E. 462; Pacific Exp. Co. v. Foley, 46 Kan. 457, 26 Pac. 665, 12 L. R. A. 799, 26 Am. St. Rep. 107; Mouton v. Louisville, etc., Ry. Co., 128 Ala. 537, 29 South. 602.

[43] Kirkland v. Dinsmore, 62 N. Y. 171, 20 Am. Rep. 475; Mulligan v. Illinois Cent. R. Co., 36 Iowa, 181, 14 Am. Rep. 514; Grace v. Adams, 100 Mass. 505, 97 Am. Dec. 117, 1 Am. Rep. 131; Inman & Co. v. Seaboard Air Line R. Co. (C. C.) 159 Fed. 960; Central of Georgia R. Co. v. City Mills Co., 128 Ga. 841, 58 S. E. 197; Lansing v. New York Cent. & H. R. R. Co., 52 Misc. Rep. 334, 102 N. Y. S. 1092; Smith v. American Exp. Co., 108 Mich. 572, 66 N. W. 479; Michalitschke Bros. & Co. v. Wells, Fargo & Co., 118 Cal. 683, 50 Pac. 847; Lawrence v. New York, P. & B. R. Co., 36 Conn. 63; Cau v. Texas & P. R. Co., 194 U. S. 427, 24 Sup. Ct. 663, 48 L. Ed. 1053; Ballou v. Earle, 17 R. I. 441, 22 Atl. 1113, 14 L. R. A. 433, 33 Am. St. Rep. 881; Merchants' D. T. Co. v. Bloch, 86 Tenn. 392, 6 S. W. 881, 6 Am. St. Rep. 847; Pacific Exp. Co. v. Foley, 46 Kan. 457, 26 Pac. 665, 12 L. R. A. 799, 26 Am. St. Rep. 107; Pacific Exp. Co. v. Ross (Tex. Civ. App.) 154 S. W. 340. In Illinois and Ohio, the contrary view has been held. Chicago & N. W. Ry. Co. v. Calumet Stock Farm, 194 Ill. 9, 61 N. E. 1095, 88 Am. St. Rep. 68; Wabash Ry. Co. v. Thomas, 222 Ill. 337, 78 N. E. 777, 7 L. R. A. (N. S.) 1041; Illinois Match Co. v. Chicago, R. I. & P. R. Co., 250 Ill. 396, 95 N. E. 492; Gaines v. Union Transp. & Ins. Co., 28 Ohio St. 418; Delta Bag Co. v. Frederick Leyland & Co., 173 Ill. App. 38.

[44] Inman & Co. v. Seaboard Air Line R. Co. (C. C.) 159 Fed. 960; Steele v. Townsend, 37 Ala. 247, 79 Am. Dec. 49; Kallman v. United States Exp. Co., 3 Kan. 205; Hengstler v. Flint & P. M. R. Co., 125 Mich. 530, 84 N. W. 1067. See, also, cases cited in preceding note.

[45] Davis v. Central Vermont R. Co., 66 Vt. 290, 29 Atl. 313, 44 Am. St. Rep 852; McMillan v. Michigan S. & N. I. R. Co., 16 Mich. 79, 93 Am. Dec. 208; Mc-

ceding paragraphs, the law, in the absence of fraud or deception, presumes that the contract is binding on the shipper either because he has read it, or otherwise learned the nature of its contents, or because, in the absence of either of these, he is willing to consent to its terms. Ignorance of the stipulations in the bill of lading or failure to read it is therefore no defense to its binding force, under such circumstances, as a contract. It has even been held that the bill of lading was binding on the shipper, though, through illiteracy or ignorance of the English language, he was unable to read the bill of lading, when this inability was not known by the carrier.[46]

In order that the bill of lading may have this effect, and be binding owing to its mere acceptance by the shipper, the bill of lading must have been delivered to the shipper at the time of, or before, the shipment of the goods.[47] When the carrier accepts the goods without limiting his liability, the shipper's consent to limitations will not be presumed merely from his acceptance of a bill of lading subsequently delivered to him by the carrier.[48] The rule as to merging all prior oral negotiations in the written contract has plainly no application in such a case. Acceptance of the subsequent bill of lading would, however, be binding on the shipper, if, at the time the goods are accepted by the carrier, there was then an understanding between the parties, express or implied, that the shipment was to be governed by the terms of the bill of lading which the carrier was to deliver later.[49]

Fadden v. Missouri Pac. Ry. Co., 92 Mo. 343, 4 S. W. 689, 1 Am. St. Rep. 721; Atchison, T. & S. F. Ry. Co. v. Dill, 48 Kan. 210, 29 Pac. 148; Hill v. Syracuse, B. & N. Y. R. Co., 73 N. Y. 351, 29 Am. Rep. 163; St. Louis, I. M. & S. Ry. Co. v. Weakly, 50 Ark. 397, 8 S. W. 134, 7 Am. St. Rep. 104.

[46] Jones v. Cincinnati, S. & M. R. Co., 89 Ala. 376, 8 South. 61; Fibel v. Livingston, 64 Barb. (N. Y.) 179.

[47] Gage v. Tirrell, 9 Allen (Mass.) 299; Southard v. Minneapolis, St. P. & S. S. M. R. Co., 60 Minn. 382, 62 N. W. 442, 619; Harris v. Great Northern R. Co., 48 Wash. 437, 93 Pac. 908, 96 Pac. 224; McGregor v. Oregon R. & Nav. Co., 50 Or. 527, 93 Pac. 465, 14 L. R. A. (N. S.) 668; Illinois Cent. R. Co. v. Craig, 102 Tenn. 298, 52 S. W. 164; The Arctic Bird (D. C.) 109 Fed. 167; Farnsworth v. National Exp. Co., 166 Mich. 676, 132 N. W. 441.

[48] Wilde v. Merchants' Despatch Transp. Co., 47 Iowa, 247, 29 Am. Rep. 479; Pruitt v. Hannibal & St. J. R. Co., 62 Mo. 527; Merchants' Dispatch & Transp. Co. v. Cornforth, 3 Colo. 280, 25 Am. Rep. 757; Union P. Ry. Co., v. Marston, 30 Neb. 241, 46 N. W. 485; Galveston, H. & S. A. Ry. Co. v. Botts, 22 Tex. Civ. App. 609, 55 S. W. 514; Central R. R. v. Dwight Mfg. Co. 75 Ga. 609.

[49] Shelton v. Merchants' Dispatch Transp. Co., 59 N. Y. 258; Leitch v. Union R. Transp. Co., Fed. Cas. No. 8,224; Union Pac. Ry. Co. v. Beardwell, 79 Kan. 40, 99 Pac. 214; Richmond, N., I. & B. R. Co. v. Richardson, 66 S. W. 1035, 23 Ky. Law Rep. 2234.

Where it was disputed whether the goods in controversy had been carried

Again, this presumption of assent by the shipper to the stipulations contained in the bill of lading does not attach, unless it is clear that the particular stipulation was so arranged as clearly to form a part of the contract which the bill of lading is presumed to embody Thus, mere acceptance alone does not import assent on the part of a shipper to stipulations printed on the back of a bill of lading,[60] or stipulations so covered by stamps as to make them illegible.[61]

Express Receipts

Express receipts stand upon the same general footing as bills of lading. When accepted without objection, they, too, constitute the contract between the parties.[62] In some of the earlier cases, it

under an original agreement between the consignee and the carrier, or whether such alleged agreement was a mere preliminary negotiation, and that the actual shipping agreement was between the defendant and the consignors, that question was for the jury. Henry J. Perkins Co. v. American Exp. Co., 199 Mass. 561, 85 N. E. 895.

60 Inman & Co. v. Seaboard Air Line R. Co. (C. C.) 159 Fed. 960; Michigan Cent. R. Co. v. Mineral Springs Mfg. Co., 16 Wall. (U. S.) 318, 21 L. Ed. 297; Newell v. Smith, 49 Vt. 255; Baltimore & O. R. Co. v. Doyle, 142 Fed. 669, 74 C. C. A. 245; St. Louis & S. F. Ry. Co. v. Tribbey, 6 Kan. App. 467, 50 Pac. 458; Merchants' Despatch Transp. Co. v. Furthmann, 149 Ill. 66, 36 N. E. 624, 41 Am. St. Rep. 265.

61 Perry v. Thompson, 98 Mass. 249.

62 Huntington v. Dinsmore, 4 Hun (N. Y.) 66; Id., 6 Thomp. & C. (N. Y.) 195; Snider v. Adams Exp. Co., 63 Mo. 376; Soumet v. National Exp. Co., 66 Barb. (N. Y.) 284; Brehme v. Dinsmore, 25 Md. 328; Christenson v. American Exp. Co., 15 Minn. 270 (Gil. 208), 2 Am. Rep. 122; Kirkland v. Dinsmore, 62 N. Y. 171, 20 Am. Rep. 475; Belger v. Dinsmore, 51 N. Y. 166, 10 Am. Rep. 575; Magnin v. Dinsmore, 56 N. Y. 168; Westcott v. Fargo, 61 N. Y. 542, 19 Am. Rep. 300; Adams Exp. Co. v. Haynes, 42 Ill. 89; Merchants' Despatch Transp. Co. v. Leysor, 89 Ill. 43; Grace v. Adams, 100 Mass. 505, 97 Am. Dec. 117, 1 Am. Rep. 131; Boorman v. American Exp. Co., 21 Wis. 152. But see Adams Exp. Co. v. Stettaners, 61 Ill. 184, 14 Am. Rep. 57; American Merchants' Union Exp. Co. v Schier, 55 Ill. 140; Bennett v. Virginia Transfer Co., 80 Misc. Rep. 222, 140 N. Y. Supp. 1055; Jonasson v. Weir, 130 App. Div. 528, 115 N. Y. Supp. 6; Wells, Fargo & Co. v. Neiman-Marcus Co., 227 U. S. 469, 33 Sup. Ct. 267, 57 L. Ed. 600. Where a person delivers a package to an express company and accepts a receipt, it is presumed to contain the terms of the contract, and if he desires to avoid such terms the burden is on the person accepting the receipt to show that he was misled by misrepresentations or fraud, and mere failure to examine the receipt is not sufficient. Porteous v. Adams Exp. Co., 115 Minn. 281, 132 N. W. 296. Delivery by an express company to a shipper, and his acceptance without dissent, of a shipping receipt containing a clause of limited liability, raises a presumption that the shipper knew of the restriction and would be bound thereby; but such presumption may be rebutted by evidence negativing knowledge and assent. Hill v. Adams Exp. Co., 80 N. J. Law, 604, 77 Atl. 1073. Plaintiff, a guest at a hotel, gave a bell boy a package addressed to plaintiff in another city, instruct-

was held that the mere delivery of such receipts did not amount to a contract, unless the terms contained in the receipts were read and assented to by the shipper.[53] But the practice of embodying the terms of shipment in such receipts has become so general that they are no longer distinguishable in this respect from bills of lading.

A distinction, however, must be observed between the great express companies of the country, operating on fast passenger trains and boats, and local express companies that make a business of receiving baggage from travelers for transportation to their immediate destination. In the latter case, there is nothing in the nature of the transaction which should naturally lead the traveler to suppose that he was receiving and accepting the written evidence of a contract, rather than a mere identifying voucher, and therefore he is not bound by the terms of the receipt received, in the absence of other evidence that he assented thereto.[54]

Tickets, Baggage Checks, Receipts, Etc.

Assent to conditions and limitations printed on railroad and steamboat tickets, baggage checks, receipts, and the like, is not presumed from a mere acceptance of these without objection.[55]

ing the boy to "take this to Adams Express." The boy did as directed, neglected to value the package, and received an express receipt containing a stipulation limiting the carrier's liability on unvalued packages to $50. Held, that the boy was plaintiff's agent, and, being authorized to deliver the package for shipment, was authorized to bind plaintiff by his acceptance of such limited liability contract, under the rule that an agent to whom the owner intrusts goods for delivery to a carrier must be regarded as having authority to stipulate for the ordinary terms of transportation. Addoms v. Weir, 56 Misc. Rep. 487, 108 N. Y. Supp. 146. In an action against an express company, it appeared that at the time of the shipment a receipt limiting the carrier's liability to fraud and gross negligence was delivered to the shipper. Plaintiff testified that he did not read the receipt at the time of shipment, but upon cross-examination stated that the receipt came out of his own book of receipts, in his possession at the time of the shipment. Held, insufficient to support a finding that the shipper did not have notice of the limitation of liability contained in the receipt. Fried v. Wells, Fargo & Co., 51 Misc. Rep. 669, 100 N. Y. Supp. 1007. In Dakota and Michigan the shipper's assent is by statute required to be shown by his signature. Hartwell v. Northern Pacific Exp. Co., 5 Dak. 463, 41 N. W. 732, 3 L. R. A. 342; Feige v. Michigan Cent. R. Co., 62 Mich. 1, 28 N. W. 685. And see Southern Exp. Co. v. Newby, 36 Ga. 635, 91 Am. Dec. 783.

53 Kirkland v. Dinsmore, 2 Hun (N. Y.) 46; Id., 4 Thomp. & C. (N. Y.) 304, reversed 62 N. Y. 171, 20 Am. Rep. 475; Belger v. Dinsmore, 51 Barb. (N. Y.) 69, reversed 51 N. Y. 166, 10 Am. Rep. 575; Adams Exp. Co. v. Nock, 2 Duv. (Ky.) 562, 87 Am. Dec. 510; Kember v. Southern Exp. Co., 22 La. Ann. 158, 2 Am. Rep. 719.

54 BLOSSOM v. DODD, 43 N. Y. 264, 3 Am. Rep. 701, Dobie Cas. Bailments and Carriers, 208. See, also, cases cited in the note following.

55 Prentice v. Decker, 49 Barb. (N. Y.) 21; Limburger v. Westcott, 49 Barb. (N. Y.) 283; Sunderland v. Westcott, 2 Sweeney (N. Y.) 260; Isaacson v.

The reason for this is that the nature of such instruments is not such as to convey to the mind of the shipper the idea of a contract, in such a manner as to raise the presumption that he knew it was a contract expressive of the terms upon which the goods are carried, or an agreement limiting the liability of the carrier.

A railroad ticket, for example, is not the contract between the carrier and passenger, but is merely evidence of such contract.[56] Such ticket is primarily a convenient voucher or token showing that the passenger has paid for the privilege of being carried between two places. Therefore a passenger is not bound by a notice printed on his ticket, unless he in some way assents to it.[57] When the passenger's attention is called to the notice, however, such assent could be implied from acceptance without objection.[58] So tokens given in exchange for baggage checks are not of such a nature as to put persons on notice as to memoranda printed upon

New York Cent. & H. R. R. Co., 94 N. Y. 278, 46 Am. Rep. 142, and cases cited infra. In the absence of fraud, the rights of a carrier and shipper are controlled by the contract made on receipt of the property for transportation, and a contract limiting the liability to a specified sum in case of loss is valid; but this rule does not apply to carriers of baggage, the receipt for baggage being only a voucher enabling the owner to follow and identify his property. Baum v. Long Island R. Co., 58 Misc. Rep. 34, 108 N. Y. Supp. 1113. See post, § 194.

[56] See post, p. 624; Rawson v. Pennsylvania R. Co., 48 N. Y. 212, 217, 8 Am. Rep. 543; Sleeper v. Pennsylvania R. Co., 100 Pa. 259, 45 Am. Rep. 380; Chollette v. Omaha & R. V. R. Co., 26 Neb. 159, 41 N. W. 1106, 4 L. R. A. 135; New York, L. E. & W. R. Co. v. Winter, 143 U. S. 60, 12 Sup. Ct. 356, 36 L. Ed. 71; Burke v. S. E. Ry. Co., 5 C. P. D. (Eng.) 1, 49 L. J. C. P. 107.

[57] Louisville & N. R. Co. v. Turner, 100 Tenn. 213, 47 S. W. 223, 43 L. R. A. 140; The Majestic (D. C.) 56 Fed. 244; Boyd v. Spencer, 103 Ga. 828, 30 S. E. 841, 68 Am. St. Rep. 146; San Antonio & A. P. Ry. Co. v. Newman, 17 Tex. Civ. App. 606, 43 S. W. 915; Rawson v. Pennsylvania R. Co., 48 N. Y. 212, 8 Am. Rep. 543; Mauritz v. New York, L. E. & W. R. Co. (C. C.) 23 Fed. 765. But one who accepts and travels on a "contract ticket" issued by a steamship company for the voyage from England to America, which ticket contained two quarto papers of printed matter, describing the rights and liabilities of the parties, is bound by the stipulations therein, though he has not read or signed. FONSECA v. CUNARD S. S. CO., 153 Mass. 553, 27 N. E. 665, 12 L. R. A. 340, 25 Am. St. Rep. 660, Dobie Cas. Bailments and Carriers, 353. The principle of this last case applies whenever the ticket purports to express the complete contract and express or implied notice of this is brought to the passenger. BOYLAN v. HOT SPRINGS R. CO., 132 U. S. 146, 10 Sup. Ct. 50, 33 L. Ed. 290, Dobie Cas. Bailments and Carriers, 355; Eastman v. Maine Cent. R. R., 70 N. H. 240, 46 Atl. 54; Wenz v. Savannah, F. & W. Ry. Co., 108 Ga. 290, 33 S. E. 970. See post, p. 625.

[58] Baltimore & O. R. Co. v. Campbell, 36 Ohio St. 647, 38 Am. Rep. 617; Rawson v. Pennsylvania R. Co., 48 N. Y. 212, 8 Am. Rep. 543.

them, and persons receiving them are not presumed to know their contents, or to assent to them.[59]

The bill of lading, too, unlike the ticket or check, plays an important part in commercial transactions as a method of transferring title or otherwise dealing with the goods for which it stands.

SAME—CONSIDERATION OF THE CONTRACT

126. Like other contracts, the contract limiting the carrier's liability must be founded upon a consideration. This consideration is usually found in the reduction of the rate charged for carrying the goods.

The contract limiting the carrier's liability must possess the ordinary elements of contractual validity, and, to be effectual, must hence be supported by a consideration.[60] But as common carriers are bound, owing to their public profession, to carry without any contract limiting their liability, their mere agreement to carry does not furnish any consideration for a contract to limit their liability.[61] In order, therefore, that such contracts must be valid, some other consideration must be found, moving from the carrier to the shipper.

It is a sufficient consideration, however, if the carrier agrees to carry for a reduced compensation because of the limitation of his liability.[62] The same is true when the carrier agrees to do

[59] BLOSSOM v. DODD, 43 N. Y. 264, 3 Am. Rep. 701, Dobie Cas. Bailments and Carriers, 208; Madan v. Sherard, 73 N. Y. 329, 29 Am. Rep. 153; Indianapolis, & C. R. Co. v. Cox, 29 Ind. 360, 95 Am. Dec. 640.

[60] Southard v. Minneapolis, St. P. & S. S. M. Ry. Co., 60 Minn. 382, 62 N. W. 442, 619; Gardner v. Southern R. Co., 127 N. C. 293, 37 S. E. 328; York Mfg. Co. v. Illinois C. R. Co., 3 Wall. 107, 18 L. Ed. 170; Louisville & N. R. Co. v. Gilbert, 88 Tenn. 430, 12 S. W. 1018, 7 L. R. A. 162; Mouton v. Louisville & N. R. Co., 128 Ala. 537, 29 South. 602; Wilcox v. Chicago G. W. R. Co., 135 Mo. App. 193, 115 S. W. 1061; Inman & Co. v. Seaboard Air Line R. Co. (C. C.) 159 Fed. 960; St. Louis, I. M. & S. R. Co. v. Furlow, 89 Ark. 404, 117 S. W. 517; Jones v. Southern Exp. Co. (Miss.) 61 South. 165.

[61] St. Louis, I. M. & S. R. Co. v. Caldwell, 89 Ark. 218, 116 S. W. 210; McFadden v. Missouri Pac. Ry. Co., 92 Mo. 343, 4 S. W. 689, 1 Am. St. Rep. 721; Illinois Cent. R. Co. v. Lancashire Ins. Co., 79 Miss. 114, 30 South. 43; Bissell v. New York Cent. R. Co., 25 N. Y. 442, 82 Am. Dec. 369; McMillan v. Michigan S. & N. I. R. Co., 16 Mich. 79, 93 Am. Dec. 208; German v. Chicago & N. W. R. Co., 38 Iowa, 127. See, also, cases cited in preceding note.

[62] Louisville & N. R. Co. v. Gilbert, 88 Tenn. 430, 12 S. W. 1018, 7 L. R. A. 162; Carter & Co. v. Southern R. Co., 3 Ga. App. 34, 59 S. E. 209; Scott County Milling Co. v. St. Louis, I. M. & S. Ry. Co., 127 Mo. App. 80, 104 S. W. 924; Johnstone v. Richmond & D. R. Co., 39 S. C. 55, 17 S. E. 512;

something he is not already bound to do,[63] such as receiving a passenger on freight trains,[64] or carrying a customer free of charge.[65] If the rate of compensation is fixed by law, so that the carrier can charge neither more nor less than a given amount for the transportation of goods, an agreement to carry for such rate would not be any consideration for an agreement on the part of the shipper limiting the carrier's liability.[66] So, also, an agreement to carry at the highest rate allowed by law furnishes no consideration for a contract limiting the carrier's liability.[67]

St. Louis, I. M. & S. R. Co. v. Furlow, 89 Ark. 404, 117 S. W. 517; Jones v. Southern Exp. Co. (Miss.) 61 South. 165; Bissell v. New York Cent. R. Co., 25 N. Y. 442, 82 Am. Dec. 369; Nelson v. Hudson River R. Co., 48 N. Y. 498; Jennings v. Grand Trunk Ry. Co., 52 Hun, 227, 5 N. Y. Supp. 140; Dillard v. Louisville & N. R. Co., 2 Lea (Tenn.) 288. A stipulation in a bill of lading exempting the receiving carrier from his common-law liability for the loss of goods while in its warehouse, at the end of its line, and before delivering to the connecting carrier, is void, unless there is a special consideration for such exemption, other than the mere receipt of the goods and the undertaking to carry them. Wehmann v. Minneapolis, St. P. & S. S. M. Ry. Co., 58 Minn. 22, 59 N. W. 546.

[63] California Powder Works v. Atlantic & P. R. Co., 113 Cal. 329, 45 Pac. 691, 36 L. R. A. 648 (accepting dangerous articles which carrier was not bound to carry); Robertson v. Old Colony R. Co., 156 Mass. 525, 31 N. E. 650, 32 Am. St. Rep. 482 (unique contract for transportation of a circus train).

[64] Arnold v. Illinois Cent. R. Co., 83 Ill. 273, 25 Am. Rep. 386.

[65] Carter & Co. v. Southern R. Co., 3 Ga. App. 34, 59 S. E. 209; Bissell v. New York Cent. R. Co., 25 N. Y. 442, 82 Am. Dec. 369.

[66] Wehmann v. Minneapolis, St. P. & S. S. M. R. Co., 58 Minn. 22, 59 N. W. 546. Where a statute requires a railroad carrying United States mail to carry a postal clerk with the mail without charge, a limitation of the carrier's liability, contained in a pass issued to such postal clerk, is without consideration and void. Seybolt v. New York, L. E. & W. R. Co., 95 N. Y. 562, 47 Am. Rep. 75. Where a carrier had but one regular rate applicable to a given class of property, it is not a reduced or a special rate that will serve as a consideration for an owner's risk contract, as the word "reduced" implies a comparison, and it is not permissible to go outside the subject-matter to seek the comparison; but it must be made with another higher rate on the same class of property, and where there is no such rate there can be no reductions. Leas v. Quincy, O. & K. C. R. Co., 157 Mo. App. 455, 136 S. W. 963. A railroad, in compliance with the Interstate Commerce Act (Act Feb. 4, 1887, c. 104, 24 Stat. 379 [U. S. Comp. St. 1901, p. 3154]) placed on file with the Interstate Commerce Commission a schedule of tariffs, showing two rates. The railroad subsequently contracted to carry goods. No freight rate was agreed to, either verbally or in the bill of lading, the latter not reciting that a reduced rate was charged. Held, that no consideration was shown for a contract limiting the liability of the railroad on account of carrying the property for the lower rate. Phœnix Powder Mfg. Co. v. Wabash R. Co., 120 Mo. App. 566, 97 S. W. 256.

[67] McMillan v. Michigan S. & N. I. R. Co., 16 Mich. 79, 93 Am. Dec. 208;

When, however, the carrier actually carries for a lower rate than he would charge, were his responsibility as at common law, then the contract is based on a real consideration.[68] The shipper grants, and the carrier benefits by, a diminished liability; the carrier grants, and the shipper benefits by, a reduced rate. Here is the quid pro quo, a mutual and sufficient consideration.

In the absence of proof to the contrary, there is a prima facie presumption of a sufficient consideration.[69] The basis of this presumption is the practice of carriers to graduate their rates according to the risk that they run and the responsibilities they incur.[70]

Shipper's Option of Carrier's Full Responsibility

A corollary to the principle that the contract limiting liability must be based on a consideration is the rule that the shipper has a right to insist that the goods be carried under the full common-law liability if a commensurate and reasonable rate be paid.[71] Were it not for this option on the part of the shipper, not only would there be no real consideration for the contract limiting liability, but

Bissell v. New York Cent. R. Co., 25 N. Y. 442, 82 Am. Dec. 369; German v. Chicago & N. W. R. Co., 38 Iowa, 127.

[68] See cases cited in note 62.

[69] Schaller v. Chicago & N. W. Ry. Co., 97 Wis. 31, 71 N. W. 1042; Cau v. Texas & P. R. Co., 194 U. S. 427, 24 Sup. Ct. 663, 48 L. Ed. 1053; Wehman v. Minneapolis, St. P. & S. S. M. Ry. Co., 58 Minn. 22, 59 N. W. 546; Arthur v. Texas & P. R. Co., 139 Fed. 127, 71 C. C. A. 391; Stewart v. Cleveland, C., C. & St. L. Ry. Co., 21 Ind. App. 218, 52 N. E. 89. Particularly is this true when the contract recites that it is based on a consideration. Georgia Southern & F. R. Co. v. Greer, 2 Ga. App. 516, 58 S. E. 782; Mires v. St. Louis & S. F. R. Co., 134 Mo. App. 379, 114 S. W. 1052. A declaration contained in a bill of lading to the effect that a limitation of liability expressed in the bill was in consideration of a reduced rate is prima facie evidence of such reduction; and it was error to tell the jury in an action for damages for failure to transport safely, that they could not consider the contract as to the limitation without other evidence of consideration. Wabash R. Co. v. Curtis, 134 Ill. App. 409. This presumption is, of course, a prima facie one, and it may be rebutted (even when there is a recital of a consideration) by evidence showing that the contract limiting the carrier's liability is in reality supported by no consideration. McFadden v. Missouri Pac. Ry. Co., 92 Mo. 343, 4 S. W. 689, 1 Am. St. Rep. 721; Lake Erie & W. R. Co. v. Holland, 162 Ind. 406, 69 N. E. 138, 63 L. R. A. 948; Georgia Railroad & Banking Co. v. Reid, 91 Ga. 377, 17 S. E. 934.

[70] St. Louis, I. M. & S. Ry. Co. v. Lesser, 46 Ark. 236; Schaller v. Chicago & N. W. Ry. Co., 97 Wis. 31, 71 N. W. 1042; Courteen v. Kanawha Dispatch, 110 Wis. 610, 86 N. W. 176, 55 L. R. A. 182. See, also, cases cited in the preceding note.

[71] St. Louis Southwestern R. Co. v. Phœnix Cotton Oil Co., 88 Ark. 594, 115 S. W. 393; Illinois Cent. R. Co. v. Lancashire Ins. Co., 79 Miss. 114, 30 South. 43; Paddock v. Missouri Pac. Ry. Co., 155 Mo. 524, 56 S. W. 453; Atchison, T. & S. F. R. Co. v. Dill, 48 Kan. 210, 29 Pac. 148.

it could not be said that the shipper had freely and voluntarily entered into the contract. If the carrier had a right to force the shipper into a contract limiting liability or else refuse to carry the goods, then the element of choice on the part of the shipper, from which such contracts derive their binding force, would be utterly lacking. But when the carrier offers the shipper the alternative of full responsibility at the full price, or reduced responsibility at a reduced price, and the shipper, after weighing the comparative advantages of the two schemes, voluntarily accepts the latter, then clearly there is the freest choice.

Accordingly, when the carrier refuses to carry the goods unless the shipper accepts a contract of limited liability, this contract would not then be binding on the shipper, though he sent his goods under it.[72] Nor, in such a case, would it be a defense for the carrier to say that the shipper could have declined to ship the goods and sued the carrier for his refusal to carry.[73] When, however, the option really existed, it is not essential that, in each case, the carrier must expressly offer to the shipper his choice of the two liabilities with the attendant difference in rates.[74] As has already been seen, for the full insuring responsibility, the carrier cannot charge more than is reasonable under the circumstances.[75]

SAME—CONSTRUCTION OF THE CONTRACT

127. Contracts limiting the common-law liability of the carrier of goods are to be construed strictly against the carrier.

Perhaps it should first be indicated that the common carrier of goods does not lose his character as such merely by means of con-

72 Stewart v. Cleveland, C., C. & St. L. Ry. Co., 21 Ind. App. 218, 52 N. E. 89; Kimball v. Rutland & B. R. Co., 26 Vt. 247, 62 Am. Dec. 567; McFadden v. Missouri Pac. Ry. Co., 92 Mo. 343, 4 S. W. 689, 1 Am. St. Rep. 721; Pacific Exp. Co. v. Wallace, 60 Ark. 100, 29 S. W. 32; Atchison, T. & S. F. R. Co. v. Mason, 4 Kan. App. 391, 46 Pac. 31.

73 Little Rock & Ft. S. Ry. Co. v. Cravens, 57 Ark. 112, 20 S. W. 803, 18 L. R. A. 527, 38 Am. St. Rep. 230.

74 Louisville & N. Ry. Co. v. Sowell, 90 Tenn. 17, 15 S. W. 837. Such option must be real, however, and not merely colorable. Illinois Cent. R. Co. v. Craig, 102 Tenn. 298, 52 S. W. 164; Little Rock & Ft. S. Ry. Co. v. Cravens, 57 Ark. 112, 20 S. W. 803, 18 L. R. A. 527, 38 Am. St. Rep. 230. Where a carrier did not refuse to transport freight, except under a special contract limiting liability for gross negligence, and then only to the extent of a valuation fixed in the contract, but such contract was thoroughly discussed before executed, and no objection was made to it by the shipper, who inserted in the contract in his own handwriting the valuation on the property, the contract was not imposed on the shipper and the carrier's liability was as fixed by it. Mering v. Southern Pac. Co., 161 Cal. 297, 119 Pac. 80.

75 See ante, pp. 284, 319; post, § 147.

tracts limiting his liability.[76] These contracts do not serve to rid the carrier of his public employment, and he remains as before a common and not a private carrier. This is none the less true, though the liability of the common carrier has been, as to the particular shipment, so reduced by contract as to correspond exactly to the liability of a private carrier.[77]

Contracts limiting liability are by the courts uniformly construed against the carrier.[78] All doubts and ambiguities will be resolved in favor of the shipper; and when the contract is capable of two meanings, the courts incline to the one least beneficial to the carrier.[79] Specific exemptions will not be enlarged by the use of general language in the same connection. For example, a release from liability for loss arising from "leakage or decay, chafing or breakage, or from any other cause," does not exempt the carrier from lia-

[76] Terre Haute & L. R. Co. v. Sherwood, 132 Ind. 129, 31 N. E. 781, 17 L. R. A. 339, 32 Am. St. Rep. 239; Crawford v. Southern Ry. Co., 56 S. C. 136, 34 S. E. 80; Liverpool & G. W. S. Co. v. Phœnix Ins. Co., 129 U. S. 397, 9 Sup. Ct. 469, 32 L. Ed. 788; Gaines v. Union Transp. & Ins. Co., 28 Ohio St. 418; Hull v. Chicago, St. P., M. & O. Ry. Co., 41 Minn. 510, 43 N. W. 391, 5 L. R. A. 587, 16 Am. St. Rep. 722.

[77] See cases cited in preceding note.

[78] Magnin v. Dinsmore, 56 N. Y. 168; Edsall v. Camden & A. R. & Transp. Co., 50 N. Y. 661; Hooper v. Wells, Fargo & Co., 27 Cal. 11, 85 Am. Dec. 211; Levering v. Union Transp. & Ins. Co., 42 Mo. 88, 97 Am. Dec. 320; Rosenfeld v. Peoria, D. & E. Ry. Co., 103 Ind. 121, 2 N. E. 344, 53 Am. Rep. 500; St. Louis & S. E. Ry. Co. v. Smuck, 49 Ind. 302; Gronstadt v. Witthoff (D. C.) 15 Fed. 265; Marx v. National Steamship Co. (D. C.) 22 Fed. 680; Ayres v. Western R. Corp., 14 Blatchf. 9, Fed. Cas. No. 689; Hoye v. Pennsylvania R. Co., 191 N. Y. 101, 83 N. E. 586, 17 L. R. A. (N. S.) 641, 14 Ann. Cas. 414; Estes v. Denver & R. G. R. Co., 49 Colo. 378, 113 Pac. 1005; E. O. Stanard Milling Co. v. White Line Cent. Transit Co., 122 Mo. 258, 26 S. W. 704; Cream City R. Co. v. Chicago, M. & St. P. Ry. Co., 63 Wis. 93, 23 N. W. 425, 53 Am. Rep. 267; Galloway v. Erie R. Co., 116 App. Div. 777, 102 N. Y. Supp. 25; MYNARD v. SYRACUSE, B. & N. Y. R. CO., 71 N. Y. 180, 27 Am. Rep. 28, Dobie Cas. Bailments and Carriers, 213.

[79] Munn v. Baker, 2 Starkie (Eng.) 255. And see Edsall v. Camden & A. R. & Transp. Co., 50 N. Y. 661; Airey v. Merrill, 2 Curt. 8, Fed. Cas. No. 115; Kansas City, M. & B. R. Co. v. Holland, 68 Miss. 351, 8 South. 516; Black v. Goodrich Transp. Co., 55 Wis. 319, 13 N. W. 244, 42 Am. Rep. 713; Little Rock, M. R. & T. R. Co. v. Talbot, 39 Ark. 523. A bill of lading provided that "no carrier shall be liable for loss or damage not accruing on its portion of the route, nor after said property is ready for delivery to the consignee." Held that, the stipulation being intended to qualify or limit the common-law liability and therefore to be strictly construed against the carrier and in favor of the shipper, the term "carrier" should be taken as referring, not merely to the transportative capacity of the company, but to the contracting entity in its dual capacity of common carrier and warehouseman. Central of Georgia Ry. Co. v. Merrill & Co., 153 Ala. 277, 45 South. 628. Clauses in a bill of lading, exempting the carrier from liability for

bility for loss by fire.[30] An exemption from liability for loss through any particular cause does not include losses of that character due to the carrier's negligence.[31]

For this rule of construction as to such contracts, two reasons are usually given: An ambiguity in a written contract is ordinarily resolved against the person who made it possible; that is, the one who drew the contract and determined in what language it should be couched. The contract limiting liability is usually, as has been seen, embodied in the bill of lading drawn by, and pri-

delay in transportation arising from specified causes, did not relieve it, when delay occurred, from the obligation which it assumed to re-ice a refrigerator car from point of shipment to destination. Geraty v. Atlantic Coast Line R. Co., 81 S. C. 367, 62 S. E. 444. A clause in a bill of lading, providing that no carrier or party in possession of all or any of the property shall be liable for any loss thereof or damage thereto by fire, was applicable only in case the carrier at the time of the fire which destroyed the goods was "in possession" thereof. Bolles v. Lehigh Valley R. Co., 159 Fed. 694, 86 C. C. A. 562. Deviation by a carrier from the route described in the contract of shipment makes him liable as an insurer of the goods shipped, though the contract of shipment exempts him from liability under the circumstances under which the goods were lost or damaged. McKahan v. American Express Co., 209 Mass. 270, 95 N. E. 785, 35 L. R. A. (N. S.) 1046, Ann. Cas. 1912B, 612.

30 Menzell v. Chicago & N. W. Ry. Co., 1 Dillon, 531, Fed. Cas. No. 9,429. See, also, Hawkins v. Great Western R. Co., 17 Mich. 57, 97 Am. Dec. 179.

31 Insurance Co. of North America v. Lake Erie & W. R. Co., 152 Ind. 333, 53 N. E. 382; McFadden v. Missouri Pac. Ry. Co., 92 Mo. 343, 4 S. W. 689, 1 Am. St. Rep. 721; Ashmore v. Pennsylvania Steam Towing & Transp. Co., 28 N. J. Law, 180; MYNARD v. SYRACUSE, B. & N. Y. R. CO., 71 N. Y. 180, 27 Am. Rep. 28, Dobie Cas. Bailments and Carriers, 213. An exemption from liability for delay does not cover a negligent delay. McKay v. New York Cent. & H. R. R. Co., 50 Hun, 563, 3 N. Y. Supp. 708. General words in a contract of carriage are not sufficient to release a carrier from negligence, but, if such a result is intended, it must be expressly provided for; and hence, where a bill of lading in a shipment of glass contained a condition that defendant would not be liable for damages to glass by breakage or for any cause, if it should be necessary or was usual to carry such property upon open cars, and the words "Loaded and secured by shipper, released," were written upon the face of it, the defendant's liability for negligence remained unaffected. Brewster v. New York Cent. & H. R. R. Co., 145 App. Div. 51, 129 N. Y. Supp. 368. Where a connecting carrier permitted flour to remain in its warehouse for 49 days before forwarding the same because of a shortage of cars, without notifying the shipper, knowing that the detention would be unusual, thereby preventing the shipper from protecting itself by insurance, and the flour was totally or partially destroyed by the burning of the warehouse, the carrier was chargeable with such negligence as made it responsible for the loss of the flour, notwithstanding a provision in the bill of lading that no carrier should be liable for the loss of the goods or damage thereto by fire. Erie R. Co. v. Star & Crescent Mill. Co., 162 Fed. 879, 89 C. C. A. 569.

marily in the interest of, the carrier.[82] A second reason is found in the fact that, when the law fixes the measure of the responsibility of one engaged in a public employment, the courts are inclined, if not to regard with disfavor, at least to scrutinize with great nicety and no friendly eye, attempts by the one engaged in such public employment to lessen this responsibility by contract.[83]

When Contract Inures to Benefit of Connecting Lines

As will be seen hereafter, a common carrier may, by special contract in particular instances, bind himself for transportation over connecting lines to points beyond his own line; and in such a case, he is liable as a carrier for the whole route, even though the loss of, or injury to, the goods occurs on the line of one of the connecting carriers.[84] In the absence of a contract thus extending his liability, the responsibility of the initial carrier is limited to his own line, and ceases entirely when the goods are delivered to the connecting carrier.[85]

When the initial carrier has by his contract undertaken to transport the goods through to their destination, beyond the end of his line, then the stipulations in the special contract between the shipper and the first carrier inure to the benefit of the connecting carrier.[86] This is upon the theory that since the compensation is fixed

[82] See Amory Mfg. Co. v. Gulf, C. & S. F. Ry. Co., 89 Tex. 419, 37 S. W. 856, 59 Am. St. Rep. 65: "To no class of contracts has this rule been applied with more stringency than to those in which common carriers seek to limit their liability as it exists at common law."

[83] Pierce v. Southern Pac. Co., 120 Cal. 156, 47 Pac. 874, 52 Pac. 302, 40 L. R. A. 350; The Queen of the Pacific, 180 U. S. 49, 21 Sup. Ct. 278, 45 L. Ed. 419; Gwyn Harper Mfg. Co. v. Carolina Cent. R. Co., 128 N. C. 280, 38 S. E. 894, 83 Am. St. Rep. 675; Alabama G. S. R. Co. v. Thomas, 89 Ala. 294, 7 South. 762, 18 Am. St. Rep. 119; MYNARD v. SYRACUSE, B. & N. Y. R. CO., 71 N. Y. 180, 27 Am. Rep. 28, Dobie Cas. Bailments and Carriers, 213.

[84] Quimby v. Vanderbilt, 17 N. Y. 306, 72 Am. Dec. 469; Hill Mfg. Co. v. Boston & L. R. Corp., 104 Mass. 122, 6 Am. Rep. 202; Bennett v Steamboat Co., 6 C. B. (Eng.) 775; Ogdensburg & L. C. R. Co. v. Pratt, 22 Wall. (U. S.) 123, 22 L. Ed. 827. This subject is discussed later at some length. See post, § 145.

[85] Miller Grain & Elevator Co. v. Union Pac. Ry. Co., 138 Mo. 658, 40 S. W. 894; Fremont E. & M. V. R. Co. v. Waters, 50 Neb. 592, 70 N. W. 225; Post v. Southern Ry. Co., 103 Tenn. 184, 52 S. W. 301, 55 L. R. A. 481; Harris v. Grand Trunk Ry. Co., 15 R. I. 371, 5 Atl. 305; Seasongood v. Tennessee & O. R. Transp. Co., 54 S. W. 193, 21 Ky. Law Rep. 1142, 49 L. R. A. 270. See post, § 145.

[86] Maghee v. Camden & A. R. Transp. Co., 45 N. Y. 514, 6 Am. Rep. 124; Bird v. Southern R. Co., 99 Tenn. 719, 42 S. E. 451, 63 Am. St. Rep. 856; Mears v. New York, N. H. & H. R. Co., 75 Conn. 171, 52 Atl. 610, 56 L. R. A. 884, 96 Am. St. Rep. 192; Kiff v. Atchison, T. & S. F. R. Co., 32 Kan.

with reference to the liability assumed, and since the first carrier is liable for the entire transportation, such carrier has an interest in making the exception commensurate with the scope and duration of the contract, and the connecting lines acting under its employment are entitled as agents of the initial carrier to the benefits of the contract.[87] The contract, since it is one providing for through shipment, covers the entire transportation. Hence the diminution of liability is equally effective all through the transit and protects all the carriers, both initial and connecting, engaged in such transit.

When, however, there is no contract for through transportation, since the liability of the initial carrier is limited to its own line, any contract it makes with the shipper prima facie is made for its own protection only, and the security afforded to the carrier under the contract would cease when the carrier's responsibility ceases, namely, when the goods are delivered to the connecting carrier.[88] The initial carrier, having no interest in the subsequent transportation, is not supposed to have made a contract operative in a transit as to which it receives no benefit and incurs no liability.[89] The

263, 4 Pac. 401; Central Railroad & Banking Co. v. Bridger, 94 Ga. 471, 20 S. E. 349; Pittsburg, C., C. & St. L. R. Co. v. Viers, 113 Ky. 526, 68 S. W. 469, 24 Ky. Law Rep. 356; White v. Weir, 33 App. Div. 145, 53 N. Y. Supp. 465. See, also, Kansas City Southern R. Co. v. Carl, 227 U. S. 639, 33 Sup. Ct. 391, 57 L. Ed. 683; Bird v. Southern R. Co., 99 Tenn. 719, 42 S. W. 451, 63 Am. St. Rep. 856; Kansas City, Ft. S. & M. Ry. Co. v. Sharp, 64 Ark. 115, 40 S. W. 781. The cases are far from clear on this subject, and many conflicting opinions are found.

87 Evansville & C. R. Co. v. Androscoggin Mills, 22 Wall. 594, 22 L. Ed. 724; Manhattan Oil Co. v. Camden & A. R. & Transp. Co., 54 N. Y. 197; Whitworth v. Erie Ry. Co., 87 N. Y. 413; Halliday v. St. Louis, K. C. & N. Ry. Co., 74 Mo. 159, 41 Am. Rep. 309; Levy v. Southern Exp. Co., 4 S. C. 234. Whenever the carrier is bound, by contract or by law, to carry to destination, all carriers who engage in the transportation for any portion of the route are entitled to all the protection which the first carrier has secured by his contract with the shipper. Whitworth v. Erie Ry. Co., supra; Kiff v. Atchison, T. & S. F. R. Co., 32 Kan. 263, 4 Pac. 401. See cases cited in preceding note.

88 Babcock v. Lake Shore & M. S. Ry. Co., 49 N. Y. 491; Merchants' Despatch Transp. Co. v. Bolles, 80 Ill. 473; Bancroft v. Merchants' Despatch Transp. Co., 47 Iowa, 262, 29 Am. Rep. 482; Adams Exp. Co. v. Harris, 120 Ind. 73, 21 N. E. 340, 7 L. R. A. 214, 16 Am. St. Rep. 315; Martin v. American Exp. Co., 19 Wis. 336; Camden & A. R. Co. v. Forsyth, 61 Pa. 81; Ætna Ins. Co. v. Wheeler, 49 N. Y. 616; Western & A. R. Co. v. Exposition Cotton Mills, 81 Ga. 523, 7 S. E. 916, 2 L. R. A. 102. See, also, Taylor v. Little Rock, M. R. & T. R. Co., 39 Ark. 148.

89 See 1 Hutch. Carr. § 471: "The connecting carrier, in such case, is not only a stranger to the contract, but to its consideration. There can be no presumption that there has been, on his part, any abatement of his charges

immunities provided in the contract made by the initial carrier are not extended beyond the transportation imposed by this contract on such initial carrier who made it. The connecting carriers, in such a case, carry not on behalf of the first carrier, but on behalf of the owner, and these must in turn protect themselves by contracts which they themselves make with such owner or his authorized agent.

These contracts, for transporting the goods over the lines beyond that of the initial carrier, however, are frequently made by the initial carrier, acting on behalf of the shipper, with the connecting carrier. In such cases it is generally held that the initial carrier has the authority to make with such connecting carriers a contract similar in terms to that made by the shipper with the first carrier, and providing for the same limitations as to the liability of such connecting carrier.[90] Or such contract might be binding on the shipper, even though differing from the contract with the original carrier, when the contract in question with the connecting carrier is the one usually made by the connecting carrier in like cases and the shipper has knowledge of this fact.[91]

SAME—BURDEN OF PROOF

128. When the carrier seeks to escape liability on the ground that the loss of or injury to the goods was due to causes as to which he is exempt under his contract, the burden of proof rests upon the carrier to bring such loss or injury within his contractual exemption.

We have already seen that at common law the shipper makes out a prima facie case against the carrier by showing a delivery of the goods to, and their acceptance by, the carrier, and the carrier's failure to deliver the goods or his delivery of them in a damaged condition.[92] When the carrier's defense is that the loss or injury falls within the exemption or limitation contained in the contract with the shipper, the law properly imposes upon the car-

as a consideration for exemption from liability on the part of the owner of the goods; and, there being no express contract with him, the law will not imply one for his benefit."

90 Lamb v. Camden & A. R. & Transp. Co., 46 N. Y. 271, 7 Am. Rep. 327.

91 As to the authority of a carrier to bind the shipper by a contract with a connecting carrier limiting the liability of the latter, see, in favor of such authority, The St. Hubert, 107 Fed. 727, 46 C. C. A. 603; Rawson v. Holland, 59 N. Y. 611, 17 Am. Rep. 394; Levy v. Southern Exp. Co., 4 S. C 234.

92 Ante, § 118.

rier the duty of affirmatively proving this.[93] There is certainly no ground, in the absence of such proof on the part of the carrier, for any presumption that the loss or injury was due to a cause which the contract excepts. If, for example, the contract released the carrier from responsibility for losses "due to fire not caused by carrier's negligence," the shipper need not show that the loss was due to some cause other than fire, but the carrier must prove that the loss was the result of the specific exception—fire.[94] Since the means of knowledge as to the causes of loss or injury are peculiarly the carrier's, this rule imposes no undue burden on the carrier and is consistent with both justice and convenience.

Negligence of Carrier

As we shall soon see,[95] the carrier is not permitted to absolve himself from liability for his negligence. When, therefore, not only a peril excepted by contract, but also the negligence of the carrier, is involved in the loss or injury, the question as to the burden of proof is more complicated. In such cases, the holdings of the courts are utterly at variance with one another.

According to what is perhaps the majority view, the carrier is prima facie relieved of liability when he proves that the loss or injury was due to a cause exempted by his contract, and the burden of showing the negligence of the carrier (thus fixing liability on him in spite of the contractual exemption) rests on the shipper.[96]

[93] Southern Exp. Co. v. Newby, 36 Ga. 635, 91 Am. Dec. 783; Georgia Southern & F. R. Co. v. Greer, 2 Ga. App. 516, 58 S. E. 782; Carter & Co. v. Southern R. Co., 3 Ga. App. 34, 59 S. E. 209; Browning v. Goodrich Transp. Co., 78 Wis. 391, 47 N. W. 428, 10 L. R. A. 415, 23 Am. St. Rep. 414; The Niagara v. Cordes, 21 How. 7, 16 L. Ed. 41; Johnson v. Alabama & V. Ry. Co., 69 Miss. 191, 11 South. 104, 30 Am. St. Rep. 534; Schaller v. Chicago & N. W. Ry. Co., 97 Wis. 31, 71 N. W. 1042; U. S. Exp. Co. v. Bachmann, 28 Ohio St. 144; Bonfiglio v. Lake Shore & M. S. Ry. Co., 125 Mich. 476, 84 N. W. 722; Hall v. Cheney, 36 N. H. 26; Mitchell v. Carolina Cent. R. Co., 124 N. C. 236, 32 S. E. 671, 44 L. R. A. 515. Of course the carrier, relying on the contract as a defense, must prove this contract, with the elements of contractual validity. Deierling v. Wabash R. Co., 163 Mo. App. 292, 146 S. W. 814; Adams Express Co. v. Adams, 29 App. D. C. 250; Illinois Match Co. v. Chicago, R. I. & P. R. Co., 250 Ill. 396, 95 N. E. 492.

[94] Louisville & N. R. Co. v. Manchester Mills, 88 Tenn. 653, 14 S. W. 314; Little Rock, M. R. & T. Ry. Co. v. Talbot, 39 Ark. 523.

[95] Post, § 130.

[96] The conflict here is the same, whether the particular exemption be one implied by law (e. g., act of God) or whether it be one created by contract (e. g., fire). The considerations set forth and cases cited in discussing this question as to the exceptions implied by law are also applicable here. See ante, p. 349, notes 60, 61. See, also, Insurance Co. of North America v. Lake & W. R. Co., 152 Ind. 333, 53 N. E. 382; Smith v. American Exp. Co., 108 Mich. 572, 66 N. W. 479; Clark v. Barnwell, 12 How. 272, 13 L. Ed. 985; The Lennox (D. C.) 90 Fed. 308; Buck v. Pennsylvania R. Co., 150 Pa. 170,

The basis of this holding seems to be that the law presumes that one has lived up to his duty rather than that there has been a failure in this respect. According, too, to some of the courts, the conditions of modern transportation do not require any stricter rule as to the carriers.

A great many courts, however, hold that the carrier must go further than showing merely that the loss or injury was due to a cause excepted by his contract and that he must also prove that such loss or injury was in no way due to his negligence.[97] This rule has, to commend it, the strong consideration of convenience, since the carrier's means of showing the absence of negligence are at hand, while the shipper, having no control over the goods or first-hand knowledge of the methods and details of transportation, has great difficulty in proving affirmatively the negligence of the carrier.[98]

Very much the same considerations apply here as in the case (already discussed)[99] of the burden of proof as to the carrier's negligence when loss or injury is due to one of the perils excepted from the carrier's insuring liability by the common law, such as, for example, the act of God.

24 Atl. 678, 30 Am. St. Rep. 800; Sager v. Portsmouth S. & P. & E. R. Co., 31 Me. 228, 50 Am. Dec. 659; St. Louis, I. M. & S. Ry. Co. v. Bone, 52 Ark. 26, 11 S. W. 958; Lancaster Mills v. Merchants' Cotton-Press Co., 89 Tenn. 1, 14 S. W. 317, 24 Am. St. Rep. 586; Kelham v. The Kensington, 24 La. Ann. 100; Standard, etc., Co. v. White Line Cent. Transit Co., 122 Mo. 258, 26 S. W. 704.

97 Georgia Southern & F. R. Co. v. Greer, 2 Ga. App. 516, 58 S. E. 782; Carter & Co. v. Southern R. Co., 3 Ga. App. 34, 59 S. E. 209; Baltimore & O. R. Co. v. Oriental Oil Co., 51 Tex. Civ. App. 336, 111 S. W. 979; Hinton v. Eastern Ry. Co., 72 Minn. 339, 75 N. W. 373; Crawford v. Southern Ry. Co., 56 S. C. 136, 34 S. E. 80; Johnson v. Alabama & V. Ry. Co., 69 Miss. 191, 11 South. 104, 30 Am. St. Rep. 534; Union Exp. Co. v. Graham, 26 Ohio St. 595; Brown v. Adams Exp. Co., 15 W. Va. 812; Hinkle v. Southern Ry. Co., 126 N. C. 932, 36 S. E. 348, 78 Am. St. Rep. 685. See cases cited, p. 349, note, 61.

98 Pittsburgh, C., C. & St. L. Ry. Co. v. Racer, 5 Ind. App. 209, 31 N. E. 853; Mitchell v. Carolina Cent. R. Co., 124 N. C. 236, 32 S. E. 671, 44 L. R. A. 515; Johnstone v. Richmond & D. R. Co., 39 S. C. 55, 17 S. E. 512. See cases cited in preceding note.

99 See ante, § 118.

VALIDITY OF SPECIFIC STIPULATIONS—STIPULATIONS RELIEVING CARRIER OF LIABILITY SAVE FOR NEGLIGENCE

129. The carrier may validly stipulate for entire relief from liability for all loss or damage that is not due to the negligence of the carrier or that of his agents or servants.

It is clear, from what has been said, that the carrier may by contract limit the insuring liability imposed on him by the common law. It is equally clear that the carrier cannot, even by express contract, relieve himself of all liability for loss or damage, regardless of the means by which it was caused. It is far from clear, however, just what these limitations are on the power of the carrier thus to diminish his responsibility. How far a sound public policy, considering the public nature of the carrier's employment, may permit the carrier to go in this respect, is a question which has caused the courts no end of trouble, and has given rise to many and conflicting doctrines.

There is substantial agreement, however, that there is no objection, on the score of public policy, to contracts which make the carrier liable for his negligence, or that of his agents or servants, but which afford the carrier complete exemption from liability for loss or damage due to any other causes.[1] In other words, the

[1] South & N. A. R. Co. v. Henlein, 52 Ala. 606, 23 Am. Rep. 578; Id., 56 Ala. 368; East Tennessee, V. & G. R. Co. v. Johnston, 75 Ala. 596, 51 Am. Rep. 489; Little Rock, M. R. & T. Ry. Co. v. Talbot, 47 Ark. 97, 14 S. W. 471; Taylor v. Little Rock, M. R. & T. R. Co., 39 Ark. 148; Overland M. & E. Co. v. Carroll, 7 Colo. 43, 1 Pac. 682; Merchants' Dispatch & Transp. Co. v. Cornforth, 3 Colo. 280, 25 Am. Rep. 757; Union Pac. R. Co. v. Rainey, 19 Colo. 225, 34 Pac. 986; Camp v. Hartford & N. Y. Steamboat Co., 43 Conn. 333; Welch v. Boston & A. R. Co., 41 Conn. 333; Central R. R. v. Bryant, 73 Ga. 722, 726; Berry v. Cooper, 28 Ga. 543; Flinn v. Philadelphia, W. & B. R. Co., 1 Houst. (Del.) 469, 502; Boscowitz v. Adams Exp. Co., 93 Ill. 523, 34 Am. Rep. 191; Erie Ry. Co. v. Wilcox, 84 Ill. 239, 25 Am. Rep. 451; Rosenfeld v. Peoria, D. & E. Ry. Co., 103 Ind. 121, 2 N. E. 344, 53 Am. Rep. 500; Bartlett v. Pittsburgh, C. & St. L. Ry. Co., 94 Ind. 281; Ohio & M. Ry. Co. v. Selby, 47 Ind. 471, 17 Am. Rep. 719; Sprague v. Missouri Pac. Ry. Co., 34 Kan. 347, 8 Pac. 465; St. Louis, K. C. & N. Ry. Co. v. Piper, 13 Kan. 505; Louisville & N. R. Co. v. Brownlee, 14 Bush (Ky.) 590; Louisville, C. & L. R. Co v. Hedger, 9 Bush (Ky.) 645, 15 Am. Rep. 740; New Orleans Mut. Ins. Co. v. New Orleans, J. & G. N. R. Co., 20 La. Ann. 302; Roberts v. Riley, 15 La. Ann. 103, 77 Am. Dec. 183; Little v. Boston & M. R. R., 66 Me. 239; Willis v. Grand Trunk Ry. Co., 62 Me. 488; McCoy v. Erie & W. Transp. Co., 42 Md. 498; Brehme v. Dinsmore, 25 Md. 328; Hoadley v. Northern Transportation Co., 115 Mass. 304, 15 Am. Rep. 106; Pemberton Co. v. New York Cent. R. Co., 104

carrier can by contract validly stipulate that his liability is to be measured, not in terms of insurance, but in terms of negligence. For the insuring liability which the law affixes to him as an extraordinary bailee, he can contractually substitute the liability

Mass. 144, 151; School District in Medfield v. Boston, H. & E. R. Co., 102 Mass. 552, 3 Am. Rep. 502; Grace v. Adams, 100 Mass. 505, 97 Am. Dec. 117, 1 Am. Rep. 131; Squire v. New York Cent. R. Co., 98 Mass. 239, 93 Am. Dec. 162; Feige v. Michigan Cent. R. Co., 62 Mich. 1, 28 N. W. 685; Michigan Cent. R. Co. v. Ward, 2 Mich. 538, overruled in Michigan Cent. R. Co. v. Hale, 6 Mich. 243; Boehl v. Chicago, M. & St. P. Ry. Co., 44 Minn. 191, 46 N. W. 333; Hull v. Chicago, St. P., M. & O. Ry. Co., 41 Minn. 510, 43 N. W. 391, 5 L. R. A. 587, 16 Am. St. Rep. 722; Ortt v. Minneapolis & St. L. Ry. Co., 36 Minn. 396, 31 N. W. 519; Chicago, St. L. & N. O. R. Co. v. Moss, 60 Miss. 1003, 1011, 45 Am. Rep. 428; Chicago, St. L. & N. O. R. Co. v. Abels, 60 Miss. 1017; New Orleans, St. L. & C. R. Co. v. Faler, 58 Miss. 911; McFadden v. Missouri Pac. Ry. Co., 92 Mo. 343, 4 S. W. 689, 1 Am. St. Rep. 721; Ball v. Wabasha, St. L. & P. Ry. Co., 83 Mo. 574; Craycroft v. Atchison, T. & S. F. Ry. Co., 18 Mo. App. 487; Atchison & N. R. Co. v. Washburn, 5 Neb. 117, 121; Chicago, R. I. & P. R. Co. v. Witty, 32 Neb. 275, 49 N. W. 183, 29 Am. St. Rep. 436; Rand v. Merchants' Dispatch Transp. Co., 59 N. H. 363; Moses v. Boston & M. R. R., 24 N. H. 71, 55 Am. Dec. 222; Id., 32 N. H. 523, 64 Am. Dec. 381; Ashmore v. Pennsylvania Steam Towing & Transp. Co., 28 N. J. Law, 180; Phifer v. Carolina Cent. R. Co., 89 N. C. 311, 45 Am. Rep. 687; Smith v. North Carolina R. Co., 64 N. C. 235; Gaines v. Union Transp. & Ins. Co., 28 Ohio St. 418; U. S. Exp. Co. v. Backman, 28 Ohio St. 144; Union Exp. Co. v. Graham, 26 Ohio St. 595; Armstrong v. United States Exp. Co., 159 Pa. 640, 28 Atl. 448; Merchants' D. T. Co. v. Bloch, 86 Tenn. 392, 397, 6 S. W. 881, 6 Am. St. Rep. 847; Coward v. East Tennessee V. & G. R. Co., 16 Lea (Tenn.) 225, 57 Am. Rep. 227; Gulf, C. & S. F. Ry. Co. v. Trawick, 68 Tex. 314, 4 S. W. 567, 2 Am. St. Rep. 494 (under statute); Gulf, C. & S. F. Ry. Co. v. McGown, 65 Tex. 640; Houston & T. C. R. Co. v. Burke, 55 Tex. 323, 40 Am. Rep. 808; Mann v. Birchard, 40 Vt. 326, 94 Am. Dec. 398; Blumenthal v. Brainerd, 38 Vt. 402, 91 Am. Dec. 349; Virginia & T. R. Co. v. Sayers, 26 Grat. (Va.) 328; Wilson v. Chesapeake & O. R. Co., 21 Grat. (Va.) 654, 671; Brown v. Adams Exp. Co., 15 W. Va. 812; Maslin v. Baltimore & O. R. Co., 14 W. Va., 180, 35 Am. Rep. 748; Abrams v. Milwaukee, L. S. & W. Ry. Co., 87 Wis. 485, 58 N. W. 780, 41 Am. St. Rep. 55. And see Black v. Goodrich Transp. Co., 55 Wis. 319, 13 N. W. 244, 42 Am. Rep. 713; Thomas v. Wabash, St. L. & P. R. Co. (C. C.) 63 Fed. 200; New York C. R. Co. v. Lockwood, 17 Wall. 357, 21 L. Ed. 627; Michigan C. R. Co. v. Mineral Springs Mfg. Co., 16 Wall. 318, 328, 21 L. Ed. 297; Ogdensburg & L. C. R. Co. v. Pratt, 22 Wall. 123, 22 L. Ed. 827; New Jersey Steam Nav. Co. v. Merchants' Bank, 6 How. 344, 12 L. Ed. 465; Liverpool & G. W. Steam Co. v. Phenix Ins. Co., 129 U. S. 397, 9 Sup. Ct. 469, 32 L. Ed. 788; Thomas v. Lancaster Mills, 71 Fed. 481, 19 C. C. A. 88. See, also, the following recent cases: Hix v. Eastern S. S. Co., 107 Me. 357, 78 Atl. 379; George N. Pierce Co. v. Wells Fargo & Co., 189 Fed. 561, 110 C. C. A. 645; Mobile & O. R. Co. v. Brownsville Livery & Live Stock Co., 123 Tenn. 298, 130 S. W. 788; Penn. Clothing Co. v. United States Exp. Co., 48 Pa. Super. Ct. 520; Russell v. Erie R. Co., 70 N. J. Law, 808, 59 Atl. 150, 67 L. R. A. 433, 1 Ann. Cas. 672; Louisville, etc., Ry. Co. v. Landers, 135 Ala. 504, 33 South. 482.

attaching to the ordinary bailee for hire.[2] He can agree that, instead of being responsible at all hazards for loss or injury not due to one of the five excepted causes, he shall be liable only when the loss or injury is attributable to his failure to exercise due care. Though there are many practical objections to it, this rule is firmly established,[3] in the absence of statute[4] limiting the right of the carrier thus to restrict his liability by contract.

SAME—STIPULATIONS SEEKING TO RELIEVE THE CARRIER FROM LIABILITY FOR NEGLIGENCE

130. The carrier cannot by contract relieve himself from liability for loss or injury due to his negligence, or that of his agents or servants.

The American courts have with substantial unanimity consistently refused to permit the carrier to stipulate against the consequences of his negligence.[5] The public nature of the employment in

[2] As we have seen, however (ante, pp. 383–384), the common carrier continues a common carrier, however, even though by his contract he reduces his liability to that of an ordinary bailee.

[3] This is apparent even from a casual inspection of the cases cited in note 1.

[4] For discussion of statutory regulation of contracts limiting the carrier's liability, see post, § 135.

[5] Alabama G. S. R. Co. v Thomas, 89 Ala. 294, 7 South. 762, 18 Am. St. Rep. 119; Pacific Exp. Co. v. Wallace, 60 Ark. 100, 29 S. W. 32; Insurance Co. of North America v. Lake Erie & W. R. Co., 152 Ind. 333, 53 N. E. 382; Louisville & N. R. Co. v. Plummer, 35 S. W. 1113, 18 Ky. Law Rep. 228; Hudson v. Northern Pac. Ry. Co., 92 Iowa, 231, 60 N. W. 608, 54 Am. St. Rep. 550; Cox v. Central Vermont R. Co., 170 Mass. 129, 49 N. E. 97; Ortt v Minneapolis & St. L. Ry. Co., 36 Minn. 396, 31 N. W. 519; McFadden v. Missouri Pac. Ry. Co., 92 Mo. 343, 4 S. W. 689, 1 Am. St. Rep. 721; Pittsburgh, C. C. & St. L. Ry. Co. v. Sheppard, 56 Ohio St. 68, 46 N. E. 61, 60 Am. St. Rep. 732; Willock v. Pennsylvania R. Co., 166 Pa. 184, 30 Atl. 948, 27 L. R. A. 228, 45 Am. St. Rep. 674; Norfolk & W. R. Co. v. Harman, 91 Va. 601, 22 S. E. 490, 44 L. R. A. 289, 50 Am. St. Rep. 855; Liverpool & G. W. S. Co. v. Phenix Ins. Co., 129 U. S. 397, 9 Sup. Ct. 469, 32 L. Ed. 788; Thomas v. Wabash, St. L. & P. R. Co. (C. C.) 63 Fed. 200. See, also, the following recent cases: P. Garvan v. New York Cent. & H. R. R. Co., 210 Mass. 275, 96 N. E. 717; Central of Georgia R. Co. v. City Mills Co., 128 Ga. 841, 58 S. E. 197; St. Louis & S. F. R. Co. v. Phillips, 17 Okl. 264, 87 Pac. 470; Jolliffe v Northern Pac. R. Co., 52 Wash. 433, 100 Pac. 977; Merchants' & Miners' Transp. Co. v. Eichberg, 109 Md. 211, 71 Atl. 993, 130 Am. St. Rep. 524; Inman & Co. v. Seaboard Air Line R. Co. (C. C.) 159 Fed. 960; St. Louis Southwestern R. Co. v. Wallace, 90 Ark. 138, 118 S. W. 412, 22 L. R. A. (N. S.) 379; Checkley v. Illinois Cent. Ry. Co., 257 Ill. 491, 100 N. E. 942, 44 L. R. A. (N. S.) 1127, Ann Cas. 1914A, 1202.

which the carrier is engaged, the tremendous part that he plays in the commercial and economic life of a country, the fact that the carrier and shipper do not stand on a footing of equality as to contracts between them, would require that such contracts, which unquestionably tend to a deterioration in the service of the carrier, should be prohibited by sound public policy. These considerations completely outweigh the sanctity which would otherwise attach to the freedom of contract between persons who are under no disability.

In New York C. R. Co. v. Lockwood,[6] a leading American case, it was said, as to contracts attempting to relieve the carrier from the consequences of his negligence: "The proposition to allow a public carrier to abandon altogether his obligations to the public, and to stipulate for exemptions that are unreasonable and improper, amounting to an abdication of the essential duties of his employment, would never have been entertained by the sages of the law. * * * And then the inequality of the parties, the compulsion under which the customer is placed, and the obligations of the carrier to the public, operate with full force to divest the transaction of validity."

Anomalous Doctrines of a Few States

While the sound doctrine just stated very generally prevails, this doctrine has been qualified by the peculiar holdings of a few states.

Thus, in Illinois, it has been held that the carrier may validly contract for exemption from liability for ordinary negligence, but not for gross negligence.[7] Not only is any attempt to restrict the salutary doctrine, as above outlined, regrettable, but any attempt to distinguish here between grades of negligence is particularly objectionable. The so-called Illinois doctrine has, accordingly, met with scant favor at the hands of the courts of other states.[8]

The New York courts recognized a distinction between the carrier's own negligence and that of his servants or agents. The carrier was then permitted to contract against the negligence of his

[6] 17 Wall. (U. S.) 357, 21 L. Ed. 627.

[7] Illinois Cent. R. Co. v. Morrison, 19 Ill. 136; Wabash Ry. Co. v. Brown, 152 Ill. 484, 39 N. E. 274; Chicago & N. W. Ry. Co. v. Calumet Stock Farm, 194 Ill. 9, 61 N. E. 1095, 88 Am. St. Rep. 68. Language to the same effect is found also in Cooper v. Raleigh & G. R. Co., 110 Ga. 659, 36 S. E. 240; Galt v. Adams Exp. Co., MacArthur & M. (D. C.) 124, 48 Am. Rep. 742; Rhodes v. Louisville & N. R. Co., 9 Bush (Ky.) 688.

[8] See, particularly, criticism of Christian, J., in Virginia & T. R. Co. v. Sayers, 26 Grat. (Va.) 328. See, also, Alabama G. S. R. Co. v. Thomas, 83 Ala. 343, 3 South. 802; New York C. R. Co. v. Lockwood, 17 Wall. 357, 21 L. Ed. 627; Sager v. Portsmouth, S. & P. & E. R. Co., 31 Me. 228, 50 Am. Dec. 659; Wyld v. Pickford, 8 Mees. & W. (Eng.) 442.

servants, but this right was denied as to his own negligence.[9] This distinction is perhaps even more unfortunate, in that it attempts to set at naught a fundamental principle of the law of master and servant, that the master, receiving the benefits of the service, is responsible for the acts of the servant within the scope of his authority. This anomalous New York doctrine, therefore, has gained little currency elsewhere.[10]

SAME—STIPULATIONS LIMITING LIABILITY AS TO AMOUNT RECOVERABLE—IN THE ABSENCE OF THE CARRIER'S NEGLIGENCE

131. Stipulations limiting the recovery for loss or damage to a specified amount are clearly valid, in the absence of negligence on the part of the carrier or his servants.

It has already been shown [11] that the carrier may by contract relieve himself from any liability whatsoever not due to negligence. If, then, the carrier in such cases may validly stipulate for a total exemption from responsibility, clearly he can in like manner secure a partial exemption. The greater includes the less, and the carrier's contracts limiting his liability to stated amounts (however short these may fall of the actual loss or injury) are valid as to losses not caused by negligence.[12] Such contracts, however,

[9] The argument for this rule is perhaps best stated by Woodruff, J., in French v. Buffalo, N. Y. & E. R. Co., *43 N. Y. 108. See, also, Bissell v. New York Cent. R. Co., 25 N. Y. 442, 82 Am. Dec. 369; Perkins v. New York Cent. R. Co., 24 N. Y. 196, 82 Am. Dec. 281; Wells v. New York Cent. R. Co., 24 N. Y. 181; Smith v. New York Cent. R. Co., 24 N. Y. 222. Later New York cases seem to permit the carrier generally to contract against even his own negligence. Cragin v. New York Cent. R. Co., 51 N. Y. 61, 10 Am. Rep. 559; Zimmer v. New York Cent. & H. R. R. Co., 137 N. Y. 460, 33 N. E. 642.

[10] "A carrier who stipulates not to be bound to the exercise of care and diligence seeks to put off the essential duties of his employment. Nor can those duties be waived in respect to his agents or servants, especially where the carrier is an artificial being, incapable of acting except by agents and servants. The law demands of the carrier carefulness and diligence in performing the service, not merely an abstract carefulness and diligence in proprietors and stockholders, who take no active part in the business. To admit such a distinction in the law of common carriers, as the business is now carried on, would be subversive of the very object of the law." Liverpool & G. W. Steam Co. v. Phenix Ins. Co., 129 U. S. 397, 9 Sup. Ct. 469, 32 L. Ed. 788. See, also, Gulf, C. & S. F. Ry. Co. v. McGown, 65 Tex. 640.

[11] Ante, § 129.

[12] Brehme v. Dinsmore, 25 Md. 328; Chesapeake & O. R. Co. v. Beasley, Couch & Co., 104 Va. 788, 52 S. E. 566, 3 L. R. A. (N. S.) 183; Boorman v.

are somewhat rare, as it is usual for the carrier, in stipulating for exemptions in the absence of negligence, to stipulate, as he validly may, for the total exemption already discussed.

SAME—SAME—CARRIER NEGLIGENT—AMOUNT FIXED WITHOUT REGARD TO THE VALUE OF THE GOODS

132. Limitations of the carrier's liability to a fixed amount, where the loss or injury is due to the carrier's negligence, are invalid when such amount is fixed without regard to the value of the goods.

By the great weight of authority, a stipulation limiting recovery to an arbitrary sum is utterly void, when loss or injury is traceable to the negligence of the carrier.[13] Since here the amount is fixed capriciously by the carrier, it is in no way based on the value of the goods shipped, and bears no essential relation to the actual or even probable amount of damage sustained by the shipper, owing to the loss of, or injury to, the goods. As such amount is purely arbitrary, the carrier might, by placing it low enough, practically escape the consequences of his negligence, if such contracts were permissible.

The courts, then, have very generally viewed such contracts as mere attempts by the carrier to exempt himself, to a greater or less degree, from liability for his negligence. These contracts have been accordingly repudiated under the general rule forbidding the carrier from contracting against his negligence, and, when a loss

American Exp. Co., 21 Wis. 152; Snider v. Adams Exp. Co., 63 Mo. 376; Louisville & N. R. Co. v. Oden, 80 Ala. 38.

[13] Louisville & N. R. Co. v. Wynn, 88 Tenn. 320, 14 S. W. 311; ALAIR v. NORTHERN PAC. R. CO., 53 Minn. 160, 54 N. W. 1072, 19 L. R. A. 764, 39 Am. St. Rep. 588, Dobie Cas. Bailments and Carriers, 215; Gardner v. Southern R. Co., 127 N. C. 293, 37 S. E. 328; Central of Georgia Ry. Co. v. Murphey, 113 Ga. 514, 38 S. E. 970, 53 L. R. A. 720; Woodburn v. Cincinnati, N. O. & T. P. R. Co. (C. C.) 40 Fed. 731; Baltimore & O. S. W. Ry. Co. v. Ragsdale, 14 Ind. App. 406, 42 N. E. 1106; Ruppel v. Allegheny Valley Ry. Co., 167 Pa. 166, 31 Atl. 478, 46 Am. St. Rep. 666; Southern Exp. Co. v. Moon, 39 Miss. 822; Ohio & M. Ry. Co. v. Tabor, 98 Ky. 503, 32 S. W. 168, 36 S. W. 18, 34 L. R. A. 685; Galveston, H. & S. A. Ry. Co. v. Ball, 80 Tex. 602, 16 S. W. 441. See, also, Louisville & N. R. Co. v. Woodford, 152 Ky. 398, 153 S. W. 722; L. & N. Ry. Co. v. Tharpe, 11 Ga. App. 465, 75 S. E. 677. Where there is an arbitrary fixing of value by a carrier, accepting goods for transportation before an inspection and without any regard to their real worth, the assumed valuation may be treated as a mere attempt in advance to limit liability. Central of Georgia Ry. Co. v. Butler Marble & Granite Co., 8 Ga. App. 1, 68 S. E. 775.

or injury occurs attributable to the carrier's negligence, the shipper may, in spite of the stipulation limiting the carrier's liability to an arbitrary amount, recover the full amount of damage that he has suffered by virtue of such negligent loss or injury.[14]

SAME—SAME—SAME—AGREED VALUATION OF THE GOODS

133. When the amount fixed is honestly accepted by the carrier as a fair and bona fide valuation of the goods for shipment, then, by the weight of authority, even when loss or injury is caused by the carrier's negligence, there can be no recovery beyond the amount thus fixed.

There is much confusion and conflict in the cases as to the carrier's limiting the amount of his liability for negligent loss or injury by fixing in the contract a specified sum as the value of the goods. It is believed, however, that the rule given in the black letter text is supported by both reason and authority.[15] In order that he may determine what precautions and methods of transportation are proper, and in order that he may graduate his charges according to the risk assumed, the carrier is entitled to know the value of the goods he carries. When, therefore, the stipulation is honestly regarded by the carrier as a real valuation of the goods, and he arranges accordingly, it would seem that every consideration of fairness would demand the rule that, however valuable the goods may actually be, the liability of the carrier, even for

[14] See cases cited in preceding note.

[15] Hart v. Pennsylvania Ry. Co., 112 U. S. 331, 5 Sup. Ct. 151, 28 L. Ed. 717; Doyle v. Baltimore & O. R. Co. (C. C.) 126 Fed. 841; Louisville & N. R. Co. v. Sherrod, 84 Ala. 178, 4 South. 29; Western Ry. Co. v. Harwell, 91 Ala. 340, 8 South. 649; Coupland v. Housatonic R. Co., 61 Conn. 531, 23 Atl. 870, 15 L. R. A. 534; Russell v. Pittsburgh, C., C. & St. L. Ry. Co., 157 Ind. 311, 61 N. E. 678, 55 L. R. A. 253, 87 Am. St. Rep. 214; Graves v. Lake Shore & M. S. R. Co., 137 Mass. 33, 50 Am. Rep. 282; O'Malley v. Great Northern Ry. Co., 86 Minn. 380, 90 N. W. 974; Ballou v. Earle, 17 R. I. 441, 22 Atl. 1113, 14 L. R. A. 433, 33 Am. St. Rep. 881; Ullman v. Chicago & N. W. R. Co., 112 Wis. 150, 88 N. W. 41, 88 Am. St. Rep. 949; ADAMS EXP. CO. v. CRONINGER, 226 U. S. 491, 33 Sup. Ct. 148, 57 L. Ed. 314, 44 L. R. A. (N. S.) 257, Dobie Cas. Bailments and Carriers, 228; American Silk Dyeing & Finishing Co. v. Fuller's Exp. Co., 82 N. J. Law, 654, 82 Atl. 894. Some cases, however, refuse to permit such valuation and grant a full recovery of damages suffered by the carrier's negligence. Kansas City, St. J. & C. B. R. Co. v. Simpson, 30 Kan. 645, 2 Pac. 821, 46 Am. Rep. 104; Hughes v. Pennsylvania R. Co., 202 Pa. 222, 51 Atl. 990, 63 L. R. A. 513, 97 Am. St. Rep. 713; Cincinnati, N. O. & T. P. Ry. Co. v. Graves, 52 S. W. 961, 21 Ky. Law Rep. 684.

negligent loss or injury, should be limited to the stipulated amount.[16]

Such a stipulation is not a limitation of the carrier's liability for negligence, but is merely an attempt, on the part of the carrier, to arrive at the value of the goods, so that he may know for what amount he may be held responsible in case of loss due to his negligence. Information, not limitation, is sought by the carrier when such valuations are real and what the term primarily signifies. The rule, too, is based upon, and limited by, an honest attempt to arrive at the value of the goods; and in the amount fixed as the value the carrier must genuinely believe.[17] If, in such a case, the shipper is allowed to recover a sum beyond a valuation thus fixed by shipper

[16] A limitation on the value of the goods shipped in consideration of a reduced rate of carriage is binding in the event of loss, and the shipper cannot recover above the value fixed, where the contract is fairly made. Windmiller v. Northern Pac. Ry. Co., 52 Wash. 613, 101 P. 225. A shipping contract voluntarily entered into, which fixes an agreed valuation of the property which forms the basis for the freight charges, is an agreement fixing the valuation of the property, and not a contract limiting the liability of the carrier, and under the contract the carrier is only liable as stipulated, and then only to the extent of the valuation fixed. Mering v. Southern Pac. Co., 161 Cal. 297, 119 Pac. 80. Plaintiff shipped a package of furs, worth $2,000 by defendant express company. Plaintiff marked no value on the package and gave none in her communications to the express company; but the box had been previously used, and a $150 valuation was marked thereon, and this amount was stated by the express company in the receipt as the value of the package. Plaintiff accepted the receipt without demur, and after the loss of the package made no claim of mistake in valuation, but claimed the right to recover the full value of the furs in spite of the limitation of liability contained in the receipt. Held, that plaintiff's recovery was limited to $150. Taylor v. Weir (C. C.) 162 Fed. 585. A contract limiting a carrier's liability to the value of the shipment given by the shipper for obtaining a concession in rates is not invalid, under Const. Ky. § 196, prohibiting any carrier from contracting "for relief against common-law liability." Barnes v. Long Island R. Co., 115 App. Div. 44, 100 N. Y. Supp. 593, reversing judgment (1905) 47 Misc. Rep. 318, 93 N. Y. Supp. 616. Where a shipper and carrier fairly and honestly agree as to the value of the property to be shipped, as the basis of the carrier's charges and responsibility, and not for the purpose of limiting the amount for which the carrier shall be liable for losses resulting from its negligence, such agreement is valid, and the values so agreed upon will be the limit of recovery. Cole v. Minneapolis, St. P. & S. S. M. Ry. Co., 117 Minn. 33, 134 N. W. 296. Parties may agree on the value of property to be shipped by express, and limit the carrier's liability to the agreed valuation, where the agreement as to limitation is fairly made, on a good consideration. Adams Exp. Co. v. Byers, 177 Ind. 33, 95 N. E. 513. A shipper who by special contract agrees on a value of the goods in case of loss, and in consideration thereof obtains a reduced rate, is estopped from showing that the real value of the goods was greater than that contracted. Faulk v. Columbia, N. & L. R. Co., 82 S. C. 369, 64 S. E. 383.

[17] See post, p. 400.

and carrier, not only would it impose an unfair burden on the carrier, but it would also permit the shipper to profit by his own wrong.

In Hart v. Pennsylvania R. Co.,[18] the leading American case, this language is used by the United States Supreme Court: "The limitation as to value has no tendency to exempt from liability for negligence. It does not induce want of care. It exacts from the carrier the measure of care due to the value agreed on.[19] The carrier is bound to respond in that value for negligence. The compensation for carriage is based on that value. The shipper is estopped from saying that the value is greater. The articles have no greater value for the purposes of the contract of transportation between the parties to that contract. The carrier must respond for negligence, up to that value. It is just and reasonable that such a contract, fairly entered into, and where there is no deceit practiced on the shipper, should be upheld. There is no violation of public policy. On the contrary, it would be repugnant to the soundest principles of fair dealing, and of the freedom of contracting, and thus in conflict with public policy, if a shipper should be allowed to reap the benefit of the contract if there is no loss, and to repudiate it in case of loss."

In the same case it was held that there is no difference in legal effect between the case of the shipper fixing the value, to which the carrier assents, and the case of the carrier, in the bill of lading, fixing the value at a figure which is reasonable for ordinary goods of the class in question, to which value the shipper gives his assent.[20] Of course, if the value were fixed by the carrier, this would in no case be binding on the shipper, unless expressly or impliedly [21] he consents thereto.

Accordingly, though some courts dissent from the rule, where the contract between the shipper and carrier is fairly made, agree-

18 112 U. S. 331, 5 Sup. Ct. 151, 28 L. Ed. 717.

19 See Graves v. Lake Shore & M. S. R. Co., 137 Mass. 33, 50 Am. Rep. 282; Squire v. New York Cent. R. Co., 98 Mass. 239, 93 Am. Dec. 162; Rosenfeld v. Peoria, D. & E. Ry. Co., 103 Ind. 121, 2 N. E. 344, 53 Am. Rep. 500; Hopkins v. Westcott, 6 Blatchf. 64, Fed. Cas. No. 6,692; The Aline (C. C.) 25 Fed. 562; The Hadji (D. C.) 18 Fed. 459.

20 The language of Mitchell, J., in ALAIR v. NORTHERN PAC. R. CO., 53 Minn. 160, 54 N. W. 1072, 19 L. R. A. 764, 39 Am. St. Rep. 588, Dobie Cas. Bailments and Carriers, 215, is almost identical with that used in the Hart Case.

21 As by accepting a bill of lading or express receipt with a clause fixing the value of the goods, in the absence of any fraud, concealment, or unfair dealing. Michalitschke Bros. & Co. v. Wells, Fargo & Co., 118 Cal. 683, 50 Pac. 847; Graves v. Adams Exp. Co., 176 Mass. 280, 57 N. E. 462. See ante, § 125.

ing on a valuation of the goods to be carried, the carrier entertaining a genuine belief that the amount thus fixed is a fair value of the goods, then, even in case of negligence, the contract is binding.[22] Such a contract is upheld as a proper and lawful method of securing a due proportion between the amount for which the carrier may be responsible and the freight he receives. It also serves as a protection to the carrier against exaggerated and fanciful valuations of the goods on the part of the shipper after the loss or injury.

When Valuation is Known by Carrier to be Far Below the Real Value of the Goods

The courts again differ sharply when the valuation in the contract is known by the carrier to be utterly disproportionate to the real value of the goods. In such case some courts hold that even then the carrier, for loss due to his negligence, is liable only for the amount fixed by the contract.[23] The better view, however, seems to be that the contract valuation is then not a real valuation at all, and is hence invalid, thus permitting the shipper to recover the full amount of damage he has suffered.[24] The first of these holdings

[22] See cases cited in note 15.

[23] Donlon Bros. v. Southern Pac. Co., 151 Cal. 763, 91 Pac. 603, 11 L. R. A. (N. S.) 811, 12 Ann. Cas. 1118 (stipulation held valid limiting value of horses to $20 each); D'Arcy v. Adams Exp. Co., 162 Mich. 363, 127 N. W. 261 (limitation to $50, though carrier knew that the contents of the package were valuable opals); George N. Pierce Co. v. Wells Fargo & Co., 189 Fed. 561, 110 C. C. A. 645 (automobiles worth $15,000, valued at $50). See, also, Greenwald v. Barrett, 199 N. Y. 170, 92 N. E. 218, 35 L. R. A. (N. S.) 971; In re Released Rates, 13 Interst. Com. 550; Bernard v. Adams Exp. Co., 205 Mass. 254, 91 N. E. 325, 28 L. R. A. (N. S.) 292, 18 Ann. Cas. 351. Many cases fail to make the distinction indicated, and treat together stipulations as to the value of goods, regardless of the carrier's knowledge that such value is far below the real value of the goods. For discriminating comments on this subject, see the brief, but excellent, notes of Prof. Goddard, 9 Mich. L. Rev. 233, 10 Mich. L. Rev. 317. In this latter note the decision in the case of George N. Pierce Co. v. Wells Fargo & Co., supra, is severely, but justly, criticised. See, also, American Silver Mfg. Co. v. Wabash R. Co., 174 Mo. App. 184, 156 S. W. 830 (holding that a limitation to ten times the freight paid was valid, though the carrier had notice that the property was worth nearly $5,000). See, also, the recent decisions of the United States Supreme Court as to limitations on interstate shipments under the Carmack amendment to the Interstate Commerce Act (Act Feb. 4, 1887, c. 104, 24 Stat. 386 [U. S. Comp. St. 1901, p. 3169], as amended by Act June 29, 1906, c. 3591, § 7, pars. 11, 12, 34 Stat. 595 [U. S. Comp. St. Supp. 1911, p. 1307]): ADAMS EXP. CO. v. CRONINGER, 226 U. S. 491, 33 Sup. Ct. 148, 57 L. Ed. 314, 44 L. R. A. (N. S.) 257, Dobie Cas. Bailments and Carriers, 228; Missouri, K. & T. R. Co. v. Harriman, 227 U. S. 657, 33 Sup. Ct. 397, 57 L. Ed. 690; Kansas City Southern R. Co. v. Carl, 227 U. S. 639, 33 Sup. Ct. 391, 57 L. Ed. 683.

[24] A contract limiting a carrier's liability to $5 per hundredweight, or to a maximum of $120, is invalid, where the freight is worth over $900 and the

permits the carrier to know two values—one, the real value of the goods; the other, a purely fictitious one, that exists only for the purpose of that particular transportation. The more acceptable doctrine, however, is the second, that recognizes only one method of valuation—that of determining the real value of the goods—and views an attempt by the carrier to fix by contract the value of the goods at a figure far below what is really known to be their value, as an attempt by the carrier to limit, in the guise of a valuation, his liability for his negligent acts.

If no limit is placed on the carrier's power to fix the amount of his liability for negligence by so-called agreed valuations, then by fixing this valuation low enough the carrier can, to all practical purposes, entirely absolve himself from the consequences of his negligence.[25] If there is a limit to this objectionable practice, it would be hard to define its precise limits, and still more difficult to apply it practically.

When goods of the actual value of $1,000 are shipped at an agreed valuation of $500, there are not a few courts, as has been indicated, that hold the carrier, even though the real value of the goods is known to him, liable only for $500 when the goods are lost through his negligence. Yet some of these courts would refuse to permit the carrier to contract that, for loss due to his negligence, the carrier's liability shall be limited to one-half the value of the goods. Still the same result would always flow from the stipulation as to half liability and an agreed valuation which the carrier, after as-

carrier had knowledge thereof. Colorado & S. Ry. Co. v. Manatt, 21 Colo. App. 593, 121 Pac. 1012. A shipper signed a printed receipt and agreed that an express company should not be liable beyond the sum of $50, at which sum the property shipped was valued. The freight paid was $330, and the testimony showed that the value of the shipment was $2,000. This was held an invalid stipulation. MURPHY v. WELLS FARGO & CO. EXPRESS, 99 Minn. 230, 108 N. W. 1070, Dobie Cas. Bailments and Carriers, 218. A carrier having an opportunity to see and know the nature and value of freight to be carried cannot by contract relieve itself from liability for full value for loss through its negligence. Galveston, H. & S. A. R. Co. v. Crippen (Tex. Civ. App.) 147 S. W. 361. See, also, Kember v. Southern Exp. Co., 22 La. Ann. 158, 2 Am. Rep. 719; Southern Exp. Co. v. Crook, 44 Ala. 468, 4 Am. Rep. 140; Powers Mercantile Co. v. Wells Fargo & Co., 93 Minn. 143, 100 N. W. 735; HANSON v. GREAT NORTHERN R. CO., 18 N. D. 324, 121 N. W. 78, 138 Am. St. Rep. 768, Dobie Cas. Bailments and Carriers, 220; Baughman v. Louisville, E. & St. L. R. Co., 14 Ky. Law Rep. 108; U. S. Exp. Co. v. Backman, 28 Ohio St. 144; Overland M. & E. Co. v. Carroll, 7 Colo. 43, 1 Pac. 682; Southern Exp. Co. v. Rothenberg, 87 Miss. 656, 40 South. 65, 112 Am. St. Rep. 466.

25 See dissenting opinion of Shaw, J., in Donlon Bros. v. Southern Pac. Co., 151 Cal. 763, 91 Pac. 603, 11 L. R. A. (N. S.) 811, 12 Ann. Cas. 1118. See, also, 10 Mich. Law Rev. 317.

certaining the real value, was careful to fix at exactly one-half of such real value.[26]

It is therefore suggested, as the better doctrine, that a keen distinction be drawn between honest attempts at valuation, which seek information, and stipulations which, placing a value on the goods far below their known value, in effect seek limitation.[27] When the carrier is negligent, the first should be upheld and the second condemned. The rule, then, which permits no recovery against the carrier for negligence beyond the valuation in the contract, should be qualified by requiring that this contract valuation must be honestly believed by the carrier to be the real value of the goods. Knowledge, on the part of the carrier, of the higher valuation should indicate to the carrier the measure of his responsibility for negligence, and he should arrange and charge accordingly.

Limitation to Fixed Amount Unless Real Value is Stated

Stipulations have been generally upheld limiting the carrier's liability for negligence to a specified amount unless the real value of the goods, in excess of such amount, is given by the shipper.[28] If, with knowledge of such stipulation, the shipper delivers the goods for shipment, the carrier is thus deceived into thinking that their value is not in excess of the amount fixed, and his liability should be determined accordingly. Such conduct on the part of the shipper is legally equivalent to the shipper's assent to such valuation, and practically conveys to the carrier the information that the value of the goods is not above the amount fixed.

If the carrier knows, however, that the value of the goods actually exceeds the amount fixed, then, in accordance with principles just discussed, it would seem that such a stipulation would afford him no protection against liability for his negligence; [29] and this is true,

[26] Says Lurton, J., in Kansas City Southern Ry. Co. v. Carl, 227 U. S. 639, at page 650, 33 Sup. Ct. 391, 57 L. Ed. 683: "An agreement to release such a carrier for part of a loss due to negligence is no more valid than one whereby there is complete exemption. Neither is such a contract more valid because it rests upon a consideration than if it was without consideration."

[27] See authorities cited in note 24.

[28] De Wolff v. Adams Exp. Co., 106 Md. 472, 67 Atl. 1099; ALAIR v. NORTHERN PAC. RY. CO., 53 Minn. 160, 54 N. W. 1072, 19 L. R. A. 764, 39 Am. St. Rep. 588, Dobie Cas. Bailments and Carriers, 215; Durgin v. American Exp. Co., 66 N. H. 277, 20 Atl. 328, 9 L. R. A. 453; Rappaport v. White's Express Co., 146 App. Div. 576, 131 N. Y. Supp. 131; Norton v. Adams Exp. Co., 123 Mo. App. 233, 100 S. W. 502; Smith v. American Exp. Co., 108 Mich. 572, 66 N. W. 479; Graves v. Adams Exp. Co., 176 Mass. 280, 57 N. E. 462; Michalitschke Bros. & Co. v. Wells Fargo & Co., 118 Cal. 683, 50 Pac. 847; Pacific Exp. Co. v. Ross (Tex. Civ. App.) 154 S. W. 340.

[29] MURPHY v. WELLS FARGO & CO. EXPRESS, 99 Minn. 230, 108 N. W. 1070, Dobie Cas. Bailments and Carriers, 218; Powers Mercantile Co. v.

whether this knowledge be gained from outside sources, or whether the appearance of the goods reasonably suggests their real value. The failure of the shipper to state what the carrier already knows does not, of course, deceive the carrier; while the carrier, knowing the real value, should not be permitted, even partially, to escape full liability for his negligent acts.

The stipulation in question is of particular importance in express receipts,[30] as the goods sent by express are usually of comparatively great value in proportion to their bulk.

Stipulations Limiting Recovery to Value of Goods at Time and Place of Shipment

In many bills of lading a stipulation is found providing that, in case of loss even by negligence, the value of the goods at the time and place of shipment shall constitute the measure of damages which the shipper may recover. The usual measure of damages, as we shall see,[31] when the goods are lost, is their value at their destination at the time the goods should have arrived in good condition. Such stipulations, though repudiated by some courts,[32] have for the most part been sustained as both reasonable and valid.[33]

These stipulations do not seek, in case of loss by negligence, to limit the carrier's liability to an amount less than the value of the goods. They simply specify the time and place at which this value shall be reckoned. The value of the goods at the destination is ordinarily greater than at the place of shipment, since this usually

Wells Fargo & Co., 93 Minn. 143, 100 N. W. 735; Orndorff v. Adams Exp. Co., 3 Bush. (Ky.) 194, 96 Am. Dec. 207; Kember v. Southern Exp. Co., 22 La. Ann. 158, 2 Am. Rep. 719; Southern Exp. Co. v. Crook, 44 Ala. 468, 4 Am. Rep. 140. There are cases, however, holding this stipulation valid in spite of the carrier's knowledge of a real value far exceeding the stipulated amount. See George N. Pierce Co. v. Wells Fargo & Co., 189 Fed. 561, 110 C. C. A. 645; D'Arcy v. Adams Exp. Co., 162 Mich. 363, 127 N. W. 261.

30 This is indicated by the mere titles of the cases. See, for example, the cases cited in the preceding note.

31 Post, § 160.

32 Illinois Cent. R. Co. v. Bogard, 78 Miss. 11, 27 South. 879; McConnell Bros. v. Southern R. Co., 144 N. C. 87, 56 S. E. 559; Southern Pac. Ry. Co. v. D'Arcais, 27 Tex. Civ. App. 57, 64 S. W. 813; Ruppel v. Allegheny Valley Ry., 167 Pa. 166, 31 Atl. 478, 46 Am. St. Rep. 666.

33 Gratiot St. Warehouse Co. v. Missouri, K. & T. R. Co., 124 Mo. App. 545, 102 S. W. 11; Inman & Co. v. Seaboard Air Line R. Co. (C. C.) 159 Fed. 960; Merchants' & Miners' Transp. Co. v. Eichberg, 109 Md. 211, 71 Atl. 993, 130 Am. St. Rep. 524; MATHESON v. SOUTHERN RY., 79 S. C. 155, 60 S. E. 437, Dobie Cas. Bailments and Carriers, 290; Zouch v. Chesapeake & O. Ry. Co., 36 W. Va. 524, 15 S. E. 185, 17 L. R. A. 116; Pierce v. Southern Pac. Co., 120 Cal. 156, 47 Pac. 874, 52 Pac. 302, 40 L. R. A. 350; Squire v. New York Cent. R. Co., 98 Mass. 239, 93 Am. Dec. 162; Tibbits v. Rock Island & P. Ry. Co., 49 Ill. App. 567.

supplies the reason for the shipment, and some courts on this ground have considered these stipulations in the light of contracts attempting to limit the carrier's liability for negligent loss.[84] The courts upholding these contracts lay stress on the advantage and convenience, as to proof, in thus fixing a definite time and place as of which the value of the goods is to be reckoned.[85]

Even by these courts, upholding the validity of such stipulations, these stipulations are limited to loss or injury by the carrier, whether with or without negligence. They do not apply when the carrier is guilty of a conversion of the goods.[86]

Effect of Agreed Valuation in Cases of Injury or Partial Loss

Another question involving cordial disagreement on the part of the courts arises when, in cases of agreed valuation, the goods are injured or a part of the shipment is lost. The difficulty lies in determining the measure of recovery in such cases. According to some courts, the shipper recovers the full amount of damage suffered up to the amount of the agreed valuation, on the theory that the valuation fixes merely the limit of recovery, and that the shipper recovers all damage actually incurred, provided it does not exceed the valuation fixed.[87] The doctrine of another line of authorities is that the shipper recovers only that proportion of the actual damage which the agreed valuation bears to the actual value of the goods.[88] The latter rule is believed to be preferable, since it is in better accord with the theory of a real valuation accepted by the carrier as such.

SAME—LIMITATIONS AS TO TIME AND MANNER OF PRESENTING CLAIMS

134. The carrier may by contract require that claims for damages be presented in a certain manner and within a specified time, and this contract will be valid, provided such stipulations as to time and manner be reasonable.

[84] See cases cited in note 32.

[85] See cases cited in note 33.

[86] Erie Dispatch v. Johnson, 87 Tenn. 490, 11 S. W. 441; Shelton v. Canadian Northern R. Co. (C. C.) 189 Fed. 153.

[87] Michalitschke Bros. & Co. v. Wells, Fargo & Co., 118 Cal. 683, 50 Pac. 847; Nelson v. Great Northern R. Co., 28 Mont. 297, 72 Pac. 642; Brown v. Cunard S. S. Co., 147 Mass. 58, 16 N. E. 717; Visanska v. Southern Exp. Co., 92 S. C. 573, 75 S. E. 962.

[88] O'Malley v. Great Northern Ry. Co., 86 Minn. 380, 90 N. W. 974; United States Exp. Co. v. Joyce, 36 Ind. App. 1, 69 N. E. 1015; Shelton v. Canadian Northern R. Co. (C. C.) 189 Fed. 153; Goodman v. Missouri, K. & T. Ry. Co., 71 Mo. App. 460; Greenfield v. Wells Fargo & Co. (Sup.) 134 N. Y. Supp. 913.

Such stipulations have nothing to do with limiting the carrier's liability for negligence.[39] They do not even attempt to limit the amount for which the carrier may be held responsible. The purpose of this stipulation is to give the carrier notice of the claim at a time when it is still fresh, and when the carrier may by diligent inquiry learn the facts and circumstances surrounding such claim.[40] The difficulties of such an inquiry increase tremendously when it is started long after the loss or injury upon which the claim is based. Especially is this true of a carrier daily engaged in hundreds or thousands of similar transactions.

In order that such a stipulation may be valid, however, the time in which the claim can be presented must be reasonable.[41] If the time stipulated is unreasonable, then the stipulation is of no effect.[42] What is a reasonable time is a relative question, depending on the circumstances of each particular case.[43] Thus, thirty hours after

[39] Liquid Carbonic Co. v. Norfolk & W. R. Co., 107 Va. 323, 58 S. E. 569, 13 L. R. A. (N. S.) 753; Cooke v. Northern Pac. R. Co., 22 N. D. 266, 133 N. W. 303.

[40] See cases cited in note 41. "This is a very reasonable and proper provision, to enable the defendants, while the matter is still fresh, to institute proper inquiries and furnish themselves with evidence on the subject. The defendants do a large business, and to allow suits to be brought against them, without such notice, at any length of time, would be to surrender them, bound hand and foot, to almost every claim which might be made. It would be next to impossible, when a thousand packages, large and small, are forwarded by them daily, to ascertain anything about the loss of one of them, at a distance of six months or a year." Weir v. Express Co., 5 Phila. (Pa.) 355.

[41] Deaver-Jeter Co. v. Southern Ry., 91 S. C. 503, 74 S. E. 1071, Ann. Cas. 1914A, 230; St. Louis & S. F. R. Co. v. Phillips, 17 Okl. 264, 87 Pac. 470; Pennsylvania Co. v Shearer, 75 Ohio St. 249, 79 N E. 431, 116 Am. St. Rep. 730, 9 Ann. Cas. 15; The Queen of the Pacific, 180 U. S. 49, 21 Sup. Ct. 278, 45 L. Ed. 419; Engesether v. Great Northern Ry. Co., 65 Minn. 168, 68 N. W. 4; St. Louis & S. F R. Co. v Hurst, 67 Ark. 407, 55 S. W. 215; Gulf, C. & S. F. Ry. Co. v Trawick, 68 Tex. 314, 4 S. W. 567, 2 Am. St. Rep. 494; Southern Exp. Co. v. Hunnicutt, 54 Miss. 566, 28 Am. Rep. 385; SOUTHERN EXP. CO. v. CALDWELL, 21 Wall. 264, 22 L. Ed. 556, Dobie Cas. Bailments and Carriers, 226; Weir v. Express Co., 5 Phila. (Pa.) 355; U. S. Exp. Co. v. Harris, 51 Ind. 127; Southern Exp. Co. v. Glenn, 16 Lea (Tenn.) 472, 1 S. W. 102; Lewis v. Railroad Co., 5 Hurl. & N. (Eng.) 867. Similar stipulations contained in insurance policies are sustained. Steen v. Niagara Fire Ins. Co., 89 N. Y. 315, 42 Am. Rep. 297. Likewise in telegraph contracts. Cole v. Western U. Tel. Co., 33 Minn. 227, 22 N. W. 385.

[42] Dixie Cigar Co. v. Southern Express Co., 120 N. C. 348, 27 S. E. 73, 58 Am. St. Rep. 795; Central Vermont R. Co. v. Soper, 59 Fed. 879, 8 C. C. A. 341; Southern Exp. Co. v. Bank of Tupelo, 108 Ala. 517, 18 South. 664; Osterhoudt v. Southern Pac. Co., 47 App. Div. 146, 62 N. Y. Supp. 134; Norfolk & W. Ry. Co. v. Reeves, 97 Va. 284, 33 S. E. 606.

[43] This is usually a question of fact for the jury. Kansas & A. V. R. Co.

delivery was in one case held reasonable;[44] while thirty days from the date of the bill of lading was in another case held unreasonable.[45] A stipulation requiring a consignee of cattle to present any claim for damages at the time of the receipt of the cattle, and before they are unloaded and mingled with other cattle, was held reasonable and valid.[46] But a stipulation requiring goods to be examined

v. Ayers, 63 Ark. 331, 38 S. W. 515; St. Louis & S. F. R. Co. v. Phillips, 17 Okl. 264, 87 Pac. 470; International & G. N. Ry. Co. v. Garrett, 5 Tex. Civ. App. 540, 24 S. W. 354. The following periods have been held reasonable: Ninety days, SOUTHERN EXP. CO. v. CALDWELL, 21 Wall. 264, 22 L. Ed. 556, Dobie Cas. Bailments and Carriers, 226. Thirty days, Hirshberg v. Dinsmore, 12 Daly (N. Y) 429; Smith v. Dinsmore, 9 Daly (N. Y.) 188; Kaiser v. Hoey (City Ct. N. Y.) 1 N. Y. Supp. 429; Southern Exp. Co. v. Hunnicutt, 54 Miss. 566, 28 Am. Rep. 385; Glenn v. Southern Exp. Co., 86 Tenn. 594, 8 S. W. 152; Weir v Express Co., 5 Phila. (Pa.) 355. Five days, Chicago & A. R. Co. v. Simms, 18 Ill. App. 68; Dawson v. St. Louis, K. C. & N. Ry. Co., 76 Mo. 514. Sixty days, Thompson v Chicago & A. R. Co. 22 Mo. App. 321. Seven days, Lewis v. Railway Co., 5 Hurl & N (Eng.) 867. The following periods have been held unreasonable: Sixty days from date of contract, Pacific Exp. Co. v. Darnell (Tex.) 6 S. W 765. Thirty days from date of contract, Adams Exp. Co. v. Reagan, 29 Ind. 21, 92 Am. Dec. 332, Southern Exp. Co. v. Caperton, 44 Ala. 101, 4 Am. Rep. 118. Where the period is fixed without reference to the time of loss or length of journey, it is unreasonable. Porter v. Southern Exp. Co., 4 S. C. 135, 16 Am. Rep. 762; Southern Exp. Co. v. Caperton, 44 Ala. 101, 4 Am. Rep. 118. But see SOUTHERN EXP. CO. v. CALDWELL, 21 Wall. 264, 22 L. Ed. 556, Dobie Cas. Bailments and Carriers, 226; and cf. Central Vermont R. Co. v. Soper, 8 C. C. A. 341, 59 Fed. 879. Stipulation, in a contract for carriage of freight, that as a condition to recovery for injury to the property the carrier shall be given notice within a certain time of claim for damages, must be reasonable, and whether it is reasonable, where the notice is required to be given within a day after delivery at destination, is a question for the jury; the stock shipped having arrived at 2 p. m., there having been no agent at such station, and the nearest agent to whom notice might have been given having been 35 miles away. St. Louis, I. M. & S. R. Co. v. Furlow, 89 Ark. 404, 117 S. W. 517. Where shippers had ample time and opportunity to notify the carriers of damage to cotton which occurred before ocean transportation began, a provision in the bills of lading requiring notice of damage within 30 days after delivery of the cotton at destination was not unreasonable. Inman & Co. v. Seaboard Air Line R. Co. (C. C.) 159 Fed. 960. A provision of a bill of lading that the carrier should not be liable in any suit to recover for loss or damage to the property, unless suit was brought within one year, was reasonable. Ingram v. Weir (C. C.) 166 Fed. 328.

[44] St. Louis & S. F. R. Co. v. Hurst, 67 Ark. 407, 55 S. W. 215.

[45] Southern Exp. Co. v. Bank of Tupelo, 108 Ala. 517, 18 South. 664.

[46] Rice v. Kansas Pac. Ry., 63 Mo. 314; Sprague v. Missouri Pac. Ry. Co., 34 Kan. 347, 8 Pac. 465; Owen v. Louisville & N. R. Co., 87 Ky. 626, 9 S. W. 698; Wood v. Southern Ry. Co., 118 N. C. 1056, 24 S. E. 704; Western Ry. Co. v. Harwell, 91 Ala. 340, 8 South. 649. This is held reasonable, in order that the carrier may inform himself as to these injuries before the injured cattle are no longer capable of identification.

before leaving the station, as applied to a car load of cotton, was held not to be reasonable.[47] So, likewise, a contract regulating the manner of presenting claims is valid, provided it is reasonable.[48] For example, a contract requiring notice of loss to be made in writing,[49] or at the place of shipment, is valid.[50] These limitations as to time or manner may, of course, be waived by the carrier.[51]

[47] Capehart v. Seaboard & R. R. Co., 81 N. C. 438, 31 Am. Rep. 505. See, also, Owen v. Louisville & N. R. Co., 87 Ky. 626, 9 S. W. 698; Rice v. Kansas Pac. Ry., 63 Mo. 314; Sprague v. Missouri Pac. Ry. Co., 34 Kan. 347, 8 Pac. 465. Such a stipulation does not apply to latent injuries, which could not be discovered at the time of delivery. Ormsby v. Union Pac. R. Co. (C. C.) 4 Fed. 170; Id. (C. C.) 4 Fed. 706; Capehart v. Seaboard & R. R. Co., 77 N. C. 355.

[48] A requirement that the claim be verified by affidavits is valid. Black v. Wabasha, St. L. & P. Ry. Co., 111 Ill. 351, 53 Am. Rep. 628. Cf. International & G. N. Ry. Co. v. Underwood, 62 Tex. 21. Notice in writing to a particular officer may be required. Dawson v. St. Louis, K. C. & N. Ry. Co., 76 Mo. 514. Cf. Baltimore & O. Exp. Co. v. Cooper, 66 Miss. 558, 6 South. 327, 14 Am. St. Rep. 586.

[49] Hirshberg v. Dinsmore, 12 Daly (N. Y.) 429; Chicago & A. R. Co. v. Simms, 18 Ill. App. 68. But see Smitha v. Louisville & N. R. Co., 86 Tenn. 198, 6 S. W. 209. The filing of suit and service of citation are sufficient to meet requirements of a shipping contract whereby the shipper agrees to give definite notice in writing of his claim to the carrier within a certain time after date of injury. Houston & T. C. R. Co. v. Davis, 50 Tex. Civ. App. 74, 109 S. W. 422.

[50] The requirement is waived where the carrier has no officer at the place named to whom notice could be given. Missouri Pac. Ry. Co. v. Harris, 67 Tex. 166, 2 S. W. 574.

[51] Chicago & E. I. R. Co. v. Katzenbach, 118 Ind. 174, 20 N. E. 709; Rice v. Kansas Pac. Ry., 63 Mo. 314; Owen v. Louisville & N. R. Co. (Ky.) 9 S. W. 841; Hudson v. Northern Pac. Ry. Co., 92 Iowa, 231, 60 N. W. 608, 54 Am. St. Rep. 550. Receipt and consideration of an unverified claim is a waiver of a stipulation requiring a verified one. Wabash Ry. Co. v. Brown, 152 Ill. 484, 39 N. E. 273. See, also, Bennett v. Northern Pac. Exp. Co., 12 Or. 49, 6 Pac. 160. Where a bill of lading contains a provision that claims for loss or damage must be made in writing within 30 days, this provision is waived where the railroad company deliberated on a claim made after the expiration of the thirty days, and placed its refusal to pay the claim on the merits. Isham v. Erie R. Co., 191 N. Y. 547, 85 N. E. 1111, affirming 112 App. Div. 612, 98 N. Y. Supp. 609. A provision of a bill of lading requiring any claim for loss or damage to be made in writing within 30 days after delivery was waived where no objection was raised on that ground to a claim filed after that time. Merchants' & Miners' Transp. Co. v. Eichberg, 109 Md. 211, 71 Atl. 993, 130 Am. St. Rep. 524. Though a contract of shipment requires written notice of claim for damages to be made within 30 days, a notice is unnecessary where the carrier's agent attended the opening of the car with the consignee, listed the damaged goods and made report thereof to the carrier, who entered upon an investigation of the damages, and did not object to the form of notice. Nairn v. Missouri, K. & T. R. Co., 126 Mo. App. 707, 106 S. W. 102. Where a carrier without objection to the form of notice receives and acts on an

Such stipulations as to notice of loss or damage do not apply to a misdelivery by the carrier.[62]

STATUTORY REGULATION OF CONTRACTS LIMITING CARRIER'S LIABILITY

135. In the federal congress and in the legislatures of many states, statutes have been passed regulating the power of the carrier to limit his common-law liability by contract. The effect of these statutes is to restrict, or take away entirely, the carrier's right thus to diminish his responsibility.

The discussion, in the preceding sections, of the carrier's right to limit his common-law liability presumes, of course, that this right on the part of the carrier is not affected by statute. In many states, however, this right is restricted or absolutely denied, either by statutes or the state Constitution. It is beyond the scope of this book to discuss these statutes in detail; but it is important to note that these statutory and constitutional provisions do exist, and that, in cases falling within their terms, they seriously affect the principles which, in the absence of such provisions, ordinarily govern the carrier's right by contract to diminish the rigorous responsibility imposed on him by the common law.

In Kentucky[63] and Nebraska,[64] the state Constitutions prohibit the carrier from limiting in any respect by contract his responsi-

oral notice of damage given by a shipper, a waiver of the requirement of the contract of shipment that the shipper shall give notice in writing results. Carter & Co. v. Southern Ry. Co., 3 Ga. App. 34, 59 S. E. 209. The act of a carrier in sending at the request of the consignee tracers for a lost shipment after the time fixed in the bill of lading for service of notice on it of a claim for loss essential to hold the carrier liable does not amount to a waiver of its right to rely on its exemption if the goods are not located; there being nothing to indicate that the carrier did not intend to insist on its contract rights nor anything to show that the consignee was prejudiced. Old Dominion S. S. Co. v. C. F. Flanary & Co., 111 Va. 816, 69 S. E. 1107.

62 Ridgway Grain Co. v. Pennsylvania R. Co., 228 Pa. 641, 77 Atl. 1007, 31 L. R. A. (N. S.) 1178; Sheldon v. N. Y. Cent. & H. R. R. Co., 61 Misc. Rep. 274, 113 N. Y. Supp. 676.

63 Const. Ky. § 196. For cases involving this provision, see The City of Clarksville (D. C.) 94 Fed. 201; Barnes v. Long Island R. Co., 191 N. Y. 528, 84 N. E. 1108; Southern Exp. Co. v. Fox & Logan, 131 Ky. 257, 115 S. W. 184, 117 S. W. 270, 133 Am. St. Rep. 241.

64 Const. Neb. art. 11, § 4; Missouri Pac. Ry. Co. v. Vandeventer, 26 Neb. 222, 41 N. W. 998, 3 L. R. A. 129; Pennsylvania Co. v. Kennard Glass & Paint Co., 59 Neb. 435, 81 N. W. 372; Wabash R. Co. v. Sharpe, 76 Neb. 424, 107 N. W. 758, 124 Am. St. Rep. 823.

bility, as imposed by the common law. In Iowa,[55] Texas,[56] and, it seems, Virginia,[57] a like result is obtained through statutes. In other states, the statutes either restrict the carrier's right to qualify his liability by contract,[58] or require that the contract, to be valid, must be in a specified form or entered into with designated formalities,[59] such as, for example, the signature of the shipper.[60]

Federal Interstate Commerce Act—Carmack Amendment

By far the most important of all the statutory provisions concerning the carrier's limitation of his liability by contract is the Carmack amendment to the Interstate Commerce Act.[61] This provides: "That any common carrier, railroad or transportation company receiving property for transportation from a point in one state to a point in another state shall issue a receipt or bill of lading therefor and shall be liable to the lawful holder thereof for any loss, damage, or injury to such property caused by it or by any common carrier, railroad, or transportation company to which such property may be delivered or over whose line or lines such property may pass, and *no contracts, receipt, rule or regulation shall exempt such common carrier, railroad or transportation company from the liability hereby imposed: Provided, that nothing in this section*

[55] Code Iowa 1897, § 2074; Lucas v. Burlington, C. R. & N. Ry. Co., 112 Iowa, 594, 84 N. W. 673; Winn v. American Express Co., 149 Iowa, 259, 128 N. W. 663; Blair & Jackson v. Wells Fargo & Co., 155 Iowa, 190, 135 N. W. 615.

[56] Rev. St. 1895, art. 320; British & Foreign Marine Ins. Co. v. Gulf, C. & S. F. Ry. Co., 63 Tex. 475, 51 Am. Rep. 661; Houston & T. C. R. Co. v. Burke, 55 Tex. 323, 40 Am. Rep. 808; Missouri Pac. Ry. Co. v. International Marine Ins. Co., 84 Tex. 149, 19 S. W. 459; Texas & P. Ry. Co. v. Richmond, 94 Tex. 571, 63 S. E. 619.

[57] Code 1904, § 1294c, subsec. 24; Chesapeake & O. R. Co. v. Pew, 109 Va. 288, 64 S. E. 35; Southern Exp. Co. v. Keeler, 109 Va. 459, 64 S. E. 38; Adams Exp. Co. v. Green, 112 Va. 527, 72 S. E. 102.

[58] St. Louis & S. F. R. Co. v. Sherlock, 59 Kan. 23, 51 Pac. 899; Cutter v. Wells Fargo & Co., 237 Ill. 247, 86 N. E. 695; Baum v. Long Island R. Co., 58 Misc. Rep. 34, 108 N. Y. Supp. 1113; Morgan v. Woolverton, 203 N. Y. 52, 96 N. E. 354, 36 L. R. A. (N. S.) 640.

[59] Chicago & N. W. Ry. Co. v. Chapman, 133 Ill. 96, 24 N. E. 417, 8 L. R. A. 508, 23 Am. St. Rep. 587; Coats v. Chicago, R. I. & P. R. Co., 239 Ill. 154, 87 N. E. 929; Central of Georgia Ry. Co. v. Kavanaugh, 92 Fed. 56, 34 C. C. A. 203; Atlanta & W. P. R. Co. v. Jacobs' Pharmacy Co., 135 Ga. 113, 68 S. E. 1039; Atchison, T. & S. F. R. Co. v. Rodgers, 16 N. M. 120, 113 Pac. 805.

[60] Feige v. Michigan Cent. Ry. Co., 62 Mich. 1, 28 N. W. 685; Richmond & A. R. Co. v. R. A. Patterson Tobacco Co., 92 Va. 670, 24 S. E. 261, 41 L. R. A. 511, affirmed 169 U. S. 311, 18 Sup. Ct. 335, 42 L. Ed. 759.

[61] This is a part of section 20 of the act (Act Feb. 4, 1887, c. 104, 24 Stat. 386 [U. S. Comp. St. 1901, p. 3169], as amended by Act June 29, 1906, c. 3591, § 7, pars. 11, 12, 34 Stat. 595 [U. S. Comp. St. Supp. 1911, p. 1307]).

shall deprive any holder of such receipt or bill of lading of, any remedy or right of action which he has under existing law." It is with the italicized portion that we are here chiefly concerned; the portion fixing liability on the initial carrier for the defaults of connecting carriers will be subsequently discussed in connection with connecting carriers.[62]

In connection with the portion italicized it will be seen that it contains two provisions. One of these prevents the initial carrier from relieving himself by contract, rule, or regulation of the liability imposed on him by the amendment for the defaults of connecting carriers. Another provision secures to the holder of the receipt or bill of lading "any remedy or right of action which he has under existing law."

The history of the amendment led many courts to the view that by "existing law" was meant here state laws, under which construction shippers secured the full benefit of state statutes and Constitutions forbidding any limitation by contract on the carrier's part of his full common-law liability.[63] In recent cases, however, "existing law" is held by the United States Supreme Court to mean, not state law, but federal law.[64] It is further held that the effect of the Carmack amendment is to withdraw contracts for interstate shipments entirely from the influence of state regulation and to bring them under one uniform rule or law.[65]

The following language is used by Justice Lurton in a very recent case:[66] "The liability sought to be enforced is the 'liability' of an interstate carrier for loss or damage under an interstate contract of shipment declared by the Carmack amendment of the Hepburn Act of 1906 [Act June 29, 1906, c. 3591, § 7, pars. 11, 12, 34 Stat. 595 (U. S. Comp. St. Supp. 1911, p. 1307)]. The validity of any stipulation in such a contract which involves a construction

[62] See post, pp. 451–452.

[63] See article contending strongly for this view in 11 Mich. Law Rev. 460, by Prof. E. C. Goddard; Atchison, T. & S. F. R. Co. v. Rodgers, 16 N. M. 120, 113 Pac. 805; Uber v. Chicago, M. & St. P. Ry. Co., 151 Wis. 431, 138 N. W. 57; Latta v. Chicago, St. P., M. & O. R. Co., 172 Fed. 850, 97 C. C. A. 198; Adams Exp. Co. v. Green, 112 Va. 527, 72 S. E. 102.

[64] ADAMS EXP. CO. v. CRONINGER, 226 U. S. 491, 33 Sup. Ct. 148, 57 L. Ed. 314, 44 L. R. A. (N. S.) 257, Dobie Cas. Bailments and Carriers, 228; Chicago, St. P., M. & O. R. Co. v. Latta, 226 U. S. 519, 33 Sup. Ct. 155, 57 L. Ed. 328; Chicago, B. & Q. R. Co. v. Miller, 226 U. S. 513, 33 Sup. Ct. 155, 57 L. Ed. 323; Kansas City Southern R. Co. v. Carl, 227 U. S. 639, 33 Sup. Ct. 391, 57 L. Ed. 683; Missouri, K. & T. R. Co. v. Harriman, 227 U. S. 657, 33 Sup. Ct. 397, 57 L. Ed. 690.

[65] See cases cited in preceding note, particularly the last two cases.

[66] Missouri, K. & T. R. Co. v. Harriman, 227 U. S. 657, 672, 33 Sup. Ct. 397, 57 L. Ed. 690.

of the statute, and the validity of a limitation thereby imposed, is a *federal question, to be determined under the general common law, and, as such, is withdrawn from the field of state law or legislation.* The liability imposed by the statute is the liability imposed by the common law upon a common carrier, and may be limited or qualified by special contract with the shipper, provided the limitation or qualification be just and reasonable and does not exempt from loss or responsibility due to negligence." [67]

It is held that the Carmack amendment does not forbid the limitation of liability, in case of loss or damage, to a valuation agreed on for the purpose of determining which of two lawful alternative rates shall be applied to the particular shipment.[68] The amendment also permits reasonable contracts as to the time within which suit must be brought after the happening of the loss or injury.[69]

[67] To sustain this, the court cited the following cases: ADAMS EXP. CO. v. CRONINGER, 226 U. S. 491, 33 Sup. Ct. 148, 57 L. Ed. 314, 44 L. R. A. (N. S.) 257, Dobie Cas. Bailments and Carriers, 228; Michigan Cent. R. Co. v. Vreeland, 227 U. S. 59, 33 Sup. Ct. 192, 57 L. Ed. 417; York Mfg. Co. v. Illinois C. R. Co., 3 Wall. 107, 18 L. Ed. 170; New York C. R. Co. v. Lockwood, 17 Wall. 357, 21 L. Ed. 627; SOUTHERN EXP. CO. v. CALDWELL, 21 Wall. 264, 267, 22 L. Ed. 556, Dobie Cas. Bailments and Carriers, 226; Hart v. Pennsylvania R. Co., 112 U. S. 331, 5 Sup. Ct. 151, 28 L. Ed. 717.

[68] Kansas City Southern R. Co. v. Carl, 227 U. S. 639, 33 Sup. Ct. 391, 57 L. Ed. 683. See, also, cases cited in note 64.

[69] Missouri, K. & T. R. Co. v. Harriman, 227 U. S. 657, 33 Sup. Ct. 397, 57 L. Ed. 690.

CHAPTER XII

COMMENCEMENT AND TERMINATION OF THE LIABILITY OF THE COMMON CARRIER OF GOODS

COMMENCEMENT OF THE COMMON CARRIER'S LIABILITY—DELIVERY TO THE CARRIER

136. The extraordinary liability of the common carrier attaches only from the time when the goods are delivered to, and accepted by, the carrier for immediate transportation.

Delivery for Immediate Transportation

We have already seen that the duties of the ordinary bailment, arising from that relation, begin only when there has been a delivery of the goods to such bailee.[1] In the case of the common carrier, though, in order that his unusual liability may attach, there must be, not only a delivery of the goods to the carrier, but also a delivery for immediate transportation.[2] This delivery must, in

[1] Ante, § 10.

[2] Michigan Southern & N. I. R. Co. v. Shurtz, 7 Mich. 515; Grand Tower Mfg. & Transp. Co. v. Ullman, 89 Ill. 244; Clarke v. Needles, 25 Pa. 338; Merriam v. Hartford & N. H. R. Co., 20 Conn. 354, 52 Am. Dec. 344; Blossom v. Griffin, 13 N. Y. 569, 67 Am. Dec. 75; Evershed v. Railway Co., 47 Law J. Q. B. (Eng.) 284, 3 Q. B. Div. 134; St. Louis, I. M. & S. Ry. Co. v. Murphy, 60 Ark. 333, 30 S. W. 419, 46 Am. St. Rep. 202; London & L. Fire Ins. Co. v. Rome, W. & O. R. Co., 144 N. Y. 200, 39 N. E. 79, 43 Am. St. Rep. 752; Id., 68 Hun, 598, 23 N. Y. Supp. 231; Stewart v. Gracy, 93 Tenn. 314, 27 S. W. 664; Gulf, C. & S. F. Ry. Co. v. Trawick, 80 Tex. 270, 15 S. W. 568, 18 S. W. 948; McCullough v. Wabash Western Ry. Co., 34 Mo. App. 23; Barron v. Eldredge, 100 Mass. 455, 1 Am. Rep. 126; Illinois Cent. R. Co. v. Smyser, 38 Ill. 354, 87 Am. Dec. 301; TATE v. YAZOO & M. V. R. CO., 78 Miss. 842, 29 South. 392, 84 Am. St. Rep. 649, Dobie Cas. Bailments and Carriers, 232; St. Louis & S. F. R. Co. v. Cavendar, 170 Ala. 601, 54 South.

addition, be accepted by the carrier;[3] but the subject of delivery alone will be discussed in this section, while the next section will deal with such acceptance.

The strict responsibility of the common carrier, then, dates only from a delivery to him for the purpose of immediate transportation.[4] A delivery for any other purpose will not have this effect. The strict liability attaches after a delivery for immediate transportation, however, though the goods, after such delivery, may remain in the carrier's storehouse,[5] though he may then have no car or vehicle ready to take the goods, or even though they are not loaded on such car or vehicle for several days.[6]

The delivery, however, is not one for immediate transportation if anything remains to be done by the shipper before the goods can be sent on their way.[7] If by the usage and course of business, and especially if by express request, the shipment is delayed for further orders from the shipper as to the destination of the goods, or for the convenience of the shipper, then, during the time of such delay,

54; St. Louis, I. M. & S. R. Co. v. Citizens' Bank of Little Rock, 87 Ark. 26, 112 S. W. 154, 128 Am. St. Rep. 17. See, also, cases cited in notes 4–8.

[3] See cases cited in § 137.

[4] See cases cited in note 2; Dixon v. Central of Georgia Ry. Co., 110 Ga. 173, 35 S. E. 369; Schmidt v. Chicago & N. W. Ry. Co., 90 Wis. 504, 63 N. W. 1057; Basnight v. Atlantic & N. C. R. Co., 111 N. C. 592, 16 S. E. 323; St. Louis, I. M. & S. R. Co. v. Knight, 122 U. S. 79, 7 Sup. Ct. 1132, 30 L. Ed. 1077; Pittsburg, C., C. & St. L. R. Co. v. American Tobacco Co., 126 Ky. 582, 104 S. W. 377, 31 Ky. Law Rep. 1013; Milne v. Chicago, R. I. & P. R. Co., 155 Mo. App. 465, 135 S. W. 85; Central of Georgia R. Co. v. Sigma Lumber Co., 170 Ala. 627, 54 South. 205, Ann. Cas. 1912D, 965; Murray v. International S. S. Co., 170 Mass. 166, 48 N. E. 1093, 64 Am. St. Rep. 290.

[5] Rogers v. Wheeler, 52 N. Y. 262; Fitchburg & W. R. Co. v. Hanna, 6 Gray (Mass.) 539, 66 Am. Dec. 427; London & L. Fire Ins. Co. v. Rome, W. & O. R. Co., 144 N. Y. 200, 39 N. E. 79, 43 Am. St. Rep. 752; White v. Goodrich Transp. Co., 46 Wis. 493, 1 N. W. 75.

[6] Meloche v. Chicago, M. & St. P. R. Co., 116 Mich. 69, 74 N. W. 301; St. Louis, I. M. & S. Ry. Co. v. Murphy, 60 Ark. 333, 30 S. W. 419, 46 Am. St. Rep. 202; Gregory v. Wabash Ry. Co., 46 Mo. App. 574; Grand Tower Mfg. & Transp. Co. v. Ullman, 89 Ill. 244; Clarke v. Needles, 25 Pa. 338.

[7] ST. LOUIS, A. & T. H. R. CO. v. MONTGOMERY, 39 Ill. 335, Dobie Cas. Bailments and Carriers, 234; Michigan Southern & N. I. R. Co. v. Shurtz, 7 Mich. 515; Moses v. Boston & M. R. R., 4 Fost. (24 N. H.) 71, 55 Am. Dec. 222; Rogers v. Wheeler, 52 N. Y. 262; O'Neill v. New York Cent. & H. R. R. Co., 60 N. Y. 138; Wade v. Wheeler, 3 Lans. (N. Y.) 201; Barron v. Eldredge, 100 Mass. 455, 1 Am. Rep. 126; Fitchburg & W. R. Co. v. Hanna, 6 Gray (Mass.) 539, 66 Am. Dec. 427; St. Louis, I. M. & S. Ry. Co. v. Knight, 122 U. S. 79, 7 Sup. Ct. 1132, 30 L. Ed. 1077; Louisville & N. R. Co. v. United States, 39 Ct. Cl. 405; Dixon v. Central of Georgia Ry. Co., 110 Ga. 173, 35 S. E. 369.

the carrier's liability is merely that of a warehouseman.[8] The more stringent liability of a common carrier attaches only when the duty of immediate transportation arises.

SAME—ACCEPTANCE BY THE CARRIER

137. The acceptance of the goods by the carrier may be, and usually is, express; but it may also be implied, as where the goods are left in a certain place in accordance with the contract of the carrier thus to receive them.

Acceptance by Carrier

It has been seen that a bailment cannot arise in the absence of the bailee's consent.[9] Liability as a common carrier, therefore, does not attach until the goods have been accepted for immediate transportation by the carrier.[10] No act of the shipper alone

[8] ST. LOUIS, A. & T. H. R. CO. v. MONTGOMERY, 39 Ill. 335, Dobie Cas. Bailments and Carriers, 234; Barron v. Eldredge, 100 Mass. 455, 1 Am. Rep. 126; Mt. Vernon Co. v. Alabama G. S. R. Co., 92 Ala. 296, 8 South. 687; O'Neill v. New York Cent. & H. R. R. Co., 60 N. Y. 138; Schmidt v. Chicago & N. W. Ry. Co., 90 Wis. 504, 63 N. W. 1057; St. Louis, I. M. & S. R. Co. v. Citizens' Bank of Little Rock, 87 Ark. 26, 112 S. W. 154, 128 Am. St. Rep. 17; American Lead Pencil Co. v. Nashville, C. & St. L. Ry., 124 Tenn. 57, 134 S. W. 613, 32 L. R. A. (N. S.) 323; St. Louis & S. F. R. Co. v. Cavender, 170 Ala. 601, 54 South. 54; Missouri Pac. Ry. Co. v. Riggs, 10 Kan. App. 578, 62 Pac. 712.

[9] Ante, § 11.

[10] Missouri Pac. R. Co. v. McFadden, 154 U. S. 155, 14 Sup. Ct. 990, 38 L. Ed. 944. "There must be either an actual or constructive acceptance by the carrier, or the contract of bailment will not arise. The essential element of such a contract is that the bailee is to be trusted with the goods, and if he is not made aware of the intention of the party to trust the goods to his keeping, or if the party, instead of trusting the goods to him, still retains the care of them, the bailment to the carrier evidently does not arise, or arises only in a modified form. Thus, where a wharfinger delivered goods, which were sent to a wharf, to go on board a vessel, to one of the crew, and did not deliver them to the captain of the vessel, or to some other person that he might reasonably presume to be in authority, it was held that he had not discharged his duty, and he, and not the shipper [the carrier], was liable for the loss which occurred owing to his negligence." Wood, Browne, Carr. § 90. And see Leigh v. Smith, 1 Car. & P. (Eng.) 638; TATE v. YAZOO & M. V. R. CO., 78 Miss. 842, 29 South. 392, 84 Am. St. Rep. 649, Dobie Cas. Bailments and Carriers, 232; St. Louis, I. M. & S. Ry. Co. v. Murphy, 60 Ark. 333, 30 S. W. 419, 46 Am. St. Rep. 202; Illinois Cent. R. Co. v. Smyser, 38 Ill. 354, 87 Am. Dec. 301; Southern Exp. Co. v. McVeigh, 20 Grat. (Va.) 264; Williams v. Southern R. Co., 155 N. C. 260, 71 S. E. 346. A carrier's liability begins when it receives freight, and does not depend upon issuance of a bill of lading. St. Louis, I. M. & S. R. Co. v. C. C. Burrow & Co., 89 Ark. 178, 116 S. W. 198.

can impose the strict liability on the common carrier. The acceptance of the goods by the carrier, though, may be either express or implied.[11] When it is express, after a delivery of the goods, there is little difficulty, so the question of implied acceptance will next be discussed.

Implied Acceptance—Contract, Custom, and Usage

The carrier, for his own protection, may make reasonable regulations as to the place and manner of delivery. The parties may themselves agree upon the place and manner of delivery, and their agreement will govern. So, if they agree that goods for transportation may be deposited at any particular place without notice to the carrier, a deposit in that place will constitute a sufficient delivery.[12] The acceptance by the carrier is then presumed, if, indeed, it cannot be said to have been made in advance.

So, also, an established custom and usage in regard to receiving goods for transportation will bind the parties. Where goods are left in the usual manner at the usual place, in accordance with the established custom of the carrier to receive them there, acceptance is presumed.[13] "It is well settled by a series of adjudications

[11] TATE v. YAZOO & M. V. R. CO., 78 Miss. 842, 29 South. 392, 84 Am. St. Rep. 649, Dobie Cas. Bailments and Carriers, 232; Merriam v. Hartford & N. H. R. Co., 20 Conn. 354, 52 Am. Dec. 344; Converse v. Norwich & N. Y. Transp. Co., 33 Conn. 166; Ford v. Mitchell, 21 Ind. 54; GREEN v. MILWAUKEE & ST. P. R. CO., 38 Iowa, 100; Id., 41 Iowa, 410, Dobie Cas. Bailments and Carriers, 235; Wright v. Caldwell, 3 Mich. 51; Packard v. Getman, 6 Cow. (N. Y.) 757, 16 Am. Dec. 475; Freeman v. Newton, 3 E. D. Smith (N. Y.) 246; Illinois Cent. R. Co. v. Smyser, 38 Ill. 354, 87 Am. Dec. 301; O'Bannon v. Southern Exp. Co., 51 Ala. 481; Evansville & T. H. R. Co. v. Keith, 8 Ind. App. 57, 35 N. E. 296. See, also, Clara Turner Co. v. New York, N. H. & H. R. Co., 86 Conn. 71, 84 Atl. 298; Colorado & S. R. Co. v. Breniman, 22 Colo. App. 1, 125 Pac. 855.

[12] Merriam v. Hartford & N. H. R. Co., 20 Conn. 354, 52 Am. Dec. 344; Montgomery & E. Ry. Co. v. Kolb, 73 Ala. 396, 49 Am. Rep. 54; Georgia S. & F. R. Co. v. Marchman, 121 Ga. 235, 48 S. E. 961. Where goods were loaded in a car upon a side track as to which the shipper and carrier had a contract providing that as to cars so loaded delivery to the carrier should be deemed to have taken place when the carrier should remove the cars from the side track and place them in its freight train for shipment, the carrier was not liable for loss of the goods in an accidental fire, started after they were loaded and while the car was standing on the side track, where the fire was not occasioned by the carrier's negligence, though its agent had issued bills of lading for the goods; delivery thereof to the carrier not having been consummated in view of the agreement. Bainbridge Grocery Co. v. Atlantic Coast Line R. Co., 8 Ga. App. 677, 70 S. E. 154.

[13] Lake Shore & M. S. Ry. Co. v. Foster, 104 Ind. 293, 4 N. E. 22, 54 Am. Rep. 319; Wright v. Caldwell, 3 Mich. 51; Converse v. Norwich & N. Y. Transp. Co., 33 Conn. 166; Merriam v. Hartford & N. H. R. Co., 20 Conn. 354, 52 Am. Dec. 344; GREEN v. MILWAUKEE & ST. P. R. CO., 38 Iowa

of high authority that if a uniform custom is established and recognized by the carrier, and is known to the public, that property intended for carriage may be deposited in a particular place, without express notice to him, that a deposit of property for that purpose, in accordance with the custom, is constructive notice, and would render any other form of delivery unnecessary. The rule is founded in reason, as the usage, if habitual, is a declaration by the carrier to the public that a delivery of property in accordance with the usage will be deemed an acceptance of it by him for the purpose of transportation. To allow a carrier, when property is thus delivered, to set up by way of defense the general rule which requires express notice, would operate as a fraud upon the public, and lead to manifest injustice." [14]

Thus, a deposit of cotton in the street adjacent to a railroad platform, in accordance with a well-established custom to deposit it there for carriage, is sufficient.[15] So, where goods were delivered, in conformity with a clear usage, in the usual manner, for transportation by a common carrier, on his private dock, which was in his exclusive use for the purpose of receiving property to be transported by him, it was held that such delivery was a good delivery to the carrier, to render him liable as a common carrier for the loss of the goods, although neither he nor his agent was otherwise notified of such delivery.[16] The custom or usage must be strictly followed, however, or the carrier will not be bound. Nor is the doctrine of implied acceptance one to be unduly extended. The courts, therefore, apply it with caution.[17]

Agents

The delivery of the goods to, and their acceptance by, the carrier may, of course, be by duly-authorized agents.[18] In such cases, the ordinary rules of agency apply. An authority given by the shipper to an agent to deliver goods to a common carrier for trans-

100; Id., 41 Iowa, 410, Doble Cas. Bailments and Carriers, 235; Lackland v. Chicago & A. R. Co., 101 Mo. App. 420, 74 S. W. 505; Washburn Crosby Co. v. Boston & A. R. Co., 180 Mass. 252, 62 N. E. 590; Evansville & T. H. R. Co. v. Keith, 8 Ind. App. 57, 35 N. E. 296.

14 Whipple, J., in Wright v. Caldwell, 3 Mich. 51.

15 Montgomery & E. Ry. Co. v. Kolb, 73 Ala. 396, 49 Am. Rep. 54.

16 Merriam v. Hartford & N. H. R. Co., 20 Conn. 354, 52 Am. Dec. 344. See, also, Converse v. Norwich & N. Y. Transp. Co., 33 Conn. 166.

17 1 Hutch. Carr. § 118.

18 Rogers v. Long Island R. Co., 2 Lans. (N. Y.) 269; Harrell v. Wilmington & W. R. Co., 106 N. C. 258, 11 S. E. 286; Nelson v. Hudson River R. Co., 48 N. Y. 498; Squire v. New York Cent. R. Co., 98 Mass. 239, 93 Am. Dec. 162; Springer v. Westcott, 166 N. Y. 117, 59 N. E. 693; Outland v. Seaboard Air Line R. Co., 134 N. C. 350, 46 S. E. 735.

portation includes all the necessary and usual means of carrying it into effect. It can only be executed by obtaining the consent of the carrier to receive them, and the agent is therefore authorized to make the usual contract containing the ordinary terms on which such goods are transported by the carrier.[19]

When the goods are accepted by an agent of the carrier with actual authority, his acceptance is, of course, binding on the carrier. Even if the agent has not such actual authority, his acts will, under the doctrine of agency by estoppel, still be binding on the carrier, if the latter has clothed him with such apparent authority. Accordingly a shipper is justified in assuming that a person in charge of the carrier's usual place for receiving goods has authority to accept such goods and contract for the carrier.[20] This would be

[19] Nelson v. Hudson River R. Co., 48 N. Y. 498; Jennings v. Grand Trunk Ry. Co., 52 Hun, 227, 5 N. Y. Supp. 140; Squire v New York Cent. R. Co., 98 Mass. 239, 93 Am. Dec. 162; York Co. v. Illinois Cent. R. Co., 3 Wall. 113, 18 L. Ed. 170; London & N. W. R. Co. v. Bartlett, 7 Hurl. & N. (Eng.) 400; Shelton v. Merchants' Dispatch Transp. Co., 59 N. Y. 258.

[20] Cronkite v. Wells, 32 N. Y. 247, 253; Rogers v. Long Island R. Co., 2 Lans. (N. Y.) 269; Ouimit v. Henshaw, 35 Vt. 605, 84 Am. Dec. 646; Witbeck v. Schuyler, 44 Barb. (N. Y.) 469. But not where the apparent scope of his employment shows it to be clearly beyond his authority. Ford v. Mitchell, 21 Ind. 54; Trowbridge v. Chapin, 23 Conn. 595. "It is the duty of a railway company to have servants capable of giving directions, and of dealing with everything that the exigency of the traffic may require (Taff Vale Rail Co. v. Giles, 23 Law J. Q. B. [Eng.] 43, 2 El. & Bl. 823); and their servants, acting in the ordinary scope of their employment, would have authority to receive goods, and enter into contracts as to the forwarding of them (Long v. Horne, 1 Car. & P. [Eng.] 610; Winkfield v. Packington, 2 Car. & P. [Eng.] 599). As a rule the officials at a railway station (Pickford v. Railroad Co., 12 Mees. & W. [Eng.] 766; Wilson v. Railroad Co., 17 Law T. [Eng.] 223); the company's draymen, where such are employed to collect, or usually collect, goods on the road, or at the houses of the consignors (Davey v. Mason, Car. & M. [Eng.] 45; Baxendale v. Hart, 21 Law J. Exch. 123, 6 Exch. [Eng.] 769); the servants of another carrier, engaged by the company, under a subcontract, to deliver and collect goods (Machin v. Railroad Co., 17 Law J. Exch. 271, 2 Exch. [Eng.] 415); a person accustomed to book for the company, although the servant of, and deriving his authority from, another and separate carrier, who undertakes the transit during a stage of the journey anterior to the goods actually coming into the company's possession (McCourt v. Railroad Co., 3 Ir. C. L. 107, 402),—would be considered persons to whom a good delivery might be made, and who would be competent to enter into a contract, ordinary or special, for the carriage of the goods. But a servant could not bind the company beyond the authority presumed from his employment (Great Western R. Co. v. Willis, 34 Law J. C. P. 195, 18 C. B. N. S. [Eng.] 748; Horn v. Railroad Co., 42 Law J. C. P. 59, L. R. 8 C. P. [Eng.] 131; per Blackburn, J.); nor even to the extent of the authority presumable from his employment, if the customer have notice of a more limited authority (Walker v. Railroad Co., 23 Law J. Q. B. [Eng.] 73, 2 El. & Bl. 750); nor when acting in

true, even though it subsequently appeared that the carrier had given no such authority to such person, but that another employé had charge of this department of the carrier's business at the place in question.

Delivery may be made to a carrier wherever he or his authorized agent will accept the goods.[21] But if the delivery is not made at the place appointed by the carrier, or at his regular office or place of business, it must be accepted by the carrier himself, or his duly authorized agent, or the carrier will not be bound.[22] The presumption that one in charge of the usual place of receiving goods has authority to accept them does not apply where the delivery is made elsewhere.[23]

SAME—EVIDENCE OF DELIVERY AND ACCEPTANCE

138. The delivery of the goods to, and their acceptance by, the carrier can be proved by any evidence that is relevant and proper. Such evidence, however, is usually incorporated in the Bill of Lading.

Bills of Lading

The general nature of the bill of lading has already been discussed.[24] As the issuance of these instruments by the carrier is almost universal, they form the readiest and most available means of proving the delivery and acceptance necessary to charge the carrier.

It has already been noted, too, that the bill of lading is not only a receipt, but also a contract,[25] and its importance as an instrument standing for, and as a means of dealing with, the goods has also been mentioned. These dealings are not confined to the consignee,

defiance of the known course of business of the company" (Redm. Ry. Carr. p. 42). See, also, in general, Stoner v. Chicago G. W. Ry. Co., 109 Iowa, 551, 80 N. W. 569; Lowenstein v. Lombard, Ayres & Co., 164 N. Y. 324, 58 N. E. 44; Rudell v. Ogdensburg Transit Co., 117 Mich. 568, 76 N. W. 380, 44 L. R. A. 415; Pecos & N. T. R. Co. v. Cox (Tex. Civ. App.) 150 S. W. 265.

[21] Phillips v. Earle, 8 Pick. (Mass.) 182.

[22] Cronkite v. Wells, 32 N. Y. 247; Southern Exp. Co. v. Newby, 36 Ga. 635, 91 Am. Dec. 783. Cf. Witbeck v. Schuyler, 44 Barb. (N. Y.) 469; Missouri Coal & Oil Co. v. Hannibal & St. J. R. Co., 35 Mo. 84.

[23] Blanchard v. Isaacs, 3 Barb. (N. Y.) 388. See cases cited in preceding note.

[24] Ante, pp. 196, 211–214.

[25] See, also, Mears v. New York, N. H. & H. R. Co., 75 Conn. 171, 52 Atl. 610, 56 L. R. A. 884, 96 Am. St. Rep. 192; Chicago & N W. Ry. Co. v Simon, 160 Ill. 648, 43 N. E. 596; Pollard v. Vinton, 105 U. S. 7, 26 L. Ed. 998.

but the consignor, by taking the bill of lading to his own order, reserves the disposal of the goods, and may even prevent the passing of title to the consignee, for whom the goods are ultimately destined.[26] Thus since, under such a bill of lading, the carrier can deliver the goods to no one save the holder of the bill of lading properly indorsed, the consignor frequently uses it to secure the payment of the purchase price of the goods.[27]

This is usually done by the so-called "bill of lading with draft attached."[28] After the issuance of the bill of lading to shipper's order, this is sent to a bank at the destination of the goods, with a draft on the buyer for the purchase price of the goods shipped. Upon the payment of this draft (or its acceptance, as the case may be) by the buyer, he obtains the bill of lading. If the carrier, in such case, delivers the goods to the consignee, who has not the bill of lading, the carrier would be responsible to the holder of the bill of lading, properly indorsed.[29]

TERMINATION OF THE COMMON CARRIER'S LIABILITY—IN GENERAL

139. The common carrier's liability is terminated when the transportation is completed and the carrier has delivered the goods either to the consignee or to a connecting carrier according to the terms of the contract. There are also certain excuses for nondelivery by the carrier which operate in addition to relieve him of all responsibility. Under

[26] North Pennsylvania R. Co. v. Commercial Nat. Bank, 123 U. S. 727, 8 Sup. Ct. 266, 31 L. Ed. 287; Thompson v. Alabama Midland R. Co., 122 Ala. 378, 24 South. 931; Midland Nat. Bank v. Missouri Pac. Ry. Co., 132 Mo. 492, 33 S. W. 521, 53 Am. St. Rep. 505; Union Stockyards Co. v. Westcott, 47 Neb. 300, 66 N. W. 419; Libby v. Ingalls, 124 Mass. 503.

[27] Boatmen's Sav. Bank v. Western & A. R. Co., 81 Ga. 221, 7 S. E. 125; Joslyn v. Grand Trunk R. Co., 51 Vt. 92; The Thames, 14 Wall. 98, 20 L. Ed. 804; North Pennsylvania R. Co. v Commercial Nat. Bank, 123 U. S. 727, 8 Sup. Ct. 266, 31 L. Ed. 287; FORBES v. BOSTON & L. R. CO., 133 Mass. 154, Dobie Cas. Bailments and Carriers, 236.

[28] See, on this subject, 1 Hutch. Carr §§ 183–191; FORBES v. BOSTON & L. R. CO., 133 Mass. 154, Dobie Cas. Bailments and Carriers, 236.

[29] National Newark Banking Co. v. Delaware, L. & W. R. Co., 70 N. J. Law, 774, 58 Atl. 311, 66 L. R. A. 595, 103 Am. St. Rep. 825; Walters v. Western & A. R. Co., 66 Fed. 862, 14 C. C. A. 267; Tishomingo Sav. Inst. v. Johnson, Nesbitt & Co., 146 Ala. 691, 40 South. 503; Vaughn v. New York, N. H. & H. R. Co., 27 R. I. 235, 61 Atl. 695; Libby v. Ingalls, 124 Mass. 503; FORBES v. BOSTON & L. R. CO., 133 Mass. 154, Dobie Cas. Bailments and Carriers, 236.

certain circumstances, the liability of the carrier is not terminated, but his extraordinary insuring liability gives way to that of the ordinary warehouseman.

Analysis

The termination of the common carrier's liability can conveniently be considered under the following heads:

(1) Delivery to the consignee.

(2) Delivery to a connecting carrier.

(3) Excuses for nondelivery by the carrier.

These will be discussed in this order, in the remaining seven sections of this chapter. The termination by the third method (excuses for nondelivery) requires only very brief mention; but termination by the first and second methods will necessitate, owing both to the difficulties of these topics and their practical importance, more extended treatment.

SAME—DELIVERY TO CONSIGNEE

140. The duty of a proper delivery to the consignee resting on the common carrier, which terminates his liability, is usually held to involve four requisites, viz.: A delivery—

(a) To the proper person;

(b) At a proper time;

(c) At the proper place;

(d) In a proper manner.

When the carrier tenders a delivery of the goods involving the four requisites above set out, he is relieved of his rigorous responsibility, even though the tender be not accepted.[80] Of course, a delivery failing in some of the above requisites may be accepted as a good delivery by the consignee, who thus waives his right to insist on a proper delivery.[81] In such case the carrier is relieved of all liability.[82]

[80] See 2 Hutch. Carr. §§ 662, 664, 686; Gregg v. Illinois Cent. R. Co., 147 Ill. 550, 35 N. E. 343, 37 Am. St. Rep. 238; Gulf, C. & S. F. R. Co. v. A. B. Frank Co. (Tex. Civ. App.) 48 S. W. 210.

[81] Cleveland & P. R. Co. v. Sargent, 19 Ohio St. 438; Jewell v. Grand Trunk Ry., 55 N. H. 84; The Mohawk, 8 Wall. 153, 19 L. Ed. 406; Normile v. Northern Pac. R. Co., 36 Wash. 21, 77 Pac. 1087, 67 L. R. A. 271.

[82] Sweet v. Barney, 23 N. Y. 335; Bartlett v The Philadelphia, 32 Mo. 256; Anchor Mill Co. v. Burlington, C. R. & N. Ry. Co., 102 Iowa, 262, 71 N. W. 255.

If, however, the consignee refuses, as he has a right to refuse, the imperfect delivery, then the carrier is not relieved from his strict liability as to the goods.[33] The four requisites of a good delivery to the consignee will next be discussed in the order above set out.

SAME—SAME—DELIVERY TO THE PROPER PERSON

141. The common carrier of goods is an insurer as to delivery of the goods to the person to whom they are consigned. For any mistake in this respect the carrier is absolutely liable, regardless of the question of the care or diligence he has used.

Delivery to Wrong Person

A carrier, by accepting goods for transportation, agrees to deliver them according to the terms in the contract of shipment, and for a delivery to any person other than the consignee the carrier is liable.[34] The reasons for this rule have already been discussed.[35] If the carrier has, through fraud, mistake, or any other cause, delivered the goods to the wrong person, the fact that there has been no negligence on his part is not an excuse. The carrier is ab-

[33] Hill v Humphreys, 5 Watts & S. (Pa.) 123, 39 Am. Dec. 117; Houston & T. C. R. Co. v. Trammell, 28 Tex. Civ App. 312, 68 S. W. 716.

[34] PACIFIC EXP. CO. v. SHEARER, 160 Ill. 215, 43 N. E. 816, 37 L. R. A. 177, and note, 52 Am. St. Rep. 324, Dobie Cas. Bailments and Carriers, 239; Merchants' & Miners' Transp. Co. v. Moore & Co., 124 Ga. 482, 52 S. E. 802; McEntee v. New Jersey Steamboat Co., 45 N. Y. 34, 6 Am. Rep. 28; Price v. Oswego & S. Ry Co., 50 N. Y. 213, 10 Am. Rep. 475; Powell v. Myers, 26 Wend. (N. Y.) 591; Hawkins v. Hoffman, 6 Hill (N. Y.) 586, 41 Am. Dec. 767; American Merchants' Union Exp. Co. v. Milk, 73 Ill. 224; Samuel v. Cheney, 135 Mass. 278, 46 Am. Rep. 467; Claflin v. Boston & L. R. Co., 7 Allen (Mass.) 341; Hall v. Boston & W. R. Corp., 14 Allen (Mass.) 443, 92 Am. Dec. 783; Wernwag v. Philadelphia, W. & B. R. Co., 117 Pa. 46, 11 Atl. 868; American Exp. Co. v. Stack, 29 Ind. 27; American Exp. Co. v. Fletcher, 25 Ind. 492; Winslow v. Vermont & M. R. Co., 42 Vt. 700, 1 Am. Rep. 365; Southern Exp. Co. v. Van Meter, 17 Fla. 783, 35 Am. Rep. 107; Gosling v. Higgins, 1 Camp. 451; Lubbock v. Inglis, 1 Starkie (Eng.) 104. Where a carrier, on refusal of the consignee to receive goods, delivers them to one who represents himself to be the agent of the consignor, without notice to the latter, and the agent converts the goods to his own use, the carrier is liable therefor. American Sugar-Refining Co. v. McGhee, 96 Ga. 27, 21 S. E. 383. See, also, Adrian Knitting Co. v. Wabash R. Co., 145 Mich. 323, 108 N. W. 706; Security Trust Co. v. Wells, Fargo & Co. Exp., 178 N. Y. 620, 70 N. E. 1109.

[35] This principle is applicable to bailees in general and was discussed in that connection. See ante, § 19.

solutely liable as an insurer for delivery to the right person, and the question of diligence is immaterial.[86]

This idea is admirably expressed in the following language from Hutchinson on Carriers (section 668), adopted by the Supreme Court of Illinois in the leading case of PACIFIC EXPRESS CO. v. SHEARER:[87] "No circumstances of fraud, imposition, or mistake will excuse the common carrier for a delivery to the wrong person. The law exacts of him absolute certainty that the person

[86] PACIFIC EXP. CO. v. SHEARER, 160 Ill. 215, 43 N. E. 816, 37 L. R. A. 177, and note, 52 Am. St. Rep. 324, Dobie Cas. Bailments and Carriers, 239; McEntee v. New Jersey Steamboat Co., 45 N. Y. 34, 6 Am. Rep. 28; Price v. Oswego & S. Ry. Co., 50 N. Y. 213, 10 Am. Rep. 475; Guillaume v. Hamburgh & A. Packet Co., 42 N. Y. 212, 1 Am. Rep. 512; Viner v. New York, A. G. & W. S. S. Co., 50 N. Y. 23; Claflin v. Boston & L. R. Co., 7 Allen (Mass.) 341; Shenk v. Philadelphia Steam Propeller Co., 60 Pa. 109, 100 Am. Dec. 541; Pennsylvania R. Co. v. Stern, 119 Pa. 24, 12 Atl. 756, 4 Am. St. Rep. 626; Wernwag v. Philadelphia, W. & B. R. Co., 117 Pa. 46, 11 Atl. 868; American Merchants' Union Exp. Co. v. Milk, 73 Ill. 224; Ela v. American Merchants' Union Exp. Co., 29 Wis. 611, 9 Am. Rep. 619; McCulloch v. McDonald, 91 Ind. 240; Merchants' Despatch & Transp. Co. v. Merriam, 111 Ind. 5, 11 N. E. 954; McEwen v. Jeffersonville, M. & I. R. Co., 33 Ind. 368, 5 Am. Rep. 216; Howard v. Old Dominion S. S. Co., 83 N. C. 158, 35 Am. Rep. 571; Adams v. Blankenstein, 2 Cal. 413, 56 Am. Dec. 350; Hayes v. Wells, Fargo & Co., 23 Cal. 185, 83 Am. Dec. 89; Southern Exp. Co. v. Crook, 44 Ala. 468, 4 Am. Rep. 140. A carrier who makes a mistake in delivery of goods is liable in damages for any diminution in value between the date of miscarriage and the time of their coming into the hands or under the control of the consignees. Vincent v. Rather, 31 Tex. 77, 98 Am. Dec. 516. Existence of local custom to deliver goods to person holding unindorsed bill of lading, unknown to the consignor when the goods were shipped, is no defense to an action for the value of goods so delivered. Weyand v. Atchison, T. & S. F. Ry. Co., 75 Iowa, 573, 39 N W. 899, 1 L. R. A. 650, 9 Am. St. Rep. 504. An agent sold goods on credit. His principal sent them marked C. O. D. The carrier, on a written order of the agent, delivered the goods without receiving the cash. Held, that it was a question for the jury whether the mark "C. O. D." was notice to the carrier of the agent's want of authority. Daylight Burner Co. v. Odlin, 51 N. H. 56, 12 Am. Rep. 45. Where consignor of goods is guilty of negligence in not properly marking their destination upon them, carriers are not liable for injuries arising from their being missent. Congar v. Chicago & N. W. Ry. Co., 24 Wis. 157, 1 Am. Rep. 164. See, also, Cavallaro v. Texas & P. Ry. Co., 110 Cal. 348, 42 Pac. 918, 52 Am. St. Rep. 94; Southern R. Co. v. Webb, 143 Ala. 304, 39 South. 262, 111 Am. St. Rep. 45, 5 Ann. Cas. 97; Dudley v. Chicago, M. & St. P. R. Co., 58 W. Va. 604, 52 S. E. 718, 3 L. R. A. (N. S.) 1135, 112 Am. St. Rep. 1027; Brown v. Cleveland, C., C. & St. L. Ry. Co., 155 Ill. App. 187; Seaboard Air Line Ry. Co. v. Phillips, 108 Md. 285, 70 Atl. 232; Equitable Powder Mfg. Co. v. St. Louis & S. F. R. Co., 99 Ark. 497, 138 S. W. 964. See cases cited in notes 34, 38–41.

[87] PACIFIC EXP. CO. v. SHEARER, 160 Ill. 215, 43 N. E. 816, 37 L. R. A. 177, and note, 52 Am. St. Rep. 324, Dobie Cas. Bailments and Carriers, 239.

to whom the delivery was made is the party rightfully entitled to the goods, and puts upon him the entire risks of mistakes in this respect, no matter from what cause occasioned, however justifiable the delivery may seem to have been, or however satisfactory the circumstances or proof of the identity may have been to his mind; and no excuse has ever been allowed for a delivery to a person for whom the goods were not directed or consigned."

Thus, if an impostor induces the consignor to ship goods to a fictitious person or firm, the carrier is liable for a delivery to the impostor.[38] So, too, the carrier is liable if an impostor procures a consignment of goods to be made to a real person, and then secures the goods from the carrier by representing himself to be that person.[39] A like result follows when the goods are delivered by the carrier on a forged order,[40] or when there is a delivery by mistake of the carrier to the wrong person, regardless of how the mistake was made.[41]

The case in this connection about which there is probably the greatest conflict of authority is when a swindler assumes (exactly or substantially) the name and address of a real firm or person in good standing and writes to a dealer in another city, asking that goods be shipped to him. If this is done, and the goods are delivered to the swindler, is the carrier responsible? Was the consignee the person who ordered the goods (the swindler), or the firm or person in good standing? Samuel v. Cheney [42] is probably the leading case exempting the carrier from liability The opposite view, holding the carrier liable (which seems to be the better doc-

[38] Price v. Oswego & S. Ry. Co., 50 N. Y. 213, 10 Am. Rep. 475; Winslow v. Vermont & M. R. Co., 42 Vt. 700, 1 Am. Rep. 365; Stephenson v. Hart, 4 Bing. (Eng.) 476. But see McKean v. McIvor, L. R. 6 Exch. (Eng.) 36; Fulton Bag & Cotton Mills v. Hudson Nav. Co. (D. C.) 157 Fed. 987.

[39] Houston & T. C. Ry. Co. v. Adams, 49 Tex. 748, 30 Am. Rep. 116; American Exp. Co. v. Fletcher, 25 Ind. 492; American Exp. Co. v. Stack, 29 Ind. 27; Duff v. Budd, 3 Brod. & B. (Eng.) 177. But see Heugh v. Railroad Co., L. R. 5 Exch. (Eng.) 50.

[40] Southern Exp. Co. v. Van Meter, 17 Fla. 783, 35 Am. Rep. 107; American Merchants' Union Exp. Co. v. Milk, 73 Ill. 224; Leibbock v. Ingles, 1 Starkie (Eng.) 104. In New York Cent. & H. R. R. Co. v. Bank of Holly Springs, 195 Fed. 456, 115 C. C. A. 358, the bill of lading on which the carrier delivered the goods was forged and the carrier was held liable.

[41] Guillaume v. Hamburgh & A. Packet Co., 42 N. Y. 212, 1 Am. Rep. 512; Devereux v. Barclay, 2 Barn. & Ald. (Eng.) 702. See, also, Cleveland, C., C. & St. L. Ry. Co. v. Wright, 25 Ind. App. 525, 58 N. E. 559. See, also, cases cited in notes 34, 36.

[42] 135 Mass. 278, 46 Am. Rep. 467. See discussion of this case in 2 Hutch. Carr. § 672.

trine), is admirably set forth in PACIFIC EXPRESS CO. v. SHEARER.[43]

Of course, the carrier would not be responsible for a delivery to the wrong person, if this is due to the wrong of the shipper.[44] Thus the carrier's misdelivery is excused when it was either caused, induced, or ratified by the shipper or owner.[45]

SAME—SAME—DELIVERY AT A PROPER TIME

142. A delivery by the carrier, to be proper, must be at a reasonable time.

A reasonable time here involves both a reasonable day and a reasonable hour of the day. A reasonable day ordinarily would exclude a delivery on the Sabbath and also a delivery on a legal holiday, on which labor is forbidden.[46] By a reasonable hour [47] is meant an hour at which business is usually transacted, and this would exclude a delivery out of business hours, such as, for example, a delivery at a late hour of the night.

SAME—SAME—DELIVERY AT THE PROPER PLACE

143. At common law, the common carrier of goods was obliged to make a personal delivery to the consignee, unless excused from such delivery by custom or usage. By custom or usage carriers by water and railroads (but not express companies) are exempted from the necessity of a personal delivery.

[43] 160 Ill. 215, 43 N. E. 816, 37 L. R. A. 177, and note, 52 Am. St. Rep. 324, Dobie Cas. Bailments and Carriers, 239. See analysis of this case in 2 Hutch. Carr. § 673. See, also, in support of this view (citing both the Shearer Case and the Samuel Case), the recent case of Southern Exp. Co. v. C. L. Ruth & Son, 5 Ala. App. 644, 59 South. 538. See, also, Southern Exp. Co. v. Van Meter, 17 Fla. 783, 35 Am. Rep. 107.

[44] Stimson v. Jackson, 58 N. H. 138; Congar v. Chicago & N. W. Ry. Co., 24 Wis. 157, 1 Am. Rep. 164; Erie Ry. Co. v. Wilcox, 84 Ill. 239, 25 Am. Rep. 451; Treleven v. Northern Pac. R. Co., 89 Wis. 598, 62 N. W. 536.

[45] Schwarzschild & Sulzberger Co. v. Savannah, F. & W. Ry. Co., 76 Mo. App. 623; Dobbin v. Michigan Cent. Ry. Co., 56 Mich. 522, 23 N. W. 204; Carroll v. Southern Exp. Co., 37 S. C. 452, 16 S. E. 128; Converse v. Boston & M. R. R., 58 N. H. 521; Cleveland & P. R. Co. v. Sargent, 19 Ohio St. 438.

[46] Gates v. Ryan (D. C.) 37 Fed. 154; Scheu v. Benedict, 116 N. Y. 510, 22 N. E. 1073, 15 Am. St. Rep. 426; Richardson v. Goddard, 23 How. 28, 16 L. Ed. 412.

[47] Marshall v. American Exp. Co., 7 Wis. 1, 73 Am. Dec. 381; Merwin v. Butler, 17 Conn. 138. Delivery to the teller of a bank after banking hours

The common-law rule, imposing the duty of a personal delivery on the common carrier,[48] placed no very great hardship when the carrying was for the most part done in wagons. It was easy and practicable for the carrier to go about with his wagon anywhere for the purpose of making deliveries.[49] When, however, other modes of carriage arose, in which a personal delivery was either impracticable or impossible, such carriers were by custom or usage excused from this duty. In modern times, the question of whether the carrier is obliged to make a personal delivery presents little difficulty. In the case of the more important classes of carriers, the question is settled by so many adjudications that it is more a question of settled law than of custom. Of course, any common carrier may by contract, express or implied, agree to make a personal delivery.[50] In such event, he is bound by his contract and must live up to it.

When personal delivery is necessary, it must be made to the consignee himself, or to some one having authority to receive the goods for the consignee.[51] Such delivery should be at the consignee's office or residence.[52] A delivery at the foot of the stairs, when the consignee's office was in the fourth story, has been held insufficient.[53] If personal delivery to the consignee is tendered,

has been held a good delivery, where a custom was shown to receive express packages at such time. Marshall v. American Exp. Co., supra. If the carrier tenders them at consignee's store after business hours, when store is closed and hands have gone away, consignee may refuse to receive them and carrier will remain liable as carrier. Hill v. Humphreys, 5 Watts & S. (Pa.) 123, 39 Am. Dec. 117. See, also, Young v. Smith, 3 Dana (Ky.) 91, 28 Am. Dec. 57.

48 To the effect that personal delivery was the common-law rule, unless the carrier was exempted therefrom by usage, see Bartlett v. The Philadelphia, 32 Mo. 256; Schroeder v. Hudson R. R. Co., 5 Duer (N. Y.) 55; Hemphill v. Chenie, 6 Watts & S. (Pa.) 62; Loveland v. Burke, 120 Mass. 139, 21 Am. Rep. 507; Birket v. Willar, 2 Barn. & Ald. (Eng.) 356.

49 Fenner v. Buffalo & S. L. R. Co., 44 N. Y. 505, 4 Am. Rep. 709.

50 Hyde v. Trent & M. Navigation Co., 5 Term R. (Eng.) 389. A carrier and shipper could contract that property, destined to a station at which there was no regular agent or depot, when delivered on the siding, should be considered delivered to the consignee and afterwards held at his risk. Southern R. Co. v. Barclay, 1 Ala. App. 348, 56 South. 26.

51 Southern Exp. Co. v. Everett, 37 Ga. 688; Sullivan v. Thompson, 99 Mass. 259.

52 Gibson v. Culver, 17 Wend. (N. Y.) 305, 31 Am. Dec. 297; Fisk v. Newton, 1 Denio (N. Y.) 45, 43 Am. Dec. 649; Duff v. Budd, 3 Brod. & B. (Eng.) 177; Storr v. Crowley, 1 McClel. & Y. (Eng.) 129; Hyde v. Navigation Co., 5 Term R. (Eng.) 389; Bansemer v. Toledo & W. Ry. Co., 25 Ind. 434, 87 Am. Dec. 367. See, also, Banner Grain Co. v. Great Northern R. Co., 119 Minn. 68, 137 N. W. 161, 41 L. R. A. (N. S.) 678.

53 Haslam v. Adams Exp. Co., 6 Bosw. (N. Y.) 235.

and he refuses to accept such delivery, or fails to pay the carrier's proper charges, the carrier has performed his duty, and his exceptional liability is at an end.[54] The carrier may then store the goods for the owner.[55] So, when the consignee is dead, or cannot be found after a reasonable endeavor to do so, the carrier is no longer responsible for the goods as a carrier.[56]

If the carrier knows that the goods are the property of the consignor, the latter should be notified of their nondelivery.[57] Even when the carrier is not informed that the consignor is the owner, though there are cases to the contrary,[58] the better rule would seem to be that the consignor should be presumed to be the owner when the consignee refuses to receive the goods, and the carrier should give notice to the consignor.[59]

[54] Manhattan Rubber Shoe Co. v. Chicago, B. & Q. R. Co., 9 App. Div. 172, 41 N. Y. Supp. 83. See, also, Gregg v. Illinois Cent. R. Co, 147 Ill. 550, 35 N. E. 343, 37 Am. St. Rep. 238; Storr v. Crowley, 1 McClel. & Y. (Eng.) 129; United States Exp. Co. v. Keefer, 59 Ind. 263. See, also, Illinois Cent. Ry. Co. v. Carter, 165 Ill. 570, 46 N. E. 374, 36 L. R. A. 527.

[55] See 2 Hutch. Carr. § 685; Landsberg v. Dinsmore, 4 Daly (N. Y.) 490. The carrier may even go further and sell the goods under some circumstances. E. L. Hasler Co. v. Griffing Florida Orchard Co., 133 Ill. App. 635; Hull v. Missouri Pac. Ry. Co., 60 Mo. App. 593. A sale of goods by a carrier, on the refusal of the consignee to accept them, is unauthorized, where the sale is for much less than the market value and is made without notice of sale, and immediate sale is unnecessary to protect the carrier in its freight charges, and it is liable for the fair market value at the time of sale. Missouri, K. & T. Ry. Co. of Texas v. Groce (Tex. Civ. App.) 106 S. W. 720. In case of refusal of the consignee to accept perishable goods, it may be the carrier's duty to sell them for the owner's account, in order to make the loss as light as possible, and he has implied authority to do so. Arthur v. The Cassius, 2 Story, 81, Fed. Cas. No. 564; Rankin v. Memphis & C. Packet Co., 9 Heisk. (Tenn.) 564, 24 Am. Rep. 339.

[56] Adams Exp. Co. v. Darnell, 31 Ind. 20, 99 Am. Dec. 582; Marshall v. American Exp. Co., 7 Wis. 1, 73 Am. Dec. 381; Clendaniel v. Tuckerman, 17 Barb. (N. Y.) 184; Roth v. Buffalo & S. L. R. Co., 34 N. Y 548, 90 Am. Dec. 736; Alabama & T. R. R. Co. v. Kidd, 35 Ala. 209; Hasse v American Exp. Co., 94 Mich. 133, 53 N. W. 918, 34 Am. St. Rep. 328; American Sugar Refining Co. v. McGhee, 96 Ga. 27, 21 S. E. 383.

[57] American Merchants' Union Exp. Co. v. Wolf, 79 Ill. 430; Stephenson v. Hart, 4 Bing. (Eng.) 476, 484.

[58] Fenner v. Buffalo & S. L. R. Co., 44 N. Y. 505, 4 Am. Rep. 709; Kremer v. Southern Exp. Co., 6 Cold. (Tenn.) 356.

[59] Alabama Great Southern R. Co. v. McKenzie, 139 Ga. 410, 77 S. E. 647, 45 L. R. A. (N. S.) 18; American Merchants' Union Exp. Co. v. Wolf, 79 Ill. 430; American Sugar Refining Co. v. McGhee, 96 Ga. 27, 21 S. E. 383. See 2 Hutch. Carr. § 721. When, however, there is no duty to make a personal delivery, it seems that the carrier is under no legal duty when the consignee refuses to receive the goods or cannot be found, to give notice to the consignor. 2 Hutch. Carr. § 725; Merchants' Dispatch Transp. Co. v. Hallock, 64 Ill. 284.

Carriers by Water

Carriers by water have never been required to make a personal delivery.[60] This exemption by immemorial usage is naturally due to the fact that this mode of transportation makes such a delivery absolutely impracticable. To make such a delivery, since the operation of his ships is confined to navigable waters, it would be necessary for the water carrier to become also a carrier by land.

When the transportation contract provides for delivery at a particular wharf or landing, such provision is, of course, binding.[61] In the absence of a provision in the contract of carriage as to the place of delivery, the carrier is to deliver at the usual wharf.[62] In the absence of a usage to the contrary, if the carrier has no wharf at the port of delivery, the consignee may require delivery at any convenient wharf.[63] In such cases, if there are several consignees, and they are not unanimous in selecting a wharf, it seems that a majority—that is, those who pay more than half the freight—have the right to choose the wharf.[64]

Railroads

Since the cars of railroad companies cannot leave the rails on which they are operated, personal delivery by them would also be impossible without the employment of additional means of transportation. By virtue of custom and usage they are, therefore, not bound to make a personal delivery.[65] The usual place of delivery, in case of railroads, is at the yard, siding, or warehouse of the rail-

[60] Richardson v. Goddard, 23 How. 28, 16 L. Ed. 412; Chickering v. Fowler, 4 Pick. (Mass.) 371; McAndrew v. Whitlock, 52 N. Y. 40, 11 Am. Rep. 657; Cope v. Cordova, 1 Rawle (Pa.) 203.

[61] Stricker v. Leathers, 68 Miss. 803, 9 South. 821, 13 L. R. A. 600; Johnston v. Davis, 60 Mich. 56, 26 N. W. 830.

[62] Richmond v. Union Steamboat Co., 87 N. Y. 240; The Boston, 1 Low. 464, Fed. Cas. No. 1,671; The E. H. Fittler, 1 Low. 114, Fed. Cas. No. 4,311; Montgomery v. The Port Adelaide (D. C.) 38 Fed. 753; Devato v. 823 Barrels of Plumbago (D. C.) 20 Fed. 510; Gatliffe v. Bourne, 4 Bing. N. C. (Eng.) 314; Salmon Falls Mfg. Co. v. The Tangier, 1 Cliff. 396, Fed. Cas. No. 12,266.

[63] Richmond v. Union Steamboat Co., 87 N. Y. 240.

[64] See Richmond v. Union Steamboat Co., 87 N. Y. 240.

[65] South & N. A. R. Co. v. Wood, 66 Ala. 167, 41 Am. Rep. 749; Michigan Cent. R. Co. v. Ward, 2 Mich. 538; Buddy v. Wabash, St. L. & P. Ry. Co., 20 Mo. App. 206; Bansemer v. Toledo & W. Ry. Co., 25 Ind. 434, 87 Am. Dec. 367; Merchants' Dispatch Transp. Co. v. Hallock, 64 Ill. 284; Thomas v. Boston & P. R. Corp., 10 Metc. (Mass.) 472, 43 Am. Dec. 444; Norway Plains Co. v. Boston & M. R., 1 Gray (Mass.) 263, 61 Am. Dec. 423; Fenner v. Buffalo & S. L. R. Co., 44 N. Y. 505, 4 Am. Rep. 709. So a transportation company engaged in carrying freight over railroads not owned by it is not bound to make a personal delivery. Merchants' Dispatch Transp. Co. v Hallock, 64 Ill. 284; See, also, Jackson v. New York Cent. & H. R. R. Co., 167 Ill. App. 461, and cases cited in note 66.

road company.[66] When goods were shipped to a station at which, to the knowledge of the shipper, the railroad had no warehouse, it was held that merely placing the goods on the station platform, according to usage and course of dealing between the parties, was a delivery at a proper place.[67]

Express Companies

It has frequently been said that the inconvenience caused by the carrier's being excused from making a personal delivery is largely responsible for the existence of express companies. To avoid this inconvenience, and at the same time to secure speed and a higher degree of safety in the carriage of goods, the greatly increased cost of sending goods by express is paid. Hence a personal delivery to the consignee is a part of the duty of an express company.[68] This is certainly true as to all the larger places at which an express company carries on its business.[69] But at small places, where the volume of business will not justify the company in maintaining a service of personal delivery, it may show a custom

[66] Where a car load of freight is consigned to a place where there is a side track, but no depot platform or agent of the carrier, which is known to the parties, leaving the car on the side track is a good delivery, and relieves the carrier of further responsibility. Reid & Beam v. Southern R. Co., 149 N. C. 423, 63 S. E. 112. A railroad company may have yards for its convenience in handling, storing, and distributing freight, and will not be obliged as a common carrier to transport freight from one point in the yards to another for the convenience of shippers. Louisville & N. R. Co. v. Higdon, 149 Ky. 321, 148 S. W. 26. See, also, Atchison, T. & S. F. R. Co. v. Interstate Commerce Commission (Com. C.) 188 Fed. 229; Davies v. Michigan Cent. R. Co., 131 Ill. App. 649; Newby v. Ford, 36 Pa. Super. Ct. 634; Kirk v. Chicago, St. P., M. & O. Ry. Co., 59 Minn. 161, 60 N. W. 1084, 50 Am. St. Rep. 397; Kenny Co. v. Atlanta & W. P. R. Co., 122 Ga. 365, 50 S. E. 132.

[67] McMasters v. Pennsylvania R. Co., 69 Pa. 374, 8 Am. Rep. 264.

[68] Packard v. Earle, 113 Mass. 280; Baldwin v. American Exp. Co., 23 Ill. 197, 74 Am. Dec. 190; Union Exp. Co. v. Ohleman, 92 Pa. 323; BULLARD v. AMERICAN EXP. CO., 107 Mich. 695, 65 N. W. 551, 33 L. R. A. 66, 61 Am. St. Rep. 358, Dobie Cas. Bailments and Carriers, 244; State v. Adams Exp. Co., 171 Ind. 138, 85 N. E. 337, 966, 19 L. R. A. (N. S.) 93. There is a distinction in the liability of a carrier in the handling of express and freight shipments. Express carriers are required to make personal delivery, and until such delivery is made they are liable as carriers, unless a reasonable excuse for nondelivery exists, while carriers of freight are exempt from the duty of personal delivery Baum v. Long Island R. Co., 58 Misc. Rep. 34, 108 N. Y. Supp. 1113.

[69] American Merchants' Union Exp. Co. v Schier, 55 Ill. 140; American Merchants' Union Exp. Co. v Wolf, 79 Ill. 430; Witbeck v. Holland, 45 N. Y. 13, 6 Am. Rep. 23; American Union Exp. Co. v. Robinson, 72 Pa. 274, Marshall v. American Exp. Co., 7 Wis. 1, 73 Am. Dec. 381; Southern Exp. Co. v. Armstead, 50 Ala. 350; Sullivan v Thompson, 99 Mass. 259, Bennett v. Northern Pac. Exp. Co., 12 Or. 49, 6 Pac. 160.

not to make a personal delivery to the consignee, but to send him prompt notice of the arrival of the goods.[70] It has also been held that an express company, in good faith and on first giving seasonable notice to the public may fix limits or zones in cities beyond or outside of which it cannot be compelled to make personal delivery.[71]

C. O. D. Shipments

The business of the express companies in C. O. D. ("collect on delivery") shipments has attained tremendous proportions. In such shipments it is the duty of the express company, not only safely to carry the goods and deliver them to the consignee, but also to collect, on behalf of the shipper, the price of the goods and to return the money so collected to the shipper.[72] The company, having accepted such a shipment, must comply with the consignor's instructions, under which the delivery of the goods and the payment of the price are to be concurrent. If, therefore, the goods are delivered to the consignee without the payment of the price, the express company becomes liable therefor to the consignor.[73]

By the better opinion, an opportunity to inspect the goods before paying for them should be given to the consignee.[74] It has even been held proper to permit the consignee, on depositing the price, to take the goods for the purpose of trying or inspecting them, on

[70] Gulliver v. Adams Exp. Co., 38 Ill. 503; State v. Adams Exp. Co., 171 Ind. 138, 85 N. E. 337, 966, 19 L. R. A. (N. S.) 93; American Standard Jewelry Co. v. Witherington, 81 Ark. 134, 98 S. W. 695; Southern Exp. Co. v. Holland, 109 Ala. 362, 19 South. 66; BULLARD v. AMERICAN EXP. CO., 107 Mich. 695, 65 N. W. 551, 33 L. R. A. 66, 61 Am. St. Rep. 358, Dobie Cas. Bailments and Carriers. 244.

[71] BULLARD v. AMERICAN EXP. CO., 107 Mich. 695, 65 N. W. 551, 33 L. R. A. 66, 61 Am. St. Rep. 358, Dobie Cas. Bailments and Carriers, 244; State v. Adams Exp. Co., 171 Ind. 138, 85 N. E. 337, 966, 19 L. R. A. (N. S.) 93. As to custom and usage in affecting the question of substitutes for, or equivalents of, personal delivery by express companies, see Southern Exp. Co. v. Everett, 37 Ga. 688, Haslam v. Adams Exp. Co., 6 Bosw. (N. Y.) 235.

[72] American Exp. Co. v. Lesem, 39 Ill. 312; United States Exp. Co. v. Keefer, 59 Ind. 263. As to what is a contract for shipment C. O. D., see Adams Exp. Co. v. Ten Winkel, 44 Colo. 59, 96 Pac. 818; Smith v. Southern Exp. Co., 104 Ala. 387, 16 South. 62.

[73] Murray v. Warner, 55 N. H. 546, 20 Am. Rep. 227; Meyer v. Lemcke, 31 Ind. 208; Felber v. Manhattan Dist. Tel. Co. (Com. Pl.) 3 N. Y. Supp. 116; Libby v. Ingalls, 124 Mass. 503. The consignor may, however, ratify a delivery not in accordance with his instructions. Rathbun v. Citizens' Steamboat Co. of Troy, 76 N. Y. 376, 32 Am. Rep. 321; Southern Ry. Co. v. Kinchen, 103 Ga. 186, 29 S. E. 816.

[74] Hutch. Carr. § 733; Lyons v. Hill, 46 N. H. 49, 88 Am. Dec. 189; Brand v. Weir, 27 Misc. Rep. 212, 57 N. Y. Supp. 731; Sloan v. Carolina Cent. R.

the condition that, if they are not satisfactory, he may return them to the express company and recover back the price.[75] Some courts, however, deny the right of inspection on the part of the consignee.[76] The reason usually given for this view is that it is the practice of the express companies not to permit such an inspection, and that C. O. D. contracts will be assumed to have been made with this practice in the minds of the parties.[77] The right of inspection here is expressly denied by the American Sales Act.[78]

If the consignee is not able to pay for the goods immediately, the express company should keep the goods a reasonable time in order to give the consignee a suitable opportunity to secure the purchase price of the goods.[79] When the consignee refuses to receive the goods, the shipper should be notified.[80] The carrier is then no longer an insurer, but a mere warehouseman.[81]

The common law places upon the common carrier no obligation whatsoever to engage in the business of C. O. D. shipments.[82] Under that law, he is required merely to be a carrier, and not a collector. These obligations are assumed, on the part of the carrier, entirely by contract; but, when thus assumed, as we have just seen, they must be carried out.[83] If, however, the common carrier holds himself out to the public as willing to accept C. O. D. shipments, then he must undertake the service according to his holding out.[84]

Co., 126 N. C. 487, 36 S. E. 21; Herrick v. Gallagher, 60 Barb. (N. Y.) 566; Thick v. Detroit, U. & R. Ry., 137 Mich. 708, 101 N. W. 64, 109 Am. St. Rep. 694.

[75] Lyons v. Hill, 46 N. H. 49, 88 Am. Dec. 189. In Hardy v. American Exp. Co., 182 Mass. 328, 65 N. E. 375, 59 L. R. A. 731, the carrier was held liable to the consignee for demanding and receiving payment without informing the consignee that the goods were damaged; such fact being well known to the carrier.

[76] Wiltse v. Barnes, 46 Iowa, 210.

[77] See Williston on Sales, § 479, for able exposition of this view and its qualifications. The question is also discussed in 18 Harvard Law Rev. 386.

[78] § 47 (3).

[79] Great Western Ry. Co. v. Crouch, 3 Hurl. & N. (Eng.) 183; 2 Hutch. Carr. § 729.

[80] American Merchants' Union Exp. Co. v. Wolf, 79 Ill. 430; Adams Exp. Co. v. McConnell, 27 Kan. 238.

[81] American Merchants' Union Exp. Co. v. Wolf, 79 Ill. 430; Weed v. Barney, 45 N. Y. 344, 6 Am. Rep. 96; Gibson v. American Merchants' Union Exp. Co., 1 Hun (N. Y.) 387.

[82] American Exp. Co. v. Lesem, 39 Ill. 318; Chicago & N. W. R. Co. v. Merrill, 48 Ill. 425.

[83] See cases cited in note 73.

[84] 2 Hutch. Carr. § 726.

SAME—SAME—DELIVERY IN A PROPER MANNER

144. As to what manner of delivery will substitute for the common carrier's insuring liability that of a mere warehouseman, the courts, though agreeing as to carriers by water, have evolved three different rules as to railroads.

In the case of carriers by water, after the arrival of the goods, the carrier must give notice of such arrival to the consignee, and also give him a reasonable time for the removal of the goods.

As to railroads, the insuring liability ends

(a) By the Massachusetts rule, when the goods have arrived at their destination and have been stored by the carrier.

(b) By the New Hampshire rule, when, after the arrival and storage of the goods, a reasonable time has elapsed within which the consignee could have removed the goods.

(c) By the Michigan rule, only when, after the arrival of the goods, notice has been given to the consignee, and a reasonable time for their removal has elapsed after such notice.

A delivery by any common carrier must, in order to be a proper delivery, be made in a reasonable manner.[85] Thus the goods must be in such a place that the consignee has ready access to them.[86] Again, they must be set apart in such a way that the consignee can take them away without the necessity of having to separate them from other goods.[87] The situation of the goods must also be such that the consignee can remove them with due speed, and without expending unusual effort or incurring any unusual danger, either to himself or to the goods.[88]

[85] Sonia Cotton Oil Co. v. The Red River, 106 La. 42, 30 South. 303, 87 Am. St. Rep. 293; Scheu v. Benedict, 116 N. Y. 510, 22 N. E. 1073, 15 Am. St. Rep. 426; Morgan v. Dibble, 29 Tex. 107, 94 Am. Dec. 264.

[86] Independence Mills Co. v. Burlington, C., R. & N. Ry. Co., 72 Iowa, 535, 34 N. W. 320, 2 Am. St. Rep. 258; Bachant v. Boston & M. R. R., 187 Mass. 392, 73 N. E. 642, 105 Am. St. Rep. 408; Russell Grain Co. v. Wabash R. Co., 114 Mo. App. 488, 89 S. W. 908.

[87] The Titania, 131 Fed. 229, 65 C. C. A. 215; The Eddy, 5 Wall. 481, 18 L. Ed. 486.

[88] East Tennessee, V. & G. R. Co. v. Hunt, 15 Lea (Tenn.) 261; Reynolds v. Great Northern R. Co., 40 Wash. 163, 82 Pac. 161, 111 Am. St. Rep. 883; Frasier v. Charlestown & W. C. Ry. Co., 73 S. C. 140, 52 S. E. 964.

Carriers by Water

As to carriers by water, the rule is well established that the strict liability of the common carrier continues until, after the arrival of the goods at their destination, the carrier has given notice of such arrival to the consignee and then a reasonable time has elapsed, since this notice, within which the consignee might have removed the goods.[89] The reason usually given by the courts for this rule is the uncertainty of the arrival of boats, which would make it unreasonable to require the consignee to watch hourly for the arrival of the boat and to be on hand at such arrival, ready to receive the goods.

If the consignee is present, the goods may be tendered or delivered to him personally, and he is bound to remove them within a reasonable time. If he is not present, he is entitled both to reasonable notice from the carrier of the arrival of the goods and a fair opportunity to receive and remove them.[90] If the consignee is unknown to the carrier, the latter must use proper and reasonable diligence to find him; in such cases, due effort to find the consignee is a condition precedent to the carrier's right to warehouse the goods.[91] What is a due and a reasonable effort, and what is proper and reasonable diligence, must depend largely upon the circumstances of each case, and, in the nature of things, is a question of fact, for the jury, and not of law, for the court.[92] The necessity, on the carrier's part, of giving notice may be dispensed with by contract,[93] or it may be waived by a custom or usage to the contrary.[94]

[89] Turner v. Huff, 46 Ark. 222, 55 Am. Rep. 580; Goodwin v. Baltimore & O. R. Co., 50 N. Y. 154, 10 Am. Rep. 457; The Titania, 131 Fed. 229, 65 C. C. A. 215; Crawford v. Clark, 15 Ill. 561; Blin v. Mayo, 10 Vt. 56, 33 Am. Dec. 175; Morgan v. Dibble, 29 Tex. 107, 94 Am. Dec. 264.

[90] Ostrander v. Brown, 15 Johns. (N. Y.) 39, 8 Am. Dec. 211; Zinn v. New Jersey Steamboat Co., 49 N. Y. 442, 10 Am. Rep. 402; Price v. Powell, 3 N. Y. 322; Russell Mfg. Co. v. New Haven Steamboat Co., 50 N. Y. 121; McAndrew v. Whitlock, 52 N. Y. 40, 11 Am. Rep. 657; Gleadell v. Thomson, 56 N. Y. 194; Crawford v. Clark, 15 Ill. 561; Salmon Falls Mfg. Co. v. The Tangier, 1 Cliff. 396, Fed. Cas. No. 12,266. This notice must be actual. Publication in newspapers has been held insufficient. Kohn v. Packard, 3 La. 224, 23 Am. Dec. 453; Segura v. Reed, 3 La. Ann. 695.

[91] Zinn v. New Jersey Steamboat Co., 49 N. Y. 442, 10 Am. Rep. 402; Sherman v. Hudson River R. Co., 64 N. Y. 254; Union Steamboat Co. v. Knapp, 73 Ill. 506.

[92] Zinn v. New Jersey Steamboat Co., 49 N. Y. 442, 10 Am. Rep. 402.

[93] The Boskenna Bay (C. C.) 40 Fed. 91, 6 L. R. A. 172; Henshaw v. Rowland, 54 N. Y. 242.

[94] Russell Mfg. Co. v. New Haven Steamboat Co., 50 N. Y. 121; Ely v. New Haven Steamboat Co., 53 Barb. (N. Y.) 207; Gibson v. Culver, 17 Wend.

Railroad Companies—Massachusetts Rule

By what is known as the "Massachusetts rule," the liability of a railroad company as a common carrier terminates, and its responsibility as a warehouseman commences, when the goods have arrived at the point of destination, and have been deposited there to await the convenience of the consignee, without notice of the arrival of the goods being given to the consignee.[95] In the leading case supporting this rule,[96] the decision was put upon the ground that from the necessary conditions of the business of railroad corporations, and from their practice to have platforms on which to place goods from the cars in the first instance, and warehouse accommodations by which they may be securely stored, the placing of the goods of each consignment by themselves, in accessible places, ready to be delivered, completes the whole duty assumed by the railroad corporation as a carrier. The distinctive duty of the carrier is to carry the goods safely to the place of destination, and there discharge them upon the platform, and then and there deliver them to the consignee or party entitled to receive them, if he is there ready to take them forthwith, or, if he is not there, ready to take them, then to place them securely, and keep them a reasonable time, ready to be delivered when called for. Delivery from themselves as common carriers to themselves as keepers for hire discharges their responsibility as common carriers; so that they are responsible as common carriers only until the goods are removed from the cars and placed on the platform. In short, the railroad corporation ceases to be a common carrier, and becomes a warehouseman, as a matter

(N. Y.) 305, 31 Am. Dec. 297; McMasters v. Pennsylvania R. Co., 69 Pa. 374, 8 Am. Rep. 264; Dixon v. Dunham, 14 Ill. 324; Crawford v. Clark, 15 Ill. 561; Farmers' & Mechanics' Bank v. Champlain Transp. Co., 16 Vt. 52, 42 Am. Dec. 491; Id., 23 Vt. 186, 56 Am. Dec. 68; Sleade v. Payne, 14 La. Ann. 457; Stone v. Rice, 58 Ala. 95; Gatliffe v. Bourne, 4 Bing. N. C. (Eng.) 314, 329; Garside v. Navigation Co., 4 Term R. (Eng.) 581. This usage need not be shown to have been known to the shipper, as he is presumed to contract with reference to all the usages of the particular trade. Van Santvoord v. St. John, 6 Hill (N. Y.) 157, 167.

[95] Thomas v. Boston & P. R. Corp., 10 Metc. (Mass.) 472, 43 Am. Dec. 444; Kight v. Wrightsville & T. R. Co., 127 Ga. 204, 56 S. E. 363; Schumacher v. Chicago & N. W. R. Co., 207 Ill. 199, 69 N. E. 825; Bansemer v. Toledo & W. Ry. Co., 25 Ind. 434, 87 Am. Dec. 367; Stanard Milling Co. v. White Line Cent. Transit Co., 122 Mo. 258, 26 S. W. 704; Shenk v. Philadelphia Steam Propeller Co., 60 Pa. 109, 100 Am. Dec. 541; Spears v. Spartanburg, U. & C. R. Co., 11 S. C. 158; Francis v. Dubuque & S. C. R. Co., 25 Iowa, 60, 95 Am. Dec. 769; Chalk v. Charlotte, C. & A. R. Co., 85 N. C. 423.

[96] Norway Plains Co. v. Boston & M. R. R., 1 Gray (Mass.) 263, 61 Am Dec. 423.

of law, when it has completed the duty of transportation, and assumed the position of warehouseman, as a matter of fact.

This rule, in the opinion of Shaw, C. J., in the case in question,[97] is held "to afford a plain, precise, and practical rule of duty, well adapted to the security of all persons interested." Of its simplicity there can be little question; but, as it is manifestly impossible for the consignee to anticipate the arrival of freight trains and be present then to receive the goods, it is believed that it unduly favors the carrier.

Same—New Hampshire Rule

Under the New Hampshire rule, the strict liability of the common carrier continues until the expiration of a reasonable time after the arrival of the goods.[98] It is held, though, that the "reasonable time" is not to be affected by the peculiar circumstances and conditions in the case of the individual consignee.[99] Thus the time is not extended in favor of one living at a distance from the railroad warehouse as against one living in its immediate vicinity. The New Hampshire rule, owing to the hazardous uncertainty of the arrival of freight trains at unearthly and unusual hours, is fairer to the consignee and is more nearly in accord, than the Massachusetts rule, with what is believed to be a sounder public policy.

Same—Michigan Rule

The Michigan rule applies the same rule to railroads that obtains as to carriers by water. In order to relieve itself of its strict common-law liability, the railroad company must first give notice to the consignee of the arrival of the goods, and must then give the consignee a reasonable time for the removal of the goods. Until the lapse of a reasonable time after such notice, the liability of the carrier remains in all its strictness.[1]

[97] Norway Plains Co. v. Boston & M. R. R., 1 Gray (Mass.) 263, 61 Am. Dec. 423.

[98] Moses v. Boston & M. R. R., 32 N. H. 523, 64 Am. Dec. 381; Tallassee Falls Mfg. Co. v. Western Ry. of Alabama, 128 Ala. 167, 29 South. 203; Leavenworth, L. & G. R. Co. v. Maris, 16 Kan. 333; Jeffersonville R. Co. v. Cleveland, 2 Bush (Ky.) 468; Winslow v. Vermont & M. R. Co., 42 Vt. 700, 1 Am. Rep. 365; Backhaus v. Chicago & N. W. Ry. Co., 92 Wis. 393, 66 N. W. 400; Berry v. West Virginia & P. R. Co., 44 W. Va. 538, 30 S. E. 143, 67 Am. St. Rep. 781.

[99] Moses v. Boston & M. R. R., 32 N. H. 523, 64 Am. Dec. 381. See, also, other cases cited in preceding note.

[1] Hutchison (section 708) calls this the New York rule. The doctrine is supported by the following cases: McMillan v. Michigan S. & N. I. R. Co., 16 Mich. 79, 93 Am. Dec. 208; Pinney v. First Division of St. Paul & P. R. Co., 19 Minn. 251 (Gil. 211); Gulf & C. R. Co. v. Fuqua & Horton, 84 Miss. 490, 36 South. 449; Lake Erie & W. R. Co. v. Hatch, 52 Ohio St. 408, 39 N.

This is believed to be the best of the three rules.[2] The same conditions that obtain in the case of water carriers are applicable here to justify the same test in the case of railroads. Any difference is one of degree, not of kind, and hardly warrants a different rule. This is particularly true as to transcontinental traffic, or even that traversing the lines of several railroads. Then the consignee can never know with even approximate certainty of the expected arrival of the goods. It might also be pointed out that by requiring the railroad company, in possession of immediate and exact knowledge, to give notice of the arrival of the goods, the carrier is relieved of the burden of answering any number of inquiries. The requirement of notice, therefore, usually by postal, though a great advantage to the consignee, imposes little, if any, hardship on the railroad company.

Duty of Common Carrier When Consignee Refuses to Receive the Goods

The duty of the consignee to receive the goods, upon the tender of a proper delivery, is as clear as the carrier's duty to deliver. The strict liability of the common carrier cannot be prolonged at the option of the consignee merely to suit his convenience. The consignee must act with reasonable promptness in taking the goods. If he fails to do so, whatever other duty may rest on the carrier as to the goods, the carrier's insuring liability is thereby terminated.[3]

Even though a consignee may neglect to accept or receive the goods, the carrier is not thereby justified in abandoning them, or in negligently exposing them to injury.[4] The law enables the car-

E. 1042; Fenner v. Buffalo & S. L. R. Co., 44 N. Y. 505, 4 Am. Rep. 709. The English cases also favor this rule. Chapman v. Great, etc., Ry. Co., 5 Q. B. Div. 278; Mitchell v. Railway Co., 10 L. R. Q. B. 256.

2 The essential fairness of this rule has so commended itself to many state Legislatures that it has been expressly enacted by statutes. Cavallaro v. Texas & P. Ry. Co., 110 Cal. 348, 42 Pac. 918, 52 Am. St. Rep. 94; Collins v. Alabama G. S. R. Co., 104 Ala. 390, 16 South. 140; Pennsylvania Ry. Co. v. Naive, 112 Tenn. 239, 79 S. W. 124, 64 L. R. A. 443; Missouri Pac. Ry. Co. v. Haynes, 72 Tex. 175, 10 S. W. 398.

3 Redmond v. Liverpool, N. Y. & P. Steamboat Co., 46 N. Y. 578, 7 Am. Rep. 390; Hedges v. Hudson River R. Co., 49 N. Y. 223; Liverpool & G. W. Steam Co. v. Suitter (D. C.) 17 Fed. 695; De Grau v. Wilson (D. C.) 17 Fed. 698. See, also, Manhattan Rubber Shoe Co. v. Chicago, B. & Q. R. Co., 9 App. Div. 172, 41 N. Y. Supp. 83; Arkansas S. R. Co. v. German Nat. Bank, 77 Ark. 482, 92 S. W. 522, 113 Am. St. Rep. 160. As to notice to the consignor, see cases cited in notes 56–59.

4 Hermann v. Goodrich, 21 Wis. 536, 94 Am. Dec. 562; Merwin v. Butler, 17 Conn. 138; Chickering v. Fowler, 4 Pick. (Mass.) 371; Dean v. Vaccaro, 2 Head (Tenn.) 488, 75 Am. Dec. 744; Shenk v. Philadelphia Steam Propeller

rier to exempt himself wholly from responsibility in such a contingency, by giving him the right to warehouse the goods. When this is done, he is no longer liable in any capacity, and if they are subsequently lost by the negligence of the warehouseman the carrier is not liable.[5] But so long as the carrier has the custody of the goods, although exempted from liability as carrier, there supervenes upon the original contract of carriage, by implication of law, a duty, as bailee or warehouseman, to take ordinary care of the property.[6]

SAME—DELIVERY TO A CONNECTING CARRIER

145. Where goods are received by a carrier to be transported over connecting lines, the initial carrier is not liable for loss or injury occurring beyond its own line, unless, by special contract, he undertakes to convey the goods to their destination.

In England and a few of the American states, such a contract (rendering the initial carrier responsible for loss or dam-

Co., 60 Pa. 109, 100 Am. Dec. 541; Northern v. Williams, 6 La. Ann. 578; Segura v. Reed, 3 La. Ann. 695; Tarbell v. Royal Exch. Shipping Co., 110 N. Y. 170, 17 N. E. 721, 6 Am. St. Rep. 350; Redmond v. Liverpool, N. Y. & P. Steamboat Co., 46 N. Y. 578, 7 Am. Rep. 390; McAndrew v. Whitlock, 52 N. Y. 40, 11 Am. Rep. 657; The City of Lincoln (D. C.) 25 Fed. 835, 839; Richardson v. Goddard, 23 How. 28, 39, 16 L. Ed. 412; The Grafton, 1 Blatchf. 173, Fed. Cas. No. 5,655. Where consignee is unable, or refuses, to accept goods, carrier must secure them in place of safety, and will not be justified in leaving them exposed on wharf. Ostrander v. Brown, 15 Johns. (N. Y.) 39, 8 Am. Dec. 211. See, also, The Keystone v. Moies, 28 Mo. 243, 75 Am. Dec. 123; Illinois Cent. R. Co. v. Carter, 165 Ill. 570, 46 N. E. 374, 36 L. R. A. 527. The carrier (when the consignee refuses or fails to receive the goods) may sell perishable freight, when that is necessary to prevent a total loss to the shipper, though, if practicable, notice should be given to the consignor before the sale. Missouri, K. & T. R. Co. of Texas v. C. H. Cox & Co. (Tex. Civ. App.) 144 S. W. 1196; Dudley v. Chicago, M. & St. P. R. Co., 58 W. Va. 604, 52 S. E. 718, 3 L. R. A. (N. S.) 1135, 112 Am. St. Rep. 1027. In some states, this right is expressly given by statute. St. Louis & S. F. R. Co. v. Dreyfus, 37 Okl. 492, 132 Pac. 491.

[5] Redmond v. Liverpool, N. Y. & P. Steamboat Co., 46 N. Y. 578, 7 Am. Rep 390; Manhattan Rubber Shoe Co. v. Chicago, B. & Q. R. Co., 9 App. Div. 172, 41 N. Y. Supp. 83. In such case, whatever remedy the owner has is against the warehouseman.

[6] Tarbell v. Royal Exch. Shipping Co., 110 N. Y. 170, 17 N. E. 721, 6 Am. St. Rep. 350; Hasse v. American Exp. Co., 94 Mich. 133, 53 N. W. 918, 34 Am. St. Rep. 328; Welch v. Concord R. R., 68 N. H. 206, 44 Atl. 304; Byrne v. Fargo, 36 Misc. Rep. 543, 73 N. Y. Supp. 943; Bryan v. Chicago & A. R. Co., 169 Ill. App. 181; Seaboard Air Line R. Co. v. A. R. Harper Piano Co., 63 Fla. 264, 58 South. 491.

age occurring on the lines of connecting carriers) is presumed from the acceptance of the goods by the initial carrier, when the goods are consigned to a point beyond the terminus of the initial carrier's line.

In the great majority of the American states, however, this mere acceptance of goods consigned beyond its own line does not render the initial carrier responsible beyond its own line. Such acceptance is held not to constitute, of itself, a contract to transport the goods to their destination.

The question is further complicated by statutes, both state and federal, most of which, like the federal Interstate Commerce Act (Carmack Amendment), render the initial carrier liable for loss or damage occurring on the lines of the connecting carrier.

Who are Connecting Carriers

According to the judicial definition most frequently approved, "a connecting carrier is one whose route, not being the first one, lies somewhere between the point of shipment and the point of destination." [7] The carrier to whom the goods are originally delivered for transportation by the consignor is called the initial carrier. All other carriers engaged in transporting the goods between the place of shipment and their destination are connecting carriers. The initial carrier receives the goods from the consignor and starts the transportation; the connecting carrier receives the goods either from the initial carrier or from another connecting carrier, and a particular connecting carrier either may or may not complete the transportation. There is but one initial carrier; there may be any number of connecting carriers. A transfer company from the depot at the station of destination to the consignee's business house was held not to be a connecting carrier, on the ground that the goods had already reached their destination and were not being carried by the transfer company under the original transportation contract.[8]

When Initial Carrier is Liable for Through Transportation

The duty of a common carrier at common law is limited to receiving and transporting goods over its own line—a duty which it must perform, or respond in damages. But it is not its duty to

[7] Nanson v. Jacob, 12 Mo. App. 125.

[8] Nanson v. Jacob, 12 Mo. App. 125. For interesting contrast as to whether a railroad company, hauling cars from the depot to consignee's store or mill, is a connecting carrier, see Western & A. R. Co. v. Exposition Cotton Mills, 81 Ga. 522, 7 S. E. 916, 2 L. R. A. 102; Missouri Pac. Ry. Co. v. Wichita Wholesale Grocery Co., 55 Kan. 525, 40 Pac. 899.

transport such goods over the line of any other carriers, or even to contract for such transportation, and it cannot be compelled to assume such an obligation. Its entire common-law duty is limited to its own line. It owes nothing to the public beyond that.[9] Any further liability is therefore self-imposed by the voluntary act of the carrier.

A carrier, however, if it so wishes, may assume an additional obligation of this kind and become an insurer of the goods throughout the whole course of the transportation; that is, the initial carrier may make its liability as a common carrier continue, even while the goods are being transported over the lines of connecting carriers, until the goods have reached their ultimate destination. This the initial carrier does by contracting to carry the goods to their destination.[10] By so doing the initial carrier voluntarily makes the succeeding carriers its agents, and thereby assumes responsibility for their defaults.

As was well said by the United States Supreme Court:[11] "Each road, confining itself to its common-law liability, is only bound, in the absence of a special contract, to safely carry over its own route and safely to deliver to the next connecting carrier; but * * * any one of the companies may agree that over the whole route its liability shall extend. In the absence of a special agreement to that effect, such liability will not attach, and the agreement will not be inferred from doubtful expressions or loose language, but only from clear and satisfactory evidence."

9 See ante, §§ 110-111. See, also, Missouri, K. & T. R. Co. v. McCann, 174 U. S. 580, 19 Sup. Ct. 755, 43 L. Ed. 1093; Perkins v. Portland, S. & P. R. Co., 47 Me. 573, 74 Am. Dec. 507; Seasongood v. Tennessee & O. R. Transp. Co., 54 S. W. 193, 21 Ky. Law Rep. 1142, 49 L. R. A. 270; Post v. Southern Ry. Co., 103 Tenn. 184, 52 S. W. 301, 55 L. R. A. 481; Coats v. Chicago, R. I. & P. R. Co., 239 Ill. 154, 87 N. E. 929; Quimby v. Vanderbilt, 17 N. Y. 306, 72 Am. Dec. 469; Ogdensburg & L. C. R. Co. v. Pratt, 22 Wall. 123, 22 L. Ed. 827.

10 Berg v. Atchison, T. & S. F. R. Co., 30 Kan. 561, 2 Pac. 639; Miller Grain & Elevator Co. v. Union Pac. Ry. Co., 138 Mo. 658, 40 S. W. 894; Griffith v. Atchison, T. & S. F. R. Co., 114 Mo. App. 591, 90 S. W. 408; Inman v. St. Louis S. W. Ry. Co., 14 Tex. Civ. App. 39, 37 S. W. 37; St. Louis S. W. R. Co. v. Wallace, 90 Ark. 138, 118 S. W. 412, 22 L. R. A. (N. S.) 379; Earnest v. Delaware, L. & W. R. Co., 149 App. Div. 330, 134 N. Y. Supp. 323; Hansen v. Flint & P. M. R. Co., 73 Wis. 346, 41 N. W. 529, 9 Am. St. Rep. 791. Such a contract, by a railroad company or other corporation doing business as a common carrier, is not ultra vires. Swift v. Pacific Mail S. S. Co., 106 N. Y. 206, 12 N. E. 583; Buffett v. Troy & B. R. Co., 40 N. Y. 168; Bissell v. Michigan Southern & N. I. R. Co., 22 N. Y. 258; Hill Mfg. Co. v. Boston & L. R. Corp., 104 Mass. 122, 6 Am. Rep. 202; Baltimore & P. Steamboat Co. v. Brown, 54 Pa. 77.

11 Myrick v. Michigan Cent. R. Co., 107 U. S. 102, 1 Sup. Ct. 425, 27 L. Ed. 325.

The courts, then, agree, both in England and America, that only by contract is responsibility imposed on the common carrier beyond the end of the line. There is grave conflict, however, as to what constitutes such a contract, or from what acts such a contract will be implied. This conflict will be discussed in detail.

From what has been said it follows a fortiori that the liability of the initial carrier is confined to its own line when such initial carrier in an express contract clearly stipulates that its liability shall not extend beyond its own line.[12] Since it requires a contract affirmatively to impose this added liability, the initial carrier by a contract expressly repudiating that responsibility is merely, in the matter of exemption from such liability, making assurance doubly sure. No court (in the absence of statute) has gone so far as to hold the initial carrier liable for loss or damage on the lines of connecting carriers, when the contract of the initial carrier stipulates that its responsibility shall cease on a delivery of the goods to the connecting carrier. Such a contract, far from attempting to limit the initial carrier's common-law liability, is no more than a definite refusal on this carrier's part to extend its common-law liability.

Same—The English Rule

In the leading English case of MUSCHAMP v. LANCASTER & P. J. RY. CO.[13] it was held that the mere acceptance by the initial carrier of goods consigned to a point beyond the end of its line was prima facie evidence of an undertaking to carry the goods to their destination. Unless, therefore, the initial carrier could offset this prima facie presumption, it was liable for loss or damage occurring on the lines of connecting carriers. This is known as the "rule of Muschamp's Case."

According, then, to the English rule (an evolution from Muschamp's Case), the mere acceptance of goods consigned to a point on the line of a connecting carrier renders the initial carrier liable for through transportation, unless such carrier has relieved itself of such liability by its contract.[14] The English cases also go to

[12] Keller v. Baltimore & O. R. Co., 174 Pa. 62, 34 Atl. 455; Myrick v. Michigan Cent. R. Co., 107 U. S. 102, 1 Sup. Ct. 425, 27 L. Ed. 325; Harris v. Minneapolis, St. P. & S. Ste. M. Ry. Co., 36 Misc. Rep. 181, 73 N. Y. Supp. 159; Post v. Southern Ry. Co., 103 Tenn. 184, 52 S. W. 301, 55 L. R. A. 481; McConnell v. Norfolk & W. Ry. Co., 86 Va. 248, 9 S. E. 1006.

[13] 8 Mees. & W. 421, Dobie Cas. Bailments and Carriers, 246.

[14] Watson v. Railway Co., 3 Eng. Law & Eq. 497; Mytton v. Railway Co., 28 Law J. Exch. 385; Coxon v. Railway Co., 5 Hurl. & N. 274; Bristol & E.

the extent of holding that when, under the rule stated, the initial carrier is responsible for through transportation, such carrier (and it alone) is liable to the shipper or consignee. Even though the loss or damage occurs, in such a case, on the line of a connecting carrier, the initial carrier is solely responsible.[15] Owing to a lack of privity, it is held the connecting carrier cannot be sued by the consignor or consignee.

A few American states have adopted the English rule of presumptive liability in the initial carrier from mere acceptance of goods consigned to points beyond the end of its line.[16] In only one state, however, has it been held that, when the loss or damage occurs on the connecting carrier's line, the initial carrier alone was liable to the consignor or consignee. The right of suing the connecting, as well as the initial, carrier has been everywhere conceded save in Georgia.[17] Even there, however, the connecting carrier, too, was made liable by statute.[18]

It should be noted that when (under any of the rules discussed) the initial carrier is held liable for loss or damage occurring on the line of a connecting carrier, the initial carrier has a remedy

Ry. Co. v. Collins, 5 Hurl. & N. 969, 29 L. J. Exch. 41; Crouch v. Railway Co., 2 Hurl. & N. 491.

15 Collins v. Railway Co., 11 Exch. 790; Coxon v. Railway Co., 5 Hurl. & N. 274; Mytton v. Railway Co., 4 Hurl. & N. 615.

16 Mobile & G. R. Co. v. Copeland, 63 Ala. 219, 35 Am. Rep. 13; Louisville & N. R. Co. v. Meyer, 78 Ala. 597; Falvey v. Georgia R. Co., 76 Ga. 597, 2 Am. St. Rep. 58; Rome R. Co. v. Sullivan, 25 Ga. 228; Mosher v. Southern Exp. Co., 38 Ga. 37; Southern Exp. Co. v. Shea, 38 Ga. 519; Cohen v. Southern Exp. Co., 45 Ga. 148; Illinois Cent. R. Co. v. Copeland, 24 Ill. 332, 76 Am. Dec. 749; Illinois Cent. R. Co. v. Johnson, 34 Ill. 389; Illinois Cent. R. Co. v. Frankenberg, 54 Ill. 88, 5 Am. Rep. 92; CHICAGO & N. W. RY. CO. v. PEOPLE, 56 Ill. 365, 8 Am. Rep. 690, Dobie Cas. Bailments and Carriers, 183; United States Exp. Co. v. Haines, 67 Ill. 137; Adams Exp. Co. v. Wilson, 81 Ill. 339; Erie Ry. Co. v. Wilcox, 84 Ill. 239, 25 Am. Rep. 451; Angle v. Mississippi & M. R. Co., 9 Iowa, 487; Mulligan v. Illinois Cent. Ry. Co., 36 Iowa, 181, 14 Am. Rep. 514; Cincinnati, H. & D. R. Co. v. Spratt, 2 Duv. (Ky.) 4; Nashua Lock Co. v. Worcester & N. R. Co., 48 N. H. 339, 2 Am. Rep. 242; Western & A. R. Co. v. McElwee, 6 Heisk. (Tenn.) 208; East Tennessee & V. R. Co. v. Rogers, 6 Heisk. (Tenn.) 143, 19 Am. Rep. 589; Louisville & N. R. Co. v. Campbell, 7 Heisk. (Tenn.) 253; Carter v. Peck, 4 Sneed (Tenn.) 203, 67 Am. Dec. 604; East Tennessee & G. R. R. v. Nelson, 1 Cold. (Tenn.) 272; Bekins Household Shipping Co. v. Grand Trunk Ry. System, 162 Ill. App. 497; Chicago, R. I. & P. R. Co. v. Cotton, 87 Ark. 339, 112 S. W. 742; Allen & Gilbert-Ramaker Co. v. Canadian Pac. R. Co., 42 Wash. 64, 84 Pac. 620; Hansen v. Flint & P. M. R. Co., 73 Wis. 346, 41 N. W. 529, 9 Am. St. Rep. 791.

17 Southern Exp. Co. v. Shea, 38 Ga. 519.

18 Code Ga. 1882, § 2084; Western & A. R. Co. v. Exposition Cotton Mills, 81 Ga. 522, 7 S. E. 916, 2 L. R. A. 102.

over against such connecting carrier on whose line the loss or injury actually occurred.[19]

Same—The American Rule

Though the English rule has the merit of convenience and simplicity, it has been repudiated by a great majority of the American courts, which hold the mere acceptance insufficient to charge the initial carrier for through transportation to the destination of the goods on the connecting carrier's line.[20] Under the American rule,

[19] Powhatan S. B. Co. v. Appomattox R. Co., 24 How. 247, 16 L. Ed. 682; Chicago & N. W. R. Co. v. Northern Line Packet Co., 70 Ill. 217; Conkey v. Milwaukee & St. P. Ry. Co., 31 Wis. 619, 11 Am. Rep. 630.

[20] Elmore v. Naugatuck R. Co., 23 Conn. 457, 470, 63 Am. Dec. 143; Hood v. New York & N. H. R. Co., 22 Conn. 502; Naugatuck R. Co. v. Waterbury Button Co., 24 Conn. 468; Converse v. Norwich & N. Y. Transp. Co., 33 Conn. 166; Savannah, F. & W. Ry. Co. v. Harris, 26 Fla. 148, 7 South. 544, 23 Am. St. Rep. 551; Pittsburgh, C. & St. L. Ry. Co. v. Morton, 61 Ind. 539, 28 Am. Rep. 682; Hill v. B., C. R. & N. R. Co., 60 Iowa, 196, 14 N. W 249; Perkins v. Portland S. & P. R. Co., 47 Me. 573, 74 Am. Dec. 507; Skinner v. Hall, 60 Me. 477; Inhabitants of Plantation No. 4, R. 1, v. Hall, 61 Me. 517; Baltimore & O. R. Co. v. Schumacher, 29 Md. 168, 176, 96 Am. Dec. 510; Nutting v. Connecticut River R. Co., 1 Gray (Mass.) 402; Darling v. Boston & W. R. Corp., 11 Allen (Mass.) 295; Burroughs v. Norwich & W. R. Co., 100 Mass. 26, 1 Am. Rep. 78; Lowell Wire Fence Co. v. Sargent, 8 Allen (Mass.) 189; Pendergast v. Adams Exp. Co., 101 Mass. 120; Pratt v. Ogdensburg & L. C. R. Co., 102 Mass. 557; Crawford v. Southern R. Ass'n, 51 Miss. 222, 24 Am. Rep. 626; McMillan v. Michigan S. & N. I. R. Co., 16 Mich. 79, 93 Am. Dec. 208; Detroit & B. C. R. Co. v. McKenzie, 43 Mich. 609, 5 N. W. 1031; Rickerson Roller-Mill Co. v. Grand Rapids & I. R. Co., 67 Mich. 110, 34 N. W. 269; Irish v. Milwaukee & St. P. Ry. Co., 19 Minn. 376 (Gil. 323), 18 Am. Rep. 340; Lawrence v. Winona & St. P. R. Co., 15 Minn. 390 (Gil. 313), 2 Am. Rep. 130; Grover & Baker Sewing Mach. Co. v. Missouri Pac. Ry. Co., 70 Mo. 672, 35 Am. Rep. 444; Van Santvoord v. St. John, 6 Hill (N. Y.) 157; Lamb v. Camden & A. R. & Transp. Co., 46 N. Y. 271, 7 Am. Rep. 327; Condict v. Grand Trunk Ry. Co., 54 N. Y. 500; Rawson v. Holland, 59 N. Y. 611, 17 Am. Rep. 394; Reed v. United States Exp. Co., 48 N. Y. 462, 8 Am. Rep. 561; Phillips v. North Carolina R. Co., 78 N. C. 294; Lindley v. Richmond & D. R. Co., 88 N. C. 547; Knott v. Raleigh & G. R. Co., 98 N. C. 73, 3 S. E. 735, 2 Am. St. Rep. 321; Camden & A. R. Co. v. Forsyth, 61 Pa. 81; American Exp. Co. v. Second Nat. Bank, of Titusville, 69 Pa. 394, 8 Am. Rep. 268; Pennsylvania Cent. R. Co. v. Schwarzenberger, 45 Pa. 208, 84 Am. Dec. 490; Clyde v. Hubbard, 88 Pa. 358; Knight v. Providence & W. R. Co., 13 R. I. 572, 43 Am. Rep. 46; Harris v. Grand Trunk Ry. Co., 15 R. I. 371, 5 Atl. 305; Piedmont Mfg. Co. v. Columbia & G. R. Co., 19 S. C. 353 (but see Kyle v. Laurens R. Co., 10 Rich. [S. C.] 382, 70 Am. Dec. 231); McConnell v. Norfolk & W. R. Co., 86 Va. 248, 9 S. C. 1006; Myrick v. Michigan Cent. R. Co., 107 U. S. 102, 1 Sup. Ct. 425, 27 L. Ed. 325; Stewart v. Terre Haute & I. R. Co. (C. C.) 1 McCrary, 312, 3 Fed. 768; Michigan Cent. R. Co. v. Mineral Springs Mfg. Co., 16 Wall. 318, 21 L. Ed. 297; Ogdensburg & L. C. R. Co. v. Pratt, 22 Wall. 123, 22 L. Ed. 827; St. Louis Ins. Co. v. St. Louis, V. T. H.

other facts besides the acceptance are necessary to charge the initial carrier for loss or damage not occurring on its line. To extend this liability beyond the initial carrier's own line, the shipper must, by other facts than the acceptance, standing alone, prove some positive contract of the initial carrier by which it agrees to assume responsibility for the carrying of the goods to their destination. Unless this burden is met by the shipper, the initial carrier's liability ceases when the goods are delivered by it to a connecting carrier. In spite of the hardship imposed on the shipper of ascertaining the particular carrier on whose line the loss or damage occurred, the American rule commends itself by its essential fairness to the initial carrier. Even when the contract is for through carriage, it is universally held in America that the shipper, when loss or damage occurs on the line of a connecting carrier, is not confined to his remedy against the initial carrier. In such case, the shipper has the option, which he may or may not exercise, of holding the connecting carrier responsible.[21]

What Constitutes a Contract for Through Carriage

Even in those states holding to the American rule, the question of what does, and what does not, constitute a contract for through shipment, is frequently one of great difficulty. When the contract of shipment clearly and expressly provides either for or against through transportation, there is no trouble.

The contract which will make a carrier liable for through transportation, however, need not contain express words to that effect. The assumption of liability for losses beyond the carrier's line may be implied from the surrounding facts and circumstances of each shipment. In doubtful cases, great importance may attach to the words used in the receipt or bill of lading.[22] In the states following

& I. R. Co., 104 U. S. 146, 26 L. Ed. 679. See, also, Cavallaro v. Texas & P. Ry. Co., 110 Cal. 348, 42 Pac. 918, 52 Am. St. Rep. 94; Chesapeake & O. R. Co. v. O'Gara, King & Co., 144 Ky. 561, 139 S. W. 803; Taffe v. Oregon R. Co., 41 Or. 64, 67 Pac. 1015, 68 Pac. 732, 58 L. R. A. 187; Vincent & Hayne v. Yazoo & M. V. R. Co., 114 La. 1021, 38 South. 816; Virginia Coal & Iron Co. v. Louisville & N. R. Co., 98 Va. 776, 37 S. E. 310; McLendon v. Wabash R. Co., 119 Mo. App. 128, 95 S. W. 943; Shockley v. Pennsylvania R. Co., 109 Md. 123, 71 Atl. 437.

21 United States Mail Line Co. v. Carrollton Furniture Mfg. Co., 101 Ky. 658, 42 S. W. 342; Johnson v. East Tennessee, V. & G. Ry. Co., 90 Ga. 810, 17 S. E. 121; Cavallaro v. Texas & P. Ry. Co., 110 Cal. 348, 42 Pac. 918, 52 Am. St. Rep. 94; Halliday v. St. Louis, K. C. & N. Ry. Co., 74 Mo. 159, 41 Am. Rep. 309; Barter v. Wheeler, 49 N. H. 9, 6 Am. Rep. 434.

22 JOHNSON v. TOLEDO, S. & M. R. CO., 133 Mich. 596, 95 N. W. 724 103 Am. St. Rep. 464, Doble Cas. Bailments and Carriers, 248; Berg v. Narragansett Steamship Co., 5 Daly (N. Y.) 394; Robinson v. Merchants' Despatch

the American rule the following circumstances have been held to be evidence, though not conclusive, from which a contract for through transportation may be inferred:[23] The use of the words "to forward," or "to be forwarded," in the carrier's receipt;[24] a receipt or bill of lading which purports to be a through contract;[25] the giving of a through rate;[26] the prepayment of freight for the whole transportation;[27] the carrier's holding out to carry over

Transp. Co., 45 Iowa, 470; Piedmont Mfg. Co. v. Columbia & G. R. Co., 19 S. C. 353; Illinois Cent. R. Co. v. Kerr, 68 Miss. 14, 8 South. 330; Candee v. Pennsylvania R. Co., 21 Wis. 582, 94 Am. Dec. 566; International & G. N. Ry. Co. v. Tisdale, 74 Tex. 8, 11 S. W. 900, 4 L. R. A. 545; Evansville & C. R. Co. v. Androscoggin Mills, 22 Wall. 594, 22 L. Ed. 724. And see Camden & A. R. Co. v. Forsyth, 61 Pa. 81.

[23] Root v. Great Western R. Co., 45 N. Y. 524, 532; Hill Mfg. Co. v. Boston & L. R. Corp., 104 Mass. 122, 6 Am. Rep. 202; Camden & A. R. Co. v. Forsyth, 61 Pa. 81; Piedmont Mfg. Co. v. Columbia & G. R. Co., 19 S. C. 353; Woodward v. Illinois Cent. R. Co., 1 Biss. 403, Fed. Cas. No. 18,006; Buffington & Lee v. Wabash R. Co., 118 Mo. App. 476, 94 S. W. 991.

[24] Reed v. United States Exp. Co., 48 N. Y. 462, 8 Am. Rep. 561; Mercantile Mut. Ins. Co. v. Chase, 1 E. D. Smith (N. Y.) 115; Wilcox v. Parmelee, 3 Sandf. (N. Y.) 610; Schroeder v. Hudson R. R. Co., 5 Duer (N. Y.) 55; BUCKLAND v. ADAMS EXP. CO., 97 Mass. 124, 93 Am. Dec. 68, Dobie Cas. Bailments and Carriers, 177; Nashua Lock Co. v. Worcester & N. R. Co., 48 N. H. 339, 2 Am. Rep. 242; Cutts v. Brainerd, 42 Vt. 566, 1 Am. Rep. 353; East Tennessee & V. R. Co. v. Rogers, 6 Heisk. (Tenn.) 143, 19 Am. Rep. 589; St. Louis, K. C. & N. Ry. Co. v. Piper, 13 Kan. 505; Colfax Mountain Fruit Co. v. Southern Pac. Co., 118 Cal. 648, 50 Pac. 775, 40 L. R. A. 78.

[25] Helliwell v. Grand Trunk Ry. of Canada (C. C.) 7 Fed. 68; Richardson v. The Charles P. Chouteau (C. C.) 37 Fed. 532; Harp v. The Grand Era, 1 Woods, 184, Fed. Cas. No. 6,084; Myrick v. Michigan Cent. R. Co., 9 Biss. 44, Fed. Cas. No. 10,001; Houston & T. C. R. Co. v. Park, 1 White & W. Civ. Cas. Ct. App. (Tex.) § 332; Texas & P. R. Co. v. Parrish, 1 White & W. Civ. Cas. Ct. App. (Tex.) § 942; Loomis v. Wabash, St. L. & P. Ry. Co., 17 Mo. App. 340; Moore v. Henry, 18 Mo. App. 35; Wiggins Ferry Co. v. Chicago & A. R. Co., 73 Mo. 389, 39 Am. Rep. 519; Ireland v. Mobile & O. R. Co., 105 Ky. 400, 49 S. W. 188, 453; Buffington & Lee v. Wabash R. Co., 118 Mo. App. 476, 94 S. W. 991.

[26] Weed v. Saratoga & S. R. Co., 19 Wend. (N. Y.) 534; Berg v. Narragansett S. S. Co., 5 Daly (N. Y.) 394; Clyde v. Hubbard, 88 Pa. 358; Candee v. Pennsylvania R. Co., 21 Wis. 589, 94 Am. Dec. 566; Aiken v. Chicago, B. & Q. Ry. Co., 68 Iowa, 363, 27 N. W. 281; Evansville & C. R. Co. v. Androscoggin Mills, 22 Wall. 594, 22 L. Ed. 724. But see McCarthy v. Terre Haute & I. R. Co., 9 Mo. App. 159; East Tennessee & G. R. Co. v. Montgomery, 44 Ga. 278; Farmers' Loan & Trust Co. v. Northern Pac. R. Co., 120 Fed. 873, 57 C. C. A. 533.

[27] Berg v. Narragansett S. S. Co., 5 Daly (N. Y.) 394; Candee v. Pennsylvania R. Co., 21 Wis. 589, 94 Am. Dec. 566; Weed v. Saratoga & S. R. Co., 19 Wend. (N. Y.) 534; Piedmont Mfg. Co. v. Columbia & G. R. Co., 19 S. C. 353; Illinois Cent. R. Co. v. Kerr, 68 Miss. 14, 8 South. 330; Scott County Milling Co. v. St. Louis, I. M. & S. R. Co., 127 Mo. App. 80, 104 S. W. 924.

the whole distance;[28] or an agreement that the goods be carried through in a particular car.[29]

Authority of Agents to Make Through Contracts

In jurisdictions in which the English rule obtains, it is usually held that the agent of the initial carrier, with authority to receive goods for shipment, has authority to bind such carrier for through shipments over the lines of other carriers.[30] This seems to follow, since, under this rule, a presumptive contract for through shipment arises when goods are received, consigned to points beyond the line of the initial carrier.

Under the American rule, requiring a positive contract besides such acceptance, somewhat different considerations are applicable. The general freight agent of a railroad company has unquestioned power to bind the company by a contract for transportation to points beyond its own line.[31] A mere station agent, however, has ordinarily no such power.[32] Nor is the power to bind the railroad by through contracts over the lines of connecting carriers to be inferred as vesting in station agents merely because these are authorized by a railroad to accept goods for shipment over its own line and in such cases to issue bills of lading for the goods thus received.[33]

The authority to make through contracts, however, may have been expressly conferred on station agents by the proper superior officer, or there may have been previous dealings from which the

[28] Root v. Great Western R. Co., 45 N. Y. 524; Collender v. Dinsmore, 55 N. Y. 200, 14 Am. Rep. 224; Toledo, P. & W. Ry. Co. v. Merriman, 52 Ill. 123, 4 Am. Rep. 590; Hill Mfg. Co. v. Boston & L. R. Corp., 104 Mass. 122, 6 Am. Rep. 202; Robinson v. Merchants' Despatch Transp. Co., 45 Iowa, 470; Harris v. Cheshire R. Co. (R. I.) 16 Atl. 512; St. John v. Southern Exp. Co., 1 Woods, 612, Fed. Cas. No. 12,228.

[29] International & G. N. Ry. Co. v. Tisdale, 74 Tex. 8, 11 S. W. 900, 4 L. R. A. 545. JOHNSON v. TOLEDO, S. & M. R. CO., 133 Mich. 596, 95 N. W. 724, 103 Am. St. Rep. 464, Dobie Cas. Bailments and Carriers, 248. For other examples of what constitutes a through contract, see 1 Hutch. Carr. §§ 238, 239.

[30] Scotthorn v. South Staffordshire R. Co., 8 Exch. (Eng.) 341; Nichols v. Oregon Short Line R. Co., 24 Utah, 83, 66 Pac. 768, 91 Am. St. Rep. 778; Southern Exp. Co. v. Boullemet, 100 Ala. 275, 13 South. 941; Hansen v. Flint & P. M. R. Co., 73 Wis. 346, 41 N. W. 529, 9 Am. St. Rep. 791.

[31] Grover & Baker Sewing Mach. Co. v. Missouri Pac. Ry. Co., 70 Mo. 672, 35 Am. Rep. 444; White v. Missouri Pac. Ry. Co., 19 Mo. App. 400.

[32] Turner v. St. Louis & S. F. Ry. Co., 20 Mo. App. 632; Burroughs v. Norwich & W. R. Co., 100 Mass. 26, 1 Am. Rep. 78; Sutton v. Chicago & N. W. Ry. Co., 14 S. D. 111, 84 N. W. 396; Pittsburgh, C., C. & St. L. Ry. Co. v. Bryant, 36 Ind. App. 340, 75 N. E. 829.

[33] McLagan v. Chicago & N. W. R. Co., 116 Iowa, 183, 89 N. W. 233; Hoffman v. Cumberland Valley R. Co., 85 Md. 391, 37 Atl. 214; Page v. Chicago, St. P., M. & O. Ry. Co., 7 S. D. 297, 64 N. W. 137.

authority may be reasonably inferred.[34] Thus, where other similar contracts had been made by the station agent, and such contracts had been recognized and carried out by the carrier, this was said to be a course of dealing between the shipper and the carrier's agent from which the authority of the agent to make the contract might well be inferred.[35] By a holding out on the part of the railroad company, or by custom, the station agent may have such authority,[36] and usually does when the station is a large and important one, at which the volume of traffic is sufficiently great.

Partnership Liability

If two or more connecting carriers enter into a partnership agreement for the transportation of freight or baggage over a through route, each partner becomes liable for the defaults of the others.[37] The result is the same as to third persons if the carriers hold themselves out as partners, though they are not such in fact. They are thereby estopped to deny the partnership as to one who has intrusted goods to their care in reliance on such representation.[38] Both as to what constitutes a partnership between such carriers and as to the legal results flowing from such a partnership, when it is once established, the same general considerations gov-

[34] Burroughs v. Norwich & W. R. Co., 100 Mass. 26, 1 Am. Rep. 78; Turner v. St. Louis & S. F. Ry. Co., 20 Mo. App. 632; Grover & Baker Sewing Mach. Co. v. Missouri Pac. Ry. Co., 70 Mo. 672, 35 Am. Rep. 444.

[35] White v. Missouri Pac. Ry. Co., 19 Mo. App. 400.

[36] Faulkner v. Chicago, R. I. & P. R. Co., 99 Mo. App. 421, 73 S. W. 927.

[37] Rocky Mount Mills v. Wilmington & W. R. Co., 119 N. C. 693, 25 S. E. 854, 56 Am. St. Rep. 682; Eckles v. Missouri Pac. R. Co., 112 Mo. App. 240, 87 S. W. 99; Cobb v. Abbot, 14 Pick. (Mass.) 289; Briggs v. Vanderbilt, 19 Barb. (N. Y.) 222, 237; Hart v. Rensselaer & S. R. Co., 8 N. Y. 37, 59 Am. Dec. 447; Bostwick v. Champion, 11 Wend. (N. Y.) 571, affirmed Champion v. Bostwick, 18 Wend. (N. Y.) 175, 31 Am. Dec. 376; Montgomery & W. P. R. Co. v. Moore, 51 Ala. 394; Ellsworth v. Tartt, 26 Ala. 733, 62 Am. Dec. 749; Weyland v. Elkins, Holt, N. P. (Eng.) 227, 1 Starkie, 272; Fromont v. Coupland, 2 Bing. (Eng.) 170. Though a railroad company or other corporation doing business as a carrier may have no power to form such a partnership, it is still liable to third persons when it has attempted to do so and has held itself out as such. Swift v. Pacific Mail S. S. Co., 106 N. Y. 206, 12 N. E. 583; Wylde v. Northern R. Co. of New Jersey, 53 N. Y. 156; Block v. Fitchburg R. Co., 139 Mass. 308, 1 N. E. 348; Barter v. Wheeler, 49 N. H. 9, 6 Am. Rep. 434. Where a traffic agreement between initial and connecting carriers made them partners in the carriage of freight or agents of each other, the connecting carrier is estopped from denying the recitals in a bill of lading in any case the initial carrier is estopped. Smith v. Southern Ry., 89 S. C. 415, 71 S. E. 989. See, also, R. E. FUNSTEN DRIED FRUIT & NUT CO. v. TOLEDO, ST. L. & W. R. CO., 163 Mo. App. 426, 143 S. W. 839, Dobie Cas. Bailments and Carriers, 196.

[38] Pattison v. Blanchard, 5 N. Y. 186; Bostwick v. Champion, 11 Wend. (N. Y.) 571, affirmed Champion v. Bostwick, 18 Wend. (N. Y.) 175, 31 Am. Dec. 376.

ern as in other partnership cases.[39] In some of the cases the relation is rather one of simple agency than of partnership.[40]

Though the cases are not entirely harmonious,[41] a partnership is usually inferred when the carriers stipulate that the profits of the entire transportation are to be shared according to a certain ratio.[42] The same result does not follow, though, from an apportionment of the gross returns according to the distances the goods have been transported by the several carriers.[43] Nor does a part-

[39] 1 Hutch. Carr. § 251.

[40] Wells Fargo & Co. v. Battle, 5 Tex. Civ. App. 532, 24 S. W. 353; Gulf, C. & S. F. Ry. Co. v. Williams, 4 Tex. Civ. App. 294, 23 S. W. 626.

[41] For admirable summary of what the cases seem to establish, see 1 Hutch. Carr. § 263.

[42] Peterson v. Chicago, R. I. & P. Ry. Co., 80 Iowa, 92, 45 N. W. 573; Carter v. Peck, 4 Sneed (Tenn.) 203, 67 Am. Dec. 604; Hart v. Rensselaer & S. R. Co., 8 N. Y. 37, 59 Am. Dec. 447; Cincinnati, H. & D. R. Co. v. Spratt, 2 Duv. (Ky.) 4; Block v. Fitchburg R. Co., 139 Mass. 308, 1 N. E. 348; Hill Mfg. Co. v. Boston & L. R. Corp., 104 Mass. 122, 6 Am. Rep. 202; Wyman v. Chicago & A. R. Co., 4 Mo. App. 35. But see Smith v. Missouri, K. & T. Ry. Co., 58 Mo. App. 80. Where the owners of stage lines each provided their own carriages and horses, employed their own drivers, and paid the expenses of their separate sections of the route, except the tolls at turnpike gates, and the moneys received as the fare of passengers, after deducting such tolls, were divided among the occupants of the several sections, in proportion to the number of miles of the route run by each, they were held liable as partners. Bostwick v. Champion, 11 Wend. (N. Y.) 571, affirmed Champion v. Bostwick, 18 Wend. (N. Y.) 175, 31 Am. Dec. 376. But the fact that the connecting carriers transact their true business by means of a joint committee or a common agent will not make them liable as such. Straiton v. New York & N. H. R. Co., 2 E. D. Smith (N. Y.) 184; Ellsworth v. Tartt, 26 Ala. 733, 62 Am. Dec. 749; Watkins v. Terre Haute & I. R. Co., 8 Mo. App. 570. An agreement to share pro rata losses that cannot be located does not make the connecting carriers partners. Aigen v. Boston & M. R., 132 Mass. 423. An arrangement between a dispatch company of St. Louis, Mo., and sundry railroad companies whose lines terminated at New York, whereby the latter separately agreed to carry all goods for the transportation of which the former should contract, does not involve joint liability upon the part of the railroad companies, nor make them partners either inter sese or as to third persons. St. Louis Ins. Co. v. St. Louis, V. T. H. & I. R. Co., 104 U. S. 146, 26 L. Ed. 679.

[43] Ellsworth v. Tartt, 26 Ala. 733, 62 Am. Dec. 749; Montgomery & W. P. R. Co. v. Moore, 51 Ala. 394; St. Louis Ins. Co. v. St. Louis V. T. H. & I. R. Co., 104 U. S. 146, 26 L. Ed. 679; Briggs v. Vanderbilt, 19 Barb. (N. Y.) 222; Gass v. New York, P. & B. R. Co., 99 Mass. 220, 96 Am. Dec. 742; Converse v. Norwich & N. Y. Transp. Co., 33 Conn. 166. Where several persons were engaged in running a line of stages, and, by the agreement between them, one was to run at his own expense a certain portion of the route, and the others, in like manner, the residue, each being authorized to receive fare from passengers over the whole or any part of the route, and the fare so received to be divided between them in proportion to the distance which they respectively transported such passengers, held, that this did not constitute a partnership between the

nership liability as to third persons necessarily result from the mere fact, standing alone, of the employment of common agents acting on behalf of all the carriers involved in the shipment in question.[44] Added to other favoring circumstances, however, this fact might well turn the scale in favor of the partnership relation.

When Delivery to Connecting Carrier is Complete

When goods are received by a carrier to be transported to a point beyond its own line, under circumstances which, according to principles discussed in the preceding paragraphs, make the initial carrier liable as an insurer only to the end of its own line, there is nevertheless superadded to its duty as a common carrier over its own line that of delivering the goods safely to the connecting carrier. This duty on the part of the initial carrier is an obligation implied in receiving the goods consigned to a point beyond its own line.[45] Until this duty is performed, the first carrier continues liable as an insurer.[46] The delivery to the connecting carrier, too,

parties. Pattison v. Blanchard, 5 N. Y. 186. See, also, Post v. Southern Ry. Co., 103 Tenn. 184, 52 S. W. 301, 55 L. R. A. 481.

[44] Gulf, C. & S. F. Ry. Co. v. Baird, 75 Tex. 256, 12 S. W. 530; Kansas City S. R. Co. v. Embry, 76 Ark. 589, 90 S. W. 15. But see Cobb v. Abbot, 14 Pick. (Mass.) 289; Schutter v. Adams Exp. Co., 5 Mo. App. 316; Wilson v. Chesapeake & O. R. Co., 21 Grat. (Va.) 654; Carter v. Peck, 4 Sneed (Tenn.) 203, 67 Am. Dec. 604.

[45] Fremont, E. & M. V. R. Co. v. Waters, 50 Neb. 592, 70 N. W. 225; Hooper v. Chicago & N. W. Ry. Co., 27 Wis. 81, 9 Am. Rep. 439; Myrick v. Michigan Cent. R. Co., 107 U. S. 102, 1 Sup. Ct. 425, 27 L. Ed. 325. If the first carrier disregards the shipper's orders, and forwards the goods by a different carrier, it is liable for any loss sustained by the shipper. Isaacson v. New York Cent. & H. R. R. Co., 94 N. Y. 278, 46 Am. Rep. 142; Johnson v. New York Cent. R. Co., 33 N. Y. 610, 88 Am. Dec. 416; Georgia R. Co. v. Cole, 68 Ga. 623; Langdon v. Robertson, 13 Ont. (Canada) 497. A common carrier who undertakes to transport goods over his own route, and then to forward them to a designated destination beyond, is bound to transmit, with their delivery to the carrier next en route, all special instructions received by him from the consignor, and, in default thereof, make good any loss resulting from failure to do so. Marks or labels on the packages delivered will not supply the omission of such instructions from the accompanying shipping bills, where they are shown not to have come to the actual knowledge of the next succeeding carrier, or his agent, charged with the duty of receiving and forwarding such bills. Little Miami R. Co. v. Washburn, 22 Ohio St. 324; Danna v. New York Cent. & H. R. R. Co., 50 How. Prac. (N. Y.) 428. A carrier who acts as the forwarding agent of the owner of goods, in giving directions, by way bills or otherwise, to the successive lines of transportation over which they are to be carried, beyond the termination of his own route, is responsible, as such forwarding agent, only for want of reasonable diligence and care. Northern R. Co. v. Fitchburg R. Co., 6 Allen (Mass.) 254.

[46] Reynolds v. Boston & A. R. Co., 121 Mass. 291; Texas & P. R. Co. v. Clayton, 173 U. S. 348, 19 Sup. Ct. 421, 43 L. Ed. 725; Chicago, I. & L. R. Co. v. Woodward, 164 Ind. 360, 72 N. E. 558, 73 N. E. 810.

must be an actual delivery, or acts which are so far equivalent to a delivery as make the next line assume the relation of a carrier to the goods.[47] The first carrier does not, by unloading the goods at the end of its line, become a mere warehouseman.[48] The shipper who delivers his goods to a common carrier has a right to understand that the liability of an insurer is upon some carrier during the whole period of the transit. The duty of one carrier is not discharged, therefore, until it has been imposed upon the succeeding carrier,[49] and this is not done until there is an actual delivery of the goods, or at least such acts as are in law equivalent to a tender of delivery.

The owner loses sight of his goods when he delivers them to the first carrier, and has no means of learning their whereabouts till

[47] Wehmann v. Minneapolis, St. P. & S. S. M. Ry. Co., 58 Minn. 22, 59 N. W. 546. Notifying second carrier to take goods, which he does not do, is not a discharge. Goold v. Chapin, 20 N. Y. 259, 75 Am. Dec. 398. If carrier of freight to be transferred to another carrier merely stores it in warehouse of its own, whence the other is in habit of taking it at its convenience, and freight, while so stored, is destroyed, first carrier is liable for its value. Condon v. Marquette, H. & O. R. Co., 55 Mich. 218, 21 N. W. 321, 54 Am. Rep. 367; Lawrence v. Winona & St. P. R. Co., 15 Minn. 390 (Gil. 313), 2 Am. Rep. 130; Wood v. Milwaukee & St. P. Ry. Co., 27 Wis. 541, 9 Am. Rep. 465; Conkey v. Milwaukee & St. P. Ry. Co., 31 Wis. 619, 11 Am. Rep. 630. If a carrier is ready to deliver goods to succeeding carrier, yet it is liable as common carrier for a reasonable time, until, according to usual course of business, the vessel of the succeeding carrier can arrive to take the goods. Mills v. Michigan Cent. R. Co., 45 N. Y. 622, 6 Am. Rep. 152. Compare Barter v. Wheeler, 49 N. H. 9, 6 Am. Rep. 434. Taking of part of a lot of goods by a railroad company from a steamboat company, and fact that rest were pointed out and ready to be taken from the boat, does not necessarily constitute constructive delivery of the whole. Gass v. New York, P. & B. R. Co., 99 Mass. 220, 96 Am. Dec. 742. Carrier is not discharged of his liability where he receives goods for transportation to point beyond end of his route, and there are public means of transportation from there to place of destination, by delivering them to mere wharfinger at end of his route, in absence of established usage to that effect, but he must deliver them to some proper carrier to be taken further. But, when there are no public means of further transportation, such point must be regarded as place of destination, and he may properly deliver to warehouseman or wharfinger. Hermann v. Goodrich, 21 Wis. 536, 94 Am. Dec. 562. See, also, Palmer v. Chicago, B. & Q. R. Co., 56 Conn. 137, 13 Atl. 818; Lewis v. Chesapeake & O. Ry. Co., 47 W. Va. 656, 35 S. E. 908, 81 Am. St. Rep. 816; Mt. Vernon Co. v. Alabama G. S. R. Co., 92 Ala. 296, 8 South. 687.

[48] Conkey v. Milwaukee & St. P. R. Co., 31 Wis. 619, 11 Am. Rep. 630; Barter v. Wheeler, 49 N. H. 9, 6 Am. Rep. 434; Michigan Cent. R. Co. v. Mineral Springs Mfg. Co., 16 Wall. 318, 21 L. Ed. 297; In re Petersen (C. C.) 21 Fed. 885; Texas & P. R. Co. v. Clayton, 84 Fed. 305, 28 C. C. A. 142.

[49] Condon v. Marquette, H. & O. R. Co., 55 Mich. 218, 21 N. W. 321, 54 Am. Rep. 367. And see Louisville, St. L. & T. R. Co. v. Bourne (Ky.) 29 S. W. 975; Buston v. Pennsylvania R. Co., 119 Fed. 808, 56 C. C. A. 320.

he or the consignee is informed of their arrival at the place of destination. At each successive point of transfer from one carrier to another, the goods are liable to be placed in warehouses, and during this storage the danger of injury to, or loss of, the goods, either from collusion of the carrier or other cause, is equally as great as while the goods are actually in transit. Again, the storing of the goods under such circumstances is to be regarded solely as an incident of, and accessory to, their actual transportation.[50]

If a connecting carrier, to whom the goods are properly tendered by another carrier, refuses to receive the goods for transportation, such other carrier, tendering the goods, should store the goods and notify either the consignor or consignee of the situation.[51] During such storage, the liability of the carrier storing the goods is merely that of a warehouseman.[52]

Presumptions and Burden of Proof

When goods are lost or injured in the course of transportation over connecting lines, the consignor or consignee (plaintiff in the action brought for such loss or injury) has ordinarily no means of showing on the line of which carrier the loss or injury occurred. In such cases, therefore, the law resorts to certain prima facie presumptions in his favor.[53]

50 McDonald v. Western R. Corp., 34 N. Y. 497; Fenner v. Buffalo & S. L R. Co., 44 N. Y. 505, 4 Am. Rep. 709.

51 Fisher v. Boston & M. R. Co., 99 Me. 338, 59 Atl. 532, 68 L. R. A. 390, 105 Am. St. Rep. 283. Without instructions from the consignor, there is no right to forward the goods by another route. Johnson v. New York Cent. R. Co., 33 N. Y. 610, 88 Am. Dec. 416; Rawson v. Holland, 59 N. Y. 611, 17 Am. Rep. 394; Nutting v. Connecticut River R. Co., 1 Gray (Mass.) 502; Louisville & N. R. Co. v. Campbell, 7 Heisk. (Tenn.) 253; Lesinsky v. Great Western Dispatch Co., 10 Mo. App. 134; Michigan Cent. R. Co. v. Mineral Springs Mfg. Co., 16 Wall. 318, 21 L. Ed. 297; In re Petersen (C. C.) 21 Fed. 885; Deming v. Norfolk & W. R. Co. (C. C.) 21 Fed. 25. But, in Regan v. Grand Trunk Ry., 61 N. H. 579, where perishable goods were shipped, and the connecting carrier designated was unable to receive them, it was held that the first carrier exercised reasonable care by forwarding the goods over another route. It may be provided, by agreement or custom between connecting carriers, that a constructive delivery shall terminate the first carrier's liability, without an actual change of possession. See McDonald v. Western R. Corp., 34 N. Y. 497; Condon v. Marquette, H. & O. R. Co., 55 Mich. 218, 21 N. W. 321, 54 Am. Rep. 367; Converse v. Norwich & N. Y. Transp. Co., 33 Conn. 166; Pratt v. Grand Trunk R. Co., 95 U. S. 43, 24 L. Ed. 336. The owner may take advantage of such a usage, and recover against the carrier to whom the goods have been constructively delivered. Ætna Ins. Co. v. Wheeler, 49 N. Y. 616.

52 Johnson v. New York Cent. R. Co., 33 N. Y. 610, 88 Am. Dec. 416; Nutting v. Connecticut River R. Co., 1 Gray (Mass.) 502; Michigan Cent. R. Co. v. Mineral Springs Mfg. Co., 16 Wall. 318, 21 L. Ed. 297.

53 Laughlin v. Chicago & N. W. Ry. Co., 28 Wis. 204, 9 Am. Rep. 493;

In the case of injury to the goods, or loss of a part of them, such partial loss or injury is prima facie attributable to that carrier in whose possession the goods are found either in a damaged condition or with part of the goods missing.[54] This presumption is most frequently invoked against the last carrier, who delivers the goods to the consignee in a damaged condition or with part of them missing. In an action, in such cases, against the last carrier, when it is shown that all the goods were delivered by the shipper to the initial carrier in good condition, unless the last carrier can show that the goods when he received them were in the same injured condition as when he delivered them, the last carrier is liable.[55] The basis of this presumption is that the condition once shown to exist (all of the goods in proper condition in the hands of the initial carrier) is presumed to continue until the contrary is shown by affirmative evidence.[56]

It is sometimes said that the rule just stated applies even when the goods are entirely lost and there is no showing where such

MOORE v. NEW YORK, N. H. & H. R. CO., 173 Mass. 335, 53 N. E. 816, 73 Am. St. Rep. 298, Dobie Cas. Bailments and Carriers, 251.

[54] Sheble v. Oregon R. & Nav. Co., 51 Wash. 359, 98 Pac. 745; Laughlin v. Chicago & N. W. Ry. Co., 28 Wis. 204, 9 Am. Rep. 493; Mobile & O. R. Co. v. Tupelo Furniture Mfg. Co., 67 Miss. 35, 7 South. 279, 19 Am. St. Rep. 262; MOORE v. NEW YORK, N. H. & H. R. CO., 173 Mass. 335, 53 N. E. 816, 73 Am. St. Rep. 298, Dobie Cas. Bailments and Carriers, 251; Beede v. Wisconsin Cent. R. Co., 90 Minn. 36, 95 N. W. 454, 101 Am. St. Rep. 390; Yesbik v. Macon, D. & S. R. Co., 11 Ga. App. 298, 75 S. E. 207.

[55] MOORE v. NEW YORK, N. H. & H. R. CO., 173 Mass. 335, 53 N. E. 816, 73 Am. St. Rep. 298, Dobie Cas. Bailments and Carriers, 251; Laughlin v. Chicago & N. W. Ry. Co., 28 Wis. 204, 9 Am. Rep. 493; Mobile & O. R. Co. v. Tupelo Furniture Mfg. Co., 67 Miss. 35, 7 South. 279, 19 Am. St. Rep. 262; Texas & P. Ry. Co. v. Barnhart, 5 Tex. Civ. App. 601, 23 S. W. 801, 24 S. W. 331; Texas & P. R. Co. v. Adams, 78 Tex. 372, 14 S. W. 666, 22 Am. St. Rep. 56; Lin v. Terre Haute & I. R. R., 10 Mo. App. 125; Central Railroad & Banking Co. v. Bayer, 91 Ga. 115, 16 S. E. 953; International & G. N. Ry. Co. v. Foltz, 3 Tex. Civ. App. 644, 22 S. W. 541; Faison v. Alabama & V. Ry. Co., 69 Miss. 569, 13 South. 37, 30 Am. St. Rep. 577. But see International & G. N. R. Co. v. Wolf, 3 Tex. Civ. App. 383, 22 S. W. 187; Western Ry. Co. v. Harwell, 97 Ala. 341, 11 South. 781; Georgia, F. & A. R. Co. v. W. H. Stanton & Co., 5 Ga. App. 500, 63 S. E. 655; Philadelphia, B. & W. R. Co. v. Diffendal, 109 Md. 494, 72 Atl. 193, 458; Connelly v. Illinois Cent. R. Co., 133 Mo. App. 310, 113 S. W. 233; New York & B. Transp. Line v. Lewis Baer & Co., 118 Md. 73, 84 Atl. 251; St. Louis, I. M. & S. R. Co. v. Carlile, 35 Okl. 118, 128 Pac. 690; Williamsport Hardwood Lumber Co. v. Baltimore & O. R. Co., 71 W. Va. 741, 77 S. E. 333.

[56] Smith v. New York Cent. R. Co., 43 Barb. (N. Y.) 225; Laughlin v. Chicago & N. W. Ry. Co., 28 Wis. 204, 9 Am. Rep. 493; Forrester v. Georgia Railroad & Banking Co., 92 Ga. 699, 19 S. E. 811. See, also, cases cited in preceding notes.

total loss occurred; in other words, when the shipper delivers the goods to the initial carrier and never hears of them again. The cases cited, however, are practically all of them cases of delivery of the goods in a damaged condition. It hardly seems fair, in the absence of any showing that the goods ever came into its possession, to hold that carrier responsible which forms the last link in the intended chain of transportation. A fairer rule, on proof of delivery to the initial carrier, is to hold such carrier prima facie liable for the total loss, unless it can show delivery to the second carrier and so on.[57] Here that carrier should be responsible into whose possession the goods can last be traced. A carrier, then, to whom possession of the goods can be traced, is prima facie liable for the total loss, and escapes liability by showing (as it can easily do when that is the real situation) a delivery to the next carrier. Under this scheme, in cases of total loss, liability (instead of starting with the last carrier and working backward) begins with the initial carrier and moves forward (on proof of possession) through the intermediate carriers towards the last carrier.

Statutes—State and Federal

The question of the liability of the initial carrier for loss or damage occurring on the lines of connecting carriers has been further complicated by statutes passed in many of the states. The trend of these statutes has unquestionably been towards imposing such liability on the initial carrier. In some states, the rule of Muschamp's Case is adopted.[58] In other states, even more stringent rules affecting the liability of the initial carrier have been enacted by the Legislatures. The particular statutes should, of course, in each case be consulted.[59]

By what is known as the Carmack Amendment to the federal Interstate Commerce Act,[60] a common carrier, receiving property

[57] See Brintnall v. Saratoga & W. R. Co., 32 Vt. 665. But in Glazer v. Old Dominion S. S. Co. (Sup.) 113 N. Y. Supp. 979, it was held that, in an action against an initial carrier for loss of goods, the burden was on the plaintiff to show a failure to deliver to the connecting carrier. And in Mobile, J. & K. C. R. Co. v. T. J. Phillips & Co. (Miss.) 60 South. 572, it was held that the connecting carrier is not liable for the loss of a package, when it was not shown that the initial carrier delivered this package to the connecting carrier.

[58] McCann v. Eddy, 133 Mo. 59, 33 S. W. 71, 35 L. R. A. 110, affirmed in Missouri, K. & T. R. Co. v. McCann, 174 U. S. 580, 19 Sup. Ct. 755, 43 L. Ed. 1093; Dimmitt v. Kansas City, St. J. & C. B. R. Co., 103 Mo. 440, 15 S. W. 761.

[59] See note, 2 Ann. Cas. 517.

[60] Interstate Commerce Act Feb. 4, 1887, c. 104, § 20, 24 Stat. 386 (U. S. Comp. St. 1901, p. 3169) as amended by Act June 29, 1906, c. 3591, § 7, pars.

for transportation from a point in one state to a point in another state, is liable for injury or loss occurring either on its own line or that of a connecting carrier, and from this liability the initial carrier cannot exempt itself by express contract to that effect. This statute, of course, applies only to interstate commerce. In imposing this liability on the initial carrier, and then in prohibiting such carrier from relieving itself, even by express contract, from responsibility for loss or damage on the lines of connecting carriers, the Carmack Amendment goes far beyond the English rule. Its constitutionality has been expressly upheld by the United States Supreme Court.[61]

Though, in the absence of statute, it is believed that the American rule is the better one, considerations of practical expediency seem to justify the wisdom of the Carmack Amendment, which, without imposing undue hardship on the initial carrier, has worked well in practice. The amendment expressly gives the initial carrier a remedy over against the connecting carrier on whose line the loss or injury actually occurred.

SAME—EXCUSES FOR NONDELIVERY BY THE CARRIER

146. The common carrier is excused for a failure to deliver the goods to the consignee:

(a) When the goods are demanded by one having paramount title to them.

(b) When the consignor, owing to the insolvency of the buyer, has exercised the right of stoppage in transitu.

(c) When the goods, in the absence of negligence on the part of the carrier, have been lost, owing to one of the excepted perils.

There still remain for discussion those cases in which the responsibility of the common carrier of the goods is terminated, though he makes no delivery either to a consignee or to a connecting carrier. In the first two of the three cases outlined in the

11, 12, 34 Stat. 595 (U. S. Comp. St. Supp. 1911, p. 1307). See this discussed in Judson on Interstate Commerce (2d Ed.) § 407.

[61] Atlantic Coast Line R. Co. v. Riverside Mills, 219 U. S. 186, 31 Sup. Ct. 164, 55 L. Ed. 167, 31 L. R. A. (N. S.) 7. For recent decisions construing the Carmack amendment, see Galveston, H. & S. A. R. Co. v. Wallace, 223 U. S. 481, 32 Sup. Ct. 205, 56 L. Ed. 516; De Winter & Co. v. Texas Cent. R. Co., 150 App. Div. 612, 135 N. Y. Supp. 893; Shultz v. Skaneateles R. Co., 145 App. Div. 906, 129 N. Y. Supp. 1146; St. Louis, I. M. & S. R. Co. v. Furlow, 89 Ark. 404, 117 S. W. 517.

black letter text, it will readily be seen that the carrier, in delivering the goods to a person other than the consignee, has merely performed a positive duty imposed on him by law. And, on his making such delivery, he is exempted from all liability in the premises. In the third case, no delivery is made to any one by the carrier, owing to the loss of the goods through agencies for which the carrier is not legally responsible; so that necessarily here a delivery is impossible and no liability is imposed on the carrier. In all these cases, it will be noted, the duty of the carrier is not merely changed into that of a warehouseman, but it thereby escapes all liability whatsoever.

Demand of Paramount Owner

The questions of the estoppel of the bailee to deny the title of his bailor, and the insuring liability of the bailee to make a proper delivery when he has notice of the claim of a third person adverse to the bailor, have already been discussed as to ordinary bailments.[62] The same considerations apply in the case of the extraordinary bailment for carriage. The liability of the bailee is the same in both classes of bailments.

Thus, not only is the carrier estopped from setting up in himself any title to the goods which denies the title of the bailor at the creation of the bailment but he is also prevented from setting up, of his own motion, the claims of third persons to defeat the title of the bailor.[63] Still, when such third person gives notice to the carrier of an adverse claim, then must the carrier (just as other bailees) deliver to such third person if his claim be well founded.[64] When, therefore, the claims of the third person are in fact paramount, then is the carrier not only justified in delivering to such claimant, but is bound to make such delivery. Hence, in yielding to the paramount owner by delivering the goods to him,

[62] Ante, §§ 14, 19.

[63] Wells v. American Exp. Co., 55 Wis. 23, 11 N. W. 537, 12 N. W. 441, 42 Am. Rep. 695; Sheridan v. New Quay Co., 4 C. B. N. S. (Eng.) 618; Lacouch v. Powell, 3 Esp. (Eng.) 115.

[64] Western Transp. Co. v. Barber, 56 N. Y. 544; Bates v. Stanton, 1 Duer (N. Y.) 79; Floyd v. Bovard, 6 Watts & S. (Pa.) 75; King v. Richards, 6 Whart. (Pa.) 418, 37 Am. Dec. 420; The Idaho, 93 U. S. 575, 23 L. Ed. 978; Rosenfield v. Express Co., 1 Woods, 131, Fed. Cas. No. 12,060; Great Western Ry. Co. v. Crouch, 3 Hurl. & N. (Eng.) 183; Boroughs v. Bayne, 5 Hurl. & N. (Eng.) 296; Taylor v. Plumer, 3 Maule & S. (Eng.) 562. A refusal to deliver would constitute a conversion. Shellenberg v. Fremont, E. & M. V. R. Co., 45 Neb. 487, 63 N. W. 859, 50 Am. St. Rep. 561. If the carrier delivers the goods according to the contract of carriage without any notice of the claim of the real owner, the carrier is not liable. Sheridan v. New Quay Co., 4 C. B. N. S. (Eng.) 618.

the carrier has performed his full legal duty in the premises. He is then, of course, excused from making a delivery to the consignee. Thus the carrier, when sued by the consignee for nondelivery, has a perfect defense in delivery of the goods to one having a paramount title to them.[65]

Stoppage in Transitu

According to a well-known principle of the law of sales, when the buyer of goods becomes or is insolvent, the unpaid seller, who has parted with the possession of the goods, can stop the goods in transit and thus regain possession of the goods. The seller then becomes for practical purposes, entitled to the same rights in regard to the goods which he would have had, had he never parted with the possession. This right is known as the "right of stoppage in transitu." [66]

Any extended discussion of the right of stoppage in transitu belongs more properly to the law of sales. The right, however, is highly favored by the law, on the ground that it is inequitable that what are essentially the goods of one should be taken to pay the debts of another. The right arises only on the insolvency of the buyer; such insolvency constituting a condition not in the contemplation of the seller when he turned the goods over to the carrier, consigned to the buyer.[67]

[65] Hentz v. The Idaho, 93 U. S. 575, 23 L. Ed. 978; National Bank of Commerce v. Chicago, B. & N. R. Co., 44 Minn. 224, 46 N. W. 342, 560, 9 L. R. A. 263, 20 Am. St. Rep. 566; Sheridan v. New Quay Co., 4 C. B. N. S. (Eng.) 618; Hardman v. Willcock, 9 Bing. 382; Biddle v. Bond, 6 Best & S. (Eng.) 225; Cheesman v. Exall, 6 Exch. (Eng.) 341; Dixon v. Yates, 5 Barn & Adol. (Eng.) 340; American Exp. Co. v. Greenhalgh, 80 Ill. 68; Young v. East Alabama Ry. Co., 80 Ala. 100; Wolfe v. Missouri Pac. Ry. Co., 97 Mo. 473, 11 S. W. 49, 3 L. R. A. 539, 10 Am. St. Rep. 331. To justify delivery to the true owner, contrary to or without the shipper's orders, the carrier has the burden of proving the ownership and immediate right of possession in the person to whom such delivery is made. Wolfe v. Missouri Pac. Ry. Co., 97 Mo. 473, 11 S. W. 49, 3 L. R. A. 539, 10 Am. St. Rep. 331.

[66] See American Sales Act, § 57. For excellent discussion of stoppage in transitu, see Williston on Sales, §§ 517-522. See, also, Gibson v. Carruthers, 8 Mees. & W. (Eng.) 321; Jeffris v. Fitchburg R. Co., 93 Wis. 250, 67 N. W. 424, 33 L. R. A. 351, 57 Am. St. Rep. 919; Walsh v. Blakely, 6 Mont. 194, 9 Pac. 809; Rowley v. Bigelow, 12 Pick. (Mass.) 307, 313, 23 Am. Dec. 607; Durgy Cement & Umber Co. v. O'Brien, 123 Mass. 12; Seymour v. Newton, 105 Mass. 272; Muller v. Pondir, 55 N. Y. 325, 14 Am. Rep. 259; Gossler v. Schepeler, 5 Daly (N. Y.) 476; Gwyn v. Richmond & D. R. Co., 85 N. C. 429, 39 Am. Rep. 708; Benedict v. Schaettle, 12 Ohio St. 515; Reynolds v. Boston & M. R. R., 43 N. H. 580; Loeb v. Peters, 63 Ala. 243, 35 Am. Rep. 17; Secomb v. Nutt, 14 B. Mon. (Ky.) 324; Millard v. Webster, 54 Conn. 415, 8 Atl. 470. For a case where the right does not exist, see Lester v. Delaware, L. & W. R. Co., 73 Hun, 398, 26 N. Y. Supp. 206.

[67] See cases cited in preceding note. A person is insolvent (according to

This right of the seller continues only while the goods are in transit.[68] A delivery to the buyer ends the transit, as does a delivery to one who is the agent of the buyer to hold and accept the goods.[69] A delivery, though, to one who is the buyer's agent merely for the transportation of the goods, does not operate as a termination of the transit.[70] The mere arrival of the goods at their destination is not an end of the transit;[71] but when, after such arrival, the carrier acknowledges that he holds the goods as a warehouseman for the buyer, the transit ceases.[72]

While the goods are in transit, the seller's right of stopping them is in no way affected by any resale of the goods or other act of the buyer.[73] The seller may, however, waive his right, or he may

American Sales Act, § 76 [3]) "who either has ceased to pay his debts in the ordinary course of business or cannot pay his debts as they become due." The seller may stop the goods whether the buyer's insolvency existed at the time of the sale or was subsequent to the sale. Bayonne Knife Co. v. Umbenhauer, 107 Ala. 496, 18 South. 175, 54 Am. St. Rep. 114; Kingman & Co. v. Denison, 84 Mich. 608, 48 N. W. 26, 11 L. R. A. 347, 22 Am. St. Rep. 711; Farrell v. Richmond & D. R. Co., 102 N. C. 390, 9 S. E. 302, 3 L. R. A. 647, 11 Am. St. Rep. 760.

[68] See American Sales Act, § 58, which defines the transit in great detail.

[69] Seymour v. Newton, 105 Mass. 272; Kingman & Co. v. Denison, 84 Mich. 608, 48 N. W. 26, 11 L. R. A. 347, 22 Am. St. Rep. 711; White v. Mitchell, 38 Mich. 390; Jenks v. Fulmer, 160 Pa. 527, 28 Atl. 841; Greve v. Dunham, 60 Iowa, 108, 14 N. W. 130; Symns v. Schotten, 35 Kan. 310, 10 Pac. 828; Whitehead v. Anderson, 9 Mees. & W. (Eng.) 518; Crawshay v. Eades, 1 Barn. & C. (Eng.) 182; Bolton v. Railway Co., L. R. 1 C. P. (Eng.) 431; James v. Griffin, 2 Mees. & W. (Eng.) 623.

[70] Bethell v. Clark, 20 Q. B. Div. (Eng.) 615; Harris v. Pratt, 17 N. Y. 249; Newhall v. Vargas, 13 Me. 93, 29 Am. Dec. 489.

[71] Seymour v. Newton, 105 Mass. 272; Whitehead v. Anderson, 9 Mees. & W. (Eng.) 518; Farrell v. Richmond & D. R. Co., 102 N. C. 390, 9 S. E. 302, 3 L. R. A. 647, 11 Am. St. Rep. 760; Jeffris v. Fitchburg R. Co., 93 Wis. 250, 67 N. W. 424, 33 L. R. A. 351, 57 Am. St. Rep. 919.

[72] McFetridge v. Piper, 40 Iowa, 627; Langstaff v. Stix, 64 Miss. 171, 1 South. 97, 60 Am. Rep. 49; Williams v. Hodges, 113 N. C. 36, 18 S. E. 83; James v. Griffin, 2 Mees. & W. (Eng.) 623; Ex parte Cooper, L. R. 11 Ch. Div. (Eng.) 68. There is no constructive possession on the part of the vendee, unless the relation in which the carrier stood before, as a mere instrument of conveyance to an appointed place of destination, has been altered by a contract, between the vendee and the carrier, that the latter should hold or keep the goods as the agent of the vendee. Foster v. Frampton, 6 Barn. & C. (Eng.) 107; Whitehead v. Anderson, 9 Mees. & W. (Eng.) 518; Reynolds v. Boston & M. R. R., 43 N. H. 580. Such is the relation when the consignee calls for the goods, and the carrier agrees that he will hold them for him. Richardson v. Goss, 3 Bos. & P. (Eng.) 119, 127; Scott v. Pettit, 3 Bos. & P. (Eng.) 469; Morley v. Hay, 3 Man. & R. (Eng.) 396; Rowe v. Pickford, 1 Moore, 526; Allan v. Gripper, 2 Cromp. & J. (Eng.) 218.

[73] Ilsley v. Stubbs, 9 Mass. 65, 73, 6 Am. Dec. 29; Pattison v. Culton, 33 Ind. 240, 5 Am. Rep. 199.

(by his own acts) have estopped himself from asserting it.[74] Thus the seller loses the right when he assents to such resale to the third person without reserving the right, or where the seller, with knowledge of the resale, ships the goods directly to the second buyer.[75] Again, when the seller transfers a document of title to the goods (such as a bill of lading), then, if the buyer transfers such document to one taking it in good faith for a valuable consideration, this defeats the right of stoppage in transitu.[76] And this is true by the better authority, whether such negotiation be prior or subsequent to the seller's notification to the carrier to stop the goods in transit.[77]

The unpaid seller ordinarily exercises his right of stoppage in transitu by giving notice of his claim to the carrier, or to an appropriate agent of the latter, and directing that the goods be stopped.[78] On receipt of this notice, it is the carrier's duty to respect it and to redeliver the goods according to the seller's directions.[79] The expenses of such redelivery must, of course, be borne by the seller.[80] If the carrier has notice of any legal defeasance of this right of the seller, he should, of course, not deliver the goods to the seller.[81] In the absence of such knowledge, though, it is usually held that the carrier is protected, and need not inquire into the question of the buyer's insolvency; the exercise of the right of stoppage in transitu being at the peril of the seller.[82]

[74] Knights v. Wiffen, L. R. 5 Q. B. (Eng.) 660; Voorhis v. Olmstead, 66 N. Y. 113.

[75] Eaton v. Cook, 32 Vt. 58; Shepard & Morse Lumber Co. v. Burroughs, 62 N. J. Law, 469, 41 Atl. 695; Neimeyer Lumber Co. v. Burlington & M. R. R. Co., 54 Neb. 321, 74 N. W. 670, 40 L. R. A. 534.

[76] Lickbarrow v. Mason, 2 Term R. (Eng.) 63; Branan v. Atlanta & W. P. R. Co., 108 Ga. 70, 33 S. E. 836, 75 Am. St. Rep. 26; National Bank of Bristol v. Baltimore & O. R. Co., 99 Md. 661, 59 Atl. 134, 105 Am. St. Rep. 321.

[77] Newhall v. Central Pac. R. Co., 51 Cal. 345, 21 Am. Rep. 713. This is expressly provided by the American Sales Act, § 62.

[78] American Sales Act, § 59 (1); Whitehead v. Anderson, 9 Mees. & W. (Eng.) 518; Reynolds v. Boston & M. R. R., 43 N. H. 580; Jones v. Earl, 37 Cal. 630, 99 Am. Dec. 338; Allen v. Maine Cent. R. Co., 79 Me. 327, 9 Atl. 895, 1 Am. St. Rep. 310.

[79] American Sales Act, § 59 (2); Pontifex v. Ry. Co., 3 Q. B. Div. (Eng.) 23, 27; The E. H. Pray (D. C.) 27 Fed. 474; Allen v. Maine Cent. R. Co., 79 Me. 327, 9 Atl. 895, 1 Am. St. Rep. 310.

[80] American Sales Act, § 59 (2). See, also, Pennsylvania R. Co. v. American Oil Works, 126 Pa. 485, 17 Atl. 671, 12 Am. St. Rep. 885; Potts v. New York & N. E. R. Co., 131 Mass. 455, 41 Am. Rep. 247.

[81] 2 Hutch. Carr. § 773. See Glyn v. Dock Co., 7 App. Cas. (Eng.) 591; The Tigress, 32 L. J. P. D. & A. (Eng.) 97, 102.

[82] The E. H. Pray (D. C.) 27 Fed. 474; The Vidette (D. C.) 34 Fed. 396; Jones v. Earl, 37 Cal. 630, 99 Am. Dec. 338; Allen v. Maine Cent. R. Co., 79

The right of the seller to stop the goods in transit implies a correlative duty on the part of the carrier to respect this right. It must therefore follow that the carrier, in redelivering the goods to a seller properly exercising such right, incurs no liability to the buyer, to whom the goods are consigned. Such a redelivery to the seller releases the carrier from all responsibility as to the goods, thus constituting a complete defense to a suit for failure to deliver the goods to the consignee.[83]

Loss of the Goods Owing to an Excepted Peril

We have already seen that the common carrier, who is not guilty of negligence, is not responsible, even under his strict common-law liability, for the loss of goods due to act of God, public enemy, inherent nature of the goods, act of owner, or public authority.[84] Loss of the goods, then, due solely to any one of these causes, exempts the carrier from all responsibility for the goods, and makes a delivery of them impossible. In such cases, then, the carrier has a sufficient excuse for nondelivery.[85]

The same result follows when the loss of the goods is due to any cause as to which the carrier has, through a valid stipulation, exempted himself by contract.[86]

Me. 327, 9 Atl. 895, 1 Am. St. Rep. 310. See, however, 2 Hutch. Carr. § 773, contending that the carrier, in such case, acts at his peril. American Sales Act, § 59 (2), provides: "If, however a negotiable document of title representing the goods has been issued by the carrier or other bailee, he shall not be obliged to deliver or justified in delivering the goods to the seller unless such document is first surrendered for cancellation." See, in that connection, Williston on Sales, § 542.

83 McFetridge v. Piper, 40 Iowa, 627; Reynolds v. Boston & M. R. R., 43 N. H. 580; Newhall v. Vargas, 13 Me. 93, 29 Am. Dec. 489; The Vidette (D. C.) 34 Fed. 396; The Tigress, 32 L. J. Adm. (Eng.) 97.

84 Ante, § 116.

85 2 Hutch. Carr. § 738; Stiles v. Davis, 1 Black, 101, 17 L. Ed. 33; Jewett v. Olsen, 18 Or. 419, 23 Pac. 262, 17 Am. St. Rep. 745.

86 As where the goods are destroyed by fire without the carrier's negligence, and the carrier has in the bill of lading contracted that he should not be responsible for the loss of the goods due to such a cause. Hoadley v. Northern Transp. Co., 115 Mass. 304, 15 Am. Rep. 106.

CHAPTER XIII

THE RIGHTS OF THE COMMON CARRIER OF GOODS

The duties of the common carrier of goods, and the consequent liabilities flowing from a breach of these duties, have been already discussed.[1] The present chapter will be devoted to the rights of the common carrier of goods. It is clear that the principal right of the carrier,[2] the practical benefit for which he undertakes the transportation, is to earn his compensation. Around this turn all of the carrier's substantial rights. This subject will be treated under three heads:

(1) The compensation of the carrier.
(2) Discrimination in the carrier's charges.
(3) The carrier's lien for his charges on the goods shipped.

COMPENSATION OF THE CARRIER

147. The common carrier of goods is entitled to a reasonable compensation, and no more, for his services. This compensation the carrier may demand in advance.

The common carrier of goods, like other laborers, is worthy of his hire, and this hire makes the bailment of goods for transportation a bailment for the mutual benefit of both bailor and bailee. As we have already seen, the carrier is never a common carrier as to a particular shipment unless he receives a compensation for such shipment.[3] The common carrier, although obliged to carry goods for all who offer, is not on the one hand obliged to do so gratis, nor even for an unreasonably low compensation. Such a requirement

[1] Ante, chapter X.

[2] Such other rights usually arise in connection with, or as qualifications of, the liabilities of the carrier. The right to make regulations has been considered in connection with the carrier's right to limit his common-law liability, with which it is often confused. The subject of regulations is treated at greater length in connection with the passenger carrier, where it assumes greater practical importance.

[3] Ante, p. 304.

would amount to a confiscation of his property.[4] Neither can he, on the other hand, demand whatever sum he sees fit; for, if that were permitted, he might practically nullify his obligation to carry for all, by asking exorbitant rates.[5] The result is that the common carrier is entitled to a reasonable compensation for his services, but to no more.[6] Under the Interstate Commerce Act (Act Feb. 4, 1887, c. 104, 24 Stat. 379 [U. S. Comp. St. 1901, p. 3154])[7] all charges must be just and reasonable, and all unjust and unreasonable charges are prohibited and declared unlawful.

[4] See Wabash, St. L. & P. R. Co. v. Illinois, 118 U. S. 557, 7 Sup. Ct. 4, 30 L. Ed. 244; Smyth v. Ames, 169 U. S. 466, 18 Sup. Ct. 418, 42 L. Ed. 819; Sandusky-Portland Cement Co. v. Baltimore & O. R. Co., 187 Fed. 583, 111 C. C. A. 439.

[5] Carr v. Railway Co., 7 Exch. (Eng.) 707.

[6] Louisville, E. & St. L. R. Co. v. Wilson, 119 Ind. 352, 21 N. E. 341, 4 L. R. A. 244; Harris v. Packwood, 3 Taunt. (Eng.) 264; London & N. W. R. Co. v. Evershed, L. R. 3 App. Cas. (Eng.) 1029; Holford v. Adams, 2 Duer (N. Y.) 471; Camblos v. Philadelphia & R. R. Co., 4 Brewst. (Pa.) 563, Fed. Cas. No. 2,331; Tift v. Southern R. Co. (C. C.) 138 Fed. 753, affirmed 148 Fed. 1021, 79 C. C. A. 536; L. & N. R. Co. v. Higdon, 149 Ky. 321, 148 S. W. 26; Louisville, E. & St. L. R. Co. v. Wilson, 119 Ind. 353, 21 N. E. 341, 4 L. R. A. 244. The shipper may maintain an action for refusal to carry upon reasonable terms. Carr v. Railway Co., 7 Exch. (Eng.) 707, per Parke, B. Unreasonable charges exacted may be recovered. Baldwin v. Liverpool & G. W. S. S. Co., 74 N. Y. 125, 30 Am. Rep. 277; Peters v. Marietta & C. R. Co., 42 Ohio St. 275, 51 Am. Rep. 814; McGregor v. Erie Ry. Co., 35 N. J. Law, 89; Atchison & N. R. Co. v. Miller, 16 Neb. 661, 21 N. W. 451; Harmony v. Bingham, 12 N. Y. 99, 62 Am. Dec. 142; Id., 1 Duer (N. Y.) 209; Mobile & M. Ry. Co. v. Steiner, 61 Ala. 559; Lafayette & I. R. Co. v. Pattison, 41 Ind. 312; Central of Georgia R. Co. v. E. G. Willingham & Sons, 8 Ga. App. 817, 70 S. E. 199; H. L. Halliday Milling Co. v. Louisiana & N. W. R. Co., 80 Ark. 536, 98 S. W. 374; Reynolds & Craft v. Seaboard Air Line Ry., 81 S. C. 383, 62 S. E. 445; Joynes v. Pennsylvania R. Co., 234 Pa. 321, 83 Atl. 318. Where a railroad constructed a bridge as a part of a through route at great expense, it was entitled to charge a reasonable arbitrary rate for the transportation of freight and passengers over the same, under the rule that, where a road or part of a road is built though a mountainous country or region requiring expensive construction, the charge for service over the same may be greater than on other portions of the road, or on roads where the cost of construction per mile is less. State v. Illinois Cent. R. Co., 246 Ill. 188, 92 N. E. 814. A railway company can fix reasonable rates for carrying freight between points on a belt line operated by it, classified according to the different kinds of freight. Crescent Coal Co. v. Louisville & N. R. Co., 143 Ky. 73, 135 S. W. 768, 33 L. R. A. (N. S.) 442. For extra services, after the arrival of the goods, the carrier may charge an extra compensation. Yazoo & M. V. R. Co. v. Searles, 85 Miss. 520, 37 South. 939, 68 L. R. A. 715.

[7] Section 1. See Judson on Interstate Commerce (2d Ed.) § 161; Interstate Commerce Commission v. Chicago G. W. R. Co., 209 U. S. 108, 28 Sup. Ct. 493, 52 L. Ed. 705; Texas & P. R. Co. v. Abilene Cotton Oil Co., 204 U. S. 426, 27 Sup. Ct. 350, 51 L. Ed. 553, 9 Ann. Cas. 1075.

As in the case of the innkeeper, the common carrier of goods, who cannot choose those with whom he deals, is permitted to demand his charges in advance.[8] This is in return for the duty, imposed on him by law, of serving indifferently all those who apply. This right of the carrier has already been briefly discussed,[9] and, as the same considerations obtain as in the case of the innkeeper,[10] no further discussion is needed here. The carrier can, of course, waive his right to require payment in advance, and this he does by receiving the goods for shipment without demanding his charges.[11] In such a case, the carrier cannot sue for his charges until he has fully performed his contract by completing the transportation of the goods.[12]

Amount of Compensation—How Fixed

The amount of the carrier's compensation may be fixed by contract, express or implied, or by statute. When the compensation is fixed by an express contract, which is lawful, that, of course, prevails.[13] When the rate is not fixed by statute or express contract, then under an implied contract the customary rate (if there is one) governs,[14] or, if there is no customary rate, the carrier may recover a reasonable compensation.[15] What is a reasonable compensation, in such cases, is a question of fact for the jury.

8 Wyld v. Pickford, 8 Mees. & W. (Eng.) 443; Randall v. Richmond & D. R. Co., 108 N. C. 612, 13 S. E. 137; Lehigh Valley Transp. Co. v. Post Sugar Co., 228 Ill. 121, 81 N. E. 819; Little Rock & M. R. Co. v. St. Louis, I. M. & S. R. Co., 63 Fed. 775, 11 C. C. A. 417, 26 L. R. A. 192.

9 Ante, § 113.

10 Ante, § 99.

11 Grand Rapids & I. R. Co. v. Diether, 10 Ind. App. 206, 37 N. E. 39, 1069, 53 Am. St. Rep. 385. The right of a common carrier to prepayment of its charges is waived if it accepts the goods for transportation without exacting such payment in advance, and liability attaches as though the freight were actually prepaid. Gratiot St. Warehouse Co. v. Missouri, K. & T. Ry. Co., 124 Mo. App. 545, 102 S. W. 11.

12 2 Hutch. on Carr. § 799. See, also, Breed v. Mitchell, 48 Ga. 533; New York Cent. & H. R. R. Co. v. Standard Oil Co., 87 N. Y. 486; Tirrell v. Gage, 4 Allen (Mass.) 245.

13 Blackshere v. Patterson, 72 Fed. 204, 18 C. C. A. 508; Atchison & N. R. Co. v. Miller, 16 Neb. 661, 21 N. W. 451; Smith v. Findley, 34 Kan. 316, 8 Pac. 871; Baldwin v. Liverpool & G. W. S. S. Co., 74 N. Y. 125, 30 Am. Rep. 277. Cf. Southern Exp. Co. v. Boullemet, 100 Ala. 275, 13 South. 941.

14 Killmer v. New York Cent. & H. R. R. Co., 100 N. Y. 395, 3 N. E. 293, 53 Am. Rep. 194; London & N. W. Ry. Co. v. Evershed, L. R. 3 App. Cas. (Eng.) 1029.

15 Louisville, E. & St. L. R. Co. v. Wilson, 119 Ind. 353, 21 N. E. 341, 4 L. R. A. 244; London, etc., Ry. Co. v. Evershed, L. R. 3 App. Cas. (Eng.) 1029; Thomas v. Frankfort & C. R. Co., 116 Ky. 879, 76 S. W. 1093, 25 Ky. Law Rep. 1051.

In recent years, the field of rate making by contract has been greatly diminished by statutes, both state and federal.[16] The state statutes apply only to intrastate commerce; the federal statutes affect only interstate commerce. Such statutes in some cases prescribe specific rates, or else fix certain limits (as maximum or minimum rates) to the fixing of rates by contract. In fixing interstate rates, the Interstate Commerce Commission has, under the Interstate Commerce Act (Act Feb. 4, 1887, c. 104, 24 Stat. 379 [U. S. Comp. St. 1901, p. 3154]),[17] large powers. In a number of the states, somewhat similar commissions have been established, with more or less extended powers in fixing rates applicable to commerce within the state.

When the rates fixed by the state statute are unreasonably low, such a rate is in effect confiscatory. These statutes are then obnoxious to the United States Constitution, in that they deprive the carrier of his property without due process of law.[18]

On What Goods Carrier may Collect Compensation

The carrier can recover his compensation only on those goods which he has (1) received; (2) carried to their destination accord-

[16] Munn v. Illinois, 94 U. S. 113, 24 L. Ed. 77; Chicago, B. & Q. R. Co. v. Iowa, 94 U. S. 155, 24 L. Ed. 94; Peik v. Chicago & N. W. R. Co., 94 U. S. 164, 24 L. Ed. 97; Chicago, M. & St. P. R. Co. v. Ackley, 94 U. S. 179, 24 L. Ed. 99; Ruggles v. Illinois, 108 U. S. 526, 2 Sup. Ct. 832, 27 L. Ed. 812; Stone v. Farmers' Loan & T. Co., 116 U. S. 307, 6 Sup. Ct. 334, 388, 1191, 29 L. Ed. 636; Dow v. Beidelman, 125 U. S. 680, 8 Sup. Ct. 1028, 31 L. Ed. 841; Georgia R. & Bkg. Co. v. Smith, 128 U. S. 174, 9 Sup. Ct. 47, 32 L. Ed. 377; Chicago, M. & St. P. Ry. Co. v. Minnesota ex rel. Railroad & W. Commission, 134 U. S. 418, 10 Sup. Ct. 462, 702, 33 L. Ed. 970; Wellman v. Chicago & G. T. Ry. Co., 83 Mich. 592, 47 N. W. 489; Pennsylvania R. Co. v. Miller, 132 U. S. 75, 10 Sup. Ct. 34, 33 L. Ed. 267. Where a shipper, under a contract with a station agent, paid freight at a rate less than the tariff rate fixed by the carrier in the schedule posted and filed with the public service commission, as required by Public Service Commission Act (Laws 1907, p. 905, c. 429) § 28, the carrier may recover from the shipper the difference between such rates. New York Cent. & H. R. R. Co. v. Smith, 62 Misc. Rep. 526, 115 N. Y. S. 838. A shipper who has obtained from a common carrier a special lower rate than the published schedule cannot maintain a claim to the special rate in opposition to the schedule rate. Foster, Glassel Co. v. Kansas City Southern R. Co., 121 La. 1053, 46 South. 1014.

[17] Section 15.

[18] Stone v. Farmers' Loan & T. Co., 116 U. S. 307, 335, 336, 6 Sup. Ct. 334, 388, 1191, 29 L. Ed. 636; Chicago, M. & St. P. Ry. Co. v. Minnesota ex rel. Railroad & W. Commission, 134 U. S. 418, 10 Sup. Ct. 462, 702, 33 L. Ed. 970; Chicago, M. & St. P. R. Co. v. Tompkins, 176 U. S. 167, 20 Sup. Ct. 336, 44 L. Ed. 417. As to whether rates fixed by state statutes or state commissions are confiscatory, and on the general subject of state regulation of interstate rates, see the important case of Simpson v. Shepard (The Minnesota Rate Cases) 230 U. S. 352, 33 Sup. Ct. 729, 57 L. Ed. 1511.

ing to his contract; and (3) delivered or offered to deliver.[19] All three conditions must concur, however, to entitle the carrier to compensation. So, if grain heats and increases in bulk during transportation, the carrier is not for that reason entitled to increased compensation.[20] Again, if part of the goods are lost during transportation (even though such loss is due to an excepted peril, for which the carrier is, of course, not responsible), the carrier is entitled to no compensation for the carriage of goods lost, unless by express contract a lump sum was to be paid, regardless of the loss of a part of the goods.[21] It is immaterial as far as the carrier's commpensation is concerned, that the goods have become damaged and worthless en route, provided it was from a cause for which the carrier was not responsible. If he carries them to their destination, and is ready to deliver, he is entitled to his freight.[22] The carrier, however, may recover full compensation, it is held, when, by the fault of the owner of the goods, he is prevented from completing the journey.[23]

Who Liable for Carrier's Compensation—Consignor or Consignee

The consignor is originally liable for the carrier's compensation, whether such consignor is, or is not, the owner of the goods.[24] It is the consignor who procures the shipment of the goods by inducing the carrier to accept them for transportation. With him the

[19] Gibson v. Sturge, 10 Exch. (Eng.) 622.

[20] Gibson v. Sturge, 10 Exch. (Eng.) 622; Shand v. Grant, 15 Com. B. N. S. (Eng.) 324.

[21] The Collenberg, 1 Black, 170, 17 L. Ed. 89; Price v. Hartshorn, 44 Barb. (N. Y.) 655; Steelman v. Taylor, 3 Ware, 52, Fed. Cas. No. 13,349; The Cuba, 3 Ware, 260, Fed. Cas. No. 3,458; Gibson v. Sturge, 10 Exch. (Eng.) 622; The Tangier (D. C.) 32 Fed. 230; Gibson v. Brown (D. C.) 44 Fed. 98; Brown v. Ralston, 4 Rand. (Va.) 504; Thibault v. Russell, 5 Har. (Del.) 293.

[22] Griswold v. New York Ins. Co., 3 Johns. (N. Y.) 321, 3 Am. Dec. 490; Whitney v. New York Ins. Co., 18 Johns. (N. Y.) 208, 210; McGaw v. Ocean Ins. Co., 23 Pick. (Mass.) 405; Steelman v. Taylor, 3 Ware, 52, Fed. Cas. No. 13,349; The Cuba, 3 Ware, 260, Fed. Cas. No. 3,458; Dakin v. Oxley, 15 C. B. N. S. (Eng.) 646; Seaman v. Adler (C. C.) 37 Fed. 268.

[23] The Gazelle, 128 U. S. 474, 9 Sup. Ct. 139, 32 L. Ed. 496; Braithwaite v. Power, 1 N. D. 455, 48 N. W. 354.

[24] WOOSTER v. TARR, 8 Allen (Mass.) 270, 85 Am. Dec. 707, Doble Cas. Bailments and Carriers, 253; Davison v. City Bank, 57 N. Y. 81; Holt v. Westcott, 43 Me. 445, 69 Am. Dec. 74; Strong v. Hart, 6 Barn. & C. (Eng.) 160; Tapley v. Martens, 8 Term R. (Eng.) 451; Great Western Ry. Co. v. Bagge, 15 Q. B. Div. (Eng.) 625; Drew v. Bird, 1 Moody & M. (Eng.) 156. The shipper named in a bill of lading is liable to the carrier for the freight, although he does not own the goods, and the carrier has waived his lien thereon. WOOSTER v. TARR, 8 Allen (Mass.) 270, 85 Am. Dec. 707, Doble Cas. Bailments and Carriers, 253. And see Union Freight R. Co. v. Winkley, 159 Mass. 133, 34 N. E. 91, 38 Am. St. Rep. 398.

contract of affreightment is made, and unless such contract clearly exempts the consignor, or unless the circumstances surrounding the acceptance of the goods indicate a clear intention on the part of the carrier and shipper to relieve the consignor of this liability, he is responsible and to him the carrier can look for his charges.[25]

There is a prima facie presumption, however, that the consignee is liable for the carrier's charges as the owner of the goods, on whose behalf the consignor was acting.[26] In accepting the goods from the carrier, the law ordinarily implies a promise on the part of the consignee to pay the freight charges.[27] It is a normal presumption on the part of the carrier that in surrendering the goods to the consignee (thus giving up his lien) the carrier can look to such consignee for his compensation.[28]

This presumption of ownership in the consignee, being merely a prima facie one, is, of course, rebuttable.[29] If the consignee is not the owner of the goods, he is not liable merely because another

[25] Spencer v. White, 23 N. C. 236; Grant v. Wood, 21 N. J. Law, 292, 47 Am. Dec. 162; Portland Flouring Mills Co. v. British & Foreign Marine Ins. Co., 130 Fed. 860, 65 C. C. A. 344; Baltimore & O. S. W. R. Co. v. New Albany Box & Basket Co., 48 Ind. App. 647, 94 N. E. 906, 96 N. E. 28; WOOSTER v. TARR, 8 Allen (Mass.) 270, 85 Am. Dec. 707, Dobie Cas. Bailments and Carriers, 253; Central R. Co. of New Jersey v. MacCartney, 68 N. J. Law, 165, 52 Atl. 575; Keeling & Field v. Walter Connally & Co. (Tex. Civ. App.) 157 S. W. 232; Pennsylvania R. Co. v. Titus, 156 App. Div. 830, 142 N. Y. Supp. 43.

[26] Davison v. City Bank, 57 N. Y. 81; O'Dougherty v. Boston & W. R. Co., 1 Thomp. & C. (N. Y.) 477; Sweet v. Barney, 23 N. Y. 335; Lawrence v. Minturn, 17 How. 100, 15 L. Ed. 58; Nebraska Meal Mills v. St. Louis S. W. Ry. Co., 64 Ark. 169, 41 S. W. 810, 38 L. R. A. 358, 62 Am. St. Rep. 183; Orange County Fruit Exchange v. Hubbell, 10 N. M. 47, 61 Pac. 121.

[27] Davison v. City Bank, 57 N. Y. 81; Philadelphia & R. R. Co. v. Barnard, 3 Ben. 39, Fed. Cas. No. 11,086; Kemp v. Clark, 12 Q. B. Div. (Eng.) 647; Young v. Moeller, 5 El. & Bl. (Eng.) 755; Sanders v. Van Zeller, 4 Q. B. Div. (Eng.) 260; Cock v. Taylor, 13 East (Eng.) 399; Gates v. Ryan (D. C.) 37 Fed. 154; North German Lloyd v. Heule (D. C.) 44 Fed. 100, 10 L. R. A. 814; Union Pac. R. Co. v. American Smelting & Refining Co., 202 Fed. 720, 121 C. C. A. 182; Pennsylvania R. Co. v. Titus, 156 App. Div. 830, 142 N. Y. Supp. 43.

[28] Abbe v. Eaton, 51 N. Y. 410; Merian v. Funck, 4 Denio (N. Y.) 110; Davis v. Pattison, 24 N. Y. 317; Hinsdell v. Weed, 5 Denio (N. Y.) 172; Scaife v. Tobin, 3 Barn. & Adol. (Eng.) 523; Coleman v. Lambert, 5 Mees. & W. (Eng.) 502; Davison v. City Bank, 57 N. Y. 81; Taylor v. Fall River Ironworks (D. C.) 124 Fed. 826; Central R. Co. of New Jersey v. MacCartney, 68 N. J. Law, 165, 52 Atl. 575; Union Pac. R. Co. v. American Smelting & Refining Co., 202 Fed. 720, 121 C. C. A. 182.

[29] Ames v. Temperly, 8 M. & W. (Eng.) 798; Elwell v. Skiddy, 77 N. Y. 282. See, also, Central R. Co. of New Jersey v. MacCartney, 68 N. J. Law, 175, 52 Atl. 575.

consigns goods to him, if he does not accept them.[80] Even acceptance of the goods does not render the consignee liable, when such acceptance is under circumstances which would not justify the carrier in presuming an intention on the part of the consignee thereby to become liable for the charges. Thus, the accepting consignee does not become responsible when he is, to the knowledge of the carrier, merely an agent of the owner.[81]

It is usual for bills of lading to state that the goods are to be delivered to the consignee or his assigns, he or they paying the freight, in which case the consignee or his assigns, by accepting the goods, become bound to pay the freight.[82] It matters not, under such a bill of lading, whether the consignee be the owner or not, or whether the consignor is also liable for the freight.[83] The provision that the consignee or his assigns shall pay the freight has been held to be for the sole benefit of the carrier, and therefore, if the carrier delivers the goods without receiving his freight, thereby waiving his lien, he may nevertheless recover of the consignor.[84] If, however, the consignee, before the goods are delivered to him, indorses the bill of lading to another, who receives the goods, it is held that the carrier must look to such assignee (and not to the consignee) for his charges, unless such assignee is acting in the capacity of an agent for the consignee.[85]

Demurrage and Storage

Carriers by water usually provide by the contract of shipment for the payment by the consignee of a certain sum for each day that the vessel of the carrier is detained by reason of the consignee's failing to receive the cargo.[86] This is called "demurrage." So, in

[80] Davis v. Pattison, 24 N. Y. 317; Central R. Co. of New Jersey v. MacCartney, 68 N. J. Law, 165, 52 Atl. 575; Pennsylvania R. Co. v. Titus, 156 App. Div. 830, 142 N. Y. Supp. 43.

[81] Dart v. Ensign, 47 N. Y. 619; Ames v. Temperley, 8 M. & W. (Eng.) 798.

[82] 2 Hutch. Carr. § 808; Dougal v. Kemble, 3 Bing. (Eng.) 383; Tobin v. Crawford, 5 M. & W. 235, Id., 9 M. & W. 716. Implied contract by consignee to pay the freight under bill of lading containing stipulation, "the consignee or consignees paying freight," arises from acceptance by the consignee of the delivery of the goods and waiver of lien by carrier. Union Pac. R. Co. v. American Smelting & Refining Co., 202 F. 720, 121 C. C. A. 182.

[83] Davison v. City Bank, 57 N. Y. 81.

[84] Shepard v. De Berrales, 13 East (Eng.) 565; Portland Flouring Mills Co. v. British & Foreign Marine Ins. Co., 130 Fed. 860, 65 C. C. A. 344; Central R. Co. of New Jersey v. MacCartney, 68 N. J. Law, 165, 52 Atl. 575; WOOSTER v. TARR, 8 Allen (Mass.) 270, 85 Am. Dec. 707, Dobie Cas. Bailments and Carriers, 253.

[85] 2 Hutch. Carr. § 808; Tobin v. Crawford, 5 M. & W. (Eng.) 235; Id. 9 M. & W. 716.

[86] Williams v. Theobald (D. C.) 15 Fed. 465, 468; Conard v. Atlantic Ins. Co., 1 Pet. 386, 446, 7 L. Ed. 189; Chicago & N. W. R. Co. v. Jenkins, 103 Ill.

the absence of an express contract as to demurrage, a carrier by water may recover for any losses sustained by him when, owing to the consignee's failure to receive the goods, the carrier's vessel is detained more than a reasonable time for discharging the cargo.[37] The term "demurrage" was formerly applicable only to the former of these cases (recovery by express contract), but as now used it is broad enough to include the damages for the detention of the vessel, even in the absence of an express stipulation on the subject.[38] Of course, no demurrage can be collected by the shipowner, when the delay is due to his fault or that of his agents.[39] The consignee, when he is the owner of the goods, is liable in that capacity for proper demurrage charges.[40] Merely by accepting the goods, however, the consignee, who is not the owner of the goods (though liable for freight charges), does not become liable for demurrage, when there are no stipulations in the bill of lading on the subject.[41]

It is sometimes said (and certainly some of the earlier cases hold) that the right to recover demurrage never exists in the case of land carriers, unless the right is given by express contract or by statute.[42] The reason usually given for thus limiting the right, in absence of statute or contract, to water carriers, is the essential differences in the methods of the two kinds of carriers.[43] The correctness of this, however, has with good reason been questioned by recent writers and nearly all the late cases.[44]

When the duty of unloading the goods from the car in which they have been shipped devolves on the railroad, then there is ordi-

588; Randall v. Lynch, 2 Camp. (Eng.) 352; Burns v. Burns (D. C.) 125 Fed. 432.

37 Huntley v. Dows, 55 Barb. (N. Y.) 310; Clendaniel v. Tuckerman, 17 Barb. (N. Y.) 184; Morse v. Pesant, *41 N. Y. 16; Horn v. Bensusan, 9 Car. & P. (Eng.) 709; Brouncker v. Scott, 4 Taunt. (Eng.) 1; Kell v. Anderson, 10 Mees. & W. (Eng.) 498.

38 2 Hutch. Carr. § 832; Black, Law Dict. "Demurrage," p. 352, and cases cited.

39 Ewan v. Tredegar Co. (D. C.) 88 Fed. 703; 2,000 Tons of Coal ex The Michigan, 135 Fed. 734, 68 C. C. A. 372.

40 2 Hutch. Carr. § 852.

41 Merritt & Chapman Derrick & Wrecking Co. v. Vogeman (D. C.) 127 Fed. 770; Dayton v. Parke, 142 N. Y. 391, 37 N. E. 642; Steamship County of Lancaster v. Sharpe & Co., 24 Q. B. D. (Eng.) 158, 59 L. J. Q. B. 22.

42 Chicago & N. W. R. Co. v. Jenkins, 103 Ill. 588.

43 "The mode of doing business by the two kinds of carriers is essentially different. Railroad companies have warehouses in which to store freights. Owners of vessels have none. Railroads discharge cargoes carried by them. Carriers by ship do not, but it is done by the consignee." Chicago & N. W. R. Co. v. Jenkins, 103 Ill. 588.

44 In favor of demurrage charges being permitted to railroads, see Miller v.

narily no occasion for demurrage.[45] This is true when in a single car are shipped the goods of many owners. Often, however (as is so frequently the case in shipments of car load lots), the duty of the carrier is simply to place the car in a convenient place in which the consignee may have reasonable access to it, and the duty of unloading the goods from the car rests upon the consignee. In such a case, there would seem to be no good reason why, even in the absence of a contract to that effect, the railroad should not be allowed to recover demurrage when the consignee detains the car for an unreasonable time, owing to his failure to unload the car with reasonable dispatch.[46] Certainly a regulation of the railroad imposing such charges seems reasonable and valid.[47]

We have already seen that on the arrival of the goods at their destination they should be stored awaiting a delivery to the consignee.[48] If the consignee does not accept delivery of the goods within a reasonable time, the carrier may either turn the goods over to a warehouseman[49] or the carrier may itself store the goods.[50] In such case either the warehouseman[51] or the carrier[52] is entitled to collect reasonable storage charges for thus storing the goods.

Georgia Railroad & Banking Co., 88 Ga. 563, 15 S. E. 316, 18 L. R. A. 323, 30 Am. St. Rep. 170; KENTUCKY WAGON MFG. CO. v. OHIO & M. RY. CO., 98 Ky. 152, 32 S. W. 595, 36 L. R. A. 850, 56 Am. St. Rep. 326, Dobie Cas. Bailments and Carriers, 255; Norfolk & W. R. Co. v. Adams, 90 Va. 393, 18 S. E. 673, 22 L. R. A. 530, 44 Am. St. Rep. 916; Swan v. Louisville & N. R. Co., 106 Tenn. 229, 61 S. W. 57; Chicago, P. & St. L. Ry. Co. v. Woolner Distilling Co., 160 Ill. App. 192; Erie R. Co. v. Waite, 62 Misc. Rep. 372, 114 N. Y. Supp. 1115.

45 2 Hutch. Carr. § 858.

46 See cases cited in note 44.

47 Miller v. Georgia Railroad & Banking Co., 88 Ga. 563, 15 S. E. 316, 18 L. R. A. 323, 30 Am. St. Rep. 170; Pennsylvania R. Co. v. Marshall, 147 App. Div. 806, 132 N. Y. Supp. 41; Yazoo & M. V. R. Co. v. Searles, 83 Miss. 520, 37 South. 939, 68 L. R. A. 715. In some states, statutes have been passed fixing demurrage charges. Ann. St. Mo. 1906, §§ 1082–1085. E. R. Darlington Lumber Co. v. Missouri Pac. R. Co., 216 Mo. 658, 116 S. W. 530.

48 Ante, § 144.

49 Alden v. Carver, 13 Iowa, 253, 81 Am. Dec. 430; Western Transp. Co. v. Barber, 56 N. Y. 544; Davidson S. S. Co., v. 119,254 Bushels of Flaxseed (D. C.) 117 Fed. 283; Gregg v. Illinois Cent. R. Co., 147 Ill. 550, 35 N. E. 343, 37 Am. St. Rep. 238.

50 Hardman v. Montana Union R. Co., 83 Fed. 88, 27 C. C. A. 407, 39 L. R. A. 300; Bickford v. Metropolitan S. S. Co., 109 Mass. 151; Southern R. Co. v. Born Steel Range Co., 126 Ga. 527, 55 S. E. 173; Tarbell v. Royal Exch. Shipping Co., 110 N. Y. 170, 17 N. E. 721, 6 Am. St. Rep. 350; Cairns v. Robbins, 8 M. & W. (Eng.) 258; Central of Georgia R. Co. v. Patterson, 6 Ala. App. 494, 60 South. 465.

51 See cases cited in note 49.

52 See cases cited in note 50; Central of Georgia R. Co. v. Turner, 143

DISCRIMINATION IN THE CARRIER'S CHARGES

148. At the common law, discrimination in rates by the common carrier of goods, in the sense of giving a lower rate to one shipper than to another, was not prohibited, provided both rates were reasonable, and provided the discrimination was not for an illegal purpose.

Modern cases, however, show a clear tendency (even in the absence of statute) to prohibit discrimination in rates by insisting strenuously on equality of rates as well as reasonableness. By sweeping statutes (both state and federal) discrimination in rates by the common carrier is now sternly forbidden under adequate penalties.

Discrimination at Common Law

Under the common law, the emphasis, in connection with the rates of the common carrier of goods, was laid upon reasonableness rather than upon equality.[53] If the rate charged to one shipper was reasonable it seems that he could not complain merely because a lower rate had been given to another shipper.[54] If, however, such

Ala. 142, 39 South. 30. A carrier, after its liability as such has ceased and its liability as warehouseman has attached, and the free time allowed by the railroad commission rules has expired, is entitled to storage charges, though the freight has not been actually placed inside the depot or freight warehouse. Seaboard Air Line Ry. v. Shackelford, 5 Ga. App. 395, 63 S. E. 252. A carrier, wrongfully refusing to deliver freight, when sued therefor, cannot counterclaim for warehouse charges. Hockfield v. Southern Ry. Co., 150 N. C. 419, 64 S. E. 181, 134 Am. St. Rep. 945.

[53] Great Western Ry. Co. v. Sutton, L. R. 4 H. L. (Eng.) 226, 238; Baxendale v. Railway Co., 5 C. B. [N. S.] (Eng.) 336; Root v. Long Island R. Co., 114 N. Y. 300, 21 N. E. 403, 4 L. R. A. 331, 11 Am. St. Rep. 643; Scofield v. Lake Shore & M. S. Ry. Co., 43 Ohio St. 571, 3 N. E. 907, 54 Am. Rep. 846; Tift v. Southern R. Co. (C. C.) 123 Fed. 789.

[54] Fitchburg R. Co. v. Gage, 12 Gray (Mass.) 393; Hoover v. Pennsylvania R. R., 156 Pa. 220, 27 Atl. 282, 22 L. R. A. 263, 36 Am. St. Rep. 43; Johnson v. Pensacola & P. R. Co., 16 Fla. 623, 26 Am. Rep. 731; Cowden v. Pacific Coast S. S. Co., 94 Cal. 470, 29 Pac. 873, 18 L. R. A. 221, 28 Am. St. Rep. 142; Parsons v. Chicago & N. W. R. Co., 167 U. S. 447, 17 Sup. Ct. 887, 42 L. Ed. 231; Christie v. Missouri Pac. Ry. Co., 94 Mo. 453, 7 S. W. 567. At common law a carrier of freight is not bound to treat all shippers alike. It must carry for every shipper at a reasonable rate. It may favor any particular shipper or class, where the circumstances warrant a distinction, subject to the limitation that the discrimination must be reasonable. A carrier cannot be charged with allowing undue preferences to a class, where the character of the shipments justify a distinction. State v. Central Vermont Ry. Co., 81 Vt. 463, 71 Atl. 194, 130 Am. St. Rep. 1065. As to discrimination as evidence of the unreasonableness of a rate, see Samuels v. Louisville & N. R. Co. (C. C.) 31 Fed. 57.

discrimination was for the purpose of fostering a monopoly or crushing an individual shipper, then even the common law would not tolerate such oppressive use of the carrier's tremendous power.[55]

[55] Scofield v. Lake Shore & M. S. Ry. Co., 43 Ohio St. 571, 3 N. E. 907, 54 Am. Rep. 846; Louisville, E. & St. L. Com. R. Co. v. Wilson, 132 Ind. 517, 32 N. E. 311, 18 L. R. A. 105; Cook v. Chicago, R. I. & P. R. Co., 81 Iowa, 551, 46 N. W. 1080, 9 L. R. A. 764, 25 Am. St. Rep. 512; McGrew v. Missouri Pac. R. Co., 230 Mo. 496, 132 S. W. 1076; Chas. H. Lilly Co. v. Northern Pac. R. Co., 64 Wash. 589, 117 Pac. 401. At common law discrimination in rates must have been fair and reasonable, and founded on grounds consistent with public interest, or it was not permitted. Hersh v. Northern Cent. Ry. Co., 74 Pa. 181; Chicago & A. R. Co. v. People ex rel. Koerner, 67 Ill. 11, 16 Am. Rep. 599; Fitchburg R. Co. v. Gage, 12 Gray (Mass.) 393. A common carrier cannot lawfully make unreasonable charges for his services, or unjust discrimination between his customers. Cook v. Chicago, R. I. & P. R. Co., 81 Iowa, 551, 46 N. W. 1080, 9 L. R. A. 764, 25 Am. St. Rep. 512. "The hinge of the question is not found in the single fact of discrimination for discrimination without partiality is inoffensive, and partiality exists only in cases where advantages are equal, and one party is unduly favored at the expense of another, who stands upon an equal footing. Many English cases support this general doctrine. Garton v. Railway Co., 1 Best & S. 112; Hozier v. Railway Co., 1 Nev. & McN. 27, 24 Law T. 339; Great Western Ry. Co. v. Sutton, L. R. 4 H. L. 226, 238; Ransome v. Railway Co., 1 C. B. (N. S.) 437; Jones v. Railway Co., 1 Nev. & McN. 45, 3 C. B. (N. S.) 718; Oxlade v. Railway Co., 1 Nev. & McN. 72, 1 C. B. (N. S.) 454; Baxendale v. Railway Co., 5 C. B. (N. S.) 336; Bellsdyke Coal Co. v. North British Ry. Co., 2 Nev. & McN. 105. The current of judicial opinion in America flows in the general channel marked out and opened by the courts of England. Bayles v. Kansas Pac. R. Co., 13 Colo. 181, 22 Pac. 341, 5 L. R. A. 480; Spofford v. Boston & M. R., 128 Mass. 326; Fitchburg R. Co. v. Gage, 12 Gray (Mass.) 393; Johnson v. Pensacola & P. R. Co., 16 Fla. 623, 26 Am. Rep. 731; Ragan v. Aiken, 9 Lea (Tenn.) 609, 42 Am. Rep. 684; McDuffee v. Portland & R. R. R., 52 N. H. 430, 13 Am. Rep. 72; Hersh v. Northern Cent. Ry. Co., 74 Pa. 181; Christie v. Missouri Pac. Ry. Co., 94 Mo. 453, 7 S. W. 567; Chicago & A. R. Co. v. People ex rel. Koerner, 67 Ill. 11, 16 Am. Rep. 599; Toledo, W. & W. Ry. Co. v. Elliott, 76 Ill. 67; Erie & P. Despatch v. Cecil, 112 Ill. 180, 185; Root v. Long Island R. Co., 114 N. Y. 300, 21 N. E. 403, 4 L. R. A. 331, 11 Am. St. Rep. 643; Killmer v. New York Cent. & H. R. R. Co., 100 N. Y. 395, 3 N. E. 293, 53 Am. Rep. 194; Stewart v. Lehigh Val. R. Co., 38 N. J. Law, 505; Union P. R. Co. v. United States, 117 U. S. 355, 6 Sup. Ct. 772, 29 L. Ed. 920; JOHN HAYS & CO. v. PENNSYLVANIA CO. (C. C.) 12 Fed. 309, Dobie Cas. Bailments and Carriers, 257. Interstate Commerce Commission v. Baltimore & O. R. Co. (C. C.) 43 Fed. 37. The cases of State v. Cincinnati, W. & B. Ry. Co., 47 Ohio St. 130, 23 N. E. 928, 7 L. R. A. 319; Scofield v. Lake Shore & M. S. Ry. Co., 43 Ohio St. 571, 3 N. E. 907, 54 Am. Rep. 846, and MESSENGER v. PENNSYLVANIA R. CO., 36 N. J. Law, 407, 13 Am. Rep. 457, Dobie Cas. Bailments and Carriers, 259, are not entirely out of line with the decisions to which we have referred, although fragmentary expressions, found in some of the opinions, seemingly pass the lines of principle." Cleveland, C., C. & I. Ry. Co. v. Closser, 126 Ind. 348, 26 N. E. 159, 9 L. R. A. 754, 22 Am. St. Rep. 593. The important point to every freighter is that the charge shall be reasonable, and a right of action will not exist in favor of any one unless it be shown that unreasonable inequality had

The individual criterion of reasonableness, then, rather than the comparative standard of impartiality, was the guiding star of the judges who worked out the common-law rule. Under the then industrial civilization and the existing economic conditions, there seems to have been no great outcry against this conception of the carrier's rate-making duty. Certainly, the whole carrying business (at least on land) then was of slight importance compared to modern world-market conditions, when the economic welfare of any important community is inseparably bound up in its transportation facilities.

been made to his detriment. A reasonable price paid by such a party is not made unreasonable by a less price paid by others. Bayles v. Kansas Pac. R. Co., 13 Colo. 181, 22 Pac. 341, 5 L. R. A. 480; Scofield v. Lake Shore & M. S. Ry. Co., 43 Ohio St. 571, 600, 3 N. E. 907, 54 Am. Rep. 846; Christie v. Missouri Pac. Ry. Co., 94 Mo. 453, 7 S. W. 567; Fitchburg R. Co. v. Gage, 12 Gray (Mass.) 393. What is a reasonable charge is ordinarily a question of fact. Root v. Long Island R. Co., 114 N. Y. 300, 21 N. E. 403, 4 L. R. A. 331, 11 Am. St. Rep. 643. The rate charged one person may be evidence in determining whether the rate charged another is reasonable. Johnson v. Pensacola & P. R. Co., 16 Fla. 623, 26 Am. Rep. 731; Menacho v. Ward (C. C.) 27 Fed. 529. As to rebates, see Cleveland, C., C. & I. R. Co. v. Closser, 126 Ind. 348, 26 N. E. 159, 9 L. R. A. 754, 22 Am. St. Rep. 593; Root v. Long Island R. Co., 114 N. Y. 300, 21 N. E. 403, 4 L. R. A. 331, 11 Am. St. Rep. 643. Discriminations based solely upon the amount of freight shipped are discriminations in favor of capital, and contrary to public policy, and therefore void. JOHN HAYS & CO. v. PENNSYLVANIA CO. (C. C.) 12 Fed. 309, Dobie Cas. Bailments and Carriers, 257; Rothschild v. Wabasha R. Co., 15 Mo. App. 242; Wood, Ry. Law, 567; Concord & P. R. R. v. Forsaith, 59 N. H. 122, 47 Am. Rep. 181; Nicholson v. Railway Co., 1 Nev. & McN. (Eng.) 121; Greenop v. Railway Co., 2 Nev. & McN. (Eng.) 319. A railroad company cannot discriminate in favor of a shipper who is able to furnish a large amount of freight, over one engaged in the same business who is unable to furnish the same quantity—at least, where both ship in carload lots. Louisville, E. & St. L. Con. R. Co. v. Wilson, 132 Ind. 517, 32 N. E. 311, 18 L. R. A. 105. In Burlington, C. R. & N. R. Co. v. Northwestern Fuel Co. (C. C.) 31 Fed. 652, a contract in which a railway company agreed to charge a rate of not less than $2.40 per ton to all persons shipping less than 100,000 tons of coal per annum, and to make a rate of $1.60 per ton to all persons shipping over 100,000 tons per annum, was held to be an unreasonable discrimination, as tending to create a monopoly, and that it was therefore void. To same effect is Scofield v. Lake Shore & M. S. Ry. Co., 43 Ohio St. 571, 3 N. E. 907, 54 Am. Rep. 846. In the absence of statute, a common carrier may discriminate in favor of longer distances. St. Louis, A. & T. H. R. Co. v. Hill, 14 Ill. App. 579; Hersh v. Northern Cent. Ry. Co., 74 Pa. 188; Shipper v. Pennsylvania R. Co., 47 Pa. 338. Common carriers may discriminate between different classes of goods, where the risk and expense of carrying such classes of goods are different. 1 Wood, Ry. Law, 570. A common carrier cannot discriminate against one who refuses to patronize him exclusively. Menacho v. Ward (C. C.) 27 Fed. 529. Discrimination on the ground that the shipper agrees to employ other lines of the company for traffic distinct from the

Among the English cases, we find such expressions as that of Byles, J.:[56] "I know no common-law reason why a carrier may not charge less than what is reasonable to one person, or even carry for him free of all charge;" or that of Crompton, J.:[57] "The charging another party too little is not charging you too much;" or that of Blackburn, J.:[58] "There was nothing in the common law to hinder a carrier from carrying for a favored individual at an unreasonably low rate, or even gratis. All that the law required was that he should not charge more than was reasonable."

Similar expressions of the common-law rule are to be found in leading American cases. Thus in an important Massachusetts case Mr. Justice Merrick[59] said: "The principle derived from that source [the common law] is very plain and simple. It requires equal justice to all. But the equality which is to be observed in relation to the public and to every individual consists in the restricted right to charge, in each particular case of service, a reasonable compensation, and no more. If the carrier confines himself to this, no wrong can be done and no cause afforded for complaint. If, for special reasons, in isolated cases, the carrier sees fit to stipulate for the carriage of goods or merchandise of any class of individuals for a certain time or in certain quantities for less compensation than what is the usual, necessary, and reasonable rate, he may undoubtedly do so without thereby entitling all other persons and parties to the same advantage and relief." And Mr. Justice Wescott, of Florida,[60] made use of the following language: "The commonness of the duty to carry for all does not involve a commonness or equality of compensation or charge; that all the shipper can

goods in question is unreasonable. Baxendale v. Railway Co., 1 Nev. & McN. (Eng.) 191; Bellsdyke Coal Co. v. North British Ry. Co., 2 Nev. & McN. (Eng.) 105. In Chicago & A. R. Co. v. People ex rel. Koerner, 67 Ill. 11, 16 Am. Rep. 599, a statute forbidding any discrimination whatever, under any circumstances, whether just or unjust, was held to be unconstitutional. As to unjust discriminations tending to injure a shipper and giving the unduly favored shipper a partial or complete monopoly, see Burlington, C. R. & N. R. Co. v. Northwestern Fuel Co. (C. C.) 31 Fed. 652; JOHN HAYS & CO. v. PENNSYLVANIA CO. (C. C.) 12 Fed. 309, Dobie Cas. Bailments and Carriers, 257; Denver & N. O. R. Co. v. Atchison, T. & S. F. R. Co. (C. C.) 15 Fed. 650; Hersh v. Northern Cent. R. Co., 74 Pa. 181; Shipper v. Pennsylvania R. Co., 47 Pa. 338: Chicago & A. R. Co. v. People ex rel. Koerner, 67 Ill. 11, 16 Am. Rep. 599; Concord & P. R. R. v. Forsaith, 59 N. H. 122, 47 Am. Rep. 181; Samuels v. Louisville & N. R. Co. (C. C.) 31 Fed. 57.

56 Baxendale v. Railway Co., 4 C. B. (N. S.) 63, 78.

57 Garton v. Railway Co., 1 Best & S. 112, 154.

58 Great Western Ry. Co. v. Sutton, L. R. 4 H. L. 226, 237.

59 Fitchburg R. Co. v. Gage, 12 Gray (Mass.) 393.

60 Johnson v. Pensacola & P. R. Co., 16 Fla. 623, 26 Am. Rep. 731.

ask of a common carrier is that for the service performed he shall charge no more than a reasonable sum to him."

Though there are many inconsistent utterances and irreconcilable expressions in the cases, it is believed that the opinion of Cooper, J., in a Tennessee case,[61] fairly states the common-law rule: "In other words, if the charge on the goods of the party complaining is reasonable, and such as the company would be required to adhere to as to all persons in like condition, it may nevertheless lower the charge of another person, if it be to the advantage of the company, not inconsistent with public interest, and based on a sufficient reason."

Even under the common law, there were limitations in the carrier's powers of discrimination in rates.[62] In many modern cases it has been held that, even in the absence of statute, all discrimina-

[61] Ragan v. Aiken, 9 Lea (Tenn.) 609, 42 Am. Rep. 684. See, also, Scofield v. Lake Shore & M. S. Ry. Co., 43 Ohio St. 571, 3 N. E. 907, 54 Am. Rep. 846; Kansas Pac. Ry. Co. v. Bayles, 19 Colo. 348, 35 Pac. 744; Cleveland, C., C. & I. R. Co. v. Closser, 126 Ind. 348, 26 N. E. 159, 9 L. R. A. 754, 22 Am. St. Rep. 593.

[62] See cases cited in note 55. In Scofield v. Lake Shore & M. S. Ry. Co., 43 Ohio St. 571, 3 N. E. 907, 54 Am. Rep. 846, a contract to carry for the Standard Oil Company at a rate 10 per cent. below that demanded from all other shippers, in consideration of their shipping all their oil over the carrier's line, was held illegal, as tending to create a monopoly. See, also, JOHN HAYS & CO. v. PENNSYLVANIA CO. (C. C.) 12 Fed. 309, Dobie Cas. Bailments and Carriers, 257; Kinsley v. Buffalo, N. Y. & P. R. Co. (C. C.) 37 Fed. 181; State v. Cincinnati, W. & B. Ry. Co., 47 Ohio St. 130, 23 N. E. 928, 7 L. R. A. 319; Louisville, E. & St. L. Con. R. Co. v. Wilson, 132 Ind. 517, 32 N. E. 311, 18 L. R. A. 105; Handy v. Cleveland & M. R. Co. (C. C.) 31 Fed. 689. A discrimination in rates for transportation of the same class of goods of different shippers under like circumstances is illegal and unreasonable. Indianapolis, D. & S. R. Co. v. Ervin, 118 Ill. 250, 8 N. E. 862, 59 Am. Rep. 369; Root v. Long Island R. Co., 114 N. Y. 300, 21 N. E. 403, 4 L. R. A. 331, 11 Am. St. Rep. 643; Scofield v. Lake Shore & M. S. Ry. Co., 43 Ohio St. 571, 3 N. E. 907, 54 Am. Rep. 846; MESSENGER v. PENNSYLVANIA R. CO., 36 N. J. Law, 407, 13 Am. Rep. 457, Dobie Cas. Bailments and Carriers, 259; Id., 37 N. J. Law, 531, 18 Am. Rep. 754; Bayles v. Kansas Pac. R. Co., 13 Colo. 181, 22 Pac. 341, 5 L. R. A. 480. A rebate secretly paid by a common carrier to certain shippers is an unjust discrimination against others shipping the same class of goods under the same conditions, and the excessive charge may be recovered back. Cook v. Chicago, R. I. & P. R. Co., 81 Iowa, 551, 36 N. W. 1080, 9 L. R. A. 764, 25 Am. St. Rep. 512. A railroad will not be permitted to charge one rate of delivery to one warehouse and a different rate to another (Vincent v. Chicago & A. R. Co., 49 Ill. 33; Chicago & A. R. Co. v. People ex rel. Koerner, 67 Ill. 11, 16 Am. Rep. 599), nor to receive and deliver exclusively at one stockyard belonging to another corporation, and charging for the use thereof in addition to the transportation a sum for the benefit of such corporation. Covington Stock-yards Co. v. Keith, 139 U. S. 128, 11 Sup. Ct. 469, 35 L. Ed. 73.

tions are illegal.[63] The temper and tone of these opinions show the necessity of such a rule under present economic conditions. The intimacy of the relation between the producer, carrier, and consumer, the attainment by the carrier of a power hitherto undreamed of, and the utter dependence of the public on the modern carrier, constitute ample warrant for this rule.

The necessity for the modern rule against discrimination in rates by the common carrier is thus admirably stated by Prof. Wyman: [64] "In last analysis, therefore, it is public opinion which has dictated this rule, although it is not too much to claim that this rule is a logical development in the law of public duty. So involved are the services of the common carrier directly or indirectly in all modern businesses that it is already felt to be unbearable if transportation is not open to all upon equal terms. And the rule must be exact. It is not enough to say that all must be given rates which are not unreasonable, for by that principle in many cases unequal rates might be justified. What public opinion requires to-day is that the rates shall be equal; if they are different by a few cents on the hundredweight, it may mean the fortune of the shipper who gets the lower rate and the ruin of the competitor who pays the higher rate. * * * It is only within the last generation, therefore, that it has been appreciated that discrimination is truly inconsistent with public duty. Indeed, it was bitter experience that forced the establishment of this law, rather than any process of logical deduction. But, now that our eyes have been opened, it is seen that this rule against discrimination is involved in the general law of public service."

Statutes

But, whatever the tone and temper of modern cases, the effect of modern statutes has been utterly to prohibit discrimination by the common carrier of goods in his rates. In England, the Railway and Canal Traffic Act of 1854 was passed to curb the carrier's power in this respect. Much more sweeping in its provisions on this sub-

63 MESSENGER v. PENNSYLVANIA R. CO., 36 N. J. Law, 407, 13 Am. Rep. 457, Dobie Cas. Bailments and Carriers, 259; Id., 37 N. J. Law, 531, 18 Am. Rep. 754 (strong opinion by Beasley, C. J.); American Exp. Co. v. U. S., 212 U. S. 522, 29 Sup. Ct. 315, 53 L. Ed. 635; Savannah, F. & W. Ry. Co. v. Bundick, 94 Ga. 775, 21 S. E. 995; Fitzgerald v. Grand Trunk R. Co., 63 Vt. 169, 22 Atl. 76, 13 L. R. A. 70; Baltimore & O. R. Co. v. Diamond Coal Co., 61 Ohio St. 242, 55 N. E. 616; Missouri, K. & T. R. Co. v. New Era Milling Co., 79 Kan. 435, 100 Pac. 273.

64 2 Wyman on Public Service Corporations, §§ 1291, 1292. Prof. Wyman's treatment of discrimination in this work (chapters 37–40) is one of the best to be found in the books.

ject, however, is our Interstate Commerce Act, enacted in 1887, amended with more and more strict provisions, until it now insists upon absolute equality of all rates to shippers.[65] What this act has done in the field of interstate commerce, state statutes have done for intrastate commerce.[66] Commissions, too, have been created to enforce the provisions of these statutes, which have been rigidly enforced. The expediency, the necessity, and the innate justice of these statutes have been amply proved by experience.

THE CARRIER'S LIEN

149. A common carrier has a lien for his proper charges on goods received from one who had authority to deliver them for transportation.

In General

Since the common carrier of goods, like the innkeeper, must serve all persons who apply, the carrier is given adequate methods of insuring the payment of his charges. Accordingly, as in the case of the innkeeper, the carrier may demand payment in advance (as we have seen),[67] and he has also a lien on the goods carried to secure the payment of his compensation.[68] This lien is governed by

[65] See particularly sections 2 and 3 of the act (Act Feb. 4, 1887, c. 104, 24 Stat. 379, 380 [U. S. Comp. St. 1901, p. 3155]). For brief résumé of the provisions of these sections, see Supplement, post, p. 687. For discussions of section 2 of the act, see 2 Hutch. Carr. §§ 535–550; Judson on Interstate Commerce (2d Ed.) §§ 192–226. As to section 3 of the act, see 2 Hutch. Carr. §§ 551–568; Judson on Interstate Commerce, §§ 227–287.

[66] See, on this subject, 2 Hutch. on Carr. §§ 574–601. Such state legislation is, of course, limited to shipments wholly within the state. Wabash, St. L. & P. R. Co. v Illinois, 118 U. S. 557, 7 Sup. Ct. 4, 30 L. Ed. 244; Interstate Commerce Commission v. Brimson, 154 U. S. 457, 155 U. S. 3, 14 Sup. Ct. 1125, 15 Sup. Ct. 19, 38 L. Ed. 1047, 39 L. Ed. 49; Minneapolis & St. L. R. Co. v. Minnesota ex rel. Railroad & W. Commission, 186 U. S. 257, 22 Sup. Ct. 900, 46 L. Ed. 1151. State statutes can prevent discrimination, not only as to persons but as to localities within the same state. Cohn v. St. Louis, I. M. & S. R. Co., 181 Mo. 30, 79 S. W. 961. For instructive cases dealing with the construction of state statutes regulating rates, see Railroad Commission of Texas v. Weld, 95 Tex. 278, 66 S. W. 1095; McGrew v Missouri Pac. Ry. Co., 114 Mo. 210, 21 S. W. 463; Conn v. Louisville & N. R. Co., 51 S. W. 617, 21 Ky. Law Rep. 469; Corporation Commission v. Seaboard Air Line System, 127 N. C. 283, 37 S. E. 266; State ex rel. Attorney General v. Pensacola & A. R. Co., 27 Fla. 403, 9 South. 89.

[67] Ante, §§ 113, 147.

[68] Skinner v. Upshaw, 2 Ld. Raym. (Eng.) 752; Lambert v. Robinson, 1 Esp. (Eng.) 119; Galena & C. U. R. Co. v. Rae, 18 Ill. 488, 68 Am. Dec. 574;

the same principles applicable to liens in general, and, for the reasons just indicated, it is even more similar to the lien of the innkeeper.

Like other liens, the lien of the carrier is a personal privilege, and therefore it cannot be assigned to another person.[69] The lien is not lost, however, by the carrier's turning the goods over to a warehouseman to be stored, until the carrying charges are paid.[70] For, in such cases, the warehouseman is merely the agent of the carrier, and his possession is treated as the possession of the carrier.

The carrier's lien is a special lien, and not a general lien, in the absence of an express contract, long-continued usage, or statute to that effect.[71] The lien, therefore, covers only the carrier's charges on the goods to which the lien attaches. The carrier cannot hold the goods to enforce the payment of a general balance arising out of a series of similar shipments.

The special lien of the carrier for transportation charges on the specific articles to which it attaches is prior to the rights of either the buyer or seller, or the creditors of either.[72] The carrier therefore may, as against any of these, insist upon retaining possession of the goods until those charges are paid.[73] But a sheriff, holding

Wilson v. Grand Trunk Ry. of Canada, 56 Me. 60, 96 Am. Dec. 435; Miami Powder Co. v. Port Royal & W. C. Ry. Co., 38 S. C. 78, 16 S. E. 339, 21 L. R. A. 123; Warehouse & Builders' Supply Co. v. Galvin, 96 Wis. 523, 71 N. W. 804, 65 Am. St. Rep. 57; Kawcabany v. Boston & M. R. R., 199 Mass. 586, 85 N. E. 846; BOGGS v. MARTIN, 13 B. Mon. (Ky.) 239, Dobie Cas. Bailments and Carriers, 260. The right and title of a shipper of goods is subordinate to the carrier's lien for its charges. Watson & Pittinger v. Hoboken Planing Mills Co., 156 App. Div. 8, 140 N. Y. Supp. 822.

69 Lempriere v. Pasley, 2 Term R. (Eng.) 485; Dewell v. Moxon, 1 Taunt. (Eng.) 391. Ames v. Palmer, 42 Me. 197, 66 Am. Dec. 271; Everett v. Saltus, 15 Wend. (N. Y.) 474; Rosencranz v. Swofford Bros. Dry Goods Co., 175 Mo. 518, 75 S. W. 445, 97 Am. St. Rep. 609.

70 Western Transp. Co. v. Barber, 56 N. Y. 544; Compton v. Shaw, 1 Hun (N. Y.) 441; Alden v. Carver, 13 Iowa, 253, 81 Am. Dec. 430; Brittan v. Barnaby, 21 How. 527, 16 L. Ed. 177; The Eddy, 5 Wall. 481, 18 L. Ed. 486.

71 Leonard's Ex'rs v. Winslow, 2 Grant Cas. (Pa.) 139; Bacharach v. Chester Freight Line, 133 Pa. 414, 19 Atl. 409; Pennsylvania R. Co. v. American Oil Works, 126 Pa. 485, 17 Atl. 671, 12 Am. St. Rep. 885; Bartlett v. Carnley, 6 Duer (N. Y.) 194; Rushforth v. Hadfield, 6 East (Eng.) 519; Butler v. Woolcott, 2 Bos. & P. N. R. (Eng.) 64; Richardson v. Goss, 3 Bos. & P. (Eng.) 119; Atlas S. S. Co. v. Columbian Land Co., 102 Fed. 358, 42 C. C. A. 398; Farrell v. Richmond & D. R. Co., 102 N. C. 390, 9 S. E. 302, 3 L. R. A. 647, 11 Am. St. Rep. 760.

72 Santa Fé Pac. R. Co. v. Bossut, 10 N. M. 322, 62 Pac. 977; Cooley v. Minnesota Transfer Ry. Co., 53 Minn. 327, 55 N. W. 141, 39 Am. St. Rep. 609; Campbell v. Conner, 70 N. Y. 424; Watson & Pittinger v. Hoboken Planing Mills Co., 156 App. Div. 8, 140 N. Y. Supp. 822.

73 Pennsylvania R. Co. v. American Oil Works, 126 Pa. 485, 17 Atl. 671,

an execution against the buyer, may lawfully advance these charges to the carrier on taking possession of the goods, and, having so advanced them, is substituted to all the carrier's rights of possession as security therefor.[74] The carrier's lien likewise is paramount to the seller's right of stoppage in transitu, and the seller, exercising this right, must, before he can take possession of the goods, pay the carrier his charges secured by the lien.[75]

The whole lien attaches to each and every part of the goods subject to it. If not discharged or waived, it remains attached, as security for the carrier's unpaid charges, to whatever part of the goods may remain within the possession of the carrier.[76] If, however, goods belonging to different owners are shipped by one bill of lading, the carrier cannot hold the goods of one for the charges upon the goods of the other. Each owner is entitled to his goods on the payment of the charges for the transportation of the goods of which he is the owner.[77]

On What Goods

A common carrier's lien will attach to all kinds of goods that are carried. Thus, the carrier of passengers being responsible, as a common carrier of goods, for the baggage of a passenger, and the transportation of the baggage being a part of the service for which the fare is charged, the carrier has a lien on this baggage.[78] But this lien does not extend to the clothing or other personal articles of the passenger, in his immediate use or actual possession.[79]

12 Am. St. Rep. 885; Potts v. New York & N. E. R. Co., 131 Mass. 455, 41 Am. Rep. 247; Rucker v. Donovan, 13 Kan. 251, 19 Am. Rep. 84; Newhall v. Vargas, 15 Me. 314, 33 Am. Dec. 617; Oppenheim v. Russell, 3 Bos. & P. (Eng.) 42; Morley v. Hay, 3 Man. & R. (Eng.) 396; Pennsylvania Steel Co. v. Georgia Railroad & Banking Co., 94 Ga. 636, 21 S. E. 577.

74 Rucker v. Donovan, 13 Kan. 251, 19 Am. Rep. 84; Potts v. New York & N. E. R. Co., 131 Mass. 455, 41 Am. Rep. 247.

75 Hays v. Mouille, 14 Pa. 48; Potts v. New York & N. E. R. Co., 131 Mass. 455, 41 Am. Rep. 247; Pennsylvania Steel Co. v. Georgia Railroad & Banking Co., 94 Ga. 636, 21 S. E. 577; Oppenheim v. Russell, 3 Bos. & P. (Eng.) 42.

76 Ware River R. Co. v. Vibbard, 114 Mass. 447; Lane v. Old Colony & F. R. R. Co., 14 Gray (Mass.) 143; New Haven & Northampton Co. v. Campbell, 128 Mass. 104, 35 Am. Rep. 360; Potts v. New York & N. E. R. Co., 131 Mass. 455, 41 Am. Rep. 247; New York Cent. & H. R. R. Co. v. Davis, 158 N. Y. 674, 52 N. E. 1125; Jeffris v. Fitchburg R. Co., 93 Wis. 250, 67 N. W. 424, 33 L. R. A. 351, 57 Am. St. Rep. 919; BOGGS v. MARTIN, 13 B. Mon. (Ky.) 239, Dobie Cas. Bailments and Carriers, 260; Dixon v. Central of Georgia Ry. Co., 110 Ga. 173, 35 S. E. 369.

77 Hale v. Barrett, 26 Ill. 195, 79 Am. Dec. 367.

78 Angell, Carr. § 375; 3 Hutch. Carr. § 1303; Wolf v. Summers, 2 Camp. (Eng.) 631; Roberts v. Koehler (C. C.) 30 Fed. 94.

79 Ramsden v. Boston & A. R. Co., 104 Mass. 117, 121, 6 Am. Rep. 200; Roberts v. Koehler (C. C.) 30 Fed. 94.

A carrier has a lien for his charges even on property of the United States, as well as on the property of an individual.[80]

No Lien When Goods are Received from One Having No Authority to Ship Them

To justify a lien upon goods for their freight, the relation of debtor and creditor must exist between the owner and the carrier, so that an action at law might be maintained for the payment of the debt secured by the lien.[81] When, however, the owner has, by his own voluntary acts, clothed the sender with an apparent authority to act for him, then the doctrine of authority by estoppel applies, and the carrier can look to the owner for his reasonable charges, and he has, further, a lien on the goods to secure the payment of these charges.[82] The carrier, in proving the authority of the person offering the goods for shipment, may make use of such evidence as is usually applied to cases of agency generally.[83]

Although the rule seems to be otherwise in England,[84] in this country a carrier has no lien on goods delivered for transportation by one who is a wrongdoer, and who has no authority to deliver the goods to the carrier.[85] This works no great hardship on the common carrier, since he is bound to receive and carry goods only when offered for carriage by their owner or his authorized agent, and

80 Union Pac. R. Co. v. U. S., 2 Wyo. 170; United States v. Wilder, 3 Sumn. 308; Fed. Cas. No. 16,694; The Davis, 10 Wall. 15, 19 L. Ed. 875.

81 Fitch v. Newberry, 1 Doug. (Mich.) 1, 40 Am. Dec. 33. This follows, since the lien is merely coextensive with the carrier's right to recover the charges which the lien secures.

82 2 Hutch. Carr. § 885; Vaughan v. Providence & W. R. Co., 13 R. I. 578; Hahl v. Laux, 42 Tex. Civ. App. 182, 93 S. W. 1080. See, also, Hoffman v. Lake Shore & M. S. Ry. Co., 125 Mich. 201, 84 N. W. 55.

83 Vaughan v. Providence & W. R. Co., 13 R. I. 578; Schneider v. Evans, 25 Wis. 241, 265, 3 Am. Rep. 56; Mallory v. Burrett, 1 E. D. Smith (N. Y.) 234. See, also, York Mfg. Co. v. Illinois C. R. Co., 3 Wall. 107, 18 L. Ed. 170.

84 Yorke v. Grenaugh, 2 Ld. Raym. 866, 867; 4 Halsbury, Laws of England, § 154, p. 92.

85 Savannah, F. & W. R. Co. v. Talbot, 123 Ga. 378, 51 S. E. 401, 3 Ann. Cas. 1092; Van Buskirk v. Purinton, 2 Hall (N. Y.) 601; Collman v. Collins, 2 Hall. (N. Y.) 609; Fitch v. Newberry, 1 Doug. (Mich.) 1, 40 Am. Dec. 33; Robinson v. Baker, 5 Cush. (Mass.) 137, 51 Am. Dec. 54; Stevens v. Boston & W. R. Corp., 8 Gray (Mass.) 262; Clark v. Lowell & L. R. Co., 9 Gray (Mass.) 231; Gilson v. Gwinn, 107 Mass. 126, 9 Am. Rep. 13; Bassett v. Spofford, 45 N. Y. 387, 6 Am. Rep. 101; Marsh v. Union Pac. R. Co. (C. C.) 3 McCrary, 236, 9 Fed. 873. Common carrier, taking property from person not authorized to direct its shipment, has no lien thereon for his services, and no right to retain the property. Pingree v. Detroit, L. & N. R. Co., 66 Mich. 143, 33 N. W. 298, 11 Am. St. Rep. 479. One who carries property for the convenience and at the request of a bailee thereof has no lien thereon for services, as against owner. Gilson v. Gwinn, 107 Mass. 126, 9 Am. Rep. 13.

he can always insist on payment for the carriage of the goods in advance. What has already been said, in discussing the innkeeper's lien, of the spirit of our jurisprudence as prohibiting the creation of hostile rights in the property of an owner, without his consent, express or implied, is equally applicable here.[86]

For What Charges

A carrier's lien covers all charges rightfully due for transportation of the goods to which the lien attaches.[87] It covers also charges for freight which the carrier holding the goods has advanced to preceding carriers,[88] unless the last of the connecting carriers had notice from the bill of lading, or otherwise, that the other carriers had been prepaid.[89] A carrier's lien on baggage is held to cover charges for carrying the owner as a passenger.[90] On these points there is general agreement among the authorities.

The earlier cases favored the limitation of the carrier's lien strict-

[86] Ante, p. 288. See, also, 2 Hutch. Carr. §§ 883, 884.

[87] Barker v. Havens, 17 Johns. (N. Y.) 234, 8 Am. Dec. 393; Clarkson v. Edes, 4 Cow. (N. Y.) 470; Langworthy v. New York & H. R. R. Co., 2 E. D. Smith (N. Y.) 195; Western Transp. Co. v. Hoyt, 69 N. Y. 230, 25 Am. Rep. 175; Bowman v. Hilton, 11 Ohio, 303; Wilson v. Grand Trunk Ry. of Canada, 56 Me. 60, 96 Am. Dec. 435; Lickbarrow v. Mason, 2 Term R. (Eng.) 63. And see Bacharach v. Chester Freight Line, 133 Pa. 414, 19 Atl. 409; Seaboard Air Line Ry. Co. v. Shackelford, 5 Ga. App. 395, 63 S. E. 252; Kawcabany v. Boston & M. R. R., 199 Mass. 586, 85 N. E. 846.

[88] Potts v. New York & N. E. R. Co., 131 Mass. 455, 41 Am. Rep. 247; Briggs v. Boston & L. R. Co., 6 Allen (Mass.) 246, 83 Am. Dec. 626; Crossan v. New York & N. E. R. Co., 149 Mass. 196, 21 N. E. 367, 3 L. R. A. 766, 14 Am. St. Rep. 408; Galena & C. U. R. Co. v. Rae, 18 Ill. 488, 68 Am. Dec. 574; Union Exp. Co. v. Shoop, 85 Pa. 325; Schneider v. Evans, 25 Wis. 241, 3 Am. Rep. 56; White v. Vann, 6 Humph. (Tenn.) 70, 44 Am. Dec. 294; Wells v. Thomas, 27 Mo. 17, 72 Am. Dec. 228; Georgia Railroad & Banking Co. v. Murrah, 85 Ga. 343, 11 S. E. 779; Bird v. Georgia R. R., 72 Ga. 655; Knight v. Providence & W. R. Co., 13 R. I. 572, 43 Am. Rep. 46; Wolf v. Hough, 22 Kan. 659; Travis v. Thompson, 37 Barb. (N. Y.) 236; Hoffman v. Lake Shore & M. S. Ry. Co., 125 Mich. 201, 84 N. W. 55; Thomas v. Frankfort & C. R. Co., 116 Ky. 879, 76 S. W. 1093, 25 Ky. Law Rep. 1051; THE VIRGINIA v. KRAFT, 25 Mo. 76, Dobie Cas. Bailments and Carriers, 262. See, also, Caye v. Pool's Assignee, 108 Ky. 124, 55 S. W. 887, 49 L. R. A. 251, 94 Am. St. Rep. 348.

[89] Marsh v. Union Pac. R. Co. (C. C.) 3 McCrary, 236, 9 Fed. 873; Converse Bridge Co. v. Collins, 119 Ala. 534, 24 South. 561. A railroad company receiving goods from a connecting line has a lien for the freight charges, but only to the extent of the contract price as set forth in the bill of lading; and, if it claims a lien for a larger sum, it does so at its own peril. Beasley v. Baltimore & P. R. Co., 27 App. D. C. 595, 6 L. R. A. (N. S.) 1048. Nor is the lien of the last carrier lost, owing to the default of the previous carrier. Thomas v. Frankfort & C. R. Co., 116 Ky. 879, 76 S. W. 1093, 25 Ky. Law Rep. 1051.

[90] See ante, note 78.

ly to cover transportation charges, and such charges alone.[91] The later cases, though, extend the carrier's lien to cover the other legitimate charges which the carrier can impose, such as storage [92] and demurrage.[93] When these charges are proper, there seems to be no good reason why they should not be secured by a lien on the goods.[94] If, for example, as most courts hold, the carrier can, after a reasonable time, turn the goods over to a warehouseman and give him a lien for storage charges, why, when the carrier stores the goods, should not the carrier have a similar lien on the goods to secure his charges for storing them?

Waiver of Lien

As in the case of other liens, the carrier's lien may be waived by contract,[95] or by conduct [96] inconsistent with its continuance. Since the very essence of the lien is possession, an unconditional delivery of the goods by the carrier (save to some person other than the consignee, who is to hold the goods as the carrier's

[91] THE VIRGINIA v. KRAFT, 25 Mo. 76, Dobie Cas. Bailments and Carriers, 262; Lambert v. Robinson, 1 Esp. (Eng.) 119. The lien does not cover damages for breach of a collateral contract. Birley v. Gladstone, 3 Maule & S. (Eng.) 205; Gray v. Carr, L. R. 6 Q. B. (Eng.) 522; Phillips v. Rodie, 15 East (Eng.) 547. Or for repairs on an engine. Kimmar v. Railway Co., 19 Law T. N. S. (Eng.) 387. That a railroad has no lien for demurrage, see Wallace v. B. & O. R. Co., 216 Pa. 311, 65 Atl. 665.

[92] Kawcabany v. Boston & M. R. R., 199 Mass. 586, 85 N. E. 846; Dixon v. Central of Georgia Ry. Co., 110 Ga. 173, 35 S. E. 369; Western Transp. Co. v. Barber, 56 N. Y. 544; Seaboard Air-Line Ry. Co. v. Shackelford, 5 Ga. App. 395, 63 S. E. 252.

[93] KENTUCKY WAGON MFG. CO. v. OHIO & M. RY. CO., 98 Ky. 152, 32 S. W. 595, 36 L. R. A. 850, 56 Am. St. Rep. 326, Dobie Cas. Bailments and Carriers, 255; Schumacher v. Chicago & N. W. R. Co., 207 Ill. 199, 69 N. E. 825; Yazoo & M. V. R. Co. v. Searles, 85 Miss. 520, 37 South. 939, 68 L. R. A. 715; Southern R. Co. v. Lockwood, 142 Ala. 322, 37 South. 667, 68 L. R. A. 227, 110 Am. St. Rep. 32, 4 Ann. Cas. 12. But see contra, East Tennessee, V. & G. R. Co. v. Hunt, 15 Lea (Tenn.) 261; Wallace v. Baltimore & O. R. Co., 216 Pa. 311, 65 Atl. 665.

[94] See 2 Hutch. Carr. § 862.

[95] Raymond v. Tyson, 17 How. 53, 15 L. Ed. 47; Chandler v. Belden, 18 Johns. (N. Y.) 157, 9 Am. Dec. 193; Crawshay v. Homfray, 4 B. & Ald. (Eng.) 50; Alsager v. Dock Co., 14 M. & W. (Eng.) 794. A waiver of a lien on freight for charges is not shown by a recital in the contract of shipment that all prior agreements concerning facilities for such shipments or concerning the transportation of such goods are merged in the written contract, and that such contract contains all the provisions relating to the transportation of such goods. Atchison, T. & S. F. Ry. Co. v. Hinsdell, 76 Kan. 74, 90 Pac. 800, 13 L. R. A. (N. S.) 94, 13 Ann. Cas. 981.

[96] Adams Exp. Co. v. Harris, 120 Ind. 73, 21 N. E. 340, 7 L. R. A. 214, 16 Am. St. Rep. 315; Gregg v. Illinois Cent. R. Co., 147 Ill. 550, 35 N. E. 343, 37 Am. St. Rep. 238.

agent [97]) is a waiver of the lien.[98] But when, on a delivery to the consignee, there is an express understanding between the parties that the lien shall continue, then, as against the consignee, the carrier's lien is deemed constructively to continue.[99] There is no waiver of the carrier's lien when the delivery of the goods is obtained by fraud.[1] A delivery of part of the property does not necessarily discharge the lien, either wholly or pro tanto. It releases the part delivered from the burden of the lien, but does not discharge the part remaining from the burden of the whole lien, unless this was the clear intention of the parties.[2] A refusal to deliver the goods for some reason other than that the charges are not paid is a waiver of the carrier's lien.[3] Thus, if a person have a lien on goods, for the price of hauling them to a place of deposit, his subsequently claiming them as his own, and refusing solely on that ground to deliver them to the owner, is a waiver of the lien.[4]

[97] See cases cited in note 70.

[98] Bigelow v. Heaton, 4 Denio (N. Y.) 496; Id., 6 Hill (N. Y.) 43; Geneva, I. & S. R. Co. v. Sage, 35 Hun (N. Y.) 95; Sears v. Wills, 4 Allen (Mass.) 212; Bailey v. Quint, 22 Vt. 474; Reineman & Co. v. Covington, C. & B. R. Co., 51 Iowa, 338, 1 N. W. 619; Lake Shore & M. S. Ry. Co. v. Ellsey, 85 Pa. 283; Gregg v. Illinois Cent. R. Co., 147 Ill. 550, 35 N. E. 343, 37 Am. St. Rep. 238; Forth v. Simpson, 13 Q. B. (Eng.) 689.

[99] McBrier v. A Cargo of Hard Coal (D. C.) 69 Fed. 469; Four Thousand, Eight Hundred Eighty-Five Bags of Linseed, 1 Black, 108, 17 L. Ed. 35. See, in this connection, Lembeck v. Jarvis Terminal Cold Storage Co., 69 N. J. Eq. 781, 63 Atl. 257, 7 Ann. Cas. 960.

[1] Bigelow v. Heaton, 6 Hill (N. Y.) 43; Anchor Mill Co. v. Burlington, C. R. & N. Ry. Co., 102 Iowa, 262, 71 N. W. 255; Hays v. Riddle, 1 Sandf. (N. Y.) 248; Ash v. Putnam, 1 Hill (N. Y.) 302; One Hundred and Fifty-One Tons of Coal, 4 Blatchf. 368, Fed. Cas. No. 10,520; Bristol v. Wilsmore, 1 Barn. & C. (Eng.) 514. Nor where the owner took them from the carrier without the carrier's consent. Hahl v. Laux, 42 Tex. Civ. App. 182, 93 S. W. 1080.

[2] Lane v. Old Colony & F. R. R. Co., 14 Gray (Mass.) 143; New Haven & Northampton Co. v. Campbell, 128 Mass. 104, 35 Am. Rep. 360; New York Cent. & H. R. R. Co. v. Davis, 86 Hun, 86, 34 N. Y. Supp. 206; BOGGS v. MARTIN, 13 B. Mon. (Ky.) 239, Dobie Cas. Bailments and Carriers, 260; Pennsylvania Steel Co. v. Georgia Railroad & Banking Co., 94 Ga. 636, 21 S. E. 577; Sodergren v. Flight, cited 6 East (Eng.) 622; New York Cent. & H. R. R. Co. v. Davis, 158 N. Y. 674, 52 N. E. 1125; Jeffris v. Fitchburg R. Co., 93 Wis. 250, 67 N. W. 424, 33 L. R. A. 351, 57 Am. St. Rep. 919; Schumacher v. Chicago & N. W. Ry. Co., 108 Ill. App. 520, affirmed in 207 Ill. 199, 69 N. E. 825.

[3] Baltimore & O. R. Co. v. O'Donnell, 49 Ohio St. 489, 32 N. E. 476, 21 L. R. A. 117, 34 Am. St. Rep. 579; Louisville & N. R. Co. v. McGuire, 79 Ala. 395. Carrier waives his right to detain goods for freight, when he puts his refusal to deliver upon the ground that they are not in his possession at the place where the demand is duly made. Adams Exp. Co. v. Harris, 120 Ind. 73, 21 N. E. 340, 7 L. R. A. 214, 16 Am. St. Rep. 315.

[4] Picquet v. McKay, 2 Blackf. (Ind.) 465.

A waiver may be and frequently is implied from the terms of payment, as when the payment of the transportation charges is to be at a time after the delivery,[5] or when there are provisions in the bill of lading or charter party inconsistent with the existence of a lien.[6]

Discharge of the Lien

On the analogy of other liens on personal property, a carrier's lien is discharged by payment or even by a tender of the amount due.[7] As the consignee is permitted to recoup against the carrier's charges any rightful claim for damages to the goods suffered[8] by the consignee, it follows that the carrier cannot hold the goods, under his lien, where such damage is equal to or greater than the amount of the charges. This is for the reason that the carrier's lien is coextensive with, and dependent upon, his right to recover compensation.[9]

Sale Under the Lien

At common law, a carrier who has a lien on the goods for his charges has no right to sell the goods to enforce the lien. Like other lienors, he has a right merely to hold the goods until the

[5] The Bird of Paradise, 5 Wall. (U. S.) 545, 18 L. Ed. 662; Chandler v. Belden, 18 Johns. (N. Y.) 157, 9 Am. Dec. 193; Alsager v. St. Katherine Dock Co., 14 Mees. & W. (Eng.) 794. But for cases where the facts have been held not to show a waiver of the lien, see The Volunteer, 1 Sumn. 551, Fed. Cas. No. 16,991; Certain Logs of Mahogany, 2 Sumn. 589, Fed. Cas. No. 2,559; The Kimball, 3 Wall. 37, 18 L. Ed. 50; Pinney v. Wells, 10 Conn. 104; Howard v. Macondray, 7 Gray (Mass.) 516; Clarkson v. Edes, 4 Cow. (N. Y.) 470; Tate v. Meek, 8 Taunt (Eng.) 280; Tambaco v. Simpson, 19 C. B. N. S. (Eng.) 453; Brown v. Tanner, 3 Ch. App. (Eng.) 597; Crawshay v. Homfray, 4 Barn. & Ald. (Eng.) 50; Neish v. Graham, 8 El. & Bl. (Eng.) 505. Lien for freight and charges is lost if goods are delivered to consignee, upon his note therefor, and is not revived if carrier or his agent afterwards accidentally obtains possession of them. Hale v. Barrett, 26 Ill. 195, 79 Am. Dec. 367.

[6] See cases cited in note 95.

[7] 2 Hutch. Carr. § 887. Tender to a carrier of the correct charge for a shipment, based upon its true weight, which the carrier has ascertained, operates to discharge its lien, and thereafter its possession of the goods is wrongful. Brown v. Philadelphia, B. & W. R. Co., 36 App. D. C. 221, 32 L. R. A. (N. S.) 189.

[8] Gleadell v. Thomson, 56 N. Y. 194; Bartram v. McKee, 1 Watts (Pa.) 39; Leech v. Baldwin, 5 Watts (Pa.) 446; Edwards v. Todd, 1 Scam. (Ill.) 462; Snow v. Carruth, 1 Spr. 324, Fed. Cas. No. 13,144.

[9] Dyer v. Grand Trunk Ry. Co., 42 Vt. 441, 1 Am. Rep. 350; Humphreys v. Reed, 6 Whart. (Pa.) 435; Ewart v. Kerr, Rice (S. C.) 203; Miami Powder Co. v. Port Royal & W. C. Ry. Co., 38 S. C. 78, 16 S. E. 339, 21 L. R. A. 123; Moran Bros. Co. v. Northern Pac. R. Co., 19 Wash. 266, 53 Pac. 49, 1101; Missouri Pac. R. Co. v. Peru-Van Zandt Implement Co., 73 Kan. 295, 85 Pac. 408, 87 Pac. 80, 6 L. R. A. (N. S.) 1058, 117 Am. St. Rep. 468, 9 Ann. Cas. 790.

charges are paid.[10] If a carrier, who has a lien, thus wrongfully sells the goods to which it attaches, he is liable to an action for conversion;[11] and the measure of damages, in such a case, is the market value of the goods less the amount of the carrier's charges secured by the lien.[12]

A sale at common law could be made only by a proceeding in equity to foreclose the lien and under a decree of sale so obtained.[13] But now by statutes in practically all the states, power is given to the carrier to sell the goods held under the lien for his charges, after he has held them a reasonable time, without the necessity of resorting to a suit.[14] A sale under such statutory power must, of course, conform to all the conditions and formalities set out in the statute.[15]

Carrier's Special Property in the Goods Carried

From what has been said as to the carrier's lien, it is clear that, like other bailees for hire, he has a special property in the goods carried.[16] He may, just as other similar bailees, maintain any appropriate action for any wrongful interference with his possession, either against the owner of the goods or a third person thus interfering.[17] In suing for the conversion of, or unlawful injury to,

10 Briggs v. Boston & L. R. Co., 6 Allen (Mass.) 246, 83 Am. Dec. 626; Lecky v. McDermott, 8 Serg & R. (Pa.) 500; Indianapolis & St. L. R. Co. v. Herndon, 81 Ill. 143; Hunt v. Haskell, 24 Me. 339, 41 Am. Dec. 387; Sullivan v. Park, 33 Me. 438; Rankin v. Memphis & C. Packet Co., 9 Heisk. (Tenn.) 564, 24 Am. Rep. 339; Gracie v. Palmer, 8 Wheat. 605, 5 L. Ed. 696; Lickbarrow v. Mason, 6 East (Eng.) 22.

11 See cases cited in preceding note; Chandler v. Belden, 18 Johns. (N. Y.) 157, 9 Am. Dec. 193; Liefert v. Galveston, L. & H. R. Co. (Tex. Civ. App.) 57 S. W. 899; Jones v. Pearle, 1 Strange (Eng.) 556.

12 Briggs v. Boston & L. R. Co., 6 Allen (Mass.) 246, 83 Am. Dec. 626.

13 Hunt v. Haskell, 24 Me. 339, 41 Am. Dec. 387; Rankin v. Memphis & C. Packet Co., 9 Heisk. (Tenn.) 564, 24 Am. Rep. 339; Fox v. McGregor, 11 Barb. (N. Y.) 41.

14 Representative cases involving sales under these statutes are Western R. Co. v. Rembert, 50 Ala. 25; Hodges v. Peacock, 2 Willson, Civ. Cas. Ct. App. (Tex.) § 826; Crass v. Memphis & C. R. Co., 96 Ala. 447, 11 South. 480; Central Railroad & Banking Co. v. Sawyer, 78 Ga. 784, 3 S. E. 629; Nathan v. Shivers, 71 Ala. 117, 46 Am. Rep. 303; Gulf, C. & S. F. R. Co. v. North Texas Grain Co., 32 Tex. Civ. App. 93, 74 S. W. 567.

15 Martin v. McLaughlin, 9 Colo. 153, 10 Pac. 806; Id., 6 Pac. 137; Central of Georgia R. Co. v. Chicago Portrait Co., 122 Ga. 11, 49 S. E. 727, 106 Am. St. Rep. 87; Gulf, C. & S. F. R. Co. v. North Texas Grain Co., 32 Tex. Civ. App. 93, 74 S. W. 567.

16 State v. Intoxicating Liquors, 83 Me. 158, 21 Atl. 840; Deakins Case, 2 Leach (Eng.) 862; Nicolls v. Bastard, 2 Cr., M. & R. (Eng.) 659; Merrick v. Brainard, 38 Barb. (N. Y.) 574.

17 The Beaconsfield, 158 U. S. 303, 15 Sup. Ct. 860, 39 L. Ed. 993; Chicago

the goods, the carrier may, as against a third person (it is usually held), recover the entire damage done, being accountable, as to any excess beyond his own interest, over to the owner.[18] As against the owner, however, or any one claiming under him, the amount of the carrier's recovery is limited to his own interest in the goods.[19] If the carrier pay the owner the value of the goods lost or injured by the wrongful act of a third person, the carrier will then be subrogated to all the rights of the owner against such wrongdoer, and the carrier may recover (for the purpose of reimbursing himself) full damages against such third person.[20] The rules applicable in general to the special property of bailees for hire in the goods forming the subject-matter of the bailment are equally applicable here.[21]

The carrier, by virtue of this special property, has an insurable interest in the goods shipped, and may insure them to their full value, not only for his own benefit, but also for the benefit of the owner; and, even as against perils for which he is not liable, he may insure for the benefit of the owner.[22] The owner may, of course, insure the goods for his own benefit; but here, in case of loss, the carrier, having paid the owner, will not be subrogated to the rights of the owner against the insurance company, and can-

& A. R. Co. v. Kansas City Suburban Belt R. Co., 78 Mo. App. 245; White v. Webb, 15 Conn. 302; HICKOK v. BUCK, 22 Vt. 149, Dobie Cas. Bailments and Carriers, 63; The Torgorm (D. C.) 48 Fed. 584; Claridge v. Tramway Co., 1 Q. B. (Eng.) 422.

18 State v. Intoxicating Liquors, 83 Me. 158, 21 Atl. 840; Lyle v. Barker, 5 Bin. (Pa.) 457; Woodman v. Town of Nottingham, 49 N. H. 387, 6 Am. Rep. 526; Ingersoll v. Van Bokkelin, 7 Cow. (N. Y.) 670.

19 Young v. Kimball, 23 Pa. 193; LITTLE v. FOSSETT, 34 Me. 545, 56 Am. Dec. 671, Dobie Cas. Bailments and Carriers, 71; White v. Webb, 15 Conn. 302; Ingersoll v. Van Bokkelin, 7 Cow. (N. Y.) 670.

20 Hagerstown Bank v. Adams Exp. Co., 45 Pa. 419, 84 Am. Dec. 499.

21 The Beaconsfield, 158 U. S. 303, 15 Sup. Ct. 860, 39 L. Ed. 993; Ingersoll v. Van Bokkelin, 7 Cow. (N. Y.) 670; LITTLE v. FOSSETT, 34 Me. 545, 56 Am. Dec. 671, Dobie Cas. Bailments and Carriers, 71; Hays v. Riddle, 1 Sandf. (N. Y.) 248.

22 Phœnix Ins. Co. v. Erie & W. Transp. Co., 117 U. S. 322, 6 Sup. Ct. 750, 29 L. Ed. 873; Willock v. Pennsylvania R. Co., 166 Pa. 184, 30 Atl. 948, 27 L. R. A. 228, 45 Am. St. Rep. 674; British & Foreign Marine Ins. Co. v. Gulf, C. & S. F. Ry. Co., 63 Tex. 475, 51 Am. Rep. 661; Savage v. Corn Exchange Fire & Inland Ins. Co., 36 N. Y. 655; Van Natta v. Mutual Security Ins. Co., 2 Sandf. (N. Y.) 490; Eastern R. Co. v. Relief Fire Ins. Co., 98 Mass. 420; Com. v. Hide & Leather Ins. Co., 112 Mass. 136, 17 Am. Rep. 72. Where a carrier insures goods for full value, he is trustee of the owner for the excess over his own interest. Stillwell v. Staples, 19 N. Y. 401; Waters v. Assurance Co., 5 El. & Bl. (Eng.) 870; Home Ins. Co. of New York v. Minneapolis, St. P. & S. S. M. Ry. Co., 71 Minn. 296, 74 N. W. 140.

not hold the latter, for the reason that the carrier is primarily and not secondarily liable for the loss.[23] When the owner insures the goods for his benefit, the insurance company paying such loss is subrogated to the owner's rights against the carrier.[24] Here the carrier is primarily liable for the loss, and the insurance company is secondarily liable, though the owner may proceed against the insurance company without resorting to his remedy against the carrier. The discussion of this and similar questions belongs more properly to the subjects of equity and insurance.

Neither can the carrier require, as a condition precedent to receiving the goods, that the owner insure them for the carrier's benefit. If the contract of carriage "contained a provision that the carrier would not be liable unless the owner should insure for its benefit, such provision could not be sustained, for that would be to allow the carrier to decline the discharge of its duties and obligations as such, unless furnished with indemnity against the consequences of failure in such discharge. Refusal of the owners to enter into a contract so worded would furnish no defense to an action to compel the company to carry, and submission to such a requisition would be presumed to be the result of duress of circumstances, and not binding." [25]

[23] Gales v. Hailman, 11 Pa. 515. By contract, the carrier may have the benefit of insurance effected by the shipper. Mercantile Mut. Ins. Co. v. Calebs, 20 N. Y. 173; Jackson Co. v. Boylston Mut. Ins. Co., 139 Mass. 508, 2 N. E. 103, 52 Am. Rep. 728; British & Foreign Marine Ins. Co. v. Gulf, C. & S. F. R. Co., 63 Tex. 475, 51 Am. Rep. 661; Rintoul v. New York Cent. & H. R. R. Co. (C. C.) 17 Fed. 905; Hardman v. Brett (C. C.) 37 Fed. 803.

[24] Hall v. Nashville & C. R. Co., 13 Wall. 367, 20 L. Ed. 594; Louisville & N. R. Co. v. Manchester Mills, 88 Tenn. 653, 14 S. W. 314; H. O. Judd & Root v. New York & T. S. S. Co., 128 Fed. 7, 62 C. C. A. 515.

[25] Fuller, C. J., in Inman v. South Carolina R. Co., 129 U. S. 128, 9 Sup. Ct. 249, 32 L. Ed. 612. See, also, Willock v. Pennsylvania R. Co., 166 Pa. 184, 30 Atl. 948, 27 L. R. A. 228, 45 Am. St. Rep. 674; The Seaboard (D. C.) 119 Fed. 375.

CHAPTER XIV

QUASI CARRIERS OF GOODS—POST OFFICE DEPARTMENT

THE POST OFFICE DEPARTMENT

150. The post office department is a carrier of the mail, but, being a branch of the government, is not liable for loss of, or injury to, the mail, occurring in its transmission.

The post office department, were it judged by the accepted tests, would be considered a common, and not a private, carrier, and it is at least a quasi bailee of mail matter. Though the contrary may be true from an administrative viewpoint, in the eyes of the law there is no such separate legal entity as the post office department. It is merely a branch of the government, and the principal back of it is none other than the United States; but the United States, as a sovereign state, cannot be sued without its consent.[1]

The federal government has undertaken, as a matter of public convenience, the business of the transmission, distribution, and delivery of all mail matter. The holding out and service are public, and the post office department furnishes the administrative machinery for the conduct of the business. A very small fee, often a nominal one, is exacted for the service. Therefore, theoretically and ethically, the government owes some duties to the sender of mail as to its handling. But these duties have not been legally defined, and they cannot be legally enforced, since the government is not subject to suit at the hands of an individual. Therefore these duties can scarcely be called legal duties at all. The sender of mail is accordingly in the somewhat anomalous position of intrusting his goods to an instrumentality or agency which he cannot hold liable for its misconduct, and which he cannot haul before a court of justice.

[1] Murdock Parlor Grate Co. v. Commonwealth, 152 Mass. 28, 24 N. E. 854, 8 L. R. A. 399; United States v. Lee, 106 U. S. 196, 1 Sup. Ct. 240, 27 L. Ed. 171; Langford v. United States, 101 U. S. 341, 25 L. Ed. 1010; Gibbons v. United States, 8 Wall. 269, 19 L. Ed. 453; Hill v. United States, 149 U. S. 593, 13 Sup. Ct. 1011, 37 L. Ed. 862; German Bank of Memphis v. United States, 148 U. S. 573, 13 Sup. Ct. 702, 37 L. Ed. 564; Schillinger v. United States, 155 U. S. 163, 15 Sup. Ct. 85, 39 L. Ed. 108.

There may be, as we shall see, however, recourse for the sender against the postmaster, mail contractor, carrier, or other individual employed about the mails.[2] Recent statutes, too, afford a limited indemnity to the sender for loss of such mail as has been registered.[3] Under still more recent statutes, and the regulations of the post office department passed in pursuance thereof, provision is made, on the payment of a small fee, for the insurance up to a limited amount of packages sent under the parcel post system.[4]

On the theoretical liability of the government, Mr. Schouler[5] has this to say: "Should a common-law country ever submit to a legal exposition the rightful standard of government responsibility to individual bailors as a mail carrier, the courts would not probably reckon this at the extraordinary standard of a common carrier (since widely different considerations of public policy apply), but rather at that of ordinary bailees for hire; while perhaps, were it made to appear, from public tables, that the postage charged the injured individual served, not for actual recompense in the bailment, but merely to help defray the necessary costs of a transportation which the government carried on at a loss for the benefit of the public, the standard would fall to the register of gratuitous bailment. But that a bailment duty of some sort coexists on the part of the government, apart from the adequate means of enforcing it, we cannot reasonably doubt."

POSTMASTERS AND OTHER OFFICIALS

151. To senders of mail, postmasters and other officials of the post office department are individually liable for losses sustained only when such losses are due to:

(1) Their own immediate negligence or misconduct.

(2) Their negligence in either selecting subordinates or supervising their conduct.

(3) The acts of their private servants, who are not agents of the government.

[2] Post, §§ 151, 152.

[3] Act April 21, 1902, c. 563, 32 Stat. 117; Act March 4, 1911, c. 241, 36 Stat. 1337 (U. S. Comp. St. Supp. 1911, p. 1137); 5 Fed. St. Ann. pp. 871, 872; Fed. St. Ann. Supp. 1912, p. 301; U. S. Comp. St. 1901, pp. 2685, 2686; U. S. Comp. St. Supp. 1911, pp. 1137, 1138; Act March 3, 1903, c. 1009, § 1, 32 Stat. 1174 (U. S. Comp. St. Supp. 1911, p. 1137).

[4] Act Aug. 24, 1912, c. 389, § 8, 37 Stat. 557; U. S. P. O. Regulations Oct., 1913, c. 2, § 488 (2), p. 272.

[5] Bailments (2d Ed.) § 269.

Though the sender of mail has, ordinarily, no recourse against the government for loss that he has sustained, he can in many cases proceed against the postmaster or other officer, agent, or servant of the post office department, and hold him individually responsible for such loss. The nature of this responsibility, and its limitations, will next be discussed. It should be noted that the postmaster or other official of the department is clearly not a common carrier.[6] Again, there is no contract between the sender and the individual post office official.[7]

Own Immediate Negligence or Misconduct

We have just seen that the postmaster or other official is not a common carrier, and is not himself a party to the contract with the sender of the mail. Any duty, therefore, which is imposed upon him by law must arise out of the nature of his relation to the mail. This duty is placed at ordinary care, and for a breach of this duty, which is negligence, the postmaster is liable to the sender for the damage sustained by the latter, proximately and naturally flowing from this negligence.[8]

The sender has thus a legal right to exact of the post office official, be he postmaster, assistant, or clerk, the duty of exercising ordinary care in the handling of the mail. When the sender can trace his own loss to the negligent act or omission of a particular official, then he can hold such official personally responsible for such loss. The burden of connecting the loss and the negligence of the official rests upon the sender.[9] When the postmaster or other official specifically authorizes a particular act on the part of a clerk or deputy, that act thereby becomes the act of the official, as well as

[6] Lane v. Cotton, 1 Ld. Raym. (Eng.) 646; Schroyer v. Lynch, 8 Watts (Pa.) 453; Central R. & Banking Co. v. Lampley, 76 Ala. 357, 52 Am. Rep. 334; BANKERS' MUT. CASUALTY CO. v. MINNEAPOLIS, ST. P. & S. S. M. R. CO., 117 Fed. 434, 54 C. C. A. 608, 65 L. R. A. 397, Dobie Cas. Bailments and Carriers, 267; Id., 187 U. S. 648, 23 Sup. Ct. 847, 47 L. Ed. 348.

[7] See cases cited in preceding note. See particularly the admirable statement in Central R. & Banking Co. v. Lampley, 76 Ala. 357, 52 Am. Rep. 334.

[8] RAISLER v. OLIVER, 97 Ala. 710, 12 South. 238, 38 Am. St. Rep. 213, Dobie Cas. Bailments and Carriers, 265; Christy v. Smith, 23 Vt. 663; Danforth v. Grant, 14 Vt. 283, 39 Am. Dec. 224; Wiggins v. Hathaway, 6 Barb. (N. Y.) 632; Dunlop v. Munroe, 1 Cranch, C. C. 536, Fed. Cas. No. 4,167; Teall v. Felton, 1 N. Y. 537, 49 Am. Dec. 352; Id., 12 How. (U. S.) 284, 13 L. Ed. 990; Maxwell v. McIlvoy, 2 Bibb (Ky.) 211.

[9] Wiggins v. Hathaway, 6 Barb. (N. Y.) 632; Dunlop v. Munroe, 7 Cranch (U. S.) 242, 3 L. Ed. 329. See, also, Christy v. Smith, 23 Vt. 663; RAISLER v. OLIVER, 97 Ala. 710, 12 South. 238, 38 Am. St. Rep. 213, Dobie Cas. Bailments and Carriers, 265. These last two cases seem to establish a less stringent rule as to the evidence of the postmaster's negligence than the first two cases.

of the clerk or deputy.[10] What is negligence is to be judged by considerations which have been frequently discussed.

Negligence of Subordinates

The question of the liability of the postmaster or other official for the acts of a subordinate, when he is not himself immediately connected with such act, has been frequently before the courts and is one of no little practical importance. The leading case on the subject is Lane v. Cotton,[11] decided in 1701. It was there decided, and it has since been generally held, that officers and agents of the post office are officers and agents of the government, and not agents and servants of the postmaster, and that, accordingly, while each officer or agent, is personally liable to the sender of mail for his own negligence, his liability ends there, and he is not liable for the negligence of any other agent or servant. The rule is now well settled that a postmaster or other official, not in any way negligent himself, is not liable for the negligence or misconduct of clerks and assistants, even though these are appointed by him and under his control. The superior official, if his own record is clear, incurs no responsibility for the acts of his official subordinates in the department.[12]

When the duty of selecting subordinates rests upon the postmaster or other official, he must, in order to gain the exemption just outlined, first properly carry out this duty of selection.[13] This he does by using due care and prudence in selecting as clerks and assistants only such persons as are competent to perform the duties attached to these positions. When the postmaster or other official is negligent in selecting his assistants, and damage results from the negligence or misconduct of such assistant, this damage can be attributed to the negligence in selecting the assistant, and the selecting postmaster or other official can be held responsible accordingly.

Again, when the duty of superintending clerks or assistants as to certain acts or lines of business is placed upon the postmaster or other official, here, too, he secures the exemption only by properly

10 Fitzgerald v. Burrill, 106 Mass. 446.

11 1 Ld. Raym. (Eng.) 646, 12 Mod. 472, 1 Salk. 17.

12 Hutchins v. Brackett, 2 Fost. (22 N. H.) 252, 53 Am. Dec. 248; Whitfield v. Le Despencer, 2 Cowp. 754; Dunlop v. Munroe, 7 Cranch, 242, 3 L. Ed. 329; Schroyer v. Lynch, 8 Watts (Pa.) 453; Bishop v. Williamson, 11 Me. 495; Wilson v. Peverly, 2 N. H. 548; Wiggins v. Hathaway, 6 Barb. (N. Y.) 632; Keenan v. Southworth, 110 Mass. 474, 14 Am. Rep. 613; Bolan v. Williamson, 1 Brev. (S. C.) 181; Id., 2 Bay (S. C.) 551.

13 See cases cited in note 12.

performing his own duty of superintendence.[14] If, therefore, the postmaster or other official is negligent in supervising the clerk or assistant in the performance of the particular act or duty, the doing of which, or the failure to do which, caused the loss or injury, then also can such postmaster be held responsible.

But when the postmaster or official has properly performed such duties of selection and supervision as rest upon him, and is not himself negligent, he cannot be held to account for the neglect or misconduct of the assistant or clerk, however gross or disastrous this may have been. The sender, in this case, must look to the offending clerk or assistant, and not to the postmaster or official, who is himself innocent.[15]

Acts of Private Servants

The exemption from liability of the postmaster for the defaults of his clerks and assistants is available to the postmaster only in cases where such clerks or assistants are appointed in pursuance of some law expressly authorizing it, so that, by virtue of the law and the appointment, the appointees become, in a measure, public officers themselves. The rules and regulations of the post office department provide for employment of clerks and assistants, when necessary for a proper and speedy discharge of the business of the office. When the employment is, therefore, in pursuance of such rules and regulations, these clerks and assistants are themselves employés of the government, for whose default the postmaster himself is not responsible, unless, under proper averments, it be shown there was negligence in their selection or superintendence, as stated above. But a postmaster, who without express authority therefor employs a clerk or assistant, whom he pays out of his own salary or means, is liable for the default or misfeasance of such clerk or assistant, just as any private person would be for the acts of his agent or employé.[16] In such cases, the assistant or clerk is in no sense a public official or government employé, for the arrangement under which he is employed is purely a private one. He is therefore a mere private or personal agent of the postmaster or official, for whose acts, within the scope of his employment, the postmaster is liable under the doctrine of respondeat superior, just as he would be for the acts of any other of his private agents.

[14] See cases cited in note 12.

[15] See cases cited in note 8.

[16] RAISLER v. OLIVER, 97 Ala. 710, 12 South. 238, 38 Am. St. Rep. 213, Dobie Cas. Bailments and Carriers, 265; Bishop v. Williamson, 11 Me. 495; Ford v. Parker, 4 Ohio St. 576; Christy v. Smith, 23 Vt. 663; Coleman v. Frazier, 4 Rich. (S. C.) 146, 53 Am. Dec. 727.

CONTRACTORS FOR CARRYING THE MAILS

152. Contractors for carrying the mail are responsible for damage due to their own negligence to senders of mail. By the weight of authority, mail contractors are not themselves responsible for the negligence of their agents or assistants.

Mail contractors are those who engage in carrying mail from place to place under a contract with, and subject to the regulations of, the government. The mail contractor's contract, then, is not with any individuals who use the mails. The contractor, therefore, does not carry for individuals, and receives no compensation from them. He carries for, his contract is with, and he is compensated by, the government. Any duty arising out of contract is therefore owed by the mail contractor to the government and not to the public.[17]

By virtue of his relation to the mail, and thus in a sense to the public, the mail contractor, like the postmaster, owes the duty of exercising ordinary care about the mails. The sender, then, if he can trace his loss to the negligence of the mail contractor himself, can hold the mail contractor responsible for the damage.[18] The mail contractor, however, even though it be a railroad engaged in the regular transportation of goods for the public, is not, as to carrying the mail, a common carrier or responsible as such.[19] There is substantial agreement among the courts thus far.

As to the liability of the mail contractor for the acts of his subordinates or agents, there is grave conflict. According to the weight of authority, when the mail contractor is not negligent himself, and has used proper care in selecting his agents and assistants, he is not

[17] Foster v. Metts, 55 Miss. 77, 30 Am. Rep. 504; Hutchins v. Brackett, 22 N. H. 252, 53 Am. Dec. 248; BANKERS' MUT. CASUALTY CO. v. MINNEAPOLIS, ST. P. & S. S. M. R. CO., 117 Fed. 434, 54 C. C. A. 608, 65 L. R. A. 397, Dobie Cas. Bailments and Carriers, 267; Id., 187 U. S. 648, 23 Sup. Ct. 847, 47 L. Ed. 348; Boston Ins. Co. v. Chicago, R. I. & P. Ry. Co., 118 Iowa, 423, 92 N. W. 88, 59 L. R. A. 796.

[18] Boston Ins. Co. v. Chicago, R. I. & P. Ry. Co., 118 Iowa, 423, 92 N. W. 88, 59 L. R. A. 796; BANKERS' MUT. CASUALTY CO. v. MINNEAPOLIS, ST. P. & S. S. M. R. CO., 117 Fed. 434, 54 C. C. A. 608, Dobie Cas. Bailments and Carriers, 267, 65 L. R. A. 397; Id., 187 U. S. 648, 23 Sup. Ct. 847, 47 L. Ed. 348.

[19] Central R. & Banking Co. v. Lampley, 76 Ala. 357, 52 Am. Rep. 834; BANKERS' MUT. CASUALTY CO. v. MINNEAPOLIS, ST. P. & S. S. M.

liable to senders of mail for loss or damage caused by the negligence or misconduct of such agents or assistants, who are themselves regarded as public agents.[20] Thus, under this view, a rider or driver employed by the contractor for carrying the mails is considered an assistant about the business of the government. Though employed and paid, and liable to be discharged at pleasure, by the contractor, such rider or driver is viewed as being employed in the public service of the government rather than in the private service of the contractor. The contractor is therefore not liable to the sender of mail for the negligence of the rider or driver.[21]

This rule is sometimes difficult to apply to corporations (which now control practically all the most important contracts for carrying the mail great distances), since a corporation can act only through agents. There are certain acts, however, such as providing equipment and devising plans for the transportation of the mails, which are regarded as the acts of the corporation; while the single negligent act of a subordinate employé in actually handling the mail-bags would be regarded, for the purposes of the rule in question, as merely the individual act of the employé of the corporate mail contractor.[22]

In support of this rule it should be said that most of the contracts for carrying the mail necessarily contemplate and require the employment of subordinate agents, and the government recognizes these agents in certain ways and prescribes certain requirements that they must possess in order to engage at all in the business of carrying the mail, even as the agents of the mail contractor.

A few cases, however, refuse to recognize this exemption and hold the mail contractor responsible for the negligent acts of his

R. CO., 117 Fed. 434, 54 C. C. A. 608, Dobie Cas. Bailments and Carriers, 267, 65 L. R. A. 397; Id., 187 U. S. 648, 23 Sup. Ct. 847, 47 L. Ed. 348.

[20] Foster v. Metts, 55 Miss. 77, 30 Am. Rep. 504; Conwell v. Voorhees, 13 Ohio, 523, 42 Am. Dec. 206, and note contending for the opposite view; Hutchins v. Brackett, 22 N. H. 252, 53 Am. Dec. 248; German State Bank v. Minneapolis, St. P. & S. S. M. R. Co. (C. C.) 113 Fed. 414; BANKERS' MUT. CASUALTY CO. v. MINNEAPOLIS, ST. P. & S. S. M. R. CO., 117 Fed. 434, 54 C. C. A. 608, Dobie Cas. Bailments and Carriers, 267, 65 L. R. A. 397; Id., 187 U. S. 648, 23 Sup. Ct. 847, 47 L. Ed. 348; Boston Ins. Co. v. Chicago, R. I. & P. Ry. Co., 118 Iowa, 423, 92 N. W. 88, 59 L. R. A. 796.

[21] Conwell v. Voorhees, 13 Ohio, 523, 42 Am. Dec. 206; Hutchins v. Brackett, 22 N. H. 252, 53 Am. Dec. 248.

[22] Boston Ins. Co. v. Chicago, R. I. & P. Ry. Co., 118 Iowa, 423, 92 N. W. 88, 59 L. R. A. 796; BANKERS' MUT. CASUALTY CO. v. MINNEAPOLIS, ST. P. & S. S. M. R. CO., 117 Fed. 434, 54 C. C. A. 608, Dobie Cas. Bailments and Carriers, 267, 65 L. R. A. 397; Id., 187 U. S. 648, 23 Sup. Ct. 847, 47 L. Ed. 348.

agents and subordinates.[22] These cases insist that such agent or subordinate is a mere private employé of the mail contractor, for whose conduct the mail contractor should be responsible under the general rules of master and servant.

[22] Sawyer v. Corse, 17 Grat. (Va.) 230, 94 Am. Dec. 445; Central R. & Banking Co. v. Lampley, 76 Ala. 357, 52 Am. Rep. 334. See, also, in support of this view, note 42 Am. Dec. 208.

CHAPTER XV

ACTIONS AGAINST CARRIERS OF GOODS

IN GENERAL

153. Since the substantive rights of the carrier of goods and those with whom he deals must, if disputed, be litigated in the courts, these rights are qualified by, and are dependent upon, the principles of law governing actions against the carrier of goods.

According to the accepted classification, actions against common carriers of goods may logically and conveniently be treated under the following heads:

(1) The parties.
(2) The form of action.
(3) The pleadings.
(4) The evidence.
(5) The measure of damages.

The substantive rights of the common carrier of goods and those with whom he deals have been considered at some length. In the present chapter, the last dealing with the carrier of goods, the subject of actions against this carrier will be discussed. Apart, in a measure, from the substantive rights already discussed, many questions arise in connection with the enforcement of these rights by action in a court. For a solution of the great majority of these questions, resort must he had to books dealing with the adjective or procedural law under the three great subjects of pleading, practice and evidence. There are certain questions in this connection, however, that can be discussed, and should be discussed, in any treatment of carriers of goods. The present chapter is therefore devoted to a brief consideration of these questions.

Thus the first question arises as to the person who is the proper party plaintiff in the action in which the carrier of goods is the defendant, involving the relations of the consignor and consignee to the carrier, to each other, and to the goods. The form of action is highly important in states in which the outworn system of common-law pleading still obtains; but even in those states which have adopted the reformed procedure, known as "Code states," the theory of the case as based on contract or tort involves distinctions that cannot be overlooked. The form of the pleadings, or written statements filed by the parties to the action previous to the trial, is beyond the scope of this book. So this subject is dismissed with a few observations on the necessary allegations in these pleadings. The admissibility or relevancy of evidence is not discussed, but merely what must be proved by evidence that is both relevant and admissible. Finally, the chapter closes with a statement and very brief discussion of the rules, and reasons underlying them, determining the amount of damages for which the common carrier of goods may be held liable.

THE PARTIES

154. By the great weight of authority, the following rules apply in determining the proper party plaintiff in an action against the common carrier for loss of, injury to, or delay in transporting, the goods:

(a) Where the contract for transportation is directly with the consignor, the consignor, whether or not he retains any interest in the goods, may maintain an action on such contract in his own name for any breach of this contract; but the recovery is for the benefit of the consignee, if the latter is the real owner of the goods.

(b) Prima facie the consignee is the owner of the goods, and is therefore the person with whom, through the agency of the consignor, the contract is made, and hence the consignee can sue on this contract for any breach of it resulting in loss of, or damage to, the goods. But this presumption may be rebutted.

(c) The person at whose risk the goods are carried—that is, the person having a general or special property in the goods, and who would therefore suffer if the goods are lost or injured—may maintain an action in tort for such loss or injury.

(d) A consignee who has no property in the goods, either general or special, and incurs no risk in their transportation, cannot maintain, either in contract or tort, any action for the loss of, or damage to, the goods.

The action against the common carrier of goods may be either in contract (ex contractu), arising out of the carrier's express or implied contract for the transportation of the goods, or in tort (ex delicto), arising out of the carrier's failure to live up to the duty imposed on him by law. This subject is considered in the next section, but it greatly conduces to clearness, in discussing the question of the proper party plaintiff, if this distinction is carefully kept in mind.

Action by the Consignor on the Contract

When, as is usually the case, the contract of shipment is made by the carrier directly with the consignor, the consignor, as a party to this contract, may bring an action against the carrier for any breach of the contract.[1] Obviously, the consignor is here the person with whom the carrier has contracted to transport and deliver the goods. He, therefore, is entitled to the performance of such contractual duty and, under the rule stated, may maintain an action on the contract for a breach thereof. Whether or not the consignor makes the contract on behalf of another, or whether or not the consignor has any interest in the goods, by virtue of the fact that the contract is made in his name, he, by the well-known rules of agency, is entitled to sue on such contract, and the carrier cannot defend on the ground that the consignor is acting on behalf of an undisclosed principal.[2]

[1] CARTER v. SOUTHERN RY. CO., 111 Ga. 38, 36 S. E. 308, 50 L. R. A. 354, Dobie Cas. Bailments and Carriers, 273; Ross v. Chicago, R. I. & P. R. Co., 119 Mo. App. 290, 95 S. W. 977; Zalk v. Great Northern R. Co., 98 Minn. 65, 107 N. W. 814; Swift v. Pacific Mail S. S. Co., 106 N. Y. 206, 12 N. E. 583; Dows v. Cobb, 12 Barb. (N. Y.) 310, 316; Ohio & M. R. Co. v. Emrich, 24 Ill. App. 245; Stafford v. Walter, 67 Ill. 83; Great Western R. Co. v. McComas, 33 Ill. 185; Illinois Cent. R. Co. v. Schwartz, 11 Ill. App. 482, 487; Blanchard v. Page, 8 Gray (Mass.) 281, 295; Atchison v. Chicago, R. I. & P. Ry. Co., 80 Mo. 213; Harvey v. Terre Haute & I. R. Co., 74 Mo. 538; Cantwell v. Pacific Exp. Co., 58 Ark. 487, 25 S. W. 503; Hooper v. Chicago & N. W. Ry. Co., 27 Wis. 81, 9 Am. Rep. 439; Missouri Pac. Ry. Co. v. Smith, 84 Tex. 348, 19 S. W. 509; Carter v. Graves, 9 Yerg. (Tenn.) 446; Goodwyn v. Douglas, Cheves (S. C.) 174; Joseph v. Knox, 3 Camp. (Eng.) 320; Moore v. Wilson, 1 Term R. (Eng.) 659; Davis v. James, 5 Burrows (Eng.) 2680; Mead v. Railway Co., 18 Wkly. Rep. (Eng.) 735; Dunlop v. Lambert, 6 Clark & F. (Eng.) 600. See, also, cases cited in note 2.

[2] Blanchard v. Page, 8 Gray (Mass.) 281; Reynolds v. Chicago & A. R. Co., 85 Mo. 90; Spence v. Norfolk & W. R. Co., 92 Va. 102, 22 S. E. 815, 29 L. R.

In a very early case before Lord Mansfield (Davis v. James)[3] the decision was properly placed on the ground that the defendants were liable for the consequences to the original consignors, whether the property was in them or not, because the carrier agreed with them to carry the goods safely, and the action was for the breach of that agreement. Unfortunately, however, the authority of this case was weakened by the case of Dawes v. Peck,[4] decided not long after. In this case Lord Kenyon held that the proper party to bring the action against the carrier is the person having an interest in the goods, for he is the one who has really sustained the loss. It is generally conceded that such a person may sue in tort, but it does not follow that thereby the consignor is prevented from suing on the contract he has made.

Though there are quite a few cases holding the contrary,[5] the doctrine is now generally recognized, both on principle and authority, that, whatever the rights of others, the consignor may sue the carrier for breaches of the contract entered into between such carrier and the consignor.[6] As was well said by Livingston, J., in a New York case:[7] "It would be without example to deny a party to whom an express promise is made, whether as trustee or in his own right, a remedy for its violation. This would produce the singular case of a party's having a right to break an engagement, without responsibility to him with whom it is made, merely because it is possible some other person may have a remedy against him; or, what would be more strange, it would make the very act which consummates the bargain between the shipper and master—that is, the delivery—destroy the remedy of the former on the contract.

A. 578; Southern Exp. Co. v. Craft, 49 Miss. 480, 19 Am. Rep. 4; CARTER v. SOUTHERN RY. CO., 111 Ga. 38, 36 S. E. 308, 50 L. R. A. 354, Dobie Cas. Bailments and Carriers, 273; Gulf, C. & S. F. R. Co. v. A. B. Patterson & Co. (Tex. Civ. App.) 144 S. W. 698. See cases cited in the preceding note.

3 5 Burrows, 2680.

4 8 Term R. (Eng.) 330.

5 Green v. Clarke, 12 N. Y. 343; Griffith v. Ingledew, 6 Serg. & R. (Pa.) 429, 9 Am. Dec. 444; Pennsylvania Co. v. Holderman, 69 Ind. 18; South & N. A. R. Co. v. Wood, 72 Ala. 451; Pennsylvania Co. v. Poor, 103 Ind. 553, 3 N. E. 253; McLaughlin v. Martin, 12 Colo. App. 268, 55 Pac. 195; Union Feed Co. v. Pacific Clipper Line, 31 Wash. 28, 71 Pac. 552; Union Pac. R. Co. v. Metcalf, 50 Neb. 452, 69 N. W. 961.

6 See 3 Hutch. Carr. §§ 1308-1314. See cases cited in notes 1 and 2. See also, Northern Line Packet Co. v. Shearer, 61 Ill. 263; Pennsylvania Co. v. Clark, 2 Ind. App. 146, 27 N. E. 586, 28 N. E. 208; Finn v. Western R. Corp., 112 Mass. 524, 17 Am. Rep. 128; Davis v. Jacksonville Southeastern Line, 126 Mo. 69, 28 S. W. 965.

7 Potter v. Lansing, 1 Johns. (N. Y.) 215, 3 Am. Dec. 310.

To whom the goods belong is of no importance if it be once conceded, which cannot be controverted, that the right of property may be in one, while another, by express agreement, may have a remedy for some negligence or misconduct in relation to it."

Nor is it necessary, in order to authorize the consignor to maintain an action against a carrier, where he has neither a general nor a special property in the goods shipped, that the carrier's contract with him should be an express one. The implied contract arising out of the delivery of the goods by the consignor to the carrier for transportation is entirely sufficient.[8]

In the majority of cases, the consignor is not the owner of the goods. When this is true the consignor, who recovers on the contract against the carrier, is liable to the true owner of the goods for the amount recovered.[9] A recovery by the consignor against the carrier is a bar to a subsequent action by the owner for the same wrong.[10] The ultimate disposition of the amount recovered is no legal concern of the carrier, but is a question between the consignor and owner. The carrier, however, being in all cases liable on the contract to the consignor with whom such contract is made, must respond in damages to such consignor; but, having once fully responded, the carrier is exempt from being further sued. The action of the consignor who has no interest in the goods is an action on the contract; he cannot sue in tort.[11]

[8] Finn v. Western R. Corp., 112 Mass. 524, 528, 17 Am. Rep. 128; Texas & P. Ry. Co. v. Nicholson, 61 Tex. 491; Mobile & M. Ry. Co. v. Jurey, 111 U. S. 584, 4 Sup. Ct. 566, 28 L. Ed. 527.

[9] Illinois Cent. R. Co. v. Schwartz, 13 Ill. App. 490; Ohio & M. R. Co. v. Emrich, 24 Ill. App. 245; Finn v. Western R. Corp., 112 Mass. 524, 17 Am. Rep. 128; American Roofing Co. v. Memphis & C. Packet Co., 5 Ohio N. P. 146; CARTER v. SOUTHERN RY. CO., 111 Ga. 38, 36 S. E. 308, 50 L. R. A. 354, Dobie Cas. Bailments and Carriers, 273.

[10] CARTER v. SOUTHERN RY. CO., 111 Ga. 38, 36 S. E. 308, 50 L. R. A. 354, Dobie Cas. Bailments and Carriers, 273; Southern Exp. Co. v. Craft, 49 Miss. 480, 19 Am. Rep. 4. "The shipper is a party in interest to the contract, and it does not lie with the carrier who made the contract with him to say upon a breach of it that he is not entitled to recover the damages unless it be shown that the consignee objects, for without that it will be presumed that the action was commenced and is prosecuted with the knowledge and consent of the consignee, and for his benefit. The consignor or shipper is, by operation of the rule, regarded as a trustee of an express trust, like a factor or other mercantile agent, who contracts in his own name on behalf of his principal." Hooper v. Chicago & N. W. Ry. Co., 27 Wis. 81, 9 Am. Rep. 439. See, also, cases cited in the preceding note.

[11] See cases cited in notes 1, 2, and 6. See, also, Wetzel v. Power, 5 Mont. 214, 2 Pac. 338; Fast v. Canton, A. & N. R. Co., 77 Miss. 498, 27 South. 525; P. Garvan v. New York Cent. & H. R. R. Co., 210 Mass. 275, 96 N. E. 717.

Consignee Presumed to Have Contracted with Carrier

In the absence of a contrary showing, there is a prima facie presumption that the consignee is the owner of the goods, and hence that the contract of transportation was made by the consignor on his behalf.[12] Under these circumstances, the consignee is the real principal in such contract, and the consignor was acting merely as his agent. Therefore, under the well-known rules of agency, the consignee as the undisclosed principal may sue the carrier on the contract, although such contract was made by the carrier with the consignor and in the latter's name.[13] And this right of the consignee to sue the carrier on the contract, when it exists, is paramount to the similar right of the consignor.[14]

[12] Merchants' Despatch Co. v. Smith, 76 Ill. 542; Thompson v. Fargo, 49 N. Y. 188, 10 Am. Rep. 342; Krulder v. Ellison, 47 N. Y. 36, 7 Am. Rep. 402; Brower v. Peabody, 13 N. Y. 121; Dows v. Greene, 24 N. Y. 638; Dows v. Perrin, 16 N. Y. 325; Sweet v. Barney, 23 N. Y. 335; Frank v. Hoey, 128 Mass. 263; Rowley v. Bigelow, 12 Pick. (Mass.) 307, 23 Am. Dec. 607; Smith v. Lewis, 8 B. Mon. (Ky.) 229; Arbuckle v. Thompson, 37 Pa. 170; Decan v. Shipper, 35 Pa. 239, 78 Am. Dec. 334; Congar v. Galena & C. U. R. Co., 17 Wis. 477; Dyer v. Great Northern Ry. Co., 51 Minn. 345, 53 N. W. 714, 38 Am. St. Rep. 506; Benjamin v. Levy, 39 Minn. 11, 38 N. W. 702; McCauley v. Davidson, 13 Minn. 162 (Gil. 150); Straus v. Wessel, 30 Ohio St. 211, 214; W. & A. R. Co. v. Kelly, 1 Head (Tenn.) 158; East Tennessee & G. R. R. v. Nelson, 1 Cold. (Tenn.) 272; East Line & R. R. Ry. Co. v. Hall, 64 Tex. 615; Strong v. Dodds, 47 Vt. 348, 356; Grove v. Brien, 8 How. 429, 12 L. Ed. 1142; Lawrence v. Minturn, 17 How. 100, 15 L. Ed. 58; Blum v. The Caddo, 1 Woods, 64, Fed. Cas. No. 1,573; Pennsylvania Co. v. Holderman, 69 Ind. 18; Madison, I. & P. R. Co. v. Whitesel, 11 Ind. 55; Scammon v. Wells, Fargo & Co., 84 Cal. 311, 24 Pac. 284; Webb v. Winter, 1 Cal. 417; South & N. A. R. Co. v. Wood, 72 Ala. 451; Dawes v. Peck, 8 Term R. (Eng.) 330; Evans v. Marlett, 1 Ld. Raym. (Eng.) 271; Coleman v. Lambert, 5 Mees. & W. (Eng.) 502, 505. As to suit by consignee named in bill of lading, see Lawrence v. Minturn, 17 How. 100, 15 L. Ed. 58; Butler v. Smith, 35 Miss. 457; Griffith v. Ingledew, 6 Serg. & R. (Pa.) 429, 9 Am. Dec. 444; Bonner v. Marsh, 10 Smedes & M. (Miss.) 376, 48 Am. Dec. 754. Suit in admiralty, see McKinlay v. Morrish, 21 How. 343, 355, 16 L. Ed. 100; Houseman v. The North Carolina, 15 Pet. 40, 49, 10 L. Ed. 653. See, also, Cleveland, C., C. & St. L. Ry. Co. v. Moline Plow Co., 13 Ind. App. 225, 41 N. E. 480; Pennsylvania Co. v. Poor, 103 Ind. 553, 3 N. E. 253.

[13] New Jersey Steam Nav. Co. v. Merchants' Bank, 6 How. 344, 380, 12 L. Ed. 465; Sanderson v. Lamberton, 6 Bin. (Pa.) 129; Elkins v. Boston & M. R. Co., 19 N. H. 337, 51 Am. Dec. 184; Ames v. First Div. St. Paul & P. R. Co., 12 Minn. 412 (Gil. 295); Taintor v. Prendergast, 3 Hill (N. Y.) 72, 38 Am. Dec. 618; Ford v. Williams, 21 How. 287, 16 L. Ed. 36. See, also, Mouton v. Louisville & N. R. Co., 128 Ala. 537, 29 South. 602; Pennsylvania Co. v. Poor, 103 Ind. 553, 23 N. E. 253; Elkins v. Boston & M. R. Co., 19 N. H. 337, 51 Am. Dec. 184.

[14] See Burriss & Haynie v. Missouri Pac. R. Co., 105 Mo. App. 659, 78 S. W. 1042; Dyer v. Great Northern Ry. Co., 51 Minn. 345, 53 N. W. 714, 38 Am. St. Rep. 506; McLaughlin v. Martin, 12 Colo. App. 268, 55 Pac. 195; Potter v. Lansing, 1 Johns. (N. Y.) 215, 3 Am. Dec. 310.

This presumption, however, that the consignee is the owner of the goods on whose behalf the consignor has made the contract of transportation, is merely a prima facie one, and is hence rebuttable.[15] When it is rebutted, then, of course the consignee cannot sue the carrier on the contract.[16] Whether or not the delivery of the goods to the carrier by the consignor passes title to the goods depends primarily on the intention of the parties.[17] Such a delivery, in pursuance of previous instructions from the consignee, ordinarily passes title, and thus enables the consignee to sue on the contract.[18] This is not the case, however, when such delivery is without instructions from the consignee,[19] or when the goods are sent on approval,[20] or when the title, for any reason, does not pass to the consignee.[21] In these cases, then, the consignee is not the owner, and hence he can bring no suit against the carrier on the

[15] Sweet v. Barney, 23 N. Y. 335; Price v. Powell, 3 N. Y. 322; Everett v. Saltus, 15 Wend. (N. Y.) 474; Lawrence v. Minturn, 17 How. 100, 15 L. Ed. 58; Congar v. Galena & C. U. R. Co., 17 Wis. 477, 486; Smith v. Lewis, 3 B. Mon. (Ky.) 229; Southern Exp. Co. v. Caperton, 44 Ala. 101, 4 Am. Rep. 118; South & N. A. R. Co. v. Wood, 72 Ala. 451; Bonner v. Marsh, 10 Smedes & M. (Miss.) 376; Stanton v. Eager, 16 Pick. (Mass.) 467; Bushel v. Wheeler, 15 Q. B. (Eng.) 442. See St. Louis & S. F. R. Co. v. Allen, 31 Okl. 248, 120 Pac. 1090, 39 L. R. A. (N. S.) 309; White v. Schweitzer, 147 App. Div. 544, 132 N. Y. Supp. 644; Ft. Worth & D. C. R. Co. v. Caruthers (Tex. Civ. App.) 157 S. W. 238.

[16] Wilson v. Wilson, 26 Pa. 393; Hays v. Stone, 7 Hill (N. Y.) 128; Atchison, T. & S. F. R. Co. v. Consolidated Cattle Co., 59 Kan. 111, 52 Pac. 71; Mitchell v. Ede, 11 Adol. & E. (Eng.) 888. See, also, St. Louis & S. F. R. Co. v. Allen, 31 Okl. 248, 120 Pac. 1090, 39 L. R. A. (N. S.) 309.

[17] This and similar questions belong to the law of sales.

[18] See American Sales Act, § 19, rule 4 (2); Williston on Sales, § 278; United States v. R. P. Andrews & Co., 207 U. S. 229, 28 Sup. Ct. 100, 52 L. Ed. 185; Prince v. Boston & L. R. Corp., 101 Mass. 542, 100 Am. Dec. 129; National Bank of Bristol v. Baltimore & O. R. Co., 99 Md. 661, 59 Atl. 134, 105 Am. St. Rep. 321; Carthage v. Munsell, 203 Ill. 474, 67 N. E. 831; Pfaff v. Pacific Exp. Co., 159 Ill. App. 493; Vale v. Bayle, Cowp. (Eng.) 294; Krulder v. Ellison, 47 N. Y. 36, 7 Am. Rep. 402; People v. Haynes, 14 Wend. (N. Y.) 547, 28 Am. Dec. 530. Even though no particular carrier is named. Dutton v. Solomonson, 3 Bos. & P. (Eng.) 582; Cooke v. Ludlow, 2 Bos. & P. N. R. (Eng.) 119; Arnold v. Prout, 51 N. H. 587, 589; Garland v. Lane, 46 N. H. 245, 248; Woolsey v. Bailey, 27 N. H. 217; Smith v. Smith, Id. 244, 252; The Mary and Susan, 1 Wheat. 25, 4 L. Ed. 27; Dunlop v. Lambert, 6 Clark & F. (Eng.) 600.

[19] Coats v. Chaplin, 3 Q. B. (Eng.) 483; Wilson v. Wilson, 26 Pa. 393; Hays v. Stone, 7 Hill (N. Y.) 128; Stone v. Hayes, 3 Denio (N. Y.) 575.

[20] American Sales Act, § 19, rule 3 (2); Williston on Sales, § 372; Swain v. Shepherd, 1 Moody & R. (Eng.) 223; Cook v. Gross, 60 App. Div. 446, 69 N. Y. Supp. 924; Hickman v. Schimp, 109 Pa. 16.

[21] Coats v. Chaplin, 3 Q. B. (Eng.) 483; Coombs v. Railway Co., 3 Hurl. & N. (Eng.) 510, 27 L. J. Exch. (Eng.) 401; St. Louis & S. F. R. Co. v. Allen, 31 Okl. 248, 120 Pac. 1090, 39 L. R. A. (N. S.) 309.

contract of transportation; but this right is under the circumstances confined to the consignor.[22]

Suit in Tort by Owner or One Having an Interest in the Goods

By virtue of the fact that he is a common carrier of goods, the law imposes on such carrier certain duties.[23] For a failure to perform these duties, the common carrier is liable to any person entitled to the performance of these duties. And any person who owns the goods which are transported by the carrier, or has an interest in the goods less than ownership, can insist upon the carrier's performing such duties as are imposed on him by law. It therefore follows that for any dereliction in his duty (which is a tort) either the owner of the goods or a person having an interest in the goods may maintain an action in tort against the carrier.[24]

This action is not on the contract of transportation, but is based on the tort of the carrier in not living up to the duties which the law considers as inherent in his relation of common carrier. Manifestly those having rights in the goods which are being transported are primarily interested in the performance of these duties, and they are the ones who suffer when the carrier departs from such duty. Apart, therefore, from remedies on the contract, the law gives

[22] Atchison, T. & S. F. R. Co. v. Consolidated Cattle Co., 59 Kan. 111, 52 Pac. 71; Spence v. Norfolk & W. R. Co., 92 Va. 102, 22 S. E. 815, 29 L. R. A. 578; Savannah, F. & W. Ry. Co. v. Commercial Guano Co., 103 Ga. 590, 30 S. E. 555; Louisville & N. R. Co. v. Allgood, 113 Ala. 163, 20 South. 986.

[23] Ante, chapter X.

[24] Blanchard v. Page, 8 Gray (Mass.) 281, 289; Griffith v. Ingledew, 6 Serg. & R. (Pa.) 429, 438, 9 Am. Dec. 444; Schlosser v. Great Northern R. Co., 20 N. D. 406, 127 N. W. 502; Waters v. Mobile & O. R. Co., 74 Miss. 534, 21 South. 240; Congar v. Galena & C. U. R. Co., 17 Wis. 477; Harvey v. Terre Haute & I. R. Co., 6 Mo. App. 585; P. Garvan v. New York Cent. & H. R. R. Co., 210 Mass. 275, 96 N. E. 717; Thompson v. Fargo, 49 N. Y. 188, 10 Am. Rep. 342. Suit by those having merely a special property in the goods: Illinois Cent. R. Co. v. Miller, 32 Ill. App. 259; Illinois Cent. R. Co. v. Schwartz, 13 Ill. App. 490; Thompson v. Fargo, 44 How. Prac. (N. Y.) 176; Baltimore & P. Steamboat Co. v. Atkins, 22 Pa. 522; White v. Bascom, 28 Vt. 268; Denver, S. P. & P. R. Co. v. Frame, 6 Colo. 382. Mere borrower cannot sue. Lockhart v. Western & A. R. R., 73 Ga. 472, 54 Am. Rep. 883. Factors: Boston & M. R. Co. v. Warrior Mower Co., 76 Me. 251; Wolfe v. Missouri Pac. Ry. Co., 97 Mo. 473, 11 S. W. 49, 3 L. R. A. 539, 10 Am. St. Rep. 331. Bailees: Murray v. Warner, 55 N. H. 546, 549, 20 Am. Rep. 227; Moran v. Portland Steam Packet Co., 35 Me. 55; Elkins v. Boston & M. R. Co., 19 N. H. 337, 51 Am. Dec. 184; Great Western R. Co. v. McComas, 33 Ill. 185, 187. A laundress delivering laundry to a carrier for transportation to the owner may maintain an action for its loss. Freeman v. Birch, 1 Nevile & M. 420, 3 Q. B. (Eng.) 492, 43 E. C. L. 835. Agents: Southern Exp. Co. v. Caperton, 44 Ala. 101, 4 Am. Rep. 118.

to those having a property (general or special) in the goods the privilege of suing the carrier in tort for a breach of his duty which causes them injury.[25]

The considerations just discussed are peculiarly applicable when the common carrier wrongfully refuses to accept goods tendered to him for transportation. This is purely a tort, and there is no contract action, because there is no contract.[26] If, however (though this is very seldom the case), the carrier has expressly agreed to accept the goods, and then fails to do so, he may, of course, be sued for a breach of his contract to accept.[27]

Consignee, Having no Interest in the Goods, Cannot Sue

When the contract of shipment is made with the consignor, the consignee, who, having no interest in the goods, incurs no risk in the transportation, cannot maintain an action against the carrier.[28] He cannot sue on the contract, for the contract is not made on his behalf, nor is the consignor his agent in making the contract. Neither can he sue in tort, for the carrier's duty is not owed to him

25 See cases cited in preceding note. Either the owner (the one who has the general property in the goods) or one with a special property in the goods may sue the carrier, but a recovery by either will bar a subsequent action by the other. Green v. Clarke, 12 N. Y. 343; Illinois Cent. R. Co. v. Miller, 32 Ill. App. 259; Illinois Cent. R. Co. v. Schwartz, 13 Ill. App. 490; Murray v. Warner, 55 N. H. 546, 549, 20 Am. Rep. 227; Elkins v. Boston & M. R. Co., 19 N. H. 337, 51 Am. Dec. 184; Denver, S. P. & P. R. Co. v. Frame, 6 Colo. 382; Southern Exp. Co. v. Caperton, 44 Ala. 101, 4 Am. Rep. 118; The Farmer v. McCraw, 26 Ala. 189, 72 Am. Dec. 718. The rule is that either the bailor or the bailee may sue, and, whichever first obtains damages, it is a full satisfaction. Murray v. Warner, 55 N. H. 546, 549, 20 Am. Rep. 227; Elkins v. Boston & M. R. Co., 19 N. H. 337, 51 Am. Dec. 184; White v. Bascom, 28 Vt. 268; Nicolls v. Bastard, 2 Cromp., M. & R. (Eng.) 659.

26 Pickford v. Railway Co., 8 Mees. & W. (Eng.) 372; Galena & C. U. R. Co. v. Rae, 18 Ill. 488, 68 Am. Dec. 574; Pittsburgh, C. & St. L. Ry. Co. v. Morton, 61 Ind. 539, 28 Am. Rep. 682. Such actions are usually brought by the person offering the goods for carriage. Cobb v. Illinois Cent. R. Co., 38 Iowa, 601; Lafaye v. Harris, 13 La. Ann. 553; Pittsburgh, C. & St. L. Ry. Co. v. Morton, 61 Ind. 539, 28 Am. Rep. 682; Pittsburgh, C., C. & St. L. Ry. Co. v. Racer, 5 Ind. App. 209, 31 N. E. 853.

27 Pittsburgh, C. & St. L. Ry. Co. v. Hays, 49 Ind. 207; Texas & P. Ry. Co. v. Nicholson, 61 Tex. 491; Northwestern Fuel Co. v. Burlington, C. R. & N. R. Co. (C. C.) 20 Fed. 712.

28 Louisville & N. R. Co. v. Allgood, 113 Ala. 163, 20 South. 986; Atchison, T. & S. F. Ry. Co. v. Consolidated Cattle Co., 59 Kan. 111, 52 Pac. 71; Spence v. Norfolk & W. R. Co., 92 Va. 102, 22 S. E. 815, 29 L. R. A. 578; Jarrett v. Great Northern Ry. Co., 74 Minn. 477, 77 N. W. 304; Bergner v. Chicago & A. R. Co., 13 Mo. App. 499; Duff v. Budd, 3 B. & B. (Eng.) 177; Brown v. Hodgson, 4 Taunt. (Eng.) 189; Southern Ry. Co. v. Miko, 136 Ga. 272, 71 S. E. 241.

and he suffers no injury when there is a breach of this duty. The consignee, under these circumstances, is barred of any action against the carrier.

THE FORM OF ACTION

155. The common carrier of goods may be sued either in contract (ex contractu) on his contract of transportation, or in tort (ex delicto) for any breach of a duty imposed on him by law.

Originally, a common carrier's liability was thought to rest exclusively upon his common-law duty to receive the goods and to transport and deliver them safely. A breach of this duty constituted a tort, and an action in tort was the only proper remedy.[29] The right of a shipper, however, to sue a common carrier upon his contract, was first recognized in the case of Dale v. Hall (1750)[30] and it is now well established that there is a choice of remedies. The carrier may be sued either ex contractu for the breach of the contract of shipment, or ex delicto for the breach of his common-law duty.[31]

[29] 3 Hutch. Carr. § 1322; COGGS v. BERNARD, Ld. Raym. (Eng.) 909, Dobie Cas. Bailments and Carriers, 1.

[30] 1 Wils. (Eng.) 281.

[31] Denman v. Chicago, B. & Q. R. Co., 52 Neb. 140, 71 N. W. 967; Deierling v. Wabash R. Co., 163 Mo. App. 292, 146 S. W. 814; Orange County Bank v. Brown, 3 Wend. (N. Y.) 158; Lamb v. Camden & A. R. & Transp. Co., 2 Daly (N. Y.) 454; Catlin v. Adirondack Co., 11 Abb. N. C. (N. Y.) 377; Atlantic Mut. Ins. Co. v. McLoon, 48 Barb. (N. Y.) 27; Smith v. Seward, 3 Pa. 342; Coles v. Louisville, E. & St. L. R. Co., 41 Ill. App. 607; Wabash, St. L. & P. Ry. Co. v. McCasland, 11 Ill. App. 491; St. Louis, I. M. & S. Ry. v. Heath, 41 Ark. 476; Baltimore & O. R. Co. v. Pumphrey, 59 Md. 390; Mississippi Cent. R. Co. v. Fort, 44 Miss. 423; School Dist. in Medfield v. Boston, H. & E. R. Co., 102 Mass. 552, 555, 3 Am. Rep. 502; The Queen of the Pacific (D. C.) 61 Fed. 213; Whittenton Mfg. Co. v. Memphis & O. R. P. Co. (C. C.) 21 Fed. 896; The Grapeshot (D. C.) 22 Fed. 123; The Samuel J. Christian (D. C.) 16 Fed. 796; Ansell v. Waterhouse, 6 Maule & S. (Eng.) 385, 2 Chit. 1, 18 E. C. L. 469. A special contract with the carrier will not preclude the shipper from suing in case without referring to the contract. Clark v. Richards, 1 Conn. 54, 59; Arnold v. Illinois Cent. R. Co., 83 Ill. 273, 25 Am. Rep. 386; Clark v. St. Louis, K. C. & N. Ry. Co., 64 Mo. 440; Oxley v. St. Louis, K. C. & N. Ry. Co., 65 Mo. 629; Coles v. Louisville, E. & St. L. R. Co., 41 Ill. App. 607; Wabash, St. L. & P. Ry. Co. v. Pratt, 15 Ill. App. 177. But see Kimball v. Rutland & B. R. Co., 26 Vt. 247, 62 Am. Dec. 567. Generally damages for delay in shipment or loss of property while in a carrier's custody may be recovered either in an action ex contractu or one ex delicto at the option of the pleader. WERNICK v. ST. LOUIS & S. F. R. CO., 131 Mo. App. 37, 109 S. W. 1027,

The distinction between actions ex contractu and actions ex delicto was formerly of more importance than it now is. In states in which the antiquated common-law forms of action still obtain, the proper contract action is assumpsit; in tort, the action is trespass on the case.[32] Under the system of Code pleading, there is but one form of civil action. Even in Code states, however, there are differences as to the pleadings between a cause of action in contract and one in tort, which make it frequently important to distinguish between the two. The considerations which prompt a pleader in making his election between proceeding ex contractu or ex delicto will be briefly discussed.

Advantages of an Action Ex Contractu

Under the common-law maxim "actio personalis moritur cum persona," tort actions perished on the death of either party.[33] Actions on contract, however, survived, so that the action ex contractu, on the death of the plaintiff, passed to his personal representative.[34] Again, the contract action of assumpsit was desirable against the carrier when the pleader wished to join the common counts in assumpsit, which could not be joined in an action ex delicto.[35] Under the system of Code pleading, which permits the joinder in a single complaint of any number of causes of action arising out of contract, the carrier should be sued on the contract, if the pleader wishes to join other causes of action founded on contract.[36] Statutes of limitations, which prescribe the time within

Dobie Cas. Bailments and Carriers, 278. Where goods transported under a bill of lading were injured by fire, alleged to have resulted from the carrier's negligence, plaintiff was entitled to go to the jury on a count alleging a cause of action in contract, as well as on a count in tort, though it could not recover on both. P. Garvan v. New York Cent. & H. R. R. Co., 210 Mass. 275, 96 N. E. 717. A shipper whose goods are lost during transit may sue in tort for a breach of the common-law duty of the carrier to deliver, which originates at the place of delivery, or he may sue for breach of the contract of transportation, or he may treat the carrier as a bailee and allege the specific tortious act by which the goods were lost, and found his right to recover thereon which originates at the place where the tortious act occurred. Merritt Creamery Co. v. Atchison, T. & S. F. Ry. Co., 128 Mo. App. 420, 107 S. W. 462.

32 Holden v. Rutland R. Co., 72 Vt. 156, 47 Atl. 403, 82 Am. St. Rep. 926; Waters v. Mobile & O. R. Co., 74 Miss. 534, 21 South. 240. See cases cited in the preceding note.

33 Chamberlain v. Williamson, 2 M. & S. (Eng.) 408; Stebbins v. Palmer, 1 Pick. (Mass.) 71, 11 Am. Dec. 146. Under modern statutes and modern decisions, it is usually held that tort actions to property survive. See 1 Woerner on Administration, §§ 290–303. See, in general, as to the advantages of an action ex contractu, 3 Hutch. Carr. § 1327.

34 Hambly v. Trott, Cowp. 371, 375.

35 1 Chitty on Pl. 114; 3 Hutch. Carr. § 1327.

36 Bliss on Code Pleading (3d Ed.) §§ 127, 128.

which actions must be brought, usually designate a shorter limitation on tort actions, so that it may, on this account, be sometimes necessary to sue ex contractu.

When the contract imposes on the carrier some duty or obligation not imposed by the common law, then, of course, for a breach of this duty, the carrier must be sued ex contractu.[37] Thus, if the carrier should agree to provide a special groom to attend the shipper's horse during the entire period of shipment, and the carrier fails to provide such a groom, then must the carrier be sued on his contract, for he owes no such duty apart from that contract.

Advantages of an Action Ex Delicto

Where there are two or more defendants, and there is any doubt as to the parties liable, it is always safer to sue ex delicto, for in tort the plaintiff may sue any or all of the defendants who are liable,[38] while the rules as to proper parties defendant in actions ex contractu are exceedingly strict.[39] In actions ex delicto, less definiteness and precision is required in the plaintiff's statement of his cause of action, and hence the danger of a variance between the pleadings and the proof is not so great as in actions ex contractu.[40] In the matter of joinder, when the common-law action of trespass on the case is brought, a count in trover (which is also an action ex delicto) may be joined;[41] but this joinder in an action ex con-

[37] WERNICK v. ST. LOUIS & S. F. R. CO., 131 Mo. App. 37, 109 S. W. 1027, Dobie Cas. Bailments and Carriers, 278; Masters v. Stratton, 7 Hill (N. Y.) 101; Legge v. Tucker, 1 Hurl. & N. (Eng.) 500; Bliss on Code Pleading (3d Ed.) § 14.

[38] Orange County Bank v. Brown, 3 Wend. (N. Y.) 158; Cabell v. Vaughan, 1 Saund. (Eng.) 291a, 291e; Jones v. Pitcher, 3 Stew. & P. (Ala.) 135, 24 Am. Dec. 716; Holsapple v. Rome, W. & O. R. Co., 86 N. Y. 275; Mitchell v. Tarbutt, 5 Term R. (Eng.) 649; Smith v. Seward, 3 Pa. 342, 345; Patton v. Magrath, Rice (S. C.) 162, 33 Am. Dec. 98; Pozzi v. Shipton, 8 Adol. & E. (Eng.) 963, 35 E. C. L. 931. Connecting carriers, see Baker v. Michigan, S. & N. I. R. Co., 42 Ill. 73; Ansell v. Waterhouse, 6 Maule & S. (Eng.) 385, 18 E. C. L. 469. See, also, Merchants' & Miners' Transp. Co. v. Eichberg, 109 Md. 211, 71 Atl. 993, 130 Am. St. Rep. 524.

[39] Smith v. Seward, 3 Pa. 342; Mershon v. Hobensack, 22 N. J. Law, 372; Patton v. Magrath, Rice (S. C.) 162, 33 Am. Dec. 98; Pozzi v. Shipton, 8 Adol. & E. (Eng.) 963.

[40] Weed v. Saratoga & S. R. Co., 19 Wend. (N. Y.) 534; Wylde v. Pickford, 8 M. & W. (Eng.) 443.

[41] Dickon v. Clifton, 2 Wils. (Eng.) 319; Dwight v. Brewster, 1 Pick. (Mass.) 50, 11 Am. Dec. 133; Wylde v. Pickford, 8 Mees. & W. (Eng.) 443; Govett v. Radnidge, 3 East (Eng.) 62, 69. Trover is not the proper remedy for loss of goods. Ross v. Johnson, 5 Burrows (Eng.) 2825; Kirkman v. Hargreaves, 1 Selw. N. P. 10th Ed. (Eng.) 411; Anon., 2 Salk. (Eng.) 665; Bowlin v. Nye, 10 Cush. (Mass.) 416. Trover lies for wrongful delivery to third person. Viner v. New York, A. G. & W. S. S. Co., 50 N. Y. 23; Bush v. Romer, 2 Thomp. &

tractu would not be permissible.[42] The measure of damages, too, is more elastic than in actions ex contractu; punitive damages being sometimes allowed in ex delicto actions.[43] Finally, in this connection, an action ex delicto is more desirable, when the contract of shipment restricts the common-law liability of the carrier; for, in such an action, the burden of alleging these special limitations and proving that the loss or injury was included within such limitations falls affirmatively on the carrier.[44]

THE PLEADINGS

156. The pleadings should indicate clearly the plaintiff's theory of the case, whether this be ex contractu or ex delicto. They should state facts constituting a complete cause of action against the carrier, consistent with this theory, and in harmony with the evidence to be adduced at the trial.

Either under the common law or Code system of pleading, the plaintiff should make it perfectly clear in his first pleading whether he is attempting to state a cause of action ex contractu or ex delicto.[45] When this is made clear, all subsequent pleadings must be

C. (N. Y.) 597; Hawkins v. Hoffman, 6 Hill (N. Y.) 586, 41 Am. Dec. 767; Libby v. Ingalls, 124 Mass. 503; Humphreys v. Reed, 6 Whart. (Pa.) 435; Shenk v. Philadelphia Steam Propeller Co., 60 Pa. 109, 100 Am. Dec. 541; Bullard v. Young, 3 Stew. (Ala.) 46; Stephenson v. Hart, 4 Bing. 476; Illinois Cent. R. Co. v. Parks, 54 Ill. 294; Indianapolis & St. L. R. Co. v. Herndon, 81 Ill. 143; St. Louis & T. H. R. Co. v. Rose, 20 Ill. App. 670. Also for refusal to deliver. Northern Transp. Co. of Ohio v. Sellick, 52 Ill. 249; Adams v. Clark, 9 Cush. (Mass.) 215, 57 Am. Dec. 41; Richardson v. Rich, 104 Mass. 156, 159, 6 Am. Rep. 210; Packard v. Getman, 6 Cow. (N. Y.) 757, 16 Am. Dec. 475; Long v. Mobile & M. R. Co., 51 Ala. 512; Hunt v. Haskell, 24 Me. 339, 41 Am. Dec. 387; Louisville & N. R. Co. v. Lawson, 88 Ky. 496, 11 S. W. 511; Erie Dispatch v. Johnson, 87 Tenn. 490, 11 S. W. 441; Lewis v. St. Paul & S. C. R. Co., 20 Minn. 260 (Gil. 234); Marsh v. Union Pac. R. Co. (C. C.) 9 Fed. 873. See, also, Ostrander v. Brown, 15 Johns. (N. Y.) 39, 8 Am. Dec. 211. Trover lies where carrier has sold goods for freight. Sullivan v. Park, 33 Me. 438; Briggs v. Boston & L. R. Co., 6 Allen (Mass.) 246, 83 Am. Dec. 626.

[42] Coryton v. Lithebye, 2 Saund. (Eng.) 115, and note. See, also, Hoagland v. Hannibal & St. J. R. Co., 39 Mo. 451; Colwell v. New York & E. R. Co., 9 How. Prac. (N. Y.) 311.

[43] See Mills v. Southern Ry., 90 S. C. 366, 73 S. E. 772; MATHESON v. SOUTHERN R. CO., 79 S. C. 155, 60 S. E. 437, Dobie Cas. Bailments and Carriers, 290.

[44] SOUTHERN EXP. CO. v. CALDWELL, 21 Wall. 264, 22 L. Ed. 556, Dobie Cas. Bailments and Carriers, 226.

[45] For forms of declarations at common law, both in assumpsit (when the

appropriate to the theory of his case thus adopted by the plaintiff. As has just been indicated, when this theory is ex contractu, much greater particularity of statement is required.[46] There are no peculiar rules of pleading applicable only to actions against carriers.[47]

As in other cases, the plaintiff must allege every fact necessary to show a cause of action against the carrier, entitling the plaintiff to recover. Thus there must be allegations of fact showing (a) the duty owed to the plaintiff (whether arising ex contractu or ex delicto); (b) the violation of that duty; and (c) the resulting damage to the plaintiff.[48] The plaintiff's pleadings must also be drawn with reference to the evidence to be adduced at the trial. The plaintiff's case must be proved as alleged; the allegata and probata must correspond, or a variance between the two might prove fatal to the plaintiff's case.[49]

action is on the contract) and in trespass on the case (when the action is on the tort), see any of the standard works on pleading. These are also given in all form books. In the Code states there are no forms of action, but the pleader in his first pleading makes it clear whether he is stating a case ex contractu or ex delicto. See WERNICK v. ST. LOUIS & S. F. RY. CO., 131 Mo. App. 37, 109 S. W. 1027, Dobie Cas. Bailments and Carriers, 278.

46 Weed v. Saratoga & S. R. Co., 19 Wend. (N. Y.) 534; Wylde v. Pickford, 8 M. & W. (Eng.) 443.

47 In an action against a railroad company to recover damages for loss and injury to property in shipment, based on its common-law liability as a common carrier, it cannot defend on the ground that plaintiff failed to give notice of the loss within a reasonable time unless such defense is specifically pleaded. Southern Ry. Co. v. Mooresville Cotton Mills, 187 Fed. 72, 109 C. C. A. 390.

48 In 3 Hutch. Carr. § 1334, the following cases are cited in which the plaintiff's statement was held sufficient: Williams v. Baltimore & O. R. Co., 9 W. Va. 33; Missouri Pac. Ry. Co. v. Edwards, 78 Tex. 307, 14 S. W. 607; LANG v. BRADY, 73 Conn. 707, 49 Atl. 199, Dobie Cas. Bailments and Carriers, 283; Independence Mills Co. v. Burlington, C. R. & N. Ry. Co., 72 Iowa, 535, 34 N. W. 320, 2 Am. St. Rep. 258; McFadden v. Missouri Pac. Ry. Co., 92 Mo. 343, 4 S. W. 689, 1 Am. St. Rep. 721. And the following cases when the pleading was held insufficient: Cox v. Columbus & W. Ry. Co., 91 Ala. 392, 8 South. 824; Pennsylvania Co. v. Clark, 2 Ind. App. 146, 27 N. E. 586, 28 N. E. 208; Richardson v. Chicago & N. W. Ry. Co., 61 Wis. 596, 21 N. W. 49. The failure of a carrier to deliver property received for transportation constitutes, in the absence of proof that the loss was occasioned by an act of God or the public enemy, or resulted from inevitable accident or from inherent defects in the property, a cause of action; and the shipper need not allege or prove the specific misconduct that incapacitated the carrier from delivering the goods. Merritt Creamery Co. v. Atchison, T. & S. F. R. Co., 128 Mo. App. 420, 107 S. W. 462. In an action by a shipper against a carrier for damage to goods in transit, particular acts of negligence need not be alleged. Louisville & N. R. Co. v. Warfield & Lee, 129 Ga. 473, 59 S. E. 234; Id., 3 Ga. App. 187, 59 S. E. 604.

49 R. E. FUNSTEN DRIED FRUIT & NUT CO. v. TOLEDO, ST. L. & W.

THE EVIDENCE

157. The plaintiff's evidence, consistent with his pleadings, in actions for loss of, or injury to, the goods, must show:
(a) Delivery of the goods to the carrier.
(b) The carrier's undertaking to transport them safely.
(c) The carrier's failure in this undertaking.
(d) The resulting damage.

The plaintiff must prove, consistent with the allegations in his pleadings, facts necessary to make out a cause of action against the carrier. This must be done by evidence that is relevant and admissible according to the accepted doctrines of evidence. These facts have been repeatedly stated and require no further discussion here.

When the plaintiff thus proves the delivery to the carrier, the carrier's undertaking, and the latter's failure in this undertaking, which results in damage to the goods or loss of them, he has made out a prima facie case.[60] This the carrier may rebut (as we have

R. CO., 163 Mo. App. 426, 148 S. W. 839, Dobie Cas. Bailments and Carriers, 196. There was a variance between an allegation that the damage was caused from delay in transportation and proof that it arose from lack of refrigeration, which was not alleged. Missouri, K. & T. Ry. Co. of Texas v. McLean, 55 Tex. Civ. App. 130, 118 S. W. 161. A variance in an action for damage to goods shipped in that the initials of the consignee on the waybill were different from those of plaintiff, though the surname was the same, was not necessarily material or fatal. Georgia S. & F. R. Co. v. Barfield, 1 Ga. App. 203, 58 S. E. 236.

[60] This the plaintiff does by showing delivery to the carrier and the carrier's failure to deliver the goods, as to a loss. Cooper v. Georgia Pac. Ry. Co., 92 Ala. 329, 9 South. 159, 25 Am. St. Rep. 59; The Priscilla (D. C.) 106 Fed. 739; Saleeby v. Central R. Co. of New Jersey, 99 App. Div. 163, 90 N. Y. Supp. 1042; Magnus v. Platt, 62 Misc. Rep. 499, 115 N. Y. Supp. 824; Taugher v. Northern Pac. R. Co., 21 N. D. 111, 129 N. W. 747. As to damage, a prima facie case is made out by showing a delivery of the goods to the carrier in good condition, and redelivery by the carrier in a damaged condition. St. Louis Southwestern R. Co. v. Phœnix Cotton Oil Co., 88 Ark. 594, 115 S. W. 393; FOCKENS v. UNITED STATES EXP. CO., 99 Minn. 404, 109 N. W. 834; Dobie Cas. Bailments and Carriers, 284; Nairn v. Missouri, K. & T. R. Co., 126 Mo. App. 707, 106 S. W. 102; Michigan Cent. R. Co. v. Osmus, 129 Ill. App. 79; Vuille v. Pennsylvania R. Co., 42 Pa. Super. Ct. 567. On proof that a carrier received goods in good condition, the burden rests on defendant to show delivery in the same condition to the next carrier or to the consignee; such proof being within its power. Orem Fruit & Produce Co. of Baltimore City v. Northern Cent. R. Co., 106 Md. 1, 66 Atl. 436, 124 Am. St. Rep. 462. In an action for breakage of goods in transit, the plaintiff must prove that the goods were delivered in good condition and properly packed. E. C. Fuller Co. v. Pennsylvania R. Co., 61 Misc. Rep. 599, 113 N. Y. Supp. 1001.

seen) by showing that such loss or damage was due either to one of the excepted perils or to a cause from which he has exempted himself by a valid contract.[51] The conflict of opinion as to whether the carrier must, in the case of an excepted peril, go further and show the absence of negligence on his part, has also been adverted to.[52] The subject of the burden of proof has also been discussed in the specific treatment of the various questions in connection with which it has arisen.

THE MEASURE OF DAMAGES—IN GENERAL

158. In determining the amount of damages to which the plaintiff is entitled in an action for the breach of the duty of the carrier, the law, in general, seeks to put the plaintiff in the position in which he would have been had the carrier fully lived up to his duty. Punitive damages are rarely given.

The consideration in detail of the measure of damages belongs more properly to a work on damages; but it seems advisable to

[51] See ante, §§ 118, 128. See, also, Gulf, C. & S. F. R. Co. v. Belton Oil Co., 45 Tex. Civ. App. 44, 99 S. W. 430; Lloyd v. Haugh & Keenan Storage & Transfer Co., 223 Pa. 148, 72 Atl. 516, 21 L. R. A. (N. S.) 188; McCord v. Atlantic Coast Line R. Co., 76 S. C. 469, 57 S. E. 477; Union Pac. R. Co. v. Stupeck, 50 Colo. 151, 114 Pac. 646. Where a box in which an overcoat was shipped was allowed to remain with the carrier at its destination until its liability became merely that of warehouseman, it was presumed negligent, and under the burden of explaining disappearance of the coat. Levine v. Delaware, L. & W. R. Co., 74 Misc. Rep. 348, 134 N. Y. Supp. 217. Where, in an action for the value of a puncheon of molasses which burst while in the custody of a carrier, there is evidence that the cause was the fermentation of the molasses, defendant is entitled to have it considered by the jury under a proper charge, as the carrier is not liable for loss or damage resulting from defects inherent in the goods. Currie v. Seaboard Air Line R. Co., 156 N. C. 432, 72 S. E. 493. As to the effect on the burden of proof when the shipper or his agent accompanies the shipment, see St. Louis, I. M. & S. R. Co. v. Pape, 100 Ark. 269, 140 S. W. 265; Winn v. American Exp. Co., 149 Iowa, 259, 128 N. W. 663. The right of a carrier to sue for the freight due and the right of the shipper to sue for damages to the shipment are independent, and it is no defense to an action for damages that the freight has not been paid. Cleveland, C., C. & St. L. Ry. Co. v. Rudy (Ind. App.) 87 N. E. 555. That a rate given to a shipper may be in violation of the rates fixed by the Interstate Commerce Commission does not affect the carrier's liability to respond or the shipper's right to recover for loss of the goods, though both the carrier and the shipper might be subject to criminal prosecution, and though the carrier might recover the charges fixed by the commission. Central of Georgia R. Co. v. Butler Marble & Granite Co., 8 Ga. App. 1, 68 S. E. 775.

[52] Ante, §§ 118, 128.

state the broad rules which govern in the more frequent actions against the carrier of goods. These are actions for the carrier's refusal to accept and transport the goods, actions for loss of, or injury to, the goods, and actions for delay in transporting the goods.

In this connection it should be noted that in actions on contract the law is stricter in limiting the recovery to the natural, direct, and proximate damages resulting from the carrier's breach of duty. In general, too, the carrier of goods is liable only for compensatory, and not for punitive, damages.[53] In other words, the general theory governing the award of damages is merely to compensate the plaintiff for the injury he has suffered, and not to go beyond this and give damages for the purpose of punishing the carrier or making such an example of him that he and other carriers will be less likely to sin again in that respect. Though punitive or exemplary damages are more usual in the case of passenger carriers, there are rare instances in which the courts feel justified in awarding such damages against the common carrier of goods.[54] In general, though, the law contents itself in granting only such damages as are necessary to place the plaintiff in a position as advantageous as the one that he would have occupied, had the carrier completely performed his duty in the transportation of the goods.

SAME—ACTIONS FOR CARRIER'S REFUSAL TO ACCEPT AND TRANSPORT THE GOODS

159. The ordinary measure of damages, in an action against the carrier for his wrongful refusal to accept and transport the goods, is the difference between what would have been the value of the goods at the place where and the time when they should have been delivered and their value at the time and place of refusal, less the transportation charges.

[53] This is borne out by the cases cited in the sections that follow.

[54] Mills v. Southern Ry. Co., 90 S. C. 366, 73 S. E. 772. For discussion of the compensatory and punitive damages recoverable against the carrier by a husband for injuries to the dead body of his wife, see Wilson v. St. Louis & S. F. R. Co., 160 Mo. App. 649, 142 S. W. 775. Where, in an action for the loss of freight, reckless or willful disregard of consignee's rights or even indifference to them does not appear, but all the testimony tends to show a loss by theft from the carrier or some mistake, which after diligent effort it cannot account for, the carrier is not liable for punitive damages. MATHESON v. SOUTHERN RY. CO., 79 S. C. 155, 60 S. E. 437, Dobie Cas. Bailments and Carriers, 290. To entitle a shipper to punitive damages for delay in transportation, gross negligence, or willful or wanton disregard of its duty, on the part of the carrier, must be shown. American Exp. Co. v. Burke & McGuire (Miss.) 61 South. 312.

If another reasonable mode of conveying the goods can readily be procured after such refusal, then the measure of damages would be the increased cost of transportation by such other mode.

The primary object of transportation is to have the use of the goods or an opportunity to sell them at the place of destination. The damages for a wrongful refusal to transport goods is, therefore, the value to the shipper of his right of having them at the point of destination. For this right the shipper must be ready, of course, to pay the carrier's lawful charges. Ordinarily, then, the measure of damages for the carrier's wrongful refusal would be the difference between the value of the goods at the time and place of refusal and their value at the place of destination at the time they should have been delivered there, less the charges of transportation.[55] Thus, suppose a carrier at Albany wrongfully refuses to accept and transport goods to Boston, the value of the goods at Albany at the time of refusal being $100, their value at Boston when they should have been delivered being $125, and the lawful charges for such a shipment being $5. Then it is clear that $20 will exactly cover the loss caused to the shipper by the carrier's unjustifiable refusal.

The general duty, however, rests on a plaintiff to minimize the damages, at least in so far as this can be done without undue effort or trouble on his part. Hence he cannot recover damages for consequences that might clearly have been avoided by the exercise of reasonable diligence on his part. Therefore, if other suitable means of transportation may readily be had, and the circumstances are such that a reasonably prudent man would forward the goods by those means, then the damages recoverable would not exceed what he would suffer who does make use of such available means. In such cases, the damages would be the excess of the cost of such transportation over the lawful charges of the carrier wrongfully refusing to accept the goods, together with the damages resulting from the delay in securing such transportation.[56] If the cost of transporting the goods by these other suitable means which the plaintiff either has adopted, or should have adopted, does not ex-

[55] Pennsylvania R. Co. v. Titusville & P. P. R. Co., 71 Pa. 350; Galena & C. U. R. Co. v. Rae, 18 Ill. 488, 68 Am. Dec. 574; Harvey v. Connecticut & P. R. R. Co., 124 Mass. 421, 26 Am. Rep. 673; Bridgman v. The Emily, 18 Iowa, 509; Ward's Cent. & P. Lake Co. v. Elkins, 34 Mich. 439, 22 Am. Rep. 544; O'Conner v. Forster, 10 Watts (Pa.) 418; Inman v. St. Louis S. W. Ry. Co., 14 Tex. Civ. App. 39, 37 S. W. 37.

[56] O'Conner v. Forster, 10 Watts (Pa.) 418; Ogden v. Marshall, 8 N. Y. 340, 59 Am. Dec. 497; Grund v. Pendergast, 58 Barb. (N. Y.) 216; Higginson v. Weld, 14 Gray (Mass.) 165; Crouch v. Railway Co., 11 Exch. (Eng.) 742.

ceed the charges which the carrier refusing might have exacted, then only nominal damages can be recovered, unless the plaintiff suffered damage due to the delay in securing such other means, when such delay is not attributable to his fault.

SAME—ACTIONS FOR TOTAL LOSS OR NONDELIVERY OF THE GOODS

160. The measure of damages in actions for total loss or nondelivery of the goods is the value of the goods at the time when and at the place where they should have been delivered, less any unpaid transportation charges.

Obviously, the natural and probable consequences of a failure to deliver the goods at their destination is a loss to the owner, amounting to the value of the goods at that point, at the time when they should have been delivered, and such value is therefore the measure of damages.[57] The plaintiff, though, can secure the transportation, or the beneficial damages worked out on the basis of the loss to him because the goods have not been so transported, only on the payment of the carrier's charges; hence any unpaid charges of the carrier must to that extent reduce the plaintiff's recovery.[58] Ordinarily the value of the goods means their market value unless that is unduly and irregularly inflated or depressed.[59] If the goods have no market price, then their value is usually held to be the value of the goods to the owner, taking into account such practical considerations as its cost and the expense of replacing it, but disregarding any pretium affectionis or fanciful and sentimental valuations.[60]

[57] Mobile & M. Ry. Co. v. Jurey, 111 U. S. 584, 4 Sup. Ct. 566, 28 L. Ed. 527; Louisville & N. R. Co. v. Kelsey, 89 Ala. 287, 7 South. 648; Pfaff v. Pacific Exp. Co., 251 Ill. 243, 95 N. E. 1089; Marshall Medicine Co. v. Chicago & A. R. Co., 126 Mo. App. 455, 104 S. W. 478; Brown v. North Western R. R., 75 S. C. 20, 54 S. E. 829; O'Hanlan v. Ry. Co., 6 Best & S. (Eng.) 484; Rodocanachi v. Milburn, 18 Q. B. Div. (Eng.) 67. Cf. Magnin v. Dinsmore, 56 N. Y. 168; Id., 62 N. Y. 35, 20 Am. Rep. 442; Id., 70 N. Y. 410, 26 Am. Rep. 608. See, also, Faulkner v. Hart, 82 N. Y. 413, 37 Am. Rep. 574; Spring v. Haskell, 4 Allen (Mass.) 112; Sangamon & M. R. Co. v. Henry, 14 Ill. 156.

[58] See cases cited in preceding note; Wilson v. St. Louis & S. F. R. Co., 129 Mo. App. 347, 108 S. W. 612; Chesapeake & O. R. Co. v. F. W. Stock & Sons, 104 Va. 97, 51 S. E. 161.

[59] See cases cited in note 57; Pfaff v. Pacific Exp. Co., 251 Ill. 243, 95 N. E. 1089; MOBILE, J. & K. C. R. CO. v. ROBBINS COTTON CO., 94 Miss. 351, 48 South. 231, Dobie Cas. Bailments and Carriers, 286.

[60] Lloyd v. Haugh & Keenan Storage & Transfer Co., 223 Pa. 148, 72 Atl 516, 21 L. R. A. (N. S.) 188; Pennsylvania R. Co. v. John Arda Co., 131 Ill.

SAME—ACTIONS FOR INJURY TO THE GOODS

161. The measure of damages for injury to goods in transit is the difference between the value of the goods at the time and place of delivery in their damaged condition and what their value would have been had they been duly delivered in good order, less any unpaid transportation charges.

When there is a total failure to deliver the goods, as we have just seen, the owner's loss is their real value when and where they should have been delivered. It is obvious that if the goods are delivered to the consignee, but in a damaged condition, the damage that would have been suffered from a total loss is diminished by an amount equal to the value of the damaged goods received, and the difference between this value and what the value would have been had the goods been delivered uninjured is the measure of damages, after the payment of any unpaid charges for the transportation.[61]

App. 426; International & G. N. Ry. Co. v. Nicholson, 61 Tex. 550; Mitchell v. Weir, 19 App. Div. 183, 45 N. Y. Supp. 1085; Cooney v. Pullman Palace-Car Co., 121 Ala. 368, 25 South. 712, 53 L. R. A. 690.

[61] St. Louis Southwestern R. Co. v. Phœnix Cotton Oil Co., 88 Ark. 594, 115 S. W. 393; Reason v. Detroit, G. H. & M. Ry. Co., 150 Mich. 50, 113 N. W. 596; Ruddell v. Baltimore & O. R. Co., 152 Ill. App. 218; R. E. FUNSTEN DRIED FRUIT & NUT CO. v. TOLEDO, ST. L. & W. R. CO., 163 Mo. App. 426, 143 S. E. 839, Dobie Cas. Bailments and Carriers, 196; Notara v. Henderson, L. R. 7 Q. B. (Eng.) 225; Chicago, B. & Q. R. Co. v. Hale, 83 Ill. 360, 25 Am. Rep. 403; Brown v. Cunard S. S. Co., 147 Mass. 58, 16 N. E. 717; Louisville & N. R. Co. v. Mason, 11 Lea (Tenn.) 116; Magdeburg General Ins. Co. v. Paulson (D. C.) 29 Fed. 530; The Mangalore (D. C.) 23 Fed. 463. See Morrison v. I. & V. Florio S. S. Co. (D. C.) 36 Fed. 569, 571; The Compta, 5 Sawy. 137, Fed. Cas. No. 3,070. Where property is injured in transportation through the negligence of the carrier, but is not entirely worthless, the owner cannot refuse to accept it and sue for its market value, but may recover only for the injury. Missouri, K. & T. Ry. Co. of Texas v. Moore, 47 Tex. Civ. App. 531, 105 S. W. 532; McGRATH BROS. v. CHARLESTON & W. C. RY. CO., 91 S. C. 552, 75 S. E. 44, 42 L. R. A. (N. S.) 782, Ann. Cas. 1914A, 64, Dobie Cas. Bailments and Carriers, 288. The rule that, on injury to goods in transportation, the value at the destination is the basis for determining the damages, the measure being the difference between the value of the goods at destination as injured and their value if delivered in good order, also applies where goods are taken for transportation to a point beyond the initial carrier's line. Southern Exp. Co. v. Jacobs, 109 Va. 27, 63 S. E. 17. Where, in an action against a carrier for injuries to a shipment of potatoes, it appeared that the shipper had sold the potatoes for delivery at a distant point, that the buyer at the point of delivery, because of the damaged condition of the shipment, refused to accept the potatoes, but there was

Thus, butterine shipped to New Orleans was damaged in transit, through the carrier's negligence. On its arrival its market value in its damaged condition was 7½ cents per pound, at which price it was sold. Had it been in good order, its market value at New Orleans would have been 15 or 16 cents a pound. It was held that plaintiff was entitled to the difference between these prices.[63]

SAME—ACTIONS FOR DELAY IN TRANSPORTATION OR DELIVERY OF THE GOODS

162. The measure of damages for delay in the transportation or delivery of the goods is the difference between the value of the goods at the time when and the place where they should have been delivered and their value at the time and place of actual delivery, less any unpaid transportation charges.

When, however, the value of the goods is not diminished by such delay, the measure of damages, after unpaid transportation charges are deducted, is the value of the use of the goods during the period of delay.

These rules indicate the normal measure of damages when the goods are delivered safely, but when, owing to the negligence of the carrier, the goods are not delivered at the proper time. Since the usual reason for shipping goods is to realize their value (after the payment of the carrier's charges) at the destination when they should have been delivered, the usual loss caused to the shipper by the delay is their value then less their value when they are ac-

no evidence to show what the sound potatoes were sold for at the place of delivery, or that diligence had been used to secure their market price, the shipper's measure of damages was the difference between the total amount of the contract price of the whole shipment agreed to be paid by the buyer, less the freight charges paid by the shipper and the amount for which the sound potatoes, in the exercise of ordinary care to obtain on their delivery at the point of delivery the market price, were sold. Texarkana & Ft. S. R. Co. v. Shivel & Stewart (Tex. Civ. App.) 114 S. W. 196. In an action against a carrier for damages to peaches consigned to Boston or Springfield, evidence of the price paid for the peaches in the orchard or point of shipment one or two weeks before they were sold at destination, was properly excluded as too remote. Henry J. Perkins Co. v. American Exp. Co., 199 Mass. 561, 85 N. E. 895.

[63] Western Mfg. Co. v. The Guiding Star (C. C.) 37 Fed. 641.

tually delivered.[63] Interest is also allowed on such sum from the time the goods should have been delivered.[64]

When there is no difference between the value of the goods when they were delivered and when they should have been delivered, then the loss is limited to the value of the use of the goods between the two dates; that is, during the period of the delay. Thus, in an action against the carrier for delay in delivering machinery (the value of which was not affected by the delay) the damages were the value of the use of the machinery during the period of its delay, or the sum for which the plaintiff might for this period have hired similar machinery.[65]

[63] Gulf, C. & S. F. Ry. Co. v. McCarty, 82 Tex. 608, 18 S. W. 716; Hudson v. Northern Pac. Ry. Co., 92 Iowa, 231, 60 N. W. 608, 54 Am. St. Rep. 550; Western & A. R. Co. v. Summerour, 139 Ga. 545, 77 S. E. 802; Newport News & M. V. R. Co. v. Mercer, 96 Ky. 475, 29 S. W. 301; Atlanta & W. P. R. Co. v. Texas Grate Co., 81 Ga. 602, 9 S. E. 600; McGRATH BROS. v. CHARLESTON & W. C. RY. CO., 91 S. C. 552, 75 S. E. 44, 42 L. R. A. (N. S.) 782, Ann. Cas. 1914A, 64, Dobie Cas. Bailments and Carriers, 288; Wilson v. Ry. Co., 9 C. B. N. S. (Eng.) 632. See, also, Cutting v. Grand Trunk Ry. Co., 13 Allen (Mass.) 381; Weston v. Grand Trunk Ry. Co., 54 Me. 376, 92 Am. Dec. 552; Sherman v. Hudson River R. Co., 64 N. Y. 254; Scott v. Boston & N. O. S. S. Co., 106 Mass. 468; Collard v. Railway Co., 7 Hurl. & N. (Eng.) 79; Ayres v. Chicago & N. W. Ry. Co., 75 Wis. 215, 43 N. W. 1122; Ingledew v. Northern R., 7 Gray (Mass.) 86. Money spent looking for goods may be recovered. Hales v. Railway Co., 4 Best & S. (Eng.) 66. Cf. Woodger v. Railway Co., L. R. 2 C. B. (Eng.) 318. Where goods have been resold and the carrier notified of the price, such price is to be taken as their true value, Deming v. Grand Trunk R. Co., 48 N. H. 455, 470, 2 Am. Rep. 267; but where the carrier is not notified of such price, the market price is considered their true value, Horne v. Midland Ry. Co., L. R. 8 C. P. (Eng.) 131. Cf. Illinois Cent. R. Co. v. Cobb, 64 Ill. 128, where shipper was allowed to recover on basis of contract price. Where goods have been sold "to arrive," and the market value at the time when they should have arrived was greater than the contract price, recovery has been allowed on the basis of market value. Rodocanachi v. Milburn, L. R. 18 Q. B. Div. (Eng.) 67. Incidental expenses proximately flowing from the negligent delay may also be recovered. Murrell v. Pacific Exp. Co., 54 Ark. 22, 14 S. W. 1098, 26 Am. St. Rep. 17; Deming v. Grand Trunk R. Co., 48 N. H. 455, 2 Am. Rep. 267.

[64] New York, L. E. & W. R. Co. v. Estill, 147 U. S. 591, 13 Sup. Ct. 444, 37 L. Ed. 292; Houston & T. C. Ry. Co. v. Jackson, 62 Tex. 209.

[65] Priestly v. Northern Indiana & C. R. Co., 26 Ill. 206, 79 Am. Dec. 369. So, in forwarding money, the measure of damages was held to be interest on the money during the period of delay. United States Exp. Co. v. Haines, 67 Ill. 137.

SAME—SPECIAL DAMAGES

163. Special damages arising from the carrier's default are ordinarily not allowed unless the peculiar circumstances out of which these damages arise are communicated to, or known by, the carrier, and unless these damages are also the natural and probable consequences of the carrier's breach of duty.

In all the rules heretofore stated, with reference to the measure of damages, the damages allowed have been for losses directly flowing from the carrier's breach of duty. In addition, these losses are such as would normally arise, without regard to any distinctive details surrounding any individual shipment. It frequently happens, however, that by virtue of these peculiar facts in a particular shipment the loss suffered is far greater than that granted under the general rules already stated. It then becomes important to determine whether such unique or special damages are recoverable, or whether the shipper is limited to a recovery under the general rule appropriate to all cases of that kind.

The accepted doctrine is that such unique and special damages cannot be recovered unless the peculiar consequences of a default (or circumstances from which such consequences should properly be inferred) are communicated to, or known by, the carrier at the time the contract of carriage was made.[66] Only such losses can

[66] International & G. N. R. Co. v. Hatchell, 22 Tex. Civ. App. 498, 55 S. W. 186; Hamilton v. Western N. C. R. Co., 96 N. C. 398, 3 S. E. 164; Norfolk & W. Ry. Co. v. Reeves, 97 Va. 284, 33 S. E. 606; The Caledonia, 157 U. S. 124, 15 Sup. Ct. 537, 39 L. Ed. 644; Missouri, K. & T. R. Co. of Texas v. McLean, 55 Tex. Civ. App. 130, 118 S. W. 161. The owner of machinery lost in transportation could not recover from the carrier special damages for time lost and expense incurred in making successive calls for the freight at the carrier's office without proof of notice to the carrier's agent of the value of the time or attendant expense or the distance that would have to be traveled in making such calls. Pacific Exp. Co. v. Jones, 52 Tex. Civ. App. 367, 113 S. W. 952. Where, on shipment of fertilizer, there was no notice to the carrier of any special use to which it was to be applied or of such scarcity of fertilizer as to prevent another purchase of a like amount by consignee, consignee was not entitled to special damages for failure to deliver the fertilizer. MATHESON v. SOUTHERN RY. CO., 79 S. C. 155, 60 S. E. 437, Dobie Cas. Bailments and Carriers, 290. Where a carrier contracting for the transportation of a musical instrument did not have notice of the shipper's intention to use the instrument for any particular purpose, the measure of damages for injuries to the instrument during transportation was the difference in its value at the time and in the condition in which it arrived at the point of destination, and its value at the time and in the condition in which it

be recovered as were reasonably contemplated by both parties, at the time the contract was made, as likely to arise from the carrier's breach, and not losses due to circumstances which were then wholly unknown to the carrier. Damages, too, are awarded only for the reasonable and proximate, and not for the speculative and remote, consequences of the breach of the carrier's duty.[67]

Thus, when the carrier delayed the delivery of a shaft for a flour mill, it was held that, when the special circumstances were not communicated to the carrier, there could be no recovery for the loss of profits due to the fact that the mill was idle during such delay.[68] Again, in the absence of special knowledge by the carrier, it was held, where there was a delay in delivering a package containing samples, that there could be no recovery of the shipper's hotel expenses during such period of delay, when he was waiting for the package.[69] But when the carrier agreed to deliver the goods at their destination at a specified time, knowing that, unless the

should have arrived there. Missouri, K. & T. Ry. Co. v. Harris (Tex. Civ. App.) 138 S. W. 1085. A carrier, informed by a shipper that tents were intended to be used during severe weather as a stable for the protection of his horses, etc., had sufficient notice to render it liable for the expenses and damages which might result by reason of its failure to deliver them within a reasonable time. Pecos & N. T. Ry. Co. v. Maxwell (Tex. Civ. App.) 156 S. W. 548.

[67] Gulf, C. & S. F. Ry. Co. v. Hodge, 10 Tex. Civ. App. 543, 30 S. W. 829; Harvey v. Connecticut & P. R. R. Co., 124 Mass. 421, 26 Am. Rep. 673; Vicksburg & M. R. Co. v. Ragsdale, 46 Miss. 458. See, on the recovery of special damages in general, the great leading case of Hadley v. Baxendale, 9 Exch. (Eng.) 341. Where a carrier lost goods in its possession for transportation to plaintiff intended for resale in the course of plaintiff's business, and no freight had ever been paid, the carrier was only liable for the fair market value of the goods at the time and place of delivery, and not for profits which plaintiff might have made had he resold the goods in the ordinary course of his business. Cincinnati, N. O. & T. P. R. Co. v. Hansford & Son, 125 Ky. 37, 100 S. W. 251, 30 Ky. Law Rep. 1105. Where a shipper of household goods notifies the agent that she needs the goods immediately, there is not a sufficient notice of special damages to authorize a recovery for a cold contracted by the shipper, caused by the lack of the household goods shipped. Alabama & V. Ry. Co. v. McKenna (Miss.) 61 South. 823.

[68] Hadley v. Baxendale, 9 Exch. (Eng.) 341 (leading case). See, also, the recent case of Harper Furniture Co. v. Southern Exp. Co., 148 N. C. 87, 62 S. E. 145, 30 L. R. A. (N. S.) 483, 128 Am. St. Rep. 588, in which the facts (delay by carrier in transporting an engine shaft for a furniture factory) were strikingly similar in many respects to those of Hadley v. Baxendale. In the Harper Case a divided court (three judges to two) held that special damages were proper and that the facts and circumstances surrounding the shipment were sufficient to give notice to the carrier that these damages might reasonably be expected as the result of the delay.

[69] Woodger v. Ry. Co., L. R. 2 C. P. (Eng.) 318.

goods were then delivered, the owner would lose the profits of a splendid sale he had made, then the carrier for its negligent delay was held liable for the difference between the price stipulated in the plaintiff's advantageous contract of sale and the market value of the goods at the time of their actual delivery.[76]

[76] Deming v. Grand Trunk R. Co., 48 N. H. 455, 2 Am. Rep. 267.

PART THREE

CARRIERS OF PASSENGERS

CHAPTER XVI

THE NATURE OF THE RELATION

WHO ARE CARRIERS OF PASSENGERS

164. Carriers of passengers are carriers engaged in the transportation of human beings.

Like carriers of goods they are divided into:

(a) Common carriers, who hold themselves out to carry all proper persons who apply.

(b) Private carriers, who carry only on special contracts in individual cases.

In General

Practically, the passenger carrier differs from the carrier of goods as to what is carried. From this difference, however, flow necessarily legal consequences that must be in many respects utterly dissimilar. And yet there are still so many analogies between the two that the study of either throws light on the other, which is in itself sufficient justification for treating the two in a single book.

The carrier of passengers is engaged in the transportation, not of goods, but of human beings. Human beings have reason, volition, and intelligence. They can move about and incur danger or avoid it when it is impending. It is clear, too, that the carrier of passengers as such is in no sense a bailee. The control of the carrier over the passenger is not, and cannot be, as complete as the measure of control which the carrier can exercise over the goods. Even in the carrier's regulations, the human aspect is predominant as a limitation on what regulations are reasonable.

Though from an economic standpoint the carriage of goods is of relatively more importance than the transportation of passengers, yet the wonderful development of passenger traffic in modern times is such that the subject merits the most careful consideration. The value set by the state on the lives and safety of its citizens has lent, too, an element of very grave responsibility (to which that of the carrier of goods is in no way comparable) to the undertaking of the carrier of passengers.

Common and Private Carriers of Passengers

The same considerations that distinguish the common from the private carrier of goods apply to set apart the common and the private carrier of passengers. As these considerations have already been treated at some length,[1] no extended comment will be required here. There, as here, the holding out is the distinctive feature. The common carrier of passengers holds himself out to carry all proper persons who apply.[2] The private carrier makes no such profession, and engages in the transportation of passengers only by virtue of special contract made in each individual case,[3] into

[1] Ante, §§ 106-107.

[2] Murch v. Concord R. Corp., 29 N. H. 9, 61 Am. Dec. 631; Davis v. Button, 78 Cal. 247, 18 Pac. 133, 20 Pac. 545; Thompson Houston Electric Co. v. Simon, 20 Or. 60, 25 Pac. 147, 10 L. R. A. 251, 23 Am. St. Rep. 86; Central of Georgia Ry. Co. v. Lippman, 110 Ga. 665, 36 S. E. 202, 50 L. R. A. 673; Gillingham v. Ohio River R. Co., 35 W. Va. 588, 14 S. E. 243, 14 L. R. A. 798, 29 Am. St. Rep. 827. Among the important common carriers of passengers are: The proprietors of omnibuses, Brien v. Bennett, 8 Car. & P. (Eng.) 724; or stage coaches, Bretherton v. Wood, 3 Brod. & B. (Eng.) 54; Hollister v. Nowlen, 19 Wend. (N. Y.) 234, 32 Am. Dec. 455; BENNETT v. DUTTON, 10 N. H. 481, Dobie Cas. Bailments and Carriers, 322; Peixotti v. McLaughlin, 1 Strob. (S. C.) 468, 47 Am. Dec. 563; Lovett v. Hobbs, 2 Show. (Eng.) 127; railroad companies, Hanley v. Harlem R. Co., 1 Edm. Sel. Cas. (N. Y.) 359; Eaton v. Boston & L. R. Co., 11 Allen (Mass.) 500, 87 Am. Dec. 730; McElroy v. Nashua & L. R. Corp., 4 Cush. (Mass.) 400, 50 Am. Dec. 794; New Orleans, J. & G. N. R. Co. v. Hurst, 36 Miss. 660, 74 Am. Dec. 785; Union Pac. Ry. Co. v. Nichols, 8 Kan. 505, 12 Am. Rep. 475; Nashville & C. R. Co. v. Messino, 1 Sneed (Tenn.) 220; Caldwell v. Richmond & D. R. Co., 89 Ga. 550, 15 S. E. 678; street car companies, Holly v. Atlanta St. R. R., 61 Ga. 215, 34 Am. Rep. 97; Chicago City Ry. Co. v. Mumford, 97 Ill. 560; Isaacs v. Third Ave. R. Co., 47 N. Y. 122, 7 Am. Rep. 418; Spellman v. Lincoln Rapid Transit Co., 36 Neb. 890, 55 N. W. 270, 20 L. R. A. 316, 38 Am. St. Rep. 753; Jackson v. Grand Ave. Ry. Co., 118 Mo. 199, 24 S. W. 192; steamboat companies, White v. McDonough, 3 Sawy. 311, Fed. Cas. No. 17,552; Benett v. Steamboat Co., 6 C. B. (Eng.) 775, 16 C. B. 29; Jencks v. Coleman, 2 Sumn. 221, Fed. Cas. No. 7,258; ferrymen, Le Barron v. East Boston Ferry Co., 11 Allen (Mass.) 312, 87 Am. Dec. 717; Slimmer v. Merry, 23 Iowa, 90.

[3] "A wagoner who occasionally carries a passenger upon his wagons, as a matter of special accommodation and agreement, does not thereby become a common carrier of passengers. He only becomes such when the carrying of passengers becomes an habitual business." Murch v. Concord R. Corp., 29 N. H. 9, 61 Am. Dec. 631. See, also, cases cited in preceding note. See Atlantic City v. Dehn, 69 N. J. Law, 233, 54 Atl. 220.

which contract the private passenger carrier can enter or not, as he chooses. He can refuse, either for a bad reason or no reason at all, to transport individuals without incurring any liability for such refusal. As the passenger traffic of the civilized world is practically controlled by common carriers, the private carrier will be dismissed with a paragraph, and only the common carrier of passengers will be considered.

The private passenger carrier is in no sense affected with a public interest, and his rights and duties are solely those of one engaged in a business in which the public, as such, has no interest or concern. He exercises no extraordinary rights, and incurs no extraordinary responsibility. He carries by special contract, and this usually is the measure of his rights and duties. Pursuing no public calling, he can, without contravening public policy, make contracts in a wider range than is permitted to the common carrier of passengers. In the absence of a contract provision on that point, the private carrier owes to his passenger only the duty of exercising due or ordinary care.

Of course, one may be a common carrier of goods and a private carrier of passengers, and vice versa. Thus one holding himself out to carry goods for all who apply (but without such holding out as to passengers) may occasionally take a passenger in special instances. As to the passenger, the carrier in such cases is only a private carrier. Likewise one whose public profession is limited to the transportation of passengers may in an individual case undertake to carry goods (not the passenger's baggage) for hire, and yet the carrier here is merely a private carrier of goods.

The most important common carriers of modern times are railway and steamboat companies, street railways (whether surface, elevated, or underground), and the proprietors of omnibuses, hacks, and taxicabs.[4] The cases are not entirely clear as to the proprietors of passenger elevators. Though a sound public policy seems to require the same degree of care as to those carried,[5] it is believed to be the better view not to hold these as being (at least for all purposes) common carriers of passengers.

4 See cases cited in note 2.

5 Fox v. Philadelphia, 208 Pa. 127, 57 Atl. 356, 65 L. R. A. 214; Chicago Exch. Bldg. Co. v. Nelson, 197 Ill. 334, 64 N. E. 369; Mitchell v. Marker, 62 Fed. 139, 10 C. C. A. 306, 25 L. R. A. 33; Goldsmith v. Holland Building Co., 182 Mo. 597, 81 S. W. 1112; Perrault v. Emporium Dept. Store Co., 71 Wash. 523, 128 Pac. 1049. Many cases decline to impose the high degree of care required of common carriers of passengers. Seaver v. Bradley, 179 Mass. 329, 60 N. E. 795, 88 Am. St. Rep. 384; Phillips Co. v. Pruitt, 82 S. W. 628, 26 Ky. Law Rep. 831; Hall v. Murdock, 114 Mich. 233, 72 N. W. 150.

SLEEPING CAR COMPANIES

165. Sleeping car companies are not carriers. They pursue a public calling, however, and incur the attendant liabilities of such callings. They are also liable for their negligence in protecting the person of the passenger or his hand baggage properly brought into the car.

Not a Carrier

The sleeping car company is not a carrier, either common or private.[6] It carries no one. The transportation, not only of sleeping car passengers, but of the sleeping car itself, is done by the railway company, which controls the operation and management of the train. It, and not the sleeping car company, contracts for the carriage, issues the ticket to the passenger, and receives the compensation therefor. The railway company alone should therefore assume the responsibilities of a carrier. Neither, as we have already seen, is the sleeping car company an innkeeper.[7] The obviously close connection, both legal and practical, between the passenger carrier and the sleeping car company, however, is ample reason, both on the score of convenience and of clearness, for treating sleeping car companies in this connection. The rules applicable to sleeping car companies apply mutatis mutandis to parlor car companies. In the Interstate Commerce Act[8] it is expressly provided that the term "common carrier" shall include sleeping car companies.

Liability for Goods of Passenger

As the sleeping car company is not a common carrier, it is not liable as an insurer for the goods of the passenger brought within its car.[9] Its duty in this respect is limited to the exercise of ordi-

[6] Dawley v. Wagner Palace Car Co., 169 Mass. 315, 47 N. E. 1024; PULLMAN PALACE CAR CO. v. GAVIN, 93 Tenn. 53, 23 S. W. 70, 21 L. R. A. 298, 42 Am. St. Rep. 902, Dobie Cas. Bailments and Carriers, 294; Pullman's Palace Car Co. v. Hall, 106 Ga. 765, 32 S. E. 923, 44 L. R. A. 790, 71 Am. St. Rep. 293; Pullman Palace Car Co. v. Adams, 120 Ala. 581, 24 South. 921, 45 L. R. A. 767, 74 Am. St. Rep. 53. See, also, Pullman Palace Car Co. v. Lawrence, 74 Miss. 782, 22 South. 53; Calhoun v. Pullman Palace Car Co. (C. C.) 149 Fed. 546.

[7] Ante, p. 247.

[8] Section 1.

[9] Voss v. Wagner Palace-Car Co., 16 Ind. App. 271, 43 N. E. 20, 44 N. E. 1010; Pullman Palace Car Co. v. Hatch, 30 Tex. Civ. App. 303, 70 S. W. 771; Whicher v. Boston & A. R. Co., 176 Mass. 275, 57 N. E. 601, 79 Am. St. Rep. 814; Pullman Palace Car Co. v. Freudenstein, 3 Colo. App. 540, 34 Pac. 578;

nary or reasonable care, and it is liable only for negligence, which is the breach of that duty.[10] What is reasonable care is here, as elsewhere, purely a relative term and is ordinarily a question for the jury.[11]

In solving this question, the jury takes into consideration all the surrounding circumstances, and great stress is laid on the inability of the passenger himself to guard his property.[12] He has no room which he can lock, and while he is asleep he must rely on the efforts of the company's servants to protect his goods. The company must therefore provide servants, sufficient in number and capability, and these, during the night, must maintain a reasonably continuous and effective watch over the car and the persons and things within it.[13]

The mere loss of goods from a sleeping car does not, it is usually held, fix liability on the company.[14] There must be some affirma-

LEWIS v. NEW YORK SLEEPING CAR CO., 143 Mass. 267, 9 N. E. 615, 58 Am. Rep. 135, Dobie Cas. Bailments and Carriers, 295; Dings v. Pullman Co., 171 Mo. App. 643, 154 S. W. 446.

10 Pullman Palace Car Co. v. Pollock, 69 Tex. 120, 5 S. W. 814, 5 Am. St. Rep. 31; Pullman Palace Car Co. v. Martin, 92 Ga. 161, 18 S. E. 364; Dawley v. Wagner Palace Car Co., 169 Mass. 315, 47 N. E. 1024; Pullman Co. v. Green, 128 Ga. 142, 57 N. E. 233, 119 Am. St. Rep. 368, 10 Ann. Cas. 893; Godfrey v. Pullman Co., 87 S. C. 361, 69 S. E. 666, Ann. Cas. 1912B, 971; Springer v. Pullman Co., 234 Pa. 172, 83 Atl. 98; LEWIS v. NEW YORK SLEEPING CAR CO., 143 Mass. 267, 9 N. E. 615, 58 Am. Rep. 135, Dobie Cas. Bailments and Carriers, 295. A passenger on a sleeping car may recover damages for money and personal effects stolen from him through the negligence of the sleeping car company in failing to keep such constant watch over passengers asleep as will protect them from robbery or unwarranted intrusion. Hill v. Pullman Co. (C. C.) 188 Fed. 497. It is the duty of a sleeping car company to exercise reasonable care to guard the personal effects of the passengers from theft, and if through want of such care they are lost, the company is liable therefor. Pullman Co. v. Schaffner, 126 Ga. 609, 55 S. E. 933, 9 L. R. A. (N. S.) 407.

11 Hatch v. Pullman Sleeping Car Co. (Tex. Civ. App.) 84 S. W. 246; Godfrey v. Pullman Co., 87 S. C. 361, 69 S. E. 666, Ann. Cas. 1912B, 971.

12 Pullman Palace Car Co. v. Hall, 106 Ga. 765, 32 S. E. 923, 44 L. R. A. 790, 71 Am. St. Rep. 293; Pullman Palace Car Co. v. Hunter, 107 Ky. 519, 54 S. W. 845, 47 L. R. A. 286; Morrow v. Pullman Palace Car Co., 98 Mo. App. 351, 73 S. W. 281.

13 Carpenter v. New York, N. H. & H. R. Co., 124 N. Y. 53, 26 N. E. 277, 11 L. R. A. 759, 21 Am. St. Rep. 644; LEWIS v. NEW YORK SLEEPING CAR CO., 143 Mass. 267, 9 N. E. 615, 58 Am. Rep. 135, Dobie Cas. Bailments and Carriers, 295; Scaling v. Pullman Palace Car Co., 24 Mo. App. 29.

14 Pullman Palace Car Co. v. Hatch, 30 Tex. Civ. App. 303, 70 S. W. 771; Carpenter v. New York, N. H. & H. R. Co., 124 N. Y. 53, 26 N. E. 277, 11 L. R. A. 759, 21 Am. St. Rep. 644; Cohen v. New York Cent. & H. R. R. Co., 121 App. Div. 5, 105 N. Y. Supp. 483; Godfrey v. Pullman Co., 87 S. C. 361, 69 S. E. 666, Ann. Cas. 1912B, 971. But see Kates v. Pullman's Palace Car Co.,

tive showing of negligence, but this may easily be inferred from the facts and circumstances surrounding the loss.[15] The contributory negligence of the passenger, as where he recklessly leaves valuable articles in an exposed position, is a good defense to the company's liability.[16] The company is liable when the goods are stolen by its servants.[17] The duty of the company continues while the passenger is reasonably absent from his berth, as when he goes to the dining car or to the toilet or wash room.[18]

The liability of the sleeping car company does not extend to all objects taken into the car, but is limited to the proper hand baggage of the passenger.[19] This includes those articles which the passenger would reasonably keep with him for his comfort and convenience during the trip.[20] The social position, sex, wealth,

95 Ga. 810, 23 S. E. 186; Pullman Co. v. Schaffner, 126 Ga. 609, 55 S. E. 933, 9 L. R. A. (N. S.) 407; Dings v. Pullman Co., 171 Mo. App. 643, 154 S. W. 446.

15 Hill v. Pullman Co. (C. C.) 188 Fed. 497; Springer v. Pullman Co., 234 Pa. 172, 83 Atl. 98; Cooney v. Pullman Palace Car Co., 121 Ala. 368, 25 South. 712, 53 L. R. A. 690. If a porter neglected to watch a bag which he received from a passenger on her retiring, and permitted its contents to be stolen, or himself stole it, the sleeping car company would be liable therefor. Sherman v. Pullman Co., 79 Misc. Rep. 52, 139 N. Y. S. 51.

16 Kates v. Pullman's Palace Car Co., 95 Ga. 810, 23 S. E. 186; Pullman Palace Car Co. v. Matthews, 74 Tex. 654, 12 S. W. 744, 15 Am. St. Rep. 873; Pullman Palace Car Co. v. Adams, 120 Ala. 581, 24 South. 921, 45 L. R. A. 767, 74 Am. St. Rep. 53.

17 Pullman's Palace Car Co. v. Martin, 95 Ga. 314, 22 S. E. 700, 29 L. R. A. 498; Morrow v. Pullman Palace Car Co., 98 Mo. App. 351, 73 S. W. 281; PULLMAN PALACE CAR CO. v. GAVIN, 93 Tenn. 53, 23 S. W. 70, 21 L. R. A. 298, 42 Am. St. Rep. 902, Dobie Cas. Bailments and Carriers, 294. Here the contributory negligence of the passenger is no defense. Morrow v. Pullman Palace Car Co., 98 Mo. App. 351, 73 S. W. 281; Pullman Co. v. Vanderhoeven, 48 Tex. Civ. App. 414, 107 S. W. 147.

18 Morrow v. Pullman Palace Car Co., 98 Mo. App. 351, 73 S. W. 281.

19 Cooney v. Pullman Palace Car Co., 121 Ala. 368, 25 South. 712, 53 L. R. A. 690; Barrott v. Pullman's Palace Car Co. (C. C.) 51 Fed. 796; Kates v. Pullman's Palace Car Co., 95 Ga. 810, 23 S. E. 186; Blum v. Southern Pullman Palace Car Co., 1 Flip. 500, Fed. Cas. No. 1,574.

20 Pullman's Palace Car Co. v. Martin, 95 Ga. 314, 22 S. E. 700, 29 L. R. A. 498; Blum v. Southern Pullman Palace Car Co., 1 Flip. 500, Fed. Cas. No. 1,574. The personal effects which a passenger may carry on his journey so as to render a sleeping car company liable for their loss through its negligence may include jewelry, and if a piece of jewelry becomes injured during his travels so that he cannot use it in the ordinary way, it does not lose its character as an article which may properly be carried on the person, so as to relieve the carrier of the duty of reasonable diligence in protecting the passenger in its possession. Pullman Co. v. Schaffner, 126 Ga. 609, 55 S. E. 933, 9 L. R. A. (N. S.) 407. While a passenger is entitled to carry with her and retain in her immediate custody as baggage a reasonable

etc., of the passenger, and the length of the occupancy of the car, are all important in this connection. Clothing, toilet articles, and a reasonable sum of money most clearly would be included.[21] Though the meaning of the term in the case of the sleeping car company is necessarily much more restricted, further light on the question will be thrown by the subsequent discussion of the meaning of baggage as to carriers of passengers.[22]

Liability for Safety and Comfort of Passenger

It is the duty of the sleeping car company to use at least reasonable care to make proper provision for the safety and comfort of the passenger.[23] Thus, as to the former, the company must furnish suitable means for entering and leaving the berth.[24] It must supply reasonable toilet facilities,[25] and see that the car is properly heated and ventilated.[26] It must also awake the sleeping passenger a reasonable time before he is to arrive at his destination.[27]

The mechanical facilities must be such that they afford reasonable protection and are reasonably safe, or the sleeping car company will be liable.[28] Thus, where the falling of a berth injured a passenger, the company was held liable.[29] For negligent acts of

quantity of personal effects for her use, comfort, and adornment during the journey, according to her station in life, a carrier or sleeping-car company owes her no duty with respect to valuable jewelry carried by her in a hand bag for transportation merely, without any intention or purpose of using it during the journey; the jewelry under such circumstances not being regarded as baggage. Bacon v. Pullman Co., 159 Fed. 1, 89 C. C. A. 1, 16 L. R. A. (N. S.) 578, 14 Ann. Cas. 516.

21 See cases cited in two preceding notes.

22 See post, chapter XX.

23 NEVIN v. PULLMAN PALACE CAR CO., 106 Ill. 222, 46 Am. Rep. 688, Dobie Cas. Bailments and Carriers, 297; Hughes v. Pullman's Palace Car Co. (C. C.) 74 Fed. 499; Houston, E. & W. T. Ry. Co. v. Perkins, 21 Tex. Civ. App. 508, 52 S. W. 124; Piper v. New York Cent. & H. R. R. Co., 76 Hun, 44, 27 N. Y. Supp. 593; St. Louis, I. M. & S. R. Co. v. Hatch, 116 Tenn. 580, 94 S. W. 671.

24 Pullman's Palace Car Co. v. Fielding, 62 Ill. App. 577.

25 NEVIN v. PULLMAN PALACE CAR CO., 106 Ill. 222, 46 Am. Rep. 688, Dobie Cas. Bailments and Carriers, 297.

26 Hughes v. Pullman's Palace Car Co. (C. C.) 74 Fed. 499; Edmundson v. Pullman Palace Car Co., 92 Fed. 824, 34 C. C. A. 382.

27 Airey v. Pullman Palace Car Co., 50 La. Ann. 648, 23 South. 512; McKeon v. Chicago, M. & St. P. Ry. Co., 94 Wis. 477, 69 N. W. 175, 35 L. R. A. 252, 59 Am. St. Rep. 910.

28 Pullman's Palace Car Co. v. Fielding, 62 Ill. App. 577; NEVIN v. PULLMAN PALACE CAR CO., 106 Ill. 222, 46 Am. Rep. 688, Dobie Cas. Bailments and Carriers, 297.

29 Jenkins v. Louisville & N. R. Co., 104 Ky. 673, 47 S. W. 761.

its servants, too, exposing the passenger to injury, the company is liable, as where obstructions were left in a dimly lighted aisle, over which a passenger fell and was injured.[30]

The passenger can claim also reasonable protection from assault, annoyance, and insult at the hands of fellow passengers or trespassers. If this could reasonably have been prevented by the servants of the sleeping car company, it is liable.[31] If, however, the assault was, owing to its suddenness and unforeseen character, not preventable by reasonable action on the part of servants of the company, then it is not responsible.[32] The company is liable when the assault is an unjustified one committed by the servant himself, as where the porter made an indecent attack on a woman, who was a passenger in the car.[33] For wrongful ejection from the car, or even from a berth, by its agents, the sleeping car company is in like manner liable.[34]

Public Employment

Though the sleeping car company is neither a common carrier nor an innkeeper, its employment is none the less a public one. It therefore must serve all members of the traveling public according to the profession which it makes.[35] As to the class which it will

[30] Levien v. Webb, 30 Misc. Rep. 196, 61 N. Y. Supp. 1113.

[31] Houston, E. & W. T. Ry. Co. v. Perkins, 21 Tex. Civ. App. 508, 52 S. W. 124; Hill v. Pullman Co. (C. C.) 188 Fed. 497. The failure of the servants of a sleeping car company to keep watch while a passenger was asleep in her berth is a reckless disregard of her safety, and where the passenger was assaulted and robbed the company is liable for punitive and compensatory damages. Calder v. Southern Ry. Co., 89 S. C. 287, 71 S. E. 841, Ann. Cas. 1913A, 894.

[32] Connell's Ex'rs v. Chesapeake & O. Ry. Co., 93 Va. 44, 24 S. E. 467, 32 L. R. A. 792, 57 Am. St. Rep. 786.

[33] Campbell v. Pullman Palace Car Co. (C. C.) 42 Fed. 484; Pullman Palace Car Co. v. Lawrence, 74 Miss. 782, 22 South. 53. See, also, Pullman Palace Car Co. v. Lawrence, 74 Miss. 782, 22 South. 53, holding the sleeping car company liable when the porter assaulted a man passenger who had called the porter and asked for food.

[34] Mann Boudoir Car Co. v. Dupre, 54 Fed. 646, 4 C. C. A. 540, 21 L. R. A. 289; NEVIN v. PULLMAN PALACE CAR CO., 106 Ill. 222, 46 Am. Rep. 688, Dobie Cas. Bailments and Carriers, 297; Pullman Co. v. Custer (Tex. Civ. App.) 140 S. W. 847. A sleeping car company is liable for expulsion of a passenger, due to selling him a sleeping car ticket over a route between two points other than that called for by his railroad ticket, where the ticket was in the possession of the sleeping car company's agent and subject to inspection. Nashville, C. & St. L. Ry. Co. v. Price, 125 Tenn. 646, 148 S. W. 219.

[35] NEVIN v. PULLMAN PALACE CAR CO., 106 Ill. 222, 46 Am. Rep. 688, Dobie Cas. Bailments and Carriers, 297; Lawrence v. Pullman's Palace Car Co., 144 Mass. 1, 10 N. E. 723, 59 Am. Rep. 58. Sleeping car service of car-

serve, the company may make reasonable regulations, both as to berth coupons and railroad tickets, and it may limit its facilities to those holding first-class tickets.[36] But, within the class, no arbitrary or unreasonable distinctions will be permitted. If the company has a vacant berth, this must be furnished to one properly applying for it.[37]

Liability of Railroad Company

The passenger in the sleeping car becomes none the less a passenger of the railroad company and loses none of his rights as such passenger.[38] The sleeping car is made by the carrier a part of its train, so that for what goes on in the sleeping car, the carrier also is responsible and thus a cumulative remedy is afforded to the passenger.[39] The carrier cannot escape liability by contracting with another party to supply facilities for transporting the passenger.[40] Hence the carrier is liable practically as if it owned and operated the sleeping car. The employés of the sleeping car company are for the time the servants of the carrier, for whose acts the carrier, too, may be compelled to answer. Hence, in the case of negligence or willful wrong of the porter, resulting in injury to the person of the passenger, or loss of his proper baggage, or even

riers is a public service, on which the state may impose reasonable regulations for the common good, subject to the constitutional limitations for protection of rights to life, liberty, and property. State v. Chicago, M. & St. P. R. Co., 152 Wis. 341, 140 N. W. 70.

[36] Lemon v. Pullman Palace Car Co. (C. C.) 52 Fed. 262; Lawrence v. Pullman's Palace Car Co., 144 Mass. 1, 10 N. E. 723, 59 Am. Rep. 58.

[37] Searles v. Mann Boudoir Car Co. (C. C.) 45 Fed. 330; NEVIN v. PULLMAN PALACE CAR CO., 106 Ill. 222, 46 Am. Rep. 688, Dobie Cas. Bailments and Carriers, 297.

[38] Pennsylvania Co. v. Roy, 102 U. S. 451, 26 L. Ed. 141; Jones v. St. Louis S. W. Ry. Co., 125 Mo. 666, 28 S. W. 883, 26 L. R. A. 718, 46 Am. St. Rep. 514; Cleveland, C., C. & I. R. Co. v. Walrath, 38 Ohio St. 461, 43 Am. Rep. 433.

[39] Kinsley v. Lake Shore & M. S. R. Co., 125 Mass. 54, 28 Am. Rep. 200; Robinson v. Chicago & A. R. Co., 135 Mich. 254, 97 N. W. 689; Missouri, K. & T. R. Co. v. Maxwell (Tex. Civ. App.) 130 S. W. 722. Agents and servants of a sleeping car company on its cars, which are attached to and become part of the system of transportation used by a railroad company, are agents of the railroad company; and if a passenger on such a car is injured by the negligence of servants of the sleeping car company, the railroad company is liable in the same way and to the same extent as if the injury had occurred on its ordinary passenger coaches. Nelson v. Illinois Cent. R. Co., 98 Miss. 295, 53 So. 619, 31 L. R. A. (N. S.) 689.

[40] Pullman Co. v. Norton (Tex. Civ. App.) 91 S. W. 841; Kinsley v. Lake Shore & M. S. R. Co., 125 Mass. 54, 28 Am. Rep. 200.

when the injury is due to insufficient mechanical facilities, as in the case of the falling of the berth, the passenger may, at his option, sue either the sleeping car company or the carrier.[41]

WHO ARE PASSENGERS

166. All persons who ride in the vehicles of the carrier, with the latter's consent, either express or implied, are passengers, except those who are in the carrier's employment.

In General

While the generally accepted definitions of a passenger vary somewhat, they usually contain two essential elements: (1) A person presenting himself for immediate transportation; and (2) the acceptance of the person in that capacity by the carrier.[42] The discussion of these two elements is left for subsequent consideration under the subject of the commencement of the relation.[43] In the present section, the only question to be considered is this: What persons riding on the conveyances of the carrier are to be regarded as passengers? Later sections will treat of the time of the commencement and termination of the relation of passenger and carrier.[44] As the duty owed by the carrier to its passengers (that of exercising the highest degree of practicable care) is much greater than the duty owed to any other class of persons, the importance of the question becames obvious.

In general, it may be said of persons riding on the carrier's conveyances that they alone are passengers who fulfill two conditions,

[41] Pennsylvania Co. v. Roy, 102 U. S. 451, 26 L. Ed. 141; Louisville & N. R. Co. v. Ray, 101 Tenn. 1, 46 S. W. 554; Dwinelle v. New York Cent. & H. R. R. Co., 120 N. Y. 117, 24 N. E. 319, 8 L. R. A. 224, 17 Am. St. Rep. 611; (assault by porter); Robinson v. Chicago & A. R. Co., 135 Mich. 254, 97 N. W. 689; Cleveland, C., C. & I. R. Co. v. Walrath, 38 Ohio St. 461, 43 Am. Rep. 433 (falling berth). A carrier must exercise the utmost care for the safety of a passenger on a Pullman car, and where the passenger, while asleep in her berth, was assaulted and robbed, the carrier and the sleeping car company were both liable for a negligent failure to protect the passenger. Calder v. Southern Ry. Co., 89 S. C. 287, 71 S. E. 841, Ann. Cas. 1913A, 894.

[42] Fetter on Passenger Carriers, § 210; 2 Hutch. Carr. § 997; Bricker v. Philadelphia & R. R. Co., 132 Pa. 1, 18 Atl. 983, 19 Am. St. Rep. 585; Woolsey v. Chicago, B. & Q. R. Co., 39 Neb. 798, 58 N. W. 444, 25 L. R. A. 79; Fitzgibbon v. Chicago & N. W. Ry. Co., 108 Iowa, 614, 79 N. W. 477; Exton v. Central R. Co., 63 N. J. Law, 356, 46 Atl. 1099, 56 L. R. A. 508; Barth v. Kansas City El. Co., 142 Mo. 535, 44 S. W. 778; Louisville & E. R. Co. v. McNally, 105 S. W. 124, 31 Ky. Law Rep. 1357; Schuyler v. Southern Pac. Co., 37 Utah, 612, 109 Pac. 1025.

[43] Post, § 167.

[44] Post, chapter XVII.

the one positive and the other purely negative. Positively, they must ride with the carrier's consent, either express or implied; negatively, they must not be in the employment of the carrier. The mere transportation under these conditions makes one a passenger.[45]

In the overwhelming majority of cases, the person riding has no connection officially with the carrier, duly presents himself with no other end in view than the mere transportation, is accepted by the carrier, and the proper fare is paid. These cases, of course, are so clear as to present no difficulty. Therefore only the somewhat exceptional or unusual cases call for any extended treatment.

Those Engaged in Business, but Not Employed by the Carrier

In addition to the employés of the carrier, there are a number of persons on the carrier's conveyances engaged in business thereon. To these, or to some of them, the term of quasi passengers is sometimes applied; but the distinction is of little practical importance, as it is held that in either case the carrier owes to them the same duty that is owed to a passenger. The fact that these seek, not transportation, but an opportunity to pursue their calling, does not affect the carrier's duty; nor does it matter, in this connection, whether they pay fare themselves or whether this is paid by those in whose employ they are.

Thus the following have been held to be passengers according to the principles just stated: Postal clerks carried under contract between the carrier and the federal government;[46] express mes-

[45] Woolsey v. Chicago, B. & Q. R. Co., 39 Neb. 798, 58 N. W. 444, 25 L. R. A. 79; Pennsylvania R. Co. v. Price, 96 Pa. 256; Gillshannon v. Stony Brook R. Corp., 10 Cush. (Mass.) 228; Ryan v. Cumberland Val. R. Co., 23 Pa. 384; O'Donnell v. Allegheny Valley R. Co., 59 Pa. 239, 98 Am. Dec. 336; Russell v. Hudson River R. Co., 17 N. Y. 134; Vick v. New York Cent. & H. R. R. Co., 95 N. Y. 267, 47 Am. Rep. 36; Wright v. Northampton & H. R. Co., 122 N. C. 852, 29 S. E. 100; Minty v. Union Pac. R. Co., 2 Idaho (Hasb.) 471, 21 Pac. 660, 4 L. R. A. 409; TRAVELERS' INS. CO. v. AUSTIN, 116 Ga. 266, 42 S. E. 522, 59 L. R. A. 107, 94 Am. St. Rep. 125, Dobie Cas. Bailments and Carriers, 305.

[46] Pennsylvania R. Co. v. Price, 96 Pa. 256; Nolton v. Western R. Corp., 15 N. Y. 444, 69 Am. Dec. 623; Seybolt v. New York, L. E. & W. R. Co., 95 N. Y. 562, 47 Am. Rep. 75; Hammond v. North Eastern R. Co., 6 S. C. 130, 24 Am. Rep. 467; Houston & T. C. Ry. Co. v. Hampton, 64 Tex. 427; Arrowsmith v. Nashville & D. R. Co. (C. C.) 57 Fed. 165; Collett v. Railway Co., 16 Q. B. (Eng.) 984; Gulf, C. & S. F. Ry. Co. v. Wilson, 79 Tex. 371, 15 S. W. 280, 11 L. R. A. 486, 23 Am. St. Rep. 345; Norfolk & W. R. Co. v. Shott, 92 Va. 34, 22 S. E. 811; Schuyler v. Southern Pac. Co., 37 Utah, 612, 109 Pac. 1025; Illinois Cent. R. Co. v. Porter, 117 Tenn. 13, 94 S. W. 666, 10 Ann. Cas. 789; Lindsey v. Pennsylvania R. Co., 26 App. D. C. 503, 6 Ann. Cas. 862.

sengers, when the express company contracts with the carrier;[47] pop corn sellers and vendors of newspapers, refreshments, and the like, whether working for themselves or employed by others;[48] a person leasing a room on a boat for the sale of cigars and liquors.[49] The same rule has been held to apply to persons in charge of a private car[50] and to employés of the sleeping car company.[51]

Trespassers—Fraud or Wrong of Person Riding

We have seen that the carrier's consent, freely and fairly given, either expressly or impliedly, is necessary to create the relation of passenger as to the person who is being carried. Otherwise, such person is not lawfully in the carrier's conveyance.[52] It is manifest, therefore, that one who stealthily gets upon the conveyance of a carrier, and secretes himself, for the purpose of passing from one place to another without payment of fare, is in no sense a passenger. In such a case, by virtue of his wrongful act he is a mere trespasser, and the carrier owes him no duty, except to abstain from willful injury.[53] In the same way, one attempting to defraud a carrier by

[47] Fordyce v. Jackson, 56 Ark. 594, 20 S. W. 528, 597; Voight v. Baltimore & O. S. W. R. Co. (C. C.) 79 Fed. 561; Missouri, K. & T. R. Co. of Texas v. Blalack, 105 Tex. 296, 147 S. W. 559; Blair v. Erie Ry. Co., 66 N. Y. 313, 23 Am. Rep. 55; Chamberlain v. Milwaukee & M. R. Co., 11 Wis. 238. Cf. Pennsylvania Co. v. Woodworth, 26 Ohio St. 585; Yeomans v. Contra Costa Steam Nav. Co., 44 Cal. 71; San Antonio & A. P. Ry. Co. v. Adams, 6 Tex. Civ. App. 102, 24 S. W. 839.

[48] Com. v. Vermont & M. R. Co., 108 Mass. 7, 11 Am. Rep. 301; Yeomans v. Contra Costa Steam Nav. Co., 44 Cal. 71.

[49] Yeomans v. Contra Costa Steam Nav. Co., 44 Cal. 71.

[50] Lockhart v. Lichtenthaler, 46 Pa. 151, 159; Cumberland Valley R. Co. v. Myers, 55 Pa. 288. See Torpy v. Railway Co., 20 U. C. Q. B. (Canada) 446; Lackawanna & B. R. Co. v. Chenewith, 52 Pa. 382, 91 Am. Dec. 168.

[51] Jones v. St. Louis S. W. Ry. Co., 125 Mo. 666, 28 S. W. 883, 26 L. R. A. 718, 46 Am. St. Rep. 514. Contra, Hughson v. Richmond & D. R. Co., 2 App. D. C. 98.

[52] Bricker v. Philadelphia & R. R. Co., 132 Pa. 1, 8 Atl. 983, 19 Am. St. Rep. 585; Haase v. Oregon Ry. & Nav. Co., 19 Or. 354, 24 Pac. 238; Fitzgibbon v. Chicago & N. W. Ry. Co., 108 Iowa, 614, 79 N. W. 477, 93 N. W. 276.

[53] Gardner v. New Haven & Northampton Co., 51 Conn. 143, 50 Am. Rep. 12; Hendryx v. Kansas City, Ft. S. & G. R. Co., 45 Kan. 377, 25 Pac. 893; Toledo, W. & W. Ry. Co. v. Brooks, 81 Ill. 245; Chicago & A. R. Co. v. Michie, 83 Ill. 427; Chicago, B. & Q. R. Co. v. Mehlsack, 131 Ill. 61, 22 N. E. 812, 19 Am. St. Rep. 17; Bricker v. Philadelphia & R. R. Co., 132 Pa. 1, 18 Atl. 983, 19 Am. St. Rep. 585; Haase v. Oregon Ry. & Nav. Co., 19 Or. 354, 24 Pac. 238; Condran v. Chicago, M. & St. P. R. Co., 14 C. C. A. 506, 67 Fed. 522, 28 L. R. A. 749. And see Reary v. Louisville, N. O. & T. Ry. Co., 40 La. Ann. 32, 3 South. 390, 8 Am. St. Rep. 497; Higley v. Gilmer, 3 Mont. 90, 35 Am. Rep. 450; O'Brien v. Boston & W. R. Co., 15 Gray (Mass.) 20, 77 Am. Dec. 347; Austin v. Railway Co., L. R. 2 Q. B. (Eng.) 442, 446; Lygo v. Newbold, 9 Exch. (Eng.) 302.

the use of a false ticket is a trespasser, not a passenger.[54] Thus, one who is injured by the mere negligence of a railway company while traveling on one of its trains upon a pass or ticket issued to another person, and by its terms not transferable, has no remedy against the company.[55] So where a person fraudulently imposed himself upon the conductor as an express messenger, and obtained the conductor's consent to carry him without fare, it was held that he did not become entitled to the rights of a passenger.[56] And it was held that a railway company was not liable for the accidental death of a boy permitted by the conductor, in excess of the authority given to him by the company and against its rules, to ride gratuitously on the train to sell newspapers.[57] The same is true of one riding on the train with the intention of beating his way or defrauding the carrier of his lawful fare,[58] or one riding by a clandestine and fraudulent private arrangement with one of the carrier's employés, even though money is paid to such employé.[59]

A person, however, intending to become a passenger, who gets on the wrong train by mistake, is none the less a passenger while he is on such train; for he is neither a wrongdoer, a trespasser, nor one seeking to work a fraud on the carrier.[60] One, too, is a pas-

[54] Toledo, W. & W. Ry. Co. v. Beggs, 85 Ill. 80, 28 Am. Rep. 613; Lillis v. St. Louis, K. C. & N. Ry. Co., 64 Mo. 464, 27 Am. Rep. 255; Brown v. Missouri, K. & T. Ry. Co., 64 Mo. 536. And see Robertson v. New York & E. R. Co., 22 Barb. (N. Y.) 91; Gulf, C. & S. F. Ry. Co. v. Campbell, 76 Tex. 174, 13 S. W. 19; Prince v. International & G. N. Ry. Co., 64 Tex. 144; McVeety v. St. Paul, M. & M. Ry. Co., 45 Minn. 268, 47 N. W. 809, 11 L. R. A. 174, 22 Am. St. Rep. 728; Toledo, W. & W. Ry. Co. v. Brooks, 81 Ill. 245; Union Pac. Ry. Co. v. Nichols, 8 Kan. 505, 12 Am. Rep. 475; Great Northern Ry. Co. v. Harrison, 10 Exch. (Eng.) 376.

[55] Toledo, W. & W. Ry. Co. v. Beggs, 85 Ill. 80, 28 Am. Rep. 613; WAY v. CHICAGO, R. I. & P. R. CO., 64 Iowa, 48, 19 N. W. 828, 52 Am. Rep. 431, Dobie Cas. Bailments and Carriers, 300; Planz v. Boston & A. R. Co., 157 Mass. 377, 32 N. E. 356, 17 L. R. A. 835; McVeety v. St. Paul, M. & M. Ry. Co., 45 Minn. 268, 47 N. W. 809, 11 L. R. A. 174, 22 Am. St. Rep. 728.

[56] Union Pac. Ry. Co. v. Nichols, 8 Kan. 505, 12 Am. Rep. 475. And see Higgins v. Hannibal & St. J. R. Co., 36 Mo. 418.

[57] Duff v. Allegheny Valley R. Co., 91 Pa. 458, 36 Am. Rep. 675; Fleming v. Brooklyn City R. Co., 1 Abb. N. C. (N. Y.) 433. A man shoveling coal for his passage by agreement with the fireman was held not a passenger. Woolsey v. Chicago, B. & Q. R. Co., 39 Neb. 798, 58 N. W. 444, 25 L. R. A. 79.

[58] Pledger v. Chicago, B. & Q. R. Co., 69 Neb. 456, 95 N. W. 1057.

[59] McNamara v. Great Northern Ry. Co., 61 Minn. 296, 63 N. W. 726; Mendenhall v. Atchison, T. & S. F. R. Co., 66 Kan. 438, 71 Pac. 846, 61 L. R. A. 120, 97 Am. St. Rep. 380.

[60] Cincinnati, H. & I. Ry. Co. v. Carper, 112 Ind. 26, 13 N. E. 122, 14 N. E. 352, 2 Am. St. Rep. 144; Patry v. Chicago, St. P., M. & O. Ry. Co., 77 Wis. 218, 46 N. W. 56; Gary v. Gulf, C. & S. F. Ry. Co., 17 Tex. Civ. App. 129, 42 S. W. 576; Lake Shore & M. S. Ry. Co. v. Rosenzweig, 113 Pa. 519, 6

senger who for pleasure travels on Sunday, though a statute prohibits such travel save for necessity or charity.[61] The wrong in such case is against the state (which might prosecute the wrongdoer), not against the carrier, who, by accepting the person as a passenger incurs the duties due to persons belonging to that class. Nor can the carrier escape the duty owed to the passenger by showing that the person was traveling on a pass issued by it in violation of a statute,[62] or that the intention of the traveler was to engage in criminal or illegal acts after arriving at his destination.[63]

Gratuitous Passengers

There is a striking difference between the liability of common carriers of goods and the liability of common carriers of passengers when the carrier receives no compensation for the service rendered. As has been seen, where goods are carried gratuitously, the carrier is not a common carrier, but is merely a private carrier, and liable, as are other gratuitous bailees, only for a failure to exercise even slight care.[64] But, in respect to common carriers of passengers, the rule is entirely different. Even though such passengers are carried gratuitously, if they have been accepted by the carrier as passengers, all the extraordinary liabilities of the relation attach. Having admitted him to the rights of a passenger, the carrier owes to him the same measure of duty which is owed to those who have paid for the service.[65]

Atl. 545; Ham v. Delaware & H. Canal Co., 142 Pa. 617, 21 Atl. 1012; Lewis v. President, etc., of Delaware & H. Canal Co., 145 N. Y. 508, 40 N. E. 248.

[61] Carroll v. Staten Island R. Co., 58 N. Y. 126, 17 Am. Rep. 221; Masterson v. Chicago & N. W. Ry. Co., 102 Wis. 571, 78 N. W. 757; Opsahl v. Judd, 30 Minn. 126, 14 N. W. 575.

[62] Buffalo, P. & W. R. Co. v. O'Hara, 3 Penny. (Pa.) 190.

[63] 1 Fetter on Passenger Carriers, § 220. See interesting cases there cited holding contra, during reconstruction times, as to those engaged in the military service of the Confederacy. Martin v. Wallace, 40 Ga. 52; Turner v. North Carolina R. Co., 63 N. C. 522.

[64] Ante, p. 304.

[65] Todd v. Old Colony & F. R. R. Co., 3 Allen (Mass.) 18, 80 Am. Dec. 49; Com. v. Vermont & M. R. Co., 108 Mass. 7, 11 Am. Rep. 301; Littlejohn v. Fitchburg R. Co., 148 Mass. 478, 20 N. E. 103, 2 L. R. A. 502; Files v. Boston & A. R. Co., 149 Mass. 204, 21 N. E. 311, 14 Am. St. Rep. 411; Philadelphia & R. R. Co. v. Derby, 14 How. (U. S.) 468, 14 L. Ed. 502; The New World v. King, 16 How. (U. S.) 469, 14 L. Ed. 1019; Quimby v. Boston & M. R. Co., 150 Mass. 365, 368, 23 N. E. 205, 5 L. R. A. 846; Waterbury v. New York C. & H. R. R. Co. (C. C.) 17 Fed. 671; Nolton v. Western R. Corp., 15 N. Y. 444, 69 Am. Dec. 623; Indianapolis Traction & Terminal Co. v. Lawson, 143 Fed. 834, 74 C. C. A. 630, 5 L. R. A. (N. S.) 721, 6 Ann. Cas. 666; Russell v. Pittsburgh, C., C. & St. L. Ry. Co., 157 Ind. 305, 61 N. E. 678, 55 L. R. A. 253, 87 Am. St. Rep. 214; McNeill v. Durham & C. R. Co., 135 N. C. 682, 47 S. E. 765, 67 L. R. A. 227; Rogers v. Kennebec Steamboat Co., 86 Me. 261, 29 Atl.

This duty, imposed by law by virtue of the relation of passenger and common carrier, has for its basis a sound public policy in the high regard which the state has for the lives and safety of its citizens. The sanctity of human life and limb which obtains in the case of carriers of passengers, as contrasted with the mere economic basis of the carrier's relation to a shipper of goods, is ample warrant for a different rule as to the two carriers, when no reward is received for the service. The passenger carrier is not compellable any more than the carrier of goods to carry gratuitously; but, having voluntarily elected so to do, its duty is in no wise affected by the nonpayment of fare.

Thus, in a leading case, the president of a railroad company, injured while riding by invitation on the line of another company, recovered as a passenger from the latter for the damage sustained, though his carriage was gratuitous.[66] So a man riding free under a custom to carry "steamboat men" without charge,[67] and a child riding with its mother under a rule of the company which permitted children under three to travel without payment of fare,[68] are passengers who can claim the same duties owed by the carrier to passengers who pay.

A person in good faith accepting an invitation to ride free, given by an authorized agent of the carrier, is a passenger.[69] But if he accepts an invitation to ride free, given by an agent not having authority to invite, he is not a passenger.[70] The invitation in such

1069, 25 L. R. A. 491; Indianapolis Traction & Terminal Co. v. Klentschy, 167 Ind. 598, 79 N. E. 908, 10 Ann. Cas. 869.

66 Philadelphia & R. R. Co. v. Derby, 14 How. (U. S.) 468, 14 L. Ed. 502.

67 The New World v. King, 16 How. (U. S.) 469, 14 L. Ed. 1019.

68 Austin v. Railway Co., 8 Best & S. (Eng.) 327, L. R. 2 Q. B. 442. In this case the child was three years and three months old, and should have paid half fare, yet a recovery was permitted. See, also, Littlejohn v. Fitchburg R. Co., 148 Mass. 478, 20 N. E. 103, 2 L. R. A. 502; Ball v. Mobile Light & Power Co., 146 Ala. 309, 39 South. 584, 119 Am. St. Rep. 32, 9 Ann. Cas. 962; Rawlings v. Wabash R. Co., 97 Mo. App. 511, 71 S. W. 535; Id., 97 Mo. App. 515, 71 S. W. 534.

69 Little Rock Traction & Electric Co. v. Nelson, 66 Ark. 494, 52 S. W. 7; Todd v. Old Colony & F. R. R. Co., 3 Allen (Mass.) 18, 80 Am. Dec. 49; Id., 7 Allen (Mass.) 207, 83 Am. Dec. 679; Rose v. Des Moines Valley R., 39 Iowa, 246; Jacobus v. St. Paul & C. Ry. Co., 20 Minn. 125 (Gil. 110), 18 Am. Rep. 360; Philadelphia & R. R. Co. v. Derby, 14 How. (U. S.) 468, 14 L. Ed. 502; Wilton v. Middlesex R. Co., 107 Mass. 108, 9 Am. Rep. 11; Grand Trunk R. Co. v. Stevens, 95 U. S. 655, 24 L. Ed. 535. Contra, Kinney v. Central R. Co., 34 N. J. Law, 513, 3 Am. Rep. 265.

70 Hoar v. Maine Cent. R. Co., 70 Me. 65, 35 Am. Rep. 299; Eaton v. Delaware, L. & W. R. Co., 57 N. Y. 382, 15 Am. Rep. 513; Houston & T. C. Ry. Co. v. Moore, 49 Tex. 31, 30 Am. Rep. 98; Waterbury v. New York C. & H. R. R. Co. (C. C.) 17 Fed. 671, and note; Clark v. Colorado & N. W. R. Co., 165

cases is binding on the carrier provided it is within the scope of the employment of such agent or employé. The term "scope of employment" has here, as elsewhere in such connection, a very broad meaning.[71] Accordingly, if within the scope of the agent's employment, the invitation is none the less binding on the carrier, to create one a passenger who accepts it, though given in violation of the carrier's rules or instructions. This was held in the case of the driver of a horse car inviting a girl to ride on the car without pay.[72]

One traveling on a "drover's pass," issued in order that he may accompany cattle on which freight has been paid, is not a *gratuitous* passenger, even though the contract of transportation may contain recitals to that effect.[73] Nor is he a servant of the railroad company.[74]

Persons Riding on Freight Trains and Other Vehicles Not Intended for Passengers

A common carrier of passengers is not necessarily such as to all the conveyances operated by it. Thus a railroad company, though it holds itself out as a common carrier of passengers, is not bound to carry them upon its hand cars,[75] pay cars,[76] nor, in all cases,

Fed. 408, 91 C. C. A. 358, 19 L. R. A. (N. S.) 988; O'Donnell v. Kansas City, St. L. & C. R. Co., 197 Mo. 110, 95 S. W. 196, 114 Am. St. Rep. 753; Rathbone v. Oregon R. Co., 40 Or. 225, 66 Pac. 909; Grimshaw v. Lake Shore & M. S. R. Co., 205 N. Y. 371, 98 N. E. 762, 40 L. R. A. (N. S.) 563, Ann. Cas. 1913E, 571.

71 Ramsden v. Boston & A. R. Co., 104 Mass. 117, 6 Am. Rep. 200. See, also, Fitzgibbon v. Chicago & N. W. R. Co., 119 Iowa, 261, 93 N. W. 276; St. Louis Southwestern R. Co. v. Fowler (Tex. Civ. App.) 93 S. W. 484.

72 Wilton v. Middlesex R., 107 Mass. 108, 9 Am. Rep. 11; Metropolitan St. R. Co. v. Moore, 83 Ga. 453, 10 S. E. 730. See, also, Pittsburg, A. & M. Pass. Ry. Co. v. Caldwell, 74 Pa. 421; Danbeck v. New Jersey Traction Co., 57 N. J. Law, 463, 31 Atl. 1038.

73 New York C. R. Co. v. Lockwood, 17 Wall. 357, 21 L. Ed. 627; Sprigg's Adm'r v. Rutland R. Co., 77 Vt. 347, 60 Atl. 143; Saunders v. Southern Pac. Co., 13 Utah, 275, 44 Pac. 932; Solan v. Chicago, M. & St. P. Ry. Co., 95 Iowa, 260, 63 N. W. 692, 28 L. R. A. 718, 58 Am. St. Rep. 430; Rowdin v. Pennsylvania R. Co., 208 Pa. 623, 57 Atl. 1125; Feldschneider v. Chicago, M. & St. P. R. Co., 122 Wis. 423, 99 N. W. 1034; New York, C. & St. L. R. Co. v. Blumenthal, 160 Ill. 40, 43 N. E. 809. In general, shippers or their agents accompanying the goods, who travel with the carrier's consent, are passengers: Chicago, B. & Q. R. Co. v. Williams, 200 Fed. 207, 118 C. C. A. 393; St. Louis, I. M. & S. R. Co. v. Loyd, 105 Ark. 340, 140 S. W. 864; Szezepanski v. Chicago & N. W. R. Co., 147 Wis. 180, 132 N. W. 989.

74 Omaha & R. V. Ry. Co. v. Crow, 54 Neb. 747, 74 N. W. 1066, 69 Am. St. Rep. 741; Missouri Pac. Ry. Co. v. Ivy, 71 Tex. 409, 9 S. W. 346, 1 L. R. A. 500, 10 Am. St. Rep. 758.

75 Hoar v. Maine Cent. R. Co., 70 Me. 65, 35 Am. Rep. 299; Gulf, C. & S. F. Ry. Co. v. Dawkins, 77 Tex. 228, 13 S. W. 982.

76 Southwestern R. R. v. Singleton, 66 Ga. 252.

upon its freight trains.[77] When a railroad company makes other suitable provision for passenger travel, no one has the right to demand that he shall be allowed to ride in its trains devoted exclusively to the carrying of freight. Not infrequently, however, persons do travel on such trains or vehicles, and the question when such persons are passengers has been frequently before the courts, particularly as to persons riding on freight trains.

When the railroad company makes a clear and well-defined separation between its freight and passenger traffic and the conveyances devoted thereto, and its regulations (up to which it lives) forbid the transportation of passengers on freight trains, then the conductors and other officials have no authority to permit persons to ride on such trains. Under such circumstances, these persons, even though they ride with the conductor's consent, are not to be considered as passengers of the carrier.[78] Particularly is this true when these trains, by their appearance and lack of facilities for passengers, clearly indicate that they are intended by the company solely for the transportation of freight and the company's servants engaged in handling this.[79]

If, however, in spite of the apparent separation of freight and passenger transportation, the company habitually permits persons to travel on its freight trains, or even if the company sits silent with knowledge that its regulations forbidding such practices are habitually broken, then a person may reasonably infer that the company permits the practice. If, under these circumstances, a person boards the freight train with the conductor's consent, believing that

77 Jenkins v. Chicago, M. & St. P. Ry. Co., 41 Wis. 112; Gardner v. New Haven & Northampton Co., 51 Conn. 143, 50 Am. Rep. 12; POWERS v. BOSTON & M. R. CO., 153 Mass. 188, 26 N. E. 446, Dobie Cas. Bailments and Carriers, 303.

78 POWERS v. BOSTON & M. R. CO., 153 Mass. 188, 26 N. E. 446, Dobie Cas. Bailments and Carriers, 303; Stalcup v. Louisville, N. A. & C. Ry. Co., 16 Ind. App. 584, 45 N. E. 802; Baltimore & O. S. W. Ry. Co. v. Cox, 66 Ohio St. 276, 64 N. E. 119, 90 Am. St. Rep. 583; Eaton v. Delaware, L. & W. R. Co., 57 N. Y. 382, 15 Am. Rep. 513; Houston & T. C. Ry. Co. v. Moore, 49 Tex. 31, 30 Am. Rep. 98; Arnold v. Illinois Cent. R. Co., 83 Ill. 273, 25 Am. Rep. 386; Thomas v. Chicago & G. T. Ry. Co., 72 Mich. 355, 40 N. W. 463; Murch v. Concord R. Corp., 29 N. H. 9, 61 Am. Dec. 631; Hobbs v Texas & P. Ry. Co., 49 Ark. 357, 5 S. W. 586; Louisville & N. R. Co. v. Hailey, 94 Tenn. 383, 29 S. W. 367, 27 L. R. A. 549; San Antonio & A. P. Ry. Co. v. Lynch, 8 Tex. Civ. App. 513, 28 S. W. 252. And see Illinois Cent. R. Co. v. Nelson, 59 Ill. 110.

79 Houston & T. C. Ry. Co. v. Moore, 49 Tex. 31, 30 Am. Rep. 98; Dysart v. Missouri, K. & T. R. Co., 122 Fed. 228, 58 C. C. A. 592.

the conductor has the power thus to accept him for transportation, then he is a passenger.[80]

When the separation of passenger and freight traffic is not distinctly made, and the carrier customarily carries persons on its freight trains, then somewhat different considerations apply. Here one boarding the freight train, with the conductor's consent, honestly believing in the authority of the conductor, when the train itself does not give him notice to the contrary, is to be considered a passenger.[81] By making its freight trains lawful passenger trains, a railroad company, so far as the public is concerned, apparently gives the conductors of its freight trains authority to carry passengers,[82] and, if a particular freight conductor has orders not to carry passengers upon his train, they are in the nature of secret instructions limiting his apparent authority, and third persons are not bound by such instructions without notice.[83]

In general, it may be said that one riding on a train or conveyance, which by its appearance indicates that it is not used for carrying passengers, is presumed prima facie not to be a passenger, even though he is permitted to ride by the agent in charge of such train or conveyance.[84] The burden of proving the authority of such

80 Greenfield v. Detroit & M. R. Co., 133 Mich. 557, 95 N. W. 546; Berry v. Missouri Pac. Ry. Co., 124 Mo. 223, 25 S. W. 229; Mobile & O. R. Co. v. McArthur, 43 Miss. 180; Houston & T. C. Ry. Co. v. Moore, 49 Tex. 31, 30 Am. Rep. 98; Lucas v. Milwaukee & St. P. Ry. Co., 33 Wis. 41, 14 Am. Rep. 735; Dunn v. Grand Trunk Ry. Co. of Canada, 58 Me. 187, 4 Am. Rep. 267; Alabama G. S. R. Co. v. Yarbrough, 83 Ala. 238, 3 South. 447, 3 Am. St. Rep. 715; St. Joseph & W. R. Co. v. Wheeler, 35 Kan. 185, 10 Pac. 461; Burke v. Missouri Pac. Ry. Co., 51 Mo. App. 491.

81 Lucas v. Milwaukee & St. P. Ry. Co., 33 Wis. 41, 14 Am. Rep. 735; Whitehead v. St. Louis, I. M. & S. Ry. Co., 99 Mo. 263, 11 S. W. 751, 6 L. R. A. 409; Fitzgibbon v. Chicago & N. W. Ry. Co., 108 Iowa, 614, 79 N. W. 477; Everett v. Oregon S. L. & U. N. Ry. Co., 9 Utah, 340, 34 Pac. 289; Illinois Cent. R. Co. v. Sutton, 53 Ill. 397; Simmons v. Oregon R. Co., 41 Or. 151, 69 Pac. 440, 1022; Boggess v. Chesapeake & O. Ry. Co., 37 W. Va. 297, 16 S. E. 525, 23 L. R. A. 777.

82 Dunn v. Grand Trunk Ry. Co. of Canada, 58 Me. 187, 4 Am. Rep. 267; St. Joseph & W. R. Co. v. Wheeler, 35 Kan. 185, 10 Pac. 461; Brown v. Kansas City, Ft. S. & G. R. Co., 38 Kan. 634, 16 Pac. 942; Wagner v. Missouri Pac. Ry. Co., 97 Mo. 512, 10 S. W. 486, 3 L. R. A. 156; Texas & P. Ry. Co. v. Black, 87 Tex. 160, 27 S. W. 118. See, also, as to construction trains, St. Joseph & W. R. Co. v. Wheeler, 35 Kan. 185, 10 Pac. 461.

83 Lawson v. Chicago, St. P., M. & O. Ry. Co., 64 Wis. 447, 456, 24 N. W. 618, 54 Am. Rep. 634; St. Joseph & W. R. Co. v. Wheeler, 35 Kan. 185, 10 Pac. 461; Illinois Cent. R. Co. v. Axley, 47 Ill. App. 307. See, also, Simmons v Oregon R. Co., 41 Or. 151, 69 Pac. 440, 1022.

84 Eaton v. Delaware, L. & W. R. Co., 57 N. Y. 382, 15 Am. Rep. 513; Atchison, T. & S. F. R. Co. v. Headland, 18 Colo. 477, 33 Pac. 185, 20 L. R. A. 822; Houston & T. C. Ry. Co. v. Moore, 49 Tex. 31, 30 Am. Rep. 98.

agent to create one a passenger rests upon the person thus riding.[85] If such person knows that the agent has no such actual authority, and that in riding he violates the company's regulations, then he is not a passenger as to the company; and this is true even though he is received by the agent's express assent and pays for his transportation.[86]

Employés of the Carrier

Employés of the passenger carrier, if engaged in the performance of their duties as such employés while riding, are not passengers. They are servants of the carrier, and the duties and liabilities of the carrier towards them are those which the master owes or incurs towards the servant.[87] The relation, then, is that of master and servant, not that of passenger and carrier. The distinction is important, in that, while the carrier owes to a passenger the highest degree of practicable care,[88] to a servant the carrier owes the duty of exercising merely ordinary care.[89] There are defenses, too, such as the fellow servant doctrine, which a carrier can set up against a servant, but which are not available against a passenger.[90]

Not only are those persons not passengers who are actually engaged in operating the train on which they are riding, such as the conductor, brakeman, or engineer, but the rule is of much broader application. Those are servants, and not passengers, when the transportation grows out of, and is immediately connected with, the service of the carrier by whom they are employed.[91] Thus

[85] Waterbury v. New York C. & H. R. R. Co. (C. C.) 17 Fed. 671.

[86] Whitehead v. St. Louis, I. M. & S. Ry. Co., 22 Mo. App. 60; Louisville & N. R. Co. v. Hailey, 94 Tenn. 383, 29 S. W. 367, 27 L. R. A. 549; Gulf, C. & S. F. Ry. Co. v. Campbell, 76 Tex. 174, 13 S. W. 19; Sands v. Southern R. Co., 108 Tenn. 1, 64 S. W. 478.

[87] Vick v. New York Cent. & H. R. R. Co., 95 N. Y. 267, 47 Am. Rep. 36; Gillshannon v. Stony Brook R. Corp., 10 Cush. (Mass.) 228; O'Donnell v. Allegheny Valley R. Co., 59 Pa. 239, 98 Am. Dec. 336; Howland v. Milwaukee, L. S. & W. Ry. Co., 54 Wis. 226, 11 N. W. 529; Kumler v. Junction R. Co., 33 Ohio St. 150. See cases cited in note 89.

[88] Post, § 179.

[89] Norfolk & W. R. Co. v. Jackson's Adm'r, 85 Va. 489, 8 S. E. 370; Washington & G. R. Co. v. McDade, 135 U. S. 554, 10 Sup. Ct. 1044, 34 L. Ed. 235; Allen v. Union Pac. Ry. Co., 7 Utah, 239, 26 Pac. 297; Louisville & N. R. Co. v. Johnson, 81 Fed. 679, 27 C. C. A. 367.

[90] Chicago & E. I. R. Co. v. Kneirim, 152 Ill. 458, 39 N. E. 324, 43 Am. St. Rep. 259; Farwell v. Boston & W. R. Corp., 4 Metc. (Mass.) 49, 38 Am. Dec. 339; Baltimore & O. R. Co. v. Baugh, 149 U. S. 368, 13 Sup. Ct. 914, 37 L. Ed. 772.

[91] Vick v. New York Cent. & H. R. R. Co., 95 N. Y. 267, 47 Am. Rep. 36; Wright v. Northampton & H. R. Co., 122 N. C. 852, 29 S. E. 100; Chattanooga Rapid Transit Co. v. Venable, 105 Tenn. 460, 58 S. W. 861, 51 L. R. A. 886;

painters and switch cleaners,[92] riding, after completing one job, to another, and a foreman,[93] carpenter,[94] or civil engineer [95] employed by the carrier and traveling in connection with their duties are all servants.

Where one is carried to and from his work by the carrier in whose service he is, and no charge is made for this service, he is while being thus carried merely a servant of the company.[96] When, however, the carrier is paid for this service, as when the wages of the person are reduced for such transportation, then he is a passenger.[97] If, however, though transported free on an employé's pass, such employé is riding in connection with his own business or pleasure, and his traveling is not in connection with his duties as an employé of the carrier, then he is a passenger, and not a servant of the carrier.[98]

TRAVELERS' INS. CO. v. AUSTIN, 116 Ga. 266, 42 S. E. 522, 59 L. R. A. 107, 94 Am. St. Rep. 125, Doble Cas. Bailments and Carriers, 305.

[92] McQueen v. Central Branch U. P. Ry. Co., 39 Kan. 689, 1 Pac. 139; Shannon v. Union R. Co., 27 R. I. 475, 63 Atl. 488.

[93] Louisville & N. R. Co. v. Stuber, 108 Fed. 934, 48 C. C. A. 149, 54 L. R. A. 696.

[94] Seaver v. Boston & M. R., 14 Gray (Mass.) 466.

[95] Texas & P. R. Co. v. Smith, 67 Fed. 524, 14 C. C. A. 509, 31 L. R. A. 321.

[96] Ionnone v. New York, N. H. & H. R. Co., 21 R. I. 452, 44 Atl. 592, 46 L. R. A. 730, 79 Am. St. Rep. 812; Gillshannon v. Stony Brook R. Corp., 10 Cush. (Mass.) 228; St. Louis, C. & St. P. Ry. Co. v. Waggoner, 90 Ill. App. 556; McNulty v. Pennsylvania R. Co., 182 Pa. 479, 38 Atl. 524, 38 L. R. A. 376, 61 Am. St. Rep. 721; Higgins v. Hannibal & St. J. R. Co., 36 Mo. 418; McDonough v. Lanpher, 55 Minn. 501, 57 N. W. 152, 43 Am. St. Rep. 541; St. Louis, I. M. & S. R. Co. v. Harmon, 85 Ark. 503, 109 S. W. 295; Walsh v. Cullen, 235 Ill. 91, 85 N. E. 223, 18 L. R. A. (N. S.) 911.

[97] O'Donnell v. Allegheny R. Co., 50 Pa. 490; Id., 59 Pa. 239, 98 Am. Dec. 336; Downey v. Chesapeake & O. Ry. Co., 28 W. Va. 732; Harris v. Puget Sound Electric Ry., 52 Wash. 289, 100 Pac. 838; Hebert v. Portland R. Co., 103 Me. 315, 69 Atl. 266, 125 Am. St. Rep. 297, 13 Ann. Cas. 886.

[98] Ohio & M. R. Co. v. Muhling, 30 Ill. 9, 81 Am. Dec. 336; Doyle v. Fitchburg R. Co., 162 Mass. 66, 37 N. E. 770, 25 L. R. A. 157, 44 Am. St. Rep. 335; Rosenbaum v. St. Paul & D. R. Co., 38 Minn. 173, 36 N. W. 447, 8 Am. St. Rep. 653; Carswell v. Macon, D. & S. R. Co., 118 Ga. 826, 45 S. E. 695; Williams v. Oregon Short Line R. Co., 18 Utah, 210, 54 Pac. 991, 72 Am. St. Rep. 777; Whitney v. New York, N. H. & H. R. Co., 102 Fed. 850, 43 C. C. A. 19, 50 L. R. A. 615; State, to Use of Abell, v. Western Maryland R. Co., 63 Md. 433.

CHAPTER XVII

COMMENCEMENT AND TERMINATION OF THE RELATION

COMMENCEMENT OF THE RELATION

167. A person becomes a passenger, entitled to the exercise of the care due to passengers, when, after he has offered himself for immediate transportation, he is accepted expressly or impliedly by the carrier.

The degree of care which the passenger carrier owes to any person is determined by the relation existing between the carrier and such person. The highest degree of practicable care is the measure of the common carrier's duty to a passenger,[1] but this duty, coincident with the relation of passenger, arises only at the moment that one becomes a passenger.[2] It is, therefore, a matter of no little importance to determine just when the relation of passenger and carrier commences. When it has once begun, it continues until it is terminated in one of the ways mentioned in the next section.

One becomes a passenger when he puts himself into the care of the carrier to be transported, and is received and accepted as a passenger by the carrier.[3] There is hardly ever any formal act of delivery of one's person into the care of the carrier, or of acceptance

[1] Post, § 179.

[2] Dodge v. Boston & B. S. S. Co., 148 Mass. 207, 19 N. E. 373, 2 L. R. A. 83, 12 Am. St. Rep. 541.

[3] Berry v. Missouri Pac. Ry. Co., 124 Mo. 223, 25 S. W. 229; Brien v. Bennett, 8 Car. & P. (Eng.) 724; Smith v. St. Paul City Ry. Co., 32 Minn. 1, 18 N. W. 827, 50 Am. Rep. 550; North Chicago St. Ry. Co. v. Williams, 140 Ill. 275, 29 N. E. 672; Bricker v. Philadelphia & R. R. Co., 132 Pa. 1, 18 Atl. 983, 19 Am. St. Rep. 585; Schaefer v. St. Louis & S. Ry. Co., 128 Mo. 64, 30 S. W. 331; Exton v. Central R. Co., 63 N. J. Law, 356, 46 Atl. 1099, 56 L. R. A. 508; WEBSTER v. FITCHBURG R. CO., 161 Mass. 298, 37 N. E. 165, 24 L. R. A. 521, Dobie Cas. Bailments and Carriers, 309; Strong v. North Chicago St. R. Co., 116 Ill. App. 246.

by the carrier of one who presents himself for transportation, and so the existence of the relation of passenger and carrier is commonly to be implied from the surrounding facts and circumstances These circumstances must be such as to warrant an implication that the one has offered himself to be carried on a trip about to be made, and that the other has accepted his offer, and has received him either to be properly cared for until the trip is begun, or to be then and there carried.[4] There is manifestly lacking here the clear and unequivocal acts which attend ordinarily the offer and acceptance of goods for transportation, so that the question of what constitutes an offer on the part of the passenger and what an acceptance by the carrier is one of much greater difficulty.

A railroad company, as a common carrier of passengers, holds itself out as ready to receive as passengers all persons who present themselves for the purpose of being carried, in a proper condition and in a proper manner, at a proper place. It invites everybody to come who is willing to be governed by its rules and regulations, and ordinarily provides platforms, waiting rooms, and other stational facilities to accommodate those properly responding to this invitation. The question is whether the person has presented himself, in readiness to be carried, under such circumstances, in reference to time, place, manner, and condition, that the railroad company must be deemed to have accepted him as a passenger.[5] Was his conduct such as to bring him within the invitation of the railroad company? The same considerations are also applicable to steamboat companies.[6]

When there is no formal offer or acceptance, these will be presumed or implied subject to the limitations just set out. Thus the intending passenger must offer himself at a reasonable time for

[4] Barth v. Kansas City El. Ry. Co., 142 Mo. 535, 44 S. W. 778; Baltimore & O. R. Co. v. State, to Use of Chambers, 81 Md. 371, 32 Atl. 201; Atchison, T. & S. F. Ry. Co. v. Holloway, 71 Kan. 1, 80 Pac. 31, 114 Am. St. Rep. 462; Maxfield v. Maine Cent. Ry. Co., 100 Me. 79, 60 Atl. 710; Busch v. Interborough Rapid Transit Co., 110 App. Div. 705, 96 N. Y. Supp. 747.

[5] Chicago & A. R. Co. v. Walker, 217 Ill. 605, 75 N. E. 520; NORFOLK & W. R. CO. v. GALLIHER, 89 Va. 639, 16 S. E. 935, Dobie Cas. Bailments and Carriers, 311; Exton v. Central R. Co. of New Jersey, 62 N. J. Law, 7, 42 Atl. 486, 56 L. R. A. (N. S.) 508; Grimes v. Pennsylvania Co. (C. C.) 36 Fed. 72; Young v. New York, N. H. & H. R. Co., 171 Mass. 33, 50 N. E. 455, 41 L. R. A. 193; WEBSTER v. FITCHBURG R. CO., 161 Mass. 298, 37 N. E. 165, 24 L. R. A. 521, Dobie Cas. Bailments and Carriers, 309; Lapin v. Northwestern El. R. Co., 162 Ill. App. 296.

[6] Dodge v. Boston & B. S. S. Co., 148 Mass. 207, 19 N. E. 373, 2 L. R. A. 83, 12 Am. St. Rep. 541; Rogers v. Kennebec Steamboat Co., 86 Me. 261, 29 Atl. 1069, 25 L. R. A. 491; The Eugene, 87 Fed. 1001, 31 C. C. A. 345.

immediate transportation, and one is not deemed to be a passenger who comes to the station an unreasonable length of time before the scheduled time for the departure of his train.[7] The carrier's invitation as to place is ordinarily limited to its platforms, vehicles, stations, or waiting rooms, and its acceptance will not be implied by the mere presence of the intending passenger at any other place.[8] The person must offer himself in a proper manner, which was not the case when a person was running rapidly, without taking precautions for his safety, directly in front of an oncoming train.[9] The actual purchase of a ticket, or the entering of the carrier's vehicle, is not necessary to establish the relation of passenger and carrier.[10] Thus, a person who is injured while attempting to board a train under the direction of the carrier's servants is a passenger, whether a ticket has been purchased[11] or not.[12] One on his way to the station is ordinarily not a passenger,[13] but where a per-

[7] Heinlein v. Boston & P. R. Co., 147 Mass. 136, 16 N. E. 698, 9 Am. St. Rep. 676. And see Harris v. Stevens, 31 Vt. 79, 73 Am. Dec. 337; Andrews v. Yazoo & M. V. R. Co., 86 Miss. 129, 38 South. 773.

[8] Archer v. Union Pac. R. Co., 110 Mo. App. 349, 85 S. W. 934; Eakins v. Chicago, R. I. & P. R. Co., 126 Iowa, 324, 102 N. W. 104; Spannagle v. Chicago & A. R. Co., 31 Ill. App. 460; Haase v. Oregon Ry. & Nav. Co., 19 Or. 354, 24 Pac. 238.

[9] Chicago & N. W. Ry. Co. v. Weeks, 99 Ill. App. 518, affirmed in Weeks v. Chicago & N. W. Ry. Co., 198 Ill. 551, 64 N. E. 1039; WEBSTER v. FITCHBURG R. CO., 161 Mass. 298, 37 N. E. 165, 24 L. R. A. 521, Dobie Cas. Bailments and Carriers, 309. That persons boarding moving cars are not passengers, see Illinois Cent. R. Co. v. Cotter (Ky.) 103 S. W. 279; Baltimore Traction Co. of Baltimore City v. State, 78 Md. 409, 28 Atl. 397; Perry v. Central R. R., 66 Ga. 746; Schaefer v. St. Louis & S. Ry. Co., 128 Mo. 64, 30 S. W. 331.

[10] Norfolk & W. R. Co. v. Groseclose's Adm'r, 88 Va. 267, 13 S. E. 454, 29 Am. St. Rep. 718; Western & A. R. Co. v. Voils, 98 Ga. 446, 26 S. E. 483, 35 L. R. A. 655; Phillips v. Southern Ry. Co., 124 N. C. 123, 32 S. E. 388, 45 L. R. A. 163; Rogers v. Kennebec Steamboat Co., 86 Me. 261, 29 Atl. 1069, 25 L. R. A. 491; Allender v. Chicago, R. I. & P. R. Co., 37 Iowa, 264; Gordon v. Grand St. & N. R. Co., 40 Barb. (N. Y.) 546. But see Gardner v. New Haven & Northampton Railroad Co., 51 Conn. 143, 50 Am. Rep. 12; Indiana Cent. Ry. Co. v. Hudelson, 13 Ind. 325, 74 Am. Dec. 254.

[11] Warren v. Fitchburg R. Co., 8 Allen (Mass.) 227, 85 Am. Dec. 700. See, also, cases cited in preceding note.

[12] Albin v. Chicago, R. I. & P. R. Co., 103 Mo. App. 308, 77 S. W. 153; Illinois Cent. R. Co. v. Laloge, 24 Ky. Law Rep. 693, 69 S. W. 795; McDonald v. Chicago & N. W. R. Co., 26 Iowa, 124, 95 Am. Dec. 114; Allender v. Chicago, R. I. & P. R. Co., 37 Iowa, 264; Norfolk & W. R. Co. v. Groseclose's Adm'r, 88 Va. 267, 13 S. E. 454, 29 Am. St. Rep. 718. Contra, Indiana Cent. Ry. Co. v. Hudelson, 13 Ind. 325, 74 Am. Dec. 254.

[13] June v. Boston & A. R. Co., 153 Mass. 79, 26 N. E. 238; Tingley v. Long Island R. Co., 109 App. Div. 793, 96 N. Y. Supp. 865; Southern R. Co. v. Smith, 86 Fed. 292, 30 C. C. A. 58, 40 L. R. A. 746; Chicago & E. I. R. Co. v. Jennings, 190 Ill. 478, 60 N. E. 818, 54 L. R. A. 827.

son was riding to a railway station in a sleigh furnished by the carrier, he was held to be a passenger.[14] If a street car or omnibus stops even on a public street at the signal of an intending passenger, he is deemed to be a passenger while boarding such car or omnibus.[15] A person entering the train before it was ready to start, by the carrier's consent, was held to be a passenger.[16]

There are expressions in some of the books that the person seeking to be carried must announce his intention to the carrier before he can be deemed to be a passenger.[17] The advisability of doing this in a way that is unmistakable (as by the purchase of a ticket) is unquestioned. But when the carrier has provided waiting rooms or platforms, to which it invites those to come who intend to become passengers, it is believed that an intending passenger, properly presenting himself at such a place at a proper time, becomes a passenger without buying a ticket, or without any further notice to the servants of the carrier of his intentions than his mere presence at the platform or waiting room under such circumstances as would, of themselves, normally indicate that he was presenting himself for immediate transportation.[18] Certainly the holder of a mileage book, who, with a satchel in his hand, took a seat in the carrier's waiting room five minutes before the departure of his

[14] Buffett v. Troy & B. R. Co., 40 N. Y. 168.

[15] Benjamin v. Metropolitan St. R. Co., 245 Mo. 598, 151 S. W. 91; Maguire v. St. Louis Transit Co., 103 Mo. App. 459, 78 S. W. 838; DUCHEMIN v. BOSTON ELEVATED R. CO., 186 Mass. 353, 71 N. E. 780, 66 L. R. A. 980, 104 Am. St. Rep. 580, 1 Ann. Cas. 603, Dobie Cas. Bailments and Carriers, 312; West Chicago St. R. Co. v. James, 69 Ill. App. 609; Gordon v. West End St. Ry. Co., 175 Mass. 181, 55 N. E. 990; Smith v. St. Paul City Ry. Co., 32 Minn. 1, 18 N. W. 827, 50 Am. Rep. 550; Brien v. Bennett, 8 Car. & P. (Eng.) 724. And see McDonough v. Metropolitan R. Co., 137 Mass. 210; Donovan v. Hartford St. Ry. Co., 65 Conn. 201, 32 Atl. 350, 29 L. R. A. 297.

[16] Hannibal & St. J. R. Co. v. Martin, 111 Ill. 219; Lent v. New York Cent. & H. R. R. Co., 120 N. Y. 467, 24 N. E. 653. And see Poucher v. New York Cent. R. Co., 49 N. Y. 263, 10 Am. Rep. 364; Gardner v. Waycross Air-Line R. Co., 94 Ga. 538, 19 S. E. 757; Missouri, K. & T. R. Co. of Texas v. Byrd, 40 Tex. Civ. App. 315, 89 S. W. 991.

[17] See 2 Hutch. Carr. § 1015, and cases cited; 6 Cyc. pp. 538, 539, and cases cited.

[18] Phillips v. Southern Ry. Co., 124 N. C. 123, 32 S. E. 388, 45 L. R. A. 163; Grimes v. Pennsylvania Co. (C. C.) 36 Fed. 72; Texas & P. R. Co. v. Jones (Tex. Civ. App.) 39 S. W. 124; Chicago & A. R. Co. v. Walker, 217 Ill. 605, 75 N. E. 520; Metcalf v. Yazoo & M. V. R. Co., 97 Miss. 455, 52 South. 355, 28 L. R. A. (N. S.) 311; Roberts v. Atlantic Coast Line R. Co., 155 N. C. 79, 70 S. E. 1080 (here passenger purchased his ticket, left the station, and later returned to the station); Mitchell v. Augusta & A. R. Co., 87 S. C. 375, 69 S. E. 664, 31 L. R. A. (N. S.) 442. See Elliott on Railroads, § 1597; note in 24 L. R. A. 521. See, also, Albin v. Chicago, R. I. & P. R. Co., 103 Mo. App. 308, 77 S. W. 153.

train, would be a passenger, though he took no steps formally to announce to the carrier's servants his intention to be carried, or even if none of these had noticed his presence.

TERMINATION OF THE RELATION—IN GENERAL

168. The relation of passenger and carrier may be terminated, after it has once begun:

(a) When the carrier has fully performed the contract of transportation.

(b) When the carrier ejects the passenger from its vehicle.

(c) When the passenger abandons the journey, though it is not completed.

As the duties owed to the passenger by the carrier arise in the commencement of the relation, so do they cease when that relation ends.[19] It is therefore necessary to discuss what will serve to terminate this relation after it has once lawfully been established. Those acts, therefore, on the part of the carrier or the passenger which will have the legal effect of terminating an existing relation of carrier and passenger, will next be discussed.

SAME—FULL PERFORMANCE BY CARRIER—ALIGHTING AT STATION

169. The passenger does not cease to be such, after arriving at his destination, until he has been afforded a reasonable time and opportunity to alight from the carrier's vehicle and leave the premises of the carrier.

Even though the carrier has transported the passenger to the destination indicated in the contract of carriage, the relation of carrier and passenger is not thereby terminated.[20] The passenger retains his character as such until the carrier has given to him a

19 Creamer v. West End St. Ry. Co., 156 Mass. 320, 31 N. E. 391, 16 L. R. A. 490, 32 Am. St. Rep. 456; Hendrick v. Chicago & A. R. Co., 136 Mo. 548, 38 S. W. 297; Smith v. City Ry. Co., 29 Or. 539, 46 Pac. 136, 780; King v. Central of Georgia Ry. Co., 107 Ga. 754, 33 S. E. 839; Lemery v Great Northern Ry. Co., 83 Minn. 47, 85 N. W. 908.

20 Chicago, R. I. & P. Ry. Co. v. Wood, 104 Fed. 663, 44 C. C. A. 118; Gulf, C. & S. F. Ry. Co. v. Glenk, 9 Tex. Civ. App. 599, 30 S. W. 278; Wandell v. Corbin, 49 Hun, 608, 1 N. Y. Supp. 795. See, also, cases cited in notes 21 and 22.

reasonable time and opportunity to alight from the carrier's vehicle and to leave the carrier's premises.[21] Until such time and opportunity are afforded, the passenger relation still continues.[22] When these have been given, however, the relation ceases, for the passenger will not be permitted to prolong it by his wrong in failing to take seasonable advantage of the opportunity granted to him.[23]

To terminate the relation, after the destination is reached, the carrier must first stop his train or vehicle long enough to permit the passengers duly to alight.[24] If this time is unreasonably short, it will not have this effect. A reasonable opportunity to alight involves, too, a safe place.[25] When, therefore, a carrier stops its

[21] McKimble v. Boston & M. R. R., 139 Mass. 542, 2 N. E. 97; South Covington & C. St. Ry. Co. v. Beatty, 50 S. W. 239, 20 Ky. Law Rep. 1845; Pennsylvania Co. v. McCaffery, 173 Ill. 169, 50 N. E. 713; Chesapeake & O. R. Co. v. King, 99 Fed. 251, 40 C. C. A. 432, 49 L. R. A. 102; BRUNSWICK & W. R. CO. v. MOORE, 101 Ga. 684, 28 S. E. 1000, Dobie Cas. Bailments and Carriers, 314; Williamson v. Grand Trunk Western R. Co., 159 Ill. App. 443.

[22] Pittsburgh, C., C. & St. L. R. Co. v. Gray (Ind. App.) 59 N. E. 1000; Texas & P. R. Co. v. Dick, 26 Tex. Civ. App. 256, 63 S. W 895; Hartzig v. Lehigh Val. R. R., 154 Pa. 365, 26 Atl. 310; Chicago, R. I. & P. Ry. Co. v. Wood, 104 Fed. 663, 44 C. C. A. 118; Keefe v. Boston & A. R. R., 142 Mass. 251, 7 N. E. 874; BRUNSWICK & W. R. CO. v. MOORE, 101 Ga. 684, 28 S. E. 1000, Dobie Cas. Bailments and Carriers, 314.

[23] Chicago, K. & W. R. Co. v. Frazer, 55 Kan. 582, 40 Pac. 923; Hurt v. St. Louis, I. M. & S. Ry. Co., 94 Mo. 255, 7 S. W. 1, 4 Am. St. Rep. 374; Imhoff v. Chicago & M. R. Co., 22 Wis. 681; St. Louis, I. M. & S. Ry. Co. v. Beecher, 65 Ark. 64, 44 S. W. 715; Chattanooga Electric R. Co. v. Boddy, 105 Tenn. 666, 58 S. W. 646, 51 L. R. A. 885; Central Ry. Co. v. Peacock, 69 Md. 257, 14 Atl. 709, 9 Am. St. Rep. 425.

[24] Keller v. Sioux City & St. P. R. Co., 27 Minn. 178, 6 N. W. 486; Raben v. Central Iowa Ry. Co., 73 Iowa, 579, 35 N. W. 645, 5 Am. St. Rep. 708; Hurt v. St. Louis, I. M. & S. Ry. Co., 94 Mo. 255, 7 S. W. 1, 4 Am. St. Rep. 374; Straus v. Kansas City, St. J. & C. B. R. Co., 75 Mo. 185; Mississippi & T. R. Co. v. Gill, 66 Miss. 39, 5 South. 39; Fairmount & Arch St. Pass. Ry. Co. v. Stutler, 54 Pa. 375, 93 Am. Dec. 714; Pennsylvania R. Co. v. Kilgore, 32 Pa. 292, 72 Am. Dec. 787; Mulhado v. Brooklyn City R. Co., 30 N. Y. 370; Ferry v. Manhattan Ry. Co., 118 N. Y. 497, 23 N. E. 822; Baker v. Manhattan R. Co., 118 N. Y. 533, 23 N. E. 885; Wood v. Lake Shore & M. S. Ry. Co., 49 Mich. 370, 13 N. W. 779; Finn v. Valley City Street & Cable Ry. Co., 86 Mich. 74, 48 N. W. 696. If one about to alight is injured by the premature starting of a train, he may recover. Washington & G. R. Co. v. Harmon, 147 U. S. 571, 13 Sup. Ct. 557, 37 L. Ed. 284; Hill v. West End St. Ry. Co., 158 Mass. 458, 33 N. E. 582; Gilbert v. West End St. Ry. Co., 160 Mass. 403, 36 N. E. 60; Onderdonk v. New York & B. Ry. Co., 74 Hun, 42, 26 N. Y. Supp. 310; Bernstein v. Dry Dock, E. B. & B. R. Co., 72 Hun, 46, 25 N. Y. Supp. 669; CHICAGO & A. R. CO. v. ARNOL, 144 Ill. 261, 33 N. E. 204, 19 L. R. A. 313, Dobie Cas. Bailments and Carriers, 332; Illinois Cent. R. Co. v. Taylor, 46 Ill. App. 141; Chicago & A. Ry. Co. v. Meyer. 127 Ill. App. 314.

[25] Louisville, N. A. & C. Ry. Co. v. Lucas, 119 Ind. 583, 21 N. E. 968, 6 L.

train and invites the passengers to alight at a place at which it would be extremely inconvenient or unsafe to alight, the passenger relation still continues.[26]

Even after he has alighted, the passenger continues as such until he has had the time and opportunity to leave the premises of the carrier.[27] Thus one who, after leaving the carrier's train, is immediately crossing the station platform on his way to the street, is still a passenger.[28] But when one remains at the station for purely social purposes (as to loiter and chat with friends), then he is no longer a passenger, and cannot claim the duties owed only to passengers.[29] In the case of street cars, which ply the public streets and have no premises thereon, the passenger ceases to be such immediately after he has alighted.[30]

SAME—SAME—CONNECTING CARRIERS

170. A person received for transportation over the lines of connecting carriers is ordinarily a passenger of the initial carrier only to the end of its own line; but he may continue a passenger of the initial carrier throughout the entire journey, either by contract to that effect or by virtue of a partnership arrangement between the connecting carriers.

R. A. 193; Richmond City Ry. Co. v. Scott, 86 Va. 902, 11 S. E. 404; Weller v. Railway Co., L. R. 9 C. P. (Eng.) 126; Bridges v. Railway Co., L. R. 7 H. L. (Eng.) 213.

26 Philadelphia, W. & B. R. Co. v. McCormick, 124 Pa. 427, 16 Atl. 848; Griffith v. Missouri Pac. Ry. Co., 98 Mo. 168, 11 S. W. 559; Lewis v. Ry. Co., L. R. 9 Q. B. (Eng.) 66; Cockle v. Ry. Co., L. R. 5 C. P. (Eng.) 457. As to carrying the passenger past the usual depot, see International & G. N. Ry. Co. v. Terry, 62 Tex. 380, 50 Am. Rep. 529; Illinois Cent. R. Co. v. Able, 59 Ill. 131; Illinois Cent. R. Co. v. Chambers, 71 Ill. 519; Reed v. Duluth, S. S. & A. Ry. Co., 100 Mich. 507, 59 N. W. 144; East Tennessee, V. & G. R. Co. v. Lockhart, 79 Ala. 315; White Water R. Co. v. Butler, 112 Ind. 598, 14 N. E. 599; Alabama G. S. R. Co. v. Sellers, 93 Ala. 9, 9 South. 375, 30 Am. St. Rep. 17; Georgia R. & Banking Co. v. McCurdy, 45 Ga. 288, 12 Am. Rep. 577; Mobile & O. R. Co. v. McArthur, 43 Miss. 180; New Orleans, J. & G. N. R. Co. v. Hurst, 36 Miss. 660, 74 Am. Dec. 785; Southern R. Co. v. Kendrick, 40 Miss. 374, 90 Am. Dec. 332. As to compelling passenger to alight before reaching the depot, see Brulard v. The Alvin (C. C.) 45 Fed. 766; Miller v. East Tennessee, V. & G. Ry. Co., 93 Ga. 630, 21 S. E. 153.

27 Keefe v. Boston & A. R. R., 142 Mass. 251, 7 N. E. 874; Glenn v. Lake Erie & W. R. Co., 165 Ind. 659, 75 N. E. 282, 2 L. R. A. (N. S.) 872, 112 Am. St. Rep. 255, 6 Ann. Cas. 1032.

28 Gulf, C. & S. F. Ry. Co. v. Glenk, 9 Tex. Civ. App. 599, 30 S. W. 278; Keefe v. Boston & A. R. R., 142 Mass. 251, 7 N. E. 874.

29 Glenn v. Lake Erie & W. R. Co., 165 Ind. 659, 75 N. E. 282, 2 L. R. A. (N. S.) 872, 112 Am. St. Rep. 255, 6 Ann. Cas. 1032.

30 Smith v. City Ry. Co., 29 Or. 539, 46 Pac. 136, 780; Nelson v. Metropol

In considering the termination of a passenger carrier's liability where connecting carriers are concerned, much the same principles are applicable as in the case of the carrier of goods.[31] The duties imposed by law upon the carrier are limited to the carrier's own line. Any liability, therefore, resting on the passenger carrier beyond his own line is self-imposed.[32] In the absence, then, of any liability thus imposed, the carrier is bound to transport only to the end of his own line, and when that is reached, and a reasonable time and opportunity are given to the passenger for alighting and leaving the carrier's premises, the traveler is no longer a passenger of the initial carrier.[33] When, however, the initial carrier operates its own trains and transports its own passengers over the line of a connecting carrier, according to its contract with these passengers, then the initial carrier for the time being makes the connecting line its own.[34] The initial carrier is therefore liable for any negligence of the connecting line in the operation of the road or in the maintenance or repair of the track and roadbed.[35] It cannot escape liability by saying that these matters are entirely in the management and control of the connecting carrier, over whose line the cars of the initial carrier are being carried.

The initial carrier may, and frequently does, contract to carry the passenger through to his destination, though that be beyond the end of its own line. When this is true, the passenger remains a passenger of the initial carrier, even though passing over the lines

itan St. R. Co., 113 Mo. App. 702, 88 S. W. 1119; Chattanooga Electric Ry. Co. v. Boddy, 105 Tenn. 666, 58 S. W. 646, 51 L. R. A. 885; Poland v. United Traction Co., 107 App. Div. 561, 95 N. Y. Supp. 498; Lee v. Boston El. Ry. Co., 182 Mass. 454, 65 N. E. 822.

31 See ante, § 145.

32 Kerrigan v. South Pac. R. Co., 81 Cal. 248, 22 Pac. 677; Hartan v. Eastern R. Co., 114 Mass. 44. See, also, cases cited in the succeeding notes.

33 Hartan v. Eastern R. Co., 114 Mass. 44; Pennsylvania R. Co. v. Connell, 112 Ill. 295, 54 Am. Rep. 238; Kerrigan v. South Pac. R. Co., 81 Cal. 248, 22 Pac. 677; Atchison, T. & S. F. R. Co. v. Roach, 35 Kan. 740, 12 Pac. 93, 57 Am. Rep. 199.

34 Chollette v. Omaha & R. V. R. Co., 26 Neb. 159, 41 N. W. 1106, 4 L. R. A. 135; Chicago & A. R. Co. v. Gates, 61 Ill. App. 211; Great Western Ry. Co. v. Blake, 7 Hurl. & N. (Eng.) 987; Buxton v. Railway Co., L. R. 3 Q. B. (Eng.) 549; Thomas v. Railway Co., L. R. 5 Q. B. (Eng) 226. And see, as to a bridge, Birmingham v. Rochester City & B. R. Co., 59 Hun, 583, 14 N. Y. Supp. 13.

35 Washington v. Raleigh & G. R. Co., 101 N. C. 239, 7 S. E. 789, 1 L. R. A. 830; McLean v. Burbank, 11 Minn. 277 (Gil. 189); Chicago & A. R. Co. v. Dumser, 161 Ill. 190, 43 N. E. 698; Eaton v. Boston & L. R. Co., 11 Allen (Mass.) 500, 87 Am. Dec. 730; Seymour v. Chicago, B. & Q. Ry. Co., 3 Biss. 43, Fed. Cas. No. 12,685.

of connecting carriers, until he arrives at the specified destination.[36] The question naturally arises as to what constitutes such a contract.

This question, we have already seen, plays a large part in the law of connecting carriers of goods, when courts have shown themselves eager to affix liability to the initial carrier for acts occurring on the lines of connecting carriers.[37] Statutes, too, have been active in this endeavor.[38] The reason given, an eminently practical one, is the exceedingly great difficulty that the shipper has in determining on which line the loss or injury occurred; the goods having passed beyond his control and means of information. No such considerations obtain as to the carrier of passengers. The passenger, who is injured, is necessarily present when the accident happens by which he is injured, and there is ordinarily no difficulty whatsoever in determining on which line the accident happened.

Accordingly the courts seem to require more or stronger evidence in the case of the passenger carrier than in the case of the carrier of goods, from which a contract for through transportation is to be inferred.[39] Thus, while a through bill of lading will ordinarily make the carrier of goods responsible for the entire transportation over its own and connecting lines,[40] yet a through ticket sold by the first carrier to a passenger is held ordinarily not to have this effect.[41] But such a ticket usually makes the initial carrier re-

[36] Omaha & R. V. Ry. Co. v. Crow, 54 Neb. 747, 74 N. W. 1066, 69 Am. St. Rep. 741; Talcott v. Wabash R. Co., 159 N. Y. 461, 54 N. E. 1; Quimby v. Vanderbilt, 17 N. Y. 306, 72 Am. Dec. 469; Van Buskirk v. Roberts, 31 N. Y. 661; Bussman v. Western Transit Co., 9 Misc. Rep. 410, 29 N. Y. Supp. 1066; Cary v. Cleveland & T. R. Co., 29 Barb. (N. Y.) 35; Candee v. Pennsylvania R. Co., 21 Wis. 582, 94 Am. Dec. 566; Cherry v. Kansas City, Ft. S. & M. R. Co., 1 Mo. App. Rep. 253, 61 Mo. App. 303; Nashville & C. R. Co. v. Sprayberry, 9 Heisk. (Tenn.) 852; Watkins v. Railroad Co., 21 D. C. 1. That such a contract is not ultra vires, see Buffett v. Troy & B. R. Co., 40 N. Y. 168; Bissell v. Michigan Southern & N. I. R. Co., 22 N. Y. 258.

[37] Ante, § 145.

[38] Ante, p. 451.

[39] Baltimore & O. R. Co. v. Campbell, 36 Ohio St. 647, 38 Am. Rep. 617; Moore v. Missouri, K. & T. Ry. Co., 18 Tex. Civ. App. 561, 45 S. W. 609; Auerbach v. New York & H. R. R. Co., 89 N. Y. 281, 42 Am. Rep. 290.

[40] Ante, p. 443.

[41] Pennsylvania Ry. Co. v. Jones, 155 U. S. 333, 15 Sup. Ct. 136, 39 L. Ed. 176; Nicholls v. Southern Pac. Co., 23 Or. 123, 31 Pac. 296, 18 L. R. A. 55, 37 Am. St. Rep. 664; Hartan v. Eastern R. Co., 114 Mass. 44; Pennsylvania R. Co. v. Connell, 112 Ill. 295, 54 Am. Rep. 238; Young v. Pennsylvania R. Co., 115 Pa. 112, 7 Atl. 741; Nashville & C. R. Co. v. Sprayberry, 9 Heisk. (Tenn.) 852; Knight v. Portland S. & P. R. Co., 56 Me. 234, 96 Am. Dec. 449; Hood v. New York & N. H. R. Co., 22 Conn. 1. And see Brooke v. Grand Trunk Ry. Co., 15 Mich. 332; Kessler v. New York Cent. & H. R. R. Co., 61 N. Y. 538.

sponsible only to the end of its own line, and it is held to be merely the agent of the connecting carriers in issuing tickets good for transportation over their lines.[42] Other evidence, however, taken in connection with the through ticket, might well show that the contract was one for through carriage, by which the initial carrier does remain responsible to one who is considered its passenger throughout the entire journey.[43] Even under such contracts, however, the passenger, for injury or delay occurring on the line of a connecting carrier, is not limited to his remedy against the first carrier. The passenger, in such cases, may, if he so prefers, sue the particular carrier on whose line the delay or injury actually occurred.[44]

As is true of carriers of goods,[45] the initial carrier of passengers may incur liability beyond the end of his own line, not only by contract with the passenger, but also by partnership agreements made with the connecting carriers.[46] Where there is such a partnership agreement between the carriers engaged in carrying the passenger, each carrier becomes liable for the defaults of any of the members of the partnership. In such case, the initial carrier would be liable to the passenger, even though he was injured on the line of the connecting carrier, due entirely to the negligence of the servants of the latter.[47]

[42] Myrick v. Michigan C. R. Co., 107 U. S. 102, 1 Sup. Ct. 425, 27 L. Ed. 325; Pool v. Delaware, L. & W. R. Co., 35 Hun (N. Y.) 29; St. Clair v. Kansas City, M. & B. R. Co., 77 Miss. 789, 28 South. 957; Kansas City, M. & B. R. Co. v. Foster, 134 Ala. 244, 32 South. 773, 92 Am. St. Rep. 25; Chicago & A. R. Co. v. Mulford, 162 Ill. 522, 44 N. E. 861, 35 L. R. A. 599. The contrary is held, however, by the English cases and some of the American courts. Najac v. Boston & L. R. Co., 7 Allen (Mass.) 329, 83 Am. Dec. 686; Wilson v. Chesapeake & O. R. Co., 21 Grat. (Va.) 654; Candee v. Pennsylvania R. Co., 21 Wis. 582, 94 Am. Dec. 566; Great Western Ry. Co. v. Blake, 7 Hurl. & N. (Eng.) 987; Mytton v. Railroad Co., 4 Hurl. & N. (Eng.) 614.

[43] Quimby v. Vanderbilt, 17 N. Y. 306, 72 Am. Dec. 469; Wheeler v. San Francisco & A. R. Co., 31 Cal. 46, 89 Am. Dec. 147; Chicago & A. R. Co. v. Gates, 162 Ill. 98, 44 N. E. 1118; Talcott v. Wabash R. Co., 159 N. Y. 461, 54 N. E. 1; Cherry v. Kansas City, Ft. S. & M. Ry. Co., 61 Mo. App. 303; Omaha & R. V. Ry. Co. v. Crow, 54 Neb. 747, 74 N. W. 1066, 69 Am. St. Rep. 741.

[44] Austin v. Ry. Co., L. R. 2 Q. B. (Eng.) 442; Schopman v. Boston & W. R. Corp., 9 Cush. (Mass.) 24, 55 Am. Dec. 41; Chicago & R. I. R. Co. v. Fahey, 52 Ill. 81, 4 Am. Rep. 587; Johnson v. West Chester & P. R. Co., 70 Pa. 357.

[45] See ante, p. 445.

[46] Bostwick v. Champion, 11 Wend. (N. Y.) 571; Champion v. Bostwick, 18 Wend. (N. Y.) 175, 35 Am. Dec. 376; Wylde v. Northern R. Co. of New Jersey, 53 N. Y. 156; Croft v. Baltimore & O. R. Co., 8 D. C. 492; Waland v. Elkins, 1 Starkie (Eng.) 272; Atchison, T. & S. F. R. Co. v. Roach, 35 Kan. 740, 12 Pac. 93, 57 Am. Rep. 199.

[47] Howe v. Gibson, 3 Tex. Civ. App. 263, 22 S. W. 826; Wabash, St. L. & P. Ry. Co. v. Wolff, 13 Ill. App. 437. See, also, cases cited in preceding note.

In determining what constitutes such a partnership arrangement, the same principles are applicable as in the case of the carrier of goods.[48] These dealings, by which it is sought to establish such a partnership, are between the carriers themselves, and not between the carrier and the shipper or the carrier and the passenger. Quite striking is this similarity in the two different kinds of common carriers, those carrying goods and those transporting passengers, in the cases when the evidence tending to prove the partnership is concerned with the sharing of profits,[49] or the employment of common agents by the initial and connecting carriers.[50]

SAME—EJECTION OF PASSENGER BY CARRIER—CAUSES OF EJECTION

171. The carrier may eject the passenger from its vehicle, thereby terminating the relation of carrier and passenger, when the passenger:

(1) Refuses to pay the proper fare, or to show or to surrender his ticket.

(2) Violates the reasonable regulations of the carrier.

(3) Is guilty of improper or disorderly conduct.

Fare and Tickets

The common carrier of passengers is, of course, entitled to his compensation before the completion of the journey.[51] As the whole conduct of his business is built up on this right, it is only fair that it should be properly safeguarded. Accordingly, if the passenger wrongfully refuses to pay the proper fare, the carrier may eject such passenger from its train or vehicle, thereby terminating the relation of carrier and passenger.[52] If this were not the

[48] See ante, pp. 445–447, and cases cited.

[49] See, also, Collins v. Texas & P. Ry. Co., 15 Tex. Civ. App. 169, 39 S. W. 643.

[50] See, also, Texas & P. R. Co. v. Dye (Tex. Civ. App.) 83 S. W. 551.

[51] See chapter XIX.

[52] BROWN v. CHICAGO, R. I. & P. R. CO., 51 Iowa, 235, 1 N. W. 487, Dobie Cas. Bailments and Carriers, 318; Ohio & M. R. Co. v. Muhling, 30 Ill. 9, 81 Am. Dec. 336; Pittsburgh, C. & St. L. Ry. Co. v. Dewin, 86 Ill. 296; Great Western Ry. Co. of Canada v. Miller, 19 Mich. 305; Gibson v. East Tennessee, V. & G. R. Co. (C. C.) 30 Fed. 904; O'Brien v. Boston & W. R. Co., 15 Gray (Mass.) 20, 77 Am. Dec. 347; State v. Campbell, 32 N. J. Law, 309; Wyman v. Northern Pac. R. Co., 34 Minn. 210, 25 N. W. 349; Lillis v. St. Louis, K. C. & N. Ry. Co., 64 Mo. 464, 27 Am. Rep. 255; Braymer v. Seattle, R. & S. R. Co., 35 Wash. 346, 77 Pac. 495; Shular v. St. Louis, I. M. & S. Ry. Co., 92 Mo. 339, 2 S. W. 310; Texas Pac. Ry. Co. v. James, 82

rule, and persons could insist on traveling without fear of ejection, though no fare was paid, the carrier's right to fare would in many cases be an empty one, and the successful continuance of his business might be impossible.

The passenger carrier's business is usually conducted by tickets, which are given to the passenger as evidence of the service for which he has paid and to which he is therefore entitled. These tickets must necessarily be shown to the conductor, in order that he may know the extent of this service, and they must be surrendered when the journey is completed. The carrier may therefore eject a passenger who, failing to comply with its regulation requiring that tickets be shown on reasonable demand of the conductor or other like official, refuses to exhibit his ticket[53] or to surrender it at the completion of the journey.[54] This rule, too, is essential to the proper handling of passenger traffic by the carrier.

Ordinarily one person may not be ejected by the carrier for his failure to pay the fare of another.[55] But it is properly held that the passenger traveling in charge of a child is liable for the fare of such child. Hence, if such person refuses to pay the fare for the child, both he and the child may be ejected, though he has paid fare for himself.[56]

Tex. 306, 18 S. W. 589, 15 L. R. A. 347; Pickens v. Richmond & D. R. Co., 104 N. C. 312, 10 S. E. 556; Nye v. Marysville & Yuba City Ry. Co., 97 Cal. 461, 32 Pac. 530; Bolles v. Kansas City Southern R. Co., 134 Mo. App. 696, 115 S. W. 459; McKinley v. Louisville & N. R. Co., 137 Ky. 845, 127 S. W. 483, 28 L. R. A. (N. S.) 611; Tarrant v. St. Louis, I. M. & S. R. Co., 237 Mo. 555, 141 S. W. 600; Adams v. Chicago Great Western R. Co. (Iowa) 135 N. W. 21, 42 L. R. A. (N. S.) 373.

53 Hibbard v. New York & E. R. Co., 15 N. Y. 455; White v. Grand Rapids & I. R. Co., 107 Mich. 681, 65 N. W. 521; Nutter v. Southern Ry. in Kentucky, 78 S. W. 470, 25 Ky. Law Rep. 1700; Rogers v. Atlantic City R. Co., 57 N. J. Law, 703, 34 Atl. 11. The conductor cannot compel repeated exhibitions of the ticket at unreasonably short intervals. Louisville, N. A. & C. Ry. Co. v. Goben, 15 Ind. App. 123, 42 N. E. 1116, 43 N. E. 890.

54 Havens v. Hartford & N. H. R. Co., 28 Conn. 69; People v. Caryl, 3 Parker, Cr. R. (N. Y.) 326; White v. Evansville & T. H. R. Co., 133 Ind. 480, 33 N. E. 273. The passenger, however, may insist on a check or some evidence that his fare has been paid before surrendering his ticket. State v. Thompson, 20 N. H. 250; East Tennessee, V. & G. Ry. Co. v. King, 88 Ga. 443, 14 S. E. 708; Indianapolis & St. L. Ry. Co. v. Howerton, 127 Ind. 236, 26 N. E. 792.

55 See Philadelphia, W. & B. R. Co. v. Hoeflich, 62 Md. 300, 50 Am. Rep. 223; Cox v. Los Angeles Terminal Ry., 109 Cal. 100, 41 Pac. 794.

56 Braun v. Northern Pac. R. Co., 79 Minn. 404, 82 N. W. 675, 49 L. R. A. 319, 79 Am. St. Rep. 497. See, also, Philadelphia, W. & B. R. Co. v. Hoeflich, 62 Md. 300, 50 Am. Rep. 223; Lake Shore & M. S. R. Co. v. Orndorff, 55 Ohio St. 589, 45 N. E. 447, 38 L. R. A. 140, 60 Am. St. Rep. 716. It has also been held that on the wrongful ejection of the child, where the mother in charge

Before ejecting the passenger, the conductor should give the passenger reasonable time and opportunity to pay his fare, or to exhibit or surrender his ticket, as the case may be.[57] Thus, when the passenger told the conductor that he needed only a very small sum, which he could borrow from a fellow passenger, to make up his fare, an opportunity thus to borrow the sum should be given to the passenger.[58] Nor should the conductor refuse a tender of the fare made by another passenger.[59]

Same—Offer to Pay Fare After Ejection has Begun

Although a passenger wrongfully refuses to pay his fare, he may nevertheless tender the sum demanded, or offer compliance with the regulation at any time before the carrier or his servant has actually begun to eject him. In such case the carrier is bound to accept the passenger's tender of his fare, and to permit him to continue his journey.[60] But when the passenger persists in his refusal until steps are taken to eject him—such as by stopping a train—an offer to comply with the carrier's demand comes too late, and the carrier may complete the expulsion.[61] The reason of this rule is obvious. If the passenger, after the train had been stopped for the purpose of ejecting him, could then tender his fare and insist

of the child leaves the train also, the mother may recover. Gibson v. East Tennessee, V. & G. R. Co. (C. C.) 30 Fed. 904.

57 Ferguson v. Michigan Cent. R. Co., 98 Mich. 533, 57 N. W. 801; Maples v. New York & N. H. R. Co., 38 Conn. 557, 9 Am. Rep. 434; Knowles v. Norfolk S. R. Co., 102 N. C. 59, 9 S. E. 7; Seaboard Air Line Ry. Co. v. Scarborough, 52 Fla. 425, 42 South. 706.

58 Curl v. Chicago, R. I. & P. Ry. Co., 63 Iowa, 417, 16 N. W. 69, 19 N. W. 308.

59 Baltimore & O. R. Co. v. Norris, 17 Ind. App. 189, 46 N. E. 554, 60 Am. St. Rep. 166; Louisville & N. R. Co. v. Garrett, 8 Lea (Tenn.) 438, 41 Am. Rep. 640.

60 Ham v. Delaware & H. Canal Co., 142 Pa. 617, 21 Atl. 1012; O'Brien v. New York Cent. & H. R. R. Co., 80 N. Y. 236; Louisville & N. R. Co. v. Garrett, 8 Lea (Tenn.) 438, 41 Am. Rep. 640; Texas & P. Ry. Co. v. Bond, 62 Tex. 442, 50 Am. Rep. 532; South Carolina R. Co. v. Nix, 68 Ga. 572; Texas & Pac. Ry. Co. v. James, 82 Tex. 306, 18 S. W. 589, 15 L. R. A. 347.

61 Hibbard v. New York & E. R. Co., 15 N. Y. 455; O'Brien v. New York Cent. & H. R. R. Co., 80 N. Y. 236; Pease v. Delaware, L. & W. R. Co., 101 N. Y. 367, 5 N. E. 37, 54 Am. Rep. 699; Hoffbauer v. D. & N. W. R. Co., 52 Iowa, 344, 3 N. W. 121, 35 Am. Rep. 278; State v. Campbell, 32 N. J. Law, 309; Cincinnati, S. & C. R. Co. v. Skillman, 39 Ohio St. 444; Pickens v. Richmond & D. R. Co., 104 N. C. 312, 10 S. E. 556; Clark v. Wilmington & W. R. Co., 91 N. C. 506, 49 Am. Rep. 647; Atchison, T. & S. F. R. Co. v. Dwelle, 44 Kan. 394, 24 Pac. 500; Louisville, N. & G. S. R. Co. v. Harris, 9 Lea (Tenn.) 180, 42 Am. Rep. 668; Harrison v. Fink (C. C.) 42 Fed. 787; Garrison v. United Railways & Electric Co., 97 Md. 347, 55 Atl. 371, 99 Am. St. Rep. 452.

on being carried, a few obstinate and self-willed passengers could render impossible the operation of trains on scheduled time.[62]

The reason for the rule, in this form, does not apply (as to stopping trains) when the train is stopped at a regular station. In such case, the fare may be tendered and must be accepted, at any time before the actual process of ejection has begun.[63] Of course, in all these cases, the proper fare must be for the entire trip, and not merely fare from the point of threatened ejection to the passenger's destination.[64] It has been held that any ticket given by the passenger, though this is claimed by the conductor to be invalid, should be returned to the passenger before the ejection.[65]

Same—Re-Entry after Ejection

If the ejection was at some point not a station, the passenger ejected from the carrier's vehicle for nonpayment of fare cannot re-enter the carrier's vehicle, tender the proper fare, and insist on being carried.[66] If, however, the expulsion takes place at a station, the rightfully expelled person may enter again the vehicle with other passengers;[67] but, as a condition precedent to his right of

[62] Georgia South. & F. R. Co. v. Asmore, 88 Ga. 529, 15 S. E. 13, 16 L. R. A. 53.

[63] O'Brien v. New York Cent. & H. R. R. Co., 80 N. Y. 236; Choctaw, O. & G. R. Co. v. Hill, 110 Tenn. 396, 75 S. W. 963. See, also, Wardwell v. Chicago, M. & St. P. Ry. Co., 46 Minn. 514, 49 N. W. 206, 13 L. R. A. 596, 24 Am. St. Rep. 246.

[64] Manning v. Louisville & N. R. Co., 95 Ala. 392, 11 South. 8, 16 L. R. A. 55, 36 Am. St. Rep. 225; Swan v. Manchester & L. R. Co., 132 Mass. 116, 42 Am. Rep. 432; Stone v. Chicago & N. W. R. Co., 47 Iowa, 82, 29 Am. Rep. 458; Pennington v. Philadelphia, W. & B. R. Co., 62 Md. 95; O'Brien v. New York Cent. & H. R. R. Co., 80 N. Y. 236. But see Ward v. New York Cent. & H. R. R. Co., 56 Hun, 268, 9 N. Y. Supp. 377. In State v. Campbell, 32 N. J. Law, 309, the passenger had an excursion ticket from New Brunswick to New York, good for a single day, which had passed, and the ticket was thus exhausted. He had also a regular ticket, which entitled him to a passage between the same points. The latter ticket he kept in his pocket, refused to exhibit any other than the exhausted ticket, and was ejected from the cars at Newark, a station on the road. He then exhibited the regular ticket, which would have entitled him to the passage if previously shown, and claimed a right to re-enter the cars. His previous conduct was held to fully justify his exclusion from the same train.

[65] Vankirk v. Pennsylvania R. Co., 76 Pa. 66, 18 Am. Rep. 404. See post, § 172.

[66] O'Brien v. Boston & W. R. Co., 15 Gray (Mass.) 20, 77 Am. Dec. 347; North Chicago St. R. Co. v. Olds, 40 Ill. App. 421.

[67] Chicago, B. & Q. Ry. Co. v. Bryan, 90 Ill. 126; Swan v. Manchester & L. R. Co., 132 Mass. 116, 42 Am. Rep. 432. But see Phillips v. Atlantic Coast Line R. Co., 90 S. C. 187, 73 S. E. 75, 38 L. R. A. (N. S.) 1151, Ann. Cas. 1913C, 1244.

being carried, he must tender the fare, not only for the remainder of the journey, but for the distance already traveled.[68]

Violation of the Carrier's Regulations

Like the carrier of goods, the passenger carrier has the right of making regulations for the conduct of his business, and these regulations, when reasonable, are valid and binding.[69] To enforce these regulations, the passenger carrier is given the power to eject passengers who refuse to comply with them.[70] Without such power, the enforcement of these necessary regulations would be difficult and in many cases impossible, while the prompt and successful conduct of the business of all important carriers would be seriously menaced.

Thus persons have been properly ejected who persisted in violating the carrier's reasonable regulations by riding in a part of the carrier's vehicle not intended for passengers,[71] by bringing dogs into passenger coaches and refusing to remove them on request to the baggage coach,[72] or by occupying more space than was permitted and refusing to remove baggage from seats intended for passengers.[73]

Misconduct of the Passenger

The right of the carrier to eject passengers guilty of misconduct is in general similar to the right of the innkeeper [74] to expel a guest for the same cause. The underlying considerations are similar, as is the basis of the right in the duty owed by such innkeeper[75] or

[68] See cases cited in note 64.

[69] Hoffbauer v. D. & N. W. R. Co., 52 Iowa, 342, 3 N. W. 121, 35 Am. Rep. 278; Brown v. Memphis & C. R. Co. (C. C.) 4 Fed. 37; Id., 7 Fed. 51; Faber v. Chicago Great Western Ry. Co., 62 Minn. 433, 64 N. W. 918, 36 L. R. A. 789; Coyle v. Southern Ry. Co., 112 Ga. 121, 37 S. E. 163. See post.

[70] Illinois Cent. R. Co. v. Whittemore, 43 Ill. 420, 92 Am. Dec. 138; McClure v. Philadelphia, W. & B. R. Co., 34 Md. 532, 6 Am. Rep. 345; Denver Tramway Co. v. Reed, 4 Colo. App. 500, 36 Pac. 557; Dobbins v. Little Rock, R. & Electric Co., 79 Ark. 85, 95 S. W. 794, 9 Ann. Cas. 84; Gregory v. Chicago & N. W. Ry. Co., 100 Iowa, 345, 69 N. W. 532; Decker v. Atchison, T. & S. F. R. Co., 3 Okl. 553, 41 Pac. 610; GULF, C. & S. F. R. CO. v. MOODY, 3 Tex. Civ. App. 622, 22 S. W. 1009, Dobie Cas. Bailments and Carriers, 315; Texas & P. R. Co. v. Diefenbach, 167 Fed. 39, 92 C. C. A. 501; Hull v. Boston & M. R. R., 210 Mass. 159, 96 N. E. 58, 36 L. R. A. (N. S.) 406, Ann. Cas. 1912C, 1147.

[71] McMillan v. Federal St. & P. V. Pass. Ry. Co., 172 Pa. 523, 33 Atl. 561.

[72] Gregory v. Chicago & N. W. Ry. Co., 100 Iowa, 345, 69 N. W. 532; Hull v. Boston & M. R. R., 210 Mass. 159, 96 N. E. 58.

[73] GULF, C. & S. F. R. CO. v. MOODY, 3 Tex. Civ. App. 622, 22 S. W. 1009, Dobie Cas. Bailments and Carriers, 315.

[74] See ante, p. 293.

[75] See ante, § 95.

carrier[76] to protect guests or passengers from the acts of one of their number. When, therefore, a passenger so wrongfully conducts himself as to cause annoyance, discomfort, or danger to his fellow passengers, it is both the right and duty of the carrier, in a proper case, to expel the offender.[77]

Though the carrier's right and duty, in a proper case, is unquestioned, yet the carrier and his servants act at their peril when they decide whether or not the case is a proper one justifying expulsion. If, therefore, the passenger does some act which is not serious enough to justify his ejection, or if the carrier, when a sufficiently serious act has been committed, ejects one who was not the perpetrator of the act, the carrier is liable.[78] Good faith is not a defense in such cases.

The carrier, too, can eject only for misconduct on its vehicle. The mere fact that the passenger was a bad character, whom the carrier might have refused to carry, is not sufficient, when such person is properly conducting himself or herself while on the carrier's vehicle.[79] If, however, the passenger's conduct is such that serious misconduct on his part is either inevitable or very highly probable, then the carrier may expel, without waiting for some overt outburst.[80]

There are many cases of ejection for drunkenness and the disorderly conduct so frequently flowing therefrom.[81] But the mere fact

[76] See post, § 184.

[77] VINTON v. MIDDLESEX R. CO., 11 Allen (Mass.) 304, 87 Am. Dec. 714, Dobie Cas. Bailments and Carriers, 316; Sullivan v. Old Colony R. Co., 148 Mass. 119, 18 N. E. 678, 1 L. R. A. 513; Murphy v. Union Ry. Co., 118 Mass. 228; Baltimore, P. & C. R. Co. v. McDonald, 68 Ind. 316; Peavy v. Georgia Railroad Banking Co., 81 Ga. 485, 8 S. E. 70, 12 Am. St. Rep. 334; Chicago City Ry. Co. v. Pelletier, 134 Ill. 120, 24 N. E. 770; Louisville & N. Ry. Co. v. Logan, 88 Ky. 232, 10 S. W. 655, 3 L. R. A. 80, 21 Am. St. Rep. 332; Robinson v. Rockland, T. & O. St. Ry. Co., 87 Me. 387, 32 Atl. 994, 29 L. R. A. 530; Thayer v. Old Colony St. R. Co., 214 Mass. 234, 101 N. E. 368, 44 L. R. A. (N. S.) 1125; Edgerly v. Union St. R. Co., 67 N. H. 312, 36 Atl. 558.

[78] Seaboard Air-Line Ry. v. O'Quin, 124 Ga. 357, 52 S. E. 427, 2 L. R. A. (N. S.) 472; Lowe v. Ry. Co., 62 L. J. Q. B. (Eng.) 524; Regner v. Glens Falls, S. H. & Ft. E. St. R. Co., 74 Hun, 202, 26 N. Y. Supp. 625.

[79] Pearson v. Duane, 4 Wall. 605, 18 L. Ed. 447; Brown v. Memphis & C. R. Co. (C. C.) 7 Fed. 51.

[80] VINTON v. MIDDLESEX R. CO., 11 Allen (Mass.) 304, 87 Am. Dec. 714, Dobie Cas. Bailments and Carriers, 316; Edgerly v. Union St. Ry. Co., 67 N. H. 312, 36 Atl. 558.

[81] Louisville & N. R. Co. v. Logan, 88 Ky. 232, 10 S. W. 655, 3 L. R. A. 80, 21 Am. St. Rep. 332; Baltimore, P. & C. R. Co. v. McDonald, 68 Ind. 316; Korn v. Chesapeake & O. R. Co., 125 Fed. 897, 62 C. C. A. 417, 63 L. R. A. 872; Sullivan v. Old Colony R. Co., 148 Mass. 119, 18 N. E. 678, 1 L. R. A.

that one has drunk too much, or is somewhat intoxicated, does not justify his ejection, unless his conduct is fraught with annoyance, discomfort, or danger to the other passengers or to the carrier and his servants.[82] A wise discretion, in such cases, on the part of the carrier's servants, is demanded. Passengers have been rightfully expelled for the loud use of profane and obscene language.[83] One affected with a highly contagious disease could also be ejected,[84] and a study of the cases would reveal other acts for which a passenger might be rightfully ejected.

There are statutes in some of the states giving the carrier the right to eject a passenger for nonpayment of fare,[85] violation of the carrier's regulations, or misconduct.[86] These statutes, however, are usually merely declaratory of the common law and ordinarily give the carrier no right to eject when he would not have had the right even in the absence of the statute. Sometimes the right to arrest is conferred on the conductor.

SAME—SAME—CIRCUMSTANCES SURROUNDING THE EJECTION

172. At common law, the ejection may be at any place at which the ejection is not fraught with danger to the passenger. In some states, by statute, however, the ejection must be either at a station or near a dwelling house.

In ejecting a passenger no more force is to be used than is necessary to accomplish that purpose, and the ejection must be carried out in a manner which will not endanger the passenger's safety.

Place of Ejection

By the common law, when a cause exists for which a carrier may eject a passenger, the carrier is not bound to wait until his vehicle

513; Atchison, T. & S. F. R. Co. v. Weber, 33 Kan. 543, 6 Pac. 877, 52 Am. Rep. 543; Hudson v. Lyon & B. R. Co., 178 Mass. 64, 59 N. E. 647; Chesapeake & O. R. Co. v. Saulsberry, 112 Ky. 915, 66 S. W. 1051, 56 L. R. A. 580.

[82] Putnam v. Broadway & S. A. R. Co., 55 N. Y. 108, 14 Am. Rep. 190; Louisville & N. R. Co. v. Logan, 88 Ky. 232, 10 S. W. 655, 3 L. R. A. 80, 21 Am. St. Rep. 332; Edgerly v. Union St. R. Co., 67 N. H. 312, 36 Atl. 558.

[83] Peavy v. Georgia Railroad & Banking Co., 81 Ga. 485, 8 S. E. 70, 12 Am. St. Rep. 334; Robinson v. Rockland, T. & C. St. Ry. Co., 87 Me. 387, 32 Atl. 994, 29 L. R. A. 530.

[84] Paddock v. Atchison, T. & S. F. R. Co. (C. C.) 37 Fed. 841, 4 L. R. A. 231.

[85] See 1 Fetter on Passenger Carriers, § 312, for citations to numerous statutes of this kind.

[86] See 1 Fetter on Passenger Carriers, § 331; Nashville, C. & St. L. R. Co. v. Moore, 148 Ala. 63, 41 South. 984.

has reached a regular stopping place. For instance, a railway train may be stopped anywhere between stations, and an offending passenger put off.[87] The carrier in such cases is under no obligation to consult the convenience of the passenger to be ejected.[88]

There is, however, this well-defined limitation to the carrier's selecting the place of ejection: The place must not be one at which the ejection would be fraught with personal danger to the passenger.[89] There can be no wanton disregard for the passenger's rights in this respect, whatever may have been the cause of his ejection.[90] Thus it seems clear that a passenger could not be ejected in the middle of a dangerous trestle on a dark night, nor in a lonely and deserted spot in the midst of a severe snowstorm. In considering what is a dangerous place, regard must be had, not only to the general surrounding circumstances, but also to the condition of the passenger, whether male or female, old or young, healthy or sick, sober or intoxicated.[91]

[87] Illinois Cent. R. Co. v. Whittemore, 43 Ill. 420, 92 Am. Dec. 138; O'Brien v. Boston & W. R. Co., 15 Gray (Mass.) 20, 77 Am. Dec. 347; BROWN v. CHICAGO, R. I. & P. R. CO., 51 Iowa, 235, 1 N. W. 487, Dobie Cas. Bailments and Carriers, 318; Wyman v. Northern Pac. R. Co., 34 Minn. 210, 25 N. W. 349; Lillis v. St. Louis, K. C. & N. Ry. Co., 64 Mo. 464, 27 Am. Rep. 255; Great Western Ry. Co. of Canada v. Miller, 19 Mich. 305; McClure v. Philadelphia, W. & B. R. Co., 34 Md. 532, 6 Am. Rep. 345; Scott v. Cleveland, C., C. & St. L. Ry. Co., 144 Ind. 125, 43 N. E. 133, 32 L. R. A. 154; Everett v. Chicago, R. I. & P. Ry. Co., 69 Iowa, 15, 28 N. W. 410, 58 Am. Rep. 207; Louisville & N. R. Co. v. Johnson, 92 Ala. 204, 9 South. 269, 25 Am. St. Rep. 35; Atchison, T. & S. F. R. Co. v. Gants, 38 Kan. 608, 17 Pac. 54, 5 Am. St. Rep. 780.

[88] Magee v. Oregon R. & Nav. Co. (C. C.) 46 Fed. 734; Moore v. Columbia & G. R. Co., 38 S. C. 1, 16 S. E. 781; Rudy v. Rio Grande W. Ry. Co., 8 Utah, 165, 30 Pac. 366; Atchison, T. & S. F. Ry. Co. v. Gants, 38 Kan. 608, 17 Pac. 54, 5 Am. St. Rep. 780.

[89] Illinois Cent. R. Co. v. Latimer, 128 Ill. 163, 21 N. E. 7; BROWN v. CHICAGO, R. I. & P. R. CO., 51 Iowa, 235, 1 N. W. 487, Dobie Cas. Bailments and Carriers, 318; Louisville, C. & L. R. Co. v. Sullivan, 81 Ky. 624, 50 Am. Rep. 186; Toledo, W. & W. Ry. Co. v. Wright, 68 Ind. 586, 34 Am. Rep. 277; Hall v. South Carolina Ry. Co., 28 S. C. 261, 5 S. E. 623; Young v. Texas & P. Ry. Co., 51 La. Ann. 295, 25 South. 69; Lake Shore & M. S. Ry. Co. v. Rosenzweig, 113 Pa. 519, 6 Atl. 545; Hudson v. Lynn & B. R. Co., 178 Mass. 64, 59 N. E. 647.

[90] Gulf, C. & S. F. Ry. Co. v. Kirkbride, 79 Tex. 457, 15 S. W. 495; Johnson v. Louisville & N. R. Co., 104 Ala. 241, 16 South. 75, 53 Am. St. Rep. 39; Haug v. Great Northern Ry. Co., 8 N. D. 23, 77 N. W. 97, 42 L. R. A. 664, 73 Am. St. Rep. 727; McKinley v. Louisville & N. Ry. Co., 137 Ky. 845, 127 S. W. 483, 28 L. R. A. (N. S.) 611.

[91] Louisville & N. R. Co. v. Ellis' Adm'r, 97 Ky. 330, 30 S. W. 979; Gill v. Rochester & P. R. Co., 37 Hun (N. Y.) 107; Jackson v. Alabama & V. Ry. Co., 76 Miss. 703, 25 South. 353; Eldson v. Southern R. Co. (Miss.) 23 South. 369; Roseman v. Carolina Cent. R. Co., 112 N. C. 709, 16 S. E. 776, 19 L. R.

Statutes have been passed restricting the carrier's rights as to the place of ejection, and requiring that the ejection must be at some station of the carrier or in the neighborhood of some dwelling house.[92] The carrier must, of course, comply, in a state having such a law, with the terms of the particular statute, else the ejection, however safe and proper, will be unlawful.[93]

Manner of Ejection

The manner of ejection adopted by the carrier's servants must never be such as to imperil the passenger's safety. What has just been said as to the place of ejection is equally applicable to the manner of ejection. Therefore, even though the ejection is proper, if it is done in a dangerous manner, the carrier will be liable to the ejected passenger.[94] A flagrant trespasser, even, cannot be ejected in a dangerous mode.[95] Thus, to take a stock example, the car-

A. 327, 34 Am. St. Rep. 524; BROWN v. CHICAGO, R. I. & P. R. CO., 51 Iowa, 235, 1 N. W. 487, Dobie Cas. Bailments and Carriers, 318; Bragg's Adm'r v. Norfolk & W. R. Co., 110 Va. 867, 67 S. E. 593.

[92] Boehm v. Duluth, S. S. & A. Ry. Co., 91 Wis. 592, 65 N. W. 506; Durfee v. Union Pac. Ry. Co., 9 Utah, 213, 33 Pac. 944; Chicago, R. I. & P. R. Co. v. Radford, 36 Okl. 657, 129 Pac. 834; Wright v. Central R. Co., 78 Cal. 360, 20 Pac. 740; Terre Haute v. Vanatta, 21 Ill. 187, 188, 74 Am. Dec. 96; Illinois Cent. R. Co. v. Latimer, 128 Ill. 163, 21 N. E. 7 (but see Illinois Cent. R. Co. v. Whittemore, 43 Ill. 420, 92 Am. Dec. 138; Toledo, W. & W. R. Co. v. Wright, 68 Ind. 586, 34 Am. Rep. 277); Texas & P. R. Co. v. Casey, 52 Tex. 112; Baldwin v. Grand Trunk Ry. Co., 64 N. H. 596, 15 Atl. 411; South Florida R. Co. v. Rhodes, 25 Fla. 40, 5 South. 633, 3 L. R. A. 733, 23 Am. St. Rep. 506; Hobbs v. Texas & P. R. Co., 49 Ark. 357, 5 S. W. 586. A commutation railway ticket, conditioned to be "good for 1,000 miles," and "within six months," is not good after six months, although the holder has not traveled 1,000 miles on it; and where, after the expiration of that period, he enters the baggage car of the company, and refuses to pay his fare except by presenting such ticket, he is a trespasser, and may be ejected at any point, and is not entitled to the benefit of a statute which prohibits the ejection of passengers except near a dwelling house or at a station. Lillis v. St. Louis, K. C. & N. R. Co., 64 Mo. 464, 27 Am. Rep. 255.

[93] Nichols v. Union Pac. Ry. Co., 7 Utah, 510, 27 Pac. 693; Phettiplace v. Northern Pac. R. Co., 84 Wis. 412, 54 N. W. 1092, 20 L. R. A. 483.

[94] Haman v. Omaha Horse Ry. Co., 35 Neb. 74, 52 N. W. 830; Planz v. Boston & A. R. Co., 157 Mass. 377, 32 N. E. 356, 17 L. R. A. 835; CHICAGO, ST. L. & P. R. CO. v. BILLS, 104 Ind. 13, 3 N. E. 611, Dobie Cas. Bailments and Carriers, 320; Hayter v. Brunswick Traction Co., 66 N. J. Law, 575, 49 Atl. 714; Denver Tramway Co. v. Reed, 4 Colo. App. 500, 36 Pac. 557; Mills v. Seattle R. & S. R. Co., 50 Wash. 20, 96 Pac. 520, 19 L. R. A. (N. S.) 704; Louisville & N. R. Co. v. Tuggle's Adm'r, 151 Ky. 409, 152 S. W. 270; Quigley v. Gulf, C. & S. F. R. Co. (Tex. Civ. App.) 142 S. W. 633. See, also, Drogmund v. Metropolitan St. R. Co., 122 Mo. App. 154, 98 S. W. 1091.

[95] Lake Erie & W. R. Co. v. Matthews, 13 Ind. App. 355, 41 N. E. 842; Arnold v. Pennsylvania R. Co., 115 Pa. 135, 8 Atl. 213, 2 Am. St. Rep. 542; Rounds v. Delaware, L. & W. R. Co., 64 N. Y. 129, 21 Am. Rep. 597; Drogmund v. Metropolitan St. R. Co., 122 Mo. App. 154, 98 S. W. 1091.

rier is liable for injuries received by one who was ejected from a rapidly moving train.[96]

When there is a right to eject a passenger, no more force is to be used than is necessary to accomplish that purpose, and for any excessive force or willful injury the carrier is liable.[97] If the passenger resists, sufficient force to overcome his resistance may be used.[98] And this is true, even as to a female passenger, for it is "not a question of gallantry or sex, but simply of legal right."[99] When, therefore, both the ejection itself and the place and manner thereof are proper, the resistance is unlawful, and for any force used in overcoming this resistance by the carrier's servants, that is not disproportionate to the resistance, there can be no recovery from the carrier.[1] For the added injuries, in such cases, the passenger has only his own wrong and folly to blame. Even when the passenger resists a proper ejection, however, the carrier would be liable if undue force is employed and if the passenger be used with

[96] Oppenheimer v. Manhattan Ry. Co., 63 Hun, 633, 18 N. Y. Supp. 411; Sanford v. Eighth Ave. R. Co., 23 N. Y. 343, 80 Am. Dec. 286; State v. Kinney, 34 Minn. 311, 25 N. W. 705; Brown v. Hannibal & St. J. R. Co., 66 Mo. 588; Gulf, C. & S. F. R. Co. v. Kirkbride, 79 Tex. 457, 15 S. W. 495; Fell v. Northern Pac. R. Co. (C. C.) 44 Fed. 248; Law v. Illinois Cent. R. Co., 32 Iowa, 534; Lake Erie & W. R. Co. v. Matthews, 13 Ind. App. 355, 41 N. E. 842; Williams v. Louisiana R. & Nav. Co., 121 La. 438, 46 South. 528.

[97] New Jersey Steamboat Co. v. Brockett, 121 U. S. 637, 7 Sup. Ct. 1039, 30 L. Ed. 1049; Holmes v. Wakefield, 12 Allen (Mass.) 580, 90 Am. Dec. 171; Pennsylvania R. Co. v. Vandier, 42 Pa. 365, 82 Am. Dec. 520; Bass v. Chicago & N. W. R. Co., 36 Wis. 450, 17 Am. Rep. 495; Mykleby v. Chicago, St. P., M. & O. Ry. Co., 39 Minn. 54, 38 N. W. 763; Evansville & I. R. Co. v. Gilmore, 1 Ind. App. 468, 27 N. E. 992; Knowles v. Norfolk & S. R. Co., 102 N. C. 59, 9 S. E. 7; Jardine v. Cornell, 50 N. J. Law, 485, 14 Atl. 590; Brown v. Hannibal & St. J. R. Co., 66 Mo. 588; Philadelphia, W. & B. R. Co. v. Larkin, 47 Md. 155; Texas Pac. Ry. Co. v. James, 82 Tex. 306, 18 S. W. 589, 15 L. R. A. 347; Gill v. Rochester & P. R. Co., 37 Hun (N. Y.) 107; Klenk v. Oregon Short Line R. Co., 27 Utah, 428, 76 Pac. 214; CHICAGO, ST. L. & P. R. CO. v. BILLS, 104 Ind. 13, 3 N. E. 611, Doble Cas. Bailments and Carriers, 320.

[98] Townsend v. New York Cent. & H. R. R. Co., 56 N. Y. 295, 15 Am. Rep. 419; Murphy v. Union Ry. Co., 118 Mass. 228; Atchison, T. & S. F. Ry. Co. v. Gants, 38 Kan. 608, 17 Pac. 54, 5 Am. St. Rep. 780; Norfolk & W. R. Co. v. Brame, 109 Va. 422, 63 S. E. 1018; Chesapeake & O. Ry. Co. v. Robinett, 151 Ky. 778, 152 S. W. 976, 45 L. R. A. (N. S.) 433.

[99] Chicago, R. I. & P. Ry. Co. v. Herring, 57 Ill. 59.

[1] Lillis v. St. Louis, K. C. & N. Ry. Co., 64 Mo. 464, 27 Am. Rep. 255; McCullen v. New York & N. S. Ry. Co., 68 App. Div. 269, 74 N. Y. Supp. 209; Coleman v. New York & N. H. R. Co., 106 Mass. 160; Atchison, T. & S. F. R. Co. v. Gants, 38 Kan. 608, 17 Pac. 54, 5 Am. St. Rep. 780; Moore v. Columbia & G. R. Co., 38 S. C. 1, 16 S. E. 781; CHICAGO, ST. L. & P. R. CO. v. BILLS, 104 Ind. 13, 3 N. E. 611, Doble Cas. Bailments and Carriers, 320.

roughness altogether disproportionate to his resistance.[2] Even resistance to a lawful ejection is not warrant for wanton injury or brutality.

If the ejection itself (regardless of the mode and place) is improper, by the better opinion, the passenger can resist and for injuries received by him as a result of his resistance he can recover from the carrier.[3] According to some courts, however, the passenger must tamely submit to the wrongful ejection and sue for damages, and he cannot increase the damages by his obstinate (?) resistance.[4] It may well be that imperative circumstances may require that he continue his journey without interruption.[5] Or, if ejected, he may suffer special damages, which he may not be able to collect. It hardly seems fair, then, to expect such vicarious submission by one who is in the right in favor of the one who is doing him a wrong. As was said in a leading case:[6] "The law does not, under such circumstances, place the passenger within the power of the conductor, and, when lawfully in the cars, he is authorized to vindicate such right to the full extent which might be required for its protection." It may well be, as is often said, that resistance here is not a prudent[7] remedy; but whether a right exists and whether it is prudent to exercise an existing right are somewhat different questions.

Again, when the ejection itself is lawful, but the manner or place of it are such as to expose the passenger to imminent peril of life or

[2] Sanford v. Eighth Ave. R. Co., 23 N. Y. 343, 80 Am. Dec. 286; CHICAGO, ST. L. & P. R. CO. v. BILLS, 104 Ind. 13, 3 N. E. 611, Dobie Cas. Bailments and Carriers, 320.

[3] Zagelmeyer v. Cincinnati S. & M. R. Co., 102 Mich. 214, 60 N. W. 436, 47 Am. St. Rep. 514; Pittsburgh, C., C. & St. L. R. Co. v. Russ, 67 Fed. 662, 14 C. C. A. 612; Ellsworth v. Chicago, B. & Q. Ry. Co., 95 Iowa, 98, 63 N. W. 584, 29 L. R. A. 173; Louisville, N. A. & C. Ry. Co. v. Wolfe, 128 Ind. 347, 27 N. E. 606, 25 Am. St. Rep. 436; Denver Tramway Co. v. Reed, 4 Colo. App. 500, 36 Pac. 557; New York, L. E. & W R. Co. v. Winter, 143 U. S. 60, 12 Sup. Ct. 356, 36 L. Ed. 71; Indianapolis Traction & Terminal Co. v. Lockman, 49 Ind. App. 143, 96 N. E. 970; English v. Delaware & H. Canal Co., 66 N. Y. 454, 23 Am. Rep. 69; Louisville, N. A. & C. Ry. Co. v. Wolfe, 128 Ind. 347, 27 N. E. 606, 25 Am. St. Rep. 436. In the last two cases the passenger had paid his fare, and was ejected for refusal to pay again. He was in each case permitted to recover for injuries due to his resistance.

[4] Atchison, T. & S. F. R. Co. v. Hogue, 50 Kan. 40, 31 Pac. 698; Pennsylvania R. Co. v. Cornell, 112 Ill. 295, 54 Am. Rep. 238; Gibson v. East Tennessee, V. & G. R. Co. (C. C.) 30 Fed. 904; Monnier v. New York Cent. & H. R. R. Co., 175 N. Y. 281, 67 N. E. 569, 62 L. R. A. 357, 96 Am. St. Rep. 619; Randell v. Chicago, R. I. & P. R. Co., 102 Mo. App. 342, 76 S. W. 493.

[5] English v. Delaware & H. Canal Co., 66 N. Y. 454, 23 Am. Rep. 69.

[6] English v. Delaware & H. Canal Co., 66 N. Y. 454, 23 Am. Rep. 69.

[7] Hufford v. Grand Rapids & T. Ry. Co., 53 Mich. 118, 18 N. W. 580.

limb, the passenger is within his rights by resisting to the utmost. It was admirably said by Comstock, C. J.,[8] in a case when an attempt was made to eject a passenger at night from a rapidly moving car: "The passenger has the same right to repel an attempt to eject him, when such an attempt will thus endanger him, that he has to resist a direct attempt to take his life. The great law of self-preservation so plainly establishes this conclusion that no further argument can be necessary."

Tender Back of Fare by Carrier before Ejection

It is usually held, though there are cases to the contrary,[9] that the carrier, before ejecting the passenger, must tender to the passenger any fare received by the carrier in excess of that required to pay for the passenger's transportation from the point at which his journey began to the point of his ejection.[10] The carrier thus is paid only for the distance the passenger is actually carried. For the carrier to eject the passenger and then retain the fare collected on the basis of transporting the passenger to his destination hardly seems fair. It has even been held that the conductor, ejecting the passenger holding a ticket claimed by the conductor to be worthless, should return such ticket, as a piece of evidence that would be valuable to the passenger in a subsequent suit against the carrier.[11]

SAME—ABANDONMENT OF INCOMPLETED JOURNEY BY PASSENGER

173. The passenger may terminate his relation as such to the carrier, at any time he chooses, by leaving the carrier's vehicle with the intention of permanently abandoning his rights as a passenger.

Another analogy between the innkeeper and passenger carrier is found in the fact that, while the innkeeper[12] and carrier[13] may terminate the relation as to guest or passenger only in a few well-

[8] Sanford v. Eighth Ave. R. Co., 23 N. Y. 343, 80 Am. Dec. 286.

[9] Gregory v. Chicago & N. W. Ry. Co., 100 Iowa, 345, 69 N. W. 532; Rahilly v. St. Paul & D. R. Co., 66 Minn. 153, 68 N. W. 853.

[10] Hoffbauer v. D. & N. W. R. Co., 52 Iowa, 344, 3 N. W 121, 35 Am. Rep. 278; Bland v. Southern Pac. R. Co., 55 Cal. 570, 36 Am. Rep. 50; Braun v. Northern Pac. R. Co., 79 Minn. 404, 82 N. W. 675, 984, 49 L. R. A. 319, 79 Am. St. Rep. 497; Burnham v Grand Trunk Ry. Co., 63 Me. 298, 18 Am. Rep. 220; Baltimore, P. & C. R. Co. v. McDonald, 68 Ind. 316.

[11] Vankirk v. Pennsylvania R. Co., 76 Pa. 66, 18 Am. Rep. 404.

[12] Ante, § 104.

[13] Ante, §§ 168-172.

defined cases, the guest [14] or passenger [15] may terminate the relation at any time, either for a poor reason or no reason at all.

At any time, then, and for any reason, the passenger may terminate the relation to the carrier by leaving the carrier's vehicle with the intention of permanently renouncing his rights as a passenger.[16] This he may do at any point, even though he is far from the destination to which his ticket, for which he has paid, entitles him to be carried.[17]

The relation is not terminated, however, when the passenger leaves the carrier's vehicle, intending to return thereto, for a mere temporary purpose,[18] as, for example, to procure refreshments.[19] Nor does the passenger cease to be such merely by rendering assistance to the carrier or his servants in case of an accident,[20] as where, on request by the conductor, he aided in moving an ill passenger from one car to another.[21] Nor does the passenger terminate the relation merely by riding in a dangerous place or posi-

[14] Ante, § 104.

[15] See cases cited in the succeeding note.

[16] Frost v. Grand Trunk R. Co., 10 Allen (Mass.) 387, 87 Am. Dec. 668; Commonwealth v. Boston & M. R. Co., 129 Mass. 500, 37 Am. Rep. 382; Buckley v. Old Colony R. Co., 161 Mass. 26, 36 N. E. 583.

[17] See cases cited in preceding note.

[18] Parsons v. New York Cent. & H. R. R. Co., 113 N. Y. 355, 21 N. E. 145, 3 L. R. A. 683, 10 Am. St. Rep. 450; Keokuk Northern Line Packet Co. v. True, 88 Ill. 608; Watson v. East Tennessee, V. & G. R. Co., 92 Ala. 320, 8 South. 770; Dice v Willamette Transportation & Locks Co., 8 Or. 60, 34 Am. Rep. 575; Jeffersonville, M. & I. R. Co. v Riley, 39 Ind. 568; Dodge v. Boston & B. S. S. Co., 148 Mass. 207, 19 N. E. 373, 2 L. R. A. 83, 12 Am. St. Rep. 541; Galveston, H. & S. A. R. Co. v. Mathes (Tex. Civ. App.) 73 S. W. 411; Conroy v. Chicago, St. P., M. & O. R. Co., 96 Wis. 243, 70 N. W. 486, 38 L. R. A. 419. But see Lemery v. Great Northern Ry. Co., 83 Minn. 47, 85 N. W. 908; Chicago, R. I. & P. R. Co. v. Sattler, 64 Neb. 636, 90 N. W. 649, 57 L. R. A. 890, 97 Am. St. Rep. 666. The passenger, however, can no longer claim to be such on leaving the station. Johnson v. Boston & M. R. R., 125 Mass. 75; King v. Central of Georgia Ry. Co., 107 Ga. 754, 33 S. E. 839.

[19] Parsons v. New York Cent. & H. R. R. Co., 113 N. Y. 355, 363, 21 N. E. 145, 3 L. R. A. 683, 10 Am. St. Rep. 450; Dodge v. Boston & B. S. S. Co., 148 Mass. 207, 19 N. E. 373, 2 L. R. A. 83, 12 Am. St. Rep. 541; Hrebrik v. Carr (D. C.) 29 Fed. 298; Peniston v. Chicago, St. L. & N. O. R. Co., 34 La. Ann. 777, 44 Am. Rep. 444; Jeffersonville, M. & I. R. Co. v. Riley, 39 Ind. 568; Pitcher v. Lake Shore & M. S. R. Co., 55 Hun, 604, 8 N. Y. Supp. 389; Alabama G. S. R. Co. v. Coggins, 88 Fed. 455, 32 C. C. A. 1; Atchison, T. & S. F. R. Co. v. Shean, 18 Colo. 368, 33 Pac. 108, 20 L. R. A. 729.

[20] McIntyre Ry. Co. v. Bolton, 43 Ohio St. 224, 1 N. E. 333; Ormond v. Hayes, 60 Tex. 180; Chicago & A. Ry. Co. v. Rayburn, 153 Ill. 290, 38 N. E. 558.

[21] Lake Shore & M. S. Ry. Co. v. Salzman, 52 Ohio St. 558, 40 N. E. 891, 31 L. R. A. 261.

tion.[22] He still, in such case, remains a passenger, though, if injured, any recovery might be barred by a plea of contributory negligence.[23]

[22] New Jersey Steamboat Co. v. Brockett, 121 U. S. 637, 7 Sup. Ct. 1039, 30 L. Ed. 1049; New York, L. E. & W. R. Co. v. Ball, 53 N. J. Law, 283, 21 Atl. 1052; Brown v. Scarboro, 97 Ala. 316, 12 South. 289; Willmott v. Corrigan Consol. St. Ry. Co., 106 Mo. 535, 17 S. W. 490.

[23] Brown v. Scarboro, 97 Ala. 316, 12 South. 289; New Jersey Steamboat Co. v. Brockett, 121 U. S. 637, 9 Sup. Ct. 1039, 30 L. Ed. 1049. For extended discussion of contributory negligence in riding in dangerous places, see 1 Fetter on Passenger Carriers, §§ 167–177.

CHAPTER XVIII

LIABILITIES OF THE COMMON CARRIER OF PASSENGERS

INTRODUCTORY

174. The law imposes upon the common carrier of passengers various duties, with a corresponding liability on the part of the carrier for a breach of these duties to the person to whom the duty is owed and who is injured by the breach.

The present chapter is devoted to the discussion of the liabilities of the common carrier of passengers under the following heads:

(1) Duty to accept and carry passengers.
(2) Duty to furnish equal accommodations to passengers.
(3) Liability for delay in transporting passengers.
(4) Liability for injuries to passengers.
(5) Contracts limiting the liability of the passenger carrier.
(6) Liability of the carrier to persons other than passengers.

The nature of the relation between the common carrier and the passenger has already been discussed,[1] as well as the commencement and termination of this relation.[2] The duties imposed on the carrier by this relation, and the consequent liability resulting from any breach of such duties next require attention. These can be conveniently treated according to the classification given above. In this classification the liability of the carrier in the first class

[1] Ante, chapter XVI.

[2] Ante, chapter XVII.

affects passengers or intending passengers; in the sixth class, the liabilities concern those who are not in any sense passengers; in the other classes, the liabilities affect only those who are passengers of the carrier. One very important liability of the carrier, that relating to the baggage of the passenger, is so unique and requires such extended notice that it is discussed in a subsequent chapter[3] devoted entirely to that subject.

DUTY TO ACCEPT AND CARRY PASSENGERS

175. The common carrier of passengers must accept and carry all proper persons who suitably apply, provided there is room in his conveyance and they are able and willing to pay for the transportation.

The primary duty of the common carrier of passengers is to accept for transportation all proper persons who suitably apply.[4] By engaging in a public calling, and by holding himself out as ready to serve all without discrimination, the common carrier of passengers must make good this holding out. He is therefore required by law to serve the public which he proposes to serve, and in this public calling to know no individuals and to make no unreasonable and arbitrary distinctions between classes of people.[5] The privileges which he exercises as a public servant, the essential dependence of the public on the carrier for the rendering of such

[3] Post, chapter XX.

[4] West Chester & P. R. Co. v. Miles, 55 Pa. 209, 93 Am. Dec. 744; Sanford v. Catawissa, W. & E. R. Co., 2 Phila. (Pa.) 107; Day v. Owen, 5 Mich. 520, 72 Am. Dec. 62; Hollister v. Nowlen, 19 Wend. (N. Y.) 234, 32 Am. Dec. 455; Hannibal R. Co. v. Swift, 12 Wall. 263, 20 L. Ed. 423; Saltonstall v. Stockton, Taney, 11 Fed. Cas. No. 12,271; Indianapolis, P. & C. Ry. Co. v. Rinard, 46 Ind. 293; Lake Erie & W. R. Co. v. Acres, 108 Ind. 548, 9 N. E. 453; Mershon v. Hobensack, 22 N. J. Law, 372; Baltimore & O. R. Co. v. Carr, 71 Md. 135, 17 Atl. 1052; Story v. Norfolk & S. R. Co., 133 N. C. 59, 45 S. E. 349; Runyan v. Central R. Co. of New Jersey, 65 N. J. Law, 228, 47 Atl. 422; BENNETT v. DUTTON, 10 N. H. 481, Dobie Cas. Bailments and Carriers, 322; Winnegar's Adm'r v. Central Pass. Ry. Co., 85 Ky. 547, 4 S. W. 237. See also Birmingham Ry., Light & Power Co. v. Anderson, 3 Ala. App. 424, 57 South. 103; Louisville & N. R. Co. v. Brewer, 147 Ky. 166, 143 S. W. 1014, 39 L. R. A. (N. S.) 647, Ann. Cas. 1913D, 151; Renaud v. New York, N. H. & H. R. Co., 210 Mass. 553, 97 N. E. 98, 38 L. R. A. (N. S.) 689.

[5] BENNETT v. DUTTON, 10 N. H. 481, Dobie Cas. Bailments and Carriers, 322; Indianapolis, P. & C. Ry. Co. v. Rinard, 46 Ind. 293; Atwater v. Delaware, L. & W. Ry. Co., 48 N. J. Law, 55, 2 Atl. 803, 57 Am. Rep. 543; Zackery v. Mobile & O. R. Co., 75 Miss. 751, 23 South. 435, 41 L. R. A. 385, 65 Am. St. Rep. 617; Ford v. East Louisiana R. Co., 110 La. 414, 34 South. 585; Reasor v. Paducah & Illinois Ferry Co., 152 Ky. 220, 153 S. W. 222, 43 L. R. A. (N. S.) 820.

service, and the vital relation of such service to the general interest of the public, afford such ample warrant for this rule that the courts have not been slow in its enforcement. The analogies of the innkeeper[6] and common carrier of goods[7] are so admirably applicable here that the general right of a proper person suitably applying to sue a common carrier refusing to accept and transport him requires no extended discussion.

Who May be Refused

The right of a person to be accepted by the common carrier, as in the case of the innkeeper, is subject to the qualification that he must be a proper person.[8] Again, this right of the carrier to exclude from his vehicles those manifestly unfit is essentially a derivative right growing out of the carrier's duty to secure the comfort and safety of the other passengers. In this connection substantially the same considerations apply as in the case of the innkeeper.[9] Accordingly, it is not only the right, but the duty, of the carrier to exclude those who may be reasonably expected to injure or unduly annoy the passengers of the carrier.[10]

Thus the carrier is not bound to carry one fleeing from justice, or one going upon the vehicle to assault a passenger,[11] to commit larceny or robbery, to interfere with the proper regulations of the company, or to commit any crime. Nor is a carrier bound to carry persons who are drunk[12] and disorderly,[13] or infected with con-

[6] See ante, § 94.

[7] See ante, § 100.

[8] Freedon v. New York Cent. & H. R. R. Co., 24 App. Div. 306, 48 N. Y. Supp. 584; Story v. Norfolk & S. R. Co., 133 N. C. 59, 45 S. E. 349; Stevenson v. West Seattle Land & Imp. Co., 22 Wash. 84, 60 Pac. 51; Meyer v. St. Louis, I. M. & S. R. Co., 54 Fed. 116, 4 C. C. A. 221; Daniel v. North Jersey St. Ry. Co., 64 N. J. Law, 603, 46 Atl. 625.

[9] See ante, §§ 94, 95.

[10] O'Neill v. Lynn & B. R. Co., 155 Mass. 371, 29 N. E. 630; Freedon v. New York Cent. & H. R. R. Co., 24 App. Div. 306, 48 N. Y. Supp. 584; Story v. Norfolk & S. R. Co., 133 N. C. 59, 45 S. E. 349. See cases cited in succeeding notes. The carrier may decline to receive one who refuses to comply with its reasonable regulations. Renaud v. New York, N. H. & H. R. Co., 210 Mass. 553, 97 N. E. 98, 38 L. R. A. (N. S.) 689; Daniel v. North Jersey St. Ry. Co., 64 N. J. Law, 603, 46 Atl. 625.

[11] BENNETT v. DUTTON, 10 N. H. 481, Dobie Cas. Bailments and Carriers, 322.

[12] Pittsburgh, C. & St. L. Ry. Co. v. Vandyne, 57 Ind. 576, 26 Am. Rep. 68; Wills v. Lynn & B. R. Co., 129 Mass. 351; Story v. Norfolk & S. R. Co., 133

[13] VINTON v. MIDDLESEX R. CO., 11 Allen (Mass.) 304, 87 Am. Dec. 714, Dobie Cas. Bailments and Carriers, 316; Pittsburg & C. R. Co. v. Pillow, 76 Pa. 510, 18 Am. Rep. 424; PITTSBURGH, F. W. & C. RY. CO. v. HINDS, 53 Pa. 512, 91 Am. Dec. 224, Dobie Cas. Bailments and Carriers, 334; Pittsburgh, C. & St. L. R. Co. v. Vandyne, 57 Ind. 576, 26 Am. Rep. 68; Flint v. Norwich & N. Y. Transp. Co., 34 Conn. 554, Fed. Cas. No. 4,873.

tagious diseases.[14] The carrier is not bound to accept persons who intend to use his vehicle for an unlawful or illegitimate purpose, such as gambling.[15] And a passenger may be refused if his arrival at the place of destination would excite violence and disorder.[16] So, too, the carrier may exclude unaccompanied blind persons when they are not qualified to travel alone,[17] and insane persons under the same circumstances.[18] Nor is there any obligation to carry one whose ostensible business on the carrier's conveyance is to injure its business by soliciting for a rival line.[19] A woman, however, cannot be refused merely because of previous unchastity, when there is nothing to indicate that she will misbehave while on the carrier's vehicle.[20]

Using Vehicle of Carrier for Business

The duty of the carrier in this regard is limited to furnishing transportation; it owes no duty to furnish to any person the opportunity of carrying on his business on its conveyances.[21] A carrier of passengers is not bound to furnish traveling conveniences for those who wish to engage on their vehicles in the business of selling books, papers, or articles of food, or in the business of receiving and distributing parcels or baggage,[22] nor even to permit

N. C. 59, 45 S. E. 349; Freedon v. New York Cent. & H. R. Co., 24 App. Div. 306, 48 N. Y. Supp. 584; Putnam v. Broadway & S. A. R. Co., 55 N. Y. 108, 14 Am. Rep. 190; Pittsburg & C. R. Co. v. Pillow, 76 Pa. 510, 18 Am. Rep. 424. But not slight intoxication. Pittsburgh, C. & St. L. R. Co. v. Vandyne, 57 Ind. 576, 26 Am. Rep. 68; Putnam v. Broadway & S. A. R. Co., 55 N. Y. 108, 114, 14 Am. Rep. 190; Milliman v. New York Cent. & H. R. Co., 66 N. Y. 642.

14 Walsh v. Chicago, M. & St. P. Ry. Co., 42 Wis. 23, 24 Am. Rep. 376.

15 Thurston v. Union Pac. R. Co., 4 Dill. 321, Fed. Cas. No. 14,019.

16 Pearson v. Duane, 4 Wall. (U. S.) 605, 18 L. Ed. 447.

17 Zackery v. Mobile & O. R. Co., 75 Miss. 751, 23 South. 435, 41 L. R. A. 385, 65 Am. St. Rep. 617; Denver & R. G. R. Co. v. Derry, 47 Colo. 584, 108 Pac. 172, 27 L. R. A. (N. S.) 761; Illinois Cent. R. Co. v. Allen, 121 Ky. 138, 89 S. W. 150, 28 Ky. Law Rep. 108, 11 Ann. Cas. 970.

18 Meyer v. St. Louis, I. M. & S. R. Co., 54 Fed. 116, 4 C. C. A. 221; Owens v. Macon & B. R. Co., 119 Ga. 230, 46 S. E. 87, 63 L. R. A. 946; Louisville, & N. R. Co. v. Brewer, 147 Ky. 166, 143 S. W. 1014, 39 L. R. A. (N. S.) 647, Ann. Cas. 1913D, 151.

19 Jencks v. Coleman, 2 Sumn. 221, Fed. Cas. No. 7,258.

20 Brown v. Memphis & C. R. Co. (C. C.) 7 Fed. 51. In Reasor v. Paducah & Illinois Ferry Co., 152 Ky. 220, 153 S. W. 222, 43 L. R. A. (N. S.) 820, it was held that the carrier could not refuse a sober and orderly passenger merely because he had been disorderly on a former trip.

21 See cases cited in the two succeeding notes.

22 Jencks v. Coleman, 2 Sumn. 221, Fed. Cas. No. 7,258; Com. v. Power, 7 Metc. (Mass.) 596, 41 Am. Dec. 465; New Jersey Steam Nav. Co. v. Merchants' Bank, 6 How. 344, 12 L. Ed. 465; The D. R. Martin, 11 Blatchf. 233, Fed.

the transaction of this business in its vehicles, when this interferes with its own interests. If a profit may arise from such business, the benefit of it belongs to the carrier, which is entitled to the exclusive use of its vehicles for such purposes.[23]

The sale or leasing of these rights to individuals, and the exclusion of others besides the privileged individuals therefrom, come under the head of reasonable regulations, which the courts recognize and enforce. The right of transportation, which belongs to all who desire it, does not carry with it a right of carrying on a traffic or of conducting a business. One violating such a rule of the carrier may be ejected from the carrier's vehicle.[24]

Insufficient Accommodations,

The carrier of passengers is not bound to receive any one for transportation after his accommodations are exhausted and he has no more room.[25] But, if the carrier sells tickets to more persons than he can carry, he is liable for breach of his contract.[26] The carrier, however, must provide facilities for the traffic which he reasonably had a right to expect,[27] and there are statutes to this effect in some of the states.[28] There is no such duty, however, when the traffic is unforeseen and somewhat unprecedented.[29] And even if the traffic, though unusually large, is foreseen, and particularly if lasting but for a short time, the carrier is not liable if it would under the circumstances be unreasonable to require the carrier to provide facilities adequate for handling the traffic.[30]

The carrier, too, must attend to the quality of its vehicles and must furnish conveyances reasonably adapted to the comfort and

Cas. No. 1,030; Barney v. Oyster Bay & H. Steamboat Co., 67 N. Y. 301, 23 Am. Rep. 115; Smallman v. Whitter, 87 Ill. 545, 29 Am. Rep. 76.

23 See cases cited in preceding note.

24 The D. R. Martin, 11 Blatchf. 233, Fed. Cas. No. 1,030.

25 Chicago & N. W. R. Co. v. Carroll, 5 Ill. App. 201; Evansville & C. R. Co. v. Duncan, 28 Ind. 441, 92 Am. Dec. 322. The underlying idea here is that of the carrier's undertaking to devote merely those facilities that he has to the service. See 1 Wyman, Public Service Corporations, § 791.

26 The Pacific, 1 Blatchf. 569, Fed. Cas. No. 10,643; Hawcroft v. Railway Co., 8 Eng. Law & Eq. 362; Williams v. International & G. N. R. Co., 28 Tex. Civ. App. 503, 67 S. W. 1085.

27 Lafayette & I. R. Co. v. Sims, 27 Ind. 59. See 1 Wyman, Public Service Corporations, § 797. See, also, Harmon v. Flintham, 196 Fed. 635, 116 C. C. A. 309.

28 See 1 Fetter, Passenger Carriers, § 249.

29 Louisville, N. O. & T. Ry. Co. v. Patterson, 69 Miss. 421, 13 South. 697, 22 L. R. A. 259; Gordon v. Manchester & L. R. R., 52 N. H. 596, 13 Am. Rep. 97; 2 Hutch. Carr. § 1114.

30 Pursell v. Richmond & D. R. Co., 108 N. C. 414, 12 S. E. 954, 956, 12 L. R. A. 113; Chicago & A. R. Co. v. Dumser, 161 Ill. 190, 43 N. E. 698.

convenience of the passenger, according to the method of transportation which the carrier adopts.[31] Thus, in winter, the carrier's vehicles should be suitably heated.[32] The passenger, too, is entitled to a seat.[33] Unless a seat is given to the passenger, he may either travel and pay fare without the seat, or he may refuse to pay without a seat, in which case he must, at the first reasonable chance, leave the carrier's conveyance.[34] He can then sue the carrier.[35] He cannot, however, insist on traveling free merely because he has no seat.[36]

When, as is usually the case, the carrier has provided separate and sufficient trains or conveyances for the transportation of goods and passengers, the passenger cannot ordinarily insist on being carried on freight trains or vehicles.[37] If the carrier, though, has held itself out as carrying passengers on freight trains, then it may render itself liable by failing to live up to this holding out, in refusing to accept one suitably applying for transportation on such trains.[38] These principles are also true as to special trains,[39] or trains run owing to some emergency.[40]

Carriers are bound to carry only those who can and will pay for

[31] Hunter v. Atlantic Coast Line R. Co., 72 S. C. 336, 51 S. E. 860, 110 Am. St. Rep. 605; Wood v. Georgia Railroad & Banking Co., 84 Ga. 363, 10 S. E. 967.

[32] Ft. Worth & D. C. Ry. Co. v. Hyatt, 12 Tex. Civ. App. 435, 34 S. W. 677; Hastings v. Northern Pac. R. Co. (C. C.) 53 Fed. 224; Taylor v. Wabash R. Co. (Mo.) 38 S. W. 304, 42 L. R. A. 110.

[33] Camden & A. R. Co. v. Hoosey, 99 Pa. 492, 44 Am. Rep. 120; Louisville N. O. & T. Ry. Co. v. Patterson, 69 Miss. 421, 13 South. 697, 22 L. R. A. 259; Memphis & C. R. Co. v. Benson, 85 Tenn. 627, 4 S. W. 5, 4 Am. St. Rep. 776; New York, L. E. & W. R. Co. v. Burns, 51 N. J. Law, 340, 17 Atl. 630.

[34] Hardenbergh v. St. Paul, M. & M. Ry. Co., 39 Minn. 3, 38 N. W. 625, 12 Am. St. Rep. 610; Memphis & C. R. Co. v. Benson, 85 Tenn. 627, 4 S. W. 5, 4 Am. St. Rep. 776; Davis v. Kansas City, St. J. & C. B. R. Co., 53 Mo. 317, 14 Am. Rep. 457; St. Louis, I. M. & S. Ry. Co. v. Leigh, 45 Ark. 368, 55 Am. Rep. 558. Cf. Louisville, N. O. & T. R. Co. v. Patterson, 69 Miss. 421, 13 South. 697, 22 L. R. A. 259.

[35] Memphis & C. R. Co. v. Benson, 85 Tenn. 627, 4 S. W. 5, 4 Am. St. Rep. 776; Hardenbergh v. St. Paul, M. & M. Ry. Co., 39 Minn. 3, 38 N. W. 625, 12 Am. St. Rep. 610.

[36] Davis v. Kansas City, St. J. & C. B. R. Co., 53 Mo. 317, 14 Am. Rep. 457; St. Louis, I. M. & S. Ry. v. Leigh, 45 Ark. 368, 55 Am. Rep. 558.

[37] Cleveland, C., C., & St. L. Ry. Co. v. Best, 169 Ill. 301, 48 N. E. 684; Roberts v. Smith, 5 Ariz. 368, 52 Pac. 1120; Gardner v. St. Louis & S. F. R. Co., 117 Mo. App. 138, 93 S. W. 917.

[38] Reed v. Great Northern Ry. Co., 76 Minn. 163, 78 N. W. 974; McCook v. Northrup, 65 Ark. 225, 45 S. W. 547; Thomas v. Chicago & G. T. Ry. Co., 72 Mich. 355, 40 N. W. 463.

[39] Southwestern R. R. Co. v. Singleton, 66 Ga. 252.

[40] Du Bose v. Louisville & N. R. Co., 121 Ga. 308, 48 S. E. 913.

their transportation. This payment may be demanded in advance as a condition precedent to accepting a person as a passenger.[41] Again, the analogy of the innkeeper[42] and common carrier of goods[43] is clear, and this right is again a corollary of the carrier's duty to accept all proper persons who apply. This method of safeguarding the payment of fare is particularly important here, since, when the passenger has no baggage, there is nothing to which the carrier's lien for his fare may attach.[44]

Waiver of Right to Refuse

A carrier should, in the first place, refuse to sell tickets to persons whom it has the right to refuse to carry, when it wishes to exercise that right, and should exclude them if they attempt to enter the vehicle without tickets. If a ticket has been inadvertently sold to such person, the carrier may still rescind the contract for transportation, but it should then tender a return of the money paid for the ticket. The ticket holder, however, may, under any circumstances, recover the amount he paid for the ticket.[45] If the carrier, at the time, knew facts which would justify a refusal to carry, his selling of a ticket to such a person is a waiver of the right to refuse him,[46] and this is also true of any other acceptance of the passenger by the carrier.

DUTY TO FURNISH EQUAL ACCOMMODATIONS TO PASSENGERS

176. The common carrier of passengers is bound, not only to transport all proper persons who apply, but also, in general, to furnish accommodations that are equal.

The carrier, however, may by regulations make reasonable discriminations in the accommodations furnished, based on--

(a) Sex, kind of ticket, or length of ticket.

(b) Race or color.

41 Day v. Owen, 5 Mich. 520, 72 Am. Dec. 62; Tarbell v. Central Pac. R. Co., 34 Cal. 616; Nashville & C. R. Co. v. Messino, 1 Sneed (Tenn.) 220; Ker v. Mountain, 1 Esp. (Eng.) 27. A strict tender of fare is not necessary. Day v. Owen, supra; Nashville & C. R. Co. v. Messino, supra; Tarbell v. Central Pac. R. Co., supra; Pickford v. Railway Co., 8 Mees. & W. (Eng.) 372.

42 See ante, §§ 94, 99.

43 See ante, §§ 113, 147.

44 See Ramsden v. Boston & A. R. Co., 104 Mass. 117, 6 Am. Rep. 200; Roberts v. Koehler (C. C.) 30 Fed. 94.

45 Thurston v. Union Pac. R. Co., 4 Dill. 321, Fed. Cas. No. 14,019.

46 Hannibal & St. J. R. Co. v. Swift, 12 Wall. 262, 20 L. Ed. 423; Pearson v. Duane, 4 Wall. 605, 18 L. Ed. 447; Tarbell v. Central Pac. R. Co., 34 Cal. 616.

The separation by the carrier of the white and colored races has also, in many states, been made the subject of statutory regulation.

The general rule, applicable alike to common carriers of passengers as well as of goods, requires, as to the service furnished, not only universality, but equality. The passenger carrier does not complete its full duty merely by serving all who apply, but it must serve them equally well, without unfair discrimination in favor of one or against another.[47] This, too, arises out of the public nature of the carrier's calling, and his relation to the public that he professes to serve.

Discrimination by Carrier's Regulation Based on Sex, Kind of Ticket, or Length of Journey

The carrier's regulations frequently make differences in the accommodations furnished depend upon other classifications of the passengers save that of race or color. These regulations are valid, provided such classification be reasonable. Thus, a carrier may provide separate cars for ladies, or for ladies and their male escorts, and may exclude from these cars all other passengers.[48] A carrier, too, may properly provide more luxurious accommodations for passengers traveling on first-class tickets than for others,[49] or for persons bound for distant points.[50]

Again, carriers may provide specially equipped chair cars, besides the coaches for holders of first-class tickets, and charge an additional fee for the use of such cars.[51] And many railroads have

[47] Atwater v. Delaware, L. & W. R. Co., 48 N. J. Law, 55, 2 Atl. 803, 57 Am. Rep. 543; Indianapolis, P. & C. Ry. Co. v. Rinard, 46 Ind. 293; BENNETT v. DUTTON, 10 N. H. 481, Dobie Cas. Bailments and Carriers, 322; Zackery v. Mobile & O. R. Co., 75 Miss. 751, 23 South. 435, 65 Am. St. Rep. 617; Central R. Co. of New Jersey v. Green, 86 Pa. 427, 27 Am. Rep. 718; West Chester & P. R. Co. v. Miles, 55 Pa. 209, 93 Am. Dec. 744.

[48] Chicago & N. W. Ry. Co. v. Williams, 55 Ill. 185, 8 Am. Rep. 641; Chilton v. St. Louis & I. M. Ry. Co., 114 Mo. 88, 21 S. W. 457, 19 L. R. A. 269; Peck v. New York Cent. & H. R. R. Co., 70 N. Y. 587; Bass v. Chicago & N. W. Ry. Co., 36 Wis. 450, 17 Am. Rep. 495; Id., 39 Wis. 636, and Id., 42 Wis. 654, 24 Am. Rep. 437; Memphis & C. R. Co. v. Benson, 85 Tenn. 627, 4 S. W. 5, 4 Am. St. Rep. 776; Brown v. Memphis & C. R. Co. (C. C.) 7 Fed. 51. And see Marquette v. Chicago & N. W. R. Co., 33 Iowa, 562. Sufficient accommodations for other passengers must be provided elsewhere. Bass v. Chicago & N. W. Ry. Co., supra.

[49] Wright v. Central Ry. Co., 78 Cal. 360, 20 Pac. 740; St. Louis & A. T. Ry. Co. v. Hardy, 55 Ark. 134, 17 S. W. 711; Nolan v. New York, N. H. & H. R. Co., 41 N. Y. Super. Ct. 541.

[50] St. Louis & A. T. Ry. Co. v. Hardy, 55 Ark. 134, 17 S. W. 711.

[51] St. Louis & A. T. Ry. Co. v. Hardy, 55 Ark. 134, 17 S. W. 711; Wright v. Central Ry. Co., 78 Cal. 360, 20 Pac. 740.

put on trains of unusual speed and luxury, requiring passengers traveling on these trains to pay a special fee beyond the usual first-class fare.

Discrimination Based on Race or Color by Regulation of the Carrier

The carrier of passengers, as well as the carrier of goods,[52] has the power to make proper regulations for the conduct of his business.[53] And these regulations, when reasonable and uniform in their operation, are valid and binding.[54] The general subject of the regulations of the passenger carrier will subsequently be discussed. It is introduced here merely as affecting the separation of the races.

Many carriers have adopted regulations under which separate accommodations are provided for white and colored passengers, each race being restricted to the accommodations provided for that race. Regulations making this discrimination have been very generally upheld as being entirely reasonable, being based, not on arbitrary caprice, but rather on principles which the law recognizes as just, equitable, and founded on good public policy.[55] The accommodations provided for colored passengers, however, must be substantially equal to those provided for white passengers.[56] The validity of such a regulation has recently been upheld by the United States Supreme Court, in the absence of a federal statute on the subject, even in the case of interstate passengers.[57]

Statutes Concerning the Separation of the Races by the Carrier

A number of statutes have been passed both for and against such separation of the white and colored races. Probably the best known of these was the famous "Civil Rights Bill," passed by

52 Ante, § 124.

53 Coyle v. Southern Ry. Co., 112 Ga. 121, 37 S. E. 163; Gray v. Cincinnati & S. R. Co. (C. C.) 11 Fed. 683; Smith v. Chamberlain, 38 S. C 529, 17 S. E. 371, 19 L. R. A. 710. See post.

54 Armstrong v. Montgomery St. Ry. Co., 123 Ala. 233, 26 South. 349; McMillan v. Federal St. P. V. Pass. Ry Co., 172 Pa. 523, 33 Atl. 560; Faber v. Chicago Great Western Ry. Co., 62 Minn. 433, 64 N W. 918, 36 L. R. A. 789.

55 Day v. Owen, 5 Mich. 520, 72 Am. Dec. 62; West Chester & P. R. Co. v. Miles, 55 Pa. 209, 93 Am. Dec. 744; Chicago & N W. Ry. v. Williams, 55 Ill. 185, 8 Am. Rep. 641; Chilton v. St. Louis & I. M. Ry Co., 114 Mo. 88, 21 S. W. 457, 19 L. R. A. 269; Houck v Southern Pac. Ry. Co (C. C) 38 Fed. 226; The Sue (D. C.) 22 Fed. 843; Logwood v. Memphis & C R. Co. (C. C.) 23 Fed. 318.

56 Murphy v. Western & A. R. R. (C. C.) 23 Fed. 637; Britton v. Atlanta & C. A. L. Ry. Co., 88 N. C. 536, 43 Am. Rep. 749; Chesapeake & O. & S. W. R. Co. v. Wells, 85 Tenn. 613, 4 S. W. 5. See, also, cases cited in preceding note

57 Chiles v. Chesapeake & O. R. Co., 218 U. S. 71, 30 Sup. Ct. 667, 54 L. Ed. 936, affirming 125 Ky. 299, 101 S. W. 386, 11 L. R. A. (N. S.) 268.

the federal Congress in 1875, substantially declaring that colored citizens should have the same accommodations at inns, public conveyances, etc., that are given to white people. This act, however, the federal Supreme Court, in the celebrated "Civil Rights Cases,"[58] held to be unconstitutional and void. Somewhat similar statutes have been passed by some of the states, both in the North and South, particularly during the years immediately following the Civil War.[59] Such a statute of Louisiana was declared unconstitutional by the United States Supreme Court, when applied to a steamboat engaged in interstate commerce.[60]

In recent years, particularly in the South, many statutes have been passed by states requiring the separation of the races and the furnishing by the carrier of separate vehicles for white and colored passengers.[61] These statutes have been sustained as to intrastate commerce.[62] Their validity, though passed on by state courts,[63] seems never to have been directly passed on by the United States Supreme Court, when applicable to interstate traffic.*

[58] 109 U. S. 3, 3 Sup. Ct. 18, 27 L. Ed. 835.

[59] See 1 Fetter, Passenger Carriers, § 258.

[60] Hall v. De Cuir, 95 U. S. 485, 24 L. Ed. 547.

[61] See 1 Fetter, Passenger Carriers, § 257; 2 Hutch. Carr. § 972; Judson Interstate Commerce (2d Ed) § 30.

[62] Louisville, N. O. & T. R. Co. v. Mississippi, 133 U. S. 587, 10 Sup. Ct. 348, 33 L. Ed. 784; Chesapeake & O. R. Co. v. Kentucky, 179 U. S. 388, 21 Sup. Ct. 101, 45 L. Ed. 244; Plessy v. Ferguson, 163 U. S. 537, 16 Sup. Ct. 1138, 41 L. Ed. 256; McCabe v. Atchison, T. & S. F. R. Co., 186 Fed. 966, 109 C. C. A. 110; Smith v. State, 100 Tenn. 494, 46 S. W. 566, 41 L. R. A. 432; Ohio Val. Ry's Receiver v. Lander, 104 Ky. 431, 47 S. W. 344, 882; Id., 48 S. W. 145, 20 Ky. Law Rep. 913.

[63] Thus as to interstate commerce such statutes were held to be void in Carrey v. Spencer (Sup.) 36 N. Y. Supp. 886; State ex rel. Abbott v. Judge, 44 La. Ann. 770, 11 South. 74; Hart v State, 100 Md. 595, 60 Atl. 457. In Smith v. State, 100 Tenn. 494, 46 S. W. 566, 41 L. R. A. 432, the decision in Hall v. De Cuir, 95 U. S. 485, 24 L. Ed. 547, is reviewed, and the statute, though applicable both to intrastate and interstate passengers, is upheld.

* Such a case seems now to be pending in the United States Supreme Court in McCabe et al. v. Atchison, T. & S. F. Ry. Co., being number 111 on the October Term, 1913. In the same case in the United States Circuit Court of Appeals for the Eighth Circuit it was held that such a statute, if construed as applicable to interstate commerce, would be unconstitutional; so the statute was construed as applicable solely to intrastate commerce and was therefore held to be valid. McCabe et al. v. Atchison, T. & S. F. Ry. Co. et al., 186 Fed. 966, 109 C. C. A. 110.

LIABILITY FOR DELAY IN TRANSPORTING PASSENGERS

177. The common carrier of passengers is liable for damage proximately due to delay in transporting the passenger after the transportation has begun, when such delay is caused by the carrier's negligence, or failure to exercise reasonable care.

The carrier is also liable for his failure to exercise reasonable diligence to transport passengers in accordance with his published time-table.

Delay in Transportation

Once the transportation is begun, the carrier must use due diligence to complete it within a reasonable time.[64] What is due diligence here, and what is a reasonable time, are, of course, relative questions, depending for their solution on varying facts and circumstances, among which the method of conveyance is highly important.[65] For delays due to other causes than the carrier's negligence, which is here the failure of the carrier to use reasonable or due care, the carrier is not liable, in the absence of a special contract to that effect.[66] The carrier may, if he wishes, bind himself by special contract to carry absolutely within a certain time. In such cases (which are rare) the carrier is liable according to the tenor of his contract, so that even the act of God will not excuse him.[67]

Conforming to Published Time-Table

The carrier, by publishing his time-tables, informs the public of the time at which his conveyances may be reasonably expected to

[64] Weed v. Panama R. Co., 17 N. Y. 362, 72 Am. Dec. 474; Williams v. Vanderbilt, 28 N. Y. 217, 84 Am. Dec. 333; Hamlin v. Railway Co., 1 Hurl. & N. (Eng.) 408; Eddy v. Harris, 78 Tex. 661, 15 S. W. 107, 22 Am. St. Rep. 88; Wilsey v. Louisville & N. R. Co., 83 Ky. 511; Milwaukee & M. R. Co. v. Finney, 10 Wis. 388; Latour v. Southern Ry., 71 S. C. 532, 51 S. E. 265.

[65] See cases cited in notes 64 and 66.

[66] Quimby v. Vanderbilt, 17 N. Y. 306, 72 Am. Dec. 469; Van Buskirk v. Roberts, 31 N. Y. 661; Alabama & V. Ry. Co. v. Purnell, 69 Miss. 652, 13 South. 472; Cobb v. Howard, 3 Blatchf. 524, Fed. Cas. No. 2,924; Hobbs v. Railway Co., L. R. 10 Q. B. (Eng.) 111; Van Horn v. Templeton, 11 La. Ann. 52; Houston, E. & W. T. Ry. Co. v. Rogers, 16 Tex. Civ. App. 19, 40 S. W. 201.

[67] Walsh v. Chicago, M. & St. P. Ry. Co., 42 Wis. 23, 24 Am. Rep. 376. And see, for other instances of special contract, Williams v. Vanderbilt, 28 N. Y. 217, 84 Am. Dec. 333; Ward v. Vanderbilt, 4 Abb. Dec. (N. Y.) 521; Watson v. Duykinck, 3 Johns. (N. Y.) 335; Dennison v. The Wataga, 1 Phila. (Pa.) 468, Fed. Cas. No. 3,799; Brown v. Harris, 2 Gray (Mass.) 359; Porter v. The New England No. 2, 17 Mo. 290; West v. The Uncle Sam, 1 McAll. 505, Fed. Cas. No. 17,427.

arrive at, and depart from, the various places on his line. Upon this information the public necessarily acts. This, however, does not constitute a contract between the carrier and passenger that the carrier will live up to the schedule.[68] Nor is the carrier a warrantor as to compliance with his time-table.[69] He must, however, at least use reasonable diligence to comply with such schedule, which he has published and on which the public must rely.[70] The law on this point is thus admirably stated in the headnote to a leading case:[71] "The publication of a time-table, in common form, imposes upon the railroad company the obligation to use due care and skill to have the trains arrive and depart at the precise moments indicated in the table; but it does not import an absolute and unconditional engagement for such arrival and departure, and does not make the company liable for want of punctuality which is not attributable to their negligence."

When changes are made in a time-table, the same publicity should be given to these changes as to the original publication.[72] If the regular time-table was published in a newspaper, and no notice of a change is given except through the posting of a notice in the carrier's office, this would not be sufficient to excuse the carrier.[73] If the scheduled time is varied, and a train is detained after the appointed time, for the mere convenience of the carrier or a portion of his expected passengers, a person who presents himself at the advertised hour, and demands a passage, is not bound by the change, unless he has had reasonable notice of it. But, even after the sale of a ticket, the carrier has a right, by giving reasonable notice, to vary the time of running his trains or other vehicles.[74]

[68] SEARS v. EASTERN R. CO., 14 Allen (Mass.) 433, 92 Am. Dec. 780, Doble Cas. Bailments and Carriers, 324; Gordon v. Manchester & L. R. R. Co., 52 N. H. 596, 13 Am. Rep. 97; Houston, E. & W. T. Ry. Co. v. Rogers, 16 Tex. Civ. App. 19, 40 S. W. 201.

[69] Gordon v. Manchester & L. R. R. Co., 52 N. H. 596, 13 Am. Rep. 97. See, also, Hurst v. Railway Co., 19 C. B. N. S. (Eng.) 310, 34 L. J. C. P. 264.

[70] SEARS v. EASTERN R. CO., 14 Allen (Mass.) 433, 92 Am. Dec. 780, Doble Cas. Bailments and Carriers, 324; Savannah, S. & S. R. Co. v. Bonaud, 58 Ga. 180; Heirn v. McCaughan, 32 Miss. 17, 66 Am. Dec. 588; Coleman v. Southern R. Co., 138 N. C. 351, 50 S. E. 690. See, also, Miller v. Southern R. Co., 69 S. C. 116, 48 S. E. 99.

[71] Gordon v. Manchester & L. R. R. Co., 32 N. H. 596, 13 Am. Rep. 97.

[72] Denton v. Railway Co., 5 El. & Bl. (Eng.) 860; Van Camp v. Michigan Cent. R. Co., 137 Mich. 467, 100 N. W. 771.

[73] SEARS v. EASTERN R. CO., 14 Allen (Mass.) 433, 92 Am. Dec. 780, Doble Cas. Bailments and Carriers, 324.

[74] SEARS v. EASTERN R. CO., 14 Allen (Mass.) 433, 92 Am. Dec. 780, Doble Cas. Bailments and Carriers, 324.

LIABILITY OF CARRIER FOR INJURIES TO PASSENGERS —ANALYSIS OF DISCUSSION

178. The liability of the common carrier of passengers for injury to the passenger is both theoretically and practically the most important of the carrier's responsibilities. Though (save as to stational facilities) the standard is the same by which the carrier's duty towards the passenger is measured, the application of this standard in practical cases reveals distinctive difficulties in the varying phases of the activities of the carrier.

In spite of the uniformity of the standard, as indicated above, for judging here the duty of the passenger carrier, this duty is revealed in such widely differing fields of the carrier's activities that, after a discussion of this duty in general, these fields require separate and distinctive notice. Thus the duty of the carrier to furnish proper instrumentalities of transportation and the duty to protect a passenger from the assaults of his fellow passengers necessarily present somewhat different questions, calling for separate treatment. The subject of the carrier's liability for injuries to the passenger will be discussed under the following analysis:

(a) In general.
(b) Means of transportation.
(c) Stational facilities.
(d) Duties in connection with transportation.
(e) Servants of the carrier.
(f) Protection of the passenger.
(g) Contributory negligence of the passenger.
(h) Presumption and burden of proof as to negligence.
(i) Carriers by water.

The last two sections of the chapter are devoted to the limitation by contract of the liability of the common carrier for injuries to passengers and the liability of the carrier to persons other than passengers.

SAME—IN GENERAL

179. The common carrier is not an insurer of the passenger's safety, but is liable for injuries to the passenger only when these are due to the carrier's negligence; such negligence here is the failure to exercise the highest degree of care that is reasonably consistent with the practical conduct of the carrier's business.

The common carrier of passengers, unlike the carrier of goods, is not an insurer. The former's liability is measured in terms of negligence, and not of insurance.[75] The law imposes liability on the carrier of goods, regardless of his fault, unless the loss or injury is due to one of the excepted causes.[76] The passenger carrier is liable only when he is at fault; in other words, when he is guilty of negligence. For this difference, many reasons have been assigned, including the volition and intelligence of the passenger, the absence of possible collusion between the carrier and wrongdoers (as the injury or death of the passenger involves no profit to the carrier), the probable refusal of the carrier to engage in passenger traffic if it involved an insuring liability, and the fact that while the goods are beyond the field of the carrier's knowledge, the passenger is necessarily present at, and to some extent cognizant of, the accident or wrong to which his injury is due.

The passenger carrier, accordingly, is liable for injury to the passenger only in case of negligence.[77] Here, as elsewhere, negligence implies the breach of a legal duty.[78] The extent of this duty, therefore, created by law as arising from the relation of common carrier and passenger, must next be defined. This has been done in varying language, but substantially the same idea underlies these apparently differing expressions. If the carrier lives up to the standard of care by which his duty is measured, he is not negligent, and hence not liable. If he fail in this standard, however, then he is guilty of a breach of legal duty, constituting actionable negligence, which makes him liable for the proximate damage resulting therefrom.

[75] White v. Boulton, Peake (Eng.) 113 (this is the first case on the subject); Hubbard, J., in Ingalls v. Bills, 9 Metc. (Mass.) 1, 43 Am. Dec. 346. See, also, Crofts v. Waterhouse, 11 Moore (Eng.) 133; BENNETT v. DUTTON, 10 N. H. 481, Dobie Cas. Bailments and Carriers, 322; Readhead v. Railway Co., L. R. 2 Q. B. (Eng.) 412, L. R. 4 Q. B. 379; Grand Rapids & I. R. Co. v. Huntley, 38 Mich. 537, 31 Am. Rep. 321. See, also, cases cited in the succeeding notes.

[76] Ante, § 116.

[77] Stockton v. Frey, 4 Gill (Md.) 406, 45 Am. Dec. 138; Doyle v. Boston & A. R. Co., 82 Fed. 869, 27 C. C. A. 264; Sanderson v. Frazier, 8 Colo. 80, 5 Pac. 632, 54 Am. Rep. 544; Stokes v. Saltonstall, 13 Pet. (U. S.) 181, 10 L. Ed. 115; Gilbert v. West End St. Ry. Co., 160 Mass. 403, 36 N. E. 60; Taillon v. Mears, 29 Mont. 161, 74 Pac. 421, 1 Ann. Cas. 613; Clerc v. Morgan's Louisiana & T. R. & S. S. Co., 107 La. 370, 31 South. 886, 90 Am. St. Rep. 319; South Covington & C. St. R. Co. v. Harris, 152 Ky. 750, 154 S. W. 35.

[78] See 1 Fetter on Passenger Carriers, §§ 3-7, and cases cited, giving various definitions and descriptions of the meaning of negligence in this connection.

The care or diligence exacted of the carrier in looking out for the passenger's safety is most often described by the terse and striking phrase "as far as human care and foresight will go."[79] Other expressions are: "Utmost care under the circumstances short of a warranty of the safety of the passenger;"[80] "the utmost care and diligence which human prudence and foresight will suggest."[81] These and other expressions of similar import[82] will clearly indicate how exacting is the law of the passenger carrier and how stringent his liability, though falling far short of the liability of an insurer. Ample warrant for this strictness, however, is found in considerations of public policy growing out of the interest which the state or government, as parens patriæ, has in protecting the lives and limbs of its citizens. These considerations apply with peculiar force to passengers on trolley cars, railroad trains, and steamboats, due both to the number of persons who of necessity daily employ them and the danger and speed involved in their operation. This duty is the same to gratuitous passengers as to passengers who pay.[83]

These expressions defining the carrier's duty are not to be taken literally as meaning that the carrier must for the passenger's safety provide every appliance that the human brain can originate and human brawn produce.[84] The absurdity of this is apparent in its

[79] Sir Jas. Mansfield in Christie v. Griggs, 2 Camp. (Eng.) 79.

[80] Indianapolis & St. L. R. Co. v. Horst, 93 U. S. 291, 23 L. Ed. 898.

[81] Palmer v. Delaware & H. Canal Co., 120 N. Y. 170, 24 N. E. 302, 17 Am. St. Rep. 629.

[82] For other expressions outlining the nature and extent of the duty of the common carrier of passengers, see Richmond & D. R. Co. v. Greenwood, 99 Ala. 501, 14 South. 495; Holly v. Atlanta St. R. R. Co., 61 Ga. 215, 34 Am. Rep. 97; Murray v. Lehigh Val. R. Co., 66 Conn. 512, 34 Atl. 506, 32 L. R. A. 539; VAN DE VENTER v. CHICAGO CITY R. CO. (C. C.) 26 Fed. 32, Dobie Cas. Bailments and Carriers, 377; Furnish v. Missouri Pac. Ry. Co., 102 Mo. 438, 13 S. W. 1044, 22 Am. St. Rep. 781; Spellman v. Lincoln Rapid Transit Co., 36 Neb. 890, 55 N. W. 270, 20 L. R. A. 316, 38 Am. St. Rep. 753; Pennsylvania Co. v. Roy, 102 U. S. 451, 26 L. Ed. 141; LOUISIANA & N. W. R. CO. v. CRUMPLER, 122 Fed. 425, 59 C. C. A. 51, Dobie Cas. Bailments and Carriers, 326; Haas v. Wichita R. & Light Co., 89 Kan. 613, 132 Pac. 195, 48 L. R. A. (N. S.) 974.

[83] See ante, p. 530. See, also, Philadelphia & R. R. Co. v. Derby, 14 How. (U. S.) 468, 14 L. Ed. 502 (leading case); Rose v. Des Moines Val. R. Co., 39 Iowa, 246; Simmons v. Oregon R. Co., 41 Or. 151, 69 Pac. 440, 1022; Rogers v. Kennebec Steamboat Co., 86 Me. 261, 29 Atl. 1069, 25 L. R. A. 491; Austin v. Railway Co., L. R. 2 Q. B. (Eng.) 442.

[84] Pershing v. Chicago, B. & Q. Ry. Co., 71 Iowa, 561, 32 N. W. 488; Indianapolis & St. L. R. Co. v. Horst, 93 U. S. 291, 23 L. Ed. 898; Libby v. Maine Cent. R. Co., 85 Me. 34, 26 Atl. 943, 20 L. R. A. 812; Birmingham Ry., Light & Power Co. v. Barrett (Ala.) 60 South. 262. "It sometimes happens

very statement. The rigor of the rule is necessarily tempered by considerations that are in their nature eminently practical, that are found in the carrier's pursuit of his calling. Nothing is required that is impracticable in the light of the actual conduct of the carrier's business under existing conditions. The standard, just as the circumstances under which it is to be applied, must needs be real, not Utopian. Thus the duty of the carrier is clearly expressed as the highest degree of care that is reasonably consistent with the practical conduct of the carrier's business.[85]

It is thus clear that passenger carriers are not required to use every possible precaution, for such a requirement, in many instances, would defeat the very objects of their employment. There are certain dangers that are necessarily incident to certain modes of travel, and these the passenger assumes when he elects to adopt such mode. Passenger carriers are not required, for instance, to use steel rails and iron or granite cross-ties, because such ties are less liable to decay, and hence safer than those of wood; nor need they have track walkers for each mile of road or lookouts at every bridge. All of these would make for the passenger's safety, but would probably bankrupt the railroad and make its continued operation impossible. Thus the expense is always an important item in determining whether a certain scheme or appliance should have been adopted by the carrier. But the law does emphatically require everything necessary to the security of the passenger that is rea-

that a derailed train is precipitated from a high embankment, and the lives of its passengers endangered or destroyed. Accidents of that character could be avoided by constructing all railroad embankments of such a width that a derailed train or car would come to a stop before reaching the declivity. But this would add immensely to the cost of constructing such improvements, and, if required, would in many cases prevent their construction entirely. If passenger trains were run at the rate of ten miles per hour, instead of from twenty-five to forty miles, it is probable that all danger of derailment would be avoided. But railroad companies could not reasonably be required to adopt that rate of speed. Their roads are constructed with a view to rapid transit, and the traveling public would not tolerate the running of trains at that low speed." Pershing v. Chicago, B. & Q. Ry. Co., supra.

85 Indianapolis & St. L. R. Co. v. Horst, 93 U. S. 291, 23 L. Ed. 898; Dunn v. Grand Trunk Ry. Co. of Canada, 58 Me. 187, 4 Am. Rep. 267; HEGEMAN v. WESTERN R. CORP., 13 N. Y. 9, 64 Am. Dec. 517, Dobie Cas. Bailments and Carriers, 329; Kansas Pac. Ry. Co. v. Miller, 2 Colo. 442; Pershing v. Chicago, B. & Q. Ry. Co., 71 Iowa, 561, 32 N. W. 488; Chicago, P. & St. L. Ry. Co. v. Lewis, 145 Ill. 67, 33 N. E. 960; Pittsburg, C. & St. L. Ry. Co. v. Thompson, 56 Ill. 138; Gadsden & A. U. Ry. Co. v. Causler, 97 Ala. 235, 12 South. 439; Louisville & N. R. Co. v. Kemp's Adm'r, 149 Ky. 344, 149 S. W. 835; Thayer v. Old Colony St. R. Co., 214 Mass. 234, 101 N. E. 368, 44 L. R. A. (N. S.) 1125.

sonably consistent with the practical operation of the business of the carrier, and the means of conveyance employed.[86]

The highest degree of practicable care, in the light of what has been said, is necessarily a phrase of intense relativity, for it must always be applied in the light of the peculiar conditions in each instance.[87] Thus the theoretical standard is the same in the case of passengers on freight trains as it is in the case of passengers on trains designed solely for passenger traffic.[88] But many precautions and appliances that are eminently practicable and required on passenger trains are by that same token utterly impracticable as to freight trains.[89] Again, practicable care, however high, must be judged in the light of the situation as it appeared (or should have appeared) to the carrier before the accident happened.[90] The car-

[86] Indianapolis & St. L. R. Co. v. Horst, 93 U. S. 291, 23 L. Ed. 898; Gilbert v. West End St. Ry. Co., 160 Mass. 403, 36 N. E. 60; Libby v. Maine Cent. R. Co., 85 Me. 34, 26 Atl. 943, 20 L. R. A. 812; Meyer v. St. Louis, I. M. & S. R. Co., 54 Fed. 116, 4 C. C. A. 221; Feary v. Metropolitan St. Ry. Co., 162 Mo. 75, 62 S. W. 452; Steverman v. Boston Elevated Ry. Co., 205 Mass. 508, 91 N. E. 919.

[87] Russ v. The War Eagle, 14 Iowa, 363; Budd v. United Carriage Co., 25 Or. 314, 35 Pac. 660, 27 L. R. A. 279; West Chicago St. Ry. Co. v. Kromschinsky, 185 Ill. 92, 56 N. E. 1110; Romine v. Evansville & T. H. R. Co., 24 Ind. App. 230, 56 N. E. 245; Stierle v. Union Ry. Co., 156 N. Y. 70, 50 N. E. 419; Burt v. Douglas County St. Ry. Co., 83 Wis. 229, 53 N. W. 447, 18 L. R. A. 479; Mitchell v. Marker, 62 Fed. 139, 10 C. C. A. 306, 25 L. R. A. 33; STEELE v. SOUTHERN R. CO., 55 S. C. 389, 33 S. E. 509, 74 Am. St. Rep. 756, Dobie Cas. Bailments and Carriers, 328; Kearney v. Seaboard Air Line R. Co., 158 N. C. 521, 74 S. E. 593; Thayer v. Old Colony St. R Co., 214 Mass. 234, 101 N. E. 368, 44 L. R. A. (N. S.) 1125.

[88] CHICAGO & A. R. CO. v. ARNOL, 144 Ill. 261, 33 N. E. 204, 19 L. R. A. 313, Dobie Cas. Bailments and Carriers, 332; Missouri Pac. Ry. Co. v. Holcomb, 44 Kan. 332, 24 Pac. 467; Sprague v. Southern R. Co., 92 Fed. 59, 34 C. C. A. 207; Southern Ry. Co. v. Cunningham, 123 Ga. 90, 50 S. E. 979; Indianapolis & St. L. R. Co. v. Horst, 93 U. S. 291, 23 L. Ed. 898; STEELE v. SOUTHERN R. CO., 55 S. C. 389, 33 S. E. 509, 74 Am. St. Rep. 756, Dobie Cas. Bailments and Carriers, 328.

[89] Stoody v. Detroit, G. R. & W. Ry. Co., 124 Mich. 420, 83 N. W. 26; Southern Ry. Co. v. Cunningham, 123 Ga. 90, 50 S. E. 979; Tibby v. Missouri Pac. Ry. Co., 82 Mo. 292; Pennsylvania Co. v. Newmeyer, 129 Ind. 401, 28 N. E. 860; Crine v. East Tennessee Ry. Co., 84 Ga. 651, 11 S. E. 555; Fisher v. Southern Pac. R. Co., 89 Cal. 399, 26 Pac. 894; STEELE v. SOUTHERN R. CO., 55 S. C. 389, 33 S. E. 509, 74 Am. St. Rep. 756, Dobie Cas. Bailments and Carriers, 328; Tickell v. St. Louis, I. M. & S. R. Co., 149 Mo. App. 648, 129 S. W. 727.

[90] Cleveland v. New Jersey Steamboat Co., 68 N. Y. 306; Id., 89 N. Y. 627; Id., 125 N. Y. 299, 26 N. E. 327; Fredericks v. Northern Cent. R. R., 157 Pa. 103, 27 Atl. 689, 22 L. R. A. 306; Libby v. Maine Cent. R. Co., 85 Me. 44, 26 Atl. 943, 20 L. R. A. 812; Garneau v. Illinois Cent. R. Co., 109 Ill. App. 169.

rier must provide for what he reasonably could have foreseen; he is not required either to be prophetic or to anticipate every remotely possible happening.[91]

SAME—MEANS OF TRANSPORTATION

180. The carrier must exercise the highest degree of practicable care, not only in furnishing suitable means and instrumentalities, but also in inspecting such means and instrumentalities and in keeping them in efficient repair.

Carrier's Duty to Provide Proper Instrumentalities

A highly important application of the passenger carrier's duty to exercise the highest degree of practical care lies in the furnishing of the many and varied instrumentalities of transportation.[92] Upon the concrete efficiency of these instrumentalities the safety of the passenger must depend, and for furnishing them he must necessarily rely upon the carrier, and is powerless to protect himself against the consequences, terrible indeed under the conditions of modern rapid transit, resulting from the carrier's negligence in this respect. The word "instrumentalities" is used here broadly, to include all inanimate means used by the carrier in the course of the transportation. The carrier's fault here may be one of pure omission, in utterly failing to supply an instrumentality,[93] or of commission, in supplying some instrumentality, but one that was not suitable.[94] This duty the courts strictly enforce, and the carrier

[91] Southern Transp. Co. v. Harper, 118 Ga. 672, 45 S. E. 458; Bowen v. New York Cent. R. Co., 18 N. Y. 408, 72 Am. Dec. 529; Keller v. Hestonville, M. & F. Pass. Ry. Co., 149 Pa. 65, 24 Atl. 159; Cornman v. Railway Co., 4 Hurl. & N. (Eng.) 781.

[92] Sharp v. Kansas City Cable Ry. Co., 114 Mo. 94, 20 S. W. 93; Heyward v. Boston & A. R. Co., 169 Mass. 466, 48 N. E. 773; Werbowlsky v. Fort Wayne & E. Ry. Co., 86 Mich. 236, 48 N. W. 1097, 24 Am. St. Rep. 120; Louisville, N. A. & C. Ry. Co. v. Miller, 141 Ind. 533, 37 N. E. 343; International & G. N. Ry. Co. v. Davis, 17 Tex. Civ. App. 340, 43 S. W. 540; Finkeldey v. Omnibus Cable Co., 114 Cal. 28, 45 Pac. 996; Oviatt v. Dakota Cent. Ry. Co., 43 Minn. 300, 45 N. W. 436; American S. S. Co. v. Landreth, 102 Pa. 131, 48 Am. Rep. 196; Id., 108 Pa. 264; Beiser v. Cincinnati, N. O. & T. P. R. Co., 152 Ky. 522, 153 S. W. 742, 43 L. R. A. (N. S.) 1050.

[93] Finkeldey v. Omnibus Cable Co., 114 Cal. 28, 45 Pac. 996; New York, C. & St. L. R. Co. v. Blumenthal, 160 Ill. 40, 43 N. E. 809; Mobile & M. R. Co. v. Ashcraft, 48 Ala. 15; Fordyce v. Jackson, 56 Ark. 594, 20 S. W. 528, 597.

[94] Sharp v. Kansas City Cable Ry. Co., 114 Mo. 94, 20 S. W. 93; Farley v. Philadelphia Traction Co., 132 Pa. 58, 18 Atl. 1090; Baltimore & P. R. Co.

is rigidly held for any negligence in this respect, resulting in injury to the passenger.

While the carrier must keep pace with modern science and invention, he is not required to provide every new or untried device in its experimental stage.[95] When, however, the instrumentality has been proved by experience as greatly lessening the dangers of transportation, and the price is under the circumstances reasonable (as in the case of the modern air brake [96]), then the failure to provide such instrumentality is at least prima facie evidence of negligence.[97] In such cases the length of time during which the appliance has been in use, its expense, the results accomplished, the custom and practice of carriers operating under substantially similar conditions, the comparative efficiency of the appliances used by the carrier, are all important factors in this problem.[98]

This duty of the carrier is nondelegable, and cannot be shifted to another, even an independent contractor, so as to relieve the carrier.[99] The carrier's liability remains the same, whether the instrumentalities are furnished by him or by another. In the latter case the negligence of such other person, judged by the same standard, is, as to the passenger, the negligence of the carrier. Any other rule would permit the carrier to evade perhaps his most serious liability by the simple expedient of turning the work over to another. Such a consequence the law could not for a moment tolerate.

Though this duty extends to all instrumentalities used by the passenger, the majority of actual cases are concerned with the

v. Swann, 81 Md. 400, 32 Atl. 175, 31 L. R. A. 313; Parker v. Boston & H. Steamboat Co., 109 Mass. 449.

95 Meier v. Pennsylvania R. Co., 64 Pa. 225, 3 Am. Rep. 581; Le Barron v. East Boston Ferry Co., 11 Allen (Mass.) 312, 87 Am. Dec. 717; Wynn v. Central Park, N. & E. R. R. Co., 10 App. Div. 13, 41 N. Y. Supp. 595; Merton v. Michigan Cent. R. Co., 150 Wis. 540, 137 N. W. 767; Alabama Midland Ry. Co. v. Guilford, 119 Ga. 523, 46 S. E. 655.

96 Kentucky Cent. R. Co. v. Thomas' Adm'r, 79 Ky. 160, 42 Am. Rep. 208.

97 Hodges v. Percival, 132 Ill. 53, 23 N. E. 423; Hanson v. Ry. Co., 20 Wkly. Rep. (Eng.) 297; Meier v. Pennsylvania R. Co., 64 Pa. 225, 3 Am. Rep. 581.

98 Pershing v. Chicago, B. & Q. Ry. Co., 71 Iowa, 561, 32 N. W. 488; Arkansas M. Ry. Co. v. Canman, 52 Ark. 517, 13 S. W. 280; Garoni v. Compagnie Nationale de Navigation, 131 N. Y. 614, 30 N. E. 865; Wynn v. Central Park, N. E. R. R. Co., 10 App. Div. 13, 41 N. Y. Supp. 595; Augusta Ry. Co. v. Glover, 92 Ga. 132, 18 S. E. 406.

99 Carrico v. West Virginia Cent. & P. Ry. Co., 39 W. Va. 86, 19 S. E. 571, 24 L. R. A. 50; Barrow S. S. Co. v. Kane, 88 Fed. 197, 31 C. C. A. 452; Virginia Cent. R. Co. v. Sanger, 15 Grat. (Va.) 230; Chicago, R. I. & T. R. Co. v. Rhodes, 35 Tex. Civ. App. 432, 80 S. W. 869.

carrier's roadbed[1] and vehicles.[2] Roadbed here, over which the carrier's vehicles are run, in the case of railroads is used broadly. It includes cuts and fills, ties, rails, switches, bridges, and culverts. These must be provided with reference, too, to conditions readily foreseen, with which they must contend. Thus embankments must be provided with drains suitable for at least ordinary rainfalls, and the track guarded against falls of earth and rock that may ordinarily be anticipated.[3] In the case of the carrier's vehicles, the care required extends not only to cars, engines, etc., but also to all the appliances with which these should reasonably be equipped, such as brakes, whistles, etc.[4]

Liability for Latent Defects

The carrier is not responsible for hidden defects in his instrumentalities which the highest degree of practicable care could neither have discovered nor prevented.[5] Failure to avert such a latent defect is not negligence, and the carrier is in no sense an insurer or

[1] Davis v. Chicago, M. & St. P. Ry. Co., 93 Wis. 470, 67 N. W. 16, 1132, 33 L. R. A. 654, 57 Am. St. Rep. 935; McFadden v. New York Cent. R. Co., 44 N. Y. 478, 4 Am. Rep. 705; Gleeson v. Virginia Midland R. Co., 140 U. S. 435, 11 Sup. Ct. 859, 35 L. Ed. 458; Pershing v. Chicago, B. & Q. Ry. Co., 71 Iowa, 561, 32 N. W. 488; Libby v. Maine Cent. R. Co., 85 Me. 34, 26 Atl. 943, 20 L. R. A. 812; Louisville, N. A. & C. Ry. Co. v. Miller, 141 Ind. 533, 37 N. E. 343; LOUISIANA & N. W. R. CO. v. CRUMPLER, 122 Fed. 425, 59 C. C. A. 51, Dobie Cas. Bailments and Carriers, 326; Arkansas Midland Ry. Co. v. Griffith, 63 Ark. 491, 39 S. W. 550.

[2] Louisville Ry. Co. v. Park, 96 Ky. 580, 29 S. W. 455; Baltimore & P. R. Co. v. Swann, 81 Md. 400, 32 Atl. 175, 31 L. R. A. 313; Sharp v. Kansas City Cable Ry. Co., 114 Mo. 94, 20 S. W. 93; Chicago, B. & Q. R. Co. v. Hazzard, 26 Ill. 373; Graeff v. Philadelphia & R. R., 161 Pa. 230, 28 Atl. 1107, 23 L. R. A. 606, 41 Am. St. Rep. 885; Werbowlsky v. Fort Wayne & E. Ry. Co., 86 Mich. 236, 48 N. W. 1097, 24 Am. St. Rep. 120.

[3] See Gleeson v. Virginia Midland R. Co., 140 U. S. 435, 11 Sup. Ct. 859, 35 L. Ed. 458.

[4] Sharp v. Kansas City Cable Ry. Co., 114 Mo. 94, 20 S. W. 93; Oviatt v. Dakota Cent. Ry. Co., 43 Minn. 300, 45 N. W. 436; De Cecco v. Connecticut Co., 85 Conn. 707, 83 Atl. 215.

[5] South Covington & C. St. R. Co. v. Barr, 147 Ky. 549, 144 S. W. 755; Ingalls v. Bills, 9 Metc. (Mass.) 1, 43 Am. Dec. 346; Palmer v. Delaware & H. Canal Co., 120 N. Y. 170, 24 N. E. 302, 17 Am. St. Rep. 629; Frink v. Potter, 17 Ill. 406; Galena & C. U. R. Co. v. Fay, 16 Ill. 558, 63 Am. Dec. 323; Sawyer v. Hannibal & St. J. R. Co., 37 Mo. 240, 90 Am. Dec. 382; Derwort v. Loomer, 21 Conn. 245; Mobile & O. R. Co. v. Thomas, 42 Ala. 672; Anthony v. Louisville & N. R. Co. (C. C.) 27 Fed. 724; Carter v. Kansas City Cable Ry. Co. (C. C.) 42 Fed. 37; Frink v. Coe, 4 G. Greene (Iowa) 555, 61 Am. Dec. 141. And see Alden v. New York Cent. R. Co., 26 N. Y. 102, 82 Am. Dec. 401, criticised in McPadden v. New York Cent. R. Co., 44 N. Y. 478, 4 Am. Rep. 705, and in Carroll v. Staten Island R. Co., 58 N. Y. 126, 139, 17 Am. Rep. 221. See, also, Readhead v. Railway Co., L. R. 2 Q. B. (Eng.) 412, L. R. 4 Q. B. 379; Buckland v. New York, N. H. & H. R. Co., 181 Mass. 3,

warrantor of the perfection of his appliances. This is true when such defect could not be thus detected or prevented by either the carrier or manufacturer.[6]

The carrier, by the great weight of authority, is liable, however, even though he could not have discovered the defect by the exercise of proper care after the instrumentality was delivered to him, if such defect were ascertainable by the exercise of proper care on the part of the manufacturer.[7] The negligence of the manufacturer then becomes, as far as the passenger is concerned, the negligence of the carrier. The rule is of great importance in cases (as of rails and car wheels) when such defect is not discoverable by external examination of the completed product, though it can be ascertained by reasonable and well-known tests during the manufacturing process. The question of the carrier's liability turns upon whether by the exercise of the requisite standard of care the defect is discoverable. When and at what stage of the process of making the appliance the defect can be found is not vital, and the carrier, here as before, escapes no liability by securing others to make the appliance, instead of making it himself.

Duty of Inspection and Repair

The carrier's duty as to instrumentalities by no means ceases when these are once provided. The same degree of care must be employed to keep them safe, in spite of the deterioration of use and continued physical changes that can be foreseen.[8] Thus arises

62 N. E. 955; Pittsburgh, C., C. & St. L. Ry. Co. v. Sheppard, 56 Ohio St. 68, 46 N. E. 61, 60 Am. St. Rep. 732.

6 Freisen v. Southern Pac. Co., 42 La. Ann. 673, 7 South. 800; Readhead v. Railway Co., L. R. 2 Q. B. (Eng.) 412, L. R. 4 Q. B. 379; Palmer v. Delaware & H. Canal Co., 120 N. Y. 170, 24 N. E. 302, 17 Am. St. Rep. 629.

7 HEGEMAN v. WESTERN R. CORP., 13 N. Y. 9, 64 Am. Dec. 517, Dobie Cas. Bailments and Carriers, 329; Caldwell v. New Jersey Steamboat Co., 47 N. Y. 282; Carroll v. Staten Island R. Co., 58 N. Y. 126, 17 Am. Rep. 221; Curtis v. Rochester & S. R. Co., 18 N. Y. 534, 538, 75 Am. Dec. 258; Perkins v. New York Cent. R. Co., 24 N. Y. 196, 219, 82 Am. Dec. 281; Bissell v. New York Cent. R. Co., 25 N. Y. 442, 82 Am. Dec. 369; Illinois Cent. R. Co. v. Phillips, 49 Ill. 234; Pittsburgh, C. & St. L. R. Co. v. Nelson, 51 Ind. 150; Treadwell v. Whittier, 80 Cal. 574, 22 Pac. 266, 5 L. R. A. 498, 13 Am. St. Rep. 175; Meier v. Pennsylvania R. Co., 64 Pa. 225, 3 Am. Rep. 581; Grote v. Railway Co., 2 Exch. (Eng.) 251; Readhead v. Railway Co., L. R. 2 Q. B. (Eng.) 412, L. R. 4 Q. B. 379. In some cases the liability of the carrier is denied, when the carrier is not himself at fault and when he employs a reputable manufacturer. Nashville & D. R. Co. v. Jones, 9 Heisk. (Tenn.) 27; Grand Rapids & I. R. Co. v. Huntley, 38 Mich. 537, 31 Am. Rep. 321.

8 Wynn v. Central Park, N. & E. R. R. Co., 133 N. Y. 575, 30 N. E. 721; Rutherford v. Shreveport & H. R. Co., 41 La. Ann. 793, 6 South. 644; Texas & P. Ry. Co. v. Hamilton, 66 Tex. 92, 17 S. W. 406; Stokes v. Ry. Co., 2 Fost. & F. (Eng.) 691; Chicago, P. & St. L. Ry. Co. v. Lewis, 145 Ill. 67, 33 N. E.

the duty, as to such instrumentalities, not only of preparation, but also of inspection and repair.[9]

The nature and frequency of such inspections are practical questions, to be decided according to the varying facts of each case.[10] The more severe the use and the greater the likelihood of deterioration, the more frequent should be the inspection. The greater the difficulty in discovering the defect and the more serious the result of its not being discovered, if present, the more exact and thorough should be the inspection. Ordinarily the most thorough and delicate tests known to scientists are not required, but the carrier should use such tests as can reasonably be made, and which are known in general to yield satisfactory results.[11] In many cases the time element is important as to how long a defect has existed, in determining whether the carrier was or was not negligent in failing to discover the defect.[12]

Not only is the carrier liable for his negligence in failing, through improper inspection, to discover defects, but also for his negligent failure to repair such defects properly after such defect is discovered.[13] Or it may be negligence on the carrier's part when he fails in many cases to make periodic repairs to certain instrumentalities in order to prevent defects, which, but for such repairs, can usually be expected to appear.[14]

960; Bremner v. Williams, 1 C. & P. (Eng.) 414; Proud v. Philadelphia & R. R. Co., 64 N. J. Law, 702, 46 Atl. 710, 50 L. R. A. 468; St. Louis Southwestern R. Co. v. Leflar, 104 Ark. 528, 149 S. W. 530.

9 Libby v. Maine Cent. R. Co., 85 Me. 34, 26 Atl. 943, 20 L. R. A. 812; Freissen v. Southern Pac. Co., 42 La. Ann. 673, 7 South. 800; Dorn v. Chicago, R. I. & P. R. Co., 154 Iowa, 140, 134 N. W. 855; Arkansas Midland Ry. Co. v. Griffith, 63 Ark. 491, 39 S. W. 550. See, also, cases cited in the preceding note.

10 Bremner v. Williams, 1 C. & P. (Eng.) 414; Stokes v. Railway Co., 2 Fost. & F. (Eng.) 691; Proud v. Philadelphia & R. R. Co., 64 N. J. Law, 702, 46 Atl. 710, 50 L. R. A. 468; St. Louis & S. F. Ry. Co. v. Mitchell, 57 Ark. 418, 21 S. W. 883; Keating v. Detroit, B. C. & A. R. Co., 104 Mich. 418, 62 N. W. 575; Burt v. Douglas County St. Ry. Co., 83 Wis. 229, 53 N. W. 447, 18 L. R. A. 479.

11 Stokes v. Railway Co., 2 Fost. & F. (Eng.) 691.

12 McPadden v. New York Cent. R. Co., 44 N. Y. 478, 4 Am. Rep. 705; Freissen v. Southern Pac. Co., 42 La. Ann. 673, 7 South. 800.

13 Pym v. Railway Co., 2 Fost. & F. (Eng.) 619; Peoria, P. & J. R. Co. v. Reynolds, 88 Ill. 418; McCafferty v. Pennsylvania R. Co., 193 Pa. 339, 44 Atl. 435, 74 Am. St. Rep. 690; Florida Ry. & Nav. Co. v. Webster, 25 Fla. 394, 5 South. 714; Missouri, K. & T. R. Co. of Texas v. Flood, 35 Tex. Civ. App. 197, 79 S. W. 1106.

14 As cross-ties, for example. See Rutherford v. Shreveport & H. R. Co., 41 La. Ann. 793, 6 South. 644.

SAME—STATIONAL FACILITIES

181. The carrier must provide proper stational facilities for the traveling public. In the construction, inspection, and repair of stational facilities (though some courts hold otherwise) the carrier is bound to use only ordinary care, and not the highest degree of practical care.

Duty to Provide Stational Facilities

In order that the public, entering or leaving its conveyances, may have proper means therefor, the carrier must provide proper stational facilities,[15] as well as the actual instrumentalities of transportation. This includes wharves in the case of steamboats,[16] and station platforms and approaches to the trains in the case of railroad companies.[17] Waiting rooms must also be provided, with accommodations which are reasonably adapted to the passenger's safety and comfort.[18] The nature and extent of all these must necessarily vary widely according to the traffic and the number of persons using them.[19]

Degree of Care

An important distinction is to be observed between the degree of care to be exercised in the construction and maintenance of tracks

[15] Falls v. San Francisco & N. P. R. Co., 97 Cal. 114, 31 Pac. 901; Chicago & A. R. Co. v. Walker, 217 Ill. 605, 75 N. E. 520; Keefe v. Boston & A. R. R., 142 Mass. 251, 7 N. E. 874; Stokes v. Suffolk & C. R. Co., 107 N. C. 178, 11 S. E. 991; Barker v. Ohio River R. Co., 51 W. Va. 423, 41 S. E. 148, 90 Am. St. Rep. 808; Texas & P. R. Co. v. Stewart, 228 U. S. 357, 33 Sup. Ct. 548, 57 L. Ed. 875.

[16] Dodge v. Boston & B. S. S. Co., 148 Mass. 207, 19 N. E. 373, 2 L. R. A. 83, 12 Am. St. Rep. 541; White v. Seattle, E. & T. Nav. Co., 36 Wash. 281 78 Pac. 909, 104 Am. St. Rep. 948; Strutt v. Brooklyn & R. B. R. Co., 18 App. Div. 134, 45 N. Y. Supp. 728.

[17] Elchorn v. Missouri, K. & T. Ry. Co., 130 Mo. 575, 32 S. W. 993; Toledo, St. L. & K. C. R. Co. v. Wingate, 143 Ind. 125, 37 N. E. 274, 42 N. E. 477; KELLEY v. MANHATTAN RY. CO., 112 N. Y. 443, 20 N. E. 383, 3 L. R. A. 74, Doble Cas. Bailments and Carriers, 331; Rathgebe v. Pennsylvania R. Co., 179 Pa. 31, 36 Atl. 160; Burnham v. Wabash West. Ry. Co., 91 Mich. 523, 52 N. W. 14; Young v. New York, N. H. & H. R. Co., 171 Mass. 33, 50 N. E. 455, 41 L. R. A. 193; Woodbury v. Maine Cent. R. Co., 110 Me. 224, 85 Atl. 753, 43 L. R. A. (N. S.) 682.

[18] Texas & P. R. Co. v. Humble, 97 Fed. 837, 38 C. C. A. 502; Jordan v. New York, N. H. & H. R. Co., 165 Mass. 346, 43 N. E. 111, 32 L. R. A. 101, 52 Am. St. Rep. 522; St. Louis, I. M. & S. Ry. Co. v. Wilson, 70 Ark. 136, 66 S. W. 661, 91 Am. St. Rep. 74.

[19] Brown v. Georgia, C. & N. R. Co., 119 Ga. 88, 46 S. E. 71; Taylor v. Pennsylvania Co. (C. C.) 50 Fed. 755; Sandifer's Adm'r v. Louisville & N. R. Co. (Ky.) 89 S. W. 528.

and running machinery by railroad corporations and the degree of care to be exercised along the same lines with regard to stational facilities. As to the former, the carrier is held to the use of the utmost practicable care in discovering and remedying defects therein.[20] As to the latter, the carrier is liable only for the want of ordinary care.[21] In each case, the carrier is liable for his negligence; but the duty (the breach of which constitutes negligence) is as to roadbed and running machinery fixed at the highest degree of practicable care,[22] while as to stational facilities the carrier fulfills his duty in exercising merely ordinary care.[23] The reason for this distinction is thus practically put by Mr. Justice Peckham in a leading New York case:[24] "But in the approaches to the cars, such as platforms, halls, stairways, and the like, a less degree of care is required, and for the reason that the consequences of a neglect of the highest skill and care which human foresight can attain to are naturally of a much less serious nature. The rule in such cases is that the carrier is bound simply to exercise ordinary care in view of the dangers to be apprehended." The failure to light the platform,[25] allowing snow and ice to accumulate,[26] or other obstruc-

[20] See ante, §§ 179-180.

[21] KELLEY v. MANHATTAN RY. CO., 112 N. Y. 443, 20 N. E. 383, 3 L. R. A. 74, Doble Cas. Bailments and Carriers, 331; Skottowe v. Oregon S. L. & U. N. R. Co., 22 Or. 430, 30 Pac. 222, 16 L. R. A. 593; Moreland v. Boston & P. R. R., 141 Mass. 31, 6 N. E. 225; Taylor v. Pennsylvania Co. (C. C.) 50 Fed. 755; Robertson v. Wabash R. Co., 152 Mo. 382, 53 S. W. 1082; Conroy v. Chicago, St. P., M. & O. R. Co., 96 Wis. 243, 70 N. W. 486, 38 L. R. A. 419; Falls v. San Francisco & N. P. R. Co., 97 Cal. 114, 31 Pac. 901; Mayne v. Chicago, R. I. & P. Ry. Co., 12 Okl. 10, 69 Pac. 933; Dotson v. Erie R. Co., 68 N. J. Law, 679, 54 Atl. 827; 'Parnaby v. Canal Co., 11 Adol. & E. (Eng.) 223; Texas & P. R. Co. v. Stewart, 228 U. S. 357, 33 Sup. Ct. 548, 57 L. Ed. 875; Woodbury v. Maine Cent. R. Co., 110 Me. 224, 85 Atl. 753, 43 L. R. A. (N. S.) 682.

[22] Ante, § 180.

[23] See cases cited in note 21.

[24] KELLEY v. MANHATTAN RY. CO., 112 N. Y. 443, 20 N. E. 383, 3 L. R. A. 74, Doble Cas. Bailments and Carriers, 331.

[25] Jamison v. San Jose & S. C. R. Co., 55 Cal. 593; Peniston v. Chicago, St. L. & N. O. R. Co., 34 La. Ann. 777, 44 Am. Rep. 444; Patten v. Chicago & N. W. Ry. Co., 32 Wis. 524; Id., 36 Wis. 413; Beard v. Connecticut & P. R. R. Co., 48 Vt. 101; Buenemann v. St. Paul, M. & M. Ry. Co., 32 Minn. 390, 20 N. W. 379; Dice v. Willamette Transportation & Locks Co., 8 Or. 60, 34 Am. Rep. 575; Valentine v. Northern Pac. R. Co., 70 Wash. 95, 126 Pac. 99; Texas & P. R. Co. v. Stewart, 228 U. S. 357, 33 Sup. Ct. 548, 57 L. Ed. 875.

[26] Memphis & C. R. Co. v. Whitfield, 44 Miss. 466, 7 Am. Rep. 699; Weston v. New York El. R. Co., 73 N. Y. 595; Seymour v. Chicago, B. & Q. Ry. Co., 3 Biss. 43, Fed. Cas. No. 12,685; Rodick v. Maine Cent. R. Co., 109 Me. 530, 85 Atl. 41; Waterbury v. Chicago, M. & St. P. Ry. Co., 104 Iowa, 32, 73 N.

tions [27] to remain thereon, or such a construction that part of a moving train projects over the platform,[28] have been held to constitute negligence for which the carrier is liable.[29] Some cases, however, even as to stational facilities, hold the carrier up to the highest degree of practicable care.[30]

The carrier cannot escape liability for its negligence in failing to exercise ordinary care as to stational facilities by proving that these were owned, controlled or constructed by another.[31] This duty is owed by the carrier, and to him can the passenger look always for its performance; by whom the facilities are actually provided or maintained does not affect the passenger's remedy against the carrier, and such passenger is not concerned with the rights of the carrier over against the one actually providing these facilities.

Right to Give Exclusive Rights in Station to Privileged Hackmen

A question which has given the courts no little trouble is the right of a railroad company to permit certain privileged hackmen to solicit business in its station and to forbid all others save those thus privileged from using the station for that purpose. By what is believed to be the better view, the railroad company is permitted to do this, provided the traveling public is properly served by the

W. 341; Hull v. Minneapolis, St. P. & S. S. M. R. Co., 116 Minn. 349, 133 N. W. 852. But see KELLEY v. MANHATTAN RY. CO., 112 N. Y. 443, 20 N. E. 383, 3 L. R. A. 74, Doble Cas. Bailments and Carriers, 331.

27 Martin v. Ry. Co., 16 C. B. (Eng.) 179; Osborn v. Union Ferry Co., 53 Barb. (N. Y.) 629; Denver & R. G. R. Co. v. Spencer, 27 Colo. 313, 61 Pac. 606, 51 L. R. A. 121.

28 Langan v. St. Louis, I. M. & S. Ry. Co., 72 Mo. 392; Chicago & A. R. Co. v. Wilson, 63 Ill. 167; Dobiecki v. Sharp, 88 N. Y. 203.

29 Holes in platform, Knight v. Portland, S. & P. R. Co., 56 Me. 234, 96 Am. Dec. 449; Chicago & N. W. Ry. Co. v. Fillmore, 57 Ill. 265; Liscomb v. New Jersey R. Transp. Co., 6 Lans. (N. Y.) 75; passengers obliged to cross tracks, Keating v. New York Cent. R. Co., 3 Lans. (N. Y.) 469; Baltimore & O. R. Co. v. State, to Use of Hauer, 60 Md. 449; Klein v. Jewett, 26 N. J. Eq. 474; grease on platform, Newcomb v. New York Cent. & H. R. R. Co., 182 Mo. 687, 81 S. W. 1069; failure to light station, Abbott v. Oregon R. Co., 46 Or. 549, 80 Pac. 1012, 1 L. R. A. (N. S.) 851, 114 Am. St. Rep. 885, 7 Ann. Cas. 961.

30 Cole v. Lake Shore & M. S. R. Co., 81 Mich. 156, 45 N. W. 983; Louisville Ry. Co. v. Park, 96 Ky. 580, 29 S. W. 455; Gulf, C. & S. F. Ry. Co. v. Butcher, 83 Tex. 309, 18 S. W. 583. See, also, Dodge v. Boston & B. S. S. Co., 148 Mass. 219, 19 N. E. 373, 2 L. R. A. 83, 12 Am. St. Rep. 541; Lapin v. Northwestern Elevated R. Co., 162 Ill. App. 296.

31 Owen v. Washington & C. R. R. Co., 29 Wash. 207, 69 Pac. 757; Frazier v. New York, N. H. & H. R. Co., 180 Mass. 427, 62 N. E. 731; Skottowe v. Oregon S. L. & U. N. Ry. Co., 22 Or. 430, 30 Pac. 222, 16 L. R. A. 593; Leveret v. Shreveport Belt R. Co., 110 La. 399, 34 South. 579; Buddenberg

privileged hackmen.[32] The carrier's duty is to the traveling public, so that, if the public is properly served, it hardly is reasonable for the disgruntled hackmen to complain because they are not permitted to perform this service for their own profit. A number of states, however, hold the contrary view.[33] There is general agreement, though, that the traveler's own carriage or one that he has previously engaged cannot be denied admittance to the station.[34]

SAME—DUTIES IN CONNECTION WITH TRANSPORTATION

182. The carrier must exercise the highest degree of practicable care in the operation and management of its instrumentalities and in the performance of services reasonably incident to the handling of its passenger traffic.

The same degree of care exacted of the carrier in providing and maintaining instrumentalities is required as to the operation and management of those instrumentalities.[35] The carrier is bound to

v. Charles P. Chouteau Transp. Co., 108 Mo. 394, 18 S. W. 970; Cotant v. Boone Suburban R. Co., 125 Iowa, 46, 99 N. W. 115, 69 L. R. A. 982; John v. Bacon, L. R. 5 C. P. (Eng.) 437.

[32] Donovan v. Pennsylvania Co., 199 U. S. 279, 26 Sup. Ct. 91, 50 L. Ed. 192; Brown v. New York Cent. & H. R. R. Co., 151 N. Y. 674, 46 N. E. 1145; Boston & M. R. R. v. Sullivan, 177 Mass. 230, 58 N. E. 689, 83 Am. St. Rep. 275; Kates v. Atlanta Baggage & Cab Co., 107 Ga. 636, 34 S. E. 372, 46 L. R. A. 431; Hedding v. Gallagher, 72 N. H. 377, 57 Atl. 225, 64 L. R. A. 811; Godbout v. St. Paul Union Depot Co., 79 Minn. 188, 81 N. W. 835, 47 L. R. A. 532; Griswold v. Webb, 16 R. I. 649, 19 Atl. 143, 7 L. R. A. 302; In re Beadell, 2 C. B. N. S. (Eng.) 509; Hole v. Digby, 27 Weekly Rep. (Eng.) 884; Norfolk & W. R. Co. v. Old Dominion Baggage Co., 99 Va. 111, 37 S. E. 784, 50 L. R. A. 722; New York Cent. & H. R. R. Co. v. Ryan, 71 Misc. Rep. 241, 129 N. Y. Supp. 55.

[33] Kalamazoo Hack & Bus Co. v. Sootsma, 84 Mich. 194, 47 N. W. 667, 10 L. R. A. 189, 22 Am. St. Rep. 693; State v. Reed, 76 Miss. 211, 24 South. 308, 43 L. R. A. 134, 71 Am. St. Rep. 528; McConnell v. Pedigo, 92 Ky. 465, 18 S. W. 15; Montana Union Ry. Co. v. Langlois, 9 Mont. 419, 24 Pac. 209, 8 L. R. A. 753, 18 Am. St. Rep. 745; Indianapolis Union Ry. Co. v. Dohn, 153 Ind. 10, 53 N. E. 937, 45 L. R. A. 427, 74 Am. St. Rep. 274.

[34] Donovan v. Pennsylvania Co., 199 U. S. 279, 26 Sup. Ct. 91, 50 L. Ed. 192; Griswold v. Webb, 16 R. I. 649, 19 Atl. 143, 7 L. R. A. 302; State v. Union Depot Co., 71 Ohio St. 379, 73 N. E. 633, 68 L. R. A. 792, 2 Ann. Cas. 186; New York Cent. & H. R. R. Co. v. Ryan, 71 Misc. Rep. 241, 129 N. Y. Supp. 55.

[35] Mitchell v. Marker, 62 Fed. 139, 10 C. C. A. 306, 25 L. R. A. 33; White v. Fitchburg R. Co., 136 Mass. 321; Louisville, N. A. & C. R. Co. v. Jones, 108 Ind. 551, 9 N. E. 476; Farlow v. Kelly, 108 U. S. 288, 2 Sup. Ct. 555, 27

exercise the highest degree of care, in view of all circumstances, to prevent damage to its passengers by the operation of its means of conveyance, avoiding sudden starts and stops,[36] danger from curves,[37] or a dangerous rate of speed.[38] The same is true of the make-up of a train and the position of the cars in the train.[39]

A like degree of care attaches to the carrier in connection with the receiving of passengers on,[40] and discharging them from,[41] his

L. Ed. 726; Hite v. Metropolitan St. Ry. Co., 130 Mo. 132, 31 S. W. 262, 32 S. W. 33, 51 Am. St. Rep. 555; Louisville & N. R. Co. v. Richmond, 67 S. W. 25, 23 Ky. Law Rep. 2394; Pennsylvania Co. v. Newmeyer, 129 Ind. 401, 28 N. E. 860; Union P. Ry. Co. v. Harris, 158 U. S. 326, 15 Sup. Ct. 843, 39 L. Ed. 1003; South Covington & C. St. R. Co. v. Hardy, 152 Ky. 374, 153 S. W. 474, 44 L. R. A. (N. S.) 32.

[36] Holmes v. Allegheny Traction Co., 153 Pa. 152, 25 Atl. 640; Yarnell v. Kansas City, Ft. S. & M. Ry. Co., 113 Mo. 570, 21 S. W. 1, 18 L. R. A. 599; North Chicago St. R. Co. v. Cook, 145 Ill. 551, 33 N. E. 958; Poole v. Georgia Railroad & Banking Co., 89 Ga. 320, 15 S. E. 321; Cassidy v. Atlantic Ave. R. Co., 9 Misc. Rep. 275, 29 N. Y. Supp. 724; Hill v. West End St. Ry. Co., 158 Mass. 458, 33 N. E. 582; CHICAGO & A. R. CO. v. ARNOL, 144 Ill. 261, 33 N. E. 204, 19 L. R. A. 313, Dobie Cas. Bailments and Carriers, 332. As to street cars where passengers are alighting, Cawfield v. Asheville St. Ry. Co., 111 N. C. 597, 16 S. E. 703; Chicago, B. & Q. R. Co. v. Landauer, 36 Neb. 642, 54 N. W. 976 (alighting from train); Robinson v. Northampton Ry. Co., 157 Mass. 224, 32 N. E. 1; Conway v. New Orleans & C. R. Co., 46 La. Ann. 1429, 16 South. 362; Washington & G. R. Co. v. Harmon, 147 U. S. 571, 13 Sup. Ct. 557, 37 L. Ed. 284; Jones v. Chicago City R. Co., 147 Ill. App. 640; Benjamin v. Metropolitan St. R. Co., 245 Mo. 598, 151 S. W. 91; Bobbitt v. United Rys. Co. of St. Louis, 169 Mo. App. 424, 153 S. W. 70; Illinois Cent. Ry. Co. v. Dallas' Adm'x, 150 Ky. 442, 150 S. W. 536.

[37] Lynn v. Southern Pac. Co., 103 Cal. 7, 36 Pac. 1018, 24 L. R. A. 710; Francisco v. Troy & L. R. Co., 78 Hun, 13, 29 N. Y. Supp. 247; Brusch v. St. Paul City Ry. Co., 52 Minn. 512, 55 N. W. 57. And see Highland Ave. & B. R. Co. v. Donovan, 94 Ala. 299, 10 South. 139.

[38] Lynn v. Southern Pac. Co., 103 Cal. 7, 36 Pac. 1018, 24 L. R. A. 710; Andrews v. Chicago, M. & St. P. Ry. Co., 86 Iowa, 677, 53 N. W. 399; Chicago, P. & St. L. Ry. Co. v. Lewis, 145 Ill. 67, 33 N. E. 960; Pennsylvania Co. v. Newmeyer, 129 Ind. 401, 28 N. E. 860; Willmott v. Corrigan Con. St. Ry. Co., 106 Mo. 535, 17 S. W. 490; Mexican Cent. Ry. Co. v. Lauricella, 87 Tex. 277, 28 S. W. 277, 47 Am. St. Rep. 103. As to effect of municipal ordinance, Cogswell v. West St. & N. E. Electric Ry. Co., 5 Wash. 46, 31 Pac. 411.

[39] Chattanooga, R. & C. R. Co. v. Huggins, 89 Ga. 494, 15 S. E. 848; Tillett v. Norfolk & W. R. Co., 118 N. C. 1031, 24 S. E. 111; Philadelphia & R. R. Co. v. Anderson, 94 Pa. 351, 39 Am. Rep. 787.

[40] Hickenbottom v. Delaware, L. & W. R. Co., 122 N. Y. 91, 25 N. E. 279; Allender v. Chicago, R. I. & P. R. Co., 43 Iowa, 276; Gulf, C. & S. F. Ry. Co. v. Powers, 4 Tex. Civ. App. 228, 23 S. W. 325; Chesapeake & O. Ry. Co. v. Austin, 137 Ky. 611, 126 S. W. 144, 136 Am. St. Rep. 307; San Antonio & A. P. R. Co. v. Turney, 33 Tex. Civ. App. 626, 78 S. W. 256; Moffitt v. Connecticut Co., 86 Conn. 527, 86 Atl. 16.

[41] Missouri Pac. Ry. Co. v. Long, 81 Tex. 253, 16 S. W. 1016, 26 Am. St.

conveyance. Thus the passenger should not be compelled to alight at an unsafe place,[42] and trains should be stopped for a period of time that is long enough to permit a passenger to enter the train or leave it in safety.[43] The carrier's duty not to invite the passenger expressly or impliedly to alight at an unsafe place is particularly important at night, when the passenger is less able to see the danger or to protect himself from it.[44] Though the cases are not entirely clear, it seems that the carrier ordinarily owes no duty to assist an able-bodied passenger to enter or leave the carrier's vehicle, unless this is fraught with some unusual difficulty or danger.[45] But a different rule applies when the passenger is so sick or infirm as manifestly to need such assistance.[46] As a general rule, too,

Rep. 811; Robostelli v. New York, N. H. & H. R. Co. (C. C.) 33 Fed. 796; McDonald v. Kansas City & Independence Rapid Transit Ry. Co., 127 Mo. 38, 29 S. W. 848; New York C. & St. L. Ry. Co. v. Doane, 115 Ind. 435, 17 N. E. 913, 1 L. R. A. 157, 7 Am. St. Rep. 451; CHICAGO & A. R. CO. v. ARNOL, 144 Ill. 261, 33 N. E. 204, 19 L. R. A. 313, Dobie Cas. Bailments and Carriers, 332; Ft. Smith & W. R. Co. v. Ford, 34 Okl. 575, 126 Pac. 745, 41 L. R. A. (N. S.) 745; Vine v. Berkshire St. R. Co., 212 Mass. 580, 99 N. E. 473; Donovan v. New Orleans Ry. & Light Co., 132 La. 239, 61 South. 216, 48 L. R. A. (N. S.) 109.

42 Richmond City Ry. Co. v. Scott, 86 Va. 902, 11 S. E. 404; Hartzig v. Lehigh Val. R. R. Co., 154 Pa. 364, 26 Atl. 310; Delaware L. & W. R. Co. v. Trautwein, 52 N. J. Law, 169, 19 Atl. 178, 7 L. R. A. 435, 19 Am. St. Rep. 442; Ellis v. Chicago, M. & St. P. R. Co., 120 Wis. 645, 98 N. W. 942; Nicholson v. Railway Co., 3 Hurl. & C. (Eng.) 534; Mensing v. Michigan Cent. R. Co., 117 Mich. 606, 76 N. W. 98; St. Louis Southwestern R. Co. of Texas v. Missildine (Tex. Civ. App.) 157 S. W. 245.

43 Kefauver v. Philadelphia & R. R. Co. (C. C.) 122 Fed. 966; Pennsylvania R. Co. v. Lyons, 129 Pa. 113, 18 Atl. 759, 15 Am. St. Rep. 701; Smalley v. Detroit & M. R. Co., 131 Mich. 560, 91 N. W. 1027; CHICAGO & A. R. CO. v. ARNOL, 144 Ill. 261, 33 N. E. 204, 19 L. R. A. 313, Dobie Cas. Bailments and Carriers, 332; Emery v. Boston & M. R. R. Co., 67 N. H. 434, 36 Atl. 367; Washington & G. R. Co. v. Harmon, 147 U. S. 571, 13 Sup. Ct. 557, 37 L. Ed. 284; Franklin v. Visalia Electric R. Co., 21 Cal. App. 270, 131 Pac. 776.

44 International & G. N. R. Co. v. Eckford, 71 Tex. 274, 8 S. W. 679; Miller v. East Tennessee, V. & G. Ry. Co., 93 Ga. 630, 21 S. E. 153; Philadelphia, W. & B. R. Co. v. McCormick, 124 Pa. 427, 16 Atl. 848; Leedom v. Philadelphia & R. Ry. Co., 52 Pa. Super. Ct. 598.

45 Yarnell v. Kansas City, Ft. S. & M. Ry. Co., 113 Mo. 570, 21 S. W. 1, 18 L. R. A. 599; Jarmy v. Duluth St. Ry. Co., 55 Minn. 271, 56 N. W. 813; Southern R. Co. v. Reeves, 116 Ga. 743, 42 S. E. 1015; Indianapolis Traction & Terminal Co. v. Pressell, 39 Ind. App. 472, 77 N. E. 357; Western & A. R. Co. v. Earwood, 104 Ga. 127, 29 S. E. 913.

46 Madden v. Port Royal & W. C. Ry. Co., 41 S. C. 440, 19 S. E. 951, 20 S. E. 65; Alexandria & F. R. Co. v. Herndon, 87 Va. 193, 12 S. E. 289; Werner v. Chicago & N. W. R. Co., 105 Wis. 300, 81 N. W. 416; Missouri Pac. Ry. Co. v. Wortham, 73 Tex. 25, 10 S. W. 741, 3 L. R. A. 368; Georgia Railroad & Banking Co. v. Rives, 137 Ga. 376, 73 S. E. 645, 38 L. R. A. (N. S.) 564; Young v. Missouri Pac. Ry. Co., 93 Mo. App. 267.

when a carrier accepts a passenger under physical disability rendering him unable to care for himself properly, as when he is sick or infirm, or even drunk, these facts must be considered in determining whether the carrier has exercised the requisite care in looking after such passenger.[47] There are various other duties resting on the carrier, such as announcing the stations,[48] and, when there is no dining car in the train, and the journey is long, to stop the train at reasonable intervals long enough to permit the passengers to obtain food or other refreshment.[49] The carrier should also warn passengers of impending danger.[50]

[47] Winfrey v. Missouri, K. & T. R. Co., 194 Fed. 808, 114 C. C. A. 218; Memphis St. R. Co. v. Shaw, 110 Tenn. 467, 75 S. W. 713; Weightman v. Louisville, N. O. & T. Ry. Co., 70 Miss. 563, 12 South. 586, 19 L. R. A. 671, 35 Am. St. Rep. 660, distinguishing Sevier v. Vicksburg & M. R. Co., 61 Miss. 8, 48 Am. Rep. 74; Meyer v. St. Louis, I. M. & S. R. Co., 4 C. C. A. 221, 54 Fed. 116; Sawyer v. Dulany, 30 Tex. 479; Sheridan v. Brooklyn City & N. R. Co., 36 N. Y. 39, 93 Am. Dec. 490; Philadelphia City Pass. Ry. Co. v. Hassard, 75 Pa. 367; Allison v. Chicago & N. W. R. Co., 42 Iowa, 274; Jeffersonville, M. & I. R. Co. v. Riley, 39 Ind. 568-584; Indianapolis, P. & C. Ry. Co. v. Pitzer, 109 Ind. 179, 6 N. E. 310, 10 N. E. 70, 58 Am. Rep. 387; Croom v. Chicago, M. & St. P. Ry. Co., 52 Minn. 296, 53 N. W. 1128, 18 L. R. A. 602, 38 Am. St. Rep. 557. When a child of such tender and imbecile age is brought to a railway station or to any conveyance, for the purpose of being conveyed, and is wholly unable to take care of itself, the contract of conveyance is on the implied condition that the child is to be conveyed subject to due and proper care on the part of the person having it in charge. Such care not being used, where the child has no natural capacity to judge of the surrounding circumstances, a child might get into serious danger from a state of things which would produce no disastrous consequences to an adult capable of taking care of himself. Waite v. Railway Co., El., Bl. & El. (Eng.) 719, per Cockburn, C. J., in exchequer chamber. See, also, Anderson v. Atlantic Coast Line R. Co., 161 N. C. 462, 77 S. E. 402; Indianapolis Southern R. Co. v. Wall (Ind. App.) 101 N. E. 680; Chicago, R. I. & G. R. Co. v. Sears (Tex. Civ. App.) 155 S. W. 1003.

[48] Pennsylvania Co. v. Hoagland, 78 Ind. 203; Houston & T. C. R. Co. v. Goodyear, 28 Tex. Civ. App. 206, 66 S. W. 862; Southern R. Co. v. Hobbs, 118 Ga. 227, 45 S. E. 23, 63 L. R. A. 68.

[49] Jeffersonville, M. & I. R. Co. v. Riley, 39 Ind. 568; Peniston v. Chicago, St. L. & N. O. R. Co., 34 La. Ann. 777, 44 Am. Rep. 444.

[50] Romine v. Evansville & T. H. R. Co., 24 Ind. App. 230, 56 N. E. 245; Tilden v. Rhode Island Co., 27 R. I. 482, 63 Atl. 675; Whalen v. Consolidated Traction Co., 61 N. J. Law, 606, 40 Atl. 645, 41 L. R. A. 836, 68 Am. St. Rep. 723; Nelson v. Southern Pac. Co., 18 Utah, 244, 55 Pac. 364; Previsich v. Butte Electric Ry. Co., 47 Mont. 170, 131 Pac. 25.

SAME—SERVANTS OF THE CARRIER

183. The highest practicable care must be exercised by the carrier in securing servants proper in skill and character and sufficient in number. The carrier is responsible for the acts of his servants within the scope of their authority

Employment of Proper Servants

It would be a queer rule of law that would permit the carrier to exercise a slighter degree of care in selecting its human instrumentalities than it must employ as to inanimate agencies. So the carrier must exercise the same degree of care in selecting servants [51] as it is required to use in providing machinery. The carrier must use this care in ascertaining the fitness of his servants for the duties assigned to them, or answer for such negligence. This applies, not only to the servant's mechanical fitness, but also to his character and habits.[52] It would clearly be negligence, for example, for a carrier to employ one as a passenger engineer, with knowledge of his utter lack of sobriety, just as it would be to employ one so color-blind that he cannot distinguish the color of signals. It would, of course, be negligence to retain a servant, after knowledge of his unfitness, though he was a proper servant when hired by the carrier.[53] The carrier's servants, too, must be sufficient in number for the traffic to be handled, however competent may be each individual employé.[54]

Liability of Carrier for Acts of Servant

By the well-known rules of agency and master and servant, the carrier is liable for the acts of his agents and servants within

[51] Anderson v. Scholey, 114 Ind. 553, 17 N. E. 125; Dean v. St. Paul Union Depot Co., 41 Minn. 360, 43 N. W. 54, 5 L. R. A. 442, 16 Am. St. Rep. 703; Long v. Chicago, K. & W. R. Co., 48 Kan. 28, 28 Pac. 977, 15 L. R. A. 319, 30 Am. St. Rep. 271; Pennsylvania R. Co. v. Books, 57 Pa. 339, 98 Am. Dec. 229; Stokes v. Saltonstall, 13 Pet. (U. S.) 181, 10 L. Ed. 115; Schafer v. Gilmer, 13 Nev. 330; Crofts v. Waterhouse, 3 Bing. (Eng.) 319; Olsen v. Citizens' Ry. Co., 152 Mo. 426, 54 S. W. 470; Blumenthal v. Union Electric Ry. Co., 129 Iowa, 322, 105 N. W. 588; Spooner v. Old Colony St. Ry. Co., 190 Mass. 132, 76 S. E. 660.

[52] See cases cited in preceding note.

[53] Bass v. Chicago & N. W. Ry. Co., 42 Wis. 654, 24 Am. Rep. 437; Clegnorn v. New York Cent. & H. R. R. Co., 56 N. Y. 44, 15 Am. Rep. 375; Gasway v. Atlanta & W. P. R. Co., 58 Ga. 216.

[54] See Hamline v. Houston, W. S. & P. F. R. Co., 14 Daly (N. Y.) 144; Means v. Carolina Cent. R. Co., 124 N. C. 574, 32 S. E. 960, 45 L. R. A. 164. In some of the states statutes have been passed regulating the size of train crews.

the scope of their authority.[55] And this is true, however careful the carrier may have been in selecting, training, and instructing such employé.[56] Pro hac vice, the act of the servant becomes the act of the master, who, receiving the benefits of such act, must also bear its burdens. This is true of corporate masters as well as of natural persons.[57]

The expression "scope of employment" is used in a broad sense here, and if the act in question falls within it, the master is liable for its proximate consequences, even though he may have expressly forbidden such acts.[58] Thus a passenger engineer may have been specially warned not to exceed a certain speed over a trestle, and yet if he dangerously exceed this instructed speed and the train is wrecked, the carrier is responsible to an injured passenger. The negligent act, though forbidden by the carrier master, was yet within the scope of the employment of the engineer servant. The negligence of the servant under similar circumstances is the negligence of the master. When, however, the servant's act is one entirely outside of the scope of his employment, he is, as to such act, merely an individual, and not a servant of the master, and the master thereby incurs no liability.[59]

[55] Hoffman v. New York Cent. & H. R. R. Co., 87 N. Y. 25, 41 Am. Rep. 337; Cleveland, C., C. & I. R. Co. v. Walrath, 38 Ohio St. 461, 43 Am. Rep. 433; Thorpe v. New York Cent. & H. R. R. Co., 76 N. Y. 402, 32 Am. Rep. 325; Pennsylvania Co. v. Roy, 102 U. S. 451, 26 L. Ed. 141; article, 25 Am. Law Rev. 569. See Edwards v. Railway Co., L. R. 5 C. P. (Eng.) 445; Grand Rapids & I. R. Co. v. Ellison, 117 Ind. 234, 20 N. E. 135; Philadelphia & D R. R. Co. v. Derby, 14 How. (U. S.) 468, 14 L. Ed. 502; Baltimore & O. Ry. Co. v. Leapley, 65 Md. 571, 4 Atl. 891; Taillon v. Mears, 29 Mont. 161, 74 Pac. 421, 1 Ann. Cas. 613; Texas Midland R. R. v. Monroe (Tex. Civ. App.) 155 S. W. 973.

[56] See cases cited in preceding note.

[57] See cases cited in note 55, in practically all of which the carrier was a corporation. See, also, Bass v. Chicago & N. W. Ry. Co., 36 Wis. 450, 17 Am. Rep. 495; Louisville & N. R. Co. v. Ballard, 85 Ky. 307, 3 S. W. 530, 7 Am. St. Rep. 600.

[58] Philadelphia & D. R. R. Co. v. Derby, 14 How. (U. S.) 468, 14 L. Ed. 502. Fitzsimmons v. Milwaukee, L. S. & W. Ry. Co., 98 Mich. 257, 57 N. W. 127; Baltimore & O. R. Co. v. Leapley, 65 Md. 571, 4 Atl. 891; Heenrich v. Pullman Palace Car Co. (D. C.) 20 Fed. 100; St. Louis & S. F. Ry. Co. v. Ryan, 56 Ark. 245, 19 S. W. 839.

[59] McGilvray v. West End St. Ry. Co., 164 Mass. 122, 41 N. E. 116; Owens v. Wilmington & W. R. Co., 126 N. C. 139, 35 S. E. 259, 78 Am. St. Rep. 642; Walker v. Hannibal & St. J. R. Co., 121 Mo. 575, 26 S. W. 360, 24 L. R. A. 363, 42 Am. St. Rep. 547; Goodloe v. Memphis & C. R. Co., 107 Ala. 233, 18 South. 166, 29 L. R. A. 729, 54 Am. St. Rep. 67; Candiff v. Louisville, N. O & T. Ry. Co., 42 La. Ann. 477, 7 South. 601; Cincinnati, H. & I. R. Co. v Carper, 112 Ind. 26, 13 N. E. 122, 14 N. E. 352, 2 Am. St. Rep. 144.

SAME—PROTECTION OF THE PASSENGER

184. The carrier must exercise the highest degree of practicable care to protect the passenger against the violence and assaults of his fellow passengers or outsiders.

The carrier is liable for assaults on passengers by the carrier's servants while engaged in performing their duties, even though such assaults may be, strictly speaking, outside of the scope of the servants' employment.

Assaults by Fellow Passengers or Outsiders

The carrier's high degree of care is not limited to preventing injuries due to the carrier's own operations, but this duty extends further to protecting passengers from injury and insult at the hands of others.[60] The passenger, by becoming such, places himself in the control of the carrier, and to the carrier he can and must look to safeguard him from the acts of others, whether these be his fellow passengers or strangers. For such injury, then, due to the carrier's failure to exercise the highest degree of care in protecting the passenger, the carrier becomes liable.[61]

In such cases, the fellow passenger or stranger in no sense acts for the carrier, and his acts impose no liability on the carrier; but the actionable negligence of the carrier consists in failing to prevent such person from doing violence or offering an insult to the passenger.[62] It therefore follows that if, by the use of the

[60] Evansville & I. R. Co. v. Darting, 6 Ind. App. 375, 33 N. E. 636; King v. Ohio & M. R. Co. (C. C.) 22 Fed. 413; Louisville & N. R. Co. v. McEwan, 51 S. W. 619, 21 Ky. Law Rep. 487; PITTSBURGH, FT. W. & C. RY. CO. v. HINDS, 53 Pa. 512, 91 Am. Dec. 224, Dobie Cas. Bailments and Carriers, 334; New Orleans, St. L. & C. R. Co. v. Burke, 53 Miss. 200, 24 Am. Rep. 689; Felton v. Chicago, R. I. & P. R. Co., 69 Iowa, 577, 29 N. W. 618; Britton v. Atlanta & C. A. L. Ry. Co., 88 N. C. 536, 43 Am. Rep. 749; Putnam v. Broadway & S. A. R. Co., 55 N. Y. 108, 14 Am. Rep. 190; Batton v. South & N. A. R. Co., 77 Ala. 591, 54 Am. Rep. 80; Chicago & A. R. Co. v. Pillsbury, 123 Ill. 9, 14 N. E. 22, 5 Am. St. Rep. 483; Pittsburg & C. R. Co. v. Pillow, 76 Pa. 510, 18 Am. Rep. 424; Koch v. Brooklyn Heights R. Co., 75 App. Div. 282, 78 N. Y. Supp. 99; Cobb v. Boston El. Ry. Co., 179 Mass. 212, 60 N. E. 476; Southern R. Co. v. Lee, 167 Ala. 268, 52 South. 648; Seale v. Boston Elevated R. Co., 214 Mass. 59, 100 N. E. 1020.

[61] See cases cited in preceding note. See, also, Lucy v. Chicago G. W. Ry. Co., 64 Minn. 7, 65 N. W. 944, 31 L. R. A. 551; West Memphis Packet Co. v. White, 99 Tenn. 256, 41 S. W. 583, 38 L. R. A. 427; Holly v. Atlanta St. R. R., 61 Ga. 215, 34 Am. Rep. 97; United Railways & Electric Co. of Baltimore v. State, to Use of Deane, 93 Md. 619, 49 Atl. 923, 54 L. R. A. 942, 86 Am. St. Rep. 453.

[62] Wood v. Louisville & N. R. Co., 42 S. W. 349, 19 Ky. Law Rep. 924;

requisite care such injury could not have been foreseen and prevented, then no liability attaches to the carrier.[63] Knowledge of the danger, or circumstances which should have imported such knowledge, on the part of the carrier, is thus always a condition precedent to the carrier's liability.

Thus, if a passenger, whose conduct had been entirely decorous and who gave no signs whatever to indicate that he would be disorderly, should suddenly strike a fellow passenger occupying the same seat with him, no liability would attach to the carrier. If such passenger, however, had been drunk and disorderly to an extent that the carrier knew or should have known of it, or if with threats he brandished a revolver in the presence of the carrier's servants, or showed unmistakable signs of violent insanity before the assault, this would import negligence on the carrier's part, rendering him liable for the wrong. In one case,[64] when a number of persons became disorderly on the train, it was held that this should have been quelled, even though it involved the stopping of the train and the conductor's summoning the train crew and some of the passengers to his assistance. Particularly keen is this duty of the carrier to protect female passengers from indecent assault or from insulting or immodest language.[65] There is no such privity between a railway company and a passenger or stranger so as to make it liable for the wrongful acts of the passenger or stranger.[66] But if a passenger receives injury, which might have been reasonably anticipated or naturally expected, from

Meyer v. St. Louis, I. M. & S. R. Co., 54 Fed. 116, 4 C. C. A. 221; Baltimore & O. R. Co. v. Barger, 80 Md. 30, 30 Atl. 561, 26 L. R. A. 220, 45 Am. St. Rep. 319; Partridge v. Woodland Steamboat Co., 66 N. J. Law, 290, 49 Atl. 726; Southern Ry. Co. v. O'Bryan, 112 Ga. 127, 37 S. E. 161; PITTSBURGH, FT. W. & C. RY. CO. v. HINDS, 53 Pa. 512, 91 Am. Dec. 224, Dobie Cas. Bailments and Carriers, 334; Spires v. Atlantic Coast Line R. Co., 92 S. C. 564, 75 S. E. 950.

63 Sullivan v. Jefferson Ave. Ry. Co., 133 Mo. 1, 34 S. W. 566, 32 L. R. A. 167; Connell's Ex'rs v. Chesapeake & O. Ry. Co., 93 Va. 44, 24 S. E. 467, 32 L. R. A. 792, 57 Am. St. Rep. 786; Galveston, H. & S. A. R. Co. v. Long, 13 Tex. Civ. App. 664, 36 S. W. 485; Lake Erie & W. R. Co. v. Arnold, 26 Ind. App. 190, 59 N. E. 394; Clarke's Adm'r v. Louisville & N. R. Co., 101 Ky. 34, 39 S. W. 840, 18 Ky. Law Rep. 1082, 36 L. R. A. 123; Id., 49 S. W. 1120, 20 Ky. Law Rep. 1839; Nute v. Boston & M. R. R., 214 Mass. 184, 100 N. E. 1099.

64 PITTSBURGH, FT. W. & C. RY. CO. v. HINDS, 53 Pa. 512, 91 Am. Dec. 224, Dobie Cas. Bailments and Carriers, 334.

65 Lucy v. Chicago G. W. Ry. Co., 64 Minn. 7, 65 N. W. 944, 31 L. R. A. 551; Segal v. St. Louis Southwestern R. Co., 35 Tex. Civ. App. 517, 80 S. W. 233; Batton v. South & N. A. R. Co., 77 Ala. 591, 54 Am. Rep. 80.

66 PITTSBURGH, FT. W. & C. RY. CO. v. HINDS, 53 Pa. 512, 91 Am. Dec. 224, Dobie Cas. Bailments and Carriers, 334. Nor will the wrong or neg-

one who is improperly received, or permitted to continue as a passenger, the carrier is then responsible.[67]

Assaults on Passengers by the Carrier's Servants

So keen would be the wrong otherwise resulting that the carrier is held liable when the assault is committed by the carrier's servant while engaged in performing his duties, even though the assault was prompted by malice or vindictiveness toward the passenger, and was not strictly within the scope of the servant's employment.[68] In such cases a sound public policy makes the car-

ligence of the carrier be imputed to the passenger, so as to bar his remedy against a third person. Little v. Hackett, 116 U. S. 366, 6 Sup. Ct. 391, 29 L. Ed. 652.

[67] Putnam v. Broadway & S. A. R. Co., 55 N. Y. 108, 14 Am. Rep. 190; Flint v. Norwich & N. Y. Transp. Co., 34 Conn. 554, 6 Blatchf. 158, Fed. Cas. No. 4,873; PITTSBURGH, FT. W. & C. RY. CO. v. HINDS, 53 Pa. 512, 91 Am. Dec. 224, Dobie Cas. Bailments and Carriers, 334; Spohn v. Missouri Pac. Ry. Co., 87 Mo. 74; Cobb v. Great Western Ry. Co. (1894) App. Cas. (Eng.) 419, 63 L. J. Q. B. 629. See cases cited in note 62.

[68] Fick v. Chicago & N. W. Ry. Co., 68 Wis. 469, 32 N. W. 527, 60 Am. Rep. 878; Bryant v. Rich, 106 Mass. 180, 8 Am. Rep. 311; Craker v. Chicago & N. W. Ry. Co., 36 Wis. 657, 17 Am. Rep. 504; Louisville & N. R. Co. v. Ballard, 85 Ky. 307, 3 S. W. 530, 7 Am. St. Rep. 600; Wabash Ry. Co. v. Savage, 110 Ind. 156, 9 N. E. 85; Heenrich v. Pullman Palace Car Co. (D. C.) 20 Fed. 100; Ramsden v. Boston & A. R. Co., 104 Mass. 117, 6 Am. Rep. 200; Chicago & E. R. Co. v. Flexman, 103 Ill. 546, 42 Am. Rep. 33. In some cases the fact of the retention of the employé by the carrier after knowledge of the wrongful act is deemed material, as indicating ratification. Goddard v. Grand Trunk Ry. of Canada, 57 Me. 202, 2 Am. Rep. 39; Bass v. Chicago & N. W. Ry. Co., 42 Wis. 654, 24 Am. Rep. 437. In Bryant v. Rich, 106 Mass. 180, 8 Am. Rep. 311, where the plaintiff, a passenger on a steamboat, was assaulted and injured by the steward and some of the table waiters, the defendant, as a common carrier, was held liable for the injury. In Craker v. Chicago & N. W. Ry. Co., 36 Wis. 657, 17 Am. Rep. 504, where the conductor of a railroad train kissed a female passenger against her will, the court, in an elaborate opinion, held the railroad company liable for compensatory damages. It is there said: "We cannot think there is a question of the respondent's right to recover against the appellant for a tort which was a breach of the contract of carriage." In Sherley v. Billings, 8 Bush (Ky.) 147, 8 Am. Rep. 451, where a passenger on defendant's boat was assaulted and injured by an officer on the boat, the defendant was held liable. See, also, McKinley v. Chicago & N. W. R. Co., 44 Iowa, 314, 24 Am. Rep. 748, and New Orleans, St. L. & C. R. Co. v. Burke, 53 Miss. 200, 24 Am. Rep. 689; Chicago & E. R. Co. v. Flexman, 103 Ill. 546, 42 Am. Rep. 33. In Goddard v. Grand Trunk Ry. of Canada, 57 Me. 202, 2 Am. Rep. 39, in discussing this question, the court says: "The carrier's obligation is to carry his passenger safely and properly, and to treat him respectfully; and, if he intrusts the performance of this duty to his servants, the law holds him responsible for the manner in which they execute the trust. * * * He must not only protect his passengers against the violence and insults of strangers and copassengers, but, a fortiori, against the violence and insults of his own serv-

rier's duty to the passenger practically absolute. So helpless is the passenger under such circumstances, when his natural protectors turn against him, that even though the servant turns entirely away from his employment and is actuated only by his own evil motives, this is no defense to the carrier.[69]

The rule has been most frequently applied in cases of assaults upon passengers while in trains by conductors and brakemen,[70] while in a number of cases the victims have been women.[71] In a leading case,[72] holding the carrier liable when a woman passenger was unwillingly and forcibly kissed by a conductor, the court used this striking analogy: "If one hire out his dog to guard sheep against wolves, and the dog sleep while the wolf makes way with a sheep, the owner is liable; but if the dog play wolf, and devour a sheep, the owner is not liable. The bare statement of the proposition seems a reductio ad absurdum." In flagrant cases of unjustifiable assaults on passengers, the courts have deemed the wrong so gross that not only compensatory, but punitive, damages have been granted against the carrier.[73]

ants. If this duty to the passenger is not performed,—if this protection is not furnished, but, on the contrary, the passenger is assaulted and insulted through the negligence of the carrier's servant, the carrier is necessarily responsible." Chicago & E. R. Co. v. Flexman, 103 Ill. 546, 42 Am. Rep. 33.

[69] Dennis v. Pittsburgh & C. S. R. R., 165 Pa. 624, 31 Atl. 52; Wabash Ry. Co. v. Savage, 110 Ind. 156, 9 N. E. 85; Smith v. Norfolk & W. Ry. Co., 48 W. Va. 69, 35 S. E. 834; Atchison, T. & S. F. R. Co. v. Henry, 55 Kan. 715, 41 Pac. 952, 29 L. R. A. 465; Lampkin v. Louisville & N. R. Co., 106 Ala. 287, 17 South. 448; Lafitte v. New Orleans, C. & L. R. Co., 43 La. Ann. 34, 8 South. 701, 12 L. R. A. 337; Goddard v. Grand Trunk Ry. of Canada, 57 Me. 202, 2 Am. Rep. 39; Citizens' St. Ry. Co. v. Clark, 33 Ind. App. 190, 71 N. E. 53, 104 Am. St. Rep. 249; Alexander v. New Orleans Ry. & Light Co., 129 La. 959, 57 South. 283.

[70] See cases cited in preceding note.

[71] Campbell v. Pullman Palace Car Co. (C. C.) 42 Fed. 484; Pullman's Palace Car Co. v. Campbell, 154 U. S. 513, 14 Sup. Ct. 1151, 38 L. Ed. 1069; Keene v. Lizardi, 6 La. 315, 26 Am. Dec. 478; Texas & P. R. Co. v. Tarkington, 27 Tex. Civ. App. 353, 66 S. W. 137; Louisville & N. R. Co. v. Ballard, 85 Ky. 307, 3 S. W. 530, 7 Am. St. Rep. 600.

[72] Craker v. Chicago & N. W. Ry. Co., 36 Wis. 657, 17 Am. Rep. 504.

[73] Goddard v. Grand Trunk Ry. of Canada, 57 Me. 202, 2 Am. Rep. 39; East Tennessee, V. & G. Ry. Co. v. Fleetwood, 90 Ga. 23, 15 S. E. 778; Louisville & N. R. Co. v. Ballard, 85 Ky. 307, 3 S. W. 530, 7 Am. St. Rep. 600; Baltimore & O. R. Co. v. Barger, 80 Md. 23, 30 Atl. 560, 26 L. R. A. 220, 45 Am. St. Rep. 319. See post, § 209.

SAME—CONTRIBUTORY NEGLIGENCE OF THE PASSENGER

185. Even though the carrier has been negligent, resulting in injury to the passenger, there can be no recovery when the negligence of the passenger himself has proximately contributed to the injury. Negligence of the passenger in such cases is the failure to exercise ordinary care.

In General

It is a wise principle of jurisprudence that one cannot hold another responsible for an injury which one has brought upon oneself.[74] One is in general responsible for the consequences of one's own acts, and if these acts bring injury to their author, the law properly withholds the right of recovering damages for such injury from another. The principle is a general one, but finds frequent application in actions by passengers against the carrier.

In general, therefore, though the carrier's negligence is partially responsible for the injury, the carrier escapes liability if the passenger, too, has been negligent and his negligence has proximately contributed to the injury.[75] When the negligence of the carrier and that of the passenger both concurred in producing the injury, the law will not endeavor to apportion the comparative responsibility, but will leave the passenger without remedy, viewing him as the author of his own misfortune.[76] Of course, if the car-

[74] Butterfield v. Forrester, 11 East (Eng.) 60; Gibbon v. Paynton, 4 Burr. (Eng.) 2298; Gorden v. Butts, 2 N. J. Law, 334; Rathbun v. Payne, 19 Wend. (N. Y.) 399; Victor Coal Co. v. Muir, 20 Colo. 321, 38 Pac. 378, 26 L. R. A. 435, 46 Am. St. Rep. 299.

[75] Central Ry. Co. v. Smith, 74 Md. 212, 21 Atl. 706; Odom v. St. Louis S. W. R. Co., 45 La. Ann. 1201, 14 South. 734, 23 L. R. A. 152; Renneker v. South Carolina Ry. Co., 20 S. C. 219; Little v. Hackett, 116 U. S. 366, 6 Sup. Ct. 391, 29 L. Ed. 652; Graham v. McNeill, 20 Wash. 466, 55 Pac. 631, 43 L. R. A. 300, 72 Am. St. Rep. 121; Richmond & D. R. Co. v. Pickleseimer, 85 Va. 798, 10 S. E. 44; Fisher v. West Virginia & P. R. Co., 42 W. Va. 183, 24 S. E. 570, 33 L. R. A. 69; Blevins v. Atchison, T. & S. F. R. Co., 3 Okl. 512, 41 Pac. 92; Sweet v. Birmingham R. & Electric Co., 145 Ala. 667, 39 South. 767; Weber v. Kansas City Cable Ry. Co., 100 Mo. 194, 12 S. W. 804, 13 S. W. 587, 7 L. R. A. 819, 18 Am. St. Rep. 541; PENNSYLVANIA R. CO. v. ASPELL, 23 Pa. 147, 62 Am. Dec. 323, Dobie Cas. Bailments and Carriers, 336; FLETCHER v. BOSTON & M. R. R., 187 Mass. 463, 73 N. E. 552, 105 Am. St. Rep. 414, Dobie Cas. Bailments and Carriers, 335; Ward v. International R. Co., 206 N. Y. 83, 99 N. E. 262, Ann. Cas. 1914A, 1170; Dawson v. Maryland Electric Ry., 119 Md. 373, 86 Atl. 1041.

[76] Waterbury v. Chicago, M. & St. P. Ry. Co., 104 Iowa, 32, 73 N. W. 341;

rier is not negligent, there is no liability, and the defense of the passenger's contributory negligence is unnecessary; but when the negligence of the carrier is shown, causing injury to the passenger, this makes out a case of liability, and the defense of contributory negligence is then highly important, so that upon it the whole case may turn.

Test of Passenger's Negligence

The passenger is negligent, in this connection, when he fails to exercise ordinary care, which is usually judged by that care which the reasonably prudent man would exercise for his safety under similar circumstances.[77] If the passenger fails to use such care, he is negligent; if he does exercise such care, there is no negligence, in which case the defense of contributory negligence necessarily falls to the ground. Ordinary care is, of course, a relative term, to be judged according to the varying circumstances of each case.[78]

So many varying factors enter into and complicate this problem that it is possible here to mention briefly only a few representative cases. A person in normal possession of his senses must make reasonable use of them to learn of danger, particularly if there are indications that such danger is imminent or impending.[79] Again an act on the part of one whose ability to use his limbs or whose senses of sight and hearing are impaired might be negligence, while the same act might not be negligence to one whose unim-

Conroy v. Chicago, St. P., M. & O. R. Co., 96 Wis. 243, 70 N. W. 486, 38 L. R. A. 419; Coburn v. Philadelphia, W. & B. R. Co., 198 Pa. 436, 48 Atl. 265; Chattanooga, R. & C. R. Co. v. Huggins, 89 Ga. 494, 15 S. E. 848; Ward v. International R. Co., 206 N. Y. 83, 99 N. E. 262, Ann. Cas. 1914A, 1170.

77 Galloway v. Chicago, R. I. & P. Ry. Co., 87 Iowa, 458, 54 N. W. 447; West Chicago St. R. Co. v. Manning, 170 Ill. 417, 48 N. E. 958; Bland v. Southern Pac. R. Co., 65 Cal. 626, 4 Pac. 672; Clerc v. Morgan's Louisiana & T. R. & S. S. Co., 107 La. 370, 31 So. 886, 90 Am. St. Rep. 319; Texas & P. Ry. Co. v. Best, 66 Tex. 116, 18 S. W. 224; Topp v. United Rys. & Electric Co., 99 Md. 630, 59 Atl. 52, 1 Ann. Cas. 912; Carroll v. Charleston & S. R. Co., 65 S. C. 378, 43 S. E. 870; Illinois Cent. R. Co. v. Dallas' Adm'x, 150 Ky. 442, 150 S. W. 536; Haas v. Wichita R. & Light Co., 89 Kan. 613, 132 Pac. 195, 48 L. R. A. (N. S.) 974; Illinois Cent. R. Co. v. Dallas' Adm'x, 150 Ky. 442, 150 S. W. 536.

78 Protheno v. Citizens' St. Ry. Co., 134 Ind. 431, 33 N. E. 765; Mitchell v Southern Pac. R. Co., 87 Cal. 62, 25 Pac. 245, 11 L. R. A. 130; Seymour v Citizens' Ry. Co., 114 Mo. 266, 21 S. W. 739; Highland Ave. & B. R. Co. v Donovan, 94 Ala. 299, 10 South. 139; Biggers v. New York Cent. & H. R. R Co., 157 App. Div. 245, 141 N. Y. Supp. 827.

79 Piper v. New York Cent. & H. R. R. Co., 156 N. Y. 224, 50 N. E. 851, 41 L. R. A. 724, 66 Am. St. Rep. 560; Fraser v. California St. Cable Co., 146 Cal. 714, 81 Pac. 29; Illinois Cent. R. Co. v. Davidson, 64 Fed. 301, 12 C. C. A. 118; Biggers v. New York Cent. & H. R. R. Co., 157 App. Div. 245, 141 N. Y. Supp. 827.

paired senses would inform him of danger and enable him to avert it.[80] Crossing railroad tracks would furnish an example of such an act.[81] As to children, they are to be judged according to their age,[82] and children of very tender years cannot be guilty of contributory negligence.[83] Persons who must act quickly in positions fraught with imminent danger are not necessarily guilty of negligence in adopting a perilous alternative merely because the alternative would be unreasonable to one thinking calmly and dispassionately on the subject.[84] Again, this alternative might be reasonable for the purpose of escaping danger, while it would be negligence for the passenger to adopt it merely to prevent annoyance or escape inconvenience.[85] The passenger might avoid the charge of negligence when the particular act was performed in pursuance of instructions from the carrier's servants, who are presumed to appreciate the danger.[86] When, however, the peril is so imminent

[80] Cincinnati, H. & D. Ry. Co. v. Nolan, 8 Ohio Cir. Ct. R. 347; Felton v. Horner, 97 Tenn. 579, 37 S. W. 696; Young v. Missouri Pac. Ry. Co., 93 Mo. App. 267; Talbert v. Charleston & Western C. Ry. Co., 72 S. C. 137, 51 S. E. 564; Denver & R. G. R. Co. v. Derry, 47 Colo. 584, 108 Pac. 172, 27 L. R. A. (N. S.) 761; Wilson v. Detroit United Ry., 167 Mich. 107, 132 N. W. 762.

[81] See Gonzales v. New York & H. R. Co., 33 N. Y. Super. Ct. 57; Wilson v. Detroit United Ry., 167 Mich. 107, 132 N. W. 762.

[82] Denison & S. R. Co. v. Carter, 98 Tex. 196, 82 S. W. 782, 107 Am. St. Rep. 626; Chicago & A. R. Co. v. Nelson, 153 Ill. 89, 38 N. E. 560; Kirchner v. Oil City St. R. Co., 210 Pa. 45, 59 Atl. 270; Van Natta v. People's Street Ry. & Electric Light & Power Co., 133 Mo. 13, 34 S. W. 505; Little Rock Traction & Electric Co. v. Nelson, 66 Ark. 494, 52 S. W. 7; East Tennessee, V. & G. Ry. Co. v. Hughes, 92 Ga. 388, 17 S. E. 949; Kambour v. Boston & M. R. R., 77 N. H. 33, 86 Atl. 624, 45 L. R. A. (N. S.) 1188.

[83] Erie City Pass. Ry. Co. v. Schuster, 113 Pa. 412, 6 Atl. 269, 57 Am. Rep. 471; Buck v. People's Street Ry., Electric Light & Power Co., 46 Mo. App. 555.

[84] Bischoff v. People's Ry. Co., 121 Mo. 216, 25 S. W. 908; Jones v. Boyce, 1 Starkie (Eng.) 493; Ladd v. Foster (D. C.) 31 Fed. 827; Buel v. New York Cent. R. Co., 31 N. Y. 314, 88 Am. Dec. 271; St. Joseph & G. I. R. Co. v. Hedge, 44 Neb. 448, 62 N. W. 887; Gannon v. New York, N. H. & H. R. Co., 173 Mass. 40, 52 N. E. 1075, 43 L. R. A. 833; Steverman v. Boston Elevated Ry. Co., 205 Mass. 508, 91 N. E. 919; Fulghum v. Atlantic Coast Line R. Co., 158 N. C. 555, 74 S. E. 584, 39 L. R. A. (N. S.) 558; Smith v. Chicago City R. Co., 169 Ill. App. 570.

[85] Adams v. Railway Co., L. R. 4 C. P. (Eng.) 739; Lake Shore & M. S. Ry. Co. v. Bangs, 47 Mich. 470, 11 N. W. 276; Denver & R. G. R. Co. v. Bedell, 11 Colo. App. 139, 54 Pac. 280; PENNSYLVANIA R. CO. v. ASPELL, 23 Pa. 147, 62 Am. Dec. 323, Dobie Cas. Bailments and Carriers, 336.

[86] Indianapolis & St. L. R. Co. v. Horst, 93 U. S. 291, 23 L. Ed. 898; Clinton v. Root, 58 Mich. 182, 24 N. W. 667, 55 Am. Rep. 671; Irish v. Northern Pac. R. Co., 4 Wash. 48, 29 Pac. 845, 31 Am. St. Rep. 899; Montgomery & E. R. Co. v. Stewart, 91 Ala. 421, 8 South. 708; Killmeyer v. Wheeling Traction Co. (W. Va.) 77 S. E. 908.

and obvious that no prudent man would do the particular act, even with such instructions, then the act is negligence; for such instructions can never justify an obviously foolhardy act.[87]

Passenger's Negligence Must Proximately Contribute to the Injury

The defense of contributory negligence involves two separate elements, as indicated by the two words of the expression: First, the negligence of the passenger; secondly, such negligence must have contributed to the injury.[88] Of these, the latter is just as essential as the former, in order that the defense may be a valid one. When the carrier's negligence and the injury flowing therefrom are admitted, however materially the passenger's conduct may have contributed to the injury, this is no excuse to the carrier, unless such conduct constitutes legal negligence on the part of the passenger.[89] The converse is equally true: However negligent the passenger may have been, this again does not relieve the carrier from liability unless the particular negligence of the passenger materially contributed to producing the injury.[90] The causal connection, then, between the passenger's negligence and the injury, must be shown in order that the defense of contributory negligence may be made out. The law does not bar a recovery against a negligent carrier for the consequences thereof, simply because the passenger's conduct was somewhat instrumental in bringing on such injury, nor merely because of the passenger's negligence disassociated from the injury. Both must concur. Thus, when a passenger was injured by a car backing over him after he had left the

[87] Hunter v. Cooperstown & S. V. R. Co., 126 N. Y. 18, 26 N. E. 958, 12 L. R. A. 429; Aufdenberg v. St. Louis, I. M. & S. Ry. Co., 132 Mo. 565, 34 S. W. 485; Chicago & A. R. Co. v. Gore, 202 Ill. 188, 66 N. E. 1063, 95 Am. St. Rep. 224; Southern R. Co. v. Bandy, 120 Ga. 463, 47 S. E. 923, 102 Am. St. Rep. 112.

[88] See summary, 3 Hutch. Carr. § 1239; Baltimore & P. R. Co. v. Jones, 95 U. S. 439, 24 L. Ed. 506.

[89] Chicago & A. R. Co. v. Woolridge, 32 Ill. App. 237; Western Maryland R. Co. v. Herold, 74 Md. 510, 22 Atl. 323, 14 L. R. A. 75; Chesapeake & O. Ry. Co. v. Clowes, 93 Va. 189, 24 S. E. 833; Bronson v. Oakes, 76 Fed. 734, 22 C. C. A. 520; Wylde v. Northern R. Co. of New Jersey, 53 N. Y. 156; Gee v. Ry. Co., L. R. 8 Q. B. (Eng.) 161; Hesse v. Meriden, S. & C. Tramway Co., 75 Conn. 571, 54 Atl. 299.

[90] Dewire v. Boston & M. R. R. Co., 148 Mass. 343, 19 N. E. 523, 2 L. R. A. 166; Lehigh Val. R. Co. v. Greiner, 113 Pa. 600, 6 Atl. 246; Kansas & A. V. R. Co. v. White, 67 Fed. 481, 14 C. C. A. 483; Jones v. Chicago, St. P., M. & O. Ry. Co., 43 Minn. 279, 45 N. W. 444; Distler v. Long Island R. Co., 151 N. Y. 424, 45 N. E. 937, 35 L. R. A. 762; Hickey v. Chicago City Ry. Co., 148 Ill. App. 197; Fremont, E. & M. V. R. Co. v. Root, 49 Neb. 900, 69 N. W. 397; Kearney v. Seaboard Air Line R. Co., 158 N. C. 521, 74 S. E. 593.

train, it was held that his riding on the platform (even if it be conceded to be negligent) was no defense, for this in no wise contributed to the injury later received.[91]

SAME—SAME—CONTRIBUTORY NEGLIGENCE A QUESTION OF LAW OR OF FACT

186. The question of contributory negligence is ordinarily one of fact for the jury, under general instructions from the court. When, however, (1) the facts are not disputed, and (2) the deduction to be drawn from those facts is so clear that but one conclusion could fairly be made by reasonable men, the question becomes one of law for the court.

Question of Law or of Fact

In the great majority of cases, the question of contributory negligence is one of fact for the jury; it is only in the rarer and somewhat exceptional case that the question is one of law for the court. When the testimony is conflicting, so that there is dispute as to the facts, then there is cordial agreement among the courts that it is peculiarly the province of the jury to sift and weigh the testimony, and the question is one for the jury to decide.[92] It is sometimes said that when the facts are clear the question is then solely one of law; but this is quite inaccurate. It is the jury's task to pass, not only on what are the facts, but also on this question: Do these facts constitute a failure on the passenger's part to exercise for his safety the ordinary care of a reasonably prudent man? If this question is an open one—that is, if reasonable men might be expected to differ on it—then the decision of that question is one for the particular jury in the instant case.[93] If, therefore, either the facts [94] or the deduction to

[91] Gadsden & A. U. Ry. Co. v. Causler, 97 Ala. 235, 12 South. 439.

[92] Chicago & A. R. Co. v. Byrum, 153 Ill. 131, 38 N. E. 578; Morgan v. Southern Pac. Co., 95 Cal. 501, 30 Pac. 601; Pittsburg & C. R. Co. v. Andrews, 39 Md. 329, 17 Am. Rep. 368; Cleveland v. New Jersey Steamboat Co., 53 Hun, 638, 7 N. Y. Supp. 28; Krock v. Boston Elevated R. Co., 214 Mass. 398, 101 N. E. 968.

[93] Richmond & D. R. Co. v. Powers, 149 U. S. 43, 13 Sup. Ct. 748, 37 L. Ed. 642; Normile v. Wheeling Traction Co., 57 W. Va. 132, 49 S. E. 1030, 68 L. R. A. 901; Comerford v. New York, N. H. & H. R. Co., 181 Mass. 528, 63 N. E. 936; Denver & R. G. R. Co. v. Spencer, 27 Colo. 313, 61 Pac. 606, 51 L. R. A. 121; Illinois Cent. R. Co. v. Proctor, 89 S. W. 714, 28 Ky. Law Rep. 598; Edgerly v. Union St. R. Co., 67 N. H. 312, 36 Atl. 558; Coburn v. Philadel-

[94] See cases cited in note 92.

be drawn from those facts[95] be not clear, then the question is for the jury.

When, though, the facts are clear (being admitted or proved by uncontradicted evidence), and in addition the question of whether those facts do or do not constitute contributory negligence is also clear, then the question of contributory negligence becomes one of law for the court.[96] If a single conclusion alone can reasonably be drawn, there is then nothing to be submitted to the jury, for it is the function of the court to declare this conclusion as the only one that is under the circumstances permissible. Whether this deduction, however, is so clear as to make the question one of law has in a veritable horde of cases given the courts no end of trouble.[97]

Specific Instances

So vast is the passenger traffic of the modern carrier (particularly the railroad), so prolific has this been of personal injury litigation, and so frequent is the defense of contributory negligence, that a vast body of case law has arisen denying or affirming that certain acts or classes of acts are contributory negligence as a matter of law. This is of great practical importance, and very frequently is of controlling importance, in settling the question of contributory negligence. The cases, though, as might be expected, in the various jurisdictions are frequently far from harmonious. Some brief mention is therefore in order of a few of the most frequent and important of these cases.

The courts have split on the question of whether boarding a

phia, W. & B. R. Co., 198 Pa. 436, 48 Atl. 265; JACKSON v. CRILLY, 16 Colo. 103, 26 Pac. 331, Dobie Cas. Bailments and Carriers, 338; Burnside v. Minneapolis & St. L. R. Co., 110 Minn. 401, 125 N. W. 895; Thorne v. Philadelphia Rapid Transit Co., 237 Pa. 20, 85 Atl. 25; Ft. Worth & D. C. R. Co. v. Taylor (Tex. Civ. App.) 153 S. W. 355.

[95] See cases cited in note 93.

[96] Smith v. Chicago, R. I. & P. R. Co., 55 Iowa, 33, 17 N. W. 398; Goodlett v. Louisville & N. R. Co., 122 U. S. 391, 7 Sup. Ct. 1254, 30 L. Ed. 1230; Shelton's Adm'r v. Louisville & N. R. Co. (Ky.) 39 S. W. 842; Chaffee v. Old Colony R. Co., 17 R. I. 658, 24 Atl. 141; Ricketts v. Birmingham St. Ry. Co., 85 Ala. 600, 5 South. 353; Jacob v. Flint & P. M. R. Co., 105 Mich. 450, 63 N. W. 502; Baltimore Traction Co. of Baltimore City v. State, 78 Md. 409, 28 Atl. 397; JACKSON v. CRILLY, 16 Colo. 103, 26 Pac. 331, Dobie Cas. Bailments and Carriers, 338; Sigl v. Green Bay Traction Co., 149 Wis. 112, 135 N. W. 506, 39 L. R. A. (N. S.) 65; Alabama Great Southern R. Co. v. Gilbert, 6 Ala. App. 372, 60 South. 542; Chapman v. Capital Traction Co., 37 App. D. C. 479.

[97] See cases cited in notes 98, 99, 1-9.

moving train [98] or alighting therefrom [99] is contributory negligence as a matter of law. As the circumstances in this connection vary so widely, depending largely on the person, place, and speed of the train, the better view seems not to regard it as contributory negligence as a matter of law. The same seems to be true of passing from car to car while the train is in motion,[1] of standing in the car under similar circumstances,[2] and of a passenger

[98] Among the representative cases holding that this is contributory negligence as a matter of law are Tobin v. Pennsylvania R. R., 211 Pa. 457, 60 Atl. 999; Denver Ry. Co. v. Pickard, 8 Colo. 163, 6 Pac. 149; Knight v. Pontchartrain R. Co., 26 La. Ann. 402; Pence v. Wabash R. Co., 116 Iowa, 279, 90 N. W. 59; Chaffee v. Old Colony St. R. Co., 17 R. I. 658, 24 Atl. 141. That this is not contributory negligence as a matter of law, see South Chicago City R. Co. v. Dufresne, 200 Ill. 456, 65 N. E. 1075; McKee v. St. Louis Transit Co., 108 Mo. App. 470, 83 S. W. 1013; Atchison, T. & S. F. Ry. Co. v. Holloway, 71 Kan. 1, 80 Pac. 31, 114 Am. St. Rep. 462; Creech v. Charleston & W. C. Ry. Co., 66 S. C. 528, 45 S. E. 86.

[99] That this is contributory negligence as a matter of law is held in Brown v. New York, N. H. & H. R. Co., 181 Mass. 365, 63 N. E. 941; Schiffler v. Chicago & N. W. R. Co., 96 Wis. 141, 71 N. W. 97, 65 Am. St. Rep. 35; Evansville & T. H. R. Co. v. Athon, 6 Ind. App. 295, 33 N. E. 469, 51 Am. St. Rep. 303; Mearns v. Central R. R., of New Jersey, 139 Fed. 543, 71 C. C. A. 331; Boulfrois v. United Traction Co., 210 Pa. 263, 59 Atl. 1007, 105 Am. St. Rep. 809, 2 Ann. Cas. 938. Alighting from a moving car or train is not necessarily contributory negligence as a matter of law: Carr v. Eel River & E. R. Co., 98 Cal. 366, 33 Pac. 213, 21 L. R. A. 354; Hecker v. Chicago & A. R. Co., 110 Mo. App. 162, 84 S. W. 126; New Jersey Traction Co. v. Gardner, 60 N. J. Law, 571, 38 Atl. 669; Pennsylvania Co. v. Marion, 123 Ind. 415, 23 N. E. 973, 7 L. R. A. 687, 18 Am. St. Rep. 330; Simmons v. Seaboard Air-Line Ry., 120 Ga. 255, 47 S. E. 570, 1 Ann. Cas. 777; Wallace v. Third Ave. R. Co., 36 App. Div. 57, 55 N. Y. Supp. 132; Mills v. Missouri, K. & T. Ry. Co. of Texas, 94 Tex. 242, 59 S. W. 874, 55 L. R. A. 497; Chesapeake & O. R. Co. v. Robinson, 149 Ky. 258, 147 S. W. 886; Harris v. Pittsburgh, C., C. & St. L. R. Co., 32 Ind. App. 600, 70 N. E. 407; Louisville & N. R. Co. v. Dilburn (Ala.) 59 South. 438.

[1] This is usually held not to be contributory negligence per se. Chesapeake & O. Ry. Co. v. Clowes, 93 Va. 189, 24 S. E. 833; Bronson v. Oakes, 76 Fed. 734, 22 C. C. A. 520; McIntyre v. New York Cent. R. Co., 37 N. Y. 287; Louisville & N. R. Co. v. Berg's Adm'r, 32 S. W. 616, 17 Ky. Law Rep. 1105. Particularly is this true on modern vestibuled trains. Bronson v. Oakes, 76 Fed. 734, 22 C. C. A. 520; Costikyan v. Rome, W. & O. R. Co., 58 Hun, 590, 12 N. Y. Supp. 683, affirmed 128 N. Y. 633, 29 N. E. 147. In the following cases it is either suggested that passing from car to car while a train is in motion is contributory negligence per se, or held such under the circumstances of the instant case: Bemiss v. New Orleans City & Lake R. Co., 47 La. Ann. 1671, 18 So. 711; Choate v. San Antonio & A. P. Ry. Co., 90 Tex. 82, 36 S. W. 247, 37 S. W. 319; Sawtelle v. Railway Pass. Assur. Co., 15 Blatchf. 216, Fed. Cas. No. 12,392; Hill v. Birmingham Union Ry. Co., 100 Ala. 447, 12 South. 201; Hunter v. Atlantic Coast Line R. R., 72 S. C. 336, 51 S. E. 860, 110 Am. St. Rep. 605.

[2] Not contributory negligence. Gee v. Railway Co., L. R. 8 Q. B. (Eng.)

projecting his arm beyond the window of the car.[3] Crossing railroad tracks to reach a train or leave it is not necessarily contributory negligence;[4] but a passenger is thus negligent who for the same purpose crawls under cars attached to a locomotive.[5] Protruding one's head from a car window is negligence,[6] however, as is one's occupying uselessly and voluntarily an exposed position,[7] and riding, under similar circumstances, on the platform of a moving train.[8] There may be circumstances, however, in the

161; CHICAGO & A. R. CO. v. ARNOL, 144 Ill. 261, 33 N. E. 204, 19 L. R. A. 313, Dobie Cas. Bailments and Carriers, 332; Wylde v. Northern R. Co. of New Jersey, 53 N. Y. 156; Trumbull v. Erickson, 97 Fed. 891, 38 C. C. A. 536; Yazoo & M. V. R. Co. v. Humphrey, 83 Miss. 721, 36 South. 154; Lane v. Spokane Falls & N. Ry. Co., 21 Wash. 119, 57 Pac. 367, 46 L. R. A. 153, 75 Am. St. Rep. 821. But see De Soucey v. Manhattan R. Co. (Com. P. L.) 15 N. Y. Supp. 108; Harris v. Hannibal & St. J. R. Co., 89 Mo. 233, 1 S. W. 325, 58 Am. Rep. 111; Felton v. Horner, 97 Tenn. 579, 37 S. W. 696; Wallace v. Western N. C. R. Co., 98 N. C. 494, 4 S. E. 503, 2 Am. St. Rep. 346; East Tennessee, V. & G. Ry. Co. v. Green, 95 Ga. 736, 22 S. E. 658.

3 Contributory negligence as a matter of law. Georgia Pac. Ry. Co. v. Underwood, 90 Ala. 49, 8 South. 116, 24 Am. St. Rep. 756; Clark's Adm'r v. Louisville & N. R. Co., 101 Ky. 34, 39 S. W. 840, 36 L. R. A. 123; Richmond & D. R. Co. v. Scott, 88 Va. 958, 14 S. E. 763, 16 L. R. A. 91; Union Pac. R. Co. v. Roeser, 69 Neb. 62, 95 N. W. 68. Question for the jury. Clerc v. Morgan's Louisiana & T. R. & S. S. Co., 107 La. 370, 31 South. 886, 90 Am. St. Rep. 319; Georgetown & T. Ry. Co. v. Smith, 25 App. D. C. 259, 5 L. R. A. (N. S.) 274; Spencer v. Milwaukee & P. du C. R. Co., 17 Wis. 487, 84 Am. Dec. 758; McCord v. Atlanta & C. Air Line R. Co., 134 N. C. 53, 45 S. E. 1031; Tucker v. Buffalo Ry. Co., 169 N. Y. 589, 62 N. E. 1101.

4 Baltimore & O. R. Co. v. State to Use of Chambers, 81 Md. 371, 32 Atl. 201; Warner v. Baltimore & O. R. Co., 168 U. S. 339, 18 Sup. Ct. 68, 42 L. Ed. 491; Atchison, T. & S. F. R. Co. v. Shean, 18 Colo. 368, 33 Pac. 108, 20 L. R. A. 729; Betts v. Lehigh Val. R. Co., 191 Pa. 575, 43 Atl. 362, 45 L. R. A. 261.

5 Smith v. Chicago, R. I. & P. R. Co., 55 Iowa, 33, 7 N. W. 398; Memphis & C. R. Co. v. Copeland, 61 Ala. 376.

6 Shelton v. Louisville & N. R. Co., 39 S. W. 842, 19 Ky. Law Rep. 215; Union Pac. Ry. Co. v. Roeser, 69 Neb. 62, 95 N. W. 68; Benedict v. Minneapolis & St. L. R. Co., 86 Minn. 224, 90 N. W. 360, 57 L. R. A. 639, 91 Am. St. Rep. 345; Christensen v. Metropolitan St. Ry. Co., 137 Fed. 708, 70 C. C. A. 657; Huber v. Cedar Rapids & M. C. R. Co., 124 Iowa, 556, 100 N. W. 478.

7 JACKSON v. CRILLY, 16 Colo. 103, 26 Pac. 331, Dobie Cas. Bailments and Carriers, 338; Hewes v. Chicago & E. I. R. Co., 217 Ill. 500, 75 N. E. 515; Garguzza v. Anchor Line, 97 App. Div. 352, 89 N. Y. Supp. 1049; Renaud v. New York, N. H. & H. R. Co., 210 Mass. 553, 97 N. E. 98, 38 L. R. A. (N. S.) 689.

8 Benedict v. Minneapolis & St. L. R. Co., 86 Minn. 224, 90 N. W. 360, 57 L. R. A. 639, 91 Am. St. Rep. 345; Jammison v. Chesapeake & O. Ry. Co., 92 Va. 327, 23 S. E. 758, 53 Am. St. Rep. 813; Meyere v. Nashville, C. & St. L. R., 110 Tenn. 166, 72 S. W. 114; Denny v. North Carolina R. Co., 132 N. C. 340, 43 S. E. 847; Alabama Great Southern R. Co. v. Gilbert, 6 Ala. App. 372, 60 South. 542.

last case, when this is not negligence, as when there is no apparent danger, and the car is full or poorly ventilated, and the passenger needs fresh air.[9]

SAME—SAME—LAST CLEAR CHANCE AND IMPUTATION OF NEGLIGENCE

187. The passenger's contributory negligence is not available as a defense, when the carrier, after knowledge of the peril of the passenger, failed to exercise proper care to avert the injury. This is the doctrine of the "last clear chance."

When the carrier's negligence proximately results in injury to the passenger, the fact that the wrong of a third person also contributed to the injury is no defense. The doctrine of the imputation of the negligence of the father or custodian to a child, that of a husband to the wife, or that of a carrier to a passenger, has been very generally discredited.

Last Clear Chance

The contributory negligence of the passenger is ordinarily a complete defense to the carrier, when the latter is sued for injuries due to the carrier's negligence.[10] This defense ceases to be such, however, when, after the discovery of the danger to which the passenger's negligence has exposed him, the carrier still had an opportunity to avoid the accident by the exercise of requisite care, and yet failed to take advantage of this last clear chance.[11] This doctrine is usually rested on one or both of two grounds. One is that under such circumstances the passenger's negligence becomes a remote cause of the injury, and that the carrier's subsequent negligence is here the proximate cause of the harm, to which

[9] Morgan v. Lake Shore & M. S. R. Co., 138 Mich. 626, 101 N. W. 836, 70 L. R. A. 609.

[10] See ante, § 185.

[11] Radley v. Railway Co., 1 App. Cas. (Eng.) 754; Cincinnati, H. & D. R. Co. v. Kassen, 49 Ohio St. 230, 31 N. E. 282, 16 L. R. A. 674; Chicago City Ry. Co. v. Schmidt, 117 Ill. App. 213, affirmed 217 Ill. 396, 75 N. E. 383; Eikenberry v. St. Louis Transit Co., 103 Mo. App. 442, 80 S. W. 360; Hensler v. Stix, 113 Mo. App. 162, 88 S. W. 108; Woodward v. West Side St. Ry. Co., 71 Wis. 625, 38 N. W. 347; Holmes v. South Pac. Coast Ry. Co., 97 Cal. 161, 31 Pac. 834; Louisville City R. Co. v. Hudgins, 124 Ky. 79, 98 S. W. 275, 30 Ky. Law Rep. 316, 7 L. R. A. (N. S.) 152; Wheeler v. Grand Trunk Ry. Co., 70 N. H. 607, 50 Atl. 103, 54 L. R. A. 955; Townsend v. Houston Electric Co. (Tex. Civ. App.) 154 S. W. 629; Norfolk & A. Terminal Co. v. Rotolo, 195 Fed. 231, 115 C. C. A. 183.

cause alone the law will look. The second ground considers the carrier's negligence in such a case to be, not mere negligence, but rather a willful and wanton wrong; and, in the case of willful or wanton acts (as distinguished from mere negligent acts) it is a general principle that the contributory negligence of the person injured is not a defense.[12] The prior imprudent conduct of the passenger is properly held not to permit any relaxation of the carrier's duty, after the discovery of the danger to which the passenger is thereby exposed.

This doctrine of the last clear chance (originating in Davies v. Mann[13] [1842], the celebrated case of the donkey negligently fettered in the highway injured by the subsequent negligence of the defendant) is of general application. It finds a fruitful field, however, in suits against passenger carriers in spite of strenuous attempts by the latter either to discredit the doctrine or to narrow the field in which it may be applied. Thus, when a passenger negligently places his hand in a place in which it is apt to be injured by a door, he may still recover, if he can show that the carrier's servants with knowledge of his danger, negligently closed the door and injured his hand.[14] Again, the passenger's negligence in boarding a street car was held to be no defense when the carrier's servant negligently failed to stop the car, after knowledge that the passenger was being dragged by the moving car.[15] The doctrine is very frequently invoked against the carrier by nonpassengers injured on the right of way of a railroad.[16]

Imputation of Negligence

It is a sound principle that, when the passenger or other person is injured by the carrier's negligence, the latter cannot escape liability on the ground that the wrong of a third person also concurred in producing the injury.[17] Under such circumstances, the wrong of the third person does not serve to diminish the rights of

[12] That contributory negligence is no defense to the carrier's willful wrong, see Chicago, St. L. & P. R. Co. v. Bills, 118 Ind. 221, 20 N. E. 775; Alabama G. S. R. Co. v. Frazier, 93 Ala. 45, 9 South. 303, 30 Am. St. Rep. 28.

[13] 10 Mees. & W. (Eng.) 546.

[14] Texas & P. Ry. Co. v. Overall, 82 Tex. 247, 18 S. W. 142.

[15] Woodward v. West Side St. Ry. Co., 71 Wis. 625, 38 N. W. 347.

[16] Ward v. Maine Cent. R. Co., 96 Me. 136, 51 Atl. 947; Galveston, H. & S. A. R. Co. v. Zantzinger, 93 Tex. 64, 53 S. W. 379, 47 L. R. A. 282, 77 Am. St. Rep. 829; Reid v. Atlantic & C. Air Line R. Co., 140 N. C. 146, 52 S. E. 307; Sites v. Knott, 197 Mo. 684, 96 S. W. 206; Wall v. New York Cent. & H. R. R. Co., 56 App. Div. 599, 67 N. Y. Supp. 519.

[17] Baltimore & O. R. Co. v. Friel, 77 Fed. 126, 23 C. C. A. 77; Malmsten v. Marquette, H. & O. R. Co., 49 Mich. 94, 13 N. W. 373; O'Rourke v. Lindell Ry. Co., 142 Mo. 342, 44 S. W. 254.

the passenger or other person against such carrier, but, on the contrary, operates to add to these rights that also of suing such third person.[18] Of course, if such third person is the agent or servant of the passenger or other plaintiff, then his acts, within the scope of his employment, are not legally those of a third person, but rather of the passenger or such other plaintiff himself.[19]

Both in the case of passengers and nonpassengers, under the doctrine of the imputation of negligence (which somehow crept into our jurisprudence), it was sought to impute to a child the negligence of a parent or one having the child in charge, in order to bar a recovery by a child; to impute the husband's negligence to the wife, and to impute the negligence of one in charge of the vehicle of a third person to those riding in such vehicle. This was done as to the child in an early New York case[20] (1839); and in England the negligence of an omnibus driver was imputed to one traveling in such omnibus, so as to bar a recovery for injuries due also to the negligence of a third person.[21] The doctrine of this latter English case was expressly overruled in England,[22] and the whole doctrine of the imputation of negligence has been very generally discredited by the later American cáses.[23]

When the parent sues the carrier for injuries to the child for loss of services to which the parent has a legal right, then the parent's negligence ought to be a defense, for otherwise the parent

18 Louisville & C. Packet Co. v. Mulligan, 77 S. W. 704, 25 Ky. Law Rep. 1287; Baltimore & O. S. W. R. Co. v. Kleesples, 39 Ind. App. 151, 76 N. E. 1015, 78 N. E. 252; Chicago & E. I. R. Co. v. Hines, 183 Ill. 482, 56 N. E. 177.

19 Central Pass. Ry. Co. v. Chatterson, 14 Ky. Law Rep. 663; Markowitz v. Metropolitan St. R. Co., 186 Mo. 350, 85 S. W. 351, 69 L. R. A. 389; Read v. City & Suburban Ry. Co., 115 Ga. 366, 41 S. E. 629.

20 Hartfield v. Roper, 21 Wend. (N. Y.) 615, 34 Am. Dec. 273. The imputation of the negligence of one having the child in charge to the child has been upheld in Waite v. Railway Co., El. Bl. & El. (Eng.) 719; McGeary v. Eastern R. Co., 135 Mass. 363; Reed v. Minneapolis St. Ry. Co., 34 Minn. 557, 27 N. W. 77; McQuilken v. Central Pac. R. Co., 64 Cal. 463, 2 Pac. 46; Kyne v. Wilmington & N. R. Co., 8 Houst. (Del.) 185, 14 Atl. 922; Brown v. European & N. A. R. Co., 58 Me. 384.

21 Thorogood v. Bryan (1849) 8 C. B. (Eng.) 115.

22 The Bernina (1888) 13 App. Cas. (Eng.) 1.

23 Little v. Hackett, 116 U. S. 366, 6 Sup. Ct. 391, 29 L. Ed. 652; Markham v. Houston Direct Nav. Co., 73 Tex. 247, 11 S. W. 131; State v. Boston & M. R. Co., 80 Me. 430, 15 Atl. 36; Becke v. Missouri Pac. Ry. Co., 102 Mo. 544, 13 S. W. 1053, 9 L. R. A. 157; Tompkins v. Clay St. R. Co., 66 Cal. 163, 4 Pac. 1165; Philadelphia, W. & B. R. Co. v. Hogeland, 66 Md. 149, 7 Atl. 105, 59 Am. Rep. 159; Frank Bird Transfer Co. v. Krug, 30 Ind. App. 602, 65 N. E. 309; Little Rock & M. R. Co. v. Harrell, 58 Ark. 454, 25 S. W. 117; New York, P. & N. R. Co. v. Cooper, 85 Va. 939, 9 S. E. 321.

profits by his own wrong.[24] It is believed, however, that there is no sound reason in law or morals why, when the infant sues himself, the negligence of his parent or custodian, concurring with the carrier's wrong to produce the injury, should be a defense to the carrier.[25] So, too, the husband's negligence should be a bar to his own suit, or when he joins with the wife as plaintiff and has an interest in the amount recovered,[26] but not to the wife's own suit [27] to recover on her own behalf for the injuries she has received.

SAME—PRESUMPTION AND BURDEN OF PROOF AS TO NEGLIGENCE

188. The mere fact of injury to the passenger, standing alone, does not create a presumption of negligence against the carrier; but when the proof of the injury shows that, according to ordinary human experience, the injury would not have been received, had the proper degree of care been exercised by the carrier, then proof of the injury gives rise to a prima facie presumption of negligence on the part of the carrier.

[24] Norfolk & W. R. Co. v. Groseclose's Adm'r, 88 Va. 267, 13 S. E. 454, 29 Am. St. Rep. 718; Winters v. Kansas City Cable Ry. Co., 99 Mo. 509, 12 S. W. 652, 6 L. R. A. 536, 17 Am. St. Rep. 591; Chicago City Ry. Co. v. Wilcox, 138 Ill. 370, 27 N. E. 899, 21 L. R. A. 76; St. Louis, I. M. & S. R. Co. v. Colum, 72 Ark. 1, 77 S. W. 596; City Pass. Ry. Co. v. Schuster, 113 Pa. 412, 6 Atl. 269, 57 Am. Rep. 471; O'Shea v. Lehigh Valley R. Co., 79 App. Div. 254, 79 N. Y. Supp. 890; Mattson v. Minnesota & N. W. R. Co., 95 Minn. 477, 104 N. W. 443, 70 L. R. A. 503, 111 Am. St. Rep. 483, 5 Ann. Cas. 498; Williams v. South & N. A. R. Co., 91 Ala. 635, 9 South. 77.

[25] Norfolk & W. Ry. Co. v. Groseclose's Adm'r, 88 Va. 267, 13 S. E. 454, 29 Am. St. Rep. 718; Warren v. Manchester St. Ry. Co., 70 N. H. 352, 47 Atl. 735; Chicago G. W. R. Co. v. Kowalski, 92 Fed. 310, 34 C. C. A. 1; Westbrook v. Mobile & O. R. Co., 66 Miss. 560, 6 South. 321, 14 Am. St. Rep. 587; Nashville R. R. Co. v. Howard, 112 Tenn. 107, 78 S. W. 1098, 64 L. R. A. 437; South Covington & C. St. Ry. Co. v. Herrklotz, 104 Ky. 400, 47 S. W. 265; St. Louis, I. M. & S. Ry. Co. v. Rexroad, 59 Ark. 180, 26 S. W. 1037; Newman v. Phillipsburg Horse-Car R. Co., 52 N. J. Law, 446, 19 Atl. 1102, 8 L. R. A. 842; Texas & P. R. Co. v. Kingston, 30 Tex. Civ. App. 24, 68 S. W. 518.

[26] Pennsylvania R. Co. v. Goodenough, 55 N. J. Law, 577, 28 Atl. 3, 22 L. R. A. 460; Horandt v. Central R. Co. of New Jersey, 78 N. J. Law, 190, 73 Atl. 93; McFadden v. Santa Ana, O. & T. St. Ry. Co., 87 Cal. 468, 25 Pac. 681, 11 L. R. A. 252.

[27] Finley v. Chicago, M. & St. P. Ry. Co., 71 Minn. 471, 74 N. W. 174; Louisville, N. A. & C. Ry. Co. v. Creek, 130 Ind. 139, 29 N. E. 481, 14 L. R. A. 733; Lewin v. Lehigh Valley R. Co., 41 App. Div. 89, 58 N. Y. Supp. 113; Atlanta & C. Air Line Ry. Co. v. Gravitt, 93 Ga. 369, 20 S. E. 550, 26 L. R. A. 553, 44 Am. St. Rep. 145.

As to contributory negligence, the better rule is that this is an affirmative defense to be proved by the carrier; but many courts hold that the passenger must himself show that he was exercising due care when injured.

Presumption of Carrier's Negligence

Though there are statements in the books to the contrary,[28] it is now well-settled that the mere proof of an accident, resulting in injury to the passenger, does not necessarily create a presumption of negligence against the carrier.[29] The rule is different, as we have seen,[30] in the case of the carrier of goods; but the carrier there is an insurer, and other striking differences exist between the two kinds of carriers. Thus proof of injury to a passenger by a brick thrown through the car window by an outsider would not of itself make out a case of prima facie liability against the carrier.

"But where the thing is shown to be under the management of the defendant or his servants, and the accident be such as, in the ordinary course of things, does not happen if those who have the management use proper care, it affords reasonable evidence, in the absence of explanation by the defendant, that the accident arose from want of care." [31] Perhaps the clearest example of this is a railroad collision,[32] which, ordinarily, the use of the highest de-

[28] Laing v. Colder, 8 Pa. 479, 49 Am. Dec. 533; Cooper v. Georgia, C. & N. Ry. Co., 61 S. C. 345, 39 S. E. 543; Southern Pac. Co. v. Cavin, 144 Fed. 348, 75 C. C. A. 350; Galena & C. U. R. Co. v. Yarwood, 15 Ill. 471; Id., 17 Ill. 509, 65 Am. Dec. 682.

[29] Dennis v. Pittsburg & C. S. R. R., 165 Pa. 624, 31 Atl. 52; Saunders v. Chicago & N. W. Ry. Co., 6 S. D. 40, 60 N. W. 148; Chicago City Ry. Co. v. Rood, 163 Ill. 477, 45 N. E. 238, 54 Am. St. Rep. 478; Faulkner v. Boston & M. R. R., 187 Mass. 254, 72 N. E. 976; Spencer v. Chicago, M. & St. P. Ry. Co., 105 Wis. 311, 81 N. W. 407; Reynolds v. Richmond & M. Ry. Co., 92 Va. 400, 23 S. E. 770; Paynter v. Bridgeton & M. Traction Co., 67 N. J. Law, 619, 52 Atl. 367; WILLIAMS v. SPOKANE FALLS & N. R. CO., 39 Wash. 77, 80 Pac. 1100, Dobie Cas. Bailments and Carriers, 341; Rist v. Philadelphia Rapid Transit Co., 236 Pa. 218, 84 Atl. 687; Allen v. Northern Pac. R. Co., 35 Wash. 221, 77 Pac. 204, 66 L. R. A. 804; Louisville & N. R. Co. v. Cornelius, 6 Ala. App. 386, 60 South. 740.

[30] Ante, § 118.

[31] Erle, C. J., in Scott v. Docks Co., 3 Hurl. & C. (Eng.) 601. See, also, LOUISIANA & N. W. R. CO. v. CRUMPLER, 122 Fed. 425, 59 C. C. A. 51, Dobie Cas. Bailments and Carriers, 326; WILLIAMS v. SPOKANE FALLS & N. R. CO., 39 Wash. 77, 80 Pac. 1100, Dobie Cas. Bailments and Carriers, 341; Wayne v. St. Louis & N. E. Ry. Co., 165 Ill. App. 353; Moore v. Greeneville Traction Co., 94 S. C. 249, 77 S. E. 928.

[32] Skinner v. Ry. Co., 5 Exch. (Eng.) 786; Louisville, N. A. & C. Ry. Co. v. Faylor, 126 Ind. 126, 25 N. E. 869; Copson v. New York, N. H. & H. R. Co., 171 Mass. 233, 50 N. E. 613; Larkin v. Chicago & G. W. Ry. Co., 118 Iowa, 652, 92 N. W. 891; Graham v. Burlington, C. R. & N. Ry. Co., 39 Minn. 81,

gree of practicable care can unquestionably prevent. The same is true when the carrier's conveyance breaks down[33] or turns over,[34] when the locomotive boiler explodes,[35] when a rail breaks,[36] a switch is wrongly thrown over,[37] a bridge goes down with a train,[38] or the brakes fail to work.[39] Since these and similar cases probably embrace a majority of accidents, it is true that in more than half of the cases proof of the injury makes out a prima facie case against the carrier. This, however, is not the same as saying that in all cases the prima facie presumption thus arises.

This presumption against the carrier, even when it does arise, is at best a mere prima facie one, which the carrier can rebut.[40] This he does by affirmatively showing that the accident was in no way due to his negligence in the premises.[41] No liability then attaches to the carrier. By proving the exercise of the highest degree of practicable care as to the apparent causes of the acci-

38 N. W. 812; Wedenkind v. Southern Pac. Co., 20 Nev. 292, 21 Pac. 682; WILLIAMS v. SPOKANE FALLS & N. R. CO., 39 Wash. 77, 80 Pac. 1100, Dobie Cas. Bailments and Carriers, 341; Kirkendall v. Union Pac. R. Co., 200 Fed. 197, 118 C. C. A. 383; Nagel v. United Rys. Co. of St. Louis, 169 Mo. App. 284, 152 S. W. 621.

33 Lawrence v. Green, 70 Cal. 417, 11 Pac. 750, 59 Am. Rep. 428; Feldschneider v. Chicago, M. & St. P. R. Co., 122 Wis. 423, 99 N. W. 1034.

34 Boyce v. California Stage Co., 25 Cal. 460; Farish v. Reigle, 11 Grat. (Va.) 697, 62 Am. Dec. 666.

35 Kelly v. Chicago & A. R. Co., 113 Mo. App. 468, 87 S. W. 583; Illinois Cent. R. Co. v. Phillips, 49 Ill. 234; Id., 55 Ill. 194.

36 Arkansas Midland Ry. Co. v. Griffith, 63 Ark. 491, 39 S. W. 550.

37 Baltimore & O. R. Co. v. Worthington, 21 Md. 275, 83 Am. Dec. 578.

38 Louisville, N. A. & C. R. Co. v. Snyder, 117 Ind. 435, 20 N. E. 284, 3 L. R. A. 434, 10 Am. St. Rep. 60.

39 Sharp v. Kansas City Cable Ry. Co., 114 Mo. 94, 20 S. W. 93.

40 McCafferty v. Pennsylvania R. Co., 193 Pa. 339, 44 Atl. 435, 74 Am. St. Rep. 690; Eureka Springs Ry. Co. v. Timmons, 51 Ark. 459, 11 S. W. 690; Pershing v. Chicago, B. & Q. Ry. Co., 71 Iowa, 561, 32 N. W. 488; Major v. Oregon Short Line R. Co., 21 Utah, 141, 59 Pac. 522; Louisville & C. Packet Co. v. Smith, 60 S. W. 524, 22 Ky. Law Rep. 1323; Eldridge v. Minneapolis & St. L. Ry. Co., 32 Minn. 253, 20 N. W. 151; Illinois Cent. R. Co. v. Porter, 117 Tenn. 13, 94 S. W. 666, 10 Ann. Cas. 789; Terre Haute & I. R. Co. v. Sheeks, 155 Ind. 74, 56 N. E. 434.

41 Fleming v Pittsburgh, C, C. & St. L. Ry., 158 Pa. 130, 27 Atl. 858, 22 L. R. A. 351, 38 Am. St. Rep 835; Fordyce v. Jackson, 56 Ark. 594, 20 S. W. 528, 597; Norfolk & W. Ry. Co. v. Marshall's Adm'r, 90 Va. 836, 20 S. E. 823; WILLIAMS v. SPOKANE FALLS & N. R. CO., 39 Wash. 77, 80 Pac. 1100, Dobie Cas. Bailments and Carriers, 341; McCurrie v. Southern Pac. Co., 122 Cal. 558, 55 Pac. 324; O'Clair v. Rhode Island Co., 27 R. I. 448, 63 Atl. 238; Illinois Cent. R. Co. v Kuhn, 107 Tenn. 106, 64 S. W. 202; St. Louis & S. F. R. Co. v. Posten, 31 Okl. 821, 124 Pac. 2.

dent, the presumption is overcome and the carrier is relieved of responsibility.

Burden of Proof as to Contributory Negligence

By the better rule, supported by the weight of authority, the passenger need go no further than proving the carrier's negligence and the resulting injury; it then devolves upon the carrier to prove the passenger's contributory negligence.[42] The passenger need not, in order to recover, show the absence of negligence in his part. This rule seems sound, for the law does not as a rule presume one to be negligent, and particularly as every prompting of human nature is in favor of the passenger's exercising due care in the interest of self-preservation. If, however, in proving the carrier's negligence, the passenger establishes by his own evidence a prima facie case of contributory negligence on his part, he must by his evidence further overcome this presumption (which he has himself raised), in order that he may recover against the carrier.[43]

Some of the courts, however, require the passenger to prove affirmatively that he was, when injured, exercising due care—in other words, that he was not guilty of contributory negligence.[44] According to this holding not only must the passenger convict the carrier, but he must also exonerate himself by showing that his own conduct was legally blameless. He must negatively relieve himself of negligence, as well as positively fix it upon the carrier.

[42] Washington & G. R. Co. v. Harmon, 147 U. S. 571, 13 Sup. Ct. 557, 37 L. Ed. 284; Mobile, J. & K. C. R. Co. v. Bromberg, 141 Ala. 258, 37 South. 395; Mares v. Northern Pac. R. Co., 3 Dak. 336, 21 N. W. 5; Carrico v. West Virginia Cent. & P. R. Co., 35 W. Va. 389, 14 S. E. 12; Bradwell v. Pittsburgh & W. E. P. Ry. Co., 139 Pa. 404, 20 Atl. 1046; Jones v. United Rys. & Electric Co., 99 Md. 64, 57 Atl. 620; Mississippi Cent. R. Co. v. Hardy, 88 Miss. 732, 41 South. 505; Durrell v. Johnson, 31 Neb. 796, 48 N. W. 890; Berry v. Pennsylvania R. Co., 48 N. J. Law, 141, 4 Atl. 303; Hughes v. Chicago & A. R. Co., 127 Mo. 447, 30 S. W. 127; Harmon v. United Rys. Co. of St. Louis, 163 Mo. App. 442, 143 S. W. 1114.

[43] Patterson v. Central Railroad & Banking Co., 85 Ga. 653, 11 S. E. 872; North Birmingham St. Ry. Co. v. Calderwood, 89 Ala. 247, 7 South. 360, 18 Am. St. Rep. 105.

[44] Tumalty v. New York, N. H. & H. R. Co., 170 Mass. 164, 49 N. E. 85; Sosnofski v. Lake Shore & M. S. R. Co., 134 Mich. 72, 95 N. W. 1077; Waldron v. Boston & M. R. R., 71 N. H. 362, 52 Atl. 443; Brockett v. Fair Haven & W. R. Co., 73 Conn. 428, 47 Atl. 763; Louisville, N. A. & C. Ry. Co. v. Miller, 141 Ind. 533, 37 N. E. 343; Owens v. Richmond & D. R. Co., 88 N. C. 502; Illinois Cent. R. Co. v. Nowicki, 148 Ill. 29, 35 N. E. 358; Tolman v. Syracuse, B. & N. Y. R. Co., 98 N. Y. 198, 50 Am. Rep. 649; Maercker v. Brooklyn Heights R. Co., 137 App. Div. 49, 122 N. Y. Supp. 87.

SAME—CARRIERS BY WATER

189. In general, the rules governing the liability of land carriers for injury to a passenger are also applicable to carriers by water, though, of necessity, difference in the two methods of transportation must result in some differences in liability.

The federal Congress in the exercise of its admiralty jurisdiction over navigable waters, has general control of the water carrier, and has enacted innumerable statutes affecting his liability.

In General

The measure of care, as the test of negligence, is the same as to carriers by water as to carriers by land.[45] The same is true of the broad general principles of the common law affecting the carrier's liability for injuries to the passenger.[46] There are, however, not a few unique rules applicable to the water carrier alone. Thus in a marine tort, when the passenger is guilty of contributory negligence, this need not bar a recovery against the carrier; but the damages are worked out by comparing the respective negligence of the passenger with that of the carrier.[47] Again, the passenger injured by the negligence of the water carrier may proceed directly against the ship (instead of against the owner) to fix an in rem liability against the ship.[48] From the very nature of the case, the master of a vessel is vested with an authority far more arbitrary and far-reaching than that possessed by any single person connected with the transportation on land.[49] Intrusted with

[45] American S. S. Co. v. Landreth, 108 Pa. 264; Yerkes v. Keokuk Northern Line Packet Co., 7 Mo. App. 265; Memphis & C. Packet Co. v. Buckner, 57 S. W. 482, 22 Ky. Law Rep. 401; Hughes v. New Jersey Steamboat Co., 11 Misc. Rep. 65, 31 N. Y. Supp. 1012; Miller v. Ocean Steam-Ship Co., 118 N. Y. 199, 23 N. E. 462; The Pilot Boy (D. C.) 23 Fed. 103; White v. Seattle, E. & T. Nav. Co., 36 Wash. 281, 78 Pac. 909, 104 Am. St. Rep. 948.

[46] Croft v. Northwestern S. S. Co., 20 Wash. 175, 55 Pac. 42; Van Buskirk v. Roberts, 31 N. Y. 661; Hoboken Ferry Co. v. Feiszt, 58 N. J. Law, 198, 38 Atl. 299; The Oriflamme, 3 Sawy. 397, Fed. Cas. No. 10,572; Rosen v. City of Boston, 187 Mass. 245, 72 N. E. 992, 68 L. R. A. 153; Trabing v. California Nav. & Imp. Co., 121 Cal. 137, 53 Pac. 644.

[47] The Max Morris, 137 U. S. 1, 11 Sup. Ct. 29, 34 L. Ed. 586.

[48] The Wasco (D. C.) 53 Fed. 546; The Pacific, 1 Blatchf. 569, Fed. Cas. No. 10,643; McGuire v. The Golden Gate, 1 McAll. 104, Fed. Cas. No. 8,815; The Glide, 167 U. S. 606, 17 Sup. Ct. 930, 42 L. Ed. 296.

[49] See particularly the language of Mr. Justice Story in Chamberlain v. Chandler, 3 Mason, 242, Fed. Cas. No. 2,575. See, also, Block v. Bannerman,

a terrible responsibility for the lives and safety of those on board, he must, owing to his necessarily isolated position, be vested with commensurate powers.

Regulation by Congress under Admiralty Jurisdiction

The exclusive admiralty jurisdiction of the United States Congress has resulted in the regulation of the passenger traffic by a number of statutes affecting many minute details of water transportation.[60] The discussion of these belongs to a work on admiralty. Reference has already been made to the Harter Act (Act Feb. 13, 1893, c 105, 27 Stat. 445 [U. S. Comp. St. 1901, p. 2946])[61] and the Limited Liability Act (Act March 3, 1851, c. 43, § 3, 9 Stat. 635 [U. S. Comp. St. 1901, p. 2943]),[62] passed to encourage the upbuilding of a merchant marine by limiting the shipowner's liability to the value of the vessel and freight.

A large number of statutes regulate precautions for the safety of passengers,[63] by requiring inspection of the hull and boilers of passenger steamers, by requiring that the masters, mates, pilots, and engineers be licensed, by limiting the number of passengers a vessel may carry, by requiring a proper supply of life preservers and lifeboats, by providing as to the carrying of explosives, the precautions necessary against fire, and hundreds of other details covering the many aspects of passenger traffic by water.

CONTRACTS LIMITING THE LIABILITY OF THE PASSENGER CARRIER

190. By the weight of authority, the common carrier cannot, even by express contract, limit or restrict his liability for injuries received by a pay passenger. This rule, however, is absolutely denied by some courts and variously qualified by others.

As to gratuitous passengers, and as to express messengers, Pullman porters, etc., whom the carrier is under no legal duty to transport, the weight of authority sanctions contracts limiting the carrier's liability.

10 La. Ann. 1; The Hammonia, 10 Ben. 512, Fed. Cas. No. 6,006; Boyce v. Bayliffe, 1 Camp. (Eng.) 58.

[60] For brief enumeration of, and comment on, some of the more important of these statutes, see 2 Fetter, Passenger Carriers, §§ 413-416.

[61] Ante, § 120.

[62] Ante, § 120.

[63] For brief summary as to these, see 2 Hutch. Carr. § 1148.

Pay Passengers

As to limitation of the carrier's liability by contract, there is much the same conflict of opinion as in the case of the carrier of goods. Certainly the reasons against such contracts are much stronger in the case of the passenger carrier. A sane public policy relieves him of insuring liability, and holds him liable only for negligence, judged by a rational standard of care under the circumstances. Life and limb are of more transcendent importance than property. The safety of its citizens is, and must be, of primary importance to the state. The great majority of the cases, then, unite in holding that as to the pay passenger (whom the carrier must transport) the duty and liability of the common carrier for injuries to the passenger is fixed by law as necessarily inhering in the relation, and that this cannot be lowered or restricted by contract, however definite, however freely it may have been entered into, or however clear the consideration.[54] Reduced rates are thus held not to be a consideration for which these safeguards of the law may in any way be diminished.[55] These courts, therefore, hold that any contract attempting to limit the liability of the carrier for injuries to the passenger, when the passenger is carried for hire, is utterly and absolutely void. And one is a pay passenger who is really, but not ostensibly, paying for his transportation, as where one was carried on a so-called "drover's pass" issued to one accompanying cattle on which freight is duly paid.[56]

A few of the courts have flatly denied the proposition just

[54] New York C. R. Co. v. Lockwood, 17 Wall. 357, 21 L. Ed. 627; Grand Trunk R. Co. v. Stevens, 95 U. S. 655, 24 L. Ed. 535; Doyle v. Fitchburg R. Co., 166 Mass. 492, 44 N. E. 611, 33 L. R. A. 844, 55 Am. St. Rep. 417; The Oregon, 133 Fed. 609, 68 C. C. A. 603; Rowdin v. Pennsylvania Ry. Co., 208 Pa. 623, 57 Atl. 1125; Davis v. Chicago, M. & St. P. Ry. Co., 93 Wis. 470, 67 N. W. 16, 33 L. R. A. 654, 57 Am. St. Rep. 935; Saunders v. Southern Pac. Co., 13 Utah, 275, 44 Pac. 932; Louisville, N. A. & C. Ry. Co. v. Faylor, 126 Ind. 126, 25 N. E. 869; Central of Georgia Ry. Co. v. Lippman, 110 Ga. 665, 36 S. E. 202, 50 L. R. A. 673; Louisville & N. R. Co. v. Bell, 100 Ky. 203, 38 S. W. 3; Checkley v. Illinois Cent. R. Co., 257 Ill. 491, 100 N. E. 942, 44 L. R. A. (N. S.) 1127, Ann. Cas. 1914A, 1202; Kirkendall v. Union Pac. R. Co., 200 Fed. 197, 118 C. C. A. 383.

[55] Richmond v. Southern Pac. Co., 41 Or. 54, 67 Pac. 947, 57 L. R. A. 616, 93 Am. St. Rep. 694; The Oregon, 133 Fed. 609, 68 C. C. A. 603. See, also, cases cited in the preceding note.

[56] New York C. R. Co. v. Lockwood, 17 Wall. 357, 21 L. Ed. 627; Louisville & N. R. Co. v. Bell, 100 Ky. 203, 38 S. W. 3; Saunders v. Southern Pac. Co., 13 Utah, 275, 44 Pac. 932; Rowdin v. Pennsylvania R. Co., 208 Pa. 623, 57 Atl. 1125; Chicago, B. & Q. R. Co. v. Williams, 200 Fed. 207, 118 C. C. A. 393. In the following cases, too, though traveling on a so-called pass, the passenger has been held a pay passenger: Williams v. Oregon Short Line R. Co., 18 Utah, 210, 54 Pac. 991, 72 Am. St. Rep. 777; Nickles v. Seaboard Air Line

stated.[57] Thus in a leading New York case[58] it was said: "A common carrier, in consideration of an abatement, in whole or in part, of his legal fare, may lawfully contract with a passenger that the latter will take upon himself the risk of damage from the negligence of agents or servants, for which the carrier would otherwise be liable; that public policy is satisfied by holding a railroad corporation bound to take the risk when the passenger chooses to pay the fare established by the Legislature. If he voluntarily and for any valuable consideration waives the right to indemnity, the contract is binding."

Some cases seek a middle ground, and permit the carrier by contract to exempt itself from liability for the negligence of its servants, provided such negligence be not gross.[59] Gross negligence means here (as it does elsewhere, when the extremely unfortunate terminology of degrees of negligence is employed) the failure to exercise even slight care.[60] This doctrine, however, has justly met with little favor.

In some states, the question is controlled by statutes.[61] The general tenor of these is to hold the carrier rigidly to the accepted standard of the highest practicable care, and to permit no limitations whatsoever by contract.

Gratuitous Passengers—Express Messengers, etc.

In the absence of special contract, the carrier owes the same duty to the gratuitous passenger as to the one for hire.[62] Somewhat different considerations apply, however, as to the two classes of passengers, in determining the question of the limitation of the carrier's liability by contract. By the weight of authority, it is held that, as to the gratuitous passenger, the carrier may by contract relieve itself from all liability due to negligence,[63] though a number of courts make no distinction between pay passengers

Ry., 74 S. C. 102, 54 S. E. 255; Doyle v. Fitchburg R. Co., 166 Mass. 492, 44 N. E. 611, 33 L. R. A. 844, 55 Am. St. Rep. 417.

[57] McCawley v. Ry. Co., L. R. 8 Q. B. (Eng.) 57; Kenney v. New York Cent. & H. R. R. Co., 125 N. Y. 422, 26 N. E. 626.

[58] Bissell v. New York Cent. R. Co., 25 N. Y. 442, 82 Am. Dec. 369.

[59] Arnold v. Illinois Cent. R. Co., 83 Ill. 273, 25 Am. Rep. 386; Higgins v. New Orleans, M. & C. R. Co., 28 La. Ann. 133.

[60] Jacksonville S. E. Ry. Co. v. Southworth, 135 Ill. 250, 25 N. E. 1093.

[61] See, for example, Code Va. 1887, § 1296; Rev. St. Tex. 1895, art. 320; Code Iowa 1873, § 1308.

[62] Ante, p. 530.

[63] NORTHERN PAC. RY. CO. v. ADAMS, 192 U. S. 440, 24 Sup. Ct. 408, 48 L. Ed. 513, Dobie Cas. Bailments and Carriers, 344; Muldoon v. Seattle City Ry. Co., 7 Wash. 528, 35 Pac. 422, 22 L. R. A. 794, 38 Am. St. Rep. 901; Boering v. Chesapeake Beach R. Co., 20 App. D. C. 500, affirmed 193 U. S. 442, 24 Sup. Ct. 515, 48 L. Ed. 742; Rogers v. Kennebec Steamboat Co., 86

and those traveling free, and deny the carrier's right to lessen his liability as much in the one case as in the other.[64]

The majority holding, sanctioned by the United States Supreme Court,[65] seems to be sound. The carrier owes no legal duty to carry one gratuitously, and, having the right to refuse him utterly, the carrier should by contract be permitted to relieve himself of liability for his negligence. Free passengers constitute a very small part of the traveling public, and they offer no temptation to the carrier's servants to relax their care upon which must depend the safety of the pay passengers and usually that of the servants themselves. It would therefore seem that the carrier, in fixing the terms on which it will carry one whom it can refuse to carry, can validly stipulate that those accepting the favor of gratuitous transportation shall exempt the carrier from all liability for injuries due to the carrier's negligence.

On somewhat the same basis as in the case of gratuitous passengers, the absence of any duty on the part of the carrier to transport them, contracts have been upheld relieving the carrier from liability for injuries due to his negligence in the case of express messengers,[66] news vendors,[67] and sleeping car porters.[68]

Me. 261, 29 Atl. 1069, 25 L. R. A. 491; Holly v. Southern R. Co., 119 Ga. 767, 47 S. E. 188; Griswold v. New York & N. E. R. Co., 53 Conn. 371, 4 Atl. 261, 55 Am. Rep. 115; Payne v. Terre Haute & I. Ry. Co., 157 Ind. 616, 62 N. E. 472, 56 L. R. A. 472; Quimby v. Boston & M. R. R. Co., 150 Mass. 365, 23 N. E. 205, 5 L. R. A. 846.

64 Missouri, K. & T. R. Co. of Texas v. Flood, 35 Tex. Civ. App. 197, 79 S. W. 1106; Jacobus v. Ry. Co., 20 Minn. 125 (Gil. 110), 18 Am. Rep. 360; Farmers' Loan & Trust Co. v. Baltimore & O. S. W. R. Co. (C. C.) 102 Fed. 17; Huckstep v. St. Louis & H. R. Co., 166 Mo. App. 330, 148 S. W. 988. In some states, statutes have been interpreted as requiring a similar holding. Norfolk & W. R. Co. v. Tanner, 100 Va. 379, 41 S. E. 721; Rose v. Des Moines Val. R. Co., 39 Iowa, 246.

65 NORTHERN PAC. RY. CO. v. ADAMS, 192 U. S. 440, 24 Sup. Ct. 408, 48 L. Ed. 513, Dobie Cas. Bailments and Carriers, 344; Boering v. Chesapeake Beach R. Co., 193 U. S. 442, 24 Sup. Ct. 515, 48 L. Ed. 742.

66 Baltimore & O. S. W. R. Co. v. Voigt, 176 U. S. 498, 20 Sup. Ct. 385, 44 L. Ed. 560; Blank v. Illinois Cent. R. Co., 182 Ill. 332, 55 N. E. 332; Bates v. Old Colony R. Co., 147 Mass. 255, 17 N. E. 633; Peterson v. Chicago & N. W. R. Co., 119 Wis. 197, 96 N. W. 532, 100 Am. St. Rep. 879; Pittsburgh, C., C. & St. L. Ry. Co. v. Mahoney, 148 Ind. 196, 46 N. E. 917, 47 N. E. 464, 40 L. R. A. 101, 62 Am. St. Rep. 503. Such a contract was held invalid under the Virginia statute prohibiting carriers from lessening their common-law liability by contract. Shannon's Adm'r v. Chesapeake & O. R. Co., 104 Va. 645, 52 S. E. 376.

67 Griswold v. New York & N. E. R. Co., 53 Conn. 371, 4 Atl. 261, 55 Am. Rep. 115. See, also, as condemning such contracts, Starr v. Great Northern Ry. Co., 67 Minn. 18, 69 N. W. 632.

68 McDermon v. Southern Pac. Co. (C. C.) 122 Fed. 669; Chicago, R. I. &

LIABILITY OF THE CARRIER TO PERSONS OTHER THAN PASSENGERS

191. The duty of exercising the highest degree of practicable care is owed by the carrier only to those who are technically passengers. To invitees, the carrier owes the duty of ordinary care; to licensees and trespassers, the carrier owes the duty to refrain from injuring them wantonly or willfully, and to exercise reasonable care to avoid hurting them after their danger is discovered.

Invitees

The invitee is one who is on the carrier's premises by virtue of the invitation of the latter, which may be either express or implied.[69] Involved in such invitation is the carrier's duty to exercise ordinary care to keep the premises reasonably safe, and for any violation of this duty (which is legal negligence) the carrier is liable to the invitee for any damage proximately resulting therefrom.[70]

Thus one who comes to the station to escort a passenger to the train,[71] a hackman driving a passenger to the station,[72] one who

P. R. Co. v. Hamler, 215 Ill. 525, 74 N. E. 705, 1 L. R. A. (N. S.) 674, 106 Am. St. Rep. 187, 3 Ann. Cas. 42; Russell v. Pittsburgh, C., C. & St. L. Ry. Co., 157 Ind. 305, 61 N. E. 678, 55 L. R. A. 253, 87 Am. St. Rep. 214. That such contracts are invalid, see Jones v. St. Louis S. W. Ry. Co., 125 Mo. 666, 28 S. W. 883, 26 L. R. A. 718, 46 Am. St. Rep. 514.

[69] Wright v. Boston & A. R. R., 142 Mass. 300, 7 N. E. 866; Turess v. New York, S. & W. Ry. Co., 61 N. J. Law, 314, 40 Atl. 614; Texas & P. Ry. Co. v. Best, 66 Tex. 116, 18 S. W. 224; Wilson v. New York, N. H. & H. R. Co., 18 R. I. 491, 29 Atl. 258; Whitley v. Southern Ry. Co., 122 N. C. 987, 29 S. E. 783; Morrow v. Atlanta & C. Air Line R. Co., 134 N. C. 92, 46 S. E. 12.

[70] Cherokee Packet Co. v. Hilson, 95 Tenn. 1, 31 S. W. 737; Berry v. Louisville & N. R. Co., 60 S. W. 699, 22 Ky. Law Rep. 1410; Yarnell v. Kansas City, Ft. S. & M. Ry. Co., 113 Mo. 570, 21 S. W. 1, 18 L. R. A. 599; Dowd v. Chicago, M. & St. P. Ry. Co., 84 Wis. 105, 54 N. W. 24, 20 L. R. A. 527, 36 Am. St. Rep. 917; Texas & P. Ry. Co. v. Best, 66 Tex. 116, 18 S. W. 224; McKone v. Michigan Cent. R. Co., 51 Mich. 601, 17 N. W. 74, 47 Am. Rep. 596; Stiles v. Atlanta & W. P. R. R., 65 Ga. 370; Tobin v. Portland, S. & P. R. Co., 59 Me. 183, 8 Am. Rep. 415; Lucas v. New Bedford & T. R. Co., 6 Gray (Mass.) 64, 66 Am. Dec. 406; Griswold v. Chicago & N. W. R. Co., 64 Wis. 652, 26 N. W. 101; Gautret v. Egerton, L. R. 2 C. P. (Eng.) 371; Watkins v. Railway Co., 37 L. T. N. S. (Eng.) 193; Blaisdell v. Long Island R. Co., 152 App. Div. 218, 136 N. Y. Supp. 768.

[71] Little Rock & Ft. S. Ry. Co. v. Lawton, 55 Ark. 428, 18 S. W. 543, 15 L. R. A. 434, 29 Am. St. Rep. 48; Davis v. Seaboard Air Line R. Co., 132 N. C. 291, 43 S. E. 840; Chesapeake & O. R. Co. v. Paris' Adm'r, 111 Va. 41, 68 S. E. 398, 28 L. R. A. (N. S.) 773.

[72] Tobin v. Portland, S. & P. R. Co., 59 Me. 183, 8 Am. Rep. 415.

goes to the station to procure a time-table,[73] a consignee of goods who is at the station in connection with receiving the goods,[74] are all on the carrier's premises by virtue of either an express or implied invitation of the carrier. They are not passengers, but invitees, and to them is owed by the carrier the duty of exercising ordinary care for their protection and safety.[75]

Licensees and Trespassers

The licensee is one on the carrier's premises, without objection on the part of the carrier, by its mere sufferance or permission, but without invitation.[76] He has no business with the carrier, but is there entirely on his own personal concerns. The trespasser is a sheer intruder, for whose presence there is no warrant whatsoever.[77] It is clear that, on simple principles of humanity, the carrier cannot willfully or wantonly injure either licensee[78] or

[73] Bradford v. Boston & M. R. R., 160 Mass. 392, 35 N. E. 1131.

[74] Holmes v. Ry. Co., L. R. 2 Exch. (Eng.) 254, 6 Exch. 123.

[75] See, also, Atlantic & B. R. Co. v. Owens, 123 Ga. 393, 51 S. E. 404; Hutchins v. Penobscot Bay & River Steamboat Co., 110 Me. 369, 86 Atl. 250; Catawissa R. Co. v. Armstrong, 49 Pa. 186; Philadelphia, W. & B. R. Co. v. State to Use of Bitzer, 58 Md. 374; Illinois Cent. R. Co. v. Frelka, 110 Ill. 498; Zeigler v. Danbury & M. R. Co., 52 Conn. 543, 2 Atl. 462; Pennsylvania Co. v. Gallagher, 40 Ohio St. 637, 48 Am. Rep. 689; In re Merrill, 54 Vt. 200; Vose v. Railway Co., 2 Hurl. & N. (Eng.) 728; Swainson v. Railway Co., L. R. 3 Exch. (Eng.) 341; Warburton v. Railway Co., L. R. 2 Exch. (Eng.) 30. And see, as to consignors, consignees, and their agents personally assisting in the reception or delivery of their freight, Wright v. Railway Co., L. R. 10 Q. B. (Eng.) 298, 1 Q. B. Div. 252; Foss v. Chicago, M. & St. P. R. Co., 33 Minn. 392, 23 N. W. 553; Watson v. Wabash, St. L. & P. R. Co., 66 Iowa, 164, 23 N. W. 380; Illinois Cent. R. Co. v. Hoffman, 67 Ill. 287; Newson v. New York Cent. R. Co., 29 N. Y. 383; New Orleans, J. & G. N. R. Co. v. Bailey, 40 Miss. 395; Shelbyville Lateral Branch R. Co. v. Lewark, 4 Ind. 471; Shelbyville Lateral Branch R. Co. v. Lynch, 4 Ind. 494; Dufour v. Central Pac. R. Co., 67 Cal. 319, 7 Pac. 769; Mark v. St. Paul, M. & M. R. Co., 32 Minn. 208, 20 N. W. 131; Blakemore v. Railway Co., 8 El. & Bl. (Eng.) 1035; Goldstein v. Chicago, M. & St. P. R. Co., 46 Wis. 404, 1 N. W. 37; Burns v. Boston & L. R. Co., 101 Mass. 50; Rogstad v. St. Paul, M. & M. R. Co., 31 Minn. 208, 17 N. W. 287.

[76] Bennett v. Louisville & N. R. Co., 102 U. S. 580, 26 L. Ed. 235; Poling v. Ohio River R. Co., 38 W. Va. 645, 18 S. E. 782, 24 L. R. A. 215; Weldon v. Philadelphia, W. & B. R. Co., 2 Pennewill (Del.) 1, 43 Atl. 159; Benson v. Baltimore Traction Co., 77 Md. 535, 26 Atl. 973, 20 L. R. A. 714, 39 Am. St. Rep. 436; Wagner v. Chicago & N. W. R. Co., 124 Iowa, 462, 100 N. W. 332.

[77] Planz v. Boston & A. R. Co., 157 Mass. 377, 32 N. E. 356, 17 L. R. A. 835; Handley v. Missouri Pac. Ry. Co., 61 Kan. 237, 59 Pac. 271; Littlejohn v. Richmond & D. R. Co., 49 S. C. 12, 26 S. E. 967; Holmes v. Cromwell & Spencer Co., 51 La. Ann. 352, 25 South. 265; Rickert v. Southern Ry. Co., 123 N. C. 255, 31 S. E. 497.

[78] Gillis v. Pennsylvania R. Co., 59 Pa. 129, 98 Am. Dec. 317; Pittsburgh, Ft. W. & C. Ry. Co. v. Bingham, 29 Ohio St. 364; Illinois Cent. R. Co. v. Godfrey, 71 Ill. 500, 22 Am. Rep. 112; Strong v. North Chicago St. R. Co.,

trespasser.[79] Again, it seems that, after the peril of the licensee or trespasser is perceived, the duty then arises on the carrier's part to use reasonable care to avert any injury to them.[80] The carrier owes them, however, not even ordinary care as to keeping the premises safe.[81] Coming for their own convenience, they are held to take the risks in this respect. The following were held to be licensees: One who took refuge in a station during a storm;[82] one who was on the carrier's platform merely as a sight-seer;[83] one going to a railroad telegraph office to pay a social visit to the operator.[84]

Trespassing Children

In general, the rules set out above apply to children as well as to adults. Many courts make an exception, however, as to trespassing children, under the doctrine of "alluring danger." This doctrine imposes on the carrier the duty not to leave exposed any instrumentality that is dangerous to young children, which would naturally attract them, in a place to which they might be expected to resort.[85] Most of the cases are concerned with railroad turntables.[86] This doctrine is questionable, at best. Some courts are

116 Ill. App. 246; Jenkins v. Central of Georgia R. Co., 124 Ga. 986, 53 S. E. 379; Burbank v. Illinois Cent. R. Co., 42 La. Ann. 1156, 8 South. 580, 11 L. R. A. 720. See, also, cases cited in note 76.

79 Massell v. Boston El. R. Co., 191 Mass. 491, 78 N. E. 108; Chicago, B. & Q. R. Co. v. Mehlsack, 131 Ill. 61, 22 N. E. 812, 19 Am. St. Rep. 17; Farber v. Missouri Pac. Ry. Co., 116 Mo. 81, 22 S. W. 631, 20 L. R. A. 350; MORGAN v. OREGON SHORT LINE R. CO., 27 Utah, 92, 74 Pac. 523, Dobie Cas. Bailments and Carriers, 346; Alabama G. S. R. Co. v. Harris, 71 Miss. 74, 14 South. 263.

80 Johnson v. Chicago, St. P., M. & O. R. Co., 123 Iowa, 224, 98 N. W. 642; Wilson v. Atchison, T. & S. F. R. Co., 66 Kan. 183, 71 Pac. 282; Pettit v. Great Northern Ry. Co., 58 Minn. 120, 59 N. W. 1082; Farber v. Missouri Pac. Ry. Co., 116 Mo. 81, 22 S. W. 631, 20 L. R. A. 350.

81 See cases cited in note 78.

82 Pittsburgh, Ft. W. & C. Ry. Co. v. Bingham, 29 Ohio St. 364.

83 Gillis v. Pennsylvania R. Co., 59 Pa. 129, 98 Am. Dec. 317.

84 Woolwine's Adm'r v. Chesapeake & O. Ry. Co., 36 W. Va. 329, 15 S. E. 81, 16 L. R. A. 271, 32 Am. St. Rep. 859.

85 Barrett v. Southern Pac. Co., 91 Cal. 296, 27 Pac. 666, 25 Am. St. Rep. 186; Holt v. Spokane & P. R. Co., 3 Idaho (Hasb.) 703, 35 Pac. 39; Consolidated Electric Light & Power Co. v. Healy, 65 Kan. 798, 70 Pac. 884; Louisville & N. R. Co. v. Popp, 96 Ky. 99, 27 S. W. 992; Wynn v. City & Suburban Ry. of Savannah, 91 Ga. 344, 17 S. E. 649.

86 Sioux City & P. R. Co. v. Stout, 17 Wall. 657, 21 L. Ed. 745; Ilwaco Ry. & Nav. Co. v. Hedrich, 1 Wash. 446, 25 Pac. 335, 22 Am. St. Rep. 169; Chicago, B. & Q. R. Co. v. Krayenbuhl, 65 Neb. 889, 91 N. W. 880, 59 L. R. A. 920; Twist v. Winona & St. P. R. Co., 39 Minn. 164, 39 N. W. 402, 12 Am. St. Rep. 626; Callahan v. Eel River & E. R. Co., 92 Cal. 89, 28 Pac. 104.

inclined to limit strictly its application,[87] while others, it seems with even better reason, have repudiated altogether the entire doctrine, and recognize no such exception to the general rule of the liability of the carrier to trespassers.[88]

[87] Sullivan v. Boston & A. R. Co., 156 Mass. 378, 31 N. E. 128; Moran v. Pullman Palace Car Co., 134 Mo. 641, 36 S. W. 659, 33 L. R. A. 755, 56 Am. St. Rep. 543; Ann Arbor R. Co. v. Kinz, 68 Ohio St. 210, 67 N. E. 479; Missouri, K. & T. R. Co. v. Edwards, 90 Tex. 65, 36 S. W. 430, 32 L. R. A. 825; Chicago, K. & W. R. Co. v. Bockhoven, 53 Kan. 279, 36 Pac. 322.

[88] Frost v. Eastern R. R. Co., 64 N. H. 220, 9 Atl. 790, 10 Am. St. Rep. 396; Bates v. Ry. Co., 90 Tenn. 36, 15 S. W. 1069, 25 Am. St. Rep. 665; Delaware, L. & W. R. Co. v. Reich, 61 N. J. Law, 635, 40 Atl. 682, 41 L. R. A. 831, 68 Am. St. Rep. 727; Walsh v. Fitchburg R. Co., 145 N. Y. 301, 39 N. E. 1068, 27 L. R. A. 624, 45 Am. St. Rep. 615; Daniels v. New York & N. E. R. Co., 154 Mass. 349, 28 N. E. 283, 13 L. R. A. 248, 26 Am. St. Rep. 253; Walker's Adm'r v. Potomac, F. & P. R. Co., 105 Va. 226, 53 S. E. 113, 4 L. R. A. (N. S.) 80, 115 Am. St. Rep. 871, 8 Ann. Cas. 862.

CHAPTER XIX

THE RIGHTS OF THE COMMON CARRIER OF PASSENGERS

THE CARRIER'S RIGHT TO MAKE REGULATIONS

192. The common carrier of passengers has a right to make and enforce regulations for the conduct of his business, provided these regulations be reasonable.

Basis of the Right

The same general considerations obtain here that are applicable to the regulations of the common carrier of goods. The nature of passenger traffic, the movement and volition of the passenger, the speed of the modern passenger train or boat, the added danger, and the comparative seriousness of accidents, all, however, tend to bring the regulations of the carrier of passengers into greater prominence and importance than those of the companion carrier of goods.

The real basis of this right lies in this fact: That only in this way can the passenger carrier properly live up to the very high degree of care imposed on him by law. Hence the right is not so much an independent as a derivative one. In a broad sense, then, this right on the carrier's part exists as a means of conferring a benefit on the traveling public, rather than as giving the carrier the opportunity to impose burdens on them. The efficiency, the promptness, and the safety of passenger traffic are in no small degree bound up in the carrier's right to prescribe suitable regulations for the conduct of his business, and to enforce these regulations promptly, and often summarily, after they are made. Thus the carrier's power here grows out of, as it is limited by, his responsibility, and the relation between the two is really that of means and end.

Regulations Must be Reasonable

The test of any regulation is its reasonableness. Unless, in the light of what has just been said, the particular regulation is reasonable, it is not valid and binding on the passenger.[1] In considering reasonableness, in this connection, the courts take into consideration the purpose of the regulation, and its effectiveness in accomplishing that purpose, as well as its general relation to the broad object of affording comfort and safety to the passenger, or of protecting the carrier against fraud, wrong, or imposition.[2] Reasonableness is a relative term, and the size of the traffic and the method of conveyance are factors of general import, while there may be local and unique circumstances to be taken into consideration. Subject to the test of reasonableness, however, the field of the carrier's regulations is unusually broad,[3] covering the many details in connection with the management of its conveyances, the

[1] Day v. Owen, 5 Mich. 520, 72 Am. Dec. 62; Chicago & N. W. Ry. Co. v. Williams, 55 Ill. 185, 8 Am. Rep. 641; Hoffbauer v. D. & N. W. R. Co., 52 Iowa, 342, 3 N. W. 121, 35 Am. Rep. 278; State v. Chovin, 7 Iowa, 204; Hibbard v. New York & E. R. Co., 15 N. Y. 455; Vedder v. Fellows, 20 N. Y. 126; Pennsylvania R. Co. v. Langdon, 92 Pa. 21, 37 Am. Rep. 651; Du Laurans v. First Division of St. Paul & P. R. Co., 15 Minn. 49 (Gil. 29), 2 Am. Rep. 102; Gleason v. Goodrich Transp. Co., 32 Wis. 85, 14 Am. Rep. 716; Bass v. Chicago & N. W. Ry. Co., 36 Wis. 450, 17 Am. Rep. 495; State v. Overton, 24 N. J. Law, 435, 61 Am. Dec. 671; Brown v. Memphis & C. R. Co. (C. C.) 4 Fed. 37; Id., 7 Fed. 51; Ft. Scott, W. & W. Ry. Co. v. Sparks, 55 Kan. 288, 39 Pac. 1032; Coyle v. Southern Ry. Co., 112 Ga. 121, 37 S. E. 163; South Fla. R. Co. v. Rhodes, 25 Fla. 40, 5 South. 633, 3 L. R. A. 733, 23 Am. St. Rep. 506; Gregory v. Chicago & N. W. Ry. Co., 100 Iowa, 345, 69 N. W. 532; Brown v. Kansas City, Ft. S. & G. R. Co., 38 Kan. 634, 19 Pac. 942; Deery v. Camden & A. R. Co., 163 Pa. 403, 30 Atl. 162; Ohage v. Northern Pac. R. Co., 200 Fed. 128, 118 C. C. A. 302; Birmingham Ry., Light & Power Co. v. Anderson, 3 Ala. App. 424, 57 South. 103; BIRMINGHAM R., LIGHT & POWER CO. v. McDONOUGH, 153 Ala. 122, 44 South. 960, 13 L. R. A. (N. S.) 445, 127 Am. St. Rep. 18, Dobie Cas. Bailments and Carriers, 349; FORSEE v. ALABAMA G. S. R. CO., 63 Miss. 66, 56 Am. Rep. 801, Dobie Cas. Bailments and Carriers, 351; Norman v. East Carolina R. Co., 161 N. C. 330, 77 S. E. 345; Renaud v. New York, N. H. & H. R. Co., 210 Mass. 553, 97 N. E. 98, 38 L. R. A. (N. S.) 689.

[2] Hibbard v. New York & E. R. Co., 15 N. Y. 455; Church v. Chicago, M. & St. P. Ry. Co., 6 S. D. 235, 60 N. W. 854, 26 L. R. A. 616; Louisville, N. A. & C. Ry. Co. v. Wright, 18 Ind. App. 125, 47 N. E. 491; Cherry v. Chicago & A. R. Co., 191 Mo. 489, 90 S. W. 381, 2 L. R. A. (N. S.) 695, 109 Am. St. Rep. 830; Faber v. Chicago Great Western Ry. Co., 62 Minn. 433, 64 N. W. 918, 36 L. R. A. 789; Gregory v. Chicago & N. W. Ry. Co., 100 Iowa, 345, 69 N. W. 532; McCook v. Northup, 65 Ark. 225, 45 S. W. 547.

[3] See Dowd v. Albany Ry., 47 App. Div. 202, 62 N. Y. Supp. 179 (taking dangerous articles into the cars); Armstrong v. Montgomery St. Ry. Co., 123 Ala. 233, 26 South. 349 (leaving street cars while they are in motion); McCook v. Northup, 65 Ark. 225, 45 S. W. 547 (tickets on freight trains); Rowe v. Brooklyn Heights R. Co., 71 App. Div. 474, 75 N. Y. Supp. 893 (employés off duty riding in front seat of street car); Central of Georgia R. Co. v. Motes, 117 Ga. 923, 43 S. E. 990, 62 L. R. A. 507, 97 Am. St. Rep. 223 (patrons sleeping on benches in waiting rooms).

carrier's dominion over its right of way and stations, and the conduct of carrier's servants and passengers. The right to enforce these reasonable regulations by the ejection of the person breaking them has already been considered.[4]

When there is no dispute as to the facts, the reasonableness of a regulation is held to be a question of law for the court.[5] "The necessity of holding this to be a question of law, and therefore within the province of the court to settle, is apparent from the consideration that it is only by so holding that fixed and permanent regulations can be established. If this question is to be left to juries, one rule would be applied by them to-day and another tomorrow. * * * A fixed system for the control of the vast interests connected with railways would be impossible, while such a system is essential equally to the roads and to the public."[6]

A regulation has been held reasonable that requires passengers to ride in the passenger cars, and not in the baggage cars or on the engine;[7] also one declining to admit passengers to the coaches until half an hour before the time scheduled for starting,[8] one forbidding passengers from riding on the platform of a car,[9] one prohibiting the presence of dogs in passenger coaches,[10] and one prohibiting the checking of baggage until the passenger has procured a ticket.[11] A regulation, however, forbidding passengers to

4 Ante, p. 551.

5 Gregory v. Chicago & N. W. Ry. Co., 100 Iowa, 345, 69 N. W. 532; St. Louis, A. & T. Ry. Co. v. Hardy, 55 Ark. 134, 17 S. W. 711; State v. Lake Roland El. Ry. Co., 84 Md. 163, 34 Atl. 1130; Central of Georgia Ry. Co. v. Motes, 117 Ga. 923, 43 S. E. 990, 62 L. R. A. 507, 97 Am. St. Rep. 223; South Florida Ry. Co. v. Rhodes, 25 Fla. 40, 5 South. 633, 3 L. R. A. 733, 23 Am. St. Rep. 506; Montgomery v. Buffalo Ry. Co., 24 App. Div. 454, 48 N. Y. Supp. 849, affirmed 165 N. Y. 139, 58 N. E. 770; Ohage v. Northern Pac. R. Co., 200 Fed. 128, 118 C. C. A. 302; BIRMINGHAM R., LIGHT & POWER CO. v. McDONOUGH, 153 Ala. 122, 44 South. 960, 13 L. R. A. (N. S.) 445, 127 Am. St. Rep. 18, Dobie Cas. Bailments and Carriers, 349.

6 Lawrence, J., in Illinois Cent. R. Co. v. Whittemore, 43 Ill. 420, 92 Am. Dec. 138.

7 O'Donnell v. Allegheny Valley R. Co., 59 Pa. 239, 98 Am. Dec. 336; Kentucky Cent. R. Co. v. Thomas' Adm'r, 79 Ky. 160, 42 Am. Rep. 208; Houston & T. C. R. Co. v. Clemmons, 55 Tex. 88, 40 Am. Rep. 799.

8 Decker v. Atchison, T. & S. F. R. Co., 3 Okl. 553, 41 Pac. 610.

9 Macon & W. R. Co. v. Johnson, 38 Ga. 409; Wills v. Lynn & B. R. Co., 129 Mass. 351; Renaud v. New York, N. H. & H. R. Co., 210 Mass. 553, 97 N. E. 98, 38 L. R. A. (N. S.) 689.

10 Gregory v. Chicago & N. W. Ry. Co., 100 Iowa, 345, 69 N. W. 532; O'Gorman v. New York & Q. C. R. Co., 96 App. Div. 594, 89 N. Y. Supp. 589; Hull v. Boston & M. R. R., 210 Mass. 159, 96 N. E. 58, 36 L. R. A. (N. S.) 406, Ann. Cas. 1912C, 1147.

11 Coffee v. Louisville & N. R. Co., 76 Miss. 569, 25 South. 157, 45 L. R. A. 112, 71 Am. St. Rep. 535.

change their seats in a car would be unreasonable,[12] and one forbidding passengers to wear the cap or uniform of an opposition line of steamers.[13] Further examples are given under the subject of "Tickets," discussed in another section.

THE RIGHT TO COMPENSATION

193. Like the carrier of goods, the common carrier of passengers is entitled to a reasonable compensation, which he may collect in advance; but the carrier cannot make any unjust discriminations in the rates charged.

The general principles as to the compensation of the carrier of passengers are those governing the carrier of goods.[14] The compensation is the benefit received by the carrier, and his right to this is the primary right upon which his very life as a carrier must necessarily depend. For the same reasons, here as there, this compensation of the passenger carrier must be a reasonable one.[15] The right of the passenger carrier to demand his compensation in advance has already been mentioned.[16] A reasonable opportunity to pay his fare must be afforded to the passenger,[17] and the latter is not required to tender the exact fare; but, to a reasonable amount, at least, the carrier must be ready to make change.[18]

In many states, statutes have been passed fixing the compensation of the passenger carrier.[19] These statutes are valid, provided they do not attempt to regulate interstate commerce, and provided these rates are not fixed so low as to be confiscatory.[20]

12 Green, C. J., in State v. Overton, 24 N. J. Law, 435, 441, 61 Am. Dec. 671.

13 South Florida R. Co. v. Rhodes, 25 Fla. 40, 5 South. 633, 3 L. R. A. 733, 23 Am. St. Rep. 506.

14 See ante, § 147.

15 Spofford v. Boston & M. R., 128 Mass. 326; McDuffee v. Portland & R. R. R., 52 N. H. 430, 13 Am. Rep. 72; Johnson v. Pensacola & P. R. Co., 16 Fla. 623, 26 Am. Rep. 731.

16 See ante, p. 567.

17 Clark v. Wilmington & W. Ry. Co., 91 N. C. 506, 49 Am. Rep. 647.

18 Barrett v. Market St. Ry. Co., 81 Cal. 296, 22 Pac. 859.

19 For example, see Rev. St. Mo. 1889, § 2673; Comp. St. Neb. 1893, c. 72, art. 9, §§ 1, 2; 1 How. Ann. St. Mich. 1882, § 3323, subd. 9; Const. Va. 1902, § 156, subsec. b; Const. Mich. art. 19a, § 1; Act N. J. March 11, 1880 (Gen. St. 1895, p. 2701, § 270); Rev. St. Ohio 1906, § 3374.

20 Chicago, B. & Q. R. Co. v. Iowa, 94 U. S. 155, 24 L. Ed. 94; Chicago, M. & St. P. R. Co. v. Minnesota ex rel. Railroad & W. Commission, 134 U. S. 418, 10 Sup. Ct. 462, 702, 33 L. Ed. 970; Atchison, T. & S. F. R. Co. v.

Discrimination in rates by the passenger carrier[21] is forbidden, according to the principles discussed under carriers of goods.[22] It is also prohibited by statutes in some of the states,[23] and by the second section of the Interstate Commerce Act. As to the amounts involved and its importance from an economic standpoint, discrimination by the passenger carrier is not nearly so serious as in the case of the carrier of goods.

TICKETS

194. Ordinarily a ticket is not the contract between the carrier and the passenger, but is merely evidence of the contract. But when the ticket purports to be the contract between the parties, the passenger accepting and using the ticket, whether he reads it or not, is presumed to have assented to the stipulations contained in the ticket.

Ordinarily, a passenger ticket is not the contract between the carrier and passenger, but serves only as a receipt for the payment of fare, and as a token to indicate to the servants of the carrier the nature and extent of the transportation to which the passenger is entitled.[24] When, therefore, the ticket is merely such a token or

Campbell, 61 Kan. 439, 59 Pac. 1051, 48 L. R. A. 251, 78 Am. St. Rep. 328; Beardsley v. New York, L. E. & W. R. Co., 15 App. Div. 251, 44 N. Y. Supp. 175; Storrs v. Pensacola & A. R. Co., 29 Fla. 617, 11 South. 226; St. Louis & S. F. R. Co. v. Gill, 54 Ark. 101, 15 S. W. 18, 11 L. R. A. 452; Norfolk & W. R. Co. v. Pendleton, 86 Va. 1004, 11 S. E. 1062, affirmed 156 U. S. 667, 15 Sup. Ct. 413, 39 L. Ed. 574; Pingree v. Michigan Cent. Ry. Co., 118 Mich. 314, 76 N. W. 635, 53 L. R. A. 274.

21 Atwater v. Delaware, L. & W. R. Co., 48 N. J. Law, 55, 2 Atl. 803, 57 Am. Rep. 543; Spofford v. Boston & M. R., 128 Mass. 326; Phillips v. Southern Ry. Co., 114 Ga. 284, 40 S. E. 268.

22 Ante, § 148.

23 Civ. Code Ga. 1895, § 2188; Laws N. C. 1891, c. 320, § 4; Acts Iowa 22d Gen. Assem. c. 28; Fla. Const. 1885, art. 16, § 30; Const. Ky. § 196; St. Mass. 1874–75, c. 372, § 138. See, also, Spofford v. Southern Ry. Co., 128 Mass. 326; Chamberlain v. Lake Shore & M. S. Ry. Co., 122 Mich. 477, 81 N. W. 339; State v. Southern Ry. Co., 122 N. C. 1052, 30 S. E. 133, 41 L. R. A. 246; Phillips v. Southern Ry. Co., 114 Ga. 284, 40 S. E. 268.

24 Rawson v. Pennsylvania R. Co., 48 N. Y. 212, 8 Am. Rep. 543; Quimby v. Vanderbilt, 17 N. Y. 306, 72 Am. Dec. 469; Boice v. Hudson River R. Co., 61 Barb. (N. Y.) 611; Elmore v. Sands, 54 N. Y. 512, 13 Am. Rep. 617; Johnson v. Concord R. Corp., 46 N. H. 213, 88 Am. Dec. 199; Gordon v. Manchester & L. R. R., 52 N. H. 596, 13 Am. Rep. 97; State v. Overton, 24 N. J. Law, 435, 61 Am. Dec. 671; Henderson v. Stevenson, L. R. 2 H. L. Sc. (Eng.) 470; Cincinnati, N. O. & T. P. R. Co. v. Harris, 115 Tenn. 501, 91 S. W. 211, 5 L. R. A. (N. S.) 779; Gulf, C. & S. F. Ry. Co. v. Copeland, 17 Tex.

check, the passenger is under no obligation to read stipulations on the ticket, nor is he bound by these unless he has in some way expressly assented to them.[25] Such a memorandum does not fall strictly within the "parol evidence rule," and other evidence is admissible to show what was the real contract between the carrier and passenger.[26]

Not infrequently, however, the ticket is made a convenient instrument in which this contract is embodied. When this is the case, and when the ticket brings this home to the passenger, then it is no longer a memorandum or token, but a contract.[27] The passenger, by then accepting it and using it, is presumed to have assented to its terms. Even though he does not sign it, or even read it, by the acceptance and use of what purports to be a contract by its form, size, etc., or what is expressly tendered to him as a contract, he becomes bound by its terms.[28] Then the analogy of the bill of lading is apt. Here, too, as there, parol evidence

Civ. App. 55, 42 S. W. 239; Norman v. East Carolina R. Co., 161 N. C. 330, 77 S. E. 345; Illinois Cent. R. Co. v. Fleming, 148 Ky. 473, 146 S. W. 1110.

[25] Henderson v. Stevenson, L. R. 2 H. L. Sc. (Eng.) 470; FONSECA v. CUNARD S. S. CO., 153 Mass. 553, 27 N. E. 665, 12 L. R. A. 340, 25 Am. St. Rep. 660, Dobie Cas. Bailments and Carriers, 353; Indianapolis & C. R. Co. v. Cox, 29 Ind. 360, 95 Am. Dec. 640; Norman v. Southern R. Co., 65 S. C. 517, 44 S. E. 83, 95 Am. St. Rep. 809; Louisville & N. R. Co. v. Turner, 100 Tenn. 213, 47 S. W. 223, 43 L. R. A. 140; San Antonio & A. P. Ry. Co. v. Newman, 17 Tex. Civ. App. 606, 43 S. W. 915; Hutchins v. Pennsylvania R. Co., 181 N. Y. 186, 73 N. E. 972, 106 Am. St. Rep. 537.

[26] Van Buskirk v. Roberts, 31 N. Y. 661; Northern R. Co. v. Page, 22 Barb. (N. Y.) 130; Barker v. Coflin, 31 Barb. 556; Nevins v. Bay Steamboat Co., 4 Bosw. (N. Y.) 225; Rawson v. Pennsylvania R. Co., 48 N. Y. 212, 8 Am. Rep. 543; Elmore v. Sands, 54 N. Y. 512, 13 Am. Rep. 617; Brown v. Eastern R. Co., 11 Cush. (Mass.) 97; Johnson v. Concord R. Corp., 46 N. H. 213, 88 Am. Dec. 199; Crosby v. Maine Cent. R. Co., 69 Me. 418; Burnham v. Grand Trunk Ry. Co., 63 Me. 298, 18 Am. Rep. 220; Peterson v. Chicago, R. I. & P. Ry. Co., 80 Iowa, 92, 45 N. W. 573; Lexington & E. Ry. Co. v. Lyons, 46 S. W. 209, 20 Ky. Law Rep. 516; Dixon v. New England R. Co., 179 Mass. 242, 60 N. E. 581.

[27] FONSECA v. CUNARD S. S. CO., 153 Mass. 553, 27 N. E. 665, 12 L. R. A. 340, 25 Am. St. Rep. 660, Dobie Cas. Bailments and Carriers, 353; Abram v. Gulf, C. & S. F. Ry. Co., 83 Tex. 61, 18 S. W. 321; Rolfs v. Atchison, T. & S. F. R. Co., 66 Kan. 272, 71 Pac. 526; Perkins v. New York Cent. R. Co., 24 N. Y. 196, 82 Am. Dec. 281; Burke v. Ry. Co., 5 C. P. Div. (Eng.) 1.

[28] Watson v. Louisville & N. R. Co., 104 Tenn. 194, 56 S. W. 1024, 49 L. R. A. 454; Quimby v. Boston & M. R. Co., 150 Mass. 365, 23 N. E. 205, 5 L. R. A. 846; St. Clair v. Kansas City, M. & B. R. Co., 77 Miss. 789, 28 South. 957; Boling v. St. Louis & S. F. R. Co., 189 Mo. 219, 88 S. W. 35; Rogers v. Atlantic City R. Co., 57 N. J. Law, 703, 34 Atl. 11; Sanden v. Northern Pac. R. Co., 43 Mont. 209, 115 Pac. 408, 34 L. R. A. (N. S.) 711; FONSECA v. CUNARD S. S. CO., 153 Mass. 553, 27 N. E. 665, 12 L. R. A. 340, 25 Am. St. Rep. 660, Dobie Cas Bailments and Carriers, 353.

cannot vary or alter the provisions of the contract.[29] Of course, though, to be valid these provisions must contravene no rule of public policy (e. g., relieving the carrier of liability for negligence),[30] and they must be supported by a valuable consideration, which is usually a reduced rate.[31] These contracts, like those of the carrier of goods, are construed most strongly against the carrier.[32]

Legal Incidents of Tickets

The almost universal use of tickets in modern passenger transportation justifies some brief reference to their more usual legal incidents. In the absence of provisions to the contrary, tickets are assignable,[33] and can be used at any time within the period prescribed for such contracts by the statute of limitations.[34] Contract stipulations are binding, however, which provide that tickets shall be nontransferable,[35] and that the ticket must be used within a cer-

[29] Simis v. New York L. E. & W. R. Co., 1 Misc. Rep. 179, 20 N. Y. Supp. 639; Eastman v. Maine Cent. R. R., 70 N. H. 240, 46 Atl. 54; FONSECA v. CUNARD S. S. CO., 153 Mass. 553, 27 N. E. 665, 12 L. R. A. 340, 25 Am. St. Rep. 660, Dobie Cas. Bailments and Carriers, 353; Dietrich v. Pennsylvania R. Co., 71 Pa. 432, 10 Am. Rep. 711; Rolfs v. Atchison, T. & S. F. R. Co., 66 Kan. 272, 71 Pac. 526.

[30] Ante, § 190.

[31] Spiess v. Erie R. Co., 71 N. J. Law, 90, 58 Atl. 116; Watson v. Louisville & N. R. Co., 104 Tenn. 194, 56 S. W. 1024, 49 L. R. A. 454; Boling v. St. Louis & S. F. R. Co., 189 Mo. 219, 88 S. W. 35; Southern R. Co. v. De Saussare, 116 Ga. 53, 42 S. E. 479.

[32] Cleveland, C., C. & St. L. Ry. Co. v. Kinsley, 27 Ind. App. 135, 60 N. E. 169, 87 Am. St. Rep. 245; Georgia Railroad & Banking Co. v. Clarke, 97 Ga. 706, 25 S. E. 368; Ann Arbor R. Co. v. Amos, 85 Ohio St. 300, 97 N. E. 978, 43 L. R. A. (N. S.) 587; Norman v. East Carolina R. Co., 161 N. C. 330, 77 S. E. 345.

[33] International & G. N. R. Co. v. Ing, 29 Tex. Civ. App. 398, 68 S. W. 722; CARSTEN v. NORTHERN PAC. R. CO., 44 Minn. 454, 47 N. W. 49, 9 L. R. A. 688, 20 Am. St. Rep. 589, Dobie Cas. Bailments and Carriers, 381; The Willamette Valley (D. C.) 71 Fed. 712; Sleeper v. Pennsylvania R. Co., 100 Pa. 259, 45 Am. Rep. 380; Spencer v. Lovejoy, 96 Ga. 658, 23 S. E. 836, 51 Am. St. Rep. 152.

[34] Cassiano v. Galveston, H. & S. A. R. Co. (Tex. Civ. App.) 82 S. W. 806; Boyd v. Spencer, 103 Ga. 828, 30 S. E. 841, 68 Am. St. Rep. 146.

[35] Schubach v. McDonald, 179 Mo. 163, 78 S. W. 1020, 65 L. R. A. 136, 101 Am. St. Rep. 452; Delaware, L. & W. R. Co. v. Frank (C. C.) 110 Fed. 689; Davis v. South Carolina & G. R. Co., 107 Ga. 420, 33 S. E. 437; Rahilly v. St. Paul & D. R. Co., 66 Minn. 153, 68 N. W. 853; WAY v. CHICAGO, R. I. & P. R. CO., 64 Iowa, 48, 19 N. W. 828, 52 Am. Rep. 431, Dobie Cas. Bailments and Carriers, 300; Post v. Chicago & N. W. R. Co., 14 Neb. 110, 15 N. W. 225, 45 Am. Rep. 100; Walker v. Wabash, St. L. & P. Ry. Co., 15 Mo. App. 333; Drummond v. Southern Pac. R. Co., 7 Utah, 118, 25 Pac. 733. And see, as to forfeiture of the ticket, Freidenhich v. Baltimore & O. R. Co., 53 Md. 201; Pittsburgh, C., C. & St. L. R. Co. v. Russ, 6 C. C. A. 597, 57 Fed.

tain time.[36] In this latter case, unless the stipulation clearly specifies the completion of the journey, it is sufficient if the journey be commenced before midnight of the day on which the ticket expires.[37] Other valid stipulations are that coupons are not good if detached,[38] that a ticket is good only on certain trains,[39] and that a return trip coupon will not be honored unless it is stamped and validated.[40]

Regulations of the carrier have been upheld requiring that tickets be exhibited on a reasonable demand by the conductor or similar

822; Kirby v. Union Pac. R. Co., 51 Colo. 509, 119 Pac. 1042, Ann. Cas. 1913B, 461.

[36] Hill v. Syracuse, B. & N. Y. R. Co., 63 N. Y. 101; Barker v. Coflin, 31 Barb. (N. Y.) 556; Boice v. Hudson River R. Co., 61 Barb. (N. Y.) 611; Wentz v. Erie R. Co., 3 Hun (N. Y.) 241; Boston & L. R. Co. v. Proctor, 1 Allen (Mass.) 267, 79 Am. Dec. 729; State v. Campbell, 32 N. J. Law, 309; Pennington v. Philadelphia, W. & B. R. Co., 62 Md. 95; Lewis v. Western & A. R. Co., 93 Ga. 225, 18 S. E. 650; Johnson v. Concord R. Corp., 46 N. H. 213, 88 Am. Dec. 199; Rawitzky v. Louisville & N. R. Co., 40 La. Ann. 47, 3 South. 387; Hanlon v. Illinois Cent. R. Co., 109 Iowa, 136, 80 N. W. 223; Elliott v. Southern Pac. Co., 145 Cal. 441, 79 Pac. 420, 68 L. R. A. 393; Burn v. Chicago, B. & Q. R. Co., 153 Ill. App. 319.

[37] Auerback v. New York Cent. & H. R. R. Co., 89 N. Y. 281, 42 Am. Rep. 290; Lundy v. Central Pac. R. Co., 66 Cal. 191, 4 Pac. 1193, 56 Am. Rep. 100; Gulf, C. & S. F. Ry. Co. v. Wright, 10 Tex. Civ. App. 179, 30 S. W. 294; Evans v. St. Louis, I. M. & S. R. Co., 11 Mo. App. 463. And see Georgia Southern R. Co. v. Bigelow, 68 Ga. 219; Pennsylvania Co. v. Hine, 41 Ohio St. 276; Morningstar v. Louisville & N. R. Co., 135 Ala. 251, 33 South. 156.

[38] Boston & M. R. R. v. Chipman, 146 Mass. 107, 14 N. E. 940, 4 Am. St. Rep. 293; Norfolk, N. & W. R. Co. v. Wysor, 82 Va. 250; Louisville, N. & G. S. R. Co. v. Harris, 9 Lea (Tenn.) 180, 42 Am. Rep. 668; Houston & T. C. R. Co. v. Ford, 53 Tex. 364. But see, where the coupons are detached by mistake, Wightman v. Chicago & N. W. Ry. Co., 73 Wis. 169, 40 N. W. 689, 2 L. R. A. 185, 9 Am. St. Rep. 778. And compare Chicago, St. L. & P. R. Co. v. Holdridge, 118 Ind. 281, 20 N. E. 837; Rouser v. North Park St. Ry. Co., 97 Mich. 565, 56 N. W. 937; Thompson v. Truesdale, 61 Minn. 129, 63 N. W. 259, 52 Am. St. Rep. 579.

[39] Lake Shore & M. S. Ry. Co. v. Rosenzweig, 113 Pa. 519, 6 Atl. 545; Thorp v. Concord R. Co., 61 Vt. 378, 17 Atl. 791; MacRae v. Wilmington & W. R. Co., 88 N. C. 526, 43 Am. Rep. 745; New York & N. E. R. Co. v. Feeley, 163 Mass. 205, 40 N. E. 20.

[40] Mosher v. St. Louis, I. M. & S. R. Co., 127 U. S. 390, 8 Sup. Ct. 1324, 32 L. Ed. 249; BOYLAN v. HOT SPRINGS R. CO., 132 U. S. 146, 10 Sup. Ct. 50, 33 L. Ed. 290, Dobie Cas. Bailments and Carriers, 355; Edwards v. Lake Shore & M. S. Ry. Co., 81 Mich. 364, 45 N. W. 827, 21 Am. St. Rep. 527; Bowers v. Pittsburgh, Ft. W. & C. R. R., 158 Pa. 302, 27 Atl. 893; Central Trust Co. v. East Tennessee, V. & G. Ry. Co. (C. C.) 65 Fed. 332; Central of Georgia R. Co. v. Cannon, 106 Ga. 828, 32 S. E. 874; Dangerfield v. Atchison, T. & S. F. Ry. Co., 62 Kan. 85, 61 Pac. 405; Central of Georgia Ry. Co. v. Bagley, 173 Ala. 611, 55 South. 894.

official,[41] and that they be surrendered;[42] but, in this last case, the passenger can validly insist that some token or receipt be given to him as evidence that he has paid his fare.[43] When a ticket is lost or mislaid, this is therefore the misfortune of the passenger, and if, after a reasonable time, the ticket cannot be found, the passenger must pay his fare under penalty of ejection.[44] A rule of the carrier is also valid providing that no one will be admitted to his conveyance save those who have already purchased tickets,[45] or one exacting a higher fare on the train from those who have no tickets,[46] if in both cases the carrier has given the passenger a reasonable opportunity to purchase a ticket before entering the conveyance of the carrier.[47]

[41] Rogers v. Atlantic City R. Co., 57 N. J. Law, 703, 34 Atl. 11; White v. Grand Rapids & I. R. Co., 107 Mich. 681, 65 N. W. 521.

[42] Baltimore & O. R. Co. v. Blocher, 27 Md. 277; White v. Evansville & T. H. R. Co., 133 Ind. 480, 33 N. E. 273; Central of Georgia Ry. Co. v. Dorsey, 106 Ga. 826, 32 S. E. 873; Rogers v. Atlantic City R. Co., 57 N. J. Law, 703, 34 Atl. 11; Van Dusan v. Grand Trunk Ry. Co. of Canada, 97 Mich. 439, 56 N. W. 848, 37 Am. St. Rep. 354.

[43] State v. Thompson, 20 N. H. 250; Illinois Cent. R. Co. v. Whittemore, 43 Ill. 420, 92 Am. Dec. 138. See, also, East Tennessee, V. & G. Ry. Co. v. King, 88 Ga. 443, 14 S. E. 708, as to ejection when passenger has surrendered ticket without a receipt.

[44] Ripley v. New Jersey R. & Transp. Co., 31 N. J. Law, 388; Harp v. Southern R. Co., 119 Ga. 927, 47 S. E. 206, 100 Am. St. Rep. 212; Louisville, N. & G. S. R. Co. v. Fleming, 14 Lea (Tenn.) 128; Downs v. New York & N. H. R. Co., 36 Conn. 287, 4 Am. Rep. 77; Standish v. Narragansett S. S. Co., 111 Mass. 512, 15 Am. Rep. 66; Cresson v. Philadelphia & R. R. Co., 11 Phila. (Pa.) 597; Crawford v. Cincinnati, H. & D. R. Co., 26 Ohio St. 580; Atwater v. Delaware, L. & W. R. Co., 48 N. J. Law, 55, 2 Atl. 803, 57 Am. Rep. 543; International & G. N. R. Co. v. Wilkes, 68 Tex. 617, 5 S. W. 491, 2 Am. St. Rep. 515; Cooper v. Railway Co., 4 Exch. Div. (Eng.) 88.

[45] Mills v. Missouri, K. & T. Ry. Co. of Texas, 94 Tex. 242, 59 S. W. 874, 55 L. R. A. 497; McCook v. Northrup, 65 Ark. 225, 45 S. W. 547; Illinois Cent. Ry. Co. v. Louthan, 80 Ill. App. 579; Poole v. Northern Pac. R. Co., 16 Or. 261, 19 Pac. 107, 8 Am. St. Rep. 289; Dickerman v. St. Paul Union Depot Co., 44 Minn. 433, 46 N. W. 907.

[46] Swan v. Manchester & L. R. Co., 132 Mass. 116, 42 Am. Rep. 432; St. Louis, A. & T. H. R. Co. v. South, 43 Ill. 176, 92 Am. Dec. 103; Illinois Cent. R. Co. v. Johnson, 67 Ill. 312; Indianapolis, P. & C. Ry. Co. v. Rinard, 46 Ind. 293; Du Laurans v. First Division of St. Paul & P. R. Co., 15 Minn. 49 (Gil. 29), 2 Am. Rep. 102; Cleveland, C., C. & St. L. Ry. Co. v. Beckett, 11 Ind. App. 547, 39 N. E. 429; Snellbaker v. Paducah, T. & A. R. Co., 94 Ky. 597, 23 S. W. 509; Coyle v. Southern Ry. Co., 112 Ga. 121, 37 S. E. 163; FORSEE v. ALABAMA G. S. R. CO., 63 Miss. 66, 56 Am. Rep. 801, Dobie Cas. Bailments and Carriers, 351.

[47] St. Louis, A. & T. H. R. Co. v. South, 43 Ill. 176, 92 Am. Dec. 103; Chicago & A. R. Co. v. Flagg, 43 Ill. 364, 92 Am. Dec. 133; Illinois Cent. R. Co. v. Johnson, 67 Ill. 312; Jeffersonville R. Co. v. Rogers, 28 Ind. 1, 92 Am. Dec. 276; Indianapolis, P. & C. Ry. Co. v. Rinard, 46 Ind. 293; Du Laurans

When the passenger has begun his journey, he has no right, in the absence of a stipulation to that effect, to stop over at intermediate points, and then to insist on being carried to his destination on the same ticket.[48] But a coupon ticket over several roads entitles the passenger to stop at the end of each carrier's line, in the absence of any express limitation.[49] The passenger cannot use a ticket to travel between the points named, but in an opposite direction to that specified.[50]

WRONG TICKET GIVEN TO PASSENGER BY THE CARRIER

195. The ticket, as between the passenger and conductor, is conclusive as to the former's right to travel. When, by the fault of the carrier's agent, an improper ticket is given to the passenger, the latter may recover damages from the carrier, based on the wrong of such agent. There is, however, grave conflict on these points among the cases.

v. First Division of St. Paul & P. R. Co., 15 Minn. 49 (Gil. 29), 2 Am. Rep. 102; Swan v. Manchester & L. R. Co., 132 Mass. 116, 42 Am. Rep. 432; Everett v. Chicago, R. I. & P. Ry. Co., 69 Iowa, 15, 28 N. W. 410, 58 Am. Rep. 207; Cross v. Kansas City, Ft. S. & M. Ry. Co., 56 Mo. App. 664; FORSEE v. ALABAMA G. S. R. CO., 63 Miss. 66, 56 Am. Rep. 801, Dobie Cas. Bailments and Carriers, 351; Phillips v. Southern Ry. Co., 114 Ga. 284, 40 S. E. 268; Rivers v. Kansas City & M. B. R. Co., 86 Miss. 571, 38 South. 508; Phettiplace v. Northern Pac. R. Co., 84 Wis. 412, 54 N. W. 1092, 20 L. R. A. 483.

48 Hamilton v. New York Cent. R. Co., 51 N. Y. 100; Beebe v. Ayres, 28 Barb. (N. Y.) 275; Terry v. Flushing, N. S. & C. R. Co., 13 Hun (N. Y.) 359; Cheney v. Boston & M. R. Co., 11 Metc. (Mass.) 121, 45 Am. Dec. 190; Oil Creek & A. R. Ry. Co. v. Clark, 72 Pa. 231; Dietrich v. Pennsylvania R. Co., 71 Pa. 432, 10 Am. Rep. 711; Vankirk v. Pennsylvania R. Co., 76 Pa. 66, 18 Am. Rep. 404; Wyman v. Northern Pac. R. Co., 34 Minn. 210, 25 N. W. 349; Pennsylvania R. Co. v. Parry, 55 N. J. Law, 551, 27 Atl. 914, 22 L. R. A. 251, 39 Am. St. Rep. 654; Cleveland, C. & C. R. Co. v. Bartram, 11 Ohio St. 457; Drew v. Central Pac. R. Co., 51 Cal. 425; Breen v. Texas & P. R. Co., 50 Tex. 43; Johnson v. Philadelphia, W. & B. R. Co., 63 Md. 106; Roberts v. Koehler (C. C.) 30 Fed. 94; Ashton v. Railway Co., [1904] 2 K. B. (Eng.) 313, 73 L. J. K. B. 701; International & G. N. R. Co. v. Best, 93 Tex. 344, 55 S. W. 315. Contra, by statute, Carpenter v. Grand Trunk Ry. Co., 72 Me. 388, 39 Am. Rep. 340; Robinson v. Southern Pac. Co., 105 Cal. 526, 541, 38 Pac. 94, 108, 722, 28 L. R. A. 773.

49 Brooke v. Grand Trunk Ry. Co., 15 Mich. 332; Little Rock & F. S. R. Co. v. Dean, 43 Ark. 529, 51 Am. Rep. 584; Spencer v. Lovejoy, 96 Ga. 657, 23 S. E. 836, 51 Am. St. Rep. 152; Auerbach v. New York Cent. & H. R. R. Co., 89 N. Y. 281, 42 Am. Rep. 290; Nichols v. Southern Pac. Co., 23 Or. 123, 31 Pac. 296, 18 L. R. A. 55, 37 Am. St. Rep. 664.

50 Godfrey v. Ohio & M. R. Co., 116 Ind. 30, 18 N. E. 61; Pease v. Delaware, L. & W. R. Co., 101 N. Y. 367, 5 N. E. 37, 54 Am. Rep. 699. For a qualifica-

There are few questions in the law which have given rise to more real conflict on almost every point involved than that of the liability of the carrier for the ejection of a passenger traveling on a wrong ticket furnished to him through the fault of the carrier's agent. In addition, great confusion has arisen through failure to differentiate even the factors that enter into the problem. The typical case is when a ticket agent negligently fails to give the passenger the proper ticket, for which the passenger has asked and paid, and the passenger, presenting this ticket and declining to pay again, is ejected from the train by the conductor.[51]

Though there are many cases to the contrary,[52] both authority and reason establish the rule that, as between the passenger and conductor, the ticket is conclusive as to the former's right to travel.[53] This rule is demanded by the exigencies of the business;

tion of this principle, see Pennsylvania Co. v. Bray, 125 Ind. 229, 25 N. E. 439.

[51] For discussions of this perplexing problem, see 2 Hutch. Carr. §§ 1061–1066; 1 Fetter on Passenger Carriers, §§ 317–326. See, also, note 9 Ann. Cas. 889.

[52] St. Louis, A. & T. Ry. Co. v. Mackie, 71 Tex. 491, 9 S. W. 451, 1 L. R. A. 667, 10 Am. St. Rep. 766; Watkins v. Pennsylvania R. Co., 21 D. C. 1; Illinois Cent. R. Co. v. Harper, 83 Miss. 560, 35 South. 764, 64 L. R. A. 283, 102 Am. St. Rep. 469; EVANSVILLE & T. H. R. CO. v. CATES, 14 Ind. App. 172, 41 N. E. 712, Dobie Cas. Bailments and Carriers, 360; Hufford v. Grand Rapids & I. R. Co., 64 Mich. 631, 31 N. W. 544, 8 Am. St. Rep. 859; Indianapolis St. R. Co. v. Wilson, 161 Ind. 153, 66 N. E. 950, 67 N. E. 993, 100 Am. St. Rep. 261 (this case, in the principal and dissenting opinions, presents both sides of this question, with elaborate citation and discussion of the cases).

[53] FREDERICK v. MARQUETTE, H. & O. R. CO., 37 Mich. 342, 26 Am. Rep. 531, Dobie Cas. Bailments and Carriers, 357; Bradshaw v. South Boston R. Co., 135 Mass. 407, 46 Am. Rep. 481; Mosher v. St. Louis & I. M. & T. R. Co. (C. C.) 23 Fed. 326; Hall v. Memphis & C. R. Co. (C. C.) 15 Fed. 57; Petrie v. Pennsylvania R. Co., 42 N. J. Law, 449; Atchison, T. & S. F. R. Co. v. Gants, 38 Kan. 608, 17 Pac. 54, 5 Am. St. Rep. 780; McKay v. Ohio River Ry. Co., 34 W. Va. 65, 11 S. E. 737, 9 L. R. A. 132, 26 Am. St. Rep. 913; Rose v. Wilmington & W. R. Co., 106 N. C. 168, 11 S. E. 526; Townsend v. New York Cent. & H. R. R. Co., 56 N. Y. 295, 15 Am. Rep. 419; Chicago, B. & Q. R. Co. v. Griffin, 68 Ill. 499; McClure v. Philadelphia, W. & B. R. Co., 34 Md. 532, 6 Am. Rep. 345; Shelton v. Lake Shore & M. S. Ry. Co., 29 Ohio St. 214; Yorton v. Milwaukee, L. S. & W. Ry. Co., 54 Wis. 234, 11 N. W. 482, 41 Am. Rep. 23; Brown v. Rapid R. Co., 134 Mich. 591, 96 N. W. 925; Morse v. Southern Ry. Co., 102 Ga. 308, 29 S. E. 865; Peabody v. Oregon Ry. & Nav. Co., 21 Or. 121, 26 Pac. 1053, 12 L. R. A. 823; Kansas City, M. & B. R. Co. v. Foster, 134 Ala. 244, 32 South. 773, 92 Am. St. Rep. 25; Kleven v. Great Northern Ry. Co., 70 Minn. 79, 72 N. W. 828; Illinois Cent. R. Co. v. Jackson, 117 Ky. 900, 79 S. W. 1187; Rolfs v. Atchison, T. & S. F. R. Co., 66 Kan. 272, 71 Pac. 526; Maxson v. Pennsylvania R. Co., 49 Misc. Rep. 502, 97 N. Y. Supp. 962; Pennsylvania Co. v. Lenhart, 120 Fed. 61, 56 C. C. A. 467; Wilson v. West Jersey & S. R. Co.,

for if the conductor were compelled to rely on the passenger's statement as to the ticket he ought to have, rather than on the ticket he actually has, this would seriously cripple the efficiency of passenger service, as well as expose the carrier to countless frauds. The conductor, then, merely performs his duty in ejecting the passenger whose ticket does not entitle him to travel on the train in question. The conductor's act, of itself, is therefore not tortious.[54]

This, however, does not mean that the ejected passenger is without remedy. He recovers damages against the carrier for the ejection, but his right of action is based, not on the act of the conductor in performing his duty, but on the wrongful act of the ticket agent in failing to supply the passenger with the proper ticket, for which he both asked and paid.[55] The passenger thereby became entitled to a ticket on which he could make the journey in question. The ticket actually furnished him did not give that right, and thus the ticket agent failed in his duty. Again, the more rigid and scrupulous the conductor is in ejecting passengers whose tickets are not proper, the keener is the wrong of the ticket agent and the clearer the causal connection between his wrong and the resulting ejection.

Similar considerations apply when, by the act of one conductor, the passenger is deprived of a proper ticket for presentation to a second conductor, by whom the passenger is ejected. In such case the actionable wrong is that of the first conductor.[56] This

83 N. J. Law, 755, 85 Atl. 347, 43 L. R. A. (N. S.) 1148; Loy v. Northern Pac. R. Co., 68 Wash. 33, 122 Pac. 372.

54 See cases cited in preceding note. See particularly Illinois Cent. R. Co. v. Jackson, 117 Ky. 900, 79 S. W. 1187.

55 Murdock v. Boston & A. R. Co., 137 Mass. 293, 50 Am. Rep. 307; Muckle v. Rochester Ry. Co., 79 Hun, 32, 29 N. Y. Supp. 732; Townsend v. New York Cent. & H. R. R. Co., 56 N. Y. 295, 15 Am. Rep. 419; Elliott v. New York C. & H. R. R. Co., 53 Hun, 78, 6 N. Y. Supp. 363; FREDERICK v. MARQUETTE, H. & O. R. CO., 37 Mich. 342, 26 Am. Rep. 531, Dobie Cas. Bailments and Carriers, 357; Lake Erie & W. R. Co. v. Fix, 88 Ind. 381, 45 Am. Rep. 464; Pennsylvania Co. v. Bray, 125 Ind. 229, 25 N. E. 439; Pittsburgh, C., C. & St. L. Ry. Co. v. Berryman, 11 Ind. App. 640, 36 N. E. 728; Appleby v. St. Paul City R. Co., 54 Minn. 169, 55 N. W. 1117, 40 Am. St. Rep. 308; Puckett v. Southern Ry. Co., 9 Ga. App. 589, 71 S. E. 944; Krueger v. Chicago, St. P., M. & O. Ry. Co., 68 Minn. 445, 71 N. W. 683, 64 Am. St. Rep. 487; Holden v. Rutland R. Co., 72 Vt. 156, 47 Atl. 403, 82 Am. St. Rep. 926; Trice v. Chesapeake & O. Ry. Co., 40 W. Va. 271, 21 S. E. 1022. See, also, giving the ejected passenger a right of recovery, New York, L. E. & W. R. Co. v. Winter, 143 U. S. 60, 12 Sup. Ct. 356, 36 L. Ed. 71; Ellsworth v. Chicago, B. & Q. Ry. Co., 95 Iowa, 98, 63 N. W. 584, 29 L. R. A. 173; Randall v. New Orleans & N. E. R. Co., 45 La. Ann. 778, 13 South. 166.

56 Lovings v. Norfolk & W. Ry. Co., 47 W. Va. 582, 35 S. E. 962; Louisville, N. A. & C. Ry. Co. v. Conrad, 4 Ind. App. 83, 30 N. E. 406; Shelton v. Lake

is clearly brought out when the conductors are in the employ of different railroads. In this case, the suit must be brought against the railroad employing the first conductor, for it alone has committed a wrong against the passenger.[57]

Negligence of the Passenger

The cases are not entirely clear and harmonious as to the effect on such recovery of the passenger's conduct. Of course, there is no difficulty when the ticket is on its face apparently good.[58] It would seem, too, that when there is some doubt as to its validity on the face of the ticket, the passenger should clearly recover who has exercised due care to satisfy himself of the ticket's validity.

Even when the ticket on its face shows obviously that it is the wrong ticket, the majority of the courts seem disposed to hold that this fact alone will not necessarily serve to bar a recovery.[59] When, however, the passenger knew that the ticket was a wrong one, or when he is negligent in not knowing that, then this should be a defense to the carrier.[60] The passenger is not bound, though, to exercise more than ordinary care, while in judging negligence by this standard the courts are inclined to be liberal to the passenger, and all the surrounding facts and circumstances are to be taken into consideration.[61]

Shore & M. S. Ry. Co., 29 Ohio St. 214. But see East Tennessee, V. & G. R. Co. v. King, 88 Ga. 443, 14 S. E. 708; Scofield v. Pennsylvania Co., 112 Fed. 855, 50 C. C. A. 553, 56 L. R. A. 224.

57 Louisville, N. A. & C. Ry. Co. v. Conrad, 4 Ind. App. 83, 30 N. E. 406.

58 Murdock v. Boston & A. R. Co., 137 Mass. 293, 50 Am. Rep. 307; Ellsworth v. Chicago, B. & Q. Ry. Co., 95 Iowa, 98, 63 N. W. 584, 29 L. R. A. 173; New York, L. E. & W. R. Co. v. Winter, 143 U. S. 60, 12 Sup. Ct. 356, 36 L. Ed. 71; Jevons v. Union Pac. R. Co., 70 Kan. 491, 78 Pac. 817; Indianapolis St. R. Co. v. Wilson, 161 Ind. 153, 66 N. E. 950, 67 N. E. 993, 100 Am. St. Rep. 261; Pittsburgh, C., C. & St. L. Ry. Co. v. Reynolds, 55 Ohio St. 370, 45 N. E. 712, 60 Am. St. Rep. 706.

59 Kansas City, M. & B. R. Co. v. Foster, 134 Ala. 244, 32 South. 773, 92 Am. St. Rep. 25; Chase v. Atchison, T. & S. F. R. Co., 70 Kan. 546, 79 Pac. 153; Illinois Cent. R. Co. v. Jackson, 117 Ky. 900, 79 S. W. 1187; Georgia Railroad & Banking Co. v. Dougherty, 86 Ga. 744, 12 S. E. 747, 22 Am. St. Rep. 499; McKay v. Ohio River Ry. Co., 34 W. Va. 65, 11 S. E. 737, 9 L. R. A. 132, 26 Am. St. Rep. 913; Illinois Cent. Ry. Co. v. Moore, 79 Miss. 766, 31 South. 436; Peabody v. Oregon Ry. & Nav. Co., 21 Or. 121, 26 Pac. 1053, 12 L. R. A. 823; Krueger v. Chicago, St. P., M. & O. Ry. Co., 68 Minn. 445, 71 N. W. 683, 64 Am. St. Rep. 487.

60 Western Maryland Ry. Co. v. Stocksdale, 83 Md. 245, 34 Atl. 880; Callaway v. Mellett, 15 Ind. App. 366, 44 N. E. 198, 57 Am. St. Rep. 238; Parish v. Ulster & D. R. Co., 99 App. Div. 10, 90 N. Y. Supp. 1000; Pouilin v. Canadian Pac. R. Co., 52 Fed. 197, 3 C. C. A. 23, 17 L. R. A. 800; Gulf, C. & S. F. R. Co. v. Daniels (Tex. Civ. App.) 29 S. W. 426; Pittsburgh, C., C. & St. L. Ry. Co. v. Daniels, 90 Ill. App. 154.

61 See cases cited in preceding note.

Damages

As to the measure of damages, in cases of the kind under discussion, the usual rule is to give to the passenger the usual compensatory damages for his ejection.[62] In the computation of these damages, the following elements have been held to be proper: Increased expense, delay, inconvenience, suffering, both physical and mental, including humiliation and indignity.[63] In a few exceptional cases, punitive damages have been held proper.[64]

When the ticket, on its face, shows that it is not good for the trip in question, it is generally and properly held that the passenger cannot resist the ejection. If he does, he cannot recover for injuries due to resistance, when only sufficient force is used to eject him.[65] When, however, the ticket is apparently good, it is held that he can lawfully resist any attempts to eject him.[66]

Form of Action

Many courts have insisted that the passenger's action must be in contract, for the breach of the carrier's contract.[67] With better reason, however, other courts have declined thus to limit the

[62] Hot Springs R. Co. v. Deloney, 65 Ark. 182, 45 S. W. 351, 67 Am. St. Rep. 913; Lexington & E. Ry. Co. v. Lyons, 104 Ky. 23, 46 S. W. 209; Georgia R. R. v. Olds, 77 Ga. 673; Lake Erie & W. Ry. Co. v. Fix, 88 Ind. 381, 45 Am. Rep. 464.

[63] Kansas City, M. & B. R. Co. v. Foster, 134 Ala. 244, 32 South. 773, 92 Am. St. Rep. 25; Southern Kansas Ry. Co. v. Rice, 38 Kan. 398, 16 Pac. 817, 5 Am. St. Rep. 766; Baltimore & O. R. Co. v. Bambrey (Pa.) 16 Atl. 67; Moore v. Central of Georgia R. Co., 1 Ga. App. 514, 58 S. E. 63; Illinois Cent. Ry. Co. v. Jackson, 117 Ky. 900, 79 S. W. 1187; Cincinnati, N. O. & T. P. R. Co. v. Carson, 145 Ky. 81, 140 S. W. 71. In a few cases the recovery is limited to nominal damages. Brown v. Rapid R. Co., 134 Mich. 591, 96 N. W. 925; Burn v. Chicago, B. & Q. R. Co., 153 Ill. App. 319.

[64] Illinois Cent. R. Co. v. Harper, 83 Miss. 560, 35 South. 764, 64 L. R. A. 283, 102 Am. St. Rep. 469; Cowen v. Winters, 96 Fed. 929, 37 C. C. A. 628; Calloway v. Mellett, 15 Ind. App. 366, 44 N. E. 198, 57 Am. St. Rep. 238; Southern Ry. Co. v. Wood, 114 Ga. 140, 39 S. E. 894, 55 L. R. A. 536; Delaware, L. & W. R. Co. v. Walsh, 47 N. J. Law, 548, 4 Atl. 323.

[65] FREDERICK v. MARQUETTE, H. & O. R. CO., 37 Mich. 342, 26 Am. Rep. 531, Dobie Cas. Bailments and Carriers, 357; Pennsylvania R. Co. v. Connell, 112 Ill. 295, 54 Am. Rep. 238; Peabody v. Oregon Ry. & Nav. Co., 21 Or. 121, 26 Pac. 1053, 12 L. R. A. 823.

[66] Ellsworth v. Chicago, B. & Q. Ry. Co., 95 Iowa, 98, 63 N. W. 584, 29 L. R. A. 173. See, also, New York, L. E. & W. R. Co. v. Winter, 143 U. S. 60, 12 Sup. Ct. 356, 36 L. Ed. 71; Louisville, N. A. & C. Ry. Co. v. Wolfe, 128 Ind. 347, 27 N. E. 606, 25 Am. St. Rep. 436; Denver Tramway Co. v. Reid, 4 Colo. App. 500, 36 Pac. 557.

[67] Western Maryland R. Co. v. Stocksdale, 83 Md. 245, 34 Atl. 880; McKay v. Ohio River Ry. Co., 34 W. Va. 65, 11 S. E. 737, 9 L. R. A. 132, 26 Am. St. Rep. 913; FREDERICK v. MARQUETTE, H. & O. R. CO., 37 Mich. 342, 26 Am. Rep. 531, Dobie Cas. Bailments and Carriers, 357.

scope of the passenger's action and have permitted it to be brought in tort [68] for the negligent act of the ticket agent, or other servant of the carrier, to whose wrong is due the fact that the ticket furnished to the passenger is not a proper one.

Another question presented to the courts with varying results is the duty of the passenger to avoid ejection by paying again his fare. This he must do, according to some courts, even though the wrong of the carrier is admitted, in order to minimize the damages flowing from such wrong.[69] That this is a prudent line of action is unquestioned; but is the passenger obliged to adopt it? It is believed that it is unfair to compel a passenger to pay again, when he is not at fault in having the wrong ticket.[70] He should not be required thus to anticipate the carrier's wrong, which is somewhat different from minimizing the consequences after the wrong has been committed. Nor should he be thus vicariously compelled to purchase a right that should already be his. This doctrine of compelling the passenger to pay again his fare under penalty of being denied a recovery for his ejection, it has been said,[71] is analogous to "a claim of exemption from liability for an assault because the wrongdoer first offered his victim a choice between assault and extortion."

[68] SLOANE v. SOUTHERN CAL. RY. CO., 111 Cal. 668, 44 Pac. 320, 32 L. R. A. 193, Dobie Cas. Bailments and Carriers, 378; Pittsburgh, C., C. & St. L. Ry. Co. v. Street, 26 Ind. App. 224, 59 N. E. 404; Hot Springs Ry. Co. v. Deloney, 65 Ark. 177, 45 S. W. 351, 67 Am. St. Rep. 913; Central Railroad & Banking Co. v. Roberts, 91 Ga. 513, 18 S. E. 315; Louisville & N. R. Co. v. Hine, 121 Ala. 234, 25 South. 857.

[69] White v. Grand Rapids & I. R. Co., 107 Mich. 681, 65 N. W. 521; Pouilin v. Canadian Pac. R. Co., 52 Fed. 197, 3 C. C. A. 23, 17 L. R. A. 800; Southern Pac. Co. v. Patterson, 7 Tex. Civ. App. 451, 27 S. W. 194; Pennsylvania R. Co. v. Connell, 112 Ill. 295, 54 Am. Rep. 238; Atchison, T. & S. F. R. Co. v. Hogue, 50 Kan. 40, 31 Pac. 698; Bradshaw v. South Boston R. Co., 135 Mass. 409, 46 Am. Rep. 481; Burn v. Chicago, B. & Q. R. Co., 153 Ill. App. 319.

[70] Lake Erie & W. Ry. Co. v. Fix, 88 Ind. 381, 45 Am. Rep. 464; Zagelmeyer v. Cincinnati S. & M. R. Co., 102 Mich. 214, 60 N. W. 436, 47 Am. St. Rep. 514; Krueger v. Chicago, St. P., M. & O. Ry. Co., 68 Minn. 445, 71 N. W. 683, 64 Am. St. Rep. 487; Ellsworth v. Chicago, B. & Q. Ry. Co., 95 Iowa, 98, 63 N. W. 584, 29 L. R. A. 173; Sprenger v. Tacoma Traction Co., 15 Wash. 660, 47 Pac. 17, 43 L. R. A. 706; St. Louis, A. & T. Ry. Co. v. Mackie, 71 Tex. 491, 9 S. W. 451, 1 L. R. A. 667, 10 Am. St. Rep. 766; Head v. Georgia Pac. Ry. Co., 79 Ga. 358, 7 S. E. 217, 11 Am. St. Rep. 434; Louisville & N. R. Co. v. Breckinridge, 99 Ky. 1, 34 S. W. 702; Yorton v. Milwaukee, L. S. & W. Ry. Co., 62 Wis. 367, 21 N. W. 516, 23 N. W. 401.

[71] 43 L. R. A. 716, note.

CHAPTER XX

THE BAGGAGE OF THE PASSENGER

DUTY AND LIABILITY OF THE CARRIER AS TO THE BAGGAGE OF THE PASSENGER

196. The common carrier of passengers is bound, without other compensation than the payment of fare, to receive and to carry a reasonable amount of baggage for the passenger.

As to such baggage, the carrier is liable as a carrier of goods; that is, subject to the same exceptions, he is liable as an insurer for any loss of, or injury to, such baggage.

Duty to Carry the Passenger's Baggage

As an incident of his own transportation, the passenger has a right to have a reasonable amount of baggage carried with him.[1]

[1] Hasbrouck v. New York Cent. & H. R. R. Co., 202 N. Y. 363, 95 N. E. 808, 35 L. R. A. (N. S.) 537, Ann. Cas. 1912D, 1150; Wells v. Great Northern R. Co., 59 Or. 165, 114 Pac. 92, 116 Pac. 1070, 34 L. R. A. (N. S.) 818, 825; McIntosh v. Augusta & A. R. Co., 87 S. C. 181, 69 S. E. 159, 30 L. R. A. (N. S.) 889; Wood v. Maine Cent. R. Co., 98 Me. 98, 56 Atl. 457, 99 Am. St. Rep. 339; Runyan v. Central R. Co. of New Jersey, 61 N. J. Law, 537, 41 Atl. 367, 43 L. R. A. 284, 68 Am. St. Rep. 711; Gomm v. Oregon R. & Nav. Co., 52 Wash. 685, 101 Pac. 361, 28 L. R. A. (N. S.) 537; Burnes v. Chicago, R. I. & P. R. Co., 167 Mo. App. 62, 150 S. W. 1100. A carrier may refuse to carry merchandise as personal baggage, or anything except what is useful and necessary, or useful for the passenger's personal comfort and convenience. Collins v. Boston & M. R. R., 10 Cush. (Mass.) 506; Smith v. Boston & M. R. R., 44 N. H. 325. It follows that the carrier may require information as to value and kind as a condition precedent to the transportation of articles offered as baggage. Norfolk & W. R. Co. v. Irvine, 84 Va. 553, 5 S. E. 532; Id., 85 Va. 217, 7 S. E. 233, 1 L. R. A. 110; RAILROAD CO. v. FRALOFF, 100 U. S. 24, 25 L. Ed. 531, Dobie Cas. Bailments and Carriers, 364. It was at first held that carriers were not liable for the traveler's baggage unless a distinct price had been paid, on the ground that the carrier is liable only in respect to his reward, and that the compensation should be in proportion to the risk. Middleton v. Fowler, 1 Salk. (Eng.) 282. Subse-

The obligation to transport the passenger, resting on the carrier, implies an equal obligation to carry his baggage. Thus arises the carrier's duty to receive and carry, to a reasonable amount, the passenger's baggage. Nor can the carrier demand for this any extra compensation save the regular fare for the passenger's transportation, which is supposed to be fixed at a rate that will include the transportation both of the baggage and the passenger.[2]

Liability of Carrier as to the Passenger's Baggage

Though there was at one time some doubt on the subject,[3] the carrier is, as to his liability for the passenger's baggage, a common carrier of goods, and his responsibility is measured accordingly.[4] The carrier is therefore an insurer of the goods against loss or injury, with the same exceptions that obtain as to the carrier of goods—act of God; public enemy; inherent nature of the goods; act of owner; law.[5] Those principles and analogies

quently, by common usage, a reasonable amount of baggage was deemed to be included with the fare of the passenger; but the courts should not allow this custom to be abused, and, under pretense of baggage, include articles not within the scope of the term, or intent of the parties, thereby defrauding the carrier of his just compensation, besides subjecting him to unknown hazards. Pardee v. Drew, 25 Wend. (N. Y.) 459; Orange County Bank v. Brown, 9 Wend. (N. Y.) 85, 24 Am. Dec. 129. The traveling public have the right to stop and receive their baggage at any regular station or stopping place for the train on which they may be traveling, and any regulation that deprives them of that right is necessarily arbitrary, unreasonable, and illegal. Pittsburgh, C. & St. L. Ry. Co. v. Lyon, 123 Pa. 140, 16 Atl. 607, 2 L. R. A. 489, 10 Am. St. Rep. 517.

[2] Wells v. Great Northern R. Co., 59 Or. 165, 114 Pac. 92, 116 Pac. 1070, 34 L. R. A. (N. S.) 818, 825; Hasbrouck v. New York Cent. & H. R. R. Co., 202 N. Y. 363, 95 N. E. 808, 35 L. R. A. (N. S.) 537, Ann. Cas. 1912D, 1150; Wood v. Maine Cent. R. Co., 98 Me. 98, 56 Atl. 457, 99 Am. St. Rep. 339; Orange County Bank v. Brown, 9 Wend. (N. Y.) 85, 24 Am. Dec. 129; Hollister v. Nowlen, 19 Wend. (N. Y.) 234, 32 Am. Dec. 455; Cole v. Goodwin, 19 Wend. (N. Y.) 251, 32 Am. Dec. 470. A carrier is liable for the loss of the luggage of a passenger whose fare was paid by another. The fare paid by a passenger to a carrier includes transportation of his baggage. Roberts v. Koehler (C. C.) 30 Fed. 94.

[3] Stewart v. Railway Co., 8 Hurl. & C. (Eng.) 138.

[4] Dill v. South Carolina R. Co., 7 Rich. (S. C.) 158, 62 Am. Dec. 407; Ranchau v. Rutland R. Co., 71 Vt. 142, 43 Atl. 11, 76 Am. St. Rep. 761; Ringwalt v. Wabash R. Co., 45 Neb. 760, 64 N. W. 219; Indiana, D. & W. R. Co. v. Zilly, 20 Ind. App. 569, 51 N. E. 141; Hubbard v. Mobile & O. R. Co., 112 Mo. App. 459, 87 S. W. 52; Wood v. Maine Cent. R. Co., 98 Me. 98, 56 Atl. 457, 99 Am. St. Rep. 339; Lewis v. Ocean S. S. Co., 12 Ga. App. 191, 76 S. E. 1073; Hollister v. Nowlen, 19 Wend. (N. Y.) 234, 32 Am. Dec. 455. Carriers are liable for the loss of baggage by theft, even when shipped as freight. The State of New York, 7 Ben. 450, Fed. Cas. No. 13,328; Walsh v. The H. M. Wright, Newb. 494, Fed. Cas. No. 17,115.

[5] Ford v. Atlantic Coast R. Co., 8 Ga. App. 295, 68 S. E. 1072; Saunders

that determine the insuring liability of the common carrier of goods, which have been discussed at some length,[6] are equally applicable here. So true is this that, though one carried free is a passenger,[7] yet as to his baggage, no compensation being received for its carriage, the carrier is a mere gratuitous bailee, and liable accordingly only for its negligence,[8] which is here its failure to exercise even slight care. Again, the whole subject of limitation of the carrier's liability as to baggage is governed by the rules controlling such limitations by common carriers of goods.[9]

v. Southern R. Co., 128 Fed. 15, 62 C. C. A. 523; Brick v. Atlantic Coast Line R. Co., 145 N. C. 203, 58 S. E. 1073, 122 Am. St. Rep. 440, 13 Ann. Cas. 328; Oakes v. Northern Pac. R. R. Co., 20 Or. 392, 26 Pac. 230, 12 L. R. A. 318, 23 Am. St. Rep. 126; Wolf v. Grand Rapids, Holland & Chicago Ry., 149 Mich. 75, 112 N. W. 732; McKibbin v. Great Northern Ry. Co., 78 Minn. 232, 80 N. W. 1052; Springer v. Pullman Co., 234 Pa. 172, 83 Atl. 98; Macrow v. Railway Co., L. R. 6 Q. B. (Eng.) 612; Southern R. Co. v. Foster, 7 Ala. App. 487, 60 So. 993. As to delay in transporting the baggage, see Brooks v. Northern Pac. R. Co., 58 Or. 387, 114 Pac. 949; Sperry v. Consolidated R. Co., 79 Conn. 565, 65 Atl. 962, 10 L. R. A. (N. S.) 907, 118 Am. St. Rep. 169, 9 Ann. Cas. 199. At common law a carrier was liable as bailee for negligence in the loss of baggage, even though the relation of passenger and carrier did not exist. Robinson v. New York Cent. & H. R. R. Co., 203 N. Y. 627, 97 N. E. 1115, affirming order 145 App. Div. 391, 129 N. Y. Supp. 1030. Where a passenger shows delivery of his baggage to a carrier and the carrier's failure to deliver the same, he makes out a prima facie case, and the burden is on the carrier to show that it has not converted the property. Fleischman, Morris & Co. v. Southern Ry., 76 S. C. 237, 56 S. E. 974, 9 L. R. A. (N. S.) 519.

6 See ante, §§ 116–118.

7 Ante, p. 530.

8 White v. St. Louis Southwestern R. Co. of Texas (Tex. Civ. App.) 86 S. W. 962; Holly v. Southern R. Co., 119 Ga. 767, 47 S. E. 188; Rice v. Illinois Cent. R. Co., 22 Ill. App. 644.

9 The distinction heretofore discussed (section 194) between the mere function of a ticket as a voucher or receipt (when its receipt alone does not make its stipulations binding on the passenger) and the ticket which on its face purports to be a contract (when it becomes binding on the passenger) is of great importance here; for limitations on the carrier's part, either as to weight or value of the baggage, or reducing the carrier's liability from that of an insurer to that of the ordinary bailee for hire, are usually contained in the passenger's ticket. A ticket limiting the carrier's liability for loss of baggage is ineffective, where the passenger does not know of the stipulation and is excusable for not knowing. Martin v. Central R. Co. of New Jersey, 121 App. Div. 552, 106 N. Y. Supp. 226. A provision in a ticket sold at a reduced rate limiting baggage to wearing apparel only and the liability of the carrier therefor to $50 is not unreasonable or unjust as matter of law. Gardiner v. New York Cent. & H. R. R. Co., 201 N. Y. 387, 94 N. E. 876, 34 L. R. A. (N. S.) 826, Ann. Cas. 1912B, 281. A ticket issued to a person at a reduced rate and limiting liability for baggage to wearing apparel not exceeding $100 in value does not relieve the carrier from accountability for the

Commencement and Termination of Insuring Liability

The carrier's insuring liability commences when the passenger, at a reasonable time before the departure of the conveyance on which the passenger and baggage are to be transported, delivers the baggage to, and it is accepted by, the carrier.[10] When the baggage is delivered and kept by the carrier in advance of such reasonable time, for the passenger's convenience, the carrier's liability would seem to be that merely of an ordinary bailee, liable only for his negligence.[11] The purchase of a ticket or checking the

value of the baggage lost through the negligence of its agents. Wells v. Great Northern Ry. Co., 59 Or. 165, 114 Pac. 92, 116 Pac. 1070, 34 L. R. A. (N. S.) 818, 825. Where plaintiff was traveling on a pass under an agreement thereon that the railroad company should not be liable for damage to property of such person by negligence of its agents or otherwise, such person could not recover for loss of baggage, except for willful misconduct. Hutto v. Southern Ry. Co., 75 S. C. 295, 55 S. E. 445. In the absence of fraud, a passenger signing a ticket containing stipulations limiting the liability of the carrier cannot urge that she was not aware of the stipulations. Rose v. Northern Pac. Ry. Co., 35 Mont. 70, 88 Pac. 767, 119 Am. St. Rep. 836. A carrier of passengers may bona fide agree on the value of baggage; but a mere general limitation as to value in a printed form applicable to the baggage of all passengers, though signed by the carrier and the passenger, is not a bona fide agreement, but an arbitrary preadjustment of damages. Southern Ry. Co. v. Dinkins & Davidson Hardware Co., 139 Ga. 332, 77 S. E. 147, 43 L. R. A. (N. S.) 806. See, also, on this subject, Hasbrouck v. New York Cent. & H. R. R. Co., 202 N. Y. 363, 95 N. E. 808, 35 L. R. A. (N. S.) 537, Ann. Cas. 1912D, 1150; Wells v. Great Northern R. Co., 59 Or. 165, 114 Pac. 92, 116 Pac. 1070, 34 L. R. A. (N. S.) 818, 825; Hooker v. Boston & M. R. R. Co., 209 Mass. 598, 95 N. E. 945, Ann. Cas. 1912B, 669; Gomm v. Oregon R. & Nav. Co., 52 Wash. 685, 101 Pac. 361, 25 L. R. A. (N. S.) 537; Black v. Atlantic Coast Line R. Co., 82 S. C. 478, 64 S. E. 418. For interesting recent cases as to the Carmack Amendment to the Interstate Commerce Act (Act Feb. 4, 1887, c. 104, § 20, 24 Stat. 386 [U. S. Comp. St. 1901, p. 3169] as amended by Act June 29, 1906, c. 3591, § 7, pars. 11, 12, 34 Stat. 595 [U. S. Comp. St. Supp. 1911, p. 1307]), and limitation of the carriers' liability as to baggage, see Ford v. Chicago, R. I. & P. R. Co. (Minn.) 143 N. W. 249, and Barstow v. New York, N. H. & H. R. R. Co., 158 App. Div. 665, 143 N. Y. Supp. 983. See, also, note on these cases, 1 Va. Law Review, 405.

10 Williams v. Southern R. Co., 155 N. C. 260, 71 S. E. 346; Shaw v. Northern Pac. R. Co., 40 Minn. 144, 41 N. W. 548; Hofford v. New York Cent. & H. R. R. Co., 43 Pa. Super. Ct. 303; Goodbar v. Wabash Ry. Co., 53 Mo. App. 434; Moffat v. Long Island R. Co., 123 App. Div. 719, 107 N. Y. Supp. 1118. As a rule, notice must be given to an authorized agent of a carrier when baggage is taken to a railroad station or other place where baggage is usually received, in order to make the carrier liable, but the carrier may bind itself by a custom of treating baggage as received when left at a given place, without other notice. Williams v. Southern Ry. Co., 155 N. C. 260, 71 S. E. 346; Houston, E. & W. T. R. Co. v. Anderson (Tex. Civ. App.) 147 S. W. 353. See, also, Lennon v. Illinois Cent. R. Co., 127 Iowa, 431, 103 N. W. 343.

11 Fleischman, Morris Co. v. Southern Ry., 76 S. C. 237, 56 S. E. 974, 9 L. R. A. (N. S.) 519; Houston, E. & W. T. Ry. Co. v. Anderson (Tex. Civ. App.

baggage on such ticket is not essential to the commencement of the carrier's insuring liability.[12]

The exceptional liability of a carrier of baggage as an insurer is terminated when the passenger has had a reasonable time to remove it after it has been unloaded by the carrier, and placed in a situation for delivery.[13] No notice to the passenger of the arrival of the baggage has been held necessary in any state, since it arrives, in the ordinary course of transportation, on the same train as the owner.[14] In actual practice, the passenger is required to take his baggage away almost immediately.[15] In other words, a reasonable time, as to the passenger's baggage, is a very short time. Thus it has been held in several cases that, when the train carrying the passenger and his baggage arrived at night, it was an unreasonable delay to permit it to remain until the next morning.[16] Of course, any longer delay would relieve the carrier of his in-

147 S. W. 353; Hofford v. New York Cent. & H. R. R. Co., 43 Pa. Super. Ct. 303; Williams v. Southern R. Co., 155 N. C. 260, 71 S. E. 346.

12 Lake Shore & M. S. Ry. Co. v. Foster, 104 Ind. 293, 4 N. E. 20, 54 Am. Rep. 319; Houston, E. & W. T. Ry. Co. v. Anderson (Tex. Civ. App.) 147 S. W. 353; Green v. Milwaukee & St. P. R. Co., 41 Iowa, 410.

13 Kaplan v. Titus, 140 App. Div. 416, 125 N. Y. Supp. 397; Charlotte Trouser Co. v. Seaboard Air Line Ry. Co., 139 N. C. 382, 51 S. E. 973; Tallman v. Chicago, M. & St. P. R. Co., 136 Wis. 648, 118 N. W. 205, 16 Ann. Cas. 711; Central of Georgia R. Co. v. Jones, 150 Ala. 379, 43 South. 575, 9 L. R. A. (N. S.) 1240, 124 Am. St. Rep. 71; Blackmore v. Missouri Pac. Ry. Co., 162 Mo. 455, 62 S. W. 993; Moyer v. Pennsylvania R. Co., 31 Pa. Super. Ct. 559; Patsheider v. Ry. Co. (1878) 3 Exch. Div. (Eng.) 153. See, also, Milwaukee Mirror & Art Glass Works v. Chicago, M. & St. P. R. Co., 148 Wis. 173, 134 N. W. 379, 38 L. R. A. (N. S.) 383; Levi v. Missouri, K. & T. R. Co., 157 Mo. App. 536, 138 S. W. 699.

14 Moffatt v. Long Island R. Co., 123 App. Div. 719, 107 N. Y. Supp. 1113; Indiana, D. & W. R. Co. v. Zilly, 20 Ind. App. 569, 51 N. E. 141.

15 Tallman v. Chicago, M. & St. P. R. Co., 136 Wis. 648, 118 N. W. 205, 16 Ann. Cas. 711; Central R. Co. v. Wiegand, 79 Fed. 991, 25 C. C. A. 681; Moyer v. Pennsylvania R. Co., 31 Pa. Super. Ct. 559; Southern Ry. Co. v. Rosenheim & Sons, 1 Ga. App. 766, 58 S. E. 81; Campbell v. Missouri Pac. R. Co., 78 Neb. 479, 111 N. W. 126; Church v. New York Cent. & H. R. R. Co. (Sup.) 116 N. Y. Supp. 560; St. Louis & S. F. R. Co. v. Terrell (Tex. Civ. App.) 72 S. W. 430.

16 Campbell v. Missouri Pac. R. Co., 78 Neb. 479, 111 N. W. 126; Southern R. Co. v. Rosenheim & Sons, 1 Ga. App. 766, 58 S. E. 81; Jacobs v. Tutt (C. C.) 33 Fed. 412; Louisville, C. & L. R. Co. v. Mahan, 8 Bush (Ky.) 184; Roth v. Buffalo & S. L. R. Co., 34 N. Y. 548, 90 Am. Dec. 736; Ross v. Missouri, K. & T. R. Co., 4 Mo. App. 582. The fact that the arrival is on Sunday, and there is a statute prohibiting travel on that day, will not excuse the delay. Jones v. Norwich & N. Y. Transp. Co., 50 Barb. (N. Y.) 193. Nor will the illness of the passenger. Chicago, R. I. & P. R. Co. v. Boyce, 73 Ill. 510, 24 Am. Rep. 268.

suring liability.[17] But, if the fault of the carrier has caused the delay, its liability as such is not terminated.[18] If the passenger has not removed his baggage within a reasonable time, the carrier is not relieved of all liability, but continues responsible as a warehouseman,[19] and thus liable only for negligence.

Connecting Carriers

Considerations similar to those affecting the liability of the carrier of goods [20] govern the liability of the initial carrier and connecting carriers for the passengers' baggage. It is perfectly clear that the carrier on whose line the loss or injury occurred is responsible.[21] In the absence of a contract assuming such liability, the responsibility of the initial carrier is limited to its own line.[22]

[17] Hoeger v. Chicago, M. & St. P. Ry. Co., 63 Wis. 100, 23 N. W. 435, 53 Am. Rep. 271; Burnell v. New York Cent. R. Co., 45 N. Y. 184, 6 Am. Rep. 61; Indiana, D. & W. R. Co. v. Zilly, 20 Ind. App. 569, 51 N. E. 141.

[18] Georgia Railroad & Banking Co. v. Phillips, 93 Ga. 801, 20 S. E. 646; Wald v. Louisville, E. & St. L. R. Co., 92 Ky. 645, 18 S. W. 850; Dininny v. New York & N. H. R. Co., 49 N. Y. 546; Kansas City, Ft. S. & G. R. Co. v. Morrison, 34 Kan. 502, 9 Pac. 225, 55 Am. Rep. 252; Prickett v. New Orleans Anchor Line, 13 Mo. App. 436. But see Chicago & A. R. Co. v. Addizoat, 17 Ill. App. 632. Where a boat was delayed, and arrived in port during the night, it was held that the voyage was not ended until passengers who remained on board by the master's permission had had a reasonable time on the next morning to leave the boat and to remove their baggage, and that the carrier was liable to passengers so remaining on board for loss of baggage occasioned by the accidental burning of the vessel during the night. Prickett v. New Orleans Anchor Line, supra.

[19] Central of Georgia R. Co. v. Jones, 150 Ala. 379, 43 South. 575, 9 L. R. A. (N. S.) 1240, 124 Am. St. Rep. 71; Kressin v. Central R. Co. of New Jersey, 119 App. Div. 86, 103 N. Y. Supp. 1002; Burnell v. New York Cent. R. Co., 45 N. Y. 184, 6 Am. Rep. 61; Mattison v. New York Cent. R. Co., 57 N. Y. 552; Fairfax v. New York Cent. & H. R. R. Co., 67 N. Y. 11; Chicago, R. I. & P. R. Co. v. Fairclough, 52 Ill. 106; Bartholomew v. St. Louis, J. & C. R. Co., 53 Ill. 227, 5 Am. Rep. 45; Mote v. Chicago & N. W. R. Co., 27 Iowa, 22, 1 Am. Rep. 212; Rome R. R. v. Wimberly, 75 Ga. 316, 58 Am. Rep. 468. As to what is a proper place to store the baggage, see Hoeger v. Chicago, M. & St. P. Ry. Co., 63 Wis. 100, 23 N. W. 435, 53 Am. Rep. 271; St. Louis & C. R. Co. v. Hardway, 17 Ill. App. 321. See, also, cases cited in note 13.

[20] See ante, § 145.

[21] Glasco v. New York Cent. R. Co., 36 Barb. (N. Y.) 557; Barter v. Wheeler, 49 N. H. 9, 6 Am. Rep. 434; Atchison, T. & S. F. R. Co. v. Roach, 35 Kan. 740, 12 Pac. 93, 57 Am. Rep. 199; Hooper v. Ry. Co., 50 L. J. C. P. (Eng.) 103; Toledo, P. & W. Ry. Co. v. Merriman, 52 Ill. 123, 4 Am. Rep. 590.

[22] Lessard v. Boston & M. R. R., 69 N. H. 648, 45 Atl. 712; Mauritz v. New York, L. E. & W. R. Co. (C. C.) 23 Fed. 765; Soviero v. Westcott Exp. Co., 47 Misc. Rep. 596, 94 N. Y. Supp. 375; Talcott v. Wabash R. Co., 188 N. Y. 608, 81 N. E. 1176; Burnes v. Chicago, R. I. & P. R. Co., 167 Mo. App. 62, 150 S. W. 1100. As to the effect of the Carmack Amendment to the Interstate Commerce Act in making the initial carrier responsible for the de-

By contract,[23] however, and this is usually held to be the case when the initial carrier sells a through ticket and checks the passenger's baggage all the way to his destination, the first carrier is liable for loss or injury occurring on any of the connecting lines.[24] One carrier, too, may become liable, as to default on the part of another carrier, by virtue of partnership arrangements between the carriers.[25]

Liability of Carrier for Articles Not Baggage and Not Accepted as Such

The liability of the carrier for articles not technically baggage is a mooted question, when no notice is given to the carrier of the nature of such articles. That, under such circumstances, the carrier is not an insurer, is universally agreed.[26] Some courts, however, hold the carrier liable as a bailee, in which case it is usually held that he is liable as a gratuitous bailee for his failure to exercise even slight care.[27] Other courts, however, hold that the carrier is not liable for his negligence or failure to exercise even the slightest degree of care.[28]

faults of connecting carriers, see House v. Chicago & N. W. R. Co., 30 S. D. 321, 138 N. W. 809.

23 Little Rock & H. S. W. R. Co. v. Record, 74 Ark. 125, 85 S. W. 421, 109 Am. St. Rep. 67; Maskos v. American Steamship Co. (C. C.) 11 Fed. 698; Hubbard v. Mobile & O. R. Co., 112 Mo. App. 459, 87 S. W. 52. Where an initial carrier was authorized to and did sell a through ticket over other connecting roads, notice to the agent of the initial carrier of the contents of one of plaintiff's trunks was notice to the other connecting carriers. Southern Ry. Co. v. Foster, 7 Ala. App. 487, 60 South. 993.

24 Atchison, T. & S. F. R. Co. v. Roach, 35 Kan. 740, 12 Pac. 93, 57 Am. Rep. 199; Kansas City, Ft. S. & M. R. Co. v. Washington, 74 Ark. 9, 85 S. W. 406, 69 L. R. A. 65, 109 Am. St. Rep. 61; Hutchins v Pennsylvania R. Co., 181 N. Y. 186, 73 N. E. 972, 106 Am. St. Rep. 537; Baltimore & O. R. Co. v. Campbell, 36 Ohio St. 647, 38 Am. Rep. 617.

25 Wolf v. Grand Rapids, Holland & Chicago Ry., 149 Mich. 75, 112 N. W. 732; Najac v. Boston & L. R. Co., 7 Allen (Mass.) 329, 83 Am. Dec. 686; Texas & N. O. R. Co. v. Berry, 31 Tex. Civ. App. 3, 71 S. W. 326; Hart v. Rensselaer & S. R. Co., 8 N. Y. 37, 59 Am. Dec. 447.

26 See cases cited in notes 27 and 28.

27 Brick v. Atlantic Coast Line R. Co., 145 N. C. 203, 58 S. E. 1073, 122 Am. St. Rep. 440, 13 Ann. Cas. 328; Toledo & Ohio Cent. Ry. Co. v. Bowler & Burdick Co., 9 O. C. D. 465; St. Louis, I. M. & S. R. Co. v. Miller, 103 Ark. 37, 145 S. W. 889, 39 L. R. A. (N. S.) 634; Illinois Southern R. Co. v. Antoon, 122 Ill. App. 359; Smith v. Boston & M. R. R., 44 N. H. 325.

28 Dunlap v. International Steamboat Co., 98 Mass. 371; Nathan v. Woolverton, 149 App. Div. 791, 134 N. Y. Supp. 469; Gurney v. Grand Trunk Ry. Co., 59 Hun, 625, 14 N. Y. Supp. 321; Blumenthal v. Maine Cent. R. Co., 79 Me. 550, 11 Atl. 605; Denver & R. G. R. Co. v. Johnson, 50 Colo. 187, 114 Pac. 650, Ann. Cas. 1912C, 627. See, also, Humphreys v. Perry, 148 U. S. 627, 13 Sup. Ct. 711, 37 L. Ed. 587 (though here there was no allegation or proof of "gross negligence").

The latter rule seems to be sound, for, in the absence of notice to the contrary, the carrier is justified in believing that only technical baggage is offered to him; that only does he accept, and for that only is he paid. This is the rule adopted by the courts of both New York[29] and Massachusetts.[30] The passenger's silence in a measure works an imposition on the carrier, and it hardly seems fair, under such circumstances, to impose a bailment responsibility on the carrier as to articles which he did not know that he was receiving. When the passenger affirmatively deceives the carrier, there is, of course, not even a bailment responsibility.[31] Most of the cases, in which these questions arise, involve the transportation of merchandise.

Carrier's Lien on Passenger's Baggage

Reference has already been made to the carrier's lien on the passenger's baggage to secure the payment of fare.[32] This lien, however, does not extend to articles in the actual possession of the passenger, or to the clothing that he is wearing.[33] Nor can the passenger be detained by the carrier to compel the payment of fare.[34]

WHAT IS BAGGAGE

197. Baggage, in its technical sense, includes such articles of convenience or necessity, delivered to the carrier for transportation, as are carried by the passenger for his personal use, either during the journey or his stay at his destination, which are also fit and proper for the personal use of persons in the same condition of life as the passenger.

In General

The definition of baggage just given is one, sometimes with unimportant changes of phraseology, in general use.[35] Practically

[29] See cases cited in note 28.

[30] See cases cited in note 28.

[31] The Ionic, 5 Blatchf. 538, Fed. Cas. No. 7,059.

[32] Ante, p. 475. See, also, Kressin v. Central R. Co. of New Jersey, 119 App. Div. 86, 103 N. Y. Supp. 1002; Cantwell v. Terminal R. Ass'n of St. Louis, 160 Mo. App. 393, 140 S. W. 966.

[33] Ramsden v. Boston & A. R. Co., 104 Mass. 117, 6 Am. Rep. 200; Wolf v. Summers, 2 Camp. (Eng.) 631.

[34] Lynch v. Metropolitan El. R. Co., 90 N. Y. 77, 43 Am. Rep. 141. But when a passenger refused to surrender his ticket on leaving a boat, claiming that he had lost it, the carrier may detain the passenger long enough to investigate the circumstances of the case. Standish v. Narragansett S. S. Co., 111 Mass. 512, 15 Am. Rep. 66.

[35] Other definitions follow: "Such articles of personal convenience or ne-

to the same effect is Mr. Lawson's definition: "The term 'baggage' means such goods and chattels as the convenience or comfort, the taste, the pleasure, or the protection, of passengers generally makes it fit and proper for the passenger in question to take with him for his personal use, according to the wants or habits of the class to which he belongs, either with reference to the period of the transit, or the ultimate purpose of the journey." [26]

It will readily be seen that these definitions involve two distinct elements, both of which must concur, as to a particular article, in order that it may be baggage: (1) The article must be for the passenger's own personal use; and (2) it must in addition be

cessity as are usually carried by passengers for their personal use, and not merchandise and other valuables." 3 Hutch. Carr. § 1242, substantially following Story, Bailments, § 499. Of this definition it was said in Dibble v. Brown, 12 Ga. 217, 226, 56 Am. Dec. 460: "When we settle down with Judge Story, upon the proposition that by baggage is to be understood 'such articles of necessity or personal convenience as are usually carried by passengers, for their personal use,' we are still without a rule for determining what articles are included in baggage. For such things as would be necessary to one man would not be necessary to another. Articles which would be held but ordinary conveniences by A. might be considered incumbrances by B. One man, from choice or habit, or from educational incapacity to appreciate the comforts or conveniences of life, needs, perhaps, a portmanteau, a change of linen, and an indifferent razor; while another, from habit, position, and education, is unhappy without all the appliances of comfort which surround him at home. The quantity and character of baggage must depend very much upon the condition in life of the traveler—his calling, his habits, his tastes, the length or shortness of his journey, and whether he travels alone or with a family. If we agree, further, with Judge Story, and say that the articles of necessity or of convenience must be such as are usually carried by travelers for their personal use, we are still at fault, because there is, in no state of this Union, nor in any part of any one state, any settled usage as to the baggage which travelers carry with them for their personal use. The quantity and character of baggage found to accompany passengers are as various as are the countenances of the travelers." "All articles which it is usual for persons traveling to carry with them, whether from necessity, or for convenience or amusement." Angell Carriers, § 115. "Only such articles as a traveler usually carries with him for his comfort or convenience, both during the journey and during his stay at the place of his destination." Wood Ry. Law, § 401. See, further, on this subject, the following modern cases: Hasbrouck v. New York Cent. & H. R. R. Co., 202 N. Y. 363, 95 N. E. 808, 35 L. R. A. (N. S.) 537, Ann. Cas. 1912D, 1150; Godfrey v. Pullman Co., 87 S. C. 361, 69 S. E. 666, Ann. Cas. 1912B, 971; Kansas City Southern R. Co. v. Skinner, 88 Ark. 189, 113 S. W. 1019, 21 L. R. A. (N. S.) 850; St. Louis & S. F. R. Co. v. Dickerson, 29 Okl. 386, 118 Pac. 140; Pullman Co. v. Green, 128 Ga. 142, 57 S. E. 233, 119 Am. St. Rep. 368, 10 Ann. Cas. 693; Denver & R. G. R. Co. v. Johnson, 50 Colo. 187, 114 Pac. 650, Ann. Cas. 1912C, 627; Wingate v. Pere Marquette R. Co., 172 Ill. App. 314; House v. Chicago & N. W. R. Co., 30 S. D. 321, 138 N. W. 809.

[26] Lawson, Bailments, § 272.

such an article as is fit and proper to be taken for such use under similar conditions by persons in the same station of life as the passenger.

Personal Use of Passenger

The passenger's personal use excludes, of course, articles for the use of some other person,[37] and also merchandise carried for sale or to be used in effecting sales, or for purely mercantile purposes.[38] The term "personal use," however, would include "not only all articles of apparel, whether for use or ornament, but also the gun case or fishing apparatus of the sportsman, the easel of the artist on a sketching tour, or the books of a student, and other articles of an analogous character, the use of which is personal to the traveler, and the taking of which has arisen from his journeying." [39] But the term in this same opinion was held not to include "what is carried * * * for larger or ulterior purposes such as articles of furniture or household goods." Again, this term includes the tools of a mechanic [40] and the instruments of a surgeon,[41]

[37] See post, § 199. See, also, Andrews v. Ft. Worth & D. C. R. Co. (Tex. Civ. App.) 25 S. W. 1040; Brick v. Atlantic Coast Line R. Co., 145 N. C. 203, 58 S. E. 1073, 122 Am. St. Rep. 440, 13 Ann. Cas. 328; Chicago, R. I. & P. R. Co. v. Boyce, 73 Ill. 510, 24 Am. Rep. 268; Hudston v. Railway Co., L. R. 4 Q. B. (Eng.) 366; Metz v. California South R. Co., 85 Cal. 329, 24 Pac. 610, 9 L. R. A. 431, 20 Am. St. Rep. 228; Dunlap v. International Steamboat Co., 98 Mass. 371; Hurwitz v. Hamburg-American Packet Co., 27 Misc. Rep. 814, 56 N. Y. Supp. 379.

[38] Wunsch v. Northern Pac. R. Co. (C. C.) 62 Fed. 878; St. Louis, I. M. & S. R. Co. v. Miller, 103 Ark. 37, 145 S. W. 889, 39 L. R. A. (N. S.) 634; Kansas City, P. & G. R. Co. v. State, 65 Ark. 363, 46 S. W. 421, 41 L. R. A. 333, 67 Am. St. Rep. 933; Haines v. Chicago, St. P., M. & O. Ry. Co., 29 Minn. 160, 12 N. W. 447, 43 Am. Rep. 199; McElroy v. Iowa Cent. R. Co., 133 Iowa, 544, 110 N. W. 915; Brick v. Atlantic Coast Line R. Co., 145 N. C. 203, 58 S. E. 1073, 122 Am. St. Rep. 440, 13 Ann. Cas. 328; Mexican Cent. R. Co. v. De Rosear (Tex. Civ. App.) 109 S. W. 949.

[39] Cockburn, C. J., in Macrow v. Railway Co., L. R. 6 Q. B. (Eng.) 612. See, also, House v. Chicago & N. W. R. Co., 30 S. D. 321, 138 N. W. 809.

[40] Wells v. Great Northern R. Co., 59 Or. 165, 114 Pac. 92, 116 Pac. 1070, 34 L. R. A. (N. S.) 818, 825; Grzywacz v. New York Cent. & H. R. R. Co., 74 Misc. Rep. 343, 134 N. Y. Supp. 209 (razors of barber); Davis v. Cayuga & S. R. Co., 10 How. Prac. (N. Y.) 330; Porter v. Hildebrand, 14 Pa. 129. A reasonable quantity of his tools is proper baggage for a mechanic working as a watchmaker and jeweler. What such a reasonable quantity is, is a question for the jury. Kansas City, Ft. S. & G. R. Co. v. Morrison, 34 Kan. 502, 9 Pac. 225, 55 Am. Rep. 252; Texas & N. O. R. Co. v. Russell (Tex. Civ. App.) 97 S. W. 1090.

[41] Hannibal & St. J. R. Co. v. Swift, 12 Wall. 262, 20 L. Ed. 423. A dentist's instruments. Brock v. Gale, 14 Fla. 523, 14 Am. Rep. 356.

but not the costumes and properties of a theatrical company.[42] Clothing [43] and jewelry [44] are included in the term, as also money,[45] provided all of these be for the passenger's own use and be reasonable in quantity.

Articles Such as are Usually Carried by Similar People under Like Circumstances

Besides being for the passenger's personal use, the article, as we have seen, must be one that could be usually and properly carried by persons in the same station of life and conditions as the pas-

[42] Oakes v. Northern Pac. R. R. Co., 20 Or. 392, 26 Pac. 230, 12 L. R. A. 318, 23 Am. St. Rep. 126; Saunders v. Southern R. Co., 128 Fed. 15, 62 C. C. A. 523.

[43] Pettigrew v. Barnum, 11 Md. 434, 69 Am. Dec. 212; Dexter v. Syracuse, B. & N. Y. R. Co., 42 N. Y. 326, 1 Am. Rep. 527; Toledo, W. & W. Ry. Co. v. Hammond, 33 Ind. 379, 382, 5 Am. Rep. 221; Dibble v. Brown, 12 Ga. 217, 225, 56 Am. Dec. 460; Baltimore Steam Packet Co. v. Smith, 23 Md. 402, 87 Am. Dec. 575; RAILROAD CO. v. FRALOFF, 100 U. S. 24, 25 L. Ed. 531, Dobie Cas. Bailments and Carriers, 364; Yazoo & M. V. R. Co. v. Baldwin, 113 Tenn. 205, 81 S. W. 599; Galveston, H. & S. A. R. Co. v. Fales, 33 Tex. Civ. App. 457, 77 S. W. 234.

[44] Hasbrouck v. New York Cent. & H. R. R. Co., 202 N. Y. 363, 95 N. E. 808, 35 L. R. A. (N. S.) 537, Ann. Cas. 1912D, 1150; Pullman Co. v. Green, 128 Ga. 142, 57 S. E. 233, 119 Am. St. Rep. 368, 10 Ann. Cas. 893; Hubbard v. Mobile & O. R. Co., 112 Mo. App. 459, 87 S. W. 52; Godfrey v. Pullman Co., 87 S. C. 361, 69 S. E. 666, Ann. Cas. 1912B, 971. See, also, cases cited in note 54.

[45] Texas & N. O. R. Co. v. Lawrence, 42 Tex. Civ. App. 318, 95 S. W. 663; Godfrey v. Pullman Co., 87 S. C. 361, 69 S. E. 666, Ann. Cas. 1912B, 971; Illinois Cent. R. Co. v. Copeland, 24 Ill. 332, 76 Am. Dec. 749 (but cf. Davis v. Michigan Southern & N. I. R. Co., 22 Ill. 278, 74 Am. Dec. 151); Merrill v. Grinnell, 30 N. Y. 594; Orange County Bank v. Brown, 9 Wend. (N. Y.) 85, 24 Am. Dec. 129; Hutchings v. Western & A. R. Co., 25 Ga. 61, 71 Am. Dec. 156; Bomar v. Maxwell, 9 Humph. (Tenn.) 621, 51 Am. Dec. 682; Doyle v. Kiser, 6 Ind. 242. In Grant v. Newton, 1 E. D. Smith (N. Y.) 95, it was held that the liability of a passenger carrier for baggage lost through his negligence does not extend to money, even if no more than sufficient for traveling expenses, contained in the trunk of a passenger. In Merrill v. Grinnell, 30 N. Y. 594, upon the question of a reasonable amount of money for traveling purposes, it was held that the "amount must be measured, not alone by the requirements of the transit over a particular part of the entire route to which the line of one class of carriers extends, but must embrace the whole of the contemplated journey, and includes such an allowance for accidents or sickness, and for sojourning by the way, as a reasonably prudent man would consider it necessary to make." In this case, $800 in gold coin in the passenger's trunk was not considered to be too large an amount, the intended journey being from Hamburg to New York and San Francisco. But money to be used in business is not baggage. Levins v. New York, N. H. & H. R. Co., 183 Mass. 175, 66 N. E. 803, 97 Am. St. Rep. 434; Pfister v. Central Pac. R. Co., 70 Cal. 169, 11 Pac. 686, 59 Am. Rep. 404. And see, on this point, cases cited in note 61.

senger.[46] This is always a question of intense relativity,[47] and in solving it all the surrounding circumstances must be taken into consideration, including particularly sex, age, wealth, social position, and nationality of the passenger and the length of the journey, its object, the season when it is undertaken, and the localities to be visited. Thus a razor might well be baggage for a man, but not for a woman, while quite the contrary would be the case as to a tortoise shell hairpin. An instructive case on this subject is the FRALOFF CASE,[48] in which $10,000 worth of lace was held to be baggage. This sounds startling, but the passenger was a Russian lady, of great wealth and high social position in a country given to wearing expensive lace, and she was making a long journey through many countries, expecting to attend various social functions calling for equally as varied costumes.

Articles Held to be Baggage

The following articles have been held, ***under the peculiar circumstances of each case,*** to come within the definition of baggage: Cloth and materials intended for clothing;[49] rifles;[50] pistols;[51]

[46] Spooner v. Hannibal & St. J. R. Co., 23 Mo. App. 403; Galveston, H. & S. A. R. Co. v. Fales, 33 Tex. Civ. App. 457, 77 S. W. 234; St. Louis S. W. Ry. Co. v. Berry, 60 Ark. 433, 30 S. W. 764, 28 L. R. A. 501, 46 Am. St. Rep. 212; Hasbrouck v. New York Cent. & H. R. R. Co., 202 N. Y. 363, 95 N. E. 808, 35 L. R. A. (N. S.) 537, Ann. Cas. 1912D, 1150; Godfrey v. Pullman Co., 87 S. C. 361, 69 S. E. 666, Ann. Cas. 1912B, 971; Werner v. Evans, 94 Ill. App. 328.

[47] Denver & R. G. R. Co. v. Johnson, 50 Colo. 187, 114 Pac. 650, Ann. Cas. 1912C, 627; Curtis v. Delaware, L. & W. R. Co., 74 N. Y. 116, 30 Am. Rep. 271; Hawkins v. Hoffman, 6 Hill (N. Y.) 586, 41 Am. Dec. 767; Johnson v. Stone, 11 Humph. (Tenn.) 419; Amory v. Wabash R. Co., 130 Mich. 404, 90 N. W. 22; Runyan v. Central R. Co. of New Jersey, 61 N. J. Law, 537, 41 Atl. 367, 43 L. R. A. 284, 68 Am. St. Rep. 711.

[48] RAILROAD CO. v. FRALOFF, 100 U. S. 24, 25 L. Ed. 531, Dobie Cas. Bailments and Carriers, 364.

[49] Mauritz v. New York, L. E. & W. R. Co. (C. C.) 23 Fed. 765, 21 Am. & Eng. Ry. Cas. 286, 292; Van Horn v. Kermit, 4 E. D. Smith (N. Y.) 453; Duffy v. Thompson, Id. 178; Kansas City Southern R. Co. v. Skinner, 88 Ark. 189, 113 S. W. 1019, 21 L. R. A. (N. S.) 850.

[50] Bruty v. Railroad Co., 32 U. C. Q. B. (Canada) 66; Davis v. Cayuga & S. R. Co., 10 How. Prac. (N. Y.) 330.

[51] Davis v. Michigan Southern & N. I. R. Co., 22 Ill. 278, 74 Am. Dec. 151. Where a Chicago grocer, who went into the country in quest of butter, sought to recover of a carrier the value of two revolvers as part of his baggage, which was lost by the company, it was held, with due regard to the habits and condition in life of the passenger, that more than one revolver was not reasonably necessary for his personal use and protection. Chicago, R. I. & P. R. Co. v. Collins, 56 Ill. 212. But, in Woods v. Devin, 13 Ill. 746, 56 Am. Dec. 483, a passenger was allowed to recover for the loss of a pocket pistol and a pair of dueling pistols contained in his carpetbag with other baggage.

guns, when for sporting purposes;[52] bedding, when passenger is required to provide it;[53] watches and jewelry, when intended to be worn;[54] opera glasses or telescopes;[55] dressing cases;[56] books and manuscripts of a student;[57] a commercial traveler's price book;[58] a camera.[59]

Articles Held Not to Constitute Baggage

Under the circumstances of each particular case, the following articles have been held not to constitute baggage: Bedding, household goods, etc.;[60] money not intended for personal use;[61]

[52] Van Horn v. Kermit, 4 E. D. Smith (N. Y.) 453. See, also, House v. Chicago & N. W. R. Co., 30 S. D. 321, 138 N. W. 809.

[53] Hirschsohn v. Hamburg American Packet Co., 34 N. Y. Super. Ct. 521; Ouimit v. Henshaw, 35 Vt. 604, 84 Am. Dec. 646.

[54] See cases cited in note 44. See, also, Sherman v. Pullman Co., 79 Misc. Rep. 52, 139 N. Y. Supp. 51; McCormick v. Hudson River R. Co., 4 E. D. Smith (N. Y.) 181; Torpey v. Williams, 3 Daly (N. Y.) 162; McGill v. Rowand, 3 Pa. 451, 45 Am. Dec. 654: Jones v. Voorhees, 10 Ohio, 145; Coward v. East Tennessee, V. & G. R. Co., 16 Lea (Tenn.) 225, 57 Am. Rep. 227; American Contract Co. v. Cross, 8 Bush (Ky.) 472, 8 Am. Rep. 471. A man traveling alone, and carrying in his trunk, for transportation, a quantity of lady's jewelry, cannot recover for the loss thereof against a common carrier. Metz v. California Southern R. Co., 85 Cal. 329, 24 Pac. 610, 9 L. R. A. 431, 20 Am. St. Rep. 228.

[55] Toledo, W. & W. Ry. Co. v. Hammond, 33 Ind. 379, 5 Am. Rep. 221; Cadwallader v. Grand Trunk R. Co., 9 L. C. (Canada) 169; Hubbard v. Mobile & O. R. Co., 112 Mo. App. 459, 87 S. W. 52.

[56] Cadwallader v. Ry. Co., 9 L. C. (Canada) 169.

[57] Gleason v. Goodrich Transp. Co., 32 Wis. 85, 14 Am. Rep. 716; Hopkins v. Westcott, 6 Blatchf. 64, Fed. Cas. No. 6,692; Doyle v. Kiser, 6 Ind. 242. See, also, holding manuscript music baggage of a traveling company, Texas & P. Ry. Co. v. Morrison Faust Co., 20 Tex. Civ. App. 144, 48 S. W. 1103.

[58] Gleason v. Goodrich Transp. Co., 32 Wis. 85, 14 Am. Rep. 716; Staub v. Kendrick, 121 Ind. 226, 23 N. E. 79, 6 L. R. A. 619. See, also, Wingate v. Pere Marquette Ry. Co., 172 Ill. App. 314.

[59] Atwood v. Mohler, 108 Ill. App. 416.

[60] Connolly v. Warren, 106 Mass. 146, 8 Am. Rep. 300; Macrow v. Railroad Co., L. R. 6 Q. B. (Eng.) 612; Texas & P. Ry. Co. v. Ferguson, 1 White & W. Civ. Cas. Ct. App. (Tex.) § 1253, 9 Am. & Eng. R. Cas. 395; Mexican Cent. R. Co. v. De Rosear (Tex. Civ. App.) 109 S. W. 949; Mauritz v. New York, L. E. & W. R. Co. (C. C.) 23 Fed. 765.

[61] Levins v. New York, N. H. & H. R. Co., 183 Mass. 175, 66 N. E. 803, 97 Am. St. Rep. 434; Pfister v. Central Pac. R. Co., 70 Cal. 169, 11 Pac. 686, 59 Am. Rep. 404; Orange County Bank v. Brown, 9 Wend. (N. Y.) 85, 24 Am. Dec. 129; Weed v. Saratoga & S. R. Co., 19 Wend. (N. Y.) 534; Whitmore v. The Caroline, 20 Mo. 513; Jordan v. Fall River R. Co., 5 Cush. (Mass.) 69, 51 Am. Dec. 44; Dunlap v. International Steamboat Co., 98 Mass. 371; Dibble v. Brown, 12 Ga. 217, 56 Am. Dec. 460; Davis v. Michigan Southern & N. I. R. Co., 22 Ill. 278, 74 Am. Dec. 151; Hutchings v. Western & A. R. R., 25 Ga. 61, 71 Am. Dec. 156. Money carried in a passenger's trunk for transportation merely, and not for traveling expenses, is not baggage; and,

cloth for a dress intended for a third person;[62] presents;[63] toys;[64] handcuffs and locks;[65] quantities of watches;[66] bullion, jewelry, etc., not intended to be worn;[67] samples of traveling salesmen;[68] deeds and documents;[69] valuable papers;[70] engravings;[71] silverware;[72] bicycles.[73]

Question for Jury or Court

The question whether certain articles are technically baggage is usually one of fact for the jury.[74] This is always true when

if the carrier is not informed of its presence, he is not liable for its loss. Orange County Bank v. Brown, 9 Wend. (N. Y.) 85, 24 Am. Dec. 129. Compare the cases cited in note 45.

[62] Dexter v. Syracuse, B. & N. Y. R. Co., 42 N. Y. 326, 1 Am. Rep. 527.

[63] Nevins v. Bay Steamboat Co., 4 Bosw. (N. Y.) 225; The Ionic, 5 Blatchf. 538, Fed. Cas. No. 7,059.

[64] Hudston v. Railway Co., L. R. 4 Q. B. (Eng.) 366 (rocking horse as a present for a child).

[65] Bomar v. Maxwell, 9 Humph. (Tenn.) 621, 51 Am. Dec. 682.

[66] Belfast, etc., Ry. Co. v. Keys, 9 H. L. Cas. (Eng.) 556; Mississippi Cent. Ry. Co. v. Kennedy, 41 Miss. 671.

[67] Cincinnati & C. Air Line R. Co. v. Marcus, 38 Ill. 219; Nevins v. Bay Steamboat Co., 4 Bosw. (N. Y.) 225; Steers v. Liverpool, N. Y. & P. S. S. Co., 57 N. Y. 1, 15 Am. Rep. 453; MICHIGAN CENT. R. CO. v. CARROW, 73 Ill. 348, 24 Am. Rep. 248, Dobie Cas. Bailments and Carriers, 369. Contrast cases cited in note 44.

[68] Hawkins v. Hoffman, 6 Hill (N. Y.) 586, 41 Am. Dec. 767; Pennsylvania Co. v. Miller, 35 Ohio St. 541, 35 Am. Rep. 620; Alling v. Boston & A. R. Co., 126 Mass. 121, 30 Am. Rep. 667; Stimson v. Connecticut River R. Co., 98 Mass. 83, 93 Am. Dec. 140; Southern Kansas Ry. Co. v. Clark, 52 Kan. 398, 34 Pac. 1054; Humphreys v. Perry, 148 U. S. 627, 13 Sup. Ct. 711, 37 L. Ed. 587; Rossier v. Wabash R. Co., 115 Mo. App. 515, 91 S. W. 1018; Hoeger v. Chicago, M. & St. P. Ry. Co., 63 Wis. 100, 23 N. E. 435, 53 Am. Rep. 271; Cahill v. Railway Co., 10 C. B. N. S. (Eng.) 154, 100 E. C. L. 154.

[69] Phelps v. Railway Co., 19 C. B. N. S. (Eng.) 321.

[70] Phelps v. Railway Co., 19 C. B. N. S. (Eng.) 321; Thomas v. Railway Co., 14 U. C. Q. B. (Canada) 389. Compare and contrast the cases cited in note 57. See, also, Yazoo & M. V. R. Co. v. Georgia Home Ins. Co., 85 Miss. 7, 37 South. 500, 67 L. R. A. 646, 107 Am. St. Rep. 265, holding the papers relating to the business of a principal not to be baggage in the trunk of the agent.

[71] Nevins v. Bay Steamboat Co. 4 Bosw. (N. Y.) 225.

[72] Giles v. Fauntleroy, 13 Md. 126.

[73] State ex rel. Bettis v. Missouri Pac. Ry. Co., 71 Mo. App. 385.

[74] RAILROAD CO. v. FRALOFF, 100 U. S. 24, 25 L. Ed. 531, Dobie Cas. Bailments and Carriers, 364; Texas & N. O. R. Co. v. Russell (Tex. Civ. App.) 97 S. W. 1090; Little Rock & H. S. W. R. Co. v. Record, 74 Ark. 125, 85 S. W. 421, 109 Am. St. Rep. 67; Mauritz v. New York, L. E. & W. R. Co. (C. C.) 23 Fed. 765; Knieriem v. New York Cent. & H. R. R. Co., 109 App. Div. 709, 96 N. Y. Supp. 902; Missouri, K. & T. R. Co. of Texas v. Meek, 33 Tex. Civ. App. 47, 75 S. W. 317; Oakes v. Northern Pac. R. R. Co., 20 Or. 392, 26 Pac. 230, 12 L. R. A. 318, 23 Am. St. Rep. 126; Wingate v. Pere Marquette Ry. Co., 172 Ill. App. 314.

the facts are in dispute.[75] Even when these are admitted, however, the questions of whether the article is for the passenger's personal use or is suitable for persons in his station to carry under the circumstances ordinarily should be determined by the jury.[76] When, however, both the facts and the solution of these questions on the facts are clear and obvious, the question becomes one of law for the court.[77]

LIABILITY OF CARRIER FOR MERCHANDISE SHIPPED AS BAGGAGE

198. If the carrier, with full knowledge, voluntarily accepts as baggage, for transportation with the passenger, articles which are not actually baggage, then the carrier thereby incurs an insuring liability as to such articles, just as if they were technically baggage.

While common carriers of passengers are bound to carry the passenger's baggage, they are not bound to carry with the passenger anything that is not, in a technical legal sense, baggage.[78] Freight trains and express facilities are provided for the transportation of such articles, and the carrier is entitled to compensation therefor. The carrier's liability, when he carries such articles as baggage, *without knowledge of their true character,* has just been discussed.[79]

A different question is presented, however, when the carrier knows the nature of the articles, which indicates that these are

[75] Since the jury is primarily the trier of facts, this would naturally follow. See cases cited in previous note; also Godfrey v. Pullman Co., 87 S. C. 361, 69 S. E. 666, Ann. Cas. 1912B, 971.

[76] Knieriem v. New York Cent. & H. R. R. Co., 109 App. Div. 709, 96 N. Y. Supp. 602; RAILROAD CO. v. FRALOFF, 100 U. S. 24, 25 L. Ed. 531, Doble Cas. Bailments and Carriers, 364; Oakes v. Northern Pac. R. R. Co., 20 Or. 392, 26 Pac. 230, 12 L. R. A. 318, 23 Am. St. Rep. 126; Godfrey v. Pullman Co., 87 S. C. 361, 69 S. E. 666, Ann. Cas. 1912B, 971; Texas & N. O. R. Co. v. Russell (Tex. Civ. App.) 97 S. W. 1090; Missouri, K. & T. R. Co. of Texas v. Meek, 33 Tex. Civ. App. 47, 75 S. W. 317; Kansas City, Ft. S. & G. R. Co. v. Morrison, 34 Kan. 502, 9 Pac. 225, 55 Am. Rep. 252.

[77] Godfrey v. Pullman Co., 87 S. C. 361, 69 S. E. 666, Ann. Cas. 1912B, 971; Jones v. Priester, 1 White & W. Civ. Cas. Ct. App. (Tex.) § 613; Connolly v. Warren, 106 Mass. 146, 8 Am. Rep. 300.

[78] Smith v. Boston & M. R. R., 44 N. H. 325; Collins v. Boston & M. R., 10 Cush. (Mass.) 506; Pfister v. Central Pac. R. Co., 70 Cal. 169, 11 Pac. 686, 59 Am. Rep. 404; Norfolk & W. R. Co. v. Irvine, 84 Va. 553, 5 S. E. 532; Id., 85 Va. 217, 7 S. E. 233, 1 L. R. A. 110.

[79] Ante, pp. 641–642.

merchandise rather than baggage, and still accepts and transports the articles as baggage. There is substantial agreement among the courts that, when the carrier has knowingly and voluntarily treated the goods as baggage, these are thereby impressed with that character in so far as the carrier's liability is concerned. His liability, then, as to such articles thus received, is that of an insurer, just as if these articles came technically within the definition of baggage.[80] The doctrine of estoppel may well be applied here against the carrier.

Where the carrier or his agent is expressly notified that the articles are not baggage, and nevertheless receives them, no question as to notice can arise. But, even without express notice, knowledge that the articles are not baggage may be implied where the goods are so packed that their nature is obvious.[81] Thus, where a roll of carpet was received as baggage, the carrier was held liable

[80] Jacobs v. Tutt (C. C.) 33 Fed. 412. In Stoneman v. Erie Ry. Co., 52 N. Y. 429, Peckham, J., said: "I think it safe to say that, if the carrier knew or had notice of the character of the goods taken as baggage, and still undertook to transport them, he is liable for their loss, although they are not travelers' baggage." See Waldron v. Chicago & N. W. R. Co., 1 Dak. 351, 46 N. W. 456; St. Louis, I. M. & S. R. Co. v. Green, 44 Tex. Civ. App. 13, 97 S. W. 531; Bergstrom v. Chicago, R. I. & P. R. Co., 134 Iowa, 223, 111 N. W. 818, 10 L. R. A. (N. S.) 1119, 13 Ann. Cas. 239; Fleischman Morris & Co. v. Southern Ry. Co., 76 S. C. 237, 56 S. E. 974, 9 L. R. A. (N. S.) 519; St. Louis & S. F. Ry. Co. v. Lilly, 1 Ala. App. 320, 55 South. 937; Wells v. Great Northern R. Co., 59 Or. 165, 114 Pac. 92, 116 Pac. 1070, 34 L. R. A. (N. S.) 818, 825; Honeyman v. Oregon & C. R. Co., 13 Or. 352, 10 Pac. 628, 57 Am. Rep. 20; St. Louis S. W. Ry. Co. v. Berry, 60 Ark. 433, 30 S. W. 764, 28 L. R. A. 501, 46 Am. St. Rep. 212; MICHIGAN CENT. R. CO. v. CARROW, 73 Ill. 348, 24 Am. Rep. 248, Dobie Cas. Bailments and Carriers, 369; Southern R. Co. v. Dinkins & Davidson Hardware Co., 139 Ga. 332, 77 S. E. 147, 43 L. R. A. (N. S.) 806. An agent who is charged with receiving and checking baggage has ordinarily authority (by virtue of his position) to accept merchandise as baggage, rendering the carrier liable accordingly. Charlotte Trouser Co. v. Seaboard Air Line R. Co., 139 N. C. 382, 51 S. E. 973; Chicago, R. I. & P. R. Co. v. Conklin, 32 Kan. 55, 3 Pac. 762; Toledo & O. C. Ry. Co. v. Dages, 57 Ohio St. 38, 47 N. E. 1039.

[81] Dahrooge v. Pere Marquette R. Co., 144 Mich. 544, 108 N. W. 283; Illinois Cent. R. Co. v. Matthews, 114 Ky. 973, 72 S. W. 302, 60 L. R. A. 846, 102 Am. St. Rep. 316; Amory v. Wabash R. Co., 130 Mich. 404, 90 N. W. 22; Trimble v. New York Cent. & H. R. R. Co., 162 N. Y. 84, 56 N. E. 532, 48 L. R. A. 115; Kansas City Ft. S. & M. Ry. Co. v. McGahey, 63 Ark. 344, 38 S. W. 659, 36 L. R. A. 781, 58 Am. St. Rep. 111. The fact that a package was marked "Glass," and resembled a package of merchandise, is insufficient to show an undertaking to carry such merchandise as baggage. Cahill v. Railway Co., 10 C. B. N. S. (Eng.) 154, 13 C. B. N. S. 818. The packing of articles, not baggage, in a laundry basket, does not give notice to the carrier of the character of the articles. St. Louis, I. M. & S. R. Co. v. Miller, 103 Ark. 37, 145 S. W. 889, 39 L. R. A. (N. S.) 634.

for its loss.[82] And, where poles, ropes, and canvas constituting a tent belonging to a passenger were accepted as baggage for transportation, it was held that the carrier must account for them as if they were personal luggage.[83] But the mere fact that a box is tendered, instead of a trunk,[84] or that a trunk is of the kind usually used by commercial travelers,[85] is not notice that they contain merchandise or samples; for baggage may well be carried in that manner, though the size and number of these trunks and other circumstances might constitute implied notice to the carrier that the trunks do contain merchandise rather than baggage. Custom and usage of the carrier are frequently relevant on this point.[86]

A passenger, by tendering a package to be carried as baggage, impliedly represents that it contains only baggage.[87] The carrier has a right to rely upon this representation without making any inquiries, in the absence of facts putting the carrier on notice, even though there may be single suspicious circumstances.[88] If the carrier inquires as to the contents, the passenger must, of course, answer truly; and, if he refuses to answer, the carrier may refuse to transport the articles as baggage.[89]

[82] Minter v. Pacific R. R., 41 Mo. 503, 97 Am. Dec. 288.

[83] Chicago, R. I. & P. R. Co. v. Conklin, 32 Kan. 55, 3 Pac. 762.

[84] Belfast, etc., Ry. Co. v. Keys, 9 H. L. Cases (Eng.) 556. See, also, St. Louis, I. M. & S. R. Co. v. Green, 44 Tex. Civ. App. 13, 97 S. W. 531. But compare when the box obviously contained merchandise and was carried with the passenger's baggage. Waldron v. Chicago & N. W. R. Co., 1 Dak. 351, 46 N. W. 456.

[85] MICHIGAN CENT. R. CO. v. CARROW, 73 Ill. 348, 24 Am. Rep. 248, Dobie Cas. Bailments and Carriers, 369; Alling v. Boston & A. R. Co., 126 Mass. 121, 30 Am. Rep. 667; Rossier v. Wabash R. Co., 115 Mo. App. 515, 91 S. W. 1018; Humphreys v. Perry, 148 U. S. 627, 13 Sup. Ct. 711, 37 L. Ed. 587.

[86] See cases cited in note 81; Trimble v. New York Cent. & H. R. R. Co., 162 N. Y. 84, 56 N. E. 532, 48 L. R. A. 115; Sloman v. Great Western R. Co., 67 N. Y. 208.

[87] MICHIGAN CENT. R. CO. v. CARROW, 73 Ill. 348, 24 Am. Rep. 248, Dobie Cas. Bailments and Carriers, 369; Humphreys v. Perry, 148 U. S. 627, 13 Sup. Ct. 711, 37 L. Ed. 587; Haines v. Chicago, St. P., M. & O. Ry. Co., 29 Minn. 160, 12 N. W. 447, 43 Am. Rep. 199.

[88] Cahill v. Railway Co., 10 C. B. N. S. (Eng.) 154, 13 C. B. N. S. 818; MICHIGAN CENT. R. CO. v. CARROW, 73 Ill. 348, 24 Am. Rep. 248, Dobie Cas. Bailments and Carriers, 369; Pennsylvania Co. v. Miller, 35 Ohio St. 541, 35 Am. Rep. 620. See, also, Blumenthal v. Maine Cent. R. Co., 79 Me. 550, 11 Atl. 605.

[89] RAILROAD CO. v. FRALOFF, 100 U. S. 24, 25 L. Ed. 531, Dobie Cas. Bailments and Carriers, 364; Norfolk & W. R. Co. v. Irvine, 84 Va. 553, 5 S. E. 532; Id., 85 Va. 217, 7 S. E. 233, 1 L. R. A. 110.

PASSENGER MUST EITHER OWN THE BAGGAGE OR HAVE A SPECIAL INTEREST IN IT

199. One, to recover against the carrier for loss of, or damage to, articles as baggage, must be a passenger, and must also either own these articles or have a special interest in them.

Baggage Implies Passenger

Since it is an incident to the transportation of the passenger, the very term "baggage" implies the relation of passenger and carrier. Unless, therefore, one is a passenger, strictly speaking, he can have no baggage. Only a passenger, therefore, can sue the carrier for loss or damage as to articles on the score of the carrier's liability arising out of the fact that these articles were technically baggage.[90] Accordingly, if one secures the transportation of articles on the representation that he will become a passenger and he does not become one, then clearly he cannot hold the carrier liable for these articles as baggage.[91] Again, if the carrier transports the goods, knowing that there was not even an intention on the part of the owner to become a passenger, such carrier is a carrier of goods, whose liability is to be worked out accordingly without reference to the subject of baggage.[92]

Passenger Must Own or Have a Special Interest in the Baggage

Ordinarily the person accompanying the baggage is its owner, in which case there is little difficulty as to the liability of the carrier. The carrier, though, is not responsible for articles as baggage when the passenger for whom they are carried has neither the ownership of, nor a special interest in, these articles; for in such

[90] Marshall v. Pontiac, O. & N. R. Co., 126 Mich. 45, 85 N. W. 242, 55 L. R. A. 650; Beers v. Boston & A. R. Co., 67 Conn. 417, 34 Atl. 541, 32 L. R. A. 535, 52 Am. St. Rep. 293 (mistake). Cases in which the plaintiff is a passenger, but his baggage is not transported on the same train or boat, present somewhat different problems, and these cases are treated in section 200. See Wood v. Maine Cent. R. Co., 98 Me. 98, 56 Atl. 457, 99 Am. St. Rep. 339. See, also, 3 Hutch. Carr. § 1274.

[91] Marshall v. Pontiac, O. & N. R. Co., 126 Mich. 45, 85 N. W. 242, 55 L. R. A. 650. This case held the carrier liable only as a gratuitous bailee, though the plaintiff checked the "baggage" on a ticket that he bought solely for that purpose, and did not use the ticket save to check the baggage. Such cases are exceedingly rare. See criticism of this case in the note appended to the case in 55 L. R. A. 650. See, when the carrier had notice of the situation, the interesting case of Adger v. Blue Ridge Ry., 71 S. C. 213, 50 S. E. 783, 110 Am. St. Rep. 568.

[92] There would then be no occasion for invoking the law of passenger carriers.

case these would not be carried for the passenger's personal use.[93] Thus it has been held that a carrier is not liable on the score of baggage for the loss of money of one passenger contained in a valise which another passenger, with the knowledge of the first, delivers as his own baggage, and the carrier receives as such.[94] So where the plaintiff's servant goes on in advance, taking with him what might properly have been the master's baggage, it was held in Becher v. Great Eastern Ry. Co. that the carrier is not liable for its loss, if it was accepted as the baggage of the servant.[95]

If, however, the articles are personal to the passenger accompanying them and otherwise satisfy the definition of baggage as to him, it seems that these are none the less baggage by virtue of the fact that the passenger does not own the articles, but has only a special interest in them.[96] Thus, as to the rod of the fisherman on a fishing trip, it would hardly be a defense to the carrier's liability for baggage that the rod was not owned by the fishing passenger, but that he had hired the use of the rod for the trip from another. The bailee of the rod could accordingly sue the carrier for loss of, or damage to, the rod, as to which the carrier owes to such bailee the full insuring liability on the score that the rod is a part of the bailee's baggage. Particularly is this true, for the owner of the rod could not claim this same responsibility, since he is not a passenger.[97]

93 Southern Kansas Ry. Co. v. Clark, 52 Kan. 398, 34 Pac. 1054; Stimson v. Connecticut River R. Co., 98 Mass. 83, 93 Am. Dec. 140; Gurney v. Grand Trunk R. Co. of Canada, 138 N. Y. 638, 34 N. E. 512; Pennsylvania R. Co. v. Knight, 58 N. J. Law, 287, 33 Atl. 845.

94 Dunlap v. International Steamboat Co., 98 Mass. 371.

95 BECHER v. GREAT EASTERN R. CO., L. R. 5 Q. B. (Eng.) 241, Dobie Cas. Bailments and Carriers, 372.

96 See dictum of Smith, L. J., in Meux v. Ry. Co. [1895] 2 Q. B. (Eng.) 387, 394. See, also, Illinois Cent. Ry. Co. v. Matthews, 114 Ky. 973, 72 S. W. 302, 60 L. R. A. 846, 102 Am. St. Rep. 316; PULLMAN PALACE-CAR CO. v. GAVIN, 93 Tenn. 53, 23 S. W. 70, 21 L. R. A. 298, 42 Am. St. Rep. 902, Dobie Cas. Bailments and Carriers, 294.

97 In Battle v. Columbia, Newberry & Laurens R. R., 70 S. C. 329, 49 S. E. 849, it was held that the father (who was not a passenger) was the proper party to sue the carrier for loss of the baggage of an infant child. On the same subject, see, also, the following cases, upholding the father's right to sue for loss or damage to the child's baggage: Baltimore Steam Packet Co. v. Smith, 23 Md. 402, 87 Am. Dec. 575; Withey v. Pere Marquette R. Co., 141 Mich. 412, 104 N. W. 773, 1 L. R. A. (N. S.) 352, 113 Am. St. Rep. 533, 7 Ann. Cas. 57; Richardson v. Louisville & N. R. Co., 85 Ala. 559, 5 South. 308, 2 L. R. A. 716. In Brick v. Atlantic Coast Line R. Co., 145 N. C. 203, 58 S. E. 1073, 122 Am. St. Rep. 440, 13 Ann. Cas. 328, it was held that the owner could sue the carrier, though the goods were not the baggage of the passenger traveling with them, holding the carrier liable as a gratuitous bailee only.

In Meux v. Railway Co.[98] plaintiff's footman bought a ticket and checked as his baggage a valise containing his livery, which belonged to his mistress. She brought suit when the livery was injured by the carrier's carelessness. She was permitted to recover on the score that her property was lawfully in the custody of the carrier, the negligence of whose servants had injured it. There was no claim that the livery was the baggage of the plaintiff. Indeed, in his opinion granting her a recovery, Smith, L. J., took occasion to remark: "It did not render it any the less the luggage[99] of the footman because the property in the clothes remained in the plaintiff. * * * Of this I am clear that, in the circumstances of the case, the footman who had taken the ticket could have sued the company either in contract or tort."[1]

In the Becher Case,[2] supra, the articles tendered by the servant were the master's property, as to which the servant had no interest whatsoever, so that they were not technically the baggage of the servant. On that score as contrasted with the Meux Case, it was held there could be no recovery by the owner for the loss of these articles.

PASSENGER ACCOMPANYING THE BAGGAGE

200. While baggage seems to be transported by the carrier on the presumption that the passenger accompanies it, even if he fails to do so, the carrier is still liable by the better opinion (though there is conflict) as an insurer. If the carrier consents to this arrangement, or if the baggage is not transported with the passenger owing to the fault of the carrier, then it is generally agreed that the full insuring liability attaches.

The passenger cannot demand the transportation of his baggage unless he accompanies it. When, to the knowledge of the carrier, the passenger does not accompany it, the carrier, in the absence of an agreement to the contrary, transports the articles as a carrier of goods, and may charge freight for the transportation.

98 [1895] 2 Q. B. (Eng.) 387.

99 This term is synonymous with baggage.

1 [1895] 2 Q. B. (Eng.) 393, 394.

2 BECHER v. GREAT EASTERN R. CO., L. R. 5 Q. B. (Eng.) 241, Dobie Cas. Bailments and Carriers, 372.

Acceptance of Baggage by Carrier on Presumption that Passenger Accompanies It

There is confusion rather than conflict in the books, due largely to a failure to analyze the real problem involved, on the general subject of the passenger's accompanying his baggage. The first case to be considered is when the owner of the baggage makes, as a passenger, the same journey as the baggage; but, though the carrier carries the baggage on the presumption that the owner accompanies it, the passenger and baggage fail to go together, without fault of the carrier.

In this case the important element is that the carrier's contract, his acceptance, and his transportation seem to be based on the presumption that the passenger and baggage go together.[3] This presumption, without fault of the carrier is not true, for the passenger does not accompany the baggage. It is then held by some courts that the carrier is liable not as an insurer for the baggage, but merely as a gratuitous bailee, liable only for failure to exercise even slight care.[4] In such cases it is said that the handling of the baggage and the watch kept over it is on the basis that the passenger accompanies the baggage and that it might well be that the presence of the passenger, particularly in an emergency, ready to help in caring for his baggage may be of very real importance.[5] Under modern methods of handling baggage, however, it is believed that the better rule is to hold the carrier liable as an insurer, even though the passenger does not accompany the baggage.[6]

Members of the same family, traveling together, may carry each other's effects.[7] And it has been held that where the plaintiff

[3] Indeed, it is generally held that the passenger can ordinarily require that his baggage be carried on the same train with him. Runyan v. Central R. Co. of New Jersey, 61 N. J. Law, 537, 41 Atl. 367, 43 L. R. A. 284, 68 Am. St. Rep. 711; Conheim v. Chicago Great Western R. Co., 104 Minn. 312, 116 N. W. 581, 17 L. R. A. (N. S.) 1091, 124 Am. St. Rep. 623, 15 Ann. Cas. 389; Wald v. Pittsburg, C., C. & St. L. R. Co., 162 Ill. 545, 44 N. E. 888, 35 L. R. A. 356, 53 Am. St. Rep. 332.

[4] Collins v. Boston & M. R., 10 Cush. (Mass.) 506. See, also, Wood v. Maine Cent. R. Co., 98 Me. 98, 56 Atl. 457, 99 Am. St. Rep. 339 (though here the passenger did not make the trip in the same way as the baggage).

[5] Collins v. Boston & M. R., 10 Cush. (Mass.) 506.

[6] Moffat v. Long Island R. Co., 123 App. Div. 719, 107 N. Y. Supp. 1113; McKibbin v. Wisconsin Cent. R. Co., 100 Minn. 270, 110 N. W. 964, 8 L. R. A. (N. S.) 489, 117 Am. St. Rep. 689; LARNED v. CENTRAL R. CO. of NEW JERSEY, 81 N. J. Law, 571, 79 Atl. 289, Dobie Cas. Bailments and Carriers, 373; Logan v. Pontchartrain R. Co., 11 Rob. (La.) 24, 43 Am. Dec. 199; Adger v. Blue Ridge Ry., 71 S. C. 213, 50 S. E. 783, 110 Am. St. Rep. 568.

[7] Dexter v. Syracuse, B. & N. Y. R. Co., 42 N. Y. 326, 1 Am. Rep. 527; Yazoo & M. V. R. Co. v. Baldwin, 113 Tenn. 205, 81 S. W. 599; Battle v. Columbia, Newberry & Laurens R. R., 70 S. C. 329, 49 S. E. 849; Brick v. Atlantic

went on in advance, leaving his baggage to be brought seven days later by his wife, with her own baggage, the carrier was liable to plaintiff for its loss.[8]

Fault or Consent of Carrier

If the fact that the baggage does not go with the passenger is due to the fault of the carrier, there is general agreement that the latter incurs the full insuring liability.[9] Any other rule would operate to lessen the carrier's liability by his own wrong. If, therefore, the baggage goes on an earlier or later train than the passenger, on account of the negligent act of the servants of the carrier, the passenger can hold the latter fully responsible as an insurer. There is no duty resting on the passenger, after a proper delivery of his baggage to the carrier, to see that it is deposited in the conveyance by which he is to travel.

Again, if the carrier consents to sending the baggage, as baggage and not as freight, on a train or boat other than the one that carries the passenger, the full liability attaches.[10] The carrier, then, is bound by its consent to take the baggage as baggage, and cannot claim compensation, either, besides the regular fare for the transportation of the passenger.[11]

Transportation of Baggage as Freight

When the carrier knowingly transports the baggage, which the passenger does not accompany, unless the carrier agrees to carry it as baggage, it is carried as freight. The carrier is then, as to such transportation, a carrier of goods, whose charges and liabilities are to be worked out on that basis.[12] The fare paid by a passenger over a railroad is the compensation for his carriage, and for the transportation at the same time of such baggage as he may require for his personal convenience and necessity during his journey. Baggage subsequently forwarded by his direction, in the

Coast Line R. Co., 145 N. C. 203, 58 S. E. 1073; 122 Am. St. Rep. 440, 13 Ann. Cas. 328.

8 Curtis v. Delaware, L. & W. R. Co., 74 N. Y. 116, 30 Am. Rep. 271.

9 Toledo, St. L. & K. C. R. Co. v. Tapp, 6 Ind. App. 304, 33 N. E. 462. See, also, Wald v. Pittsburg, C., C. & St. L. R. Co., 162 Ill. 545, 44 N. E. 888, 35 L. R. A. 356, 53 Am. St. Rep. 332; Tewes v. North German Lloyd S. S. Co., 42 Misc. Rep. 148, 85 N. Y. Supp. 994; Southern R. Co. v. Foster, 7 Ala. App. 487, 60 South. 993.

10 Warner v. Burlington & M. R. R. Co., 22 Iowa, 166, 92 Am. Dec. 389.

11 Warner v. Burlington & M. R. R. Co., 22 Iowa, 166, 92 Am. Dec. 389.

12 Wilson v. Grand Trunk Ry. Co. of Canada, 57 Me. 138, 2 Am. Dec. 26; Graffam v. Boston & M. R. Co., 67 Me. 234; The Elvira Harbeck, 2 Blatchf. 336, Fed. Cas. No. 4,424; Wright v. Caldwell, 3 Mich. 51.

absence of any special agreement of the carrier, or of negligence on its part, is liable, like any other article of merchandise, to the payment of the usual freight.[13]

PASSENGER'S CUSTODY OF THE BAGGAGE

201. (a) When the passenger retains in his possession, without notice to the carrier, articles which would not fall within the technical definition of baggage, even if delivered to the carrier, the carrier owes to the passenger, as to these articles, no affirmative degree of care whatsoever.

(b) When articles which are properly baggage are delivered to the carrier, but which, for the convenience of the passenger, are carried in the stateroom or car with him, so he can have access to the articles, resulting in a mixed custody of passenger and carrier, the carrier is liable only for his negligence, or failure to exercise ordinary care. The English rule, favored by some of the American courts, however, holds the carrier in such cases liable as an insurer.

(c) As to articles which would properly be baggage if delivered to the carrier, but which the passenger retains in or about his person with the intention of exercising complete custody over them, the carrier is not an insurer, but is liable only for his negligence, or failure to exercise ordinary care.

In any case, the negligence of the passenger, contributing to the loss of, or injury to, the articles, is a complete defense to the carrier.

In General

In all the cases heretofore considered, it has been assumed that the baggage, or articles claimed to be such, had been delivered into the complete and exclusive custody of the carrier. In the present section the carrier's liability is discussed in connection with a more or less complete custody of the articles by the passenger himself. It has already been seen that common carriers of goods are liable as insurers only when the goods have been delivered into their exclusive custody.[14] The question in the case of the passenger carrier most frequently arises in respect to baggage retained in the custody of the passenger, or at least carried in the same car or stateroom with him, and more or less under his supervision. On analysis, these cases will be found to fall into one of

13 See cases cited in preceding note.

14 See ante, p. 327.

three classes, as indicated in the black letter text, and the whole subject can best be discussed on that basis.

Articles Not Technically Baggage in Exclusive Custody of the Passenger

In the first class of cases, the articles are not even potential baggage, for they would not fall within the technical definition of baggage, even on the most perfect delivery to the carrier. Besides this fact, however, these articles are retained in the absolute and exclusive custody of the passenger, who, in addition, gives no notice whatsoever to the carrier as to the articles.

Under the ordinary contract of carriage, a carrier of passengers makes no contract and enters into no duty as to articles not forming part of a passenger's ordinary baggage.[15] It seems pretty clear, then, that as to such articles, of which the carrier has no notice, and over which the passenger exercises exclusive custody, the carrier owes no duty of affirmative care, and is therefore not liable even for negligence.[16]

Where, therefore, a passenger carried $16,000 worth of bonds on his person, without notice to, or knowledge by, the carrier, and they were violently taken from him by robbers, without gross negligence or fraud on the part of the carrier, the latter was held not liable.[17] So, also, there was no liability where a passenger went upon defendant's train, carrying $4,000 with him, and during the transit the train fell through a bridge, and the passenger and

[15] See Henderson v. Louisville & N. R. Co., 123 U. S. 61, 8 Sup. Ct. 60, 31 L. Ed. 92, holding that the carrier was not liable for the loss by a woman passenger of her handbag out of the car window, though the carrier refused to stop the train to recover the bag, which she informed the conductor contained property of great value. Where a passenger on a subway lost a violin, due to a sudden jerk of the car, but without negligence of the carrier, it was under no duty to stop the car between stations to permit him to regain it. Bursteen v. Boston Elevated Ry. Co., 211 Mass. 459, 98 N. E. 27, 39 L. R. A. (N. S.) 313, Ann. Cas. 1913B, 558.

[16] Mexican Cent. R. Co. v. De Rosear (Tex. Civ. App.) 109 S. W. 949; First Nat. Bank of Greenfield v. Marietta & C. R. Co., 20 Ohio St. 259, 5 Am. Rep. 655; Del Valle v. The Richmond, 27 La. Ann. 90; Weeks v. New York, N. H. & H. R. Co., 72 N. Y. 50, 28 Am. Rep. 104. Some of the cases use expressions that indicate that the carrier, though not held liable in the instant case, might be held liable for "gross negligence"; that is, the failure to exercise even slight care.

[17] Weeks v. New York, N. H. & H. R. Co., 72 N. Y. 50, 56, 28 Am. Rep. 104. "It is apparent that, if the carrier is liable, in such case, for a loss by robbery, it is liable also for a loss by theft by strangers (see Abbott v. Bradstreet, 55 Me. 530), or for loss resulting from negligence in any way, no matter what the character of the valuables, or the amount of them borne upon the person, and in the sole care and custody of the passenger. It is, then, seen that the carrier of passengers, against its will, with no knowledge or

the $4,000 were burned in the wreck.[18] In this last case, Scott, J., used the following language: "We do not call in question the right of a passenger to carry about his person, for the mere purpose of transportation, large sums of money, or small parcels of great value, without communicating the fact to the carrier, or paying anything for the transportation. But he can only do so at his own risk, in so far as the act of third persons, or even ordinary negligence on the part of the carrier or his servants, is concerned. For this secret method of transportation would be fraud upon the carrier, if he could thereby be subjected to an unlimited liability for the value of the parcels never delivered to him for transportation, and of which he has no knowledge, and has therefore no opportunity to demand compensation for the risk incurred. No one could reasonably suppose that a liability which might extend indefinitely in amount would be gratuitously assumed, even though the danger to be apprehended should arise from the inadvertent negligence of the carrier himself."

Articles Technically Baggage in Mixed Custody of Passenger and Carrier

Cases falling under the present class, involving the mixed custody of both passenger and carrier, have been frequent and troublesome. Though courts have often failed to make the distinction, it should be noted that in the present class of cases (b), the articles are delivered to the carrier, while in the other two classes, (a) and (c), there is no delivery to the carrier, the passenger's custody remaining complete and exclusive. The instant discussion accordingly relates to those cases in which the articles, which are technically baggage are delivered to the carrier, so that the articles are, on the one hand, in the carrier's custody, but these articles are also carried, for the passenger's convenient access, in the stateroom or car with him, so that the articles are, on the other hand, to some extent in the custody of the passenger. What, then, in these cases of mixed custody of articles falling within the technical definition of baggage, is the measure by which the carrier's responsibility is to be judged?

In England the cases hold the carrier under such circumstances still liable as an insurer.[19] The reason for this rule has thus been

notice of the charge and risk put upon it, becomes more, in fact, than a carrier of passengers—it becomes an 'express' carrier with unusual burdens." Id.

18 First Nat. Bank of Greenfield v. Marietta & C. R. Co., 20 Ohio St. 259, 5 Am. Rep. 655.

19 Leconteur v. Railway Co., L. R. 1 Q. B. 54, 6 Best & S. 961; Bunch v. Railway Co., 17 Q. B. Div. 215; s. c., 13 App. Cas. H. of L. 31; Richards v.

stated in an early leading case [20] by Cockburn, C. J.: "Nothing could be more inconvenient than that the practice of placing small articles, which it is convenient to the passenger to have about him in the carriage in which he travels, should be discontinued; and if the company were, from the mere fact of articles of this description being placed in a carriage with the passenger, to be at once relieved from the obligation of safe carriage, it would follow that no one who has occasion to leave the carriage temporarily could do so consistently with the safety of his property." The doctrine of this case, though some cases have dissented from it,[21] states the English rule under which the carrier's full insuring liability is not diminished by the carrier's diminished control of the articles.[22]

While the cases are far from harmonious in the United States, the majority of our courts hold the carrier liable only for negligence and discard the high standard of insurance.[23] These courts, while admitting the convenience to the passenger of having access to the articles, co-ordinate responsibility and power by holding the carrier to his insuring liability only when he can effectively secure the safety of the articles by having them in his complete and exclusive custody. This rule, on the whole, seems fair to the carrier, without imposing undue hardship on the passenger. Some American cases, however, uphold the English rule.[24]

In a number of cases, the carrier has been one by water, and the articles lost were stolen from the stateroom occupied by the passenger. Here it has been sought to hold the water carrier to his insuring liability not only as a carrier, but also as an innkeeper. This

Railway Co., 62 E. C. L. 839; Butcher v. Railway Co., 16 C. B. 13; Great Northern Ry. Co. v. Shepherd, 8 Exch. 30; Robinson v. Dunmore, 2 Bos. & P. 416, 419.

[20] Leconteur v. Railway Co., L. R. 1 Q. B. 54, 6 Best & S. 961.

[21] Bergheim v. Railway Co., 3 C. P. Div. 221. See, also, Talley v. Railway Co., L. R. 6 C. P. 44.

[22] See cases cited in note 19.

[23] Sperry v. Consolidated R. Co., 79 Conn. 565, 65 Atl. 962, 10 L. R. A. (N. S.) 907, 118 Am. St. Rep. 169, 9 Ann. Cas. 199; Gleason v. Goodrich Transp. Co., 32 Wis. 85, 14 Am. Rep. 716; The R. E. Lee, 2 Abb. U. S. 49, Fed. Cas. No. 11,690; Del Valle v. The Richmond, 27 La. Ann. 90; Hasbrouck v. New York Cent. & H. R. R. Co., 202 N. Y. 363, 95 N. E. 808, 35 L. R. A. (N. S.) 537, Ann. Cas. 1912D, 1150; American S. S. Co. v. Bryan, 83 Pa. 446; THE HUMBOLDT (D. C.) 97 Fed. 656, Dobie Cas. Bailments and Carriers, 374. In many of the cases cited in this note and in succeeding notes, the question in reality turned upon whether or not there was a delivery to the carrier.

[24] Mudgett v. Bay State Steamboat Co., 1 Daly (N. Y.) 151; Van Horn v. Kermit, 4 E. D. Smith (N. Y.) 453; Nashville, C. & St. L. R. Co. v. Lillie, 112 Tenn. 331, 78 S. W. 1055, 105 Am. St. Rep. 947 (baggage taken into sleeping car).

analogy of the steamboat and the inn was approved by the New York courts,[25] and the water carrier was held to the rigorous responsibility of the insurer. The majority of the courts, however, hold that there is no difference here between those who carry by land and those who carry by water, and both are held liable, in cases of mixed custody, only when they have failed to exercise ordinary care.[26] Negligence, not insurance, is thus, by the accepted American doctrine, the standard by which, in these cases, the liability of the carrier is to be determined.

Articles Technically Baggage in Exclusive Custody of the Passenger

Here the case differs from the first class (a), in that the articles are such as to come technically within the definition of baggage; it differs from the second class (b), in that the custody is not mixed, for the articles are not delivered to the carrier. The character of the articles is proper, for they would have been baggage imposing the insuring liability if delivered to the carrier's exclusive custody; but these articles are kept by the passenger in or about the person of the passenger animo custodiendi.

The courts generally agree that the carrier who has not even a mixed custody cannot be held as an insurer.[27] To hold otherwise would be obviously unfair. Since, however, the articles are such as are contemplated by the parties to be within the contract of transportation, the carrier does owe a duty of affirmative care, which is fixed at ordinary care. The carrier, then, is liable only for negligence and ordinary care on the carrier's part is the duty by which negligence should be judged.[28] Having exercised ordinary

[25] Macklin v. New Jersey Steamboat Co., 7 Abb. Prac. N. S. (N. Y.) 229; Dunn v. New Haven Steam-Boat Co., 58 Hun, 461, 12 N. Y. Supp. 406; Gore v. Norwich & New York Transp. Co., 2 Daly (N. Y.) 254; Adams v. New Jersey Steamboat Co., 151 N. Y. 163, 45 N. E. 369, 34 L. R. A. 682, 56 Am. St. Rep. 616.

[26] The Crystal Palace v. Vanderpool, 16 B. Mon. (Ky.) 302; Gleason v. Goodrich Transp. Co., 32 Wis. 85, 14 Am. Rep. 716; THE HUMBOLDT (D. C.) 97 Fed. 656, Dobie Cas. Bailments and Carriers, 374; The R. E. Lee, 2 Abb. U. S. 49, Fed. Cas. No. 11,690; Del Valle v. The Richmond, 27 La. Ann. 90; American S. S. Co. v. Bryan, 83 Pa. 446. In McKee v. Owen, 15 Mich. 115, the court was evenly divided on this question.

[27] See cases cited in the succeeding note.

[28] Tower v. Utica & S. R. Co., 7 Hill (N. Y.) 47, 42 Am. Dec. 36; Carpenter v. New York, N. H. & H. R. R. Co., 124 N. Y. 53, 26 N. E. 277, 11 L. R. A. 759, 21 Am. St. Rep. 644; Knierlem v. New York Cent. & H. R. R. Co., 109 App. Div. 709, 96 N. Y. Supp. 602; Pullman Palace Car Co. v. Pollock, 69 Tex. 120, 5 S. W. 814, 5 Am. St. Rep. 31; Abbot v. Bradstreet, 55 Me. 530; Clark v. Burns, 118 Mass. 275, 19 Am. Rep. 456; Nashville, C. & St. L. R. Co. v. Lillie, 112 Tenn. 331, 78 S. W. 1055, 105 Am. St. Rep. 947 (baggage taken into day coach); Kinsley v. Lake Shore & M. S. R. Co., 125 Mass. 54, 28 Am.

care, the carrier is relieved of liability; having failed to exercise it, for loss of or injury to the articles proximately resulting from such failure, the carrier is liable.[29]

Contributory Negligence of the Passenger

Under all of the cases just discussed, when the carrier is sought to be held on the score of his negligence, the contributory negligence of the passenger is a complete defense. When the negligence of the passenger and that of the carrier both concur in producing the loss or injury as to the articles in question, there can be no recovery.[30] When the articles are in the passenger's exclusive custody, or even when this custody is shared with the carrier, the duty of exercising ordinary care in looking after the articles rests on the passenger. What constitutes such care is, of course, to be judged in the light of all the surrounding circumstances.[31]

Here, as elsewhere, it is also true that such contributory negligence, while a bar to a recovery based on negligence, is not a defense to a suit based on the willful or wanton act of the carrier. Thus the passenger, negligently exposing his property, can still recover when the property is stolen by the carrier's servants.[32]

Rep. 200; WHITNEY v. PULLMAN'S PALACE CAR CO., 143 Mass. 243, 9 N. E. 619, Doble Cas. Bailments and Carriers, 375.

29 See cases cited in preceding note, especially Kinsley v. Lake Shore & M. S. R. Co., 125 Mass. 54, 28 Am. Rep. 200; Knieriem v. New York Cent. & H. R. R. Co., 109 App. Div. 709, 96 N. Y. Supp. 602.

30 Gleason v. Goodrich Transp. Co., 32 Wis. 85, 14 Am. Rep. 716; Illinois Cent. Ry. Co. v. Handy, 63 Miss. 609, 56 Am. Rep. 846: WHITNEY v. PULLMAN'S PALACE CAR CO., 143 Mass. 243, 9 N. E. 619, Doble Cas. Bailments and Carriers, 375; Talley v. Railway Co., L. R. 6 C. P. (Eng.) 44; Kinsley v. Lake Shore & M. S. Ry. Co., 125 Mass. 54, 28 Am. Rep. 200.

31 See cases cited in preceding note.

32 Pullman Palace Car Co. v. Matthews, 74 Tex. 654, 12 S. W. 744, 15 Am. St. Rep. 873.

CHAPTER XXI

ACTIONS AGAINST CARRIERS OF PASSENGERS

IN GENERAL

202. When suit is necessary to enforce substantive rights against carriers of passengers, these rights exist only in connection with, and are therefore qualified by, the rules of law governing actions against carriers of passengers.

Actions against carriers of passengers will be considered with reference to—

(1) The parties.
(2) The form of action.
(3) The pleadings.
(4) The evidence.
(5) The measure of damages.

The subject of actions against carriers remains to be considered, along the lines indicated, and according to the same analysis used, in the discussion of actions against carriers of goods. Many of the principles there discussed[1] are equally applicable here, such, for example, as the form of action; while essential differences between the two carriers sometimes call for different rules, such, for example, as the measure of damages. Only a brief discussion is here given, as an extended treatment of the questions involved is proper only in works on Pleading, Evidence, and Damages.

[1] Ante, chapter XV.

THE PARTIES

203. Ordinarily the injured passenger is the proper plaintiff. In some cases, persons may sue by virtue by their relationship to the injured passenger, as when a husband sues for injury to the wife, or a parent for injury to the minor child.

In the usual case, the injured passenger is the proper person to sue, and this question presents none of the difficulty found in suits against the carrier of goods, involving the relative rights of consignor and consignee to sue the carrier.

Husband and Wife—Parent and Child

When the injured passenger is a married woman, in addition to her own right to sue for her injuries, the husband has a right to bring a separate suit to recover against the carrier for the loss of the wife's companionship and society.[2] By virtue of the marriage, he is entitled to the wife's consortium, and when this right is impaired by the carrier's negligence, a cause of action accrues to the husband, quite apart from the wife's own cause of action, though both are based on the same negligent act.[3] To the husband's suit, either his own negligence or that of the wife contributing to the injury is a defense.[4] As we have already seen, by the weight of authority, the husband's contributory negligence does not

[2] Filer v. New York Cent. R. Co., 49 N. Y. 47, 10 Am. Rep. 327; Blair v. Chicago & A. R. Co., 89 Mo. 334, 1 S. W. 367; Southern Kansas Ry. Co. v. Pavey, 57 Kan. 521, 46 Pac. 969; Skoglund v. Minneapolis St. Ry. Co., 45 Minn. 330, 47 N. W. 1071, 11 L. R. A. 222, 22 Am. St. Rep. 733; Kelley v. New York, N. H. & H. R. Co., 168 Mass. 308, 46 N. E. 1063, 38 L. R. A. 631, 60 Am. St. Rep. 397; Baltimore & O. R. Co. v. Glenn, 66 Ohio St. 395, 64 N. E. 438; Washington & G. R. Co. v. Hickey, 12 App. D. C. 269; Birmingham Southern R. Co. v. Lintner, 141 Ala. 420, 38 South. 363, 109 Am. St. Rep. 40, 3 Ann. Cas. 461.

[3] See cases cited in preceding note.

[4] As to wife's contributory negligence, see Chicago, B. & Q. R. Co. v. Honey, 63 Fed. 39, 12 C. C. A. 190, 26 L. R. A. 42; Cleveland, C. & C. R. Co. v. Terry, 8 Ohio St. 570; Accousi v. G. A. Stowers Furniture Co. (Tex. Civ. App.) 87 S. W. 861. In the analogous case of the parent's suit for injury to his child, the parent's contributory negligence is a defense. See cases cited in note 8. Here, when the husband sues, he should not be permitted to profit by his own wrong. See Pennsylvania Ry. Co. v. Goodenough, 55 N. J. Law, 577, 28 Atl. 3, 22 L. R. A. 460. By the same token, the parent, whose negligence contributes to the injury, cannot recover for loss of the services of the child. See cases cited in note 9.

defeat the wife's recovery,[5] though her own contributory negligence is, of course, a defense to her own suit.[6]

The parent, entitled to the services of a minor child, likewise has, besides the child's right to sue the carrier, a cause of action when the parent loses partially or completely these services, owing to the carrier's negligence.[7] As above, contributory negligence of either parent[8] or child[9] will defeat the parent's action; but, by the better rule, when the child sues, there is no imputation of the parent's negligence to him,[10] and only the child's own contributory negligence will bar his recovery.[11]

Death by Wrongful Act

Under the common law, if the carrier's negligence resulted in the death of the passenger, there was no right of action.[12] Whatever right of action the passenger had died with him under the maxim, "Actio personalis moritur cum persona." The manifest injustice in allowing a heavy recovery when a passenger was severely injured, but lived, and denying a recovery when the injury was much more severe and resulted in death, presented a situation calling for statutory relief.

This defect of the common law was remedied in England by Lord Campbell's Act,[13] which enacted that, "wherever the death of a

5 Ante, p. 607.

6 Just as the contributory negligence of the plaintiff is in general a defense, when the plaintiff sues in his (or her) own right for injuries to the plaintiff. See ante, § 185.

7 Wilton v. Middlesex R. Co., 125 Mass. 130; Drew v. Sixth Ave. R. Co., 26 N. Y. 49; Pennsylvania R. Co. v. Kelley, 31 Pa. 372; Citizens' St. R. Co. v. Willoeby, 15 Ind. App. 312, 43 N. E. 1058; Scamell v. St. Louis Transit Co., 103 Mo. App. 504, 77 S. W. 1021.

8 Williams v. South & N. A. R. Co., 91 Ala. 635, 9 South. 77; Mattson v. Minnesota & N. W. R. Co., 98 Minn. 296. 108 N. W. 517; Pollack v. Pennsylvania R. Co., 210 Pa. 634, 60 Atl. 312, 105 Am. St. Rep. 846; Galveston, H. & H. R. Co. v. Scott, 34 Tex. Civ. App. 501, 79 S. W. 642; St. Louis, I. M. & S. R. Co. v. Colum, 72 Ark. 1, 77 S. W. 596; Winters v. Kansas City Cable Ry. Co., 99 Mo. 509, 12 S. W. 652, 6 L. R. A. 536, 17 Am. St. Rep. 591.

9 Chicago & G. E. Ry. Co. v. Harney, 28 Ind. 28, 92 Am. Dec. 282; Burke v. Broadway & Seventh Ave. R. Co., 34 How. Prac. (N. Y.) 239; Raden v. Georgia R. R., 78 Ga. 47.

10 See ante, p. 607.

11 See ante, § 185. See, also, Brown v. European & N. A. Ry. Co., 58 Me. 384; Masser v. Chicago, R. I. & P. Ry. Co., 68 Iowa, 602, 27 N. W. 776; Illinois Cent. Ry. Co. v. Johnson, 221 Ill. 42, 77 N. E. 592.

12 Grosso v. Delaware, L. & W. R. Co., 50 N. J. Law, 317, 13 Atl. 233; Louisville & N. R. Co. v. Jones, 45 Fla. 407, 34 South. 246; Connecticut Mut. Life Ins. Co. v. New York & N. H. R. Co., 25 Conn. 265, 65 Am. Dec. 571; Seney v. Chicago, M. & St. P. R. Co., 125 Iowa, 290, 101 N. W. 76; Jackson v. Pittsburgh, C., C. & St. L. Ry. Co., 140 Ind. 241, 39 N. E. 663, 49 Am. St. Rep. 192; Bligh v. Biddeford & S. R. Co., 94 Me. 499, 48 Atl. 112.

13 9 & 10 Vict. c. 93.

person shall be caused by wrongful act, neglect, or default, and the act, neglect, or default is such as would (if death had not ensued) have entitled the party injured to maintain an action and recover damages in respect thereof, then and in every such case the person who would have been liable if death had not ensued shall be liable to an action for damages, notwithstanding the death of the person injured, and although the death shall have been caused under such circumstances as amount in law to a felony"; that "every such action shall be for the benefit of the wife, husband, parent, and child of the person whose death shall have been so caused, and shall be brought by and in the name of the executor or administrator of the person deceased; that in every such action the jury may give such damages as they may think proportioned to the injury resulting from such death to the parties respectively for whose benefit such action shall be brought; and that the amount so recovered, and deducting the costs not recovered from the defendant, shall be divided amongst the before-mentioned parties in such shares as the jury by their verdict shall find and direct."

Statutes similar to Lord Campbell's Act have been enacted in all the states of this country. In their purpose and general tenor, these statutes are similar; but they vary infinitely as to their details. By virtue of the fact that such statutes are in derogation of the common law, and since, when a statute creating a right also prescribes the remedy, that remedy is exclusive, the courts have shown a tendency to construe these statutes strictly.[14] Particularly is this true as to the person bringing the suit.[15] The peculiar words of each statute, and the decisions of the courts of that particular state construing such statute should always be carefully consulted. To discuss these statutes in detail is beyond the scope of this book.

Proper Party Defendant

There is seldom any difficulty as to the proper party defendant. This is, of course, the carrier whose negligence causes the injury.[16]

[14] Chicago & E. R. Co. v. La Porte, 33 Ind. App. 691, 71 N. E. 166; Vaughn v. Bunker Hill & Sullivan Mining & Concentrating Co. (C. C.) 126 Fed. 895; In re California Nav. & Imp. Co. (D. C.) 110 Fed. 678.

[15] Howell v. Board of Com'rs of Yancey County, 121 N. C. 362, 28 S. E. 362; Alabama & V. Ry. Co. v. Williams, 78 Miss. 209, 28 So. 853, 51 L. R. A. 836, 84 Am. St. Rep. 624; Louisville & N. R. Co. v. Coppage, 13 S. W. 1086, 12 Ky. Law Rep. 200.

[16] See Bryce v. Southern R. Co. (C. C.) 125 Fed. 958; Penfield v. Cleveland, C., C. & St. L. Ry. Co., 26 App. Div. 413, 50 N. Y. Supp. 79; Kansas City, M. & B. Ry. Co. v. Foster, 134 Ala. 244, 32 South. 773, 92 Am. St. Rep. 25; Atchison, T. & S. F. R. Co. v. Cochran, 43 Kan. 225, 23 Pac. 151, 7 L. R. A. 414, 19 Am. St. Rep. 129. As to liability of the initial carrier for injuries due to the negligence of the connecting carrier, see ante, § 170.

When the injury is due to the negligence of more than one carrier, one, all, or any intermediate number of these may be sued at the option of the injured party.[17]

Suits by Persons Who are Not Passengers

The principles just discussed apply equally to persons injured by the carrier's negligence, who are not passengers. Thus, the invitee on the carrier's premises, injured by the latter's failure to exercise ordinary care, is the proper plaintiff in a suit against the carrier in control of the premises.[18] If such invitee is a married woman or minor child, what has just been said as to the husband or parent is applicable.[19] When the carrier wrongfully refuses to accept as a passenger a person who lawfully applies, such person is, of course, the proper plaintiff to sue the carrier for the carrier's breach of duty in thus failing to accept and transport him.[20]

THE FORM OF ACTION

204. As in the case of the carrier of goods, the carrier of passengers negligently injuring a passenger may be sued either in an action of assumpsit, based on the contract to carry, or in action of trespass on the case, based on the breach of duty imposed by the relation of carrier and passenger.

In general, the advantages and disadvantages of the passenger's suing ex contractu or ex delicto are the same as in actions against carriers of goods.

A passenger injured by the carrier's negligence has the same choice of remedies as exists in the case of carrier of goods, and the action brought may be either one of assumpsit, based on the express or implied contract of carriage, or one of trespass on the case, for the tort.[21] The different forms of actions have the same

[17] Matthews v. Delaware, L. & W. Ry. Co., 56 N. J. Law, 34, 27 Atl. 919, 22 L. R. A. 261; Flaherty v. Minneapolis & St. L. Ry. Co., 39 Minn. 328, 40 N. W. 160, 1 L. R. A. 680, 12 Am. St. Rep. 654; Lucas v. Pennsylvania Co., 120 Ind. 205, 21 N. E. 972, 16 Am. St. Rep. 323; Cuddy v. Horn, 46 Mich. 596, 10 N. W. 32, 41 Am. Rep. 178.

[18] See ante, § 191. See, also, Indiana, B. & W. Ry. Co. v. Barnhart, 115 Ind. 400, 16 N. E. 121; Little Rock & Ft. S. Ry. Co. v. Lawton, 55 Ark. 428, 18 S. W. 543, 15 L. R. A. 434, 29 Am. St. Rep. 48.

[19] See ante, pp. 664-665.

[20] See ante, § 175. See, also, BENNETT v. DUTTON, 10 N. H. 481, Dobie Cas. Bailments and Carriers, 322; Brown v. Memphis & C. R. Co. (C. C.) 7 Fed. 51; Zackery v. Mobile & O. R. Co., 74 Miss. 520, 21 South. 246, 36 L. R. A. 546, 60 Am. St. Rep. 529.

[21] Patterson v. Augusta & S. R. Co., 94 Ga. 140, 21 S. E. 283; Saltonstall v. Stockton, Fed. Cas. No. 12,271, affirmed 13 Pet. 181, 10 L. Ed. 115; Balti-

advantages and disadvantages when the action is for injury to a passenger as when it is for an injury to goods.[22] In general, the tort action is preferable, so that the majority of suits against the passenger carrier are brought in that form.[23] Where it is doubtful whether the action in any particular case is to be regarded as one of assumpsit or trespass on the case, the leaning of the courts is to consider the action one of trespass on the case founded on the breach of duty inhering in the relation of carrier and passenger.[24] Where exemplary damages are sought, the declaration must be on the tort, and not in assumpsit, on the contract.[25]

THE PLEADINGS

205. As in the case of actions against carriers of goods, the pleadings in an action against the passenger carrier should show clearly whether the action is one of contract or of tort. The pleadings should state facts stating a complete cause of action, consistent with the evidence to be adduced at the trial.

more City Pass. Ry. Co. v. Kemp, 61 Md. 619, 48 Am. Rep. 134; NEVIN v. PULLMAN PALACE CAR CO., 106 Ill. 222, 46 Am. Rep. 688, Dobie Cas. Bailments and Carriers, 297; Willson v. Northern Pac. Ry. Co., 5 Wash. 621, 32 Pac. 468, 34 Pac. 146; Serwe v. Northern Pac. R. Co., 48 Minn. 78, 50 N. W. 1021; Pennsylvania Ry. Co. v. Peoples, 31 Ohio St. 537; Knights v. Quarles, 2 Brod. & B. (Eng.) 102; Boster v. Chesapeake & O. Ry. Co., 36 W. Va. 318, 15 S. E. 158; Hansley v. Jamesville & W. R. Co., 115 N. C. 602, 20 S. E. 528, 32 L. R. A. 543, 44 Am. St. Rep. 474.

22 See ante, § 155. The differences are chiefly concerned with statutes of limitation, the parties who may sue and be sued, strictness of allegation and proof, and damages.

23 See ante, p. 503. See, also, Heirn v. McCaughan, 32 Miss. 17, 66 Am. Dec. 588; Denver Tramway Co. v. Cloud, 6 Colo. App. 445, 40 Pac. 779; Willson v. Northern Pac. Ry. Co., 5 Wash. 621, 32 Pac. 468, 34 Pac. 146; Kelly v. Ry. Co., [1895] 1 Q. B. (Eng.) 944; Atlantic & P. R. Co. v. Laird, 164 U. S. 393, 17 Sup. Ct. 120, 41 L. Ed. 485.

24 See Chitty on Pleading, 135; Burnett v. Lynch, 5 Barn. & C. (Eng.) 589; New Orleans, J. & G. N. R. Co. v. Hurst, 36 Miss. 660, 74 Am. Dec. 785; Gorman v. Southern Pac. Co., 97 Cal. 1, 31 Pac. 1112, 33 Am. St. Rep. 157; Boling v. St. Louis & S. F. R. Co., 189 Mo. 219, 88 S. W. 35; McKeon v. Chicago, M. & St. P. Ry. Co., 94 Wis. 477, 69 N. W. 175, 35 L. R. A. 252, 59 Am. St. Rep. 910.

25 See ante, p. 504. See, also, Purcell v. Richmond & D. R. Co., 108 N. C. 414, 12 S. E. 954, 956, 12 L. R. A. 113; New Orleans, J. & G. N. R. Co. v. Moore, 40 Miss. 39; Craker v. Chicago & N. W. Ry. Co., 36 Wis. 657, 17 Am. Rep. 504; Norfolk & W. R. Co. v. Wysor, 82 Va. 250; Pullman Co. v. Lutz, 154 Ala. 517, 45 South. 675, 14 L. R. A. (N. S.) 904, 129 Am. St. Rep. 67; Richardson v. Wilmington & W. R. Co., 126 N. C. 100, 35 S. E. 235; Sedgwick on Damages (9th Ed.) §§ 603, 670.

Particularly striking is the analogy between the carrier of goods and the passenger carrier as to the pleadings in actions against the carrier.[26] It is the peculiar function of the plaintiff's pleading to indicate whether the case is one ex contractu or ex delicto.[27] Then the plaintiff's pleading should contain, consistent with his theory of the case, a statement of every essential fact in the cause of action against the passenger carrier. These facts should indicate: (a) The establishment of the relation of passenger and carrier.[28] (b) The duty owed by the carrier.[29] (c) The breach of that duty.[30] (d) The damage to the passenger resulting proximately from this breach, and when special damages are sought these should be duly pleaded.[31] Finally, the pleader should remember that he must prove his case as alleged, and therefore he must so shape his pleadings as to prevent any variance between the facts alleged and the facts proved.[32] The allegata and probata must correspond.

[26] See ante, § 156.

[27] As just indicated, the courts lean toward considering the action as one ex delicto. See cases cited in note 24.

[28] North Birmingham Ry. Co. v. Liddicoat, 99 Ala. 545, 13 South. 18; Breese v. Trenton Horse R. Co., 52 N. J. Law, 250, 19 Atl. 204; Smith v. Louisville, E. & St. L. R. Co., 124 Ind. 394, 24 N. E. 753; Powell v. East Tennessee, V. & G. R. Co. (Miss.) 8 South. 738.

[29] This is the least important, since, if the proper facts be alleged from which the duty springs, the duty duly follows, largely as a matter of course, so that the court will take judicial notice of the nature and extent of the duty. See Evansville & C. R. Co. v. Duncan, 28 Ind. 441, 92 Am. Dec. 322; Atlantic & P. R. Co. v. Laird, 58 Fed. 760, 7 C. C. A. 489; Lemon v. Chanslor, 68 Mo. 340, 30 Am. Rep. 799.

[30] The modern decisions are quite liberal to the plaintiff, in not requiring great particularity here, and in upholding allegations of negligence in general and sometimes quite indefinite forms. Gulf, C. & S. F. Ry. Co. v. Wilson, 79 Tex. 371, 15 S. W. 280, 11 L. R. A. 486, 23 Am. St. Rep. 345; Louisville & N. R. Co. v. Crunk, 119 Ind. 542, 21 N. E. 31, 12 Am. St. Rep. 443; McCaslin v. Lake Shore & M. S. Ry. Co., 93 Mich. 553, 53 N. W. 724; Lavis v. Wisconsin Cent. Ry. Co., 54 Ill. App. 636; Searle v. Kanawha & O. Ry. Co., 32 W. Va. 370, 9 S. E. 248.

[31] Wabash Ry. Co. v. Savage, 110 Ind. 156, 9 N. E. 85; Southern Pac. Co. v. Hall, 100 Fed. 760, 41 C. C. A. 50; Missouri, K. & T. Ry. Co. v. Cook, 8 Tex. Civ. App. 376, 27 S. W. 769; Wabash Western Ry. Co. v. Friedman, 146 Ill. 583, 30 N. E. 353, 34 N. E. 1111.

[32] Highland Ave. & B. R. Co. v. Winn, 93 Ala. 306, 9 South. 509; Buck v. People's Street Railway & Electric Light & Power Co., 108 Mo. 179, 18 S. W. 1090; Lombard & S. S. Pass. Ry. Co. v. Christian, 124 Pa. St. 114, 16 Atl. 628; Flint & P. M. Ry. Co. v. Stark, 38 Mich. 714; Indiana, B. & W. Ry. Co. v. Burdge, 94 Ind. 46; Richmond Ry. & Electric Co. v. West, 100 Va. 184, 40 S. E. 643.

THE EVIDENCE

206. The plaintiff's evidence, that is consistent with his pleadings, as well as relevant and admissible, must, in the light of legal presumptions, establish the facts necessary to make out a cause of action against the passenger carrier.

Here, as elsewhere, the duty of proving his case rests upon the passenger plaintiff. The evidence adduced for this purpose must of course be relevant and such as is admissible according to the doctrines of evidence as applied by the courts.[33] By a preponderance of such evidence, the passenger must prove the essential facts in his case on which the recovery is based.[34]

The burden of proof upon the various questions that may arise in actions against passenger carriers has already been discussed in connection with the specific treatment of each of these questions. Particularly important are the presumptions as to the carrier's negligence [35] and the passenger's contributory negligence.[36] It therefore may not be amiss to state again that proof of the mere happening of an accident causing injury does not necessarily raise a presumption of the carrier's negligence. But such presumption does arise when the proof shows that the accident was due to instrumentalities peculiarly in the carrier's control and that ordinary experience demonstrates that such accidents can be avoided by the use of the highest degree of practicable care. As to contributory negligence, the better doctrine, supported by the weight of authority, is that this is a defense to be affirmatively proved by the carrier. A number of courts, however, require the passenger to negative his contributory negligence, by proving the exercise of ordinary care on his part, as an element of his case against the carrier.

[33] See 2 Fetter on Passenger Carriers, §§ 447–472, for discussion of this subject, with practical reference to actions against carriers of passengers.

[34] Cleveland, C., C. & I. R. Co. v. Newell, 104 Ind. 264, 3 N. E. 836, 54 Am. Rep. 312; Yarnell v. Kansas City, Ft. S. & M. Ry. Co., 113 Mo. 570, 21 S. W. 1, 18 L. R. A. 599; Hawkins v. Front St. Cable Ry. Co., 3 Wash. 592, 28 Pac. 1021, 16 L. R. A. 808, 28 Am. St. Rep. 72; Dennis v. Pittsburg & C. S. R. R., 165 Pa. 624, 31 Atl. 52; Murphy v. Atlanta & W. P. R. Co., 89 Ga. 832, 15 S. E. 774; Donovan v. Hartford St. Ry. Co., 65 Conn. 201, 32 Atl. 350, 29 L. R. A. 297.

[35] See ante, § 188, and cases cited in notes.

[36] See ante, § 188, and cases cited in notes.

THE MEASURE OF DAMAGES—ACTIONS FOR PERSONAL INJURIES

207. In actions brought by the passenger for personal injuries, the damages are such as will reasonably compensate the passenger for the damage suffered as a proximate and natural consequence of such injury. Among the important elements of the damage are mental and physical pain, inconvenience, loss of time, medical expenses, and diminution of earning power.

The measure of damages for personal injuries which the passenger may recover against the carrier is in general the same as in personal injury cases in other fields of the law.[37] A very striking difference is necessarily found here, however, between carriers of goods and passenger carriers. As to the former, the most important element is the more or less definite market value of the goods;[38] as to the latter, other and subtler considerations must apply in compensating the injured passenger, with a wide field for the personal equation as to the passenger and the varying judgment of juries. Damages are, of course, allowed only for the proximate and natural consequences of the injury, though these may be quite varied.[39] When the consequences, however, are proximate and natural, it is no defense to the carrier that these injuries were aggravated by, or even would not have been suffered had it not been for, the previous sickness of the passenger,[40] as in the case of a pregnant woman.[41]

[37] RICKETTS v. CHESAPEAKE & O. R. CO., 33 W. Va. 433, 10 S. E. 801, 7 L. R. A. 354, 25 Am. St. Rep. 901, Dobie Cas. Bailments and Carriers, 378; Milwaukee & St. P. R. Co. v. Arms, 91 U. S. 489, 23 L. Ed. 374; Cone v. Central R. Co., 62 N. J. Law, 99, 40 Atl. 780; Smedley v. Hestonville, M. & F. Pass. Ry. Co., 184 Pa. 620, 39 Atl. 544; Florida Ry. & Nav. Co. v. Webster, 25 Fla. 394, 5 South. 714; Kral v. Burlington, C. R. & N. Ry. Co., 71 Minn. 422, 74 N. W. 166; Southern Pac. Co. v. Maloney, 136 Fed. 171, 69 C. C. A. 83; VAN DE VENTER v. CHICAGO CITY R. CO. (C. C.) 26 Fed. 32, Dobie Cas. Bailments and Carriers, 377.

[38] See ante, §§ 160–161.

[39] Hobbs v. Railway Co., L. R. 10 Q. B. (Eng.) 111; Bell v. Gulf & C. R. Co., 76 Miss. 71, 23 South. 268; Baltimore & O. R. Co. v. Blocher, 27 Md. 277; Boothby v. Grand Trunk Ry. Co., 66 N. H. 342, 34 Atl. 157; Rosted v. Great Northern Ry. Co., 76 Minn. 123, 78 N. W. 971.

[40] Baltimore City Pass. Ry. Co. v. Kemp, 61 Md. 74; Kral v. Burlington, C. R. & N. Ry. Co., 71 Minn. 422, 74 N. W. 166; Spade v. Lynn & B. R. Co.,

[41] St Louis S. W. R. Co. of Texas v. Ferguson, 26 Tex. Civ. App. 460, 64 S. W. 797.

Physical Pain and Medical Expenses

Physical pain suffered by the injured passenger is always an important element in fixing the damages.[42] Though it is always difficult to reckon this in dollars and cents, the anguish of bodily suffering is one of the most terrible and real consequences of a personal injury, for which compensation should unquestionably be given. The duration and severity of such pain are always prominent, when the amount of such damages is to be determined, in the minds of the jury. Not only past, but future, pain may be considered, when such future pain is reasonably certain to follow the injury, but not when this is speculative, or merely probable.[43] This rule is essential, since the injury is a single cause of action, for which only one suit can be brought.

Money spent for medical expenses, such as medicines, nurses, doctors, and treatment at a hospital, is a clear element of damages.[44] The causal connection between these and the injury is too obvious for comment. And especially should these expenses be recoverable, since the law imposes upon the injured passenger the duty of reasonable care in minimizing the damages.[45]

172 Mass. 488, 52 N. E. 747, 43 L. R. A. 832, 70 Am. St. Rep. 298; Denver & R. G. R. Co. v. Harris, 122 U. S. 597, 7 Sup. Ct. 1286, 30 L. Ed. 1146; Ohio & M. R. Co. v. Hecht, 115 Ind. 443, 17 N. E. 297.

42 Morse v. Auburn & S. R. Co., 10 Barb. (N. Y.) 621; O'Donnel v. St. Louis Transit Co., 107 Mo. App. 34, 80 S. W. 315; Alabama G. S. R. Co. v. Hill, 93 Ala. 514, 9 South. 722, 30 Am. St. Rep. 65; Cone v. Central R. Co., 62 N. J. Law, 99, 40 Atl. 780; Hickenbottom v. Delaware, L. & W. R. Co., 122 N. Y. 91, 25 N. E. 279; Keegan v. Minneapolis & St. L. R. Co., 76 Minn. 90, 78 N. W. 965; Goodhart v. Pennsylvania R. Co., 177 Pa. 1, 35 Atl. 191, 55 Am. St. Rep. 705; Pence v. Wabash R. Co., 116 Iowa, 279, 90 N. W. 59; VAN DE VENTER v. CHICAGO CITY R. CO. (C. C.) 26 Fed. 32, Dobie Cas. Bailments and Carriers, 377.

43 Curtis v. Rochester & S. R. Co., 18 N. Y. 534, 75 Am. Dec. 258; Hamilton v. Great Falls Street Ry. Co., 17 Mont. 334, 42 Pac. 860, 43 Pac. 713; Cleveland, C., C. & I. R. Co. v. Newell, 104 Ind. 264, 3 N. E. 836, 54 Am. Rep. 312; White v. Milwaukee City Ry. Co., 61 Wis. 536, 21 N. W. 524, 50 Am. Rep. 154. Damages have also been allowed for disfigurement. The Oriflamme, 3 Sawy. 397, Fed. Cas. No. 10,572; Kalen v. Terre Haute & I. R. Co., 18 Ind. App. 202, 47 N. E. 694, 63 Am. St. Rep. 343; St. Louis S. W. Ry. Co. v. Dobbins, 60 Ark. 481, 30 S. W. 887, 31 S. W. 147.

44 Parker v. South Carolina & G. R. R., 48 S. C. 364, 26 S. E. 669; Smith v. Chicago & A. R. Co., 108 Mo. 244, 18 S. W. 971; Sherwood v. Chicago & W. M. Ry. Co., 82 Mich. 374, 46 N. W. 773; Pennsylvania R. Co. v. Books, 57 Pa. 339, 98 Am. Dec. 229; North Chicago St. Ry. Co. v. Cotton, 140 Ill. 486, 29 N. E. 899; Eckerd v. Chicago & N. W. Ry. Co., 70 Iowa, 353, 30 N. W. 615; Montgomery St. Ry. Co. v. Mason, 133 Ala. 508, 32 South. 261; VAN DE VENTER v. CHICAGO CITY R. CO. (C. C.) 26 Fed. 32, Dobie Cas. Bailments and Carriers, 377.

45 Texas & P. R. Co. v. White, 101 Fed. 928, 42 C. C. A. 86, 62 L. R. A. 90;

Damages for Mental Suffering

On this subject the cases are far from harmonious. Without an attempt to reconcile them, it may at least be said that the earlier cases are rather illiberal, while the later cases have dealt with the subject in a spirit of increasing liberality. When the passenger receives an actual physical injury, there is general agreement that to the physical pain may be added any mental suffering proximately resulting from the injury.[46] There is disagreement, however, among the cases when the mental suffering is unaccompanied by any physical injury. If the accident or other event to which the mental suffering is attributed does not inflict a physical injury, and if, in addition, the mental suffering is not followed by, or manifested in, physical injury, the great majority of the cases decline to allow damages.[47] Such a rule seems justified, for the evidence of such damage is highly intangible and unsatisfactory, and the opportunity for fraud against the carrier, if such damage were allowed, would be almost limitless. Particularly is this true in cases of fright and so-called nervous shock.[48] When, however, though the accident or other event to which the mental suffering is attributed does not at that time inflict physical injury, this mental suffering does result in concrete, determinable physical injury, different con-

Galveston, H. & S. A. R. Co. v. Zantzinger, 93 Tex. 64, 53 S. W. 379, 47 L. R. A. 282, 77 Am. St. Rep. 829, Id., 92 Tex. 365, 48 S. W. 563, 44 L. R. A. 553, 71 Am. St. Rep. 859.

[46] Smitson v. Southern Pac. Co., 37 Or. 74, 60 Pac. 907; Gallagher v. Bowie, 66 Tex. 265, 17 S W. 407; Philadelphia, B. & W. R. Co. v Mitchell, 107 Md. 600, 69 Atl. 422, 17 L. R. A. (N. S.) 974; Homans v. Boston El. Ry. Co., 180 Mass. 456, 62 N. E. 737, 57 L. R. A. 291, 91 Am. St. Rep. 324; Shay v. Camden & S. Ry. Co., 66 N. J. Law, 334, 49 Atl. 547; Denver & R. G. R. Co. v. Roller, 100 Fed. 738, 41 C. C. A. 22, 49 L. R. A. 77; Lofink v. Interborough Rapid Transit Co., 102 App. Div 275, 92 N. Y. Supp. 386; Southern Pac. Co. v. Hetzer, 135 Fed. 272, 68 C. C. A. 26, 1 L. R. A. (N. S.) 288; Richmond Passenger & Power Co. v. Robinson, 100 Va. 394, 41 S. E. 719.

[47] Morse v. Chesapeake & O. Ry. Co., 117 Ky. 11, 77 S. W. 361; Kalen v. Terre Haute & I. R. Co., 18 Ind. App. 202, 47 S. E. 694, 63 Am. St. Rep. 343; Spohn v. Missouri Pac. Ry. Co., 116 Mo. 617, 22 S. W. 690; Chicago City R. Co. v. Anderson, 182 Ill. 298, 55 N. E. 366; Texarkana & Ft. S. Ry. Co. v. Anderson, 67 Ark. 123, 53 S. W. 673; Dorrah v. Illinois Cent. R. Co., 65 Miss. 14, 3 South. 36, 7 Am. St. Rep. 629; Atchison, T. & S. F. R. Co. v. McGinnis, 46 Kan. 109, 26 Pac. 453; Turner v. Great Northern R. Co., 16 Wash. 213, 46 Pac. 243, 55 Am. St. Rep. 883; SLOANE v. SOUTHERN CAL. R. CO., 111 Cal. 668, 44 Pac. 320, 32 L. R. A. 193, Dobie Cas. Bailments and Carriers, 378.

[48] Haile's Curator v. Texas & P. R. Co., 60 Fed. 557, 9 C. C. A. 134, 23 L. R. A. 774; Judice v. Southern Pac. Co., 47 La. Ann. 255, 16 South. 816; Spade v. Lynn & Boston R. Co., 168 Mass. 285, 47 N. E. 88, 38 L. R. A. 512, 60 Am. St. Rep. 393; Newton v. New York, N. H. & H. R. Co., 106 App. Div. 415, 94 N. Y. Supp. 825.

siderations apply. Here the weight of modern decision wisely permits damages therefor to be recovered.[49] When the causal connection here is clear, and when the resulting physical injury is definite (as in the case of a miscarriage),[50] the objections above urged against mere mental suffering, neither accompanied by nor resulting in physical injury, are no longer valid. Some courts, however, deny any recovery in such cases.[51]

Loss of Time and Earnings and Diminution of Earning Power

Another clear element of damages is the time lost from work by the passenger, with the attendant loss of wages, salary, or earnings. This is a definite pecuniary loss, it can be more accurately calculated than pain, and, when due proximately to the injury, is always recoverable.[52] To determine the amount of damages already suffered, evidence is of course admissible as to the character of the passenger's trade, employment, or profession and the amount of his wages, salary, or earnings.[53]

In this connection, reference must be had, not only to wages or earnings already lost, but to those, too, that the passenger will lose in the future as the result of his impaired earning capacity, due to his injuries.[54] Particularly important in this connection, to

[49] SLOANE v. SOUTHERN CAL. R. CO., 111 Cal. 668, 44 Pac. 320, 32 L. R. A. 193, Dobie Cas. Bailments and Carriers, 378; Simone v. Rhode Island Co., 28 R. I. 186, 66 Atl. 202, 9 L. R. A. (N. S.) 740; Stewart v. Arkansas Southern R. Co., 112 La. 764, 36 South. 676; Taber v. Seaboard Air Line Ry., 81 S. C. 317, 62 S. E. 311; Louisville & N. R. Co. v. Wilson, 123 Ga. 62, 51 S. E. 24, 3 Ann. Cas. 128; Purcell v. St. Paul City Ry. Co., 48 Minn. 134, 50 N. W. 1034, 16 L. R. A. 203.

[50] Fitzpatrick v. Ry. Co., 12 U. C. Q. B. (Canada) 645.

[51] Haile's Curator v. Texas & P. R. Co., 60 Fed. 557, 9 C. C. A. 134, 23 L. R. A. 774; Mitchell v. Rochester Ry. Co., 151 N. Y. 107, 45 N. E. 354, 34 L. R. A. 781, 56 Am. St. Rep. 604; Morris v. Lackawanna & W. V. R. Co., 228 Pa. 198, 77 Atl. 445; Miller v. Baltimore & O. S. W. R. Co., 78 Ohio St. 309, 85 N. E. 499, 18 L. R. A. (N. S.) 949, 125 Am. St. Rep. 699.

[52] Mateer v. Missouri Pac. Ry. Co., 105 Mo. 320, 16 S. W. 839; Glenn v. Philadelphia & W. C. Traction Co., 206 Pa. 135, 55 Atl. 860; Chicago, R. I. & P. R. Co. v. Hoover, 3 Ind. T. 693, 64 S. W. 579; Kentucky Cent. R. Co. v. Ackley, 87 Ky. 278, 8 S. W. 691, 12 Am. St. Rep. 480; Bridger v. Asheville & S. R. Co., 27 S. C. 456, 3 S. E. 860, 13 Am. St. Rep. 653; Stynes v. Boston Elevated R. Co., 206 Mass. 75, 91 N. E. 998, 30 L. R. A. (N. S.) 737; VAN DE VENTER v. CHICAGO CITY R. CO. (C. C.) 26 Fed. 32, Dobie Cas. Bailments and Carriers, 377.

[53] Simonin v. New York, L. E. & W. R. Co., 36 Hun (N. Y.) 214; Alabama G. S. R. Co. v. Yarbrough, 83 Ala. 238, 3 South. 447, 3 Am. St. Rep. 715; Phillips v. Ry. Co., 5 C. P. Div. (Eng.) 280; Parshall v. Minneapolis & St. L. R. Co. (C. C.) 35 Fed. 649; Ohio & M. R. Co. v. Hecht, 115 Ind. 443, 17 N. E. 297; Hanover R. Co. v. Coyle, 55 Pa. 396.

[54] Karczewski v. Wilmington City R. Co., 4 Pennewill (Del.) 24, 54 Atl. 746; Duffy v. St. Louis Transit Co., 104 Mo. App. 235, 78 S. W. 831; San

determine the difference between what the passenger could earn, were he uninjured, and what he will be able to earn, with his injury, is the nature of the passenger's occupation.[55] Other relevant and important circumstances are the passenger's health, age, industry, character, and opportunities for promotion and advancement.[56] Nor can the carrier offset such damages by proving the amounts realized on accident and life insurance policies.[57]

SAME—ACTIONS OTHER THAN THOSE FOR PERSONAL INJURIES

208. In actions against the carrier other than those for the personal injury to the passenger, the damages are also such as will compensate the passenger for the proximate and natural consequences of the carrier's wrong. As to these actions, compared to those for personal injuries, the damages are usually far less in amount and somewhat different considerations attach in fixing them.

Actions against passenger carriers for personal injuries are more numerous and more serious than the others to which the carrier is subject, yet the importance of the latter is such as to require some treatment as to the measure of damages. The most important of these actions are those arising out of the (1) ejection of the passenger; (2) failure to accept one as passenger; (3) delay in transportation; and (4) failure to carry the passenger to his destination.

Antonio & A. P. R. Co. v. Turney, 33 Tex. Civ. App. 626, 78 S. W. 256; Florida Ry. & Nav. Co. v. Webster, 25 Fla. 394, 5 South. 714; St. Louis S. W. Ry. Co. v. Dobbins, 60 Ark. 481, 30 S. W. 887, 31 S. W. 147; Delaware, L. & W. R. Co. v. Devore, 114 Fed. 155, 52 C. C. A. 77.

[55] Storrs v. Los Angeles Traction Co., 134 Cal. 91, 66 Pac. 72; Pennsylvania R. Co. v. Dale, 76 Pa. 47; Illinois Cent. R. Co. v. Davidson, 76 Fed. 517, 22 C. C. A. 306; Chicago, R. I. & P. Ry. Co. v. Posten, 59 Kan. 449, 53 Pac. 465; St. Louis S. W. Ry. Co. v. Dobbins, 60 Ark. 481, 30 S. W. 887, 31 S. W. 147.

[56] Richmond & D. R. Co. v. Allison, 86 Ga. 145, 12 S. E. 352, 11 L. R. A. 43; Louisville N. A. & C. Ry. Co. v. Miller, 141 Ind. 533, 37 N. E. 343; Texas & P. R. Co. v. Humble, 181 U. S. 57, 21 Sup. Ct. 526, 45 L. Ed. 747; Thomas v. Union Ry. Co., 18 App. Div. 185, 45 N. Y. Supp. 920; Vicksburg & M. R. Co. v. Putnam, 118 U. S. 545, 7 Sup. Ct. 1, 30 L. Ed. 257.

[57] Ephland v. Missouri Pac. Ry. Co., 57 Mo. App. 147; Louisville & N. R. Co. v. Carothers, 65 S. W. 833, 66 S. W. 385, 23 Ky. Law Rep. 1673; Missouri, K. & T. R. Co. v. Flood, 35 Tex. Civ. App. 197, 79 S. W. 1106; Harding v. Town of Townsend, 43 Vt. 536, 5 Am. Rep. 304; Illinois Cent. R. Co. v. Prickett, 210 Ill. 140, 71 N. E. 435; Lipscomb v. Houston & T. C. R. Co., 95 Tex. 5, 64 S. W. 923, 55 L. R. A. 869, 93 Am. St. Rep. 804.

Proximate Consequences of Carrier's Wrong

In the class of cases now under discussion, there is conflict among the cases in deciding the question of when the injury to the passenger is the proximate, probable, and natural consequence of the carrier's wrong. The question usually arises when the damage is directly caused by an event subsequent to such wrong. It then becomes necessary to determine whether such intervening cause is an independent one, for which no responsibility attaches to the carrier, or one arising out of, and so intimately connected with, the wrong as to render the carrier responsible. A tendency is clear, among the recent decisions, to disregard as far as is practicable any distinction here between contract and tort actions. And a further tendency towards increasing liberality to the passenger is also discernible.[58]

Thus in Hobbs v. Railway Co.[59] it appeared that plaintiff, his wife and children, were set down at the wrong station, and, being unable to get a conveyance, they were obliged to walk, during which walk the wife contracted a severe cold. It was held that there could be no recovery for the expense of the illness, because it was neither within the contemplation of the parties, nor a probable consequence of her having to walk home. The action was on the contract. The authority of this decision, however, was much shaken by the strong opinions of Bramwell and Brett, L. J., in McMahon v. Field,[60] and the practical influence of the Hobbs Case has been practically neutralized in most states by decisions holding that it does not apply where the action sounds in tort; and cases of this character have been almost always treated as sounding in tort.[61] Thus, in an action for neglect to transport a passenger across the isthmus of Panama according to contract, the plaintiff was allowed to recover the expense of a subsequent illness caused by

[58] See cases cited in notes 61 and 64. See, also, Tilburg v. Northern Cent. R. Co., 217 Pa. 618, 66 Atl. 846, 12 L. R. A. (N. S.) 359; Seaboard Air Line R. Co. v. Scarborough, 52 Fla. 425, 42 South. 706; Chicago, B. & Q. R. Co. v. Spirk, 51 Neb. 167, 179, 70 N. W. 926; Brown v. Georgia, C. & N. R. Co., 119 Ga. 88, 46 S. E. 71.

[59] L. R. 10 Q. B. (Eng.) 111.

[60] L. R. 7 Q. B. Div. (Eng.) 591 (though this was a case of an innkeeper, the judges referred to the Hobbs Case and disapproved it).

[61] Delmonte v. Southern Pac. Co., 2 Cal. App. 211, 83 Pac. 269; Rosted v. Great Northern Ry. Co., 76 Minn. 123, 78 N. W. 971; Alabama G. S. R. Co. v. Heddleston, 82 Ala. 218, 3 South. 53; Baltimore City Pass. Ry. Co. v. Kemp, 61 Md. 74, Id., 61 Md. 619, 48 Am. Rep. 134; Heirn v. McCaughan, 32 Miss. 17, 66 Am. Dec. 588; Yorton v. Milwaukee, L. S. & W. Ry. Co., 62 Wis. 367, 21 N. W. 516, 23 N. W. 401. It has been fully followed in some jurisdictions. Pullman Palace Car Co. v. Barker, 4 Colo. 344, 34 Am. Rep. 89; Murdock v. Boston & A. R. Co., 133 Mass. 15, 43 Am. Rep. 480.

being left in that unhealthy country.[62] Brown v. Chicago, M. & St. P. Ry. Co.[63] was a case very similar to the Hobbs Case, and in an elaborate opinion the court reached a conclusion directly opposite to that reached in the Hobbs Case. The authority of the Hobbs Case has been further weakened by a number of modern cases permitting the passenger to recover for sickness caused by exposure to the weather or walking to the destination, when the passenger has been either ejected from the train or carried to a point other than his destination.[64]

Damages for Wrongful Ejection

When the passenger is wrongfully ejected from the carrier's vehicle, he may recover for the increased expense in reaching his destination, the inconvenience resulting from the ejection, as well as for the time that is lost.[65] Not only may the passenger recover for physical suffering proximately resulting from his expulsion, but even for mental suffering due to the humiliation and mortification of being ejected in the presence of his fellow passengers.[66] And for such mental suffering even though unaccompanied by, or resulting in, physical suffering, the passenger (as is not the case in the ordinary personal injury suit) may recover against the car-

[62] Williams v. Vanderbilt, 28 N. Y. 217, 84 Am. Dec. 333.

[63] 54 Wis. 342, 11 N. W. 356, 911, 41 Am. Rep. 41.

[64] Cincinnati, H. & I. R. Co. v. Eaton, 94 Ind. 474, 48 Am. Rep. 179; Serwe v. Northern Pac. R. Co., 48 Minn. 78, 50 N. W. 1021; Haug v. Great Northern Ry. Co., 8 N. D. 23, 77 N. W. 97, 42 L. R. A. 664, 73 Am. St. Rep. 727; Pickens v. South Carolina & G. R. Co., 54 S. C. 498, 32 S. E. 567; Mobile & O. R. Co. v. McArthur, 43 Miss. 180; International & G. N. R. Co. v. Addison (Tex. Civ. App.) 93 S. W. 1081.

[65] Boehm v. Duluth, S. S. & A. Ry. Co., 91 Wis. 592, 65 N. W. 506; Yorton v. Milwaukee, L. S. & W. Ry. Co., 62 Wis. 367, 21 N. W. 516, 23 N. W. 401; Pullman Palace Car Co. v. McDonald, 2 Tex. Civ. App. 322, 21 S. W. 945; Pennsylvania R. Co. v. Connell, 127 Ill. 419, 20 N. E. 89; SLOANE v. SOUTHERN CAL. RY. CO., 111 Cal. 668, 44 Pac. 320, 32 L. R. A. 193, Dobie Cas. Bailments and Carriers, 378; Hamilton v. Third Ave. R. Co., 53 N. Y. 25; Central Railroad & Banking Co. v. Strickland, 90 Ga. 562, 16 S. E. 352; Paddock v. Atchison, T. & S. F. R. Co. (C. C.) 37 Fed. 841, 4 L. R. A. 231; Quigley v. Central Pac. R. Co., 11 Nev. 350, 21 Am. Rep. 757; Cincinnati, N. O. & T. P. R. Co. v. Carson, 145 Ky. 81, 140 S. W. 71. See also cases cited ante, chapter XIX, notes 62, 63.

[66] CARSTEN v. NORTHERN PAC. R. CO., 44 Minn. 454, 47 N. W. 49, 9 L. R. A. 688, 20 Am. St. Rep. 589, Dobie Cas. Bailments and Carriers, 381; Coine v. Chicago & N. W. R. Co., 123 Iowa, 458, 99 N. W. 134; Perry v. Pittsburg Union Pass. Ry. Co., 153 Pa. 236, 25 Atl. 772; Lucas v. Michigan Cent. R. Co., 98 Mich. 1, 56 N. W. 1039, 39 Am. St. Rep. 517; Kansas City, M. & B. R. Co. v. Foster, 134 Ala. 244, 32 South. 773, 92 Am. St. Rep. 25; Norfolk & W. R. Co. v. Neely, 91 Va. 539, 22 S. E. 367; Delaware, L. & W. R. Co. v. Walsh, 47 N. J. Law, 548, 4 Atl. 323.

rier.[67] Damages for the ejection may be increased by any added insult, due to the language and conduct of the carrier's servants.[68] Not only may the passenger recover for physical injuries inflicted in wrongfully ejecting him, but, even when the ejection is lawful, if excessive force is used to eject him, the passenger may recover for injuries received as the proximate result of the use of force beyond that which is reasonably necessary to complete the ejection.[69]

Wrongful Refusal to Accept One as Passenger

Here the damages, ordinarily, are confined to those naturally flowing from the carrier's wrongful refusal, which would include the added expense of going by another route or by different means of conveyance, inconvenience, and also for the loss of time, and even hotel expenses, when these are made necessary by the refusal.[70] The person refused must exercise reasonable care to minimize the damages; so that one who declined to hire a conveyance to take him to his destination, but walked, was denied a recovery for damages resulting from his eight-mile walk.[71]

Unreasonable Delay in Transporting Passenger

To compensate the passenger properly for the damage suffered by the carrier's negligent delay in transporting him, his recovery should be based on the value of the time lost, and also any necessary expenses that he has reasonably incurred as a proximate result of the delay.[72] The first of these is to be determined with ref-

[67] Curtis v. Sioux City & H. P. Ry. Co., 87 Iowa, 622, 54 N. W. 339; Lucas v. Michigan Cent. R. Co., 98 Mich. 1, 56 N. W. 1039, 39 Am. St. Rep. 517; Willson v. Northern Pac. R. Co., 5 Wash. 621, 32 Pac. 468, 34 Pac. 146; Gorman v. Southern Pac. Co., 97 Cal. 1, 31 Pac. 1112, 33 Am. St. Rep. 157; St. Louis & S. F. Ry. Co. v. Trimble, 54 Ark. 354, 15 S. W. 899; Chicago, St. L. & P. R. Co. v. Holdridge, 118 Ind. 281, 20 N. E. 837. See, also, Chicago & E. I. R. Co. v. Conley, 6 Ind. App. 9, 32 N. E. 96, 865, in which damages for humiliation were allowed, when the passenger was compelled to pay another fare to avoid ejection.

[68] Shepard v. Chicago, R. I. & P. Ry. Co., 77 Iowa, 55, 41 N. W. 564; Pennsylvania Co. v. Bray, 125 Ind. 229, 25 N. E. 439; Southern Kan. Ry. Co. v. Hinsdale, 38 Kan. 507, 16 Pac. 937; Atchison, T. & S. F. R. Co. v. Cuniffe (Tex. Civ. App.) 57 S. W. 692.

[69] See ante, pp. 555–558. See, also, Texas Pac. Ry. Co. v. James, 82 Tex. 306, 18 S. W. 589, 15 L. R. A. 347; Klenk v. Oregon Short Line R. Co., 27 Utah, 428, 76 Pac. 214; Alabama G. S. R. Co. v. Frazier, 93 Ala. 45, 9 South. 303, 30 Am. St. Rep. 28; Atchison, T. & S. F. R. Co. v. Brown, 2 Kan. App. 604, 42 Pac. 588.

[70] Northern Cent. Ry. Co. v. O'Conner, 76 Md. 207, 24 Atl. 449, 16 L. R. A. 449, 35 Am. St. Rep. 422; Pleasants v. North Beach & M. R. Co., 34 Cal. 586.

[71] Gulf, C. & S. F. R. Co. v. Cleveland (Tex. Civ. App.) 33 S. W. 687.

[72] Turner v. Great Northern Ry. Co., 15 Wash. 213, 46 Pac. 243, 55 Am. St. Rep. 883; Illinois Cent. R. Co. v. Head, 119 Ky. 809, 84 S. W. 751; Hansley

erence to the passenger's normal wages or earnings at his usual occupation.[73] As to the latter, it was held that the expense of a special train was unreasonable.[74]

Damages for Wrongful Failure to Carry Passenger to his Destination

Normal damages here, if the journey is partly completed, would be the added expense of reaching the destination, and compensation for the inconvenience, and for the time lost as a result of such failure.[75] But in a leading New York case, when the carrier agreed to transport the passenger from New York to San Francisco, by way of Nicaragua, and the passenger was detained on the Isthmus of Panama, the passenger (who abandoned the trip and returned to New York) was permitted to recover for his entire fare paid to the carrier, the expenses of his journey back, his loss of time, and the expenses of his detention and his sickness contracted on the Isthmus.[76] Practically the same considerations are applicable when the passenger is wrongly carried past his destination and set down at another station.[77]

SAME—EXEMPLARY OR PUNITIVE DAMAGES

209. Exemplary or punitive damages may be granted against the carrier for negligence so great as to amount to a reckless disregard of human rights, or for the wanton, willful, or malicious conduct of the carrier or his servants. Some courts, as a condition of the recovery of punitive damages, require that the act of the servant must be either authorized or ratified by the carrier.

v. Jamesville & W. R. Co., 115 N. C. 603, 20 S. E. 528, 32 L. R. A. 543, 44 Am. St. Rep. 474; Illinois Cent. R. Co. v. Byrne, 205 Ill. 9, 68 N. E. 720; Norfolk & W. R. Co. v. Lipscomb, 90 Va. 137, 17 S. E. 809, 20 L. R. A. 817; International & G. N. R. Co. v. Doolan, 56 Tex. Civ. App. 503, 120 S. W. 1118; Hamlen v. Railway Co., 1 H. & N. (Eng.) 408.

73 Cooley v. Pennsylvania R. Co., 40 Misc. Rep. 239, 81 N. Y. Supp. 692. See, also, Yonge v. Pacific Mail S. S. Co., 1 Cal. 353.

74 Le Blanche v. Railway Co., 1 C. P. Div. (Eng.) 286.

75 North American Transp. Co. v. Morrison, 178 U. S. 262, 20 Sup. Ct. 869, 44 L. Ed. 1061; Pennsylvania R. Co. v. Connell, 127 Ill. 419, 20 N. E. 89; Bullock v. White Star S. S. Co., 30 Wash. 448, 70 Pac. 1106; Miller v. Baltimore & O. R. Co., 89 App. Div. 457, 85 N. Y. Supp. 883; Trigg v. St. Louis, K. C. & N. Ry. Co., 74 Mo. 147, 41 Am. Rep. 305.

76 Williams v. Vanderbilt, 28 N. Y. 217, 84 Am. Dec. 333.

77 Dalton v. Kansas City, F. S. & M. R. Co., 78 Kan. 232, 96 Pac. 475, 17 L. R. A. (N. S.) 1226, 16 Ann. Cas. 185; Carter v. Illinois Cent. R. Co. (Ky.) 34 S. W. 907; St. Louis, I. M. & S. R. Co. v. Williams, 100 Ark. 356, 140 S. W. 141; Judice v. Southern Pac. Co., 47 La. Ann. 255, 16 South. 816; Martin v. Southern Ry., 89 S. C. 32, 71 S. E. 236.

In actions by the passenger against the carrier, the damages are usually compensatory only, such as are designed to do no more than compensate the passenger for the damage he has suffered.[78] In addition to these damages, however, punitive or exemplary damages are given in exceptional cases. The theory of such damages, sometimes called "smart money," is not to compensate the passenger, but to punish the carrier, as an example to discourage the repetition of flagrant wrongs.[79]

As a rule, the awarding of punitive damages is limited to the active and positive wrongs of the carrier, so that they are rarely given for mere negligence, or the more or less negative failure to live up to a required standard of care.[80] In cases, however, of negligence so great and glaring as to amount to a reckless disregard of human safety, such damages may be given.[81] Thus, where a statute required a train to be brought to a stop at a crossing, and the engineer ran by the crossing at an unabated speed exceeding thirty miles an hour, this was held to be a case for punitive damages.[82]

The more typical cases of punitive damages are those in which the wrong treatment of the passenger has been active and positive. For such wanton and willful wrong, punitive damages have, in a number of cases, been held to be proper.[83] Many of these have

[78] See cases cited under §§ 207, 208.

[79] Louisville & N. R. Co. v. Street, 164 Ala. 155, 51 South. 306, 20 Ann. Cas. 877; Chiles v. Southern R. Co., 69 S. C. 327, 48 S. E. 252; Missouri P. R. Co. v. Humes, 115 U. S. 512, 6 Sup. Ct. 110, 29 L. Ed. 463; Atchison, T. & S. F. R. Co. v. Chamberlain, 4 Okl. 542, 46 Pac. 499; Norfolk & W. R. Co. v. Neely, 91 Va. 539, 22 S. E. 367; Caldwell v. New Jersey Steamboat Co., 47 N. Y. 282; Philadelphia Traction Co. v. Orbann, 119 Pa. 37, 12 Atl. 816.

[80] Southern R. Co. v. Davis, 132 Ga. 812, 65 S. E. 131; Southern R. Co. in Kentucky v. Lee, 101 S. W. 307, 30 Ky. Law Rep. 1360, 10 L. R. A. (N. S.) 837; St. Louis, I. M. & S. R. Co. v. Dysart, 89 Ark. 261, 116 S. W. 224; St. Louis & S. F. R. Co. v. Garner, 96 Miss. 577, 51 South. 273; Alabama G. S. R. Co. v. Arnold, 84 Ala. 159, 4 South. 359, 5 Am. St. Rep. 354; Hill v. New Orleans, O. & G. W. R. Co., 11 La. Ann. 292; Missouri Pac. Ry. Co. v. Mitchell, 72 Tex. 171, 10 S. W. 411.

[81] Hansley v. Jamesville & W. R. Co., 115 N. C. 602, 20 S. E. 528, 32 L. R. A. 543, 44 Am. St. Rep. 474; Texas Trunk Ry. Co. v. Johnson, 75 Tex. 158, 12 S. W. 482; Milwaukee & St. P. Ry. Co. v. Arms, 91 U. S. 489, 23 L. Ed. 374; Lexington R. Co. v. Johnson, 139 Ky. 323, 122 S. W. 830; Chattanooga, R. & C. R. Co. v. Liddell, 85 Ga. 482, 11 S. E. 853, 21 Am. St. Rep. 169; Alabama G. S. Ry. Co. v. Hill, 93 Ala. 514, 9 South. 722, 30 Am. St. Rep. 65.

[82] Richmond & D. R. Co. v. Greenwood, 99 Ala. 501, 14 South. 495.

[83] Baltimore & O. R. Co. v. Barger, 80 Md. 23, 30 Atl. 560, 26 L. R. A. 220, 45 Am. St. Rep. 319; Schwartz v. Missouri, K. & T. R. Co., 83 Kan. 30, 109 Pac. 767; Gardner v. St. Louis & S. F. R. Co., 117 Mo. App. 138, 93 S. W. 917; Gorman v. Southern Pac. Co., 97 Cal. 1, 31 Pac. 1112, 33 Am. St.

arisen in connection with the ejection of,[84] and assaults upon, passengers.[85] Abuse, indecency, insulting language, oppression, and undue force are among the elements that influence the awarding of punitive damages in such cases.[86]

Necessity for Authorization or Ratification by the Carrier of the Servant's Act

A great many courts refuse to grant punitive damages when the act complained of is that of a servant, unless this act was previously authorized or subsequently ratified by the carrier.[87] Other courts, however, by what is believed to be the fairer rule, award punitive damages for the reckless negligence or the active wrong of such servant, in the absence of any authorization or ratification on the carrier's part.[88]

Rep. 157; East Tennessee, V. & G. Ry. Co. v. Fleetwood, 90 Ga. 23, 15 S. E. 778; Springer Transp. Co. v. Smith, 84 Tenn. 498, 1 S. W. 280; LEXINGTON RY. CO. v. COZINE, 111 Ky. 799, 64 S. W. 848, 98 Am. St. Rep. 430, Dobie Cas. Bailments and Carriers, 383; McCauley v. Chicago City Ry. Co., 163 Ill. App. 176.

[84] See cases cited in preceding note. See, also, Illinois Cent. R. Co. v. Reid, 93 Miss. 458, 46 South. 146, 17 L. R. A. (N. S.) 344; Little Rock R. & Electric Co. v. Goerner, 80 Ark. 158, 95 S. W. 1007, 7 L. R. A. (N. S.) 97, 10 Ann. Cas. 273; Kibler v. Southern R. R., 64 S. C. 242, 41 S. E. 977; Citizens' St. R. Co. of Indianapolis v. Willoeby, 134 Ind. 563, 33 N. E. 627; Ann Arbor R. Co. v. Amos, 85 Ohio St. 300, 97 N. E. 978, 43 L. R. A. (N. S.) 587.

[85] Shelby v. Metropolitan St. R. Co., 141 Mo. App. 514, 125 S. W. 1189; Bass v. Chicago & N. W. Ry. Co., 36 Wis. 450, 17 Am. Rep. 495; Goddard v. Grand Trunk Ry. of Canada, 57 Me. 202, 2 Am. Rep. 39; East Tennessee, V. & G. Ry. Co. v. Fleetwood, 90 Ga. 23, 15 S. E. 778; Baltimore & O. R. v. Barger, 80 Md. 23, 30 Atl. 560, 26 L. R. A. 220, 45 Am. St. Rep. 319; LEXINGTON RY. CO. v. COZINE, 111 Ky. 799, 64 S. W. 848, 98 Am. St. Rep. 430, Dobie Cas. Bailments and Carriers, 383.

[86] St. Louis, I. M. & S. Ry. Co. v. Davis, 56 Ark. 51, 19 S. W. 107; Chicago, B. & Q. R. Co. v. Bryan, 90 Ill. 126; Citizens' St. R. Co. of Indianapolis v. Willoeby, 134 Ind. 563, 33 N. E. 627; LEXINGTON RY. CO. v. COZINE, 111 Ky. 799, 64 S. W. 848, 98 Am. St. Rep. 430, Dobie Cas. Bailments and Carriers, 383; Louisville & N. R. Co. v. Maybin, 66 Miss. 83, 5 South. 401; McNamara v. St. Louis Transit Co., 182 Mo. 676, 81 S. W. 880, 66 L. R. A. 486.

[87] Lake Shore & M. S. R. Co. v. Prentice, 147 U. S. 101, 13 Sup. Ct. 261, 37 L. Ed. 97; Trabing v. California Nav. & Imp. Co., 121 Cal. 137, 53 Pac. 644; Cleghorn v. New York Cent. & H. R. R. Co., 56 N. Y. 44, 15 Am. Rep. 375; Hagan v. Providence & W. R. Co., 3 R. I. 88, 62 Am. Dec. 377; Gulf, C. & S. F. Ry. Co. v. Reed, 80 Tex. 362, 15 S. W. 1105, 26 Am. St. Rep. 749; Sullivan v. Oregon Ry. & Nav. Co., 12 Or. 392, 7 Pac. 508, 53 Am. Rep. 364; Philadelphia Traction Co. v. Orbann, 119 Pa. 37, 12 Atl. 816; Wells v. Boston & M. R. R., 82 Vt. 108, 71 Atl. 1103, 137 Am. St. Rep. 987; Quingley v. Central Pac. R. Co., 11 Nev. 350, 21 Am. Rep. 757; Rueping v. Chicago & N. W. R. Co., 116 Wis. 625, 93 N. W. 843, 96 Am. St. Rep. 1013; Id., 123 Wis. 319, 101 N. W. 710; Topolewski v. Plankinton Packing Co., 143 Wis. 52, 126 N. W. 554.

[88] Knoxville Traction Co. v. Lane, 103 Tenn. 376, 53 S. W. 557, 46 L. R. A. 549; Hart v. Railroad Co., 33 S. C. 427, 12 S. E. 9, 10 L. R. A. 794; High-

ACTIONS RELATING TO BAGGAGE

210. Though brought against the passenger carrier, those actions relating to delay, injury, or loss as to the baggage follow in general the rules applicable to actions against carriers of goods. Particularly is this true as to evidence and measure of damages.

We have seen that the passenger carrier's liability for baggage is that of a carrier of goods.[89] Actions pertaining to baggage, therefore, follow as a rule the same rules governing actions against carriers of goods.[90] The form of such action may be either in tort or contract, usually the former.[91] The evidence, too, is similar to actions against carriers of goods, save that the relation of passenger and carrier should be established.[92] A prima facie case is made out against the carrier by showing delivery of the baggage in good condition to the carrier, and the latter's failure to redeliver, or delivery in an injured condition.[93]

land Ave. & B. R. Co. v. Robinson, 125 Ala. 483, 28 South. 28; Palmer v. Maine Cent. R. Co., 92 Me. 399, 42 Atl. 800, 44 L. R. A. 673, 69 Am. St. Rep. 513; Southern Kansas Ry. Co. v. Rice, 38 Kan. 398, 16 Pac. 817, 5 Am. St. Rep. 766; Wheeler & Wilson Mfg. Co. v. Boyce, 36 Kan. 350, 13 Pac. 609, 59 Am. Rep. 571; Ammons v. Southern R. Co., 138 N. C. 555, 51 S. E. 127, 3 Ann. Cas. 886; Baltimore & O. R. Co. v. Strube, 111 Md. 119, 73 Atl. 697; East Tennessee, V. & G. Ry. Co. v. Fleetwood, 90 Ga. 23, 15 S. E. 778; Southern R. Co. v. Lanning, 83 Miss. 161, 35 South. 417; Berg v. St. Paul City R. Co., 96 Minn. 513, 105 N. W. 191; Baltimore & O. S. W. R. Co. v. Davis, 44 Ind. App. 375, 89 N. E. 403; LEXINGTON RY. CO. v. COZINE, 111 Ky. 799, 64 S. W. 848, 98 Am. St. Rep. 430, Dobie Cas. Bailments and Carriers, 383.

89 Ante, p. 636.

90 See ante, chapter XV.

91 Weed v. Saratoga & S. R. Co., 19 Wend. (N. Y.) 534; Atchison, T. & S. F. R. Co. v. Wilkinson, 55 Kan. 83, 39 Pac. 1043; Spencer v. Wabash R. Co., 36 App. Div. 446, 55 N. Y. Supp. 948. See, also, Flint & P. M. Ry. Co. v. Wier, 37 Mich. 111, 26 Am. Rep. 499; Corry v. Pennsylvania Ry. Co., 194 Pa. 516, 45 Atl. 341; Lake Shore & M. S. Ry. Co. v. Warren, 3 Wyo. 134, 6 Pac. 724.

92 See ante, § 118.

93 Zeigler v. M. R. Co., 87 Miss. 367, 39 South. 811; The New England (D. C.) 110 Fed. 415; Cleveland, C., C. & St. L. Ry. Co. v. Tyler, 9 Ind. App. 689, 35 N. E. 523; Hubbard v. Mobile & O. R. Co., 112 Mo. App. 459, 87 S. W. 52; McCormick v. Pennsylvania Cent. R. Co., 99 N. Y. 65, 1 N. E. 99, 52 Am. Rep. 6; Meyer v. Atlantic Coast Line R. R., 92 S. C. 101, 75 S. E. 209. A passenger to whom a carrier delivers a baggage check need not prove that the carrier actually received the baggage until the carrier has rebutted the constructive delivery evidenced by the check by proof that it never received the baggage. Lewis v. Ocean S. S. Co., 12 Ga. App. 191, 76 S. E. 1073.

The measure of damages, too, is the same as against carriers of goods.[94] For loss of baggage, the measure is ordinarily the value of the baggage to the passenger at his destination when the baggage should have arrived.[95] For injury to his baggage, the passenger recovers the difference between what the baggage would have been worth at his destination, had it been uninjured, and what it is worth in its injured condition.[96] For delay, the value of the use of the baggage to the passenger during such delay forms the measure of damages.[97]

As to parties, the proper plaintiff, in an action pertaining to baggage as such, is the passenger.[98] This, of course, is different from actions against carriers of goods. The pleadings, of course, should set out the facts showing the relation of passenger and carrier, the duty arising therefrom, its breach, and the consequent damage.[99] Such pleadings, too, should be consistent with the plaintiff's theory of the case, and should harmonize with the evidence.[100]

[94] See ante, §§ 158-163.

[95] Turner v. Southern Ry., 75 S. C. 58, 54 S. E. 825, 7 L. R. A. (N. S.) 188; Galveston, H. & S. A. R. Co. v. Fales, 33 Tex. Civ. App. 457, 77 S. W. 234; Fairfax v. New York Cent. & H. R. R. Co., 73 N. Y. 167, 29 Am. Rep. 119; Lake Shore & M. S. Ry. Co. v. Warren, 3 Wyo. 134, 6 Pac. 724. In Brock v. Gale, 14 Fla. 523, 14 Am. Rep. 356, a dentist, whose instruments were lost by the carrier, was denied special damages in the shape of profits and earnings he might have made, had the instruments not been lost.

[96] Missouri, K. & T. R. Co. of Texas v. Hailey (Tex. Civ. App.) 156 S. W. 1119; Wall v. Atlantic Coast Line R. R., 71 S. C. 337, 51 S. E. 95; St. Louis & S. F. R. Co. v. Dickerson, 29 Okl. 386, 118 Pac. 140.

[97] Texas & N. O. R. Co. v. Russell (Tex. Civ. App.) 97 S. W. 1090; Conheim v. Chicago Great Western R. Co., 104 Minn. 312, 116 N. W. 581, 17 L. R. A. (N. S.) 1091, 124 Am. St. Rep. 623, 15 Ann. Cas. 389; Ford v. Atlantic Coast Line R. Co., 8 Ga. App. 295, 68 S. E. 1072; Brooks v. Northern Pac. R. Co., 58 Or. 387, 114 Pac. 949. In an action against a carrier for delay of the samples of a salesman traveling on commission, he could not recover profits lost, because he was unable to make sales during the delay; such profits being speculative and contingent, and incapable of being proved with the certainty required to constitute recoverable damages. St. Louis & S. F. R. Co. v. Lilly, 1 Ala. App. 320, 55 South. 937. Punitive damages, in an action for delay in delivery of baggage, are recoverable where the negligence is so gross and reckless as to assume the nature of wantonness and willfulness. Webb v. Atlantic Coast Line R. Co., 76 S. C. 193, 56 S. E. 954, 9 L. R. A. (N. S.) 1218, 11 Ann. Cas. 834.

[98] See ante, § 199.

[99] See Cleveland, C., C. & St. L. Ry. Co. v. Tyler, 9 Ind. App. 689, 35 N. E. 523; Ranchau v. Rutland R. Co., 71 Vt. 142, 43 Atl. 11, 76 Am. St. Rep. 761; Hubbard v. Mobile & O. R. Co., 112 Mo. App. 459, 87 S. W. 52; Southern Pac. Co. v. Maloney, 136 Fed. 171, 69 C. C. A. 83.

[100] Montgomery & E. Ry. Co. v. Culver, 75 Ala. 587, 51 Am. Rep. 483.

SUPPLEMENT

THE FEDERAL INTERSTATE COMMERCE ACT, THE SAFETY APPLIANCE ACTS, AND THE EMPLOYERS' LIABILITY ACTS

So important are the acts affecting interstate commerce that it is deemed advisable to add a brief supplement dealing with them. To reproduce the text of these acts, or even to treat them in detail, would require more space than the scope of this book would permit. All that is attempted, then, is a brief summary of the most striking provisions of three of the most important of these acts: The Interstate Commerce Act, the Safety Appliance Acts, and the Employers' Liability Acts.

THE INTERSTATE COMMERCE ACT[1]

Introductory

Constitutional warrant for the Interstate Commerce Act is found in the United States Constitution (article 1, § 8, par. 3), which gives Congress the power "to regulate commerce with foreign nations, among the several states, and with the Indian tribes."

The original Interstate Commerce Act was passed in 1887, but this act has been amended by the acts of 1889, 1893, 1903, 1906, 1908, and 1910. Of these amendatory acts, the most important were the Hepburn Act of 1906, and the Mann-Elkins Act of 1910. The act is discussed as it now stands, with all of these amendments.

The principal objects of the act, according to the United States Supreme Court,[2] were "to secure just and reasonable charges for

[1] For an excellent discussion of the Interstate Commerce Act, see Judson on Interstate Commerce (second edition), from which generous assistance has been received in preparing this brief supplement. For a compilation of the act, with its amendments and supplementary provisions down to December 31, 1913, with full historical and explanatory annotations, see U. S. Comp. St. 1913, §§ 8563–8604.

[2] Interstate Commerce Commission v. Baltimore & O. R. Co., 145 U. S. 263, 12 Sup. Ct. 844, 36 L. Ed. 699.

transportation, to prohibit unjust discriminations in the rendition of like services under similar conditions, to prevent unreasonable preferences to persons, corporations, or localities, to inhibit greater compensation for a shorter than for a longer distance over the same line, and to abolish combinations for pooling freights."

A brief summary of the more important provisions of the act is given under the sections of the act in which such provisions are found.

Section 1. Scope of Act. Passes Prohibited. Commodities Clause

The first section of the act limits its application to common carriers and interstate or foreign commerce. A broad definition of common carriers is given, however, and within this definition are included oil pipe lines, sleeping car companies, express companies, interstate electric railroads,[3] and telegraph, telephone, and cable companies. But the act does not apply to transportation entirely by water.[4]

This section then provides that the carrier's charges must be just and reasonable, and requires, too, that his classifications, regulations, and practices shall be subjected to the same test. Such a provision is practically only an affirmation of the common law.

Section 1 also prohibits "any free ticket, free pass or free transportation for passengers," subject to a long list of specific exceptions. Both giving and using a prohibited pass are made misdemeanors. In this connection should be considered the qualifying provisions of section 22 of the act.

Under the celebrated "commodities clause," the carrier is forbidden to transport "any article or commodity" (timber and its manufactured products excepted), not intended for the carrier's use, "manufactured, mined or produced by it, or under its authority, or which it may own in whole or in part, or in which it may have any interest direct or indirect." The Supreme Court upheld the constitutionality of this clause,[5] and has also had occasion to pass on its evasion by the carrier's holding stock in the producing corporation.[6]

This section concludes by requiring the carrier to make switch

[3] Willson v. Rock Creek Ry. Co. of Dist. of Columbia, 7 Interst. Com. Com'n R. 83; Boyle v. Great Falls & Old Dominion R. Co., 20 Interst. Com. Com'n R. 232; Judson, Interstate Commerce (2d Ed.) § 143.

[4] Cary v. Eureka Springs Ry. Co., 7 Interst. Com. Com'n R. 286.

[5] United States v. Delaware & Hudson Co., 213 U. S. 366, 29 Sup. Ct. 527, 53 L. Ed. 836.

[6] United States v. Delaware & Hudson Co., 213 U. S. 366, 29 Sup. Ct. 527. 53 L. Ed. 836; United States v. Lehigh Val. R. Co., 220 U. S. 257, 31 Sup. Ct. 387, 55 L. Ed. 458.

connections with lateral lines and private tracks, when this is economical and practicable.

Section 2. Discrimination in the Carrier's Charges

Section 2 defines and forbids any unjust discrimination in the carrier's charges. If such discrimination is real, it makes no difference whether it be done by "special rate, rebate, drawback or other device." Whatever lack of clearness there may be as to the common law of discrimination, this section is definite and explicit in its sweeping prohibitions. Such a discrimination occurs when more is charged one person than is charged another for the "transportation of a like kind of traffic *under substantially similar circumstances and conditions.*" The practical application of the italicized phrase, the key of the whole section, has however, given rise to no little difficulty.

Section 3. Discriminatory Preferences and Advantages

Discrimination is also the subject of section 3, prohibiting "any undue or unreasonable preference or advantage to any particular person, company, firm, corporation or locality." It will readily be seen that the scope of this section is far wider than that of section 2. While section 2 is confined to discrimination in rates, section 3 covers any form of undue preference or unreasonable preference by the carrier in favor of persons, firms, corporations, or localities. Within this prohibition would fall car service,[7] the operation of stations and warehouses,[8] side tracks, and similar connections.[9]

Section 4. Long and Short Haul

This section contains the famous "long and short haul provision" which makes it unlawful for the carrier to charge "any greater compensation in the aggregate for the transportation of passengers, or of like kind of property, for a shorter than for a longer distance over the same line or route in the same direction, the shorter being included within the longer distance, or to charge any greater compensation as a through route than the aggregate of the intermediate rates subject to the provisions of this act." By the act of 1910, the qualifying words "under substantially similar circumstances and provisions" were stricken out, thus broadening the application of the provision against the carrier. This fact must be considered in connection with cases decided before this amendment. The Interstate Commerce Commission may, on application from a carrier, "prescribe the extent to which such des-

[7] See Judson, Interstate Commerce, § 250.
[8] See Judson, Interstate Commerce, § 249.
[9] See Judson, Interstate Commerce, § 262.

ignated common carrier may be relieved from the operation of this section."

Section 5. Pooling of Freights

Here provision is made against contracts and combinations of common carriers "for the pooling of freights of *different and competing* railroads, or to divide between them the aggregate or net proceeds of the earnings of such railroads or any portion thereof." According to the charge of a district judge,[10] "the statute contemplates two methods of pooling, both of which are prohibited: First, a physical pool, which means a distribution by the carriers of property offered for transportation among different and competing railroads in proportions and on percentages previously agreed upon; and, secondly, a money pool, which is described best in the language of the statute, 'To divide between them [different and competing railroads] the aggregate or net proceeds of the earnings of such railroads, or any portion thereof.'"

Section 6. Filing and Printing of Schedules of Rates

This requires the carrier to file with the Interstate Commerce Commission and to print and publicly post "schedules showing all the rates, fares and charges for transportation between different points on its own route and between points on its own route and points on the route of any other carrier by railroad, by pipe-line or by water when a through route and joint rate have been established." These schedules must specify "terminal charges, storage charges, icing charges and all other charges which the commission may require." There can be no deviation from the published rates, and these cannot be changed except on thirty days' notice to the public and to the Interstate Commerce Commission. This section is the great publicity provision of the act.

Section 7. Interruption of Transit

In a brief section here the carrier is forbidden to break the continuity of the carriage of freight "unless such break, stoppage, or interruption was made in good faith for some necessary purpose, and without any intent to avoid or unnecessarily interrupt such continuous carriage or to evade any of the provisions of this act."

Section 8. Civil Remedy for Violations of the Act

A civil remedy is given by this section against the carrier failing to comply with the act, for it is provided, in case of a violation of the act by the carrier, "such common carrier shall be liable to the person or persons injured thereby for the full amount of damage

10 Hammond, J., In re Pooling Freights (D. C.) 115 Fed. 588, 589.

sustained in consequence of any such violation of the provisions of this act, together with a reasonable counsel or attorney's fee."

Section 9. Election of Remedies against the Carrier

An election is given here to the person damaged by a carrier subject to the provisions of the act either to file a complaint before the Interstate Commerce Commission or to bring suit in a federal court. He cannot do both, but may choose either remedy. Provision is also made to compel the officers of the defendant to testify and to produce the carrier's books.

Section 10. Criminal Penalties for Violation of the Act

Penalties for violations of the act are covered by this section. It is first provided, in general, that any carrier subject to the act, or, when such carrier is a corporation, any officer, agent, or person employed by such corporation, who shall *willfully* do anything prohibited by the act, or fail *willfully* to do something required by the act, or who shall aid or abet therein, or shall be guilty of any infraction of the act for which no penalty is otherwise provided, shall be guilty of a misdemeanor and subject to a fine not to exceed five thousand dollars for each offense. Besides this general provision, the first paragraph of the section makes specific provision that "when the offense for which any person shall be convicted as aforesaid shall be unlawful discrimination in rates, fares or charges" such person may in addition to the fine, be imprisoned for a term not exceeding two years.

The second and third paragraphs are concerned with false billing, false weighing, false classification, etc., either by the carriers, the officers or agents of such carrier, or by shippers and other persons. The penalty for this is the same as for unlawful discrimination—fine not to exceed five thousand dollars or imprisonment not to exceed two years, or both.

Paragraph 4 is the complement of the last part of paragraph 1. It makes it a misdemeanor for any person to induce or to attempt to induce the carrier to make unjust discriminations, or to aid or abet the carrier in such unjust discrimination. A similar penalty of a fine not exceeding five thousand dollars or imprisonment not over two years is provided. Such person, together with the carrier, is also made liable for the damages caused by such discrimination to the consignor or consignee discriminated against.

Section 11. Constitution of the Interstate Commerce Commission

The Interstate Commerce Commission is created by this section. Its provisions as to the number of commissioners, etc., have been largely superseded by the provisions of section 24.

Section 12. Powers and Duties of the Commission

The powers and duties of this Commission are outlined here. As to carriers subject to the act, the Commission has "authority to inquire into the management of the business of all common carriers," and "shall have the right to obtain from such common carriers full and complete information necessary to enable the commission to carry out the objects for which it was created." It is further provided: "The Commission is hereby authorized and required to execute and enforce the provisions of this Act."

To aid the Commission, it may apply to the various United States district attorneys to institute proceedings under the direction of the Attorney General. The Commission also has the power to require "the attendance and testimony of witnesses" and the production of documentary evidence. In enforcing this last provision, the aid of the United States Courts may be invoked. Ample provision is also made for taking the depositions of witnesses.

In order to secure the full and free testimony of witnesses, the section includes the following provision: "The claim that any such testimony or evidence may tend to criminate the person giving such evidence shall not excuse such person from testifying; but such evidence or testimony shall not be used against such person on the trial of any criminal proceeding."

Section 13. Complaints to, and Investigations by, the Commission

Complaints to the Commission form the subject of this section. It provides that persons complaining of violations of the act "may apply to said Commission by petition, which shall briefly state the facts." A statement of the complaint is sent by the Commission to the carrier, who must make reparation, or answer the complaint in writing. If the carrier fails to make reparation, the Commission proceeds to investigate the matters complained of.

Provision is also made for investigations by the Commission on the complaint of the railroad commission or commissioner of any state or territory. In addition, and what is much more important, the Commission may institute inquiries on its own motion and may proceed with these with full power and authority. This section concludes: "No complaint shall at any time be dismissed because of the absence of direct damage to the complainant."

Section 14. Reports and Decisions of the Commission

This short section makes it the duty of the Commission to make a report in writing of all investigations which shall be made. Copies of these reports shall be furnished to the complainant and carrier, while provision is also made for the publication of the reports and decisions of the Commission.

Section 15. Prescribing of Rates by the Commission

Under this section, the Commission has power, after a full hearing, when a rate is deemed to be discriminatory, unreasonable, preferential, or otherwise in violation of this act, to determine and prescribe what will be a just and reasonable rate "to be thereafter observed in such case as the maximum to be charged." The Commission also has the power to investigate new schedules of rates filed by the carrier and to suspend the operation of such new schedules; the burden resting on the carrier of justifying the reasonableness of increased rates.

Under the third and fourth paragraphs of the section, through routes and joint rates and classifications may, with certain limitations, be established by the Commission. Paragraph 5 gives the shipper a restricted right as to the selection of the route. The sixth paragraph forbids the carrier to give, or a competitor of the shipper or consignee to receive, information as to the business of such shipper or consignee with the carrier, which information might be used to the detriment of such shipper or consignee; and paragraph 7 makes this a misdemeanor punishable by fine. Under paragraph 8, when the owner of the property transported renders any service, or furnishes any instrumentality, connected with the transportation, the Commission may determine what is a just and reasonable allowance to be made by the carrier for such service or instrumentality.

Section 15 wisely ends with a safeguarding paragraph: "The foregoing enumeration of powers shall not exclude any power which the Commission would otherwise have in the making of an order under this act."

Section 16. Enforcement of Commission's Orders Awarding Damages

The Commission, after hearing on a proper complaint, may make an order directing the carrier to pay to the complainant the sum to which he is entitled on or before a day named. If the carrier fails, within the time set, to comply with the order, the complainant may bring suit by filing "in *any state court of general jurisdiction* having jurisdiction of the parties a petition setting forth briefly the causes for which he claims damages, and the order of the Commission."

This section further provides that suit may be brought in the United States Circuit Court, the complainant being able to choose either that court or the state court just mentioned. As the United States Circuit Court has been abolished, and its powers vested in the United States District Court, it would seem that the District Court would have this jurisdiction; and particularly does this seem true since the orders of the Commission for the payment of money were expressly excepted from the jurisdiction of the former Commerce Court of the United States.[11] And later in this section of the act, provision was made for application by the Commission or injured party to this Commerce Court to enforce orders of the Commission "other than for the payment of money."

Further provision, in suits brought to enforce orders of the Commission for the payment of money, is made in this section as to attorney's fees, limitation of time within which suits must be brought, and service of process.

The section contains a provision inflicting a forfeiture of five thousand dollars when the carrier or an agent "knowingly fails or neglects to obey an order made under section fifteen of this act."

Section 16a. Rehearings by the Commission

Express power is given by this section to the Commission to grant rehearings "if sufficient reason therefor be made to appear." After such rehearing, the Commission may reverse, change or modify its original order.

Section 17. Form of Procedure by the Commission

Authority is given to the Commission under this section to "conduct its proceedings in such manner as will best conduce to the proper dispatch of business and the ends of justice." A majority of the Commission is made a quorum, any party is allowed to appear before the Commission in person or by attorney, and the Commission may make and amend its rules and regulations governing its procedure.

Section 18. Former Salary of Commissioners and Secretary—Expenses

Provision is here made for the expenses of the Commission. The provisions as to salaries have been superseded, largely by section 24 of the act.

Section 19. Principal Office of Commission—Places of General and Special Sessions

The principal office of the Commission is fixed in Washington, in which the general sessions of the Commission are held. Special Sessions of the Commission, however, and inquiries by one or more of the commissioners, may be held in any part of the United States.

[11] See sections 289–291 of the Judicial Code (Act March 3, 1911, c. 231, 36 Stat. 1167 [U. S. Comp. St. Supp. 1911, p. 243]), abolishing the United States Circuit Court, and conferring its powers on the United States District Court. The Commerce Court was abolished by Deficiency Appropriation Bill Dec. 22, 1913, and its jurisdiction vested in the United States District Courts.

Section 20. Annual Reports of Carriers—Liability of Initial Carrier

By this section the Commission is authorized "to require annual reports from all common carriers subject to the provisions of this act, * * * to prescribe the manner in which such reports shall be made and to require from such carriers specific answers to all questions upon which the Commission may need information." Elaborate provisions are also made relating to various phases of these reports, such as their contents, time of filing, special reports, system of keeping accounts, method of compelling the filing of such reports, and the mutilation and destruction of records.

The last part of this section contains the celebrated "Carmack Amendment," making the initial carrier of goods received for transportation to a point in another state liable for loss or injury to these goods, even though such loss or injury occur on the line of a connecting carrier. From this liability, the initial carrier cannot relieve himself by contract or regulation. Provision is made that the holder of the bill of lading shall not be deprived of any "remedy or right of action which he has under existing law." When such loss or damage occurs on the line of the connecting carrier, the initial carrier is given a remedy over against such connecting carrier. The constitutionality of this "Carmack Amendment" was sustained by the Supreme Court.[12] Reference has already been made to this amendment, in discussing the rule of Muschamp's Case [13] and the situation in America, and also in treating the limitation by contract [14] of the carrier's common-law responsibility.

Section 21. Annual Reports of the Commission to Congress

Annual reports of the Commission to Congress are required by this section. These reports contain valuable data and information collected by the Commission, recommendations as to additional legislation deemed necessary by the Commission, and "the names and compensation of the persons employed by said Commission." An admirable epitome of the value and volume of the work done by the Commission is contained in these annual reports.

Section 22. Persons and Property that may be Carried Free or at Reduced Rates

This section permits certain freight and passenger traffic to be handled by the carrier, either free or at reduced rates. It should be read in connection with that part of section 1 of the act prohibit-

[12] Atlantic Coast Line R. Co. v. Riverside Mills, 219 U. S. 186, 31 Sup. Ct. 164, 55 L. Ed. 167, 31 L. R. A. (N. S.) 7.

[13] See ante, § 145.

[14] Ante, p. 409.

ing "free ticket, free pass, or free transportation to passengers." Permissive provision is made as to "joint interchangeable five thousand mile tickets, with special privileges as to the amount of free baggage." The cases enumerated in this section, as to which this indulgence is permitted, have been held to be illustrative, and not exclusive.[15]

Section 23. Jurisdiction of United States Courts to Issue Writs of Mandamus

Under this section, jurisdiction was given to the United States courts to issue peremptory writs of mandamus commanding the movement of interstate traffic at rates and under conditions as favorable as those existing as to other shippers.

Section 24. Constitution of the Commission

This section enlarged the Commission to seven members, with seven-year terms and annual salaries of $10,000. The appointment of these Commissioners is by the President, by and with the advice and consent of the Senate, and "not more than four Commissioners shall be appointed from the same political party."

THE SAFETY APPLIANCE ACTS[16]

These acts consist of the Safety Act of 1893, entitled "An act to promote the safety of employés and travelers upon railroads by compelling common carriers engaged in interstate commerce to equip their cars with automatic couplers and continuous brakes and their locomotives with driving wheel brakes, and for other purposes," the amendments of 1896 and 1903, and the supplementary Safety Act of 1910. The general tenor of these acts is to compel common carriers by railroad, engaged in interstate commerce (or in commerce in the territories or in the District of Columbia), to equip their locomotives with driving wheel brakes and appliances for operating the train-brake system, and to equip their cars with automatic couplers, grabirons, handholds, sill steps and hand brakes. "All cars requiring secure ladders and secure running boards shall be equipped with such ladders and such running boards." Provision is also made for fixing a standard height for the drawbars on freight cars.

[15] Interstate Commerce Commission v. Baltimore & O. R. Co. (Party Rate Case) 145 U. S. 263, 12 Sup. Ct. 844, 36 L. Ed. 699.

[16] See Judson, Interstate Commerce, §§ 497–526. For a compilation of the act, with its amendments and supplementary provisions down to December 31, 1913, with full historical and explanatory annotations, see U. S. Comp. St. §§ 8605–8650.

The act provides penalties for its violation, and gives the Interstate Commerce Commission varied powers for its enforcement. It further provides that, when the statute is violated, the carrier's servant, by continuing in the service with knowledge of such violation, does not assume the risk of injuries thereby occasioned. This provision was wisely inserted to prevent the carrier from escaping liability to the servant, when the act has been violated to the servant's injury, by pleading the well-known, but eminently unfair, defense of assumption of risk.

THE EMPLOYERS' LIABILITY ACTS [17]

These acts comprise the Employers' Liability Act approved June 11, 1906, and declared unconstitutional by the Supreme Court in the Employers' Liability Cases; [18] the Employers' Liability Act approved April 22, 1908, declared constitutional by the Supreme Court in Second Employers' Liability Cases; [19] and the amendatory act of April 5, 1910. The brief summary given below covers the act of 1908, as amended in 1910.

The act applies to common carriers by railroad engaged in interstate or foreign commerce (section 1), and to "Every common carrier by railroad in the territories, the District of Columbia, the Panama Canal Zone, or other possessions of the United States" (section 2). The carrier is liable in damages to any person suffering injury "while he is employed by such carrier in such [interstate and foreign] commerce" (under section 1), or is "employed by such carrier in any of said jurisdictions" (District of Columbia, etc., under section 2). Such injury must, in addition, be one resulting wholly or in part (a) "from the negligence of any of the officers, agents or employés of such carrier," or (b) "by reason of any defect or insufficiency due to its negligence in its cars, engines, appliances, machinery, track, roadbed, works, boats, wharves, or other equipment." It will be seen that of these (a) is broad enough to abrogate the fellow servant rule, and there is a recovery by the injured employé when the injury is due to the negligence of a fellow servant.

Under section 1 of the act, ample provision is made for suit by the personal representative of the injured employé, for the benefit

[17] See Judson, Interstate Commerce, §§ 527–540. For a compilation of the act, with its amendments and supplementary provisions down to December 31, 1913, with full historical and explanatory annotations, see U. S. Comp. St. §§ 8657–8665.

[18] Brooks v. Southern Pac. Co., 207 U. S. 463, 28 Sup. Ct. 141, 52 L. Ed. 297.

[19] Mondou v. New York, N. H. & H. R. Co., 223 U. S. 1, 32 Sup. Ct. 169. 56 L. Ed. 327, 38 L. R. A. (N. S.) 44.

of specified relatives, when the employé's death results from the carrier's negligence; while section 9 (added by the amendment of 1910) provides for the survival to the personal representative of the right of action for the injury given to the injured employé.

The third section, on contributory negligence, first provides that contributory negligence of the employé shall not be a complete defense to actions brought under the act, "but the damages shall be diminished by the jury in proportion to the amount of negligence attributable to such employé." Then the section even more sweepingly provides that the employé cannot be held guilty of contributory negligence at all, when his injury or death was in any way due to the carrier's violation of "any statute enacted for the safety of employés." The Safety Appliance Acts, just discussed, are excellent examples of such statutes.

In suits brought under this act, section 4, when the death or injury is wholly or partly due to the carrier's violation "of any statute enacted for the safety of employés," takes away the carrier's defense of assumption of risk. The employé does not, in such cases, assume the risk of death or injury resulting from the carrier's violations of these statutes.

Section 5 wisely safeguards the practical value of the act by providing that no contract, rule, or device of the carrier can exempt the carrier from the liabilities imposed by the act. The carrier, however, in suits brought under the act, may diminish the recovery by setting off "any insurance, relief, benefit or indemnity" paid by the carrier on account of the death or injury.

A time limitation is imposed by the provision of section 6 "that no action shall be maintained under this act unless commenced within two years from the day the cause of action accrued." This section (as amended by the act of 1910) also provides, as to suits brought under the act: "The jurisdiction of the courts of the United States under this act shall be concurrent with that of the courts of the several states, and no case arising under this act and brought in any state court of competent jurisdiction shall be removed to any court of the United States."

Under section 7, "the term 'common carrier,' as used in this act, shall include the receiver or receivers or other persons or corporations charged with the duty of the management and operation of the business of a common carrier."

The cumulative aspect of the act is emphasized by section 8, which provides that the act shall not be construed as in any way limiting either the duty of the carrier or the rights of the employé under any other acts of Congress.

TABLE OF CASES CITED

[THE FIGURES REFER TO PAGES]

A

[The figures refer to pages]

[The figures refer to pages]

B

[The figures refer to pages]

[The figures refer to pages]

[The figures refer to pages]

[The figures refer to pages]

[The figures refer to pages]

C

[The figures refer to pages]

[The figures refer to pages]

[The figures refer to pages]

[The figures refer to pages]

D

[The figures refer to pages]

[The figures refer to pages]

E

[The figures refer to pages]

[The figures refer to pages]

[The figures refer to pages]

G

[The figures refer to pages]

[The figures refer to pages]

[The figures refer to pages]

H

[The figures refer to pages]

[The figures refer to pages]

[The figures refer to pages]

[The figures refer to pages]

[The figures refer to pages]

I

[The figures refer to pages]

J

[The figures refer to pages]

[The figures refer to pages]

K

[The figures refer to pages]

L

[The figures refer to pages]

[The figures refer to pages]

[The figures refer to pages]

[The figures refer to pages]

[The figures refer to pages]

M

[The figures refer to pages]

[The figures refer to pages]

[The figures refer to pages]

[The figures refer to pages]

[The figures refer to pages]

[The figures refer to pages]

[The figures refer to pages]

N

[The figures refer to pages]

[The figures refer to pages]

O

P

[The figures refer to pages]

[The figures refer to pages]

Q

R

[The figures refer to pages]

[The figures refer to pages]

[The figures refer to pages]

S

[The figures refer to pages]

[The figures refer to pages]

[The figures refer to pages]

[The figures refer to pages]

[The figures refer to pages]

[The figures refer to pages]

[The figures refer to pages]

T

[The figures refer to pages]

[The figures refer to pages]

[The figures refer to pages]

U

V

[The figures refer to pages]

W

[The figures refer to pages]

[The figures refer to pages]

[The figures refer to pages]

[The figures refer to pages]

[The figures refer to pages]

Y

Z

INDEX

[THE FIGURES REFER TO PAGES]

A

[The figures refer to pages]

[The figures refer to pages]

[The figures refer to pages]

[The figures refer to pages]

[The figures refer to pages]

[The figures refer to pages]

[The figures refer to pages]

[The figures refer to pages]

[The figures refer to pages]

[The figures refer to pages]

[The figures refer to pages]

[The figures refer to pages]

[The figures refer to pages]

D

[The figures refer to pages]

[The figures refer to pages]

E

[The figures refer to pages]

[The figures refer to pages]

F

[The figures refer to pages]

G

[The figures refer to pages]

H

[The figures refer to pages]

I

[The figures refer to pages]

[The figures refer to pages]

[The figures refer to pages]

[The figures refer to pages]

L

M

[The figures refer to pages]

[The figures refer to pages]

O

P

[The figures refer to pages]

[The figures refer to pages]

[The figures refer to pages]

[The figures refer to pages]

S

[The figures refer to pages]

[The figures refer to pages]

[The figures refer to pages]

U

[The figures refer to pages]

V

W

WEST PUBLISHING CO., PRINTERS, ST. PAUL, MINN.

CPSIA information can be obtained
at www.ICGtesting.com
Printed in the USA
BVHW011309161121
621774BV00009B/171

9 781248 447697